Nation of Nations

Volume II: Since 1865
Chapters 17-33

Nation of Nations

A Narrative History of the American Republic

Fourth Edition

James West Davidson

William E. Gienapp
Harvard University

Christine Leigh Heyrman
University of Delaware

Mark H. Lytle
Bard College

Michael B. Stoff
University of Texas, Austin

Here is not merely a nation but a teeming nation of nations

Walt Whitman

Boston   Burr Ridge, IL   Dubuque, IA   Madison, WI   New York   San Francisco   St. Louis
Bangkok   Bogotá   Caracas   Lisbon   London   Madrid
Mexico City   Milan   New Delhi   Seoul   Singapore   Sydney   Taipei   Toronto

McGraw-Hill Higher Education

A Division of The **McGraw-Hill** Companies

NATION OF NATIONS: A NARRATIVE HISTORY OF THE AMERICAN REPUBLIC,
VOLUME II: SINCE 1865, FOURTH EDITION

Published by McGraw-Hill, an imprint of The McGraw-Hill Companies, Inc., 1221 Avenue of the Americas, New York, NY 10020. Copyright © 2001, 1998, 1994, 1990 by The McGraw-Hill Companies, Inc. All rights reserved. No part of this publication may be reproduced or distributed in any form or by any means, or stored in a database or retrieval system, without the prior written consent of The McGraw-Hill Companies, Inc., including, but not limited to, in any network or other electronic storage or transmission, or broadcast for distance learning.

Some ancillaries, including electronic and print components, may not be available to customers outside the United States.

This book is printed on acid-free paper.

4 5 6 7 8 9 0 VNH/VNH 0 9 8 7 6 5 4 3 2

ISBN 0–07–231509–1

Vice president and editor-in-chief: *Thailia Dorwick*
Editorial director: *Jane E. Vaicunas*
Senior sponsoring editor: *Lyn Uhl*
Developmental editor: *Kristen Mellitt*
Marketing manager: *Janise A. Fry*
Project manager: *Mary E. Powers*
Senior media producer: *Sean Crowley*
Production supervisor: *Enboge Chong*
Cover designer: *Gino Cieslik*
Interior designer: *Maureen McCutcheon*
Photo research coordinator: *John C. Leland*
Photo research: *PhotoSearch, Inc.*
Supplement coordinator: *Brenda A. Ernzen*
Compositor: *York Graphic Services, Inc.*
Typeface: *10/12 Berkley*
Printer: *Von Hoffmann Press, Inc.*

Photo credits: At the top of the cover, ©*PhotoDisc.* Bottom left to right; ©*Corbis;* center ©*National Archives,* right ©*Bob Fitch/Take Stock.*

The credits section for this book begins on page P–1 and is considered an extension of the copyright page.

Permissions Acknowledgments
939, 1058: From Frank Levy, *Dollars and Dreams: The Changing American Income Distribution.* ©1987 Russell Sage Foundation. Used with permission of the Russell Sage Foundation. Reprinted with permission; **648:** From "I Am Changing My Name to Chrysler," by Tom Paxton. Copyright ©1980 Pax Music. All rights reserved. Used by permission; **805:** From Charles P. Kindleberg, *The World in Depression, 1929–1939* (revised ed., 1986), p.170. Copyright ©1986 The Regents of the University of California. Reprinted by permission from University of California Press.

Library of Congress has cataloged the combined version as follows:

Nation of nations : a narrative history of the American republic / James West Davidson,
William E. Gienapp, Christine Leigh Heyrman. — 4th ed.
     p. cm.
 Includes bibliographical references and index.
   ISBN 0–07–231502–4 (combined : acid-free paper) — ISBN 0–07–231507–5 (v. 1 :
acid-free paper) — ISBN 0–07–231509–1 (v. 2 : acid-free paper)
   1. United States—History. I. Davidson, James West. II. Gienapp, William E.
III. Heyrman, Christine Leigh.

E178.1 .N346 2001
973—dc21   00–036152
                                                                              CIP
www.mhhe.com

brief contents

List of Maps and Charts xv

Preface to the Fourth Edition xvii

Introduction xxvii

Map of the World xxx

Map of the United States xxxii

17 Reconstructing the Union 532

Part Four

The United States in an Industrial Age 561

18 The New South and the Trans-Mississippi West 566

19 The New Industrial Order 608

20 The Rise of an Urban Order 640

21 The Political System under Strain 668

22 The Progressive Era 706

23 The United States and the Old World Order 738

Part Five

The Perils of Democracy 771

24 The New Era 776

25 The Great Depression and the New Deal, 1929–1939 810

26 America's Rise to Globalism 852

Part Six

The United States in a Nuclear Age 899

27 Cold War America 904

28 The Suburban Era 934

29 Civil Rights and the Crisis of Liberalism 970

30 The Vietnam Era 1002

31 The Age of Limits 1036

32 The Conservative Challenge 1068

33 Nation of Nations in a Global Community 1096

Appendix A-2

contents

List of Maps and Charts   xv

Preface to the Fourth Edition   xvii

Introduction   xxvii

Map of the World   xxx

Map of the United States   xxxii

Chapter 17

Reconstructing the Union   532

Preview   532

Presidential Reconstruction   533
Lincoln's 10 Percent Plan   534
The Mood of the South   534
Johnson's Program of Reconstruction   535
The Failure of Johnson's Program   536
Johnson's Break with Congress   537
The Fourteenth Amendment   538
The Elections of 1866   538

Congressional Reconstruction   539
Post-Emancipation Societies in the Americas   540
The Land Issue   540
Impeachment   541

Reconstruction in the South   542
Black Officeholding   542
White Republicans in the South   543
The New State Governments   544
Economic Issues and Corruption   545

Black Aspirations   545
Experiencing Freedom   545
The Black Family   547
The Schoolhouse and the Church   548
New Working Conditions   549
The Freedmen's Bureau   550
Planters and a New Way of Life   551

The Abandonment of Reconstruction   552
The Election of Grant   552
The Grant Administration   553
Growing Northern Disillusionment   554
The Triumph of White Supremacy   555
The Disputed Election of 1876   556
Racism and the Failure of Reconstruction   557

Chapter Summary   558

Significant Events   559

Additional Reading   560

Counterpoint: Should Johnson Have Been Removed from Office?   542

Daily Lives: The Black Sharecropper's Cabin   546

Part Four

The United States in an Industrial Age   561

Chapter 18

The New South and the Trans-Mississippi West   566

Preview   566

The Southern Burden   568
Agriculture in the New South   568
Tenancy and Sharecropping   569
Southern Industry   570
Timber and Steel   571
The Sources of Southern Poverty   573

Life in the New South   573
Rural Life   574
The Church   575
Segregation   576

Western Frontiers   578
Western Landscapes   579
Indian Peoples and the Western Environment   580
Whites and the Western Environment: Competing Visions   581

The War for the West   582
Contact and Conflict   583
Custer's Last Stand—and the Indians'   584
Killing with Kindness   586
Borderlands   587
Ethno-Racial Identity in the New West   588

Boom and Bust in the West   589
Mining Sets a Pattern   589

The Transcontinental Railroad 591
Cattle Kingdom 592
The Final Frontier 594
A Rush for Land 594
Farming on the Plains 595
A Plains Existence 595
The Urban Frontier 597

The West and the World Economy 598
Chapter Summary 601
Significant Events 602
Additional Reading 601

Counterpoint: How to Define the Frontier? 579

Daily Lives: The Frontier Kitchen of the Plains 598

AFTER THE FACT
Historians Reconstruct the Past:
Where Have All the Bison Gone? 603

Chapter 19

The New Industrial Order 608

Preview 608
The Development of Industrial Systems 610
Natural Resources and Industrial Technology 610
Systematic Invention 611
Transportation and Communication 612
Finance Capital 613
The Corporation 615
An International Pool of Labor 616
Global Labor Network 616
Railroads: America's First Big Business 618
A Managerial Revolution 618
Competition and Consolidation 619
The Challenge of Finance 620
The Growth of Big Business 621
Growth in Consumer Goods 621
Carnegie Integrates Steel 623
Rockefeller and the Great Standard Oil Trust 624
The Mergers of J. Pierpont Morgan 624
Corporate Defenders 625
Corporate Critics 626
The Costs of Doing Business 627
The Workers' World 628
Industrial Work 629
Children, Women, and African Americans 630

The American Dream of Success 632
The Systems of Labor 632
Early Unions 632
The Knights of Labor 633
The American Federation of Labor 633
The Limits of Industrial Systems 634
Management Strikes 636
Chapter Summary 638
Significant Events 639
Additional Reading 638

Daily Lives: The Rise of Information Systems 614

Counterpoint: American Business Leaders: Robber Barons or Captains of Industry? 628

Chapter 20

The Rise of an Urban Order 640

Preview 640
A New Urban Age 641
The Urban Explosion 642
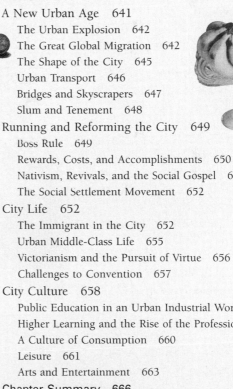
The Great Global Migration 642
The Shape of the City 645
Urban Transport 646
Bridges and Skyscrapers 647
Slum and Tenement 648
Running and Reforming the City 649
Boss Rule 649
Rewards, Costs, and Accomplishments 650
Nativism, Revivals, and the Social Gospel 651
The Social Settlement Movement 652
City Life 652
The Immigrant in the City 652
Urban Middle-Class Life 655
Victorianism and the Pursuit of Virtue 656
Challenges to Convention 657
City Culture 658
Public Education in an Urban Industrial World 658
Higher Learning and the Rise of the Professional 659
A Culture of Consumption 660
Leisure 661
Arts and Entertainment 663
Chapter Summary 666
Significant Events 667
Additional Reading 666

Counterpoint: The "New" Immigrant: Who Came and Why? 654

Daily Lives: The Vaudeville Show 664

Chapter 21

The Political System under Strain   668

Preview   668
The Politics of Paralysis   670
  Political Stalemate   670
  The Parties   671
  The Issues   672
  The White House from Hayes to Harrison   674
  Ferment in the States and Cities   676
The Revolt of the Farmers   676
  The Harvest of Discontent   677
  The Origins of the Farmers' Alliance   677
  The Alliance Peaks   678
  The Election of 1892   679
The New Realignment   680
  The Depression of 1893   680
  The Rumblings of Unrest   681
  The Battle of the Standards   681
  The Rise of Jim Crow Politics   684
  The African American Response   685
  McKinley in the White House   687
Visions of Empire   687
  European Expansion Worldwide   688
  The Shapers of American Imperialism   688
  Dreams of a Commercial Empire   693
  Prelude in the Pacific   694
The Imperial Moment   694
  Mounting Tensions   695
  The Imperial War   696
  War in Cuba   697
  Peace and Debate over Empire   698
  America's First Asian War   700
  An Open Door in China   701
Chapter Summary   703
Significant Events   704
Additional Reading   703

Counterpoint: Origins of the Welfare State 672

Daily Lives: The New Navy   690

Chapter 22

The Progressive Era   706

Preview   706
The Roots of Progressive Reform   708
  The Progressive System of Beliefs   709
  The Pragmatic Approach   709
  The Progressive Method   710

The Search for the Good Society   711
  Poverty in a New Light   712
  Expanding the "Woman's Sphere"   712
  Social Welfare   714
  Woman Suffrage   714
  Militant Suffragettes   715
Controlling the Masses   716
  Stemming the Immigrant Tide   717
  The Curse of Demon Rum   718
  Prostitution   720
The Politics of Municipal and State Reform   720
  The Reformation of the Cities   721
  Progressivism in the States   721
Progressivism Goes to Washington   723
  TR   723
  A Square Deal   724
  Bad Foods and Pristine Wilds   727
  The Troubled Taft   728
  Roosevelt Returns   729
  The Election of 1912   730
Woodrow Wilson and the Politics of Morality   731
  Early Career   731
  The Reforms of the New Freedom   732
  Labor and Social Reform   733
  The Limits of Progressive Reform   734
Chapter Summary   734
Significant Events   736
Additional Reading   735

Counterpoint: What Was Progressivism? 709

Daily Lives: "Amusing the Million"   718

Chapter 23

The United States and the Old World Order   738

Preview   738
Progressive Diplomacy   740
  Big Stick in the Caribbean   741
  A "Diplomatist of the Highest Rank"   741
  Dollar Diplomacy   742
Woodrow Wilson and Moral Diplomacy   743
  Missionary Diplomacy   743
  Intervention in Mexico   744
The Road to War   746
  The Guns of August   747
  Neutral but Not Impartial   748
  The Diplomacy of Neutrality   749

Peace, Preparedness, and the Election
    of 1916   750
  Wilson's Final Peace Offering   751
War and Society   752
  The Slaughter of Stalemate   752
  "You're in the Army Now"   753
  Mobilizing the Economy   755
  War Work   756
  Great Migrations   757
  Propaganda and Civil Liberties   757
  Over There   759

  The Influenza Pandemic of 1918–1919   760
The Lost Peace   762
  The Treaty of Versailles   762
  The Battle for the Treaty   763
  Red Scare   766
Chapter Summary   769
Significant Events   770
Additional Reading   769

Counterpoint: Why Did the United States
Go to War?   752

Daily Lives: The Doughboys Abroad   764

Part Five

The Perils of Democracy   771

Chapter 24

The New Era   776

Preview   776
The Roaring Economy   778
  Technology and Consumer Spending   778
  The Booming Construction Industry   779
  The Automobile   779
  The Business of America   782
  Welfare Capitalism   782
  The Consumer Culture   783
A Mass Society   784
  The New Woman   784
  Mass Media   787
  A Youth Culture   789
  "Ain't We Got Fun?"   790
  The Art of Alienation   791
  A "New Negro"   791
Defenders of the Faith   792
  Nativism and Immigration Restriction   793
  The "Noble Experiment"   794
  Fundamentalism versus Darwinism   795
  KKK   796

Republicans Ascendant   797
  The Politics of "Normalcy"   798
  The Policies of Mellon and Hoover   798
  Distress Signals at Home and Abroad   800
  The Election of 1928   801
The Great Bull Market   803
  The Rampaging Bull   803
  The Great Crash   804
  The Sickening Slide in Global Perspective   804
  The Causes of the Great Depression   805
Chapter Summary   807
Significant Events   808
Additional Reading   807

Daily Lives: The Beauty Contest   802

Counterpoint: Were the 1920s a Sharp
Break with the Past?   802

Chapter 25

The Great Depression and the New Deal, 1929–1939   810

Preview   810
The Human Impact of the Great Depression   811
  Hard Times   812
  The Golden Age of Radio and Film   813
  "Dirty Thirties": An Ecological Disaster   814
  Mexican Americans and Repatriation   815
  African Americans in the Depression   816
The Tragedy of Herbert Hoover   817

  The Failure of Relief   818
  The Hoover Depression Program   819
  Stirrings of Discontent   820
  The Bonus Army   821
  The Election of 1932   822
The Early New Deal (1933–1935)   823
  The Democratic Roosevelts   823
  Saving the Banks   824
  Relief for the Unemployed   825
  Planning for Industrial Recovery   827
  Planning for Agriculture   828
A Second New Deal (1935–1936)   829
  Voices of Protest   829
  The Second Hundred Days   831
  The Election of 1936   832
The American People under the New Deal   833
  The New Deal and Western Water   833
  The Limited Reach of the New Deal   834
  Tribal Rights   836

A New Deal for Women   837
The Rise of Organized Labor   838
Campaigns of the CIO   840
"Art for the Millions"   840
The End of the New Deal (1937–1940)   841
Packing the Courts   842
The New Deal at Bay   844
Recovery Abroad   844
The Legacy of the New Deal   845
Chapter Summary   848
Significant Events   850
Additional Reading   848

Daily Lives: Post Office Murals   842

Counterpoint: Assessing the New Deal   847

Chapter 26

America's Rise to Globalism   852

Preview   852
The United States in a Troubled World   854
Pacific Interests   854
Becoming a Good Neighbor   855
The Diplomacy of Isolationism   855
Neutrality Legislation   856
Inching toward War   858
Hitler's Invasion   858
Retreat from Isolationism   860
Disaster in the Pacific   862
A Global War   863
Strategies for War   863
Gloomy Prospects   864
A Grand Alliance   865
The Naval War in the Pacific   866
Turning Points in Europe   867
Those Who Fought   868
Uneasy Recruits   868
Women at War   870
War Production   870
Finding an Industrial Czar   871
Science Goes to War   872
War Work and Prosperity   873
Organized Labor   874
Women Workers   874
Global Labor Migrations   876
A Question of Rights   876
Concentration Camps   877
Minorities on the Job   879
At War with Jim Crow   880
The New Deal in Retreat   881

Winning the War and the Peace   882
The Fall of the Third Reich   882
Two Roads to Tokyo   883
Big Three Diplomacy   885
The Road to Yalta   885
The Fallen Leader   888
The Holocaust   888
A Lasting Peace   890
Atom Diplomacy   890
Chapter Summary   892
Significant Events   893
Additional Reading   894

Counterpoint: Did Roosevelt Deliberately Invite War?   863

Daily Lives: Air Power Shrinks the Globe   886

AFTER THE FACT
Historians Reconstruct the Past:
Did the Atomic Bomb Save Lives?   895

Part Six

The United States in a Nuclear Age   899

Chapter 27

Cold War America   904

Preview   904
The Rise of the Cold War   906
Cracks in the Alliance   906
The View from West and East   907
Toward Containment   908
The Truman Doctrine   909
The Marshall Plan   910
The Fall of Eastern Europe   910
The Atomic Shield versus the Iron Curtain   912
Atomic Deterrence   912
Postwar Prosperity   913
Postwar Adjustments   914
The New Deal at Bay   918
A Welfare Program for GIs   918
The Election of 1948   919
The Fair Deal   920
The Cold War at Home   920
The Shocks of 1949   922
The Loyalty Crusade   922

HUAC, Hollywood, and Unions   923
The Ambitious Senator McCarthy   924
From Cold War to Hot War and Back   924
Police Action   925
The Chinese Intervene   927
Truman versus MacArthur   928
The Global Implications of the Cold War   928
K1C2: The Election of 1952   929
The Fall of McCarthy   930
Chapter Summary   932
Significant Events   932
Additional Reading   933

Counterpoint: What Were Stalin's Intentions?   907

Daily Lives: Jackie Robinson Integrates Baseball   916

Chapter 28
The Suburban Era   934

Preview   934
The Rise of the Suburbs   936
A Boom in Babies and in Housing   936
The Boom Worldwide   936
Cities and Suburbs Transformed   938
The Culture of Suburbia   940
American Civil Religion   941
"Homemaking" Women in the Workaday World   942
A Revolution in Sexuality?   944
The Flickering Gray Screen   945
The Politics of Calm   946
Eisenhower's Modern Republicanism   946
The Conglomerate World   948
Cracks in the Consensus   949
Critics of Mass Culture   949
The Rebellion of Young America   950
Nationalism in an Age of Superpowers   951
To the Brink?   952
Brinksmanship in Asia   952
The Covert Side of the New Look   954
Nationalism Unleashed   955
The Response to *Sputnik*   956
Thaws and Freezes   957
The Cold War along a New Frontier   958
The Election of 1960   958

The Hard-Nosed Idealists of Camelot   959
The (Somewhat) New Frontier at Home   960
Kennedy's Cold War   961
Cold War Frustrations   961
Confronting Khrushchev   963
The Missiles of October   964
Chapter Summary   967
Significant Events   968
Additional Reading   967

Daily Lives: The New Suburbia   942

Counterpoint: Assessing Eisenhower   947

Chapter 29
Civil Rights and the Crisis of Liberalism   970

Preview   970
The Civil Rights Movement   972
The Changing South and African Americans   973
The NAACP and Civil Rights   974
The *Brown* Decision   975
Latino Civil Rights   976
A New Civil Rights Strategy   977
Little Rock and the White Backlash   978
A Movement Becomes a Crusade   979
Riding to Freedom   980
Civil Rights at High Tide   981
The Fire Next Time   983
Black Power   984
Violence in the Streets   984
Lyndon Johnson and the Great Society   986
The Origins of the Great Society   987
The Election of 1964   988
The Great Society   988
Immigration Reform   989
Evaluating the Great Society   990
The Reforms of the Warren Court   990
The Counterculture   992
Activists on the New Left   992
The Rise of the Counterculture   994
The Rock Revolution   995
The West Coast Scene   998
Chapter Summary   999

Significant Events 1000

Additional Reading 1001

Counterpoint: What Triggered the
Upheavals of the 1960s? 993

Daily Lives: The Politics of Dress 996

Chapter 30

The Vietnam Era 1002

Preview 1002

The Road to Vietnam 1005
Lyndon Johnson's War 1006
Rolling Thunder 1007

Social Consequences of the War 1009
The Soldiers' War 1009
The War at Home 1011

The Unraveling 1012
Tet Offensive 1012
The Shocks of 1968 1015
Chicago 1016
Revolutionary Clashes Worldwide 1017
Whose Silent Majority? 1017

Nixon's War 1019
Vietnamization—and Cambodia 1019
Fighting a No-Win War 1020
The Move toward Détente 1021

The New Identity Politics 1024
Latino Activism 1024
The Choices of American Indians 1027
Asian Americans 1028
Gay Rights 1028
Feminism 1029
Equal Rights and Abortion 1030
The Legacy of Identity Politics 1031

The End of an Era 1031

Chapter Summary 1033

Significant Events 1034

Additional Reading 1033

Counterpoint: Whose War? 1015

Daily Lives: The Race to the Moon 1022

Chapter 31

The Age of Limits 1036

Preview 1036

The Limits of Reform 1038
Consumerism 1038
Environmentalism 1039

Watergate and the Politics of Resentment 1043
Nixon's New Federalism 1043
Stagflation 1044
Social Policies and the Court 1044
Us versus Them 1045
Triumph 1046
The President's Enemies 1046
Break-In 1047
To the Oval Office 1047
Resignation 1049

A Ford, Not a Lincoln 1049
Kissinger and Foreign Policy 1049
Global Competition and the Limits of American
Influence 1050
Shuttle Diplomacy 1052
Détente 1052
The Limits of a Post-Watergate President 1053
Fighting Inflation 1054
The Election of 1976 1054

Jimmy Carter: Restoring the Faith 1056
The Search for Direction 1056
A Sick Economy 1057
Leadership, Not Hegemony 1058
The Wavering Spirit of Détente 1059
The Middle East: Hope and Hostages 1060
A President Held Hostage 1061

Chapter Summary 1062

Significant Events 1063

Additional Reading 1062

Daily Lives: Fast-Food America 1040

Counterpoint: Interpreting the
Environmental Movement 1042

AFTER THE FACT
Historians Reconstruct the Past:
The Contested Ground of Collective
Memory 1064

Chapter 32

The Conservative Challenge 1068

Preview 1068

The Conservative Rebellion 1070
The Conservative Tide Worldwide 1071
Born Again 1071
The Catholic Conscience 1072
The Media as Battleground 1073
The Election of 1980 1074

Prime Time with Ronald Reagan   1075
    The Great Communicator   1075
    The Reagan Agenda   1076
    The Reagan Revolution in Practice   1077
    The Supply-Side Scorecard   1077
    The Military Buildup   1079
Standing Tall in a Chaotic World   1080
    Terrorism in the Middle East   1080
    Mounting Frustrations in Central America   1081
    The Iran-Contra Connection   1081
    Cover Blown   1083
    From Cold War to Glasnost   1084
    The Election of 1988   1085
An End to the Cold War   1085
    A Post–Cold War Foreign Policy   1086
    The Gulf War   1086
    Domestic Doldrums   1088
    The Conservative Court   1088
    Disillusionment and Anger   1090
    The Election of 1992   1092
Chapter Summary   1094
Significant Events   1095
Additional Reading   1094

Counterpoint: Defining the New
Conservatism   1073

Daily Lives: Life in the Underclass
1090

Chapter 33

Nation of Nations in a Global Community   1096

Preview   1096
The New Immigration   1098
    The New Look of America—Asian Americans
        1099
    The New Look of America—Latinos   1102
    Illegal Immigration   1103
    Links with the Home Country   1103
    Religious Diversity   1104
The Clinton Presidency: Managing a New Global
Order   1105
    Clinton: Ambitions and Character   1105
    The New World Disorder   1106
    Yugoslavian Turmoil   1107
    Middle East Peace   1108

    Global Financial Disorder   1109

The Clinton Presidency on Trial   1110
    Recovery without Reform   1110
    The Conservative Revolution Reborn   1111
    Conservatives and the
        Feminist Agenda   1113
    Scandal   1114
    The Politics of Surplus   1115
The United States in a
Networked World   1116
    The Internet Revolution   1116
    American Workers in a
        Two-Tiered Economy   1118

Multiculturalism and Contested American Identity
1120
    African Americans and the Persistence of the Racial
        Divide   1120
    African Americans in a Full-Employment Economy
        1121
    Global Pressures in a Multicultural America   1123
Chapter Summary   1125
Significant Events   1127
Additional Reading   1126

Daily Lives: Motels as an Ethnic Niche
1100

Counterpoint: The Significance of
Impeachment   1115

Appendix   A-2

    The Declaration of Independence   A-2
    The Constitution of the United States of America
    A-5
    Presidential Elections   A-15
    Presidential Administrations   A-19
    Justices of the Supreme Court   A-30
    A Social Profile of the American Republic
    A-32
        Population   A-32
        Vital Statistics   A-32
        Life Expectancy   A-33
        The Changing Age Structure   A-33
        Regional Origin of Immigrants   A-34
        Recent Trends in Immigration   A-34
        American Workers and Farmers   A-35
        The Economy and Federal Spending   A-36
        American Wars   A-36

Bibliography   B-1
Photo Credits   P-1
Index   I-1

list of maps & charts

The Southern States during Reconstruction   540

A Georgia Plantation after the War   550

Election of 1876   556

Tenant Farmers, 1900   570

Spending on Education in the South before and after Disfranchisement   578

Natural Environment of the West   581

The Indian Frontier   585

The Mining and Cattle Frontiers   590

Steel Production, 1880 and 1914   611

Occupational Distribution, 1880 and 1920   617

Railroads, 1870–1890   620

Boom and Bust Business Cycle, 1865–1900   627

Immigration and Population, 1860–1920   643

Growth of New Orleans to 1900   646

The Voting Public, 1860–1912   670

Election of 1896   684

Balance of U.S. Imports and Exports, 1870–1910   688

Imperialist Expansion, 1900   689

The Spanish-American War   698

The United States in the Pacific   699

Woman Suffrage   716

Republican and Democratic Parties' Share of Popular Vote, 1860–1912   730

Election of 1912   731

Panama Canal—Old and New Transoceanic Routes   739

American Interventions in the Caribbean, 1898–1930   743

The Course of War in Europe, 1914–1917   748

Election of 1916   750

The Final German Offensive and Allied Counterattack, 1918   758

Areas of Population Growth   793

Election of 1928   801

Declining World Trade, 1929–1933   000

Election of 1932   822

Unemployment Relief, 1934   825

The Tennessee Valley Authority   826

Unemployment, 1925–1945   831

Federal Budget and Surplus/Deficit, 1920–1940   845

What the New Deal Did . . . 846

World War II in Europe and North Africa   859

The U-Boat War   864

The Impact of World War II on Government Spending   881

The Pacific Campaigns of World War II   884

Cold War Europe   911

Election of 1948   920

The Korean War   926

The United States Birthrate, 1900–1989   937

Average Annual Regional Migration, 1947–1960   939

Asian Trouble Spots   953

Election of 1960   958

The World of the Superpowers   962

The Spontaneous Spread of Sit-ins, February 1960   980

Civil Rights: Patterns of Protest and Unrest   985

Growth of Government, 1955–1990   990

The War in Vietnam   1008

Levels of U.S. Troops in Vietnam (at Year End)   1013

Election of 1968   1018

Oil and Conflict in the Middle East, 1948–1988   1051

OPEC Oil Prices, 1973–1987   1054

Income Projections of Two-Income Families, 1967–1984   1058

Election of 1980   1075

Poverty in America, 1970–1993   1078

The Federal Budget and Surplus/Deficit, 1945–1995   1079

Central American Conflicts, 1974–1990   1082

War with Iraq: Operation Desert Storm   1087

Election of 1992   1093

Projected Population Shifts, 1980–2050   1099

Election of 1996   1112

Map of the World

Map of the United States

preface
to the fourth edition

All good history begins with a good story: that has been the touchstone of *Nation of Nations*. Narrative is embedded in the way we understand the past; hence it will not do simply to compile an encyclopedia of American history and pass it off as a survey.

Yet the narrative keeps changing. As we constantly revalue the past, searching for more revealing ways to connect *then and there* with *here and now,* the story shifts, sometimes in subtle ways and other times more boldly. The fourth edition of this text has been significantly revised.

Changes to the Fourth Edition

Most broadly, the changes in this edition arise from our conviction that it is difficult to understand the American past without linking its story to events worldwide. Half a millennium ago, the societies of Europe, Africa, and Asia first began a sustained interaction with the civilizations of the Americas, and the interplay between newcomers and natives, between old cultures and new, continues to this day. We still introduce each of the book's six parts with Global Essays and Global Timelines. But for this edition we have also woven into the text of every chapter additional shorter narratives underscoring the global links. These narratives are not separate special features. Sometimes only a paragraph in length, sometimes an entire section, they integrate an international perspective whether we are discussing the trans-Atlantic culture of the early slave trade, the rise of postal networks, the influenza pandemic of 1918–1919, or international influences on the student rebellions of the 1960s. As the title of the book's new final chapter makes clear, we have become a "Nation of Nations in a Global Community." This narrative of the 1990s views events through twin engines of social change: the recent wave of immigration, whose upsurge rivals the influx at the beginning of the century; and the global culture being wrought by the communications revolution of the Internet and the World Wide Web.

In addition, a number of structural changes help the narrative flow as well as reflect recent scholarship.

- A new prologue, "Settling and Civilizing the Americas," is devoted to the Pre-Columbian Americas. It highlights all major regional cultures of North America by focusing on the influence of Mesoamerican classical civilizations on North American societies.

- Part 4 employs a new chapter order. Chapter 18, following our treatment of Reconstruction, now covers the New South and the trans-Mississippi West. The chapter's narrative opening (on the Exodusters) provides a useful bridge between the two chapters. Chapter 19 is now "The New Industrial Order" and Chapter 20 is "The Rise of an Urban Order."

- The coverage of the 1920s and 1930s has been consolidated into two chapters, down from three. Chapter 24, "The New Era," takes the narrative through the Great Crash, and Chapter 25 has become "The Great Depression and the New Deal, 1929–1939."

- Part 6 (the post–World War II material) has been thoroughly revised to create a more coherent, thematic story—always a challenge in narrating the most recent years of the American survey.

  - Chapter 28, "The Suburban Era," extends its political and foreign policy narrative through the Kennedy administration, ending with (and incorporating new scholarship about) the Cuban missile crisis of 1962. This approach delineates more clearly the arc of the first half of the cold war, culminating in the confrontation that brought the world the closest it has yet come to a full-scale nuclear war.

  - Chapter 29—now titled "Civil Rights and the Crisis of Liberalism"—is more strongly focused on the civil rights crusade as the era's defining social movement. Coverage begins with the social and economic background of the 1950s and is followed by *Brown v. Board of Education,* the Montgomery bus boycott, and the crisis at Little Rock—materials originally treated in "The Suburban Era." New material emphasizes the grassroots elements of the crusade and provides coverage of *Hernandez v. Texas,* the 1954 Supreme Court decision that proved as pivotal for Latino civil rights as was *Brown v. Board of Education* for African Americans. Lyndon Johnson's Great Society and the counterculture remain in this chapter, as does the material on the Warren Court.

- Chapter 30, "The Vietnam Era," reorients its coverage of minority activism by focusing on the theme of identity group politics. Coverage of the feminist movement, the Equal Rights Amendment, and abortion rights has been moved to this chapter to join expanded coverage of Latino protests (Chavez and the farmworkers, Mexican American student activists) as well as the campaigns of Native Americans, Asian Americans, and gay activists.

- Chapter 32 now focuses, as its new name suggests, on the conservative rebellion. It covers the years from 1980 to 1992.

- And, as already indicated, Chapter 33 examines the renewed immigration of the 1980s and 1990s, the rise of the Internet and its social implications, and the influence of multiculturalism on the contested nature of American identity. Of course, the chapter also recounts the turbulent events of the Clinton administration, both foreign and domestic.

New Pedagogy

Significant pedagogical changes appear in this edition. Building on the popularity of our marginal headings, we now include a succinct preview of each chapter's themes as well as bulleted summaries, which make student review easier. These and other features of the text are described on page xx–xxv.

Taken together, these revisions are substantial; indeed, they entailed a good deal of elbow grease to put into place. But we believe that a text is unlikely to remain useful to its readers unless it strives continually to rethink the ways in which history is presented. For all that, we trust that the essential character of *Nation of Nations* remains.

Acknowledgments

We are grateful to the many reviewers who were generous enough to offer comments and suggestions at various stages in our development of this manuscript. Our thanks go to:

Wayne Ackerson, *Salisbury State University*
Anita Ashendel, *Indiana University*
Rosalind Beiler, *University of Central Florida*
David Bernstein, *California State University–Long Beach*
Jo Tice Bloom, *New Mexico State University*
Jamie Bronstein, *New Mexico State University*
Randolph "Mike" Campbell, *University of North Texas*
Paul H. Carlson, *Texas Tech University*
Tom Dicke, *Southwest Missouri State University*
Vincent A. Clark, *Johnson County Community College*
Tom Dicke, *Southwest Missouri State University*
James E. Fell Jr., *University of Colorado–Denver*
Randy Finley, *Georgia Perimeter College*
Paul Gilje, *University of Oklahoma*
B. Merrielyn Ginn, *Southwest Mississippi Community College*
Laura Graves, *South Plains College*
Robert H. Greenblatt, *Massachusetts Bay Community College*
Kenneth D. Hairgrove, *San Antonio College*
April Hatfield, *Texas A&M University*
Marianne Holdzkom, *Ohio State University*
Troy R. Johnson, *California State University–Long Beach*
Beryl Graham Kalisa, *DeKalb Community College*
Perry Kaufman, *Burlington County College*
Lisa M. Lane, *Mira Costa College*
Joanne Maypole, *Front Range Community College*
Pete Meintsma, *Anoka Ramsey Community College*
Matthew Oyos, *Radford University*
Robert C. Pierce, *Foothill College*
Linda Reese, *University of Oklahoma*
John B. Reid, *Truckee Meadows Community College*
Janet E. Roberts, *California State University–San Marcos*
J. Kelly Robison, *Indiana University*
Yolanda Romero, *North Lake College*
Gail S. Rowe, *University of Northern Colorado*
Ronald Schultz, *University of Wyoming*
Rebecca S. Shoemaker, *Indiana State University*
C. Calvin Smith, *Arkansas State University*
Tom Spencer, *Northwest Missouri State University*
William Stueck, *University of Georgia*
Paul D. Travis, *Texas Woman's University*
Carol Weisenberger, *University of Northern Iowa*
Julie Willett, *Texas Tech University.*

In addition, friends and colleagues contributed their advice and constructive criticism in ways both small and large. We owe a debt to Michael Bellesiles, Lawrence A. Cardoso, Dinah Chenven, Christopher Collier, James E. Crisp, R. David Edmunds, George Forgie, Erica Gienapp, Richard John, Virginia Joyner, Philip Kuhn, Stephen E. Maizlish, Drew McCoy, James McPherson, Walter Nugent, Vicki L. Ruiz, Harold Selesky, Jim Sidbury, David J. Weber, Devra Weber, and John Womack.

The division of labor for this book was determined by our respective fields of scholarship: Christine Heyrman, the colonial era, in which Europeans, Africans, and Indians participated in the making of both a new America and a new republic; William Gienapp, the 90 years in which the young nation first flourished, then foundered on the issues of section and slavery; Michael Stoff, the post–Civil War era, in which industrialization and urbanization brought the nation more centrally into an international system regularly disrupted by depression and war; and Mark Lytle, the modern era, in which Americans finally faced the reality that even the boldest dreams of national greatness are bounded by the finite nature of power and resources both natural and human. Finally, because the need to specialize inevitably imposes limits on any project as broad as this one, our fifth author, James Davidson, served as a general editor and writer, with the intent of fitting individual parts to the whole as well as providing a measure of continuity, style, and overarching purpose. In producing this collaborative effort, all of us have shared the conviction that the best history speaks to a larger audience.

James West Davidson
William E. Gienapp
Christine Leigh Heyrman
Mark H. Lytle
Michael B. Stoff

Global Essay

Each of the book's six parts begins with an essay that sets American events into a global context.

Global Time Line

Each global essay includes a time line comparing political and social events in the United States with developments elsewhere.

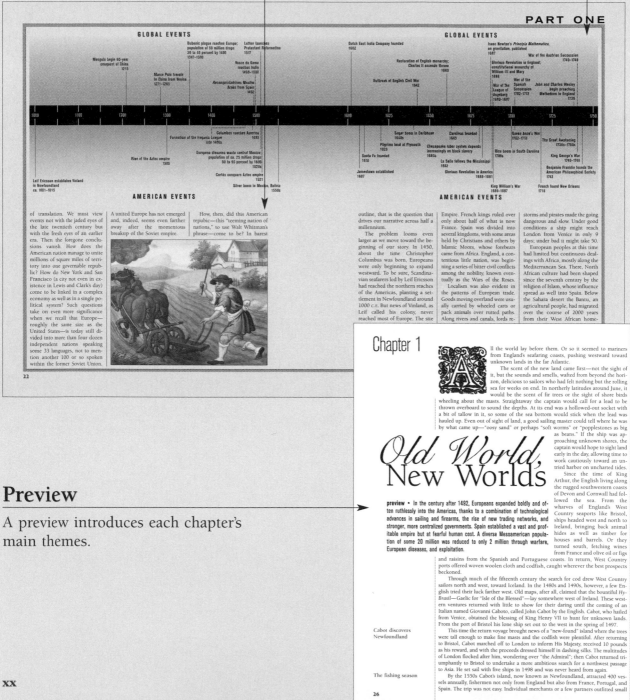

Preview

A preview introduces each chapter's main themes.

AFTER THE FACT

AFTER THE FACT
Historians Reconstruct the Past

Tracking the First Americans

Sometimes the most ordinary circumstances end in the most extraordinary discoveries. One of those times was a morning in 1908 when George McJunkin, an African American cowboy scanning the range near Folsom, New Mexico, for stray cattle, dropped his gaze into a dry gully and spotted some large bones poking through the soil. Intrigued, he began digging and found a stone spear point lodged in the skeleton. He carried the lot back to his ranch, where they remained for the next seventeen years. Then McJunkin's curiosities somehow came to the attention of archaeologists, who identified the bones as those of a long-extinct form of bison that had ranged throughout the Southwest at least ten thousand years earlier. They realized, too, that only a spear-wielding human could have killed the bison.

That discovery rocked the scientific community, which for the previous century had confidently declared that Indians had first arrived in the Americas only about 4000 years ago. Shortly thereafter, in 1932, another shock wave followed when some amateur collectors digging at Clovis, New Mexico, unearthed more bones and spearheads suspected to be even older. Finally, in 1949, scientists established the great antiquity of both finds by using "radiocarbon dating," a method for measuring decay rates of the radioactive isotope of carbon, which exists in organic matter like bone and starts to break down immediately after an organism dies. Tests revealed that the Indians whose hunting grounds were now called Folsom and Clovis had been turning bison into bones between 10,800 and 11,500 years ago.

Those conclusions pointedly raised the question of exactly how much earlier the first American an-

cestors of such hunters had come to the New World. This tantalizing mystery puzzles (and divides) archaeologists and anthropologists, geologists and historians, right down to the present. Such men and women devote their lives to the hard work of digging in remote sites or exploring the ocean's floor, to the harder work of analyzing their finds in laboratories, and to the hardest work of all —trying to make sense of what it all means. Their efforts have yielded much new evidence and increasingly sophisticated techniques for understanding its significance, but many important questions still remain unanswered.

Even so, almost all of them agree on a number of points. First, whoever the first inhabitants of the New World were, they came, originally, from the Old

Arrowheads known as Clovis points found with the skeleton of a mammoth.

World: scientists have found no fossil remains to support the view that human beings evolved into modern men and women in the Americas. Second, these first Americans were almost certainly fully evolved human beings, known as *Homo sapiens sapiens*—not the less developed forerunners, the Neanderthals, or even earlier ancestors. These *Homo sapiens sapiens* excelled at surviving anywhere, armed as they were with the intellectual ability to plan and project and the technology to sew warm clothing and to store food. About 35,000 years ago, these resourceful adapters came to predominate, edging out the Neanderthals, whose more limited skills

had restricted their settlements to the tropical and temperate parts of the world.

The new species multiplied rapidly and the pressure of its growing population pushed many into settling in less hospitable regions—including the arctic frontier of Siberia in northeastern Asia. Indeed, a third point of general agreement among scholars is that the descendants of these migrants to Siberia continued the wandering ways of their ancestors and somehow, at some time, wandered into North America by way of Alaska. The research of physical anthropologists documents key biological similarities between Siberians and American Indians. Both groups share not only certain genetic variants that suggest their descent from common ancient ancestors but also distinctive formations of the roots and crowns of their teeth known as Sinodonty.

But how did Asians get to Alaska —a region now separated from Siberia by fifty miles of ocean known as the Bering Strait? It is not impossible that they sailed across, for some *Homo sapiens sapiens* could build boats sturdy enough to navigate short stretches of open ocean. Archaeologists have discovered that Southeast Asians floated across 55 miles of ocean on rafts to reach Australia some 35,000 years ago. Could their contemporaries in northeast Asia, using bark

16

17

After the Fact: Historians Reconstruct the Past

The book includes six essays that demonstrate the methods used by historians to analyze a variety of sources, ranging from typescript drafts of presidential memoirs or handwritten notations in church records to military casualty estimates, public monuments, and even climate data derived from the analysis of tree rings.

Global Coverage

A section of the narrative in each chapter discusses American history from a global perspective, showing that the United States did not develop in a geographic or cultural vacuum and that the broad forces shaping it also influenced other nations.

---

34   Part One   The Creation of a New America

and land to rent. Wealth flowed into the coffers of sixteenth-century traders, financiers, and landlords, creating a pool of capital that those investors could plow into colonial development. Both the commercial networks and the private fortunes needed to sustain overseas trade and settlement were in place by the time of Columbus's discovery.

Political centralization   The direction of Europe's political development also paved the path for American colonization. After 1450 strong monarchs in Europe steadily enlarged the sphere of royal power at the expense of warrior lords. Henry VII, the founder of England's Tudor dynasty, Francis I of France, and Ferdinand and Isabella of Spain began the trend, forging modern nation-states by extending their political control over more territory, people, and resources. Those larger, more centrally organized states were able to marshal the resources necessary to support colonial outposts and to sustain the professional armies and navies capable of protecting empires abroad.

Europeans, Chinese, and Aztecs on the Eve of Contact

It was the growing power of monarchs as well as commercial and technological development that allowed early modern Europeans to establish permanent settlements—even empires—in another world lying an ocean away. But that conclusion raises an intriguing question: why didn't China, the most advanced civilization of the early modern world, engage in expansion and colonization? Or for that matter, if events had fallen out a little differently, why didn't the Aztecs discover and colonize Europe?

The Chinese undoubtedly possessed the capability to navigate the world's oceans and to establish overseas settlements. A succession of Ming dynasty emperors and their efficient bureaucrats marshaled China's resources to develop a thriving shipbuilding industry and trade with ports throughout southeast Asia and India. By the opening of the fifteenth century, the Chinese seemed poised for even greater maritime exploits. Seven times between 1405 and 1433, its "treasure fleet"—300 ships manned by 28,000 sailors and commanded by Zheng He (pronounced *Jung Huh*)— unfurled their red silk sails off the south China coast and sailed as far as the kingdoms of east Africa. The treasure fleet's largest craft were nine-masted junks measuring 400 feet long that boasted multiple decks and luxury cabins with balconies. By contrast, when Columbus's three ships set sail to find the Indies, the biggest was a mere 85 feet long, and the crew aboard all three totaled just 90 men.

Why China did not explore farther   Zheng He could have been another Columbus, given the resources available to him. But the Chinese had little incentive either to seek out the world's trade or to conquer and colonize new territories. Unlike western Europeans, they faced no shortages of land or food, and they led the world in producing luxury goods. On the other hand, China faced the threat of attack from the Mongols on its northwestern border—a threat so pressing that by 1433 the Ming emperor mobilized all the country's wealth and warriors to fend it off. Thus ended the great era of Chinese maritime expansion. All foreign trade was suspended, and Zheng He's treasure fleet, which would remain the world's most impressive navy until the beginning of the twentieth century, rotted away in the ports of southern China.

As for the Aztecs, their cultural development paralleled that of early modern Europe in many ways. Both societies were predominantly rural, with most inhabitants living in small villages and engaging in agriculture. In both places, merchants and specialized craftworkers clustered in cities, organized themselves into guilds, and clamored for protection from the government. Aztec noble and priestly classes, like those in Europe, took the lead in politics and religion, demanding tribute from the common people. Finally, both societies were robustly expansionist, bent on bringing new lands and peoples under their control.

Daily Lives

POPULAR ENTERTAINMENT
The Vaudeville Show

It looked like a palace or some high-toned concert hall. Patrons walked through a richly ornamented arched gateway to gold-domed, marble ticket booths. Ushers guided them through a stately lobby cushioned with velvet carpets. Large mirrors and brass ornaments hung on brocaded walls. There were "gentlemen's smoking and reading rooms" and suites with dressing cases and free toiletries for the ladies. The house seats were thick and comfortable and positioned well back from the stage. Thousands of electrical fixtures set the place aglow. When the lights dimmed, the audience sank into polite silence as the show began.

Benjamin Franklin Keith, who had worked in circuses, tent shows, and dime museums, opened the New Theatre in Boston in 1894. Seeing housewives with children as a source of new profits, resourceful theater owners such as Keith had cleaned up the bawdy variety acts of saloons and music halls, borrowed the animal and acrobat acts from circuses and Wild West shows and the comedy acts of minstrel shows, and moved them to plusher surroundings. They called the new shows "vaudeville," after the French "pieces de vaudeville" developed in eighteenth-century street fairs. In 1881 Tony Pastor opened the first vaudeville theater on Fourteenth Street in New York City. Within a decade more elegant palaces like Keith's New Theatre were opening in cities across the country.

For anywhere from a dime to two dollars, a customer could see up to nine acts—singers, jugglers, acrobats, magicians, trained animals, and comics. The mix of performers reflected the urban tempo and new urban tastes. Skits often drew on the experience of immigrants, and early comedy teams had names like "The Sport and the Jew" and "Two Funny Sauerkrauts." Divided into acts that came in rapid-fire succession, "continuous shows" ran one after another, from early morning until late at night. "After breakfast go to Proctor's," trumpeted one advertisement for F. F. Proctor's vaudeville show, "after Proctor's go to bed."

Saloon music halls had catered to a rowdy all-male, working-class clientele, who smoke, drank,

Balconies at vaudeville shows, like this one depicted by Charles Dana Gibson, attracted a wide variety of customers. Most seats cost $1, and theater owners scheduled performances from morning until night.

stomped, and jeered at the players. Vaudeville was aimed at middle-class and wealthier working-class families who could no longer afford "legitimate" theater and light opera. Keith worked diligently to make each of his theaters "as homelike" an amusement resort as it was possible to make it." Backstage he tacked signs warning performers that to say "slob" or "son-of-a-gun" or "hully-gee" unless you want to be canceled peremptorily." In the interest of good taste, all his chorus girls wore stockings. Within a few years Keith was producing the kind of show, as one comedian put it, "to which any child could bring his parents."

The audience, too, was instructed on proper behavior. No liquor was served. No cigars or cigarettes were permitted. Printed notices directed patrons to "kindly avoid the stamping of feet and pounding of canes on the floor. . . . Please don't talk during acts, as it annoys those about you, and prevents a perfect hearing of the entertainment."

Enjoying its heyday from 1890 to 1920, vaudeville became big business. Nearly one in five city dwellers went to a show once every seven days. Headliners earned $1,000 a week, theaters $20,000.

Owners like Keith and Edward Albee merged their operations into gigantic circuits. By the time of Keith's death in 1914, the Keith-Albee circuit had built an empire of 29 theaters in more than seven cities.

Vaudeville became middle-class mass entertainment. Moderate and moral, it furnished cheap recreation that also reinforced genteel values. Skits encouraged audiences to pursue success through hard work. An emerging star system made American heroes out of performers like Will Rogers and George M. Cohan and American models out of Fanny Brice and Mae West. Ethnic comics defused tensions among immigrants with spoofs that exaggerated stereotypes and stressed the common foibles of all humanity. And theatergoers learned how to behave. Order and decorum replaced the boisterous atmosphere of saloons and music halls. Vaudeville audiences adopted the middle-class ideal of behavior—passive and polite. Americans were learning to defer to experts in the realms of public conduct and popular entertainment, as elsewhere in the new urban, industrial society.

---

ambivalent about this process. Cities beckoned migrants from the countryside and immigrants from abroad with unparalleled opportunities for work and pleasure. The playwright Israel Zangwill celebrated the city's transforming power in his 1908 Broadway hit *The Melting Pot*. "The real American," one of his characters explained, "is only in the Crucible, I tell you—he will be the fusion of all the races, the coming superman."

Where Zangwill saw a melting pot with all its promise for a new superrace, champions of traditional American values, such as the widely read Protestant minister Josiah Strong, saw "a commingled mass of venomous filth and seething sin, of lust, of drunkenness, of pauperism, and crime of every sort." Both the champions and the critics of the late nineteenth century had a point. Corruption, crudeness, and disorder were no more or less a part of the cities than the vibrancy, energy, and opportunities that drew people to them. The gap between rich and poor yawned most widely in cities. As social critic Henry George observed, progress and poverty seemed to go hand in hand.

In the end moral judgments, whether pro or con, missed the point. Cities stood at the hubs of the new industrial order. All Americans, whatever they thought about the new urban world, had to search for ways to make that world work.

Daily Lives

Every chapter contains an essay focusing on one of five themes that give insight into the lives of ordinary Americans: clothing and fashion; time and travel; food, drink, and drugs; public space/private space; and popular entertainment.

Marginal Headings

Succinct notes in the margins highlight key terms and concepts.

Counterpoint

Each chapter incorporates a discussion that explores contrasting ways historians have interpreted one of the chapter's central topics. These discussions are integrated into the narrative to emphasize that such debates are an inevitable and productive part of writing history.

---

654   Part Four   The United States in an Industrial Age

Entertainment in immigrant neighborhoods often resulted in a cross-fertilization of cultures. The New Cathay Boys Club Band, a marching band of Chinese Americans (shown here), was formed in San Francisco's Chinatown in 1911. It was inspired by the Columbia Park Boys Band of Italians from nearby North Beach and played American music only.

Special situation of the Chinese

The Chinese were an exception to the pattern. The ban on the immigration of Chinese laborers in the 1880s (page 651) had frozen the sex ratio of Chinese communities into a curious imbalance. Like other immigrants, most Chinese newcomers had been single men. In the wake of the ban, those in the United States could not bring over their wives and families. Nor by law in 13 states could they marry whites. With few women, Chinese communities suffered from high rates of prostitution, large numbers of gangs and secret societies, and low birth totals. When the San Francisco earthquake and fire destroyed birth records in 1906, resourceful Chinese immigrants created "paper sons" (and less often "paper daughters") by forging American birth certificates and claiming their China-born children as American citizens.

counterpoint

The "New" Immigrants: Who Came and Why?

With so many immigrants coming to America, it is no wonder that historians have disagreed over who came and why. Early historians of immigration focused on those arriving in the United States. These newcomers were depicted as an undifferentiated mass of European peasants, striking out on their own, often poverty-stricken, sometimes persecuted, sometimes eager for opportunity. The march of so many immigrants into American life, these historians argue, both reflected and helped to create the uniqueness of the American experience.

More recently, historians have placed immigration to the United States in global perspective by examining both receiving and sending countries. In an international context, the United States moves from the center of immigration history to the fringes of the story as one of many countries attracting migrants in an expanding world economy. Immigration to the United States thus becomes part of an international labor exchange and the American experience less exceptional and more comparable to that of other receiving nations such as Argentina and Australia. As for the immigrants themselves, the international perspective underscores the diversity of the newcomers and of their motives. Landless young men from Italy hoped to return to buy plots in Italy, whereas the sons of cattle farmers from western Norway left for good because inheritance laws kept them from owning farms at home. Other immigrants to the United States, fewer in number, came not from Europe but from Latin America, Africa, the Caribbean, and Asia.

Summary

A bulleted summary reinforces each chapter's main points.

Significant Events

A chronology at the end of each chapter shows the temporal relationship among important events.

Additional Reading

Annotated references to both classic studies and recent scholarship encourage further pursuit of the topics and events covered in the chapter.

that role because they trusted that a large republic, with its millions of citizens, would yield more of that scarce resource—disinterested gentlemen dedicated to serving the public good. Such gentlemen, in Madison's words, "whose enlightened views and virtuous sentiments render them superior to local prejudices," would fill the small number of national offices.

Not all the old revolutionaries agreed. Anti-Federalists drawn from the ranks of ordinary Americans still believed that common people were more virtuous and gentlemen more interested than the Federalists allowed. "These lawyers and men of learning, and moneyed men, that talk so finely," complained one Anti-Federalist, would "get all the power and all of the money into their own hands, and then they will swallow up all us little folks." Instead of being dominated by enlightened gentlemen, the national government should be composed of representatives from every social class and occupational group.

The narrow majorities by which the Constitution was ratified reflected the continuing influence of such sentiments, as well as fear that the states were surrendering too much power. That fear made Patrick Henry so ardent an Anti-Federalist that he refused to attend the Constitutional Convention in 1787, saying that he "smelt a rat." "I am not a Virginian, but an American," Henry had once declared. Most likely he was lying. Or perhaps Patrick Henry, a southerner and a slaveholder, could see his way clear to being an "American" only so long as sovereignty remained firmly in the hands of the individual states. Henry's convictions, 70 years hence, would rise again to haunt the Union.

chapter summary

Leading Americans would give more thought to federalism, the organization of a United States, as the events of the postrevolutionary period revealed the weaknesses of the state and national governments.

- For a decade after independence, the revolutionaries were less committed to creating a single national republic than to organizing 13 separate state republics, each dominated by popularly elected legislatures.

- The Articles of Confederation provided for a government by a national legislature, but left the crucial power of the purse, as well as all final power to make and execute laws, entirely to the states.

- Many conflicts in the new republic were occasioned by westward expansion, which created both inter-

national difficulties with Britain and Spain and internal tensions over the democratization of state legislatures.

- In the wake of the Revolution, ordinary Americans struggled to define republican society; workers began to organize, some women claimed a right to greater political, legal, and educational opportunities, and religious dissenters called for disestablishment.

- In the mid-1780s the political crisis of the Confederation came to a head, prompted by the controversy over the Jay-Gardoqui Treaty and Shays's Rebellion.

- The Constitutional Convention of 1787 produced an entirely new frame of government that established a truly national republic and provided for a separation of powers among a judiciary, a bicameral legislature, and a strong executive.

- The Anti-Federalists, opponents of the Constitution, softened their objections when promised a bill of rights after ratification, which was accomplished by 1789.

- Tecumseh's movement collapsed with his death during the War of 1812.

- France and Britain both interfered with neutral rights, and the United States went to war against Britain in 1812.

- In the years after 1815 there was a surge in American nationalism.

  - The Transcontinental Treaty with Spain (1819) foreshadowed American expansion by drawing a boundary line to the Pacific.

- The Monroe Doctrine (1823) barred European intervention in the Western Hemisphere.

- Britain's recognition of American sovereignty after 1815 ended the threat of foreign interference in America's internal affairs.

additional reading

A good survey of the presidencies of Jefferson and Madison is Marshall Smelser, *The Democratic Republic* (1968). Drew R. McCoy, *The Elusive Republic* (1980) skillfully analyzes the dilemmas Jefferson and Madison confronted in power. An important study of the Federalist party is David Hackett Fischer, *The Revolution of American Conservatism* (1965). For the origins of the War of 1812, see Roger H. Brown, *The Republic in Peril* (1964). The biographies of Jefferson and Madison, listed in the bibliography, examine political developments in this period in detail.

Malcolm J. Rohrbough, *The Trans-Appalachian Frontier* (1978) traces the process of western settlement, while other

aspects of western society are treated in John Boles, *The Great Revival in the South* (1972) and R. David Edmunds, *The Shawnee Prophet* (1983). Donald Jackson, *Thomas Jefferson and the Stony Mountains: Exploring the West from Monticello* (1979) is a fascinating analysis of western exploration in this period. The journals of the Lewis and Clark expedition, which have been published in several editions, are invaluable; a recent history is Stephen E. Ambrose, *Undaunted Courage* (1996).

The first part of George Dangerfield, *The Awakening of American Nationalism* (1965), capably covers Monroe's administration. Samuel F. Bemis traces American foreign policy during and after the war in *John Quincy Adams and the Foundations of American Foreign Policy* (1949). Ernest R. May, *The Making of the Monroe Doctrine* (1976), is the best study of the subject. For a fuller list of readings, see the Bibliography.

Significant Events

Year	Event
1798	1790s Second Great Awakening begins
1800	
1801	1801 Adams's "midnight" appointments; Marshall becomes chief justice; Jefferson inaugurated in Washington; Cane Ridge revival
1802	1802 Judiciary Act of 1801 repealed
1803	1803 *Marbury v. Madison*; Louisiana Purchase; war resumes between Great Britain and France
1804	1804–1806 Lewis and Clark expedition
1805	1805 Prophet's revivals begin
1806	
1807	1807 *Chesapeake* affair; Embargo Act passed
1808	1808 Madison elected president
1809	1809 Tecumseh's confederacy organized
1810	1810 *Fletcher v. Peck*; 1810–1813 West Florida annexed
1811	1811 Battle of Tippecanoe
1812	1812 War declared against Great Britain
1813	1813 Battle of Lake Erie; Tecumseh killed; 1813–1814 Creek War
1814	1814 Washington burned; Hartford Convention; Treaty of Ghent signed
1815	1815 Battle of New Orleans
1816	1816 Monroe elected president
1817	
1818	1818 United States–Canada boundary fixed to the Rockies; joint occupation of Oregon established
1819	1819 Transcontinental Treaty with Spain; United States acquires Florida
1823	1823 Monroe Doctrine proclaimed

Initial Blocks and Printer Ornaments

History records change over time in countless ways. The flow of history is reflected not only in the narrative of this text, but in the decorative types used in its design.

 Over the years printers have used ornamental designs to enliven their texts. Each chapter of *Nation of Nations* incorporates an ornament created during the period being written about. Often these ornaments are from printers' specimen books, produced by type manufacturers so printers could buy such designs. In other chapters the ornaments are taken from printed material of the era.

The initial blocks—the large decorative initials beginning the first word of every chapter—are drawn from type styles popular during the era covered by each of the book's six parts.

Part 1 uses hand-engraved initials of the sort imported from England and Europe by colonial printers in the seventeenth and eighteenth centuries.

 Part 2 displays mortised initial blocks. These ornaments had holes cut in the middle of the design so a printer could insert the initial of choice. These holes provided greater flexibility when the supply of ornaments was limited.

Part 3 features initial blocks cut from wood, an approach common in the early and middle nineteenth century. This design, Roman X Condensed, allowed more letters to be squeezed into a limited space.

Part 4 makes use of a more ornamental initial block common in the late nineteenth and early twentieth century. Some Victorian designs became quite ornate. This font, a style that is relatively reserved, is Latin Condensed.

Part 5 illustrates an initial block whose clean lines reflect the Art Deco movement of the 1920s and 1930s. Printers of the New Era turned away from the flowery nineteenth-century styles. This font is Beverly Hills.

Part 6 features an informal style, Brush Script Regular. First introduced during World War II, this typeface reflects the more casual culture that blossomed during the postwar era.

Information about Supplements

The supplements listed here accompany *Nation of Nations: A Narrative History of the American People,* fourth edition. Please contact your local McGraw-Hill representative for details concerning policies, prices, and availability, as some restrictions may apply.

For the Student

Packaged free with every copy of the book, an **Interactive Study Guide CD-ROM** (0072373792) includes quizzes containing multiple-choice, true-false, and fill-in questions for every chapter; an Internet primer; and more.

The **Student Study Guide with Map Exercises** (Volume I: 0072315040; Volume II: 0072315059) includes for each chapter a list of learning objectives, key events, quizzes, map identifications, primary source documents, and other resources to help students master the material covered in the text.

Located on the book's Web site www.mhhe.com/davidson4, the **Student Online Learning Center** offers interactive maps with exercises, extensive Web links, quizzes, and more.

For the Instructor

The **Instructor's Manual/Test Bank** (0072373725) offers a variety of resources for instructors, including ideas for classroom discussions and lecture strategies. Numerous multiple-choice, fill-in, and essay questions are provided for instructors to use in constructing exams.

Computerized Test Banks for both the Mac (007237375X) and PC (0072373768) are also available.

A set of **Overhead Transparencies** (0072315067) includes maps and images from the textbook.

A **Presentation Manager CD-ROM** (0072373733) provides materials for instructors to use in the classroom, including PowerPoint presentations and electronic versions of the maps in the textbook.

A set of **Audiotapes** (Volume I: 0072373776; Volume II: 0072373784) features conversations with the authors about topics covered in the text.

about the authors

James West Davidson received his Ph.D. from Yale University. A historian who has pursued a full-time writing career, he is the author of numerous books, among them *After the Fact: The Art of Historical Detection* (with Mark H. Lytle), *The Logic of Millennial Thought: Eighteenth-Century New England,* and *Great Heart: The History of a Labrador Adventure* (with John Rugge).

William E. Gienapp has a Ph.D. from the University of California, Berkeley. He taught at the University of Wyoming before going to Harvard University, where he is Professor of History. In 1988 he received the Avery O. Craven Award for his book *The Origins of the Republican Party, 1852–1856*. His essay on "The Antebellum Era" appeared in the *Encyclopedia of Social History* (1992). Currently he is at work on *Abraham Lincoln and Civil War America.*

Christine Leigh Heyrman is Professor of History at the University of Delaware. She received a Ph.D. in American Studies from Yale University and is the author of *Commerce and Culture: The Maritime Communities of Colonial Massachusetts, 1690–1750*. Her book *Southern Cross: The Beginnings of the Bible Belt* was awarded the Bancroft Prize in 1998.

Mark H. Lytle, who received a Ph.D. from Yale University, is Professor of History and Environmental Studies and Chair of the American Studies Program at Bard College. He was recently appointed a Fulbright Scholar to teach at University College, Dublin, in Ireland. His publications include *The Origins of the Iranian-American Alliance, 1941–1953* and *After the Fact: The Art of Historical Detection* (with James West Davidson) and "An Environmental Approach to American Diplomatic History," in *Diplomatic History*. He is at work on *The Uncivil War: America in the Vietnam Era.*

Michael B. Stoff is Associate Professor of History at the University of Texas at Austin. The recipient of a Ph.D. from Yale University, he has received many teaching awards, most recently the Friars' Centennial Teaching Excellence Award. He is the author of *Oil, War, and American Security: The Search for a National Policy on Foreign Oil, 1941–1947* and coeditor (with Jonathan Fanton and R. Hal Williams) of *The Manhattan Project: A Documentary Introduction to the Atomic Age.*

introduction

History is both a discipline of rigor, bound by rules and scholarly methods, and something more: the unique, compelling, even strange way in which we humans define ourselves. We are all the sum of the tales of thousands of people, great and small, whose actions have etched their lines upon us. History supplies our very identity—a sense of the social groups to which we belong, whether family, ethnic group, race, class, or gender. It reveals to us the foundations of our deepest religious beliefs and traces the roots of our economic and political systems. It explores how we celebrate and grieve, how we sing the songs we sing, how we weather the illnesses to which time and chance subject us. It commands our attention for all these good reasons and for no good reason at all, other than a fascination with the way the myriad tales play out. Strange that we should come to care about a host of men and women so many centuries gone, some with names eminent and familiar, others unknown but for a chance scrap of information left behind in an obscure letter.

Yet we do care. We care about Sir Humphrey Gilbert, "devoured and swallowed up of the Sea" one black Atlantic night in 1583; we care about George Washington at Kips Bay, red with fury as he takes a riding crop to his retreating soldiers. We care about Octave Johnson, a slave fleeing through Louisiana swamps trying to decide whether to stand and fight the approaching hounds or take his chances with the bayou alligators; we care about Clara Barton, her nurse's skirts so heavy with blood from the wounded, that she must wring them out before tending to the next soldier. We are drawn to the fate of Chinese laborers, chipping away at the Sierras' looming granite; of a Georgian named Tom Watson seeking to forge a colorblind political alliance; and of desperate immigrant mothers, kerosene lamps in hand, storming Brooklyn butcher shops that had again raised prices. We follow, with a mix of awe and amusement, the fortunes of the quirky Henry Ford ("Everybody wants to be somewhere he ain't"), turning out identical automobiles, insisting his factory workers wear identical expressions ("Fordization of the Face").

We trace the career of young Thurgood Marshall, crisscrossing the South in his own "little old beat-up '29 Ford," typing legal briefs in the back seat, trying to get black teachers to sue for equal pay, hoping to get his people somewhere they weren't. The list could go on and on, spilling out as it did in Walt Whitman's *Leaves of Grass:* "A southerner soon as a northerner, a planter nonchalant and hospitable, / A Yankee bound my own way . . . a Hoosier, a Badger, a Buckeye, a Louisianian or Georgian. . . ." Whitman embraced and celebrated them all, inseparable strands of what made him an American and what made him human:

> In all people I see myself, none more and not one a barleycorn less, And the good or bad I say of myself I say of them.

To encompass so expansive an America, Whitman turned to poetry; historians have traditionally chosen *narrative* as their means of giving life to the past. That mode of explanation permits them to interweave the strands of economic, political, and social history in a coherent chronological framework. By choosing narrative, historians affirm the multicausal nature of historical explanation—the insistence that events be portrayed in context. By choosing narrative, they are also acknowledging that, although long-term economic and social trends shape societies in significant ways, events often take on a logic (or an illogic) of their own, jostling one another, being deflected by unpredictable personal decisions, sudden deaths, natural catastrophes, and chance. There are literary reasons, too, for preferring a narrative approach, because it supplies a dramatic force usually missing from more structural analyses of the past.

In some ways, surveys such as this text are the natural antithesis of narrative history. They strive, by definition, to be comprehensive: to furnish a broad, orderly exposition of their chosen field. Yet to cover so much ground in so limited a space necessarily deprives readers of the context of more detailed accounts. Then, too, the resurgence of social history—with its concern for class and race, patterns of rural and urban life, the spread of market and industrial economies—lends itself to more analytic, less chronological treatments. The challenge facing historians is to incorporate these areas of research without losing the story's narrative drive or the chronological flow that orients readers to the more familiar events of our past.

With the cold war of the past half-century at an end, there has been increased attention to the worldwide breakdown of so many nonmarket economies and, by inference, to the greater success of the market societies of the United States and other capitalist nations. As our own narrative makes clear, American society and politics have indeed come together centrally in the marketplace. What Americans produce, how and where they produce it, and the desire to buy cheap and sell dear have been defining elements in every era. That market orientation has created unparalleled abundance and reinforced striking inequalities, not the least a society in which, for two centuries, human beings themselves were bought and sold. It has made Americans powerfully provincial in protecting local interests and internationally adventurous in seeking to expand wealth and opportunity.

It goes without saying that Americans have not always produced wisely or well. The insistent drive toward material plenty has levied a heavy tax on the global environment. Too often quantity has substituted for quality, whether we talk of cars, education, or culture. When markets flourish, the nation abounds with confidence that any problem, no matter how intractable, can be solved. When markets fail, however, the fault lines of our political and social systems become all too evident.

In the end, then, it is impossible to separate the marketplace of boom and bust and the world of ordinary Americans from the corridors of political maneuvering or the ceremonial pomp of an inauguration. To treat political and social history as distinct spheres is counterproductive. The primary question of this narrative—how the fledgling, often tumultuous confederation of "these United States" managed to transform itself into an enduring republic—is not only political but necessarily social. In order to survive, a republic must resolve conflicts between citizens of different geographic regions and economic classes, of diverse racial and ethnic origins, of competing religions and ideologies. The resolution of these conflicts has produced tragic consequences, perhaps, as often as noble ones. But tragic or noble, the destiny of these states cannot be understood without comprehending both the social and the political dimensions of the story.

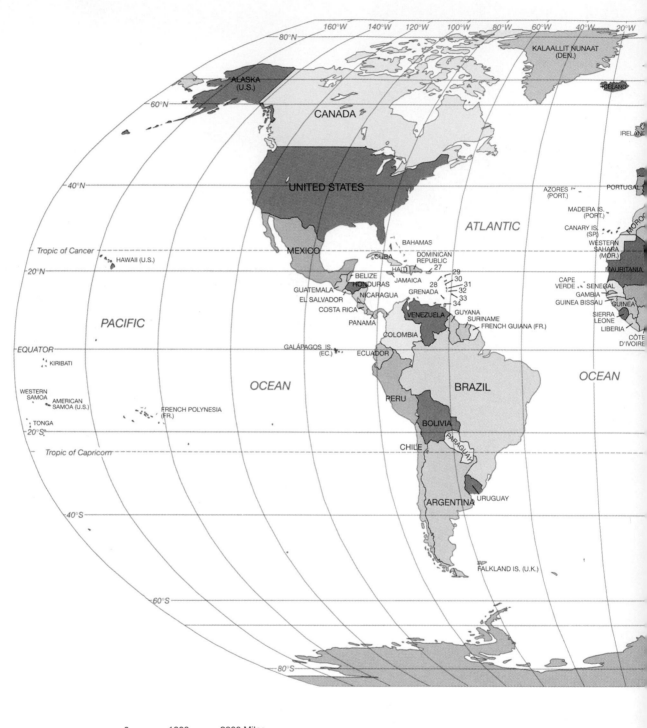

160°W 140°W 120°W 100°W 80°W 60°W 40°W 20°W

80°N

KALAALLIT NUNAAT
(DEN.)

ALASKA
(U.S.)

ICELAND

60°N

CANADA

IRELAND

40°N

UNITED STATES

ATLANTIC

AZORES
(PORT.)

PORTUGAL

MADEIRA IS.
(PORT.)

CANARY IS.
(SP.)

MOROCCO

Tropic of Cancer

HAWAII (U.S.)

MEXICO

BAHAMAS

CUBA

DOMINICAN
REPUBLIC

WESTERN
SAHARA
(MOR.)

MAURITANIA

20°N

HAITI

27

29

CAPE
VERDE

SENEGAL

BELIZE

JAMAICA

28

30

31

GAMBIA

GUATEMALA
EL SALVADOR

HONDURAS

NICARAGUA

GRENADA

32

33

GUINEA BISSAU

GUINEA

COSTA RICA

34

SIERRA
LEONE

LIBERIA

PANAMA

VENEZUELA

GUYANA
SURINAME

FRENCH GUIANA (FR.)

CÔTE
D'IVOIRE

PACIFIC

COLOMBIA

GALÁPAGOS IS.
(EC.)

ECUADOR

EQUATOR

KIRIBATI

OCEAN

BRAZIL

OCEAN

WESTERN
SAMOA

AMERICAN
SAMOA (U.S.)

FRENCH POLYNESIA
(FR.)

PERU

TONGA

20°S

BOLIVIA

Tropic of Capricorn

CHILE

PARAGUAY

40°S

ARGENTINA

URUGUAY

FALKLAND IS. (U.K.)

60°S

80°S

0   1000   2000 Miles

0   1000   2000 Kilometers

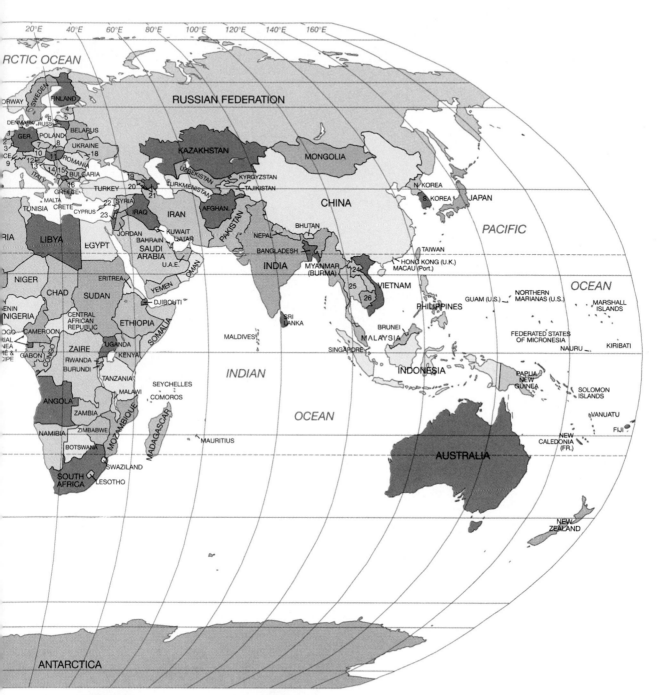

1. NETHERLANDS
2. BELGIUM
3. LUXEMBOURG
4. ESTONIA
5. LATVIA
6. LITHUANIA
7. CZECH REPUBLIC
8. SLOVAKIA
9. SWITZERLAND
10. AUSTRIA
11. HUNGARY
12. SLOVENIA
13. CROATIA
14. BOSNIA AND HERCEGOVINA
15. YUGOSLAVIA
16. MACEDONIA
17. ALBANIA
18. MOLDOVA
19. GEORGIA
20. ARMENIA
21. AZERBAIJAN
22. LEBANON
23. ISRAEL
24. LAOS
25. THAILAND
26. CAMBODIA
27. PUERTO RICO (U.S.)
28. ST. KITTS AND NEVIS
29. ANTIGUA AND BARBUDA
30. DOMINICA
31. ST. LUCIA
32. ST. VINCENT AND THE GRENADINES
33. BARBADOS
34. TRINIDAD AND TOBAGO

Chapter 17

Reconstructing the UNION

Joseph Davis had had enough. Well on in years and financially ruined by the war, he decided to quit farming. In November 1866, he sold his Mississippi plantations Hurricane and Brierfield to Benjamin Montgomery and his sons. The sale of southern plantations was common enough after the war, but this transaction was bound to attract attention, since Joseph Davis was the elder brother of Jefferson Davis. Indeed, before the war the Confederate president had operated Brierfield as his own plantation, although his brother retained legal title to it. In truth, the sale was so unusual that the parties involved agreed to keep it secret, since the Montgomerys were black, and Mississippi law prohibited African Americans from owning land.

Though a slave, Montgomery had been the business manager of the two Davis plantations before the war. He had also operated a store on Hurricane Plantation for white as well as black customers with his own line of credit in New Orleans. In 1863 Montgomery fled to the North, but when the war was over, he returned to Davis Bend, where the federal government was leasing plots of the land on confiscated plantations, including Hurricane and Brierfield, to black farmers. Montgomery quickly emerged as the leader of the African American community at the Bend.

Then, in 1866, President Andrew Johnson pardoned Joseph Davis and restored his lands. By then Davis was over 80 years old and lacked the will and stamina to rebuild, yet unlike many ex-slaveholders, he still felt bound by obligations to his former slaves. Convinced that with proper encouragement African Americans could succeed economically in freedom, he sold his land secretly to Benjamin Montgomery. Only when the law prohibiting African Americans from owning land was overturned in 1867 did Davis publicly confirm the sale to his former slave.

For his part, Montgomery undertook to create a model society at Davis Bend based on mutual cooperation. He rented land to black farmers, hired others to work his own fields, sold supplies on credit, and ginned and marketed the crops. To the growing African American community, he preached the gospel of hard work, self-reliance, and education.

Various difficulties dogged these black farmers, including the destruction caused by the war, several disastrous floods, insects, droughts, and declining cotton prices. Yet before long, cotton production exceeded that of the prewar years, and in 1870 the black families at Davis Bend produced 2500 bales. The Montgomerys eventually acquired another plantation and owned 5500 acres, which made them reputedly the third largest planters in the state. They won national and international awards for the quality of their cotton. Their success demonstrated what African Americans, given a fair chance, might accomplish.

The experiences of Benjamin Montgomery during the years after 1865 were not those of most black southerners, who did not own land or have a powerful white benefactor. Yet Montgomery's dream of economic independence was shared by all

preview • Reconstruction became the battleground of attempts to define the new shape of the Union. Congress rejected Andrew Johnson's lenient terms for the South's reentry and enacted a program that included the principle of black suffrage. African Americans asserted their freedom by uniting divided families, establishing churches, and seeking education and land. But when northern whites became disillusioned with reform, the ideology of white supremacy brought Reconstruction to an end.

A Visit from the Old Mistress, by Winslow Homer, captures the conflicting, often awkward, emotions felt by both races after the war.

African Americans. As one black veteran noted, "Every colored man will be a slave, and feel himself a slave until he can raise him own bale of cotton and put him own mark upon it and say dis is mine!" Blacks could not gain effective freedom simply through a proclamation of emancipation. They needed economic power, including their own land that no one could unfairly take away.

For nearly two centuries the laws had prevented slaves from possessing such economic power. If those conditions were to be overturned, black Americans needed political power too. Thus the Republic would have to be reconstructed to give African Americans political power that they had been previously denied.

War, in its blunt way, had roughed out the contours of a solution, but only in broad terms. Clearly, African Americans would no longer be enslaved. The North, with its industrial might, would be the driving force in the nation's economy and retain the dominant political voice. But beyond that, the outlines of a reconstructed Republic remained vague. Would African Americans receive effective power? How would the North and the South readjust their economic and political relations? These questions lay at the heart of the problem of Reconstruction.

Presidential Reconstruction

Throughout the war Abraham Lincoln had considered Reconstruction his responsibility. Elected with less than 40 percent of the popular vote in 1860, he was acutely aware that once the states of the Confederacy were restored to the Union, the Republicans would be weakened unless they ceased to be a sectional party. By a generous peace, Lincoln hoped to attract former Whigs in the South, who supported many of the Republicans' economic policies, and build up a southern wing of the party.

Lincoln's 10 Percent Plan

Lincoln outlined his program in a Proclamation of Amnesty and Reconstruction issued in December 1863. When a minimum of 10 percent of the qualified voters from 1860 took a loyalty oath to the Union, they could organize a state government. The new state constitution had to be republican in form, abolish slavery, and provide for black education, but Lincoln did not insist that high-ranking Confederate leaders be barred from public life. Once these requirements had been met, the president would recognize the new civilian state government.

Disavowing any thought of trying prominent Confederate leaders, Lincoln indicated that he would be generous in granting pardons and did not rule out compensation for slave property. Moreover, while he privately suggested permitting some black men to vote in the disloyal states, "as for instance, the very intelligent and especially those who have fought gallantly in our ranks," he did not demand social or political equality for black Americans, and he recognized pro-Union governments in Louisiana, Arkansas, and Tennessee that allowed only white men to vote.

Radical Republicans   The Radical Republicans found Lincoln's approach much too lenient. Strongly antislavery, Radical members of Congress had led the struggle to make emancipation a war aim. Now they were in the forefront in advocating rights for the freedpeople. They were also disturbed that Lincoln had not enlisted Congress in devising Reconstruction policy. Lincoln argued that the executive branch should bear the responsibility for restoring proper relations with the former Confederate states. The Radicals, on the other hand, believed that it was the duty of Congress to set the terms under which states would regain their rights in the Union. Though the Radicals often disagreed on other matters, they were united in a determination to readmit southern states only after slavery had been ended, black rights protected, and the power of the planter class destroyed.

Wade-Davis bill   Under the direction of Senator Benjamin Wade of Ohio and Representative Henry Winter Davis of Maryland, Congress formulated a much stricter plan of Reconstruction. It proposed that Confederate states would be ruled temporarily by a military governor, required half the white adult males to take an oath of allegiance before drafting a new state constitution, and restricted political power to the hard-core Unionists in each state. When the Wade-Davis bill passed on the final day of the 1864 congressional session, Lincoln exercised his right of a pocket veto.* Still, his own program could not succeed without the assistance of Congress, which refused to seat Unionist representatives who had been elected from Louisiana or Arkansas. As the war drew to a close, Lincoln appeared ready to make concessions to the Radicals. He suggested that he might favor different—and conceivably more rigorous—Reconstruction plans for different states. At his final cabinet meeting, he approved placing the defeated South temporarily under military rule. But only a few days later Booth's bullet found its mark, and Lincoln's final approach to Reconstruction would never be known.

The Mood of the South

Northerners worried about the attitude of ex-Confederates at war's end. In the wake of defeat, the immediate reaction among white southerners was one of shock, despair, and hopelessness. Some former Confederates, of course, were openly antagonistic. A North Carolina innkeeper remarked bitterly that Yankees had stolen his slaves, burned his house, and killed all his sons, leaving him only one privilege: "To

---

*If a president does not sign a bill after Congress has adjourned, it has the same effect as a veto.

hate 'em. I git up at half-past four in the morning, and sit up till twelve at night, to hate 'em." Most Confederate soldiers were less defiant, having had their fill of war. Even among hostile civilians the feeling was widespread that the South must accept northern terms. A South Carolina paper admitted that "the conqueror has the right to make the terms, and we must submit."

This psychological moment was critical. To prevent a resurgence of resistance, the president needed to lay out in unmistakable terms what white southerners had to do to regain their old status in the Union. Any confusion in policy, or wavering on the peace terms, could only increase the likelihood of resistance. Perhaps even a clear and firm policy would not have been enough. But with Lincoln's death, the executive power came to rest in far less capable hands.

Johnson's Program of Reconstruction

Andrew Johnson, the new president, had been born in North Carolina and eventually moved to Tennessee, where he worked as a tailor. Barely able to read and write when he married, he rose to political power by portraying himself as the champion of the people against the wealthy planter class. "Some day I will show the stuck-up aristocrats who is running the country," he vowed as he began his political career. He had not opposed slavery before the war—in fact, he hoped to disperse slave ownership more widely in southern society. Although he accepted emancipation as one consequence of the war, Johnson remained a confirmed racist. "Damn the negroes," he said during the war, "I am fighting these traitorous aristocrats, their masters."

Johnson's character and values

Andrew Johnson's contentious personality masked a deep-seated insecurity.

Because Johnson disliked the planter class so strongly, Republican Radicals in Congress expected him to uphold their views on Reconstruction. In fact, the new president did speak of trying Confederate leaders and breaking up planters' estates. Unlike most Republicans, however, Johnson strongly supported states' rights and opposed government aid to business. Given such differences, conflict between the president and the majority in Congress was inevitable, but Johnson's personality and political shortcomings made the situation worse. Scarred by his humble origins, he remained throughout his life an outsider. When challenged or criticized, he became tactless and inflexible, alienating even those who sought to work with him.

At first, Johnson seemed to be following Lincoln's policy of quickly restoring the southern states to their rightful place in the Union. He prescribed a loyalty oath ordinary white southerners would have to take to have their property, except for slaves, restored and to regain their civil and political rights. Like Lincoln, Johnson excluded high Confederate officials from this group, but he added those with property worth over $20,000, which included his old foes in the planter class. These groups had to apply to the president for individual pardons.

Johnson's program

Loyal state governments could be formed after a provisional governor, appointed by the president, called a convention to draft a new state constitution. Voters and delegates had to qualify under the 1860 state election laws and take the new loyalty oath. Once elections were held to choose a governor, legislature, and members of Congress, Johnson announced he would recognize the new state government, revoke martial law, and withdraw Union troops. Again, the plan was similar to Lincoln's, though more lenient. Unlike the formula Lincoln adopted, Johnson spoke only informally of requiring southern states to repeal their ordinances of secession, repudiate the Confederate debt, and ratify the proposed Thirteenth Amendment abolishing slavery.

The Failure of Johnson's Program

Southern defiance

The southern delegates who met to construct new governments soon demonstrated that they were in no frame of mind to follow Johnson's recommendations. Several states merely repealed instead of repudiating their ordinances of secession, rejected the Thirteenth Amendment, or refused to repudiate the Confederate debt.

Nor did any of the new governments allow African Americans any political rights or make any effective provisions for black education. In addition, each state passed a series of laws, often modeled on its old slave code, that applied only to African Americans. These "black codes" did grant African Americans some rights that had not been enjoyed by slaves. They legalized marriages from slavery and allowed black southerners to hold and sell property and to sue and be sued in state courts. Yet their primary purpose was to keep African Americans as propertyless agricultural laborers with inferior legal rights. The new freedpeople could not serve on juries, testify against whites, or work as they pleased. South Carolina forbade blacks from engaging in anything other than agricultural labor without a special license; Mississippi prohibited them from buying or renting farmland. Most states ominously provided that black people who were vagrants could be arrested and hired out to landowners. Many northerners were incensed by the restrictive black codes, which violated their conception of freedom.

Black codes

Elections in the South

Southern voters under Johnson's plan also defiantly elected prominent Confederate military and political leaders to office, headed by Alexander Stephens, the vice president of the Confederacy, who was elected senator from Georgia. At this point, Johnson could have called for new elections or admitted that a different program of Reconstruction was needed. Instead he caved in. For all his harsh rhetoric, he shrank

The black codes enacted under presidential Reconstruction provided for fines for unemployed blacks. If they were unable to pay the fine, their services could be sold to the highest bidder. Here a Florida freedman watches as white landlords bid for his labor at an auction. Critics charged that this system constituted quasi-slavery.

SELLING A FREEDMAN TO PAY HIS FINE, AT MONTICELLO, FLORIDA.—FROM A SKETCH BY JAS. E. TAYLOR.—SEE PAGE 275.

from the prospect of social upheaval, and he found it enormously gratifying when upper-class planters praised his conduct and requested pardons. As the lines of ex-Confederates waiting to see him lengthened, he began issuing special pardons almost as fast as they could be printed. In the next two years he pardoned some 13,500 former rebels.

In private, Johnson warned southerners against a reckless course. Publicly he put on a bold face, announcing that Reconstruction had been successfully completed. But many members of Congress were deeply alarmed, and the stage was set for a serious confrontation.

Johnson's Break with Congress

The new Congress was by no means of one mind. A small number of Democrats and a few conservative Republicans backed the president's program of immediate and unconditional restoration. At the other end of the spectrum, a larger group of Radical Republicans, led by Thaddeus Stevens, Charles Sumner, Benjamin Wade, and others, was bent on remaking southern society in the image of the North. Reconstruction must "revolutionize Southern institutions, habits, and manners," thundered Representative Stevens, ". . . or all our blood and treasure have been spent in vain."

Thaddeus Stevens, Radical leader in the House

As a minority, the Radicals could accomplish nothing without the aid of the moderate Republicans, the largest bloc in Congress. Led by William Pitt Fessenden and Lyman Trumbull, the moderates hoped to avoid a clash with the president, and they had no desire to foster social revolution or promote racial equality in the South. But they wanted to keep Confederate leaders from reassuming power, and they were convinced that the former slaves needed federal protection. Otherwise, Trumbull declared, the freedpeople would "be tyrannized over, abused, and virtually reenslaved."

The central issue dividing Johnson and the Radicals was the place of African Americans in American society. Johnson accused his opponents of seeking "to Africanize the southern half of our country," while the Radicals championed civil and political rights for African Americans. Convinced that southern white Unionists were too small a nucleus to build a party around, Radicals believed that the only way to maintain loyal governments and develop a Republican party in the South was to give black men the ballot. Moderates agreed that the new southern governments were too harsh toward African Americans, but they feared that too great an emphasis on black civil rights would alienate northern voters.

Issue of black rights

In December 1865, when southern representatives to Congress appeared in Washington, a majority in Congress voted to exclude them. Congress also appointed a joint committee, chaired by Senator Fessenden, to look into Reconstruction.

The growing split with the president became clearer when Congress passed a bill extending the life of the Freedmen's Bureau. Created in March 1865, the Bureau provided emergency food, clothing, and medical care to war refugees (including white southerners) and took charge of settling freedpeople on abandoned lands. The new bill gave the Bureau the added responsibilities of supervising special courts to resolve disputes involving freedpeople and establishing schools for black southerners. Although this bill passed with virtually unanimous Republican support, Johnson nevertheless vetoed it, and Congress failed to override his veto.

Johnson's vetoes

Johnson also vetoed a civil rights bill designed to overturn the more flagrant provisions of the black codes. The law made African Americans citizens of the United States and granted them the right to own property, make contracts, and have access to courts as parties and witnesses. For most Republicans Johnson's action was the last straw, and in April 1866 Congress overrode his veto, the first major legislation in American history to be enacted over a presidential veto. Congress then approved a slightly revised Freedmen's Bureau bill in July and promptly overrode the president's veto. Johnson's refusal to compromise drove the moderates into the arms of the Radicals.

The Fourteenth Amendment

To prevent unrepentant Confederates from taking over the reconstructed state governments and denying African Americans basic freedoms, the Joint Committee on Reconstruction proposed an amendment to the Constitution, which passed both houses of Congress with the necessary two-thirds vote in June 1866. The amendment, coupled with the Freedmen's Bureau and civil rights bills, represented the moderates' terms for Reconstruction.

Provisions of the amendment

The Fourteenth Amendment put a number of matters beyond the control of the president. The amendment guaranteed repayment of the national war debt and prohibited repayment of the Confederate debt. To counteract the president's wholesale pardons, it disqualified prominent Confederates from holding office and provided that only Congress by a two-thirds vote could remove this penalty. Because moderates, fearful of the reaction of white northerners, balked at giving the vote to African Americans, the amendment merely gave Congress the right to reduce the representation of any state that did not have impartial male suffrage. The practical effect of this provision, which Radicals labeled a "swindle," was to allow northern states to restrict suffrage to whites if they wished, since unlike southern states they had few African Americans and thus would not be penalized.

The amendment's most important provision, Section 1, defined an American citizen as anyone born in the United States or naturalized, thereby automatically making African Americans citizens. Section 1 also prohibited states from abridging "the privileges or immunities" of citizens, depriving "any person of life, liberty, or property, without due process of law," or denying "any person . . . equal protection of the laws." The framers of the amendment probably intended to prohibit laws that applied to one race only, such as the black codes, or that made certain acts felonies when committed by black but not white people, or that decreed different penalties for the same crime when committed by white and black lawbreakers. The framers probably did not intend to prevent African Americans from being excluded from juries or to forbid segregation (the legal separation of the races) in schools and public places.

Nevertheless, Johnson denounced the proposed amendment and urged southern states not to ratify it. Ironically, of the seceded states only the president's own state ratified the amendment, and Congress readmitted Tennessee with no further restrictions. The telegram sent to Congress by a longtime foe of Johnson announcing Tennessee's approval ended, "Give my respects to the dead dog in the White House." The amendment was ratified in 1868.

The Elections of 1866

When Congress blocked his policies, Johnson undertook a speaking tour of the East and Midwest in the fall of 1866 to drum up popular support. But the president found it difficult to convince northern audiences that white southerners were fully repentant. News that summer of major race riots in Memphis and New Orleans heightened northern concern. Forty-six African Americans died when white mobs invaded the black section of Memphis, burning homes, churches, and schoolhouses. About the same number were killed in New Orleans when whites attacked both black and white delegates to a convention supporting black suffrage. "The negroes now know, to their sorrow, that it is best not to arouse the fury of the white man," boasted one Memphis newspaper. When the president encountered hostile audiences during his northern campaign, he only made matters worse by trading insults and ranting that the Radicals were traitors. Even supporters found his performance humiliating.

Antiblack riots

Not to be outdone, the Radicals vilified Johnson as a traitor aiming to turn the country over to rebels and Copperheads. Resorting to the tactic of "waving the bloody shirt," they appealed to voters by reviving bitter memories of the war. In a classic example of such rhetoric, Governor Oliver Morton of Indiana proclaimed that "every bounty jumper, every deserter, every sneak who ran away from the draft" was a Democrat; everyone "who murdered Union prisoners," every "New York rioter in 1863 who burned up little children in colored asylums called himself a Democrat. In short, the Democratic party may be described as a common sewer. . . ."

Voters soundly repudiated Johnson, as the Republicans won more than a two-thirds majority in both houses of Congress, every northern gubernatorial contest, and control of every northern legislature. The Radicals had reached the height of their power, propelled by genuine alarm among northerners that Johnson's policies would lose the fruits of the Union's victory. Johnson was a president virtually without a party.

Repudiation of Johnson

Congressional Reconstruction

With a clear mandate in hand, congressional Republicans passed their own program of Reconstruction, beginning with the first Reconstruction Act in March 1867. Like all later pieces of Reconstruction legislation, it was repassed over Johnson's veto.

Placing the 10 unreconstructed states under military commanders, the act provided that in enrolling voters, officials were to include black adult males but not former Confederates who were barred from holding office under the Fourteenth Amendment. Delegates to the state conventions would frame constitutions that provided for black suffrage and that disqualified prominent ex-Confederates from office. The first state legislatures to meet under the new constitution were required to ratify the Fourteenth Amendment. Once these steps were completed and Congress approved the new state constitution, a state could send representatives to Congress.

White southerners found these requirements so obnoxious that officials took no steps to register voters. Congress then enacted a second Reconstruction Act, also in March, ordering the local military commanders to put the machinery of Reconstruction into motion. Johnson's efforts to limit the power of military commanders produced a third act, passed in July, that upheld their superiority in all matters. When elections were held to ratify the new state constitutions, white southerners boycotted them in large numbers. Undaunted, Congress passed the fourth Reconstruction Act (March 1868), which required ratification of the constitution by only a majority of those voting rather than those who were registered.

Resistance of southern whites

By June 1868 Congress had readmitted the representatives of seven states. Georgia's state legislature expelled its black members once it had been readmitted, granting seats to those barred by Congress from holding office. Congress ordered the military commander to reverse these actions, and Georgia was then admitted a second time in July 1870. Texas, Virginia, and Mississippi did not complete the process until 1869.

Post-Emancipation Societies in the Americas

With the exception of Haiti's revolution (1791–1804), the United States was the only society in the Americas in which the destruction of slavery was accomplished by violence. But the United States, uniquely among these societies, enfranchised former slaves almost immediately after the emancipation. Thus in the United States former masters and slaves battled for control of the state in ways that did not occur in other post-emancipation societies. In most of the Caribbean, property requirements for voting left the planters in political control. Jamaica, for example, with a population of 500,000 in the 1860s, had only 3,000 voters.

Moreover, in reaction to political efforts to mobilize disfranchised black peasants, Jamaican planters dissolved the assembly and reverted to being a Crown colony governed from London. Of the sugar islands, all but Barbados adopted the same policy, thereby blocking the potential for any future black peasant democracy. Nor did any of these societies have the counterparts of the Radical Republicans, a group of outsiders with political power that promoted the fundamental transformation of the post-emancipation South. These comparisons highlight the radicalism of Reconstruction in the United States, which alone saw an effort to forge an interracial democracy.

The Land Issue

Blacks' desire for land

While the political process of Reconstruction proceeded, Congress confronted the question of whether land should be given to former slaves to foster economic independence. At a meeting with Secretary of War Edwin Stanton near the end of the

The Southern States during Reconstruction

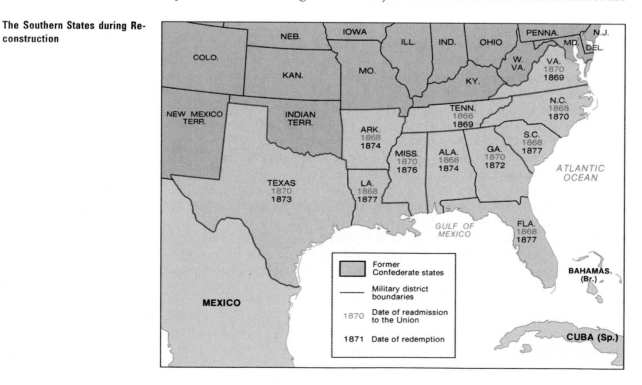

war, African American leaders declared, "The way we can best take care of ourselves is to have land, and till it by our own labor." During the war, the Second Confiscation Act of 1862 had authorized the government to seize and sell the property, including land, of supporters of the rebellion. In June 1866, however, President Johnson ruled that confiscation laws applied only to wartime.

Congress debated land confiscation off and on from December 1865 until early 1867. Thaddeus Stevens, a leading Radical in the House, advocated confiscating 394 million acres of land from about 70,000 of what he termed the "chief rebels" in the South, who comprised less than 5 percent of the South's white families. He proposed to give 40 acres to every adult male freedperson and then sell the remaining land, which would amount to nine-tenths of the total, to pay off the public debt, compensate loyal southerners for losses they suffered during the war, and fund Union veterans' pensions. Land, he insisted, would be far more valuable to African Americans than the right to vote.

But in the end Congress rejected all proposals. Even some Radicals were opposed to land redistribution. Given Americans' strong belief in self-reliance, little sympathy existed for the idea that government should support any group. In addition, land redistribution represented an attack on property rights, another cherished American value. "A division of rich men's lands amongst the landless," argued the *Nation*, a Radical journal, "would give a shock to our whole social and political system from which it would hardly recover without the loss of liberty." By 1867 land reform was dead.

Few freedpeople acquired land after the war, a development that severely limited African Americans' economic independence and left them vulnerable to white coercion. It is doubtful, however, that this decision was the basic cause of the failure of Reconstruction. In the face of white hostility and institutionalized racism, African Americans probably would have been no more successful in protecting their property than they were in maintaining the right to vote.

Failure of land redistribution

Impeachment

Throughout 1867 Congress routinely overrode Johnson's vetoes. Still, the president had other ways of undercutting congressional Reconstruction. He interpreted the new laws as narrowly as possible and removed military commanders who vigorously enforced them. Congress responded by restricting Johnson's power to issue orders to military commanders in the South. It also passed the Tenure of Office Act, which forbade Johnson from removing any member of the cabinet without the Senate's consent. The intention of this law was to prevent him from firing Secretary of War Edwin Stanton, the only Radical in the cabinet.

Tenure of Office Act

Facsimile of a ticket of admission to the impeachment trial of President Andrew Johnson

When Johnson tried to dismiss Stanton in February 1868, the determined secretary of war barricaded himself in his office (where he remained night and day for about two months). Angrily, the House of Representatives approved articles of impeachment. The articles focused on the violation of the Tenure of Office Act, but the charge with the most substance was that Johnson had conspired to systematically obstruct Reconstruction legislation. In the trial before the Senate, his lawyers argued that a president could be impeached only for an indictable crime, which Johnson clearly had not committed. The Radicals countered that impeachment applied to political offenses and not merely criminal acts.

Johnson acquitted

In May 1868 the Senate voted 36 to 19 to convict, one vote short of the two-thirds majority needed. The seven Republicans who joined the Democrats in voting for acquittal were uneasy about using impeachment as a political weapon. Their vote against conviction established the precedent that a president could be removed from office only for indictable offenses, which greatly lessened the effectiveness of the threat of impeachment.

counterpoint

Should Johnson Have Been Removed from Office?

For the first half of the twentieth century, most historians viewed Reconstruction as an undertaking that was tragically flawed at best or vindictive and misconceived at worst. Beginning in the 1960s historians increasingly found much to praise in the experiment of Reconstruction and much to condemn in Andrew Johnson's leadership. (It is no coincidence that the reevaluation gained momentum just as the civil rights movement was forcing Americans to rethink attitudes about segregation, racism, and equality.)

Controversy persists, however, over the narrower issue of whether congressional Republicans were wise to pursue impeachment. Some historians point out that when the Constitution was first drafted, James Madison argued that impeachment should apply to political misdeeds as well as crimes. Johnson, after all, had never been elected president in his own right. In 1866 the voters in congressional elections had rejected his clumsy attempts to gain support. Furthermore, as president he had taken an oath to uphold the laws of the nation. Yet time after time Johnson interpreted those laws as narrowly as possible, refusing to enforce them in the manner that Congress clearly intended. When Congress voted to not convict the president, these historians argue, it lessened the threat of impeachment ever being used. Yet impeachment was one of the legislative branch's most important weapons to control an abuse of power by a president.

Other historians, while not sympathetic to Johnson's policies, believe that his acquittal was fortunate. The Constitution states that the president could be removed only for "Treason, Bribery, or other high Crimes and Misdemeanors." Johnson's lawyers ably argued that whatever his "misdeeds" in the eyes of Congress, he had not committed "high Crimes." Historians who sympathize with that view argue that a conviction would have upset the constitutional doctrine of separation of powers. Removing Johnson from office would have seriously weakened the presidency, placed too much power in the hands of Congress, and provided a dangerous precedent for the future. The best course, they conclude, was the one Congress actually followed: to let Johnson finish his term as an ineffective president.

Reconstruction in the South

The refusal of Congress to convict Johnson sent a clear signal: the power of the Radicals in Congress was waning. Increasingly the success or failure of Reconstruction hinged on developments not in Congress but in the southern states themselves. Power there rested with the new Republican parties, representing a coalition of black and white southerners and transplanted northerners.

Black Office Holding

Almost from the beginning of Reconstruction, African Americans had lobbied for the right to vote. After they received the franchise, black men constituted as much as 80 percent of the Republican voters in the South. They steadfastly opposed the

Democratic party with its appeal to white supremacy. As one Tennessee Republican explained, "The blacks know that many conservatives [Democrats] hope to reduce them
again to some form of peonage. Under the
impulse of this fear they will roll up their
whole strength and will go entirely for the
Republican candidate whoever he may be."

Throughout Reconstruction, African
Americans never held office in proportion to
their voting strength. No African American
was ever elected governor, and only in South
Carolina, where more than 60 percent of the
population was black, did they control even
one house of the legislature. During Reconstruction between 15 and 20 percent of the
state officers and 6 percent of members of
Congress (2 senators and 15 representatives) were black. Only in South Carolina
did black officeholders approach their proportion of the population.

Hiram Revels, a minister and educator, became the first African American to serve in the U.S. Senate, representing Mississippi. Later he served as president of Alcorn University.

Blacks who held office generally came from the top levels of African American
society. Among state and federal officeholders, perhaps four-fifths were literate, and
more than a quarter had been free before the war, both marks of distinction in the
black community. Their occupations also set them apart: two-fifths were professionals (mostly clergy), and of the third who were farmers, nearly all owned land.
Among black members of Congress, all but three had a secondary school education,
and four had gone to college. In their political and social values, African American
leaders were more conservative than the rural black population was, and they showed
little interest in land reform.

Background of black political leaders

White Republicans in the South

Black citizens were a majority of the voters only in South Carolina, Mississippi, and
Louisiana. Thus in most of the South the Republican party had to secure white votes
to stay in power. Opponents scornfully labeled white southerners who allied with
the Republican party scalawags, yet an estimated quarter of white southerners at
one time voted Republican. Although the party appealed to some wealthy planters,
they were outnumbered by Unionists from the upland counties and hill areas who
were largely yeoman farmers. Such voters were attracted by Republican promises to
rebuild the South, restore prosperity, create public schools, and open isolated areas
to the market with railroads.

The other group of white Republicans in the South were known as carpetbaggers. Originally from the North, they allegedly had arrived with all their worldly
possessions stuffed in a carpetbag, ready to loot and plunder the defeated South.
Some did, certainly, but northerners moved south for a variety of reasons. Those in
political office were especially well educated. Though carpetbaggers made up only
a small percentage of Republican voters, they controlled almost a third of the offices. More than half of all southern Republican governors and nearly half of Republican members of Congress were originally northerners.

The Republican party in the South had difficulty agreeing on a program or maintaining unity. Scalawags were especially susceptible to the race issue and social

Divisions among southern Republicans

From the beginning of Reconstruction, African Americans demanded the right to vote as free citizens. The Fifteenth Amendment, ratified in 1870, secured that right for black males. In New York, black citizens paraded in support of Ulysses Grant for president. Parades played a central role in campaigning: this parade exhibits the usual banners, flags, costumes, and a band. Blacks in both the North and the South voted solidly for the Republican party as the party of Lincoln and emancipation, although white violence in the South increasingly reduced black turnout.

pressure. "Even my own kinspeople have turned the cold shoulder to me because I hold office under a Republican administration," testified a Mississippi white Republican. As black southerners pressed for greater recognition and a greater share of the offices, white southerners increasingly defected to the Democrats. Carpetbaggers, by contrast, were less sensitive to race, although most felt that their black allies needed guidance and should be content with minor offices. The friction between scalawags and carpetbaggers, which grew out of their rivalry for party honors, was particularly intense.

The New State Governments

New state constitutions

The new southern state constitutions enacted several significant reforms. They put in place fairer systems of legislative representation, allowed voters to elect many officials who before had been appointed, and abolished property requirements for officeholding. In South Carolina, for the first time, voters were allowed to vote for the president, governor, and other state officers.* The Radical state governments also assumed some responsibility for social welfare and established the first statewide systems of public schools in the South. Although the Fourteenth Amendment prevented high Confederate officials from holding office, only Alabama and Arkansas temporarily forbade some ex-Confederates from voting.

Race and social equality

All the new constitutions proclaimed the principle of equality and granted black adult males the right to vote. On social relations they were much more cautious. No state outlawed segregation, and South Carolina and Louisiana were the only states that required integration in public schools (a mandate that was almost universally ignored). Sensitive to status, mulattoes pushed for prohibition of social discrimination, but white Republicans refused to adopt such a radical policy.

---

*Previously, presidential electors as well as the governor had been chosen by the South Carolina legislature.

Economic Issues and Corruption

The war left the southern economy in ruins, and problems of economic reconstruction were as difficult as those of politics. The new Republican governments encouraged industrial development by providing subsidies, loans, and even temporary exemptions from taxes. These governments also largely rebuilt the southern railroad system, often offering lavish aid to railroad corporations. These investments in the South's industrial base helped: in the two decades after 1860, the region doubled its manufacturing establishments. Yet the harsh reality was that the South steadily slipped further behind the booming industrial economy of the North. Between 1854 and 1879, 7000 miles of railroad track were laid in the South, but in the same period 45,000 miles were constructed in the rest of the nation.

The expansion of government services offered temptations for corruption. In many southern states, officials regularly received bribes and kickbacks for their award of railroad charters, franchises, and other contracts. By 1872 the debts of the 11 states of the Confederacy had increased by $132 million, largely because of railroad grants and new social services such as schools. The tax rate grew as expenditures went up, so that by the 1870s it was four times the rate of 1860.

Corruption, however, was not only a southern problem: the decline in morality affected the entire nation. During these years in New York City alone, the Democratic Tweed Ring stole more money than all the Radical Republican governments in the South combined. Moreover, corruption in the South was hardly limited to Republicans. Many Democrats and white business leaders participated in these corrupt practices both before and after the Radical governments were in power. Louisiana Governor Henry Warmoth, a carpetbagger, told a congressional committee that the legislature was as good as the people it represented. "Everybody is demoralizing down here. Corruption is the fashion."

Corruption in Radical governments undeniably existed, but southern whites exaggerated its extent for partisan purposes. Conservatives just as bitterly opposed honest Radical regimes as they did notoriously corrupt ones. In the eyes of most white southerners, the real crime of the Radical governments was that they allowed black citizens to hold some offices and tried to protect the civil rights of African Americans. Race was the conservatives' greatest weapon. And it would prove the most effective means to undermine Republican power in the South.

Corruption

Emancipation came to slaves in different ways and at different times. For some it arrived during the war when Union soldiers entered an area; for others it came some time after the Confederacy's collapse, when Union troops or officials announced that they were free. Whatever the timing, freedom meant a host of precious blessings to people who had been in bondage all their lives.

Black Aspirations

Experiencing Freedom

The first impulse was to think of freedom as a contrast to slavery. Emancipation immediately released slaves from the most oppressive aspects of bondage—the whippings, the breakup of families, the sexual exploitation. Freedom also meant movement,

Daily Lives

PUBLIC SPACE/ PRIVATE SPACE

The Black Sharecropper's Cabin

On the plantations of the Old South, slaves had lived in cabins along a central path in the shadow of the white master's "big house." These quarters were the center of their community, where marriages and other festivals were celebrated and family life went on. But with the coming of emancipation, freedpeople looked to leave the old quarters, which stood as a symbol of bondage and of close white supervision. African Americans either built new housing or dismantled their old cabins and hauled them to the plots of land they rented as tenants or sharecroppers. Moving enabled them to live on the land they farmed, just as white farmers and tenants did.

In selecting a cabin site, freedpeople tried to locate within a convenient distance of their fields but close to the woods as well, since cutting wood was a year-round task for boys. To improve drainage, cabins were often built on a knoll or had a floor raised above the ground. A nearby stream, spring,

or well provided not only water but a place to cool butter and other perishable dairy products.

Like slave cabins, most sharecroppers' dwellings were one story high, about 16 feet square, and usually built of logs chinked with mud. The few windows had shutters to protect against the weather; glass was rare. Though the inside walls normally lacked plaster or sheeting, they were given a coat of whitewash annually to brighten the dark interior. To provide a bit of cheer, women often covered the walls with pictures from seed catalogues and magazines. The floor, packed dirt that

was as smooth and hard as concrete, was covered with braided rugs made from scraps of cloth and worn-out clothing.

The main room served as kitchen and dining room, parlor, bathing area, and the parents' bedroom. To one side might be a homemade drop-leaf table (essential because of cramped space), which served as a kitchen work counter and a dining table. The other side of the room had a few plain beds, their slats or rope bottoms supporting corn shuck or straw mattresses. (Featherbeds were considered a remarkable luxury.) The social center of the room

Chimneys on sharecroppers' cabins were often tilted deliberately so that they could be pushed away from the house quickly if they caught fire.

the right to travel without a pass or white permission. Above all, freedom meant that African Americans' labor would be for their own benefit. One Arkansas freedman, who earned his first dollar working on a railroad, recalled that when he was paid, "I felt like the richest man in the world."

Changing employment

Freedom included finding a new place to work. Changing jobs was one concrete way to break the psychological ties of slavery. Even planters with reputations for kindness sometimes found that most of their former hands had departed. The cook who left a South Carolina family, even though they offered her higher wages than her new job, explained, "I must go. If I stays here I'll never know I'm free."

Importance of names

Symbolically, freedom meant having a full name, and African Americans now adopted last names. More than a few took the last name of some prominent individual; more common was to take the name of the first master in the family's was the fireplace, the only source of heat and the main source of light after dark. Pots and pans were hung on the wall near the fireplace, and the mother and daughters did the cooking stooped over an open fire. Clothing was hung on pegs in the wall.

The cabin's chimney was made of small logs notched together and covered with several layers of clay to protect it from the heat. It often narrowed toward the top, and sometimes its height was extended by empty flour barrels. A taller chimney drew better, which kept smoke from blowing back down into the house and kept sparks away from the roof. After the evening meal the family gathered around the fireplace, the children to play with homemade dolls and toys, the mother to sew, and the father perhaps to play the fiddle. At bedtime a trapdoor in the ceiling offered access up a ladder to the loft beneath the gabled roof, where older children slept, usually on pallets on the floor, as had been the case in slavery.

In the summer, cooking was done outdoors over an open fire. Women generally preferred to cook under a tree, which offered some protection from rain as well as relief from the sun and the high humidity. Sharecropper families rarely had separate cooking rooms attached to or next to the cabin. Separate kitchens, which were a sign of prosperity, were more common among black landowners and white tenant farmers.

Gradually, as black sharecroppers scraped together some savings, they improved their homes. By the end of the century, frame dwellings were more common, and many older log cabins had been covered with wood siding. The newer homes were generally larger, with wood floors, and often had attached rooms such as a porch or kitchen. In addition, windows had glass panes, roofs were covered with shingles instead of planking, and stone and brick chimneys were less unusual. Ceramic dishes were more frequently seen, and wood-burning stoves made cooking easier for women and provided a more efficient source of heat.

Without question, the cabins of black sharecroppers provided more space than the slave quarters had, and certainly more freedom and privacy. Still, they lacked many of the comforts that most white Americans took for granted. Such housing reflected the continuing status of black sharecroppers as poverty-stricken laborers in a caste system based on race.

oral history as far back as it could be recalled. Most, on the other hand, retained their first name, especially if the name had been given to them by their parents (as most often had been the case among slaves). It had been their form of identity in bondage, and for those separated from their family it was the only link with their parents. Whatever name they took, it was important to black Americans that they made the decision themselves without white interference.

The Black Family

African Americans also sought to strengthen the family in freedom. Because slave marriages had not been recognized as legal, thousands of former slaves insisted on being married again by proper authorities, even though a ceremony was not required

Upholding the family

547

by law. Blacks who had been forcibly separated in slavery and later remarried confronted the dilemma of which spouse to take. Laura Spicer, whose husband had been sold away in slavery, received a series of wrenching letters from him after the war. He had thought her dead, had remarried, and had a new family. "You know it never was our wishes to be separated from each other, and it never was our fault. I had rather anything to had happened to me most than ever have been parted from you and the children," he wrote. "As I am, I do not know which I love best, you or Anna." Declining to return, he closed, "Laura, truly, I have got another wife, and I am very sorry. . . ."

Like white husbands, black husbands deemed themselves the head of the family and acted legally for their wives. They often insisted that their wives would not work in the fields as they had in slavery, a decision that had major economic repercussions for agricultural labor. "The [black] women say they never mean to do any more outdoor work," one planter reported, "that white men support their wives and they mean that their husbands shall support them." In negotiating contracts, a father also demanded the right to control his children and their labor. All these changes were designed to insulate the black family from white control.

The Schoolhouse and the Church

Black education

In freedom, the schoolhouse and the black church became essential institutions in the black community. Next to ownership of land, African Americans saw education as the best hope for advancement. At first, northern churches and missionaries, working with the Freedmen's Bureau, set up black schools in the South. Tuition represented 10 percent or more of a laborer's monthly wages. Yet these schools were

After living for years in a society where teaching slaves to read and write was usually illegal, freedpeople viewed literacy as a key to securing their newfound freedom. Blacks were not merely "*anxious* to learn," a school official in Virginia reported, they were "*crazy* to learn."

full. Many parents sent their children by day and attended classes themselves at night. Eventually, the Bureau schools were replaced by the new public school systems, which by 1876 enrolled 40 percent of African American children.

Black adults had good reasons for seeking literacy. They wanted to be able to read the Bible, to defend their newly gained civil and political rights, and to protect themselves from being cheated. One elderly Louisiana freedman explained that giving children an education was better than giving them a fortune, "because if you left them even $500, some man having more education than they had would come along and cheat them out of it all." Both races saw that education would undermine the old servility that slavery had fostered.

Teachers in the Freedmen's Bureau schools were primarily northern middle-class white women sent south by northern missionary societies. "I feel that it is a precious privilege," Esther Douglass wrote, "to be allowed to do something for these poor people." Many saw themselves as peacetime soldiers, struggling to make emancipation a reality. Indeed, on more than one occasion, hostile white southerners destroyed black schools and threatened and even murdered white teachers. Teachers in urban schools often lived together in comfortable housing, which provided a social network, created a sense of sisterhood, and helped sustain morale. In rural areas, however, teachers often had to live alone or with black families because of white hostility. Then there were the everyday challenges: low pay, dilapidated buildings, lack of sufficient books, classes of 100 or more children, and irregular attendance. Meanwhile, the Freedmen's Bureau undertook to quickly train black teachers, and by 1869 a majority of the approximately 3000 teachers in freedmen's schools were black.

Teachers in black schools

Before the war, most slaves had attended white churches or services supervised by whites. Once free, African Americans quickly established their own congregations led by black preachers. In the first year of freedom, the Methodist Church South lost fully half of its black members. By 1870 the Negro Baptist Church had increased its membership threefold compared to 1850, and the African Methodist Episcopal Church expanded at an even greater rate.

Independent black churches

Black churches were so important because they were the only major organizations in the African American community controlled by blacks. A white missionary reported that "the Ebony preacher who promises perfect independence from White control and direction carried the colored heart at once." Black ministers were respected leaders, and many of the black men elected to office during Reconstruction were preachers. As it had in slavery, religion offered African Americans a place of refuge in a hostile white world and provided them with hope, comfort, and a means of self-identification.

New Working Conditions

As a largely propertyless class, blacks in the postwar South had no choice but to work for white landowners. Except for paying wages, whites wanted to retain the old system of labor, including close supervision, gang labor, and physical punishment. Determined to remove all emblems of servitude, African Americans refused to work under these conditions, and they demanded time off to devote to their own interests. Convinced that working at one's own pace was part of freedom, they simply would not work as long or as hard as they had in slavery. Because of shorter hours and the withdrawal of children and women from the fields, work output

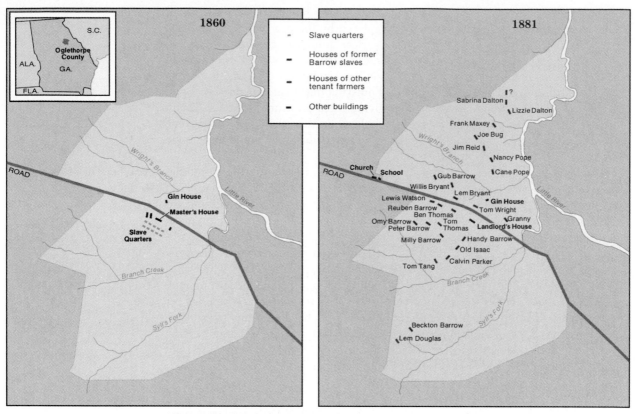

A Georgia Plantation after the War After emancipation, sharecropping became the dominant form of agricultural labor in the South. Black families no longer lived in the old slave quarters but dispersed to separate plots of land that they farmed themselves. At the end of the year each sharecropper turned over part of the crop to the white landowner.

Sharecropping

declined by an estimated 35 percent in freedom. Blacks also refused to live in the old slave quarters located near the master's house. Instead, they erected cabins on distant parts of the plantation. Wages at first were $5 or $6 a month plus provisions and a cabin; by 1867, they had risen to an average of $10 a month.

These changes eventually led to the rise of sharecropping. Under this arrangement African American families farmed separate plots of land and then at the end of the year divided the crop, normally on an equal basis, with the white landowner. Sharecropping had higher status and offered greater personal freedom than being a wage laborer. "I am not working for wages," one black farmer declared in defending his right to leave the plantation at will, "but am part owner of the crop and as [such,] I have all the rights that you or any other man has. . . ." Although black per capita agricultural income increased 40 percent in freedom, sharecropping was a harshly exploitative system in which black families often sank into perpetual debt.

The Freedmen's Bureau

The task of supervising the transition from slavery to freedom on southern plantations fell to the Freedmen's Bureau, a unique experiment in social policy supported by the federal government. Assigned the task of protecting freedpeople's economic rights, approximately 550 local agents supervised and regulated working conditions in southern agriculture after the war. The racial attitudes of Bureau agents varied widely, as did their commitment and competence. Then, too, they had to depend on the army to enforce their decisions.

Most agents encouraged or required written contracts between white planters and black laborers, specifying not only wages but also the conditions of employment. Although agents sometimes intervened to protect freedpeople from unfair treatment, they also provided important help to planters. They insisted that black laborers not desert at harvest time; they arrested those who violated their contracts or refused to sign new ones at the beginning of the year; and they preached the gospel of work and the need to be orderly and respectful. Given such attitudes, freedpeople increasingly complained that Bureau agents were mere tools of the planter class. "They are, in fact, the planters' guards, and nothing else," claimed the New Orleans *Tribune,* a black newspaper. One observer reported, "Doing justice seems to mean seeing that the blacks don't break contracts and compelling them to submit cheerfully."

Bureau's mixed record

The primary means of enforcing working conditions were the Freedmen's Courts, which Congress created in 1866 in order to avoid the discrimination African Americans received in state courts. These new courts functioned as military tribunals, and often the agent was the entire court. The sympathy black laborers received varied from state to state. In 1867 one agent summarized the Bureau's experience with the labor contract system: "It has succeeded in making the freedman work and in rendering labor secure and stable—but it has failed to secure to the Freedman his just dues or compensation."

In 1869, with the Bureau's work scarcely under way, Congress decided to shut it down, and by 1872 it had gone out of business. Despite its mixed record, it was the most effective agency in protecting blacks' civil and political rights. Its disbanding signaled the beginning of the northern retreat from Reconstruction.

End of the Bureau

Planters and a New Way of Life

Planters and other white southerners faced emancipation with dread. "All the traditions and habits of both races had been suddenly overthrown," a Tennessee planter recalled, "and neither knew just what to do, or how to accommodate themselves to the new situation."

The old ideal of a paternalistic planter, which required a facade of black subservience and affection, gave way to an emphasis on strictly economic relationships. Mary Jones, a Georgia slaveholder before the war who did more for her workers than the law required, lost all patience when two workers accused her of trickery and hauled her before a Freedmen's Bureau agent, with whom she won her case. Upon returning home, she announced to the assembled freedpeople that "I have considered them friends and treated them as such but now they were only laborers under contract, and only the law would rule between us." Only with time did planters develop new norms and standards to judge black behavior. What in 1865 had seemed insolence was viewed by the 1870s as the normal attitude of freedom.

Planters' new values

Slavery had been a complex institution that welded black and white southerners together in intimate relationships. After the war, however, planters increasingly embraced the ideology of segregation. Because emancipation significantly reduced the social distance between the races, white southerners sought psychological separation and kept dealings with African Americans to a minimum. By the time Reconstruction ended, white planters had developed a new way of life based on the institutions of sharecropping and segregation and undergirded by a militant white supremacy.

Although most planters kept their land, they did not regain the economic prosperity of the prewar years. Rice plantations, which were not suitable to tenant farming, largely disappeared after the war. In addition, southern cotton growers faced increased competition from new areas such as India, Egypt, and Brazil. Cotton prices began a long decline, and southern per capita income suffered as a result. By 1880 the value of southern farms had slid 33 percent below the level of 1860.

The Abandonment of Reconstruction

On Christmas Day 1875, a white acquaintance approached Charles Caldwell on the streets of Clinton, Mississippi, and invited him into Chilton's store to have a drink to celebrate the holiday. A former slave, Caldwell was a state senator and the leader of the Republican party in Hinds County, Mississippi. But the black leader's fearlessness made him a marked man. Only two months earlier, he had been forced to flee the county to escape an armed white mob angry about a Republican barbecue he and his fellow Republicans had organized. For four days the mob hunted down and killed nearly 40 Republican leaders for presuming to hold a political meeting. Despite that hostility, Caldwell had returned to vote in the November state election. Even more boldly, he had led a black militia company through the streets to help quell the disturbances. Now, as Caldwell and his "friend" raised their glasses in a holiday toast, a gunshot exploded through the window. Caldwell collapsed, mortally wounded from a bullet to the back of his head. He was taken outside, where his assassins riddled his body with bullets. He died in the street.

Charles Caldwell shared the fate of more than a few black Republican leaders in the South during Reconstruction. Southern whites used violence, terror, and political assassination to challenge the federal government's commitment to sustaining Reconstruction. If northerners had boldly countered such terrorism, Reconstruction might have ended differently. But in the years following President Johnson's impeachment trial in 1868, the influence of Radical Republicans steadily waned. The Republican party was being drained of the crusading idealism that had stamped its early years.

The Election of Grant

Immensely popular after the war, Ulysses S. Grant was the natural choice of Republicans to run for president in 1868. Although Grant was elected, Republicans were shocked that despite his great military stature, his popular margin was only 300,000 votes. An estimated 450,000 black Republican votes had been cast in the South, which meant that a majority of whites casting ballots had voted Democratic. The 1868 election helped convince Republican leaders that an amendment securing black suffrage throughout the nation was necessary.

Fifteenth Amendment   In February 1869 Congress sent the Fifteenth Amendment to the states for ratification. It forbade any state from denying the right to vote on grounds of race, color, or previous condition of servitude. Some Radicals had hoped to forbid literacy or property requirements to protect blacks further. Others wanted a simple declaration that all adult male citizens had the right to vote. But the moderates in the party were aware that many northerners were increasingly worried about the number of immigrants who were again entering the country and wanted to be able to restrict their voting. As a result, the final amendment left loopholes that eventually allowed southern states to disfranchise African Americans. The amendment was ratified in March 1870, aided by the votes of the four southern states that had not completed the process of Reconstruction and thus were also required to endorse this amendment before being readmitted to Congress.

Lucy Stone, a major figure in the women's rights movement.

Proponents of women's suffrage were gravely disappointed when Congress refused to prohibit voting discrimination on the basis of sex as well as race. The Women's Loyal League, led by Elizabeth Cady Stanton and Susan B. Anthony, had pressed for first the Fourteenth and then the Fifteenth Amendment to recognize women's public role. But even most Radicals, contending that black rights had to be ensured first, were unwilling to back women's suffrage. The Fifteenth Amendment ruptured the feminist movement. Although disappointed that women were not included in its provisions, Lucy Stone and the American Woman Suffrage Association urged ratification. Anthony and Stanton, on the other hand, broke with their former allies among the Radicals, denounced the amendment, and organized the National Woman Suffrage Association to work for passage of a new amendment giving women the ballot. The division hampered the women's rights movement for decades to come.

Women's suffrage rejected

The Grant Administration

Ulysses Grant was ill at ease with the political process. His simple, quiet manner, while superb for commanding armies, did not serve him as well in public life, and his well-known resolution withered when he was uncertain of his goal. Also, he lacked the moral commitment to make Reconstruction succeed.

A series of scandals wracked Grant's presidency. Although Grant did not profit personally, he remained loyal to his friends and displayed little zeal to root out wrongdoing. His relatives were implicated in a scheme to corner the gold market, and his private secretary escaped conviction for stealing federal whiskey revenues only because Grant interceded on his behalf. His secretary of war resigned to avoid impeachment. James W. Grimes, one of the party's founders, denounced the Republican party under Grant as "the most corrupt and debauched political party that has ever existed."

Corruption under Grant

Nor was Congress immune from the lowered tone of public life. In such a climate ruthless state machines, led by men who favored the status quo, came to dominate the party. Office and power became ends in themselves, and party leaders worked in close cooperation with northern industrial interests. The few Radicals still active in public life increasingly repudiated Grant and the Republican governments in the South. Congress in 1872 passed an amnesty act, removing the restrictions of the Fourteenth Amendment on officeholding except for about 200 to 300 ex-Confederate leaders.

Grant swings from a trapeze while supporting a number of associates accused of corruption. Among those holding on are Secretary of the Navy George M. Robeson (top center), who was accused of accepting bribes in the awarding of navy contracts; Secretary of War William W. Belknap (top right), who was forced to resign for selling Indian post traderships; and the president's private secretary, Orville Babcock (bottom right), who was implicated in the Whiskey Ring scandal. Although not personally involved in the scandals during his administration, Grant was reluctant to dismiss from office supporters accused of wrongdoing.

As corruption in both the North and the South worsened, reformers became more interested in cleaning up government than in protecting blacks' rights. These liberal Republicans opposed the continued presence of the army in the South, denounced the corruption of southern governments as well as the national government, and advocated free trade and civil service reform. In 1872 they broke with the Republican party and nominated for president Horace Greeley, the editor of the New York *Tribune*. A onetime Radical, Greeley had become disillusioned with Reconstruction and urged a restoration of home rule in the South as well as adoption of civil service reform. Democrats decided to back the Liberal Republican ticket. The Republicans renominated Grant, who, despite the defection of a number of prominent Radicals, won an easy victory with 56 percent of the popular vote.

Growing Northern Disillusionment

Civil Rights Act of 1875

During Grant's second term, Congress passed the Civil Rights Act of 1875, the last major piece of Reconstruction legislation. This law prohibited racial discrimination in all public accommodations, transportation, places of amusement, and juries. At the same time, Congress rejected a ban on segregation in public schools, which was almost universally practiced in the North as well as the South. Although some railroads, streetcars, and public accommodations in both sections were desegregated after the bill passed, the federal government made little attempt to enforce the law, and it was ignored throughout most of the South. In 1883 the Supreme Court struck down its provisions except the one relating to juries.

Waning northern concern

Despite passage of the Civil Rights Act, many northerners were growing disillusioned with Reconstruction. They were repelled by the corruption of the southern governments, they were tired of the violence and disorder in the South, and they had little faith in black Americans. William Dodge, a wealthy New York capitalist and an influential Republican, wrote in 1875 that the South could never develop its resources "till confidence in her state governments can be restored, and this will never be done by federal bayonets." It had been a mistake, he went on, to make black southerners feel "that the United States government was their special friend, rather than those . . . among whom they must live and for whom they must work. We have tried this long enough," he concluded. "Now let the South alone."

As the agony of the war became more distant, the Panic of 1873 diverted public attention from Reconstruction to economic issues. In the severe depression that followed over the next four years, some 3 million people found themselves out of work. Congress became caught up in the question of whether printing greenbacks would help the economy prosper. Battered by the panic and the corruption issue, the Republicans lost a shocking 77 seats in Congress in the 1874 elections, and along with them control of the House of Representatives for the first time since 1861. "The truth is our people are tired out with the worn out cry of 'Southern outrages'!!" one Republican concluded. "Hard times and heavy taxes make them wish the 'ever lasting nigger' were in hell or Africa." Republicans spoke more and more about cutting loose the unpopular southern governments.

Depression and Democratic resurgence

The Triumph of White Supremacy

As northern commitment to Reconstruction waned, southern Democrats set out to overthrow the remaining Radical governments. Already white Republicans in the South felt heavy pressure to desert their party. In Mississippi one party member justified his decision to leave on the grounds that otherwise he would have "to live a life of social oblivion" and his children would have no future.

To poor white southerners who lacked social standing, the Democratic appeal to racial solidarity offered great comfort. As one explained, "I may be poor and my manners may be crude, but . . . because I am a white man, I have a right to be treated with respect by Negroes. . . . That I am poor is not as important as that I am a white man; and no Negro is ever going to forget that he is not a white man." The large landowners and other wealthy groups that led southern Democrats objected less to black southerners voting. These well-to-do leaders did not face social and economic competition from African Americans, and in any case, they were confident that if outside influences were removed, they could control the black vote.

Racism

Democrats also resorted to economic pressure to undermine Republican power. In heavily black counties, white observers at the polls took down the names of black residents who cast Republican ballots and published them in local newspapers. Planters were urged to discharge black tenants who persisted in voting Republican. But terror and violence provided the most effective means to overthrow the Radical regimes. A number of paramilitary organizations broke up Republican meetings, terrorized white and black Republicans, assassinated Republican leaders, and prevented black citizens from voting. The most famous was the Ku Klux Klan, founded in 1866 in Tennessee. It and similar groups functioned as unofficial arms of the Democratic party.

Congress finally moved to break the power of the Klan with the Force Act of

Two Ku Klux Klan members pose in full regalia. Violence played a major role in overthrowing the Radical governments in the South. One South Carolina paper openly praised Klan attacks on blacks and the Republican Union Leagues:

> Born of the night, and
> vanish by day;
> Leaguers and niggers,
> get out of the way!

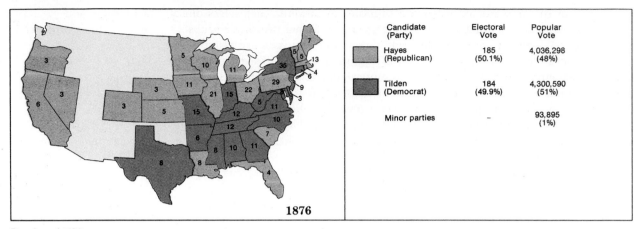

Candidate (Party)	Electoral Vote	Popular Vote
Hayes (Republican)	185 (50.1%)	4,036,298 (48%)
Tilden (Democrat)	184 (49.9%)	4,300,590 (51%)
Minor parties	–	93,895 (1%)

1876

Election of 1876

1870 and the Ku Klux Klan Act of 1871. These laws made it a felony to interfere with the right to vote; they also authorized use of the army and suspension of the writ of habeas corpus. The Grant administration eventually suspended the writ of habeas corpus in nine South Carolina counties and arrested hundreds of suspected Klan members throughout the South. Although these actions weakened the Klan, terrorist organizations continued to operate underground.

Mississippi Plan

Then in 1875 Democrats inaugurated what became known as the Mississippi Plan, the decision to use as much violence as necessary to carry the state election. Several local papers trumpeted, "Carry the election peaceably if we can, forcibly if we must." When Republican Governor Adelbert Ames requested federal troops to stop the violence, Grant's advisers warned that sending troops to Mississippi would cost the party the Ohio election. In the end the administration told Ames to depend on his own forces. Bolstered by terrorism, the Democrats swept the election in Mississippi. Violence and intimidation prevented as many as 60,000 black and white Republicans from voting, converting the normal Republican majority into a Democratic majority of 30,000. Mississippi had been "redeemed."

The Disputed Election of 1876

With Republicans on the defensive across the nation, the 1876 presidential election was crucial to the final overthrow of Reconstruction. The Republicans nominated Ohio Governor Rutherford B. Hayes to oppose Samuel Tilden of New York. Once again, violence prevented an estimated quarter of a million Republican votes from being cast in the South. Tilden had a clear majority of 250,000 in the popular vote, but the outcome in the Electoral College was in doubt because both parties claimed South Carolina, Florida, and Louisiana, the only reconstructed states still in Republican hands. Hayes needed all three states to be elected, for even without them, Tilden had amassed 184 electoral votes, one short of a majority. Republican canvassing boards in power disqualified enough Democratic votes to give each state to Hayes.

To arbitrate the disputed returns, Congress established a 15-member electoral commission: 5 members each from the Senate, the House, and the Supreme Court. By a straight party vote of 8–7, the commission awarded the disputed electoral votes—and the presidency—to Hayes.

When angry Democrats threatened a filibuster to prevent the electoral votes from being counted, key Republicans met with southern Democrats on February 26 at the Wormley Hotel in Washington. There, they reached an informal understanding, later known as the Compromise of 1877. Hayes's supporters agreed to withdraw federal troops from the South and not oppose the new Democratic state governments. For their part, southern Democrats dropped their opposition to Hayes's election and pledged to respect African American rights.

Compromise of 1877

Without federal support, the Republican governments in South Carolina and Louisiana promptly collapsed, and Democrats took control of the remaining states of the Confederacy. By 1877, the entire South was in the hands of the Redeemers, as they called themselves. Reconstruction and Republican rule had come to an end.

Redeemers take control

Racism and the Failure of Reconstruction

Reconstruction failed for a multitude of reasons. The reforming impulse that had created the Republican party in the 1850s had been battered and worn down by the war. The new materialism of industrial America inspired in many Americans a jaded cynicism about the corruption of the age and a desire to forget uncomfortable issues. In the South, African American voters and leaders inevitably lacked a certain amount of education and experience; elsewhere, Republicans were divided over policies and options.

Yet beyond these obstacles, the sad fact remains that the ideals of Reconstruction were most clearly defeated by a deep-seated racism that permeated American life. Racism was why the white South so unrelentingly resisted Reconstruction. Racism was why most white northerners had little interest in black rights except as a means to preserve the Union or to safeguard the Republic. Racism was why northerners were willing to write off Reconstruction and with it the welfare of African Americans. While Congress might pass a constitutional amendment abolishing slavery, it could not overturn at a stroke the social habits of two centuries.

Certainly the political equations of power, in the long term, had been changed. The North had fought fiercely during the war to preserve the Union. In doing so, it had secured the power to dominate the economic and political destiny of the nation. With the overthrow of Reconstruction, the white South had won back some of the power it had lost in 1865. But even with white supremacy triumphant, African Americans did not return to the social position they had occupied before the war. They were no longer slaves, and black southerners who walked dusty roads in search of family members, sent their children to school, or worshiped in churches they controlled knew what a momentous change emancipation was. Even under the exploitative sharecropping system, black income rose significantly in freedom. Then, too, the principles of "equal protection" and "due process of law" had been written into the Constitution. These guarantees would be available for later generations to use in championing once again the Radicals' goal of racial equality.

But this was a struggle left to future reformers. For the time being, the clear trend was away from change or hope—especially for former slaves like Benjamin Montgomery and his sons, the owners of the old Davis plantations in Mississippi. In the 1870s bad crops, lower cotton prices, and falling land values undermined the Montgomerys' financial position, and in 1875 Jefferson Davis sued to have the sale of Brierfield invalidated.

End of the Davis Bend experiment

Benjamin Montgomery, together with his sons, purchased Jefferson Davis's plantation along the Mississippi River after the war. A former slave, Montgomery pursued the dream of black economic independence by renting land to black farmers at Davis Bend.

A lower court ruled against Davis, since he had never received legal title to the plantation. Davis appealed to the state supreme court, which, following the overthrow of Mississippi's Radical government, had a white conservative majority. In a politically motivated decision, the court awarded Brierfield to Davis in 1878, and the Montgomerys lost Hurricane as well. The final outcome was not without bitter irony. In applying for restoration of his property after the war, Joseph Davis had convinced skeptical federal officials that he—and not his younger brother—held legal title to Brierfield. Had they decided instead that the plantation belonged to Jefferson Davis, it would have been confiscated.

But the waning days of Reconstruction were times filled with such ironies: of governments "redeemed" by violence, of Fourteenth Amendment rights designed to protect black people being used by conservative courts to protect giant corporations, of reformers taking up other causes. Disowned by its northern supporters and unmourned by public opinion, Reconstruction was over.

chapter summary

Presidents Abraham Lincoln and Andrew Johnson and the Republican-dominated Congress each developed a program of Reconstruction to quickly restore the Confederate states to the Union.

- Lincoln's 10 percent plan required that 10 percent of qualified voters from 1860 swear an oath of loyalty to begin organizing state government.

- Following Lincoln's assassination, Andrew Johnson changed Lincoln's terms and lessened Reconstruction's requirements.

- The more radical Congress repudiated Johnson's state governments and eventually enacted its own program of Reconstruction, which included the principle of black suffrage.

  - Congress passed the Fourteenth and Fifteenth Amendments and also extended the life of the Freedmen's Bureau, a unique experiment in social welfare.

  - Congress rejected land reform, however, which would have provided the freedpeople with a greater economic stake.

  - The effort to remove Johnson from office through impeachment failed.

- The Radical governments in the South, led by black and white southerners and transplanted northerners, compiled a mixed record on matters such as radical equality, education, economic issues, and corruption.

- Reconstruction was a time of both joy and frustration for former slaves.

  - Former slaves took steps to reunite their families and establish black-controlled churches.

  - They evidenced a widespread desire for land and education.

  - Black resistance to the old system of labor led to the adoption of sharecropping.

  - The Freedmen's Bureau fostered these new working arrangements and also the beginnings of black education in the South.

- Northern public opinion became disillusioned with Reconstruction during the presidency of Ulysses S. Grant.

- Southern whites used violence, economic coercion, and racism to overthrow the Republican state governments.

- In 1877 Republican leaders agreed to end Reconstruction in exchange for Rutherford B. Hayes's election as president.

- Racism played a key role in the eventual failure of Reconstruction.

Significant Events

1863 — 1863 Lincoln outlines Reconstruction program

1864 Lincoln vetoes Wade-Davis bill; Louisiana, Arkansas, and Tennessee establish governments under Lincoln's plan

1865 — 1865 Freedmen's Bureau established; Johnson becomes president; presidential Reconstruction completed; Congress excludes representatives of Johnson's governments; Thirteenth Amendment ratified; Joint Committee on Reconstruction established

1865–1866 Black codes enacted

1866 Civil rights bill passed over Johnson's veto; Memphis and New Orleans riots; Fourteenth Amendment passes Congress; Freedmen's Bureau extended; Ku Klux Klan organized; Tennessee readmitted to Congress; Republicans win decisive victory in congressional elections

1867 Congressional Reconstruction enacted; Tenure of Office Act

1867–1868 Constitutional conventions in the South; Blacks vote in southern elections

1868 Johnson impeached but acquitted; Fourteenth Amendment ratified; Grant elected president

1870 — 1870 Last southern states readmitted to Congress; Fifteenth Amendment ratified; Force Act passed

1871 Ku Klux Klan Act

1872 General Amnesty Act; Freedmen's Bureau closes down; Liberal Republican revolt

1873–1877 Panic and depression

1874 Democrats win control of the House

1875 — 1875 Civil Rights Act; Mississippi Plan

1876 Disputed Hayes-Tilden election

1877 Compromise of 1877; Hayes declared winner of electoral vote; last Republican governments in South fall

1877 —

additional reading

Historians' views of Reconstruction have dramatically changed in recent decades. Modern studies offer a more sympathetic assessment of Reconstruction and the experience of African Americans. Indicative of this trend is Eric Foner, *Reconstruction* (1988), the fullest modern treatment. Foner devotes considerable attention to black southerners' experiences but seriously neglects the North. The book is also available in an abridged edition.

Eric L. McKitrick, *Andrew Johnson and Reconstruction* (1966), while very critical of Johnson and his policies, argues that impeachment was unjustified. A different conclusion is reached by Michael Les Benedict in *The Impeachment and Trial of Andrew Johnson* (1973), which is the most thorough treatment of Congress's effort to remove Johnson from office. Political affairs in the South during Reconstruction are examined in Dan T. Carter, *When the War Was Over* (1985) and Thomas Holt, *Black over White* (1977), an imaginative study of black political leadership in South Carolina. Leon Litwack, *Been in the Storm So Long* (1979) and Willie Lee Rose, *Rehearsal for Reconstruction* (1964) sensitively analyze former slaves' transition to freedom, and James L. Roark, *Masters without Slaves* (1977) discusses former slaveholders' adjustment to the end of slavery. An excellent study of changing labor relations in southern agriculture is Julie Saville, *The Work of Reconstruction* (1995). George R. Bentley, *A History of the Freedmen's Bureau* (1955) is a sympathetic treatment of that unique institution; Donald Nieman, *To Set the Law in Motion: The Freedmen's Bureau and the Legal Rights of Blacks, 1865–1868* (1979) is more critical. Different perspectives on the overthrow of Reconstruction appear in William Gillette, *Retreat from Reconstruction, 1869–1879* (1980), which focuses on national politics and the federal government, and in Michael Perman, *The Road to Redemption* (1984), which looks at developments in the South. For a fuller list of readings, see the Bibliography

GLOBAL ESSAY

THE UNITED STATES IN AN INDUSTRIAL AGE

The Statue of Liberty has now stood watch over New York harbor for more than a hundred years. Looking back today, most Americans view the tired, huddled masses who passed beneath Liberty's torch as part of the continuing stream of immigrants stretching back to the English Pilgrims, the French fur traders of Canada, and the Spanish friars of Old California. But the tide of immigration that swelled during the mid-nineteenth century was strikingly different from the great majority of those who traveled to America in an earlier age. Innovations in transportation, communications, and industry created an international network that for the first time made possible voluntary migration on a massive scale.

In the 300 years before 1820 most new arrivals in North and South America did not come voluntarily. Nearly 8 million Africans were brought to the Americas during those years, virtually all as slaves. That number was four to five times the number of Europeans who came during the same period. In contrast, between 1820 and 1920 nearly 30 million free immigrants arrived from Europe.

Nor was this new flood directed only toward America. At least as many Europeans settled in other regions of Europe or the world. From eastern Europe millions followed the Trans-Siberian Railway (completed in 1905) into Asiatic Russia. The Canadian prairie provinces of Manitoba and Saskatchewan competed for homesteaders with Montana and the Dakotas. And as cowboys began driving American steers to railheads for shipment east, gauchos in western Argentina were rounding up cattle to be shipped to Buenos Aires. Before 1900 two out of three emigrating Italians booked passage not for the United States but for Brazil or Argentina.

This broad movement could not have taken place without a global network of communication, markets, and transportation. By midcentury, urbanization and industrialization were well under way in both America and Europe. The British, who led in revolutionizing industry, also discovered its harsh side effects. Without efficient transportation, British urban workers were forced to live within walking distance of factories. The resulting overcrowding and filth were almost stupefying. Families jammed into dark, dingy row houses built with few windows. In the streets and alleys beyond, open sewers flowed with garbage. In London one construction engineer reported that the overflow from privies had collected to the depth of three feet in the cellars of nearby houses.

Spurred by a deadly cholera epidemic in 1848, social reformer Edwin Chadwick led a campaign to install a system of cheap iron pipes and tile drains to provide running water and sewers throughout major cities. In addition, French and German research during the 1860s and 1870s established the germ theory of disease, confirming the need for better sanitation.

Other urban planners admired the radical renovation of Paris begun in the 1850s by Baron Georges Haussmann. Haussmann's workers

Darwin's *On the Origin of Species* published
1859

Suez Canal completed
1869

Franco–Prussian War;
Britain produces half the world's pig iron
1870

Refrigerated ships permit
export of beef from Argentina
1876

Pogroms against
Russian Jews
spur emigration
1880s

| 1850 | | 1860 | | 1870 | | | | 1880 | |
| GRANT | | | | | HAYES | GARFIELD | ARTHUR |

1877
Reconstruction
ends

1869
Transcontinental railroad completed

1876
Bell invents telephone

Rockefeller founds Standard Oil

1853
Commodore Perry visits Japan

1881
American Federation of Labor founded

AMERICAN EVENTS

tore down the city's medieval fortress walls, widened major streets into boulevards, and set aside land for pleasant green parks. American cities had no ancient walls and fewer narrow roads, and Americans were often more willing to rebuild and enlarge. Their innovations led Europeans to adopt horse-drawn streetcars and, later, electric trolleys. With an intracity transportation network in place, the old "walking cities" were able to add suburbs, partially easing the crush of earlier industrial crowding.

As hubs of the new industrial networks, cities needed efficient links to raw materials as well as markets for their finished products. Much of the late nineteenth century can be seen as a scramble of Western nations for those natural resources and markets.

Miners combed the hills of California for gold in 1849, as they did two years later in Victoria, Australia. In South Africa, the rush was for diamonds discovered along the Vaal and Orange rivers and gold near present-day Johannesburg. In Canada, Argentina, Australia, and New Zealand, farmers and cattle ranchers moved steadily toward larger commercial operations. All these enterprises extracted value from previously untapped natural resources.

The end result of the scramble was the age of imperialism, as the European powers sought to dominate newly acquired colonies in Africa and Asia. The United States joined the rush somewhat late, in part because it was still extracting raw materials from its own "colonial" re-

gions, the booming West and the defeated South.

European imperialists sometimes justified their rule over nonwhite races in Darwinian fashion, as the survival of the fittest. "The path of progress is

GLOBAL EVENTS

Berlin Conference concluded;
European powers partition Africa;
Indian National Congress

Slavery abolished
in Brazil
1888

Germany enacts a social security system;
Japan establishes the Meiji Constitution
1889

Boxer Rebellion in China;
Freud's *Interpretation of Dreams* published

Spanish–American War
1998

Outbreak of
Russo–Japanese War;
Social welfare legislation
in France
1904

| 1885 | 1890 | | 1895 | | 1900 | |
| CLEVELAND | HARRISON | CLEVELAND | | McKINLEY | | ROOSEVELT |

Sherman Antitrust Act

1897
First U.S. subway opens
(Boston)

1901
J. P. Morgan creates
U.S. Steel

1896
Plessy v. Ferguson
upholds segregation

Carnegie Steel produces
more steel than all Great
Britain

Twain's *Huckleberry Finn* published

1893
Three-year depression begins

AMERICAN EVENTS

strewn with the wreck . . . of inferior races," one English professor proclaimed in 1900. British poet Rudyard Kipling even suggested that Europeans were making a noble sacrifice on behalf of their subject peoples. "Take up the White Man's Burden," he exhorted them. "Send forth the best ye breed— / Go bind your sons to exile / To serve your captives' need."

But the burdens were far greater for the coolie laborers of Kipling's India, who died by the thousands clearing jungles for tea plantations. Imperialism's costs were also harsh for black miners laboring in South Africa and for Chinese workers in Australia and the United States who found themselves excluded and segregated after both gold rushes. A similar racialism—the widely ac-

cepted practice of categorizing and ranking people according to race—thwarted southern black sharecroppers in the United States and made it easier for successive waves of prospectors, cowhands, and sodbusters to drive American Indians off their lands.

The racial undercurrent of both European imperialism and American expansion was something most white Americans of the era ignored. But farmers in both the South and the West did lash out at industrial "robber barons" and railroad "monopolists." These business leaders seemed to epitomize the abuses of the new industrial order. As we shall see, the underlying causes of the era's social strain could not be so conveniently placed at the door of a few greedy villains. Industrialization created

a whole new order of complex, interlocking systems that fostered an increasingly stratified society.

The social strains arising out of such wrenching changes forced political systems to adjust

PART FOUR

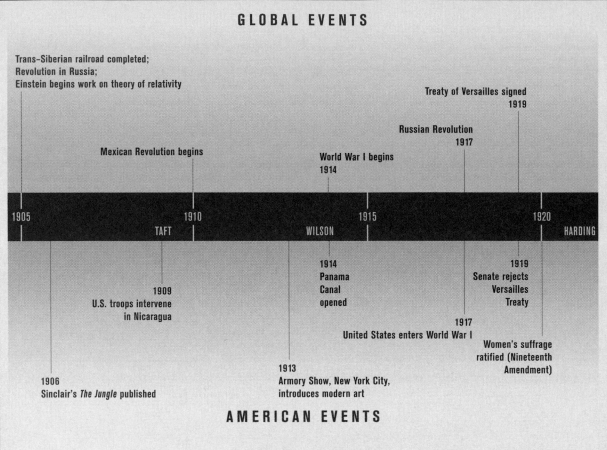

GLOBAL EVENTS

Trans–Siberian railroad completed;
Revolution in Russia;
Einstein begins work on theory of relativity

Treaty of Versailles signed
1919

Russian Revolution
1917

Mexican Revolution begins

World War I begins
1914

1905   1910   1915   1920

TAFT   WILSON   HARDING

1914
Panama
Canal
opened

1919
Senate rejects
Versailles
Treaty

1909
U.S. troops intervene
in Nicaragua

1917
United States enters World War I

Women's suffrage
ratified (Nineteenth
Amendment)

1906
Sinclair's *The Jungle* published

1913
Armory Show, New York City,
introduces modern art

AMERICAN EVENTS

as well. In the United States both Populist and Progressive reformers called on the government to play a more active part in managing the excesses of the new industrial order. In Europe, both radical reformers like Karl Marx and more moderate socialists pushed for change. As strikes became more common and labor unions more powerful, industrializing nations passed social legislation that included the first social security systems and health insurance. In the end, however, the political system was unable to manage the new global order of commerce and imperialism. With the coming of World War I, it was shaken to its roots.

The news spread across the South during the late 1870s. Perhaps a man came around with a handbill telling of cheap land, or a letter might arrive from friends or relatives and be read aloud at church. The news spread in different ways, but in the end, the talk always spelled Kansas.

Few black farmers had been that far west themselves. But more than a few knew that the abolitionist Old John Brown had lived in Kansas before coming east to raid Harpers Ferry. Black folks, it seemed, might be able to live more freely in Kansas. "You can buy land at from a dollar and a half to two dollars an acre," wrote one settler to his friend in Louisiana. There was another distinct advantage: "They do not kill Negroes here for voting."

In 1878 such prospects excited hundreds of black families already stretched to their limits by hardship and violence. With Rutherford Hayes president, Reconstruction was at an end. Southern state governments had been "redeemed" by conservative whites, and the future seemed uncertain. "COME WEST," concluded *The Colored Citizen,* a newspaper in Topeka. "COME TO KANSAS."

The New South & The Trans-Mississippi West

preview • In the decades following Reconstruction, the South and the West became more tightly linked to the economy of the Northeast. Both regions supplied the agricultural goods and raw materials that fueled urban and industrial growth in the northeastern and north central states. Tragically, both were also racially divided societies in which whites often used violence to assert their dominance.

St. Louis learned of these rumblings in the first raw days of March 1879, as steamers from downriver began unloading freedpeople in large numbers. Some came with belongings and money; others, with only the clothes on their backs. While the weather was still cold, they sought shelter beneath tarpaulins along the river levee, built fires by the shore, and got out frying pans to cook meals while their children jumped rope nearby. By the end of 1879, more than 20,000 had arrived.

When the crowds overwhelmed the wharves and temporary shelters, the city's black churches banded together to house the "refugees," feed them, and help them continue toward Kansas. Repeated rumors that rail passage would not be free failed to shake their hopes. "We's like de chilun ob Israel when dey was led from out o' bondage by Moses," one explained, referring to the Bible's tale of exodus from Egypt. "If we sticks together an' keeps up our faith we'll git to Kansas and be out o' bondage for shuah." So the "Exodusters," as they became known, pressed westward.

In the end, more black emigrants settled in growing towns like Topeka, Lincoln, and Kansas City. Men worked as hired hands; women did laundry. With luck, couples made $350 a year, saved a bit for a home, and put down roots. Bill Sims, an emigrant who settled in Ottawa, Kansas, put down roots literally—working at tree husbandry for a living. By the 1930s, when he was in his nineties, he could boast that his oldest daughter had been the "first colored girl to ever graduate" from Ottawa University. On the courthouse grounds at the center of town, the trees he had planted years before were still standing, a silent monument to his place in the community.

The Exodusters

Ho for Kansas!

Brethren, Friends, & Fellow Citizens:
I feel thankful to inform you that the
REAL ESTATE
AND
Homestead Association,
Will Leave Here the
15th of April, 1878,
In pursuit of Homes in the Southwestern Lands of America, at Transportation Rates, cheaper than ever was known before.

For full information inquire of
Benj. Singleton, better known as old Pap,
NO. 5 NORTH FRONT STREET.
Beware of Speculators and Adventurers, as it is a dangerous thing to fall in their hands.
Nashville, Tenn., March 18, 1878.

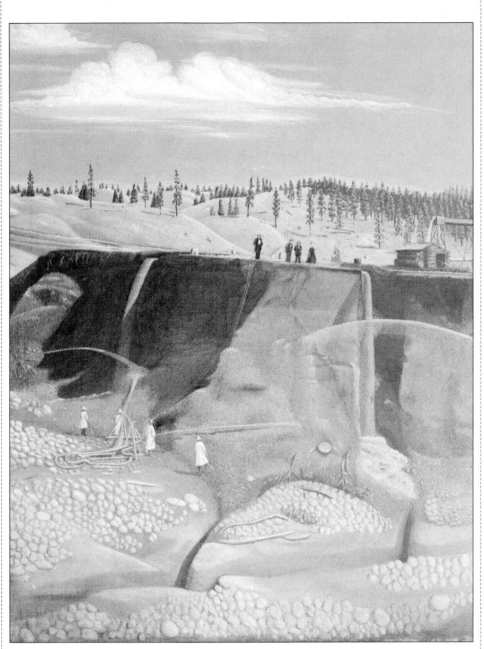

Blasting away with pressurized water jets, miners loosen gold-bearing gravel. Such techniques damaged the environment in the rush to exploit western resources. The artist, Mrs. Jonas Brown, lived in Idaho City during the height of its gold rush.

Sims and the host of Exodusters who poured into Kansas were part of a human flood westward. It had many sources—played-out farms of New England and the South, crowded cities, all of Europe. In 1879, as African Americans traveled up the Mississippi to St. Louis, 1000 white emigrants arrived in Kansas every week. Special trains brought settlers to the plains, all eager to start anew. During the 1880s the number of Kansans jumped from a million to a million and a half. Other western states experienced similar booms.

Yet the boomers' optimistic spirits could not mask serious strains in the rapidly expanding nation, especially in the South and West. The boom economies of cotton, cattle, and grain all depended on city markets in the Northeast. Often, especially during hard times, westerners and southerners saw themselves as the victims of a colonial economic system, in which their fortunes were controlled by the industries of northeastern cities and their hardships ignored by Washington.

Relations between the South, West, and Northeast

But these self-styled victims themselves exploited people and land. Whether locking former slaves into new forms of economic bondage such as sharecropping and tenancy or taking land from Indian peoples and Latinos by conquest or purchase, white Americans in the South and the West built societies of violence and racial caste. As largely agricultural regions, both areas struggled to find their place in the new age of industry emerging from Reconstruction. In the South, the pull of custom and a racial system valuing white supremacy over economic growth hampered the process. In the West, the wave of newcomers—human, plant, and animal—clashed with natives and strained resources as never before. In both regions, the adjustments were often wrenching. Yet by the end of the nineteenth century, the South and the West had taken their place as sources of raw materials for factories, as providers of foodstuffs for growing cities, and as markets for finished goods. Most of the value added to those goods, it should be noted, ended up outside the South and the West and enriched the rest of the country at the expense of those regions.

The Southern Burden

It was just such inequities that infuriated Henry Grady, the editor of the *Atlanta Constitution*. Grady often liked to tell the story of the poor cotton farmer buried in a pine coffin in the pine woods of Georgia. Except the coffin hadn't been made in Georgia but in Cincinnati. The nails in the coffin had been forged in Pittsburgh, though an iron mine lay near the cemetery. Even the farmer's cotton coat was made in New York and his trousers in Chicago. The "South didn't furnish a thing on earth for that funeral but the corpse and the hole in the ground!" fumed Grady. The irony of the story was the tragedy of the South. The region had human and natural resources aplenty but, alas, few factories to manufacture the goods it needed.

The gospel of a "New South"

In the 1880s Grady campaigned to bring about a "New South" of bustling industry, cities, and commerce. The business class and its values would displace the old planter class as southerners raced "to out-Yankee the Yankee." Grady and other publicists recognized the South's potential. Extending from Delaware south to Florida and west to Texas, the region took in a third of the nation's total area. It held a third of its arable farmlands, vast tracts of lumber, and rich deposits of coal, iron, oil, and fertilizers. To overcome the destruction of the Civil War and the loss of slaveholding wealth, apostles of the New South campaigned to catch up with the industrial North.

Yet no amount of hopeful talk could change the economic structure of southern society that had emerged from the Civil War—decentralized, rural, and agricultural. As late as 1890 the census counted less than 10 percent of all southerners as urban dwellers, compared with more than 50 percent in the North Atlantic states. Well into the twentieth century, Grady's New South remained the poorest section of the country. And the South suffered as well the burden of an unwieldy labor system that was often unskilled, usually underpaid, and always divided along lines of race.

Agriculture in the New South

A cotton-dominated economy

For all the talk of industry, the economy of the postwar South remained agricultural, tied to crops like tobacco, rice, sugar, and especially cotton. By using fertilizers, planters were able to introduce cotton into areas once considered marginal. The number of acres planted in cotton more than doubled between 1870 and 1900. Some southern farmers sought prosperity in crops other than cotton. George Washington Carver, of Alabama's Tuskegee Institute (page 686), persuaded many poor black farmers to plant peanuts. But most southern soils were too acidic and the spring rains too heavy for other legumes and grains to flourish. Parasites and diseases plagued cattle herds. Work animals like mules were raised more cheaply in other regions. Try as southerners might to diversify, cotton still dominated their economy. "When southern cotton prices drop, every man feels the blow," noted one observer. "When southern cotton prices advance, every industry thrives with vigor."

From 1880 to 1900 world demand for cotton grew slowly, and prices fell. As farms in other parts of the country were becoming larger and more efficient and were tended by fewer workers per acre, southern farms decreased in size. This decrease reflected the breakup of large plantations, but it also resulted from a high birthrate. Across the country, the number of children born per mother was dropping, but in the South, large families remained common because more children meant more farmhands. Each year, fewer acres of land were available for each person to cultivate. Even though the southern economy kept pace with national growth, per capita income fell behind.

After the Civil War, African Americans marked their freedom by ending field labor for most women and children. The women instead played a vital role in the domestic economy. Home garden plots supplemented the family food supply.

Tenancy and Sharecropping

To freedpeople across the South, the end of slavery brought hopes of economic independence. John Solomon Lewis was one such farmer. After the war Lewis rented land to grow cotton in Tensas Parish, Louisiana. A depression in the 1870s dashed his dreams. "I was in debt," Lewis explained, "and the man I rented land from said every year I must rent again to pay the other year, and so I rents and rents and each year I gets deeper and deeper in debt."

The dream of economic independence was rooted in a theory of landholding called the "agricultural ladder," in vogue after the Civil War. According to this theory, any poor man could work his way up, rung by rung, until he finally owned his own land. Each rung in the agricultural ladder brought greater autonomy and with it, the chance to achieve self-sufficiency and independence. At the bottom was the hired hand, who simply worked for wages on someone else's farm. On the next rung, the sharecropper worked the land of another but owned none of the crop and was paid no wages. Instead, he received a share of the proceeds when the owner sold the harvest, about half minus whatever debts had been incurred. The tenant, higher still, literally rented a parcel of land, had his own tools and work animals, and owned the crop itself. As rent, the tenant turned over part of the harvest, usually a quarter of the cotton crop and a third of any grains, to the landowner. Through ruthless penny-pinching, the tenant eventually could purchase land and rise finally to the status of independent farmer. So the theory went.

In practice, harsh realities overwhelmed theory, as John Solomon Lewis and other poor farmers learned. Most of the best land in the South remained in the hands of large plantation owners. Few freedpeople or poor whites ever had enough money to acquire property. The problem lay in a ruinous system of credit. The harvest, whether

Agricultural ladder

Crop-lien system

produced by croppers or tenants or even small, independent farmers, was rarely enough for the worker to make ends meet, let alone to pay off debts and move up the agricultural ladder. Most farmers had to borrow money in the spring just to buy seeds, tools, or necessities such as food and clothing. Usually the only source of supplies and credit was the country store. When John Solomon Lewis and other tenants entered the store, they saw two prices, one for cash and one for credit. The credit price might be as much as 60 percent higher. (By contrast, merchants in New York charged around 6 percent to buy on credit.) As security for the loan, independent farmers mortgaged their land and soon slipped into tenancy as debts mounted and creditors foreclosed on their farms. The only asset tenants had was the crop they owned or the share they received. So they put up a mortgage or "lien" on the crop. The lien gave the shopkeeper first claim on the crop until the debt was paid.

Across the South, sharecropping and crop liens reduced many farmers to virtual slavery by shackling them to perpetual debt. Year after year, they rented or worked the land and borrowed against their future returns until they found themselves so deeply in debt that they could never escape. This economic dependence, known as debt peonage, turned the agricultural ladder into an agricultural slide, robbing small farmers of their land and sending them to the bottom rungs of tenancy, sharecropping, and migrant farm work. By the 1880s three of every four African American farmers in the black belt states of Mississippi, Alabama, and Georgia were croppers. Twenty years later, a majority of southern white farmers had fallen into sharecropping. Few had the freedom to move up. The landlord or shopkeeper (often the same person) could insist that tenants grow only cash crops such as cotton rather than produce they could eat. Most landlords also required that cotton be ginned, baled, and marketed through their mills—at rates they controlled. Sharecropping, crop liens, and monopolies on ginning and marketing added up to inequality and crushing poverty for the small farmers of the South, black or white.

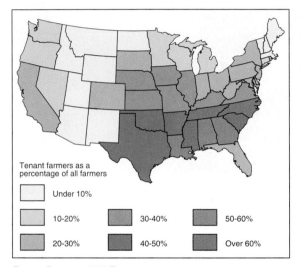

Tenant farmers as a percentage of all farmers

☐ Under 10%

☐ 10-20%   ☐ 30-40%   ☐ 50-60%

☐ 20-30%   ☐ 40-50%   ☐ Over 60%

Tenant Farmers, 1900 Tenant farming dominated southern agriculture after the Civil War. But notice that by 1900 it also accounted for much of the farm labor in the trans-Mississippi West, where low crop prices, high costs, and severe environmental conditions forced independent farmers into tenancy.

Southern Industry

The crusade for a New South did bring change. From 1869 to 1909, industrial production grew faster than the national rate. So did productivity for southern workers. A boom in railroad building after 1879 furnished the region with good transportation. In two areas, cotton textiles and tobacco, southern advances were striking. With cotton fiber and cheap labor close at hand, 400 cotton mills were humming by 1900, when they employed almost 100,000 workers.

Boom in textiles

Most new textile workers were poor white southerners escaping competition from black farm laborers or fleeing the hardscrabble life of the mountains. Entire families worked in the mills. Older men had the most trouble adjusting. They lacked the experience, temperament, and dexterity to tend spindles and looms in cramped mills. Only over time, as farm folk adapted to the tedious rhythm of factories, did southerners become competitive with workers from other regions of the United States and western Europe.

Tobacco and cigarettes

The tobacco industry also thrived in the New South. Before the Civil War, American tastes had run to cigars, snuff, and chewing tobacco. In 1876, James Bonsack, an 18-year-old Virginian, invented a machine to roll cigarettes. That was just the

This girl had been working in a cotton mill in Whitnel, North Carolina, for about a year, sometimes on the night shift. She made 48 cents a day. When asked how old she was, she hesitated, then said, "I don't remember." But then she added, confidentially, "I'm not old enough to work, but do just the same."

device Washington Duke and his son James needed to boost the fortunes of their growing tobacco business. Cigarettes suited the new urban market in the North. Unlike chewing tobacco and snuff, they were, according to one observer, "clean, quick, and potent."

Between 1860 and 1900, the annual rate of tobacco consumption nearly quadrupled. Americans spent more money on tobacco than on clothes or shoes. The sudden interest in smoking offered southerners a rare opportunity to control a national market. But the factories were so hot, the stench of tobacco so strong, and the work so exhausting that native-born white southerners generally refused the jobs. Duke solved the labor problem by hiring Jewish immigrants, expert cigar makers, to train black southerners in the techniques of tobacco work. Then he promoted cigarettes in a national advertising campaign, using gimmicks like collectible picture cards. By the 1890s his American Tobacco Company led the industry.

The growth of the textile and tobacco industries encouraged urbanization and investment in regional development. But investment and urbanization could not by themselves lift the region from poverty. Low wages reflected the pattern of southern agriculture rather than the higher wage patterns of industries in the Northeast and upper Midwest. As immigrants flooded into those regions, they created skilled workforces and expanded markets. Low wages discouraged them from settling in the South. Isolated from the international labor pool, the southern labor force grew almost exclusively from natural increase.

Timber and Steel

The realities of southern economic life were more accurately reflected in lumber and steel than in tobacco and textiles. After the Civil War, the South possessed more than 60 percent of the nation's timber resources. With soaring demand from towns and cities, lumber and turpentine became the South's chief industries and employers. If anything, however, aggressive lumbering left the South far poorer. Corruption of state officials and a relaxed federal timber policy allowed northerners and foreigners to acquire huge forest tracts at artificially low prices. The timber was then sold as raw lumber rather than as more profitable finished products such as cedar shingles or newsprint (or the coffins Henry Grady liked to mention). Only in North Carolina did the manufacture of furniture flourish.

Aggressive logging added little to local economies. Logging camps were isolated and temporary. Visitors described the lumberjacks as "single, homeless, and possessionless." Once loggers leveled the forests around their camps, they moved on to other sites. Most sawmills operated for only a few years before the owners followed the loggers to a new area. Thus loggers and millers had little time to put down roots and invest their cash in the community.

Environmental costs

The environmental costs were equally high. In the South, as elsewhere, overcutting and other logging practices stripped hillsides bare. As spring rains eroded soil and unleashed floods, forests lost their capacity for self-renewal. By 1901 a Georgian complained that "from most of the visible land the timber is entirely gone." With it went the golden eagles, the peregrine falcons, and other native species.

Turpentine mills, logging, and lumber milling provided young black southerners with their greatest source of employment. Occasionally an African American rose to be a supervisor, though most supervisors were white. Because the work was dirty and dangerous and required few skills, turnover was high and morale low. Southerners often blamed the workers, not the operators, for the industry's low standards. As one critic complained, "The sawmill negro is rather shiftless and is not inclined to stay in any one location and consequently there is little incentive on the part of the owner or operator to carry on welfare work in any extensive manner." In fact, most black workers left the mills in search of higher wages or to settle down to sharecropping in order to marry and support families.

Birmingham steel

The iron and steel industry most disappointed promoters of the New South. The availability of coke as a fuel made Chattanooga, Tennessee, and Birmingham, Alabama, major centers for foundries. By the 1890s the Tennessee Coal, Iron, and Railway Company (TCI) of Birmingham was turning out iron pipe for gas, water, and sewer lines vital to cities. Unfortunately Birmingham's iron deposits were

This railroad served a lumber mill. The lumber industry in the South exploited large stands of timber, but overcutting led to erosion and tended to impoverish the region.

ill-suited for the kinds of steel in demand. In 1907 the financially strapped TCI was sold to the giant U.S. Steel Corporation, controlled by northern interests.

The pattern of lost opportunity was repeated in other southern industries—mining, chemical fertilizers, cottonseed oil, and railroads. Under the campaign for a New South, all grew dramatically in employment and value, but not enough to end poverty or industrialize the region. The South remained largely rural, agricultural, and poor.

The Sources of Southern Poverty

Why did poverty persist in the New South? Many southerners claimed that the region was exploited by outside interests. In effect, they argued, the South became a colonial economy controlled by business interests in New York or Pittsburgh rather than Atlanta or New Orleans. Raw materials such as minerals, timber, and cotton were shipped to other regions, which earned larger profits by turning them into finished goods. Profits that might have been used to foster development in the South were thereby siphoned off to other regions.

This theory alone does not explain the South's lagging development. Three other factors contributed to the region's poverty. First, the South began to industrialize later than the Northeast, so northerners had a head start on learning new manufacturing techniques. Northern workers produced more not because they were more energetic or disciplined but because they were more experienced. Once southern workers overcame their inexperience, they competed well. Second, the South commanded only a small technological community to guide its industrial development. Northern engineers and mechanics seldom followed northern capital into the region. Few people were available to adapt modern technology to southern conditions or to teach southerners how to do it themselves.

Late start in industrializing

Education might have overcome the problem by upgrading the region's workforce. But no region in the nation spent less on schooling than the South did. Southern leaders, drawn from the ranks of the upper class, cared little about educating ordinary white residents and openly resisted educating black southerners. Education, they contended, "spoiled" otherwise contented workers by leading them to demand higher wages and better conditions. In fact, the region's low wages encouraged educated workers to leave the South in search of higher pay. Few southern states invested in technical colleges and engineering schools, and so none could match those of the North.

Undereducated labor

Lack of education aggravated a third source of southern poverty: the isolation of its labor force. In 1900 agriculture still dominated the southern economy. It required unskilled, low-paid sharecroppers and wage laborers. Southerners feared outsiders, whether capitalists, industrialists, or experts in technology, who might spread discontent among workers. So southern states discouraged social services and opportunities that might have attracted human and financial resources. The South remained poor because it received too little, not too much, outside investment.

The isolated southern labor market

Many a southern man, noted a son of the region, loved "to toss down a pint of raw whiskey in a gulp, to fiddle and dance

Life in the New South

all night, to bite off the nose or gouge out the eye of a favorite enemy, to fight harder and love harder than the next man, to be known far and wide as a hell of a fellow." Life in the New South was a constant struggle to balance this love of the vigorous life with an equally powerful pull: Christian piety.

Divided in its soul, the South was also divided by race. Even after the Civil War ended slavery, some 90 percent of African Americans continued to live in the rural South. Without slavery, however, southerners lost the system of social control that had defined race relations. Over time they substituted a new system of racial separation that eased, but never eliminated, white fear of African Americans.

Rural Life

Pleasure, piety, race—all divided southern life, in town and country alike. And life separated along lines of gender as well, especially in rural areas, where most southerners lived.

Hunting

Southern males found one source of pleasure in hunting. Hunting offered welcome relief from heavy farm work. One South Carolinian recalled that possum hunting "gave you a wild feeling of being free, of standing alone against darkness and all the forces that cramped you." For rural people a successful hunt could also add meat and fish to a scanty diet. And through hunting many boys found a path to manhood. Seeing his father and brothers return with wild turkeys, young Edward McIlhenny longed "for the time when I would be old enough to hunt this bird." The prospect of danger, perhaps a fall from a horse, only added to the excitement.

The thrill of illicit pleasure also drew many southern men to events of violence and chance, including cockfighting. They valued combative birds and were convinced that their champions fought more boldly than did northern bantams. The longer blades or gaffs attached to the birds' heels cut more deeply, producing more blood and quicker deaths. Gambling between bird owners and among spectators doubtless heightened the thrills. Such sport offended churchgoing southerners. They condemned as sinful "the beer garden, the base ball, the low theater, the dog fight and cock fight and the ring for the pugilist and brute."

Farm entertainments

Many southern customs involved no such disorderly behavior. Work-sharing festivals celebrated the harvest and offered relief from the daily burdens of farm life. A Mississippian spoke of "neighborhood gatherings such as house raisings, log rollings, quiltings, and road workings." These events, too, were generally segregated along gender lines. Men did the heavy chores and competed in contests of physical prowess. Women shared more domestic tasks. Quilting was a favorite, for it brought women an opportunity to work together and enjoy one another's company. Community gatherings also offered young southerners a relaxed place for courtship. In one courting game, the young man who found a rare red ear of corn "could kiss the lady of his choice"—although in the school, church, or home under adult supervision, such behavior was discouraged.

Town

For rural folk, a trip to town brought special excitement, along with a bit of danger. Saturdays, court days, and holidays provided an occasion to mingle. Once again, there were male and female domains. For men the saloon, the blacksmith shop, or the storefront was a place to do business and to let off steam. Few men went to town without participating in social drinking, but when men turned to roam the streets, the threat of brawling and violence drove most women away. One Tennessee woman claimed that "it was never considered safe for a lady to go down on the streets on Saturdays."

Court week, when a district judge arrived to mete out justice, drew the biggest crowds. Some people came to settle disputes; most came to enjoy the spectacle or do some business like horse trading. Peddlers and entertainers worked the crowds with magic tricks, patent medicines, and other wares. Town also offered a chance to attend the theater or a traveling circus.

The Church

At the center of southern life stood the church as a great stabilizer and custodian of social order. "When one joined the Methodist church," a southern woman remembered, "he was expected to give up all such things as cards, dancing, theatres, in fact all so called worldly amusements." Many devout southerners pursued these ideals, although such restraint asked more of people, especially men, than most were willing to show, except perhaps on Sunday.

Congregations were often so small and isolated that they could attract a preacher only once or twice a month. Evangelicals counted on the Sunday sermon to steer them from sin. In town, a sermon might last 30 to 45 minutes, but in the country, a preacher could go on for two hours or more, whipping up his congregation until "even the little children wept."

Rural religion

By 1870 southern churches were segregated by race (see page 549). Within them, the congregation, particularly in rural areas, was separated by gender too. Upon seeing a man and woman seated together, a Virginia Baptist claimed "they were from Richmond or Lynchburg, or some other city where folks did not know any better." As a boy entered manhood, he moved from the female to the male section. Yet churches were, at base, female domains. Considered guardians of virtue, more women were members, attended services, and ran church activities.

Church was a place to socialize as well as worship. Many of the young went simply to meet those of the opposite sex. Church picnics and all-day sings brought as many as 30 or 40 young people together for hours of eating, talk, services, and hymn singing. Still, these occasions could not match the fervor of a weeklong camp meeting. In the late summer or early fall, town and countryside alike emptied as folks set up tents in shady groves and listened to two or three ministers preach day and night in the largest event of the year. The camp meeting refired evangelical faith while celebrating traditional values of home and family.

For Baptists in the South, both white and black, the ceremony of adult baptism included total immersion, often in a nearby river. The ritual symbolized the waters of newfound faith washing away sins that had been forgiven by God's free grace. Here, a black congregation looks on, some holding umbrellas to protect against the sun.

Segregation

Nothing challenged tradition in the post–Civil War South more than race. With the abolition of slavery and the end of Reconstruction, white northerners and southerners achieved sectional harmony by sacrificing the rights of black citizens. White southerners were assured that in matters of race they would be "left alone" by the federal government. The hands-off, or laissez-faire, approach suited even the white northerners who once championed black rights. The editor of one magazine published in New York told northern readers that he doubted whether former slaves were capable of participating in "a system of government for which you and I have much respect." In the New South, African Americans would remain free but scarcely equal.

During the 1880s, Redeemer governments (pages 557–558) moved to formalize a new system of segregation or racial separation. Redeemers were Democratic politicians who came to power in southern states to end the Republican rule established during Reconstruction. They were eager to reap the benefits of economic expansion and to attract the business classes—bankers, railroad promoters, industrial operators. As their part of the bargain, the Redeemers assured anxious northerners that Redeemer rule would not mean political disfranchisement of the freedpeople. That promise they would not keep.

Pressure to reach a new racial accommodation in the South increased as more African Americans moved into southern towns and cities, competing for jobs with poor whites. One way to preserve the social and economic superiority of white southerners, poor as well as rich, was to separate blacks as an inferior caste. But federal laws designed to enforce the Civil Rights Act of 1866 and the Fourteenth Amendment stood in the way. In effect, these laws established social equality for all races in public gathering places such as hotels, theaters, and railroads.

In 1883, however, the Supreme Court ruled (in the *Civil Rights Cases*) that hotels and railroads were not "public" institutions because private individuals owned them. The Fourteenth Amendment was thus limited to protecting citizens from

Laissez-faire race relations

A long line of African American voters waits to cast ballots in Caddo Parish, Louisiana, in 1894. Clearly, interest in voting remained high among black citizens. Two years later Louisiana followed the lead of other Southern states in disfranchising most of its black voters (as well as many poor whites).

violations of their civil rights by states, not by private individuals. The national policy of laissez faire in race relations could not have been made any clearer.

Within 20 years every southern state had enacted segregation as law. The earliest laws legalized segregation in trains and other such public conveyances where blacks and whites were likely to mingle. Soon a complex web of Jim Crow statutes had drawn an indelible color line separating the races in prisons, parks, hotels, restaurants, hospitals, and virtually all public gathering places except streets and stores. (The term *Jim Crow*, used to denote a policy of segregation, originated in a song of the same name sung in minstrel shows of the day.)

Jim Crow laws

Was such state-sponsored separation an act of discrimination that violated civil rights? Only the Supreme Court could decide. In 1896, the Court gave its full blessing to the policy of segregation. *Plessy v. Ferguson* upheld a Louisiana law requiring segregated railroad facilities. Segregation did not constitute discrimination, the Court argued, so long as accommodations for both races were equal. The doctrine of separate but equal thus became embedded in the fabric of American law and would govern race relations for more than half a century. In reality, of course, such separate facilities were seldom equal and always stigmatized African Americans.

Plessy v. Ferguson

By the turn of the century segregation was firmly in place, stifling economic competition between the races and reducing African Americans to second-class citizenship. Many kinds of employment, such as work in the textile mills, went largely to whites. Skilled and professional black workers generally served black clients. African Americans could enter some white residences only as servants and hired help, and usually by the back door only. They were barred from juries and usually received far stiffer penalties than whites for the same crimes.

As Jim Crow laws became entrenched, so did social custom. Black southerners always addressed white southerners as Mister, Miss, and Ma'am—even those of lower status. But white southerners called black southerners by their first names or more simply Sister or Boy, no matter their age or profession. Any African American who

Spending on Education in the South before and after Disfranchisement With disfranchisement and segregation, education was separate, but hardly equal, for blacks and whites. In these states, after blacks were disfranchised, spending on white students rose while spending on black students decreased.

[*Source:* Data from Robert A. Margo, *Disfranchisement, School Finance, and the Economics of Segregated Schools in the U.S. South, 1890–1910* (New York: Garland Press, 1985), table I-1.]

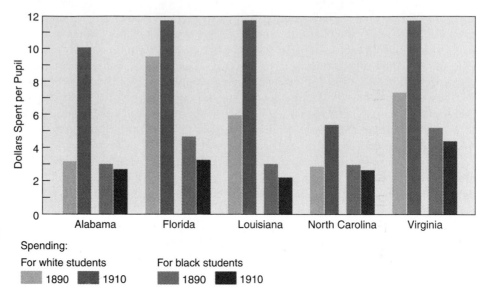

Spending:

For white students   For black students
■ 1890 ■ 1910   ■ 1890 ■ 1910

crossed the color line risked violence. Some were tarred and feathered, others whipped and beaten, and many lynched. Of the 187 lynchings averaged each year of the 1890s, some 80 percent occurred in the South. The victims were almost always African Americans.

Western Frontiers

The black Exodusters flooding into Kansas in the 1870s and 1880s were only part of the vast migration west. Looking beyond the Mississippi in the 1840s and 1850s, white "overlanders" had set their sights on California and Oregon and the promise of land. They headed across the Mississippi River, pushing the frontier of Anglo settlement from east to west to the edge of the continent. They rolled over the Great Plains, through the snow-capped Rockies, and across the Great Basin, with deserts so dry that rain sometimes evaporated before hitting the ground. When they reached the fertile valleys of the West Coast, they stopped, ready, as one Oregonian emigrant proclaimed, "to seek their fortunes and settle an empire."

The overlanders went west in search of opportunity and "free" land. In the trans-Mississippi West, however, opportunity proved elusive to those without money or power. They also found Indians—perhaps as many as 360,000—and "Hispanos," settlers of Spanish descent. The Indians and Hispanos hardly considered the land free for use by Anglos. The overlanders discovered as well that the West was not one region but many, each governed by a different ecology. And its frontiers moved in many directions, not just from east to west. Before the Civil War, the frontier for easterners had moved beyond the Mississippi to the timberlands of Missouri but skipped over the Great Plains, as the overlanders settled in California and Oregon. But another frontier then pushed east from the Pacific coast, following miners into the Sierra Nevadas. For Texans, the frontier moved from south to north as cattle ranchers sought new grazing land, as had the ancestors of the Spanish rancheros of the Southwest. And for American Indians, the frontier was constantly shifting and disrupting their ways of life.

Moving frontiers

How to Define the Frontier?

For historian Frederick Jackson Turner, writing in the 1890s, the West was not many frontiers but one, a westward-moving line he defined as "the meeting point of savagery and civilization." The frontier represented the march of progress into isolated areas of "free land." Its significance in American history—as a safety valve for unhappy easterners, as a cradle of democracy, as a fountain of American self-reliance and sense of community—could no longer be ignored.

Most historians have rejected the "Turner thesis," though not the significance of the West in American history. In the ethnocentric fashion of his age, Turner ignored the presence of rich tribal cultures beyond the point of Anglo settlement. Nor did he acknowledge the Hispanic tradition or the role of women. Where Turner saw civilization meeting savagery, social historians see a "new West" of conflict, opportunity, and cultural interplay, and ecological historians see a web of delicate environments shaping and being shaped by their human and nonhuman inhabitants.

Western Landscapes

Whatever perspective one adopts, the West is, first and foremost, a place of varied landscapes. Early travelers from the United States labeled the vast region beyond the Mississippi the "Great American Desert," and with good reason. Most of the land between the 98th meridian and the lush lowlands of the West Coast receives less than 20 inches of rain a year, making the Great Plains a treeless expanse of prairie grass and dunes. Infrequent stands of timber cluster along river bottoms, and wood for housing and fences is scarce. To eastern farmers accustomed to all the water, timber, and tillable land they needed, the region at first seemed suitable for neither humans nor domesticated animals. Many overlanders of the 1840s and 1850s compared its vast windy spaces to the oceans: a "sea of grass" stretching to the horizon and crossed by "prairie schooners."

But the plains are only part of the trans-Mississippi West. And even they can be divided. The Great Plains west of the 98th meridian are semiarid, but the eastern Prairie Plains are favored with good soil and abundant rain. Beyond the plains the jagged peaks of the Rocky Mountains stretch from Alaska to New Mexico. And west of the mountains lies the Great Basin of Utah, Nevada, and eastern California. There temperatures climb above 100 degrees and the ground cracks. Near the coast rise the Sierra Nevadas and Cascades, rich in minerals and lumber and sloping to the temperate shores and fertile valleys of the Pacific.

Easterners who watched the wagons roll west liked to conjure up the image of a "trackless wilderness." In truth, even in the 1840s, the Great Plains and mountain frontier comprised a complex web of cultures and environments in which Spanish, Anglo-American, and Indian cultures interacted and often produced swift change. One example is the horse, introduced into North America by the colonial Spanish. By the eighteenth century horses were grazing on prairie grass across the Great Plains. By the nineteenth century the Comanche, Cheyenne, Apache, and other tribes had become master riders and hunters who could shoot their arrows with deadly accuracy at a full gallop. The new mobility of the Plains Indians far extended the area in which they could hunt buffalo, which soon became a staple of their existence. Their lives shifted from settled, village-centered agriculture to nomadic hunting.

Indian Peoples and the Western Environment

Some whites embraced the myth of the Indian as "noble savage" who lived in perfect harmony with the natural world. To be sure, Plains Indians were inventive in using scarce resources. Cottonwood bark fed horses in winter, and the buffalo supplied not only meat but also bones for tools, fat for cosmetics, sinews for thread, even dung for fuel. Yet Indians could not help but shape their environment. Plains Indians hunted buffalo by stampeding herds over cliffs, which often led to waste. They irrigated crops and set fires to improve vegetation and game. By the mid-nineteenth century some tribes had become so enmeshed in trade with whites, that they overtrapped their own hunting grounds. In these and other ways, Indians altered the ecological systems around them.

Variety of Indian cultures

Ecosystems, in turn, helped to shape Indian cultures. Although big-game hunting was common among many western tribes, the nomadic buffalo culture of the Great Plains Indians was hardly representative. In the lush forests and mountain ranges of the Pacific Northwest, Yuroks, Chinook, and other tribes hunted bear, moose, elk, and deer. Along the rocky coast they took whales, seals, and a variety of fish from the ocean. The Yakimas and Walla Wallas moved into the river valleys for the great salmon runs. Where the land was less bountiful, Indian tribes lived close to starvation. Utes, Shoshones, Paiutes, and Pavistos scoured the deserts of the Great Basin to eke out a diet of rabbits, snakes, insects, roots, and berries. The early Hohokams and later the Pima and other tribes in New Mexico and Arizona developed irrigation to allow farming of beans, squash, and corn in the arid climate.

The cultures of western Indians were remarkably varied, ranging from the nomadic Plains tribes to the more settled peoples of the northwest coast who lived off the sea. This Sioux woman gathers firewood; the photograph was taken by Edward Curtis, who spent many years recording the faces and lives of native peoples of the West.

Despite their diversity, Indian peoples shared certain values. Most tribes were small extended kinship groups of 300 to 500 people in which the well-being of all outweighed the needs of each member. Although some tribes were better off than others, the gap between rich and poor within tribes was seldom large. Such small material differences often promoted communal decision making. The Cheyenne, for example, employed a council of 44 to advise the chief.

Most of all, Indians shared a reverence for nature, whatever their actual impact on the natural world. They believed human beings were part of an interconnected world of animals, plants, and other natural elements. All had souls of their own but were bound together, as if by contract, to live in balance through the ceremonial life of the tribe and the customs related to specific plants and animals. The Taos of New Mexico thought that each spring the pregnant earth issued new life. To avoid disturbing "mother" earth, they removed the hard shoes from their horses, while they themselves walked in bare feet or soft moccasins. Whites were mystified by the attitude of Chief Smohalla of the Wanapun tribe, who explained why his people refused to farm: "You ask me to plow the ground! Shall I take a knife and tear my mother's bosom? . . . You ask me to cut grass and make hay and sell it, and be rich like white men! But how dare I cut off my mother's hair?"

Regard for the land endowed special places with religious meaning. The Taos centered their spiritual and economic life on Blue Lake in northwest New Mexico, the source of life and the revelations of the great spirit of the universe. Where the Sioux saw in the Black Hills the sacred home of Wakan Tanka—the burial place of the dead and the site of their vision quests—whites saw grass for grazing and gold for the taking. From such contrasting views came conflict.

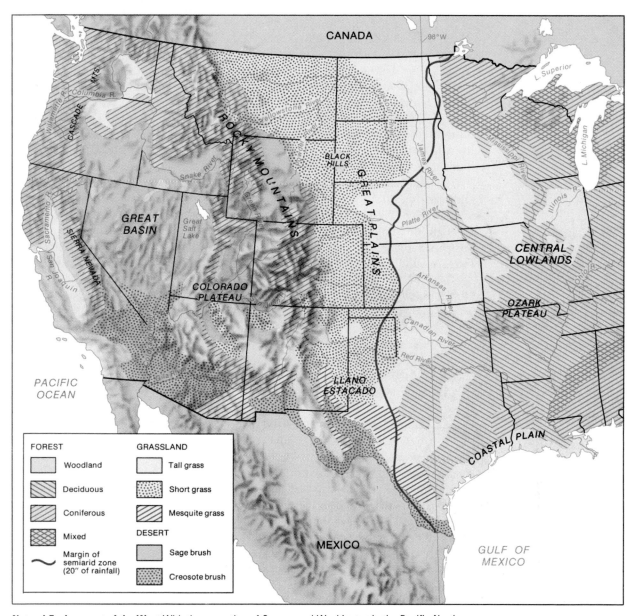

Natural Environment of the West With the exception of Oregon and Washington in the Pacific North-west, few areas west of the 20-inch rainfall line receive enough annual precipitation to support agriculture without irrigation. Consequently, water has been the key to growth and development in the area west of the 98th meridian, which encompasses more than half the land area of the continental United States. The dominance of short grasses and coniferous (evergreen) trees reflects the rainfall patterns.

Whites and the Western Environment: Competing Visions

As discoveries of gold and silver lured whites into Indian territory, many adopted the confident outlook of Missouri politician William Gilpin. Only a lack of vision prevented the opening of the West for exploitation, Gilpin told an Independence, Missouri, audience in 1849. What was most needed were cheap lands and a railroad linking the two coasts "like ears on a human head." Distance, climate, and even the Indians were just obstacles to overcome.

William Gilpin, a western booster

By 1868 a generous Congress had granted western settlers their two greatest wishes: free land under the Homestead Act of 1862 and a transcontinental railroad. As the new governor of Colorado, Gilpin crowed about the region's limitless resources. One day, he believed, the West would support more than a billion people. Scarce rainfall and water did not daunt him, for in his eyes the West was an Eden-like garden, not "the great American Desert." Once the land had been planted, Gilpin assured listeners, the rains would develop naturally. He subscribed to the popular notion that "rain follows the plow," a myth sustained by an unusually wet cycle from 1878 to 1886. When the dry weather returned in the late 1880s, not rain but hardship followed those farmers who moved west.

John Wesley Powell

Unlike the visionary Gilpin, John Wesley Powell knew something about water and farming. After losing an arm in the Civil War, geologist Powell went west. In 1869 and 1871 he led scientific expeditions down the Green and Colorado rivers through the Grand Canyon. Navigating the swirling rapids that blocked his way, he returned to warn Congress that developing the West required more scientific planning. Much of the region had not yet been mapped or its resources identified.

In 1880 Powell became director of the recently formed U.S. Geological Survey. He too had a vision of the West, but one based on the limits of its environment.

Water as a key resource

The key was water, not land. In the water-rich East, the English legal tradition of river rights prevailed. Whoever owned the banks of a river or stream controlled as much water as they might take, regardless of the consequence for those downstream. Such a practice in the West, Powell recognized, would enrich the small number with access to water while spelling ruin for the rest.

The alternative was to treat water as community property. The practice would benefit many rather than a privileged few. To that end Powell suggested that the federal government establish political boundaries defined by watersheds and regulate the distribution of the scarce resource. But his scientific realism could not overcome the popular vision of the West as the American Eden. Powerful interests ensured that development occurred with the same helter-skelter, laissez-faire credo that captivated the East. The first to feel the effects of this unrestrained expansion would be the Indian and Latino residents of the region.

 # The War for the West

So marginal did federal officials consider the Great Plains that they left the lands to the Indians. By the end of the Civil War, some two-thirds of all Indian peoples lived on the Great Plains. Even before the war, a series of gold and silver discoveries beginning in 1848 signaled the first serious interest by white settlers in the arid and semiarid lands beyond the Mississippi. To open more land, federal officials introduced in 1851 a policy of "concentration," pressuring tribes to sign treaties limiting the boundaries of their hunting grounds—the Sioux to the Dakotas, the Crows to Montana, the Cheyenne to the foothills of Colorado.

Policy of concentration

Such treaties often claimed that their provisions would last "as long as waters run," but time after time, land-hungry pioneers broke the promises of their government by squatting on Indian lands and demanding federal protection. The government, in turn, forced more restrictive agreements on the western tribes. This cycle of promises made and broken continued, until a full-scale war for the West raged between whites and Indians.

Contact and Conflict

In the Pacific Northwest many Indians had welcomed the first white overlanders, but by the 1850s, in an oft-repeated pattern, the pressures from the newcomers had become disruptive. Territorial governor Isaac Stevens persuaded representatives of the Cayuse, Yakima, Walla Walla, and Nez Percé to cede millions of acres of land on which they had once freely hunted.

In similar fashion, by 1862 the lands of the Santee Sioux had been whittled down to a strip 10 miles wide and 150 miles long along the Minnesota River. Lashing out in frustration, the tribe attacked several undefended white settlements along the Minnesota frontier. In response, General John Pope arrived in St. Paul declaring his intention to wipe out the Sioux. "They are to be treated as maniacs or wild beasts and by no means as people," he instructed his officers. When Pope's forces captured 1800 Sioux, white Minnesotans were outraged that President Lincoln ordered only 38 hanged.

The campaign under General Pope was the opening of a guerrilla war that continued on and off for some 30 years. The conflict gained momentum in 1864, when Governor John Evans of Colorado sought to end all land treaties with Indian peoples in eastern Colorado. In November, a force of 700 Colorado volunteers under Colonel John Chivington fell upon a band of friendly Cheyenne gathered at Sand Creek under army protection. Chief Black Kettle raised an American flag to signal friendship, but Chivington would have none of it. "Kill and scalp all, big and little," he told his men. The troops massacred at least 150, including children holding white flags of truce and mothers with babies in their arms. A joint congressional investigation later condemned Chivington. In 1865 virtually all Plains Indians joined in the First Sioux War to drive whites from their lands.

Chivington massacre

Among the soldiers who fought the Plains Indians were African American veterans of the Civil War. In 1866 two regiments of black soldiers were organized into the Ninth and Tenth Calvary under the command of white officers. Their Indian foes dubbed them "buffalo soldiers," reflecting the similarity they saw between the hair of African Americans and that of the buffalo. It was also a sign of hard-won respect. The buffalo soldiers fought Indians across the West for more than 20 years. They also subdued bandits, cattle thieves, and gunmen—from the rugged country of Big Bend to the badlands of South Dakota. And they helped to prepare the way for white settlement by laying the foundations for posts such as Fort Sill in Oklahoma and by locating water, wood, and grasslands for eager homesteaders.

Buffalo soldiers

War was only one of several ways in which white settlement undermined tribal cultures. Over the course of centuries only an estimated 4000 Indians (and about 7000 whites) were killed in direct warfare—a paltry few compared to the casualty lists of the Civil War. Far more devastating forces were at work. Disease, including smallpox, measles, and cholera, killed more Indians than combat did. Liquor furnished by white traders entrapped many a brave in a deadly cycle of alcoholism. Trading posts altered traditional ways of life with metal pots and pans, traps, coffee, and sugar but furnished no employment and thus few ways for their Indian customers to pay for these goods. Across the West mines, crops, grazing herds, and fences disturbed traditional hunting and farming lands of many tribes.

On the Great Plains the railroad disrupted the migratory patterns of the buffalo and thus the patterns of the hunt. When buffalo robes became popular in the East in the 1870s and hides became a source of leather for industrial belts, commercial companies hired hunters, who could kill more than 100 bison an hour. Military commanders promoted the butchery as a way of undermining Indian resistance. By 1883 bison had nearly disappeared from the plains (see After the Fact, "Where Have All the Bison Gone?" on pages 603–606). With them went a way of life that left the Plains Indians more vulnerable to white expansion.

Custer's Last Stand—and the Indians'

The Sioux War ended in 1868 with the signing of the Treaty of Fort Laramie. It established two large Indian reservations, one in Oklahoma and the other in the Dakota Badlands. Only six years later, however, in the summer of 1874, Colonel George Armstrong Custer led an expedition into *Pa Sapa,* the sacred Black Hills of the Sioux. In doing so, he flagrantly disregarded the treaty of 1868. Custer, a Civil War veteran, already had a reputation as a "squaw killer" for his cruel warfare against Indians in western Kansas. To open the Black Hills to whites, his expedition spread rumors of gold "from the grass roots down." Prospectors poured into Indian country. Once again, federal authorities tried to force a treaty to gain control of the Black Hills. When negotiations failed, President Grant ordered all "hostiles" in the area rounded up and driven onto the reservations.

Battle of Little Big Horn   In reaction the Cheyenne for the first time allied with the Sioux, who were led by a young war chief named Crazy Horse and medicine man Sitting Bull. Against them marched several army columns, including Custer's Seventh Cavalry, a force of about 600 troops. Custer, eager for glory, arrived at the Little Big Horn River a day earlier than the other columns. Hearing of a native village nearby, he attacked, only to discover that he had stumbled onto an encampment of more than 12,000 Sioux and Cheyenne extending for almost 3 miles. From a deep ravine Crazy Horse charged Custer, killing him and some 250 soldiers.

As he led the attack, Crazy Horse yelled "It is a good day to die!"—the traditional war cry. Even in the midst of victory he spoke truly. Although Custer had been conquered, railroads stood ready to extend their lines, prospectors to make fortunes, and soldiers to protect them. By late summer the Sioux were forced to split into small bands in order to evade the army. Sitting Bull barely escaped to Canada; Crazy Horse and 800 with him surrendered in 1876 after a winter of suffering and starvation.

The battles along the Platte and upper Missouri rivers did not end the war between whites and Indians, but never again would it reach such proportions. Even peaceful tribes like the Nez Percé of Idaho found no security once whites began to hunger for their land. The Nez Percé had become breeders of livestock, rich in horses and cattle that they grazed in the meadows west of the Snake River canyon. Their business enterprise did not prevent the government from trying to force them onto a small reservation in 1877.

Chief Joseph   Rather than see his people humiliated, Chief Joseph led almost 600 Nez Percé toward Canada, pursued by the U.S. Army. In just 75 days they traveled more than 1300 miles. Every time the army closed to attack, Chief Joseph and his warriors drove them off. But before the Nez Percé could reach the border, they were trapped and forced to surrender. Chief Joseph's words still ring with eloquence: "Hear me, my chiefs, I am tired; my heart is sick and sad. From where the sun now stands I will fight no more forever." The government then shipped the defeated tribe to the bleak Indian Country of Oklahoma. There disease and starvation finished the destruction begun by the army.

The Indian Frontier As conflict erupted between Indian and white cultures in the West, the government sought increasingly to concentrate tribes on reservations. Resistance to the reservation concept helped unite the Sioux and Cheyenne, traditionally enemies, in the Dakotas during the 1870s. Along the Little Big Horn River, the impetuous Custer underestimated the strength of his Indian opponents and attacked before the supporting troops of Reno and Benteen were in a position to aid him.

Killing with Kindness

Over these same years Indians saw their legal sovereignty being whittled away. Originally, federal authorities had treated various tribes as autonomous nations existing within the United States, with whom treaties could be made. That tribal status began shrinking in 1831, when the Supreme Court declared Indians "domestic dependent nations." Although the United States continued to negotiate treaties with the tribes, government officials began treating Indians as wards, with as little regard for them as for inept children. In 1869 President Grant created the Board of Indian Commissioners, whose members were chosen by Protestant churches to help settle conflicts with local tribes and to spread Christian values and white styles of living. Finally, in 1871, Congress abandoned the treaty system altogether and with it the legal core of Indian autonomy.

La Fleche and Jackson

Some whites and Indians spoke out against the tragedy taking place on the Great Plains. In the 1870s, Susette La Fleche, daughter of an Omaha chief, lectured eastern audiences about the mistreatment of Indian peoples and inspired reformers to action. Similarly moved, the poet Helen Hunt Jackson turned her energies to lobbying for Indian rights and attacking government policy. In 1881, she published *A Century of Dishonor*. The best-selling exposé detailed government fraud and corruption in dealing with Indians, as well as the many treaties broken by the United States.

Reformers began pressing for assimilation of Indians into white society, ironically as the only means of preserving Indians in a society that seemed bent on destroying them. The Women's National Indian Association, created in 1874, and the later Indian Rights Association, joined by Helen Hunt Jackson, sought to end the Indian way of life by suppressing communal activities, reeducating Indian children, and establishing individual homesteads.

The Dawes Act

Reformers also recognized that the policy of concentrating Indians on reservations had failed. Deprived of their traditional lands and culture, reservation tribes became dependent on government aid. In any case, whites who coveted Indian lands were quick to violate treaty terms. With a mix of good intentions and unbridled greed, Congress adopted the Dawes Severalty Act in 1887. It ended reservation policy by permitting the president to distribute land to Indians who had severed their attachments to their tribes. The goals of the policy were simple: to draw Indians into white society as farmers and small property owners and (less high-mindedly) to bring Indian lands legally into the marketplace.

In practice, the Dawes Act was more destructive than any blow struck by the army. It undermined the communal structure on which Indian tribal life was based. Lands held by tribes would now be parceled out to individuals: 160 acres to the head of a family and 80 acres to single adults or orphans. But as John Wesley Powell had warned, small homestead farms in the West could not support a family—white or Indian—unless the farms were irrigated. Most Indians, moreover, had no experience with farming, managing money, or other white ways.

The sponsors of the Dawes Act, knowing that whites might swindle Indians out of their private holdings, arranged for the government to hold title to the land for 25 years. That arrangement did not stop unscrupulous speculators from "leasing" lands. Furthermore, all reservation lands not allocated to Indians were opened to non-Indian homesteaders. In 1881, Indians held more than 155 million acres of land. By 1890 the figure had dropped to 104 million and by 1900 to just under 78 million.

Against such a dismal future, some Indians sought solace in the past. In 1890 a religious revival swept the Indian nations when word came from the Nevada desert that a humble Paiute named Wovoka had received revelations from the Great Spirit. Wovoka preached that if his followers adopted his mystical rituals and lived together in love and harmony, the Indian dead would come back, whites would be driven from the land, and game would be thick again. As the rituals spread, alarmed settlers referred to the strange shuffling and chanting as the "Ghost Dance." The army moved to stop the proceedings among the Sioux for fear of another uprising. At Wounded Knee in South Dakota the cavalry fell upon one band and with devastating machine-gun fire killed some 146 men, women, and children.

Wounded Knee

Wounded Knee was a final act of violence against an independent Indian way of life. After 1890 the battle was over assimilation, not extinction. The system of markets, rail networks, and extractive industries was linking the Far West with the rest of the nation. Free-roaming bison were being replaced by herded cattle and sheep, nomadic tribes by prairie sodbusters, and sacred hunting grounds with gold fields. Reformers relied on education, citizenship, and allotments to move Indians from their communal lives into white society. Most Indians were equally determined to preserve their tribal ways and separateness as a people.

Borderlands

The coming of the railroad in the 1880s and 1890s brought wrenching changes to the Southwest as well, especially to the states and territories along the old border with Mexico. But here there was a twist. As new markets and industries sprang up, new settlers poured in not only from the East but also from the South, across the Mexican border. Indians such as the Navajo and the Apache thus faced the hostility of newcomers—Anglos and Mexicans alike—as well as of Hispanos, those settlers of Spanish descent already in the region. Before the Mexican War of 1846, the governors of northern Mexico had offered bounties for Indian scalps.

Like Indians, Hispanos discovered that they had either to accommodate or to resist the flood of new Anglos. The elite, or *Ricos*, often aligned themselves with Anglos against their countryfolk to protect their status and property. Others,

Western cities attracted ethnically diverse populations. This chili stand in San Antonio served the city's large Latino population.

Juan José Herrera and the White Caps

including Juan José Herrera, resisted the newcomers. When Anglo cattle ranchers began forcing Hispanos off their lands near Las Vegas, Herrera assembled a band of masked nightriders known as *Las Gorras Blancas* (the White Caps). In 1889 and 1890 as many as 700 White Caps burned Anglo fences, haystacks, and occasionally barns and houses. Herrera's followers also set thousands of railroad ties afire when the Atchison, Topeka and Santa Fe Railroad refused to raise the low wages it paid Hispano workers.

New Anglos frequently fought Hispanos. But it was western lawyers and politicians, using legal tactics, who deprived Hispanos of most of their property. Thomas Catron, an ambitious New Mexico lawyer, squeezed out many Hispanos by contesting land titles so aggressively that his holdings grew to 3 million acres. In those areas of New Mexico and California where they remained a majority, Hispanos continued to play a role in public life. During the early 1890s Herrera and his allies formed a "People's Party," swept local elections, and managed to defeat a bid by Catron to represent the territory in Congress.

Mexican immigrants

With the railroads came more white settlers as well as Mexican laborers from south of the border. Just as the southern economy depended on African American labor, the Southwest grew on the labor of Mexicans. Mexican immigrants worked mostly as contract and seasonal laborers for railroads and large farms. Many of them settled in the growing cities along the rail lines: El Paso, Albuquerque, Tucson, Phoenix, and Los Angeles. They lived in segregated barrios, Spanish towns, where their cultural traditions persisted. But by the late nineteenth century, most Hispanics, whether in barrios or on farms and ranches, had been excluded from power.

Formation of regional communities

Yet to focus on cities alone would distort the experience of most southwesterners of Spanish descent, such as those who lived in the small villages of northern New Mexico and southern Colorado. In those areas emerged a pattern of adaptation and resistance to Anglo penetration. As the market economy advanced, Hispanic villagers turned to migratory labor to adapt. Women continued to work in the old villages, whereas men traveled from job to job in mining, in farming, and on the railroads. The resulting network of villages and migrant workers furnished a base from which Hispanics could seek employment and a haven to which they could return. This "regional community" allowed for both the preservation of the communal life of the old Hispanic village and an entry into the new world of market capitalism that was transforming the West.

Ethno-Racial Identity in the New West

The New West met the Old South in the diamond-shaped Blackland Prairie of central Texas. Before the Civil War, King Cotton had thrived in its rich soil. Afterward, Texas became the leading cotton-producing state in the country. Having embraced the slave system of the Old South, Texas also adopted the New South's system of segregation, with its racial separation, restrictions on black voting, and biracial labor force of African Americans and poor whites.

Yet Texas was also part of the borderlands of the American West, where the Anglo culture of European Americans met the Latino culture of Mexicans and Mexican Americans. Many *Mexicanos* had lived in Texas since before the 1840s, when it had been part of Mexico. In the late nineteenth and early twentieth centuries, more newcomers crossed the Rio Grande in search of work. Between 1890 and 1910, the Spanish-speaking population of the Southwest nearly doubled. In central Texas, the presence of this large and growing force of *Mexicano* laborers complicated racial matters. The black-and-white poles of European and African Americans that had defined identity in the Old South was now replaced by a new racial triad of black, white, and brown that negotiated identity and status among themselves.

Like African Americans, Mexican Americans and Mexican immigrants in Texas were separated from Anglos by a color line and were considered inferior by most whites. Unlike African Americans, however, Texans of Mexican descent sometimes found themselves swinging between the white world of privilege and the black world of disadvantage. In 1914, for example, Mexicans gained status by joining Anglos in the Land League, a radical organization of Texas renters dedicated to land reform. Its secretary, frustrated over the reluctance of whites to sign on, extolled the virtues of Mexican members: "Mexican tenants not only join the League but will starve before they will submit to a higher rent than the League and the law says is just." And whites could lose status, as had the many Texans who sank into landlessness and poverty on the eve of the First World War. White landowners disdained them as "white trash" and a "white scourge," found them to be more expensive tenants, and thus were more likely to rent to what they now regarded as "hard-working" Mexican Americans and Mexican immigrants.

Such complex bargaining over racial status and privilege occurred within a New West of corporate enterprise and wage labor. As small white operators lost their farms and ranches to large corporations, they saw the social distance shrink between themselves and black and brown laborers, sharecroppers, and tenants. By the 1920s, a multiracial labor force of landless wage earners worked on giant ranches and large farms across the Southwest. In Texas, the labor force was triracial, but in California it also included Asian Americans and, elsewhere, American Indians as well. Thus racial identity in the New West would be more complicated and, for Mexicans and Mexican Americans, more fluid.

Opportunity in the West lay in land and resources, but wealth also accumulated in the towns and cities. Each time a spec-

Boom and Bust in the West

ulative fever hit a region, new communities sprouted to serve those who rushed in. The western boom began in mining—with the California gold rush of 1849 and the rise of San Francisco (see page 442). In the decades that followed, new hordes threw up towns in Park City in Utah, Tombstone in Arizona, Deadwood in the Dakota Territories, and other promising sites. All too often, busts followed booms, transforming boom towns into ghost towns.

Mining Sets a Pattern

The gold and silver strikes of the 1840s and 1850s set a pattern that was followed by other booms. Stories of easy riches attracted single prospectors with their shovels and wash pans. Almost all were male, and nearly half were foreign born. Someone entering the local saloon could expect to hear English, the Irish brogue, German, French, Spanish, Chinese, Italian, Hawaiian, and various Indian dialects. Muddy mining camps sprang up in which a prospector could register a claim, get provisions, bathe, and buy a drink or a companion.

Prostitution flourished openly in mining towns (as it did in cattle towns). Such communities provided ideal conditions: large numbers of rootless men, few women, and money enough to buy sexual favors. In the booming towns of Gold Hill and Virginia City near the Comstock Lode of Nevada, men outnumbered women by a

Prostitution

The Mining and Cattle Frontiers
In the vast spaces of the West, railroads, cattle trails, and gold mining usually preceded the arrival of enough settlers to establish towns and cities. The railroads forged a crucial link between the region's natural resources and urban markets in the East and in Europe, but by transecting the plains they also disrupted the migratory patterns of the buffalo herds, undermining Plains Indian cultures while opening the land to cattle grazing and farming.

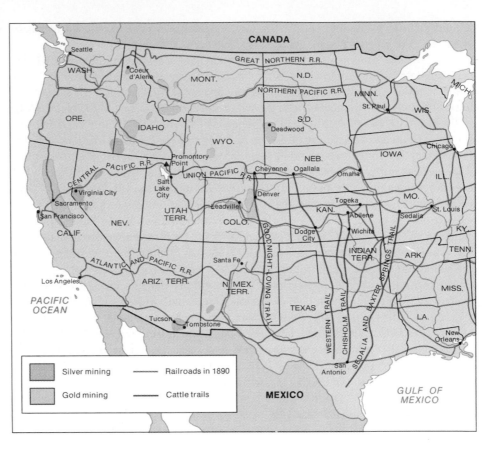

ratio of 2 to 1 in 1875. Almost 1 woman in 12 was a prostitute. Usually the prostitutes were young, in their teens and twenties. They walked the streets and plied their trade in one-room shacks called "cribs." If young and in demand, they worked in dance halls, saloons, and brothels. Pay varied by race, with Anglos at the top of the scale, followed by African Americans, Mexicans, and Indians. All told, as many as 50,000 women worked as prostitutes in the trans-Mississippi West before the turn of the century.

A few succeeded well enough at their trade to accumulate property. In Helena, Montana, Josephine Hensley (known among her patrons as "Chicago Jo") started as a madame. By the 1880s, she controlled most of the tenderloin district of saloons and brothels. Throughout the town, prostitutes earned from $179 to $339 a month at a time when saleswomen made no more than $65 a month. But in a common trend, independent prostitutes in Helena became renters rather than property owners. Hard times and competition undermined their relative prosperity, and by the 1890s, men had seized control of the business. Most prostitutes found themselves mired in a life of alcoholism, drug addiction, disease, and violence. Many ended as suicides.

Prostitution was one source of revenue, but a far more profitable one came from outfitting these boom societies with the equipment they needed. Such sales siphoned riches into the pockets of store owners and other suppliers. Once the quick profits were gone, a period of consolidation brought more order to towns. Police departments replaced vigilantes. Brothels, saloons, and gambling dens were limited to certain districts. And larger scale came to regional businesses. In the mine fields, that meant corporations with the capital for hydraulic water jets to blast ore loose and for other heavy equipment to crush rock and extract silver and gold from deeper veins.

In their quest for quick profits, such operations often led to environmental disaster. With each snow melt and rain, the gravel from hydraulic mining worked its way down into river systems. The resulting floods, mudslides, and dirty streams threatened the livelihood of farmers in the valleys below. Outside Sacramento, 39,000 acres of farmland lay under the debris by the 1890s, and another 14,000 acres were nearly ruined. In 1893 Congress created the Sacramento River Commission to eliminate flooding with series of dams and canals, effectively ending free-flowing rivers in California. Meanwhile underground mining consumed so much timber that one observer called the Comstock Lode in Nevada "tomb of the forest of the Sierras." In Butte, Montana, the smoke from sulfur-belching smelters turned the air so black that by the 1880s townsfolk had trouble seeing even in daylight.

Environmental costs of mining

In corporate mining operations, paid laborers replaced the independent prospectors of earlier days. As miners sought better wages and working conditions, shorter hours, and the right to unionize, management fought back. In Coeur d'Alene, Idaho, troops crushed a strike in 1892, killing seven miners. The miners then created the Western Federation of Miners. In the decade after 1893 the union attracted some 50,000 members and gained a reputation for militancy. In a cycle repeated elsewhere, the rowdy mining frontier of small-scale prospectors was integrated into the industrial system of wage labor, large-scale resource extraction, and high-finance capital.

The Transcontinental Railroad

As William Gilpin predicted in 1849, the development of the West awaited the railroads. Before the Central and Union Pacific railroads were joined to span the continent in 1869, travel across the West was slow and dusty. Vast distances and sparse population gave entrepreneurs little chance to follow the eastern practice of building local railroads from city to city.

In 1862 Congress granted the Central Pacific Railroad the right to build the western link of the transcontinental railroad eastward from Sacramento. To the Union Pacific Corporation fell responsibility for the section from Omaha westward. Generous loans and gifts of federal and state lands made the venture wildly profitable. For every mile of track completed, the rail companies received between 200 and 400 square miles of land—some 45 million acres by the time the route was completed. Fraudulent stock practices, corrupt accounting, and wholesale bribery (involving a vice president of the United States and at least two members of Congress) swelled profits even more. More than 75 western railroads eventually benefited from such government generosity.

Railroad land grants

General Grenville Dodge, an army engineer on leave to the Union Pacific, recruited his immense labor force from Irish and other European immigrants. He drove them with ruthless army discipline, completing as much as 10 miles of track in a single day. Charles Crocker of the Central Pacific had no similar source of cheap labor in California. Worse yet, he faced the formidable task of cutting through the Sierra Nevadas. When his partner Leland Stanford suggested importing workers from China, Crocker dismissed him with a laugh—at first. But it was some 10,000 Chinese laborers who accomplished the feat. With wheelbarrows, picks, shovels, and baskets they inched eastward, building trestles like the one at Secrettown (page 592) and chipping away at the Sierras' looming granite walls. On the worst stretches they averaged only eight inches a day.

Once Chinese crews had broken into the flat country of the desert basin, the two railroads raced to claim as much federal land as possible. In the resulting scramble, both sides passed each other, laying more than 200 miles of parallel track before the government ordered them to join. On May 10, 1869, at Promontory Point, Utah, a silver hammer pounded a gold spike into the last tie. East and West were finally linked by rail.

As the railroads pushed west in the 1860s, they helped spawn cities like Denver and later awakened sleepy communities such as Los Angeles. Railroads opened the Great Plains to cattle drives that in the 1870s brought great herds to "cow towns" like Sedalia, Missouri, and Cheyenne, Wyoming, where cattle could be shipped to market. Fast behind the cattle boom came the "sodbusters" in the late 1870s to till the hard prairie soils left open by the destruction of the buffalo. By the 1890s the once barren Great Plains were crisscrossed by rails, dotted with towns, and divided into farms, ranches, and Indian reservations.

The rail companies recognized early the strategic value of their enterprise. If a key to profiting from the gold rush was supplying miners, one way to prosper from the West was to control transportation. Just by threatening to bypass a town, a railroad could extract concessions on rights of way, taxes, and loans. That coercion was one reason why westerners developed such mixed feelings toward the railroads.

Cattle Kingdom

Westerners recognized that railroads were crucial components of the cattle industry. Cow towns like Abilene, Denver, and Cheyenne flourished from the business of the growing cattle kingdom. By 1860, some 5 million head of longhorn cattle were wandering the grassy plains of Texas. Ranchers allowed their herds to roam the unbroken or "open" range freely, identified only by a distinctive mark on their hides. Each spring cowboys rounded up the herds, branded the calves, and selected the steers to send to market.

Anglo Americans who came to Texas readily adopted the Mexican equipment: the tough mustangs and broncos (horses suited to managing mean-spirited longhorns), the branding iron for marking the herds, the corral for holding cattle, and the riata, or lariat, for roping. The cowboys also wore Mexican chaps, spurs, and broad-brimmed sombreros, or "hats that provide shade." But at least a third of all cowboys were Mexicans and black freedmen after the Civil War. And sometimes rivalries developed among them. One Mexican *corrido,* or ballad, boasted of a herd of 500 steers that could not be corralled by 30 Anglo cowboys, when suddenly five Mexican *vaqueros* arrived: *"Esos cinco mexicanos al momento los echaron/y los trienta americanos se quedaron azorados."* ("Those five Mexicans in a moment put in the steers/and the thirty Americans were left astonished.")

Clara Williamson painted this herd on the long drive north from Texas. Cowboys normally worked in pairs, opposite each other, as shown here; the chuck wagon can be seen at the rear of the train. So strenuous was the work that each cowboy brought with him about eight horses so that fresh mounts would always be available.

In 1866, as rail lines swept west, Texas ranchers began driving their herds north to railheads for shipment to market. These "long drives" lasted two to three months and sometimes covered more than 1000 miles. When early routes to Sedalia, Missouri, proved unfriendly, ranchers scouted alternative paths. The Chisholm Trail led from San Antonio to Abilene and Ellsworth in Kansas. More westerly routes soon ran to Dodge City and even Denver and Cheyenne.

Because cattle grazed on the open range, early ranches were primitive. Most had a house for the rancher and family, a bunkhouse for the hired hands, and about 30 to 40 acres of grazing land per animal. Women were scarce in the masculine world of the cattle kingdom. Most were ranchers' wives, strong and resourceful women who cooked, nursed the sick, and helped run the ranch. Some women ranched themselves. When Helen Wiser Stewart of Nevada learned in July 1884 that her husband had been murdered, she took over the ranch. Her life was an endless round of buying and selling cattle, managing the hands, and tending to family and crops.

Home on the range

Farmers looking for their own homesteads soon became rivals to the cattle ranchers. The "nesters," as ranchers disdainfully called them, fenced off their lands, thus shrinking the open range. Vast grants to the railroads also limited the area of free land, and ranchers intent on breeding heavier cattle with more tender beef began to fence in their stock to prevent them from mixing with inferior strays.

Conflicts also arose between cattle ranchers and herders of another animal introduced by the Mexicans—sheep. Cattle ranchers had particular contempt for the sheep raiser and the "woolies." Sheep cropped grasses so short that they ruined land for cattle grazing. To protect the range they saw as their own from the "hooved locust," cattle ranchers attacked shepherds and their flocks. On one occasion enraged cattle ranchers clubbed 8000 sheep to death along the Green River in Wyoming. The feuds often burst into range wars, some more violent than those between farmers and ranchers.

Western boom and bust

The cattle boom that began with the first long drive of 1866 reached its peak from 1880 to 1885. Ranchers came to expect profits of 25 to 40 percent a year. Millions of dollars poured into the West from eastern and foreign interests eager to cash in on soaring cattle prices. Ranching corporations extended the open range from Texas into Wyoming and Montana.

As in all booms, forces were at work bringing the inevitable bust. High profits soon swelled the size of the herds and led to overproduction. Increased competition from cattle producers in Canada and Argentina caused beef prices to fall. And nature imposed its own limits. On the plains, nutritious buffalo and gamma grasses were eaten to the nub, only to be replaced by unpalatable species. In the Great Basin, overgrazing destroyed the delicate balance between sagebrush and an understory of perennial bunch grasses. In their place came Russian thistle and cheatgrass that could support only small herds. When overgrazing combined with drought, as in New Mexico in the 1880s and 1890s, the results could be disastrous. In all these regions, as vegetation changed, erosion increased, further weakening the ecosystem. In 1870, 5 acres of plains land were needed to feed a steer. By the mid-1880s, 50 acres were required.

There was, moreover, simply not enough grass along the trails to support the millions of head on their way to market. Diseases like "Texas fever" sometimes wiped out entire herds. Then in 1886 and 1887 came two of the coldest winters in recorded history. The winds brought blizzards that drove wandering herds up against fences, where they either froze or starved to death. Summer brought no relief. Heat and drought scorched the grasslands and dried up waterholes. In the Dakotas, Montana, Colorado, and Wyoming, losses ran as high as 90 percent.

By the 1890s the open range and the long drives had largely vanished. What prevailed were the larger cattle corporations such as the King Ranch of Texas. Only the large corporations had enough capital to acquire and fence vast grazing lands, hire ranchers to manage herds, and pay for feed during winter months. As for the cowboys, most became wage laborers employed by the ranching corporations. Like the mining industry, the cattle industry in the West was succumbing to the eastern pattern of economic concentration and labor specialization.

The Final Frontier

In the 1860s they had come in a trickle; in the 1870s they came in a torrent. They were farmers from the East and Midwest, black freedpeople from the rural South, and peasant-born immigrants from Europe. What bound them together was a craving for land. They had read railroad and steamship advertisements and heard stories from friends about millions of free acres in the plains west of the 98th meridian. Hardier strands of wheat like the "Turkey Red" from Russia, improved machinery, and new farming methods made it possible to raise crops in what once had been called the "Great American Desert." The number of farms in the United States jumped from around 2 million on the eve of the Civil War to almost 6 million in 1900.

A Rush for Land

So intense was the desire for land that in the spring of 1889 nearly 100,000 people made their way by wagon, horseback, carriage, buckboard, mule, and on foot to a line near present-day Oklahoma City, in the center of land once reserved for the

Indians. These people were "Boomers," gathered for the last great land rush in the trans-Mississippi West. At noon on April 22, 1889, the Boomers raced across the line to claim some 2 million acres of Indian territory just opened for settlement. Beyond the line lay the "Sooners"—those who had jumped the gun and hidden in gullies and thickets, ready to leap out an instant after noon to claim a stake in prosperity.

Boomers and Sooners

Yet even as the hopefuls lined up in Oklahoma, thousands of other settlers were abandoning their farms to escape mounting debts. The dream of the West as a garden paradise was already being shaken by harsh weather, overproduction, and competition from abroad. Wheat sold for $1.60 a bushel during the Civil War. It fell to 49 cents in the 1890s. Holding on as best they could, plains farmers braved a harsh climate in isolation.

Farming on the Plains

Farmers looking to plow the plains faced a daunting task. Under the Homestead Act (1862), government land could be bought for $1.25 an acre or claimed free if a homesteader had worked it for 5 years. But the best parcels—near a railroad line, with access to eastern markets—were owned by the railroads themselves or by speculators and sold for around $25 an acre. Furthermore, successful farming on the plains demanded expensive machinery. Steel-tipped plows and harrows (which left a blanket of dust to keep moisture from evaporating too quickly) permitted "dry farming" in arid climates. Threshers, combines, and harvesters brought in the crop, and powerful steam tractors pulled the heavy equipment.

Homestead Act

With little rain, many farmers had to install windmills and pumping equipment to draw water from deep underground. The threat of cattle trampling the fields forced farmers to erect fences. Lacking wood, they found the answer in barbed wire, first marketed by Illinois farmer Joseph Glidden in 1874. To get started, the average farmer spent what was for the poor a small fortune, about $785 on machinery and another $500 for land. Bigger operators invested 10 or 20 times as much.

Tracts of 160 acres granted under the Homestead Act might be enough for eastern farms, but in the drier West more land was needed to produce the same harvest. Farms of more than 1000 acres, known as "bonanza farms," were most common in the wheat lands of the northern plains. A steam tractor working a bonanza farm could plow, harrow, and seed up to 50 acres a day—20 times more than a single person could do without machinery. Against such competition, small-scale farmers could scarcely survive. Like the southerners, many westerners became tenants on land owned by someone else. Bonanza farmers hired as many as 250 laborers to work each 10,000 acres in return for room, board, and 50 cents a day in wages.

Bonanza farms

A Plains Existence

For poor farm families, life on the plains meant sod houses or dugouts carved from hillsides for protection against the wind. Tough, root-bound sod was cut into bricks a foot wide and three feet long and laid edgewise to create walls. Sod bricks covered rafters for a roof. The average house was seldom more than 18 by 24 feet, and in severe weather it had to accommodate animals as well as people. One door and often a single window provided light and air. The thick walls kept the house warm in winter and cool in summer, but a heavy, soaking rain or snow could bring the roof down or drip mud and water into the living area. As soon as a home was established, armies of flies, gnats, mosquitoes, and fleas moved in. Katherine Gibson

Sod houses could often make living difficult. It might be dry in a downpour, but afterward, the soaked roof would begin to drip and rain for hours. This Kansas sod house, built in 1899, looks simple enough from the outside, but the four windows hint that it was better furnished than most. For its interior, see below.

of the Dakota territories went to light her stove one cold morning only to be attacked by a rattlesnake and its offspring.

The heaviest burdens fell to women. With stores and supplies scarce, they spent long days over hot tubs preparing tallow wax for candles or soaking ashes and boiling lye with grease and pork rinds to make soap. In the early years of settlement wool was in such short supply that resourceful women used hair from wolves and other wild animals to make cloth. Buttons had to be fashioned from old wooden spoons.

Nature added its hardships. In summer, searing winds blasted the plains for weeks. Grasses grew so dry that a single spark could ignite thousands of acres. Farmers in the Southwest lived in dread of stinging centipedes and scorpions that inhabited wall cracks. From Missouri to Oregon, nothing spelled disaster like locusts. They descended without warning in swarms 100 miles long. Beating against houses like hailstones, they stripped all vegetation, including the bark of trees. An entire year's labor might be destroyed in a day. Winter held special horrors. Blizzards swept the plains, piling snow to the rooftops and halting all travel. Settlers might awaken to find their food frozen and snow on their beds. Weeks would pass before farm families saw an outsider.

The interior of the sod house shown above. Mr. and Mrs. Bartholomew sit proudly amid their possessions, including two ample bookcases, a pedal organ (note the fancy swiveled seat), wallpapered walls, pictures, and rugs on the floor.

In the face of such hardships many westerners found comfort in religion. Indians turned to traditional spiritualism and Hispanics to the Catholic church as a means of coping with nature and change. Though Catholics and Jews came West, evangelical Protestants dominated the Anglo frontier in the mining towns and in other western communities. Worship offered an emotional outlet and some intellectual stimulation as well as a means of preserving old values and sustaining hope. In the West, as in the rural South, circuit riders compensated for the shortage of preachers, while camp meetings offered the chance to socialize. Both brought contact with a world beyond the prairie. In many communities it was the churches that first instilled order on public life. Through church committees westerners could deal with local problems like the need for schools or charity for the poor.

Religion

The Urban Frontier

Not all westerners lived in isolation. By 1890 the percentage of those in cities of 10,000 or more was greater than in any other section of the country except the Northeast. Usually unruly, often chaotic and unplanned, western cities were mostly the products of history, geography, technology, and commerce.

Some western cities—San Antonio, El Paso, and Los Angeles—were old Spanish towns whose growth had been sparked by the westward march of Anglo migrants, the northward push of Mexican immigrants, and the spread of railroad lines. Other cities profited from their location near commercial routes, such as Portland near the Columbia River in Oregon. Still others, such as Witchita, Kansas, arose to serve the cattle and mining booms of the West. And as technology freed people from the need to produce their own food and clothing, westerners turned to the business of supplying goods and services, enterprises that required the labor of more densely populated cities.

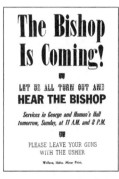

The Bishop Is Coming!

LET US ALL TURN OUT AND
HEAR THE BISHOP

Services in George and Human's Hall
tomorrow, Sunday, at 11 A.M. and 8 P.M.

PLEASE LEAVE YOUR GUNS
WITH THE USHER

Wallace, Idaho. Miner Print.

The town of Wallace, Idaho, in the Coeur d'Alene mining region, illustrates the difficult transition from a raw frontier community to a settled town with churches and family life. ("Please leave your guns with the usher," notes the 1890 circular.) When the first church was finally built, it was competing for attention with more than 60 saloons.

Most newer cities had wide streets and large blocks. Whereas the streets of eastern cities measured 30 to 60 feet across, street widths of 80 feet or more were typical in the West. Streets had to be broad enough to allow ox-drawn wagons to turn, but they also bespoke the big plans of town promoters. "Every town in the West," marveled one European, "is laid out on a plan as vast as though it were destined, at no distant future, to contain a million of inhabitants."

Denver, Colorado, was typical. Founded in 1859, Denver's growth was boosted by the discovery of gold at the mouth of Cherry Creek. It catered largely to miners with a mix of supply stores, saloons, gambling parlors, and brothels. As it grew, so did its reputation for violence. "A city of demons," said one disgusted visitor, where "a man's life is of no more worth than a dog's." Until the early 1860s, when the city hired its first police force, vigilante committees kept the peace with "the rope and the revolver."

In the 1870s Denver embarked on a new phase of growth. The completion of the Denver Pacific and Kansas Pacific railroads made it the leading city on the eastern slope of the Rocky Mountains. Its economy diversified, and its population soared from about 5000 in 1870 to more than 100,000 by 1890. It soon ranked behind only Los Angeles and Omaha among western cities.

Like much of the urban West, Denver grew outward rather than upward, spreading across the open landscape. Such sprawling patterns of growth produced a city with sharply divided districts for business, government, and industry. Workers lived in one section of town; managers, owners, and other wealthier citizens lived in another.

Daily Lives

FOOD/DRINK/ DRUGS

The Frontier Kitchen of the Plains

Out on the treeless plains the Indians had adjusted to scarcity of food, water, and other necessities by adopting a nomadic way of life. Their small kinship groups moved each season to wherever nature supplied the food they needed. Such mobility discouraged families from acquiring extensive material possessions. Tools and housing had to be light and portable. Even tribes that raised crops as part of their subsistence cycle often moved with the seasons.

White settlement was different. Farmers, ranchers, and townspeople rooted themselves to a single place. What the surrounding countryside could not supply had to be brought from afar, generally at great effort and expense. In areas distant from the railroad or other transportation links, families generally had to learn either to do without or to improvise from materials at hand. Keeping food on the table was nearly impossible some seasons of the year. Coffee and sugar were staples in such short supply that resourceful women invented a variety of substitutes. "Take a gallon of bran, two tablespoonsful of molasses, scald and parch in an oven until it is somewhat browned and charred," one woman suggested. Something as simple as finding water suitable for drinking or cooking became a problem in many western areas, where the choice might be between "the strong alkaline water of the Rio Grande or the purchase of melted manufactured ice (shipped by rail) at its great cost."

Gardening, generally a woman's responsibility, brought variety to the diet and color to the yard. The legume family of peas and beans, in particular, provided needed protein. Flowers were much prized but seldom survived the winds, heat, and dry periods. Dishwater and laundry water helped keep flowers alive. One woman was so excited by the discovery of a hardy dandelion that she cultivated it with care and planted its seeds each spring. To prepare for the lean winter months, women stocked their cellars and made wild fruits into leathery cakes eaten to ward off the scurvy that resulted from vitamin deficiency.

Until rail lines made the shipment of goods cheap and until Sears, Roebuck "wishbooks" brought mail order to the frontier, a woman's kitchen was fairly modest. A cast iron stove that sold for $25 in the East was in such demand and so expensive to ship that it fetched $200 in some areas of the West. One miner's wife in Montana during the 1870s

Like southern women, women in the West played an essential role in the family economy. This woman has found a rather remarkable way to feed her cat.

Development was so rapid that Denver struggled to keep up with itself. Within a decade of plotting its initial tracts, the city began construction of the first of several horse-drawn railways. In 1891 the electrified trolley made its first appearance. By 1900, the city contained 800 miles of streets, but only 24 of them were paved. A British observer marveled at "how [Denver's] future vast proportions seem to exist already in the minds of its projectors. Instead of its new streets and buildings being huddled as with us in our urban beginnings, they are placed here and there at suitable points, with confidence that the connecting links will soon be established." So, too, with the rest of the urban West.

The West and the World Economy

In its cities or on its open ranges, deep in its mine shafts or on the sun-soaked fields of its bonanza farms, the West was being linked to the world economy. Longhorn cattle that grazed on Texas prairies fed city dwellers in the eastern United States and in Europe as well. Wood from the forests of the Pacific Northwest found its way considered her kitchen "well-furnished" with two kettles, a cast iron skillet, and a coffeepot. A kitchen cupboard might be little more than a box nailed to a log. One "soddie" recalled that her kitchen remained snug and dry during a rainstorm, but after the sun came out, the water trapped in the thick sod roof seeped slowly down. She ended up frying pancakes on her stove under the protection of an umbrella while the sun shone brightly outside.

Without doctors, women learned how to care for the hurt and sick. Most folk remedies did little more than ease pain. Whiskey and patent medicines were often more dangerous than the disease, but they were used to treat a range of ills from frostbite to snakebite and from sore throats to burns and rheumatism. Settlers believed that onions and gunpowder had valuable medicinal properties. Cobwebs could bandage small wounds; turpentine served as a disinfectant. Mosquitoes were repelled with a paste of vinegar and salt. Most parents thought the laxative castor oil could cure any childhood malady. And if a family member had a fever, one

treatment was to bind the head with a cold rag, wrap the feet in cabbage leaves, and then force down large doses of sage tea, rhubarb, and soda. Some women adapted remedies used on their farm animals. Sarah Olds, a Nevada homesteader whose family was plagued by fleas and lice, recalled that "we all took baths with plenty of sheep dip in the water. . . . I had no disinfectant . . . so I boiled all our clothing in sheep dip and kerosene."

Gradually, as the market system penetrated the West, families had less need to improvise in matters of diet and medicine. Through catalogs one might order spices like white pepper or poultry seasoning and appliances like grinders for real coffee. If a local stagecoach passed by the house, a woman might send her eggs and butter to town to be exchanged for needed store-bought goods like thread and needles. It took a complex commercial network to bring all that the good life required to a land that produced few foods and necessities in abundance.

into the hulls of British schooners and the furniture that adorned the parlors of Paris. Wheat grown on the Great Plains competed with grain from South America and Australia. Gold and silver mined in the Rockies were minted into coins around the world.

The ceaseless search for western resources depended ultimately on money. As raw materials flowed out of the region, capital flowed in, most of it from the East and from Europe. With it, westerners built great railroads, sank mine shafts, cut towering forests, and raised cattle and crops that found their way to national and international markets. Foreign investments varied from industry to industry but generally came in two forms: direct stock purchases, and loans to western corporations and individuals. The great open-range cattle boom of the 1870s and 1880s, for example, brought an estimated $45 million into the western livestock industry from Great Britain alone. The Scottish-owned Prairie Cattle Company owned nearly 8000 square miles of western cattle land in three huge tracts. By 1887, Congress had become so alarmed at foreign ownership that it enacted the Alien Land Law, which prohibited the purchase of any land in western territories by foreign corporations or by individuals who did not intend to become citizens. Capital-hungry western-ers paid little attention. A decade later, there had been virtually no forfeitures of land under the law.

Like southerners, westerners rarely consumed what they took from the ground. In most instances, they located the resources, extracted them, and sent them outside the region to be turned into finished products. Only when manufactured goods re-turned to the West did westerners finally consume them. But westerners were more than consumers. They were part of a vast network of production and trade that spanned the globe. Between 1865 and 1915, world population increased by more than 50 percent, and demand mushroomed. Better and cheaper transportation, fed by a new industrial order, allowed westerners to supply raw materials and agricul-tural goods to places they knew only as exotic names on a map. Still, global reach came at a price. Decisions made elsewhere—in London and Paris, in Tokyo and Buenos Aires—now determined the prices that westerners charged and the profits they made.

Examining the census records of 1890, the superintendent of the census noted that landed settlements stretched so far that "there can hardly be said to be a fron-tier line." One after another, territories became states: Nebraska in 1867; Colorado in 1876; North Dakota, South Dakota, Montana, and Washington in 1889; Wyoming in 1890; Utah in 1896; Oklahoma in 1907; and New Mexico and Arizona in 1912. A new West was emerging as a mosaic of ethnicities, races, cultures, and climates but with the shared identity of a single region.

That sense of a regional identity was heightened for both westerners and south-erners because so many of them felt isolated from the mainstream of industrial Amer-ica. Ironically, it was not their isolation from northern industry but their links to it that marginalized them. The campaign for a New South to out-Yankee the indus-trial Yankee could not overcome the low wages and high fertility rates of an older South. The promoters of the West had greater success in adapting large-scale in-dustry and investment to mining, cattle ranching, and farming. Still, they too con-fronted the limits of their region, whose resources were not endless and whose rain-fall did not follow the plow. Like easterners, citizens of the West found that large corporations with near-monopoly control over markets and transportation bred in-equality, corrupt politics, and resentment.

What beggared the South and conquered the West was a vast new industrial or-der that was reshaping the entire Western world. It first took hold in Great Britain at the end of the eighteenth century, then spread to Europe and abroad. In the United States, the new machine age engulfed the North and the East after the Civil War, nourished industrial cities from Pittsburgh to Chicago, and pulled millions of im-migrants from Europe, Latin America, and Asia to work in its factories. By the turn of the twentieth century, the new industrial order would enrich the United States beyond imagining. The country would stand as the mightiest industrial power on earth. But the attending conflicts of race, class, region, and ethnicity would bedevil Americans for the next hundred years and beyond.

chapter summary

In the years after the Civil War, both regions became more closely linked to the industrial Northeast.

- Despite differences in geography and history, the South and the West shared many features.
  - Both became sources of agricultural goods and raw materials that fed urban and industrial growth in the northeastern and north central states.
  - Both were racially divided societies in which whites often used violence to assert their dominance.
  - Both looked beyond their regions for the human and financial resources needed to boost their economies.
  - Southerners embraced the philosophy of the "New South" that industrialization would bring prosperity.

- The South nonetheless remained wedded to agriculture, especially cotton, and to a system of labor that exploited poor whites and blacks.
  - Important in the South were the *crop-lien system,* which shackled poor southerners to the land through debt, and *Jim Crow segregation,* which kept blacks and whites apart.

- White westerners too exploited people of other races and ethnicities through settlement, conquest, and capture.
  - By 1890, the emergence of the Ghost Dance and the closing of the frontier signaled that Indians must adapt to life within the boundaries set by white culture despite their efforts at resistance.
  - Latinos were increasingly subjected to similar exploitation but resisted and adapted more effectively to the intrusions of white culture and market economy.
  - In a pattern that became typical for western mining, ranching, and agriculture, small operators first grabbed quick profits and then were followed by large corporations that increased both the scale and the wealth of these industries.

additional reading

The themes of change and continuity have characterized interpretations of southern history after Reconstruction. For years C. Vann Woodward's classic *The Origins of the New South* (1951) dominated thinking about the region with its powerful argument for a changing South. Edward Ayers, *The Promise of the New South* (1992) offers a fresh, comprehensive synthesis that sees both change and continuity. Gavin Wright, *Old South, New South* (1986) destroys the myth of the southern colonial economy. Ted Ownby, *Subduing Satan* (1990) provides a valuable discussion of southern social life, especially the role of religion. On the issue of race relations see Joel Williamson, *The Crucible of Race: Black-White Relations in the South since Emancipation* (1984).

The contours of western history were first mapped by Fredrick Jackson Turner in his famous address "The Significance of the Frontier in American History" (1893) but have been substantially reshaped by Richard White, "*It's Your Own Misfortune and None of My Own*": A New History of the American West (1992); Patricia Limerick, *A Legacy of Conquest: The Unbroken Past of the American West* (1987); and Donald Worster, *Rivers of Empire* (1985). Each describes the history of the West less as a traditional saga of frontier triumphs than as an analysis of how the region and its resources have been exploited by various peoples and cultures. Sarah Deutsch, *No Separate Refuge: Culture, Class, and Gender on an Anglo-Hispanic Frontier in the American Southwest, 1880–1940* (1987) develops the concept of regional community to depict the interpenetration of cultures and their impact on gender in New Mexico and Colorado, and Robert M. Utley offers an excellent survey of American Indians in *The Indian Frontier of the American West 1846–1890* (1984). On the growing literature of ethno-racial identity in the West, see Neil Foley, *White Scourge: Mexicans, Blacks, and Poor Whites in Texas Cotton Culture* (1997) and David Gutiérrez, *Walls and Mirrors: Mexican Americans, Mexican Immigrants, and the Politics of Ethnicity* (1995). For an excellent account of the African American experience in shaping the West, see Quintard Taylor, *In Search of the Racial Frontier: African Americans in the American West, 1528–1990* (1998). For a fuller list of readings, see the Bibliography.

Significant Events

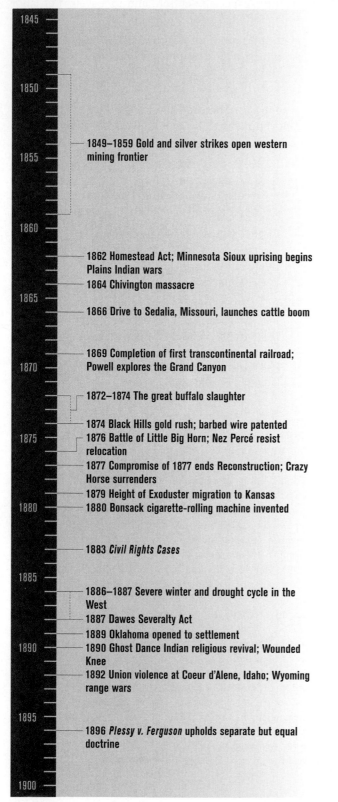

1845

1850

1849–1859 Gold and silver strikes open western mining frontier

1855

1860

1862 Homestead Act; Minnesota Sioux uprising begins Plains Indian wars
1864 Chivington massacre

1865

1866 Drive to Sedalia, Missouri, launches cattle boom

1869 Completion of first transcontinental railroad; Powell explores the Grand Canyon

1870

1872–1874 The great buffalo slaughter

1874 Black Hills gold rush; barbed wire patented
1876 Battle of Little Big Horn; Nez Percé resist relocation
1875
1877 Compromise of 1877 ends Reconstruction; Crazy Horse surrenders
1879 Height of Exoduster migration to Kansas
1880
1880 Bonsack cigarette-rolling machine invented

1883 *Civil Rights Cases*

1885

1886–1887 Severe winter and drought cycle in the West
1887 Dawes Severalty Act
1889 Oklahoma opened to settlement
1890
1890 Ghost Dance Indian religious revival; Wounded Knee
1892 Union violence at Coeur d'Alene, Idaho; Wyoming range wars

1895

1896 *Plessy v. Ferguson* upholds separate but equal doctrine

1900

AFTER THE FACT
Historians Reconstruct the Past

Where Have All the Bison Gone?

In late summer of 1875 a herd of great American bison—the largest animals in North America—grazed lazily along a shallow creek bed. Summering on the highlands of the southern plains, they fed on the mid and tall grasses of early spring and the late-sprouting short grasses of summer. They groomed, played, and mated before beginning their slow trek down to the river bottoms, where naturally cured short grasses and cottonwood bark nourished them during the winter months.

So the cycle had spun for thousands of years. But on this day in 1875 the bison of this herd began mysteriously to die. One by one, they dropped to the ground as if swatted by a huge, invisible hand. Those at the herd's edges went first. Occasionally the animals gathered about a carcass and sniffed at the warm blood. Or they raised their heads to scent the wind for trouble. With the poorest eyesight on the plains, the bison could see little—certainly not the puff of smoke that appeared downwind as each new bison staggered and fell.

The hunter lay perfectly still. No need to move—his powerful .50-caliber Sharps rifle could drop a "shaggy" at 600 feet. No need for horses—they would only spook the herd. The man lay quietly downwind, ideally firing one, maybe two rounds a minute, keeping the pace of killing slow and steady. With care, a good hunter might bag as many as a hundred bison a day. And Tom Nixon was a good hunter, a professional in it for profit.

On this day in 1875, legend has it, Nixon killed 120 bison in 40 minutes. The barrel of his Sharps

The buffalo robe of a Hidatsa warrior. Kiowa Indians kept calendars on buffalo skin robes, which historians have used to help estimate bison populations.

grew so hot that his bullets wobbled in flight. He forgot about the slow and steady kill, forgot even about his rifle, which was ruined in the hunt. That day he was out for a record, and he got it. The season was as profitable as the day. From September 15 to October 20, Nixon killed 2127 bison.

Other hunters fared well too. A buffalo robe fetched as much as $5 in the East. Operating in bands of three or four—a shooter, two skinners, and a cook—professional hunters wreaked havoc with the southern herd of the Great Plains in the 1870s. And within a decade, the northern herd had nearly vanished. By some counts, the 30 million bison that roamed the plains in the early nineteenth century shrank to 5000 by the mid-1880s.

Where had all the bison gone? Popular historical accounts have focused almost entirely on the gun-toting white hunters of legend and the smoke-belching railroad: symbols of a market economy penetrating the West. Without doubt, the market economy played a role in eliminating the vast herds. As far back as the 1830s and 1840s, fur trappers and traders were eating buffalo meat; so too were the railroad crews who extended tracks west. More to the point, the new rail lines provided easy transport of bulky robes and skins to the East. Railroad companies also brought whole trainloads of tourists to shoot at the herd from open windows or atop the cars. In all, the great hunts brought about 10 million bison hides to market.

Ten million is an immense number. But even conservative estimates have suggested that 30 million buffalo had been roaming the plains. What other factors can account for the precipitous drop?

Understanding the fate of the bison herds has required historians to analyze the entire ecology of the plains, of which the bison were an integral part. In many ways, the decades of the 1870s and 1880s represent the end of a process begun much earlier. In reconstructing that process, historians have assembled evidence ranging from traditional accounts of traders and trappers to Indian oral traditions, agricultural census data for livestock, and meteorology reports. They have even found ingenious ways to evaluate the rings of trees and pollen sediment.

One piece of the bison puzzle appears in the 1850s, nearly 20 years before the great white hunts. Starving Indians began to appear across the central and southern plains. Traders reported that the Cheyenne were eating their treasured horses, and other

This Blackfoot robe records the history of one warrior's exploits. It also shows the importance in plains culture of the horse, which competed with the bison for food, especially during the winter. Dozens of horseshoes record animals stolen from enemies.

tribes were raiding Mexico for stock. Historians are also able to catch a glimpse of these hard times in the painted robe calendars of the Kiowa. The calendars show the sign for "few or no bison" for four successive years beginning in 1849.

Contemporaries blamed white emigrants headed overland to the Pacific coast. But the pressures of overland migration alone were not enough to bring the Indians to starvation. From accounts in their diaries and letters, overlanders themselves admitted to being poor hunters of bison. Few recorded ever killing more than a handful at a time. More puzzling, many overlanders reported seeing the "blanched skulls and bones" of bison in the early 1840s, *before* the height of the overland migration. Most puzzling, bison were disappearing first from the western portion of the central plains, where whites were most scarce.

Here, in the western plains, was precisely where Indians were plentiful. Since the seventeenth century, Indian peoples had been lured to the bison-rich plains. The bison became a staple of Indian life, providing a "grocery store on the hoof," hides for clothing and shelter, and a source of powerful religious symbols. Most Plains Indians followed the herds for their subsistence, but as the commercial trade in buffalo robes grew in the 1870s, tribes such as the Blackfeet were being drawn into the hunt for profit. In the first half of the nineteenth century, moreover, new Indian peoples had come to the plains, pushed by the westward advance of European Americans and by hostile tribes from the Great Lakes region. The Indian population in the central plains grew from perhaps 8000 in 1820 to as many as 20,000 in the 1850s.

For a time, the competition between tribes actually helped protect the bison. Warring groups created buffer zones between them. These contested spaces served as refuges for bison, because hunting could be conducted only sporadically for fear of enemy attack. But after 1840 Indian diplomacy brought peace among many rival tribes. The bison began to disappear as Indians stepped up the hunt across the former buffer zones of the western range. They especially favored two-to five-year-old bison cows for their tender meat and their thinner, more easily processed hides. The death of these cows, the most fertile members of the herd, sharply reduced the number of new births.

Yet more was at work on the plains than the onslaught of hunters, white or Indian. A broader biotic invasion was under way. Incoming whites and Indians carried animals with them. Indians brought tens of thousands of horses, while the Pacific-bound overlanders brought oxen, cattle, mules, and sheep. These ungulates carried diseases new to the plains—brucellosis, tuberculosis, and a variety of parasites. Later in the century, bison in refuges were found to be riddled with these deadly ailments. The new species also competed for grazing land. So overlanders and Indians were weakening the herds less through slaughter than by occupying the *habitats* of the bison and consuming their food.

Then, beginning in the late 1840s, two decades of unusually heavy rainfall were followed by years of drought. Scientists can deduce these conditions using the science of dendrochronology, which focuses on reading tree rings to provide clues about the weather of a particular era. Around 1850 tree rings began to shrink, indicating the onset of a cycle with more frequent droughts. As highland springs and creeks dried up and summer short grasses grew poorly, more bison began to disappear.

Earlier cycles of drought had led to the virtual disappearance of bison from the plains. No bison bones appear, for example, at archaeological levels that match pollen data indicating droughts between 5000 and 2500 C.E. and 500 to 1300 B.C.E. Thereafter a cycle of above-average rainfall and cooler weather created a more hospitable climate for bison. Unusually abundant rains in the early nineteenth century allowed the herds to grow much larger than normal, as Indian calendars also noted. When drought set in, the herds started to shrink.

By comparing the rings from this pine tree taken from the Grand Canyon, historians can date the years of its growth. The widest ring, indicating the wettest year, was 1767.

In contrast, 1754 was extremely dry.

In the end, the bison were brought low not by one factor but many. Drought, Indian population increases, and Indian market hunting weakened the great herds. The disturbances created by overlanders and their animals, the appearance of new bovine diseases, and the increased competition for grazing land only made matters worse. By the time the great white hunts began, the bison, though still numerous, were already in crisis.

BIBLIOGRAPHY. Mari Sandoz, *The Buffalo Hunters: The Story of the Hide Men* (1954) provides a vivid description of white hunters in the 1870s and 1880s. Dan Flores sets that traditional tale in a broader context in his pathbreaking article "Bison Ecology and Bison Diplomacy: The Southern Plains from 1800 to 1840," *Journal of American History* (September 1991): 465–485. Flores focuses on the southern plains, but more recently, Elliott West has come to similar conclusions about the central plains in *The Way to the West: Essays on the Central Plains* (1995). His essays move beyond the bison and include broader discussions of the interplay of climate, animals, plants, and people in the region.

I t was so dark, Robert Ferguson could not see his own feet. Inching along the railroad tracks, he suddenly pitched forward and felt his breath taken away as the ground vanished beneath him. To his dismay, he found himself wedged between two railroad ties, his legs dangling in the air. Scrambling back to solid ground, he retreated along the tracks to the railroad car, where he sat meekly until dawn.

Ferguson, a Scot visiting America in 1866, had been in Memphis, Tennessee, only two days earlier, ready to take the "Great Southern Mail Route" east some 850 miles to Washington. Things had gone badly from the start. About 50 miles outside of town, a broken river bridge forced him to take a ferry and spend 10 miles bumping along in a mule-drawn truck before learning that the rail line did not resume for another 40 miles. Disheartened, he decided to return to Memphis to try again.

The train to Memphis arrived six hours late, dawdled its way home, and then, barely three miles from the city, derailed in the middle of the night. When a few passengers decided to hike the remaining distance into town, Ferguson tagged along. It was then that he had fallen between the tracks and retreated to the railcar. At dawn he discovered to his horror that the tracks led onto a flimsy, high river bridge. Ferguson had trouble managing the trestle even in daylight.

Before he finally reached Washington, Robert Ferguson faced six more days of difficult travel. One line would end, and passengers and freight would be forced onto another because rail gauges—the width of the track—differed from line to line. Or a bridge would be out, or there would be no bridge at all. Trains had no meals "on board" or any sleeping cars. "It was certainly what the Americans would call 'hard travelling,'" Ferguson huffed; "—they do not make use of the word 'rough,' because roughness may be expected as a natural condition in a new country."

The New Industrial Order

preview • At the heart of the new order reshaping American society was not just industry but *systems* of industry—systems of transportation and communication, systems for managing large corporations and raising the money to finance them. Workers fought to create systems of labor as well, by forming unions. Industrialization came at a price that was often steep, but by 1890 the United States had transformed itself into the most industrialized nation in the world.

Cross-country travel proved so rough that it inspired even an American to fantasy. In 1859, the *Southern Literary Messenger* carried the first of several installments describing Miss Jane Delaware Peyton's trip to Washington, D.C., from Rasselas, Oregon, in 2029, 170 years in the future. Elegant trains whisked her from one end of the country to the other in only 8 days at speeds of 60 miles an hour. While this "immense velocity" presented no physical problems, Miss Peyton had to guard against "Tourbilliere," an all-too-common mental disorder of the twenty-first century. After 10 or more hours on a speeding train, quick-witted passengers found perception accelerating but memory lapsing. "The mind loses an idea almost as soon as it has been formed," Miss Peyton reported. The only cure was to stop and let the mind catch up to its changing surroundings. So every few days Miss Peyton and her fellow travelers disembarked from their train to sit quietly at a depot until their symptoms subsided. Such persons were said to be "waiting for their brains."

By the 1880s, some of our writer's fantasies had come true, as T. S. Hudson discovered in 1882 when he launched a self-proclaimed "Scamper Through America." Hudson, another British tourist, did not cross the continent in quite 8 days, but it took him just 60 days to go from England to San Francisco and back. And he booked his rail ticket from a single agent in Boston. Such centralization would have been unthinkable in 1859, when a transcontinental railroad was still a decade from completion.

Giant egg-shaped Bessemer converters remove carbon from molten iron ore to make steel at Andrew Carnegie's steelworks in Pittsburgh. Factory temperatures soared to over 100 degrees, and Carnegie ran his mills 24 hours a day, every day a year except for July 4th.

Hudson's trains had Pullman Palace cars with luxury sleeping quarters and a full breakfast of coffee, iced milk, eggs, "game in their season," and fresh fruits. Newly installed air brakes made trains safer and their stops smoother. Bridges appeared where none had been before, including a "magnificent" span over the Mississippi at St. Louis. He also found himself in the midst of a communications revolution. Traveling across the plains, he was struck by the number of telephone poles along the route.

What made America in the 1880s so different from just a few decades earlier was not the speed and comfort of travel or the wonders of the new technology. The true marvel was the emerging industrial order that underlay those technologies and made them possible. Because this order was essentially in place by the beginning of the twentieth century, we tend to take its existence for granted. Yet its growth in scale and complexity was at first slow and required innovations in many different areas of society in order to achieve its effects.

The process of industrialization began in the United States at least three decades before the Civil War, with small factories producing light consumer goods like clothing, shoes, and furniture. Despite these early national markets, much of the economy remained local. Only after the 1850s did the industrial economy develop a set of interlocking systems that allowed larger factories, using more and bigger machines, to produce goods with greater efficiency and market them on a national and international scale.

The transformation, remarkable as it was, brought pain along with progress. The demand for natural resources led to virgin forests being cut down and open-pit mines spewing hazardous runoffs. Factories along the rivers of the Northeast were left toxic with industrial wastes. In 1882, the year Hudson scampered by rail across America, an average of 675 people were killed on the job every week. Like most people, workers scrambled—sometimes literally—to adjust. Few Americans anywhere had time to "wait for their brains" to catch up to the dizzying pace of change.

The Development of Industrial Systems

The new industrial order can best be understood as a web of complex industrial systems woven together in the second half of the nineteenth century. By "industrial system," we mean a set of orderly arrangements or processes—whether of extraction, production, transportation, distribution, or finance—organized to make the whole industrial order function smoothly. Look, for example, at the industrial systems required to build the bridge across the Mississippi that T. S. Hudson so admired. When James B. Eads constructed its soaring arches in 1874, he needed steel, most likely made from iron ore mined in northern Michigan. Giant steam shovels scooped up the ore and loaded whole freight cars in a few strokes. A transportation system—railroads, boats, and other carriers—probably moved the ore to Pittsburgh, where the factory system furnished the labor and machinery to finish the steel. The capital to create such factories came itself from a system of finance that linked investment banks and stock markets to entrepreneurs in need of money. Only with such a national network of industrial systems could the Eads bridge be built and a new age of industry arise.

Natural Resources and Industrial Technology

The earliest European settlers had marveled at the "merchantable commodities" of America, from the glittering silver mines of the Spanish empire to the continent's hardwood forests. What set the new industrial economy apart from that older America was

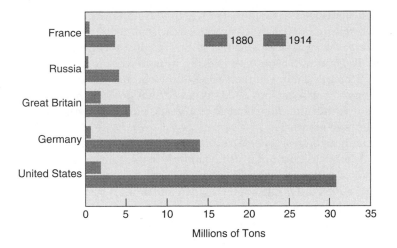

Steel Production, 1880 and 1914
While steel production jumped in western industrial nations from 1880 to 1914, it skyrocketed in the United States because of rich resources, cheap labor, and aggressive management.

the scale and efficiency of using such natural resources. New technologies made it possible to exploit them in ways undreamed of only decades earlier.

Steel, for example, had been made from iron and carbon alloyed with other metals and forged into swords as far back as the Middle Ages. In the 1850s, inventors in England and America discovered a cheaper way—called the Bessemer process after its British developer—to convert large quantities of iron into steel. By the late 1870s, the price of steel had dropped by more than half. Steel was lighter than iron, could support 20 times as much weight, and lasted 20 years instead of 3. Steel tracks soon carried most rail traffic; steel girders replaced the old cast iron frames; steel cables supported new suspension bridges.

Bessemer process

Industrial technology made some natural resources more valuable. New distilling methods transformed a thick, smelly liquid called petroleum into kerosene for lighting lamps, oil for lubricating machinery, and paraffin for making candles. Beginning in 1859, new drilling techniques began to tap vast pools of petroleum below the surface. About the same time, Frenchman Etienne Lenoir constructed the first practical internal combustion engine. After 1900, new vehicles like the gasoline-powered carriage turned the oil business into a major industry.

Petroleum industry

The vast scale of these operations used equally vast amounts of resources and produced equally huge quantities of waste. Coal mining, logging, and the industrial toxins of factories led to only the most obvious forms of environmental degradation—scarred land, vanishing forests, contaminated waters. As giant water cannons blasted away hillsides in search of gold in California, rock and gravel washed into rivers, raising their beds and threatening populations downstream with floods. When engineers tried to cleanse the Chicago River by reversing its flow, they succeeded only in shifting pollution to rivers downstate. But some industrialists did succeed in limiting pollution, often to turn a profit as much as to protect the environment. Chicago meat packers stretched their imaginations to use every conceivable part of the animals that came into their plants. Straight-length bones were turned into cutlery, hoofs and feet into glue and oil, fat into oleomargarine.

Environmental costs

Systematic Invention

Industrial technology rested on invention. For sheer inventiveness, the 40 years following the Civil War have rarely been matched in American history. Between 1790 and 1860, 36,000 patents had been registered with the government. Over the next three decades, the U.S. Patent Office granted more than half a million. The process of invention became systematized as small-scale inventors were replaced by orderly "invention factories"—forerunners of expensive research labs.

Edison's contributions

No one did more to bring system, order, and profitability to invention than Thomas Alva Edison. In 1868, at the age of 21, Edison went to work for a New York brokerage house and promptly improved the design of the company's stock tickers. Granted a $40,000 bonus (worth perhaps $400,000 in current dollars), he set himself up as an independent inventor. For the next five years, Edison patented a new invention almost every five months.

Edison was determined to bring system and order to the process of invention. Only then could breakthroughs come in a steady and profitable stream. He moved 15 of his workers to Menlo Park, New Jersey, where in 1876 he created an "invention factory." Like a manufacturer, Edison subdivided the work among gifted inventors, engineers, toolmakers, and others.

The spread of an electrical power system

This orderly bureaucracy soon evolved into the Edison Electric Light Company. Its ambitious owner aimed at more than perfecting his new electric light bulb. Edison wanted to create a unified electrical power system—central stations to generate electric current, wired to users, all powering millions of small bulbs in homes and businesses. To launch his enterprise, Edison won the backing of several large banking houses by lighting up the Wall Street district in 1882. It was like "writing by daylight," recorded one reporter. Soon Edison power plants sprang up in major cities across the country.

Electricity was more flexible than earlier sources of energy. Factories no longer had to be built near rivers and falls to make use of water power. Before the end of the century, electricity was running automatic looms, trolley cars, subways, and factory machinery. Electricity not only revolutionized industry; it also worked in the homes of ordinary citizens. The electric motor, developed commercially by George Westinghouse and Nikola Tesla in 1886, powered everything from sewing machines to Edison's "gramophone," later known as the record player.

George Eastman revolutionized photography by making the consumer a part of his inventive system. In 1888 Eastman marketed the "Kodak" camera. The small black box weighed just over two pounds and contained a strip of celluloid film that replaced hundreds of pounds of photography equipment. After 100 snaps of the shutter, the owner simply sent the camera back to the store or factory and waited for the developed photos, along with a reloaded camera, to return by mail. "You press the button—we do the rest" was Eastman Kodak's apt slogan.

What united these innovations was the notion of rationalizing inventions—of making a systematic process out of them. By 1913, Westinghouse Electric, General Electric, U.S. Rubber Company, and other firms had set up research laboratories. And by the middle of the century research laboratories had spread beyond business to the federal government, to universities, to trade associations, and to labor unions.

Thomas Edison, unkempt and wrinkled, in his research lab

Transportation and Communication

The problem of scale

Abundant resources and new inventions remained worthless to industry until they could be moved to processing plants, factories, and offices. With more than 3.5 million square miles of land in the United States, distance alone was daunting. Where 100 miles of railroad track would do for shipping goods in Germany and England, 1000 miles was necessary in America.

An efficient transportation system tied the United States into an emerging international network. By the 1870s railroads crisscrossed the country, and steam-powered ships (introduced before the Civil War) were pushing barges down rivers and carrying passengers and freight across the oceans. The time of transatlantic travel was cut in half, to about 10 days. Between 1870 and 1900, the value of American exports tripled. Eventually the rail and water transportation systems fused. By 1900 railroad companies owned nearly all the country's domestic steamship lines.

A thriving industrial nation also required effective communication. Information was a precious commodity, as essential to industry as were resources or technology. In the early 1840s, it took newspapers as many as 10 days to reach Indiana from New York and 3 months to arrive by ship in San Francisco. In 1844 Samuel Morse succeeded in sending the first message over an electrical wire between cities. By 1861 the Western Union Company had strung 76,000 miles of telegraph lines across the country. If a bank collapsed in Chicago, bankers in Dallas knew of it that day. Railroads could keep traffic unsnarled through the dots and dashes of Morse's code. So useful to railroads was the telegraph that they allowed poles and wires to be set along their rights of way in exchange for free telegraphic service. By the turn of the century a million miles of telegraph wire handled some 63 million messages a year, not to mention those flashing across underwater cables to China, Japan, Africa, and South America.

> **Telegraph**

A second innovation in communication, the telephone, vastly improved on the telegraph. Alexander Graham Bell, a Scottish immigrant, was teaching the deaf when he began experimenting with ways to transmit speech electrically. In 1876, he transmitted his famous first words to a young assistant: "Mr. Watson, come here! I want you." No longer did messages require a telegraph office, the unwieldy Morse code, and couriers to deliver them.

> **Telephone**

President Rutherford B. Hayes installed the first telephone in the White House in 1878, when the instrument was still a curiosity. The same year, the city of New Haven, Connecticut, opened the first telephone exchange in America. By 1895 there were 310,000 of Bell's machines in America. Five years later there were 1.5 million. The telephone patent proved to be the most valuable ever granted. In the scramble for profits, the Bell Telephone Company fought off challenges from competitors and suits from rivals who claimed that their contributions were worth a share of the rights.

Along with other innovations in communication (see Daily Lives, "The Rise of Information Systems," pages 614–615), telephones modernized offices and eased business transactions. In 1915 the American Telephone and Telegraph Company opened the first transcontinental line. A business executive in New York now could speak personally to an associate in San Francisco. When commercial rates dropped after the turn of the century, the telephone became part of a social revolution. Like the railroad and the telegraph, it compressed distances and reduced differences across the country. In time, remote farms and isolated villages would be connected to distant neighbors and vital hospitals and fire departments.

Finance Capital

As industry grew, so did the demand for investment capital—the money spent on land, buildings, and machinery. The scale of industry required more funds than ever. Between 1870 and 1900, the number of workers in an average iron and steel firm grew from 100 to 400, and the capital invested jumped to nearly $1 million, about seven times what it had been in 1870.

The need for capital was great especially because so many new industrial systems were being put into place at once. A railroad, for example, had enormous start-up

Daily Lives

TIME AND TRAVEL
The Rise of Information Systems

In 1877, a year after its invention, advertisements were already touting Alexander Graham Bell's "speaking telegraph": "Conversation can easily be carried on after slight practice and occasional repetition of a word or sentence. . . . [A]fter a few trials the ear becomes accustomed to the peculiar sound."

It was not so for everyone. Some people had great difficulty understanding the strange sounds. Others reported terrifying "stage fright" that left them speechless. Still others had no idea how to greet callers. Bell answered with a chipper "Ahoy!" Operators at the first public telephone exchange used the old-fashioned "What is wanted?" But it was Thomas Edison's melodious "Hello" (derived from "Halloo," the traditional call to bring hounds to the chase) that won out by 1880.

At first Bell's electrical toys could be rented only in pairs by individuals who wanted to connect two places. In 1877 the advantages of such direct communication led to the first intercity hookup, between New York and Boston. Before the turn of the century, the Bell-organized American Telephone and Telegraph Company had combined more than 100 local telephone companies to furnish business and government with long-distance service. When rates dropped after 1900, telephones found their way into ordinary American homes.

The telephone revolutionized communications, cutting time and obliterating distances. It also liberated social relations by freeing people from the nineteenth-century convention of addressing only those to whom they had been properly introduced. And it acted as a great social leveler. Almost overnight, telephone operators (called "hello girls") began connecting people of different locales and classes who might never have spoken to each other at all, let alone as peers.

The telephone and other innovations were the basis of the information system required of any thriving industrial nation. The increased specialization at all stages of production required information about markets, prices, and supply sources—and required it quickly.

During the first half of the nineteenth century, information had traveled mostly through the

Systems of finance and communications intersected at Wall Street, New York, where the nation's most important investment banks and markets were located. The Great Blizzard of 1888 buried the district with snow and also shadowed in white the crisscrossing "blizzard" of wires needed for the communications networks.

---

costs. Miles of track had to be laid, workers hired, engines and cars bought, depots constructed. Industrial processes involving so many expensive systems could not take shape until someone raised the necessary funds.

Sources of capital

Where did the money come from? For the first three-quarters of the nineteenth century, investment capital came mostly from the savings of firms. In the last half of the century "capital deepening"—a process essential for industrialization—took place. Simply put, as national wealth increased, people began to save and invest more of their money, which meant that more funds could be loaned to companies seeking to start up or expand.

Savings and investment grew more attractive with the development of a complex network of financial institutions. Commercial and savings banks, investment houses, and insurance companies gave savers new opportunities to channel money mails. In 1844 Samuel F. B. Morse sent the first intercity message across electrical wires, thereby achieving instantaneous communication. But the telegraph had drawbacks. Instantaneous communication was hardly direct. Messages had to be taken to a telegraph office, where trained clerks could translate them into Morse code, an unwieldy system of dots and dashes. Only then could they be transmitted by electrical impulse. When they arrived at the receiving station, messages were recast into understandable language, then carried by hand to their precise destination. This system was a far cry from the telephone, which was both instantaneous and direct.

Another device that helped businesses was the typewriter. C. Latham Sholes, a Milwaukee printer and editor, had been tinkering with an automatic numbering machine when a friend suggested he develop a mechanical letter-writing device. In 1868 he patented the "Type-Writer." In the 1870s the Remington Arms Company began mass-producing them. By the early twentieth century the typewriter had taken its modern shape—a keyboard with upper- and lowercase letters and a carriage that allowed typists to see the output.

At first typewriters were used mainly by writers, editors, ministers, and others from the world of letters. (Legend has it that Mark Twain's *The Adventures of Tom Sawyer* was the first book manuscript to be typed.) Early critics charged that "machine-made" letters were too impersonal. When farmers complained about receiving them, Sears, Roebuck hired secretaries to write their business letters by hand. Nevertheless, machine writing soon became standard business practice.

The need for speed and efficiency in the office led to other breakthroughs. Carbon paper, designed for making a typewritten copy along with the original, was patented in 1872. In 1890 Alfred Dick invented the mimeograph to reproduce many copies of a single document cheaply, a communications boon not only to businesses but also to churches, reform organizations, and political groups. Communications, like the rest of the new industrial order, were steadily becoming more orderly and efficient, permitting the rapid distribution of information to those people who desired it.

to industry. The New York Stock Exchange, in existence since 1792, linked eager investors with money-hungry firms. By the end of the nineteenth century the stock market had established itself as the basic means of making capital available to industry.

The Corporation

For those business leaders with the skill to knit the industrial pieces together, large profits awaited. This was the era of the "robber barons," entrepreneurs who bulled their way to success at the expense of competitors and employees. To be sure, sheer ruthlessness went a long way in the fortune-building game. "Law? Who cares about law!" railroad magnate Cornelius Vanderbilt once boasted. "Hain't I got the power?"

But to survive in the long term, business leaders could not depend on ruthlessness alone. They had to have ingenuity, an eye for detail, and the gift of foresight. The growing scale of enterprise and need for capital led them to adapt an old device, the corporation, to new needs. Corporations had existed since colonial times, when governments granted charters of incorporation to organizations that ran public facilities such as turnpikes, canals, and banks. After the Civil War the modern corporation came into use for raising money and protecting business holdings.

Advantages of the corporation

The corporation had several advantages over more traditional forms of ownership: the single owner and the partnership. A corporation could raise large sums quickly by selling "stock certificates," or shares in its business. It could also outlive its owners (or stockholders) because it required no legal reorganization if one of the owners died. It limited liability because owners were no longer personally responsible for corporate debts. And it separated owners from day-to-day management of the company. Professional managers could now operate complex businesses. So clear were these advantages that before the turn of the century, corporations were making two-thirds of all manufactured products in the United States.

An International Pool of Labor

Last, but hardly least important for the new industrial order, was a pool of labor. In the United States the demand for workers was so great that the native-born could not fill it. In 1860 it took about 4.3 million workers to run all the factories, mills, and shops in the United States. By 1900 there were approximately 20 million workers in industrial and associated enterprises.

Global labor network

In part, the United States relied on a vast global network to fill its need for workers. In Europe as well as Latin America, Asia, Africa, and the Middle East, seasonal migrations provided a rich source of workers for many nations, including the United States. Beginning in the 1870s, for example, rural laborers and tenant farmers from the Mezzogiorno in Italy traveled throughout Europe seeking wage work in construction during the building season that stretched from spring through early fall. Poor Irish workers migrated to Great Britain, where they constituted a reserve source of industrial labor during the nineteenth century. Mechanization, poverty, oppression, and ambition pushed many of these rural laborers from farms into industrial cities and, more and more, to other continents once steamships made transoceanic travel easier.

To draw these workers to the United States, industrialists advertised in newspapers, distributed pamphlets, and sent agents fanning out across the globe. Between 1870 and 1890, more than 8 million immigrants arrived in the United States, another 14 million by 1914. Some came from Asia and Latin America, but most came from Europe and settled in industrial cities. Like migratory laborers elsewhere, they hoped to find work, fatten their purses, and go home. According to one estimate, between 25 and 60 percent of all immigrants returned to their homelands from the United States during these years.

Migration chains

In the United States as in other countries, immigrants relied on well-defined migration chains of family and friends to get jobs. A brother might find work with other Slavs in the mines of Pennsylvania; or the daughter of Greek parents, in a New England textile mill filled with relatives. Labor contractors also served as a funnel to industry. Tough and savvy immigrants themselves, they met newcomers at the docks and train stations with contracts to work in local factories, mines, and other industries. For their trouble they took a fee or a slice of the new workers' wages. Among

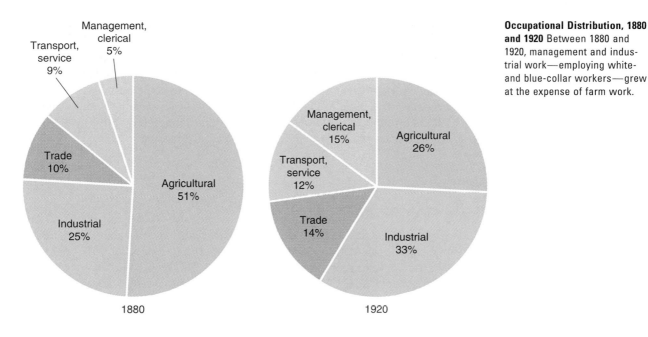

Occupational Distribution, 1880 and 1920 Between 1880 and 1920, management and industrial work—employing white- and blue-collar workers—grew at the expense of farm work.

Italians they were known as *padrones;* among Mexicans, as *enganchistas.* By the end of the nineteenth century such contractors controlled two-thirds of the labor in New York.

Mexicans, too, formed part of this transnational labor pool, streaming across the border especially after the Mexican Revolution in 1910. But even before, seasonal migration of Mexican laborers to plant and pick crops from Texas to California was common enough to spawn cross-border family networks. One man was responsible for bringing 27 families from Mexico to California. "Come! Come! Come over," a Mexican migrant remembered being told by friends. Mexican laborers also helped build the transcontinental railroad and, after the turn of the century, moved farther north for jobs in the tanneries, meatpacking plants, foundries, and rail yards of Chicago, St. Louis, and other centers of industry.

Rural Americans—some 11 million between 1865 and 1920—provided a home-grown source of labor, similar in the roots and patterns of their movements to migrants from abroad. Driven from the farm by machines and bad times or just following dreams of a new life, they moved first to small, then to larger cities in search of work. Most lacked the skills for high-paying jobs. But unlike their foreign counterparts, they spoke English, many could read and write, and few were certain of returning home. In iron and steel cities as well as in coal-mining towns, the better industrial jobs and supervisory positions often went to them. Other rural migrants found work in retail stores or offices and slowly entered the new urban middle class of white-collar workers.

Most African Americans continued to work the fields of the South. About 300,000 moved to northern cities between 1870 and 1910, perhaps more to southern cities. Between 1880 and 1910, the black urban population across the South jumped, more than doubling in industrial cities such as Birmingham. In some instances, black migrants were escaping domineering fathers; in others, seeking the excitement of the city; and in still others, following a husband or fleeing the prejudices of the Old South. These migrants too relied on family migration chains in their journey, sometimes traveling in

Domestic sources

Chicago laborer

groups, sometimes alone. On occasions, they brought siblings or spouses and children, often one by one, after they had found work.

All came in search of opportunity, and all faced the burden of continued discrimination when they arrived. Newer industries such as textile manufacturing and railroad shop work refused to hire African Americans, but some businesses, like Andrew Carnegie's steel mills in Pittsburgh, employed blacks as janitors and wage laborers. Women found jobs as domestic servants and laundresses. Still, by 1890 an average of less than one black man in ten worked in industry.

Railroads: America's First Big Business

The system was a mess: any good railroad executive knew as much. Along the tracks that spanned the country, each town—each rail station—set its clocks separately by the sun. In 1882, the year T. S. Hudson scampered across America, New York and Boston were 11 minutes and 45 seconds apart. Stations often had several clocks showing the time on different rail lines, along with one displaying "local mean time." In 1883, without consulting anyone, the railroad companies organized time by dividing the country into four zones, each an hour apart. One Chicago newspaper compared the feat to Joshua's making the sun stand still. Cities and towns soon adjusted, but Congress did not get around to making the division official until 1918.

Railroad time

At the center of the new industrial systems were the railroads, moving people and freight, spreading communications, reinventing time, ultimately tying the nation together. Railroads also stimulated economic growth, simply because the sheer building of them required so many resources—coal, wood, glass, rubber, brass, and by the 1880s 75 percent of all U.S. steel. By lowering transportation costs, railroads allowed manufacturers to reduce prices, attract more buyers, and increase business. Perhaps most important, as America's first big business they devised new techniques of management, soon adopted by other companies.

A Managerial Revolution

To the men who ran them, railroads provided a challenge in organization and finance. In the 1850s the Pepperell textile mills of Maine, one of the largest industrial enterprises in America, employed about 800 workers. By the early 1880s the Pennsylvania Railroad had nearly 50,000 people on its payroll. From setting schedules and rates to determining costs and profits, everything required a level of coordination unknown in earlier businesses.

Pioneering trunk lines

The so-called trunk lines pioneered in devising new systems of management. Scores of early companies had serviced local networks of cities and communities, often with less than 50 miles of track. During the 1850s longer trunk lines emerged east of the Mississippi to connect the shorter branches, or "feeder" lines. By the outbreak of the Civil War, four great trunk lines linked the eastern seaboard with the Great Lakes and western rivers. After the war, trunk lines grew in the South and West.

The new managers

The operations of large lines spawned a new managerial elite, beneath owners but with wide authority over operations. Cautious by nature, they preferred to negotiate and administer rather than compete. In the 1850s, Daniel McCallum, superintendent of the New York and Erie Railroad, laid the foundation for this system by drawing up the first table of organization for an American company. A tree trunk with roots represented the president and board of directors; five branches consti-tuted the main operating divisions; leaves stood for the local agents, train crews, and other workers. Information moved up and down the trunk so that managers could get daily reports to and from the separate parts.

By the turn of the century, these managerial techniques had spread to other in-dustries. Local superintendents were responsible for daily activities. Central offices served as corporate nerve centers, housing divisions for purchases, production, trans-portation, sales, and accounting. A new class of middle managers ran them and im-posed new order on business operations. Executives, managers, and workers were being taught to operate in increasingly precise and coordinated ways.

Competition and Consolidation

Although managers made operations more systematic, the struggle among railroad companies to dominate the industry was anything but precise and rational. In the 1870s and 1880s the pain of railroad progress began to tell.

By their nature, railroads were saddled with enormous fixed costs—expensive equipment, huge payrolls, high debts. These remained constant regardless of the volume of traffic. To generate added revenue, railroads constructed more lines in hopes of increasing their traffic. Soon the railroads had overbuilt. With so much extra capacity, railroad owners schemed to win new accounts. They gave free passes to fa-vored shippers, promised them free sidings at their plants, offered free land to lure businesses to their territory.

The most savage and costly competition came over the rates charged for shipping goods. Managers lowered rates for freight that was shipped in bulk, on long hauls, or on return routes (since the cars were empty anyway). They used "re-bates"—secret discounts to preferred customers—to drop prices below the posted rates of competitors (and then re-couped the losses by overcharging small shippers like farm-ers). When the economy plunged or a weak line sought to improve its position, rate wars broke out. By 1880, 65 lines had declared bankruptcy.

One way to prevent the ravages of competition was to buy up competing lines. It was often expensive and could ignite even fiercer war-fare. From 1866 to 1868 Cornelius Vanderbilt of the New York Central waged a fu-tile battle to gain control of the Erie Railroad. The Erie was headed by a trio of rail-road sharks: the corporate buccaneer Daniel Drew, the flamboyant speculator James Fisk Jr. and the unscrupulous Jay Gould. Vanderbilt fought the trio in the courts, where each side bought its own judges. He fought them in the legislature, where both sides bribed legislators (for $15,000 apiece, some said). He fought them on the streets with gangs of hired toughs and on the seas, where Fisk himself served as admiral of a Hudson River fleet armed with riflemen.

The "Erie Wars" ended in a standoff. The Erie paid Vanderbilt a huge ransom to end his attack. Gould and Drew retained control of the company, until they turned against each other. By 1877, the Erie was bankrupt, mismanaged, and drowned in a sea of "watered stock." (Such stock, issued in excess of the company's assets, de-rived its name from the rancher's trick of having cattle drink water before weighing

An 1886 office furniture catalog underlines the need for effi-ciency that was a hallmark of the rising middle-level office manager. Filing cabinets and one of Edison's mimeograph machines are near at hand. Workers dress in a more digni-fied style reserved for profes-sionals, while framed pictures on the wall lend a homey air.

in for sale.) Gould emerged unscathed from the fight. When he died of tuberculosis at the age of 56 in 1892, his estate totaled $74 million.

Cooperation worked better than competition. During the 1870s railroad managers created regional federations to pool traffic, set prices, and divide profits among members. Pooling—informal agreements among competing companies to act together—was designed to remove the competition that led to rate wars. Without the force of law, however, pools failed. Members broke ranks by cutting prices in hopes of quick gain. In the end, rate wars died down only when weaker lines failed or stronger ones bought up competitors.

Pooling

The Challenge of Finance

Earlier in the nineteenth century, many railroads relied on state governments for financial help. Backers also looked to counties, cities, and towns for bonds and other forms of aid. People living near the ends of rail lines, who stood to gain from construction, were persuaded to take railroad stock in exchange for land or labor. In the 1850s and 1860s western promoters went to Washington for help and returned with $65 million in loans to six western railroads and some 131 million acres of land.

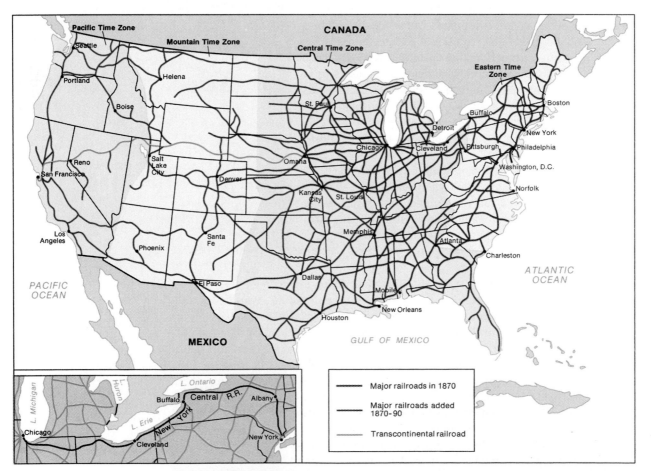

Railroads, 1870–1890 By 1890, the railroad network stretched from one end of the country to the other, with more miles of track than all of Europe combined. New York and Chicago, linked by the New York Central trunk line, became the new commercial axes.

Federal aid helped to build only part of the nation's railroads. Most of the money came from private investors. The New York Stock Exchange expanded rapidly as railroad corporations began to trade their stocks and bonds. Large investment banks developed financial networks to track down money at home and abroad. By 1898 a third of the assets of American life insurance companies had gone into railroads, while Europeans owned nearly a third of all American railroad stocks.

New ways of raising money

Because investment bankers played such large roles in funding railroads, they found themselves advising companies about their business affairs. If a company fell into bankruptcy, bankers sometimes served as the "receivers" who oversaw the property until financial health returned. By absorbing smaller lines into larger ones, eliminating rebates, and stabilizing rates, the bankers helped reduce competition and impose order and centralization. In the process, they often came to control the companies they counseled.

By 1900, the new industrial systems had transformed American railroads. Some 200,000 miles of track were in operation, 80 percent of it owned by only six groups of railroads. Time zones coordinated schedules; standardized track made cross-country freighting easier. Soon passengers were traveling 16 billion miles a year. To that traffic could be added farm goods, raw materials, and factory-finished products. Everything moved with a new regularity that allowed businesses to plan and prosper.

In 1865, 26-year-old John D. Rockefeller sat stone-faced in the office of his Cleveland oil refinery, about to conclude the

The Growth of Big Business

biggest deal of his life. Rockefeller's business was flourishing, but not his partnership with Maurice Clark. The two had fallen out over how quickly to expand. Rockefeller was eager to grow fast; the cautious Clark was not. They dissolved their partnership and agreed to bid for the company. Bidding opened at $500, rocketed to $72,500, and abruptly stopped. "The business is yours," said Clark. The men shook hands and a thin smile crept across Rockefeller's face.

Twenty years later, Rockefeller's Standard Oil Company controlled 90 percent of the nation's refining capacity and an empire that stretched well beyond Cleveland. Around the clock, trains sped Standard executives to New York, Philadelphia, and other eastern cities. The railroads were a fitting form of transportation for Rockefeller's company; in many ways they were the key to his oil empire. They carried his oil products, and discounted his rates, giving him the edge to squeeze out rivals. And they pioneered the business systems on which Rockefeller was building. Like other American firms, Standard Oil was improving on the practices of the railroads to do bigger and bigger business.

Growth in Consumer Goods

But first a great riddle had to be solved: How to control the ravages of competition? In Michigan in the 1860s, salt producers found themselves fighting for their existence. The presence of too many salt makers had begun an endless round of price-cutting that was driving them all out of business. Seeing salvation in combination, they drew together in the nation's first pool. In 1869 they formed the Michigan Salt Association. They voluntarily agreed to divide production, assign markets, and set prices—at double the previous rate.

The pool

Horizontal growth

Competition often plagued salt processing and other manufacturers of consumer goods because their start-up costs were low. Horizontal combination—joining loosely together with rivals—had saved Michigan salt producers. The railroads were among the first big businesses to employ pools. By the 1880s there was a whiskey pool, a cordage pool, and countless others. Such informal arrangements ultimately proved unenforceable and therefore unsatisfactory. (After 1890 they were also considered illegal restraints on trade.) But other forms of horizontal growth, such as formal mergers, spread in the wake of an economic panic in the 1890s.

Vertical integration

Some makers of consumer products worried less about direct competition and concentrated on boosting efficiency and sales. They adopted a strategy called "vertical growth" that integrated several different activities—from acquiring raw materials all the way up to marketing their products to consumers—under one company. Gustavus Swift, a New England butcher, saw the advantages of such integration when he arrived in Chicago in the mid-1870s. Aware of the demand for fresh beef in the East, he acquired new refrigerated railcars to ship meat from western slaughterhouses and a network of ice-cooled warehouses in eastern cities to store it. By 1885 he had created the first national meatpacking enterprise, Swift and Company.

Swift moved upward, closer to consumers, by putting together a fleet of wagons to distribute his beef to retailers. He moved down toward raw materials, extending and coordinating the purchase of cattle at the Chicago stockyards. By the 1890s Swift and Company was a fully integrated, vertically organized corporation operating on a nationwide scale. Soon Swift, Armour and Company, and three other giants—together called the "Big Five"—controlled 90 percent of the beef shipped across state lines.

Vertical growth generally brought producers of consumer goods closer to the marketplace. For them, profit came from high-volume sales. The Singer Sewing

Carnegie Furnaces, Braddock, Pennsylvania

Machine Company and the McCormick Harvester Company created their own retail sales arms. Manufacturers began furnishing ordinary consumers with technical information, credit, and repair services in an effort to expand sales. Advertising expenditures grew, to some $90 million by 1900, to identify markets, shape buying habits, and drum up business.

Carnegie Integrates Steel

Industrialization encouraged vertical integration in heavy industry but more often downward, toward reliable sources of raw materials. These firms made heavy machinery and materials for big users like railroads and factory builders. Their markets were easily identified and changed little. For them, profits lay in securing limited raw materials and in holding down costs.

Andrew Carnegie led the way in steel. A Scottish immigrant, he worked his way up from bobbin boy in a textile factory to expert telegrapher to superintendent of the western division of the Pennsylvania Railroad at the age of 24. A string of wise investments paid off handsomely. He owned a share of the first sleeping car, the first iron railroad bridge, a locomotive factory, and finally an iron factory that became the nucleus of his steel empire.

In 1872, on a trip to England, Carnegie chanced to see the new Bessemer process for making steel. Awestruck by its fiery display, he rushed home to build the biggest steel mill in the world. The J. Edgar Thomson Mills (shrewdly named in honor of the president of the Pennsylvania Railroad) opened in 1875, in the midst of a severe depression. Over the next 25 years, Carnegie added mills at Homestead and elsewhere in Pennsylvania and moved from railroad building to city building. He supplied steel for the Brooklyn Bridge, New York City's elevated railway, and the Washington Monument.

Keys to Carnegie's
success

Carnegie succeeded, in part, by taking advantage of the boom-and-bust business cycle. He jumped in during hard times, building and buying when equipment and businesses were cheap. But he also found skilled managers who employed the administrative techniques of the railroads. And Carnegie knew how to compete. He scrapped machinery, workers, even a new mill to keep costs down and undersell competitors.

The final key to Carnegie's success was expansion. His empire spread horizontally by purchasing rival steel mills and constructing new ones. It spread vertically, buying up sources of supply, transportation, and eventually sales. Controlling such an integrated system, Carnegie could ensure a steady flow of materials from mine to mill and market as well as a steady stream of profits. In 1900 his company turned out more steel than Great Britain and netted him $40 million.

Integration of the kind Carnegie employed expressed the logic of the new industrial age. More and more, the industrial activities of society were being linked together in one giant, interconnected process.

Rockefeller and the Great Standard Oil Trust

John D. Rockefeller began his career as a refiner of petroleum and soon accomplished in oil what Carnegie achieved in steel. And he went further, developing an innovative business structure—the trust—that promised greater control than even Carnegie's integrated system. At first Rockefeller grew horizontally by buying out or joining competing oil refiners. To cut costs, he expanded vertically, with oil pipelines, warehouses, and barrel factories. By 1870, when he and five partners formed the Standard Oil Company of Ohio, his high-caliber, low-cost products could compete with any other.

Rockefeller's methods
of expansion

Because the oil refining business was a jungle of competitive firms, Rockefeller proceeded to twist arms. He bribed rivals, spied on them, created phony companies, and slashed prices. His decisive edge came from the railroads. Desperate for business, they granted Standard Oil not only rebates on shipping rates but also "drawbacks," a fee railroaders paid Standard for any product shipped by a rival. Within a decade Standard dominated the oil business with a vertically integrated empire that stretched from drilling to selling.

Throughout the 1870s Rockefeller kept his empire stitched together through informal pools and other business combinations. But they were weak and afforded him too little control. He could try to expand further, except that corporations were restricted by state law. In Rockefeller's home state of Ohio, for example, corporations could not own plants in other states or own stock in out-of-state companies.

The trust

In 1879 Samuel C. T. Dodd, chief counsel of Standard Oil, came up with a solution, the "trust." Under the trust, the stockholders of a corporation surrendered their shares "in trust" to a central board of directors with the power to control all property. In exchange, stockholders received certificates of trust that paid hefty dividends. Because it did not literally own other companies, the trust violated no state law.

In 1882 the Standard Oil Company of Ohio formed the country's first great trust. It brought Rockefeller what he sought so fiercely—centralized management of the oil industry. Other businesses soon created trusts of their own—in meatpacking, wiremaking, farm machinery, and elsewhere. Just as quickly, trusts became notorious for crushing rivals and fixing prices.

The Mergers of J. Pierpont Morgan

The trust was only a stepping-stone to an even more effective means of avoiding competition, managing people, and controlling business: the corporate merger. The idea of two corporations merging—one buying out another—remained impossible until 1889, when New Jersey began to permit corporations to own other corporations.

In 1890, the need to find a substitute for the trust grew urgent. Congress outlawed trusts under the Sherman Antitrust Act (page 627). The Sherman Act specifically banned business from "restraining trade" by setting prices, dividing markets, or engaging in other unfair practices. The ever-inventive Samuel Dodd came up with a new idea, the "holding company," a corporation of corporations that had the power to hold shares of other companies. Many industries converted their trusts into holding companies, including Standard Oil, which moved to New Jersey in 1899.

The holding company

Two years later came the biggest corporate merger of the era, created by a financial wizard named J. Pierpont Morgan. His orderly mind detested the chaotic competition that threatened his profits. "I like a little competition," Morgan used to say, "but I like combination more." After the Civil War he had taken over his father's powerful investment bank. For the next 50 years, the House of Morgan played a part in consolidating almost every major industry in the country.

Morgan's greatest triumph was in steel, where for years Carnegie had refused to combine with rivals. In January 1901, with the threat of a colossal steel war looming, Morgan convinced Carnegie to put a price tag on his company. When a messenger brought back the scrawled reply—more than $400 million—Morgan merely nodded and said, "I accept this price." He then bought Carnegie's eight largest competitors and announced the formation of the United States Steel Corporation.

U.S. Steel gobbled up more than 200 manufacturing and transportation companies, 1000 miles of railways, and the whole Mesabi iron range of Minnesota. The mammoth holding company produced nearly two-thirds of all American steel. Its value of $1.4 billion exceeded the national debt and made it the country's first billion-dollar corporation.

What Morgan helped to create in steel was rapidly coming to pass in other industries. A wave of mergers swept through American business after the depression of 1893. As the economy plunged, cutthroat competition bled businesses until they were eager to sell out. Giants sprouted almost overnight. By 1904, in each of 50 industries one firm came to account for 60 percent or more of the total output.

The merger movement

Corporate Defenders

As Andrew Carnegie's empire grew, his conscience turned troubled. Preaching a "gospel of wealth," he urged the rich to act as stewards for the poor, "doing for them better than they would or could do for themselves." He devoted his time to philanthropy by creating foundations and endowing libraries and universities with some $350 million in contributions.

The gospel of wealth

Defenders of the new corporate order were less troubled than Carnegie was about the rough-and-tumble world of big business. They justified the system by stressing the opportunity created for individuals by economic growth. Through frugality, acquisitiveness, and discipline—the sources of cherished American individualism—anyone could rise like Andrew Carnegie.

When most ordinary citizens failed to follow in Carnegie's footsteps, defenders blamed the individual. Failures were lazy, ignorant, or morally depraved, they said. British philosopher Herbert Spencer added the weight of science by applying Charles Darwin's theories of evolution where naturalist Darwin had never intended—to society. Spencer maintained that in society, as in biology, only the "fittest" survived. The competitive social jungle doomed the unfit to poverty and rewarded the most fit with property and privilege.

Social Darwinism

The cartoon satirizes Andrew Carnegie as a little boy playing at building libraries. Before he died in 1919, Carnegie gave away $350 million of his $400 million fortune. He built not just libraries but also museums and colleges as well as public-spirited institutions, including the Carnegie Endowment for Peace. "The wealthy person who dies without giving away money," Carnegie wrote, "dies disgraced."

Spencer's American apostle, William Graham Sumner, argued that competition was natural and had to proceed without any interference, including government regulation. Millionaires were simply the "product of natural selection." Such "social Darwinism" found strong support among turn-of-the-century business leaders. The philosophy of ruthless competition certified their success even as they worked to destroy the very competition it celebrated.

Corporate Critics

Andrew Carnegie invoked the gospel to wealth to justify his millions, but a group of radical critics looked on his libraries and foundations as desperate attempts to buy peace of mind. For all the contemporary celebrations of wealth and big business, they saw the new industrial order as exploitative, divisive, and immoral. It was built on the backs of ordinary "toilers," whose labors profited the few Carnegies of the world.

Henry George, a journalist and self-taught economist, began his critique with a simple question. How could poverty exist when industrial progress had created such wealth? George pointed to greedy landowners who bought property when it was cheap and then held it until the forces of society—labor, technology, and speculation on nearby sites—had increased its value. They reaped most of the rewards, despite the hard work of others. In his best-selling book *Progress and Poverty* (1879), George proposed a single tax on these "unearned" profits to end monopoly landholding. With all other taxes abolished, income would be slowly redistributed. "Single-tax" clubs sprang up throughout the country, and George nearly won the race for mayor of New York in 1886.

The journalist Edward Bellamy tapped the same popular resentment against the inequalities of industrial capitalism. In his best-selling novel *Looking Backward* (1888) Julian West, a fictional Bostonian, falls asleep in 1887 and awakens Rip Van Winkle–like in the year 2000. In place of the competitive, class-ridden society of the nineteenth century is an orderly utopia managed by a benevolent government trust. "Fraternal cooperation," shared abundance, and "nationalism," which puts the interests of the community above those of the individual, are the guiding principles. By 1892, Bellamy's philosophy had spawned over 160 clubs in 27 states with followers demanding redistribution of wealth, civil service reform, and nationalization of railroads and utilities.

Socialist Labor party

Less popular but equally hostile to capitalism was the Socialist Labor party, formed in 1877. Under Daniel De Leon, a West Indian immigrant, it stressed class conflict and called for a revolution to give workers control over production. De Leon refused to compromise his radical beliefs, and the socialists ended up attracting more intellectuals than workers. Some immigrants found its class consciousness appealing, but most rejected its radicalism and rigidity. A few party members, bent on gaining greater support, revolted and in 1901 founded the more successful Socialist Party of America. Workers were beginning to organize their own responses to industrialism.

By the mid-1880s, in response to the growing criticism of big business, several states in the South and West enacted laws limiting the size of corporations. But these laws proved all too easy to evade when states such as New Jersey and Delaware eased their rules to allow corporations to grow nationwide.

In 1890, the public clamor against trusts finally forced Congress to act. The Sherman Antitrust Act relied on the only constitutional authority the federal government had over business: its right to regulate interstate commerce. The act outlawed "every contract, combination in the form of trust or otherwise, or conspiracy, in restraint of trade or commerce." The United States stood practically alone among industrialized nations in regulating such business combinations.

Sherman Antitrust Act

Its language was purposefully vague, but the Sherman Antitrust Act did give the government the power to break up trusts and other big businesses. So high was the regard for the rights of private property, however, that few in Congress expected the government to exercise that power or the courts to uphold it. They were right. Before 1901, the Justice Department filed only 14 antitrust suits against big businesses, virtually none of them successful. And in 1895, the Supreme Court dealt the law a major blow by severely limiting its scope when the government brought suit against the E. C. Knight Company, which controlled over 90 percent of sugar refining in the country. *United States v. E. C. Knight Co.* held that businesses involved in manufacturing (as opposed to "trade or commerce") lay outside the authority of the Sherman Act. The ruling thus excluded most firms other than transportation companies that carried goods across state lines. Not until after the turn of the century would the law be used to bust a trust.

United States v. *E. C. Knight Co.*

The Costs of Doing Business

The heated debates between the critics and defenders of industrial capitalism made clear that the changes in American society were two-edged. Big businesses certainly helped to order or rationalize production, increase national wealth, and tie the country together. Yet they also concentrated power, corrupted politics, and made the gap between rich and poor more apparent than ever. In 1890, the richest 9 percent of Americans held nearly three-quarters of all wealth in the United States. But by 1900, one American in eight (nearly 10 million people) lived below the poverty line.

More to the point, the practices of big business subjected the economy to enormous disruptions. The banking system could not always keep pace with the demand for capital, and businesses failed to distribute enough profits to sustain the purchasing

The boom-and-bust cycle

Boom and Bust Business Cycle, 1865–1900 Between 1865 and 1900, industrialization produced great economic growth but also wild swings of prosperity and depression. During booms, productivity soared and near-full employment existed. But the rising number of industrial workers meant high unemployment during deep busts.

power of workers. The supply of goods regularly outstripped the demand for them, and then the wrenching cycle of boom and bust set in. Three severe depressions—1873–1879, 1882–1885, and 1893–1897—rocked the economy in the last third of the nineteenth century. With hard times came fierce competition as managers searched frantically to cut costs, and the industrial barons earned their reputations for ruthlessness.

counterpoint

American Business Leaders: Robber Barons or Captains of Industry?

Attacks and celebrations have continued to characterize portraits of entrepreneurs such as Carnegie and Rockefeller. Some historians, following the lead of nineteenth-century critics, have depicted them as unscrupulous hypocrites who extolled the virtues of competition while ruthlessly crushing it. A lust for profits alone drove them, and they cared little for the needs of society, according to this portrait. The leaders of big business resembled nothing so much as medieval barons who had oppressed their serfs and robbed them of the fruits of their labors. Using corporations, trusts, and other devices, these nineteenth-century "robber barons" similarly exploited their workers and concentrated wealth and power in the hands of a relatively small elite. Such centralization, these historians argue, threatened the fundamentals of democracy.

Standing in sharp contrast to the image of business leaders as robber barons is the notion of them as "captains of industry." Some business historians, interested in examining the growth of industry, concede that the Rockefellers and Carnegies employed methods of doubtful morality. But in their eyes business leaders were not greedy robber barons. Instead they are depicted as industrial statesmen whose creativity and ambition helped to promote an economy of mass-produced abundance. Still other business historians have shown little interest in questions of morality or the tension between democracy and economic concentration. They emphasize less the people than the processes by which new strategies, structures, and forms of doing business increased efficiency and productivity.

The Workers' World

At seven in the morning, Sadie Frowne sat at her sewing machine in a Brooklyn garment factory. The boss, a man she barely knew, dropped a pile of unfinished skirts next to her. She pushed one under the needle and began to rock her foot quickly on the pedal that powered her machine. Sometimes Sadie pushed the fabric too hastily, and the needle pierced her finger. "The machines go like mad all day because the faster you work the more money you get," Sadie explained of the world of industrial work in 1902.

The cramped sweatshops, the vast steel mills, the dank tunnels of the coal fields—all demanded workers and required them to work in new ways. Farmers or peasants who had once timed themselves by the movement of the sun now lived by the clock and labored in the twilight of gaslit factories. Instead of being self-employed, they had to deal with supervisors and were paid by the piece or hour. Not the seasons but the relentless cycle of machines set their pace. Increasingly, workers bore the brunt of depressions, faced periodic unemployment, and toiled under dangerous conditions as they struggled to bring the new industrial processes under their control.

Industrial Work

In 1881, the Pittsburgh Bessemer Steel Company opened its new mill in Homestead, Pennsylvania. Nearly 400 men and boys went to work in its 60 acres of sheds. They kept the mill going around the clock by working in two shifts: 12 hours a day the first week, 12 hours a night the next. In the furnace room, some men fainted from the heat, while the vibration and screeching of machinery deafened others. There were no breaks, even for lunch. "Home is just the place where I eat and sleep," said a steelworker. "I live in the mills."

Few industrial workers labored under conditions quite so harsh, but the Homestead mill reflected the common characteristics of industrial work: the use of machines for mass production; the division of labor into intricately organized, menial tasks; and the dictatorship of the clock. At the turn of the century, two-thirds of all industrial work came from large-scale mills.

Pattern of industrial work

Under such conditions labor paid dearly for industrial progress. By 1900, most of those earning wages in industry worked 6 days a week, 10 hours a day. They held jobs that required more machines and fewer skills. Repetition of small chores replaced fine craftwork. In the 1880s, for example, almost all the 40 different steps that had gone into making a pair of shoes by hand could be performed by a novice or "green hand" with a few days of instruction at a simple machine.

With machines also came danger. Tending furnaces in a steel mill or plucking tobacco from cigarette-rolling machines was tedious. If a worker became bored or tired, disaster could strike. Each year from 1880 to 1900 industrial mishaps killed an average of 35,000 wage earners and injured over 500,000. Workers could expect no payment from employers or the government for death or injury. Accidents were assumed to be their own fault.

The laborers in Thomas Anschutz's painting, *Steelworkers—Noontime* were luckier than those at Homestead. They could escape the factory's stifling heat for a brief break. Workers fortunate enough to bring food used a "lunch pail" like the one at left.

Industrial workers rarely saw an owner. The foreman or supervisor exercised complete authority over the unskilled in his section, hiring and firing them, even setting their wages. Skilled workers had greater freedom, yet they too felt the pinch of technology and organization. By the 1880s, carpenters were finding that machine-made doors were replacing the ones they once constructed at the site. Painters no longer mixed their own paints. "I regard my people," said one manager, "as I regard my machinery. So long as they can do my work for what I choose to pay them, I keep getting out of them all I can."

Taylorism

Higher productivity and profits were the aims, and for Frederick W. Taylor, efficiency was the way to achieve them. During the 1870s and 1880s, Taylor undertook careful time-and-motion studies of workers' movements in the steel industry. He set up standard procedures and offered pay incentives for beating his production quotas. On one occasion, he designed 15 ore shovels, each for a separate task. One hundred forty men were soon doing the work of 600. By the early twentieth century "Taylorism" was a full-blown philosophy, complete with its own professional society. "Management engineers" prescribed routines from which workers could not vary.

For all the high ideals of Taylorism, ordinary laborers refused to perform as cogs in a vast industrial machine. In a variety of ways, they worked to maintain control. Many European immigrants continued to observe the numerous saints' days and other religious holidays of their homelands, regardless of factory rules. When the pressure of six-day weeks became too stifling, workers took an unauthorized "blue Monday" off. Or they slowed down to reduce the grueling pace. Or they simply walked off the job. Come spring and warm weather, factories reported turnover rates of 200 to 300 percent.

Worker citizens

For some laborers, seizing control of work was more than a matter of survival or self-respect. Many workers regarded themselves as citizens of a democratic republic. They expected to earn a "competence"—enough money to support and educate their families and enough time to stay abreast of current affairs. Few but highly skilled workers could realize such democratic dreams. More and more, labor was being managed as another part of an integrated system of industry.

Children, Women, and African Americans

In the mines of Pennsylvania, nimble-fingered eight- and nine-year-olds snatched bits of slate from amid the chunks of coal. In Illinois glass factories, quick-footed "dog boys" dashed with trays of red-hot bottles to the cooling ovens. By 1900, the industrial labor force included some 1.7 million children, more than double the number 30 years earlier. Parents often had no choice. As one union leader observed, "Absolute necessity compels the father . . . to take the child into the mine to assist him in winning bread for the family." On average, children worked 60 hours a week and carried home paychecks a third the size of those of adult males.

Women had always labored on family farms, but by 1870 one out of every four nonagricultural workers was female. In general they earned one-half of what men did. Nearly all were single and young, anywhere from their mid-teens to their mid-twenties. Most lived in boardinghouses or at home with their parents. Usually they contributed their wages to the family kitty. Once married, they took on a life of full-time housework and child rearing.

Only 5 percent of married women held jobs outside the home in 1900. Married black women (in need of income because of the low wages paid to their husbands) were four times more likely than married whites to work away from home.

Domestic service was by far the most common occupation for these women. But industrialization inevitably pushed women into new jobs. Mainly they worked in industries considered extensions of housework: food processing, textiles and clothing, and cigar making. And many women actually preferred factory labor, with its long hours and dirty conditions, to being a live-in servant, where they were at work over six days a week and on call 24 hours a day.

New methods of management and marketing opened positions for white-collar women as "typewriters," "telephone girls," bookkeepers, and secretaries. On rare occasions women entered the professions, though law and medical schools still regarded them as unwelcome invaders. Such discrimination drove ambitious, educated women into nursing, teaching, and library work. Their growing presence soon "feminized" these professions, pushing men upward into managerial slots or out entirely.

Injured boy from the mills

Even more than women, African American men faced discrimination in the workplace. They were paid less than whites and given menial jobs. Their greatest opportunities in industry often came as strikebreakers to replace white workers. Once a strike ended, however, black workers were replaced themselves and hated by the white regulars whom they had replaced. The service trades furnished the largest single source of jobs. Waiting on whites in restaurants or on railroads lay within the boundaries set by the prevailing color line. Craftworkers and a sprinkling of black professionals could usually be found in cities. After the turn of the century, black-owned businesses thrived in the growing black neighborhoods of the North and South.

Clerks' jobs, traditionally held by men, came to be filled by women as growing industrial networks created more managerial jobs for men. In this typical office, male managers literally oversee female clerks.

The American Dream of Success

Rising real wages

Whatever their separate experiences, working-class Americans did improve their overall lot. Though the gap between the very rich and the poor widened, most wage earners made some gains. Between 1860 and 1890 real daily wages—pay in terms of buying power—climbed some 50 percent, more the result of gradually falling prices than of increases in pay. And after 1890, the number of hours on the job began a slow decline.

Yet most unskilled and semiskilled workers in factories continued to receive low pay. In 1890, an unskilled laborer could expect about $1.50 for a 10-hour day; a skilled one, perhaps twice that amount. It took about $600 to make ends meet, but most manufacturing workers made under $500 a year. Native-born white Americans tended to earn more than immigrants, those who spoke English more than those who did not, men more than women, and all others more than African Americans, Latinos, and Asians.

Social mobility

Few workers repeated the rags-to-riches rise of Andrew Carnegie. But some did rise despite periodic unemployment and ruthless wage cuts. About one-quarter of the manual laborers in one study entered the lower middle class in their own lifetimes. More often such unskilled workers climbed in financial status within their own class. Most workers, seeing some improvement, believed in the American dream of success, even if they did not fully share in it.

 # The Systems of Labor

Putting in more hours to save a few pennies, walking out in exhaustion or disgust, slowing down on the job—in these ways individual workers coped with industrial America. Sporadic and unorganized, such actions stood little chance of bringing the new industrial order under the control of labor. For ordinary workers to begin to shape industrialization they had to combine, as businesses did. They needed to combine horizontally—organizing not just locally but on a national scale. And they needed to integrate vertically by coordinating action across a wide range of jobs and skills, as Andrew Carnegie coordinated the production of steel.

Unions were the workers' systematic response to industrialization. The most radical unions echoed the moral critics of capitalism by pointing to the oppressiveness of the new industrial order and worked to overturn it. Others embraced the new industrial order but wanted to improve the position of workers within it. Yet whatever their views, unionists believed that power had swung out of balance and only an organized response could correct it.

Early Unions

In the United States unions began forming before the Civil War. Skilled craftworkers—carpenters, iron molders, cigar makers—joined together to protect themselves against the growing power of management. Railroad "brotherhoods" also furnished insurance for those hurt or killed on the accident-plagued lines. Largely local and exclusively male, these early craft unions remained weak and unconnected to each other as well as to the growing mass of unskilled workers.

After the Civil War, a group of craft unions, brotherhoods, and reformers united skilled and unskilled workers in a nationwide organization. The National Labor Union (NLU) hailed the virtues of a simpler America, when workers controlled their workday, earned a decent living, and had time to be good citizens. NLU leaders attacked the wage system as unfair and enslaving and urged workers to manage their own factories. By the early 1870s, NLU ranks swelled to more than 600,000.

National Labor Union

The NLU pressed energetically for the eight-hour workday, the most popular labor demand of the era. Workers saw it as a way not merely of limiting their time on the job but of limiting the power of employers over their lives. "Eight hours for work; eight hours for rest; eight hours for what we will!" proclaimed a banner at one labor rally. Despite the popularity of the issue, the NLU wilted during the depression of 1873.

The Knights of Labor

More successful was a national union born in secrecy. In 1869 Uriah Stephens and nine Philadelphia garment cutters founded the Noble and Holy Order of the Knights of Labor. They draped themselves in ritual and regalia to deepen their sense of solidarity and met in secret to evade hostile owners. The Knights remained small and fraternal for a decade. Their strongly Protestant tone repelled Catholics, who made up almost half the workforce in many industries.

In 1879 the Knights elected Terence V. Powderly as their Grand Master Workman. Handsome, dynamic, Irish, and Catholic, Powderly threw off the Knights' secrecy, dropped their rituals, and opened their ranks. He called for "one big union" to embrace the "toiling millions"—skilled and unskilled, men and women, natives and immigrants, all religions, all races. By 1886, membership had leaped to over 700,000, including nearly 30,000 African Americans and 3000 women.

Terence Powderly

Like the NLU, the radical Knights of Labor looked to abolish the wage system. In its place they wanted to construct a cooperative economy of worker-owned mines, factories, and railroads. The Knights set up more than 140 cooperative workshops, where workers shared decisions and profits, and sponsored some 200 political candidates, who enjoyed only sporadic success. To tame the new industrial order, they supported the eight-hour workday and the regulation of trusts. Underlying this program was a moral vision of society. If only people renounced greed, laziness, and dishonesty, Powderly argued, corruption and class division would disappear, and democracy would flourish. To reform citizens, the Knights promoted the prohibition of child and convict labor and the abolition of liquor.

It was one thing to proclaim a national union, quite another to coordinate the activities of so many members. Powderly soon found locals resorting to strikes and violence, actions he condemned. In the mid-1880s, such stoppages wrung concessions from the western railroads, but the organization soon became associated with unsuccessful strikes and violent extremists. Even the gains against the railroads were wiped out when the Texas and Pacific Railroad broke a strike by local Knights. By 1890 the Knights of Labor, symbol of organized labor's resistance to industrial capitalism, teetered near extinction.

The American Federation of Labor

The Knights' position as the premier union in the nation was taken by the rival American Federation of Labor (AFL). The AFL reflected the practicality of its leader, Samuel Gompers. Born in a London tenement, the son of a Jewish cigar maker, Gompers had immigrated in 1863 with his family to New York's Lower East Side.

Samuel Gompers

Unlike the visionary Powderly, Gompers preached accommodation, not resistance. He urged his followers to accept capitalism and the wage system. What he wanted was "pure and simple unionism"—a worker organization that bargained for higher wages, fewer hours, improved safety, more benefits.

Gompers chose to organize highly skilled craftworkers because they were difficult to replace. He bargained with employers and used strikes and boycotts only as last resorts. With the Cigar Makers' Union as his base, Gompers helped create the first national federation of craft unions in 1881. In 1886, it was reorganized as the American Federation of Labor. Twenty-five labor groups joined, representing nearly 140,000 skilled workers.

Here was labor's answer to the corporation and the trust: a horizontal organization for consolidating competition among skilled workers. Gompers fought off radicals and allied himself with whatever candidate supported labor. Stressing gradual, concrete gains, he made the AFL the most powerful union in the country. By 1901 it had more than a million members, almost a third of all skilled workers in America.

Failure of organized labor

Despite the success of the AFL, the laboring classes did not organize themselves as systematically as did the barons of industrial America. For one thing, Gompers and the AFL were less interested in vertical integration that combined skilled and unskilled workers and had little inclination to include women and African Americans. For another, workers themselves were separated by language and culture, divided along lines of race and gender, and fearful of retaliation by management. A strong strain of individualism made many workers regard any collective action as un-American. And so they often resisted unionization. In 1900, union membership comprised less than 10 percent of industrial workers.

The Limits of Industrial Systems

It was the vagaries of the marketplace and stubbornness of owners that in the end broke the labor movement and set the limits of industrial systems for workers. As managers increased their control over the workplace, workers often found themselves at the mercy of the new industrial order. Even in boom times, one in three workers was out of a job at least three or four months a year. The word "unemployment" dates from the late nineteenth century.

Spontaneous protests

When a worker's pay dropped and frustration mounted, when a mother worked all night and fell asleep during the day while caring for her children, when food prices suddenly jumped—anger might boil over into protest. "A mob of 1,000 people, with women in the lead, marched through the Jewish quarter of Williamsburg last evening and wrecked half a dozen butcher shops," reported the *New York Times* in 1902. In the late nineteenth century a wave of labor activism swept the nation. More often than mobs, it was strikes and boycotts that challenged the authority of employers and gave evidence of working-class identity and discontent.

Most strikes broke out spontaneously, organized by informal leaders in a factory. "Malvina Fourtune and her brother Henry Fourtune it was them who started the strike," declared a company informer in Chicopee, Massachusetts. "They go from house to house and tells the people to keep up the strike." Thousands of rallies and organized strikes were staged as well, often on behalf of the eight-hour workday, in good times and bad, by union and nonunion workers alike.

Molly McGuires

Some workers resorted to terrorism to resist the new industrial order. In the coalfields of Pennsylvania, Irish miners organized a secret society called the Molly McGuires, after an earlier group of protesters in Ireland who had disguised themselves as women and roamed the Irish countryside beating and sometimes killing

In this painting by Robert Koehler, entitled *The Strike* (1886), labor confronts management in a strike that may soon turn bloody. One worker reaches for a stone as an anxious mother and her children look on.

tyrannical landlords. The American Mollys founded their society in 1866, and for the next decade the small but dedicated band resorted to intimidation, arson, and murder to combat the horrid working conditions of coal miners. In 1876, twenty Mollys were brought to trial and a year later executed for sixteen murders. For most Americans, justice was served, despite the questionable legality of the trial—and in its wake, the secret society vanished. But for those who had joined the Mollys, violence was a long-established tradition, imported from Ireland and employed as both a form of protest and a means of achieving "retributive justice" against oppressors.

Great Railroad Strike

In 1877, in the midst of a deep depression, the country's first nationwide strike opened an era of confrontation between labor and management. When the Baltimore and Ohio Railroad cut wages by 20 percent, a crew in Martinsburg, West Virginia, seized the local depot and blocked the line. President Hayes sent federal troops to enforce a court order ending the strike, but instead two-thirds of the nation's tracks were shut down in sympathy. The novel tactic suggested a growing sense of solidarity among workers. The country ground to a halt.

When owners brought in strikebreakers, workers torched rail yards, smashed engines and cars, and tore up track. Local police, state militia, and federal troops finally quashed the strike after 12 bloody days. The "Great Railroad Strike" of 1877 left 100 people dead and more than $10 million worth of railroad property in rubble. It signaled the rising power and unity of labor and sparked fears, as one newspaper warned, that "this may be the beginning of a great civil war in this country, between labor and capital."

Laundresses strike

The Civil War between North and South was still fresh in the minds of Atlantans when 3000 laundresses struck for higher wages in 1881. Over 98 percent of the city's domestic workers were black women, just a decade and a half out of slavery. Pitiful wages already had led many of them to employ informal strategies to protest. They took unauthorized breaks, pretended to be sick, or "pantoted" (stole) leftovers from the kitchens of their white employers. Washerwomen were among the most privileged domestics because they neither worked nor lived with their employers. Instead they labored together in common spaces in their neighborhoods, where they built social and political networks. In 1881 they formed the Washing Society and threatened to leave much of the city without clean clothes unless their demands for higher wages were met. Though little resulted from the strike, it nonetheless showed the growing appeal of organized protest against economic inequality and laid the groundwork for later civil rights protests.

Haymarket Square riot

In 1886, tension between labor and capital exploded in the "Great Upheaval"—a series of strikes, boycotts, and rallies. One of the most violent episodes occurred at Haymarket Square in Chicago. A group of anarchists was protesting the recent killing of workers by police at the McCormick Harvester Company. As rain drenched the small crowd, police ordered everyone out of the square. Suddenly a bomb exploded. One officer was killed; 6 others were mortally wounded. When police opened fire, the crowd fired back. Nearly 70 policemen were injured, and at least 4 civilians died.

Conservatives charged that radicals were responsible for the "Haymarket Massacre." Though the bomb thrower was never identified and though no evidence connecting the accused to the bombing was ever presented, a jury found eight anarchists guilty of conspiracy to commit murder. Four were hanged, one killed himself, and three remained in jail until they were pardoned by Governor John Peter Altgeld in 1893. He considered their conviction a miscarriage of justice, but ordinary citizens who had supported labor grew fearful of what newspapers called its "Samson-like power." Cities enlarged their police forces, and states built more National Guard armories on the borders of working-class neighborhoods.

Management Strikes

The strikes, rallies, and boycotts of 1886 were followed by a second surge of labor activism in 1892. In the remote silver mines of Coeur d'Alene, Idaho, at the Carnegie steel mill in Homestead, Pennsylvania, in the coal mines near Tracy City, Tennessee, strikes flared, only to be crushed by management. Often state and federal troops joined company guards and private detectives from the Pinkerton agency to fight workers.

Government troops were often called in to help management quell strikes. In the Pullman Strike of 1894, U.S. Regulars "give the butt" to angry laborers in this drawing by Frederick Remington.

"GIVING THE BUTT"—THE WAY THE "REGULAR" INFANTRY TACKLES A MOB.

The broadest confrontation between labor and management took place two years later. A terrible depression had shaken the economy for almost a year when George Pullman, owner of the Palace Car factory and inventor of the plush railroad car, laid off workers, cut wages (but kept rents high on company-owned housing), and refused to discuss grievances. In 1894 workers struck and managed to convince the new American Railway Union to support them by boycotting all trains that used Pullman cars. Quickly the strike spread to 27 states and territories.

Anxious railroad owners appealed to President Grover Cleveland for federal help. On the slim pretext that the strike obstructed mail delivery (strikers had actually been willing to handle mail trains without Pullman cars), Cleveland secured a court order halting the strike. He then called several thousand special deputies into Chicago to enforce it. In the rioting that followed, 12 people died and scores were arrested. But the strike was crushed.

In all labor disputes the central issue was the power to shape the new industrial systems. Employers always enjoyed the advantage. They hired and fired workers, set the terms of employment, and ruled the workplace. They fought unions with "yellow dog" contracts that forced workers to refuse to join. Blacklists circulated the names of labor agitators. Lockouts kept protesting workers from plants, and company spies infiltrated their organizations. With a growing pool of labor, employers could replace strikers and break strikes.

Management could also count on local, state, and federal authorities for troops to break strikes. In addition, businesses used a powerful new legal weapon, the injunction. These court orders prohibited certain actions, including strikes, by barring workers from interfering with their employer's business. It was just such an order that had brought federal deputies into the Pullman strike and put Eugene Debs, head of the American Railway Union, behind bars. The Indiana-born Debs, a former locomotive fireman and early labor organizer, received a six-month jail sentence for violating the court injunction. After his release, he abandoned the Democratic party to become the foremost Socialist leader in America. Yet despite the protests of workers such as Debs, employers had become masters of the mightiest industrial economy on earth.

In a matter of only 30 or 40 years, the new industrial order transformed the landscape of America. Whether rich or poor, worker, entrepreneur, or industrial baron, Americans were being drawn closer by the new industrial systems. Ore scooped from Mesabi might end up in a steel girder on James Eads's Mississippi bridge, in a steel needle for Sadie Frowne's sewing machine in Brooklyn, or in a McCormick reaper slicing across the Nebraska plains. When a textile worker in Massachusetts struck, a family in Alabama might well pay more for clothes. A man in Cleveland now set his watch to agree with the time of a man in New York, regardless of the position of the sun. Such changes might seem effortless to someone like T. S. Hudson, scampering across the rails of America in 1882. But as the nineteenth century drew to a close, material progress went hand in hand with social pain and upheaval.

Pullman strike

Management weapons

chapter summary

In the last third of the nineteenth century, a new industrial order reshaped the United States.

- New systems—of resource development, technology, invention, transportation, communications, finance, corporate management, and labor—boosted industrial growth and productivity.

- Businesses grew big, expanding vertically and horizontally to curb costs and competition and to increase control and efficiency.

- Industrialization came at a price.

  - Workers found their power, job satisfaction, and free time reduced as their numbers in factories mushroomed.

  - The environment was degraded.

  - A vicious cycle of boom and bust afflicted the economy.

- Workers both resisted and accommodated the new industrial order.

  - Some resisted through informal mechanisms such as slowdowns, absenteeism, and quitting and through spontaneous and more formal ones, including radical unions like the Knights of Labor.

  - Other workers were more accommodating, accepting low-paying jobs and layoffs and creating "pure-and-simple" unions, such as the American Federation of Labor, that accepted the prevailing system of private ownership and wage labor while bargaining for better wages and working conditions.

- The benefits of industrialization were equally undeniable.

  - Life improved materially for many Americans.

  - The real wages of even industrial workers climbed.

- The United States rocketed from fourth place among industrial nations in 1860 to first by 1890.

additional reading

For a useful introduction to the period, see Edward C. Kirland, *Industry Comes of Age: Business, Labor, and Public Policy, 1860–1897* (1967). Mechanization and its impact are the focus of Siegfried Giedion's classic *Mechanization Takes Command* (1948). The best overview of American labor is American Social History Project, *Who Built America? Working People and the Nation's Economy, Politics, Culture, & Society,* Volume Two: *From the Gilded Age to the Present* (1992). Herbert Gutman, *Work, Culture, and Society in Industrializing America: Essays in American Working-Class History* (1976) explores the development of working-class communities in the nineteenth century, especially the role of ethnicity in creating a working-class culture. David Montgomery offers a broad look at the impact of industrialization on American labor in *The Fall of the House of Labor: The Workplace, the State, and American Labor Activism, 1865–1925* (1987), and Leon Fink, *Workingmen's Democracy: The Knights of Labor and American Politics* (1983) examines early efforts of the Knights of Labor to challenge corporate capitalism by organizing workers and socializing them into a labor culture. Alice Kessler-Harris, *Out to Work: A History of Wage-Earning Women in the United States* (1982) surveys female wage earners and their effect on American culture, family life, and values. Kevin Kenny, *Making Sense of the Molly McGuires* (1998) is a superb study not only of the mysterious Mollys and their tragic end but of immigration, working-class violence, and the history of the Irish in America.

No book did more to set the idea of big business as ruthless robber barons than Matthew Josephson, *The Robber Barons: The Great American Capitalists, 1861–1901* (1934). An early revision of this bleak image can be found in Allan Nevins's biography of John D. Rockefeller, *A Study in Power: John D. Rockefeller, Industrialist and Philanthropist,* 2 vols. (1953). Business historian Alfred D. Chandler Jr.'s *Strategy and Structure: Chapters in the History of American Industrial Enterprise* (1962) and *The Visible Hand: The Managerial Revolution in American Business* (1977) are seminal accounts of business organization and management that stress the adaptations of business structures and the emergence of a new class of managers. For a comparative view of the rise of big business in the United States, Great Britain, and Germany, see his *Scale and Scope* (1988). For a fuller list of readings, see the Bibliography.

Significant Events

1855	**1859** First oil well drilled near Titusville, Pennsylvania
1860	**1866** National Labor Union founded
	1869 Knights of Labor created
	1870 John D. Rockefeller incorporates Standard Oil Company of Ohio
1865	
1870	**1873** Carnegie Steel Company founded; Panic of 1873
	1874 Massachusetts enacts first 10-hour workday law for women
1875	**1876** Alexander Graham Bell invents telephone
	1877 Railroad wage cuts lead to violent strikes; Thomas Edison invents phonograph
1880	**1879** Edison develops incandescent light bulb; Henry George's *Progress and Poverty* published
	1882 Rockefeller's Standard Oil Company becomes nation's first trust; Edison's electric company begins lighting New York City
1885	**1883** Railroads establish standard time zones
1890	**1886** American Federation of Labor organized; Haymarket Square bombing
1895	**1892** Homestead Steel strike
	1893 Panic of 1893
1900	**1894** Pullman strike
1905	**1901** U.S. Steel Corporation becomes nation's first billion-dollar company

Graziano's bootblack stand was jammed with people milling about, looking for help. Above the crowd, enthroned like an Irish king, sat George Washington Plunkitt, ward boss of Manhattan's Fifteenth Assembly District. There to help, Plunkitt asked little in return, only votes on election day. Plunkitt understood the close relationship between help and votes. "There's got to be in every ward," another boss explained, "somebody that any bloke can come to—no matter what he's done—and get help. *Help, you understand; none of your law and justice, but help.*" The reverse was also true: to maintain power, bosses like Plunkitt had to be able to count on the political support of those they helped.

For years Plunkitt had been a leader of Tammany Hall, the Democratic party organization that ruled New York City politics from 1850 to 1930. Much of Plunkitt's daily routine was taken up with helping. One typical day began when a bartender roused him at two in the morning to get a friend out of jail. Plunkitt succeeded but didn't return to bed until after three. Howling fire sirens woke him at six. Before dawn he was assisting burned-out tenants with food, clothing, and shelter. Home by eleven, he found four out-of-work men waiting for help. Within hours each had a job. A quick bite of lunch and he was off again, this time to a pair of funerals. Plunkitt brought flowers for the bereaved and offered condolences, all in full view of the assembled. From there he rushed to attend a "Hebrew confirmation." Early evening found him at district headquarters, helping his election captains plot ways of "turning out the vote."

After a quick stop at a church fair, it was back to the party clubhouse. He helped some local teams by buying tickets for their next game. Before leaving, he pledged to two dozen pushcart peddlers that he would try to stop the police from harassing them. He arrived at a wedding reception at half past ten (already having helped the bride and groom with "a handsome wedding present"). Finally, at midnight, he crawled into bed, after a day of helping all he could.

Such relentless effort helped Plunkitt as well. Born poor to Irish immigrants, he died a millionaire in 1924. His pluck and practicality would have made him the envy of any industrialist. Like the Carnegies and Rockefellers, fierce ambition fueled his rise from butcher boy to political boss. City politics was his way out of the slums in a world that favored the rich, the educated, and the well-established.

In the late nineteenth century the needs of rapidly growing cities gave political bosses like George Washington Plunkitt their chance. "I seen my opportunities and I took 'em," Plunkitt used to say. Every city contract and bond issue, every tax assessment, every charter for a new business offered Plunkitt and his cronies an opportunity to line their pockets. Money made from defrauding the public was known as "boodle," or honest graft. ("Black" graft came from vice and extortion.) How much boodle bosses collected depended on how well their organization managed to elect sympathetic officials. That explained why Plunkitt spent so much time helping his constituents.

Plunkitt's New York was the first great city in history to be ruled by ordinary people in an organized and continuing way. Bosses and their cronies came from the

A boss at work

The Rise of an Urban Order

preview • At the center of the new industrial order was the city. But to accommodate the global migration of laborers and families, to support the sprawling factories and the masses who kept them going, urban centers of the late nineteenth century had to reinvent themselves. Transportation systems, residential housing, political and social cultures all changed.

Boodle

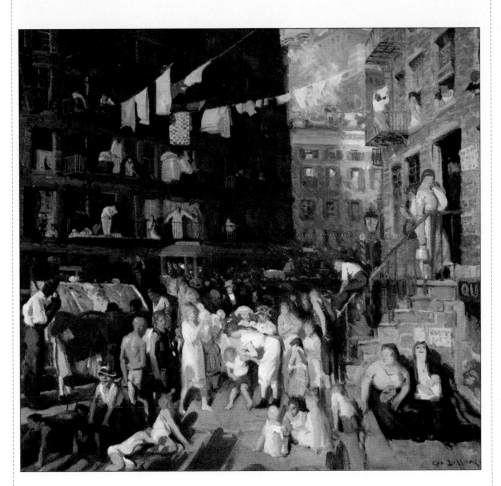

Realist painters like George Bellows, who were scorned by critics as the "Ashcan School," captured the grittiness and vibrancy of teeming urban life. *Cliff Dwellers* makes dramatic use of light and dark, relying on line, mass, and color to achieve its naturalism.

streets and saloons, the slums and tenements, the firehouses and funeral homes. Many of their families had only recently arrived in America. While the Irish of Tammany Hall ran New York, Germans governed St. Louis, Scandinavians Minneapolis, and Jews San Francisco.

In an earlier age political leadership had been drawn from the ranks of the wealthy and native-born. America had been an agrarian republic where personal relationships were grounded in small communities. By the late nineteenth century, the country was in the midst of an urban explosion. Industrial cities of unparalleled size and diversity were transforming American life. They lured people from all over the globe, created tensions between natives and newcomers, reshaped the social order. For Plunkitt, as for so many Americans, a new urban age was dawning. The golden door of opportunity opened onto the city.

A New Urban Age

The modern city was the product of industrialization. Cities contained the great investment banks, the smoky mills and dingy sweatshops, the spreading railroad yards, the grimy tenements and sparkling mansions, the new department stores and skyscrapers. People came from places as near as the countryside and as far as Italy, Russia, and Armenia. By the end of the nineteenth century America had entered a new urban age, with tens of millions of "urbanites," an urban landscape, and a growing urban culture.

The Urban Explosion

During the 50 years after the Civil War, the population of the United States quadrupled—from 23 million to 92 million. Yet the number of people living in American cities increased nearly sevenfold. In 1860, only one American in six lived in a city with a population of 8000 or more; in 1900, one in three did. By 1910 nearly half the nation lived in cities large and small.

Cities grew in every region of the country, some faster than others. In the Northeast and upper Midwest early industrialization created more cities than in the West and the South, although those regions contained big cities as well. Atlanta, Nashville, and later Dallas and Houston boomed under the influence of railroads. Los Angeles had barely 6000 people in 1870. By 1900 it trailed only San Francisco among large cities on the Pacific coast, with a population of 100,000.

Large urban centers dominated whole regions and tied the country together in a complex urban network. New York, the nation's banker, printer, and chief marketplace, ruled the East. Smaller cities operated within narrower spheres of influence and often specialized. Milwaukee was famous for its beer, Tulsa for oil, and Hershey, Pennsylvania, for chocolate.

Cities' relations to regions around them

Cities even shaped the natural environment hundreds of miles beyond their limits. Chicago became not only the gateway to the West but a powerful agent of ecological change. As its lines of commerce and industry radiated outward, the city transformed the ecosystems of the West. Wheat to feed Chicago's millions replaced sheltering prairie grasses. Great stands of white pine in Wisconsin vanished, only to reappear in the furniture and frames of Chicago houses or as fence rails shipped to prairie farms.

The Great Global Migration

Between 1820 and 1920, some 60 million people left farms and villages for cities across the globe. They formed part of a migrating pool of labor, moving from country to country in search of work (see page 616). Mushrooming population gave them a powerful push. In Europe the end of the Napoleonic Wars in 1815 launched a cycle of baby booms that continued at 20-year intervals for the rest of the century. Improved diet and sanitation, aided by Louis Pasteur's discovery that bacteria cause infection and disease, reduced deaths. Meanwhile machinery cut the need for farm workers. In 1896 one man in a wheat field could do what had taken 18 men just 60 years earlier.

Push and pull factors

Surplus farm workers formed a ragtag army of migrants both in America and in Europe. The prospect of factory work for better pay and fewer hours especially lured the young to cities. Labor agents combed Europe, pulling immigrants to the United States with often false promises of high-paying jobs and unimagined riches. "They told me that in America the streets were paved with gold," reported one immigrant. "When I got here, I found the streets were not paved with gold, they were not paved at all, and they expected me to pave them." In America, young farm women spearheaded the migration. Mechanization and the rise of commercial agriculture made them less valuable in the fields, while mass-produced goods from mail-order houses made them less useful at home.

Asia sent comparatively fewer newcomers to the United States, Canada, and other industrializing nations hungry for workers, but Asian immigrants followed migration patterns similar to the workers leaving Europe and for similar reasons. In

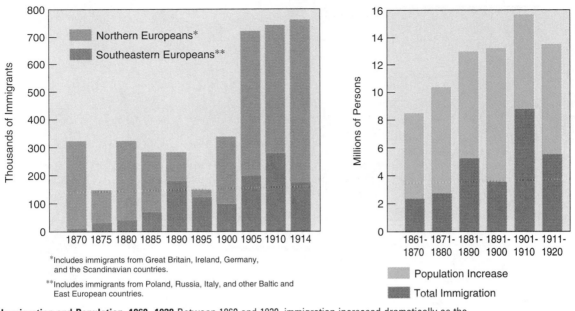

*Includes immigrants from Great Britain, Ireland, Germany, and the Scandinavian countries.

**Includes immigrants from Poland, Russia, Italy, and other Baltic and East European countries.

Immigration and Population, 1860–1920 Between 1860 and 1920, immigration increased dramatically as the sources of immigrants shifted from northern Europe to southeastern Europe. Despite fears to the contrary, the proportion of newcomers as a percentage of population increases did not show nearly the same jump.

China, for example, several factors combined to push some 370,000 people out of the country and into the United States and Hawaii between 1850 and 1882. Defeats in the Opium Wars (1839–1842) and the Anglo-Chinese War (1856–1860) forced the Chinese to pay large indemnities to Great Britain and to limit the duties charged on foreign imports. When the Chinese government raised taxes to make up the difference, small landowners unable to afford them lost their farms, tenants unable to pay higher rents lost their plots, and peasants who had turned their homes into centers of small industry lost income, for they could not compete with the now-cheaper manufactured goods from the West.

Chinese immigrants

To that international context could be added domestic upheavals, interethnic rivalries, and local wars in central and southern China that devastated those regions. Many of the people displaced by taxation and turmoil moved within the country, but those from Guandong Province in southeastern China, especially around the coastal city of Canton, often left. Canton had long been a thriving port of trade at which foreigners called and from which the Cantonese ventured abroad. Agents from America and Europe could recruit workers more easily in Canton, and ships stood ready in the harbor to transport them across the Pacific and elsewhere. In Japan and other Asian nations, similar forces of push and pull sparked migration into the United States, including some 400,000 Japanese between 1885 and 1924.

Earlier in the century, European immigrants had come to the United States from northern and western Europe. In the 1880s, "new" immigrants from southern and eastern Europe began to arrive. Some, like Russian and Polish Jews, were fleeing religious and political persecution. Others left to evade famine or diseases such as cholera, which swept across southern Italy in 1887. But most came for the same reasons as migrants from the countryside—a job, more money, a fresh start.

The "new" immigration

Ambitious, hardy, and resourceful, immigrants found themselves tested every step of the way to America. They left behind the comfort of family, friends, and old

By the 1890s, European immigrants were arriving at the new receiving center on Ellis Island in New York harbor (left). Asian immigrants came through Angel Island in San Francisco Bay (right). On both coasts, physical examinations, like the eye inspections shown, became part of standard screening practices as immigration policies stiffened. The rapid rise in immigration ignited nativist fears that immigrants were taking over the country. In the 1870s cartoon, immigrants literally gobble up Uncle Sam.

ways. The price of one-way passage by steamship—about $50 in 1904—was far too expensive for most to bring relatives, at least at first. And the trip was dangerous even before immigrants stepped on board a ship. They traveled for weeks, stealing across heavily guarded borders, just to reach a port like Le Havre in France. At dockside, shipping lines vaccinated, disinfected, and examined them to ensure against their being returned at company expense.

It took one to two weeks to cross the Atlantic aboard steam-powered ships. Immigrants spent most of the time below decks in cramped, filthy compartments called "steerage." Most arrived at New York's Castle Garden or the newer facility on nearby Ellis Island, opened in 1892. If coming from Asia, they landed at Angel Island in San Francisco Bay. Sometimes they were held in the facility for weeks. As one Chinese newcomer gazed out on San Francisco Bay, he scribbled a poem on the gray walls:

> Why do I have to languish in this jail?
> It is because my country is weak and my family poor.
> My parents wait in vain for news;
> My wife and child, wrapped in their quilt, sigh with loneliness.

Immigrants had to pass another medical examination, have their names recorded by customs officials, and pay an entry tax. At any point, they could be detained or shipped home.

Immigrants arrived in staggering numbers—over 6 million between 1877 and 1890, some 30 million by 1920. By 1900 they made up nearly 15 percent of the population. Most were young, between the ages of 15 and 40. Few spoke English or had skills or much education. Unlike earlier arrivals, who were mostly Protestant, these new immigrants worshiped in Catholic, Greek, or Russian Orthodox churches and Jewish synagogues. Almost two-thirds were men. A large number came to make money for buying land or starting businesses back home. Some changed their minds and sent for relatives, but those returning were common enough to be labeled "birds of passage."

Immigrant profile

Jews were an exception. Russian Jews escaped from Europe by the tens of thousands after the assassination of Czar Alexander II in 1881 rekindled anti-Semitic "pogroms," or riots. Between 1880 and 1914, a third of eastern Europe's Jews left. They made up 10 percent of all immigration to the United States during those years. Almost all stayed and brought their families, often one by one. They had few choices. As one Jewish immigrant wrote of his Russian homeland, "Am I not despised? Am I not urged to leave? . . . Do I not rise daily with the fear lest the hungry mob attack me?"

The Shape of the City

In colonial days, Benjamin Franklin could walk from one end of Boston to the other in an hour. Only Franklin's adopted home, Philadelphia, spilled into suburbs. Over the years these colonial "walking cities" developed ringed patterns of settlement. Merchants, professionals, and the upper classes lived near their shops and offices in the city center. As one walked outward, the income and status of the residents gradually declined.

Cities of the late nineteenth century still exhibited this ringed pattern, except that industrialization had reversed the order of settlement and increased urban sprawl. As the middle and upper classes moved out of a growing industrial core, the poor, some immigrants, African Americans, and lower-class laborers filled the void. They took over old factories and brownstones, shanties and cellars. By sheer weight of numbers they transformed these areas into the slums of the central city.

Patterns of settlement

Curled around the slums was the "zone of emergence," an income-graded band of those on their way up. It contained second-generation city dwellers, factory workers, skilled laborers, and professional mechanics. They lived in progressively better tenements and neater row houses as the distance from center city increased. Poverty no longer imprisoned them, but they could still slip back in hard times.

Farther out was the suburban fringe, home to the new class of white-collar managers and executives. They lived in larger houses with individual lots on neat, tree-lined streets. The very wealthy still maintained mansions on fashionable city avenues, but by the 1870s and 1880s, they too began to keep suburban homes.

Growth of New Orleans to 1900
Streetcars helped cities spread beyond business districts while still functioning as organic wholes. By 1900, streetcar lines in New Orleans reached all the way to Audubon Park and Tulane University, bringing these once distant points within the reach of city dwellers and creating "streetcar suburbs."

Urban Transport

For all their differences, the circles of settlement held together as a part of a massive and interdependent whole. One reason was an evolving system of urban transportation. Civic leaders came to understand that the modern city could not survive, much less grow, without improved transportation. San Francisco installed trolley cars pulled by steam-driven cables. It worked so well in San Francisco that Chicago, Seattle, and other hilly cities installed cable systems in the 1880s. Other cities experimented with elevated trestles to carry steam locomotives or cable lines high above crowded streets. But none of the breakthroughs quite did the trick. Cables remained slow and unreliable; the elevated railways, or "els," were dirty, ugly, and noisy.

Role of electricity

Electricity rescued city travelers. In 1888 Frank Julian Sprague, a naval engineer who had once worked for Thomas Edison, installed the first electric trolley line in Richmond, Virginia. Electrified streetcars were soon speeding along at 12 miles an hour, twice as fast as horses. By 1902 electricity drove nearly all city railways. Sprague's innovations also meant that "subways" could be built without having to worry about tunnels filled with a steam engine's smoke and soot. Between 1895 and 1897 Boston built the first underground electric line. New York followed in 1904 with a subway that ran from City Hall on the southern tip of Manhattan north to Harlem. Once considered too far afield, Harlem soon became dotted with new apartment and tenement developments. When the white middle class of New York refused to move so far uptown, Philip A. Peyton convinced landlords to allow his Afro-American Realty Company to handle the properties. Within a decade Harlem had become the black capital of America.

The rich had long been able to keep homes outside city limits, traveling to and fro in private carriages. New systems of mass transit freed the middle class and even the poor to live miles from work. For a nickel or two, anyone could ride from central shopping and business districts to the suburban fringes and back. A network of moving vehicles held the segmented and sprawling city together and widened its reach out to "streetcar suburbs."

Bridges and Skyscrapers

Because cities often grew along rivers and harbors, their separate parts sometimes had to be joined over water. The principles of building large river bridges had already been worked out by the railroads. It remained for a German immigrant and his son, John and Washington Roebling, to make the bridge a symbol of urban growth.

The Brooklyn Bridge, linking New York City with Brooklyn, took 13 years to complete. It cost $15 million and 20 lives, including that of designer John. When it opened in 1883, it stretched more than a mile across the East River, with passage broad enough for a footpath, two double carriage lanes, and two railroad lines. Its arches were cut like giant cathedral windows, and its supporting cables hung, said an awestruck observer, "like divine messages from above." Soon other suspension bridges were spanning the railroad yards in St. Louis and the bay at Galveston, Texas.

Even as late as 1880 church steeples dominated the urban landscape. They towered over squat factories and office buildings. But growing congestion and the increasing value of land pushed architects to search for ways to make buildings taller. In place of thick walls of brick that restricted factory floor space, builders used cast iron columns. The new "cloudscrapers" were strong, durable, and fire-resistant. Their open floors were ideal for warehouses and also for office buildings and department stores.

Steel, tougher in tension and compression, turned cloudscrapers into skyscrapers. William LeBaron Jenney first used steel in his 10-story Home Insurance Building (1885) in Chicago. By the end of the century steel frames and girders raised buildings to 30 stories or more. New York City's triangular Flatiron building (at right), named for its shape, used the new technology to project an angular yet remarkably delicate elegance. In Chicago, Daniel Burnham's Reliance Building (1890) relied so heavily on new plate glass windows that contemporaries called it "a glass tower fifteen stories high."

It was no accident that many of the new skyscrapers arose in Chicago, for the city had burned nearly to the ground in 1871. The "Chicago school" of architects helped rebuild it. The young maverick Louis H. Sullivan promised a new urban profile in which the skyscraper would be "every inch a proud and soaring thing." In the Wainwright Building (1890) in St. Louis and the Carson, Pirie, and Scott department store (1889–1904) in Chicago, Sullivan produced towering structures that symbolized the modern industrial city.

Slum and Tenement

Far below the skyscrapers lay the slums and tenements of the inner city. In cramped rooms and sunless hallways, along narrow alleys and in flooded basements lived the city poor. They often worked there, too, in "sweaters' shops" where as many as 18 people labored and slept in foul two-room flats.

Perils of the slum neighborhood

In New York, whose slums were the nation's worst, crime thrived in places called "Bandit's Roost" and "Hell's Kitchen." Bands of young toughs with names like the "Sewer Rats" and the "Rock Gang" stalked the streets in search of thrills and easy money. Gambling, prostitution, and alcoholism all claimed their victims most readily in the slums. The poor usually turned to such crime in despair. A 20-year-old prostitute supporting a sickly mother and four brothers and sisters made no apologies: "Let God Almighty judge who's to blame most, I that was driven, or them that drove me to the pass I'm in."

The poor diets of slum dwellers left them vulnerable to disease, but it was their close quarters and often filthy surroundings that raised their rates of infection to epidemic levels. Until the 1860s pigs, sheep, and other animals roamed freely in the streets of New York. Tons of manure from horse-drawn carriages and railways covered city streets, furnishing a fertile habitat for deadly microbes. Tightly packed tenements and streets piled high with refuse were also breeding grounds for microbes. Cholera, typhoid, and an outbreak of yellow fever in Memphis in the 1870s killed tens of thousands. Tuberculosis was deadlier still. As late as 1900, among infectious diseases it ranked only behind influenza and pneumonia *combined* as a killer. Slum children—all city children—were most vulnerable. Almost a quarter of children born in American cities in 1890 never lived to see their first birthday.

The installation of new sewage and water purification systems helped. The modern flush toilet came into use only after the turn of the century. Until then people relied on water closets and communal privies. Some catered to as many as 800. All too often cities dumped waste into old private vaults or rivers used for drinking water. In 1881 an exasperated mayor of Cleveland called the Cuyahoga River "an open sewer through the center of the city."

Slum housing was often more dangerous than the water. The tubercle bacillus flourished in musty, windowless tenements. In 1879 New York enacted a new housing law requiring a window in all bedrooms of new tenements. Architect James E. Ware won a competition with a design that contained an indentation on both sides of the building. When two tenements abutted each other, the indentations formed a narrow shaft for air and light. From above, the buildings looked like giant dumbbells. Up to 16 families lived on a floor, with only two toilets in the hall.

Originally hailed as an innovation, Ware's dumbbell tenement spread over such cities as Cleveland, Cincinnati, and Boston "like a scab," said an unhappy reformer. Ordinary blocks contained 10 such tenements and housed as many as 4000 people. The airshafts became giant silos for trash. They blocked what little light had entered and, worse still, carried fires from one story to the next. When the New York housing commission met in 1900, it concluded that conditions were worse than when reformers had started 33 years earlier.

"Dumbbell" tenements were designed to use every inch of available space in the standard 25-by-200-foot city lot while providing ventilation and reducing the spread of disease.

Every new arrival to the city brought dreams and altogether too many needs. Schools and houses had to be built,

Running and Reforming the City

streets paved, garbage collected, sewers dug, fires fought, utility lines laid. Running the city became a full-time job, and a new breed of professional politician rose to the task. So, too, did a new breed of reformer, determined to help the needy cope with the ravages of urban life.

The need for change was clear. Many city charters dating from the eighteenth century included a cumbersome system of checks and balances. Mayors vetoed city councils; councils ignored mayors. Jealous state legislatures allowed cities only the most limited and unpopular taxes, such as those on property. But to the cities more than the states fell responsibility for providing services. Municipal government grew into a tangle of little governments—fragmented, scattered, at odds with one another. By 1890, Chicago had 11 branches of government, each with its own regulations and taxing authority. Just as such decentralization paralyzed city governments, the traditional sources of political leadership evaporated. The middle and upper classes were being drawn into business and moving to the suburbs. As immigrants and rural newcomers flocked to factories and tenements, the structures of urban government strained to adapt.

Boss Rule

"Why must there be a boss," journalist Lincoln Steffens asked Boss Richard Croker of New York, "when we've got a mayor—and a city council?" "That's why," Croker broke in. "It's because we've got a mayor and a council and judges—*and*—a hundred other men to deal with." The boss was right. He and his system furnished cities with the centralization, authority, and services they sorely needed.

Bosses ruled through the political machine. Often, like New York's Tammany Hall, machines dated back to the late eighteenth and early nineteenth centuries. They began as fraternal and charitable organizations. Over the years they became centers of political power. In New York the machine was Democratic; in Philadelphia, Republican. Some were less centralized, as in Chicago; some less ethnically mixed, like Detroit. Machines could be found even in rural areas. In Duval County, Texas, for instance, the Spanish-speaking Anglo boss Archie Parr molded a powerful alliance with Mexican American landowners.

In an age of enterprise, the political machine operated similarly to a corporation. Like a corporate executive, the boss looked on politics as a business. His office might be a saloon, a funeral home, or like George Washington Plunkitt, a shoeshine stand. His managers were party activists, connected in a corporate-style chain of command. Local committeemen reported to district captains, captains to district leaders, district leaders to the boss or bosses who directed the machine.

The boss as entrepreneur

The stock in trade of the machine was simple: a Christmas turkey, a load of coal for the winter, jobs for the unemployed, English language classes for the recently arrived. Bosses sponsored fun, too—sports teams, glee clubs, balls and barbecues with bands playing and drink flowing. "You can't do nothin' with the people unless you do somethin' for 'em," one boss concluded. This system, rough and uneven as it was, served as a form of public welfare at a time when private charity could not cope with the crush of demands. To the unskilled, the boss doled out jobs in public construction. For bright, ambitious young men, he had places

A crude welfare system

This stereotyped depiction of the "party boss" as a larger-than-life thug has him handing out "special privilege" and "immunity from arrest," among other gifts. Cartoons such as this one could be powerful weapons. The political cartoons of Thomas Nast, which appeared in the *New York Times*, especially angered Boss William Tweed. His supporters might not have been able to read, but they surely could understand pictures. Tweed offered Nast $100,000 to "study art" in Europe. Nast refused the bribe.

in city offices or in the party. These positions represented the first steps into the middle class.

In return, citizens were expected to show their gratitude at the ballot box. Sometimes the grateful were not enough, so bosses turned elsewhere. "Little Bob" Davies of Jersey City was adept at mobilizing the "graveyard vote." He drew names from tombstones to pad lists of registered voters and hired "repeaters" to vote under the phony names. When reformers introduced the Australian (secret) ballot in the 1880s to prevent fraud, bosses pulled the "Tasmanian dodge" by premarking election tickets. Failing that, they dumped whole ballot boxes into the river or drove unpersuaded voters from the polls with hired thugs.

Rewards, Costs, and Accomplishments

Why did bosses go to such lengths? Some simply loved the game of politics. More often bosses loved money. Their ability to get it was limited only by their ingenuity or the occasional success of reform. The record for brassiness must go to Boss William Tweed. During his reign in the 1860s and 1870s, Tweed swindled the city of New York out of a fortune. His masterpiece was a chunky three-story courthouse in lower Manhattan originally budgeted at $250,000. When Tweed was through, the city had spent more than $13 million—and the building was still not finished! Tweed died in prison, but with such profits to be made, it was small wonder that bosses rivaled the pharaohs of Egypt as builders.

In their fashion bosses played a vital role in the industrial city. Rising from the bottom ranks, they guided immigrants into American life and helped some of the underprivileged up from poverty. They changed the urban landscape with massive construction programs and modernized city government by uniting it and making it perform. Choosing the aldermen, municipal judges, mayors, and administrative officials, bosses exerted new control to provide the contracts and franchises to run cities. Such accomplishments fostered the notion that government could be called on to help the needy. The welfare state, still decades away, had some of its roots here.

The toll was often outrageous. Inflated taxes, extorted revenue, and unpunished vice and crime were only the obvious costs. A woman whose family enjoyed Plunkitt's Christmas turkey might be widowed by an accident to her husband in a sweatshop kept open by timely bribes. Filthy buildings might claim her children, as corrupt inspectors ignored serious violations. Buying votes and selling favors, bosses turned democracy into a petty business—as much a "business," said Plunkitt, "as the grocery or dry-goods or the drug business." Yet they were the forerunners of the new breed of full-time, professional politicians who would soon govern the cities and the nation as well.

Nativism, Revivals, and the Social Gospel

Urban blight and the condition of the poor inspired social as well as political activism, especially within churches. Not all of it was positive. The popular Congregationalist minister Josiah Strong concluded that the city was "a menace to society." Along with anxious economists and social workers, he held immigrants responsible for everything from corruption to unemployment and urged restrictions on their entry into the country.

In the 1880s and 1890s, two depressions sharpened such anxieties. Nativism, a defensive and fearful nationalism, peaked as Americans blamed their economic woes on foreign competition and immigration. New organizations like the Immigration Restriction League attacked Catholics and the foreign-born for subverting democracy, taking jobs, and polarizing society. Already the victims of racial prejudice, the Chinese were an easy target. In 1882 Congress enacted the Chinese Exclusion Act. It banned the entry of Chinese laborers and represented an important step in the drive to restrict immigration. In 1897 the first bill requiring literacy tests for immigrants passed Congress, but President Grover Cleveland vetoed it.

Some clergy took their missions to the slums to bridge the gap between the middle class and the poor. Beginning in 1870 Dwight Lyman Moody, a 300-pound former shoe salesman, won armies of lowly converts with revivals in Boston, Chicago, and other cities. Evangelists helped to found American branches of the British Young Men's Christian Association and the Salvation Army. By the end of the century the Salvation Army had grown to 700 corps staffed by some 3000 officers. They ministered to the needy with food, music, shelter, and simple good fellowship.

A small group of ministers rejected the old ethos that weak character explained sin and that society would be perfected only as individual sinners were converted. They spread a new "Social Gospel" that focused on improving the conditions of society in order to save individuals. In *Applied Christianity* (1886), the influential Washington Gladden preached that the church must be responsible for correcting social injustices, including dangerous working conditions and unfair labor practices. Houses of worship, such as William Rainford's St. George's Episcopal Church in New York, became centers of social activity, with boys' clubs, gymnasiums, libraries, glee clubs, and industrial training programs.

The Sawdust Trail, painted by George Bellows in 1916, depicts one of the revival meetings of William Ashley ("Billy") Sunday in Philadelphia. Sunday, a hard-drinking professional baseball player turned evangelist, began his religious revivals in the 1890s and drew thousands. Here, Sunday leans down from the platform to shake the hand of an admirer. In the foreground, a swooning woman, overcome with a sense of her sins, is carried away.

The Social Settlement Movement

The settlement house

Church-sponsored programs often repelled the immigrant poor, who saw them as thinly disguised missionary efforts. Immigrants and other slum dwellers were more receptive to a bold experiment called the settlement house. Often situated in the worst slums, these early community centers were run by middle-class women and men to help the poor and foreign-born. At the turn of the century there were more than 100 of them, the most famous being Jane Addams's Hull House in Chicago. When Hull House opened in 1889, it occupied a crumbling mansion on South Halstead Street. Slowly it grew to a dozen buildings over more than a city block. In 1898 the Catholic church sponsored its first settlement house in New York, and in 1900 Bronson House opened its doors to the Latino community in Los Angeles.

High purposes inspired settlement workers. They left comfortable middle-class homes to live in settlement houses and dedicated themselves (like the "early Christians," said one) to service and sacrifice. Teaching immigrants American ways and creating a community spirit would foster "right living through social relations." But immigrants were also urged to preserve their heritages through festivals, parades, and museums. Like political bosses, settlement reformers furnished help, from day nurseries to English language and cooking classes to playgrounds and libraries. Armed with statistics and personal experiences, they also lobbied for social legislation to improve housing, women's working conditions, and public schools.

City Life

Urban social stratification

City life reflected the stratified nature of American society in the late nineteenth century. Every city had its tenements and slums but also its fashionable avenues for the rich, who constituted barely 1 percent of the population but owned a fourth of all wealth. In between tenement and mansion lived the broad middle of urban society—educated professionals, white-collar clerks and salespeople, shopkeepers, corporate managers and executives, public employees, and their families. They composed nearly a third of the population and owned about half the nation's wealth. With more money and more leisure time, their power and influence were growing.

In the impersonal city of the late nineteenth century, class distinctions continued to be based on wealth and income. But no longer were dress and manners enough to distinguish one class from another. Such differences were more often reflected in where people lived, what they bought, which organizations they joined, and how they spent their time.

The Immigrant in the City

When the ship put into port, the first thing an immigrant was likely to see was a city. Perhaps it was Boston or New York or Galveston, Texas, where an overflow of Jewish immigrants was directed after the turn of the century. Enough of the newcomers traveled inland so that by 1900 three-quarters of the residents of Minnesota and Wisconsin and nearly two-thirds in Utah had at least one foreign-born parent.* But some 70 percent of all immigrants, exhausted physically and financially, settled in cities.

*Mormons serving as missionaries in Europe and Great Britain especially swelled Utah's population with converts.

Cities developed well-defined mosaics of ethnic communities, because immigrants usually clustered together on the basis of old world villages or provinces. But these neighborhoods were constantly changing. As many as half the residents moved out every 10 years, often because they got better-paying jobs or had more family members working. Though one nationality usually dominated a neighborhood, there were always others. Despite popular misconceptions, no other immigrants lived like the Chinese, in urban ghettos of just one ethnic group. Racial prejudice forced the Chinese together, and local ordinances kept them from buying their way out.

Ethnic communities served as havens from the strangeness of American society and as springboards to a new life. From the moment they stepped off the boat, newcomers felt pressed to learn English, don American clothes, and drop their "greenhorn" ways. Yet in their neighborhoods they also found comrades who spoke their language, theaters that performed their plays and music, restaurants that served their food. Houses of worship were always at the center of neighborhood life, often reflecting the practices of individual towns or provinces.

The *Jewish Daily Forward* and scores of other foreign-language newspapers reported events from the homeland but also gave eager readers profiles of local leaders, advice on voting, and tips on adjusting to America. Immigrant aid societies like the Polish National Alliance and the Society for the Protection of Italian Immigrants furnished fellowship and assistance in the newcomers' own languages. They fostered assimilation by sponsoring baseball teams, insurance programs, libraries, and English classes.

Sometimes immigrants combined the old and new in creative adaptations. Italians developed a pidgin dialect called "Italglish." It permitted them to communicate quickly with Americans and to absorb American customs. So the Fourth of July became *"Il Forte Gelato"* (literally "The Great Freeze"), a play on the sound of the words. Other immigrant groups invented similar idioms, like *Chuco,* a dialect that developed among border Mexicans in El Paso.

The backgrounds and cultural values of immigrants often influenced the jobs they took. Because Chinese men did not scorn washing or ironing, more than 7500 of them could be found in San Francisco laundries by 1880. Sewing ladies' garments seemed unmanly to many native-born Americans but not to Russian and Italian tailors. Slavs tended to be physically robust and valued steady income over education. They worked in the mines for better pay than in factories and pulled their children from school to send them to work.

On the whole, immigrants married later and had more children than the native-born. Greeks and eastern European Jews prearranged marriages according to tradition. They imported "picture brides," betrothed by mail with a photograph. After marriage men ruled the household, but women managed it. Although child-rearing practices varied, immigrants resisted the relative permissiveness of American parents. Youngsters were expected to contribute like little adults to the welfare of the family.

In these "family economies" of working-class immigrants, key decisions—over whether and whom to marry, over work and education, over when to leave home—were made on the basis of collective rather than individual needs. Though boys were more likely to work outside the home than girls, daughters in immigrant families went to work at an early age so sons could continue their education. It was customary for one daughter to remain unmarried so she could care for younger siblings or aged parents.

Ethnic neighborhoods

Adapting to America

Family life

Entertainment in immigrant neighborhoods often resulted in a cross-fertilization of cultures. The New Cathay Boys Club Band, a marching band of Chinese Americans (shown here), was formed in San Francisco's Chinatown in 1911. It was inspired by the Columbia Park Boys Band of Italians from nearby North Beach and played American music only.

Special situation of the Chinese

The Chinese were an exception to the pattern. The ban on the immigration of Chinese laborers in the 1880s (page 651) had frozen the sex ratio of Chinese communities into a curious imbalance. Like other immigrants, most Chinese newcomers had been single men. In the wake of the ban, those in the United States could not bring over their wives and families. Nor by law in 13 states could they marry whites. With few women, Chinese communities suffered from high rates of prostitution, large numbers of gangs and secret societies, and low birth totals. When the San Francisco earthquake and fire destroyed birth records in 1906, resourceful Chinese immigrants created "paper sons" (and less often "paper daughters") by forging American birth certificates and claiming their China-born children as American citizens.

counterpoint

The "New" Immigrants: Who Came and Why?

With so many immigrants coming to America, it is no wonder that historians have disagreed over who came and why. Early historians of immigration focused on those arriving in the United States. These newcomers are depicted as an undifferentiated mass of European peasants, striking out on their own, often poverty-stricken, sometimes persecuted, sometimes eager for opportunity. The march of so many immigrants into American life, these historians argue, both reflected and helped to create the uniqueness of the American experience.

More recently, historians have placed immigration to the United States in global perspective by examining both receiving and sending countries. In an international context, the United States moves from the center of immigration history to the fringes of the story as one of many countries attracting migrants in an expanding world economy. Immigration to the United States thus becomes part of an international labor exchange and the American experience less exceptional and more comparable to that of other receiving nations such as Argentina and Australia. As for the immigrants themselves, the international perspective underscores the diversity of the newcomers and of their motives. Landless young men from Italy hoped to return to buy plots in Italy, whereas the sons of cattle farmers from western Norway left for good because inheritance laws kept them from owning farms at home. Other immigrants to the United States, fewer in number, came not from Europe but from Latin America, Africa, the Caribbean, and Asia.

Caught between past and present, immigrants from all countries clung to tradition and assimilated slowly. Their children adjusted more quickly. They soon spoke English like natives, married whomever they pleased, and worked their way out of old neighborhoods. Yet the process was not easy. Children faced heartrending clashes with parents and rejection from peers. Sara Smolinsky, the immigrant heroine of Anzia Yezierska's novel *Bread Givers* (1925), broke away from her tyrannical family, only to discover a terrible isolation: "I can't live in the old world and I'm yet too green for the new. I don't belong to those who gave me birth or to those with whom I was educated."

Assimilation

Urban Middle-Class Life

Life and leisure for the urban middle class revolved around home and family. By the turn of the century just over a third of middle-class urbanites owned their homes. Often two or three stories, made of brick or brownstone, these houses were a measure of their owners' social standing. The plush furniture, heavy drapes, antiques, and curios all signaled status and refinement.

The home as haven and status symbol

Such homes, usually on their own lots, served as havens to protect and nourish the family. Seventeenth-century notions of children as inherently sinful had given way to more modern theories about the shaping influence of environment. Calm and orderly households with nurturing mothers would launch children on the right course. "A clean, fresh, and well-ordered house," stipulated a domestic adviser in 1883, "exercises over its inmates a moral, no less than physical influence, and has a direct tendency to make members of the family sober, peaceable, and considerate of the feelings and happiness of each other."

A woman was judged by the state of her home. The typical homemaker prepared elaborate meals, cleaned, laundered, and sewed. Each task took time. Baking bread alone required several hours, and in 1890, four of five loaves were still made at home. Perhaps 25 percent of urban households had live-in servants to help with

The middle-class homemaker

Bicycling became a popular middle-class recreation as cycle designs improved. These African American cyclists, photographed around 1900, had just crossed a bridge over the South Platte River in Denver.

the work. They were on call about 100 hours a week, were off just one evening and part of Sunday, and averaged $2 to $5 a week in salary.

By the 1890s a host of new consumer products eased the burdens of housework. Brand names trumpeted a new age of commercially prepared food—Campbell's soup, Quaker oats, Pillsbury flour, Jell-O, and Cracker Jacks, to name a few. New appliances such as "self-working" washers offered mechanical assistance, but shredded shirts and aching arms testified to how far short mechanization still fell.

Toward the end of the century, Saturday became less of a workday and more of a family day. Sunday mornings remained a time for church, still an important center of family life. Afternoons had a more secular flavor. There were shopping trips (city stores often stayed open) and visits to lakes, zoos, and amusement parks (usually built at the end of trolley lines to attract more riders). Outside institutions of all kinds—fraternal organizations, uplift groups, athletic teams, and church groups—were becoming part of middle-class urban family life.

Victorianism and the Pursuit of Virtue

Middle-class life reflected a code of behavior called Victorianism, named for Britain's long-reigning Queen Victoria (1837–1901). It emerged in the 1830s and 1840s as part of an effort to tame the turbulent urban-industrial society developing in Europe.

Victorianism dictated that personal conduct be based on orderly behavior and disciplined moralism. It stressed sobriety, industriousness, self-control, and sexual modesty and taught that demeanor, particularly proper manners, was the backbone of society. According to its rules, women were "pure vessels," devoid of sexual desire. Their job was to control the "lower natures" of their husbands by withholding sex except for procreation.

Women's fashion mirrored Victorian values. Strenuously laced corsets ("an instrument of torture," one woman called them) pushed breasts up, stomachs in, and rear ends out. Internal organs pressed unnaturally against one another; ribs occasionally cracked; uteruses sagged. Fainting spells and headaches were all too common. But the resulting wasplike figure accentuated the image of women as child bearers. Ankle-length skirts were draped over bustles, hoops, and petticoats to make hips look larger and suggest fertility. Such elegant dress symbolized wealth, status, and modesty. It also set off middle- and upper-class women from those below, whose plain clothes signaled lives of drudgery and want.

When working-class Americans failed to follow Victorian guidelines, reformers helped them pursue virtue. It seemed natural to Frances Willard that women, who cared for the moral and physical well-being of their families, should lead the charge. She resigned her position as dean of women at Northwestern University and in 1879 became the second president of the newly founded Woman's Christian Temperance Union (WCTU; 1874). The very title of the organization, stressing the singular "woman," spoke for the unity of women. Under Willard's leadership, the organization grew by the 1890s to 150,000 members, all of them women and most of them middle-class and white. By the turn of the century it was the largest women's organization in the world.

Initially the WCTU focused on temperance—the movement, begun in the 1820s, to stamp out the sale of alcoholic beverages and to end drunkenness. For these women, the campaign seemed not merely a way to reform society but to protect their homes and families from abuse at the hands of drunken husbands and fathers. And in attacking the saloon, Willard also sought to spread democracy by

Woman's Christian Temperance Union

storming these all-male bastions, where political bosses conducted so much political business and where women were refused entry. Soon, under the slogan of "Do Everything," the WCTU was also promoting suffrage for women, prison reform, better working conditions, and an end to prostitution. Just as important, it offered talented, committed women an opportunity to move out of their homes and churches and into the public arena of lobbying and politics.

Anthony Comstock crusaded with equal vigor against what he saw as moral pollution ranging from pornography and gambling to the use of nude art models. In 1873 President Ulysses S. Grant signed the so-called Comstock Law, a statute banning from the mails all materials "designed to incite lust." Two days later Comstock went to work as a special agent for the Post Office. In his 41-year career, he claimed to have made more than 3000 arrests and destroyed 160 tons of vice-ridden books and photographs.

Comstock Law

Victorian crusaders like Comstock were not simply missionaries of a stuffy morality. They were apostles of a middle-class creed of social control and discipline who responded to growing alcoholism, venereal disease, gambling debts, prostitution, and unwanted pregnancies. No doubt they overreacted in warning that the road to ruin lay behind the door of every saloon, pool hall, or bedroom. Yet the new urban environment did indeed reflect the disorder of a rapidly industrializing society.

The insistence with which moralists warned against "impropriety" suggests that many people did not heed their advice. Three-quarters of women surveyed toward the turn of the century reported that they enjoyed sex. The growing variety of contraceptives—including spermicidal douches, sheaths made of animal intestines, rubber condoms, and forerunners of the diaphragm—testified to the desire for pregnancy-free intercourse. Abortion, too, was prevalent. According to one estimate, a third of all pregnancies were aborted, usually with the aid of a midwife. (By the 1880s abortion had been made illegal in most states, following the lead of the first antiabortion statute in England in 1803.) Despite Victorian marriage manuals, middle-class Americans became more conscious of sexuality as an emotional dimension of a satisfying union.

Challenges to Convention

A few bold men and women openly challenged convention. Victoria Woodhull, publisher of *Woodhull & Claflin's Weekly,* divorced her husband, ran for president in 1872 on the Equal Rights party ticket, and pressed the case for sexual freedom. "I am a free lover!" she shouted to a riotous audience in New York. "I have the inalienable, constitutional, and natural right to love whom I may, to love as long or as short a period as I can, to change that love every day if I please!" Woodhull made a strong public case for sexual freedom. But in private she believed in strict monogamy and romantic love for herself.

Victoria Woodhull

The same cosmopolitan conditions that provided protection for Woodhull's unorthodox beliefs also made possible the growth of self-conscious communities of homosexual men and women. Earlier in the century, Americans had idealized romantic friendships among members of the same sex, without necessarily attributing sexual overtones to those friendships. But for friendships with an explicitly sexual dimension, the anonymity of large cities provided new meeting grounds. Single factory workers and clerks, living in furnished rooms rather than with their families in small towns and on farms, were freer to seek others who shared their sexual orientation. Homosexual men and women began forming social networks: on the

Urban homosexual communities

streets where they regularly met or at specific restaurants and clubs, which, to avoid controversy, sometimes passed themselves off as athletic associations or chess clubs. Such places could be found in New York City's Bowery, around the Presidio military base in San Francisco, and at Lafayette Square in Washington, D.C.

Only toward the end of the century did physicians begin to notice homosexual behavior, usually to condemn it as a disease or an inherited infirmity. Indeed, not until the turn of the century did the term *homosexual* come into existence. Certainly homosexual love itself was not new. But for the first time in the United States, the conditions of urban life allowed gay men and lesbians to define themselves in terms of a larger, self-conscious community, even if they were stoutly condemned by Victorian morality.

 City Culture

"We cannot all live in cities," reformer Horace Greeley lamented just after the Civil War, "yet nearly all seemed determined to do so." Economic opportunity drew people to the teeming industrial city. But so, too, did a vibrant urban culture, boasting temples of entertainment, electrified trolleys and lights, the best schools, stores and restaurants, the biggest newspapers, and virtually every museum, library, art gallery, bookshop, and orchestra in America. In the beckoning cities of the late nineteenth century, Americans sought to realize their dreams of success.

Public Education in an Urban Industrial World

Those at the bottom and in the middle ranks of city life found one path to success in public education. Although the campaign for public education began in the Jacksonian era, it did not make real headway until after the Civil War, when industrial cities began to mushroom. As late as 1870 half the children in the country received no formal education at all, and one American in five could not read.

Between 1870 and 1900, an educational awakening occurred. As more and more businesses required workers who could read, write, and figure sums, attendance in public schools more than doubled. The length of the school term rose from 132 to 144 days. Illiteracy fell by half. At the turn of the century, nearly all the states outside the South had enacted mandatory education laws. Almost three of every four school-age children were enrolled. Even so, the average American adult still attended school for only about five years, and less than 10 percent of those eligible ever went to high school.

The average school day started early, but by noon most girls were released under the assumption that they needed less formal education. Curricula stressed the fundamentals of reading, writing, and arithmetic. Courses in manual training, science, and physical education were added as the demand for technical knowledge grew and opportunities to exercise shrank. Students learned by memorization, sitting in silent study with hands clasped or standing erect while they repeated phrases and sums. Few schools encouraged creative thinking. "Don't stop to think," barked a Chicago teacher to a class of terrified youngsters in the 1890s, "tell me what you know!"

A rigid social philosophy underlay the harsh routine. In an age of industrialization, massive immigration, and rapid change, schools taught conformity and values as much as facts and figures. Teachers acted as drillmasters, shaping their charges for the sake of society. "Teachers and books are better security than handcuffs and policemen," wrote a New Jersey college professor in 1879. In *McGuffey's Reader*, a standard textbook used in grammar schools throughout the nineteenth century, students learned not only how to read but also how to behave. Hard work, Christian ethics, and obedience to authority would lead boys to heroic command, girls to blissful motherhood, and society to harmonious progress.

As Reconstruction faded, so did the impressive start made in black education. Most of the first generation of former slaves had been illiterate. So eager were they to learn that by the end of the century nearly half of all African Americans could read. But discrimination soon took its toll. For nearly 100 years after the Civil War, the doctrine of "separate but equal," upheld by the Supreme Court in *Plessy v. Ferguson* (1896), kept black and white students apart but scarcely equal (page 577). By 1882 public schools in a half dozen southern states were segregated by law, the rest by practice. Underfunded and ill-equipped, black schools served dirt-poor families whose every member had to work. In fact, only about a third of the South's black children attended and rarely for the entire school year.

Like African Americans, immigrants saw education as a way of getting ahead. Some educators saw it as a means of Americanizing newcomers. They assumed that immigrant and native-born children would learn the same lessons in the same language and turn out the same way. Only toward the end of the century, as immigration mounted, did eastern cities begin to offer night classes that taught English, along with civics lessons for foreigners. When public education proved inadequate, immigrants established their own schools. Catholics, for example, started an elaborate expansion of their parochial schools in 1884.

Educational reformers in the 1870s pushed elementary schools to include drawing as a required subject. Their goal was not to turn out gifted artists but to train students in the practical skills needed in an industrial society. Winslow Homer's portrait of a teacher by her blackboard shows the geometric shapes behind practical design.

By the 1880s educational reforms were helping schools respond to the needs of an urban society. Opened first in St. Louis in 1873, American versions of innovative German "kindergartens" put four-to six-year-olds in orderly classrooms while parents went off to work. "Normal schools" multiplied to provide teachers with more professional training. By 1900 almost one teacher in five had a professional degree. In the new industrial age, science and manual training supplemented more conventional subjects in order to supply industry with better-educated workers. And vocational education reduced the influence of unions. Now less dependent on a system of apprenticeship controlled by labor, new workers were also less subject to being recruited into unions.

Higher Learning and the Rise of the Professional

As American society grew more organized, mechanized, and complex, the need for managerial, technical, and literary skills brought greater respect for college education. The Morrill Act of 1862 generated a dozen new state colleges and universities,

Postgraduate education

eight mechanical and agricultural colleges, and six black colleges. Private charity added more. Railroad barons like Johns Hopkins and Leland Stanford used parts of their fortunes to found colleges named after them (Hopkins in 1873, Stanford in 1890). The number of colleges and universities nearly doubled between 1870 and 1910, though less than 5 percent of college-age Americans enrolled in them.

A practical impulse inspired the founding of several black colleges. In the late nineteenth century, few institutions mixed races. Church groups and private foundations, such as the Peabody and Slater funds (supported by white donors from the North), underwrote black colleges after Reconstruction. By 1900, a total of 700 black students were enrolled. About 2000 had graduated. Through hard work and persistence, some even received degrees from institutions normally reserved for whites.

In keeping with the new emphasis on practical training, professional schools multiplied to provide training beyond a college degree. American universities adopted the German model requiring young scholars to perform research as part of their training. The number of law and medical schools more than doubled between 1870 and 1900; medical students almost tripled. Ten percent of them were women, though their numbers shrank as the medical profession became more organized and exclusive.

Professionals of all kinds—in law, medicine, engineering, business, academics—swelled the ranks of the middle class. Slowly they were becoming a new force in urban America, replacing the ministers and gentlemen freeholders of an earlier day as community leaders.

Higher education for women

Before the Civil War women could attend only three private colleges. After the war they had new ones all their own, among them Smith (1871), Wellesley (1875), and Bryn Mawr (1885). Many land-grant colleges, chartered to serve all people, admitted women from the start. By 1910 some 40 percent of college students were women, almost double the 1870 figure. Only one college in five refused to accept them.

Potent myths continued to make college life hard for women. As Dr. Edward Clarke of the Harvard Medical School told thousands of students in *Sex in Education* (1873), the rigors of a college education could lead the "weaker sex" to physical or mental collapse, infertility, and early death. Women's colleges therefore included a strict program of physical activity to keep students healthy. Many also offered an array of courses in "domestic science"—cooking, sewing, and other such skills—to counter the claim that higher education would be of no value to women.

College students, together with office workers and female athletes, became role models for ambitious young women. These "new women," impatient with custom, cast off Victorian restrictions. Fewer of them married, and more were self-supporting. They shed their corsets and bustles and donned lighter, more comfortable clothing, including "shirtwaist" blouses (styled after men's shirts) and lower-heeled shoes. Robust and active, they could be found ice-skating in the winter, riding bicycles in the fall and spring, playing golf and tennis in the summer.

A Culture of Consumption

The city spawned a new material culture built around consumption. As standards of living rose, American industries began providing "ready-made" clothing to replace garments that had once been made at home. Similarly, food and furniture were mass-produced in greater quantities. The city became a giant marketplace for these goods, where new patterns of mass consumption took hold. Radiating outward to more rural areas, this urban consumer culture helped to level American society. Increasingly, city businesses sold the same goods to farmer and clerk, rich and poor, native-born and immigrant.

Department Stores

Well-made, inexpensive merchandise in standard sizes and shapes found outlets in new palaces of consumption called "department stores" because they displayed their goods in separate sections or departments. The idea was imported from France, where shopping arcades had been built as early as the 1860s. Unlike the small exclusive shops of Europe, department stores were palatial, public, and filled with inviting displays of furniture, housewares, and clothing.

The French writer Emile Zola claimed that department stores "democratized luxury." Anyone could enter free of charge, handle the most elegant and expensive goods, and buy whatever was affordable. When consumers found goods too pricey, department stores pioneered layaway plans with deferred payments. Free delivery and free returns or exchanges were available to all, not just the favored customers of exclusive fashion makers. The department store also educated people by showing them what "proper" families owned and the correct names for things like women's wear and parlor furniture. This process of socialization was taking place not only in cities but in towns and villages across America. Mass consumption was giving rise to a mass culture.

Chain stores and mail-order houses

"Chain stores" (a term coined in America) spread the culture of consumption without frills. They catered to the working class, who could not afford department stores, and operated on a cash-and-carry basis. Owners kept their costs down by buying in volume to fill the small stores in growing neighborhood chains. Founded in 1859, the Great Atlantic and Pacific Tea Company was the first of the chain stores. By 1876 its 76 branch stores had added groceries to its original line of teas.

Far from department and chain stores, rural Americans joined the community of consumers by mail. In 1872, Aaron Montgomery Ward sent his first price sheet to farmers from a livery stable loft in Chicago. Ward eliminated the intermediary and promised savings of 40 percent on fans, needles, trunks, harnesses, and scores of other goods. By 1884, his catalog boasted 10,000 items, each illustrated by a woodcut. Similarly, Richard W. Sears and Alvah C. Roebuck built a $500 million mail-order business by 1907. Schoolrooms that had no encyclopedia used a Ward's or Sears' catalog instead. Children were drilled in reading and spelling from them. When asked the source of the Ten Commandments, one farm boy replied that they came from Sears, Roebuck.

"In the dessert I generally introduce some new importation such as bananas, sugar-cane, American Lady apples, prickly pears, etc.," advised etiquette expert Elizabeth F. Ellet in 1873. "These also give a subject for the gentlemen to talk about when the ladies have left, as freetrade, colonial policy, etc." As middle-class Americans began to include bananas in their diets, stores offered consumers a new table accessory: the banana bowl, or banana boat.

Leisure

As mechanization slowly reduced the number of hours on the job, factory workers found themselves with more free time. So did the middle class, with free weekends, evenings, and vacations. And these changes were occurring at just the moment when freedom on the job was shrinking. Although artisans earlier in the century stopped for brief diversions whenever they pleased, current discipline of factory and office allowed no such luxury. A new, stricter division between work and leisure developed. City dwellers turned their free time into a consumer item that often reflected differences in class, gender, and ethnicity.

Sports and class distinctions

Sports, for example, had been a traditional form of recreation for the rich. They continued to play polo, golf, and the newly imported English game of tennis. Croquet had more middle-class appeal because it required less skill and special equipment. Perhaps as important, it could be enjoyed in mixed company, like the new

In towns small and large, cock-fighting remained a popular spectator sport well into the twentieth century, even though it was outlawed in most states by the end of the nineteenth century. Cockfighting attracted men from a wide range of classes and races, as seen in Horace Bonham's *Nearing the Issue at the Cockpit,* painted in 1878. Journalists and cartoon-ists often used the cockpit to symbolize the political arena. By focusing on the racially mixed crowd, Bonham may well have been underscoring the new diversity of the American electorate.

craze of bicycling. Bicycles evolved from unstable contraptions with large front wheels into "safety" bikes with equal-sized wheels, a dropped middle bar, pneumatic tires, and coaster brakes. A good one cost about $100, far beyond the reach of a factory worker but within the grasp of a mechanic or a well-paid clerk. On Sunday afternoons city parks became crowded with cyclists. Women also rode the new safety bikes, although social convention forbade them from riding alone. But cycling broke down conventions too. It required looser garments, freeing women from corsets. Lady cyclists demonstrated that they were hardly too frail for physical exertion.

Spectator sports for the urban masses

Organized spectator sports attracted crowds from every walk of life. Baseball overshadowed all others. For city dwellers with dull work, tight quarters, and isolated lives, baseball offered the chance to join thousands of others for an exciting outdoor spectacle. By the 1890s it was attracting crowds of 60,000. Baseball began to take its modern form in 1869, when the first professional team, the Cincinnati Red Stockings, appeared. Slowly the game evolved: umpires began to call balls and strikes, the overhand replaced the underhand pitch, and fielders put on gloves. Teams from eight cities formed the National League of Professional Baseball Clubs in 1876, followed by the American League in 1901. League players were distinctly working class. At first, teams featured a few black players. When African Americans were barred in the 1880s, black professionals formed their own team, the Cuban Giants of Long Island, New York, looking to play anyone they could. Their name was chosen with care. In an age of racial separation, the all-black team hoped to increase its chances of playing white teams by calling itself "Cuban."

Horse racing, bicycle tournaments, and other sports of speed and violence helped to break the monotony, frustration, and routine of the industrial city. In 1869, without pads or helmets, Rutgers beat Princeton in the first intercollegiate football match. By the 1890s the service academies and state universities fielded teams. Not everyone cheered. Cornell University forbade its team from playing the University of Michigan. "I will not permit 30 men to travel 400 miles to agitate a bag of wind," said President White. Despite protests against rising death tolls (18 players died in 1905), football soon attracted crowds of 50,000 or more. Beginning in 1891 when Dr. James Naismith nailed a peach basket to the gymnasium wall at the YMCA Training School in Springfield, Massachusetts, "basketball" became the indoor interlude between the outdoor sports of spring and fall.

Arts and Entertainment

Variety also marked social life in the city. For the poor and working class, the streets offered a social carnival of vendors, neighbors and friends, games of chance and physical prowess. The saloon served as a workingman's club, a male preserve to enjoy a drink or a free lunch and uninhibited talk. Rougher saloons offered prostitutes, gambling, drugs, or almost any illicit desire. Young working women escaped the drudgery of factory, office, or sweatshop at vaudeville shows, dance halls, and the new amusement parks. Coney Island's Luna Park, opened in 1903, drew 5 million customers in a single season.

Workingmen took their dates to dance halls and boxing exhibitions staged in small rings used for variety acts between fights. Bare-knuckled prizefighting, illegal in some states, took place secretly in saloons and commercial gyms. In the rough-and-tumble world of the industrial city, the ring gave young men from the streets the chance to stand out from the crowd and to prove their masculinity. "Sporting clubs" of German, Irish, and African American boxers sprouted up in cities along the East Coast. *The National Police Gazette* and other magazines followed the bouts with sensational stories chronicling matches in detail. When the sport adopted the Marquis of Queensbury rules in the 1880s, including the use of gloves, boxing gained new respectability and appeal. Soon boxing, like other sports, was being commercialized with professional bouts, large purses, and championship titles.

Wealthier couples went to concerts given by local symphony orchestras, which played a mixture of popular tunes, John Philip Sousa marches, and the music of classical European composers. At the theater, popular melodramas gave patrons a chance to avoid the ambiguities of modern life. Theatergoers booed villains and cheered heroes, as in the illustration on page 664; they shuddered for heroines and marveled at tricky stage mechanics that made ice floes move and players float upward to heaven.

In villages and cities music of every tempo and style filled the air. Organ grinders churned out Italian airs on street corners. Steam-powered calliopes tooted spirited waltzes from amusement parks and riverboat decks. In bandstands brass ensembles played German-style concerts. By 1900 the sale of phonograph records had reached 3 million. Popular music became a big business as companies hawked sentimental ballads like "My Mother Was a Lady" or topical tunes celebrating the discovery of oil or the changing styles of women's clothing. In Scott Joplin's "Maple Leaf Rag" (1899) the lively syncopation of ragtime heralded the coming of jazz.

As the nineteenth century drew to a close the city was reshaping the country, just as the industrial system was creating a more specialized, diversified, and interlocking national and even international economy. Most Americans were

Daily Lives

POPULAR ENTERTAINMENT

The Vaudeville Show

It looked like a palace or some high-toned concert hall. Patrons walked through a richly ornamented arched gateway to gold-domed, marble ticket booths. Ushers guided them through a stately lobby cushioned with velvet carpets. Large mirrors and brass ornaments hung on brocaded walls. There were "gentlemen's smoking and reading rooms" and suites with dressing cases and free toiletries for the ladies. The house seats were thick and comfortable and positioned well back from the stage. Thousands of electrical fixtures set the place aglow. When the lights dimmed, the audience sank into polite silence as the show began.

Benjamin Franklin Keith, who had worked in circuses, tent shows, and dime museums, opened the New Theatre in Boston in 1894. Seeing housewives with children as a source of new profits, resourceful theater owners such as Keith had cleaned up the bawdy variety acts of saloons and music halls, borrowed the animal and ac-

robat acts from circuses and Wild West shows and the comedy acts of minstrel shows, and moved them to plusher surroundings. They called the new shows "vaudeville," after the French "pieces de vaudeville" developed in eighteenth-century street fairs. In 1881 Tony Pastor opened the first vaudeville theater on Fourteenth Street in New York City. Within a decade more elegant palaces like Keith's New Theatre were opening in cities across the country.

For anywhere from a dime to two dollars, a customer could see up to nine acts—singers, jugglers, acrobats, magicians, trained ani-

mals, and comics. The mix of performers reflected the urban tempo and new urban tastes. Skits often drew on the experience of immigrants, and early comedy teams had names like "The Sport and the Jew" and "Two Funny Sauerkrauts." Divided into acts that came in rapid-fire succession, "continuous shows" ran one after another, from early morning until late at night. "After breakfast go to Proctor's," trumpeted one advertisement for F. F. Proctor's vaudeville show, "after Proctor's go to bed."

Saloon music halls had catered to a rowdy all-male, working-class clientele, who smoke, drank,

Balconies at vaudeville shows, like this one depicted by Charles Dana Gibson, attracted a wide variety of customers. Most seats cost $1, and theater owners scheduled performances from morning until night.

ambivalent about this process. Cities beckoned migrants from the countryside and immigrants from abroad with unparalleled opportunities for work and pleasure. The playwright Israel Zangwill celebrated the city's transforming power in his 1908 Broadway hit *The Melting Pot*. "The real American," one of his characters explained, "is only in the Crucible, I tell you—he will be the fusion of all the races, the coming superman."

Where Zangwill saw a melting pot with all its promise for a new superrace, champions of traditional American values, such as the widely read Protestant minister Josiah Strong, saw "a commingled mass of venomous filth and seething sin, of stomped, and jeered at the players. Vaudeville was aimed at middle-class and wealthier working-class families who could no longer afford "legitimate" theater and light opera. Keith worked diligently to make each of his theaters "as 'homelike' an amusement resort as it was possible to make it." Backstage he tacked signs warning performers not to say "slob" or "son-of-a-gun" or "'hully-gee' . . . unless you want to be canceled peremptorily." In the interest of good taste, all his chorus girls wore stockings. Within a few years Keith was producing the kind of show, as one comedian put it, "to which any child could bring his parents."

The audience, too, was instructed on proper behavior. No liquor was served. No cigars or cigarettes were permitted. Printed notices directed patrons to "kindly avoid the stamping of feet and pounding of canes on the floor. . . . Please don't talk during acts, as it annoys those about you, and prevents a perfect hearing of the entertainment."

Enjoying its heyday from 1890 to 1920, vaudeville became big business. Nearly one in five city dwellers went to a show once every seven days. Headliners earned $1,000 a week, theaters $20,000.

Owners like Keith and Edward Albee merged their operations into gigantic circuits. By the time of Keith's death in 1914, the Keith-Albee circuit had built an empire of 29 theaters in more than seven cities.

Vaudeville became middle-class mass entertainment. Moderate and moral, it furnished cheap recreation that also reinforced genteel values. Skits encouraged audiences to pursue success through hard work. An emerging star system made American heroes out of performers like Will Rogers and George M. Cohan and American models out of Fanny Brice and Mae West. Ethnic comics defused tensions among immigrants with spoofs that exaggerated stereotypes and stressed the common foibles of all humanity. And theatergoers learned how to behave. Order and decorum replaced the boisterous atmosphere of saloons and music halls. Vaudeville audiences adopted the middle-class ideal of behavior—passive and polite. Americans were learning to defer to experts in the realms of public conduct and popular entertainment, as elsewhere in the new urban, industrial society.

lust, of drunkenness, of pauperism, and crime of every sort." Both the champions and the critics of the late nineteenth century had a point. Corruption, crudeness, and disorder were no more or less a part of the cities than the vibrancy, energy, and opportunities that drew people to them. The gap between rich and poor yawned most widely in cities. As social critic Henry George observed, progress and poverty seemed to go hand in hand.

In the end moral judgments, whether pro or con, missed the point. Cities stood at the hubs of the new industrial order. All Americans, whatever they thought about the new urban world, had to search for ways to make that world work.

chapter summary

The modern city was the product of industrialization, lying at the center of the new integrated systems of transportation, communications, manufacturing, marketing, and finance.

- Fed by a great global migration of laborers, cities began to grow and to assume their modern shape of ringed residential patterns around central business districts and strict divisions among different classes, races, and ethnic groups.

- The challenge for the political system was to find within its democratic traditions a way to bring order out of the seeming chaos of unchecked urban growth.

- The urban boss and the urban political machine met the needs of cities for centralized authority but at a terrible cost in corruption, while social settlement houses, the Salvation Army, and the Social Gospel churches represented only a start at coping with the problems of poverty and urban blight.

- As cities grew, the middle-class code of behavior—called Victorianism—spread, teaching the values of sobriety, hard work, self-control, and modesty that served the needs of new industrial society for efficiency and order and the middle-class need for protection against the turbulence of city life.

- Yet for all the emphasis on skills, discipline, and order, the vibrancy of city culture remained attractive, drawing millions in search of education, entertainment, and opportunity and radiating outward to almost every corner of the country.

additional reading

The best treatment of the rise of cities is Howard B. Chudacoff, *The Evolution of American Urban Society* (rev. ed., 1981). John Stilgoe, *Borderland: The Origins of the American Suburb, 1820–1929* (1988) chronicles the growth of suburban America. William Cronon, *Nature's Metropolis: Chicago and the Great West* (1991) looks at Chicago as part of the ecological landscape. In *Boss Cox's Cincinnati: Urban Politics in the Progressive Era* (1968), Zane Miller reassesses the urban political machine, and Paul Boyer explores efforts at controlling city life in *Urban Masses and Moral Order in America, 1820–1920* (1978). John F. Kasson, *Rudeness & Civility: Manners in Nineteenth-Century Urban America* (1990) and Lawrence Levine, *High-*

brow/Lowbrow: The Emergence of Cultural Hierarchy in America (1988) investigate the emerging urban culture.

Marcus Lee Hanson's classic *The Atlantic Migration, 1607–1860* (1940) began the shift in immigration history away from the national and toward a more global perspective. For richly detailed comparative examinations of the immigrant experience, see Roger Daniels, *Coming to America: A History of Immigration and Ethnicity in American Life* (1990) and Ronald Takaki, *A Different Mirror: A History of Multicultural America* (1993). Susan A. Glenn, *Daughters of the Shtetl: Life and Labor in the Immigrant Generation* (1990) throws light on the issue of gender by probing the lives and labor of immigrant women, with particular attention to the shaping effect of old world Jewish culture. Virginia Yans-McLaughlin, ed., *Immigration Reconsidered: History, Sociology, and Politics* (1990) offers a collection of penetrating essays that places American immigration in its international context. For a fuller list of readings, see the Bibliography.

Significant Events

1869 Cincinnati Red Stockings become first professional baseball team; Rutgers beats Princeton in first intercollegiate football game

1870

1870 Elevated railroad begins operation in New York City

1872 William "Boss" Tweed convicted of defrauding city of New York

1873 Comstock Law enacted

1874 Women's Christian Temperance Union founded

1875

1875 Dwight Moody begins urban evangelical revivals

1876 Central Park completed in New York City; Johns Hopkins University opens nation's first graduate school

1880

1882 Chinese Exclusion Act

1883 Brooklyn Bridge opens

1885

1885 Home Life Insurance Building, world's first skyscraper, built in Chicago; first all-black professional baseball team, the Cuban Giants, organized

1888 Nation's first electric trolley line begins operation in Richmond, Virginia

1889 Hull House opens in Chicago

1890

1892 Ellis Island opens as a receiving station for immigrants

1894 Immigration Restriction League organized

1895

1896 *Plessy v. Ferguson* lays down doctrine legitimizing segregation

1897 Boston opens nation's first subway station

On May 1, 1893, an eager crowd of nearly half a million people jostled into a dramatic plaza fronted on either side by gleaming white buildings overlooking a sparkling lagoon. Named the Court of Honor, the plaza was the center of a strange ornamental city that was at once awesome and entirely imaginary. At one end stood a building whose magnificent white dome exceeded even the height of the capitol in Washington. Unlike the marble-built capitol, however, this building was all surface: a stucco shell plastered onto a steel frame and then sprayed with white oil paint to make it glisten. Beyond the Court of Honor stretched thoroughfares encompassing over 200 colonnaded buildings, piers, islands, and watercourses. Located five miles south of Chicago's central business district, this city of the imagination proclaimed itself the "World's Columbian Exposition" in honor of the 400th anniversary of Columbus's voyage to America.

President Grover Cleveland opened the world's fair in a way that symbolized the nation's industrial transformation. He pressed a telegrapher's key. Instantly electric current set 7000 feet of shafting into motion—motion that in turn unfurled flags, set fountains pumping, and lit 10,000 electric bulbs. All told, 7000 arc lamps and 120,000 incandescent bulbs illuminated the fair, banishing darkness from the grounds. The lights played over an array of exhibition buildings soon known far and wide as the "White City."

In Cleveland's judgment the neoclassical architecture was both "magnificent" and "stupendous." Surely the sheer size was astonishing, for the buildings had been laid out not by the square foot but

The Political System Under **Strain**

preview • Struggling to come to terms with the inequalities of the new urban and industrial order, the political system ground to a near-stalemate, broken only during the turbulent 1890s when a deep depression sparked labor protests and a revolt of farmers. The needs of industry for raw materials and markets also encouraged Americans to look abroad, in order to seek their "Manifest Destiny" in a commercial and even a territorial empire.

by the acre. The Hall of Manufactures and Liberal Arts alone spread its roof over 30 acres, twice the area of Egypt's Great Pyramid.

One English visitor dismissed the displays within as little more than "the contents of a great dry goods store mixed up with the contents of museums." In a sense he was right. Visitors paraded by an unending collection of typewriters, pins, watches, agricultural machinery, cedar canoes, and refrigerators, to say nothing of a map of the United States fashioned entirely out of pickles. But this riot of mechanical marvels, gewgaws, and bric-a-brac was symbolic too of the nation's industrial transformation. The fair resembled nothing so much as a tangible version of the new mail-order catalogs whose pages were now introducing the goods of the city to the hinterlands.

The connections made by the fair were international as well. This event was the *World's* Columbian Exposition, with exhibits from 36 nations. Visitors could admire chinaware from England and a four-story high cross section of a modern new ocean liner that was making international travel easier. Germany's famous manufacturer of armaments, Krupp, had its own separate building. It housed a 120-ton rifled gun. Easily within the range of its gunsights was a replica of the U.S. battleship *Illinois*, whose own bristling turrets stood just offshore of the exposition, on Lake Michigan. At the fair's amusement park, visitors encountered exotic cultures—and not just temples, huts, and totems, but exhibits in the living flesh. The Arabian village

In 1893 the World's Columbian Exposition set the night ablaze with a towering searchlight visible 60 miles away. Here the beam spotlights the fair's theme, "The World United," just as the giant exhibition halls highlighted the way the new industrial order was reshaping the globe.

featured Saharan camels, veiled ladies, and elders in turbans. Nearby, Irish peasants boiled potatoes over turf fires while Samoan men threw axes.

Like all such fairs, the Columbian Exposition created a fantasy. Beyond its boundaries, the new industrial order was showing signs of strain. Early in 1893 the Philadelphia and Reading Railroad had gone bankrupt, setting off a financial panic. By the end of the year, nearly 500 banks and 15,000 businesses had failed. Although millions of tourists continued to marvel at the fair's wonders, crowds of worried and unemployed workers also gathered elsewhere in Chicago. On Labor Day, Governor John Altgeld of Illinois told a crowd that the government was powerless to avoid the "long dark day" of "suffering and distress" brought by this latest economic downturn.

In truth, the political system was ill equipped to cope with the economic and social revolutions reshaping America. The executive branch remained weak, while members of Congress and the courts found themselves easily swayed by the financial interests of the industrial class. The crises of the 1890s strained the political order and forced it to confront such inequities.

Strains on the political system

The political system also had to take into account developments abroad. Industrialization had sent American businesses around the world in search of raw materials and new markets. As that search intensified, many influential Americans argued that the United States needed to compete with European nations in acquiring territory overseas. By the end of the century, the nation's political system had taken its first steps toward modernization, including a major political realignment at home and a growing empire abroad. The changes launched the United States into the twentieth century and an era of prosperity and global power.

International consequences

The Politics of Paralysis

During the 1880s and 1890s, as the American political system came under strain, Moisei Ostrogorski was traveling across the United States. Part of a flood of foreign observers, the Russian political scientist had come to see the new democratic experiment in action. His verdict was as blunt as it was widely shared: "the constituted authorities are unequal to their duty." It seemed that the glorious experiment had fallen victim to greed, indifference, and political mediocrity.

In fact, there were deeper problems: a great gulf between rich and poor; a wrenching cycle of boom and bust; the unmet needs of African Americans, Indians, and women. Politics was the traditional medium of resolution, but it was grinding into a dangerous stalemate.

Political Stalemate

From 1877 to 1897 American politics rested on a delicate balance of power that left neither Republicans nor Democrats in control. Republicans inhabited the White House for 12 years; Democrats, for 8. Margins of victory in presidential elections were paper thin. No president could count on having a majority of his party in both houses of Congress for his entire term. Usually Republicans controlled the Senate and Democrats the House of Representatives.

With elections so tight, both parties worked hard to turn out the vote. Brass bands, parades, cheering crowds of flag-wavers "are the order of the day and night from end to end of the country," reported a British visitor. In cities party workers handed out leaflets and pinned campaign buttons on anyone who passed. When Election Day arrived, stores and businesses shut down. At political clubs

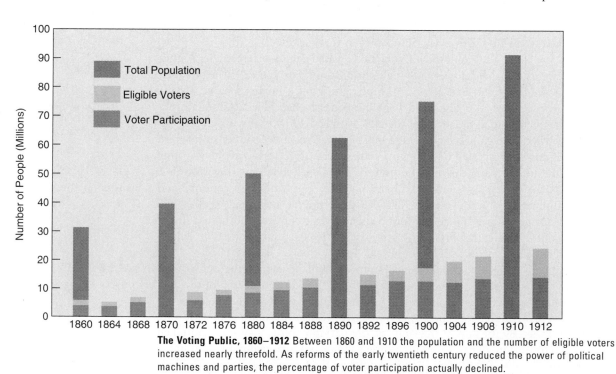

The Voting Public, 1860–1912 Between 1860 and 1910 the population and the number of eligible voters increased nearly threefold. As reforms of the early twentieth century reduced the power of political machines and parties, the percentage of voter participation actually declined.

and corner saloons men lined up to get voting orders (along with free drinks) from ward bosses. In the countryside, fields went untended as farmers took their families to town, cast their ballots, and bet on the outcome.

An average of nearly 80 percent of eligible voters turned out for presidential elections between 1860 and 1900, a figure higher than at any time since. In that era, however, the electorate made up a smaller percentage of the population. Strict voting qualifications limited participation. Only one American in four qualified to vote, and only one in five actually voted in presidential elections from 1876 to 1892. Most voters were white males. Women could vote in national elections only in a few western states, and beginning in the 1880s, the South erected barriers that eventually disfranchised many African American voters.

Party loyalty rarely wavered. In every election, 16 states could be counted on to vote Republican and 14 Democratic (the latter mainly in the South). In only six states—the most important being New York and Ohio—were the results in doubt. National victories often hung on their returns.

Voter turnout

The Parties

What inspired such loyalty? While Republicans and Democrats shared broad values, they also had differences. Both parties supported business and condemned radicalism, and neither offered embattled workers or farmers much help. Democrats believed in states' rights and limited government, while Republicans favored federal activism to foster economic growth. The stronghold of Democrats lay in the South, where they reminded voters that they had led the states of the Old Confederacy, "redeemed" them from Republican Reconstruction, and championed white supremacy. Republicans dominated the North with strong support from industry and business. They, too, invoked memories of the Civil War to secure votes, black as well as white. "Not every Democrat was a rebel," they chanted, "but every rebel was a Democrat."

Ethnicity and religion also cemented voter loyalty. Republicans relied on old-stock Protestants, who feared new immigrants and put their faith in promoting pious behavior throughout society. In the Republican party, they found support for immigration restriction, prohibition, and English-only schools. In the North, the Democratic party attracted urban political machines, their immigrant voters, and the working poor. Often Catholic, these voters saw salvation in following their own religious rituals, not in dictating the conduct of others.

"For three months processions, usually with brass bands, flags, badges, crowds of cheering spectators, are the order of the day and night from end to end of the country," commented a British observer. Here, Denver Republicans lead a nighttime parade to celebrate the election of Benjamin Harrison in the presidential contest of 1888.

Ethnic and religious factors

Region, religion, and ethnicity thus bound voters to each party. So too did the ordinary concerns of daily life. Some citizens weighed their purses and calculated the effect of their vote on their incomes. More thought of their parents, their children, or their communities when they went to the polls. Year after year, these familial and cultural loyalties shaped political allegiances.

Outside the two-party system, reformers often fashioned political organizations of their own. Some formed groups that aligned themselves behind issues rather than

Despite high voter turnout, politicians were often considered opportunists, out for the spoils of office. In this cartoon entitled "Our Stumbling Block," Thomas Nast depicts corrupt politics and the spoils system as blocking the path of business and keeping Americans from prosperity.

parties. Opponents of alcohol created the Woman's Christian Temperance Union (1874) and the Anti-Saloon League (1893). Champions of women's rights joined the National Woman Suffrage Association (1890), a reunion of two branches of the women's suffrage movement that had split in 1869.

Third political parties also crystallized around a single concern or a particular group. Advocates of temperance rallied to the Prohibition party (1869). Those who sought inflation of the currency formed the Greenback party (1874). Angry farmers in the West and South created the Populist, or People's, party (1892). All drew supporters from both conventional parties, but as largely single-interest groups they mobilized minorities, not majorities.

The Issues

In the halls of Congress, attention focused on well-worn issues: veterans' benefits, appointments, tariffs, and money. The presidency had been weakened by the impeachment of Andrew Johnson, the scandals of Ulysses S. Grant, and the contested victory of Rutherford B. Hayes in 1876 (see page 556). So Congress enjoyed the initiative in making policy. Time after time, legislators squandered it amid electioneering and party infighting.

Some divisive issues were the bitter legacy of the Civil War. Republicans and Democrats waved symbolic "bloody shirts," each tarring the other with responsibility for the war. The politics of the Civil War also surfaced in the lobbying efforts of veterans. The Grand Army of the Republic, an organization of more than 400,000 Union soldiers, petitioned Congress for pensions to make up for poor wartime pay and to support the widows and orphans of fallen comrades. By the turn of the century Union army veterans and their families were receiving $157 million annually. It was one of the largest public assistance programs in American history, which at its peak accounted for nearly half of the federal budget. It was also one of the first government programs to offer benefits to African Americans and laid the foundations of the modern welfare state.

counterpoint

Origins of the Welfare State

Historians disagree over the origins of the welfare state. Some maintain that the United States followed the lead of industrial nations in Europe, where the first social insurance laws were enacted in the 1880s and 1890s. Similar laws were not established in the United States until the 1930s (see Chapter 25). Marxist historians pointed to the emergence of these laws as a way for capitalism to control the working class and head off more radical change.

Other historians and social scientists have placed the origins of the welfare state in late nineteenth-century America. These scholars focus on the activities of interest groups, especially veterans', women's, and other voluntary organizations. Lobbying by these organizations resulted in an extensive aid program for Civil War veterans and, in the first two decades of the twentieth century, benefits for mothers and pensions for widows in over 40 states. Many of these benefits were more elaborate than those in Europe.

More important than welfare was the campaign for a new method of staffing federal offices. Since the early nineteenth century, political victors had awarded government jobs to loyal followers regardless of their qualifications. After elections, winners faced an army of office seekers, "lying in wait . . . like vultures for a wounded bison."

A growing federal bureaucracy only aggravated the problem. From barely 53,000 employees at the end of the Civil War the federal government had grown to 166,000 by the early 1890s. Far more of these new jobs required special skills. But dismantling this "spoils system" proved difficult for politicians who had rewarded faithful supporters with government jobs. Reacting to the scandals of the Grant administration, a group of independents formed the National Civil Service Reform League in 1881. The league promoted the British model of civil service based on examination and merit. But in Congress neither party was willing to take action when it held power (and thus controlled patronage).

One July morning in 1881, a frustrated office seeker named Charles Guiteau unwittingly broke the log jam. As President James Garfield hurried to catch a train, Guiteau jumped from the shadows and shot him twice. Garfield's death finally produced reform. In 1883 the Civil Service Act, or Pendleton Act, created a bipartisan civil service commission to administer competitive examinations for some federal jobs. Later presidents expanded the jobs covered. By 1896 almost half of all federal workers came under civil service jurisdiction.

Pendleton Act

The protective tariff also stirred emotions in Congress. Since 1812, tariffs, or taxes on imported goods, had been used to shield "infant industries" in the United States from foreign competition. But by the 1880s many American industries had grown into strapping adults, no longer in need of such protection. Worse still, tariff revenues had created a budget surplus so large that it could undermine prosperity by depriving the economy of money for investment in employment and productivity. While the surplus mounted, Congress debated how or whether to spend it.

As promoters of business, Republicans usually championed tariffs and were joined by industrialists, westerners who sold protected raw materials like wool and timber, and even many workers, who believed that the tariff safeguarded their jobs and their wages. Democrats, with their strength in the agricultural South, sought to reduce tariffs in order to lower the prices that farmers and other consumers paid for manufactured goods. In 1890, when Republicans controlled the House, Congress enacted the McKinley Tariff, named for its sponsor, Ohio senator William McKinley. It raised tariff rates so high that they threatened to choke off all manufactured imports. It also contained a novel twist to appease reductionists. A "reciprocity" clause allowed the president to lower rates if other countries did the same. It was not enough to soothe opponents, who helped to drive McKinley and other Republicans from office in the elections of 1890. For the next two decades and more, a national tug-of-war would be waged over the tariff.

McKinley Tariff

Just as divisive was the issue of currency. For most of the nineteenth century, currency was backed by both gold and silver. The need for more money during the Civil War had led Congress to issue "greenbacks"—currency printed on paper with a green back and not convertible to gold or silver. For the next decade and a half Americans argued over whether to print more such paper money or take it out of circulation. Farmers and other debtors favored printing greenbacks as a way of inflating prices and thus reducing their debts. For the opposite reasons, bankers and creditors stood for "sound money" backed by gold. Fear of inflation led Congress first to reduce the number of greenbacks and then in 1879 to make all remaining paper money convertible into gold.

In this cartoon, Uncle Sam sits securely behind a locked door, protected by the soon to be enacted Dingley tariff bill (1897) from the riotous clamor of foreigners seeking entry into U.S. markets. Whenever reformers tried to reduce tariffs, political support for protection made the task nearly impossible. In 1882 Congress had created a commission to consider lowering tariffs, but it was quickly captured by the interests who stood to gain most from high tariffs. Complained one senator: "There was a representative of the wool growers on the commission; . . . of the iron interest . . . of the sugar interest. . . . And those interests were very carefully looked out for."

A more heated battle was developing over silver-backed money. By the early 1870s so little silver was being used that Congress officially stopped coining it in 1873, touching off a steep economic slide as the supply of money contracted. With it came charges that a conspiracy of bankers had been responsible for "demonetizing" silver and wrecking the economy in what was widely referred to as the "Crime of '73." In truth, the money supply was inadequate. By the late nineteenth century, the supply of goods had expanded more rapidly than the amount of money in circulation. As the demand for money grew, pressure to raise interest rates, the charges for borrowing, grew as well. So, too, did deflation, or falling prices, as too little money chased too many goods. In some parts of the country prices fell so seriously that businesses found it difficult to make a profit. All added to economic instability and increased calls for enlarging the money supply.

Crime of '73

In 1878 the Bland-Allison Act inaugurated a limited form of silver coinage. But pressure for unlimited coinage of silver—coining all silver presented at U.S. mints— mounted as silver production quadrupled between 1870 and 1890. In 1890 pressure for silver peaked in the Sherman Silver Purchase Act. It obligated the government to buy 4.5 million ounces of silver every month. Paper tender called "treasury notes," redeemable in either gold or silver, would pay for it. The compromise satisfied both sides only temporarily.

Bland-Allison Act

The White House from Hayes to Harrison

From the 1870s through the 1890s a string of nearly anonymous presidents presided over the country. Not all were mere caretakers. Some tried to energize the office, but Congress continued to dominate Washington.

Republican Rutherford B. Hayes was the first of the "Ohio dynasty," which included three presidents from 1876 to 1900. He moved quickly to end Reconstruction and tried unsuccessfully to woo southern Democrats with promises of economic support. His pursuit of civil service reform ended only in splitting his party between "Stalwarts" (who favored the old spoils systems) and "Half-Breeds" (who opposed it and favored reform). Hayes left office after a single term, happy to be "out of a scrape."

In 1880, Republican James Garfield, another Ohioan, succeeded Hayes by a handful of votes. He spent his first hundred days in the White House besieged by office hunters and failing to placate the rival sections of his party. After Garfield's assassination only six months into his term, Chester A. Arthur, the "spoilsman's spoilsman," became president. To everyone's surprise, the dapper Arthur turned out to be an honest president. He broke with machine politicians, including his mentor and Stalwart leader Roscoe Conkling of New York. He worked to lower the tariff, warmly endorsed the new Civil Service act, and reduced the federal surplus by beginning construction of a modern navy. Such evenhandedness left him little chance for renomination from divided party leaders.

The election of 1884 was one of the dirtiest ever recorded. Senator James G. Blaine, leader of the reform-minded Half-Breeds in the Republican party, fought off charges of corrupt dealings with the railroads, while Democrat Grover Cleveland, the former governor of New York, admitted to fathering an illegitimate child. In the last week of the race a New York minister labeled the Democrats the party of "Rum, Romanism, and Rebellion" (alcohol, Catholicism, and the Civil War). In reaction the Irish Catholic vote swung strongly to Cleveland and with it New York and the election.

The dirty election of 1884

Cleveland was the first Democrat elected to the White House since James Buchanan in 1856, and he was more active than many of his predecessors. He pleased reformers by expanding the civil service, and his devotion to gold-backed currency, economy, and efficiency earned him praise from business. He supported the growth of federal power by endorsing the Interstate Commerce Act (1887), new agricultural research, and federal arbitration of labor disputes.

Cleveland's presidential activism nonetheless remained limited. He vetoed two of every three bills brought to him, more than twice the number of all his predecessors. Toward the end of his term, embarrassed by the large federal surplus, Cleveland finally reasserted himself by attacking the tariff, but to no avail. The Republican-controlled Senate blocked his attempt to lower it.

In 1888 Republicans nominated a sturdy defender of tariffs, Benjamin Harrison, the grandson of President William Henry Harrison. President Cleveland won a plurality of the popular vote but lost in the Electoral College. The "human iceberg" (as Harrison's colleagues called him) worked hard, rarely delegated management, and turned the White House into a well-regulated office. He helped to shape the Sherman Silver Purchase Act

A Chinese laborer, queue in hand, proudly displays patches in support of the 1888 Democratic presidential candidate Grover Cleveland and his running mate, Allen B. Thurman. Cleveland and Thurman lost to Benjamin Harrison and Levi P. Morton, a wealthy New York banker. After his victory, Harrison, a pious Presbyterian, grabbed the hand of Senator Matthew Quay and crowed, "Providence has given us the victory." "Providence hadn't a damn thing to do with it," Quay said later, irked that Harrison seemed to have no idea how many Republicans "were compelled to approach the gates of the penitentiary to make him President."

(1890), kept up with the McKinley Tariff (1890), and accepted the Sherman Antitrust Act (1890) to limit the power and size of big businesses.

At the end of Harrison's term in 1893, Congress had completed its most productive session of the era, including the first billion-dollar peacetime budget. The growing federal surplus had become an embarrassment, and Republicans spent it, mostly on giveaway and pork-barrel projects that blatantly benefited their own states and districts. To Democratic jeers of a "Billion Dollar Congress," Republican House Speaker Thomas Reed shot back, "This is a billion-dollar country!"

Ferment in the States and Cities

Despite its growing expenditures and more legislation, most people expected little from the federal government. Few newspapers even bothered to send correspondents to Washington. Public pressure to curb the excesses of the new industrial order mounted closer to home, in state and city governments. Experimental and often effective, state programs began to grapple with the problems of corporate power, discriminatory shipping rates, political corruption, and urban decay.

State commissions   Starting in 1869 with Massachusetts, states established commissions to investigate and regulate industry, especially railroads, America's first big business. By the turn of the century, almost two-thirds of the states had them. These early commissions gathered and publicized information on shipping rates and business practices and furnished advice about public policy.

In the Midwest, on the Great Plains, and in the Far West, merchants and farmers pressed state governments to rein in high railroad rates and stop the rebates given to large shippers. In California, one newspaper published a schedule of freight rates to Nevada, showing that lower rates had been charged by wagon teams before the railroads were built. On the West Coast and in the Midwest, state legislatures empowered commissions to end rebates and monitor freight rates. In 1870 Illinois became the first of several states to define railroads as public highways subject to regulation, including setting maximum rates.

Concern over political corruption and urban blight led to state municipal conventions, the first in Iowa in 1877. Philadelphia sponsored a national conference on **National Municipal** good city government in 1894. A year later reformers founded the National Mu-**League** nicipal League. It soon had more than 200 branches. Its model city charter advanced such farsighted reforms as separate city and state elections, limited contracts for utilities, and more authority for mayors. Meanwhile cities and states in the Midwest enacted laws closing stores on Sundays, prohibiting the sale of alcohol, and making English the language of public schools—all in an effort to standardize social behavior and control the habits of new immigrants.

 The Revolt of the Farmers

In 1890, the politics of stalemate cracked as the patience of farmers across the South and the western plains reached an end. Beginning in the 1880s, a sharp depression drove down agricultural prices and forced thousands from their land. But farmers suffered from a great deal more, including heavy mortgages, widespread poverty, and railroad rates that sometimes discriminated against them. In 1890 their resentment boiled over. An agrarian revolt—called Populism—swept across the political landscape and helped break the political stalemate of the previous 20 years.

The Harvest of Discontent

The revolt of the farmers stirred first on the southern frontier, spread eastward from Texas through the rest of the Old Confederacy, then moved west across the plains. Farmers blamed their troubles on obvious inequalities: manufacturers protected by the tariff, railroads with sky-high shipping rates, wealthy bankers who held their mounting debts, expensive intermediaries who stored and processed their commodities—all seemed to profit at their expense.

Targets of farm anger

The true picture was fuzzier. The tariff protected industrial goods but also supported some farm commodities such as wool and sugar. Railroad rates, however high, actually fell from 1865 to 1890. And while mortgages were heavy, most were short, no more than four years. Farmers often refinanced them and used the money to buy more land and machinery, thus increasing their debts. Millers and operators of grain elevators or storage silos earned handsome profits, yet every year more of them came under state regulation.

In hard times, of course, none of this mattered. And in the South many poor farmers seemed condemned forever to hard times. Credit lay at the root of their problem, because most southern farmers had to borrow money to plant and harvest their crops. The inequities of sharecropping and the crop-lien system (pages 569–570) forced them into debt. When the prices for their crops fell, they borrowed still more, stretching the financial resources of the South beyond their meager limits. Within a few years after the Civil War, Massachusetts's banks had five times as much money as all the banks of the Old Confederacy.

Beginning in the 1870s, nearly 100,000 debt-ridden farmers a year picked up stakes across the Deep South and fled to Texas to escape this ruinous system of credit, only to find it waiting for them. Others stood and fought, as one pamphlet exhorted in 1889, "not with glittering musket, flaming sword and deadly cannon, but with the silent, potent and all-powerful ballot."

Mary Shelley's novel of a man-made monster who turns against its creator strikes the theme for this 1874 cartoon entitled "The American Frankenstein." Here, the railroad is a monstrous creation that crushes the common people in its path. It carries the symbols of wealth and might—a cloak of ermine and a club of capital. "Agriculture, commerce, and manufacture are all in my power," the monster bellows in the caption. Figures of authority, like the policeman at the lower right, can only snap to attention and salute.

The Origins of the Farmers' Alliance

Before farmers could vote together, they had to get together. Life on the farm was harsh, drab, and isolated. Such conditions shocked Oliver Hudson Kelley as he traveled across the South after the Civil War. In 1867 the young government clerk founded the Patrons of Husbandry to brighten the lives of farmers and broaden their horizons. Local chapters, called "granges," brought farmers and their families together to pray, sing, and learn new farming techniques. The Grangers sponsored fairs, picnics, dances, lectures—anything to break the bleakness of farm life. After a slow start the Grange grew quickly. By 1875 there were 800,000 members in 20,000 locals, most in the Midwest, South, and Southwest.

At first the Grangers swore off politics. But in a pattern often repeated, socializing led to economic and then political action. By pooling their money to buy supplies and equipment to store and market their crops, Grangers could avoid the high charges of intermediaries. By the early 1870s they also were lobbying midwestern legislatures to adopt "Granger laws" regulating rates charged by railroads, grain elevator operators, and other intermediaries.

Granger cases

Eight "Granger cases" came before the Supreme Court in the 1870s to test the new regulatory measures. *Munn v. Illinois* (1877) upheld the right of Illinois to regulate private property (in this case, the giant elevators for storing grain) so long as it was "devoted to a public use." Later decisions allowed state regulation of railroads, but only within state lines. Congress responded in 1887 by creating the Interstate Commerce Commission, a federal agency that could regulate commerce across state boundaries. In practice, it had little power, but it was a key step toward establishing the public right to oversee private corporations.

Southern Alliance

Slumping prices in the 1870s and 1880s bred new farm organizations. Slowly they blended into what the press called the "Alliance Movement." The Southern Alliance, formed in Texas in 1875, spread rapidly after Dr. Charles W. Macune took command in 1886. A doctor and lawyer as well as a farmer, Macune planned to expand Texas's network of local chapters, or suballiances, into a national network of state Alliance Exchanges. Like the Grangers, the exchanges pooled their resources in cooperatively owned enterprises for buying and selling, milling and storing, banking and manufacturing.

Soon the Southern Alliance was publicizing its activities in local newspapers, publishing a journal, and sending lecturers across the country. For a brief period, between 1886 and 1892, the Alliance cooperatives grew to more than a million members throughout the South and challenged accepted ways of doing business. Macune claimed that his new Texas Exchange saved members 40 percent on plows and 30 percent on wagons. But most Alliance cooperatives were managed by farmers without the time or experience to succeed. Usually opposed by irate local merchants, the ventures eventually failed.

Although the Southern Alliance admitted no African Americans, it encouraged them to organize. A small group of black and white Texans founded the Colored Farmers' National Alliance and Cooperative Union in 1886. By 1891 a quarter of a million farmers had joined. Its operations were largely secret, because public action often brought swift retaliation from white supremacists. When the Colored Farmers' Alliance organized a strike of black cotton pickers near Memphis in 1891, white mobs hunted down and lynched 15 strikers. The murders went unpunished, and the Colored Alliance began to founder.

The Alliance Peaks

Farmer cooperation reached northward to the states of the Midwest and Great Plains in the National Farmers' Alliance, created in 1880. In June 1890 Kansas organizers formed the first People's party to compete with Democrats and Republicans. Meanwhile the Southern Alliance changed its name to the National Farmers' Alliance and Industrial Union, incorporated the strong Northern Alliances in the Dakotas and Kansas, and made the movement truly national.

The key to Alliance success was not organization but leadership, both at the top and in the middle. Alliance lecturers fanned out across the South and the Great Plains, organizing suballiances and teaching new members about finance and cooperative businesses. Membership lists, recorded in the rough script of a farmer-secretary, showed that at least one-quarter of Alliance members were women. Families had formed an essential part of the Grange, and the Alliance movement continued the practice of sponsoring family-oriented activities: songfests, parades, picnics, even burial services. Although Alliance members remained sharply divided over woman suffrage, more than a few women became speakers and organizers. "Wimmin is everywhere," noted one observer of the Alliance. The comment seemed to apply literally to Mary Elizabeth Lease, who in the summer of 1890 alone gave 160 speeches.

In 1890 members of the Alliance met in Ocala, Florida, and issued the "Ocala Demands." The manifesto reflected the Populists' deep distrust of "the money power"—large corporations and banks whose financial power gave them the ability to manipulate the "free" market. The Ocala Demands called on government to correct such abuses by reducing tariffs, abolishing national banks, regulating railroads, and coining silver money freely. The platform also demanded a federal income tax and the popular election of senators to make government more responsive to the public.

The most innovative feature of the platform came from Charles Macune. His "subtreasury system" would require the federal government to furnish warehouses for harvested crops and low-interest loans to tide farmers over until prices rose. Under such a system farmers would no longer have to sell in a glutted market, as they did under the crop-lien system. And they could exert control over the money supply, expanding it simply by borrowing at harvest time.

In the elections of 1890 the old parties faced hostile farmers across the nation. In the South, the Alliance continued to work within the Democratic party and elected 4 governors, won 8 legislatures, and sent 44 members of Congress and 3 senators to Washington. In the Great Plains, Alliance candidates drew farmers from the Republican party. Newly created farmer parties elected five representatives and two senators in Kansas and South Dakota and took over both houses of the Nebraska legislature.

Mary Elizabeth Lease, the "Kansas Pythoness," was admitted to the bar as a young woman but soon turned to radical activism. A charismatic speaker, she campaigned for Populist candidates in the 1890s, on one occasion warning the industrial Northeast that "the people are at bay, let the bloodhounds of money beware."

The People's Party

In February 1892, as the presidential election year opened, a convention of 900 labor, feminist, farm, and other reform delegates (100 of them black) met in St. Louis. They founded the People's, or Populist, party and called for another convention to nominate a presidential ticket. Initially southern Populists held back, clinging to their strategy of working within the Democratic party. But when newly elected Democrats failed to support Alliance programs, southern leaders such as Tom Watson of Georgia abandoned the party and began recruiting black and white farmers for the Populists.

The national convention of Populists met in Omaha, Nebraska, on Independence Day, 1892. Their impassioned platform promised to return government "to the hands of 'the plain people.'" More conservative southern Populists succeeded in blocking a plank for woman suffrage, though western Populists joined the campaign that would win women the right to vote in Colorado in 1893. Planks advocated the subtreasury plan, unlimited coinage of silver and expansion of the money supply, direct election of senators, an income tax, and government ownership of railroads, telegraph, and telephone. To attract wage earners the party endorsed the eight-hour workday, restriction of immigration, and a ban on the use of Pinkerton detectives in labor disputes—for the Pinkertons had engaged in a savage gun battle with strikers that year at Andrew Carnegie's Homestead steel plant. Delegates rallied behind the old greenbacker and Union general James B. Weaver, carefully balancing their presidential nomination with a one-legged Confederate veteran as his running mate.

The Election of 1892

The Populists enlivened the otherwise dull campaign of 1892, as Democrat Grover Cleveland and Republican incumbent Benjamin Harrison refought the election of 1888. This time, however, Cleveland won, and for the first session since the Civil War, Democrats gained control of both houses of Congress. The Populists, too, enjoyed success. Weaver polled over a million votes, the first third-party candidate to do so. Populists elected 3 governors, 5 senators, 10 representatives, and nearly 1500 members of state legislatures.

Longer-term weaknesses of the Populists

Despite these victories, the election revealed dangerous weaknesses in the People's party. Across the nation thousands of voters did change political affiliations, but most often from the Republicans to the Democrats, not to the Populists. No doubt a Democratic party campaign of intimidation and repression hurt the People's party in the South, where white conservatives had been appalled by Tom Watson's open courtship of black southerners. ("You are kept apart that you may be separately fleeced of your earnings," Watson had told his racially mixed audiences.) In the North, Populists failed to win over labor and most city dwellers. Both were more concerned with family budgets than with the problems of farmers and the downtrodden.

The darker side of Populism also put off many Americans. Its rhetoric was often violent; it spoke ominously of conspiracies and stridently in favor of immigration restriction. In fact, in 1892 the Alliance lost members, an omen of defeats to come. But for the present, the People's party had demonstrated two conflicting truths. It showed how far from the needs of many ordinary Americans the two parties had drifted and how difficult it would be to break their power.

The New Realignment

On May 1, 1893, President Cleveland was in Chicago to throw the switch that set ablaze 10,000 electric bulbs and opened the World's Columbian Exposition (pages 668–669). The gleaming White City with its grand displays stood as a monument to the nation's glorious progress. Four days later a wave of bankruptcies destroyed major firms across the country, and stock prices sank to all-time lows, setting off the depression of 1893. By the time the exposition closed in October, Chicago's mayor estimated the number of unemployed in the city to be near 200,000, a fraction of the millions who had already lost their jobs nationwide.

The sharp contrast between the exposition's White City and the nation's economic misery demonstrated the inability of the political system to smooth out the economy's cycle of boom and bust. In the slow recovery from the depression of 1873, the economy had overexpanded, and in 1893 the inevitable contraction began. By increasing production, opening markets, and tying Americans closer together, the new industrial order had brought soaring prosperity. But in 1893, the price of interdependence became obvious, as a downturn in one sector of the economy quickly affected others. With no way to control the swings in the business cycle, depression came on a scale as large as that of the booming prosperity.

The Depression of 1893

Railroad baron and descendant of two presidents Charles Francis Adams Jr. called the depression a "convulsion," but the country experienced it as crushing idleness. In August 1893, unemployment stood at 1 million; by the middle of 1894, it was 3 million. At the end of the year nearly one worker in five was out of a job, and one survey revealed that as late as 1901 half the heads of working-class households still had no jobs. Lining the streets of Washington stood "a vast army of unemployed, and men pleading for food who have never before been compelled to seek aid."

Working and middle-class families took in boarders, laundry, and sewing to make ends meet. With so many fathers and husbands unemployed, more and more wives and children left home to work. In the 1890s the number of laboring women actually increased, from 4 million to 5.3 million, but mainly in the exploitative fields of domestic and clerical work. In the South, where half the nation's working children were employed, child labor rose by 160 percent in textile mills during the decade. Concern for the young became so acute that middle-class women created the League for the Protection of the Family in 1896. Among other things it advocated compulsory education to keep children out of factories and mines.

Charles Dana Gibson, the Massachusetts-born illustrator famous for his portraits of well-bred young women in the 1890s, tackles a different subject in this ink drawing, a bread line of mixed classes during the depression of 1893.

The federal government had no program at all to combat the effects of the depression. "While the people should patriotically and cheerfully support their Government," President Cleveland had said at his inauguration, "its functions do not include the support of the people." The states offered little more. Relief, like poverty, was considered a private matter. The burden fell on local charities, benevolent societies, churches, labor unions, and ward bosses. In city after city, citizens organized relief committees to distribute bread and clothing until their meager resources gave out.

Others were less charitable. As the popular preacher Henry Ward Beecher told his congregation, "No man in this land suffers from poverty unless it be more than his fault—unless it be his sin." But the scale of hardship was so great, its targets so random, that anyone could be thrown out of work—an industrious neighbor, a factory foreman with 20 years on the job, a bank president. Older attitudes about personal guilt and responsibility for poverty began to give way to new ideas about its social origins and the obligation of public agencies to help.

The Rumblings of Unrest

Even before the depression, rumblings of unrest had begun to roll across the country. The Great Railroad Strike of 1877 had ignited nearly two decades of labor strife (pages 635–637). After 1893 discontent mounted as wages were cut, employees laid off, and factories closed. During the first year of the depression, 1400 strikes sent more than half a million workers from their jobs.

Uneasy business executives and politicians saw radicalism and the possibility of revolution in every strike. But the depression of 1893 had unleashed another force: simple discontent. In the spring of 1894, it focused on government inaction. On Easter Sunday, "General" Jacob Coxey, a 39-year-old Populist and factory owner, launched the "Tramps' March on Washington" from Massillon, Ohio. His "Commonweal Army   Coxey's Army of Christ"—some 500 men, women, and children—descended on Washington at the end of April to offer "a petition with boots on" for a federal program of public works. President Cleveland's staff tightened security around the White House as other "armies" of unemployed mobilized: an 800-person contingent left from Los Angeles; a San Francisco battalion of 600 swelled to 1500 by the time it reached Iowa.

On May 1, Coxey's troops, armed with "clubs of peace," massed at the foot of the capitol. When Coxey entered the capitol grounds, 100 mounted police routed the demonstrators and arrested the general for trespassing on the grass. Nothing came of the protest, other than to signal a growing demand for federal action.

Federal help was not to be found. Grover Cleveland had barely moved into the White House when the depression struck. The country blamed him; he blamed silver. In his view the Sherman Silver Purchase Act of 1890 had shaken business confidence by forcing the government to use its shrinking reserves of gold to purchase (though not coin) silver. Repeal of the act, Cleveland believed, was the way to build gold reserves, restore confidence, and achieve recovery. After bitter debate, Congress complied. But this economic tinkering only strengthened the resolve of "silverites" in the Democratic party to overwhelm Cleveland's conservative "gold" wing.

Worse for the president, repeal of silver purchases brought no economic revival. In the short run abandoning silver hurt the economy by shrinking the money supply just when expansion might have stimulated it by providing needed credit. As panic and unemployment spread, Cleveland's popularity wilted. Democrats were buried in the congressional elections of 1894. Dropping moralistic reforms and stressing national activism, Republicans won control of both the House and the Senate. With the Democrats now confined to the South, the politics of stalemate was over. All that remained for the Republican party was to capture the White House in 1896.

The Battle of the Standards

The campaign of 1896 quickly became known as the "battle of the standards"—a reference to the burning question of whether gold alone or gold and silver should become the nation's monetary standard. Most Republicans saw gold as the stable base for building business confidence and economic prosperity. They adopted a platform calling for "sound money" supported by gold alone. Their candidate, Governor William McKinley of Ohio, cautiously supported the gold plank and firmly believed in high tariffs to protect American industry.

Free silver

Silverites, on the other hand, campaigned for "free and independent" coinage of silver, in which the Treasury freely minted all the silver presented to it, independent of other nations. The supply of money would increase, prices would rise, and the economy would revive—or so their theory held. But the free silver movement was more than a monetary theory. It was a symbolic protest of region and class—of the agricultural South and West against the commercial Northeast, of debt-ridden farm folk against industrialists and financiers.

Cross of Gold speech

Silverites controlled the Democratic national convention from the start. They paraded with silver banners, wore silver buttons, and wrote a plank into the anti-Cleveland platform calling for free and unlimited coinage of the metal. The high point came when William Jennings Bryan of Nebraska stepped to the lectern, threw back his head, and offered himself to "a cause as holy as the cause of liberty—the cause of humanity." The audience rose as one, cheered wildly, then listened as the 36-year-old Bryan spoke for "the plain people of this country," for "our farms" and against "your cities," for silver and against gold. The crowd was in a near frenzy as he reached the dramatic climax and spread his arms in mock crucifixion: "You shall not crucify mankind upon a cross of gold." The next day the convention nominated him for the presidency.

Populists were in a quandary. They had expected the Democrats to stick with Cleveland and gold, sending unhappy silverites headlong into their camp. Instead, the Democrats had stolen their thunder. "If we fuse [with the Democrats] we are sunk," complained one Populist. "If we don't fuse, all the silver men we have will leave us for the more powerful Democrats." At a bitter convention, fusionists nominated Bryan for president. The best antifusionists could do was drop the Democrats' vice presidential candidate in favor of the agrarian rebel who had set Georgia aflame in 1892, Tom Watson.

Bryan knew he faced an uphill battle. Adopting a more active style that would be imitated in future campaigns, he tried to "educate" voters. He traveled 18,000 miles by train, gave as many as 30 speeches a day, and reached perhaps 3 million people in 27 states. The nomination of the People's party actually did more harm than good by labeling Bryan a Populist (which he was not) and a radical (which he definitely was not). Devoted to the "plain people," the Great Commoner spoke for rural America and Jeffersonian values: small farmers, small towns, small government.

McKinley knew he could not compete with Bryan's barnstorming, so he contented himself with sedate speeches from his front porch in Canton, Ohio. The folksy appearance of the campaign belied its reality. From the beginning, it had been engineered by Marcus Alonzo Hanna, a talented Ohio industrialist. Hanna relied on modern techniques of organization and marketing. He advertised McKinley, said Theodore Roosevelt, "as if he were patent medicine." His well-oiled campaign brought to Canton tens of thousands, who cheered the candidate's promises of a "full dinner pail." Hanna also saturated the country with millions of leaflets, along with 1400 speakers attacking free trade and free silver. Frightened conservatives poured some $4 million into McKinley's war chest.

The election also proved to be one of the most critical in the republic's history.* Over the previous three decades, political life had been characterized by vibrant campaigns, slim party margins, high voter turnout, and low-profile presidents. The election of 1896 signaled a new era of dwindling party loyalties and voter turnout, stronger presidents, and Republican rule. William McKinley's victory broke the

---

*Five elections, in addition to the contest of 1896, are often cited as critical shifts in voter allegiance and party alignments: the Federalist defeat of 1800, Andrew Jackson's rise in 1828, Lincoln's Republican triumph of 1860, Al Smith's Democratic loss in 1928, and—perhaps—Ronald Reagan's conservative tide of 1980.

William Jennings Bryan made the first of his three presidential bids in 1896, when he ran on both the Democratic and Populist tickets. Passionate in his convictions and devoted to the plain people, the "Great Commoner" is depicted in this hostile cartoon as a Populist snake devouring the Democratic party.

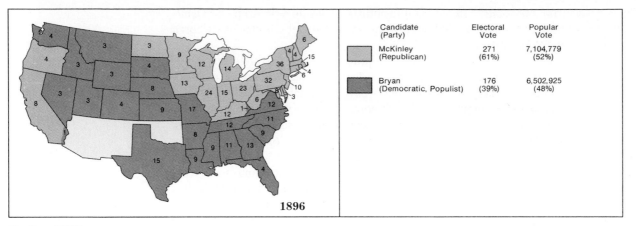

Candidate (Party)	Electoral Vote	Popular Vote
McKinley (Republican)	271 (61%)	7,104,779 (52%)
Bryan (Democratic, Populist)	176 (39%)	6,502,925 (48%)

1896

Election of 1896

Republican coalition

political stalemate and forged a powerful coalition that dominated politics for the next 30 years. It rested on the industrial cities of the Northeast and Midwest and combined old support from business, farmers, and Union army veterans with broader backing from industrial wage earners. The Democrats controlled little but the South.

The Rise of Jim Crow Politics

In 1892, despite the stumping of Populists like Tom Watson, African Americans had cast their ballots for Republicans, when they were permitted to vote freely. But increasingly, their voting rights were being curtailed across the South.

As the nineteenth century drew to a close, a long-standing racialism—categorizing people on the basis of race—deepened. The arrival of "new" immigrants from eastern and southern Europe and the acquisition of new overseas colonies highlighted differences among races and also helped to encourage prejudices that stridently justified segregation and other forms of racial control (see page 576). In the South racialism was enlisted into a political purpose—preventing an alliance of poor blacks and whites that might topple white conservative Democrats. The white supremacy campaign, on the face of it directed at African Americans, also had a broader target in the world of politics: rebellion from below, whether black or white.

Disfranchisement

Mississippi, whose Democrats had led the move to "redeem" their state from Republican Reconstruction, in 1890 took the lead in disfranchising African Americans. A new state constitution required voters to pay a poll tax and pass a literacy test, requirements that eliminated the great majority of black voters. Conservative Democrats favored the plan because it also reduced voting among poor whites, who were most likely to join opposition parties. Before the new constitution went into effect, Mississippi contained more than 250,000 eligible voters, black and white. By 1892, after its adoption, there were fewer than 77,000. Soon an all-white combination of conservatives and "reformers"—those disgusted by frequent election-stealing with blocs of black votes—passed disfranchisement laws across the South. Between 1895 and 1908, campaigns to limit voting won out in every southern state.

The disfranchisement campaign succeeded in achieving its broad aim of splitting rebellious whites from blacks, as the tragic fate of Tom Watson demonstrated. Only a dozen years after his biracial campaign of 1892, Watson was promoting black disfranchisement and white supremacy in Georgia. Like other southern Populists, Watson returned to the Democratic party still hoping to help poor whites. But under the increased atmosphere of intolerance, only by playing a powerful race card could he hope to win election. "What does civilization owe the negro?" he asked bitterly. "Nothing! Nothing!! NOTHING!!!"

The African American Response

To mount a successful campaign for disfranchisement, white conservatives inflamed racial passions. They staged "White Supremacy Jubilees" and peppered newspaper editorials with complaints of "bumptious" and "impudent" African Americans. The lynchings of blacks peaked during the 1890s, averaging over a hundred a year for the decade. Most took place in the South. White mobs in cities such as Atlanta and New Orleans terrorized blacks for days in the new, heightened atmosphere of tension.

African Americans worked out their own responses to the climate of intolerance. Ida B. Welles, a black woman born into slavery, turned her talents into a nationwide campaign against lynching when a friend, Thomas Moss, and two of his partners in the People's Grocery were brutally murdered after a fight with a white competitor in 1892. Welles meticulously documented the murders of African Americans across the South, demonstrating an increase of an astounding 200 percent between 1882 and 1892. As a teacher, journalist, and civil rights activist, she had already sued the Chesapeake, Ohio, and Southwestern Railroad for ejecting her from the ladies' car on one of their trains and had written editorials calling for improved schools for black children.

Ida B. Welles

In 1892, Welles turned antilynching into a personal crusade. She spent much of her time educating Americans about the use of lynching and other forms of mob violence as devices for terrorizing African Americans in the absence of slavery. Black men like Thomas Moss, who might want to start black-owned businesses or alter race relations in the South, were particular targets, for they threatened the prevailing racial and economic hierarchy in the South. Though her lobbying failed to produce a federal antilynching law, Welles did help organize black women, eventually into the National Association of Colored Women in 1896. It supported wide-ranging reforms, including education, housing, health care, and of course, antilynching.

Welles's campaign had focused on mob violence, but another former slave, Booker T. Washington, stressed instead the need for accepting the framework for race relations and working within it. "I love the South," Washington reassured an audience of white and black southerners in Atlanta in 1895. He conceded that white prejudice against blacks existed throughout the region but nonetheless counseled African Americans to accept what was offered them and work for their economic betterment through manual labor. Every laborer who learned a trade, every farmer who tilled the land could increase his or her savings. And those earnings would amount to "a little green ballot" that "no one will throw out or refuse to count." Toward that end, Washington organized the Tuskegee Institute and created a curriculum stressing vocational skills for farming, manual trades, and industrial work.

Booker T. Washington

Many white Americans hailed Washington's "Atlanta Compromise," for it struck the note of patient humility they were so eager to hear. For African Americans, it made the best of a bad situation. Washington, an astute politician, discovered that philanthropists across the nation hoped to make Tuskegee an example of their generosity. He was the honored guest of Andrew Carnegie at his imposing Skibo Castle. California railroad magnate Collis Huntington became his friend, as did other business executives eager to discuss "public and social questions."

Throughout, Washington preached accommodation to the racial caste system. He accepted segregation (so long as separate facilities were equal) and qualifications

In keeping with Booker T. Washington's emphasis on manual training, the Tuskegee Institute, opened in Alabama in 1881, was training 1400 students in 30 trades by 1900. Academic subjects received attention, too, as evidenced by this photograph of a history class (segregated by gender) learning about Captain John Smith and Pocahontas.

on voting (if they applied to white citizens as well). Above all Washington sought economic self-improvement for common black folk in fields and factories. In 1900 he organized the National Negro Business League to help establish African Americans in business as the leaders of their people. The rapid growth of local chapters (320 by 1907) extended his influence across the country.

W. E. B. Du Bois

Not all black leaders accepted Washington's call for accommodation. W. E. B. Du Bois, a professor at Atlanta University, leveled the most stinging attack in *The Souls of Black Folk* (1903). Du Bois saw no benefit for African Americans in sacrificing intellectual growth for narrow vocational training. Nor was he willing to abide the humiliating stigma that came from the South's discriminatory caste system. A better future would come only if black citizens struggled politically to achieve suffrage and equal rights.

Instead of exhorting African Americans to pull themselves up slowly from the bottom, Du Bois called on the "talented tenth," a cultured black vanguard, to blaze a trail of protest. In 1905 he founded what became known as the Niagara movement for political and economic equality. In 1909 a coalition of black and sympathetic whites transformed the Niagara movement into the National Association for

NAACP

the Advancement of Colored People (NAACP). Middle class and elitist, it mounted legal challenges to the Jim Crow system of segregation. But for sharecroppers in southern cotton fields and laborers in northern factories—the mass of African Americans—the strategy offered little relief, at least in the short run.

Neither accommodation nor legal agitation would suffice. But in the "Solid South" (as well as an openly racist North) it was Washington's restrained approach that set the agenda for most African Americans. The ferment of the early 1890s, among black Populists and white, was replaced by a lily-white Democratic party that dominated the region but remained in the minority on the national level.

McKinley in the White House

In William McKinley, Republicans found a skillful chief with a national agenda and personal charm. He cultivated news reporters, openly walked the streets of Washington, and courted the public with handshakes and flowers from his own lapel. Firmly but delicately, he curbed the power of old-time state bosses. When need be, he prodded Congress to action. In all these ways, he foreshadowed "modern" presidents, who would act as party leaders rather than as executive caretakers.

Fortune at first smiled on McKinley. When he entered the White House, the economy had already begun its recovery, as the cycle of economic retrenchment hit bottom. Factory orders were slowly increasing, and unemployment dropped. Farm prices climbed. New discoveries of gold in Alaska and South Africa expanded the supply of money without causing "gold bugs" to panic that currency was being destabilized by silver.

Freed from the burdens of the economic crisis, McKinley called a special session of Congress to revise the tariff. In 1897 the Dingley Tariff raised protective rates still higher but allowed the tariffs to come down if other nations lowered theirs. McKinley also sought a solution for resolving railroad strikes, like the earlier Pullman conflict, before they turned violent. The Erdman Act of 1898 set up machinery for government mediation. McKinley even began laying plans for stronger regulation of trusts.

But affairs overseas competed for his attention. The same expansive forces that had transformed the United States were also causing Americans to look increasingly beyond their borders. McKinley found himself facing a crisis with Spain that would force the nation to decide whether a democratic, industrial republic should also become an imperial nation. Regulation—and a true age of reform—would await the next century.

An 1896 Republican campaign poster features presidential hopeful William McKinley atop a giant gold coin engraved with the words "sound money" and supported by workers and businessmen alike. The poster promises domestic prosperity and respect overseas. The links between prosperity and empire as well as commerce and civilization were made not only in McKinley's campaign but also by later presidents.

The crisis with Spain was only the affair of the moment that turned American attention abroad. Underlying the conflict

Visions of Empire

were larger forces linking the destiny of the United States with international events. By the 1890s, southern farmers were exporting half their cotton crop to factories worldwide, while western wheat farmers earned some 30 to 40 percent of their income from markets abroad. John D. Rockefeller's Standard Oil Company shipped about two-thirds of its refined products overseas, and Cyrus McCormick supplied Russian farmers with the reaper.

More than these growing commercial ties turned American heads overseas. Since the 1840s expansionists had spoken of a Manifest Destiny to overspread the North American continent from the Atlantic to the Pacific. So involved with conquering the West were Americans in the nineteenth century that only slowly did they begin to look abroad. It was perhaps only natural that as they brought the West under control and the new industrial order took hold, visions of a new empire stretching all the way to Asia danced before their eyes, realized less by conquest than by opening the doors of trade to foreign markets and resources. And to the south lay Latin America, where the United States had long asserted its hegemony, or dominance, under the old Monroe Doctrine (1823) that warned European powers to stay out of the Americas. It was perhaps natural too then that as Americans spun visions of empire in Asia and Latin America they would encounter other nations—old imperial powers Great Britain, France, Belgium, and Spain and newcomers Germany and Japan—who had imperial visions of their own.

European Expansion Worldwide

The scramble for empire was well underway by the time the Americans, Germans, and Japanese entered the fray in the late nineteenth century. Spain and Portugal still clung to the remnants of their colonial empires, dating from the fifteenth and sixteenth centuries. In the early nineteenth century, England, France, and Russia accelerated their drive to control foreign peoples and lands. But the late nineteenth century became the new age of imperialism because the technology of arms and the networks of communication, transportation, and commerce brought the prospect of effective, truly global empires within much closer reach.

Ecological factors

From the very first years of settlement, the success of European expansion into colonial North America benefited from ecological factors. European diseases, animals, and plants often devastated and disrupted the new worlds they entered. The coming of smallpox and measles; of pigs, cattle, and horses; and of sugar and wheat played equally important roles in opening the Western Hemisphere and the Pacific basin to European domination. In areas like the Middle East, Asia, and Africa, where populations already possessed hardy domesticated animals and plants (as well as their own devastating disease pools), European penetration was less complete and sometimes relied on naked force alone.

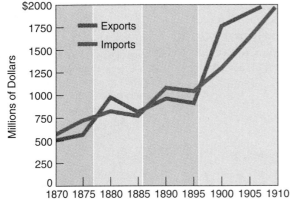

Balance of U.S. Imports and Exports, 1870–1910 After the depression of 1893, both imports and exports rose sharply, suggesting one reason why the age of imperialism was so closely linked with the emerging global industrial economy.

The speed and efficiency with which Europeans took over in the Niger and Congo basins of Africa in the 1880s prompted many Americans to argue for this European-style imperialism of conquest and possession. Germany, Japan, and Belgium were eagerly joining the hunt for colonies. But other Americans preferred a more indirect imperialism: one that exported products, ideas, and influence. To them, this American imperialism seemed somehow purer, for they could portray Americans as bearers of long-cherished values: democracy, free-enterprise capitalism, and Protestant Christianity.

While Americans tried to justify imperial control in the name of such values, social, economic, and political forces were drawing them rapidly into the imperial race. The growth of industrial networks linked them to international markets as never before, whether they were Arkansas sharecroppers dependent on world cotton prices or Pittsburgh steelworkers whose jobs were made possible by orders for Singer sewing machines for Europe, China, and the Hawaiian Islands. As economic systems became more tightly knit and political systems more responsive to industrialists and financiers, a rush for markets and distant lands was perhaps unavoidable.

Forces encouraging American imperialism

The Shapers of American Imperialism

Although the climate for expansion and imperialism was present at the end of the nineteenth century, the small farmer or steelworker was little concerned with how the United States advanced its goals abroad. An elite group—Christian missionar-

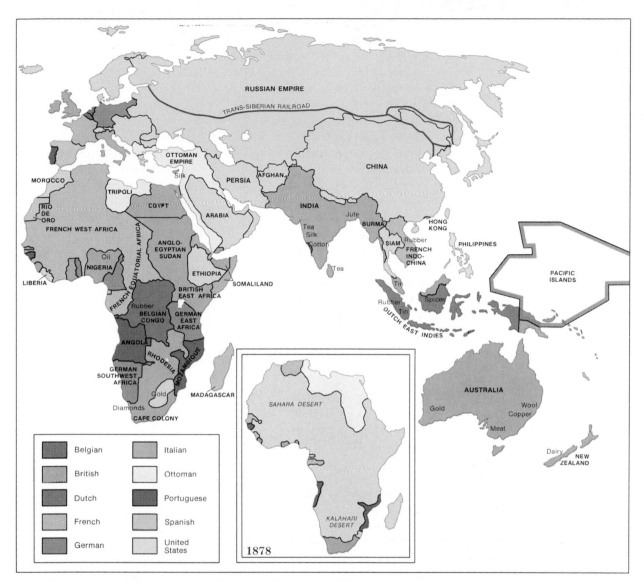

Imperialist Expansion, 1900 A comparison of Africa in 1878 (inset) and 1900 shows how quickly Europeans extended their colonial empires. Often resource-poor countries like Japan and England saw colonies as a way to acquire raw materials, such as South African diamonds and tin from Southeast Asia. Closer scrutiny shows that four of the most rapidly industrializing countries—Germany, Japan, Russia, and the United States—had few if any overseas possessions, even in 1900. And while China appears to be undivided, all the major powers were eagerly establishing spheres of influence there.

ies, intellectuals, business leaders, and commercial farmers—joined navy careerists to shape a more active American imperialism.

By 1880 the once-proud Civil War fleet of more than 600 warships was rotting with neglect. The U.S. Navy ranked twelfth in the world, behind Denmark and Chile. The United States had a coastal fleet but no functional fleet to protect its interests overseas. Discontented navy officers combined with trade-hungry business leaders to lobby Congress for a modern navy.

Alfred Thayer Mahan, a Navy captain and later admiral, formulated their ideas into a widely accepted theory of navalism. In *The Influence of Sea Power upon History* (1890), Mahan argued that great nations were seafaring powers that relied on

Mahan calls for a strong navy

Daily Lives

TIME AND TRAVEL
The New Navy

Early on February 3, 1874, a fleet of chunky monitors, steam frigates, and sloops lumbered out of Key West at a slow 4.5 knots. It was the largest assembly of American naval power since the Civil War. To the officers watching from shore, this fleet was an embarrassment. "Two modern vessels of war would have done us up in thirty minutes," a future admiral later observed.

In the era after the Civil War technology transformed the navies of Europe. Compound engines, improved armor plating, self-propelled torpedoes, and large rifled guns revolutionized naval warfare. The U.S. Navy, by contrast, sailed into the past. With 3000 miles of ocean as protection and no colonies to defend, a large blue-water fleet seemed unnecessary. Even steamships seemed impractical. The United States had no coaling stations in foreign waters to fuel them. By 1878 the navy had just 6000 sailors, the smallest force since the presidency of Andrew Jackson.

In 1873, as the U.S. Navy fell into disrepair, the British launched the *Devastation,* a single-masted, steam-driven vessel with heavy armor and powerful twin turrets. A forerunner of the modern battleship, it could steam across the Atlantic and back without stopping for coal. Less than a decade later, a British fleet smashed Alexandria, Egypt, whose fortifications were sturdier than those of American ports. That battle convinced Congress that the American coast was no longer safe. In 1883 it appropriated $1.3 million for four modern, steel-hulled vessels—the cruisers *Atlanta, Boston,* and *Chicago,* each 3000 to 4500 tons, and the 1500-ton dispatch boat *Dolphin.* These early "protected" cruisers (so named for the armored deck built over boilers, engines, and other machinery) were an odd mix of old and new. All three had full sail rigs yet were completely electrified and contained watertight compartments and double bottoms. The *Chicago* had twin propellers but engines and boilers so antiquated that one observer compared them to a

Passengers on riverboats and yachts saluted the new steel-hulled, steam-powered American fleet as it steamed triumphantly up the Hudson River after naval victories in the Spanish-American War. Within a few years, these modern ships would be obsolete because an international arms race forced rapid innovation in naval design.

foreign trade for wealth and might. In times of overproduction and depression, as had occurred repeatedly in the United States after the Civil War, overseas markets assumed even greater importance. The only way to protect foreign markets, Mahan reasoned, was with large cruisers and battleships. These ships, operating far from American shores, would need coaling stations and other resupply facilities throughout the world.

Mahan's logic was so persuasive and the profits to be reaped by American factories so great that in the 1880s Congress launched a program to rebuild the navy with steam vessels made of steel rather than the wooden sailing ships of old. By sawmill. The steel breech-loading guns were vast improvements over the iron muzzle loaders, yet gunners still aimed them the old-fashioned way, by looking down the barrels through open sights.

The naval program that began as a halfhearted effort had become a major commitment by the turn of the century. The fleet included additional protected cruisers, larger armored cruisers, and its first full-sized battleships —the *Indiana, Massachusetts,* and *Oregon,* each displacing more than 10,000 tons. (Soon after 1900 giant battleships were displacing 20,000 tons; on the eve of World War I they reached more than 30,000 tons.) With five more first-class battleships commissioned by 1896, the U.S. Navy rose to fifth place in the world. The prestige of naval service had risen, too, and with it the number of sailors: nearly 10,000 in uniform.

The new navy, unlike the civilian world, was not a democratic culture. Privileges of rank were everywhere apparent. Commanders lived in wood-paneled luxury and dined on specially prepared cuisine, capped by coffee, brandy, and cigars. The crew ate salted meats, beans, and potatoes. Officers had private quarters, while enlisted men, so the saying went, lived under the place where they slept and slept under the place where they ate. At night the tables and benches used for dining in the common quarters were stowed between overhead beams from which hammocks were hung.

Battery drill was held twice a day, but under fire American marksmanship proved poor. During one battle in the Spanish-American War, Americans fired more than 8000 shells at fleeing Spanish cruisers. An examination of their hulls later revealed only 120 hits.

By 1907 President Theodore Roosevelt decided to put American naval power on display. He sent 16 battleships on a 46,000-mile, 14-month world tour. Ironically, the Great White Fleet (named for the gleaming white hulls of its ships) was already out of date. In 1906 Great Britain had commissioned the *Dreadnought,* a warship whose new guns rendered all its competitors obsolete. Unlike conventional battleships with guns of varying sizes, the Dreadnought carried guns so powerful that the ship had twice the firepower of anything else afloat. In a single stroke the new American navy, the proud product of a quarter century of effort, was outclassed—but not for long. The United States would match the British, for it had joined a naval arms race that would lead the world down the path to war.

1900, the U.S. Navy ranked third in the world. With a modern navy, the country had the means to become an imperial power.

Protestant missionaries provided a spiritual rationale for imperialism that complemented Mahan's military and economic arguments. As devout Americans sought to convert "heathen" unbelievers in the faraway lands of China, the Middle East, and the western Pacific, they encountered people whose cultural differences often made them unreceptive to the Christian message. Many missionaries came to believe that natives first had to become Western in culture before turning Christian in belief. Although most opposed expansion through direct military or political intervention,

Missionaries

Missionaries often viewed the Chinese as uncivilized "heathen" whose souls needed saving and whose culture needed civilizing. This cartoon, published around 1900, pokes fun at the common stereotype by suggesting what the Chinese must think of American "heathen." "Contributions Received Here to Save the Foreign Devils," reads the sign of the Chinese "preacher," who laments the uncivilized behavior of corrupt American city governments, feuding backwoodsmen, rioting laborers, and mobs tormenting Chinese and black Americans.

they eagerly took up what British poet Rudyard Kipling called "the White Man's Burden" of "civilizing" the nonwhite world. Missionaries introduced Western goods, education, and systems of government administration—any "civilizing medium," as one minister remarked when he encouraged Singer to bring his sewing machines to China. Implanting Western civilization would surely "uplift" native populations but also open the way for American economic expansion.

Social Darwinism

From scholars, academics, and scientists came racial theories to justify European and American expansion. Charles Darwin's *On the Origin of Species* (1859) had popularized the notion that among animal species, the fittest survived through a process of natural selection. Social Darwinists like Herbert Spencer in England and William Graham Sumner in the United States argued that the same laws of survival governed the social order. By natural as well as divine law, the fittest people (those descended from Anglo-Saxon and Teutonic stock, said Spencer and Sumner) would assert their dominion over lesser peoples of the world.

Commercial factors

Perhaps more compelling than either religious or racial motives for American expansion was the need for trade. The business cycle of boom and bust reminded Americans of the unpredictability of their economy. In hard times, people sought salvation wherever they could, and one obvious road to recovery lay in markets abroad. With American companies outgrowing the home market, "expansion of our foreign trade is [the] only promise of relief," explained the National Association of Manufacturers. In and out of government, leading public figures called for a campaign to "find markets in every part of the habitable globe."

Dreams of a Commercial Empire

No one did more to initiate the idea of a "New Empire" for the United States than William Henry Seward, secretary of state under Lincoln and Andrew Johnson. Seward believed that "empire has . . . made its way constantly westward . . . until the tides of the renewed and decaying civilizations of the world meet on the shores of the Pacific Ocean." The United States must thus be prepared to win supremacy in the Far East—not by planting colonies or sending troops but by pursuing commerce. Equal access to foreign markets, often called the "open door," guided American policy in Asia.

William Henry Seward

While he pursued ties to Japan, Korea, and China, Seward promoted a transcontinental railroad at home and a canal across the Central American isthmus. Link by link, he was trying to connect eastern factories to western ports in the United States and, from there, to markets in the Far East. In pursuit of these goals Seward made two acquisitions in 1867: Midway Island in the Pacific and Alaska. Unimportant by itself, the value of Midway lay as a way station to Asia not far from Hawaii, where missionary planters were already establishing an American presence. Critics called Alaska "Seward's Folly," but he paid only about 2 cents an acre for a mineral-rich territory twice the size of Texas.

Acquisition of Midway and Alaska

Seward's conviction that the future of the United States lay in the Pacific and Asia flourished only in the 1890s, when Mahan provided the naval theory necessary to make the leap and the vanishing American frontier supplied an economic rationale for extending Manifest Destiny beyond the nation's continental borders. But in the 1880s, Secretary of State James G. Blaine began to look for ways to expand American trade and influence southward into Central and South America, where Great Britain had interests of its own to protect.

Blaine launched a campaign to cancel the Clayton-Bulwer Treaty (1850), which shared rights with Great Britain to any canal built in Central America. At the same time, he tried to shift Central American imports from British to U.S. goods by proposing that a "customs union" be created to reduce trade barriers in the Americas. His efforts resulted only in a weak Pan-American Union to foster peaceful understanding in the region, for Latin American nations balked at lowering their tariffs. In response, Blaine threatened to ban any export to the United States of the products of their generally single-crop economies. Dependent on such exports, only three nations—Colombia, Haiti, and Venezuela—had the will to resist.

Blaine's Pan-American Union

Gold, with its capacity to muddy the waters from which it was panned, stirred trouble in the jungles of Venezuela. In the 1880s, prospectors unearthed a 32-pound nugget along the border between Venezuela and British Guiana. Both Britain and Venezuela laid claim to the territory, which included the mouth of the Orinoco River, gateway to trade in the interior of South America's northern coast. In 1895, President Cleveland intervened, insisting on the right of the United States to mediate the dispute under the Monroe Doctrine. Great Britain and the United States rattled their sabers at each other but neither could afford war. The British finally accepted an American mediated settlement and in 1897 signed a treaty with Venezuela that left Venezuela with what it wanted most, control of access to the Orinoco, and the United States with what it wanted, the opportunity to assert its supremacy in the hemisphere.

The Venezuelan Boundary Dispute

Sugar was the key to Hawaii's English- and American-dominated plantations. Polynesians were culturally ill suited to the backbreaking labor that sugar cultivation demanded. Planters filled their labor needs by recruiting Japanese workers like this one.

Anglo-American tensions eased in the wake of the crisis and reached a new peak of friendship with a treaty concluded by Secretary of State John Hay and British Ambassador Julian Paunceforte in 1901. The Hay-Paunceforte Treaty ceded British interest in building a canal across the Central American isthmus and required the United States to leave such a canal open to ships of all nations. The campaign begun years earlier by James Blaine to pave the way for a U.S.-owned canal had finally come to an end.

Prelude in the Pacific

In the Pacific, the United States confronted Great Britain and Germany as they vied for control of the strategically located islands of Samoa. In 1878 a treaty gave America the rights to the fine harbor at Pago Pago. When the Germans sent marines to secure their interests in 1889, the British and Americans sent gunboats. As tensions rose, a typhoon struck, sinking the rival fleets and staving off conflict. Ten years later the three powers finally carved up the islands, with the United States retaining Pago Pago.

If American expansionists wanted to extend trade across the Pacific to China, Hawaii was the crucial link. It afforded a fine naval base and a way station along the route to Asia. In 1893, American sugar planters overthrew the recently enthroned Queen Liliuokalani, a Hawaiian nationalist eager to rid the island of American influence. Their success was ensured when a contingent of U.S. marines arrived ashore on the pretext of protecting American lives. Eager to avoid the McKinley Tariff's new tax on sugar imported into the United States, planters lobbied for the annexation of Hawaii, but President Cleveland refused. He was no foe of expansion but was, as his secretary of state noted, "unalterably opposed to stealing territory, or of annexing people against their consent, and the people of Hawaii do not favor annexation." The idea of incorporating the nonwhite population also troubled Cleveland. For a time, matters stood at a stalemate.

The Imperial Moment

Cuba in revolt

In 1895, after almost 15 years of planning from exile in the United States, José Martí returned to Cuba to renew the colony's struggle for independence from Spain. With cries of "Cuba libre," Martí and his rebels cut railroad lines, destroyed sugar mills, and set fire to the cane fields. Within a year, rebel forces controlled more than half the island. But even as they fought the Spanish, the rebels worried about the United States. Their island, just 90 miles off the coast of Florida, had long been a target of American expansionists and business interests. Martí had no illusions. "I have lived in the bowels of the monster," he explained of his exile in the United States, "and I know it."

The Spanish overlords struck back at Martí and his followers with brutal force. Governor-General Valeriano Weyler herded half a million Cubans from their homes into fortified camps where filth, disease, and starvation killed perhaps 200,000. Outside these "reconcentration" camps, Weyler chased the rebels across the countryside, polluting drinking water, killing farm animals, burning crops.

The revolt in Cuba was only the first round in a struggle that would eventually end in a war between the United States and Spain. By the time it was over, the Spanish-American War would leave Spain defeated and banished from the Western Hemisphere, Cuba free of Spanish rule, the United States with new colonial possessions in the Pacific and the Caribbean, and the knotty problem of what to do with them the subject of a national debate. For better or worse, America's imperial moment had arrived.

Mounting Tensions

President Cleveland had little sympathy for the Cuban revolt, but in the Republican party, expansionists such as Theodore Roosevelt and Massachusetts senator Henry Cabot Lodge urged a forceful policy of recognizing Cuban independence—a step that if taken would likely provoke war with Spain. When William McKinley entered the White House in 1897, however, his Republican supporters discovered that they had elected only a moderate expansionist. Cautiously, privately, he lobbied Spain to stop cracking down on the rebels and destroying American-owned property. With over $50 million invested in Cuban sugar and an annual trade of over $100 million, American business interest had much to lose.

In October 1897 Spain promised to remove the much-despised Weyler, end the reconcentration policy, and offer Cuba greater autonomy. The shift encouraged McKinley to resist pressure at home for more hostile action. But leaders of the Spanish army in Cuba had no desire to compromise. Although Weyler was removed, the military renewed efforts to quash the rebellion and encouraged pro-army riots in the streets of Havana. Early in 1898, McKinley dispatched the battleship *Maine* to show that the United States meant to protect its interests and its citizens.

Then in February 1898 the State Department received a stolen copy of a letter to Cuba sent by the Spanish minister in Washington, Enrique Dupuy de Lôme. So did William Randolph Hearst, a pioneer of sensationalist, or "yellow," journalism who was eager for war with Spain. "WORST INSULT TO THE UNITED STATES IN ITS HISTORY," screamed the headline of Hearst's *New York Journal*. What had de Lôme actually written? After referring to McKinley as a "would-be politician," the letter admitted that Spain had no intention of changing policy in Cuba. The Spanish planned to crush the rebels. Red-faced Spanish officials immediately recalled de Lôme, but most Americans now believed that Spain had deceived the United States.

The de Lôme letter

On February 15, 1898, as the USS *Maine* lay peacefully at anchor in the Havana harbor, explosions ripped through its hull. Within minutes the ship sank to the bottom, killing some 260 American sailors. The cause of the blasts remains unclear, but most Americans, inflamed by hysterical news accounts, concluded that Spanish agents had sabotaged the ship. McKinley sought a diplomatic solution but also a $50 million appropriation "to get ready for war."

Sinking of the Maine

Pressures for war proved too great, and on April 11, McKinley asked Congress to authorize "forceful intervention" in Cuba. Nine days later Congress recognized Cuban independence, insisted on the withdrawal of Spanish forces, and gave the president authority to use military force. In a flush of idealism, Congress also adopted the Teller Amendment, renouncing any aim to annex Cuba. Certainly both idealism and moral outrage led many Americans down the path to war. But in the end, the "splendid little war" (as Secretary of State Hay called it) resulted from less lofty ambitions—empire, trade, glory.

Teller Amendment

President McKinley sent the battleship *Maine* to Havana in January 1898. Despite a thorough investigation, the causes of the explosion that sank it remain a mystery. Nonetheless, fervent patriots turned the event into a call for war.

The Imperial War

For the 5462 men who died, there was little splendid about the Spanish-American War. Only 379 gave their lives in battle. The rest suffered from accidents, disease, and the mismanagement of an unprepared army. As war began, the American force totaled only 30,000, none of whom had been trained for fighting in tropical climates. The sudden expansion to 60,000 troops and 200,000 volunteers overtaxed the Army's graft-ridden system of supply. Rather than tropical uniforms, some troops were issued winter woolens and fed on rations that were diseased, rotten, or even lethally spoiled. Others found themselves fighting with weapons from the Civil War.

Dewey at Manila

The Navy fared better. Decisions in the 1880s to modernize the fleet now paid off handsomely. Naval battles largely determined the outcome of the war. As soon as war was declared, Admiral George Dewey ordered his Asiatic battle squadron from China to the Philippines. Just before dawn on May 1, he began shelling the Spanish ships in Manila Bay. Five hours later the entire Spanish squadron lay at the bottom of the bay. Three hundred eighty-one Spaniards were killed but only one American, a ship's engineer who died of a heart attack. Dewey had no plans to follow up his stunning victory with an invasion. His fleet carried no marines with which to take Manila. So ill-prepared was President McKinley for war, let alone victory, that only after learning of Dewey's success did he order 11,000 American troops to the Philippines.

Halfway around the globe, another Spanish fleet had slipped into Santiago harbor in Cuba just before the arrival of the U.S. Navy. The Navy, under Admiral William Sampson, blockaded the island, expecting the Spanish to flee under the cover of darkness. Instead, on July 3, the Spanish fleet made a desperate dash for the open seas in broad daylight. So startled were the Americans that several of their ships nearly collided as they rushed to attack their exposed foes. All seven Spanish ships were sunk, with 474 casualties. Only one American was killed and one wounded. With Cuba now cut off from Spain, the war was virtually won.

War in Cuba

Few Americans had heard of the Philippine Islands; fewer still could locate them on a globe. McKinley himself followed news from the Pacific front on an old textbook map. But most Americans knew the location of Cuba and how close it lay to the Florida coast.

Before the outbreak of hostilities, Tampa, Florida, was a sleepy coastal town with a single railroad line. But when it became the port of embarkation for the Cuban expeditionary force, some 17,000 troops arrived in the spring of 1898 alone. Tampa's overtaxed facilities soon broke down, spawning disease, tension, and racial violence. President McKinley had authorized the army to raise five volunteer regiments of black soldiers. By the time war was declared, over 8000 African Americans had signed up, half of them stationed around segregated Tampa. They found that although they could sail off to die freeing the peasants of Cuba, they were forbidden to buy a soda at the local drugstore. "Is America any better than Spain?" one dismayed black chaplain wondered. After drunken white troops shot at a black child, black troops in Tampa rioted. Three white and 27 black Americans were wounded in the melee.

Racial tensions

Matters were scarcely less chaotic as 17,000 disorganized troops and hundreds of reporters finally scrambled aboard ships. There they sat for a week, until sailing on June 14 for Santiago and battle. By June 30, the Americans had landed to challenge some 24,000 Spanish, many equipped with modern rifles. The following day

Black veterans of the western Indian wars along with volunteers, segregated and commanded by white officers, made up almost a quarter of the American force that invaded Cuba. Members of the Tenth Cavalry, shown here, were clearly in no mood to be subjected to the harassment they and other black troops encountered around Tampa. Later the Tenth Cavalry supported a charge by Colonel Teddy Roosevelt's Rough Riders at the battle of San Juan Hill.

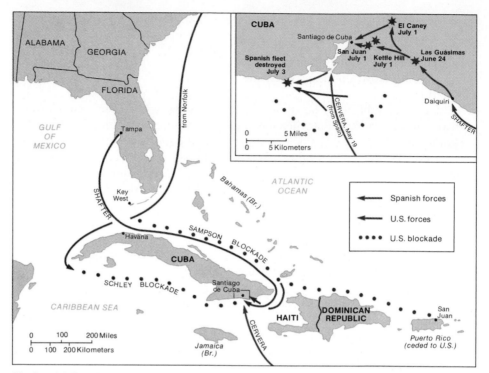

The Spanish-American War Had the Spanish-American War depended largely on ground forces, the ill-prepared U.S. Army might have fared poorly. But the key to success, in both Cuba and the Philippines, was naval warfare, in which the recently modernized American fleet had a critical edge. Proximity to Cuba also gave the United States an advantage in delivering troops and supplies and in maintaining a naval blockade that isolated Spanish forces.

7000 Americans—including the black soldiers of the Ninth and Tenth Cavalry regiments—stormed up heavily fortified San Juan and nearby Kettle hills. Their objective was the high ground north and east of Santiago.

The Rough Riders

Among them Lieutenant Colonel Theodore Roosevelt thrilled at the experience of battle. He had raised a cavalry troop of cowboys and college polo players, originally called "Teddy's Texas Tarantulas." By the time they arrived in Cuba, the volunteers were answering to the nickname "Rough Riders." As they charged toward the high ground, Roosevelt yelled: "Gentlemen, the Almighty God and the just cause are with you. Gentlemen, charge!" The withering fire drowned out his shrill, squeaky voice, so he repeated the call. Charge they did and conquer the enemy, though the battle cost more than 1500 American casualties.

Without a fleet for cover or any way to escape, the Spanish garrison surrendered on July 17. In the Philippines, a similar brief battle preceded the American taking of Manila on August 13. The "splendid little war" had ended in less than four months.

Peace and the Debate over Empire

Conquering Cuba and the Philippines proved easier than deciding what to do with them. The Teller Amendment had renounced any American claim to Cuba. But clearly the United States had not freed the island to see chaos reign or American business and military interests excluded. And what of the Philippines—and Spanish Puerto

Rico, which American forces had taken without a struggle? Powerful public and congressional sentiment pushed McKinley to claim empire as the fruits of victory.

The president himself favored such a course. The battle in the Pacific highlighted the need for naval bases and coaling stations. "To maintain our flag in the Philippines, we must raise our flag in Hawaii," the New York *Sun* insisted. On July 7 McKinley signed a joint congressional resolution annexing Hawaii, as planters had wanted for nearly a decade.

Annexing Hawaii

The Philippines presented a more difficult problem. Filipinos had greeted the American forces as liberators, not new colonizers. The popular leader of the rebel forces fighting Spain, Emilio Aguinaldo, had returned to the islands on an American ship. But to the rebels' dismay, McKinley insisted that the islands were under American authority until the peace treaty settled matters.

Aguinaldo

Such a settlement, McKinley knew, would have to include American control of the Philippines. He had no intention of leaving Spain in charge or of seeing the islands fall to other European rivals. American military advisers warned that without control of the entire island of Luzon, its capital, Manila, would be indefensible as the naval base McKinley wanted. Nor, McKinley felt certain, were the Filipinos capable of self-government. Aguinaldo and his rebels thought otherwise, and in June he declared himself president of a new Philippine republic.

The United States in the Pacific In the late nineteenth century both Germany and the United States emerged as major naval powers and as contestants for influence and commerce in China. The island groups of the central and southwest Pacific, though of little economic value, had potential strategic significance as bases and coaling stations along the routes to Asia. Rivalry (as in the case of Samoa) sometimes threatened to erupt into open conflict. Control of Hawaii, Midway, Samoa, Guam, and the Philippines gave the United States a string of strategic stepping-stones to the Orient.

Anti-imperialists

Many influential Americans—former president Grover Cleveland, steel baron Andrew Carnegie, novelist Mark Twain—opposed annexation of the Philippines. Yet even these anti-imperialists favored expansion, if only in the form of trade. Business leaders especially believed that the country could enjoy the economic benefits of the Philippines without the costs of maintaining it as a colony. Annexation would mire the United States too deeply in the quicksands of Asian politics, they argued. More important, a large, costly fleet would be necessary to defend the islands. To the imperialists that was precisely the point: a large fleet was crucial to the interests of a powerful commercial nation.

The role of racism

Racial ideas shaped both sides of the argument. Imperialists believed that the racial inferiority of nonwhites made occupation of the Philippines necessary, and they were ready to assume the "White Man's Burden" and govern. Filipinos, they argued, would gradually be taught the virtues of Western civilization, Christianity, democracy, and self-rule. (In fact, most Filipinos were already Catholic after many years under Spanish rule.) Anti-imperialists, on the other hand, feared racial intermixing and the possibility of Asian workers flooding the American labor market. They also maintained that dark-skinned people would never develop the capacity for self-government. An American government in the Philippines could be sustained only at the point of bayonets—yet the U.S. Constitution made no provision for governing people without representation or equal rights. Such a precedent abroad, the anti-imperialists warned, might one day threaten American liberties at home.

Still, when the Senate debated the Treaty of Paris ending the Spanish-American War in 1898, the imperialists had the support of the president, most of Congress, and the majority of public opinion. Even an anti-imperialist like William Jennings Bryan, defeated by McKinley in 1896, endorsed the treaty. In it Spain surrendered title to Cuba, ceded Puerto Rico and Guam to the United States, and in return for $20 million turned over the Philippines as well.

Eager to see war ended, Bryan and other anti-imperialists believed that once the United States possessed the Philippines, it could free them. The imperialists had other notions. Having acquired an empire and a modern navy to protect it, the United States could now assert its new status as one of the world's great powers.

America's First Asian War

Acquiring an empire was one thing, managing it quite another. As the Senate debated annexation of the Philippines in Washington, rebels fought with an American patrol outside of Manila. The few Americans who paid attention to the ensuing clash called it the "Filipino insurrection," but to those who fought, it was a brutal war. When it ended more than three years later, nearly 5000 Americans, 25,000 rebels, and perhaps as many as 200,000 civilians lay dead.

Racial antagonism spurred the savage fighting. American soldiers tended to dismiss Filipinos as nearly subhuman. Their armed resistance to American occupation often transformed the frustrations of ordinary troops into brutality and torture. To avenge a rebel attack, one American officer swore he would turn the surrounding countryside into a "howling wilderness." Before long the American force was resorting to a garrison strategy of herding Filipinos into concentration camps while destroying their villages and crops. The policy was embarrassingly reminiscent of the tactics of "Butcher" Weyler in Cuba. In 1902, only after the Americans captured Aguinaldo himself, did the war end.

In contrast to the bitter guerrilla war, the United States ruled the Philippines with relative benevolence. Under William Howard Taft, the first civilian governor, the Americans built schools, roads, sewers, and factories and inaugurated new farming techniques. The aim, said Taft, was to prepare the island territory for independence, and in keeping with it, he granted great authority to local officials. These advances—social, economic, and political—benefited the Filipino elite and thus earned their support. Decades later, on July 4, 1946, the Philippines were finally granted independence.

The United States played a similar role in Puerto Rico. As in the Philippines, executive authority resided in a governor appointed by the U.S. president. Under the Foraker Act of 1900 Puerto Ricans received a voice in their government as well as a nonvoting representative in the U.S. House of Representatives and certain tariff advantages. All the same, many Puerto Ricans chafed at the idea of such second-class citizenship. Some favored eventual admission to the United States as a state; others advocated independence—a division of opinion that persists even today.

Puerto Rico

An Open Door in China

Like a reciprocal equation, interest in Asia drove the United States to annex the Philippines, and annexation of the Philippines only whetted American interest in Asia. As ever, the possibility of markets in China—whether for Christian souls or consumer goods—proved an irresistible lure.

Both the British, who dominated China's export trade, and the Americans, who wanted to, worried that China might soon be carved up by other powers. Japan had defeated China in 1895, encouraging Russia, Germany, and France to join in demanding trade concessions. Each nation sought to establish an Asian "sphere of influence" in which its commercial and military interests reigned. Often such spheres resulted in restrictions against rival powers. Since Britain and the United States wanted the benefits of trade rather than actual colonies, they tried to limit foreign demands while leaving China open to all commerce.

The American decision to occupy the Philippines rather than give it independence forced Filipino nationalists to fight U.S. troops, as they had already been fighting the Spanish since 1896. Forces like the ones pictured at the right were tenacious enough to require more than 70,000 Americans (left) to put down the rebellion. Sporadic, bloody guerrilla fighting continued until 1902, and other incidents persisted until 1906.

The open-door notes

In 1899, at the urging of the British, Secretary of State Hay circulated the first of two "open-door" notes among the imperial powers. He did not ask them to give up their spheres of influence in China, only to keep them open to free trade with other nations. The United States could hardly have enforced even so modest a proposal, for it lacked the military might to prevent the partitioning of China. Still, Japan and most of the European powers agreed in broad outline with Hay's policy out of fear that the Americans might tip the delicate balance by siding with a rival. Hay seized on the tepid response and brashly announced that the open door in China was international policy.

Boxer Rebellion

Unrest soon threatened to close the door. Chinese nationalists, known to Westerners as Boxers for their clenched fist symbol, formed secret societies to drive out the *fon kwei,* or foreign devils. Encouraged by the Chinese empress, Boxers murdered hundreds of Christian missionaries and their followers and set siege to foreign diplomats and citizens at the British Embassy in Beijing. European nations quickly dispatched troops to quell the uprising and free the diplomats, while President McKinley sent 2500 Americans to join the march to the capital city. Along the way, the angry foreign armies plundered the countryside and killed civilians before reaching Beijing and breaking the siege.

Hay feared that once in control of Beijing the conquerors might never leave. So he sent a second open-door note in 1900, this time asking foreign powers to respect China's territorial and administrative integrity. They endorsed the proposal in principle only. In fact, the open-door notes together amounted to little more than an announcement of American desires to maintain stability and trade in Asia. Yet they reflected a fundamental purpose to which the United States dedicated itself across the globe: to open closed markets and to keep open those markets that other empires had yet to close. The new American empire would have its share of colonies, but in Asia as elsewhere it would be built primarily on trade.

Sense of mission

To expansionists like Alfred Thayer Mahan, Theodore Roosevelt, and John Hay, American interests would be secure only when they had been established worldwide, a course of action they believed to be blessed by divine providence. "We will not renounce our part in the mission of the race, trustee under God of the civilization of the world," declared Senator Albert Beveridge. But to one French diplomat, more accustomed to wheeling and dealing in the corridors of international power, it seemed that the Americans had tempted fate. With a whiff of Old World cynicism or perhaps a prophet's eye, he remarked, "The United States is seated at the table where the great game is played, and it cannot leave it."

On New Year's Eve at the State House in Boston a midnight ceremony ushered in the twentieth century. The crowd celebrated with psalms and hymns. There was a flourish of trumpets, and in the absence of a national anthem everyone sang "America."

Solemn and patriotic, the dawn of the new century brought an end to an era of political uncertainty and a decade of social upheaval. Prosperity returned at home; empire beckoned abroad. But deep divisions—between rich and poor, farmers and factory workers, men and women, native-born and immigrant, black and white—split the country. A younger generation of leaders stood in the wings, fearful of the schisms but confident it could bridge them. Theodore Roosevelt, who had looked eagerly toward war with Spain and the chance to expand American horizons, did not mince words with an older opponent. "You and your generation have had your chance. . . . Now let us of this generation have ours!"

chapter summary

The end of the nineteenth century witnessed a crisis arising out of years of political stalemate at home as well as the realization of dreams of empire abroad.

- Republicans and Democrats ground politics into near-gridlock over the well-worn issues of regional conflict, tariff, and monetary reform.

- Discontented Americans often fashioned political instruments of their own, whether for woman suffrage, temperance, monetary change, antilynching and civil rights, or farm issues.

- The political deadlock came finally to an end in the turbulent 1890s, when depression-spawned labor strife and a revolt of farmers produced the People's, or Populist, party and a political realignment that left the Republicans in control of national politics.

- By the 1890s too the tradition of Manifest Destiny combined powerfully with the needs of the new industrial order for raw materials and markets and the closing of the American frontier to produce a powerful drive toward empire, which rested on these two principles of American foreign policy:

  - The old Monroe Doctrine (1823), which warned European powers to stay out of the Americas.

  - The newer open-door notes of Secretary of State John Hay (1899–1900), which stressed the importance of equal commercial access to the markets of Asia.

- Most Americans favored an overseas empire for the United States but disagreed over whether it should be territorial or commercial.

- In the end America's overseas empire was both territorial and commercial. A victory in the Spanish-American War (1898) capped an era of territorial and commercial expansion by furnishing colonial possessions in the Caribbean and the Pacific and at the same time providing more stepping-stones to the markets of Asia.

additional reading

Sean Dennis Cashman, *America in the Gilded Age: From the Death of Lincoln to the Rise of Theodore Roosevelt* (1984) is a fine overview of the era. The importance of the presidential politics of the Gilded Age is stressed in H. Wayne Morgan, *From Hayes to McKinley: National Party Politics, 1877–1896* (1969), but for the importance of ethnicity and religion see Paul Kleppner, *The Cross of Culture: A Social Analysis of Midwestern Politics, 1850–1900* (1970). John Hicks's classic *The Populist Revolt* (1931) emphasizes poverty as the driving force behind Populism, while Lawrence Goodwyn points to the "movement culture" of the Alliance in reevaluating the Populists as crusaders for radical democratic change in *Democratic Promise: The Populist Movement in America* (1976). Charles Hoffman, *The Depression of the Nineties: An Economic History* (1970) furnishes a lucid account of the economy and the depression of 1893. On the spread of segregation in the post-Reconstruction South, see C. Vann Woodward's classic *The Strange Career of Jim Crow* (3d rev. ed., 1974). Woodward focuses on changes in the law, while John Cell, *The High-est Stage of White Supremacy* (1982) points to the role of the city. For Booker T. Washington's approach to race relations, see Louis Harlan, *Booker T. Washington* (1972) and *Booker T. Washington: The Wizard of Tuskegee* (1983). David Levering Lewis, *W. E. B. DuBois: Biography of a Race* (1993) is the fullest account of the early life and career of the civil rights leader.

For a conventional view of the rise of the welfare state in the 1930s, see Harold Wilensky and Charles N. Lebeaux, *Industrial Society and Social Welfare* (1958). A revision of those views can be found in Theda Skocpol's *Protecting Soldiers and Mothers: The Political Origins of Social Policy in the United States* (1994), which stresses the nineteenth-century origins of the welfare state and the interplay between the state and nongovernmental political groups.

For broad interpretive views of American foreign policy, see Michael Hunt, *Ideology and American Foreign Policy* (1984); John Dobson, *America's Ascent: The United States Becomes a Great Power, 1880–1914* (1978); and Walter LaFeber, *The American Age* (1989). LaFeber contains a rich bibliography, and his *Inevitable Revolutions* (3d ed., 1993) is good on Central America. Michael Hunt, *The Making of a Special Relationship: The United States and China to 1914* (1983) is excellent on Sino-American relations. For the Philippines, see Stanley Karnow, *In Our Image* (1989). For a fuller list of readings, see the Bibliography.

Significant Events

1850 — 1850 Clayton-Bulwer Treaty

1867 — 1867 Patrons of Husbandry ("Grange") founded; Alaska acquired

1869 Prohibition party founded; Massachusetts establishes first state regulatory commission

1870 —

1874 Greenback party organized; Women's Christian Temperance Union formed

1875 — 1875 First Farmers' Alliance organized

1877 *Munn v. Illinois* establishes the right of states to regulate private property in the public interest

1880 —

1881 President James Garfield assassinated; Chester Arthur sworn in; Booker T. Washington founds Tuskegee Normal and Industrial Institute in Alabama

1887 Interstate Commerce Commission created

1885 — 1889 First Pan-American Congress

1890 National Woman Suffrage Association created; Sherman Antitrust Act; Wyoming enters the Union as the first state to give women the vote; Sherman Silver Purchase Act; McKinley Tariff; Southern and Northwestern Alliances adopt Ocala Demands; Mahan's *The Influence of Sea Power upon History, 1660–1793* published

1890 — 1892 Populist party formed; Grover Cleveland elected president

1893 Panic of 1893; Sherman Silver Purchase Act repealed; Anti-Saloon League created; controversy over annexation of Hawaii

1895 — 1894 Coxey's Army marches on Washington to demand public works for unemployed

1895 National Municipal League founded; Venezuelan boundary dispute; Martí revives Cuban revolution

1896 League for the Protection of the Family organized; William McKinley elected president

1900 — 1898 Sinking of the USS *Maine*; war with Spain; Teller Amendment; Dewey captures the Philippines; Tampa riots; Treaty of Paris; Hawaii formally annexed; Anti-Imperialist League established

1899–1902 Philippine insurrection

1899 First open-door notes

1900 Boxer Rebellion; second open-door notes; Foraker Act establishes civil government in Puerto Rico

1905 — 1903 W. E. B. Du Bois's *The Souls of Black Folk* published

1909 National Association for the Advancement of Colored People founded

1909 —

Quitting time, March 25, 1911. The long day was about to end at the Triangle Shirtwaist Company near Washington Square at the lower end of Manhattan. The deafening whir of some 1500 sewing machines would soon be silenced as hundreds of workers—mostly young immigrant women—were set free. To some, quitting time seemed like an emancipation. Twelve-hour days in stifling, crowded workrooms, weekly paychecks of only $3 to $15, fines for the tiniest mistakes, deductions for needle and thread, even for electricity, made the young seamstresses angry. Two years earlier, their frustration had boiled over into an industrywide strike for better wages and working conditions. Despite a union victory, the only change visible at Triangle was that every morning the doors were locked to keep workers in and labor organizers out.

The fire broke out in the lofts as the workers were leaving their machines. In minutes the top stories were ablaze. Terrified seamstresses groped through the black smoke, only to find exits locked or clogged with bodies. All but one of the few working fire escapes collapsed. When the fire trucks arrived, horrified firefighters discovered that their ladders could not reach the top stories. Children, their hair on fire, jumped to their deaths. "Spectators saw again and again pitiable companionships formed in the instant of death—girls who placed their arms around each other as they leaped," read one news story. Their bodies hit the sidewalk with a sickening thud or were spiked on the iron guard rails. One hundred forty-six people died, most of them young immigrant women. In far-off Russia and Poland, news of the disaster sent families into spasms of grief. "Most of these old parents had an idea of America as one big town," explained one immigrant. "Each of them was almost sure that their daughter was a victim of that terrible catastrophe."

A few days later 80,000 New Yorkers joined the silent funeral procession snaking slowly up Fifth Avenue in the rain. A quarter of a million watched. At the Metropolitan Opera House, union leader Rose Schneiderman told a rally, "This is not the first time that girls have been burned alive in the city. Every year thousands of us are maimed." A special state commission investigated the tragedy. Over the next four years its recommendations produced 56 state laws regulating fire safety, hours, machinery, and home work. They amounted to the most far-reaching labor code in the country.

The Triangle fire shocked the nation and underscored a widespread fear: modern industrial society had created profound strains, widespread misery, and deep class divisions. Corporations grew to unimagined size, bought and sold legislators, dictated the terms of their own profit. Men, women, and children worked around the clock in unsafe factories for wages that barely supported them. In cities across America, tenement-bred diseases took innocent lives. Criminals threatened people and property, while saloons tied the working poor to dishonest political bosses. Even among the middle class, inflation was shrinking wallets at the rate of 3 percent a

The Progressive Era

preview • The first truly broad-based, national reform movement, Progressivism addressed problems arising out of industrialization, urbanization, and immigration. Led by members of the urban middle class—many of them women—progressives were moderate modernizers who looked to bring order and efficiency as well as social justice to economic and political life. During the presidencies of Theodore Roosevelt and Woodrow Wilson, they established the modern, activist state.

By 1900 a wave of corporate mergers led muckraking reformers to use imagery like this grasping octopus, by George Luks, to dramatize the evils of monopoly. Progressives sought to counter the new powers of industrial society by invigorating government.

year. "It was a world of greed," concluded one garment worker; "the human being didn't mean anything."

But human beings did mean something to followers of an influential reform movement sweeping the country. Progressivism had emerged as a political force in the mid-1890s and would continue to shape politics through World War I. The movement sprang from many impulses, mixing a liberal concern for the poor and working class with conservative efforts to stabilize business and avoid social chaos. But liberal or conservative, most progressives shared a desire to soften the harsher aspects of industrialization, urbanization, and immigration.

Progressivism thus began in the cities, where the wellspring of misery was fullest, political corruption deepest, and social division clearest. It was organized by an angry, idealistic middle class and percolated up from neighborhoods to city halls, state capitals, and finally, to Washington. Though usually pursued through politics, the goals of progressives were broadly social—to create a "good society" where people could live decently, harmoniously, and prosperously, along middle-class lines.

Unlike past reformers, progressives saw government as a protector, not an oppressor. Only government possessed the resources for the broad-based reforms they sought. Progressivism spawned the modern activist state, with its capacity to regulate the economy and manage society. And because American society had

In 1911 the fiery deaths of 146 people at the Triangle Shirtwaist Company shocked the nation. Firefighters arrived within minutes, but their ladders could not reach the top stories. Trapped by locked doors, those who failed to escape perished within or leaped to their deaths on the streets below. Following the horrifying episode, New York enacted the most ambitious labor code in the country.

become so interdependent, progressivism became the first nationwide reform movement. No political party monopolized it; no single group controlled it. It flowered in the presidencies of Republican Theodore Roosevelt and Democrat Woodrow Wilson. In 1912 it even gave birth to its own party, the Progressive, or "Bull Moose," party. But by then progressivism had filtered well beyond politics into every realm of American life.

The Roots of Progressive Reform

Families turned from their homes; an army of unemployed on the roads; hunger, strikes, and bloody violence across the country—the wrenching depression of 1893 forced Americans to take a hard look at their new industrial order. They found common complaints that cut across lines of class, religion, and ethnicity. If streetcar companies raised fares while service deteriorated, if food processors doctored their canned goods with harmful additives, if politicians skimmed money from the public till, everyone suffered. And no one could stop it alone.

Aims of progressives

The result was not a coherent progressive movement but a set of loosely connected goals. Some progressives fought to make government itself efficient and honest. Others called for greater regulation of business and a more orderly economy. Some sought social justice for the poor and working classes; others, social welfare to protect children, women, and consumers. Still other progressives looked to purify society by outlawing alcohol and drugs, stamping out prostitution and slums, and restricting the flood of new immigrants.

Paternalistic by nature, progressives often imposed their solutions, no matter what the less "enlightened" poor or oppressed saw as their own best interests. Then, too, reformers acted partly out of nostalgia. In a rapidly changing world, they wanted to redeem such traditional American values as democracy, opportunity for the individual, and the spirit of public service. Yet if the ends of progressives were traditional, their means were distinctly modern. They used the systems and methods of the new industrial order—the latest techniques of organization, management, and science—to fight its excesses.

counterpoint

Historians writing during the progressive era depicted progressivism as progressives them-selves did: an idealistic, democratic crusade of the "good people" against the "bad interests" to curb big business, fight political corruption, and promote social justice. A later generation of historians, examining individual progressives, concluded that their motives were far less idealistic. They found progressives to be a small group of once-powerful, upper-middle-class families of merchants, clergy, and landholders anxious to regain the status and power they had lost to rising industrialists, corporate executives, and urban political bosses.

To explain the often strong support of business for many progressive reforms, historians of the New Left have portrayed progressivism as the triumph of conservatism, whose aim it was to protect corporations from stricter regulation and competition. Still others have looked at pro-gressivism as a widespread effort by the new middle class of professionals, business leaders, and others to secure their power by bringing order and efficiency to the new industrial economy.

Historians with interests in women, consumers, and African Americans have all found in progressivism an opportunity for these groups to advance their separate, sometimes con-flicting goals. Perhaps the most useful interpretation comes from those historians who see progressivism as part of the broad process of adjustment to the new industrial order. They emphasize the weakening of political parties and the growing influence of interest groups of workers, industrialists, consumers, and others who campaigned for the reforms they wanted.

The Progressive System of Beliefs

Progressives were moderate modernizers—reformers, not revolutionaries. They ac-cepted the American system as sound, only in need of adjustment. Many drew on the increasingly popular Darwinian theories of evolution to buttress this gradual ap-proach to change. With its notion of slowly changing species, evolution undermined the acceptance of fixed principles that had guided social thought in the Victorian era. Progressives saw an evolving landscape and ever-shifting values. They denied the old Calvinist doctrine of inborn sinfulness and instead saw people as having a greater potential for good than for evil.

Yet progressives had seen the mean side of industrialism and somehow had to explain the existence of evil and wrongdoing. Most agreed that they were "largely, if not wholly, products of society or environment." People went wrong, wrote one progressive, because of "what happens to them." By changing what happened, the human potential for good could be released. As reformer Jane Addams explained, "what has been called 'the extraordinary pliability of human nature'" made it "im-possible to set any bounds to the moral capabilities which might unfold under ideal civic and educational conditions."

With an eye to results, progressives asked not "Is it true?" but "Does it work?" Philosopher Charles Peirce called this new way of thinking "pragmatism." William James, the Harvard psychologist, became its most famous popularizer. For James, pragmatism meant "looking towards last things, fruits, consequences, facts."

Pragmatism

The Pragmatic Approach

Pragmatism led educators, social scientists, and lawyers to adopt new approaches to reform. John Dewey, the master educator of the progressive era, believed that en-vironment shaped the patterns of human thought. Instead of demanding mindless memorization of abstract and unconnected facts, Dewey tried to "make each one of our schools an embryonic community life." At his School of Pedagogy, founded in 1896 with his wife, Alice, he let students unbolt their desks from the floor, move about, and learn by doing so they could train for real life.

Behaviorism

Psychologist John B. Watson believed that human behavior could be shaped at will. "Give me a dozen healthy infants," he wrote, ". . . and my own specified world to bring them up in, and I'll guarantee to take any one at random and train him to become any specialist I might select, doctor, lawyer, artist, merchant, chief, and yes, even beggarman and thief." "Behaviorism" swept the social sciences and later advertising, where Watson himself eventually landed.

John Dewey, progressive philosopher and educator.

Lawyers and legal theorists applied their own blend of pragmatism and behaviorism. Justice Oliver Wendell Holmes Jr., appointed to the Supreme Court in 1902, rejected the idea that the traditions of law were constant and universal. "Long ago I decided I was not God," said Holmes. Law was a living organism to be interpreted according to experience and the needs of a changing society.

That was what Denver Judge Ben Lindsey did when he handed down a verdict. Presiding over one of the first juvenile courts in the country, the "Kids' Judge" examined the home life of youthful offenders before he ruled. Often he discovered poverty, illness, and joblessness. So he used the new authority of his court to remove delinquents from dysfunctional homes and make them wards of the state. In several states, supervised probation replaced suspended sentences to ensure that bad habits stayed broken.

Sociological jurisprudence

This environmental view of the law, known as "sociological jurisprudence," found a skilled practitioner in Louis Brandeis. Shaken by the brutal suppression of the Homestead steel strike of 1892, Brandeis quit his corporate practice and proclaimed himself the "people's lawyer." The law must "guide by the light of reason," he wrote, by which he meant bringing everyday life to bear in any court case. Whereas older court opinions had been based largely on legal precedent, progressives asked courts to look at the world around them and realize that society had undergone changes so fundamental that many precedents of the past no longer applied. Past and present must stand on equal footing in interpreting the law, they said.

Brandeis Brief

Brandeis had a chance to test his practical principles when laundry owner Curt Muller challenged an Oregon law that limited his laundresses to working 10 hours a day. Brandeis defended the statute before the Supreme Court in 1908. His famous legal brief in *Muller v. Oregon* contained 102 pages describing the damaging effects of long hours on working women and only 15 pages of legal precedents. The Supreme Court upheld Oregon's right to limit the working hours of laborers and thus legitimized the "Brandeis Brief."

The Progressive Method

Seeing the nation riven by conflict, progressives tried to restore a sense of community through the ideal of a single public interest. Christian ethics were the guide, to be applied after using the latest scientific methods to gather and analyze data about a social problem. The modern corporation furnished an appealing model for organization. Like corporate executives, progressives relied on careful management, coordinated systems, and specialized bureaucracies to carry out reforms.

Between 1902 and 1912 a new breed of journalists investigated wrongdoers, named them in print, and described their misdeeds in vivid detail. Most exposés began as articles in mass-circulation magazines. *McClure's* magazine stirred controversy and boosted circulation when it sent reporter Lincoln Steffens to uncover the crooked ties between business and politics. Steffens's "Tweed Days in St. Louis" appeared in the October 1902 issue of *McClure's* and was followed in the November issue by Ida M. Tarbell's *History of the Standard Oil Company,* another stinging, well-researched indictment. Soon a full-blown literature of exposure was covering every ill from unsafe food to child labor.

A disgusted Theodore Roosevelt thought the new reporters had gone too far and called them "muckrakers," after the man who raked up filth in the seventeenth-century classic *Pilgrim's Progress.* But by documenting dishonesty and blight, muckrakers not only aroused people but educated them. No broad reform movement of American institutions would have taken place without them.

Muckrakers

To move beyond exposure to solutions, progressives stressed volunteerism, civic responsibility, and collective action. They drew on the organizational impulse that seemed everywhere to be bringing people together in new interest groups. Between 1890 and 1920 nearly 400 organizations were founded, many to combat the ills of industrial society. Some, like the National Consumers' League, grew out of efforts to promote general causes—in this case protecting consumers and workers from exploitation. Others, such as the National Tuberculosis Association, aimed at a specific problem.

Voluntary organizations

When voluntary action failed, progressives looked to government to protect the public welfare. They mistrusted legislators, who might be controlled by corporate interests or political machines. So they strengthened the executive branch by increasing the power of individual mayors, governors, and presidents. Then they watched those executives carefully.

Progressives also drew on the expertise of the newly professionalized middle class. Confident, cosmopolitan professionals—doctors, engineers, psychiatrists, city planners—mounted campaigns to stamp out venereal disease and dysentery, to reform prisons and asylums, and to beautify cities. At all levels—local, state, federal—new agencies and commissions staffed by impartial experts began to investigate and regulate lobbyists, insurance and railroad companies, public health, even government itself.

Professionals

If progressivism ended in politics, it began with social reform: the need to reach out, to do something to bring the "good

The Search for the Good Society

society" a step closer. Ellen Richards had just such ends in mind in 1890 when she opened the New England Kitchen in downtown Boston. Richards, a chemist and home economist, designed the Kitchen to sell cheap, wholesome food to the working poor. For a few pennies, customers could choose from a nutritious menu, every dish of which had been tested in Richards's laboratory at the Massachusetts Institute of Technology.

The New England Kitchen promoted social as well as nutritional reform. Women freed from the drudgery of cooking could seek gainful employment. And as a "household experiment station" and center for dietary information, the Kitchen tried to educate the poor and Americanize immigrants by showing them how the middle class prepared meals. According to philanthropist Pauline Shaw, it was also a "rival to the saloon." A common belief was that poor diets fostered drinking, especially among the lower classes.

In the end, the New England Kitchen served more as an inexpensive eatery for middle-class working women and students than as a resource for the poor or an

Pattern of reform

agency of Americanization. Still, Ellen Richards's experiment reflected a pattern typical of progressive social reform: the mix of professionalism with uplift of the poor and needy, socially conscious women entering the public arena, the hope of creating a better world along middle-class lines.

Poverty in a New Light

During the 1890s crime reporter and photographer Jacob Riis launched a campaign to introduce middle-class audiences to urban poverty. Writing in vivid detail in *How the Other Half Lives* (1890), Riis brought readers into the teeming tenement. Accompanying the text were shocking photos of poverty-stricken Americans—Riis's "other half." He also used slide shows to publicize their plight. His pictures of slum life appeared artless, merely recording the desperate poverty before the camera. But Riis used them to tell a moralistic story, much the way the earlier English novelist Charles Dickens had used his melodramatic tales to attack the abuses of industrialism in England. People began to see poverty in a new, more sympathetic light, the result less of flawed individuals than of environment.

Naturalism

A haunting naturalism in fiction and painting followed the tradition introduced by Riis's gritty photographic essays. In *McTeague* (1899) and *Sister Carrie* (1900), novelists Frank Norris and Theodore Dreiser spun dark tales of city dwellers struggling to keep body and soul intact. The "Ashcan school" painted urban life in all its grimy realism. Photographer Alfred Stieglitz and painters such as John Sloan and George Bellows chose slums, tenements, and dirty streets as subjects. Poverty began to look less ominous and more heartrending.

Between 1908 and 1914 the Russell Sage Foundation produced six large volumes of facts and figures documenting a vicious cycle of urban poverty that trapped its victims for generations. The children of paupers were likely to be paupers themselves, the reports explained, not because of heredity or sin but because of deprivation.

Social work

A new profession—social work—proceeded from this new view of poverty. Social work developed out of the old settlement house movement (page 652). Like the physicians from whom they drew inspiration, social workers studied hard data to diagnose the problems of their "clients." Unlike nineteenth-century philanthropists, the new social workers refused to do things to or for people. Instead they worked with their clients, enlisting their help to solve their own problems. A social worker's "differential casework" attempted to treat individuals case by case, each according to the way the client had been shaped by environment.

In reality poverty was but a single symptom of many personal and social ills. Most progressives continued to see it as a by-product of political and corporate greed, slum neighborhoods, and "institutions of vice" such as the saloon. Less clear to them was how deeply rooted poverty had become. Simple middle-class goodwill or even the era's most up-to-date scientific treatments were not enough to banish the alcoholism, drug addiction, and mental illness associated with poverty.

Expanding the "Woman's Sphere"

Progressive social reform attracted a great many women seeking what Jane Addams called "the larger life" of public affairs. In the late nineteenth century, women found that protecting their traditional sphere of home and family forced them to move beyond it. Bringing up children, making meals, keeping house, and caring for the sick now involved community decisions about schools, public health, and countless other matters.

By 1900 one-fourth of the non-farm labor force was female. On average, women industrial workers made $3 less a week than did unskilled men. Here, at a Labor Day parade in San Diego in 1910, women demand equal pay for equal work.

Many middle- and upper-middle-class women received their first taste of public life from women's organizations, including mothers' clubs, temperance societies, and church groups. By the turn of the century, some 500 women's clubs boasted over 160,000 members. Through the General Federation of Women's Clubs, they funded libraries and hospitals and supported schools, settlement houses, compulsory education, and child labor laws. Eventually they moved beyond the concerns of home and family to endorse such controversial causes as woman suffrage and unionization. To that list the National Association of Colored Women added the special concerns of African Americans, none more urgent than the fight against lynching.

Women's organizations

The dawn of the century saw the rise of a new generation of women. Longer lived, better educated, and less often married than their mothers, they were also willing to pursue careers for fulfillment. Usually they turned to professions that involved the traditional role of nurturer—nursing, library work, teaching, and settlement house work.

New woman

Custom and prejudice still restricted these new women. The faculty at the Massachusetts Institute of Technology, for example, refused to allow Ellen Richards to pursue a doctorate. Instead they hired her to run the gender-segregated "Woman's Laboratory" for training public school teachers. At the turn of the century, only about 1500 women lawyers practiced in the whole country, and in 1910 women made up barely 6 percent of licensed physicians. That figure rapidly declined as male-dominated medical associations grew in power and discouraged the entry of women.

Despite the often bitter opposition of families, some feminists tried to destroy, not widen, the boundaries of the woman's sphere. In *Women and Economics* (1898) Charlotte Perkins Gilman condemned femininity, marriage, maternity, and domesticity as enslaving and obsolete. She argued for a radically restructured society with large apartment houses, communal child rearing and housekeeping, and cooperative kitchens to free women from economic dependence on men.

Margaret Sanger sought to free women from the bonds of chronic pregnancy. Sanger, a visiting nurse on the Lower East Side of New York, had seen too many poor women overburdened with children, pregnant year after year, with no hope of

Margaret Sanger

escaping the cycle. The consequences were sometimes deadly but always crippling. "Women cannot be on equal footing with men until they have complete control over their reproductive functions," she argued.

The insight came as a revelation one summer evening in 1912 when Sanger was called to the home of a distraught immigrant family on Grand Street. Sadie Sachs, mother of three, had nearly died a year earlier from a self-induced abortion. In an effort to terminate another pregnancy, she had accidentally killed herself. Sanger vowed that night "to do something to change the destiny of mothers whose miseries were as vast as the sky." She became a crusader for what she called "birth control." By distributing information on contraception, she hoped to free women from unwanted pregnancies and the fate of Sadie Sachs.

Single or married, militant or moderate, professional or lay, white or black, more and more middle-class urban women thus became "social housekeepers." From their own homes they turned to the homes of their neighbors and from there to all of society.

Social Welfare

In the "bigger family of the city," as one woman reformer called it, settlement house workers found that they could not care for the welfare of the poor alone. If industrial America, with its sooty factories and overcrowded slums, was to be transformed into the good society, individual acts of charity would have to be supplemented by government. Laws had to be passed and agencies created to promote social welfare, including improved housing, workplaces, parks, and playgrounds; the abolition of child labor; and the enactment of eight-hour-day laws for working women.

By 1910 the more than 400 settlement houses across the nation had organized into a loose affiliation, with settlement workers ready to help shape government policy. Often it was women who led the way. Julia Lathrop, a Vassar College graduate, spent 20 years at Jane Addams's Hull House before becoming the first head of the new federal Children's Bureau in 1912. By then two-thirds of the states had adopted some child labor legislation, although loopholes exempted countless youngsters from coverage. Under Lathrop's leadership, Congress was persuaded to pass the Keating-Owen Act (1916), forbidding goods manufactured by children to cross state lines.*

Florence Kelley, who had also worked at Hull House, spearheaded a similar campaign in Illinois to protect women workers by limiting their workday to eight hours. As general secretary of the National Consumers' League, she also organized boycotts of companies that treated employees inhumanely. Eventually most states enacted laws restricting the number of hours women could work.

Keating-Owen Act (margin note)

Woman Suffrage

No one had ever seen pickets in front of the White House before, let alone picketing women. But there they were, starting on January 10, 1917. From ten in the morning until half past five in the evening, they stood stiff and silent at the front gates, six days a week, rain or shine. The "Silent Sentinels," as they called themselves, let their banners speak for them. "Mr. President," read one, "What Will You Do For Woman Suffrage?" Another quoted the words of Inez Milholland. Only a

---

*The Supreme Court struck down the law in 1918 as an improper regulation of local labor; nonetheless, the law focused greater attention on the abuses of child labor.

year earlier, she had collapsed at a suffrage rally in Los Angeles as she rose to speak in favor of granting women the right to vote. "Mr. President," she had said with her dying breath, "How long must women wait for liberty?"

Ever since the conference for women's rights held at Seneca Falls in 1848, women reformers had pressed for the right to vote on the grounds of equal opportunity and simple justice. Progressives embraced woman suffrage by stressing what they saw as the practical results: reducing political corruption, protecting the home, and increasing the voting power of native-born whites. The "purer sensibilities" of women—an ideal held by Victorians and progressives alike—would help cleanse the political process of selfishness and corruption, while their sheer numbers would keep the political balance tilted away from immigrant newcomers.

The suffrage movement benefited, too, from new leadership. In 1900 Carrie Chapman Catt became president of the National American Woman Suffrage Association, founded by Susan B. Anthony in 1890. Politically astute and a skilled organizer, Catt mapped a grassroots strategy of education and persuasion from state to state. She called it "the winning plan." As the map (page 716) shows, victories came first in the West, where women and men had already forged a more equal partnership to overcome the hardships of frontier life. By 1914, 10 western states (and Kansas) had granted women the vote in state elections, as Illinois had in presidential elections.

The slow pace of progress drove some suffragists to militancy. The shift in tactics had its origins abroad. In England, the campaign for woman suffrage had peaked after 1900, when Emmeline Pankhurst and her daughters Christabel and Sylvia turned to violence to make their point that women should be given the right to vote. They and their followers chained themselves to the visitors' gallery in the House of Commons and slashed paintings in museums. When those tactics failed, they invaded the time-honored bastion of British manhood—the golf course—and scrawled "VOTES FOR WOMEN" in acid on the greens. They smashed the windows of department stores, broke up political meetings, even burned the houses of members of Parliament, all in an effort to convince their opponents of the seriousness of their purpose.

British authorities responded to the violence by arresting suffragists and throwing them in jail, Emmeline Pankhurst included. When the women went on hunger strikes in prison, wardens tied them down, held open their mouths with wooden clamps, and fed them by force through tubes placed down their throats and noses. Rather than permit the protesters to die as martyrs, Parliament passed the Cat and Mouse Act, a statute of doubtful constitutionality that allowed officials to release starving prisoners, then rearrest them once they returned to health.

Among the British suffragists was a small American with large, determined eyes. In 1907, barely out of her teens, Alice Paul had gone to England to join the suffrage crusade. When asked why she had enlisted, she recalled her Quaker upbringing. "One of their principles . . . is equality of the sexes," she explained. "I never had any other idea." Paul marched arm-in-arm with British suffragists through the streets of London and more than once was imprisoned and refused to eat. In 1910, she returned to the United States and brought the aggressive tactics with her, inspiriting American suffragists with new vigor. That year, Washington state granted women the right to vote, followed by California in 1911, and Kansas, Oregon, and Arizona in 1912. In 1913, Paul organized 5000 women to parade in protest at President Woodrow Wilson's

"BEAN HIM!"*

*Note for ignorami—Hit him in the head

In this cartoon from a 1914 issue of *Life* magazine, a burly feminist catcher tells a suffragist pitcher to "bean" the male batter at the plate.

Militant suffragists

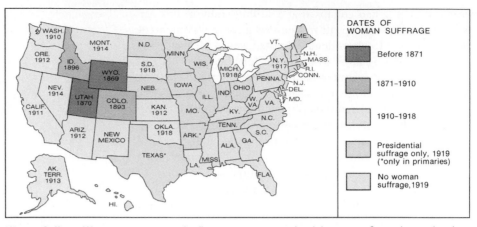

Woman Suffrage Western states were the first to grant women the right to vote. Sparsely populated and more egalitarian than the rest of the nation, the West was used to women participating fully in settlement and work. Other sections of the country, notably the Midwest, granted women partial suffrage that included voting for school boards and taxes. Suffragists encountered the most intractable resistance in the South, where rigid codes of social conduct elevated women symbolically but shackled them practically.

inauguration. Wilson himself was skeptical of women voting and favored a state-by-state approach to the issue. Half a million people watched as a near-riot ensued. Paul and other suffragists were hauled to jail, stripped naked, and thrown into cells with prostitutes.

In 1914, Paul broke with the more moderate National American Woman Suffrage Association and formed the Congressional Union, dedicated to enacting national woman suffrage at any cost through a constitutional amendment. She soon allied her organization with western women voters in the militant National Woman's party in 1917. It was also Paul who organized the Silent Sentinels at the White House the same year, when the president refused to see any more delegations of women urging a constitutional amendment. On October 20, 1917, Paul was arrested at the gates of the White House and received a seven-month sentence. Guards dragged her off to a cell block in the Washington jail, where she and others refused to eat. Prison officials declared her insane, but a public outcry over her treatment soon led to her release.

Such repression only widened public support for woman suffrage in the United States and elsewhere. So did the contributions of women to the First World War at home and abroad (see Chapter 23). In the wake of the war, Great Britain granted women (over age thirty) the right to vote in 1918, Germany and Austria in 1919, **Nineteenth Amendment** and the United States in 1920 through the Nineteenth Amendment. Overnight the number of eligible voters in the country doubled.

Controlling the Masses

"Observe immigrants," wrote one American in 1912. "You are struck by the fact that from ten to twenty percent are hirsute, low-browed, big-faced persons of obviously low mentality. . . . They clearly belong in skins, in wattled huts at the close of the Ice Age." The writer was neither an uneducated fanatic nor a stern opponent of change. He was Professor Edward A. Ross, a progressive from Madison, Wisconsin, who prided himself on his scientific study of sociology.

Faced with the chaos and corruption of urban life, more than a few progressives feared they were losing control of their country. Saloons and dance halls lured youngsters and impoverished laborers; prostitutes walked the streets; vulgar amusements pandered to the uneducated. Strange Old World cultures clashed with "all-American" customs, and races jostled uneasily. The city challenged middle-class reformers to convert this riot of diversity into a more uniform society. To maintain control progressives sometimes moved beyond education and regulation and sought restrictive laws to control the masses.

Stemming the Immigrant Tide

A rising tide of nonwhite and immigrant Americans, many settling in cities, aggravated the fears of more than a few progressives and other native-born whites. During the 1890s, segregation laws had already begun to restrict the opportunities of African Americans in the South. After 1900, the rhetoric of reform was used to support white supremacy. Southern progressives won office by promising to disfranchise black southerners, in order to break the power of corrupt political machines that rested on the black vote, much as northern machines marshaled the immigrant vote.

The South was hardly the only region in which discrimination flourished. Asians, Latinos, and Indians faced similar curbs in the West, as did the new arrivals from southern and eastern Europe in the North. The sharp increase in immigration especially troubled native-born Americans, including reformers anxious over the changing ethnic complexion of the country. In northern cities progressives often succeeded in reducing immigrant voting power by increasing residency requirements.

A new science called "eugenics" lent respectability to the idea that newcomers were biologically inferior. Eugenicists believed that heredity largely shaped all human behavior, and they therefore advocated selective breeding for human improvement. By 1914 more magazine articles discussed eugenics than slums, tenements, and living standards combined. In *The Passing of the Great Race* (1916), upper-crust New Yorker and amateur zoologist Madison Grant helped popularize the notion that the "lesser breeds" threatened to "mongrelize" America. So powerful was the pull of eugenics that it captured the support of many reformers, including birth control advocate Margaret Sanger.

Eugenics

More enlightened reformers such as Jane Addams stressed the cultural "gifts" immigrants brought with them: folk rituals, dances, music, and handicrafts. With characteristic paternalism, these reformers hoped to "Americanize" the foreign-born (the term was newly coined) by teaching them middle-class ways. Education was one key. Progressive educator Peter Roberts, for example, developed a lesson plan for the Young Men's Christian Association that taught immigrants to dress, tip, buy groceries, and vote.

Americanization

Less tolerant citizens sought to restrict immigration as a way of reasserting control and achieving social harmony. Though white, Protestant, and American-born, these nativists were usually not progressives themselves, but they did employ progressive methods of organization, investigation, education, and legislation. Active since the 1890s, the Immigration Restriction League pressed Congress in 1907 to require a literacy test for admission into the United States. Presidents Taft and Wilson vetoed it in 1913 and 1915, but Congress overrode Wilson's second veto in 1917, when war fever raised defensive nationalism to a new peak.

Literacy test

Daily Lives

PUBLIC SPACE/ PRIVATE SPACE

"Amusing the Million"

On a sunny May morning in 1903, 45,000 people poured through the gates of Luna Park at Coney Island, just south of Brooklyn. What they saw on opening day amazed them: "a storybook land of trellises, columns, domes, minarets, lagoons, and lofty aerial flights." A huge dolphin fountain gushed water from the base of the main tower. Barkers beckoned them into a Venetian city, a Japanese garden, and a bustling Asian Indian celebration. They could hop aboard the "Switchback" Railroad, a forerunner of the roller coaster, or career on flat-bottom boats down a steep incline into the "Shoot-the-Chutes" lagoon. They could even witness a disaster. In "Fire and Flames," mock firefighters doused a four-story blaze as mock residents jumped from top floors to safety nets below—all on cue. Those who spent their days in crowded tenements rolling cigars or sleeping nights in stuffy apartments might well blink in awe as a quarter of a million electric lights, strung like glittering pearls across the buildings, turned night into enchanted day. This was "a world removed—shut away from the sordid clatter and turmoil of the streets," such a place "as Aladdin never dreamed."

Coney Island was but one of a host of similar parks that popped up across the country at the turn of the century. Soaring urban populations, increases in leisure time, more spending money, and new trolley systems that made for cheap excursions from the city led to the opening of Boston's Paragon Park, Cleveland's Euclid Beach, Atlanta's Ponce de Leon Park, and Los Angeles's Venice Beach.

All traded in entertainment, but of a sort new to city dwellers. Earlier Victorian reformers had promoted two models of public entertainment: the spacious city park and the grand public exposition. Both were meant to instruct as well as amuse. Their planners hoped to reduce urban disorder by raising public taste and refining public conduct. When it opened in

Gondolas in Venice Canal, Venice, California

The Venice Amusement Park in California was meant to conjure up Venice, Italy, complete with a network of canals. (Note the gondola in the foreground.) The founders dubbed Venice Park "the Coney Island of the Pacific."

The Curse of Demon Rum

Tied closely to concern over immigrants was an attack on saloons. Part of a broader crusade to clean up cities, the antisaloon campaign drew strength from the century-old drive to lessen the consumption of alcohol. Women made up a disproportionate number of alcohol reformers. The temperance movement reflected their growing campaign to storm male domains—in this case the saloon—and to contain male violence, particularly the wife and child abuse associated with drinking.

By 1900 the dangers of an alcoholic republic seemed all too real. Alcohol consumption had risen to an annual rate of more than two gallons per person. Over half of Boston and Chicago visited a bar at least once a day. Often political bosses owned saloons or conducted their business there. To alcohol reformers, taverns and saloons thus seemed at the center of many social problems—gambling and

1858, New York City's Central Park became a model pastoral retreat in the midst of the city. Its rustic paths, tranquil lakes, and woodsy views were designed as respites from the chaos of urban life. According to designer Frederick Law Olmstead, such vistas would have "a distinctly harmonizing and refining influence" on even the rudest fellow.

The World's Columbian Exposition of 1893 in Chicago also reflected an elevating vision of society. Its neoclassical buildings were designed to instruct citizens about their country's marvelous wealth and industry (see pages 668–669). At the center of the exposition stood a 100-foot statue, "The Republic," a toga-draped figure holding an eagle perched on a globe. Some amusement parks, like Venice Beach's, mimicked the style of the exposition.

But it did not escape the amusement park operators that people wanted to have fun more than they wished to be enlightened. At the Columbian Exposition, the amusements section, a mile-long strip of theaters, restaurants, sideshows, and rides, had easily lured more people than did the free public exhibits. As one owner put it, parks were in the business of "amusing the million." Coney Island's Luna Park drew 5 million paying customers in a single season.

Jostling with crowds, eating ice cream and hot dogs, riding Shoot-the-Chutes, young working men and women, single, in couples, or married, even the newest immigrant could feel gloriously free and independent, gloriously American. A sense of solidarity drew the mostly working-class crowds together, and the zaniness of the setting loosened social restraints. "I have heard some of the high people with whom I have been living say that Coney Island is not tony," reported one 20-year-old servant girl. "The trouble is that these high people don't know how to dance. I have to laugh when I see them at their balls and parties. If only I could get out on the floor and show them how— they would be astonished." In this girl's mind, the Victorian values of sober industry, thrift, and orderly conduct could hardly compete with the democratic abandon and gaiety of the new amusement parks. The parks heralded the rise of mass culture, invading public space with the private dreams of ordinary people.

prostitution, political corruption, drug trafficking, unemployment, and poverty. Few reformers recognized the complex cycle of social decay that produced such problems, fewer still the role of saloons as "workingmen's clubs." The saloon was often the only place to cash a check, find out about jobs, eat a cheap meal, or take a bath.

Reformers considered a national ban on drinking unrealistic and intrusive. Instead they concentrated on prohibiting the sale of alcohol at local and state levels and attacked businesses that profited from it. Led by the Anti-Saloon League (1893), a massive publicity campaign bombarded citizens with pamphlets and advertisements. Doctors cited scientific evidence linking alcohol to cirrhosis, heart disease, and insanity. Social workers connected drink to the deterioration of the family; employers, to accidents on the job and lost efficiency.

Anti-Saloon League

By 1917 three out of four Americans lived in "dry" counties. Nearly two-thirds of the states had adopted laws outlawing the manufacture and sale of alcohol. Not all progressives were prohibitionists, but the many who were sighed with relief at having taken the profit out of human pain and corruption.

Prostitution

No urban vice worried reformers more than prostitution. In their eyes it was a social evil that threatened young city women with a fate much worse than death. The Chicago Vice Commission of 1910 estimated that 5000 full-time and 10,000 occasional prostitutes plied their trade in the city. Other cities, small and large, reported similar numbers.

An unlikely group of reformers united to fight the vice: feminists who wanted husbands to be as chaste as their wives, public health officials worried about the spread of sexually transmitted disease, and immigration restrictionists who regarded the growth of prostitution as yet another sign of corrupt newcomers. Progressives condemned prostitution but saw the problem in economic and environmental terms. "Poverty causes prostitution," concluded the Illinois Vice Commission in 1916. On average, prostitutes earned five times the income of factory workers.

The "Inebriate's Express," loaded with drunken riders, is heading straight for hell. This detail from a chromolithograph, published around 1900, was typical of Victorian-era responses to the problems posed by alcohol. To the all-seeing eye of the omnipotent God, faith, hope, charity, and the Bible are sufficient to cure the problems of drinking.

Some reformers saw more active agents at work. Rumors spread of a vast and profitable "white slave trade." Men armed with hypodermic needles were said to be lurking about streetcars, amusement parks, and dance halls in search of young women. Although the average female rider of the streetcar was hardly in danger of abduction, in every city there could be found cribs with locked doors where women were held captive and forced into prostitution. By conservative estimates they comprised some 10 percent of all prostitutes.

As real abuses blended with sensationalism, Congress passed the Mann Act (1910), prohibiting the interstate transport of women for immoral purposes. By 1918 reformers succeeded in banning previously tolerated red-light districts in most cities. Once again, progressives went after those businesses that, like the liquor trade, made money from misery.

 ## The Politics of Municipal and State Reform

Reform the system. In the end, so many urban problems seemed to come back to the premise that government had to be overhauled. Jane Addams learned as much outside the doors of her beloved Hull House in Chicago. For months during the early 1890s, garbage had piled up in the streets. The filth and stench drove Addams and her fellow workers to city hall in protest—700 times in one summer—but to no avail. In Chicago, as elsewhere, corrupt city bosses had made garbage collection a plum to be awarded to the company that paid them the most for it.

In desperation, Addams herself submitted a bid for garbage removal in the ward. When it was thrown out on a technicality, she won an appointment as garbage inspector. For almost a year she dogged collection carts, but boss politics kept things dirty. So Addams ran candidates in 1896 and 1898 against local ward boss Johnny Powers. They lost, but Addams kept up the fight for honest government and social reform—at city hall, in the Illinois legislature, and finally in Washington. Politics turned out to be the only way to clean things up.

The Reformation of the Cities

For middle-class reformers, the urban battleground furnished the first test of political reform. And a series of colorful and independent mayors demonstrated that cities could be run humanely without changing the structure of government.

In Detroit, shoe magnate Hazen Pingree turned the mayor's office into an instrument of reform when elected in 1889. By the end of his fourth term, Detroit had new parks and public baths, fairer taxes, ownership of the local light plant, and a work-relief program for victims of the depression of 1893. In 1901, Cleveland Mayor Tom Johnson launched a similar reform campaign. Before he was through, municipal franchises had been limited to a fraction of their previous 99-year terms and the city ran the utility company. By 1915 nearly two out of three cities in the nation had copied some form of this "gas and water socialism" to control the runaway prices of utility companies.

Jane Addams founded her settlement at Hull House in Chicago because she was convinced, like many progressives, that reform must be practical, arising out of the needs of individuals within a community. As Addams continued her campaigns, she also looked beyond the local neighborhood to reform political structures of municipal and state governments.

Tragedy dramatized the need to alter the very structure of government. On a hot summer night in 1900 a tidal wave from the Gulf of Mexico smashed the port city of Galveston, Texas. Floods killed one of every six residents. The municipal government sank into confusion and political wrangling. In reaction business leaders won approval of a new charter that replaced the mayor and city council with a powerful commission. Each of five commissioners controlled a municipal department, and together they ran the city. By 1920 nearly 400 cities had adopted the plan. Expert commissioners enhanced efficiency and helped to check party rule in municipal government.

In other cities, elected officials appointed an outside expert, or "city manager," to run things. The first was hired in Staunton, Virginia, in 1908. Within a decade, 45 cities had them. At lower levels experts took charge of services: engineers oversaw utilities; accountants, finances; doctors and nurses, public health; specially trained firefighters and police, the safety of citizens. Broad civic reforms attempted to break the corrupt alliance between companies doing business with the city and the bosses who controlled the wards. Citywide elections replaced the old ward system, and civil service laws helped create a nonpartisan bureaucracy. Political machines and ethnic voters lost power, while city government gained efficiency.

City-manager plan

Progressivism in the States

"Whenever we try to do anything, we run up against the charter," complained the reform mayor of Schenectady, New York. Charters granted by state governments defined the powers of cities. The rural interests that generally dominated state legislatures rarely gave cities adequate authority to levy taxes, set voting requirements, draw up budgets, or legislate reforms. State legislatures too found themselves under the

Weaknesses of city government

On the state level, progressives made their greatest impact in Wisconsin, where Robert La Follette led the fight to regulate railroads, control corruption, and expand the civil service. In trying to do an end run around political party bosses, he used his publication, *La Follette's Magazine*, to reach ordinary Americans directly.

influence of business interests, party machines, and county courthouse rings. Reformers therefore tried to place their candidates where they could do some good—in the governors' mansions.

State progressivism enjoyed its greatest success in the Midwest, under the leadership of Robert La Follette of Wisconsin. La Follette first won election to Congress in 1885 by toeing the Republican line of high tariffs and the gold standard. When a Republican boss offered him a bribe in a railroad case, La Follette pledged to break "the power of this corrupt influence." In 1900 he won the governorship of Wisconsin as an uncommonly independent Republican.

Over the next six years "Battle Bob" La Follette made Wisconsin, in the words of Theodore Roosevelt, "the laboratory of democracy." La Follette's "Wisconsin idea" produced the most comprehensive set of state reforms in American history. There were new laws regulating railroads, controlling corruption, and expanding the civil service. His direct primary weakened the hold of party bosses by transferring nominations from the backrooms of party conventions and caucuses to the voters at large. Among La Follette's notable "firsts" were a state income tax, a state commission to oversee factory safety and sanitation, and a Legislative Reference Bureau at the University of Wisconsin. University-trained experts poured into state government.

Other states copied the Wisconsin idea or hatched their own. By 1916 all but three had direct primary laws. To cut the power of party organizations and make officeholders directly responsible to the public, progressives worked for three additional reforms: initiative (voter introduction of legislation), referendum (voter enactment or repeal of laws), and recall (voter-initiated removal of elected officials). By 1912 a dozen states had adopted initiative and referendum, seven recall. A year later the Seventeenth Amendment to the Constitution permitted the direct election of senators, previously selected by state legislatures.

Almost every state established regulatory commissions with the power to hold public hearings and to examine company books and question officials. Some could set maximum prices and rates. Yet it was not always easy to define, let alone serve, the "public good." All too often commissioners found themselves refereeing battles within industries—between carriers and shippers, for example—rather than between what progressives called "the interests" and "the people." Regulators had to rely on the advice of experts drawn from the business community itself. Many commissions thus became captured by the industries they regulated.

Social welfare received special attention from the states. The lack of workers' compensation for injury, illness, or death on the job had long drawn fire from reformers and labor leaders. American courts still operated on the common-law assumption that employees accepted the risks of work. Workers or their families could collect damages only if they proved employer negligence. Most accident victims received nothing. In 1902 Maryland finally adopted the first workers' compensation act. By 1916, most states required insurance for factory accidents and over half had employer liability laws. Thirteen states also provided pensions for widows with dependent children.

More and more it was machine politicians and women's organizations that pressed for working-class reforms. Despite the progressive attack on machine politics, political bosses survived, in part by adapting the climate of reform to the needs of their working-class constituents. After the Triangle fire of 1911, for example, it was Tammany Democrats Robert F. Wagner and Alfred E. Smith who led the fight for a new labor code.

This working-class "urban liberalism" also found advocates among women's associations, especially those concerned with mothers, children, and working women. The Federation of Women's Clubs led the fight for mothers' pensions (a forerunner of aid to dependent children). When in 1912 the National Consumers' League and other women's groups succeeded in establishing the Children's Bureau, it was the first federal welfare agency and the only female-run national bureau in the world. At a time when women lacked the vote, they nonetheless sowed the seeds of the welfare state as they helped to make urban liberalism a powerful instrument of social reform.

Seeds of the welfare state

On September 6, 1901, at the Pan-American Exposition in Buffalo, New York, Leon Czolgosz stood nervously in line.

Progressivism Goes to Washington

He was waiting among well-wishers to meet President William McKinley. Unemployed and bent on murder, Czolgosz shuffled toward McKinley. As the president reached out, Czolgosz fired two bullets into his chest. McKinley slumped into a chair. Eight days later the president was dead. The mantle of power passed to Theodore Roosevelt. At 42 he was the youngest president ever to hold office.

Roosevelt's entry into the White House was a political accident, as he himself acknowledged. Party leaders had seen the weak office of vice president as a way of removing him from power, but the tragedy in Buffalo foiled their plans. "It is a dreadful thing to come into the presidency this way," he remarked, "but it would be a far worse thing to be morbid about it." Surely progressivism would have come to Washington without Theodore Roosevelt, and while there he was never its most daring advocate. In many ways he was quite conservative. He saw reform as a way to avoid more radical change. Yet without Roosevelt, progressivism would have had neither the broad popular appeal nor the buoyancy he gave it.

TR

TR, as so many Americans called him, was the scion of seven generations of wealthy, aristocratic New Yorkers. A sickly boy, he built his body through rigorous exercise, sharpened his mind through constant study, and pursued a life so strenuous that few could keep up. He learned to ride and shoot, roped cattle in the Dakota Badlands, mastered judo, and later in life climbed the Matterhorn, hunted African game, and explored the Amazon.

In 1880, driven by an urge to lead and serve, Roosevelt won election to the New York State Assembly. In rapid succession he became a civil service commissioner in Washington, New York City police commissioner, assistant secretary of the navy, and the Rough Rider hero of the Spanish-American War. At the age of 40 he won election as reform governor of New York and two years later as vice president. Through it all, TR remained a solid Republican, personally flamboyant but committed to mild change only.

To the Executive Mansion (he renamed it the "White House"), Roosevelt brought a passion for order, a commitment to the public, and a sense of presidential possibilities. Most presidents believed the Constitution set specific limits on their power. Roosevelt thought that the president could do anything not expressly forbidden in the document. Recognizing the value of publicity, he gave reporters the first press room in the White House and favored them with all the stories they wanted. He

Bullnecked and barrel-chested, Theodore Roosevelt was "pure act," said Henry Adams. TR may have had the attention span of a golden retriever, as one critic charged, but he also embodied the great virtues of his day—honesty, hard work, constancy, courage, and while in power, self-control.

was the first president to ride in an automobile, fly an airplane, and dive in a submarine—and everyone knew it.

To dramatize racial injustice, Roosevelt invited black educator Booker T. Washington to lunch at the White House in 1901. White southern journalists called such mingling with African Americans treason, but for Roosevelt the gesture served both principle and politics. His lunch with Washington was part of a "black and tan" strategy to build a biracial coalition among southern Republicans. He denounced lynching and appointed black southerners to important federal offices in Mississippi and South Carolina.

Sensing the limits of political feasibility, Roosevelt went no further. Perhaps his own racial narrowness stopped him too. In 1906, when Atlanta exploded in a race riot that left 12 people dead, he said nothing. Later that year he discharged "without honor" three entire companies of African American troops because some of the soldiers were unjustly charged with having "shot up" Brownsville, Texas. All lost their pensions, including six winners of the Medal of Honor. The act stained Roosevelt's record. (Congress acknowledged the wrong in 1972 by granting the soldiers honorable discharges.)

Brownsville incident

A Square Deal

Philosophy of the Square Deal

By temperament, Roosevelt was not inclined to follow the cautious course McKinley had charted. He had more energetic plans in mind. He accepted growth—whether of business, labor, or government—as natural. In the pluralistic system he envisioned, big labor would counterbalance big capital, big farm organizations would offset big food processors, and so on. Standing astride them all, mediating when needed, was a big government that could ensure fair results for all.

Later, as he campaigned for a second term in 1904, Roosevelt named this program the "Square Deal."

In a startling display of presidential initiative, Roosevelt in 1902 intervened in a strike that idled 140,000 miners and paralyzed the anthracite (hard) coal industry. As winter approached, public frustration with the mine owners mounted. They refused even to recognize the miners' union, let alone negotiate worker demands for higher wages and fewer hours. Roosevelt summoned both sides to the White House. John A. Mitchell, the young president of the United Mine Workers, agreed to arbitration, but management balked. Roosevelt leaked word to Wall Street that the army would take over the mines if the owners did not yield. *Anthracite coal strike*

Seldom had a president acted so boldly, and never on behalf of strikers. In late October 1902 the owners settled by granting miners a 10 percent wage hike and a nine-hour day in return for increases in coal prices and no recognition of the union. Roosevelt was equally prepared to intervene on the side of management, as he did when he sent federal troops to end strikes in Arizona in 1903 and Colorado in 1904. His aim was to establish a vigorous presidency ready to deal squarely with all sides.

Roosevelt especially needed to face the issue of economic concentration. Financial power had become consolidated in giant trusts following a wave of mergers at the end of the century. As large firms swallowed smaller ones, Americans feared that monopoly would destroy individual enterprise and free competition. A series of government investigations revealed a rash of corporate abuses—rebates, collusion, "watered" stock, payoffs to government officials. The conservative courts showed little willingness to break up the giants or blunt their power. In *United States v. E. C. Knight* (1895), the Supreme Court crippled the Sherman Antitrust Act by ruling that the law applied only to commerce and not to manufacturing. *U.S. v. E. C. Knight*

The decision left the American Sugar Refining Company in control of 98 percent of the nation's sugar factories.

In his first State of the Union message, Roosevelt told Congress that he did not oppose business concentration. As he saw it, large corporations were not only inevitable but more productive than smaller operations. He wanted to regulate, not destroy them, to make them fairer and more efficient. Only then would the economic order be humanized, its victims protected, and class violence avoided. Like individuals, trusts had to be held to strict standards of morality. Conduct, not size, was the yardstick TR used to measure "good" and "bad" trusts.

With a progressive's faith in the power of publicity and a regulator's need for the facts, Roosevelt moved immediately to strengthen the federal power of investigation. He called for the creation of a Department of Commerce with a Bureau of Corporations that could force companies to hand over their records. Congressional conservatives shuddered at the prospect of putting corporate books on display. Finally, in 1903, after Roosevelt charged that John D. Rockefeller was orchestrating the opposition, Congress enacted the legislation and provided the Justice Department with additional staff to prosecute antitrust cases.

Northern Securities

In 1902, to demonstrate the power of government, Roosevelt had Attorney General Philander Knox file an antitrust suit against the Northern Securities Company. The mammoth holding company virtually monopolized railroads in the Northwest. Worse still, it had bloated its stock with worthless certificates. Here, clearly, was a symbol of the "bad trust."

J. P. Morgan, one of the company's founders, rushed to the White House. "Send your man [the attorney general] to my man [Morgan's lawyer] and they can fix it up," he told Roosevelt and Knox. "We don't want to fix it up," replied the attorney general. "We want to stop it." A trust-conscious nation cheered as the Supreme Court ordered the company to dissolve in 1904. Ultimately, the Roosevelt administration brought suit against 44 giants, including the Standard Oil Company, the American Tobacco Company, and the Du Pont Corporation.

Railroad regulation

Despite his reputation for trustbusting, Roosevelt always preferred regulation. The problems of the railroads, for example, were newly underscored by a recent round of consolidation that had contributed to higher freight rates. Roosevelt pressed Congress to strengthen the weak Interstate Commerce Commission (ICC) (page 678). In 1903 Congress enacted the Elkins Act, which gave the ICC power to end rebates. Even the railroads supported the act because it saved them from the costly practice of granting special reductions to large shippers.

By the election of 1904 the president's boldness had won him broad popular support. He trounced his two rivals, Democrat Alton B. Parker, a jurist from New York, and Eugene V. Debs of the Socialist party. No longer was he a "political accident," Roosevelt boasted.

Conservatives in his own party opposed Roosevelt's meddling in the private sector. But progressives, goaded by Robert La Follette, demanded still more regulation of the railroads, in particular a controversial proposal for making public the value of all rail property. In 1906, the president finally reached a compromise typical of his restrained approach to reform. The Hepburn Railway Act allowed the ICC to set ceilings on rates and to regulate sleeping car companies, ferries, bridges, and terminals. La Follette did not gain his provision to disclose company value, but the Hepburn Act drew Roosevelt nearer to his goal of continuous regulation of business.

Bad Food and Pristine Wilds

Extending the umbrella of federal protection to consumers, Roosevelt belatedly threw his weight behind two campaigns for healthy foods and drugs. In 1905 Samuel Hopkins Adams of *Collier's Weekly* wrote that in its patent medicines "Gullible America" would get "huge quantities of alcohol, an appalling amount of opiates and narcotics," and worse—axle grease, acid, glue. Adams sent the samples he had collected to Harvey Wiley, chief chemist at the Agriculture Department. Wiley's "Poison Squad" produced scientific evidence of Adams's charges.

Several pure food and drug bills had already died at the hands of lobbyists, despite a presidential endorsement. The appearance of Upton Sinclair's *The Jungle* in 1906 spurred Congress to act. Sinclair intended to recruit people to socialism by exposing the plight of workers in the meatpacking industry. His novel contained a brief but vivid description of the slaughter of cattle infected with tuberculosis, of meat covered with rat dung, and of men falling into cooking vats and being served to the public as "Durham's Pure Leaf Lard." Readers paid scant attention to the workers, but their stomachs turned at what they might be eating for breakfast. The Pure Food and Drug Act of 1906 sailed through Congress, and the Meat Inspection Act soon followed.

Roosevelt had come late to the consumer cause, but on conservation he led the nation. An outdoors enthusiast, he galvanized public concern over the reckless use of natural resources. His chief forester, Gifford Pinchot, persuaded him that planned management under federal guidance was needed to protect the natural domain. Cutting trees must be synchronized with tree plantings, oil pumped from the ground under controlled conditions, and so on.

Conservation through planned management

In the western states water was the problem. Economic growth, even survival, depended on it. As fragmented local and state water policies sparked controversy, violence, and waste, many progressives campaigned for a federal program to replace the chaotic web of rules. Democratic Senator Frederick Newlands of Nevada introduced the Reclamation Act of 1902 to set aside proceeds from the sale of public lands for irrigation projects. The Reclamation Act signaled a progressive step toward the conservationist end of rational resource development.

Conservation often conflicted with the more radical vision of preservationists, led by naturalist and wilderness philosopher John Muir. Muir founded the Sierra Club in 1892 in hopes of maintaining such natural wonders as Yosemite and its neighboring Hetch-Hetchy valley in a state "forever wild" to benefit future generations. Many conservationists saw such valleys only as sites for dams and reservoirs. Controversy flared after 1900 when San Francisco announced plans to create a reservoir in the Hetch-Hetchy valley. For 13 years Muir waged a publicity campaign against the "devotees of ravaging commercialism." Pinchot enthusiastically backed San Francisco's claim. Roosevelt, torn by his friendship with Muir, did so less loudly. Not until 1913 did President Woodrow Wilson finally decide the issue in favor of San Francisco. Conservation had won over preservation.

John Muir and preservation

Roosevelt nonetheless advanced many of Muir's goals. Over the protests of cattle and timber interests, he added nearly 200 million acres to government forest reserves; placed coal and mineral lands, oil reserves, and water-power sites in the public domain; and enlarged the national park system. When Congress balked, he appropriated another 17 million acres of forest before the legislators could pass a bill limiting him. Roosevelt also set in motion national congresses and commissions

The Sierra Club, founded by naturalist John Muir, believed in the importance of preserving wilderness in its natural state. "In God's wildness," Muir wrote in 1890, "lies the hope of the world—the great fresh un-blighted, unredeemed wilderness." Muir helped persuade President Theodore Roosevelt to double the number of national parks. Here, some Sierra Club members lounge at the base of a giant redwood in Big Basin in 1905.

on conservation and mobilized governors across the country. Like a good progressive, he sent hundreds of experts to work applying science, education, and technology to environmental problems.

As Roosevelt acted more forcefully, conservatives lashed back. So far his record had been modest, but his chief accomplishment—invigorating the presidency—could lead to deeper reform. When another dip in the business cycle produced financial panic on Wall Street in 1907, business leaders and conservative politicians blamed the president. Roosevelt blamed the "speculative folly and the flagrant dishonesty of a few men of great wealth."

Clearly shaken, however, Roosevelt assured business leaders that he would do nothing to interfere with their efforts at recovery. That included a pledge not to file an antitrust suit if the giant U.S. Steel bought the Tennessee Coal and Iron Company. The economy recovered, and having declared he would not run in 1908, the 50-year-old Roosevelt prepared to give over his office to William Howard Taft.

The Troubled Taft

On March 4, 1909, as snow swirled outside the White House, William Howard Taft readied himself for his inauguration. Over breakfast with Roosevelt, he warmed in the glow of recent Republican victories. Taft had beaten Democrat William Jennings Bryan in the "Great Commoner's" third and last bid for the presidency. Republicans had retained control of Congress, as well as a host of northern legislatures. Reform was at high tide, and Taft was eager to continue the Roosevelt program.

"Will," as Roosevelt called him, was his handpicked successor. A distinguished jurist and public servant, the first American governor-general of the Philippines, and Roosevelt's secretary of war, Taft had great administrative skill and personal charm.

But he disliked the political maneuvering of Washington and preferred conciliation to confrontation. Even Roosevelt had doubts. "He's all right," TR had told a reporter on inauguration day. "But he's weak. They'll get around him. They'll"— and here Roosevelt pushed the reporter with his shoulder— "lean against him."

Trouble began early when progressives in the House moved to curb the near-dictatorial power of the conservative Speaker, Joseph Cannon. Taft waffled, first supporting them, then abandoning them to preserve the tariff reductions he was seeking. When progressives later broke Cannon's power without Taft's help, they scorned the president. And Taft's compromise was wasted. Senate protectionists peppered the tariff bill with so many amendments that rates jumped nearly to their old levels.

Late in 1909, the rift between Taft and the progressives reached the breaking point in a dispute over conservation. Taft had appointed Richard Ballinger secretary of the interior over the objections of Roosevelt's old friend and mentor Chief Forester Pinchot. When Ballinger opened a million acres of public lands for sale, Pinchot rebelled openly. He charged that shady dealings had led Ballinger to transfer Alaskan public coal lands to a syndicate that included J. P. Morgan. Early in 1910, Taft fired him for insubordination. Angry progressives saw the Ballinger-Pinchot controversy as another betrayal by Taft. They began to look longingly across the Atlantic, where TR was stalking big game in Africa.

Despite his failures, Taft was no conservative pawn. He ended up protecting more land than Roosevelt, and he pushed Congress to enact a progressive program regulating safety standards for mines and railroads, creating a federal children's bureau, and setting an eight-hour workday for federal employees. Taft's support of a graduated income tax—sometimes fiery, sometimes mild—was finally decisive. Early in 1913 it became the Sixteenth Amendment. Historians view it as one of the most important reforms of the century, for it eventually generated the revenue for many new social programs.

Yet no matter what Taft did, he managed to alienate conservatives and progressives alike. That spelled trouble for the Republicans as the presidential election of 1912 approached.

William Howard Taft—big, good-natured, and modest— was reluctant to run for the presidency in 1908. At the outset of the campaign, President Roosevelt sent him pointed advice: "Photographs on horseback, yes, tennis, no, and golf is fatal." But Taft played anyway. He loved golf despite its reputation as a "dude's game."

Taft's accomplishments

Roosevelt Returns

In June 1910 Roosevelt had come home laden with hunting trophies and exuberant as ever. He found Taft unhappy and progressive Republicans threatening to defect. Party loyalty kept Roosevelt quiet through most of 1911, but in October Taft pricked him personally on the sensitive matter of busting trusts. Like TR, Taft accepted trusts as natural, but he failed to make Roosevelt's distinction between "good" and "bad" ones. He demanded, more impartially, that all trusts be prevented from restraining trade. In four years as president, Taft had brought nearly twice the antitrust suits Roosevelt had in seven years.

In October 1911 the Justice Department charged U.S. Steel with having violated the Sherman Antitrust Act by acquiring the Tennessee Coal and Iron Company. Roosevelt regarded the action as a personal rebuke, because he himself had allowed U.S.

Steel to proceed with the acquisition. Taft "was playing small, mean, and foolish politics," complained TR.

New Nationalism

Roosevelt decided to play big, high-minded, and presidential. Already, in a speech at Osawatomie, Kansas, in 1910, he had outlined a program of sweeping reform. His "New Nationalism" stressed the interests of the nation as a whole and the value of government as an agent of reform. It accepted consolidation in the economy—whether big business or big labor—but insisted on protecting the interests of individuals through big government. The New Nationalism promised government planning and efficiency under a powerful executive, "a steward of the public welfare." It promoted taxes on incomes and inheritances and greater regulation of industry. And it embraced social justice, specifically workers' compensation for accidents, minimum wages and maximum hours, child labor laws, and "equal suffrage"—a nod to women and loyal black Republicans. Roosevelt, a cautious reformer as president, grew daring as he set his sights again on the White House.

The Election of 1912

"My hat is in the ring!" Roosevelt announced in February 1912, to no one's surprise. Taft responded by claiming that the New Nationalism had won support only from "radicals," "emotionalists," and "neurotics." In fact, the enormously popular Roosevelt won most of the primaries, but by the time Republicans met in Chicago in June 1912, Taft had used presidential patronage and promises to secure the nomination. A frustrated Roosevelt bolted and took progressive Republicans with him. Two months later, amid choruses of "Onward Christian Soldiers," delegates to the newly formed Progressive party nominated Roosevelt for the presidency. "I'm feeling like a bull moose!" he bellowed. Progressives suddenly had a symbol for their breakaway party.

Progressive, or "Bull Moose," party

The Democrats met in Baltimore, jubilant over the prospect of a divided Republican party. Delegates chose as their candidate Woodrow Wilson, the progressive governor of New Jersey. Wilson wisely concentrated his fire on Roosevelt. He countered the New Nationalism with his "New Freedom." It rejected the economic consolidation that Roosevelt embraced. Bigness itself was a sin, no matter how big

Woodrow Wilson's New Freedom

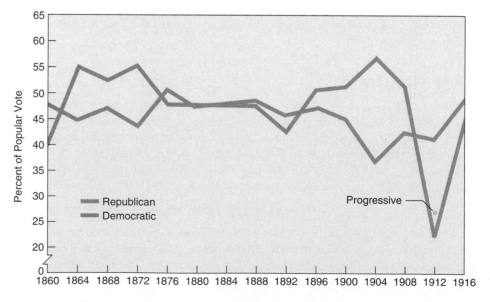

Republican and Democratic Parties' Share of Popular Vote, 1860–1912 In the last quarter of the nineteenth century the Republican and Democratic parties were deadlocked until the Republicans became the majority party in 1896. In 1912 the parties splintered. TR ran as a Progressive, and Republican fortunes plummeted.

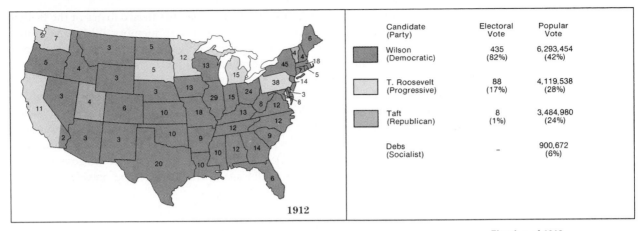

Candidate (Party)	Electoral Vote	Popular Vote
Wilson (Democratic)	435 (82%)	6,293,454 (42%)
T. Roosevelt (Progressive)	88 (17%)	4,119,538 (28%)
Taft (Republican)	8 (1%)	3,484,980 (24%)
Debs (Socialist)	–	900,672 (6%)

1912

Election of 1912

corporations acted, because it crowded out competition, thereby promoting inefficiency and reducing economic opportunity. Only by strictly limiting the size of business enterprises could the free market be preserved and Americans be released from the control of the wealthy and powerful. And only by keeping government small could individual liberty be protected. "Liberty," Wilson cautioned, "has never come from government," only from the "limitation of governmental power."

Increasingly voters found Taft beside the point. In an age of reform, even the Socialists looked good. Better led, financed, and organized than ever, the Socialist party had enlarged its membership to nearly 135,000 by 1912. Socialist mayors ran 32 cities. The party also had an appealing candidate in Eugene V. Debs, a homegrown Indiana radical. He had won 400,000 votes for president in 1904. Now, in 1912, he summoned voters to make "the working class the ruling class."

On Election Day voters gave progressive reform a resounding endorsement. Wilson won 6.3 million votes, Roosevelt 4.1 million, Taft just 3.6 million. Debs received almost a million votes. Together the two progressive candidates amassed a three to one margin. The Republican split, moreover, had broken the party's hold on national politics. For the first time since 1896, a Democrat would sit in the White House— and with his party in control of Congress.

Woodrow Wilson was not shy about his good fortune. Soon after the election he confessed to William McCombs, chair-

Woodrow Wilson and the Politics of Morality

man of the Democratic National Committee: "God ordained that I should be the next President of the United States." To the White House Wilson brought a passion for reform and the conviction that he was meant to accomplish great things. Under him, progressivism peaked.

Early Career

From the moment of his birth in 1856, Thomas Woodrow Wilson could not escape a sense of destiny. It was all around him. In the family's Presbyterian faith, in the sermons of his minister father, in dinnertime talk ran the unbending belief in a world predetermined by God and ruled by saved souls, the "elect." Wilson ached to be one of them and behaved as if he were.

To prepare to lead, young Tommy Wilson studied the fiery debates of the British Parliament and wandered the woods reciting them from memory. Like most southerners, he grew up loving the Democratic party, hating the tariff, and accepting racial separation. (Under his presidency, segregation would return to Washington for the first time since Reconstruction.)

An early career in law bored him, so he turned to political science and became a professor. His studies persuaded him that a modern president must act as a "prime minister," directing and uniting his party, shaping legislation and public opinion, exerting continuous leadership. In 1910, after a stormy tenure as head of Princeton University, Wilson was helped by Democratic party bosses to win the governorship of New Jersey. In 1912 they helped him again, this time to the presidency of the country.

The Reforms of the New Freedom

As governor, Wilson had led New Jersey on the path of progressive reform. As president, he was a model of executive leadership. More than Theodore Roosevelt, he shaped policy and legislation. He went to Congress to let members know he intended to work personally with them. He kept party discipline tight and mobilized public opinion when Congress refused to act.

Lowering the high tariff was Wilson's first order of business. Progressives had long attacked the tariff as another example of the power of trusts. By protecting American manufacturers, Wilson argued, such barriers weakened the competition he cherished. When the Senate threatened to raise rates, the new president appealed directly to the public. "Industrious" and "insidious" lobbyists were blocking reform, he cried to reporters. A "brick couldn't be thrown without hitting one of them."

Underwood-Simmons Tariff

The Underwood-Simmons Tariff of 1913 marked the first downward revision of the tariff in 19 years and the biggest since before the Civil War. To compensate for lost revenue, Congress enacted a graduated income tax under the newly adopted Sixteenth Amendment. It applied solely to corporations and the tiny fraction of Americans who earned more than $4000 a year. It nonetheless began a momentous shift

Woodrow Wilson came to the White House with promises to reform government. In this 1913 cartoon entitled "A New Captain in the District," the newly elected president strides through corrupt Washington, ready to police such abuses as easy land grants and pork barreling, the much-criticized congressional practice of voting for projects that benefit home districts and constituents.

in government revenue from its nineteenth-century base—public lands, alcohol taxes, and customs duties—to its twentieth-century base—personal and corporate incomes.

Wilson turned next to the perennial problems of money and banking. Early in 1913 a congressional committee under Arsene Pujo revealed that a few powerful banks controlled the nation's credit system. They could choke Wilson's free market by raising interest rates or tightening the supply of money. As a banking reform bill moved through Congress in 1913, Wall Street conservatives lobbied for a privately controlled, centralized banking system that could issue currency and set interest rates. Rural Democrats favored a decentralized system of regional banks run by local bankers. Populists and progressives—including William Jennings Bryan and Robert La Follette—wanted government control.

Wilson split their differences in the Federal Reserve Act of 1913. The new Federal Reserve System contained 12 regional banks scattered across the country. But it also created a central Federal Reserve Board in Washington, appointed by the president, to supervise the system. The board could regulate credit and the money supply by setting the interest rate it charged member banks, by buying or selling government bonds, and by issuing paper currency called Federal Reserve notes. Thus the Federal Reserve System sought to stabilize the existing order by increasing federal control over credit and the money supply.

Federal Reserve Act

When Wilson finally took on the trusts, he moved closer to the New Nationalism of Theodore Roosevelt. The Federal Trade Commission Act of 1914 created a bipartisan executive agency to oversee business activity. The end—to enforce orderly competition—was distinctly Wilsonian, but the means—an executive commission to regulate commerce—were pure Roosevelt.

Federal Trade Commission

Roosevelt would have stopped there, but Wilson made good on his campaign pledge to attack trusts. The Clayton Antitrust Act (1914) barred some of the worst corporate practices—price discrimination, holding companies, and interlocking directorates (directors of one corporate board sitting on others). Yet despite Wilson's bias against size, the advantages of large-scale production and distribution were inescapable. In practice his administration chose to regulate rather than break up bigness. Under Wilson the Justice Department filed fewer antitrust suits than under the Taft administration and negotiated more "gentlemen's agreements" (voluntary agreements by companies to change practices) than under Roosevelt.

Clayton Antitrust Act

Labor and Social Reform

For all of Wilson's impressive accomplishments, voters turned lukewarm toward the New Freedom. In the elections of 1914 Republicans cut Democratic majorities in the House and won important industrial and farm states. To strengthen his hand in the presidential election of 1916, Wilson began edging toward the social reforms of the New Nationalism he had once criticized as paternalistic and unconstitutional. Early in 1916 he signaled the change when he nominated his close adviser Louis D. Brandeis to the Supreme Court. The progressive Brandeis had fought for the social reforms lacking in Wilson's agenda. His appointment also broke the tradition of anti-Semitism that had previously kept Jews off the Court.

In a host of other ways, Wilson revealed his willingness to intervene more actively in the economy. He helped pass laws improving the working conditions of merchant seamen and setting an eight-hour day for workers on interstate railroads. He endorsed the Keating-Owen Child Labor Act (page 714) and threw his support to legislation providing farmers with low-interest loans. And just before the election Wilson intervened to avert a nationwide strike of rail workers.

The Limits of Progressive Reform

Woodrow Wilson's administration capped a decade and a half of heady reform. Seeing chaos in the modern industrial city, progressive reformers had worked to reduce the damage of poverty and the hazards of industrial work, control the rising immigrant tide, and spread a middle-class ideal of morality. In city halls and state legislatures, they tried to break the power of corporate interests and entrenched political machines. In Washington, they enlarged government and broadened its mission from caretaker to promoter of public welfare.

Progressivism did not always succeed. Reformers sometimes betrayed their high ideals by denying equality to African Americans, Asians, and other minorities. They preferred to Americanize foreigners rather than accept the contributions of their cultures. Too often government commissions that were designed to be "watchdog" agencies found themselves captured by the interests they were supposed to oversee. Well-meaning but cumbersome regulation crippled industries like the railroads for decades. Although the direct primary, the popular election of senators, and other reforms weakened the power of political machines, boss rule survived.

For all its claims of sweeping change, progressivism left the system of market capitalism intact. Neither the New Nationalism of Theodore Roosevelt, with its emphasis on planning and regulation, nor Woodrow Wilson's New Freedom, which promoted competition through limits on corporate size, aimed to do more than improve the system. But the Gilded Age philosophy of laissez faire—of giving private enterprise a free hand—had clearly been rejected. Both state and federal governments established their right to regulate the actions of private corporations for the public good.

The reforms thus achieved, including the eight-hour workday, woman suffrage, direct election of senators, graduated income taxes, and public ownership of utilities, began to address the problems of an urban industrial society. Under progressive leadership, the modern state—active and interventionist—was born.

American confidence was restored as the new century unfolded. A golden age of peace, prosperity, and human advancement seemed within reach, at least to progressives. But in 1914, as progressivism crested in America, the guns of a hot August shattered the uneasy calm in Europe and plunged the world into war. Few people anywhere were prepared for the bloodbath that followed.

chapter summary

Progressivism was a broad-based reform movement, the first truly national reform movement in American history, that attempted to address problems arising from industrialization, urbanization, and immigration.

- Progressive reform sprang from many impulses:
  - Desires to curb the advancing power of big business and to end political corruption.
  - Efforts to bring order and efficiency to economic and political life.
  - Attempts by new interest groups to make business and government more responsive to the needs of ordinary citizens.
  - Moralistic urges to rid society of industries such as the liquor trade that profited from human misery, to bridge the gap between immigrants and native-born Americans, and to soften the consequences of industrialization through social justice and social welfare.

- Led by members of the urban middle class, progressives were moderate modernizers, attempting to redeem such traditional American values as democracy, Judeo-Christian ethics, individualism, and the spirit of volunteerism and public service while employing the newest techniques of management and planning, coordinated systems, and specialized bureaucracies of experts.

- The twin drives for social justice and social welfare often relied on women, who extended their traditional sphere of home and family to become "social housekeepers" and crusaders for women's rights, especially the right to vote.

- Increasingly, progressivism animated politics, first at the local and state levels, then in the presidencies of Theodore Roosevelt and Woodrow Wilson.

- In the end, the weaknesses of progressivism—the fuzziness of its conception of the public interest, the exclusion of African Americans and other minorities, the ease with which its regulatory mechanisms were "captured" by those being regulated—were matched by its accomplishments in establishing the modern, activist state.

additional reading

The long interpretive debate over progressivism is best covered in Arthur Link and Richard L. McCormick, *Progressivism* (1985). Benchmarks in that debate include George Mowry, *The California Progressives* (1951) and Richard Hofstadter, *The Age of Reform: From Bryan to FDR* (1955), both of which see progressives as a small elite seeking to recapture its fading status and influence. Gabriel Kolko, *The Triumph of Conservatism: A Reinterpretation of American History 1900–1916* (1963) makes the controversial case of the New Left for business capture of reform to control competition and stave off stricter federal regulation. Richard McCormick stresses the transformation of political culture accompanying the decline of political parties and the rise of interest groups in *From Realignment to Reform: Political Change in New York State, 1893–1910* (1981).

John M. Blum, *The Republican Roosevelt* (1954) remains the most incisive rendering of TR, and Lewis L. Gould, *The Presidency of Theodore Roosevelt* (1991) is the best single-volume study of the White House years. Unsurpassed for its detail and depth is Arthur Link, *Woodrow Wilson*, 5 vols. (1947–1965). Robert Crunden, *Ministers of Reform: The Progressives' Achievements in American Civilization, 1889–1920* (1982) emphasizes the cultural origins and impact of progressivism, and Ellen Chesler, *Woman of Valor: Margaret Sanger and the Birth Control Movement in America* (1992) looks through a feminist lens at the life and times of social reformer Margaret Sanger. For a fuller list of readings, see the Bibliography.

Significant Events

1890 — 1890 New England Kitchen opens; General
Federation of Women's Clubs organized

1892 Sierra Club founded

1893 Illinois legislature enacts eight-hour workday
law for women; Anti-Saloon league created

1895 — 1895 *United States v. E. C. Knight*

1899 National Consumers League founded

1900 Robert La Follette elected governor of
Wisconsin; Galveston, Texas, creates first
commission form of government

1900 — 1901 Leon Czolgosz assassinates President
McKinley; Theodore Roosevelt becomes president;
Socialist Party of America founded

1902 Bureau of the Census created; Northern
Securities Company dissolved under Sherman
Antitrust Act; anthracite coal miners strike in
Pennsylvania; Maryland adopts first workers'
compensation law

1903 Department of Labor and Commerce created;
Elkins Act ends railroad rebates; Wisconsin first
1905 — state to enact direct primary

1904 Lincoln Steffens's *The Shame of the Cities*
published; Theodore Roosevelt elected president

1906 Hepburn Act strengthens Interstate
Commerce Commission; Upton Sinclair's *The
Jungle* published; Meat Inspection and Pure Food
and Drug act passed

1907 William James's *Pragmatism* published

1908 *Muller v. Oregon* upholds the right of states
to regulate working hours of women; William
1910 — Howard Taft elected president

1909 Ballinger-Pinchot controversy

1910 Mann Act passed

1911 Triangle Shirtwaist fire

1912 Progressive ("Bull Moose") party nominates
Theodore Roosevelt for presidency; Woodrow
Wilson elected president

1913 Sixteenth and Seventeenth amendments allow
for federal income taxes and direct election of
1915 — senators; Underwood-Simmons Tariff enacted;
Federal Reserve Act passed

1914 Clayton Antitrust Act passed; Federal Trade
Commission created

1916 Margaret Sanger organizes New York Birth
Control League; Keating-Owen Child Labor Act
passed; Woodrow Wilson reelected president

1917 Congress enacts literacy test for new
immigrants

1920 — 1920 Nineteenth Amendment grants women the
right to vote

Chapter 23

The United States &
The Old World Order

preview • With the outbreak of World War I, the old order of colonial imperialism and carefully balanced military alliances came crashing down. Wilson at first proclaimed Americans neutral, in hopes of brokering a peace settlement. But American economic and cultural ties to the Allies, along with German submarine warfare, brought Americans into the war. By its end, Woodrow Wilson's hopes for a progressive "peace without victory" and a new world order were dashed.

War! War! WAR!" The news had flashed across the country in the spring of 1898. As tens of thousands of eager young men signed up to fight the Spanish in Cuba, the USS *Oregon* left San Francisco Bay on a roundabout route toward its battle station in the Caribbean. It first headed south through the Pacific, passing Central America and leaving it thousands of miles behind. Then, in the narrow Strait of Magellan at South America's tip, the ship encountered a gale so ferocious, the shore could not be seen. All communication ceased, and Americans at home feared the worst. But the *Oregon* passed into the Atlantic and steamed north until finally, after 68 days and 13,000 miles at sea, it helped win the Battle of Santiago Bay.

The daring voyage electrified the nation but worried its leaders. Since the defeat of Mexico in 1848, the United States had stretched from the Atlantic to the Pacific without enough navy to go around. As an emerging power, the country needed a path between the seas—a canal across the narrow isthmus of Colombia's Panamanian province in Central America—to defend itself and to promote its growing trade.

"I took the isthmus," Theodore Roosevelt later told a cheering crowd. In a way he did. As president, in 1903 he negotiated an agreement with Colombia to lease the needed strip of land. Holding out for more money and greater control over the canal, the Colombian senate refused to ratify the agreement.

Privately, TR talked of seizing Panama. But when he learned of a budding independence movement in Panama, he let it be known that he would welcome a revolt. On schedule and without bloodshed, the Panamanians rebelled late in 1903. The next day a U.S. cruiser dropped anchor offshore to prevent Colombia from landing troops. The United States quickly recognized the new Republic of Panama and signed a treaty for a renewable lease on a canal zone 10 miles wide. Panama received $10 million plus an annual rent of $250,000 (the same terms offered to Colombia). One of the few critics called it "a rough-riding assault upon another republic." Roosevelt never apologized, but in 1921, after oil had been discovered in the Canal Zone, Congress voted $25 million to Colombia.

In November 1906 Roosevelt pulled into port at Panama City aboard the USS *Louisiana,* newly launched and the biggest battleship in the fleet. He spent the next three days traveling the length of the canal site in the pouring rain. Soaked from head to toe, his huge panama hat and white suit sagging about his body, he splashed through labor camps and asked workers for their complaints. He toured the hospital at Ancon and met Dr. William Gorgas, the sanitation engineer in charge of eradicating the yellow-fever-bearing mosquito. He walked railroad ties at the cuts and made speeches in the mud. "This is one of the great works of the world," he told an assembly of black diggers.

Indeed, the workers appreciated all too well the back-breaking effort that had gone into digging the largest trench yet cut into the earth's surface. Some 30,000 black laborers were brought from the West Indies to accomplish the task. Paid 10 cents an hour, they worked 10 hours a day, 6 days a week. When completed, the canal stretched some 50 miles across the Isthmus of Panama. At $352 million, its final cost was four times that of the Suez Canal. The giant locks used to raise and lower water levels were deeper than a six-story building.

African American artist Horace Pippin lost the use of his right arm in the First World War. In 1930, after three years of work, he completed *The End of the War: Starting Home*. It shows black troops, bayonets at the ready, forcing a German surrender.

Panama Canal — Old and New Transoceanic Routes Tropical forests cover three-fourths of Panama, including the Canal Zone. Vegetation is denser at high elevations but tightly packed even below 1000 feet. The terrain is rugged, but the distance saved by the canal (nearly 8000 miles) made the ordeal of construction worthwhile.

The Panama Canal embodied Roosevelt's muscular foreign policy of respect through strength. He modernized the army and tripled its size, created a general staff for planning and mobilization, and established the Army War College. As a pivot point between the two hemispheres, his canal allowed the United States to flex its strength across the globe.

These expanding horizons came about largely as an outgrowth of American commercial and industrial expansion, just as the imperialist empires of England, France, Germany, Russia, and Japan reflected the spread of their own industrial and commercial might. The Americans, steeped in democratic ideals, frequently seemed uncomfortable with the naked ambitions of European empire-builders. Roosevelt's embrace of the canal, however, showed how far some progressives had come in being willing to shape the world.

Theodore Roosevelt visited the site of the Panama Canal in 1906. Relentlessly curious, he had to know everything, from the salary of engineers to the proper techniques for operating this giant Bucyrus steam shovel. "It is greater work than you, yourselves, at the moment realize," he told workers.

Expansionist diplomats at home and abroad assured each other that global order could be maintained by balancing power through a set of carefully crafted alliances. But that system and the spheres of influence it spawned did not hold. In 1914, the year the Panama Canal opened, the old world order shattered in a terrible war.

Progressive Diplomacy

Foundations of
progressive diplomacy

As the Panama Canal was being built, progressive diplomacy was taking shape. Like progressive politics, it stressed moralism and order as it stretched presidential power to new limits in an effort to mold and remake the international environment. It rested on faith in the superiority of Anglo-American stock and institutions. "Of all our race, [God] has marked the American people as His chosen nation to finally lead in the redemption of the world," said one senator in 1900. Every western leader assumed that northern Europeans were racially superior, too. The darker peoples of the tropical zones, observed a progressive educator, dwelled in "nature's asylum for degenerates." In this global vision of Manifest Destiny, few progressives questioned the need to uplift them.

Economic expansion underlay the commitment to a "civilizing" mission. The depression of 1893 had encouraged American manufacturers and farmers to look overseas for markets, and that expansion continued after 1900. By 1918, at the end of World War I, the United States had become the largest creditor in the world, with networks of commerce that reached as far away as the deserts of Arabia and river valleys of central China. Every administration committed itself to opening doors of trade and keeping them open.

Big Stick in the Caribbean

Theodore Roosevelt liked to invoke the old African proverb "Walk softly and carry a big stick." But in the Caribbean he moved both loudly and mightily. The Panama Canal gave the United States a commanding position in the Western Hemisphere. Its importance required the country to "police the surrounding premises," explained Secretary of State Elihu Root. Before granting Cuba independence in 1902, the United States reorganized its finances and attached the Platt Amendment to the Cuban constitution. The amendment gave American authorities the right to intervene in Cuba if the independence or internal order of the country were threatened. Claiming that power, U.S. troops occupied the island twice between 1906 and 1923.

Platt Amendment

In looking to enforce a favorable environment for trade in the Caribbean, Roosevelt also worried about European intentions. The Monroe Doctrine of 1823 declared against further European colonization of the Western Hemisphere, but in the early twentieth century the rising debts of Latin Americans to Europeans invited intrusion. "If we intend to say hands off to the power of Europe, then sooner or later we must keep order ourselves," Roosevelt warned. In his balance-of-power system, it was the obligation of great powers to avoid the spheres of others while keeping order in their own. Across the globe, great powers would thus check each other, much as big government held big business in check at home.

Going well beyond Monroe's concept of resisting foreign intrusions into the Western Hemisphere, Roosevelt tightened his grip on the region. He convinced Britain and Germany to arbitrate a debt dispute with Venezuela in 1902. Two years later, when the Dominican Republic defaulted on its debts, he added the "Roosevelt Corollary" to the Monroe Doctrine by claiming the right to intervene directly if Latin Americans failed to keep their own financial households in order. Invoking its sweeping (and self-proclaimed) power, the United States assumed responsibility for several Caribbean states, including the Dominican Republic, Cuba, and Panama.

Roosevelt Corollary to the Monroe Doctrine

A "Diplomatist of the Highest Rank"

In the Far East Roosevelt exercised ingenuity rather than force, because he realized that few Americans would have supported armed intervention half a world away. Like McKinley before him, TR committed himself only to maintaining an "open door" of equal access to trade in China and to protecting the Philippines, "our heel of Achilles."

The key to success lay in offsetting Russian and Japanese ambitions in the region. When Japan attacked Russian holdings in the Chinese province of Manchuria in 1904, Roosevelt offered to mediate. He worried that if unchecked, Japan might threaten American interests in China and the Philippines. At the U.S. Naval Base near Portsmouth, Maine, Roosevelt guided the Russians and the Japanese to the Treaty of Portsmouth in 1905. It recognized the Japanese victory (the first by an Asian power over a European country) and ceded to Japan Port Arthur, the southern half of Sakhalin Island, and, in effect, control of Korea. Japan promised to leave Manchuria as part of China and keep trade open to all foreign nations. The balance of power in Asia and the open door in China thus had been preserved. For his contributions, Roosevelt received the Nobel Peace Prize in 1906.

Treaty of Portsmouth

Gentlemen's agreement

Japanese nationalists resented the peace treaty for curbing Japan's ambitions in China. Their anger surfaced in a protest lodged, of all places, against the San Francisco school board. In 1906, rising Japanese immigration led San Francisco school authorities to place the city's 93 Asian students in a separate school. In Japan citizens talked of war over the insult. Roosevelt, furious at the "infernal fools in California," summoned the mayor of San Francisco and seven school board members to the White House. In exchange for an end to the segregation order Roosevelt offered to arrange a mutual restriction of immigration between Japan and the United States. In 1907 all sides accepted his "gentlemen's agreement."

Great White Fleet

The San Francisco school crisis sparked wild rumors that Japan was bent on taking Hawaii, or the Philippines, or the Panama Canal. In case Japan or any other nation thought of upsetting the Pacific balance, Roosevelt sent 16 gleaming white battleships on a world tour. "By George, isn't it magnificent!" he crowed as the "Great White Fleet" steamed out of Hampton Roads, Virginia, in 1907 (see pages 690–691). The fleet made its most conspicuous stop in Japan. Some Europeans predicted disaster. Instead, cheering crowds turned out in Tokyo and Yokohama, where a group of Japanese children sang "The Star-Spangled Banner" in English. The show of force heralded a new age of American naval might but had an unintended consequence that haunted Americans for decades: it spurred Japanese admirals to expand their own navy.

Watching Roosevelt in his second term, an amazed London *Morning Post* honored him as a "diplomatist of the highest rank." Abroad as at home, his brand of progressivism was grounded in an enthusiastic nationalism that mixed force with finesse to achieve balance and order. Yet despite TR's efforts, imperial rivalries, an unchecked arms race, and unrest in Europe threatened to plunge the world into chaos.

Dollar Diplomacy

Instead of force or finesse, William Howard Taft stressed private investment to promote economic stability, keep peace, and tie debt-ridden nations to the United States. "Dollar diplomacy" simply amounted to "substituting dollars for bullets," Taft explained. He and Philander Knox, his prickly secretary of state, treated the restless nations of Latin America like ailing corporations, injecting capital and reorganizing management. By the time Taft left office in 1913, half of all American investments abroad were in Latin America.

In Nicaragua dollar diplomacy was not enough. In 1909, when the Nicaraguan legislature balked at American demands to take over its customshouse and national bank, a U.S. warship dropped anchor off the coast. The lawmakers hastily changed their minds, but in 1912 a revolution led Taft to dispatch 2000 marines to protect American lives and property. Sporadic American intrusions lasted more than a dozen years.

Failure dogged Taft overseas as it did at home. In the Caribbean his dollar diplomacy was linked so closely with unpopular regimes, corporations, and banks that Woodrow Wilson scrapped it as soon as he entered the White House. Taft's efforts to strengthen China with investments and trade only intensified rivalry with Japan and made China more suspicious of all foreigners, including Americans. In 1911 the southern Chinese provinces rebelled against foreign intrusion and overthrew the monarchy. Only persistent pressure from the White House kept dollar diplomacy in Asia alive at all.

The Lightfoot Club had been meeting in the Reverend Wilson's hayloft for months when the question of whether the pen was

Woodrow Wilson and Moral Diplomacy

mightier than the sword came up. Young Tommy Wilson, who had organized the debating society, jumped at the chance to argue that written words were more powerful than armies. But when the boys drew lots, Tommy ended up on the other side. "I can't argue that side," he protested. "I can't argue for something I don't believe in." Thomas Woodrow Wilson eventually dropped his first name, but he never gave up his boyhood conviction that morality, at least as he defined it, should guide all conduct. To the diplomacy of order, force, and finance, Wilson added a missionary's commitment to spreading his system of beliefs—justice, democracy, and the Judeo-Christian values of harmony and cooperation.

Missionary Diplomacy

As president, Woodrow Wilson revived and enlarged Jefferson's notion of the United States as a beacon of freedom. The country had a mission: "We are chosen, and prominently chosen, to show the way to the nations of the world how they shall walk in the paths of liberty." Such paternalism only thinly masked Wilson's assumption of Anglo-American superiority and his willingness to force others to accept American-style democracy and Christian morality through force.

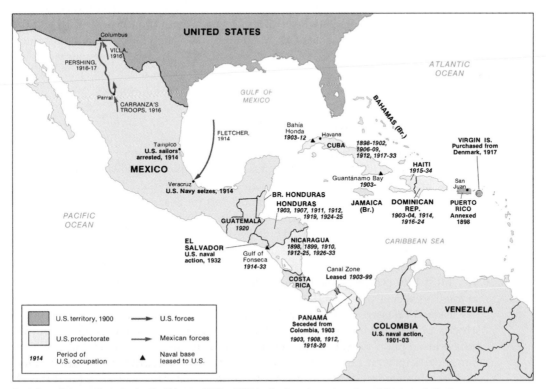

American Interventions in the Caribbean, 1898 – 1930 In the first three decades of the twentieth century, U.S. diplomacy transformed the Caribbean into an American lake as armed and unarmed intervention became part of the country's diplomatic arsenal.

Wilson's missionary diplomacy had a practical side. In the twentieth century foreign markets would serve as America's new frontier. American industries "will burst their jackets if they cannot find free outlets in the markets of the world," Wilson cautioned in 1912. His special genius lay in reconciling this commercial self-interest with a global idealism. In his eyes, exporting American democracy and capitalism would promote peace, prosperity, and human advancement throughout the world.

Solitary and self-assured, Wilson conducted foreign policy on his own. Bypassing the State Department, he sent personal emissaries to foreign leaders and often typed his own dispatches. Sometimes Secretary of State William Jennings Bryan had no idea of what was happening. In rare moments of doubt, Wilson turned to his trusted friend, Edward M. House. The honorary "Colonel" House had hooked himself to Wilson in the early days of his political career and wielded power behind the scenes.

Twenty-One Demands

In Asia and the Pacific Wilson moved to put "moral and public considerations" ahead of the "material interests of individuals." He pulled American bankers out of a six-nation railroad project in China backed by President Taft. The scheme encouraged foreign intervention and undermined Chinese sovereignty, said Wilson. The United States became the first major power to recognize the new Republic of China in 1911 when nationalists overthrew the last Manchu emperor. And in 1915 Wilson strongly opposed Japan's "Twenty-One Demands" for control of China. At the end of Wilson's first administration the Philippines gained limited self-government, the first step toward the eventual independence finally granted in 1946.

In the Caribbean and Latin America, Wilson discovered that interests closer to home could not be pursued through high-minded words alone. In August 1914 he convinced Nicaragua, already occupied by American troops, to yield control of a naval base and grant the United States an alternate canal route. Upheavals in Haiti and the Dominican Republic brought in the U.S. Marines. By the end of his administration American troops were still stationed there and also in Cuba. All four nations were economically dependent on the United States and were virtual protectorates. Missionary diplomacy, it turned out, could spread its gospel with steel as well as cash.

Intervention in Mexico

Mexican Revolution

A lingering crisis in Mexico turned Wilson's "moral diplomacy" into a mockery. A common border, 400 years of shared history, and millions of dollars in investments made what happened in Mexico of urgent importance to the United States. In 1910 a revolution overthrowing the aged dictator, Porfirio Díaz, plunged the country into turmoil. Just as Wilson was entering the White House in 1913, the ruthless general Victoriano Huerta emerged as head of the government. Wealthy landowners and foreign investors endorsed Huerta, a conservative militarist who was likely to protect their holdings. Soon a bloody civil war was raging between Huerta and his rivals.

Most European nations recognized the Huerta regime immediately, but Wilson refused to accept the "government of butchers." (Huerta had murdered the popular leader Francisco Madera with the approval of the Taft administration.) When Huerta proclaimed himself dictator, Wilson banned arms shipments to Mexico. He threw his support to rebel leader Venustiano Carranza, on the condition that Carranza participate in American-sponsored elections. No Mexican was ready to tolerate such foreign interference. Carranza and his "constitutionalists" rejected the offer. With few options, Wilson armed the rebels anyway.

Wilson's distaste for Huerta was so great that he used a minor incident as a pretext for an invasion. In April 1914 the crew of the USS *Dolphin* landed without permission in the Mexican port city of Tampico. Local police arrested the sailors, only to release them with an apology. Unappeased, their squadron commander demanded a 21-gun salute to the American flag. Agreed, replied the Mexicans, but only if American guns returned the salute to Mexico. Learning of a German shipload of weapons about to land at Veracruz, Wilson broke the impasse by ordering American troops to take the city. Instead of the bloodless occupation they expected, U.S. marines encountered stiff resistance as they stormed ashore; 126 Mexicans and 19 Americans were killed before the city fell. The intervention accomplished little, except the unlikely feat of uniting the rival Mexican factions against the United States.

Only the combined diplomacy of Argentina, Brazil, and Chile (the "ABC powers") staved off war between Mexico and the United States. When a bankrupt Huerta resigned in 1914, Carranza formed a new constitutionalist government but refused to follow Wilson's guidelines. Wilson turned to Francisco "Pancho" Villa, a wily, peasant-born general who had broken from Carranza. Together with Emiliano Zapata, another peasant leader, Villa kept a rebellion flickering.

Pancho Villa

A year later, Wilson finally recognized the Carranza regime, which only turned Villa against the United States. In January 1916 Villa abducted 18 Americans from a train in Mexico and slaughtered them. In March, he galloped into Columbus, New Mexico, killed 19 people, and left the town in flames. Wilson ordered 6000 troops into Mexico to capture Villa "dead or alive." A reluctant Carranza agreed to yet another American invasion.

For nearly two years, General John "Black Jack" Pershing (nicknamed for the all-black unit he commanded in the Spanish-American War) chased Villa on horseback, by automobile, and in airplanes. There were bloody skirmishes with government troops but not a single one with Villa and his rebels. As the chase grew wilder and wilder, Carranza withdrew his consent for U.S. troops on Mexican soil. Early in 1917 Wilson pulled Pershing home. The "punitive expedition," as the president called it, poisoned Mexican-American relations for the next 30 years.

General John J. "Black Jack" Pershing led U.S. forces into Mexico on a "punitive action" to catch rebel leader Pancho Villa "dead or alive." Villa (pictured here) eluded the Americans for several months before they abandoned the expedition. Audacious and ruthless, he was worshiped by Mexican peasants, who extolled his exploits in folktales and ballads after his assassination in 1923.

The Road to War

In early 1917, around the time Wilson recalled Pershing, the British liner *Laconia* was making a voyage across the Atlantic. As the ship steamed through the inky night, passengers below decks talked almost casually of the war raging in Europe since 1914. "What do you think are our chances of being torpedoed?" asked Floyd Gibbons, an American reporter who was aboard. Since Germany had stepped up its submarine attacks, the question was unavoidable. "I should put our chances at 250 to 1 that we don't meet a sub," replied a British diplomat.

"At that minute," recalled Gibbons, "the torpedo hit us." Suddenly whistle blasts echoed through the corridors and the passengers were forced to abandon ship. They watched in horror from lifeboats as a second torpedo struck its target. The *Laco-*

Fervent nationalism heightened the imperial rivalries that pulled European nations into World War I. Flags became important patriotic symbols, masses of morale-boosting color deployed above parades of marching troops and cheering citizens. The American artist Childe Hassam demonstrated that Americans shared this patriotic penchant. Here, flags of the Allies are featured.

nia's bow rose straight in the air as its stern sank; then the entire ship slid silently beneath icy waters. After a miserable night spent bobbing in the waves, Gibbons was rescued. But by 1917 other neutral Americans had already lost their lives at sea. And in April, despite Woodrow Wilson's best efforts at peace, the United States found itself dragged into war.

The Guns of August

For a century, profound strains had been pushing Europe toward war. Its population tripled, its middle and working classes swelled, discontent with industrial society grew. The United States had experienced many of the same strains, of course, yet in Europe these pressures played out on a field that was at once more stratified socially and more divided ethnically and culturally. As the continent's political systems adjusted to the new industrial order, both imperialism and nationalism gained sway. Abroad, European nations competed for empire, acquiring colonies that could supply industrial raw materials and cheap labor. At home, nationalism proved an equally useful political card to play. It papered over internal division and dissent by focusing ambitions and rivalries toward other nations. By 1914 empires jostled uneasily against one another across the globe.

Causes of World War I

Europe responded to the increased competition with an arms race. Great Britain became convinced that its mastery of the seas depended on maintaining a navy equal in power to the combined navies of its closest two rivals. France and Germany both doubled the size of their standing armies between 1870 and 1914. Led by Kaiser Wilhelm II, Germany aligned itself with Turkey and Austria-Hungary. The established imperial powers of England and France looked to contain Germany by supporting its foe, Russia. Soon Europe bristled with weapons, troops, and armor-plated navies. These war machines were linked to one another through a web of diplomatic alliances—all of them committed to war should someone or some nation set chaos in motion.

That moment came in 1914, in the unstable Balkan province of Bosnia. Since the 1870s the Ottoman, or Turkish, empire had been slowly disintegrating, allowing a host of smaller, ethnically based states to emerge. Serbia was one of them, and many Serbs dreamed of uniting other Slavic peoples in a "Pan-Slavic" nation. Their ambitions had been blocked in 1908, when Austria-Hungary annexed neighboring Bosnia. Tensions in the region were high when the Archduke Franz Ferdinand, heir to the Austro-Hungarian throne, visited Sarajevo, Bosnia's capital. On June 28, 1914, the Archduke and his wife were gunned down by a Serbian nationalist.

Assassination of Archduke Franz Ferdinand

Austria-Hungary mobilized to punish Serbia. In response, rival Russia called up its 6-million-soldier army to help the Serbs. Germany joined with Austria-Hungary, France with Russia. On July 28, after a month of insincere demands for apologies, Austria-Hungary declared war on Serbia. On August 1, Germany issued a similar declaration against Russia and, two days later, against France. Following a battle plan drawn up well in advance, German generals pounded neutral Belgium with siege cannons the size of freight cars. Within days, five German columns were slicing west through the Belgian countryside, determined to overrun France before Russia could position its slow-moving army on the eastern front.

The guns of August heralded the first global war. Like so many dominoes, the industrialized nations fell into line: Britain, Japan, Romania, and later Italy to the side of "Allies" France and Russia; Bulgaria and Turkey to the "Central Powers" of Germany and Austria-Hungary. Armies fought from the deserts of North Africa to the

The Course of War in Europe, 1914–1917 When World War I erupted between the Central and Allied Powers in 1914, few countries in Europe remained neutral. The armies of the Central Powers penetrated as far west as France and as far east as Russia, but by 1917, the European war had settled into a hideous standoff along the deadly line of trenches on the western front.

plains of Flanders in Belgium. Fleets battled off the coasts of Chile and Sumatra. Soldiers came from as far away as Australia and India. Nearly 8 million never returned.

Neutral but Not Impartial

The outbreak of war in Europe shocked most Americans. Few knew Serbia as anything but a tiny splotch on the map of Europe. Fewer still were prepared to go to war in its defense. President Wilson issued an immediate declaration of neutrality and approved a plan for evacuating Americans stranded in Belgium. "The more I read about the conflict," he wrote a friend, "the more open it seems to me to utter condemnation."

Wilson's neutral ideals   Wilson came to see the calamity as an opportunity. Neutral America could lead warring nations to a new world order. Selfish nationalism would give way to cooperative internationalism, power politics to collective security and Christian charity. Progressive faith in reason would triumph over violence. Everything hinged on maintaining American neutrality. Only if the United States stood above the fray could it lead the way to a higher peace. Americans must remain "impartial in thought as well as action," Wilson insisted in 1914.

True impartiality was impossible. Americans of German and Austrian descent naturally sympathized with the Central Powers, as did Irish-Americans, on the grounds of England's centuries-old domination of Ireland. But the bonds of language, culture, and history tied most Americans to Great Britain. Even Wilson, long an admirer of British institutions, could not escape the tug of loyalty. And gratitude for French aid during the American Revolution still lived. When the first American division marched through Paris years later, its commander stopped to salute Lafayette's tomb with the cry, "Nous voilà, Lafayette!"—Lafayette, we are here!

Germany aroused different sentiments. Although some progressives admired German social reforms, Americans generally saw Germany as an iron military power bent on conquest. Americans read British propaganda about spike-helmeted "Huns" raping Belgian women, bayoneting their children, pillaging their towns. Some of the stories were true, some embellished, some manufactured, but all worked against Germany.

American economic ties to Britain and France also created an investment in Allied victory. After faltering briefly in 1914, the American economy boomed with the flood of war orders. The commanding British navy ensured that the Atlantic trade went mostly to the Allies. Between 1914 and 1916 trade with the Allies rocketed from $800 million to $3 billion. The Allies eventually borrowed more than $2 billion from American banks to finance their purchases. By contrast, a British naval blockade reduced American "contraband" commerce with the Central Powers to a trickle.

The Diplomacy of Neutrality

Though Wilson insisted that all warring powers respect the right of neutrals to trade with any nation, he hesitated to retaliate against Great Britain's blockade. Embargoing arms, he feared, would weaken Britain's most powerful weapon—the navy—and tip the balance toward Germany, a land power. Meanwhile, Great Britain enforced its blockade with caution and shrewdness where the Americans were concerned. When Britain forbade the sale of cotton to the Central Powers in 1915, the British government bought American surpluses. It also agreed to compensate American firms for their losses when the war was over. By the end of 1915 the United States had all but accepted the British blockade of Germany, while American supplies continued to flow to England. True neutrality was dead. America became the quartermaster of the Allies.

Early in 1915, Germany turned to a dreadful new weapon to even the odds at sea. It mounted a counterblockade of Great Britain with two dozen submarines, or *Unterseebootes,* called U-boats. Before submarines, sea raiders usually gave crews and passengers the chance to escape. But if thin-skinned U-boats surfaced to obey these conventions, they risked being rammed or blown from the water. So submarines attacked without warning and spared no lives. Invoking international law and national honor, President Wilson threatened to hold Germany to "strict accountability" for any American losses. Germany promised not to sink any American ships, but soon a new issue grabbed the headlines: the safety of American passengers on belligerent vessels.

Submarine warfare

On the morning of May 7, 1915, the British passenger liner *Lusitania* appeared out of a fog bank off the coast of Ireland on its way from New York to Southampton. The commander of the German U-20 could hardly believe his eyes: the giant ship filled the viewfinder of his periscope. He fired a single torpedo. A tremendous roar followed as one of the *Lusitania*'s main boilers exploded. The ship stopped dead in the water and listed so badly that lifeboats could barely be launched before the vessel sank. Nearly 1200 men, women, and children perished, including 128 Americans.

Former President Theodore Roosevelt charged that such an "act of piracy" demanded war against Germany. Wilson, though horrified at this "murder on the high seas," urged restraint. "There is such a thing as a nation being so right that it does not need to convince others by force," he said a few days later. He sent notes of protest but did little more.

Secretary of State Bryan, an advocate of what he called "real neutrality," wanted equal protests lodged against both German submarines and British blockaders. He suspected that the *Lusitania* carried munitions as well as passengers and was thus a legitimate target. (Much later, evidence proved him right.) Relying on passengers for protection against attack, Bryan argued, was "like putting women and children in front of an army." Rather than endorse Wilson's policy, Bryan resigned.

Battling on two fronts in Europe, Germany wanted to keep the United States out of the war. But in February 1916 a desperate Germany declared submarine warfare on all *armed* vessels, belligerent or neutral. A month later a U-boat commander mistook the French steamer *Sussex* for a mine layer and torpedoed the unarmed vessel as it ferried passengers and freight across the English Channel. Several Americans were injured.

Sussex pledge

In mid-April, Wilson issued an ultimatum. If Germany refused to stop sinking nonmilitary vessels, the United States would break off diplomatic relations. War would surely follow. Without enough U-boats to control the seas, Germany agreed to Wilson's terms, all but abandoning its counterblockade. This *Sussex* pledge gave Wilson a great victory but carried a grave risk. If German submarines resumed unrestricted attacks, the United States would have to go to war. "Any little German [U-boat] commander can put us into the war at any time," Wilson admitted to his cabinet.

Peace, Preparedness, and the Election of 1916

While hundreds of young Yanks slipped across the border to enlist in the Canadian army, most Americans agreed neutrality was the wisest course. Before the war a peace movement had taken seed in the United States, nourished in 1910 by a gift of $10 million from Andrew Carnegie. In 1914 social reformers Jane Addams, Charlotte Perkins Gilman, and Lillian Wald founded the Women's International League for Peace and Freedom and the American Union Against Militarism. Calling on Wilson to convene a peace conference, they lobbied for open diplomacy, disarmament, an end to colonial empires, and an international organization to settle disputes. In time these aims would become the core of Wilson's peace plan.

Pacifists might condemn the war, but Republicans and corporate leaders argued that the nation was woefully unprepared to keep peace. The army numbered only 80,000 men in 1914, the navy just 37 battleships and a handful of new "dreadnoughts," or supercruisers. Advocates of "preparedness" called for a navy larger than Great Britain's, an army of millions of reservists, and universal military training.

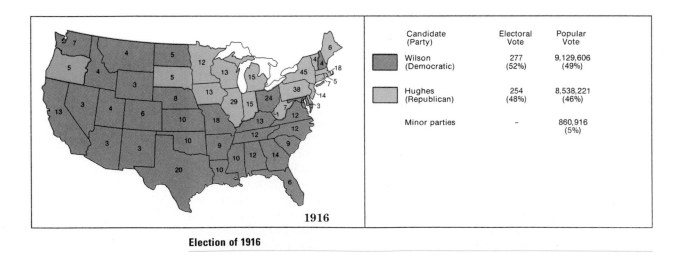

Election of 1916

By the end of 1915, frustration with German submarines led Wilson to join the preparedness cause. He toured the country promoting preparedness and promised a "navy second to none." In Washington, he pressed Congress to double the army, increase the National Guard, and begin construction of the largest navy in the world. To foot the bill progressives pushed through new graduated taxes on higher incomes and on estates as well as additional levies on corporate profits.

Whoever paid for it, most Americans were thinking of preparedness for peace, not war, in 1916. The Democrats discovered the political power of peace early in the presidential campaign. As their convention opened in St. Louis in June, the keynote speaker began what he expected to be a dull description of Wilson's recent diplomatic maneuvers—only to have the crowd roar back in each case, "What did we do? What did we do?" The speaker knew the answer and shouted it back: "We didn't go to war! We didn't go to war!" The next day Wilson was renominated by acclamation. "He Kept Us Out of War" became his campaign slogan.

The Republicans had already nominated Charles Evans Hughes, the former governor of New York. He endorsed "straight and honest" neutrality and peace. But despite his moderate stand, Democrats succeeded in painting Hughes as a warmonger, partly because Theodore Roosevelt had rattled his own sabers so loudly. As the election approached, Democrats took out full-page advertisements in newspapers across the country: "If You Want WAR, Vote for HUGHES! If You Want Peace with Honor VOTE FOR WILSON!"

As the polls closed on election day, Wilson squeaked out a paper-thin victory. He carried the South and key states in the Midwest and West on a tide of prosperity, progressive reform, and, most of all, promises of peace. As the British ambassador reported, "Americans desire nothing so much as to keep out of war."

Wilson's Final Peace Offensive

Twice since 1915 Wilson had sent his trusted adviser Edward House to Europe to negotiate a peace between the warring powers, and twice he had failed. With the election over, Wilson opened his final peace offensive. But when he asked the belligerents to state their terms for a cease-fire, neither side responded. Frustrated, fearful, and genuinely agonized, Wilson called for "peace without victory": no victor, no vanquished, no embittering division of the spoils of war, only "a peace among equals," the president told the Senate in January 1917.

As Wilson spoke, a fleet of U-boats was cruising toward the British Isles. Weeks earlier German military leaders had persuaded the Kaiser to take one last desperate gamble to starve the Allies into submission. On January 31, 1917, the German ambassador in Washington announced that unrestricted submarine warfare would resume the next day.

Wilson's dream of keeping the country from war collapsed. He asked Congress for authority to arm merchant ships and early in February severed relations with Germany. Then British authorities handed him a bombshell—an intercepted telegram from the German foreign secretary, Arthur Zimmermann, to the Kaiser's ambassador in Mexico. In the event of war with the United States, the ambassador was instructed to offer Mexico guns, money, and its "lost territory in Texas, New Mexico, and Arizona" to attack the United States. Hot with rage, Wilson released the Zimmermann telegram to the press. Soon after, he ordered gun crews aboard merchant ships and directed them to shoot U-boats on sight.

Zimmermann telegram

The momentum of events now propelled a reluctant United States toward war. On March 12 U-boats torpedoed the American merchant vessel *Algonquin*. On March

Jeannette Rankin.

15, a revolution in Russia toppled Czar Nicholas II. A key ally was crumbling from within. By the end of the month U-boats had sunk nearly 600,000 tons of Allied and neutral shipping. For the first time reports came to Washington of cracking morale in the Allied ranks.

On April 2, 1917, accompanied by armed cavalry, Wilson rode down Pennsylvania Avenue and trudged up the steps of the capitol. He delivered to Congress a stirring war message, full of idealistic purpose. "We shall fight for the things we have always carried nearest our hearts—for democracy, for the right of those who submit to authority to have a voice in their own governments, for the rights and liberties of small nations."

Pacifists held up the war resolution until it finally passed on April 6, Good Friday. Six senators and 50 House members opposed it, including the first woman in Congress, Jeannette Rankin of Montana. Cultural, economic, and historical ties to the Allies, along with the German campaign of submarine warfare, had tipped the country toward war. Wilson had not wanted it, but now the battlefield seemed the only path to a higher peace.

counterpoint

Why Did the United States Go to War?

Because the United States was never attacked, the question of why the country went to war has sparked heated debate among historians. Within a decade of victory, "revisionists" began challenging the official explanation that for moral and pragmatic reasons, Germany's campaign of submarine warfare compelled the United States to enter. They pointed instead to a conspiracy of greedy financiers, munitions makers, and others who sought to profit from Allied victory. A school of "realists," interested in demonstrating the importance of strategic, diplomatic, and other practical considerations in American foreign policy, maintained that Wilson had rightly gone to war in 1917 but for the wrong reasons—abstract moral principles such as "making the world safe for democracy."

Other historians have painted a more complex portrait, stressing that the pressures from all sides limited Wilson's choices, including the German submarine campaign and Allied blockade but also interventionists, preparedness groups, and advocates of continued trade with the Allies. New Left historians writing in the 1960s and 1970s placed the blame for American entry on capitalism, which required a stable, peaceful world for the United States to exert its commercial supremacy.

War and Society

In 1915 the German zeppelin LZ-38, hovering at 8000 feet, dropped a load of bombs that killed seven Londoners. For the first time in history, civilians died in an air attack. Few aerial bombardments occurred during the First World War, but they signaled the growing importance of the home front in modern combat. Governments not only fielded armies, they mobilized industry, controlled labor, even rationed food. In the United States, traditions of cooperation and volunteerism helped government to organize the home front and the battle front, often in ways that were peculiarly progressive.

The Slaughter of Stalemate

While the United States debated entry into the Great War, the Allies were coming perilously close to losing it. Following the German assault in 1914, the war had settled into a grisly stalemate. A continuous, immovable front stretched from Flanders in the north to the border of Switzerland in the south. Troops dug ditches, six to eight feet

Trench warfare

deep and four to five feet wide, to escape bullets, grenades, and artillery. Twenty-five thousand miles of these "trenches"—enough to circle the globe—slashed a muddy scar across Europe. Men lived in them for years, prey to disease, lice, and a plague of rats.

War in the machine age gave the advantage to the defense. When soldiers bravely charged "over the top" of the trenches, they were shredded by machine guns that fired 600 rounds a minute. Poison gas choked them in their tracks. Giant howitzers lobbed shells on them from positions too distant to see. In the Battle of the Somme River in 1916 a million men were killed in just four months of fighting, all to enable the British army to advance barely seven miles. Only late in the war did new armored "landships"—code-named "tanks"—return the advantage to the offense by surmounting the trench barriers with their caterpillar treads.

By then Vladimir Lenin was speeding home to Russia aboard a special train provided by the Germans. Lenin had been exiled to Switzerland during the early stages of the Russian Revolution but returned to lead his Bolshevik ("majority" in Russian) party to power in November 1917. Soon the Bolshevik-controlled government negotiated a separate peace with Germany, which promptly transferred a million of its soldiers to the western front for the coming spring offensive.

The ideal of neat, sharply defined spaces for living and fighting is exemplified by these model trenches in northern France (above). Trench warfare, wrote one general, was "marked by uniform formations, the regulation of space and time by higher commands down to the smallest details . . . fixed distances between units and individuals." The reality (below) was something else again.

"You're in the Army Now"

The Allies' plight forced the U.S. army into a crash program to send a million men to Europe by the spring of 1918. The United States had barely 180,000 men in uniform. Volunteers rushed to recruitment offices, especially in ethnic communities, where Mexican Americans enlisted in numbers proportionately higher than any other group. But they were not enough.

To raise the necessary force, Congress passed the Selective Service Act in May 1917. Young men between the ages of 20 and 30 would be conscripted into the armed forces. Feelings against pressing men into service ran high. "There is precious little difference between a conscript [draftee] and a convict," protested the House Speaker in 1917. Progressives were more inclined to see military service as an opportunity to unite America and promote democracy: "Universal [military] training will jumble the boys of America all together, . . . smashing all the petty class distinctions that now divide, and prompting a brand of real democracy."

When the first number was drawn in the new draft lottery in July 1917, some 24

With hostility remaining high between Mexico and the United States after President Wilson sent U.S. troops into Mexico, many Mexican laborers returned to Mexico rather than be drafted into a foreign army whose goals they did not share. On the other hand Mexican Americans, especially those whose families had long lived in the United States, enlisted in the U.S. Army. Felix Sanchez of New Mexico was one such recruit.

million men were already registered. Almost 3 million were drafted; another 2 million volunteered. Most were white and young, between the ages of 21 and 31. Some 20,000 women served as clerks, telephone operators, and nurses. In a nation of immigrants, nearly one draftee in five was born in another country. Training often aimed at educating and Americanizing ethnic recruits. In special "development battalions" drill sergeants barked out orders while volunteers from the YMCA taught American history and English.

Like Mexican Americans, African Americans volunteered in disproportionately high numbers. They quickly filled the four all-black army and eight National Guard units already in existence. They were also granted fewer exemptions from the draft than white Americans were. Only 10 percent of the population, blacks comprised 13 percent of all draftees. Abroad, where 200,000 black troops served in France, just one in five (compared with two of every three whites) was permitted in combat. Southern Democrats in Congress had opposed training African Americans to arms, fearful of the prospect of putting "arrogant, strutting representatives of black soldiery in every community." But four regiments of the all-black 93rd Division, brigaded with the French army, were among the first Americans in the trenches and among the most decorated units in the U.S. Army.

Racial violence sometimes flared among the troops, notably in Houston in the summer of 1917. Harassed by white soldiers and by the city's Jim Crow laws, seasoned black regulars rioted and killed 17 white civilians. Their whole battalion was disarmed and sent under arrest to New Mexico. Thirteen troopers were condemned to death and hanged within days, too quickly for appeals even to be filed.

Progressive reformers did not miss the chance to put the social sciences to work in the army. Most recruits had fewer than seven years of education, yet they had to be classified and assigned quickly to units. Psychologists saw the chance to use new intelligence tests to help the army and prove their own theories about the value of "IQ" (intelligence quotient) in measuring the mind. In fact, these new "scientific" IQ tests often measured little more than class and cultural origins. Questions such as "Who wrote 'The Raven'?" exposed background rather than intelligence. More than half the Russian, Italian, and Polish draftees and almost 80 percent of blacks showed up as "inferior." The army stopped the testing program in January 1919, but schools across the country adopted it after the war, reinforcing many ethnic and racial prejudices.

On the home front, moral crusaders waged a war against sin, often pursuing old reforms with the help of mushrooming patriotism. Temperance leaders pressured the War Department to prohibit the sale of liquor to anyone in uniform in the vicinity of training camps. Alcohol would only impair a soldier's ability to fight. The army also declared war on venereal disease. "A Soldier who gets a dose is a Traitor!" warned one poster. The Commission on Training Camp Activities produced thousands of pamphlets, films, and lectures on the dangers of sexual misconduct. The drive constituted the first serious sex education many young Americans had ever received.

Mobilizing the Economy

To equip, feed, and transport an army of nearly 5 million demanded a national effort. The production of even a single ammunition shell brought components from every section of the country (plus vital nitrates from Chile) to assembly plants in New Jersey, Virginia, and Pennsylvania and from there to military installations or Atlantic ports.

At the Treasury Department, Secretary William Gibbs McAdoo fretted over how to finance the war, which cost, finally, $32 billion. The old revenue base of excise (luxury) taxes and customs duties gave way to a new one of taxes on incomes and profits. And by reducing the minimum level of taxable income to $1000, the number of Americans paying taxes jumped tenfold, from 437,000 in 1916 to 4,425,000 in 1918.

New taxes financed about a third of all war costs. The rest came from the sale of "Liberty" and "Victory" bonds and war savings certificates. The Federal Reserve System expanded the money supply to make borrowing easier. The national debt, which had stood at $2 billion in 1917, jumped to $20 billion only three years later.

With sweeping grants of authority provided by Congress, President Wilson constructed a massive bureaucracy to manage the home front. What emerged was a more managed economy, ironically similar to the New Nationalism envisioned by Theodore Roosevelt. Under the leadership of Wall Street wizard Bernard Baruch, a War Industries Board (WIB) coordinated production through networks of industrial and trade associations. Though it had the authority to order firms to comply, the WIB relied instead on persuasion through publicity and "cost-plus" contracts that covered all costs, plus a guaranteed profit. When businesses balked—as when Henry Ford refused to accept government curbs on the manufacture of civilian automobiles—Baruch could twist arms. In this case, he threatened to have the army run Ford's factories. Ford quickly reversed himself. Overall, corporate profits tripled and production soared during the war years.

War Industries Board

The Food Administration encouraged farmers to grow more and citizens to eat less wastefully. Herbert Hoover, who had saved starving refugees as chairman of the Commission for Relief in Belgium in 1914, was appointed administrator. Like the WIB, the Food Administration mobilized what Hoover called "the spirit of self-sacrifice." Huge publicity campaigns promoted "wheatless" and "meatless" days each week and encouraged families to plant "victory" gardens. Stirred by high commodity prices, farmers brought more marginal lands into cultivation, and their real income increased 25 percent.

A Fuel Administration met the army's energy needs by increasing production and limiting domestic consumption. Transportation snarls required more drastic action. In December 1917 the U.S. Railroad Administration took over rail lines for the duration of the war. Government coordination, together with a new system of permits, got freight moving and kept workers happy. Federally imposed "daylight savings time" stretched the workday and saved fuel as well. Rail workers saw their wages grow by $300 million. Railroad unions won recognition, an eight-hour day, and a grievance procedure. For the first time in decades labor unrest subsided, and the trains ran on schedule.

The modern bureaucratic state received a powerful boost during the 18 months of American participation in the war. Speeding trends that were already under way, hundreds of federal agencies centralized authority as they cooperated with business

Bureaucratic state

and labor to mount an unprecedented war effort. The number of federal employees more than doubled between 1916 and 1918, to over 850,000, and thousands of business executives entered government service for a nominal dollar a year. The wartime bureaucracy was quickly dismantled at the end of the war, but it set an important precedent for the growth of government.

War Work

The war benefited working men and women, though not as much as it benefited their employers. Government contracts guaranteed high wages, an eight-hour day, and equal pay for comparable work. To encourage people to stay on the job, federal contracting agencies set up special classes to teach employers the new science of personnel management in order to supervise workers more efficiently and humanely. American industry moved one step closer to the "welfare capitalism" of the 1920s, with its promises of profit sharing, company unions, and personnel departments to forestall worker discontent.

Personnel management was not always enough to guarantee industrial peace. In 1917 American workers called over 4000 strikes, the largest annual outbreak in American history. To keep factories running smoothly, President Wilson created the National War Labor Board (NWLB) early in 1918. The NWLB arbitrated more than 1000 labor disputes, helped to increase wages, established overtime pay, and supported the principle of equal pay for women. In return for pledges not to strike, the board guaranteed the rights of unions to organize and bargain collectively. Membership in the American Federation of Labor jumped from 2.7 million in 1914 to nearly 4 million by 1919.

National War Labor Board

Women in the workforce

As doughboys went abroad, the war brought nearly a million more women into the labor force. Most were young and single. Sometimes they took over jobs once held by men as railroad engineers, drill press operators, and electric lift truck drivers. Here, too, government tried to mediate between labor and management. In 1917 the Labor Department opened the Women in Industry Service (WIS) to recommend guidelines for using female labor. Among the most important were an eight-hour day, rest periods and breaks for meals, and equal pay for equal work. Most women never worked under such conditions, but for the first time, the federal government tried to upgrade their working conditions.

The prewar trend toward higher-paying jobs for women intensified. Most still earned less than the men they replaced as they moved into clerical and light industrial work. And some of the most spectacular gains in defense and government work evaporated after the war as male veterans returned and the country demobilized. Tens of thousands of army nurses, defense workers, and war administrators lost their jobs. Agencies such as the Women's Service Section of the Railroad Administration, which fought sexual harassment and discrimination, simply went out of business.

The constraints of war brought more women than ever into the job market. These women work on a production line manufacturing bullets. The novelty of the situation seems evident from the fashionable high-heeled high-button shoes that they wear—ill suited to the conditions in an armaments plant.

Great Migrations

War work sparked massive migrations of laborers. As the fighting abroad choked off immigration and the draft depleted the workforce, factory owners scoured the country and beyond for willing workers. Pressed by railroads and large-scale farmers, Congress waived immigration requirements in 1917 for agricultural workers from Mexico. A year later, the waiver was extended to workers on railroads, in mines, and on government construction projects.

Industrial cities, no matter how small, soon swelled with newcomers, many of them Mexican and Mexican American. Between 1917 and 1920, some 50,000 Mexicans legally crossed the border into Texas, California, New Mexico, and Arizona. At least another 100,000 entered illegally. Some Mexican Americans left the segregated barrios and farmlands of the West, pushed out by this cheaper labor from Mexico, and migrated to Chicago, Omaha, and other midwestern cities. Mexican *colonias*, or communities, sprang up across the industrial heartland. But most Mexicans and Mexican Americans continued to work on the farms and ranches of the Southwest, where they were freed from military service by the deferment granted to all agricultural labor.

Northern labor agents fanned out across the rural South to recruit young African Americans, while black newspapers like the Chicago *Defender* summoned them up to the "Land of Hope." Over the war years more than 400,000 moved to the booming industrial centers of the North. Largely unskilled and semiskilled, they worked in the steel mills of Pennsylvania, the war plants of Massachusetts, the brickyards of New Jersey. Southern towns were decimated by the drain. Finally, under pressure from southern politicians, the U.S. Employment Service suspended its program to assist blacks moving north.

These migrations—of African Americans into the army as well as into the city—aggravated racial tensions. Lynching parties murdered 38 black southerners in 1917 and 58 in 1918. In 1919, after the war ended, more than 70 African Americans were hung, some still in uniform. Housing shortages and job competition helped spark race riots across the North.

In almost every city black citizens, stirred by war rhetoric of freedom and democracy, showed new militancy by fighting back. In mid-1917 some 40 black and 9 white Americans died when East St. Louis erupted in racial violence. During the "red summer" of 1919, blood flowed in the streets of Washington, D.C., Omaha, Nebraska, New York City, and Chicago, where thousands of African Americans were burned out of their homes and hundreds injured. "The Washington riot gave me the *thrill that comes once in a life time*," wrote a young black woman in 1919. "At last our men had stood like men, struck back, were no longer dumb driven cattle."

Latino migrations

African Americans

Propaganda and Civil Liberties

"Once lead this people into war," President Wilson warned before American entry into the First World War, "and they'll forget there ever was such a thing as tolerance." Americans succumbed to war hysteria, but they had help. Wilson knew how reluctant Americans had been to enter the war, and he created the Committee on Public Information (CPI) to boost American commitment to the war.

Under George Creel, a California journalist, the CPI launched "a fight for the *minds* of men, for the conquest of their convictions.'" A zealous publicity campaign produced 75 million pamphlets, patriotic "war expositions" attended by 10 million people in two dozen cities, and colorful war posters, including James Flagg's famous,

Committee on Public Information

"I Want *You* for the U.S. Army." Seventy-five thousand fast-talking "Four-Minute Men" invaded movie theaters, lodge halls, schools, and churches to keep patriotism at "white heat" with four minutes of war tirades. The CPI organized "Loyalty Leagues" in ethnic communities and sponsored parades and rallies, among them a much-publicized immigrant "pilgrimage" to the birthplace of George Washington.

100 percent Americanism

The division between patriotism and intolerance proved impossible to maintain. As war fever rose, voluntary patriotism blossomed into an orgy of "100 percent Americanism" that distrusted all aliens, radicals, pacifists, and dissenters. German Americans became special targets. In Iowa the governor made it a crime to speak German in public. Hamburgers were renamed "Salisbury steak"; German measles, "liberty measles." When a mob outside St. Louis lynched a naturalized German American who had tried to enlist in the navy, a jury found the leaders not guilty.

Espionage and Sedition acts

Congress gave hysteria more legal bite by passing the Espionage and Sedition acts of 1917 and 1918. Both set out harsh penalties for any actions that hindered the war effort or that could be viewed as even remotely unpatriotic. Following their passage, 1500 citizens were arrested for offenses that included denouncing the draft, criticizing the Red Cross, and complaining about wartime taxes.

Radical groups received especially severe treatment. The Industrial Workers of the World (IWW), a militant labor union centered in western states, saw the war as a battle among capitalists and threatened to strike mining and lumber companies in protest. Federal agents raided the Chicago headquarters of the IWW—familiarly known as the "Wobblies"—and arrested 113 of its leaders in September 1917. The crusade destroyed the union.

Similarly, the Socialist party stridently opposed the "capitalist" war. In response, the postmaster general banned a dozen Socialist publications from the mail, though

The Final German Offensive and Allied Counterattack, 1918
On the morning of March 21, 1918, the Germans launched a spring offensive designed to cripple the Allies. Sixty-three German divisions sliced through Allied lines for the first time since 1914 and plunged to within 50 miles of Paris. The tide turned in July, when the Germans were stopped at the Marne. The Allied counterattack, with notable American successes at Château-Thierry, Belleau Wood, Saint-Mihiel, and Meuse-Argonne, broke the German war effort.

the party was a legal organization that had elected mayors, municipal officials, and members of Congress. In June 1918 government agents arrested Eugene V. Debs, the Socialist candidate in the presidential election of 1912, for attacking the draft. A jury found him guilty of sedition and sentenced him to 10 years in jail. Running for the presidency from his jail cell in 1920, Debs received nearly 1 million votes.

The Supreme Court condoned the wartime assault on civil liberties. In *Schenck v. United States* (1919), the Court unanimously affirmed the use of the Espionage Act to convict a Socialist party officer who had mailed pamphlets urging resistance to the draft. Free speech had limits, wrote Justice Oliver Wendell Holmes, and the pamphlets created "a clear and present danger" to a nation at war. In *Abrams v. United States* (1919) the Court upheld the verdict against Russian immigrant Jacob Abrams, whose pamphlets had denounced an American intervention in Russia to fight the Bolsheviks. Although Holmes saw no "clear and present danger," the majority ruled that the pamphlets tended to discourage the American war effort and thus violated the Sedition Act.

Over There

The first American doughboys landed in France in June 1917, but they saw no battle. Not until November would the first Americans die in action. General John Pershing held back his raw troops until they could receive more training. He also separated them in a distinct American Expeditionary Force to preserve their identity and avoid Allied disagreements over strategy.

In the spring of 1918, as the Germans pushed within 50 miles of Paris, Pershing rushed 70,000 American troops to the front. American units helped block the Germans both at the town of Château-Thierry and a month later, in June, at Belleau Wood. At Belleau, it cost half their force to drive the enemy from the woods. Two more German attacks, one at Amiens, the other just east of the Marne River, ended in costly German retreats. On September 12, 1918, half a million American soldiers and a smaller number of French troops overran the German stronghold at Saint-Mihiel in four days.

With their army in retreat and civilian morale low, Germany's leaders sought an armistice. They hoped to negotiate terms along the lines laid out by Woodrow Wilson in a speech to Congress in January 1918. Wilson's bright vision of peace had encompassed "Fourteen Points." The key provisions called for open diplomacy, free

In September 1918 half a million Americans moved against the German stronghold at the strategic Saint-Mihiel salient. Four days of fighting produced some 8000 casualties and netted the Allied victors 15,000 German prisoners. Here, John Singer Sargent's painting *Gassed* depicts the horrid results of a poison gas attack on Allied soldiers.

Wilson's Fourteen Points

seas and free trade, disarmament, democratic self-rule, and an "association of nations" to guarantee collective security. It was nothing less than a new world order to end selfish nationalism, imperialism, and war.

Allied leaders were not impressed. "President Wilson and his Fourteen Points bore me," French Premier Georges Clemenceau said. "Even God Almighty has only ten!" But Wilson's idealistic platform was also designed to save the Allies deeper embarrassment. Almost as soon as it came to power in 1917, the new Bolshevik government in Moscow began publishing secret treaties from the czar's archives. They revealed that the Allies had gone to war for territory and colonies, not the high principles they claimed. Wilson's Fourteen Points now gave their cause a nobler purpose.

His ideals also stirred German liberals. On October 6 Wilson received a telegram from Berlin requesting an immediate truce. Within a month Turkey and Austria surrendered. Early in November the Kaiser was overthrown and fled to neutral Holland. On November 11, 1918, just before dawn, German officers filed into Allied headquarters in a converted railroad car near Compiègne, France, and signed the armistice.

Of the 2 million Americans who served in France, some 116,500 died. Over 200,000 were wounded. By comparison, the war claimed 1.8 million Germans, 1.7 million Russians, 1.4 million French, 1.2 million Austro-Hungarians, and nearly a million Britons. The American contribution had nonetheless been crucial, providing vital convoys at sea and fresh, confident troops on land. The United States emerged from the war stronger than ever. Europe, on the other hand, looked forward—as one newspaper put it—to "Disaster . . . Exhaustion . . . Revolution."

The Influenza Pandemic of 1918–1919

The truce brought an end to the killing but not to the dying. In the months before the armistice, a scourge more lethal than war had begun to engulf the globe. It started innocently enough. At Fort Riley, Kansas, on the morning of March 11, 1918, company cook Albert Mitchell reported to the infirmary on sick call. His head and muscles ached, his throat was sore, and he had a low-grade fever.

In October 1918 artist D. C. Boonzaier drew this grim cartoon of the Spanish flu—*Spaanse Griep*—when it came to South Africa. In his diary Boonzaier spoke of "the presence of some universal calamity, from which there was no escape. Death stalked by your side incessantly, you looked into its face wherever you turned."

Cartoon by D. C. Boonzaier in *De Burger*, 16/10/1918

The army doctor had seen the symptoms before. It was the flu, dangerous for the very young and the old but ordinarily no problem for a robust young man like Mitchell. By noon, however, 107 soldiers had reported similar symptoms. Within a week, the number had jumped to over 500, and cases of the flu were being reported in virtually every state in the Union, even on the isolated island of Alcatraz in San Francisco Bay.

No one knew how or where the outbreak started or even what caused influenza. The discovery that it was a virus was still years away, as was the speculation that this eruption probably had its origin in birds, who passed it to pigs, who passed it to humans. It may have been spread initially by brush fires set on the Kansas plains, which scattered microbes from fecal matter and the earthworms that ingested it.

The first wave of flu produced few deaths in the United States. But as the virus spread and mutated over the next year, its victims experienced more and more distressing symptoms: vomiting, dizziness, labored breathing, incessant sweating. Pulmonary hemorrhages brought on projectile nosebleeds and fits of coughing that produced sometimes pints of yellow-green pus. Victims literally drowned in their own bodily fluids from the pneumonia that accompanied the infection.

Soldiers and others living in close quarters were especially vulnerable, and for reasons still unknown, so were young adults 20 to 34 years old, precisely the ages of most of those in the armed services. In September 1918, when acting Surgeon General of the Army Dr. Victor Vaughn visited Camp Devens near Boston, he was shocked to find "hundreds of young men in uniform coming into the wards of the hospital. . . . The faces wore a bluish cast; a cough brought up the blood-stained sputum. In the morning, the dead bodies are stacked about the morgue like cordwood." For every 50 people infected, one died. In the United States alone, the death toll rose to at least 675,000, more than the American battle deaths in World War I, World War II, the Korean War, and the war in Vietnam combined.

Ironically, the United States was the country least affected by this worldwide epidemic, called a "pandemic." American soldiers seem to have carried the disease to Europe, where it jumped like lightning from one country to another in the spring and summer of 1918. French troops and civilians soon were suffering from it, then British and Germans. General Eric von Ludendorf counted the flu as one of the causes of the failure of the final German offensive in July 1918, which almost won the war for Germany. In Spain, it infected as many as 8 million people and killed the Spanish king. Fear of the epidemic was so strong that a young Italian newspaper publisher named Benito Mussolini suggested throwing people in jail for shaking hands (a policy actually adopted by the town of Prescott, Arizona).

Global spread of the pandemic

With steamships and railroads carrying people all over the globe, virtually no place and no one was immune from the virus. By the summer of 1918, it had leapt from North America and Europe to Asia and Japan; by fall, to Africa and South America. As far north as the Russian city of Archangel, officials were reporting 30 influenza deaths a day by October 1918. When President Woodrow Wilson traveled to Paris to convene the peace conference in January 1919, he came down with the disease and lived. In India, one account claimed that at least 12 million perished from influenza. Six of every ten Inuit died from it in the villages north of Nome, Alaska, and on the Samoan islands in the Pacific, nearly 90 percent of the population caught the flu, many succumbing to starvation because they were too weak to eat.

Sixteen months after Albert Mitchell had first reported to sick call, the flu was gone, as quickly and mysteriously as it had appeared. Conservative estimates placed the number of dead worldwide at 25 million, making the influenza pandemic of 1918–1919 the most lethal outbreak of disease on an annual basis in human history. Global war had helped spread this particular disease, but improvements in transportation that had spawned the great migrations of the previous two centuries had also spawned pandemics. As automobiles and airplanes continued to shrink the globe, similar pandemics, though less deadly, would be repeated in years to come.

The Lost Peace

As the USS *George Washington* approached the coast of France in mid-December 1918 the mist suddenly lifted in an omen of good hope. Woodrow Wilson had come to represent the United States at the Paris peace conference at Versailles, once the glittering palace of Louis XIV. A world of problems awaited him and the other Allied leaders. Europe had been shelled into ruin and scarred with the debris of war. Fifty million people lay dead or maimed from the fighting. Throughout the Balkans and the old Turkish empire, ethnic rivalries, social chaos, and revolution loomed.

With the old world order so evidently in shambles, Wilson felt the need to take vigorous action. Thus the president handpicked the peace commission of experts that accompanied him. It included economists, historians, geographers, and political scientists—but not a single member of the Republican-controlled Senate. What promised to make peace negotiations easier, however, created a crippling liability in Washington, where Republicans cast a hostile eye on the mirrored halls of Versailles.

The Treaty of Versailles

Everywhere he went, cheers greeted the president. In Paris 2 million people showered him with flowers. In Italy they hailed him as the "peacemaker from America." And everywhere he went, Wilson believed what he heard, unaware of how determined the victors were to punish the vanquished Germans. David Lloyd George of England, Georges Clemenceau of France, Vittorio Orlando of Italy, and Wilson comprised the Big Four at the conference that included some 27 nations. War had united them; now peacemaking threatened to divide them.

Wilson's sweeping call for reform had taken Allied leaders by surprise. Hungry for new colonies, eager to see Germany crushed and disarmed, their secret treaties had already divided up the territories of the Central Powers. Germany had offered to surrender on the basis of Wilson's Fourteen Points, but the Allies refused to accept them. When Wilson threatened to negotiate peace on his own, Allied leaders finally agreed—but only for the moment.

Noticeably absent when the peace conference convened in January 1919 were the Russians. None of the Western democracies had recognized the Bolshevik regime in Moscow out of fear that the communist revolution might spread. Instead, France and Britain were helping to finance a civil war to overthrow the Bolsheviks. Even Wilson had been persuaded to send a small number of American troops to join the Allied occupation of Murmansk in northern Russia and Vladivostok on the Sea of Japan. The Soviets would neither forget nor forgive this invasion of their soil.

Grueling peace negotiations forced Wilson to yield several of his Fourteen Points. Britain, with its powerful navy, refused even to discuss the issues of free trade and freedom of the seas. Wilson's "open diplomacy" was conducted behind closed doors by the Big Four. The only mention of disarmament involved Germany, which was permanently barred from rearming. Wilson's call for "peace without victory" gave way to a "guilt clause" that saddled Germany with responsibility for the war. Worse still, the victors imposed on the vanquished a impoverishing debt of $33 billion in reparations.

Wilson did achieve some successes. His pleas for national self-determination led to the creation of a dozen new states in Europe, including Yugoslavia, Hungary, and Austria. (Newly created Poland and Czechoslovakia, however, contained millions of ethnic Germans.) Former colonies gained new status as "mandates" of the victors, who were obligated to prepare them for independence. The old German and Turkish empires in the Middle East and Africa became the responsibility of France and England, while Japan took over virtually all German possessions in the Pacific north of the equator.

Wilson never lost sight of his main goal—a League of Nations. He had given so much ground precisely because he believed this new world organization would correct any mistakes in the peace settlement. As constituted, the League was composed of a general Body of Delegates, a select Executive Council, and a Court of International Justice. Members promised to submit all war-provoking disagreements to arbitration and to isolate aggressors by cutting off commercial and military trade. Article X (Wilson called it "the heart of the covenant") bound members to respect one another's independence and territory and to join together against attack. "It is definitely a guarantee of peace," the president told the delegates in February 1919.

League of Nations

The Battle for the Treaty

Wilson left immediately for home to address growing opposition in Congress. In the off-year elections of 1918, voters unhappy with wartime controls, new taxes, and attacks on civil liberties gave both houses to the Republicans. A slim Republican majority in the Senate put Wilson's archrival, Henry Cabot Lodge of Massachusetts, in the chairman's seat of the all-important Foreign Relations Committee. "I never expected to hate anyone in politics with the hatred I feel toward Wilson," Lodge confessed.

While most of the country favored the League, Lodge was against it. For decades he had fought to preserve American freedom of action in foreign affairs. Now he worried that the League would force Americans to subject themselves to "the will of other nations." And he certainly did not want Democrats to win votes by taking credit for the treaty. Securing the signatures of enough senators to block any treaty, Lodge rose in the Senate just before midnight on March 3 to read a "round robin" resolution against the League. "Woodrow Wilson's League of Nations died in the Senate tonight," concluded the New York *Sun*.

Wilson formally presented the treaty in July. "Dare we reject it and break the heart of the world?" he asked the senators. Fourteen Republicans and two Democrats were happy to do just that. "Irreconcilable" opponents of internationalism, they vowed to kill "the unholy thing with the holy name." Twenty-three "strong reservationists," led by Lodge, sought to amend the treaty with major changes requiring yet another round of Allied negotiations. Twelve "mild reservationists" wanted minimal alterations, mainly interpretive in nature.

Allied leaders convened the peace conference in the palace of Louis XIV at Versailles. Woodrow Wilson faces the painter, as British Prime Minister David Lloyd George and French Premier Georges Clemenceau confer. On June 28, 1919, representatives of the new German republic were herded into the famed Hall of Mirrors, where they glumly signed the peace treaty they had no hand in writing. The Germans, observed one reporter, suffered a "horrible humiliation."

Daily Lives

TIME AND TRAVEL

The Doughboys Abroad

At ten in the morning on July 20, 1917, Secretary of War Newton Baker tied a blindfold over his eyes, reached into a huge glass bowl at the Senate Office Building, and drew the first number in a new draft lottery. The United States, with barely 180,000 men in the service, had begun to raise an army. By the time the conflict ended in November 1918, nearly 2 million men had donned uniforms, learned the manual of arms and close order drill, and gone off to fight in Europe. For the first time the New World was invading the Old, and for most of those who went, it was their first trip from home.

Armed against the enemy, scrubbed and clothed, drilled until they dropped, the "doughboys" marched out of their training camps and up the gangplanks of the "Atlantic Ferry"—the ships that conveyed them to Europe. (Infantrymen were called "doughboys" for the "dough" of clay that soldiers had used to clean their white belts in the 1850s.) Each man was outfitted with a pack, a weapon, a set of uniforms, and a "safety" razor, a new device that quickly altered American shaving habits.

Almost half the soldiers sailed on British vessels. Some were fortunate enough to ship out on refitted luxury liners, but most made the voyage below decks in converted freighters, "the blackest, foulest, most congested hole that I ever set foot into," reported one private. A few died from anthrax in the horsehair of their new shaving brushes. It was a poignant taste of things to come. Disease killed more Americans than enemy fire did. Some 62,000 troops died of influenza and other diseases.

The first American troops, a division of army regulars and a battalion of marines, arrived in France at the end of June 1917. Two months later the first volunteers landed, wearing spring parade

After months of training stateside, the American Expeditionary Force sailed to Europe on the troop ships of the "Atlantic Ferry." Most soldiers departed from Hoboken, New Jersey, and almost half made the journey aboard British vessels.

Wilson's only hope of winning the necessary two-thirds majority for passage of the treaty lay in compromise, but temperamentally he could not abide it. Worn out by the concessions already wrung from him in Paris, afflicted increasingly by numbing headaches and a twitch in his left eye, he resisted any more changes. Despite his doctor's warnings, Wilson took his case to the people in a month-long stump across the nation.

In Pueblo, Colorado, a crowd of 10,000 heard perhaps the greatest oration of Wilson's career. He spoke of American soldiers killed in France and American boys whom the League one day would spare from death. Listeners wept openly. That evening, utterly exhausted, Wilson collapsed in a spasm of pain. On October 2, four days after being rushed to the White House, he fell to the bathroom floor, knocked unconscious by a stroke.

Wilson's stroke

uniforms and carrying just 10 rounds of ammunition apiece. They were squeezed into "40-and-8's"—French freight cars designed to hold 40 men and 8 horses—and carried inland to training areas.

With the United States at war for such a short time, most American soldiers spent more time in training and on leave than in the trenches. To keep the men from becoming restless, company commanders marched their troops against imaginary enemies in never-ending exercises. "Every hill in this vicinity has been captured or lost at least ten times," wrote one weary infantryman who had to keep training even after the armistice. Soldiers complained about "cooties" (lice) and food (so bad that many reported a 10 percent weight loss within weeks of arriving). Used to freewheeling individualism and equality, they positively hated military discipline.

Enlisted men groused about army life, but the Old World awed them. Paris was titillating, with women who danced the "Can-Can" and cried "oo-la-la." The antiquity of Europe struck the dough-boys even more: "The church here is very, very old, probably built sometime in the 12th or 13th century. Saint Louis the Crusader, King of France, attended a service there on three occasions and Jeanne d'Arc was there several times." The Europeans seemed old and old-fashioned, too. Elderly women in black shawls of mourning often were the only ones left in shattered villages. "They still harvest with cradles and sickles," noted one soldier. Everything endorsed the American myth of the Old World as hidebound and worn and the New as modern and vital.

It was as if they had become crusaders, off on what one dough-boy called "a glorious adventure" to save beleaguered Europe. Disillusion and discontent overcame British and French troops after years in the trenches, but most doughboys never fought long enough to lose their sense of wonder and delight. A year after the war ended a veteran wrote: "I know how we all cried to get back to the States. But now that we are here, I must admit for myself at least that I am lost and somehow strangely lonesome. These our own United States are truly artificial and bare. There is no romance or color here, nothing to suffer for and laugh at."

For six weeks Wilson could do no work at all and for months after worked little more than an hour a day. His second wife, Edith Bolling Wilson, handled the routine business of government along with the president's secretary and his doctor. The country knew nothing of the seriousness of his condition. Wilson recovered slowly but never fully. More and more the battle for the treaty consumed his fading energies.

On November 19 Lodge finally reported the treaty out of committee with 14 amendments to match Wilson's Fourteen Points. The most important asserted that the United States assumed no obligation under Article X to come to the aid of League members unless Congress consented. Wilson believed Lodge had delivered a "knife thrust at the heart of the treaty" and refused to accept any changes. Whatever ill will Lodge bore Wilson, his objections did not destroy the treaty but only weakened it by protecting the congressional prerogative to declare war.

Under orders from the president, Democrats joined Republicans and "Irreconcilables" to defeat the treaty with Lodge's reservations. An attempt to pass the unamended treaty failed. Although four-fifths of the senators favored it in some form, Wilson and Lodge refused to compromise. When the amended treaty came before the Senate in March 1920, enough Democrats broke from the president to produce a majority but not the required two-thirds. The Treaty of Versailles was dead, and loyal Democrats had been forced to deliver the killing blow. Not until July 1921 did Congress enact a joint resolution ending the war. The United States, which had fought separately from the Allies, made a separate peace as well.

Red Scare

Peace abroad did not bring peace at home. On May Day 1919, six months after the war ended, mobs in a dozen cities broke up Socialist parades, injured hundreds, and killed three people. Later that month, when a spectator at a Victory Loan rally in Washington refused to stand for the national anthem, a sailor shot him in the back.

In September 1919 some 350,000 steelworkers struck for higher wages, recognition of their union, and a reduction in their 70-hour workweeks. Mill owners countered by hiring black strikebreakers and armed guards and by launching a potent publicity campaign that depicted the strike as a plot of "Red agitators." Here, armed police ride down strikers in Philadelphia.

The stadium crowd applauded. On the floor of the Senate Kenneth McKellar of Tennessee advocated sending citizens with radical beliefs to a penal colony on Guam.

The spontaneous violence and extremism occurred because Americans believed they were under attack. Millions of soldiers had returned home, now unemployed and looking for jobs. With prices rising and war regulations lifted, laborers were demanding higher wages and striking when they failed to get them. In Boston even the police walked off their jobs. When a strike by conservative trade unionists paralyzed Seattle for five days in January, Mayor Ole Hanson draped his car in an American flag and led troops through the streets in a show of force. Hanson blamed radicals, while Congress ascribed the national ills to Bolshevik agents inspired by the revolution in Russia.

The menace of radical subversion was entirely overblown. With Socialist Eugene Debs in prison, his dwindling party numbered only about 30,000. Radicals at first hoped that the success of the Russian Revolution would help reverse their fortunes in the United States. But most Americans found the prospect of "Bolshevik" agitators threatening, especially after March 1919, when the new Russian government formed the Comintern to spread revolution abroad. Furthermore, the Left itself splintered. In 1919 dissidents deserted the Socialists to form the more radical

Radicals and labor unrest

Communist Labor party. About the same time, a group of mostly Slavic radicals created a separate Communist party. Both organizations counted no more than 40,000 members.

On April 28 Mayor Hanson received a small brown parcel at his office, evidently another present from an admirer of his tough patriotism. It was a homemade bomb. Within days, 20 such packages were discovered, including ones sent to John D. Rockefeller, Supreme Court Justice Oliver Wendell Holmes, and Postmaster General Albert Burleson. On June 2 bombs exploded simultaneously in eight different cities. One of them demolished the front porch of A. Mitchell Palmer, the attorney general of the United States. The bomb thrower was blown to bits, but enough remained to identify him as an Italian anarchist from Philadelphia. Already edgy over Bolshevism and labor militancy, many Americans assumed that an organized conspiracy was being mounted to overthrow the government.

Palmer raids

Palmer, a Quaker and a staunch progressive, hardened in the wake of the bombings. In November 1919 and again in January 1920, he launched raids in cities across the United States. In a single night in January, government agents invaded private homes, meeting halls, and pool parlors in 33 cities. They took 4000 people into custody without warrants, sometimes beating those who resisted. Many were Russians, some were communists, but most were victims of suspicion run amok. In Detroit, 300 innocent people were arrested and confined for a week, one day without food. Prisoners were marched through streets in chains, crammed into dilapidated jails, and held incommunicado without hearings. Over 200 aliens, most of whom had no criminal records, were deported to the Soviet Union.

Arrests continued at the rate of 200 a week through March. State after state passed new statutes outlawing radical unions. Local vigilance committees even screened the loyalty of schoolteachers. In Centralia, Washington, vigilantes spirited radical labor organizer Wesley Everest from jail, castrated him, and hanged him from the Chehalis River bridge as they riddled his body with bullets. The county coroner ruled it a suicide.

Such abuses of civil liberties finally provoked a backlash. After the New York legislature expelled five duly elected Socialists in 1919, responsible politicians—from former presidential candidate Charles Evans Hughes to Ohio Senator Warren Harding—began to denounce the action. Assistant Secretary of Labor Louis Post refused to issue more deportation orders, and the "deportation delirium" ended early in 1920.

Palmer finally overreached himself by predicting a revolutionary uprising for May 1, 1920. Buildings were put under guard and state militia called to readiness. Nothing happened. Four months later, when a wagonload of bombs exploded on Wall Street, Palmer blamed a Bolshevik conspiracy. Despite 33 deaths and more than 200 injuries, Americans saw it as the work of a few fanatic anarchists (which it probably was) and went about business as usual.

Not for another 20 years would the United States assume a leading position in international affairs. And the spirit of reform at home dimmed as well. When war came, progressivism had furnished the bureaucratic weapons to organize the fight, but the push for social justice and toleration had been overshadowed by a patriotic frenzy.

War changed Americans. They experienced a managed economy for the first time. Propaganda shaped diverse ethnic, racial, class, and gender differences into a uniform set of national issues. Such single-mindedness would not quickly disappear. War work drew millions from country to city, from farm to factory. The army mixed millions more. They learned to fight but also to read, to sleep in a bed, to eat regular meals, and to take regular baths. After seeing Europe, they returned like tourists in uniform to tell of its wonders. Provincial America became more cosmopolitan and urban. But with the war over, the nation turned from idealistic crusades to the practical business of getting and spending. At home and abroad, a dynamic new era of prosperity and peace dawned, but within a decade both prosperity and peace would vanish because of the terrible price exacted from the failure of the Treaty of Versailles to establish a new world order of international cooperation.

chapter summary

The First World War marked the beginning of the end of the old world order of colonial imperialism, military alliances, and balances of power; it also marked a failed effort to establish a new world order based on the progressive ideals of international cooperation and collective security.

- Progressive diplomacy—whether through Theodore Roosevelt's big stick diplomacy, William Taft's dollar diplomacy, or Woodrow Wilson's missionary diplomacy—stressed moralism and order, championed "uplifting" nonwhites, and stretched presidential authority to its limits.

- With the outbreak of the First World War in 1914, Woodrow Wilson saw an opportunity for the United States to lead the world to a higher peace of international cooperation by remaining neutral and brokering the peace settlement.

- However, American sympathy for the Allies, heavy American investments in the Allies, and the German campaign of unrestricted submarine warfare finally drew the country into the war in 1917.

- Progressive faith in government, planning, efficiency, and publicity produced a greatly expanded bureaucratic state that managed the war effort on the home front.

  - The darker side of progressivism also flourished as the war transformed progressive impulses for assimilation and social control into campaigns for superpatriotism and conformity that helped to produce a postwar red scare in 1919 and 1920.

  - Meanwhile, changes already underway, including more women in the labor force and migrations of African Americans and Mexican Americans from rural to urban America, vastly accelerated with the expansion of opportunities for war work.

- When the war ended, Wilson's hopes for "peace without victory" and a new world order, embodied in his Fourteen Points, were dashed when his European allies imposed a harsh settlement on Germany and the U.S. Senate failed to ratify the Treaty of Versailles.

additional reading

The diverse vectors of progressive diplomacy, as practiced by Theodore Roosevelt and Woodrow Wilson, are the subject of Howard K. Beale, *Theodore Roosevelt and the Rise of America to World Power* (1956) and Arthur Link, *Woodrow Wilson: Revolution, War, and Peace* (1968). Ernest R. May examines American prewar diplomacy and the policies of the Great Powers, especially Germany's U-boat campaign, in *The World War and American Isolation, 1914–1917* (1957). David M. Kennedy, *Over Here: The First World War and American Society* (1980) is the definitive account of mobilization and the home front, but see also Maurine W. Greenwald, *Women, War, and Work* (1980), a detailed look at the status of women, and Joel William Trotter Jr., *The Great Migration in Historical Perspective* (1991), a fine collection of essays that stresses gender and class in the wartime experience of African Americans. Frank Freidel recreates the horrors of trench warfare in *Over There: The Story of America's First Great Overseas Crusade* (1964). For African Americans on the battle front, see Arthur E. Barbeau and Henri Florette, *The Unknown Soldiers: Black American*

Troops in World War I (1974). Robert Ferrell, *Woodrow Wilson and World War I* (1985) analyzes Wilson's wartime diplomacy, the peace negotiations, and the fate of the Treaty of Versailles. The most informed account of the influenza pandemic can be found in Alfred W. Crosby, *America's Forgotten Pandemic: The Influenza of 1918* (1989).

The debate over American entry into World War I has a long history. Early revisionist accounts emphasizing a fi-

nancial conspiracy to bring the nation to war include Charles Beard, *The Open Door to War* (1934) and Charles C. Tansill, *America Goes to War* (1938). A good account from the school of realists, which is critical of Wilson's moral motives, is found in George Kennan, *American Diplomacy, 1900–1950* (rev. ed., 1971). For a fuller list of readings, see the Bibliography.

Significant Events

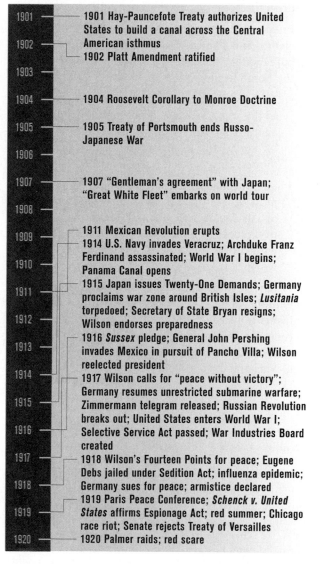

1901 **1901 Hay-Pauncefote Treaty authorizes United States to build a canal across the Central American isthmus**

1902 **1902 Platt Amendment ratified**

1903

1904 **1904 Roosevelt Corollary to Monroe Doctrine**

1905 **1905 Treaty of Portsmouth ends Russo-Japanese War**

1906

1907 **1907 "Gentleman's agreement" with Japan; "Great White Fleet" embarks on world tour**

1908

1911 Mexican Revolution erupts

1914 U.S. Navy invades Veracruz; Archduke Franz Ferdinand assassinated; World War I begins; Panama Canal opens

1915 Japan issues Twenty-One Demands; Germany proclaims war zone around British Isles; *Lusitania* torpedoed; Secretary of State Bryan resigns; Wilson endorses preparedness

1916 *Sussex* pledge; General John Pershing invades Mexico in pursuit of Pancho Villa; Wilson reelected president

1917 Wilson calls for "peace without victory"; Germany resumes unrestricted submarine warfare; Zimmermann telegram released; Russian Revolution breaks out; United States enters World War I; Selective Service Act passed; War Industries Board created

1918 Wilson's Fourteen Points for peace; Eugene Debs jailed under Sedition Act; influenza epidemic; Germany sues for peace; armistice declared

1919 Paris Peace Conference; *Schenck v. United States* affirms Espionage Act; red summer; Chicago race riot; Senate rejects Treaty of Versailles

1920 Palmer raids; red scare

THE PERILS OF DEMOCRACY

In the wake of World War I, the editors of the American progressive journal *The New Republic* despaired that "the war did no good to anybody. Those of its generation whom it did not kill, it crippled, wasted, or used up." With the specter of Russian Bolshevism looming, parliamentary governments across Europe struggled to establish what President Warren Harding in the United States called "normalcy": a mixture of material prosperity and political stability.

By the mid-1920s despair had given way to hope. The postwar recession had lifted in the United States, and Woodrow Wilson's vision of a world made safe for democracy no longer seemed a naive hope. In both political and material terms democracy seemed to be advancing almost everywhere. Great Britain eliminated restrictions on suffrage for men, and between 1920 and 1928 women gained the vote in both Britain and the United States. Hapsburg Germany transformed itself into the Weimar Republic, whose constitution provided universal suffrage and a bill of rights. Across central and eastern Europe, the new nations carved out of the old Russian and Austro-Hungarian empires attempted to create governments along similarly democratic lines. So did the previously independent Romania, Bulgaria, Greece, and Albania.

The winds of political reform blew from Europe across the Middle East through Asia. Some Asians, like Mao Zedong in China and Ho Chi Minh in Indochina (Vietnam), saw in communism the means to liberate their peoples from imperialist rule. But even Asian Marxists aligned themselves with the powerful force of nationalism. In India, the Congress party formed by Mohandas K. Gandhi united socialists and powerful industrial capitalists. Through tactics of nonviolence and boycotts of British goods, Indian nationalists pushed the British to grant them greater political representation, economic autonomy, and eventual self-government. In Turkey, Kemal Atatürk in 1923 abolished the sultanate and established the Turkish Republic, with all the trappings of a Western democratic state.

The spread of democracy had a material side as well. The credibility of parliamentary governments depended heavily on their ability to restore and maintain prosperity. In the second half of the 1920s the world economy expanded. Some optimists suggested that innovations in manufacturing, like Henry Ford's moving assembly line, would usher in an era in which plenty would replace want. Increased earnings encouraged a democratic culture of consumption, whether it was buying radios in France or Western-style fashions in Tokyo (below). Products like the automobile, once available only to the rich, were increasingly accessible to people of all classes. Ford himself became an international hero, and German and Russian engineers used the term *Fordismus* to characterize modern industrial techniques.

Along with the automobile the mass media introduced a revolution in world culture. The impact of movies, radio, and mass circulation

GLOBAL EVENTS

Inflation plagues defeated Germany
1920s

Washington Conference on naval armaments
1921

Mussolini marches on Rome;
James Joyce's *Ulysses*
1922

Atatürk establishes Turkish Republic
1923

Kellogg-Briand Pact outlaws war

| 1920 | 1921 | 1922 | 1923 | 1925 | 1928 |
| HARDING | | | COOLIDGE | | |

Stock market
boom underway

1923
Teapot Dome scandal exposed

1922
Sinclair Lewis's *Babbitt*
published

1925
F. Scott Fitzgerald's *The Great Gatsby* published;
Scopes trial debates evolution

KDKA, Pittsburgh, first commercial radio station on air;
Prohibition takes effect

AMERICAN EVENTS

magazines, while greatest in the United States, was felt around the globe. Once-remote people and places became accessible and familiar. Stories, names, phrases, images, and ideas could become the common property of all. "In short, it seems to be the nature of radio to encourage people to think and feel alike," two prominent psychologists concluded. Consumption of culture as well as manufactured goods seemed to walk hand in hand with the democracy of the masses.

But the foundations upon which democracy rested were fragile. In the new Soviet Union, communists led by Lenin and the young Joseph Stalin demonstrated how readily talk of "the masses" and "democratic socialism" could mask an iron totalitarianism. In Japan, democracy

was hampered by that nation's persistent feudal traditions and the rise of militarism. Although its parliamentary government was controlled for a time by liberal, westernized factions, nationalists from the old samurai class joined with the nation's economically powerful families in quest of a Japanese East Asian empire.

Fear of communist revolution led some nationalists in Europe to reject democracy. With Italy's parliamentary government seemingly paralyzed by postwar unrest, Benito Mussolini and his *Fasci di Combattimento,* or fascists, used terrorism, murder, and intimidation to create an "all-embracing" single-party state, outside which "no human or spiritual values can exist, let alone be desirable." They rejected both the

liberals' belief in political parties and the Marxist concept of class solidarity. Instead, they glorified the nation-state dominated by the middle class, small businesspeople, modest property owners, and small farmers.

Fascism thus gave a sinister twist to the liberal ideal of national solidarity, but one that others embraced as a no-nonsense means of blunting Marxism. Adolf Hitler, like many Germans, resented the stinging defeat that war brought in 1919 and blamed communists, among others, for the sorry state of German life. Like Mussolini, Hitler used the politics of discontent to rise to power. Having achieved it in 1933, his Nazi party destroyed democracy. Under one-party rule, the Gestapo secret political police ensured that Germans expressed

PART FIVE

GLOBAL EVENTS

Stalin's power consolidated

Civil War breaks out in Spain

Japan attacks China

Depression spreads to Europe;
Japan invades Manchuria

Hitler becomes chancellor of Germany

Italy invades Ethiopia

| 1929 | | 1931 | 1932 | 1933 | | 1935 | 1936 | 1937 |

HOOVER

ROOSEVELT

Isolationists pass
Neutrality Act

"Hundred days" of the New Deal;
Prohibition ends

"Second New Deal" program

Bonus Army arrives in Washington

FDR fails to enlarge the Supreme Court

Stock market crash

AMERICAN EVENTS

only those ideas that conformed to the views of their national leader, the Führer.

Hitler succeeded partly because the prosperity of the 1920s was shattered worldwide by the corro-

sive hardships of the Great Depression. Farmers were particularly hard hit: during the 1920s the opening of new lands to cultivation had already led to overproduction. In Java, for example, the use of scientific agricultural techniques created a glut in the sugar market. By 1930 the price of wheat, measured in gold, reached its lowest point in 400 years. And those urban unemployed who walked the street in search of a job ("I seek work of any sort," reads the German's sign at left) were often ready to believe that only the forceful leadership of one could unite the many. Even in the United States, the business newspaper *Barron's* voiced the thoughts of more than a few when it mused that "a mild species of dictatorship" might "help us over the roughest spots in the road ahead."

Still, the rise of Hitler and Mussolini shook those people who had faith in the possibilities of mass politics. While Franklin Roosevelt used his radio "fireside chats" to bring government closer to the people, Hitler's fiery speeches and mass rallies seemed bent on encouraging racist fears and manipulating public opinion. While Hollywood produced films that affirmed popular faith in democratic government, a capitalist economy, and the success ethic, the German director Leni Riefenstahl used her cinematic gifts to combine myth, symbolism, and documentary into an evocation of the Führer as a pagan god of strength and a Christian savior. The "mass" aspects of the media were a two-edged sword. Perceptive critics recognized that even in democracies,

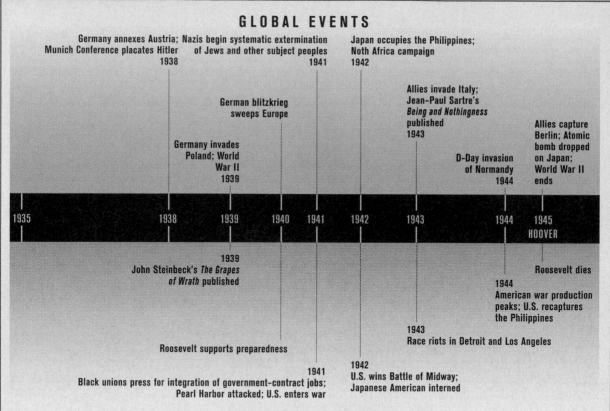

GLOBAL EVENTS

Germany annexes Austria; Nazis begin systematic extermination
Munich Conference placates Hitler   of Jews and other subject peoples
1938   1941

Japan occupies the Philippines;
Noth Africa campaign
1942

German blitzkrieg
sweeps Europe

Allies invade Italy;
Jean–Paul Sartre's
Being and Nothingness
published
1943

Allies capture
Berlin; Atomic
bomb dropped
on Japan;
World War II
ends

Germany invades
Poland; World
War II
1939

D-Day invasion
of Normandy
1944

1935   1938   1939   1940   1941   1942   1943   1944   1945
                                                                        HOOVER

1939
John Steinbeck's *The Grapes
of Wrath* published

Roosevelt dies
1944
American war production
peaks; U.S. recaptures
the Philippines

1943
Race riots in Detroit and Los Angeles

Roosevelt supports preparedness

1941
Black unions press for integration of government-contract jobs;
Pearl Harbor attacked; U.S. enters war

1942
U.S. wins Battle of Midway;
Japanese American interned

AMERICAN EVENTS

mass culture was devoted primarily to the entertainment and escapism of light comedy and melodrama rather than serious social criticism.

Thus the Depression shook both the political and the material pillars of democratic culture. On the eve of World War II the number of European democracies had been reduced from 27 to 10. Latin America was ruled by a variety of dictators and military juntas that differed little from the dictatorships of Europe. China suffered not only from invasion by Japan's militarists and civil war but also from the corrupt and ineffectual one-party dictatorship of Chiang Kai-shek. Almost alone, the New Deal attempted to combat the Depression through the methods of parliamentary democracy. The totalitarian states that had promised stability, national glory, and an end to the communist menace instead led the world to chaos and war, from which both communism and democracy emerged triumphant.

Chapter 24

The New Era

preview • The 1920s ushered in a "New Era" in which key features of modern life took hold: mass society, mass culture, and mass consumption. Urban America led the way in rejecting social conventions that had limited Americans, especially women and children, while more traditional regions defended their ways of life through immigration restriction, Prohibition, Fundamentalism, and a reborn Ku Klux Klan. In the end the roaring economy crashed, undone by underlying weaknesses.

Just before Christmas 1918 the "Gospel Car" pulled into Los Angeles. Bold letters on the side announced: "JESUS IS COMING—GET READY." Aimee Semple McPherson, the ravishing redheaded driver, had completed a cross-country drive to seek her destiny in the West. With only "ten dollars and a tambourine" to her name, Sister Aimee at first found destiny elusive. After three years of wandering the state, she landed in San Diego. With the highest rates of illness and suicide in California, it was the perfect place for Sister Aimee to preach the healing message of her "Foursquare Gospel." Her revival attracted 30,000 people, who witnessed her first proclaimed miracle: a paralytic walked.

Sister Aimee had a Pentecostal message for her flock: "Jesus is the healer. I am only the little office girl who opens the door and says, 'Come in.'" After the miracle in San Diego, her fame spread. She returned triumphantly to Los Angeles, where nearly three-quarters of a million people, many from the nation's heartland, had migrated in search of opportunity, sun, and perhaps salvation. In heading west, most had lost touch with the traditional Protestant denominations at home. Sister Aimee put her traveling gospel tent away. She would minister to the lost flock at her doorstep.

To the blare of trumpets on New Year's Day, 1923, she unveiled the $1.5 million Angelus

Temple, graced by a 75-foot, rotating electronic cross. It was visible at night from 50 miles away. Inside was a 5000-seat auditorium, radio station KFSG (Kall Four Square Gospel), a "Cradle Roll Chapel" for babies, and a "Miracle Room" filled with crutches and canes discarded by the cured faithful. Services were not simply a matter of hymn, prayer, and sermon. Sister added pageants, Holy Land slide shows, circuses, and healing sessions.

Aimee Semple McPherson succeeded because she was able to blend old and new. Her lively sermons carried the spirit of what people were calling the "New Era" of productivity and consumerism. Where country preachers menaced their congregations with visions of eternal damnation, Sister Aimee, wrote a reporter, offered "flowers, music, golden trumpets, red robes, angels, incense, nonsense, and sex appeal." Her approach revealed a nose for publicity and a sophisticated understanding of the booming media industries of the 1920s. Here was one brand of evangelism suited to a new consumer age.

Modernizing the gospel was just one symptom of the New Era. Writing in 1931, journalist Frederick Lewis Allen found the changes of the preceding decade so breathtaking that he could not believe that 1919 was *Only Yesterday*, as he titled his book. To give a sense of the transformation, Allen followed an average American couple, the fictitious "Mr. and Mrs. Smith," through the 1920s. The same revolution in industry and technology that allowed the sweet-voiced Aimee McPherson to save souls by the thousands had also transformed the Smiths' home with the sounds of radio, the miracles of canned foods, and the savings in time and energy generated by a host of new electrical gadgets. But the most striking and visible changes involved the revolution in women's fashions and behavior. By the end

Sister Aimee Semple McPherson, billed as "the world's most pulchritudinous evangelist," in her robe.

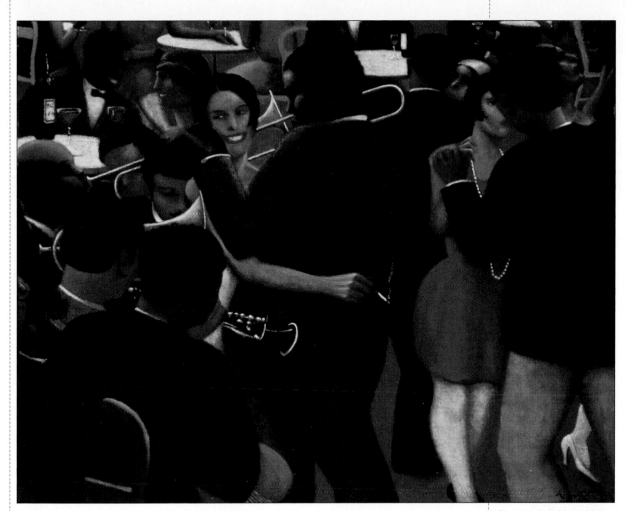

Blues, painted in 1929 by African American artist Archibald Motley Jr., evokes the improvised rhythms of the Jazz Age. New Orleans–born Motley was one of a group of black genre painters in the 1920s who became part of the Harlem Renaissance.

of the decade, Mrs. Smith's corset vanished, and her hemline jumped from her ankle to her knee. Mimicking stylish young flappers, she bobbed, or cut, her long hair to the popular, near-boyish length and flattened her breasts for greater freedom of movement.

With Prohibition in full force, Mrs. Smith and other women of her day walked into illegal speakeasy saloons as readily as men. In the trendy hotels she and her husband danced to jazz. Modern couples like the Smiths sprinkled their conversations with references to "repressed sexual drives" and the best methods of contraception. But perhaps the most striking change about these "average" Americans was that they lived in the city. The census of 1920 showed that for the first time just over half the population were urbanites. Here, in urban America, the New Era worked its changes and sent them rippling outward.

Yet the city-dwelling Smiths of Frederick Allen's imagination were hardly average. Nearly as many Americans still lived on isolated farms, in villages, and in small towns as in cities. In fact, many "city" dwellers lived there, too. By defining cities as incorporated municipalities with 2500 people or more, the Census Bureau had created hundreds of statistical illusions. New York with its millions of inhabitants ranked in the census tables alongside Sac Prairie, Wisconsin, whose population hovered barely above the mystical mark of 2500, and tiny Hyden, along the Cumberland plateau of eastern Kentucky.

Urban role in the New Era

Most citizens, the Smiths aside, dwelled in an earlier America and clung to its traditions. The technology of the New Era had yet to penetrate many urban American homes, let alone the hinterlands. As late as 1927, two-thirds of American households still had no washing machines or vacuum cleaners and half had no telephones. Nearly all American farms lacked electricity.

The poet August Derleth grew up under just such conditions in Sac Prairie. As a 10-year-old in 1919 he could hear the "howl of wolves" at night. The town observed changing seasons not with new fashions but by the appearance and disappearance of plants and animals. In Hyden, Kentucky, Main Street was still unpaved. By 1930 there were still only 10 automobiles in the county. God-fearing Baptists worshiped together as their parents had before them and still repaired to the Middle Fork of the Kentucky River for an open-air baptism when they declared their new birth in Christ. They would have nothing to do with flapper girls or the showy miracles of Aimee McPherson.

As much as some Americans resisted the transforming forces of modern life, the New Era could not be walled out. Industrial breakthroughs led to a host of new consumer goods, while large corporations developed more "modern" bureaucracies to make production more efficient and profitable. Whether Americans embraced the New Era or condemned it, change came nonetheless, in the form of a mass-produced consumer economy, a culture shaped by mass media, and a more materialistic society. A new ethic of getting and spending took hold, driving the economy to dizzying heights. Most Americans believed the New Era of peace and prosperity would last forever and ripple outward across the globe. Little did they realize that their roaring economy was honeycombed with weaknesses, and in 1929, to their astonishment, it collapsed.

The Roaring Economy

In the 1920s, the United States was in the midst of a revolution in production. Manufacturing rose 64 percent; output per workhour, 40 percent. The sale of electricity doubled; the consumption of fuel oil more than doubled. Between 1922 and 1927 the economy grew by 7 percent a year—the largest peacetime rate ever. If anything roared in the "Roaring Twenties," it was the economy.

Technology and Consumer Spending

Technology was partly responsible. Steam turbines and shovels, electric motors, belt and bucket conveyors, and countless other new machines became common at work sites. Machines replaced 200,000 workers each year, and a new phrase—"technological unemployment"—entered the vocabulary. Even so, rising demand, especially for new consumer goods, kept the labor force growing at a faster rate than the population. And pay improved. Between 1919 and 1927, average income climbed nearly $150 for each industrial worker.

As the industrial economy matured, more consumer goods appeared on store shelves—cigarette lighters, wristwatches, radios, panchromatic film. Under their impact, American customs changed, sometimes with unintended results. Electric washing machines and vacuum cleaners lightened the load of a "Blue Monday" spent washing clothes by hand and reduced the drudgery of cleaning house. At the same time these innovations boosted standards of household cleanliness and meant hours more of work for homemakers. Commercial laundries disappeared, and the long-term trend toward fewer domestic servants intensified.

The improvement in productivity helped keep prices down. The cost of a tire and an inner tube, for example, dropped by half between 1914 and 1929. Meanwhile, the purchasing power of wage earners jumped by 20 percent. Americans enjoyed the highest standard of living any people had ever known.

Yet for all the prosperity, a dangerous imbalance was developing in the economy. Most Americans saved little in the mistaken belief that prosperity was here to stay. Falling prices made many items seem like good buys, and the rapid expansion of credit (see page 784) allowed consumers to put off paying for what they purchased. As a result, personal debt was rising two and a half times faster than personal income, an unhealthy sign of consumers scrambling to spend.

The Booming Construction Industry

Along with technology and consumer spending, new "boom industries" promoted economic growth. In a rebound after the war years, construction boomed. Even cities the size of Beaumont, Texas, Memphis, Tennessee, and Syracuse, New York, were erecting buildings of 20 stories or more. New York got a new skyline of tall towers, topped in 1931 when the Empire State Building rose to the world-record height of 86 stories.

Residential construction doubled as people moved from cities to suburbs. Near Detroit, suburban Grosse Point grew by 700 percent, and Beverly Hills, on the outskirts of Los Angeles, by 2500 percent. Road construction made suburban life possible and pumped millions of dollars into the economy. In 1919 Oregon, New Mexico, and Colorado hit on a novel idea for financing roads—a tax on gasoline. Within a decade every state had one.

Construction stimulated other businesses: steel, concrete, lumber, home mortgages, and insurance. It even helped change the nation's eating habits. The limited storage space of small "kitchenettes" in new apartments boosted supermarket chains and the canning industry. As shipments of fresh fruits and vegetables sped across new roads, interest in nutrition grew. Vitamins, publicized with new zeal, appeared on breakfast tables.

The Automobile

No industry boomed more than automobile manufacturing. Although cars had first appeared on streets at the turn of the century, for many years they remained little more than expensive toys. By 1920 there were 10 million in America, a sizable number. But by 1929 the total had jumped to 26 million, one for every five people (compared to one for every 43 in Britain and one for every 7000 in Russia). Automakers bought one-seventh of the nation's steel and more rubber, plate glass, nickel, and lead than any other industry. By the end of the decade, one American in four somehow earned a living from automobiles.

Henry Ford helped to make the boom possible by pushing standardization and mass production to such ruthless extremes that the automobile became affordable. Trading on his fame as a race-car manufacturer, he founded the Ford Motor Company in 1903 with the dream of building a "motor car for the multitude." "Everybody wants to be somewhere he ain't," Ford observed. The way to succeed was to

Henry Ford

Henry Ford at the turn of the century.

drive down costs by making all the cars alike, "just like one pin is like another pin." In 1908 Ford perfected the Model T. It had a 20-horsepower engine and a body of steel. It was high enough to ride the worst roads, and it came in only one color: black.

Priced at $845, the Model T was cheap by industry standards but still too costly and too time-consuming to build. Two Ford engineers suggested copying a practice of Chicago meatpacking houses, where beef carcasses were carried on moving chains past meat dressers. In 1914 Ford introduced the moving assembly line. A conveyor belt, positioned waist high to eliminate bending or walking, propelled the chassis at six feet per minute as stationary workers put the cars together. The process cut assembly time in half. In 1925 new Model Ts were rolling off the line every 10 seconds. At $290, almost anybody could buy one. By 1927 Ford had sold 15 million of his "tin lizzies."

Doctrine of high wages

Ford was also a social prophet. Breaking with other manufacturers, he preached a "doctrine of high wages." According to it, workers with extra money in their pockets would buy enough to sustain a booming prosperity. In 1915 Ford's plants in Dearborn established the "Five-Dollar Day," twice the wage rate in Detroit. He reduced working hours from 48 to 40 a week and cut the workweek to five days. By 1926 he also employed 10,000 African Americans, many of whom had advanced far enough to hire and fire their white subordinates.

Yet Ford workers were not happy. Ford admitted that the repetitive operations on his assembly line made it scarcely possible "that any man would care to continue long at the same job." The Five-Dollar Day was designed, in part, to reduce the turnover rate of 300 percent a year at Ford plants. And Ford recouped his profits by speeding up the assembly line and enforcing ruthless efficiencies. Ford workers could not talk, whistle, smoke, or sit on the job. They wore frozen expressions called "Fordization of the Face" and communicated in the "Ford Whisper" without moving their lips. A Sociological Department spied on workers in their homes, and the Education Department taught plant procedures but also Americanization classes where immigrant workers learned English, proper dress, and even etiquette.

General Motors copied Ford's production techniques but not his business strategies. While Ford tried to sell everyone the same car, GM created "a car for every purse and purpose." There were Cadillacs for the wealthy, Chevrolets for the modest. GM cars were painted in a rainbow of colors, and every year the style changed. In a standardized society, such details made automobiles symbols of distinction as well as prestige.

A car culture

By making automobiles available to nearly everyone, the industry changed the face of America. The spreading web of paved roads fueled urban sprawl, real estate booms in California and Florida, and a new roadside culture of restaurants, service stations, and motels. Thousands of "auto camps" opened to provide tourists with tents and crude toilets. "Auto clubs" like the Tin Can Tourists Association (named for the tin can tied to the radiator cap of a member's car) sprang up to aid travelers.

Across the country the automobile gave the young unprecedented freedom from parental authority. After hearing 30 cases of "sex crimes" (19 had occurred in cars), an exasperated juvenile court judge declared that the automobile was "a house of prostitution on wheels." It was, of course, much more. The automobile was to the 1920s what the railroad had been to the nineteenth century: the catalyst for economic growth, a transportation revolution, and a cultural symbol.

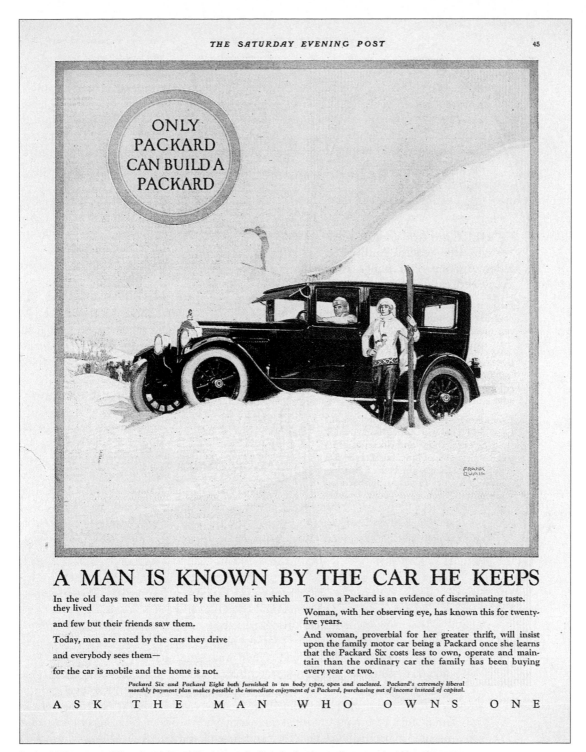

ONLY PACKARD CAN BUILD A PACKARD

A MAN IS KNOWN BY THE CAR HE KEEPS

In the old days men were rated by the homes in which they lived

and few but their friends saw them.

Today, men are rated by the cars they drive

and everybody sees them—

for the car is mobile and the home is not.

To own a Packard is an evidence of discriminating taste.

Woman, with her observing eye, has known this for twenty-five years.

And woman, proverbial for her greater thrift, will insist upon the family motor car being a Packard once she learns that the Packard Six costs less to own, operate and maintain than the ordinary car the family has been buying every year or two.

Packard Six and Packard Eight both furnished in ten body types, open and enclosed. Packard's extremely liberal monthly payment plan makes possible the immediate enjoyment of a Packard, purchasing out of income instead of capital.

A S K   T H E   M A N   W H O   O W N S   O N E

In the 1920s, automobile advertising shifted gears by broadening its audience and making the automobile a symbol of social success. Earlier advertisements had stressed the technical advantages of automobiles and were aimed strictly at men. Here an automobile advertisement from 1925 emphasizes the subliminal rewards of owning a luxury car. Prestige, power, wealth, and romantic love belong to a man who owns a Packard automobile. And women are not ignored. The advertisement points out to women that owning a Packard is not only "evidence of discriminating taste" but also a sign of cost-consciousness for family-minded females.

The Business of America

In business, said Henry Ford, the "fundamentals are all summed up in the single word, 'service.'" President Calvin Coolidge echoed the theme of service to society in 1925: "The business of America is business. The man who builds a factory builds a temple. The man who works there worships there." A generation earlier, progressives had criticized business for its social irresponsibility. But the wartime contributions of business managers and the return of prosperity in 1922 gained them a renewed respect.

Corporate consolidation   Encouraged by federal permissiveness, a wave of mergers swept the country. Between 1919 and 1930, some 8000 firms disappeared as large gobbled small. Oligopolies (where a few firms dominated whole industries) flourished in steel, meatpacking, cigarettes, and other businesses. National chains began to replace local "mom and pop" stores. By 1929, one bag of groceries in ten came from the 15,000 red-and-gold markets of the Great Atlantic and Pacific Tea Company.

Managerial elite   This expansion and consolidation meant that the capital of the nation was being controlled not by individuals but by corporations. The model of modern business was the large, bureaucratic corporation, in which those who actually managed the company had little to do with those who owned it—the shareholders. Stocks and bonds were becoming so widely dispersed that few individuals held more than 1 or 2 percent of any company.

A salaried bureaucracy of executives and plant managers formed a new elite, which no longer set their sites on becoming swashbuckling entrepreneurs like the Carnegies and Rockefellers of old. The new managers looked to work their way up a corporate ladder. They were less interested in risk than in productivity and stability. Managers subdivided operations and put experts in charge. Corporate leaders learned the techniques of "scientific management" taught at Harvard and other new schools of business through journals, professional societies, and consulting firms. They channeled earnings back into their companies to expand factories, carry on research, and grow in size and wealth. By the end of the decade, more than a thousand firms had research laboratories and half the total industrial income was concentrated in 100 corporations.

Welfare Capitalism

The new "scientific management" also stressed smooth relations between managers and employees. The rash of postwar strikes had left business leaders suspicious as ever of labor unions and determined to find ways to limit their influence.

Some tactics were more strong-armed than scientific. In 1921 the National Association of Manufacturers, the Chamber of Commerce, and other employer groups

The American Plan   launched the "American Plan," aimed at opening "closed shops," factories where only union members could work. Employers made workers sign agreements disavowing union membership. Labor organizers called them "yellow dog contracts." Companies infiltrated unions with spies, locked union members out of factories if they protested, and boycotted firms that hired union labor.

The gentler side of the American Plan involved a social innovation called "welfare capitalism." Companies like General Electric and Bethlehem Steel pledged to care for their employees and give them incentives for working hard. They built clean, safe factories, installed cafeterias, hired trained dietitians, formed baseball teams and glee clubs. Several hundred firms encouraged perhaps a million workers to buy company stock. Millions more enrolled in company unions. Called "Kiss-Me Clubs" for their lack of power, they offered what few independent unions could match: health and safety insurance; a grievance procedure; and representation for African Americans, women, and immigrants.

But welfare capitalism embraced barely 5 percent of the workforce and often gave benefits only to skilled laborers, the hardest to replace. Most companies cared more for production than for contented employees. In the 1920s a family of four could live in "minimum health and decency" on $2000 a year. The average industrial wage was $1304, and almost one family in six was labeled as "chronically destitute." Thus working-class families often needed more than one wage earner just to get by. Over a million children ages 10 to 15 still worked full-time in 1920. Some received as little as 20 cents an hour.

A shop steward.

In 1927, the most famous strike of the decade idled 2500 mill hands in Gastonia, North Carolina, where workers labored for 10- to 12-hour shifts in 90-degree heat and endured regular "stretch-outs," the textile equivalent of assembly-line speedups. Even strikebreakers walked out. Eventually, however, authorities broke the strike, presaging a national trend. A year later there were a record-low 629 strikes. Union membership sank from almost 5 million in 1921 to less than 3.5 million in 1929. "The AF of L [American Federation of Labor] machinery has practically collapsed," reported one union official.

The Consumer Culture

During the late nineteenth century the economy had boomed, too, but much of its growth had gone into producer goods: huge steel factories and rail, telephone, and electric networks. By World War I, these industrial networks had penetrated enough of the country to create mass markets for consumer goods such as refrigerators, bicycles, and other products for ordinary Americans. As an increasing percentage of the nation's industries turned out consumer goods, prosperity hinged more and more on consumption. If consumers purchased more goods, production would increase at the same time that costs would decrease. Lower production costs would allow for lower prices, which would lift sales, production, and employment still higher.

Everything in this cycle of prosperity depended on consumption. In the consumer economy, wives ceased to be homemakers and became purchasers of processed food and manufactured goods. Husbands were not merely workers but, equally important, consumers of mortgages and other forms of credit. Even vacationers became consumers—in this case, consumers of leisure time as more employees got two-week (unpaid) vacations. Consumption was the key to prosperity, and increased consumption rested on two innovations: advertising to help people buy, and credit to help them pay.

Before World War I advertising had been a grubby business, hawking the often exaggerated virtues of products. Around the turn of the century, advertisers began a critical shift from emphasizing *products* to stressing a consumer's *desires*: health, popularity, social status. During the First World War the Committee on Public Information, the federal propaganda agency, demonstrated the power of emotional appeals as an instrument of mass persuasion. Like the war propaganda, advertising copy aimed at emotions and cynically regarded the "average normal American," in the words of one executive, as having the "literate capacity of a 12- or 14-year-old." Behavioral psychologists like John B. Watson, who left Johns Hopkins University for an advertising agency in the 1920s, helped advertisers develop more sophisticated techniques for attracting customers.

Role of advertising

Earlier in the century Albert Lasker, the owner of Chicago's largest advertising firm, Lord and Thomas, created modern advertising in America. His eye-catching ads were hard-hitting, positive, and often preposterous. To expand the sales of Lucky Strike cigarettes Lord and Thomas advertisements claimed smoking made people slimmer and more courageous. "Luckies" became one of the most popular brands in America. Bogus doctors and dentists endorsed all kinds of products, including toothpaste containing potassium chloride—eight grams of which was lethal. "Halitosis" was plucked from the pages of an obscure medical dictionary and used to sell Listerine mouthwash.

Installment buying as credit

Advertisers encouraged Americans to borrow against tomorrow to purchase what advertising convinced them they wanted today. Installment buying had once been confined to sewing machines and pianos. In the 1920s it grew into the tenth biggest business in the United States. In 1919 Alfred Sloan created millions of new customers by establishing the General Motors Acceptance Corporation, the nation's first consumer credit organization. By 1929 Americans were buying most of their cars, radios, and furniture on the installment plan. Consumer debt jumped to $7 billion, almost twice the federal budget.

 # A Mass Society

In the evening after a day's work in the fields—perhaps in front of an adobe house built by one of the western sugar-beet companies—Mexican American workers might gather to chat or sing a *corrido* or two. The *corrido*, or ballad, was an old Mexican folk tradition whose subjects matched the concerns of the day. One corrido during the 1920s told of a field laborer distressed that his family had rejected old Mexican customs in favor of new American fashions. His wife, he sang, now had "a bob-tailed dress of silk" and, wearing makeup, went about "painted like a *piñata*." As for his children:

> My kids speak perfect English
> And have no use for our Spanish
> They call me "fader" and don't work
> And are crazy about the Charleston.

It was enough to make him long for Mexico.

For Americans from all backgrounds, the New Era was witness to "a vast dissolution of ancient habits," commented columnist Walter Lippmann. Mass marketing and mass distribution led not simply to a higher standard of living but to a life less regional and diverse. In the place of moral standards set by local communities and churches came "modern" fashions and attitudes, spread by the new mass media of movies, radio, and magazines. In the place of "ancient habits" came the forces of mass society: independent women, freer love, standardized culture, urban energy and impersonality, and deep alienation.

The New Woman

The "New Woman," charged critics, was at the bottom of what Frederick Lewis Allen called the "revolution in manners and morals" of the twenties. The most flamboyant of them wore close-fitting felt hats and makeup, long-waisted dresses and few undergarments, strings of beads, and unbuckled galoshes (which earned them the nickname "flappers"). Cocktail in hand, cigarette in mouth, footloose and economically free, the New Woman became a symbol of liberation and sexuality to some. To others she represented the decline of civilization.

World War I had served as a social catalyst, while the decade before it had stimulated changes for women workers. Single and married women poured into the workforce after the turn of the century. From a fifth of the labor force in 1900, women jumped to a quarter by 1930, with the greatest gains coming before the war. But most female workers remained in poor-paying jobs, and few found new freedom after quitting time. The war prompted a change in attitudes. Before, women were arrested for smoking cigarettes openly, using profanity, appearing on public beaches without stockings, and driving automobiles without men beside them. But with women bagging explosives, running locomotives, and drilling with rifles, the old taboos often seemed silly.

Disseminating birth control information by mail had also been a crime before the war. By the armistice there was a birth control clinic in Brooklyn, a National Birth Control League, and later an American Birth Control League led by Margaret Sanger. Sanger's crusade had begun as an attempt to save poor women from the burdens of unwanted pregnancies (pages 713–714). In the 1920s her message found a receptive middle-class audience. Surveys showed that by the 1930s nearly 90 percent of college-educated couples practiced contraception.

Being able to a degree to control the matter of pregnancy, women felt less guilt about enjoying sex and less fear over the consequences. In 1909 Sigmund Freud had come to America to lecture on his theories of coping with the unconscious and overcoming harmful repressions. Some of Freud's ideas, specifically his emphasis on childhood sexuality, shocked Americans, while most of his complex theories sailed blissfully over their heads. As popularized in the 1920s, however, Freudian psychology stamped sexuality as a key to health.

Such changes in the social climate were real enough, but the life of a flapper girl hardly mirrored the lives and work routines of most American women. Over the decade, the female labor force grew by only 1 percent. As late as 1930 nearly 60 percent of all working women were African American or foreign-born and generally held low-paying jobs in domestic service or the garment industry. At home, women found that even new, "labor-saving" appliances could increase their burdens by raising standards of household cleanliness.

The New Era did spawn new careers for women. The consumer culture capitalized on a preoccupation with appearance and led to the opening of some 40,000 beauty parlors staffed by hairdressers, manicurists, and cosmeticians. "Women's fields" carved out by progressive reformers expanded opportunities in education, libraries, and social welfare. Women earned a higher percentage of doctoral degrees (from 10 percent in 1910 to 15.4 percent in 1930) and held more college teaching posts than ever (32 percent). But in most areas, professional men resisted the "feminization" of the workforce. The number of female doctors dropped by half. Medical schools imposed restrictive quotas, and 90 percent of all hospitals rejected female interns.

In 1924 two women—Nellie Ross in Wyoming and Miriam ("Ma") Ferguson in Texas—were elected governors, the first female chief executives. But for the most part, women continued to be marginalized in party politics while remaining widely involved in educational and welfare programs. Operating outside male-dominated

Margaret Sanger

"Street selling was torture for me," Margaret Sanger recalled of her efforts to promote the *Birth Control Review.* Hecklers often taunted Sanger and her colleagues. "Have you never heard God's word to be fruitful and multiply and replenish the earth'?" one asked. The reply came back, "They've done that already."

Daily Lives

CLOTHING AND FASHION
The Beauty Contest

On a sunlit day early in September 1921 eight young women stood nervously on the boardwalk at Atlantic City, New Jersey. For a week the seaside resort had presented a succession of swimming exhibitions, dance contests, and automobile races. A giant parade featured clowns, bands, and a float carrying King Neptune escorted by mermaids. All the marchers except the clowns wore bathing suits, even the mayor and members of the chamber of commerce. They had been instrumental in organizing the week's central event—a national beauty contest to select the first "Miss America."

The American beauty contest drew on an old heritage. In colonial times the traditional May Day celebration crowned a Queen of the May as a symbol of fertility. Queens embodied fruitfulness and community. Though physical beauty mattered in the selection, qualities such as civic leadership and popularity also counted. By the middle of the nineteenth century many cities began holding such festivals to publicize their virtues.

In 1854 showman P. T. Barnum conceived of a competition among women to judge their beauty at his American Museum in New York. Because Victorian codes prohibited such displays, Barnum attracted only contestants of "questionable reputation." To lure middle-class women, he announced that "daguerreotypes," or photographs, could be submitted. Participants did not even have to send their names. The idea spread to newspapers and later to the new mass circulation dailies. When the promoters of the St. Louis Exposition advertised a beauty contest in 1905, some 40,000 women applied.

Promoters had conceived of the Miss America pageant as a way of extending the summer season past September 1. The contest measured physical beauty alone, with the high point being a bathing suit competition. (Only later did the pageant add a talent show.) After the turn of the century, bathing suits had grown alarmingly scant, exposing arms and discarding billowy bloomers in favor of revealing tights. Organizers worried that straitlaced visitors might balk at the sight of middle-class women

Margaret Gorman of Washington, D.C., crowned in 1921 as the first Miss America.

---

political parties, women activists succeeded in winning passage of the Sheppard-Towner Federal Maternity and Infancy Act in 1921 to fight infant mortality with rural prenatal and baby-care centers. It was the first federal welfare statute. Yet by the end of the decade the Sheppard-Towner Act had lapsed.

In the wake of its greatest success, the hard-won vote for women, feminists splintered. The National Woman Suffrage Association disbanded in 1920. In its place the new League of Women Voters encouraged informed voting with nonpartisan publicity. For the more militant Alice Paul and her allies, that was not enough. Their National Woman's party pressed for a constitutional Equal Rights Amendment (ERA). Social workers and others familiar with the conditions under which women labored opposed it. Death and injury rates for women were nearly double those for men. To them the ERA meant losing the protection as well as the benefits women derived from mothers' pensions and maternity insurance. Joined by most men and a majority of Congress, they fought the amendment to a standstill.

Equal Rights Amendment

strutting seminude before a panel of judges.

Aware of such perils, pageant officials depicted entrants as wholesome, conventional, and unsophisticated. None of the contestants was permitted to wear short bobbed hair or makeup—both symbols of the racy modern woman. Models, theatrical performers, and other "professional beauties" competed separately. Famous women's illustrators lent legitimacy by serving as judges. To underscore the lightheartedness of the pageant, local police dressed like Keystone Kops, the bumbling heroes of Mack Sennett's comedy films.

As the contestants waited anxiously, officials announced the winner—Margaret Gorman of Washington, D.C. She radiated innocence and athletic vigor. "She represents the type of womanhood America needs," observed Samuel Gompers of the American Federation of Labor, "—strong, red-blooded, able to shoulder the responsibilities of home-making and motherhood."

The Miss America pageant was an immediate success. Newspapers across the country reported the results. In 1922 representatives of 58 cities competed, and a crowd of 200,000 watched the opening parade. The much-feared protests nonetheless materialized. In 1928 organizers were forced to cancel the pageant when hotel owners objected that their middle-class clientele found the display offensive. The pageant was revived again in 1935, and a Miss America has reigned ever since.

Miss America and other beauty contests evolved as commercialism and advertising took hold and Victorianism declined in the early twentieth century. But the lengths to which pageant organizers went to gain respect demonstrated the strength of the older social ideals. The Miss America pageant in particular came to symbolize the middle-class ideal of womanhood. Physical beauty remained the chief component, marriage and motherhood the chief ends. The message was graphic: men competed in sports gear, business attire, and professional garb; women, in bathing suits. That fashion would be slow to change.

Mass Media

In balmy California, where movies could be made year-round, Hollywood helped give the New Woman notoriety as a temptress and trendsetter. When sexy Theda Bara (the "vamp") appeared in *The Blue Flame* in 1920, crowds mobbed theaters. And just as Hollywood dictated standards of physical attraction, it became the judge of taste and fashion in countless other ways because motion pictures were a virtually universal medium. There was no need for literacy or fluency, no need even for sound, given the power of the pictures parading across the screen.

Motion pictures, invented in 1889, had first been shown in tiny neighborhood theaters called "nickelodeons." For a nickel, patrons watched a silent screen flicker with moving images as an accompanist played music on a tinny piano. The audience was anything but silent. The theater reverberated with the cracking of Indian nuts, the day's equivalent of popcorn, while young cowboys shot off their Kilgore

Motion pictures

787

The vibrant energy of the New Woman is reflected in the geometric designs of this fashionable evening wrap (1928), whose jagged lines also suggest the era's newest vaulting skyscrapers. The beaded handbag (1925) conveys a similar excitement.

repeating cap pistols during dramatic scenes. Often children read the subtitles aloud to their immigrant parents, translating into Italian, Yiddish, or German.

After the first feature-length film, *The Great Train Robbery* (1903), productions became rich in spectacle, attracted middle-class audiences, and turned into America's favorite form of entertainment. By 1926 more than 20,000 movie houses offered customers lavish theaters with overstuffed seats, live music, and a celluloid dream world—all for 50 cents or less. At the end of the decade, they were drawing over 100 million people a week, roughly the equivalent of the national population.

In the spring of 1920 Frank Conrad of the Westinghouse Company in East Pittsburgh rigged up a research station in his barn and started transmitting phonograph music and baseball scores to local wireless operators. An ingenious Pittsburgh newspaper began advertising radio equipment to "be used by those who listen to Dr. Conrad's programs." Six months later Westinghouse officials opened the first licensed broadcasting station in history, KDKA, to stimulate sales of their supplies. By 1922 the number of licensed stations had jumped to 430. And by 1930 nearly one home in three had a radio ("furniture that talks," comedian Fred Allen called it).

At first radio was seen as a civilizing force. "The air is your theater, your college, your newspaper, your library," exalted one ad in 1924. But with the growing number of sets came commercial broadcasting, catering to more common tastes. By 1931 advertisers were paying $10,000 an hour for a national hookup, and the most popular show on radio was "Amos 'n' Andy," a comedy about African Americans created by two white vaudevillians in 1926. It borrowed its style from black comedians Aubrey Lyles and Flournoy Miller, who occasionally wrote dialogue for the show. A slice of black culture, often stereotyped, sometimes mocked, nonetheless entered mainstream American life.

At night families gathered around the radio instead of the hearth, listening to a concert, perhaps, rather than going out to hear music. Ticket sales at vaudeville theaters collapsed. The aged, the sick, and the isolated, moreover, could be "at home but never alone," as one radio ad declared. Linked by nothing but airwaves, Americans were finding themselves part of a vast new community of listeners.

Print journalism also broadened its audience during the 1920s. In 1923 Yale classmates Henry R. Luce and Briton Hadden rewrote news stories in a snappy style, mixed them with photographs, and created the country's first national weekly, *Time* magazine. Fifty-five giant newspaper chains distributed 230 newspapers with a combined circulation of 13 million by 1927. Though they controlled less than 10 percent of all papers, the chains pioneered modern mass news techniques. Editors relied on central offices and syndicates to prepare editorials, sports, gossip, and Sunday features for a national readership.

In a world in which Americans were rapidly being reduced to anonymous parts of mass, industrialized society, media offered them a chance to identify with the achievements of individuals by creating a world of celebrities and heroes. Sports figures, business executives, and movie stars found their exploits splashed across the front pages of newspapers and magazines and followed on radio by millions hungry for excitement and eager to project their own dreams onto others.

The Roxy, the largest theater in the world when it opened in 1926, in all its palatial glory. Such lavish movie houses sought to attract more prosperous middle-class audiences with splendor reminiscent of European cathedrals. On the night the Roxy opened, pealing chimes marked the beginning of the show, whereupon a man dressed as a monk strode onto center stage, pointed to the balcony, and declared, "Let there be light!" Blazing spotlights then set the orchestra aglow. "Does God live here?" asked a little girl in a *New Yorker* cartoon.

No hero attracted more attention than a shy, reed-thin youth named Charles Lindbergh. Early on the morning of May 20, 1927, "Lucky Lindy" streaked into the skies above Long Island aboard a silver-winged monoplane called the *Spirit of St. Louis* and headed east. Thirty-three hours and thirty minutes later he landed just outside Paris, the first flier to cross the Atlantic alone. Eight others had died trying. An ecstatic mob swamped him and nearly tore his plane to pieces in search of souvenirs.

Lindbergh, dubbed by reporters the "Lone Eagle," returned with his plane aboard the warship USS *Memphis*. In New York City alone, he was greeted by nearly 4 million cheering fans, and when he sailed up the Potomac, he received a 21-gun salute, an honor previously reserved only for heads of state. Lindbergh had "fired the imagination of mankind," observed one newspaper. Never had one person mastered a machine so completely or conquered nature so courageously. To Americans ambivalent about mass society and worried about being overwhelmed by technology and bureaucracy, Lindbergh's accomplishment was a sign. Perhaps they could control the New Era without losing their cherished individualism. For a moment, Charles Lindbergh made it seem possible, and the media lionized him for it.

Charles Lindbergh

Youth Culture

By the 1920s, the drive for public education had placed a majority of teenagers in high school for the first time in American history. College enrollment reached 10 percent of the eligible population by 1928; in 1890 it had been less than 3 percent. A full-blown "peer culture" emerged, as children and adolescents spent more time outside the family among people their own age. Revolving around school and friends, its components were remarkably modern—athletics, clubs, sororities and fraternities, dating, proms, "bull sessions," and moviegoing.

Tolerance for premarital sex among young adults seems to have grown in the 1920s ("necking" and "petting" parties replaced sedate tea parties), but the new subculture of youth still tied sexual relations to love. Casual sex remained rare; what changed was the point at which sexual intimacy occurred. A growing minority of young women reported having premarital intercourse, for example, but only with their future husbands. Unsupervised dating and "going together" replaced chaperoned courting.

For all the frivolity and rebelliousness it promoted, the new youth culture tended to fuse the young to the larger society by promoting widely held values—competitiveness, merit through association, service, prestige. Even notorious young flappers usually ended their courting days with marriages that emphasized the conventional roles of wife and mother.

"Ain't We Got Fun?"

Spectator sports

"Ev'ry morning, ev'ry evening, ain't we got fun?" ran the 1921 hit song. As the average hours on the job each week decreased from 47.2 in 1920 to 42 by 1930, spending on amusement and recreation tripled. Spectator sports came of age. In 1921, some 60,000 fans paid $1.8 million to see Jack Dempsey, the "Manassas Mauler," knock out French champion Georges Carpentier. Millions more listened as radio took them ringside for the first time in sports history. Universities constructed huge stadiums for football—a 60,000-seater at Berkeley, a 64,000-seater at Ohio State. By the end of the decade college football games were outdrawing major league baseball.

Baseball remained the national pastime but became a bigger business. An ugly World Series scandal in 1919 led owners to appoint Judge Kenesaw Mountain Landis as "czar" of the sport early in the decade. His strict rule reformed the game. In 1920 the son of immigrants revolutionized it. George Herman "Babe" Ruth hit 54 home runs and made the New York Yankees the first club to attract a million fans in one season. A heroic producer in an era of consumption, Ruth was also baseball's bad boy. He smoked, drank, cursed, and chased every skirt in sight. Under the guidance of the first modern sports agent, Christy Walsh, Ruth became the highest paid player in the game and made a fortune endorsing everything from clothing to candy bars.

At parties old diversions—charades, card tricks, recitations—faded in popularity as dancing took over. The ungainly camel walk, the sultry tango, and in 1924 the frantic Charleston were the urban standards. Country barns featured a revival of square dancing with music provided by Detroit's WBZ, courtesy of Henry Ford. And from the turn-of-the-century brothels and gaming houses of New Orleans, Memphis, and St. Louis came a rhythmic, compelling music that swept into nightclubs and over the airwaves: jazz.

Jazz

Jazz was a remarkably complex blend of several older African American musical traditions, combining the soulfulness of the blues with the brighter syncopated rhythms of ragtime music. The distinctive style of jazz bands came from a marvelous improvising as the musicians embellished melodies and played off one another. The style spread when the "Original Dixieland Jazz Band" (hardly original but possessed of the advantage of being white) recorded a few numbers for the phonograph. The music became a sensation in New York in 1917 and spread across the country. Black New Orleans stalwarts like Joe "King" Oliver's Creole Jazz Band began touring, and in 1924 Paul Whiteman inaugurated respectable "white" jazz in a concert at Carnegie

Hall. When self-appointed guardians of good taste denounced such music as "intellectual and spiritual debauchery," Whiteman disagreed: "Jazz is the folk music of the machine age."

The Art of Alienation

Before World War I a generation of young writers had begun to rebel against Victorian purity. The savagery of the war drove many of them even farther from any faith in reason or progress. Instead they embraced a "nihilism" that denied all meaning in life. When the war ended, they turned their resentment against American life, especially its small towns and big businesses, its conformity, technology, and materialism. Some led unconventional lives in New York City's Greenwich Village. Others, called expatriates, left the country altogether for the artistic freedom of London and Paris. Their alienation helped produce a literary outpouring unmatched in American history.

Expatriates

On the eve of World War I the poet Ezra Pound had predicted an "American Risorgimento" that would "make the Italian Renaissance look like a tempest in a teapot." From Europe the expatriate Pound began to make it happen. Abandoning rhyme and meter in his poetry, he decried the "botched civilization" that had produced the war. Another voluntary exile, T. S. Eliot, bemoaned the emptiness of modern life in his epic poem *The Waste Land* (1922). Ernest Hemingway captured the disillusionment of the age in *The Sun Also Rises* (1926) and *A Farewell to Arms* (1929), novels where resolution came as it had in war—by death.

At home Minnesota-born Sinclair Lewis, the first American to win a Nobel Prize in literature, sketched a scathing vision of midwestern small-town life in *Main Street* (1920). The book described "savorless people . . . saying mechanical things about the excellence of Ford automobiles, and viewing themselves as the greatest race in the world." His next novel, *Babbitt* (1922), dissected small-town businessman George Follansbee Babbitt, a peppy realtor from the fictional city of Zenith. Faintly absurd and supremely dull, Babbitt was the epitome of the average.

The novels of another Minnesotan, F. Scott Fitzgerald, glorified youth and romantic individualism but found redemption nowhere. Fitzgerald's heroes, like Amory Blaine in *This Side of Paradise* (1920), spoke for a generation "grown up to find all Gods dead, all wars fought, all faiths in man shaken." Like most writers of the decade, Fitzgerald saw life largely as a personal affair—opulent, always self-absorbing, and ultimately tragic.

A "New Negro"

As World War I seared white intellectuals, so too did it galvanize black Americans. Wartime labor shortages had spurred a migration of over a million African Americans out of the rural South into northern industrial cities. But postwar unemployment and racial violence quickly dashed black hopes for equality. Common folk in these urban enclaves found an outlet for their alienation in a charismatic nationalist from Jamaica named Marcus Garvey.

Marcus Garvey

Garvey brought his organization, the Universal Negro Improvement Association (UNIA), to America in 1916 in hopes of restoring black pride by returning African Americans to Africa and Africa to Africans. "Up you mighty race," he told his followers, "you can accomplish what you will." When Garvey spoke at the first national UNIA convention in 1920, over 25,000 supporters jammed Madison Square

Garden in New York to listen. Even his harshest critics admitted there were at least half a million members in more than 30 branches of his organization. It was the first mass movement of African Americans in history. But in 1925 Garvey was convicted of mail fraud and sentenced to prison for having oversold stock in his Black Star Line, the steamship company founded to return African Americans to Africa. His dream shattered.

Harlem Renaissance

As Garvey rose to prominence a renaissance of black literature, painting, and sculpture was brewing in Harlem. Since the completion of Manhattan's subway system in 1904, Harlem had grown increasingly black as eagerly expected white renters never appeared, despite millions of dollars invested in new apartment developments. By the end of World War I, Harlem had become the cultural capital of black America.

The first inklings of a renaissance in Harlem came in 1922 when Claude McKay, another Jamaican immigrant, published a book of poems entitled *White Shadows*. In his most famous, "If We Must Die," McKay mixed defiance and dignity: "Like men we'll face the murderous, cowardly pack/Pressed to the wall, dying but fighting back!" Often supported by white patrons, or "angels," the young black writers and artists of Harlem found their subjects in the street life of cities, the folkways of the rural South, and the primitivism of preindustrial cultures. Poet Langston Hughes reminded his readers of the ancient heritage of African Americans in "The Negro Speaks of Rivers," while Zora Neale Hurston collected folktales, songs, and prayers of black southerners.

Born in Jamaica in 1887, Marcus Garvey founded his "Back to Africa" movement in 1914. He went to prison for mail fraud in 1925, but it was like "jailing a rainbow," said one observer. President Coolidge pardoned Garvey in 1927, then deported him to Jamaica.

Though generally not a racial protest, the Harlem Renaissance drew on the new assertiveness of African Americans as well as on the alienation of white intellectuals. In 1925 Alain Locke, a black professor from Howard University, collected a sampling of their works in *The New Negro*. The New Negro, Locke wrote, was "not a cultural foundling without his own inheritance" but "a conscious contributor . . . collaborator and participant in American civilization." The title of the book reflected not only an artistic movement but a new racial consciousness.

 # Defenders of the Faith

As mass society pushed the country into a future of machines, organization, middle-class living, and cosmopolitan diversity, not everyone approved. Dr. and Mrs. Wilbur Crafts, the authors of *Intoxicating Drinks and Drugs in All Lands and Times,* set forth a litany of sins that tempted young people in this "age of cities." "Foul pictures, corrupt literature, leprous shows, gambling slot machines, saloons, and Sabbath breaking. . . . *We are trying to raise saints in hell.*"

The changing values of the New Era seemed especially threatening to traditionalists like the Crafts. Their deeply held beliefs reflected the rural roots of so many Americans: an ethic that valued neighborliness, small communities, and a sameness of race, religion, and ethnicity. Improvements in mass media—radio, movies, magazines—made it impossible for isolated communities to avoid national trends, even when they disapproved of them. Opponents of the new ways could be found among not only countryfolk but also rural migrants to cities as well as an embattled Protestant elite. All were determined to defend the older faiths against the modern age.

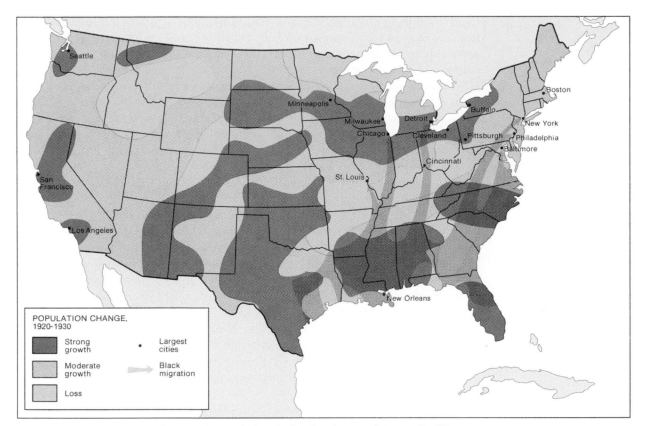

Areas of Population Growth In the 1920s the population of urban America grew by some 15 million people, at the time the greatest 10-year jump in American history. Spurred first by the industrial demands of World War I and then by declining farm income, cities grew largely by depopulating rural areas. The biggest gains were in the South and West, where farmers followed opportunity to cities in climates similar to their own. In the most dramatic manifestation of the overall trend, more than a million African Americans migrated from the rural South to the urban North in hopes of escaping poverty and discrimination.

Nativism and Immigration Restriction

In 1921, two Italian aliens, who freely admitted to being radical anarchists, presented a dramatic challenge to those older faiths. Nicola Sacco and Bartolomeo Vanzetti were sentenced to death—on the face of it, for a shoe company robbery and murder in South Braintree, Massachusetts, committed a year earlier. But the evidence against them was controversial, and critics charged that Sacco and Vanzetti were convicted primarily because they were foreign-born radicals. During the trial, the presiding judge had scorned them in private as "anarchist bastards" and later refused all motions for a retrial, in spite of a confession to the robbery by a member of a well-known gang. For protesters around the world, Sacco and Vanzetti's execution in 1927 was a symbol of American bigotry and prejudice.

By then, nativism—a rabid hostility to foreigners—had produced the most restrictive immigration laws in American history. In the aftermath of World War I immigration was running close to 1 million a year, almost as high as prewar levels. Most immigrants came from eastern and southern Europe and from Mexico; most were Catholics and Jews. Alarmed white native-born Protestants warned that if the

Sacco and Vanzetti

flood continued, Americans might become "a hybrid race of people as worthless and futile as the good-for-nothing mongrels of Central America and Southeastern Europe." Appreciating the wage benefits of a shrunken labor pool, the American Federation of Labor supported restriction.

Mexican Americans

In the Southwest, Mexicans and Mexican Americans became a target of concern. The Spanish had inhabited the region for nearly 400 years, producing a rich blend of European and Indian cultures. By 1900 about 300,000 Mexican Americans lived in the United States. In the following decade Mexicans fleeing poverty and a revolution in 1910 almost doubled the Latino population of Texas and New Mexico. In California it quadrupled. During World War I, labor shortages led authorities to relax immigration laws, and in the 1920s American farmers opened a campaign to attract Mexican farm workers.

Thousands of single young men, known as solos, also crossed the border to catch trains for Detroit, Kansas City, and other industrial cities. By the end of the 1920s, many cities had thriving communities of Mexicans. In barrios—Mexican neighborhoods—Spanish-speaking newcomers settled into an immigrant life of family and festivals, churchgoing, hard work, and slow adaptation. Like other immigrants, some returned home, but some brought their families. The census of 1930 listed nearly 1.5 million Mexicans living in the United States, not including an untold number who had entered the country illegally.

National Origins acts

In 1921 Senators Henry Cabot Lodge of Massachusetts and Hiram Johnson of California sponsored the National Origins Act to reduce the flood of immigrants to 350,000 a year. That quota parceled out available spaces by admitting up to 3 percent of each nationality living in the United States as of 1910. Asian immigration was virtually banned. In 1924 a second National Origins Act cut the quota to 150,000 and pushed the base year back to 1890, before the bulk of southern and eastern Europeans had arrived. To control the flow of illegal aliens, Congress also created the Border Patrol. Its 450 agents, stationed along the boundaries with Canada and Mexico, were scarcely enough to make anything other than a symbolic statement of restrictionist sentiment.

The National Origins Act fixed the pattern of immigration for the next four decades. Immigration from southern and eastern Europe was reduced to a trickle. The free movement of Europeans to America, a migration of classes and nationalities that had been unimpeded for 300 years, came to an end.

The "Noble Experiment"

Nativists who distrusted immigrants usually viewed alcohol as a particular problem of poor immigrants. Progressive prohibitionists stressed the need for efficiency and public health, which they contrasted with the corrupting influence of the immigrant saloon culture. German brewers and their beer gardens came under particular suspicion during World War I.

Eighteenth Amendment

For nearly a hundred years reformers had tried—with sporadic success—to reduce the consumption of alcohol. Their most ambitious campaign climaxed in January 1920 when the Eighteenth Amendment, sanctioning the prohibition of liquor, went into effect. Prohibition was not total: private citizens could still drink. They simply could not make, sell, transport, or import any "intoxicating beverage" containing 0.5 percent alcohol or more. The aim was to take the profit out of the liquor trade and reduce alcohol consumption without trampling too heavily on the rights of individuals. By some estimates, the consumption of liquor was cut in half.

From the start, however, enforcement was underfunded and understaffed. In large cities "speakeasies"—taverns operating under cover—were plentiful. Rural stills continued to turn out "moonshine." Even so, the consequences of so vast a social experiment were significant and often unexpected. Prohibition reversed the prewar trend toward beer and wine, because hard liquor brought greater profits to bootleggers. Prohibition also advanced women's rights. Whereas saloons had discriminated against "ladies," either barring them or having them enter by a separate door, speakeasies welcomed them. Prohibition helped to line the pockets and boost the fame of gangsters, including "Scarface" Al Capone. Like Capone, thousands of poor immigrants looked to illegal bootlegging to move them out of the slums. As rival gangs fought over territory, cities erupted in violence.

Consequences of Prohibition

Prohibition can be best understood as cultural and class legislation. Support had always run deepest in Protestant churches, especially the evangelical Baptists and Methodists. And there had always been a strong antiurban and anti-immigrant bias among reformers. As it turned out, the steepest decline in drinking occurred among working-class ethnics. Only the well-to-do had enough money to drink regularly without risking death or blindness, the common effects of cheap, tainted liquor. Traditionalists might celebrate the triumph of the "noble experiment," but modern urbanites either ignored or resented it.

Fundamentalism versus Darwinism

Although Aimee Semple McPherson embraced the fashions of the New Era, many Protestants, especially in rural areas, felt threatened by the secular aspects of modern life. Scientists and intellectuals spoke openly about the relativity of moral values and questioned the possibility of biblical miracles. Darwinism, pragmatism, and other philosophical and scientific theories left traditional religious teachings open to skepticism or even scorn. Pastors noted that despite an increase of nearly 13 million in church membership, church attendance was slipping. Some churches abandoned Sunday evening services altogether.

As early as the 1870s anxious conservatives had combined to combat modernist influences. Between 1909 and 1912 two wealthy Los Angeles churchgoers, Lyman and Milton Stewart, subsidized a series of booklets known as *The Fundamentals*. The 3 million copies sent across the country stressed the "verbal inerrancy" of scripture: every word of the Bible was literally true. Advocates of this view, who after 1920 were increasingly known as "fundamentalists," saw themselves as defenders of traditional religion. Yet their literal reading of scripture was hardly traditional, for over the centuries many Christian theologians had interpreted various passages of scripture symbolically.

The Fundamentals

Fundamentalists maintained effective ministries nationwide but especially among Southern Baptists. Nothing disturbed them more than Darwinian theories of evolution. By definition Darwinism denied the divine origin of humankind and made the creation story of Adam and Eve at best a parable. In 1925 a part-time schoolteacher and clerk of the Round Lick Association of Primitive Baptists convinced his fellow Tennessee legislators to make it illegal to teach that "man has descended from a lower order of animals." Oklahoma, Florida, Mississippi, and Arkansas passed similar statutes.

Encouraged by the newly formed American Civil Liberties Union, a number of skeptics in the town of Dayton, Tennessee, decided to test the law. In the spring of 1925 a bespectacled biology teacher named John T. Scopes was arrested for teaching evolution. Behind the scenes, Scopes's sponsors were as much preoccupied with boosting their town's commercial fortunes as with the defense of academic freedom.

Scopes trial

When the Scopes trial opened in July, it took on the flavor of a championship boxing match. Millions listened over the radio to the first trial ever broadcast. Inside the courtroom Clarence Darrow, the renowned defense lawyer from Chicago and a professed agnostic, acted as cocounsel for Scopes. Opposing him was William Jennings Bryan, the three-time presidential candidate who had recently joined the antievolution crusade. It was urban Darrow against rural Bryan in what Bryan described as a "duel to the death" between Christianity and evolution.

The presiding judge ruled that scientists could not be used to defend evolution. He considered their testimony "hearsay" because they had not been present at the Creation. The defense virtually collapsed until Darrow called Bryan to the stand as an "expert on the Bible." Under withering examination Bryan admitted, to the horror of his followers, that the Earth might not have been made "in six days of 24-hours." Even so, the Dayton jury took only eight minutes to find Scopes guilty of violating the law and fine him $100.

By then the excesses of the Scopes trial had transformed it into more of a national joke than a confrontation between darkness and light. Yet the debate over evolution raised a larger issue that continued to reverberate across the twentieth century. As scientific, religious, and cultural standards clashed, how much should religious beliefs influence public education in a nation where church and state were constitutionally separated?

KKK

On Thanksgiving Day 1915, just outside Atlanta, 16 men trudged up a rocky trail to the crest of Stone Mountain. There, as night fell, they set ablaze a large wooden cross and swore allegiance to the Invisible Empire, Knights of the Ku Klux Klan. The KKK was reborn.

As the Ku Klux Klan grew in influence after World War I, race riots erupted in over 25 cities beginning in 1919, including Chicago; Longview, Texas; Knoxville, Tennessee; and Omaha, Nebraska. More than 70 African Americans were lynched in the first year of peace, and 11 were burned alive. Many blacks fought back, their experience in World War I having made them determined to resist repression. In June 1921, rioting in Tulsa left 21 African Americans as well as 11 whites dead. As the billowing smoke in this photograph indicates, white mobs burned whole neighborhoods of the black community. Four companies of the National Guard were called out to reestablish order.

The modern Klan, a throwback to the hooded order of Reconstruction days (page 555), reflected the insecurities of the New Era. Klansmen worried about the changes and conflicts in American society, which they attributed to the rising tide of new immigrants, "uppity women," and African Americans who refused to "recognize their place." Whereas any white man could join the old Klan, the new one admitted only "native born, white, gentile [Protestant] Americans." And the reborn Klan was not confined to the rural South, like the hooded nightriders of old. In Texas, Klansmen fed off hatred of Mexicans; in California, of Japanese; in New York, of Jews and other immigrants. By the 1920s the capital of the Klan was Indianapolis, Indiana. More than half of its leadership and over a third of its members came from cities of more than 100,000 people.

The new Klan drew on the culture of small-town America. It was patriotic, gave to local charities, and boasted the kind of outfits and rituals adopted by many fraternal lodges. Klansmen wore white hooded sheets and satin robes, sang songs called "klodes," and even used a secret hand "klasp." The Women of the Ku Klux Klan had chapters in 36 states, including Indiana, where almost a third of all native-born white women joined. Klanswomen were often God-fearing members of their communities who saw the Klan as the keeper of traditional values. A typical gathering brought the whole family to a barbecue with fireworks and hymn singing, the evening capped by the burning of a giant cross.

Members came mostly from the middle and working classes: small businesspeople, clerical workers, independent professionals, farmers, and laborers with few skills. Some lived on the edge of poverty. The Klan offered them status, security, and the promise of restoring an older America. It touted white supremacy, chastity, fidelity, and parental authority and fought for laissez-faire capitalism and fundamental Protestantism. When boycotts and whispering campaigns failed to cleanse communities of Jews, Mexicans, Japanese, or others who offended their social code, the Klan resorted to floggings, kidnappings, acid mutilations, and murder.

Using modern methods of promotion, the Klan enrolled perhaps 3 million dues-paying members by the early 1920s. Moving into politics, Klan candidates won control of legislatures in Indiana, Texas, Oklahoma, and Oregon. The organization was instrumental in electing six governors, three senators, and thousands of local officials. In the end, however, the Klan was undone by sex scandals and financial corruption. In November 1925 David Stephenson, grand dragon of the Indiana Klan and the most powerful leader in the Midwest, was sentenced to life imprisonment for rape and second-degree murder.

Republicans Ascendant

"The change is amazing," wrote a Washington reporter shortly after the inauguration of Warren G. Harding on March 4, 1921. Woodrow Wilson had been ill, reclusive, and austere. Harding was handsome, warm, lovable. Wilson had kept his own counsel; Harding promised to bring the "best minds" into the cabinet and let them run things. Sentries disappeared from the gates of the White House, tourists again walked the halls, and reporters freely questioned the president. The reign of "normalcy," as Harding called it, had begun. "By 'normalcy,'" he explained, ". . . I mean normal procedure, the natural way, without excess."

The Politics of "Normalcy"

"Normalcy"—Harding's misreading of "normality"—turned out to be anything but normal. After eight years of Democratic rule, Republicans controlled the White House from 1921 to 1933 and both houses of Congress from 1918 to 1930. Fifteen years of bold reform gave way to eight years of cautious governing. A strengthened executive fell into weak hands. The cabinet and the Congress set the course of the nation.

Warren G. Harding

Harding and his successor, Calvin Coolidge, were content with delegating power. Harding appointed to the cabinet some men of quality, as he promised: jurist Charles Evans Hughes as secretary of state, farm leader Henry C. Wallace as secretary of agriculture, and Herbert Hoover, savior of Belgian war refugees and former head of the Food Administration, as secretary of commerce. He also made, as one critic put it, some "unspeakably bad appointments": his old crony Harry Daugherty as attorney general and New Mexico Senator Albert Fall as interior secretary. Daugherty sold influence for cash and resigned in 1923. Only a divided jury saved him from jail. In 1929 Albert Fall became the first cabinet member to be convicted of a felony. In 1922 he had accepted bribes of more than $400,000 for secretly leasing naval oil reserves at Elk Hill, California, and Teapot Dome, Wyoming, to private oil companies.

Harding died suddenly in August 1923, before most of the scandals came to light. Though he would be remembered as lackluster, his tolerance and moderation had a calming influence on the strife-ridden nation. Slowly he had even begun to lead. In 1921 he created a new Bureau of the Budget that brought modern accounting techniques to the management of federal revenues. Toward the end of his administration he cleared an early scandal from the Veterans' Bureau and set an agenda for Congress that included expanding the merchant marine.

Calvin Coolidge

To his credit Calvin Coolidge handled Harding's sordid legacy with skill and dispatch. He created a special investigatory commission, prosecuted the wrongdoers, and restored public confidence. Decisiveness, when he chose to exercise it, was one of Coolidge's hallmarks. He believed in small-town democracy and minimalist government. "One of the most important accomplishments of my administration has been minding my own business," he boasted. Above all Coolidge worshiped wealth. "Civilization and profits," he once said, "go hand in hand."

Coolidge had been in office barely a year when voters returned him to the White House by a margin of nearly two to one in the election in 1924. It was another sign that Americans had wearied of reform and delighted in surging prosperity. Whether the business-dominated policies served the economy or the nation well in the long term was open to question.

The Policies of Mellon and Hoover

Coolidge retained most of Harding's cabinet, including his powerful Treasury Secretary Andrew Mellon. The former president of aluminum giant Alcoa, Mellon believed that prosperity "trickled down" from rich to poor through investment, which would raise production, employment, and wages. For more than a decade Mellon devoted himself to encouraging investment by reducing taxes on high incomes and corporations. By the time he was through, Congress had nearly halved taxes.

Unlike Mellon, Commerce Secretary Herbert Hoover (another Harding holdover) was not a traditional Republican. Hoover promoted a progressive brand

Andrew Mellon, secretary of the treasury and the millionaire head of an aluminum monopoly, is flanked by Grace and Calvin Coolidge on the lawn of the White House. A disciple of business, President Coolidge believed that what was of "real importance to wage-earners was not how they might conduct a quarrel with their employers but how the business of the country might be so organized as to insure steady employment at a fair rate of pay. If that were done there would be no occasion for a quarrel, and if it were not done a quarrel would do no good."

of capitalism called "associationalism." It involved cooperation between business and government through trade associations, groups of private companies organized industry by industry. Approximately 2000 trade associations had come into being by 1929. The role of government, as Hoover saw it, was to promote cooperation among businesses, to advise them on how best to act in the public interest, and to ensure that everyone obeyed the rules. Through associationalism, Hoover married the individualism of the past with what progressives had seen as the efficiency, organization, and cooperation of the future. As such, he represented the best of the New Era.

Conferences sponsored by the Department of Commerce advised trade associations on how to standardize the products of member businesses, share information about pricing and costs, and develop new markets. The Bureau of Standards not only set standards for product design and manufacturing but also researched and published information about marketing and other business practices. The aim was to eliminate waste, cut costs, and end the boom-and-bust business cycle of ruthless competition. In that way, Hoover moved beyond old conservatives who had sought to fashion a healthy environment for business to directly aiding businesses by spreading the new gospel of efficiency and growth through voluntary cooperation.

Both Hoover and Mellon ended up placing government in service of business. Mellon's tax policies helped concentrate wealth in the hands of fewer individuals and corporations, while Hoover's associationalism, for all its faith in the ability of businesses to act for public good, helped them consolidate their power at the expense of the public. By the end of the decade, 200 giant corporations controlled almost half the corporate wealth and nearly a fifth of national wealth. In keeping with this government-sponsored trend, the Anti-Trust Division of the Justice Department offered few objections, while the Supreme Court affirmed the

Associationalism

constitutionality of trade associations. And for all the talk of limiting government, its role in the economy grew. So did its size, by more than 40,000 employees between 1921 and 1930. Building on their wartime partnership, government and business dropped all pretense of a laissez-faire economy. "Never before, here or elsewhere, has a government been so completely fused with business," noted the *Wall Street Journal*.

Distress Signals at Home and Abroad

Some economic groups remained outside the magic circle of Republican prosperity. Ironically, they included those people who made up the biggest business in America: farmers. In 1920 farming still had an investment value greater than manufacturing, all utilities, and all railroads combined. A third of the population relied on farming for a living.

Yet the farmers' portion of the national income shrank by almost half during the 1920s. The government withdrew wartime price supports for wheat and ended its practice of feeding refugees with American surpluses. As European farms began producing again, the demand for American exports dropped. New dietary habits meant that average Americans of 1920 ate 75 fewer pounds of food annually than they had 10 years earlier. New synthetic fibers drove down demand for natural wool and cotton fibers.

In 1921 a group of southern and western senators organized the "farm bloc" in Congress to coordinate relief for farmers. Over the next two years they succeeded in bringing stockyards, packers, and grain exchanges under federal supervision. Other legislation exempted farm cooperatives from antitrust actions and created a dozen banks for low-interest farm loans. But regulation and credit were not enough, and over the decade the purchasing power of farmers continued to slide.

For the five years that Coolidge ran a "businessman's government," workers reaped few gains in wages, purchasing power, and bargaining rights. Although welfare capitalism promised workers profit-sharing and other benefits, only a handful of companies put it into practice. Those that did often used it to weaken independent unions. As dangerous imbalances in the economy developed, Coolidge ignored them.

If most Americans paid little attention to the distress signals at home, they ignored economic unrest abroad. At the end of World War I, Europe's victors had forced Germany to take on $33 billion in war costs or reparations, partly to repay their own war debts to the United States. When Germany defaulted in 1923, French forces occupied the Ruhr valley, the center of German industry. Germany struck back by printing more money to cope with the crushing burden of debt. Runaway inflation soon wiped out the savings of the German middle class, shook confidence in the new democratic Weimar Republic, and eventually threatened the economic structure of all Europe.

The Dawes plan

In 1924 American business leader Charles G. Dawes persuaded the victorious Europeans to scale down reparations. In return the United States promised to help stabilize the German economy. Encouraged by the State Department, American bankers made large loans to Germany, with which the Germans paid their reparations. The European victors then used those funds to repay *their* war debts to the United States. It amounted to taking money out of one American vault and depositing it in another. In 1926 the United States also reduced European war debts. Canceling them altogether would have made more sense, but few Americans were that forgiving.

Two grand, if futile, diplomatic gestures reflected the twin desires for peace and economy. In 1921, in a conference held in Washington, the sea powers of the world agreed to freeze battleship construction for 10 years and to set ratios on the tonnage of each navy. The Five-Power Agreement was the first disarmament treaty in modern history. A more extravagant gesture came in 1928, when the major nations of the world (except the Soviet Union) signed the Kellogg-Briand Pact outlawing war. "Peace is proclaimed," announced Secretary of State Frank Kellogg as he signed the document with a foot-long pen of gold.

Kellog-Briand Pact

But what seemed so bold on paper proved timid in practice. The French resented the lower limits set on their battleships under the Five-Power Agreement and touched off a new arms race by building smaller warships such as submarines, cruisers, and destroyers. And with no means of enforcement, the Kellogg-Briand Pact remained a hollow proclamation.

The Election of 1928

On August 2, 1927, in a small classroom in Rapid City, South Dakota, Calvin Coolidge handed a terse, typewritten message to reporters: "I do not choose to run for President in nineteen twenty-eight." Republicans honored the request and nominated Herbert Hoover. Hoover was not a politician but an administrator who had never once campaigned for public office. It did not matter. Republican prosperity made it difficult for any Democrat to win. Hoover, perhaps the most admired public official in America, made it impossible.

The Democratic party continued to be polarized between its rural supporters in the South and West and ethnic laborers in the urban Northeast. The two factions had clashed during the 1924 convention, scuttling the presidential candidacy of New York Governor Al Smith. By 1928 the shift in population toward cities had given an edge to the party's urban wing. Al Smith won the nomination on the first ballot, even though his handicaps were evident. For one, he sounded like a city slicker. When the New York City–bred Smith spoke "poisonally" on the "rha-dio,"

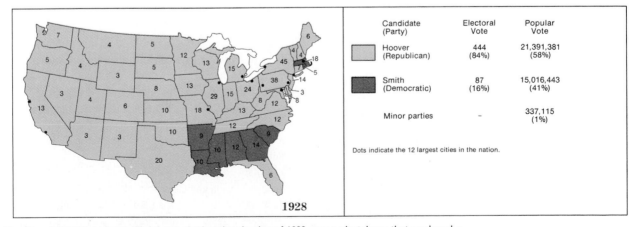

Candidate (Party)	Electoral Vote	Popular Vote
Hoover (Republican)	444 (84%)	21,391,381 (58%)
Smith (Democratic)	87 (16%)	15,016,443 (41%)
Minor parties	–	337,115 (1%)

Dots indicate the 12 largest cities in the nation.

1928

Election of 1928 Historians still debate whether the election of 1928 was a pivotal one that produced a significant political realignment. Hoover cracked the solidly Democratic South, which returned to the Democratic fold in 1932. On the other hand, Democrat Al Smith won the twelve largest cities in the country, all of which had voted Republican in 1924 but stayed in the Democratic fold in 1932.

voters across America winced. Though he pledged to enforce Prohibition, Smith campaigned against it and even took an occasional drink (which produced the false rumor that he was a hopeless alcoholic). Most damaging of all, Smith was Catholic at a time when anti-Catholicism remained strong in many areas of the country.

In the election of 1928, nearly 60 percent of the eligible voters turned out to give all but eight states to Hoover. The solidly Democratic South cracked for the first time. Still, the stirrings of a major political realignment lay buried in the returns. The 12 largest cities in the country had gone to the Republicans in 1924; in 1928 the Democrats won them. Western farmers, ignored by Republicans for a decade, also voted for Smith. The Democrats were becoming the party of the cities and of immigrants, a core around which they would build the most powerful vote-getting coalition of the twentieth century.

Just as important, a new kind of electorate was emerging. No longer were voters part of a vast partisan army whose loyalties were tied to the party, year in, year out, by barbecues, rallies, and torchlight parades. The reforms of the progressive era had restricted the power of machines and the discipline they could exert over voters. The culture of consumption that had shaped American life in the 1920s also worked to shape politics. Increasingly, parties courted voters with newspaper advertisements and persuaded them with radio "spots." In 1929 the Democrats created the first public relations department in American politics. Paradoxically, the twentieth century would witness a deterioration of party loyalty as the growing reliance on the media to communicate with "consumer/voters" weakened traditional party networks.

counterpoint

Were the 1920s a Sharp Break with the Past?

Historians have long argued over the significance of the 1920s. Initially most concluded that the decade represented a sharp break from the past as well as from the future. Wedged between two eras of reform, bounded by a world war at one end and a world depression at the other, the 1920s was depicted as a frivolous and irresponsible era that represented a period of decline in the history of the nation. Prevailing institutions and standards began to disintegrate as an orgy of consumption and speculation fueled a society bent on pleasure. Government fell into the hands of conservatives who reflected the narrow interests of business, retreated from progressive activism, and ignored danger signals in the economy.

Other historians see the 1920s as more continuous with the past, more complicated, and more important. Business historians have pointed to the trade association movement as an innovative attempt to achieve the old progressive goals of efficiency and equity in the modern industrial economy. Political historians have emphasized the remnant progressives who continued to fight for social justice and social welfare in the form of such legislation as the Sheppard-Towner Act for maternal and infant care.

Some social historians, interested in examining complex social structures, have stressed the search for continuity amid change by fastening on the theme of shared anxiety over the future and nostalgia for a mythic past. Cultural historians also have emphasized the importance of both change and continuity. Some see the origins of the intellectual revolt of the 1920s a decade earlier, while others have highlighted the emergence of a new American culture radiating outward from "mongrel Manhattan," with its hybrid mix of ethnicities, races, and sexes.

Strolling across the felt-padded floor of the New York Stock Exchange, Superintendent William Crawford greeted the

The Great Bull Market

New Year with swaggering confidence. Nineteen twenty-eight had been a record-setter, with more than 90,500,000 shares traded. The "bulls," or buyers of stock, had routed the bears, those who sell. It was the greatest bull market in history as eager purchasers drove prices to new highs. At the end of the last business day of 1928, Crawford surveyed the floor and declared flatly, "The millennium's arrived."

Veteran financial analyst Alexander Noyes had his doubts. Speculation—buying and selling on the expectation that rising prices will yield quick gains—had taken over the stock market. "Something has to give," said Noyes in September 1929. Less than a month later, the Great Bull Market fell in a heap.

The Rampaging Bull

No one knows exactly what caused the wave of speculation that boosted the stock market to dizzying heights. Driven alternately by greed and fear, the market succumbed to greed in a decade that considered it a virtue. A new breed of aggressive outsiders helped spread the speculative fever. William Durant of General Motors, the Fisher brothers from Detroit, and others like them bought millions of shares, crowded out more conservative investors from the East, and helped send prices soaring.

New blood

Money and credit to fuel the market became plentiful. From 1922 to 1929, some $900 million worth of gold flowed into the country. The money supply expanded by $6 billion. Over the decade corporate profits grew by 80 percent. At interest rates as high as 25 percent, more could be made from lending money to brokers (who then made "brokers' loans" to clients for stock purchase) than from constructing new factories. By 1929 brokers' loans had almost tripled from two years earlier.

New money

"Margin requirements," the cash actually put down to purchase stock, hovered around 50 percent for most of the decade. Thus buyers had to come up with only half the price of a share. The rest came from credit furnished by brokers' loans. As trading reached record heights in August 1929, the Federal Reserve Board tried to dampen speculation by raising the interest rates. Higher interest rates made borrowing more expensive and, authorities hoped, would rein in the galloping bull market. They were wrong. It was already too late.

ON THE FLOOR — N.Y. STOCK EXCHANGE   REGINALD MARSH

The Great Crash

On Thursday morning, October 24, 1929, the gallery of the New York Stock Exchange was packed with visitors. Trouble was in the air. The day before, a sharp break downward had accelerated a week of falling prices. Nervous speculators had begun to sell.

At the opening bell, a torrent of sell orders flooded the Exchange. Prices plunged as panic set in. By the end of "Black Thursday" nearly 13 million shares had been traded—a record. Losses stood at $3 billion, another record. Thirty-five of the largest brokerage houses on Wall Street issued a joint statement of reassurance: "The worst has passed."

The worst had just begun. Prices rallied for the rest of the week, buoyed by a bankers' buying pool organized at the House of Morgan. The following Tuesday, October 29, 1929, the bubble burst. Stockholders lost $10 billion in a single day. Within a month industrial stocks lost half of what they had been worth in September. And the downward slide continued for almost four years. At their peak in 1929 stocks had been worth $87 billion. In 1933 they bottomed out at $18 billion.

Role of the Crash

The Great Crash did not cause the Great Depression, but it did damage the economy and break the unbounded optimism on which the New Era rested. Although only about 500,000 people were actually trading stocks by the end of the decade, their investments had helped to sustain prosperity. Thousands of middle-class investors lost their savings and their futures. Commercial banks—some loaded with corporate stocks, others financing brokers' loans—reeled in the wake of the crash. As one historian put it, the shock of the stock market's fall "lowered the economy's resistance to the point where already existing defects could multiply rapidly and bring down the whole organism."

The Sickening Slide in Global Perspective

The Great Crash signaled the start of the greatest depression in the history of the modern world. In the United States, the gains of the 1920s were wiped out in a few years. In the first three years after the crash, national income fell by half, factory wages by almost half. By some estimates 85,000 businesses failed.

Although the Great Depression was less deep and less prolonged in other countries, the shock waves from the United States rippled across the globe, helping to topple already fragile economies in Europe. American loans, investments, and purchases had propped up Europe since the end of World War I. When those American resources dried up, European governments defaulted on war debts. More European banks failed; more businesses collapsed; unemployment surged to at least 30 milion worldwide by 1932.

Europeans scrambled to protect themselves. Led by Great Britain in 1931, 41 nations abandoned the gold standard. Foreign governments hoped to devalue their currencies by expanding their supplies of money. Exports would be cheaper and foreign trade would increase. But several countries did so at once, while each country raised tariffs to protect itself from foreign competition. Devaluation failed, and the resulting trade barriers only deepened the crisis. Between 1929 and 1933 world exports declined by two-thirds, from a high of nearly $3 billion to less than $1 billion. (See the chart on page 805.)

In Latin America and other regions where countries depended on exporting raw materials, the slide varied. Shrinking sales of metallic minerals, timber, and hides crippled Chile, Bolivia, Peru, and Malaya, while exports of fuel oils still needed to warm homes and run factories shielded Venezuela. Only the Soviet Union escaped catastrophe, with its limited exports and a command economy that had launched a breakneck campaign of industrialization. Even in the Soviet Union, however, bumper crops of Russian wheat forced onto the world market at deflated prices led millions of peasants to starve to death in 1932–1933. Virtually everywhere else economies cracked under the weight of slackening demand and contracting world trade.

In the United States declining sales abroad sent crop prices to new lows. Farm income dropped by more than half—to a paltry $5 billion. The epidemic of rural bank failures spread to the cities. Nervous depositors rushed to withdraw their cash. Even healthy banks could not bear the strain. In August 1930 every bank in Toledo but one closed its doors. Between 1929 and 1933 collapsing banks took more than $20 billion in assets with them. The economy was spiraling downward, and no one could stop it.

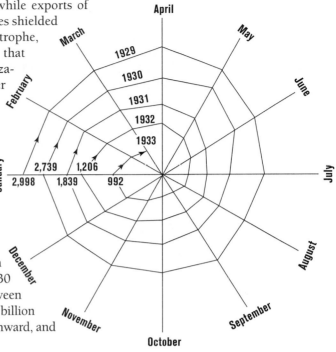

(in millions of dollars)

The Causes of the Great Depression

What, then, caused the Great Depression in the United States? In the months before the crash, with national attention riveted on the booming stock market, hardly anyone paid attention to existing defects in the American economy. But by 1928 the booming construction and automobile industries began to lose vitality as demand sagged. In fact, increases in consumer spending for all goods and services slowed to a lethargic 1.5 percent for 1928–1929. Warehouses began to fill as business inventories climbed, from $500 million in 1928 to $1.8 billion in 1929.

In one sense, businesses had done all too well. Corporations had boosted their profits by some 80 percent during the 1920s. They had done so by keeping the cost of labor and raw materials low as well as by increasing productivity (producing more, using fewer workers). But the profits that business reaped were used to expand factories rather than to pay workers higher wages. Without strong labor unions or government support, real wages never kept pace with productivity, which led to a paradox. As consumers, workers did not have enough money to buy the products they were making. The American economy was overexpanding at the same time that purchasing power was declining.

People made up the difference between earnings and purchases by borrowing. Consumers bought "on time," paying for merchandise a little each month. During the decade, consumer debt rose by 250 percent. Few could afford to keep spending at that rate. Nor could the distribution of wealth sustain prosperity. By 1929, 1 percent of the population owned 36 percent of all personal wealth. The wealthy had more money than they could possibly spend and saved too much. The working and middle classes had not nearly enough to keep the economy growing, spend though they might.

As the Great Depression deepened, world trade collapsed. Here the imports of 75 countries are tracked from 1929 to 1933. (The amounts are measured in millions of U.S. gold dollars.) The greatest annual decline occurred between 1930 and 1931 as production plummeted and nation after nation began to erect high tariff barriers to protect their domestic markets from cheaper imports. Over the four-year period, world import trade fell by almost two-thirds, only underscoring the growing interdependence of the global economy.

Consumer debt and uneven distribution of wealth

Banking system

Another problem lay with the banking system. Mismanagement, greed, and the emergence of a new type of executive—half banker, half broker—led banks to divert more funds into speculative investments. The uniquely decentralized American banking system left no way to set things right if a bank failed. At the end of the decade, half of the 25,000 banks in America lay outside the Federal Reserve System. Its controls even over member banks were weak, and during the decade, 6000 banks failed.

Corporate structure and public policy

A shaky corporate structure only made matters worse. No government agency at all monitored the stock exchanges, while big business operated largely unchecked. Insider stock trading, shady stock deals, and outright stock fraud ran rampant. Meanwhile public policy encouraged corporate consolidation and control because the government filed fewer antitrust suits. High profits and the Mellon tax program helped make many corporations wealthy enough to avoid borrowing. Thus changes in interest rates—over which the Federal Reserve exercised some control—had little influence on such corporations. Free from government regulation, fluctuating prices, and the need for loans, big businesses ruled the economy. And they ruled badly.

"Sick" industries

Unemployment began to increase as early as 1927, a sign of growing softness in the economy. By the fall of 1929 some 2 million people were out of work. Many of them were in textiles, coal mining, lumbering, and railroads. All were "sick" industries during the decade because they suffered from overexpansion, reduced demand, and weak management. Farmers were in trouble too. As European agriculture revived after World War I, farm prices tumbled. American farmers earned 16 percent of the national income in 1919 but only 9 percent in 1929. As more farmers went bust, so did many of the rural banks that had loaned them money.

Economic ignorance

Finally, plain economic ignorance contributed to the calamity. High tariffs protected American industries but discouraged European business from selling to the world's most profitable market. Because Europeans weren't profiting, they lacked the money for American goods being shipped to Europe. Only American loans and investments supported demand abroad. When the American economy collapsed, those vanished and with them went American foreign trade. Furthermore, the Federal Reserve had been stimulating the economy both by expanding the money supply and by lowering interest rates. Those moves only fed the speculative fever by furnishing investors with more money at lower costs. A decision finally to raise interest rates in 1929 to stem speculation ended up speeding the slide.

"Everyone ought to be rich," proclaimed one enthusiastic investment adviser in *The Ladies Home Journal*—at a time when the economy was still bubbling and the stock market was setting new highs. But as the economy began to collapse upon itself, the heady optimism of so many people in the New Era vanished. The United States was facing a depression more severe and more prolonged than any in its history. And no one—not the brokers of Wall Street nor the captains of industry nor the leaders of government—seemed to have any clear notion of the path toward recovery.

chapter summary

The New Era of the 1920s brought a booming economy and modern times to America, vastly accelerating the forces of change—bureaucracy, productivity, technology, advertising and consumerism, mass media, peer culture, and suburbanization. Urban-rural tensions peaked with shifts in population that gave cities new power. But as the decade wore on, weaknesses in the economy and a new ethos of getting and spending, too much of it on credit, proved to be the New Era's undoing.

- Technology, advertising and consumer spending, and such boom industries as automobile manufacturing and construction fueled the largest peacetime economic growth in American history.

- Key features of modern life—mass society, mass culture, and mass consumption—took hold, fed by mass media in the form of radio, movies, and mass-circulation newspapers and magazines.

- Modern life unsettled old ways and eroded social conventions that had limited life especially for women and children, leading to the emergence of a New Woman and a youth culture.

- Great migrations of African Americans from the rural South to the urban North and of Latinos from Mexico to the United States reshaped the social landscape.

- Traditional culture, centered in rural America, hardened and defended itself against change through immigration restriction, Prohibition, Fundamentalism, and a reborn Ku Klux Klan.

- A galloping bull market in stocks reflected the commitment of government to big business and economic growth.

- When the stock market crashed in 1929, weaknesses in the economy—overexpansion, declining purchasing power, uneven distribution of wealth, weak banking and corporate structures, "sick" industries, and economic ignorance—finally brought the economy down, and with it the New Era came to a close.

additional reading

For years, Frederick Lewis Allen, *Only Yesterday: An Informal History of the 1920s* (1931) shaped the stereotyped view of the decade as a frivolous interlude between World War I and the Great Depression. William Leuchtenburg, *The Perils of Prosperity, 1914–1932* (1958) began an important reconsideration by stressing the serious conflict between urban and rural America and the emergence of modern mass society. Ann Douglas, *Terrible Honesty: Mongrel Manhattan in the 1920s* (1995) puts Manhattan at the core of the cultural transformation in the 1920s, especially its success at bringing African American folk and popular art into the mainstream.

Roland Marchand, *Advertising the American Dream: Making Way for Modernity, 1920–1940* (1985) analyzes the role of advertising in shaping mass consumption, values, and culture, and Ellis Hawley, *The Great War and the Search for a Modern Order* (1979) emphasizes economic institutions.

Three recent studies explore continuity and change for women in the 1920s: Kathleen M. Blee, *Women of the Klan: Racism and Gender in the 1920s* (1991); Virginia Scharff, *Taking the Wheel: Women and the Coming of the Motor Age* (1991); and Jacqueline Jones, *Labor of Love, Labor of Sorrow: Black Women, Work, and Family, From Slavery to the Present* (1985).

The most thorough and readable examination of the stock market and its relation to the economy and public policy in the 1920s is still Robert Sobel, *The Great Bull Market: Wall Street in the 1920s* (1968). The best books on the disintegration of the American economy remain Lester Chandler, *America's Greatest Depression, 1929–1941* (1970) and, from a global standpoint, Charles Kindleberger, *The World in Depression, 1929–1939* (1973). For an analysis of the Great Depression from the perspective of Keynesian economics that stresses declining purchasing power and investment, see John Kenneth Galbraith, *The Great Crash* (rev. ed., 1988). For the argument of monetarists, who see the roots of the depression in the shrinking money supply, see Milton Friedman and Anna Jacobson Schwartz, *Monetary History of the United States* (1963) and Peter Temin, *Did Monetary Forces Cause the Great Depression?* (1976). For a fuller list of readings, see the Bibliography.

Significant Events

1900

1903 First feature-length film, *The Great Train Robbery*, released

1909 Sigmund Freud comes to America

1905

1914 Henry Ford introduces moving assembly line

1915 Modern Ku Klux Klan founded

1916 Marcus Garvey brings Universal Negro Improvement Association to America

1919 Eighteenth Amendment outlawing alcohol use ratified

1910

1920 First commercial radio broadcast; Nineteenth Amendment grants women right to vote; Warren Harding elected president

1921 Congresss enacts quotas on immigration; Sheppard-Towner Federal Maternity and Infancy Act; American Birth Control League organized

1915

1921–1922 Washington Naval Disarmament Conference

1922 Sinclair Lewis's *Babbitt* published; T. S. Eliot's *The Waste Land* published

1920

1923 *Time* magazine founded; Harding dies; Calvin Coolidge becomes president; Harding scandals break

1924 Dawes plan to stabilize German inflation; Coolidge elected president

1925 John T. Scopes convicted of teaching evolution in Tennessee; Alain Locke's *The New Negro* published

1925

1927 Charles Lindbergh's solo flight across the Atlantic; Sacco and Vanzetti executed; first "talking" film, *The Jazz Singer*, released

1928 Herbert Hoover elected president

1930   1929 Stock market crashes

Chapter 25

THE GREAT DEPRESSION &
The New Deal,
1929–1939

Winner, South Dakota, November 10, 1933. "Dammit, I don't WANT to write to you again tonight. It's been a long, long day, and I'm tired." All the days had been long since Lorena Hickok began her cross-country trek. Four months earlier Harry Hopkins, in charge of the federal relief program in President Franklin Roosevelt's new administration, had hired her to report on government efforts to help Americans. Forget about statistics or the "social worker angle," he told her. "Talk with the unemployed, those who are on relief and those who aren't, and when you talk to them," he added, "don't ever forget that but for the grace of God you, I, any of our friends might be in their shoes."

As she toured the country in 1933 and 1934, Hickok found that Roosevelt's relief program was falling short. Its half-billion-dollar subsidy to states, localities, and charities was still leaving out too many Americans, such as the sharecropper Hickok discovered near Raleigh, North Carolina. He and his daughters had been living in a tobacco barn for two weeks on little more than weeds and table scraps. "Seems like we just keep goin' lower and lower," said the blue-eyed 16-year-old. To Hickok's surprise, hope still flickered in those eyes. She couldn't explain it until she noticed a pin on the girl's chest. It was a campaign button from the 1932 election—"a profile of the President." Hope sprang from the man in the White House.

Before Franklin D. Roosevelt, the White House was far removed from ordinary citizens. His predecessor, President Herbert Hoover, had been distant and austere. The only federal agency with which Americans had any contact at all was the post office. And after 1929, it usually delivered bad news. The old order was widely perceived to have failed, and nothing, least of all government, seemed capable of reviving it.

preview • The Great Depression, the longest one in the history of the nation, left many Americans shaken. Rates of birth and marriage declined, and many women worked additional hours in and out of the home. Sufferings were most acute among agricultural migrants, African Americans, Latinos, and American Indians. Franklin Roosevelt's New Deal attacked the Depression along three broad fronts: recovery for the economy, relief for the needy, and reforms designed to ward off future depressions. It succeeded in all but the quest for recovery.

As Lorena Hickok traveled the country in 1933, a year after Roosevelt's election, she detected a change. Perhaps people talked about long-awaited contributions to relief or maybe reforms in securities and banking or the new recovery programs for industry and agriculture. Just as likely it was Franklin Roosevelt they mentioned. Hickok seldom heard voters call themselves "Republicans" or "Democrats" anymore. Instead, she wrote, they were "for the president."

The mail carried other signs that plain people were looking to Washington, the federal government, and the president as at no time since the Civil War. The first weekend after Roosevelt's inauguration nearly half a million letters and telegrams poured into the White House. For years the average remained a record 5000 to 8000 a day. Over half the letters came from those at the bottom of the economic heap. Most sought help, offered praise, or just expressed their gratitude.

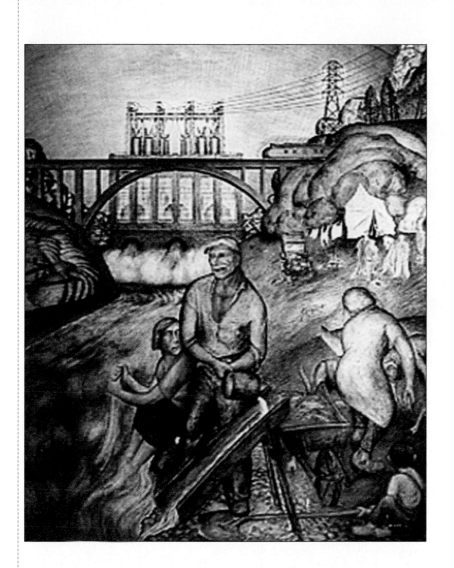

Migrants flocked to California during the Great Depression, often in jalopies like the one pictured behind these laborers in John Langley Howard's mural. By 1932 over a million homeless Americans wandered the nation. But a sign of the New Deal can be seen in the mural also: Shasta Dam along the Sacramento River, one of many dams built with federal funds that extended the power of the New Deal, quite literally in this case, all across the country.

Whatever the individual messages, their collective meaning was clear: Franklin D. Roosevelt and his "New Deal" for the American people had begun to restore hope. Though it never brought about a full recovery, the New Deal did improve economic conditions and provided relief to thousands of Americans. It reformed the economic system and committed the federal government to managing its ups and downs. Finally, the New Deal extended the progressive drive to soften the impact of industrialization and translated decades of growing concern for the disadvantaged into a federal aid program. For the first time, Americans believed Washington would help them through a terrible crisis. The liberal state came of age: active, interventionist, and committed to social welfare.

The Human Impact of the Great Depression

Long breadlines snaked around corners. Vacant-eyed apple-sellers stood shivering in the wind. A man with his hat in his hand came to the back door asking for food in exchange for work. Fewer automobiles rode the streets; more hoboes rode the rails. Between 1929 and 1932 an average of 100,000 people lost their jobs every week until some 13 million Americans were jobless. At least one worker in four could find no work at all.

Shantytowns (called "Hoover-villes" after President Herbert Hoover) sprang up around most cities as the Depression deepened. Sometimes the down-and-out turned to desperate action. In 1931 a hunger riot broke out when the unemployed stormed a grocery store in Oklahoma City. Meanwhile thousands occupied the Seattle County-City Building to protest conditions there. Two years later in Chicago, 55 citizens were arrested when they were found tearing down a four-story building and taking it away brick by brick.

The Great Depression was a great leveler that reduced differences in the face of common want. The New York seamstress without enough piecework to pay her rent felt the same pinch of frustration and anger as the Berkeley student whose college education was cut short when the bank let her father go. Not everyone was devastated. Most husbands had some job. Most wives continued as homemakers. Most Americans got by as best they could, often cooperating with one another, practicing a ruthless underconsumption to make ends meet. "We lived lean," recalled one Depression victim. So did most of the American people—northern and southern, urban and rural, black, white, brown, yellow, and red.

Hard Times

Subsistence incomes

The hard times lasted the entire decade. Even before the Great Crash many Americans were having trouble making a living. Economists calculated that for the barest necessities a family of four in the golden year of 1929 required $2000 a year—more money than 60 percent of American families earned. By 1932 the average family had an annual income of $1348, barely enough to survive.

As soup kitchens opened and bread lines formed in cities across the nation, survival often became the primary goal. Millions stayed alive by foraging like animals, and city hospitals began receiving new patients ill from starvation. Pellagra and other diseases associated with malnutrition increased. Despite official claims that "no one has starved," the New York City Welfare Council reported 29 victims of starvation and 110 dead of malnutrition in 1932. Most were children.

Unable to pay mortgages or rent, many families lived off the generosity of forgiving landlords. Some traded down to smaller quarters or simply lost their homes. By 1932 between 1 million and 2 million Americans were homeless wanderers, among them an estimated 25,000 nomadic families. For the first time, emigration out of the United States exceeded immigration into it because Americans could find no work in their own country.

Marriage and family

Marriages and births, symbols of faith in the future, decreased. For the first time in three centuries the curve of population growth began to level, as many young couples postponed having children. Experts worried about an impending "baby crop shortage." Strong families hung together and grew closer; weak ones languished or fell apart. Although divorce declined, desertion—the "poor man's divorce"—mushroomed. Under the strain, rates of mental illness and suicide rose as well.

Many fathers, whose lives had been defined by work, suddenly had nothing to do. They grew listless and depressed. Most mothers stayed home and found their traditional roles as nurturer and household manager less disrupted than the roles of their husbands. Between 1929 and 1933 living costs dropped 25 percent, but family incomes tumbled by 40 percent. Homemakers watched household budgets with a closer eye than ever, canned more food, and substituted less expensive fish for meat. When they earned extra money, they often did so within the confines of the "woman's sphere" by taking in boarders, laundry, and sewing, opening beauty parlors in their kitchens, and selling baked goods.

Fathers and mothers

Family life took on new importance, and the home emerged as the center of recreation. Surveys showed that while Americans dreamed of the outdoors—swimming, boating, or playing tennis—they spent most of their free time at home. Board games such as Monopoly and card games like contract bridge enjoyed great popularity. Between 1934 and 1937, phonograph record sales jumped a hundredfold, and reading became the number one form of entertainment.

For those women who worked outside the home, prejudice still relegated them to so-called women's work. Over half the female labor force continued to work in domestic service or the garment trades, while others found traditional employment as school teachers, social workers, and secretaries. Only slowly did the female proportion of the workforce reach pre-Depression levels, until it rose finally to 25 percent by 1940, largely because women were willing to take almost any job. Meanwhile, the middle-class dream of a wife freed from working for wages, a dream that had weakened in the 1910s and 1920s, reasserted itself because many women came to associate working outside the home with financial distress.

Whether in the renewed importance of homemaking and family life or the reemergence of home industries, the Great Depression sent ordinary Americans scurrying for the reassuring shelter of past practices and left many of them badly shaken. Shame, self-doubt, and pessimism became epidemic as people blamed themselves for their circumstances and turned their anger inward. "Shame? You tellin' me?" recalled one man. "I would go stand on the relief line [and] bend my head low so nobody would recognize me. The only scar that is left on me is my pride, my pride." The lasting legacy of humiliation and fear—that you had caused your own downfall; that the bottom would drop out again; that life would be leveled once more; that the next depression might not end—was what one writer called an "invisible scar."

Psychological impact

The Golden Age of Radio and Film

By the end of the decade almost 9 out 10 families owned radios. People depended on radios for nearly everything—news, sports, and weather; music and entertainment; advice on how to bake a cake or find God. Some programming helped change national habits. When *The Sporting News* conducted a poll about baseball in 1932, editors were surprised to discover that a "new crop of fans has been created by radio . . . the women." Many women were at home during the day when most games were played, and broadcasters went out of their way to educate these new listeners. Attendance at night games soon outran day games, in part because husbands began taking wives and daughters, whose interest in the game was sparked by radio.

Programming

Radio entered a golden age of commercialism, because advertisers hawked their products on variety programs like *Major Bowes' Amateur Hour* and comedy shows with

George Burns and Gracie Allen. Daytime melodramas, called "soap operas" because they were sponsored by soap companies, aimed at women with stories of the personal struggles of ordinary folk.

Radio continued to bind the country together. A teenager in Splendora, Texas, could listen to the same wisecracks from Jack Benny, the same music from Guy Lombardo, as kids in New York and Los Angeles. In 1938 Orson Welles broadcast H. G. Wells's classic science fiction tale *The War of the Worlds*. Americans everywhere listened to breathless reports of an "invasion from Mars," and many believed it. In Newark, New Jersey, cars jammed roads as families rushed to evacuate the city. The nation, bombarded with reports of impending war in Europe and used to responding to radio advertising, was prepared to believe almost anything, even reports about invaders from Mars.

Art Deco radio, 1930. Art Deco, popularized in the 1920s, relied on the geometrical patterns of machines arranged in decorative designs.

In Hollywood an efficient but autocratic studio system churned out a record number of feature films. Eight motion picture companies produced more than two-thirds of them. Color, first introduced to feature films in *Becky Sharp* (1935), soon complemented sound, which had debuted in the 1927 version of *The Jazz Singer.* Neither alone could keep movie theaters full. As attendance dropped early in the Depression, big studios like Metro-Goldwyn-Mayer and Universal lured audiences back with films that shocked, titillated, and just plain entertained.

By the mid-1930s more than 60 percent of Americans were going to the movies at least once a week. They saw tamer films as the industry began regulating movie content in the face of growing criticism. In 1933 the Catholic Church created the Legion of Decency to monitor features. To avoid censorship and boycotts, studios stiffened their own regulations. Producers could not depict homosexuality, abortion, drug use, or sex. (Even the word "sex" was banned, as was all profanity.) If couples were shown in bed, they had to be clothed and one foot of each partner had to touch the floor. Middle-class morality reigned on the screen, and most Depression movies, like most of popular culture, preserved traditional values.

"Dirty Thirties": An Ecological Disaster

Dust Bowl

Between 1932 and 1939 an average of nearly 50 "black blizzards" a year turned 1500 square miles between the Oklahoma panhandle and western Kansas into a gigantic "Dust Bowl," whose baleful effects were felt as far north as the Dakotas and as far south as Texas. It was one of the worst ecological disasters in modern history. Nature played its part, scorching the earth and whipping the winds. But the "dirty thirties" were mostly human-made. The semiarid lands west of the 98th meridian were not suitable for agriculture or livestock. Sixty years of intensive farming and grazing had stripped the prairie of its natural vegetation and rendered it defenseless against the elements. When the dry winds came, one-third of the Great Plains just blew away.

The dust storms lasted anywhere from hours to days. Walking into one was like walking into "a wall of dirt." "This is the ultimate darkness," despaired a Kansan in the midst of one storm. "So must come the end of the world." Winds carried the dust aloft so high that yellow grit from Nebraska collected on the windowsills of the White House, and ships 300 miles off the East Coast found bits of Montana and Wyoming on their decks. Even the fish died—from lack of oxygen in dust-coated rivers.

Impact of commercial farming

Some 3.5 million plains people abandoned their farms. Landowners or corporations forced off about half of them as large-scale commercial farming slowly spread into the heartland of America. Commercial farms were more common in California, where 10

Black blizzards dwarfed all fabricated structures. The drought that gave rise to the huge dust storms lasted from 1932 until 1936, and few who lived through a black blizzard ever forgot it. "Noon was like night," reported a conductor on the Santa Fe railroad. "There was no sun, and, at times, it was impossible to see a yard. The engineer could not see the signal lights." In a single day in 1934, 12 million tons of western dirt fell on Chicago.

percent of the farms grew more than 50 percent of the crops. As in industrial America, the strategy in agricultural America was to consolidate and mechanize. As farms grew in size, so did the number of tenants. In most Dust Bowl counties people owned less than half the land they farmed. American agriculture was turning from a way of life into an industry. And as the economy contracted, owners cut costs by cutting workers.

Relief offices around the country reported a change in migrant families. Rather than black or brown, more and more were white and native-born, typically a young married couple with one child. Most did not travel far, perhaps to the next county. Long-distance migrants—the "exodusters" from Oklahoma, Arizona, and Texas— usually set their sights on California. Handbills and advertisements promised jobs picking fruit and harvesting vegetables. If they were like the Joad family in John Steinbeck's classic novel *The Grapes of Wrath* (1939), they drove west along Route 66 through Arizona and New Mexico, their belongings piled high atop rickety jalopies, heading for the West Coast.

Exodusters

More than 350,000 Oklahomans migrated to California—so many that "Okie" came to mean any Dust Bowler, even though most of Oklahoma lay outside the Dust Bowl. The poor were only a small minority of new arrivals, but enough came to make Californians edgy. By the middle of the decade Los Angeles police had formed "bum blockades" to keep migrants out. "Negroes and Okies upstairs," read one sign in a San Joaquin Valley theater. Native-born whites had never encountered such discrimination before.

Only one in two or three migrants actually found work. The labor surplus allowed growers to set their own terms. A migrant family earned about $450 a year, less than a third the subsistence level. Families that did not work formed wretched enclaves called "little Oklahomas." The worst were located in the fertile Imperial Valley. There, at the end of the decade, relief officials discovered a family of 10 living in a 1921 Ford. When told to go, the mother responded vacantly, "I wonder where?"

Mexican Americans and Repatriation

The Chavez family lost their farm in the North Gila River valley of Arizona in 1934. They had owned a small homestead near Yuma for two generations, but the Depression pushed them out. Cesar, barely six years old at the time, remembered only

Cesar Chavez

images of the departure: a "giant tractor" leveling the corral; the loss of his room and bed; a beat-up Chevy hauling the family west; his father promising to buy another farm someday.

The elder Chavez could never keep his promise. Instead he and his family lived on the road, "following the crops" in California. In eight years Cesar went to 37 schools. The family was forced to sell their labor to unscrupulous *enganchistas,* or contractors, for less than $10 a week. The father joined strikers in the Imperial Valley in the mid-1930s, but they were crushed. "Some people put this out of their minds and forget it," said Cesar Chavez years later. "I don't." Thirty years later he founded the United Farm Workers of America, the first union of migratory workers in the country.

Repatriation

A deep ambivalence had always characterized American attitudes toward Mexicans, but the Great Depression turned most Anglo communities against them. Cities such as Los Angeles, fearing the burden of relief, found it cheaper to ship Mexicans home. Some migrants left voluntarily. Others were driven out by frustrated officials or angry neighbors. Beginning in 1931 the federal government launched a series of deportations, or "repatriations," of Mexicans back to Mexico. These deportations often included the Mexicans' American-born children, who by law were citizens of the United States. During the decade the Latino population of the Southwest dropped by 500,000. In Chicago, the Mexican community shrank almost by half. Staying in the United States turned out to be as difficult as leaving. The average income of Mexican American families in the Rio Grande valley of Texas was $506 a year. The sum represented the combined income of parents and children. Following the harvest made schooling particularly difficult: fewer than 2 Mexican American children in 10 completed five years of school.

LULAC and ethnic identity

For Americans of Mexican descent, the Great Depression only deepened anxiety over identity. Were they Mexicans, as many Anglos regarded them, or were they Americans, as they regarded themselves? In the 1920s, such questions had produced several organizations founded to assert the American identity of native-born and naturalized Mexican Americans and to pursue their civil rights. In 1929, on the eve of the Depression, many of these organizations were consolidated into the League of United Latin American Citizens (LULAC). By the early 1940s, "Flying Squadrons" of LULAC organizers had founded some 80 chapters nationwide, making it the largest Mexican American civil rights association in the country.

LULAC permitted only those Latinos who were American citizens to join, thus excluding hundreds of thousands of ethnic Mexicans who nonetheless regarded the United States as their home. It pointedly conducted meetings in English, relied heavily on the assimilated middle class for leadership, and stressed desegregation of public schools, voter registration, and an end to discrimination in public facilities and on juries.

Perhaps LULAC's clearest statement of intent in the 1930s came in its support for immigration restriction from Mexico—as a means of both establishing the "Americanness" of its members and creating more jobs for Mexican Americans already here. Still, LULAC counted small farmers, ranchers, and wage laborers among its rank and file, many of whom identified strongly with Mexico. And despite LULAC's efforts to distance itself from Mexican immigrants, women members raised funds for milk, eyeglasses, Christmas toys, and clothes for the new arrivals.

African Americans in the Depression

Hard times were nothing new to African Americans. "The Negro was born in depression," opined one black man. "It only became official when it hit the white man." Still, when the Depression struck, black unemployment surged. By 1932 it reached 50 percent, twice the national level. By 1933 several cities reported between 25 and 40 percent of their black residents with no support except relief payments. Even skilled black workers who retained their jobs saw their wages cut in half, according to one study of Harlem in 1935.

Migration out of the rural South, up 800,000 during the 1920s, dropped by 50 percent in the 1930s. As late as 1940 three of four African Americans still lived in rural areas; yet conditions there were just as bad as in cities. In 1934 one study estimated the average income for black cotton farmers at under $200 a year. Millions of African Americans made do by stretching meager incomes, as they had for years. "Our wives could go to the store and get a bag of beans or a sack of flour and a piece of fat meat, and they could cook this. And we could eat it," explained another man. "Now you take the white fella, he couldn't do this."

During the 1930s, with crop failures common, the annual income for black sharecroppers in the South averaged little more than $200 a year. This poignant drawing in charcoal, entitled *There Were No Crops*, won a first-place prize at the American Negro Exposition in Chicago in 1940 for the African American artist Charles White.

Like many African Americans, George Baker refused to be victimized by the Depression. Baker had moved from Georgia to Harlem in 1915. He changed his name to M. J. Divine and founded a religious cult that promised followers an afterlife of full equality. In the 1930s Father Divine preached economic cooperation and opened shelters, or "heavens," for regenerate "angels," black and white. In Detroit, Elijah Poole changed his name to Elijah Muhammad and in 1931 established the Black Muslims, a blend of Islamic faith and black nationalism. He exhorted African Americans to celebrate their African heritage, to live a life of self-discipline and self-help, and to strive for a separate all-black nation.

Father Divine and Elijah Muhammad

The Depression inflamed racial prejudice. "Dust has been blown from the shotgun, the whip, and the noose," reported *The New Republic* in 1931, "and Ku Klux Klan practices were being resumed in the certainty that dead men not only tell no tales but create vacancies." Lynchings tripled between 1932 and 1933. In 1932 the Supreme Court ordered a retrial in the most celebrated racial case of the decade. A year earlier nine black teenagers had been accused of raping two white women on a train bound for Scottsboro, Alabama. Within weeks all-white juries had sentenced eight of them to death. The convictions rested on the testimony of the women, one of whom later admitted that the boys had been framed. Appeals kept the case alive for almost a decade. In the end charges against four of the "Scottsboro boys" were dropped. The other five received substantial prison sentences.

Scottsboro boys

The presidency of Herbert Hoover began with great promise but soon became the worst ordeal of his life. "I have no fears

The Tragedy of Herbert Hoover

for the future of our country," he had announced at his inauguration in March 1929. "It is bright with hope." Within seven months a "depression" had struck. (Hoover himself coined the term to minimize the crisis.) Try as he might, he could not beat it and the nation turned against him. "People were starving because of Herbert Hoover," sputtered an angry mother in 1932. "Men were killing themselves because of Herbert Hoover, and their fatherless children were being packed away to orphanages . . . because of Herbert Hoover." The charge was unfair, but it stuck. For all of Hoover's promise and innovative intelligence, his was to be a transitional presidency, important as a break from the do-nothing policies of past depression presidents and as a herald of the new, more active policies of the future.

The Failure of Relief

Private charity

By the winter of 1931–1932 the story was the same everywhere: relief organizations found themselves with too little money and too few resources to make any significant headway against the Depression. Once-mighty private charity had dwindled to 6 percent of all relief funds. Hull House in Chicago, the model of progressive benevolence, was overwhelmed by the needs of its neighbors.

Ethnic charities made similar efforts to stave off disaster. Mexican Americans and Puerto Ricans turned to *mutualistas*, traditional societies that provided members with social support, life insurance, and sickness benefits. The stress of the Depression quickly bankrupted most *mutualistas*. In San Francisco, the Chinese Six Companies offered food and clothing to needy Chinese Americans. But as the head of the Federation of Jewish Charities warned, private efforts were failing. The government would be "compelled, by the cruel events ahead of us, to step into the situation and bring relief on a large scale."

City services

An estimated 30 million needy people nationwide quickly depleted city treasuries, already pressed because nearly 30 percent of city taxpayers had fallen behind in paying the taxes they owed. In Philadelphia relief payments to a family of four totaled $5.50 a week, the highest in the country. Some cities gave nothing to unmarried people or childless couples, no matter how impoverished they were. New Orleans refused all new applications for aid in 1931. Oklahoma City began arresting unemployed men, charging them with vagrancy, and ordering them out of town. By the end of 1931, Detroit, Boston, and scores of other cities were bankrupt.

Louis Ribak's *Home Relief Station* grimly portrays the failing relief efforts of private charities and the humiliation of applying for relief. A crowd of broken men and women sits anxiously as a burly administrator interrogates a frail relief applicant. To go on relief, said one man, was to endure a "crucifixion."

Cities clamored for help from state capitals, but after a decade of extravagant spending and sloppy bookkeeping, many states were already running in the red. As businesses and property values collapsed, tax bases shrank and with them state revenues. Michigan, one of the few states to provide any relief, reduced funds by more than half between 1931 and 1932. Until New York established its Temporary Emergency Relief Administration (TERA) in 1931, no state had any agency at all to handle the problem of unemployment.

TERA

Some people refused to accept help even when they qualified. Before applications could even be considered, all property had to be sold, all credit exhausted, all relatives declared flat broke. After a half-hour grilling about his family, home, and friends, one applicant left, "feeling I didn't have any business living any more." Hostile officials attached every possible stigma to aid. Ten states wrote property requirements for voting into their constitutions. The destitute were being disfranchised.

The Hoover Depression Program

From the fall of 1930 onward, President Herbert Hoover took responsibility for ending the crisis—and as humanely as possible. It was a mark of his character. Orphaned at nine, he became one of Stanford University's first graduates and before the age of 40, the millionaire head of one of the most successful mine engineering firms in the world. As a good Quaker, he balanced private gain with public service, saving starving Belgian refugees in 1915 after war broke out in Europe. He worked 14 hours a day, paid his own salary, and convinced private organizations and businesses to donate food, clothing, and other necessities. In his honor, Finns coined a new word: to "hoover" meant to help.

As secretary of commerce under Harding and Coolidge, Hoover perfected his associational philosophy (see page 799). It rested on the notion that government should foster private solutions to public problems by promoting voluntary cooperation among businesses and between businesses and government. Even so, when the Depression struck, his was not a do-nothing presidency. Past presidents had feared that any intervention at all by government would upset the natural workings of the economy and that their sole responsibility was to keep the budget balanced. But Hoover understood the vicious cycle in which rising unemployment drove down consumer demand, and he appreciated the need for stimulating investment. Thus he set in motion an unprecedented program of government activism.

Despite the president's best efforts, his program failed. As a good associationalist, Hoover rallied business leaders, who pledged to maintain employment, wages, and prices—only to see those leaders back down as the economy sputtered. He pushed a tax cut through Congress in 1930 in order to increase the purchasing power of consumers. But when the cuts produced an unbalanced federal budget, Hoover reversed course. At bottom he firmly believed that capitalism would generate its own recovery and that a balanced federal budget was required in order to restore the confidence of business. Too much government action, he worried, might destroy the very economic system he was seeking to save. So he agreed to tax increases in 1932, further undermining investment and consumption.

Herbert Hoover

Equally disastrous, the president endorsed the Smoot-Hawley Tariff (1930) to protect the United States from cheap foreign goods. That bill brought a wave of retaliation from countries abroad, which choked world trade and reduced American sales overseas. Even the $1 billion that Hoover spent on public works—more than the total spent by all his predecessors combined—did not approach the $10 billion needed to employ only half the jobless. Spending such huge sums seemed unthinkable, for the entire federal budget at the time was only $3.2 billion.

Reconstruction Finance Corporation

Under pressure from Congress, Hoover took his boldest action to save the banks. Between 1930 and 1932 some 5100 failed as panicky depositors withdrew their funds. Hoover agreed to permit the creation of the Reconstruction Finance Corporation (RFC) in 1932, an agency that could lend money to banks and their chief corporate debtors—insurance companies and railroads. Modeled on a similar agency created during World War I, the RFC had a capital stock of $500 million and the power to borrow four times that amount. Within three months bank failures dropped from 70 a week to 1 every two weeks. The Glass-Steagall Banking Act (1932) made it easier for banks to loan money by adding $2 billion of new currency to the money supply, backed by Federal Reserve government bonds.

Yet in spite of this success, Hoover drew criticism for rescuing banks and not people. From the start he rejected the idea of federal relief for the unemployed. It was not that the president was insensitive—far from it. He never visited a breadline or a relief shelter because he could not bear the sight of human suffering. He feared that a "dole," or giveaway program (of the kind being used in Britain), would damage the freedom and initiative of recipients, perhaps even create a permanent underclass. The bureaucracy that would be needed to police recipients would inevitably meddle in the private lives of citizens and bring a "train of corruption and waste." Hoover assumed that neighborliness and cooperation would be enough.

Unemployment relief

As unemployment continued to worsen, Hoover slowly softened his stand on federal relief. In 1932 he allowed Congress to pass the Emergency Relief and Construction Act. It authorized the RFC to lend up to $1.5 billion for "reproductive" public works that paid for themselves—like toll bridges and slum clearance. Another $300 million went to states as loans for the direct relief of the unemployed. Yet in this Depression, $300 million was a pittance. When the governor of Pennsylvania requested loans to furnish the destitute with 13 cents a day for a year, the RFC sent only enough for 3 cents a day.

Stirrings of Discontent

Thus Hoover's efforts were too little, too late. "The word revolution is heard at every hand," one writer warned in 1932. Some wondered if capitalism itself had gone bankrupt.

Farm Holiday Association

Here and there the desperate took matters into their own hands in 1932. In Wisconsin the Farm Holiday Association dumped thousands of gallons of milk on highways in a vain attempt to raise prices. Ten thousand striking miners formed a 48-mile motorcar "Coal Caravan" that worked its way in protest across southern Illinois. In March a demonstration turned ugly when communist sympathizers led a hunger march on Henry Ford's Rouge Assembly Plant in Dearborn, Michigan. As 3000 protesters surged toward the gates, Ford police drenched them with hoses, then opened fire at point-blank range. Four marchers were killed and more than 20 wounded.

Communist party

For all the stirrings of discontent, revolution was never a danger. In 1932 the Communist party of the United States had 20,000 members—up from 6500 only three years earlier but hardly large enough to constitute a political force. Deeply suspicious of Marxist doctrine, most Americans were unsympathetic. Fewer than 1000 African Americans joined the party in the early 1930s. At first hostile to established politics, the Communists adopted a more cooperative strategy to contain Adolf Hitler when his Nazi party won control of Germany in 1933. The Soviet Union ordered Communist parties in

Europe and the United States to join with liberal politicians in a "popular front" against Nazism. Thereafter party membership peaked in the mid-1930s at about 80,000.

Hoover sympathized with the discontented but only to a point. When 1600 Communist-led hunger marchers came to Washington in December 1931, he was determined to protect their right to protest and ordered blankets, tents, a field kitchen, and medical aid for them. Washington police stood guard over their parade. Hoover himself received their petitions at the White House. But in the summer of 1932, the "Bonus Army" received a far different reception.

The Bonus Army

The army, a ragtag collection of World War I veterans, was hungry and looking to cash in the bonus certificates they had received from Congress in 1924 as a reward for wartime service. By the time they reached Washington, D.C., in June 1932, their numbers had swelled to nearly 20,000, the largest protest in the city's history. Hoover dismissed them as a special-interest lobby and refused to see their leaders, but the House voted to pay them immediately. When the Senate blocked the bonus bill, most veterans left.

About 2000 stayed to dramatize their plight, camping with their families and parading peaceably. Despite the efforts of the Washington police to evict them, the protesters refused to leave. By the end of July, the President had had enough. He called in the U.S. Army under the command of Chief of Staff General Douglas MacArthur. MacArthur arrived with four troops of saber-brandishing cavalry, six tanks, and a column of infantry with bayonets ready for action. By the time the smoke cleared the next morning, the Bonus marchers had vanished except for 300 wounded veterans.

Though he had intended that the army only assist the police, Hoover accepted responsibility for the action. And the sight of unarmed and unemployed veterans under attack by American troops soured most Americans. In Albany, New York, Governor

In the early years of the Depression, demonstrations of the unemployed, some organized by Communists and other radicals, broke out all over the country. On March 6, 1930, a Communist-led protest at Union Square in New York turned into an ugly riot. In 1935 Communist parties, under orders from Moscow, adopted the more cooperative strategy of allying with democratic and socialist groups against fascism, proclaiming in the United States that "Communism is twentieth-century Americanism."

Franklin D. Roosevelt exploded at the president's failure: "There is nothing inside the man but jelly." Like the hero of a classical tragedy, Herbert Hoover, symbol of the New Era and the greatest humanitarian of his generation, came tumbling down.

The Election of 1932

At their convention in Chicago, Republicans still stuck with Hoover and endorsed his Depression program to the last detail. Democrats countered with Franklin D. Roosevelt, the charismatic New York governor. As a sign of things to come, Roosevelt broke all precedent by flying to Chicago and addressing the delegates in person. "I pledge you, I pledge myself to a new deal for the American people," he told them.

Without a national following, Roosevelt zigged and zagged during the campaign in an effort to appeal to the broadest possible bloc of voters. One minute he attacked Hoover as a "profligate spender" and vowed to balance the budget; the next he called for costly public works and aid to the unemployed. He promised to help business, then spoke vaguely of remembering the "forgotten man" and "distributing wealth and products more equitably." For his part, Hoover denounced Roosevelt's New Deal as a "dangerous departure" from time-honored traditions, one that would destroy American values and institutions and "build a bureaucracy such as we have never seen in our history." None of it mattered. The deepening Depression ensured that virtually any Democratic would defeat Hoover.

On Election Day, Roosevelt captured a thundering 58 percent of the popular vote and carried with him large Democratic majorities in the Congress. Just as telling as the margin of victory were its sources. Industrial workers in the North, poor farmers in the South and West, immigrants and big city dwellers everywhere were being galvanized into a broad new coalition. These people had experienced firsthand the savage effects of the boom-and-bust business cycle and wanted change. But they were not radicals and found no appeal in the presidential campaigns of Socialist Norman Thomas or Communist William Z. Foster, both of whom had called for worker ownership of businesses. The Socialists polled less than a million votes, the Communists barely over 100,000. Instead Depression-era voters turned to Roosevelt and the Democrats, who recognized that in a modern industrial state it was not enough to rally round business and hope that capitalism would right itself.

Over 30 years of nearly unbroken Republican rule had come to an end. For decades, the "Roosevelt coalition" would dominate national politics by voting its support for the Democratic party's newly active and interventionist welfare state.

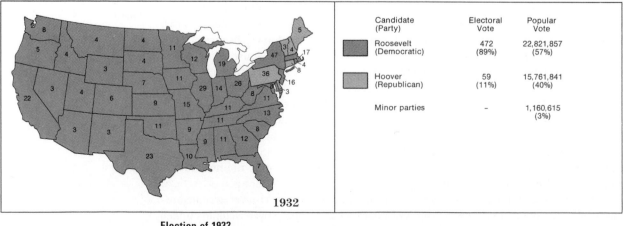

Candidate (Party)	Electoral Vote	Popular Vote
Roosevelt (Democratic)	472 (89%)	22,821,857 (57%)
Hoover (Republican)	59 (11%)	15,761,841 (40%)
Minor parties	–	1,160,615 (3%)

1932

Election of 1932

On March 4, 1933, as the clocks struck noon, Eleanor Roosevelt wondered if it were possible to "do anything to save

The Early New Deal (1933–1935)

America now." One-fourth of the workforce was unemployed. Thirty million families had no means of support. There wasn't enough money in the Treasury to meet the federal payroll.

Eleanor looked at her husband, who had just been sworn in as thirty-second president of the United States. Franklin faced the crowd of over 100,000 as millions more huddled around their radios: "Let me assert my firm belief that the only thing we have to fear is fear itself—nameless, unreasoning, unjustified terror." Heeding the nation's call for "action, and action now," he promised to exercise "broad Executive power to wage a war against the emergency." The crowd cheered. Eleanor was terrified: "One has the feeling of going it blindly because we're in a tremendous stream, and none of us know where we're going to land."

Roosevelt had no master plan. Instead, the early New Deal unfolded in the spring of 1933 with a chaotic, three-month burst of legislation known as the hundred days. It stressed recovery through planning and cooperation with business. But it also furnished relief for the unemployed and began a reform of the economic system. Above all, the early New Deal revived national confidence. With Roosevelt in the White House, most Americans believed that they were in good hands, wherever they landed.

Recovery, relief, reform

The Democratic Roosevelts

From the moment they entered it in 1933, Franklin and Eleanor—the Democratic Roosevelts—transformed the White House. No more footmen bowing and buglers playing, as they had when Hoover arrived in the dining room to partake of his customary seven-course meal. Instead visitors got fare fit for a boardinghouse. Roosevelt's lunches of hash and a poached egg cost 19 cents. With millions of Americans tightening their belts, the president joined them with a symbolic gesture that made his point of ending business as usual.

Such belt-tightening was new to Franklin Roosevelt. Born in 1882 of a old Dutch New York family, he grew up rich and pampered. He idolized his Republican cousin Theodore Roosevelt and mimicked his career, except as a Democrat. Like Theodore, Franklin was graduated from Harvard University (in 1904), won a seat in the New York State legislature (in 1910), secured an appointment as assistant secretary of the navy (in 1913), and ran for the vice presidency (in 1920). Then disaster struck. On vacation in the summer of 1921, Roosevelt fell ill with poliomyelitis. The disease paralyzed him from the waist down. For the rest of his life, he walked only with the aid of crutches and heavy steel braces.

Franklin Roosevelt

Roosevelt emerged from the ordeal with greater patience, deeper conviction, and more empathy for the unfortunates of the world. He won the governorship of New York in 1928. When the Depression struck, he created the first state relief agency in 1931, the Temporary Emergency Relief Administration. Aid to the jobless "must be extended by Government, not as a matter of charity, but as a matter of social duty," he explained. He considered himself a progressive, but moved well beyond the cautious use of federal power advocated by most progressives. A conventional budget balancer, he could abandon convention and be bold with sometimes costly social programs. He cared little about economic principles. What he wanted were results. "Take a method and try it," he instructed his staff. "If it fails, try another. But above all try something." Experimentation became a hallmark of the New Deal.

Most photographers acceded to White House wishes that President Roosevelt never be shot from the waist down. After contracting polio, Roosevelt helped transform the ramshackle resort at Warm Springs, Georgia (where this picture was taken), into a treatment center for victims of the disease.

The Brains Trust

Emergency Banking Act

Having followed a political path to the presidency, Roosevelt understood the value of public relations. As president, he held an unequaled number of press conferences (998) and hired the first press secretary. His famous "fireside chats" on radio brought him into American homes. When Roosevelt's reassuring voice came over the airwaves ("My friends, I want to tell you what has been done in the last few days, why it was done, and what the next steps are going to be"), people felt as if he had each of them in mind.

Eleanor Roosevelt redefined what it meant to be First Lady. Never had a president's wife been so visible, so much of a crusader, so cool under fire. She was the first First Lady to hold weekly press conferences. Her column, "My Day," appeared in 135 newspapers, and her twice-weekly broadcasts made her a radio personality rivaling her husband. She became his eyes, ears, and legs, traveling 40,000 miles a year. Secret Service men code-named her "Rover."

Eleanor believed that she was only a spur to her husband. But she was an activist in her own right, as a teacher and social reformer before Franklin became president and afterward as a tireless advocate of the underdog. In the White House, she pressed him to hire more women and minorities. She supported antilynching and anti-poll tax measures when he would not and experimental towns for the homeless. By 1939 more Americans approved of her than of her husband.

Before the election Roosevelt had gathered a group of lawyers and university professors called the "Brains Trust" to advise him on economic policy. Out of their recommendations came the early, or "first," New Deal of government planning, intervention, and experimentation. Brain trusters disagreed over the means of achieving their goals but shared the broad aims of economic recovery, relief for the unemployed, and sweeping reform to soften the impact of the industrial order and to guard against the return of depression. All concurred that the first step was to save the banks. By the eve of the inauguration governors in 38 states had temporarily closed their banks to stem the withdrawal of deposits by nervous depositors. Without a sound credit structure, there could be no borrowing; without borrowing, no investment; without investment, no recovery.

Saving the Banks

On March 5, the day after his inauguration, Roosevelt ordered every bank in the country closed for four days (later extended to eight). He called it a "bank holiday." Instead of panicking, Americans acted as if it were a holiday, using homemade currencies called "scrip" and bartering their services. On March 9, the president introduced emergency banking legislation. The House passed the measure, sight unseen, and the Senate endorsed it later in the day. Roosevelt signed it that night.

Rather than nationalizing the banks as radicals wanted, the Emergency Banking Act followed the modest course of extending federal assistance to them. Sound banks would reopen immediately with government support. Troubled banks would be handed over to federal "conservators," who would guide them to solvency. On Sunday, March 12, Roosevelt explained what was happening in the first of his fireside chats. When banks reopened the next day, deposits exceeded withdrawals, even though legislation to insure those deposits had yet to be enacted.

To restore confidence in government, Roosevelt pushed through the Economy Act in March 1933, slashing $400 million in veterans' payments and $100 million in salaries from the federal budget. To guard against future stock crashes, financial reforms gave government greater authority to manage the currency and regulate stock transactions. In April 1933, Roosevelt dropped the gold standard and began experimenting with the value of the dollar to boost prices. Later that spring the Glass-Steagall Banking Act restricted speculation by banks and, more important, created federal insurance for bank deposits of up to $2500. Under the Federal Deposit Insurance Corporation, fewer banks failed for the rest of the decade than in the best year of the 1920s. The Securities Exchange Act (1934) established a new federal agency, the Securities and Exchange Commission, to oversee the stock market.

Federal Deposit Insurance

Relief for the Unemployed

Saving the banks and financial markets meant little if human suffering could not be relieved. Mortgage relief for the millions who had lost their homes came eventually in 1934 in the Home Owners' Loan Act. But to meet the urgent need to alleviate starvation, Congress created the Federal Emergency Relief Administration (FERA) in May 1933. Sitting amid unpacked boxes, gulping coffee and chain-smoking, former

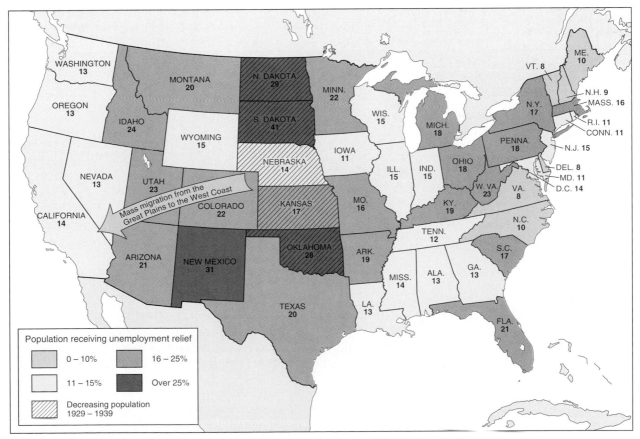

Unemployment Relief, 1934 The percentage of people receiving unemployment relief differed markedly throughout the nation. The farm belt of the plains was hit especially hard, with 41 percent of South Dakota's citizens receiving federal benefits. In the East, the percentage dropped as low as 8 percent in some states.

social worker Harry Hopkins spent $5 million of a $500 million appropriation in his first two hours on the job. In its two-year existence, FERA furnished more than $1 billion in grants to states, local areas, and private charities.

Work relief

As the winter of 1933–1934 approached, Hopkins persuaded the president to expand relief with an innovative shift from government giveaways to a work program. Paying someone "to do something socially useful preserves a man's morale," Hopkins argued. The Civil Works Administration (CWA) employed 4 million Americans on projects such as repairing schools, laying sewer pipes, and building roads. Alarmed at the high cost of the program, Roosevelt disbanded the CWA in the spring of 1934. It nonetheless furnished a new weapon against unemployment and an important precedent for future relief programs.

Another work relief program established during Roosevelt's first hundred days proved even more creative. The Civilian Conservation Corps (CCC) was Roosevelt's pet project. It combined his concern for conservation with compassion for youth. The CCC took unmarried, 18- to 25-year-olds from relief rolls and sent them into the woods and fields to plant trees, build parks, and fight soil erosion. During its 10 years, the CCC provided 2.5 million young men with jobs (which prompted critics who felt women were being neglected to chant, "Where's the she, she, she?").

Tennessee Valley Authority

New Dealers intended relief programs to last only through the crisis. But the Tennessee Valley Authority (TVA)—a massive public works project created in 1933—made a continuing contribution to regional planning. For a decade, planners had dreamed of transforming the flood-ridden basin of the Tennessee River,

The Tennessee Valley Authority The Tennessee River basin encompassed parts of seven states. Rivers honeycombed the area, which received some of the heaviest rainfall in the nation. A long-time dream of Senator George Norris, the Tennessee Valley Authority, created in 1933, constructed some 20 dams and improved 5 others over the next 20 years to control chronic flooding and erosion and to produce cheap hydroelectric power and fertilizers.

one of the poorest areas of the country, with a program of regional development and social engineering. The TVA constructed a series of dams along the seven-state basin to control flooding, improve navigation, and generate cheap electric power. In cooperation with state and local officials, it also launched social programs to stamp out malaria, provide library bookmobiles, and create recreational lakes.

Like many New Deal programs, the TVA left a mixed legacy. It saved three million acres from erosion, multiplied the average income in the valley tenfold, and repaid its original investment in federal taxes. Its cheap electricity helped bring down the rates of private utility companies and increase usage. But the experiment in regional planning also pushed thousands of families from their land, failed to end poverty, and created an agency that became one of the worst polluters in the country.

Planning for Industrial Recovery

Planning, not just for regions but for the whole economy, seemed to many New Dealers the key to recovery. Some held that if businesses were allowed to plan and cooperate, the ruthless competition that was driving down the economy might be controlled and the riddle of industrial recovery solved. Business leaders had been urging such a course since 1931. In June 1933, under the National Industrial Recovery Act (NIRA), Roosevelt put planning to work for industry.

The legislation created two new agencies. The Public Works Administration (PWA) was designed to boost consumer purchasing power and industrial activity with a $3.3 billion public works program. The workers it hired would spend their paychecks and stimulate production, while its orders for factory and other goods would send waves of capital rippling through the economy. Harold Ickes, the prickly interior secretary who headed PWA, built the Triborough Bridge and Lincoln Tunnel in New York, the port city of Brownsville, Texas, and two aircraft carriers. But he was so fearful of waste and corruption that he never spent funds quickly enough to jump-start the economy.

Public Works Administration

A second federal agency, the National Recovery Administration (NRA), aimed directly at controlling competition. Under NRA chief Hugh Johnson, representatives from government and business (and also from labor and consumer groups) drew up "codes of fair practices." Industry by industry, the codes established minimum prices and wages and maximum hours. No company could seek a competitive edge by cutting prices or wages below certain levels or by working a few employees mercilessly and firing the rest. It also required business to accept key demands of labor, including union rights to organize and bargain with management (thus ensuring that if prices jumped, so too might wages). And each code promised improvements in working conditions and outlawed such practices as child labor and sweatshops.

National Recovery Administration

No business was forced to comply, for fear that government coercion might be ruled unconstitutional. The NRA relied instead on voluntary participation. A publicity campaign of parades, posters, and massive public pledges exhorted businesses to join the NRA and consumers to buy only NRA-sanctioned products. More than two million employers eventually signed up. In store windows and on merchandise, shiny decals with blue-eagle crests alerted customers that "We Do Our Part."

For all the hoopla, the NRA failed to bring recovery. Big businesses shaped the codes to their advantage. Often they limited production and raised prices, sometimes beyond what they normally might have been. Not all businesses joined, and those that did often found the codes too complicated or costly to follow. The relatively few NRA inspectors had trouble keeping up with all the complaints. Even NRA support for labor faltered, because the agency had no way to enforce the rules granting unions the right to bargain. Business survived under the NRA, but by and large it did not grow. And without increased production and sales, there was no incentive for expansion, employment, and investment. Under such conditions hard times could last indefinitely. Despite an enthusiastic start, the NRA spawned little but evasion from businesses and criticism from consumers about "NRA prices and Hoover wages."

Schecter decision

On May 27, 1935, the Supreme Court struck down the floundering NRA in *Schecter Poultry Corp. v. United States.* The justices unanimously ruled that when the NRA regulated the Schecter brothers poultry business within the state of New York, it exceeded the power granted the federal government to regulate commerce among the states. Privately Roosevelt was relieved to be rid of the NRA. But he and other New Dealers were plainly shaken by the Court's reasoning. They were relying on federal power to regulate commerce as a means of fighting the Depression. Their distress only grew when Justice Benjamin Cardozo added a chilling afterthought: the NRA's code-making represented "an unconstitutional delegation of legislative power" to the executive branch. Without the ability to make rules and regulations, *all* the executive agencies of the New Deal might flounder.

Planning for Agriculture

Agricultural Adjustment Administration

Like planning for industry, New Deal planning for agriculture relied on private interests—the farmers—to act as the principal planners. Under the Agricultural Adjustment Act of 1933, producers of basic commodities agreed to limit their own production. The government, in turn, paid farmers for not producing, while a tax on millers, cotton ginners, and other processors financed the payments. In theory, production quotas would reduce surpluses, and demand for farm commodities would rise, as would prices. Agriculture would recover.

THE TATTOOED MAN

Despite the popularity of Roosevelt and the New Deal, there were critics. New federal agencies, designated by their initials, became easy targets of satirists and cartoonists. In this 1934 cartoon, a wincing Uncle Sam receives an unwelcomed set of tattoos, each signifying a New Deal agency.

In practice the Agricultural Adjustment Administration (AAA) did help increase prices. Unlike the code-ridden NRA, the AAA wisely confined coverage to seven major commodities. As a way to push prices even higher, the new Commodity Credit Corporation gave loans to farmers who stored their crops rather than sell them—a revival of the Populists' old subtreasury plan (see page 679). Farm income rose from $5.5 billion in 1932 to $8.7 billion in 1935.

Not all the gains in farm income were due to government actions or were free of problems. The dust storms, droughts, and floods of the mid-1930s helped reduce harvests and push up prices. The AAA, moreover, failed to distribute its benefits equally. Large landowners were in a position to decide which of the fields would be left fallow. In the South this decision frequently meant that big farmers would cut the acreage of tenants and sharecroppers or force them out. Even when big farmers reduced the acreage that they themselves plowed, they could increase yields, because they had the money and equipment to cultivate more intensively.

In 1936 the Supreme Court voided the AAA. In *Butler v. U.S.,* the six-justice majority concluded that the government had no right to regulate agriculture, either by limiting production or taxing processors. Congress hastily passed a replacement bill, the Soil Conservation and Domestic Allotment Act (1936), which addressed the Court's complaints. Farmers were now subsidized for practicing "conservation"—taking soil-depleting crops off the land—and paid from general revenues instead of a special tax. A second Agricultural Adjustment Act in 1938 returned production quotas.

Other agencies tried to help impoverished farmers. The Farm Credit Administration refinanced about a fifth of all farm mortgages. In 1935 the Resettlement Administration gave marginal farmers a fresh start by moving them to better land. Beginning in 1937 the Farm Security Administration furnished low-interest loans to help tenants buy family farms. In neither case did the rural poor have enough political leverage to obtain sufficient funds from Congress. Fewer than 5000 families (of a projected 500,000) were resettled, and less than 2 percent of tenant farmers received loans.

After years of Hoover paralysis, Roosevelt's first hundred days finally broke national despair. The economic depression proved more resistant. Though Roosevelt regarded recovery as his primary goal, the New Deal never achieved it. Conditions improved, but the economy only limped along. Perhaps no one could have solved the riddle of recovery, but Roosevelt tried, and in 1935 he began boldly to address a second riddle: how to reform the system so that the Great Depression did not return.

"Boys—this is our hour," concluded Harry Hopkins in the spring of 1935. A year earlier voters had broken precedent

A Second New Deal (1935–1936)

by returning the party in power to office, giving the Democrats their largest majorities in decades. With the presidential election of 1936 only a year away, Hopkins figured that time was short: "We've got to get everything we want—a works program, social security, wages and hours, everything—now or never."

Hopkins calculated correctly. Swept along by a torrent of protest, Roosevelt and the Congress produced a "second hundred days" of lawmaking and a "Second New Deal." The emphasis shifted from planning and cooperation with business to greater regulation of business, broader relief, and bolder reform. A limited welfare state emerged, in which government was finally committed—at least symbolically—to guaranteeing the well-being of needy Americans.

Voices of Protest

By 1934 the Great Depression was nearly five years old. Conditions were improving but not quickly enough for some Americans. In Minneapolis, a mob of 6000 stormed city hall with demands for more relief and higher-paying jobs. Longshoremen shut down the docks in San Francisco, setting off a citywide strike. Before the end of the year, 1.5 million workers had joined in 1800 strikes. Voices of protest were demanding ways to jump-start a recovery more quickly.

From the right came the charges of some wealthy business executives and conservatives that Roosevelt was an enemy of private property and a dictator in the making. In August 1934 they founded the American Liberty League. Despite spending $1 million in anti–New Deal advertising, the league won little support and only helped to convince the president that cooperation with business was not the way to achieve recovery.

Liberty League

In California discontented voters took over the Democratic party and nominated novelist Upton Sinclair, a Socialist, for governor. Running under the slogan "End Poverty in California," Sinclair proposed to confiscate idle factories and land and permit the unemployed to produce for their own use. Republicans mounted a no-holds-barred counterattack, including fake newsreels depicting Sinclair as a Bolshevik, atheist, and advocate of free love. Sinclair lost the election but won nearly one million votes.

"End Poverty in California"

Huey Long

Huey P. Long, the flamboyant senator from Louisiana, had ridden to power on a wave of rural discontent against banks, corporations, and machine politics as usual.

As governor of Louisiana, he pushed through reforms regulating utilities, building roads and schools, even distributing free schoolbooks. By turns comical and ruthless, Long used his power to feather his own financial nest, and his private police force was not above kidnapping political opponents. Detractors called him "dictator"; most Louisianans affectionately called him the "Kingfish" after a conniving character in the popular *Amos 'n' Andy* radio show.

Breaking with Roosevelt in 1933, Long pledged to bring about recovery by making "every man a king." His "Share Our Wealth" proposal was a drastic but simple plan: the government would limit the size of all fortunes and confiscate the rest. Every family would then be guaranteed an annual income of $2500 and an estate of $5000, enough to buy a house, an automobile, and a radio. (Long had already built a national following over the airwaves.)

Louisiana Governor and U.S. Senator Huey Long promised to make "every man a king," but critics predicted that only Long would wear the crown. Power-hungry and charismatic, the Kingfish made no secret of his presidential aspirations.

Despite his wild underestimates of the cost of subsidies for the have-nots, Long was addressing a real problem, the uneven distribution of wealth. By 1935, one year after his Share Our Wealth organization was begun, it boasted 27,000 clubs. Democratic National Committee members shuddered at polls showing that Long might capture up to 4 million votes in 1936, enough to put a Republican in the White House. But late in 1935, in the corridors of the Louisiana capitol, Long was shot to death by a disgruntled constituent whose family had been wronged by the Long political machine.

Charles Coughlin

Father Charles Coughlin was Long's urban counterpart. Whereas Long explained the Depression as the result of bloated fortunes, Coughlin blamed the banks. In weekly broadcasts from the Shrine of the Little Flower in suburban Detroit, the Radio Priest told his working-class, largely Catholic audience that international bankers (many of them Jewish, Coughlin also charged) had toppled the world economy by manipulating gold-backed currencies.

Across the urban North, 30 to 40 million Americans—the largest audience in the world—sat by their radios to listen. Like Long, Coughlin promised to cure the Depression with a few simple strokes: in his case, nationalizing banks, inflating the currency with silver, spreading work. When Roosevelt refused to adopt Coughlin's schemes, the priest broke with the president. In 1934 Coughlin organized the National Union for Social Justice to pressure both parties. As the election of 1936 approached, the Union loomed ominously as a third-party threat.

Francis Townsend

A less ominous challenge came from Dr. Francis Townsend, a recently retired California physician. Moved by the plight of elderly Americans without pension plans or medical insurance, Townsend set up Old Age Revolving Pensions, Limited, in 1934. He proposed to have the government pay $200 a month to Americans aged 60 years or older who quit their jobs and spent the money within 30 days. For funding, the government would levy a 2 percent tax on commercial transactions. Thus Townsendites expected to spend more than half the national income to compensate less than one-tenth of the population. By 1936 Townsend clubs counted 3.5 million members, most of them small businesspeople and farmers at or beyond retirement age.

For all their differences, Sinclair, Long, Coughlin, and Townsend struck similar chords. Each proposed simplistic solutions for serious problems: a maldistribution of goods and wealth, inadequacies in the money supply, the plight of the elderly. Each attacked the growing control of corporations, banks, and government over individuals and communities. And each created mass political movements based on social as well as economic dissatisfaction. When Sinclair supporters pledged to produce for their own use and Long's followers swore to "share our wealth," when Coughlinites damned the "monied interests" and Townsendites thumped their Bibles at foul-ups in Washington, they were all also trying to protect their freedom and their communities from what they saw as the ills and intrusions of big business and big government.

The Second Hundred Days

By the spring of 1935, the forces of discontent were pushing Roosevelt to bolder action. So was Congress. With Democrats accounting for more than two-thirds of both houses, they were prepared to outspend even the president. The 100 days from April through mid-July, the "second hundred days," produced a legislative barrage that moved the New Deal toward Roosevelt's ultimate destination—"a little to the left of center," where government would permanently seek to soften the impact of industrial excesses, protect the needy, and compensate for swings in the economy.

To help the many Americans who were still jobless, Roosevelt proposed the Emergency Relief Appropriation Act of 1935, with a record of $4.8 billion for relief and employment. Some of the money went to the new National Youth Administration for more than 4.5 million jobs for young people. But the lion's share went to the new Works Progress Administration (WPA), where Harry Hopkins mounted the largest work-relief program in history. Because his agency was not permitted to compete with private industry and stressed spending its money on wages, Hopkins showed remarkable ingenuity. WPA workers taught art classes in a Cincinnati mental hospital, drafted a Braille map for the blind in Massachusetts, and pulled a library by packhorse through the hills of Kentucky. Before its end in 1943, the WPA employed at least 8.5 million people and built or improved over 100,000 schools, post offices, and other public buildings.

Works Progress Administration

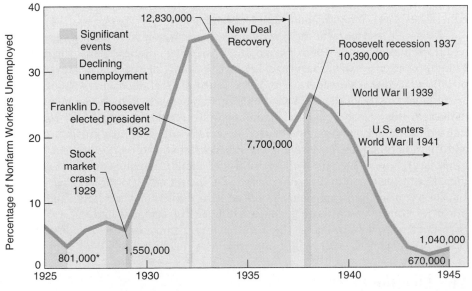

*Unemployed totals for entire labor force.

Unemployment, 1925–1945 Unemployment mushroomed in the wake of the stock market crash of 1929. It did not drop to 1929 levels until American entry into the Second World War in 1941. The colored bands indicate periods of declining unemployment.

Social Security

The ambitious Social Security Act, passed in 1935, sought to help those people who could not help themselves—the aged poor, the infirm, dependent children. But Social Security went further, extending the umbrella of protection in the form of pensions for retirees and insurance for those suddenly laid off from their jobs. Equally important, the financial assistance Social Security provided would also act as an economic stabilizer to sustain consumer purchasing power in good times and bad. A payroll tax on both employers and employees underwrote pensions given to retirees over age 65, while an employer-financed system of insurance made possible government payments to unemployed workers. To win the votes of southerners worried about race relations, the legislation excluded farm workers and domestic servants, doubtless among the neediest Americans but often black, brown, and disproportionately Southern.

Social Security marked a historic reversal in American political values. A new social contract between the government and the people replaced the gospel of self-help and the older policies of laissez faire. Government acknowledged a broad responsibility to protect the social rights of citizens. This commitment had been foreshadowed in the aid given veterans and their families after the Civil War and the temporary relief agencies of the early New Deal. But that legislation had been strictly limited. Social Security was meant to be a permanent institution, not a temporary fix for a one-time problem. In short, the Social Security Act institutionalized the welfare state.

National Labor Relations Act

Congress had whittled down Roosevelt's plan for Social Security, but its labor legislation pushed well beyond the president's paternalistic goals. Roosevelt would have been happy providing moderate aid for workers in the form of pension plans, unemployment insurance, and later, federal minimum wage standards. But New York Senator Robert Wagner, the son of a janitor, wanted to give workers the power to fight their own battles. In 1933 Wagner had included union recognition in the NRA. When the Supreme Court killed the agency in 1935, Wagner introduced what became the National Labor Relations Act. (So important had labor support become to Roosevelt that he gave the bill his belated blessing.) The "Wagner Act" created a National Labor Relations Board (NLRB) to supervise the election of unions and ensure union rights to bargain. Most vital, the NLRB had the power to enforce these policies. By 1941, union membership had doubled.

Roosevelt responded to the growing hostility of business by turning against the wealthy and powerful in 1935. The popularity of Long's tirades against the rich and Coughlin's against banks sharpened Roosevelt's points of attack. The Revenue Act of 1935 (called the "Wealth Tax Act") threatened to "soak the rich," although Congress's final version of the law levied only moderate taxes on high incomes and inheritances. To control the powerful banking industry, the Banking Act of 1935 centralized the money market in the Federal Reserve Board. By controlling interest rates and the money supply, government increased its ability to compensate for swings in the economy. Finally, the Public Utilities Holding Company Act (1935) limited the size of widely unpopular utility empires. Long the target of progressive reformers, the giant holding companies produced high profits for speculators and higher prices for consumers. Although Congress diluted the act, as it had the wealth tax, New Dealers could still claim a political victory. "I am now on your bandwagon again," a Philadelphia voter told the president as the election of 1936 approached.

The Election of 1936

In June 1936 Roosevelt traveled to Philadelphia, not to thank the loyal voter who had hopped aboard his bandwagon but to accept the Democratic nomination for a second term as president. "This generation of Americans has a rendezvous with destiny," he told a crowd of 100,000 packed into Franklin Field. Whatever destiny had in store for his generation, Roosevelt knew that the coming election would turn on a single issue: "It's myself, and people must be either for me or against me."

Roosevelt ignored his Republican opponent, Governor Alfred Landon of Kansas. Despite a bulging war chest of $14 million, Landon lacked luster as well as issues, because he favored the regulation of business and much of the New Deal. For his part Roosevelt turned the election into a contest between haves and have-nots. The forces of "organized money are unanimous in their hate for me," he told a roaring crowd at New York's Madison Square Garden, "and I welcome their hatred." The election returns shocked even experienced observers. Roosevelt won the largest electoral victory ever—523 to 8—and a whopping 60.8 percent of the popular vote. The margin of victory came from those at the bottom of the economic ladder, grateful for help furnished by the New Deal.

A dramatic political realignment was now clearly in place, one as important as the Republican rise to power in 1896. No longer did the Democratic Party depend for its strength primarily on the regional support of the "Solid South." Class replaced region as the dominant element in American politics. For the next 30 years, the Democrats would reign as the new majority party. The "Roosevelt coalition" rested on three pillars: traditional Democratic support in the South; citizens in the industrial cities, particularly ethnics and African Americans; and labor, both organized and unorganized. The minority Republicans became the party of big business and small towns.

Roosevelt coalition

Before 1939, farmers in the Hill Country of Texas spent their evenings in the light of 25-watt kerosene lamps. Their wives

The American People under the New Deal

washed eight loads of laundry a week, all by hand. Every day they hauled home 200 gallons of water—about 1500 pounds—from nearby wells. Farms had no milking machines, no washers, no automatic pumps or water heaters, no refrigerators, and no radios. "Living—just living—was a problem," recalled one woman.

The reason for this limited life was simple: the Hill Country had no electricity. Thus, no agency of the Roosevelt administration changed the way people lived more dramatically than did the Rural Electrification Administration (REA), created in 1935. At the time, less than 10 percent of American farms had electricity. Six years later, 40 percent did, and by 1950, 90 percent did. The New Deal did not always make such a dramatic impact, and its overall record was mixed. But time and again it changed the lives of ordinary people as government never had before.

Rural Electrification Administration

The New Deal and Western Water

In September 1936, President Roosevelt pushed a button in Washington, D.C., and sent electricity pulsing westward from the towering Boulder Dam on the Colorado River to cities as far away as Los Angeles. Its generators and turbines were the largest ever installed and could produce four times the electricity of Niagara Falls. The diverted waters irrigated 2.5 million acres, while the dam's floodgates protected millions in southern California, Nevada, and Arizona from the ravages of the Colorado River, the wildest in the West. In its water management programs, the New Deal further extended federal power, literally across the country.

The Boulder Dam (begun under the Hoover administration) was one of several multipurpose dams completed under the New Deal in the arid West. The aim was simple: to control whole river systems for regional use. The task, of course, was more complicated, involving strings of dams, channels, and other projects costing billions. The Buchanan Dam on the lower Colorado River, the Bonneville and Grand Coulee dams on the Columbia, and many smaller versions curbed floods, generated cheap electric power, and developed river basins from Texas to Washington state. Beginning in 1938, the All-American Canal diverted the Colorado River to the Imperial Valley in California, 80 miles away, with a 130-mile extension to the Coachella Valley. The giant Central Valley Project funneled water south from the Sacramento Valley in northern California along the 500-mile watershed of the Central Valley to the arid San Joaquin Valley in the south.

Such projects made the Bureau of Reclamation a powerful force in Washington and the West. It oversaw most water development and so provided not only employment for tens of thousands of westerners but also some of the cheapest electricity in the United States. Inexpensive power also helped to attract industry and to free regions, particularly the Pacific Northwest, from their dependence on extractive industries such as logging and mining. It was no wonder, then, that Franklin Roosevelt carried the West in every one of his four presidential elections.

The environmental price for such rewards soon became evident, as it did with the New Deal's experiment in eastern water use, the Tennessee Valley Authority. The once-mighty Columbia River, its surging waters checked by dams, flowed tamely from human-made lake to human-made lake, but without the salmon whose spawning runs were also checked. Blocked by the All-American Canal of its path to the sea, the Colorado River slowly turned salty. By 1950 its water was unfit for drinking or irrigation.

The Limited Reach of the New Deal

In the spring of 1939, the Daughters of the American Revolution (DAR) refused to permit the black contralto Marian Anderson to sing at Constitution Hall. Eleanor Roosevelt quit the DAR in protest, and Secretary of the Interior Harold Ickes began looking for another site. On a nippy Easter Sunday, in the shadow of the Lincoln Memorial, Anderson finally stepped to the microphone and sang to a crowd of 7500. Lincoln himself would not have missed the irony.

African Americans

In 1932 most African Americans cast their ballots as they had since Reconstruction—for Republicans, the party of Abraham Lincoln and emancipation. But disenchantment with decades of broken Republican promises was spreading, and by 1934 African Americans were voting for Democrats. "Let Jesus lead you and Roosevelt feed you," a black preacher told his congregation on the eve of the 1936 election. When the returns were counted, three of four black voters had cast their ballots for Roosevelt.

The New Deal accounted for this voting revolution. Sympathetic but never a champion, Roosevelt regarded African Americans as one of many groups whose interests he brokered. Even that attitude was an improvement. Federal offices had been segregated since Woodrow Wilson's day, and in the 1920s black leaders called Hoover "the man in the lily-White House." Under Roosevelt, racial integration slowly returned to government, and its doors opened a bit wider to African Americans. Supporters of civil rights, such as Eleanor Roosevelt and Secretary of the Interior Ickes, brought political scientist Clark Foreman, economist Robert C. Weaver, and other black advisers into the administration. Mary McLeod Bethune, a sharecropper's

California's multiethnic workforce

daughter and founder of Bethune-Cookman College, ran a division of the National Youth Administration. Important as both symbols and activists, African American administrators created a "Black Cabinet" to help design federal policy.

Outside of government the Urban League continued to lobby for economic advancement, and the National Association for the Advancement of Colored People pressed to make lynching a federal crime. (Though publicly against lynching and privately in favor of an antilynching bill, Roosevelt refused to make it "must" legislation for fear of losing the powerful white southern members of Congress whom he needed "to save America.") In New York's Harlem, the Reverend John H. Johnson organized the Citizens' League for Fair Play in 1933 to persuade white merchants to hire black clerks. After picketers blocked storefronts, hundreds of African Americans got jobs with Harlem retailers and utility companies. Racial tension over employment and housing continued to run high, and in 1935 Harlem exploded in the only race riot of the decade.

Racial discrimination persisted under the New Deal. Black newspapers reported hundreds of cases in which businesses, under the guise of following NRA codes, replaced black workers with white ones or paid black workers lower wages than those paid to whites. Disgusted editors renamed the agency "Negroes Ruined Again." Federal efforts to promote grassroots democracy often gave control of New Deal programs to local governments, where discrimination went unchallenged. New Deal showplaces like the TVA's model town of Norris, Tennessee, and the subsistence homestead village of Arthurdale, West Virginia, were closed to African Americans.

African Americans reaped a few benefits from the New Deal, but usually only when the programs were administered by federal officials who did not share local prejudices. The WPA hired black workers for almost 20 percent of its jobs, even though African Americans made up less than 10 percent of the population. When it was discovered that the WPA was paying black workers less than whites, Roosevelt issued an executive order to halt the practice. Public Works Administrator Ickes established the first quota system for hiring black Americans. By 1941 the number of African Americans working for the government exceeded their percentage of the population.

Mexican Americans

Civil rights never became a goal of the New Deal, but for the nearly one million Mexican Americans in the United States, Latino culture sometimes frustrated meager federal efforts to help. Mexican folk traditions of self-help inhibited some from seeking aid; others remained unfamiliar with claim procedures. Still others failed to meet residency requirements, and some feared that applying for aid might lead to deportation, even when they were legal residents. Low voter turnout hampered the political influence of Latinos, and discrimination limited economic advancement. More important, from the Rio Grande Valley in Texas to the Imperial Valley in California, the majority of Mexicans and Mexican Americans served as farm workers, picking and planting for others. As such, they lay beyond most New Deal programs.

On Capitol Hill, Dennis Chavez of New Mexico, the only Mexican American in the Senate, channeled what funds he could into Spanish-speaking communities of the Southwest, but the results of his and other federal efforts were often mixed. The CCC and the WPA furnished some jobs for Mexican Americans in the Southwest and California, though fewer of them and for less pay than Anglos received. In southern Colorado, New Deal relief measures alleviated unemployment among Latinos, but the policy of emptying relief rolls just before the beet harvest to avoid competing with the wages offered by local growers only drove wages down. Crafts programs meant to generate income and preserve village life ended up preserving a marginalized, underpaid workforce as well. Federal training programs for midwives helped to bring down high rates of infant mortality but also raised the cost to patients and threatened village control of custom and culture. Like African Americans, most Mexican Americans remained mired in poverty.

Tribal Rights

The New Deal renewed federal interest in the 320,000 Indians living on reservations in Oklahoma, New Mexico, and other western states. Among the most disadvantaged Americans, Indian families rarely earned more than $100 a year. Their infant mortality was the highest in the country; their life expectancy was the shortest;

In 1937 Artist Amy Jones painted life on an Iroquois Indian reservation in the Adirondack mountains. Indian rates for tuberculosis were high, and a doctor and nurse examine an Indian child for the disease (left side of the painting). On the right, Iroquois women and children weave baskets form wooden splints while Indian workers split logs to be made into splints for baskets. These themes of public health, manual labor, and Indian crafts formed powerful points of emphasis in the New Deal.

their education level—usually no more than five years—was the lowest. Their rate of unemployment was three times the national average.

Part of the reason for new attention from Washington was John Collier. In the 1930s, Indians had no stronger friend. For years he had fought to restore tribal lands and culture, first as a social worker among the Pueblos and later as executive secretary of the American Indian Defense Association. Appointed as the new commissioner of the Bureau of Indian Affairs in 1933, Collier hired over 4000 Indians. By the end of the decade they made up a fourth of all BIA employees. He cleaned out corruption and incompetence from the bureau, placed 77,000 young Indians in the CCC, and built Indian day schools with funds from the Public Works Administration.

The centerpiece of Collier's new program was the Indian Reorganization Act of 1934. It reversed the decades-old policy of assimilation and promoted tribal life. The 200 tribes on reservations, explained Collier, would be "surrounded by the protective guardianship of the federal government and clothed with the authority of the federal government." A special Court of Indian Affairs removed Indians from state jurisdiction. Tribal governments ruled reservations. Elders were urged to celebrate festivals, artists to work in native styles, children to learn the old languages. Perhaps most important, tribes regained control over Indian land. Since the Dawes Act of 1887, land had been allotted to individual Indians, who were often forced by poverty to sell to whites. By the end of the 1930s, Indian landholding had increased.

John Collier's Indian Reorganization Act

Indians split over Collier's policies. The Pueblos, with a strong communal spirit and already functioning communal societies, favored them. The tribes of Oklahoma and the Great Plains tended to oppose them. Individualism, the profit motive, and an unwillingness to share property with other tribe members fed their resistance. So did age-old suspicion of all government programs. And some Indians genuinely desired assimilation. The Navajos, under the leadership of J. C. Morgan, rejected the Indian Reorganization Act in 1935. Morgan saw tribal government as a step backward.

A New Deal for Women

As the tides of change rippled across the country, a new deal for women was unfolding in Washington. The New Deal's welfare agencies offered unprecedented opportunity for social workers, teachers, and other women who had spent their lives helping the downtrodden. They were already experts on social welfare. Several were also friends with professional ties, and together they formed a network of activists in the New Deal promoting women's interests and social reform. Led by Eleanor Roosevelt and Labor secretary Frances Perkins, women served on the consumers' advisory board of the NRA, helped to administer the relief program, and won appointments to the Social Security Board.

In growing numbers women became part of the Democratic party machinery. At the 1936 Democratic National Convention 219 women served as delegates while more than 300 stood by as alternates. Social worker Mary W. "Molly" Dewson led the new Women's Division of the Democratic National Committee. It played a critical role in the election. Thousands of women mounted a "mouth-to-mouth" campaign, literally traveling from door to door to drum up support for Roosevelt and other Democrats. When the ballots were finally tallied, women formed an important part of the new Roosevelt coalition.

Federal appointments and party politics broke new ground for women, but in general the New Deal abided by existing social standards. Gender equality, like racial equality, was never high on its agenda. One quarter of all NRA codes permitted women to be paid less than men, and WPA wages averaged $2 a day more for men. The New Deal gave relatively few jobs to women and when it did, the jobs were often in gender-segregated trades such as sewing. The percentage of women hired by the government fell below even that of the private sector.

Reflecting old conceptions of reform, New Dealers placed greater emphasis on aiding and protecting women than on employing them. The FERA built 17 camps for homeless women in 11 states. Social Security furnished subsidies to mothers with dependent children, and the WPA established emergency nursery schools (which became the government's first foray into early childhood education). But evenhanded protection for women was lacking. Social Security, for example, did not cover domestic servants, most of whom were women.

The Rise of Organized Labor

Although women and minorities discovered that the New Deal had limits to the changes it promoted, a powerful union movement arose in the 1930s by taking full advantage of the new climate. Workers themselves took the lead and ended up pushing Roosevelt well beyond his limits.

At the outset of the Great Depression, most workers were demoralized and languishing. Barely 6 percent belonged to a union. Though the New Deal left farm workers officially outside its coverage, its promise of support encouraged these workers, traditionally among the most unorganized laborers, to act on their own. In California, where large agribusinesses employed migrant laborers to pick vegetables, fruit, and cotton, some 37 strikes involving over 50,000 workers swept the state after Roosevelt took office.

CAWIU farm strike

The most famous strike broke out in the cotton fields of the San Joaquin Valley under the auspices of the Cannery and Agricultural Workers Industrial Union (CAWIU). Most of the strikers were Mexican, supported more by a complex network of families, friends, and coworkers than by the weak CAWIU. Before the strike was over, local farmers killed three people, and local officials threatened to cut off all relief aid to strikers and to send them back to Mexico. The government finally stepped in to arbitrate a wage settlement, which resulted in an end to the strike but at a fraction of the pay the workers sought.

During the wave of agricultural strikes in California in 1933, Mexican laborers who had been evicted from their homes settled in camps such as this one in Corcoran. The camp held well over 3000 people, each family providing an old tent or burlap bags for habitation. Makeshift streets were named in honor of Mexican towns and heros. By chance the field had been occupied previously by a Mexican circus, the Circo Azteca, which provided nightly entertainment.

Such government support was not enough to embolden the cautious American Federation of Labor, the nation's premier union. Historically bound to skilled labor and organized on the basis of craft, it ignored the unskilled workers who by the 1930s made up most of the industrial labor force, and it almost never organized women or black workers. Thus the AFL avoided major industries like rubber, automobiles, and steel. Because the NRA's regulations gave unions the right to organize and bargain, the AFL increased its membership, but its cautious president, William Green, sought cooperation with management and made no changes in its policies toward the unskilled.

The thundering, barrel-chested John L. Lewis fought, sometimes literally, to unionize unskilled laborers. The son of a Welsh miner, Lewis was tough, charismatic, practical, and dedicated to organizing all workers regardless of skill level, race, or gender. He headed the United Mine Workers (UMW), an affiliate of the AFL, and had supported Herbert Hoover in the 1932 presidential election. But when Roosevelt won, Lewis promptly paid a call on the new President to shore up his ties to the White House. He received little more than consolation from Roosevelt for his shrinking union. Yet the shrewd Lewis returned to the coalfields with a message he had never been given: "The president wants you to join a union." Within a year the UMW had 400,000 members. Raising his sights, Lewis called for the creation of a Steel Workers' Organizing Committee and for the admission of the United Auto Workers into the AFL.

At the annual AFL convention in Atlantic City in 1935, Lewis demanded a commitment to the "industrial organization of mass production workers." The delegates, mostly from craft unions, voted down the proposal. Near the end of the convention, as he passed "Big Bill" Hutcheson of the carpenters union, angry words passed between the two. Lewis spun and with a single punch sent Hutcheson sprawling in a bloody heap.

The blow signaled the determination of industrial unions to break the AFL's domination of organized labor. A few weeks later, Lewis and the heads of seven other AFL unions announced the formation of the Committee for Industrial Organization (CIO). The AFL suspended the rogue unions in 1936. The CIO, later rechristened the Congress of Industrial Organizations, turned to the unskilled and embarked on a series of organizing drives in large-scale, mass-production industries.

Congress of Industrial Organizations

Campaigns of the CIO

Sit-down strikes

CIO representatives concentrated on the mighty steel industry, which had clung to the open, or nonunion, shop since 1919. In other industries, militant members of the rank and file did not wait. Emboldened by the recent passage of the Wagner Act, a group of rubber workers in Akron, Ohio, simply sat down on the job in early 1936. Because the strikers occupied the plants, managers could not replace them with strikebreakers. Nor could the rubber companies call in the military or police without risk to their property. The leaders of the United Rubber Workers Union opposed the "sit-downs," but when the Goodyear Tire and Rubber Company laid off 70 workers, 1400 rubber workers struck on their own. An 11-mile picket line sprang up outside. Eventually Goodyear settled by recognizing the union and accepting its demands on wages and hours.

The biggest strikes erupted in the automobile industry. A series of spontaneous strikes at General Motors plants in Atlanta, Kansas City, and Cleveland spread to Fisher Body No. 2 in Flint, Michigan, late in December 1936. Singing the unionists' anthem, "Solidarity Forever," workers took over the plant while wives, friends, and fellow union members handed food and clothing through the windows. Local police tried to break up supply lines, but were driven off by a hail of nuts, bolts, coffee mugs, and bottles.

In the wake of this "Battle of Running Bulls" (a reference to the retreating police), Governor Frank Murphy finally called out the National Guard, not to arrest but to protect strikers. General Motors surrendered in February 1937. Less than a month later U.S. Steel capitulated to the Steel Workers Organizing Committee without a strike. By the end of the year every automobile manufacturer except Henry Ford had negotiated with the UAW. Not until 1941 and the pressure of an impending war did Ford finally recognize the union.

Union gains

Bloody violence accompanied some drives. On Memorial Day 1937, 10 strikers lost their lives when Chicago police fired on them as they marched peacefully toward the Republic Steel plant. Sit-down strikes often alienated an otherwise sympathetic middle class. (In 1939 the Supreme Court outlawed the tactic.) Yet a momentous transfer of power had nonetheless taken place. By 1940 nearly one worker in three belonged to a union. The unskilled had a powerful voice in the CIO. And membership in the craft unions of the AFL outnumbered CIO membership by more than a million. Women's membership in unions tripled between 1930 and 1940, and African Americans also made gains. Independent unions had become a permanent part of industrial America.

Government played an important but secondary role in the industrial union movement. Roosevelt courted workers, both organized and unorganized, but stood aside in the toughest labor battles. When the CIO tried to unionize the steel industry, the president declared "a plague o' both your houses." Yet doing nothing in favor of strikers was a vast improvement over the active hostility shown by earlier presidents. The Wagner Act afforded laborers an opportunity to organize and protection if they chose to request it. Leaders such as John L. Lewis, Walter Reuther of the United Auto Workers, and Philip Murray of the Steel Workers' Organizing Committee galvanized workers who, in the end, won their own victories.

"Art for the Millions"

No agency of the New Deal touched more Americans than Federal One, the bureaucratic umbrella of the WPA's arts program. For the first time, thousands of unemployed writers, musicians, painters, actors, and photographers went on the federal payroll, and millions of ordinary Americans saw their work. Public projects—from massive murals to tiny guidebooks—would make, as one New Dealer put it, "art for the millions."

A Federal Writers Project (FWP) produced about a thousand publications. Its 81 state, territorial, and city guides were so popular that commercial publishers happily printed them. A Depression-bred interest in American history prompted the FWP to collect folklore, study ethnic groups, and record the reminiscences of former slaves. Meanwhile, the Federal Music Project (FMP) employed some 15,000 out-of-work musicians. For a token charge, Americans could hear the music of Bach and Beethoven or the commissioned compositions of American composers such as Aaron Copland. In the Federal Art Project (FAP), watercolorists and drafters painstakingly prepared the Index of American Design, which offered elaborate illustrations of American material culture, from skillets to cigar-store Indians. At night, artists taught sculpture, painting, clay modeling, and carving in country churches, settlement houses, and schools.

The most notable contribution of the FAP came in the form of murals. Under the influence of Mexican muralists Diego Rivera and José Clemente Orozco, American artists adorned the walls of thousands of airports, post offices, and other government buildings with murals glorifying local life and work. The rare treatment of class conflict later opened the FAP to charges of communist infiltration, but most of the murals stressed the enduring qualities of American life—family, work, community.

Rivera and Orozco

The Federal Theater Project (FTP) reached the greatest number of people—some 30 million—and aroused the most controversy. As its head, Hallie Flanagan made government-supported theater vital, daring, and relevant. Living Newspapers dramatized headlines of the day in play-like form. Under the direction of Orson Welles and John Houseman, an all-black company (one of 16 "Negro Units") set Shakespeare's *Macbeth* in Haiti with voodoo priestesses and African drummers. Occasionally frank depictions of class conflict riled congressional conservatives, and beginning in 1938, the House Un-American Activities Committee investigated the FTP as "a branch of the Communistic organization." A year later Congress slashed its budget and brought government-sponsored theater to an end.

Documentary realism

The documentary impulse to record life permeated the arts in the 1930s. Novels such as Erskine Caldwell's *Tobacco Road*, feature films such as John Ford's *The Grapes of Wrath*, and such federally funded documentaries as Pare Lorentz's *The River* stirred the social conscience of the country. New Dealers had practical motives for promoting such documentary realism. They wanted to blunt criticism of New Deal relief measures. In 1937 Rexford Tugwell established an Information Division in his Resettlement Administration. He put Roy Stryker, his former Columbia University teaching assistant, in charge of its Historical Section. Stryker hired talented photographers to produce an unvarnished record of the Great Depression. Their raw and haunting photographs turned history into both propaganda and art.

"I see one-third of a nation ill-housed, ill-clad, ill-nourished," the president lamented in his second inaugural address

The End of the New Deal (1937–1940)

on January 20, 1937 (the first January inauguration under a new constitutional amendment). Industrial output had doubled since 1932; farm income had almost quadrupled. But full recovery remained elusive. Over 7 million Americans were still out of work. At the height of his popularity, with bulging majorities in Congress, Roosevelt planned to expand the New Deal. Within a year, however, the New Deal was largely over—drowned in a sea of economic and political troubles, some of them Roosevelt's own doing.

Daily Lives

PUBLIC SPACE/ PRIVATE SPACE
Post Office Murals

"How can a finished citizen be made in an artless town?" asked the postmaster of Pleasant Hill, Missouri, in 1939. Such weighty matters as citizenship and art might have seemed beyond an ordinary postmaster, but he did not think so. Neither did the New Dealers in Washington. They had just made his post office the recipient of a new painting entitled *Back Home: April 1865.* His town, like so many others across America, had been "wholly without objects of art." Now it had one that showed common people at an epic moment in American history, the end of the Civil War. Townsfolk saw it every day, and every day it made them a bit more comfortable with art, more appreciative of the heritage of democracy, more secure in the knowledge that the republic had endured other crises.

The Fine Arts Section (FAS) of the Treasury Department sponsored the artwork for Pleasant Hill. It was only one of the New Deal programs for artists. The largest and most famous, the Works Progress Administration's Federal Art Project (1935–1943), produced 18,000 easel paintings, 17,000 sculptures, and 2500 murals. It employed thousands of needy artists and placed their work in state and municipal institutions.

The Treasury Department had a similar mission but focused on federal buildings. During its nine-year existence, the FAS hired 850 artists and authorized nearly 1400 works. Unlike relief agencies, which handed out work on the basis of need, FAS artists competed for contracts. Most were for the 1100 new post offices built during the New Deal.

Post offices were an ideal medium for democratizing art because they were often at the center of town and almost everyone used them. The rectangular brick buildings reflected the solidity, permanence, and service for which government stood. Indeed, the post office was likely to be the only contact many citizens ever had with Washington.

Rather than emphasizing government might with portraits of national heroes or friezes of eagles and flags, the new post office murals depicted the daily routines of

Back Home: April 1865, presented to the Pleasant Hill, Missouri, post office in 1939, was commissioned by the Fine Arts Section of the Treasury Department as part of its program to democratize American art by adorning public buildings with it.

Packing the Courts

As Roosevelt's second term began, only the Supreme Court clouded the political horizon. In its first 76 years the Court had invalidated only two acts of Congress. Between 1920 and 1933 it struck down portions of 22 laws. This new judicial activism, spearheaded by a conservative majority, rested on a narrow view of the constitutional powers of Congress and the president. As the New Deal broadened those powers, the Supreme Court let loose a torrent of nullifications.

In 1935 the Court wiped out the NRA on the grounds that manufacturing was not involved in interstate commerce and thus lay beyond federal regulation. In 1936 it canceled the AAA, reducing federal authority that had been formerly justified under the taxing power and the general welfare clause of the Constitution.

common citizens from the community or region. Local committees helped select the artists and the subjects. And whenever possible, local artists did the work. Such regard for community participation was meant to temper the sense that people were surrendering control to an intrusive central government.

From the artists' point of view, post offices were hardly ideal settings. Muralists required space and light. Most post offices were small and dark. Available wall space was often no more than 6 by 12 feet, usually above the postmaster's door at the end of a long, cramped lobby. Hanging light fixtures and vestibules obstructed vision.

Unlike the giant muralist Diego Rivera, whose controversial work had glorified the Mexican Revolution, post office muralists were forced to paint on a smaller scale and were encouraged to avoid controversy. They drew fewer figures and arranged them in the foreground to draw the attention of viewers. Sometimes they used geometric designs that carried the eye across the disruptive door or vertical lines that broke the painting into parts.

In a decade of fear and insecurity, the murals stressed the continuity of past and present. The old virtues that had made the country great would help it overcome the current crisis. Grand themes were distilled to simple, timeless symbols embodied in everyday experiences: a family enjoying a Sunday picnic, friends picking fruit, skaters gliding across a frozen pond. Family, work, community—these lasting values bound Americans together in good times and saw them through bad.

Regionalism often influenced subject matter. Colonial and urban scenes predominated in New England and the Mid-Atlantic states; agriculture and country life in the South; the frontier and Indian and Spanish culture in the West. Artists were rarely permitted to deal with inflammatory subjects such as war, radicalism, or poverty.

The caliber of the murals varied greatly, but in the end they achieved their aim. They reached millions of common folk by combining the ordinary and the aesthetic. And almost always they communicated a harmonious vision of America, inspiring viewers with faith in progress and in themselves.

In *Moorehead v. Tipaldo* (1936) the Court ruled that a New York minimum-wage law was invalid because it interfered with the right of workers to negotiate a contract. A frustrated Roosevelt complained that the Court had thereby created a "'no-man's land,' where no government—State or Federal" could act. It seemed that no law would be safe, not the Wagner Act, not wages and hours legislation, not even Social Security.

Roosevelt was the first president since James Monroe to serve four years without having the opportunity to make a Supreme Court appointment. Among federal judges, Republicans outnumbered Democrats by more than two to one in 1933. Roosevelt intended to redress the balance by adding new judges to the federal bench, including the Supreme Court. Too many judges were "aged or infirm," Roosevelt declared early in February 1937. In the interest of efficiency he proposed to

Roosevelt's plan

843

HAROLD, I MAY WANT TO DO THIS. HOW ABOUT A PWA GRANT?

NEW DEAL PLAN for ENLARGED SUPREME COURT

Roosevelt's plan to "pack" the courts came under furious attack as a naked power grab and vindictive assault on the Supreme Court itself. Here, cartoonist John Berryman lampoons the president as Roosevelt asks Interior Secretary and Public Works Administrator Harold Ickes if he would construct a new, bigger Supreme Court building flying Roosevelt's flag.

"vitalize" the judiciary with new members. When a 70-year-old judge who had served at least 10 years failed to retire, the president would add another, up to six to the Supreme Court and 44 to the lower federal courts.

Roosevelt badly miscalculated. He unveiled his plan without warning, expecting widespread support. He regarded courts as political, not sacred, institutions and had ample precedent for altering even the Supreme Court. (As recently as 1869 Congress had increased its size to nine.) But most Americans clung to the courts as symbols of stability. Few accepted Roosevelt's efficiency argument, and no one on Capitol Hill, with its share of 70-year-olds, believed that seven decades of life made a person incompetent. Worse still, the proposal ignited conservative-liberal antagonisms within the Democratic party.

In the midst of the controversy, the Court suddenly began to reverse direction. In April 1937, *N.L.R.B. v. Jones and Laughlin Steel Corporation* upheld the Wagner Act by one vote. A month later the justices sustained the Social Security Act as a legitimate exercise of the commerce power. And when Justice Willis Van Devanter, the oldest and most conservative justice, retired later that year, Roosevelt at last made an appointment to the Supreme Court.

With Democrats deserting him, the president abandoned his proposal in favor of a substitute measure that modestly reformed the lower federal courts. Roosevelt claimed victory nonetheless. After all, the Court had finally shifted course. And over his four terms in office the president did appoint nine Supreme Court justices. But victory came at a high price. The momentum of the 1936 election was squandered, the unity of the Democratic party was destroyed, and opponents learned that Roosevelt could be beaten. A conservative coalition of Republicans and rural Democrats had joined forces in the first of several anti–New Deal causes.

The New Deal at Bay

As early as 1936 Secretary of the Treasury Henry Morgenthau began to plead for fiscal restraint. With productivity rising and unemployment falling, Morgenthau felt that it was time to reduce spending, balance the budget, and let business lead the recovery. "Strip off the bandages, throw away the crutches," he said, and let the economy "stand on its own feet."

Morgenthau was preaching to the converted. Although the president had been willing to run budget deficits in a time of crisis, he was never comfortable with

John Maynard Keynes

them. To be sure, the British economist John Maynard Keynes had actually recommended the kind of deficit spending that Roosevelt was using. Keynes's startling theory called on government not to balance the budget but to spend its way out of depression. When prosperity returned, Keynes argued, government could pay off its debts through taxes. This deliberate policy of "countercyclical" action (spending in bad times, taxing in good) was designed to compensate for swings in the economy.

Recovery abroad

Keynes's theory was precisely the path chosen by several industrial nations in which recovery came more quickly than it did to the United States. Germany, in particular built its rapid recuperation on spending. When Adolf Hitler and his National Socialist (Nazi) Party came to power in 1933, they went on a spending spree, constructing huge highways called *autobahns,* enormous government buildings, and other public works. Later they ran up deficits for rearmament as they prepared for war. Between 1933 and 1939 the German national debt almost quadrupled, while in the United States it rose by barely 50 percent. For Germans, the price in lost freedoms was incalculable, but by 1936, their depression was over.

Similarly, fascist dictator Benito Mussolini created a corporate state in partnership with business that helped lift Italy from economic ruin, in part through government financing of public works and military expansion. In Japan militarists launched a spending campaign that led to full employment by the end of 1936. When the minister of finance attempted to curb it, he was assassinated.

Not all nations relied on military spending. And many of them, such as Great Britain and France, had not shared in the economic expansion of the 1920s, which meant their economies had a shorter distance to rise in order to reach pre-Depression levels. Yet spending of one kind or another helped solve the riddle of recovery in country after country. In Great Britain, for example, low interest rates plus government assistance to the needy ignited a housing boom, while government subsidies to the automobile industry and to companies willing to build factories in depressed areas slowed the slide. In the 1930s, Britons still endured what they called the "Great Slump," but their economy was the first to surpass its performance in 1929, and by 1937 British unemployment had been cut nearly by half.

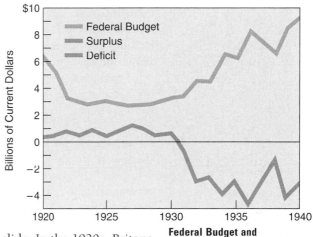

Federal Budget and Surplus/Deficit, 1920–1940 During the 1920s the federal government ran a modest surplus as spending dropped back sharply after World War I. Hoover's cautious depression spending programs led to a small deficit in the early 1930s, which grew steadily as Franklin Roosevelt's New Deal spent boldly and as revenues from taxes and tariffs continued to sink. In 1937 federal spending cuts to balance the budget reduced the deficit but brought on a recession that was quickly followed by renewed federal spending and increasing deficits.

In the United States, Roosevelt ordered cuts in federal spending early in 1937. He slashed relief rolls by half and virtually halted spending on public works. Within six months, the economy collapsed. Industrial activity plummeted to 1935 levels. At the end of the year unemployment stood at 10.5 million. The president, sounding strangely like Hoover, told his cabinet to "sit tight and keep quiet." The "Roosevelt recession" only deepened. Finally spenders convinced him to propose a $3.75 billion omnibus measure in April 1938. Facing an election, Congress happily reversed relief cuts, quadrupled farm subsidies, and embarked on a new shipbuilding program. The economy revived but never recovered. Keynesian economics was vindicated, though decades would pass before it became widely accepted.

With Roosevelt vulnerable, conservatives in Congress struck. They cut back on public housing programs and minimum wage guarantees in the South. The president, wrote Harold Ickes in August 1938, "is punch drunk from the punishment." Vainly Roosevelt fought back. In the off-year elections of 1938, he tried to purge Democrats who had deserted him. The five senators he targeted for defeat all won. Republicans posted gains in the House and Senate and won 13 governorships. Democrats still held majorities in both houses but conservatives had the votes to block new programs. With the economy limping toward recovery, the New Deal passed into history, and the nation turned to a new crisis—a looming war abroad.

The Legacy of the New Deal

The New Deal lasted only five years, from 1933 to 1938, and it never spent enough to end the Depression. Though it pledged itself to the "forgotten" Americans, it failed the neediest among them—sharecroppers, tenant farmers, migrant workers. In many ways, it was quite conservative. It left capitalism intact, even strengthened, and it overturned few cultural conventions. Even its reforms followed the old progressive formula of softening industrialism by strengthening the state.

Yet for all its conservatism and continuities, the New Deal left a legacy of change. Under it, government assumed a broader role in the economy than progressives had ever undertaken. To the progressive goal of regulation was now added the more complicated task of maintaining economic stability—compensating for swings in the business cycle. In its securities and banking regulations, unemployment insurance, and requirements for wages and hours the New Deal created stabilizers to avoid future breakdowns. Bolstering the Federal Reserve system and enhancing control over credit strengthened the means by which government could shape the economy.

Franklin Roosevelt modernized the presidency. He turned the White House into the heart of government, the place where decisions were made. Americans looked to the president to set the public agenda, spread new ideas, initiate legislation, and assume responsibility for the nation. The power of Congress diminished but the scope of government grew. In 1932 there were 605,000 federal employees; by 1939 there were nearly a million (and by 1945, after World War II, some 3.5 million). The many programs of the New Deal—home loans, farm subsidies, bank deposit insurance, relief payments and jobs, pension programs, unemployment insurance, aid to mothers with dependent children, rural electrification, western water man-

What the New Deal Did...

	RELIEF	RECOVERY	REFORM
FOR THE FARMER:	Rural Electrification Administration (1936) Farm Security Administration (1937)	Agriculture Adjustment Act (1933)	
FOR THE WORKER:		National Industrial Recovery Act (1933)	National Labor Relations Act (1935) Fair Labor Standards Act (1938)
FOR THE MIDDLE CLASS:	Home Owner's Loan Act (1934)		Revenue ("Wealth Tax") Act (1935) Public Utilities Holding Company Act (1935)
FOR THE NEEDY:	Federal Emergency Relief Act (1933) Civilian Conservation Corp (1933) Civil Works Administration (1933) National Public Housing Act (1937) Emergency Relief Appropriation Act (1935)		
FOR PROTECTION AGAINST FUTURE DEPRESSIONS:			Federal Deposit Insurance Corporation (1933) Securities Exchange Act (1934) Social Security Act (1935)

agement—touched the lives of ordinary Americans, made them more secure, and formed the outlines of the new welfare state.

The welfare state had limits. Most of its relief measures were designed to last no longer than the crisis. Millions fell through even its more nearly permanent safety nets. Yet the commitment to furnishing minimum standards of life, not the failure to do so, marked a change so dramatic that the poor and working class threw their support to Roosevelt. He was, after all, the first president to try.

At a time when dictators and militarists took hold in Germany, Italy, Japan, and Russia, the New Deal strengthened democracy in America. Roosevelt acted as a democratic broker, responding first to one group, then another. And his "broker state" embraced groups previously spurned—unions, farm organizations, ethnic minorities, women. In short, during the 1930s the United States found a middle way between the extremes of communism and fascism. Still, the broker state had limits. The unorganized, whether in city slums or in sharecroppers' shacks, too often found themselves ignored.

Under the New Deal, the Democratic party became a mighty force in politics. In a quiet revolution, African Americans came into the party's fold, as did workers and farmers. Political attention shifted to bread-and-butter issues. In 1932 people had argued about Prohibition and European war debts. By 1935 they were debating Social Security, labor relations, tax reform, public housing, and the TVA. With remarkable speed, the New Deal had become a vital part of American life.

counterpoint

Assessing the New Deal

Historians disagree sharply in assessing the New Deal. We have taken the view, shared by many liberal historians, that the New Deal was not radical or socialistic but fell within the American political tradition of pragmatic reform. Historians of the New Left, a group of radical scholars writing in the 1960s, criticized the New Deal for being too conservative and thus failing to aid those most in need—sharecroppers, for example. Instead, they say, the New Deal preserved the worst of corporate and industrial capitalism.

Other scholars have defended the New Deal, noting the obstacles faced by reformers. Some stress the absence of "state capacity," a bureaucracy of necessary size and expertise to carry out the New Deal's massive programs. Still others point out that New Dealers themselves were often skeptical of growing deficits, expanding governments, and mounting welfare initiatives.

In February 1939 Eleanor Roosevelt addressed the National Youth Congress. Only six years earlier she had stood at her husband's inauguration, chilled with worry over the future of her country. As the decade drew to a close, she could take justifiable pride in the accomplishments of Franklin and the other New Dealers, including those in Congress. During the 1930s the United States found a middle way between the extremes of communism and fascism. Blending public and private controls, the New Deal attempted to humanize industrial society and generate prosperity without sacrificing capitalism or democracy. And through it all, government—embodied in her husband—had taken the lead.

Yet New Dealers from the president down recognized that they could not do everything. "I never believed that the Federal government could solve the whole problem," Eleanor told the members of the Youth Congress. A measure of doubt crept into her voice: "It bought us time to think. . . . Is it going to be worthwhile?" Only future generations could say.

chapter summary

The Great Depression of the 1930s was the longest in the history of the nation; it forced virtually all Americans to live leaner lives and it spawned Franklin Roosevelt's New Deal.

- The Great Depression acted as a great leveler that reduced differences in income and status and left many Americans with an "invisible scar" of shame, self-doubt, and lost confidence.

  - Unemployment and suffering was especially acute among agricultural migrants, African Americans, Latinos, and American Indians.

  - Rates of marriage and birth declined, and many women found themselves working additional hours inside and outside the home to supplement family incomes.

  - Popular culture rallied to reinforce basic tenets of American life: middle-class morality, family, capitalism, and democracy.

- President Herbert Hoover represented a transition from the old, do-nothing policies of the past to the interventionist policies of the future. In the end, his program of voluntary cooperation and limited government activism failed, and in 1932 he lost the presidency to Franklin Roosevelt.

- Roosevelt's New Deal attacked the Great Depression along three broad fronts: recovery for the economy, relief for the needy, and reforms to ward off future depressions.

- The New Deal failed to achieve full recovery but did result in lasting changes:

  - The creation of economic stabilizers such as federal insurance for bank deposits, unemployment assistance, and greater control over money and banking that were designed to compensate for swings in the economy.

  - The establishment of a limited welfare state to provide minimum standards of well-being for all Americans.

  - The revitalization of the Democratic Party and the formation of a powerful new political coalition of labor, urban ethnics, women, African Americans, and the South.

  - The modernization of the presidency.

additional reading

For a comparative look at responses to the Great Depression, see John A. Garraty, *The Great Depression* (1987). Robert Sobel, *The Great Bull Market: Wall Street in the 1920s* (1968) is a brief, evenhanded study of the stock market and Republican fiscal policies in the 1920s. Caroline Bird, *The Invisible Scar* (1966) remains the most sensitive treatment of the human impact of the Great Depression, but it should not be read without Studs Terkel, *Hard Times: An Oral History of the Great Depression* (1970) and Robert McElvaine, *The Great Depression: America, 1929–1941* (1984), which are especially good on Depression culture and values. Joan Hoff Wilson, *Herbert Hoover: Forgotten Progressive* (1975) traces Hoover's progressive impulses before and during his presidency.

Frank Freide, *Franklin D. Roosevelt: A Rendezvous with Destiny* (1990) is the best single-volume biography of Roosevelt, and William Leuchtenburg, *Franklin D. Roosevelt and the New Deal, 1932–1940* (1963) is the best single-volume study of the New Deal. Both fall within the liberal tradition of New Deal scholarship and are admiringly critical of Roosevelt's use of power. They emphasize the limits of political feasibility faced by New Dealers. For sharp criticism of New Left historians, see Paul Conkin, *The New Deal* (1967). For the bureaucratic constraints faced by the New Deal and the absence of "state capacity," see Theda Skocpol and Kenneth Finegold, "State Capacity and Economic Intervention in the Early New Deal," *Political Science Quarterly* (1982), 255–278.

Eleanor Roosevelt is analyzed in rich detail and from a frankly feminist viewpoint in Blanche Wiesen Cook, *Eleanor Roosevelt, Volume One, 1884–1993* (1992) and *Eleanor Roosevelt: Volume 1933–1938* (1999). Susan Ware, *Beyond Suffrage: Women and the New Deal* (1981) locates a women's political network within the New Deal, and Harvard Sitkoff, *A New Deal for Blacks* (1978) studies a similar network of blacks and whites and surveys the mixed record of the New Deal for African Americans. The culture and politics of working men and women during the Great Depression are the subject of Lisabeth Cohen, *Making a New Deal: Industrial Workers in Chicago, 1919–1939* (1990), which depicts the erosion of ethnic communities and the acceptance among workers of federal activism and welfare capitalism during the Great Depression. Steve Fraser and Gary Gerstle, eds., *The Rise and Fall of the New Deal Order, 1930–1980* (1989) is an excellent collection of interpretive essays examining the origins, impact, and legacy of the New Deal. For a probing analysis of New Deal liberalism and its retreat from reform, see Alan Brinkley, *The End of Reform: New Deal Liberalism in Recession and War* (1995). For a fuller list of readings, see the Bibliography.

Significant Events

1928 "Great Bull Market" begins to peak; Herbert Hoover elected president

1929 Federal Farm Board created for loans to farmers; "Great Crash" of stock market ushers in Great Depression

1930 Smoot-Hawley Tariff raises rates on imports and helps choke off world trade

1931 Repatriation of Mexicans; Scottsboro boys arrested in Alabama on charges of rape; New York establishes first state welfare agency, Temporary Emergency Relief Administration

1932 Reconstruction Finance Corporation created to save banks; Emergency Relief and Construction Act passed to furnish funds for public works and for unemployment aid to states; Farm Holiday Association formed; Bonus Army marches on Washington, D.C.; Franklin Roosevelt elected president

1933 Roosevelt inaugurated; black blizzards begin to form Dust Bowl; Hundred Days legislation enacted; bank holiday shuts banks for eight days; repeal of Eighteenth Amendment ends Prohibition

1934 Securities and Exchange Commission created; Indian Reorganization Act returns Indian lands to tribes; newly founded American Liberty League begins conservative campaign against Roosevelt; Huey Long organizes Share Our Wealth Society to redistribute wealth; Father Charles Coughlin creates National Union for Social Justice

1935 Second Hundred Days legislation enacted, including Emergency Relief Appropriation Act to create Works Progress Administration for work relief; Rural Electrification Administration authorized; *Schecter Poultry Corporation v. United States* invalidates National Recovery Administration; *Becky Sharp*, first color film, released; Communist Party announces "popular front" to join in antifascist campaign

1936 *Butler v. United States* invalidates Agricultural Adjustment Administration (AAA); Soil Conservation and Domestic Allotment Act replaces AAA; Congress of Industrial Organization formed to unionize unskilled industrial workers; Roosevelt reelected; United Auto Workers begin sit-down strikes; John Maynard Keynes publishes *The General Theory of Employment, Interest, and Money*, advocating deficit spending to end the Depression

1937 Roosevelt announces his court-packing plan; Roosevelt slashes federal spending, which initiates Roosevelt recession; war between Japan and China breaks out

1938 Fair Labor Standards Act sets minimum wages and maximum work hours; Congress establishes Temporary National Economic Committee to investigate monopoly business practices; Orson Welles's radio broadcast of *The War of the Worlds*

1939 Marion Anderson gives concert at Lincoln Memorial; Executive Reorganization Act restructures and enlarges office of president; war in Europe breaks out

J ohn Garcia, a native Hawaiian, worked as a pipe fitter's apprentice at the Pearl Harbor Navy Yard in Honolulu. On Sunday, December 7, 1941, Garcia planned to enjoy a lazy day off. By the time his grandmother rushed in to wake him that morning at eight, he had already missed the worst of it. "The Japanese were bombing Pearl Harbor," he recalled her yelling at him. John listened in disbelief. "I said, 'They're just practicing.'" "No," his grandmother replied. It was real. He catapulted his huge frame from the bed, ran to the front porch, and caught sight of the antiaircraft fire in the sky. "Oh boy" were his only words.

Hopping on his motorcycle, Garcia sped the four miles to the harbor in 10 minutes. "It was a mess," he remembered. The USS *Shaw* was in flames. The battleship *Pennsylvania,* a bomb nesting one deck above the powder and ammunition, was about to blow. When ordered to put out its fires, he refused. "There ain't no way I'm gonna go down there," he told the navy officer. Instead, he spent the rest of the day pulling bodies from the water. There were so many, he lost count. He couldn't tell "how many were alive and how many were dead." Surveying the wreckage the following morning, he noted that the battleship *Arizona* "was a total washout." So was the *West Virginia.* The *Oklahoma* had "turned turtle, totally upside down." It took two weeks to get all the fires out.

The world had been at war since 1937, but Americans had largely been spared. The surprise attack at Pearl Harbor suddenly transformed the Pacific into an avenue of potential assault. Dennis Keegan, a young college student at the University of San Francisco, could not believe war had come, even though his younger brother Bill was training in Canada to fly with the Royal Air Force. "These places were so far away from us," Dennis said after hearing the radio reports on Pearl Harbor. "It just didn't seem possible that we were at war."

All along the West Coast panic spread. That night Keegan drove into downtown San Francisco. Market Street was "bedlam." "The United Artists Theater had a huge marquee with those dancing lights, going on and off," he recalled. "People were throwing everything they could to put those lights out, screaming Blackout! Blackout!" The next day a false army report of 30 Japanese planes flying toward the coast triggered air-raid sirens throughout the city. Los Angeles turned trigger happy. A young police officer named Tom Bradley (who later served as mayor of the city) heard "sirens going off, aircraft guns firing." "Here we are in the middle of the night," he said; "there was no enemy in sight, but somebody thought they saw the enemy." In January 1942 worried officials moved the Rose Bowl from Pasadena, California, to Durham, North Carolina. Though overheated, their fears were not entirely imaginary. Japanese submarines shelled Santa Barbara, while other enemy ships launched balloons carrying incendiary devices. One floated all the way to Iowa without doing any damage.

America's Rise to Globalism

preview • As the Depression accelerated the rise of militarism in Europe and Asia, most Americans hoped to remain isolated from war. Only Japan's attack on Pearl Harbor brought the United States into the conflict. Eventually American industrial might supplied the Allies in both Europe and the Pacific, bringing renewed prosperity at home. And the dropping of two atomic bombs to end the war underscored America's new role as the preeminent power in a globally interdependent world.

Images of its battleships in flames sent the United States into global war. Despite the apparent devastation, the losses at Pearl Harbor were more shocking than disabling. The *West Virginia,* shown here, settled to the bottom with guns firing and was later repaired.

Although the Japanese would never invade the mainland, in a world with long-range bombers and submarines no place seemed safe. This war was a global war, the first of its kind. Arrayed against the Axis powers of Germany, Italy, and Japan were the Allies—Great Britain, the Soviet Union, the United States, China, and the Free French. Their armies fought from the Arctic to the southwestern Pacific, in the great cities of Europe and Asia and the small villages of North Africa and Indochina, in malarial jungles and scorching deserts, on six continents and across four oceans. Perhaps as many as 100 million people took up arms; some 40 to 50 million lost their lives.

Tragedy on such a scale taught the generation of Americans who fought the war that they could no longer isolate themselves from any part of the world, no matter how remote it might seem. Manchuria, Ethiopia, and Poland had once seemed far away, yet the road to war had led from those distant places to the United States. Retreat into isolation had not cured the worldwide depression or preserved the peace. To avoid other such disasters, the United States would eventually assume a far wider role in managing the world's geopolitical and economic systems.

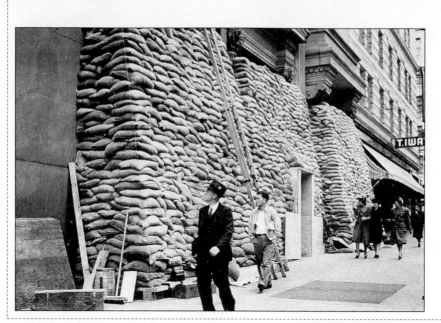

The Japanese attack on Pearl Harbor created a panic along the West Coast of the United States. Hasty defenses such as these sandbags stacked in front of the telephone company in San Francisco were thrown up to ward off an attack that never came.

The United States in a Troubled World

The outbreak of World War II had its roots in World War I. So vast was the devastation of the Great War that the victors suffered almost as much as the vanquished. Many of the victorious as well as the defeated nations were deeply dissatisfied with the peace terms adopted at Versailles. Over the next two decades Germany, the Soviet Union, Italy, Poland, and Japan all sought to achieve unilaterally what Allied leaders had denied them at Versailles. In central and eastern Europe rivalry among fascists, communists, and other political factions led to frequent violence and instability. War debts imposed at Versailles shackled Germany's economy. As Germany struggled to recover, so did all of Europe. Although the United States possessed the resources to ease international tensions, it declined to lead in world affairs. It even rejected membership in the League of Nations.

Pacific Interests

A preference for isolation did not mean the United States could simply ignore events abroad. In assuming colonial control over the Philippines, Americans acquired a major interest in the western Pacific that created a potentially dangerous rivalry with Japan. The United States had also committed itself to an open-door policy (page 702) to prevent China from being divided up by foreign powers. That temptation seemed especially great during the 1920s, because China was wracked by civil war. In 1927 the Nationalist party, led by Chiang Kai-shek, consolidated power by massacring thousands of their Communist party allies.

The Japanese had long dominated Korea, and during the 1920s they expanded their influence on the Chinese mainland. In 1931 Japanese agents staged an explosion on a rail line in Manchuria (meant to appear as if carried out by Chinese nationalists) that provided Japan with an excuse to occupy the whole province. A year later Japan converted Manchuria into a puppet state called Manchukuo.

Here was a direct threat to the Versailles system and the open door. But neither the major powers in Europe nor the United States was willing to risk a war with Japan over China. President Hoover instructed Secretary of State Henry Stimson only to protest that the United States would refuse to recognize Japan's takeover of Manchuria as legal. The policy of "nonrecognition" became known as the Stimson Doctrine, even though Stimson himself doubted its worth. He was right to doubt. Three weeks later Japan's imperial navy shelled the Chinese port city of Shanghai. When the League of Nations condemned Japan in 1933, the Japanese withdrew from the League. The seeds of war in Asia had been sown.

Stimson Doctrine

Becoming a Good Neighbor

Trouble abroad encouraged the United States to improve relations with nations closer to home. By the late 1920s the United States had intervened in Latin America so often that the Roosevelt Corollary (page 741) had become an embarrassment. Slowly, Washington began to abandon some of its highhanded policies. In 1927, when Mexico confiscated American-owned properties, President Coolidge sent an ambassador, instead of the marines, to settle the dispute. In 1933, when critics compared the American position in Nicaragua to Japan's in Manchuria, Secretary Stimson ordered U.S. troops to withdraw. In those gestures and in President Hoover's efforts to cultivate goodwill south of the border lay the roots of a "Good Neighbor" policy.

Good Neighbor policy

Franklin Roosevelt pushed the good neighbor idea. To Roosevelt being a good neighbor meant correcting the political inequities between the United States and Latin America. At the seventh Pan-American Conference in 1933, his administration accepted a resolution denying any country "the right to intervene in the internal or external affairs of another." The following year he negotiated a treaty with Cuba that renounced the American right to intervene under the Platt Amendment (page 741). Henceforth the United States would replace direct military presence with indirect (but still substantial) economic influence.

The greatest test of the Good Neighbor policy came in 1937 and 1938, when Bolivia and Mexico expropriated the property of American oil companies. Roosevelt worried that intervention would push Mexico toward closer ties with potential enemies. When an arbitration committee decided that U.S. oil companies were entitled to only $24 million (not the $450 million they demanded), Roosevelt accepted the decision.

As the threat of war increased during the 1930s, the United States found a new Latin willingness to cooperate in matters of common defense. In the first visit of an American president to the capital of Argentina, Roosevelt opened the Pan-American Conference in 1936. In a speech he declared that outside aggressors "will find a Hemisphere wholly prepared to consult together for our mutual safety and our mutual good." By the end of 1940 the administration had worked out defense agreements with every Latin American country but one. The United States faced the threat of war with the American hemisphere largely secured.

The Good Neighbor policy made Franklin Roosevelt unusually popular in Latin America, as this sheet music suggests. Roosevelt was the first American president to visit South America, and his diplomacy paid dividends when the Western Hemisphere faced the world crisis largely united.

The rise of fascism

The Diplomacy of Isolationism

During the 1920s Benito Mussolini had appealed to Italian nationalism and fear of communism to gain power in Italy. Spinning dreams of a new Roman empire, Mussolini embodied the rising force of fascism. Then on March 5, 1933, one day after the inauguration of Franklin Roosevelt, the German legislature gave Adolf Hitler control of Germany. Riding a wave of anticommunism and anti-Semitism, Hitler's Nazi party promised to unite all Germans in a Greater Third Reich that would last a thousand years. Just over a week earlier, Yosuke Matsuoka had led the Japanese withdrawal from the League of Nations. Governed by militarists, Japan began to carve out its own empire, which it called the Greater East Asia Co-Prosperity Sphere. The rise of fascism and militarism in Europe and Asia brought the world to war.

Recognition of the Soviet Union

As much as Roosevelt wanted the United States to play a leading role in world affairs, the nation proved unwilling to follow. "It's a terrible thing to look over your shoulder when you are trying to lead—and to find no one there," he commented during the mid-1930s. Only when a potential economic interest was involved could the president command wide support for foreign initiatives. For example, in 1933 Roosevelt recognized the Communist regime in Russia, hoping that the Soviet Union would help contain Japanese expansion in Asia and fascism in Europe. Business leaders saw recognition largely as an opportunity to increase Russian-American trade. For every step Roosevelt took toward internationalism, the Great Depression forced him home again. Programs to revive the economy gained broad support; efforts to resolve crises abroad provoked controversy.

Nye Committee

In 1935 Senator Gerald P. Nye of North Dakota headed investigations that revealed that bankers and munitions makers, so-called merchants of death, had made enormous profits during World War I. The Nye Committee report implied, but could not prove, that business interests had even steered the United States into war. "When Americans went into the fray," declared Senator Nye, "they little thought that they were there and fighting to save the skins of American bankers who had bet too boldly on the outcome of the war and had two billions of dollars of loans to the Allies in jeopardy."

Internationalists versus isolationists

Such charges provoked debate over how the United States should respond to the growing threats to peace. Internationalists like the League of Women Voters and former Secretary of State Henry Stimson favored a policy of collective security—working actively with other nations. "The only certain way to keep out of a great war is to prevent war," Stimson declared. "The only hope of preventing war . . . is by the earnest, intelligent, and unselfish cooperation of the nations of the world towards that end."

On the other side stood the isolationists, united by their firm opposition to war and the conviction that the United States should avoid alliances with other nations. Yet many strange bedfellows made up the isolationist movement. It included liberal reformers like George W. Norris and conservatives like Robert A. Taft of Ohio, a concentration of midwesterners as well as major leaders from both coasts, and a number of Democrats as well as leading Republicans. Pacifists added yet another element to the debate. Powerful groups like the Women's International League for Peace and Freedom insisted that disarmament was the only road to peace.

Neutrality Legislation

Roused by the Nye Committee hearings, Congress debated a proposal to prohibit the sale of arms to belligerents in time of war. Internationalists opposed the idea. The embargo, they argued, should apply only to aggressor nations. Otherwise, aggressors could strike when they were ready and their victims were ill prepared. The president, they believed, should have the authority to use the embargo selectively. The Neutrality Act of 1935 denied Roosevelt that power. At the isolationists' insistence, it required an impartial embargo of arms to all belligerents. The president had authority only to determine when a state of war existed. A troubled Roosevelt argued that the Neutrality Act might "drag us into war rather than keeping us out."

The limitations of formal neutrality became immediately apparent. In October 1935 Benito Mussolini ordered Italian forces into the North African country of Ethiopia. Against tanks and planes, the troops of Emperor Haile Selassie fought with spears and flintlock rifles. Roosevelt immediately invoked the Neutrality Act in hopes of depriving Italy of war goods. Unfortunately for Roosevelt, Italy needed not arms but oil, steel, and copper—materials not included under the Neutrality Act. When Secretary of State Cordell Hull called for a "moral embargo" on such goods, hard-pressed American businesses shipped them anyway. With no effective opposition from the League of Nations or the United States, Mussolini quickly completed his conquest. In a second Neutrality Act Congress added a ban on providing any loans or credits to belligerents.

Neutrality legislation also benefited Nazi dictator Adolf Hitler. In March 1936, two weeks after Congress renewed the Neutrality Act, German troops thrust into the demilitarized area west of the Rhine River. This flagrant act violated the Treaty of Versailles. As Hitler shrewdly calculated, Britain and France did nothing, while the League of Nations sputtered out a worthless condemnation. Roosevelt remained aloof. The Soviet Union's lonely call for collective action fell on deaf ears.

Then came a rebellion against Spain's fledgling democracy. In July 1936 Generalissimo Francisco Franco, made bold by Hitler's success, revolted against the newly elected Popular Front government. The civil war that followed became a staging ground for World War II. Hitler and Mussolini sent supplies, weapons, and troops to Franco's Fascists, while the Soviet Union and Mexico aided the left-leaning government. The war divided opinion in Europe and America. Catholics supported the anti-Communist Franco forces. Leftists embraced the Loyalists, who backed the democratic government. In the face of domestic political divisions Roosevelt refused to become involved in the conflict. By 1939 the Spanish republic had fallen to Franco.

Spanish Civil War

A flag company of Hitler youth parades past its *Führer,* Adolf Hitler (centered in the balcony doorway). Hitler's shrewd use of patriotic and party symbols, mass rallies, and marches exploited the possibilities for mass politics and propaganda.

Cash-and-carry

For its part, Congress searched for a way to allow American trade to continue (and thus to promote economic recovery at home) without drawing the nation into war itself. Under new "cash-and-carry" provisions in the Neutrality Act of 1937, belligerents could buy supplies other than munitions. But they would have to pay beforehand and carry the supplies on their own ships. If war spread, these terms favored the British, whose navy would ensure that supplies reached England.

Aggression in China

But the policy of cash-and-carry did not help China. In 1937 Japanese forces pushed into its southern regions. In order to give China continued access to American goods, Roosevelt refused to invoke the Neutrality Act, which would have cut off trade with both nations. But Japan had by far a greater volume of trade with the United States. Because the president lacked the freedom to impose a selective embargo, Japan could use American resources to support the invasion.

Inching toward War

With Italy, Germany, and Japan turning into armed camps, war seemed inevitable in both Europe and Asia. The three militant nations signed the Anti-Comintern Pact in 1937. On the face of it, the pact was merely a pledge of mutual support against the Soviet Union. But the Rome-Berlin-Tokyo axis freed those nations for further expansion. Roosevelt groped for some way to contain the Axis powers—these "bandit nations." In his first foreign policy speech in 14 months, he called for an international "quarantine" of aggressor nations. Most newspaper editorials applauded his remarks, yet Roosevelt quickly retreated. When Japanese planes sank the American gunboat *Panay* on China's Yangtze River in December, only two months later, he meekly accepted an apology for the unprovoked attack.

Quarantine speech

In truth, domestic pressures kept the president from risking a confrontation with powerful isolationists. His ill-fated plan to pack the Supreme Court in 1937 had emboldened opposition among both conservative Democrats and Republicans. In 1939, his request to Congress for flexibility in applying the arms embargo went down to defeat. "Well, Captain," Vice President John Nance Garner told him, "we may as well face the facts. You haven't got the votes, and that's all there is to it."

What made Roosevelt's impotence so frustrating was the growing Nazi menace. In 1938 German troops marched into Austria in yet another violation of the Treaty of Versailles. Hitler then insisted that the 3.5 million ethnic Germans in the Sudetenland of Czechoslovakia be brought into the Reich. With Germany threatening to invade Czechoslovakia, the leaders of France and Britain flew to Munich in September 1938, where they struck a deal to appease Hitler. Czechoslovakia would give up the Sudetenland in return for German pledges to seek no more territory in Europe. When British Prime Minister Neville Chamberlain returned to England, he told cheering crowds that the Munich Pact would bring "peace in our time." Six months later, in open contempt for the European democracies, Hitler took over the remainder of Czechoslovakia. "Appeasement" became synonymous with betrayal, weakness, and surrender.

Appeasement

Hitler's Invasion

By 1939 Hitler made little secret that he intended to recapture territory lost to Poland after World War I. Russia was the key to his success. If Soviet leader Joseph Stalin joined the Western powers, Hitler might be blocked. But Stalin suspected that the West hoped to turn Hitler against him. On August 24, 1939, the foreign ministers of Russia and Germany signed a nonaggression pact, shocking the rest of the world.

World War II in Europe and North Africa Coordination of Allied strategy was crucial to victory. Until 1944 Soviet forces engaged the bulk of the Axis armies across a huge front. The battle of Stalingrad prevented Hitler from reinforcing Rommel against the British in North Africa. After winning North Africa, the Allies turned north to knock Italy out of the war. The final key to defeating the Nazis was the invasion of western Europe at Normandy. D-Day would not have been possible had the Allies been unable to use England as a base to gather their forces. Stalin supported D-Day with a spring offensive in eastern Europe.

The secret protocols of the agreement freed Hitler to invade Poland without having to fight a war in which his enemies attacked him on two fronts. Stalin could extend his western borders by bringing eastern Poland, the Baltic states (Latvia, Estonia, and Lithuania), and parts of Romania and Finland into the Soviet sphere.

On the hot Saturday of September 1, 1939, German tanks and troops surged into Poland. "It's come at last," Roosevelt sighed. "God help us all." Within days France and England declared war on Germany. Stalin quickly moved into eastern Poland, where German and Russian armor took just three weeks to crush the Polish cavalry. As Hitler consolidated his hold on eastern Europe, Stalin invaded Finland.

Germany begins
World War II

Once spring arrived in 1940, Hitler moved to protect his sea lanes by capturing Denmark and Norway. The French retreated behind their Maginot Line, a steel and concrete fortification at the German border. Undeterred, German panzer divisions supported by air power knifed through Belgium and Holland in a blitzkrieg—a "lightning war." The Low Countries fell in 23 days, giving the Germans a route into France. By May a third of a million British and French troops had been driven back onto the Atlantic beaches of Dunkirk. Only a strenuous rescue effort, staged by the Royal Navy and a flotilla of English pleasure craft, saved them. The way was clear for the Germans to march to Paris.

On June 22, less than six weeks after the German invasion, France capitulated. Hitler insisted that the surrender come in the very railway car in which Germany had submitted in 1918. William Shirer, an American war correspondent standing 50 yards away, watched the dictator through binoculars: "He swiftly snaps his hands on his hips, arches his shoulders, plants his feet wide apart. It is a magnificent gesture of defiance, of burning contempt for this place and all that it has stood for in the twenty-two years since it witnessed the humbling of the German Empire."

Retreat from Isolationism

Now, only Britain stood between Hitler and the United States. If the Nazis defeated the British fleet, the Atlantic Ocean could easily become a gateway to America. Isolationism suddenly seemed dangerous. By the spring of 1940 Roosevelt had abandoned impartiality in favor of outright aid to the Allies. In May he requested funds to motorize the army (it had only 350 tanks) and build 50,000 airplanes a year (fewer than 3000 existed, most outmoded). Over isolationist protests he soon persuaded Congress to adopt a bill for the first peacetime draft in history.

Battle of Britain

That summer thousands of German fighter planes and heavy bombers struck targets in England. In the Battle of Britain Hitler and his air chief, Hermann Goering, sought to soften up England for a German invasion from occupied France. Radio reporters relayed graphic descriptions of London in flames and Royal Air Force pilots putting up a heroic defense. Such tales convinced a majority of Americans that the United States should help Britain win the war, though few favored military involvement. So Roosevelt adopted policies designed to help the British help themselves. In September 1940 he agreed to give Britain 50 old destroyers in return for leases on British bases in the Western Hemisphere. The destroyers-for-bases deal, Roosevelt told the nation, was the most important "reinforcement of our national defenses that has been taken since the Louisiana Purchase."

Lend-lease aid

In the 1940 election campaign both Roosevelt and his Republican opponent, Wendell Willkie, favored an internationalist course short of war. In defeating Willkie, Roosevelt promised voters that "your boys are not going to be sent into any foreign wars." He portrayed the United States, instead, as "the great arsenal of democracy." Because the British no longer could pay for arms under the provisions of cash-and-carry, Roosevelt proposed a scheme to "lease, lend, or otherwise dispose of" arms and supplies to countries whose defense was vital to the United States. That meant sending supplies to England on the dubious premise that they would be returned when the war ended. Roosevelt likened "lend-lease" to loaning a garden hose to a neighbor whose house was on fire. Isolationist Senator Robert Taft thought a comparison to "chewing gum" more apt. After a neighbor used it, "you don't want it back." In March 1941 Congress rejected isolationism, passing the Lend-Lease Act by a large majority.

By the summer of 1941 the United States and Germany were on the verge of war. American destroyers had begun to escort British ships as far as Iceland (though Roosevelt insisted it was a "patrol," not a convoy). The United States extended its defensive sphere to include Greenland and Iceland. Then Hitler, as audacious as ever, broke his alliance with the Soviet Union by launching a surprise invasion in June 1941. The Allies expected a swift Russian collapse. Soviet armies had fought poorly in the Finnish War, and Stalin in a series of purges three years earlier had executed much of his officer corps. But when the Russians threw up a heroic resistance, Roosevelt extended lend-lease to the Soviet Union.

In August 1941 Roosevelt took a secret voyage to Argentia Bay off the coast of Newfoundland. There he met Britain's new war Prime Minister, Winston Churchill. Almost every day since England and Germany had gone to war, the two men had exchanged phone calls, letters, or cables. The Argentia meetings cemented this friendship—one key to Allied victory. Roosevelt and Churchill also drew up the Atlantic Charter, a statement of principles that the two nations held in common. The Charter condemned "Nazi tyranny" and embraced the "Four Freedoms"—freedom of speech and expression, freedom of worship, freedom from want, and freedom from fear. In effect, the Atlantic Charter was an unofficial statement of war aims. It put humanitarian values ahead of narrow interests.

Atlantic Charter

By the time of the Argentia meetings, American destroyers in the North Atlantic were stalking German U-boats and reporting their whereabouts to British commanders. Given the harsh weather and aggressive American policy, incidents were inevitable. In October a U-boat sank the destroyer *Reuben James* with the loss of more than 100 American sailors. That attack increased public support for the Allied cause. Yet when interventionists criticized Roosevelt for being too cautious, isolationists charged him with being too provocative. As late as September 1941 eight of ten Americans opposed entering the hostilities. Few in the United States suspected that an attack by Japan, not Germany, would bring a unified America into the war.

During World War II, Franklin Roosevelt and British Prime Minister Winston Churchill developed the closest relationship ever between an American president and the head of another government. The two distant cousins shared a sense of the continuities of Anglo-American culture and of the global strategy of the war.

Disaster in the Pacific

Worried most by the prospect of a German victory in Europe, Roosevelt avoided a showdown with Japan. The navy, the president told his cabinet, had "not got enough ships to go round, and every little episode in the Pacific means fewer ships in the Atlantic." But precisely because American and European attention lay elsewhere, Japan was emboldened to expand militarily into Southeast Asia.

Japanese expansion

Japanese leaders were able to justify their expansion easily enough. They viewed their Greater East Asia Co-Prosperity Sphere as simply an Asian version of the Monroe Doctrine. Japan, the preeminent power in the region, would replace the Europeans as a promoter of economic development. To American leaders, however, Japan's actions threatened the principles of the open-door policy and the survival of Chinese independence. By the summer of 1941 Japanese forces controlled the China coast and all major cities. When its army marched into French Indochina (present-day Vietnam) in July, Japan stood ready to conquer all of the Southeast Asian peninsula and the oil-rich Dutch East Indies.

Japan's thrust into Indochina forced Roosevelt to act. He embargoed trade, froze Japanese assets in American banks, and barred shipments of vital scrap iron and petroleum. When the Dutch slapped a similar embargo on their oil from the East Indies, Japan faced a turning point. If the United States would not supply needed petroleum, it would be forced to attack the Dutch East Indies. Prime Minister Fumimaro Konoye still hoped to negotiate a settlement and proposed a summit meeting with Roosevelt. In fact, the two nations' goals were so at odds that no diplomatic resolution was possible. The Japanese ambassador pressed the United States to recognize recent conquests and Japanese dominance in Asia. Secretary of State Hull replied that Japan must renounce the Tripartite Pact with Italy and Germany and withdraw from China before any summit talks could begin.

In October the militant General Hideki Tojo replaced the more moderate Prime Minister Konoye. With the war party firmly in control, the military began preparing surprise attacks on American positions in Guam, the Philippines, and Hawaii. One final round of diplomacy, then war.

For their part, American military leaders urged Roosevelt to avoid conflict. The United States needed time to build up its national defenses. Massive Japanese troop movements southward indicated an assault on British and Dutch holdings. If the Japanese attacked American possessions, most expected the blow to fall on Guam or the Philippines. In late November American intelligence located, and then lost, a Japanese armada in Hitokappu Bay in Japan. Observing strict radio silence, the six carriers and their escorts steamed across the North Pacific toward the American base at Pearl Harbor in Hawaii. On Sunday morning, December 7, 1941, the first wave of Japanese planes roared down on the Pacific Fleet lying at anchor. For more than an hour the Japanese pounded the harbor and nearby airfields. Altogether 19 ships—the heart of the Pacific Fleet—were sunk or battered. Practically all of the 200 American aircraft were damaged or destroyed. Only the aircraft carriers, by chance on maneuvers, escaped the worst naval defeat in American history.

In Washington, Secretary of War Henry Stimson could not believe the news. "My God! This can't be true, this must mean the Philippines." Later that day the Japanese did attack the Philippines, along with Guam, Midway, and British forces in Hong Kong and the Malay peninsula. On December 8, Franklin Roosevelt told a stunned nation that "yesterday, December 7, 1941" was "a date which will live in infamy." America, the "reluctant belligerent," was in the war at last. Three days later Hitler declared war on the "half Judaized and the other half Negrified" people of the United States. Italy quickly followed suit.

counterpoint

Did Roosevelt Deliberately Invite War?

Had Roosevelt known the attack on Pearl Harbor was coming? Some critics have charged that the president deliberately contrived to bring war about. For months, American intelligence had been cracking some of Japan's secret codes. Much information indicated that Pearl Harbor was at risk. Yet Roosevelt left the fleet exposed, seeming almost to provoke an attack to bring the United States into the war. Was it mere coincidence that the vital aircraft carriers were at sea? That only the obsolete battleships were left at Pearl Harbor?

This argument, however, is based on circumstantial, not documentary, evidence. Roosevelt's defenders (and they include most historians) have countered that he wanted to fight Germany more than Japan. If he really had wished to provoke an incident leading to war, one in Atlantic waters would have served him far better. More important, the intelligence signals intercepted by American code-breakers were confusing. Analysts lost track of the Japanese fleet as it moved toward Hawaii. Secretary of War Stimson had good reason to be astonished when the fleet attacked Pearl Harbor.

In the end, it seems equally plausible to argue that cultural misperceptions explained the coming of war better than any conspiracy theory. American leaders were surprised by the attack on Pearl Harbor because they could not quite believe that the Japanese were daring or resourceful enough to attack an American stronghold some 4000 miles from Japan. Japanese militarists counted on a surprise attack to give them time to build a line of defense strong enough to discourage weak-willed Westerners from continuing the war. As it turned out, both calculations were wrong.

A Global War

Prime Minister Churchill greeted the news of Pearl Harbor with shock but, even more, elation. Great Britain would no longer stand alone in the North Atlantic and the Pacific wars. "We have won the war," he thought, and that night he slept "the sleep of the saved and thankful."

Japan's shocking triumph over U.S. forces united Americans in a way Roosevelt had not. And as Churchill recognized, only with the Americans fully committed to war could the Allies make full use of the enormous material and human resources of the United States. Still, the Allies needed to secure an alliance between the Anglo-American democracies and the Soviet Communist dictatorship. And they needed to find a strategy to win both the war and the peace to follow.

Strategies for War

Within two weeks, Churchill was in Washington, meeting with Roosevelt to coordinate production schedules for ships, planes, and armaments. The numbers they announced were so high that some critics openly laughed—at first. A year later combined British, Canadian, and American production boards not only met but exceeded the schedules.

Defeat Germany first

Roosevelt and Churchill also planned grand strategy. Outraged by the attack on Pearl Harbor, many Americans thought Japan should be the war's primary target. But the two leaders had always agreed that Germany posed the greater threat. The Pacific war, they decided, would be fought as a holding action, while the Allies concentrated on Europe. In a global war, in which arms and resources had to be allocated carefully, these long-range decisions would prove important. But in the short term, the Allies faced a daunting future indeed.

Gloomy Prospects

By summer's end in 1942 the Allies faced defeat. The Nazis were massed outside the Soviet Union's three major cities—Leningrad, Moscow, and Stalingrad. In North Africa General Erwin Rommel, the famed "Desert Fox," swept into Egypt with his Afrika Korps and stood within striking distance of the Suez Canal—a crucial link to the resources of the British empire. German U-boats in the North Atlantic threatened to break the ocean link between the United States and Britain. U-boat sailors called the first six months of 1942 "the American hunting season," as they sank 400 Allied ships in U.S. territorial waters. So deadly were these "Wolfpacks" that

U-boat war

The U-Boat War In the world's first truly global war, the need to coordinate and supply troops and matériel became paramount. But as German U-boats took a heavy toll on Allied shipping, it became difficult to deliver American supplies to Europe. Avoiding the North Atlantic route forced an arduous 12,000 mile journey around Africa to the Persian Gulf and then across Iran by land. The elimination of German submarines greatly eased the shipping problem and, as much as any single battle, ensured victory.

merchant sailors developed a grim humor about sleeping. Those on freighters carrying iron ore slept above decks, because the heavily laden ships could sink in less than a minute. On flammable oil tankers, however, sailors closed their doors, undressed, and slept soundly. If a torpedo hit, no one would survive.

Fall of the Philippines

In the Far East the Allies fared no better. Japanese forces had invaded the Philippines, British Malaya, and the Dutch East Indies. The supposedly impregnable British bastion of Singapore fell in just one week, and at the Battle of Java Sea, the Japanese navy destroyed almost the entire remaining Allied naval force in the western Pacific. In April 1942 General Douglas MacArthur, commander of American forces in the Philippines, fled to Australia. In what appeared to be an empty pledge, he vowed, "I shall return." Left behind with scant arms and food, American and Philippine troops on Bataan and Corregidor put up a heroic but doomed struggle. By summer no significant Allied forces stood between the Japanese and India or Australia.

The chain of spectacular victories disguised fatal weaknesses within the Axis alliance. Japan and Germany were fighting separate wars, each on two fronts. They never coordinated strategies. Vast armies in China and Russia drained them of both personnel and supplies. Brutal occupation policies made enemies of conquered populations. Axis armies had to use valuable forces to maintain control and move supplies. The Nazis were especially harsh. They launched a major campaign to exterminate Europe's Jews, Slavs, and Gypsies. Resistance movements grew as the victims of Axis aggression fought back. At the war's height 50 countries joined the Allies, who referred to themselves as the United Nations.

A Grand Alliance

Defeat at first obscured the Allies' strengths. Chief among these were the human resources of the Soviet Union and the industrial capacity of the United States. During World War II Americans would develop a global economy. Safe from the fighting, American farms and factories could produce enough food and war materials to supply two separate wars at once. By the end of the war American factories had turned out 300,000 airplanes, 87,000 ships, 400,000 artillery pieces, 102,000 tanks and self-propelled guns, and 47 million tons of ammunition.

The Big Three

The Allies benefited too from exceptional leadership. The "Big Three"—Joseph Stalin, Winston Churchill, and Franklin Roosevelt—all had shortcomings but were able to maintain a unity of purpose that eluded Axis leaders. All three understood the global nature of the war. To a remarkable degree they managed to set aside their differences in pursuit of a common goal—the defeat of Nazi Germany. The arch–anti-Communist Churchill pledged Britain's resources to assist the defense of the world's largest Communist state. The anti-imperialist Roosevelt poured American resources into the war effort of two of Europe's major imperial powers.

To be sure, each nation had its own needs. Russian forces faced 3.5 million Axis troops along a 1600-mile front in eastern Europe. To ease the pressure on those troops, Stalin repeatedly called on the Allies to open a second front in western Europe. So urgent were his demands that one Allied diplomat remarked that Stalin's foreign minister knew only four words in English: *yes, no,* and *second front.* But Churchill and Roosevelt felt compelled to turn Stalin down. In August 1942 the western Allies lacked the massive, well-trained force needed for a successful invasion of Europe. Churchill himself flew to Moscow to give Stalin the bad news: no second front in Europe until 1943. Postponed again until mid-1944, the second front became a source of festering Russian discontent.

Operation Torch

Yet after an initial surge of anger over the postponement, Stalin accepted Churchill's rationale for a substitute action. British and American forces would invade North Africa by the end of 1942. Code-named Operation Torch, the North African campaign could be mounted quickly. Equally important, it could bring British and American troops into direct combat with the Germans and stood an excellent chance of succeeding. Here was an example of how personal contact among the Big Three ensured Allied cooperation. The alliance sometimes bent but never broke.

The Naval War in the Pacific

Despite the Allied decision to concentrate on defeating Germany first, the earliest successes came in the Pacific. At the Battle of Coral Sea in May 1942 planes from the aircraft carriers *Yorktown* and *Lexington* stopped a large Japanese invading force headed for Port Moresby in New Guinea (see the map, page 884). For the first time in history two fleets fought without seeing each other. The age of naval aviation had arrived. The Japanese fleet actually inflicted greater damage but decided to turn back to nurse its wounds. Had they captured Port Moresby, the Japanese could have severed Allied shipping routes to Australia.

Midway

To extend Japan's defenses, Admiral Isoruku Yamamoto ordered the capture of Midway, a small island guarding the approach west of Hawaii. The Americans, in possession of decoded messages, knew the Japanese were coming. On June 3, as the Japanese main fleet bore down on Midway, a patrol plane from the American carrier task force spotted smoke from the ships. Aircraft from the carriers *Hornet*,

The Battle of Midway proved the importance of naval air power. The Japanese suffered major losses of aircraft carriers and pilots. Never again after Midway would the Japanese navy offer a major threat.

Enterprise, and *Yorktown* sank four enemy carriers, a cruiser, and three destroyers. The Japanese sunk only the *Yorktown.* More important, the Japanese lost many of their best carrier pilots, who were more difficult to replace than planes. The Battle of Midway broke Japanese naval supremacy in the Pacific and stalled Japan's offensive. In August 1942 American forces launched their first offensive—on the Solomon Islands, east of New Guinea. With the landing of American marines on the key island of Guadalcanal, the Allies started on the bloody road to Japan and victory.

Turning Points in Europe

By the fall of 1942 the Allies had their first successes in the European war. At El Alamein, 75 miles from the Suez Canal, British forces under General Bernard Montgomery broke through Rommel's lines. Weeks later, the Allies launched Operation Torch, the invasion of North Africa. Under the command of General Dwight D. Eisenhower, Allied forces swept eastward through Morocco and Algeria. They were halted in February 1943 at the Kasserine Pass in Tunisia, but General George S. Patton regrouped them and masterminded an impressive string of victories. By May 1943 Rommel had fled from North Africa, leaving behind 300,000 German troops.

Success in North Africa provided a stirring complement to the Russian stand at Stalingrad. From August 1942 until February 1943 Axis and Soviet armies pounded each other with more than a million troops. In one of the bloodiest engagements in history, each side suffered more casualties than the Americans did during the entire war. When it was over, the Germans had lost an army and their momentum. Stalin's

Stalingrad

forces went on the offensive, moving south and west through the Ukraine toward Poland and Romania. By the fall of 1942 the Allies had also gained the edge in the war for the Atlantic. Supplies moved easily after antisubmarine forces sank 785 out of the nearly 1200 U-boats the Germans built.

Those Who Fought

Mobilizing for war brought together Americans from all regions, social classes, and ethnic backgrounds. "The first time I ever heard a New England accent," recalled a midwesterner, "was at Fort Benning. The southerner was an exotic creature to me. The people from the farms. The New York street smarts." More than any other social institution the army acted as a melting pot. It also offered educational opportunities and job skills or suggested the need for them. "I could be a technical sergeant only I haven't had enough school," reported one Navajo soldier in a letter home to New Mexico. "Make my little brother go to school even if you have to lasso him."

In waging the world's first global war, the U.S. armed forces swept millions of Americans into new worlds and new experiences. When Pearl Harbor came, the army had 1.6 million men in uniform. By 1945 it had more than 7 million; the navy, 3.9 million; the army air corps, 2.3 million; and the marines, 600,000. Nineteen-year-olds who had never left home found themselves swept off to Europe or to the South Pacific. At basic training new recruits were subjected to forms of regimentation—the army haircut, foul-mouthed drill sergeants, and barracks life—they had seldom experienced in other areas of America's democratic culture.

In this war, as in most wars, the infantry bore the brunt of the fighting and dying. They suffered 90 percent of the battlefield casualties. In all, almost 400,000 Americans died and more than 600,000 were wounded. But service in the military did not mean constant combat. Most battles were reasonably short, followed by long periods of waiting and preparation. The army used almost 2 million soldiers just to move supplies. Yet even during the lull in battle, the soldiers' biggest enemy, disease, stalked them: malaria, dysentery, typhus, and even plague. In the Pacific theater, the thermometer sometimes rose to over 110 degrees Fahrenheit.

Wherever they fought, American soldiers usually lived in foxholes dug by hand with small shovels. Whenever possible they turned a hole in the ground into a home. "The American soldier is a born housewife," observed war correspondent Ernie Pyle. Between battles, movies were about the only entertainment many troops had. Each film was a tenuous link to a more comfortable world at home, a place American soldiers yearned for with special intensity. It was not a country or an idea for which they fought so much as a set of memories—a house, a car, Mom and Pop.

Many young GIs at first looked forward to going into battle. "I was going to gain my manhood," recalled one soldier. But combat soon hardened such troops. Donald Dickson's portrait of one such war-weary GI is titled *Too Many, Too Close, Too Long*.

Uneasy Recruits

African Americans at war

Minorities enlisted in unusually large numbers because the services offered training and opportunities unavailable in civilian life. Still, prejudice against African Americans and other minorities remained high. The army was strictly segregated and generally assigned black soldiers to noncombatant roles. The navy accepted them only as cooks and servants. At first the air corps and marines would not take them at all. The American Red Cross even kept "black" and "white" blood plasma separated, as if there were a difference. (Ironically, a black physician, Charles Drew, had invented the process allowing plasma to be stored.)

Despite the persistence of prejudice, more than a million black men and women served. As the war progressed, leaders of the black community pressured the military to ease segregation and allow black soldiers a more active role. The army did form some black combat units, usually led by white officers, as well as a black air corps unit. By mid-1942 black officers were being trained and graduated from integrated officer candidate schools at the rate of 200 a month. More than 80 black pilots won the Distinguished Flying Cross.

For both Mexican Americans and Asian Americans the war offered an opportunity to enter the American mainstream. Putting on a uniform was an essential act of citizenship. Mexican Americans had a higher enlistment rate than the population in general. A California congressional representative observed that "as I read the casualty list from my state, I find that anywhere from one-fourth to one-third of these names are names such as Gonzales and Sanchez." Chinese Americans served at the highest rate of all groups. As Harold Liu of New York's Chinatown recalled, "for the first time Chinese were accepted as being friends. . . . All of a sudden we became part of an American dream." Korean Americans were especially valuable in the Pacific theater because many could translate Japanese.

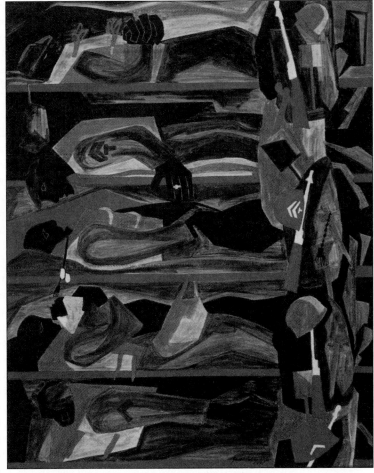

In *Shipping Out,* black artist Jacob Lawrence commemorated black troops heading overseas in the crowded confines of a troop ship. African Americans in segregated units served more often in service roles than in combat. It was ironic that, in a war against Nazi racism, race remained a central issue among Americans. Lawrence was certainly aware of such ironies; the portrayal of soldiers crowded onto their bunks recalls eerily the packing of slave transport ships from earlier centuries.

Like other Asian Americans, Filipinos had a powerful reason to enlist. Service offered an opportunity to fight for the liberation of their homeland from Japanese invaders. And like other minorities, Filipino Americans realized that in fighting for freedom abroad they were fighting for freedom at home. A Filipino soldier commented that he was doing something he had never before been allowed to do: serve "as an equal with American boys." Such loyalty had its rewards. Filipinos who volunteered became citizens. The California Attorney General reinterpreted laws that had once prevented Filipinos from owning land. Now they could buy their own farms. Jobs opened in war factories. The status of Mexican Americans and other Asian Americans improved in similar ways. Minorities who served gained useful experience in dealing with the Anglo world. After the war, minority veterans would provide new leadership in their communities.

Homosexuals who wished to join the military faced a dilemma. Few Americans of the day had any knowledge of the gays in their midst, and fewer had much tolerance for homosexuality. Still, many gays risked exposure. Charles Rowland, from Arizona, recalled that he and other gay friends "were not about to be deprived the privilege of serving our country in a time of great national emergency by virtue of some stupid regulation about being gay." Homosexuals who did pass the screening

Choices for homosexuals

test found themselves in gender-segregated bases, where life in an overwhelmingly male or female environment allowed many, for the first time in their lives, to meet like-minded gay men and women. Like other servicemen and -women, they served in a host of different roles, fighting and dying on the battlefield or doing the unglamorous jobs that kept the army going.

Women at War

World War II brought an end to the military as an exclusive male enclave that women entered only as nurses. During the prewar mobilization, Eleanor Roosevelt and other female leaders had campaigned for a regular military organization for women. The War Department came up with a compromise that allowed women to join the Women's Army Auxiliary Corps (WAAC), but only with inferior status and lower pay. By 1943 the "Auxiliary" had dropped out of the title: WAACs became WACs, with full army status, equal ranks, and equal pay. (The navy had a similar force called the WAVEs.)

WACs

Women could look with a mixture of pride and resentment on their wartime military service. Thousands served close to the battlefields, working as technicians, mechanics, radio operators, postal clerks, and secretaries. Although filling a vital need, these jobs were largely traditional female ones that implied a separate and inferior status. Until 1944 women were prevented by law from serving in war zones, even as noncombatants. There were female pilots, but they were restricted to shuttling planes behind the lines. At many posts WAVEs and WACs lived behind barbed wire and could move about only in groups under armed escort.

War Production

When Pearl Harbor brought the United States into the war, Thomas Chinn sold his publishing business and devoted himself full time to war work. Like many other Chinese Americans, he was working for the first time outside Chinatown. He served as a supervisor in the Army Quartermaster Market Center, which was responsible for supplying the armed forces with fresh food as it was harvested across California. Chinn found himself coordinating a host of cold storage warehouses all the way from the Oregon border as far south as Fresno. "At times," he recalled, "in order to catch seasonal goods such as fresh vegetables, as many as 200 or 300 railroad cars would be shuttling in and out" of the warehouses.

Food production and distribution was only one of many areas that demanded attention from the government. After Pearl Harbor, steel, aluminum, and electric power were all in short supply, creating bottlenecks in production lines. Roosevelt recognized the need for more direct government control of the economy.

Although the conversion from peace to war came slowly at first, the president used a mix of compulsory and voluntary programs to control inflation and guarantee an ever-increasing supply of food, munitions, and equipment. In the end the United States worked a miracle of production that proved every bit as important to victory as any battle fought overseas. From 1939 to 1945 the gross national product grew from $91 billion to $166 billion. (In World War I it had not changed significantly.) So successful was war production that civilians suffered little deprivation.

Finding an Industrial Czar

Roosevelt's first attempt at coordinating the production effort was to set up a War Production Board (WPB) under the direction of former Sears, Roebuck president Donald M. Nelson. On paper, Nelson's powers were impressive. The WPB had authority to allocate resources and organize factories in whatever way promoted national defense. In one of its first acts, the WPB ordered an end to all civilian car and truck production. The American people would have no new cars until the war ended.

In practice, Nelson was scarcely the dictator the economy needed. Other federal agencies with their own czars controlled petroleum, rubber, and labor resources, while military agencies continued their own procurement. To end the bottlenecks once and for all, the president in 1943 installed Supreme Court Justice James F. Byrnes as director of the new Office of War Mobilization (OWM). A canny political facilitator, Byrnes became the dictator the economy needed. His authority was so great and his access to Roosevelt so direct that he became known as the "assistant president." By assuming control over vital materials such as steel, aluminum, and copper, OWM was able to allocate them more systematically. The bottlenecks disappeared. Such centralized planning helped ease the conversion to war production of industries both large and small. While the "Big Three" automakers—Ford, General Motors, and Chrysler—generated some 20 percent of all war goods, small business also played a vital role. A manufacturer of model trains, for example, made bomb fuses.

When war cut off the United States from its rubber supply in Malaysia, old tires were recycled to help meet the shortage. Most Americans were unable to replace their car tires during the four years the United States was at war. The manufacturers of synthetic rubber eventually eased the crisis.

The career of Henry J. Kaiser, a California industrialist, illustrates how the war inspired creative financing and management. Kaiser sent his lobbyists to Washington, where they rustled up generous government loans for building factories. And because Kaiser needed steel to build new factories, they found ways around wartime restrictions. To attract workers to his new West Coast shipyards, Kaiser offered high wages and benefits, including day care for the children of working mothers. His innovative application of assembly line techniques reduced the time required to build cargo vessels, known as Liberty ships, from almost a year to only 56 days. His yards finished one in a record 14 days. Speed had its price: one Liberty ship actually split in half at its launching. Despite such occasional missteps, Kaiser built ships in the quantity the war effort demanded.

The aircraft industry also transformed the industrial landscape of the West Coast. When production of aircraft factories peaked in 1944, the industry had 2.1 million workers. Most of the new factories were located around Los Angeles, San Diego, and Seattle, where large labor pools, temperate climates, and available land made the locations attractive. The demand for workers opened opportunities for many Asian workers who had been limited to jobs within their own ethnic communities. In Los Angeles about 300 laundry workers closed their shops so that they could work on the construction of the ship *China Victory*. By 1943, 15 percent of all shipyard workers around San Francisco Bay were Chinese.

West Coast war industries

The military relied on large, established firms in part because they had more experience producing in large volume. At the same time lucrative war contracts helped big corporations increase their dominance over the economy. Workers in companies with more than 10,000 employees amounted to just 13 percent of the workforce in 1939; by 1944 they made up more than 30 percent. In agriculture a similar move toward bigness occurred. The number of people working on farms dropped by a fifth, yet productivity increased 30 percent as small farms were consolidated into larger ones. Large commercial farming by corporations rather than individuals (later called "agribusiness") came to dominate agriculture.

Productivity increased for a less tangible but equally important reason: pride in work done for a common cause. Civilians volunteered for civil defense, hospitals, and countless scrap drives. Children became "Uncle Sam's Scrappers" and "Tin-Can Colonels" as they scoured vacant lots for valuable trash. One 13-year-old in Maywood, Illinois, collected more than 100 tons of paper between Pearl Harbor and D-Day. Backyard "victory" gardens added 8 million tons of food to the harvest in 1943; car pooling conserved millions of tires. As citizens put off buying new consumer goods, they helped limit inflation. Morale ran high because people believed that every contribution, no matter how small, helped defeat the Axis.

Science Goes to War

The striking success of aircraft against ships at Coral Sea and Midway demonstrated how science and technology changed the way war was fought. The air war in Europe spurred the development of a new generation of fighter planes and long-range bombers. To combat enemy bombers and submarines, English and American scientists rushed to perfect electronic detection devices such as radar and sonar.

Without sonar the Allies might never have won the submarine war in the North Atlantic. At the same time, improved American submarines crippled Japanese shipping in the western Pacific. By 1944 the home islands faced serious shortages of vital raw materials. Above the water, the newly developed techniques of radar-controlled naval and antiaircraft gunnery gave American ships a decided edge in crucial sea battles. It became possible to hit targets obscured by darkness, fog, or smoke. One of the most critical technical advances was also one of the best kept secrets of the war, the proximity fuse. By placing a small radio device in a warhead, scientists created a shell that did not need to hit a target to destroy it. Proximity fuses accounted for the success of American antiaircraft guns against Japanese planes and German V-1 bombs.

The Manhattan Project required complex facilities to produce small amounts of nuclear materials for the first atom bombs. This plant at Oak Ridge, Tennessee, took advantage of abundant electricity from the Tennessee Valley Authority as well as the expertise of scientists from universities and private industry.

Scientific advances saved lives as well as destroyed them. Insecticides, pesticides, and drugs limited the spread of infectious diseases like malaria and syphilis. Penicillin had its first widespread use in World War II. The health of the nation actually improved during the war. Life expectancy rose by three years overall and by five years for African Americans. Infant mortality was cut by more than a third, and in 1942 the nation recorded its lowest death rate in history. Still, such discoveries sometimes had unforeseen consequences. Although the pesticide DDT helped control malaria and other insect-borne diseases, its harmful effects on the environment became clear only years later.

Science made its most dramatic advances in atomic research. In 1938 German scientists discovered the process of fission, in which atoms of uranium-235 were split, releasing an enormous amount of energy. Leading European physicists who had come to America to escape the Nazis understood all too well the military potential of the German discovery. In 1939 Enrico Fermi, Albert Einstein, and Leo Szilard warned President Roosevelt "that extremely powerful bombs of a new type may thus be constructed."

Roosevelt initiated what soon became the largest research and development effort in history, code-named the Manhattan Project. More than 100,000 scientists, engineers, technicians, and support workers from the United States, Canada, and England worked at 37 installations across the country to build an atomic bomb. The key to success was not so much secret discoveries but money (the project cost $2 billion) and industrial, scientific, and technical resources to produce nuclear fuels and a bomb design. Yet even with increased funding, scientists feared they might not win the race to produce an atomic bomb.

The Manhattan Project

War Work and Prosperity

War production revived prosperity, but not without stress. As late as 1940 unemployment stood at almost 7 million. By 1944, it had virtually disappeared. Jeff Davies, president of Hoboes of America, reported in 1942 that 2 million of his members were "off the road." In retirement communities like San Diego nearly 4 retirees in 10 returned to work. Employers, eager to overcome the labor shortage, welcomed disabled workers. The hearing impaired found jobs in deafening factories; dwarfs became aircraft inspectors because they could crawl inside wings and other cramped spaces. By the summer of 1943 nearly 3 million children aged 12 to 17 were working.

Roosevelt had to find some means to pay the war's enormous cost without undermining prosperity. His approach attempted to mix conservative and liberal elements. The Treasury Department tried to raise money voluntarily, by selling war bonds through advertising campaigns. To raise more funds, Secretary of the Treasury Henry Morgenthau also proposed a tax structure that was highly progressive—that is, it taxed higher income at a higher rate. Conservatives in Congress balked at sweeping tax reforms. After six months of wrangling, Congress passed a compromise, the Revenue Act of 1942, which levied a flat 5 percent tax on all annual incomes over $624. That provision struck hardest at low-income workers: in 1942 almost 50 million citizens paid taxes compared with 13 million the year before. The most innovative feature of the bill was a payroll deduction system. No longer would taxpayers have to set aside money to pay their total tax bill to the Internal Revenue Service at the end of the year.

Tax reform

Organized Labor

Wartime prosperity did not end the tug-of-war between business and labor. In 1941 alone more than 2 million workers walked off their jobs in protest. To end labor strife Roosevelt established the War Labor Board (WLB) in 1942. Like the similar agency Woodrow Wilson had created during World War I, the new WLB had authority to impose arbitration in any labor dispute. Its most far-reaching decision established a compromise between employers and unions that gave workers 15 days to leave the union after a contract was signed. Any worker who remained a member had to pay union dues for the life of the contract. That policy led to an almost 40 percent growth in union membership between 1941 and 1945, when a record 14.75 million workers held union cards.

Despite the efforts of the WLB, strikes did occur. Dissatisfied railroad workers tied up rail lines in a wildcat strike in 1943. General George C. Marshall cursed it as the "damnedest crime ever committed against America." To break the impasse, the government seized the railroads and then granted wage increases. That same year the pugnacious John L. Lewis allowed his United Mine Workers to go on strike. "The coal miners of America are hungry," he charged. "They are ill-fed and undernourished." Roosevelt seized the mines and ran them for a time; he even considered arresting union leaders and drafting striking miners. But as Secretary of the Interior Harold Ickes noted, a "jailed miner produces no more coal than a striking miner." In the end the government negotiated a settlement that gave miners substantial new benefits.

Most Americans were unwilling to forgive Lewis or his miners. A huge coal shortage along the East Coast had left homes dark and cold. "John L. Lewis—Damn your coal black soul," wrote the military newspaper *Stars and Stripes.* In reaction, Congress easily passed the Smith-Connolly Act of 1943. It gave the president more authority to seize vital war plants shut by strikes and required union leaders to observe a 30-day "cooling-off" period before striking. Roosevelt vetoed the bill, only to be overridden in both houses.

John L. Lewis

Despite these incidents, workers remained dedicated to the war effort. Stoppages actually accounted for only about one-tenth of one percent of total work time during the war. When workers did strike, it was usually in defiance of their union leadership, and they left their jobs for just a few days.

Women Workers

The demands of war placed a double demand for labor: not only soldiers to fight but workers to increase production. With as many as 12 million men in uniform, women (especially married women) became the nation's largest untapped source of labor. During the high-unemployment years of the Depression, both government and business had discouraged women from competing with men for jobs. With the onset of war, magazines and government bulletins suddenly began trumpeting "the vast resource of womanpower." The percentage of female workers grew from around a quarter in 1940 to more than a third by 1945. These women were no longer mostly young and single, as female workers of the past had been. A majority were either married or between 55 and 64 years old. Patriotism alone could not explain their willingness to leave families and homes for the factories.

Many women preferred the relative freedom of work and wages to the confines of home. With husbands off at war, millions of women needed additional income and had more free time. Black women in particular realized dramatic gains. Once concentrated in low-paying domestic and farm jobs with erratic hours and tedious labor, some 300,000 rushed into factories that offered higher pay and more regular hours. Given the chance to learn skills like welding, aircraft assembly, and electronics, women shattered many stereotypes about their capabilities. The diary of a ship welder in Oregon recorded both amazement and pride at what she accomplished:

> I, who hates heights, climbed stair after stair after stair till I thought I must be close to the sun. I stopped on the [tanker's] top deck. I, who hate confined spaces, went through narrow corridors, stumbling my way over rubber-coated leads. . . . I welded in the poop deck lying on the floor while another welder spattered sparks from the ceiling and chippers like giant woodpeckers shattered our eardrums. . . . I did overhead welding, horizontal, flat, vertical. . . . I made some good welds and some frightful ones. But now a door in the poop deck of an oil tanker is hanging, four feet by six of solid steel, by my welds. Pretty exciting!

Between 1940 and 1945 the female labor force increased more than 50 percent. Many women performed jobs once restricted exclusively to males. Lionized with nicknames such as "Rosie the Riveter," women such as this airplane factory worker dispelled stereotypes about the work women were able to do.

Although the demand for labor improved the economic status of women, it did not alter conventional views about gender roles. Most Americans assumed that when the war ended veterans would pick up their old jobs and women would return to the home. Surveys showed that the vast majority of Americans, whether male or female, continued to believe that child rearing was a woman's primary responsibility. The birthrate, which had fallen during the Depression, began to rise in 1943 as prosperity returned. And other traditional barriers continued to limit women's opportunities, even in wartime. Most professions admitted few women into graduate programs or other career paths. As women flooded into government bureaucracies, factory production lines, and corporate offices, few became managers. Supervision remained men's work.

The social stresses of wartime placed additional pressures on women. Alcohol abuse, teenage prostitution, divorce, and juvenile delinquency all were on the rise. Some observers blamed such trends on working mothers, who were said to neglect their families. In fact, studies showed that the families of mothers who stayed home fared no better than did those where mothers held outside jobs. The real problem lay with the extraordinary mobility created by the war. Crowded into new communities with inadequate schools and recreational facilities, young people had few outlets for their energies. Rather than build new recreational facilities, concerned public agencies were just as likely to recommend rules restricting mothers from work. Only labor shortages prevented the acceptance of such rules. The war inspired a change in economic roles for women without fomenting a revolution in attitudes about gender. That would come later.

Mobility

The war not only changed who worked and how much people earned, but also where they worked. Vine Deloria Jr., an Indian, recalled many years later that "the war dispersed the reservation people as nothing ever had. Every day, it seemed, we would be bidding farewell to families as they headed west to work in the defense plants on the coast." African Americans left the South in such large numbers that cotton growers began to buy mechanical harvesters to replace their labor. So many hill people traveled back and forth between Kentucky and Detroit, they called the bus the "Paducah Express." The Census Bureau discovered that between Pearl Harbor in 1941 and March 1945 at least 15.3 million people had changed their county of residence. That number did not include most of the men and women in the military.

Global Labor Migrations

Labor migration affected all regions and all groups of people, not only in the United States but around the world. In Europe and Asia much of this movement was necessitated by the tide of battle. After the Japanese conquered the Chinese capital at Beijing and the new capital in Nanking, Chinese leader Chiang Kai-shek moved his government a thousand miles inland to Chungking. The combination of war and civil war uprooted the Chinese on such a vast scale that numbers became almost meaningless. One historian estimated a refugee population as high as 50 million. In the face of the German invasion, the Soviet Union moved much of its heavy industry from western Russia and the Ukraine east behind the Ural Mountains. There it was safe from both the German army and the *Luftwaffe's* bombers.

War economies in Europe and Asia had voracious appetites for labor. By using conquered people to produce for the war, Japan and Germany freed their own people for military service. Both countries violated international law by forcing military prisoners and captured civilians into virtual slave labor. By war's end the Nazis had brought as many as 10 million foreign workers into German industries. Japan had no plan to eliminate or enslave whole categories of people as the Germans had for Jews and Slavs. Indeed, Japan made an effort to co-opt conquered people into voluntary service. In the Dutch East Indies, the Japanese so skillfully exploited anti-Dutch sentiment that most Javanese willingly supported the Japanese war effort. Japan eased its domestic labor shortages by bringing in hundreds of thousands of Koreans. Of these, some 100,000 were so-called comfort women who were impressed into sexual service during the war. In ways both voluntary and coercive, war economies uprooted people around the globe.

A Question of Rights

Franklin Roosevelt had been a government official during World War I. Now, presiding over a bigger world war, he was determined to avoid many of the patriotic excesses he had witnessed then: mobs menacing immigrants, the patriotic appeals to spy on neighbors, the raids on pacifist radicals. Even so, the conflicts arising over race, ethnic background, and class differences could not simply be ignored. In a society in which immigration laws discriminated against Asians by race, the war with Japan made life difficult for loyal Asian Americans of all backgrounds. Black and Hispanic workers faced as much discrimination in shipyards and airplane factories as they had in peacetime industries.

Little Italy

Aliens from enemy countries fared far better in World War II than in World War I. When the war began, about 600,000 Italian aliens and 5 million Italian Americans lived in the United States. Most still resided in Italian neighborhoods centered around churches, fraternal organizations, and clubs. Some had been proud of Mussolini and supported *Fascismo*. "Mussolini was a hero," recalled one Italian American. "A superhero. He made us feel special." Those attitudes changed abruptly after Pearl Harbor. During the war, Italian Americans pledged their loyalties to the United States.

At first the government treated Italians without citizenship (along with Japanese and Germans) as "aliens of enemy nationality." They could not travel without permission, enter strategic areas, or possess shortwave radios, guns, or maps. By 1942 few Americans believed that German Americans or Italian Americans posed any kind of danger. Eager to keep the support of Italian voters in the 1942 congressional elections, Roosevelt chose Columbus Day 1942 to lift restrictions on Italian aliens. The segregation of Italian Americans ended. Henceforth they would maintain their ethnic unity as a matter of choice, not necessity.

Concentration Camps

Americans showed no such tolerance to the 127,000 Japanese living in the United States, whether they were aliens or citizens. Ironically, tensions were least high in Hawaii, where the war with Japan had begun. Local newspapers there expressed confidence in the loyalty of Japanese Americans, who in any case were crucial to Hawaii's economy. General Delos Emmons, the military governor of the islands, rebuffed pressures from Washington to evacuate as many as 20,000 "dangerous" Japanese. He branded a Justice Department report warning of widespread sabotage to be "so fantastic it hardly needs refuting."

On the mainland, Japanese Americans remained largely separated from the mainstream of American life. State laws and local custom threw up complex barriers to integration. In the western states, where they were concentrated around urban areas, most Japanese could not vote, own land, or live in decent neighborhoods. Approximately 47,000 Japanese aliens, known as "Issei," were ineligible for citizenship under American law. Only their children could become citizens. Despite such restrictions, some Japanese achieved success in small businesses like landscaping, while many others worked on or owned farms that supplied fruits and vegetables to growing cities.

Issei

West Coast politicians pressed the Roosevelt administration to evacuate the Japanese from their communities. It did not seem to matter that about 80,000 were American citizens, called "Nisei," and that no evidence indicated that they posed any threat. "A Jap's a Jap. . . ." commented General John De Witt, commander of West Coast defenses. "It makes no difference whether he is an American citizen or not." In response, the War Department in February 1942 drew up Executive Order 9066, which allowed the exclusion of any person from designated military areas. Under De Witt's authority, the order was applied only on the West Coast against Japanese Americans. By late February Roosevelt had agreed that both Issei and Nisei would be evacuated. But where would they go?

Nisei

The army began to ship the entire Japanese community to "assembly centers." Most Nisei incurred heavy financial losses as they sold property at far below market value. Their distress became a windfall for people who had long resented their

The bleak landscape of the internment camp at Manzanar, California, was typical of the sites to which the government sent Japanese Americans. In such a harsh environment the Japanese had no real opportunity to create productive farm communities, as government officials had promised.

economic competition. "We've been charged with wanting to get rid of the Japs for selfish reasons," admitted the Grower-Shipper Vegetable Association. "We might as well be honest. We do. It's a question of whether the white man lives on the Pacific Coast or the brown man." At the assembly centers—racetracks, fairgrounds, and similar temporary locations—the army had not prepared basic sanitation, comfort, or privacy. "We lived in a horse stable," remembered one young girl. "We filled our cheesecloth with straw—for our mattress." The authorities at least had the decency to keep families together.

Internment camps

Most Japanese were interned in 10 camps in remote areas of seven western states. Notions that the camps might become self-sufficient communities proved wishful thinking. Even resourceful farmers could not raise food in arid desert soil. No claim of humane intent could change the reality—these were concentration camps. Internees were held in wire-enclosed compounds by armed guards. Temporary tar-papered barracks housed families or small groups in single rooms. Each room had a few cots, some blankets, and a single light bulb. That was home.

Some Japanese within the camps protested. Especially offensive was a government loyalty questionnaire that asked Nisei citizens if they would be willing to serve in the armed forces. "What do they take us for? Saps?" asked Dunks Oshima, a camp prisoner. "First, they change my army status to 4-C [enemy alien] because of my ancestry, run me out of town, and now they want me to volunteer for a suicide squad so I could get killed for this damn democracy. That's going some, for sheer brass!" Yet thousands of Nisei did enlist, and many distinguished themselves in combat.

Korematsu and Hirabayashi

Other Japanese Americans challenged the government through the courts. Fred Korematsu in California and Gordon Hirabayashi in Washington State were arrested when they refused to report for relocation. "As an American citizen, I wanted to uphold the principles of the Constitution," recalled Hirabayashi. But the Supreme Court let stand military policies aimed specifically at Japanese Americans. The majority opinion stated that "residents having ethnic affiliations with an invading enemy may be a greater source of danger than those of different ancestry," even though the army had never demonstrated that any danger existed. And in *Korematsu v. United States* (1944), the Court upheld the government's relocation program as a wartime necessity. Three justices dissented, criticizing relocation as the "legalization of racism."

Concentration camps in America did not perpetuate the horror of Nazi death camps, but they were built on racism and fear. Worse, they violated the traditions of civil rights and liberties for which Americans believed they were fighting.

Minorities on the Job

Minority leaders saw the irony of fighting a war for freedom in a country in which civil rights were still limited. "A jim crow army cannot fight for a free world," the NAACP declared. Such ideas of racial justice had been the driving force in the life of A. Philip Randolph, long an advocate of greater militancy. Randolph had demonstrated his gifts as an organizer and leader of the Brotherhood of Sleeping Car Porters, the most powerful black labor organization. He was determined to break down the wall of discrimination that kept minority workers out of jobs in defense industries and segregated in government agencies, unions, and the armed forces. "The Administration leaders in Washington will never give the Negro justice," Randolph argued, "until they see masses—ten, twenty, fifty thousand Negroes on the White House lawn." In 1941 he began to organize a march on Washington.

A. Philip Randolph

President Roosevelt had the power to issue executive orders ending segregation in the government, defense industries, unions, and the armed forces, as Randolph demanded. It took the threat of the march to make him act. He issued Executive Order 8802 in June, which forbade discrimination by race in hiring either government or defense industry workers. To carry out the policy, the order established the Fair Employment Practices Commission (FEPC). In some ways creating the FEPC was the boldest step toward racial justice taken since Reconstruction. Even so, the new agency had only limited success in breaking down barriers against black and Hispanic Americans. It was one thing to ban discrimination, quite another to enforce that ban in a society still deeply divided by racial prejudice.

Fair Employment Practices Commission

Still, efforts by the FEPC did open industrial jobs in California's shipyards and aircraft factories, which had previously refused to hire Hispanic Americans. Thousands migrated from Texas, where job discrimination was most severe, to California, where war work created new opportunities. Labor shortages led the southwestern states to join with the Mexican government under the bracero program to recruit Mexican labor under specially arranged contracts. In Texas, by contrast, antagonism to braceros ran so deep that the Mexican government tried to prevent workers from going there. With support from labor unions, officials in the oil and mining industries routinely blocked Hispanics from training programs and job advancement. Not until late 1943 did the FEPC investigate the situation.

Bracero program

Black Americans experienced similar frustrations. More than half of all defense jobs were closed to minorities. In the aircraft industry, for example, which offered 100,000 skilled and high-paying jobs, blacks held about 200 janitorial positions. The federal agency charged with placing workers honored local "whites only" employment practices. Unions segregated black workers or excluded them entirely. One person wrote to the president with a telling complaint: "Hitler has not done anything to the colored people—it's people right here in the United States who are keeping us out of work and keeping us down."

Eventually the combination of labor shortages, pressure from black leaders, and initiatives from government agencies opened the door to more skilled jobs and higher pay. Beginning in 1943, the U.S. Employment Service rejected requests with racial stipulations. Faced with a dwindling labor pool, many employers finally opened their doors. By 1944 African Americans, who accounted for almost 10 percent of the population, held 8 percent of the jobs.

At War with Jim Crow

At the beginning of World War II three-quarters of the 12 million black Americans lived in the South. Hispanic Americans, whose population exceeded a million, were concentrated in a belt along the United States–Mexico border. When jobs for minorities opened in war centers, blacks and Hispanics became increasingly urban. In cities, too, they encountered deeply entrenched systems of segregation that denied them basic rights to decent housing, jobs, and political participation. Competition with whites for housing and the use of public facilities like parks, beaches, and transportation produced explosive racial tensions.

To ease crowding the government funded new housing. In Detroit, federal authorities had picked a site for minority housing along the edge of a Polish neighborhood. One such project, named in honor of the black abolitionist Sojourner Truth, included 200 units for black families. When the first of them tried to move in, they faced an angry mob of whites. Local officials had to send several hundred National Guardsmen to protect the newcomers from menacing Ku Klux Klan members. Tensions increased with the approaching hot summer, and riots broke out in June 1943, as white mobs beat up African Americans riding public trolleys or patronizing movie theaters, and black protesters looted white stores. Six thousand soldiers from nearby bases finally imposed a troubled calm, but not before the riot had claimed the lives of 24 black and 9 white residents. Although wartime labor shortages gradually improved the situation for African Americans in Detroit, local officials refused to accept responsibility. Instead, they blamed the NAACP and the "militant" Negro press for stirring up trouble.

Hispanics in southern California suffered similar indignities. By 1943 overt Anglo hostility had come to focus on the pachucos, or "zoot suiters." These young Hispanic men and boys had adopted the stylish fashions of Harlem hipsters: greased hair swept back into a ducktail; broad-shouldered, long-waisted suit coats; baggy pants, pegged at the ankles, polished off with a swashbuckling keychain. The Los Angeles city council passed an ordinance making it a crime even to wear a zoot suit. For most "zooters" this style was a modest form of rebellion; for a few it was a badge of criminal behavior; for some white servicemen it was a target for racism.

In June 1943 sailors from the local navy base invaded Hispanic neighborhoods in search of zooters who had allegedly attacked servicemen. The self-appointed vigilantes grabbed innocent victims, tore their clothes, cut their hair, and beat them. When Hispanics retaliated, the police arrested them, ignoring the actions of white sailors. Irresponsible newspaper coverage made matters worse. "ZOOTERS THREATEN L.A. POLICE" charged one Hearst paper. A citizens committee created at the urging of California Governor Earl Warren rejected Hearst's inflammatory accusations. Underlying Hispanic anger were the grim realities of filthy housing, unemployment, disease, and white racism, which all added up to a level of poverty that wartime prosperity eased but did not end.

Minority leaders acted on the legal as well as the political front. The Congress of Racial Equality (CORE), a nonviolent civil rights group inspired by the Indian

Detroit riots

Zoot suit riots

leader Mohandas K. Gandhi, used sit-ins and other peaceful tactics to desegregate some restaurants and movie theaters. In 1944 the Supreme Court outlawed the "all-white primary," an infamous device used by southerners to exclude blacks from voting in primary elections within the Democratic party. Because Democratic candidates in the South often ran unopposed in the general elections, the primary elections were usually the only true political contests. In *Smith v. Allwright* the Court ruled that since political parties were integral parts of public elections, they could not deny minorities the right to vote in primaries. Thus the war sowed the seeds of future protest and reform. Asian, Hispanic, black, and Indian veterans would play leading roles in the postwar struggle for equality.

The New Deal in Retreat

After Pearl Harbor Roosevelt told reporters that "Dr. New Deal" had retired so that "Dr. Win-the-War" could get down to business. Political opposition, however, could not be eliminated even during a global conflict. The increasingly powerful anti–New Deal coalition of Republicans and rural Democrats saw in the war an opportunity to attack programs they had long resented. The president, for his part, never lost sight of the election returns. When war came, New Deal foes moved quickly. They ended the Civilian Conservation Corps, the National Youth Administration, and the largely ineffective National Resources Planning Board. They reduced the powers of the Farm Security Administration and blocked moves to extend social security and unemployment benefits. Seeming to approve such measures, voters in the 1942 elections sent an additional 44 Republicans to the House and another 9 to the Senate. The GOP began eyeing the White House.

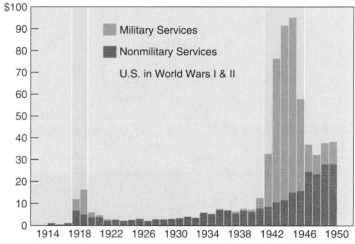

The Impact of World War II on Government Spending This chart shows that World War II more than the New Deal spurred government spending, even on nonmilitary sectors. Note that after both world wars, nonmilitary spending was higher than in the prewar years.

Roosevelt wins a fourth term

By the spring of 1944 no one knew whether Franklin Roosevelt would seek an unprecedented fourth term. The president's health had declined noticeably. Pallid skin, sagging shoulders, and shaking hands seemed open signs that he had aged too much to run. In July, one week before the Democratic convention, Roosevelt announced his decision: "All that is within me cries out to go back to my home on the Hudson River. . . . But as a good soldier . . . I will accept and serve." Conservative Democrats, however, made sure that Roosevelt's liberal vice president, Henry Wallace, would not remain on the ticket. In his place they settled on Harry S Truman of Missouri, a loyal New Dealer and party stalwart. The Republicans chose the moderate governor of New York, Thomas E. Dewey, to run against Roosevelt, but Dewey never had much of a chance. Reports of victory in Europe and the Pacific undermined his charges that Roosevelt had mismanaged the war. Always pragmatic, Roosevelt made his domestic policies more conservative as well.

At the polls, voters gave Roosevelt 25.6 million popular votes to Dewey's 22 million, a clear victory, although the election was tighter than any since 1916. Like its aging leader, the New Deal coalition was showing signs of strain.

Winning the War and the Peace

To impress upon newly arrived officers the vastness of the war theater in the Pacific, General Douglas MacArthur laid out a map of the region. Over it, he placed an outline map of the United States. Running the war from headquarters in Australia, MacArthur pointed out, the distances were about the same as if, in the Western Hemisphere, the center was located in South America. On the same scale, Tokyo would lie far up in northern Canada, Iwo Jima somewhere in Hudson Bay, Singapore in Utah, Manila in North Dakota, and Hawaii off the coast of Scotland.

In a war that stretched from one end of the globe to the other, the Allies had to coordinate their strategies on a grand scale. Which war theaters would receive equipment in short supply? Who would administer conquered territories? Inevitably, the questions of fighting a war slid into discussions of the peace that would follow. What would happen to occupied territories? How would the Axis powers be punished? If a more stable world order could not be created, the cycle of violence might never end. So as Allied armies struggled mile by mile to defeat the Axis, Allied diplomacy concentrated just as much on winning the peace.

The Fall of the Third Reich

After pushing the Germans out of North Africa in May 1943, Allied forces looked to drive Italy from the war. Late in July, two weeks after a quarter of a million British and American troops had landed on Sicily, Mussolini fled to German-held northern Italy. Although Italy surrendered early in September, Germany continued to pour in reinforcements. It took the Allies almost a year of bloody fighting to reach Rome, and

The Normandy landing involved complex problems of moving troops and matériel. The Rhino ferry allowed the landing forces to improvise docking facilities soon after the invasion forces landed. Sailors described these awkward craft as "ugly as hell, cranky as hell—but efficient as hell."

at the end of the campaign they had yet to break German lines. Along the eastern front, Soviet armies steadily pushed the Germans out of Russia and back toward Berlin.

General Dwight D. Eisenhower, fresh from battle in North Africa and the Mediterranean, took command of Allied preparations for Operation Overlord, a massive invasion of Europe striking from across the English Channel. By June 1944 all attention focused on the coast of France, for Hitler, of course, knew the Allies were preparing. He suspected they would hit Calais, the French port city closest to the British Isles. Allied planners did their best to encourage this belief, even deploying fake armaments across the Channel. On the morning of June 6, 1944, the invasion began—not at Calais but on the less fortified beaches of Normandy (see the map, page 859). Almost 3 million men, 11,000 aircraft, and more than 2000 vessels took part in D-Day.

D-Day

As Allied forces hit the beaches, luck and Eisenhower's meticulous planning favored their cause. Persuaded that the Allies still wanted Calais, Hitler delayed sending in two reserve divisions. His indecision allowed the Allied forces to secure a foothold. Over the next few days more than 1.5 million soldiers landed on the beaches—but they still had to move inland. Slowed by difficult conditions, the Allied advance from Normandy took almost two months, not several weeks as expected. Once Allied tanks broke through German lines their progress was spectacular. In August Paris was liberated, and by mid-September the Allies had driven the Germans from France and Belgium.

All went well until December 1944, when Hitler threw his reserves into a last, desperate gamble. The unexpected German onslaught drove the Allied lines back along a 50-mile bulge. There the Germans trapped the 101st Airborne Division. When asked to surrender, General Tony MacAuliffe sent back a one-word reply: "Nuts!" His troops held, General George Patton raced to the rescue, and the last German offensive collapsed. Little stood between the Allies and Berlin.

Two Roads to Tokyo

In the bleak days of 1942 General Douglas MacArthur—flamboyant and jaunty with his dark sunglasses and corncob pipe—had emerged as America's only military hero. MacArthur believed that the future of America lay in the Far East. The Pacific theater, not the European, should have top priority, he argued. In March 1943 the Combined Chiefs of Staff agreed to his plan for a westward advance along the northern coast of New Guinea toward the Philippines and Tokyo. Naval forces directed by Admiral Chester Nimitz used amphibious warfare to move up the island chains of the Central Pacific (see the map, page 884).

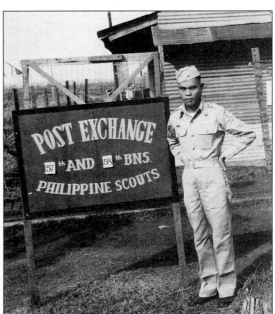

In the face of Japanese occupation, many Filipinos actively supported the American war effort. Valentine Untalan survived capture by the Japanese and went on to serve in the American army's elite Philippine Scouts. Like a growing number of Filipinos, he moved to the United States once the war was over.

By July 1944 the navy's leapfrogging campaign had reached the Marianas, east of the Philippines. From there B-29 bombers could reach the Japanese home islands. As a result, Admiral Nimitz proposed bypassing the Philippines in favor of a direct attack on Formosa (present-day Taiwan). MacArthur insisted instead on keeping his personal promise "to eighteen million Christian Filipinos that the Americans would return." President Roosevelt himself came to Hawaii to resolve the impasse, giving MacArthur the green light. Backed by more than 100 ships of the Pacific Fleet, the general splashed ashore on the island of Leyte in October 1944 to announce his return.

The Pacific Campaigns of World War II The extraordinary distances of the Pacific spurred the United States to devise a two-front strategy to defeat Japan. MacArthur's army forces used Australia as a base of operations, aiming for the Philippines and the southeast coast of China. Once those areas were secured, forces could then launch air attacks on Japan. The navy, under command of Admiral Nimitz, set out to destroy the Japanese fleet and to conduct a series of amphibious landings on island chains in the central Pacific. Meanwhile, British forces launched separate operations in Burma, forces under Chiang Kai-shek occasionally engaged Japanese forces on China's mainland, and in August 1945 Soviet troops attacked northern China.

Battle of Leyte Gulf

The decision to invade the Philippines led to savage fighting until the war ended. As retreating Japanese armies left Manila, they tortured and slaughtered tens of thousands of Filipino civilians. The United States suffered 62,000 casualties redeeming MacArthur's pledge to return. A spectacular U.S. Navy victory at the Battle of Leyte Gulf spelled the end of the Japanese Imperial Navy as a fighting force. MacArthur and Nimitz prepared to tighten the noose around Japan's home islands.

Big Three Diplomacy

While the Allies cooperated to gain military victories in both Europe and the Pacific, negotiations over the postwar peace proved knottier. Churchill believed that only a stable European balance of power, not an international agency, could preserve peace. In his view the Soviet Union was the greatest threat to upsetting that balance of power. Premier Joseph Stalin left no doubt that an expansive notion of Russian security defined his war aims. For future protection Stalin expected to annex the Baltic states, once Russian provinces, along with bits of Finland and Romania and about half of prewar Poland. In eastern Europe and other border areas such as Iran, Korea, and Turkey, he wanted "friendly" neighbors. It soon became apparent that "friendly" meant regimes dependent on Moscow.

Early on, Franklin Roosevelt had promoted his own version of an international balance of power, which he called the "Four Policemen." Under its framework, the Soviet Union, Great Britain, the United States, and China would guarantee peace through military cooperation. But by 1944 Roosevelt had rejected both this scheme and Churchill's wish to return to a balance of power that safely hemmed in the Russians. Instead, he looked to bring the Soviet Union into a peacekeeping system based on an international organization similar to the League of Nations. This time, Roosevelt intended that the United States, as well as all the great powers, would participate. Whether Churchill and Stalin—or the American people as a whole—would accept the idea was not yet clear.

The Road to Yalta

The outlines—and the problems—of a postwar settlement became clearer during several summit conferences among the Allied leaders. In November 1943, with Italy's surrender in hand and the war against Germany going well, Churchill and Roosevelt agreed to make a hazardous trip to Teheran, Iran. There, the Big Three leaders met **Teheran Conference** together for the first time and had a chance to take a personal measure of each other. ("Seems very confident," Roosevelt said of Stalin, "very sure of himself, moves slowly—altogether quite impressive.") The president tried to charm the Soviet premier, teasing Churchill for Stalin's benefit, keeping it up "until Stalin was laughing with me, and it was then that I called him 'Uncle Joe.'"

Teheran proved to be the high point of cooperation among the Big Three. It was there that Roosevelt and Churchill committed to the D-Day invasion Stalin had so long sought. In return he promised to launch a spring offensive to keep German troops occupied on the eastern front. He also reaffirmed his earlier pledge to declare war against Japan once Germany was beaten.

But thorny disagreements over the postwar peace had not been resolved. That was clear in February 1945, when the Big Three met one last time at the Russian resort city of Yalta, on the Black Sea. By then, Russian, British, and American troops **Yalta Conference** were closing in on Germany. Roosevelt arrived tired, ashen. At 62, limited by his paralysis, he had visibly aged. He came to Yalta mindful that although Germany was all but beaten, Japan still held out in the Pacific. Under no circumstances did he want Stalin to withdraw his promises to enter the fight against Japan and to join a postwar international organization. Churchill remained profoundly mistrustful of Soviet intentions. As Germany and Japan disintegrated, he saw power vacuums opening up in both Europe and Asia. These the Russians appeared only too eager to fill. Most diplomats in the American State Department and a growing number of military officers and politicians shared Churchill's fears.

Daily Lives

TIME AND TRAVEL

Air Power Shrinks the Globe

During World War I, the popular imagination thrilled to the stories of aerial dogfights and "flying aces." In reality, airplanes played only a secondary role in that war's military strategy. Short flying ranges and an inability to carry heavy loads limited what planes could do. Between the two wars, however, airframes grew stronger, engines more powerful, and payloads greater. Air-power strategists began to suggest that concerted waves of planes could attack industrial and military targets deep in enemy territory. Hitler grasped the strategic possibilities and insisted that Germany's air force as well as its army rearm and modernize.

During the blitzkriegs against Poland and France in the opening campaigns of the war, Hitler's air attacks terrorized civilian populations and disrupted enemy forces. Air Marshal Hermann Goering predicted that bombers from the German *Luftwaffe* would soon bring England to its knees. The Battle of Britain, fought during the winter of 1940–1941, signaled the start of the age of modern air warfare. For the first time in history, one nation tried to conquer another from the skies. Goering's boast failed as England continued doggedly to resist.

Despite the *Luftwaffe*'s failure, Allied air-power strategists believed heavy bombers could cripple Germany and Japan. The first test of such "strategic bombing" came in 1942, when more than 1100 planes of the British Royal Air Force (RAF) destroyed some 20,000 homes, 1500 stores and offices, and about 60 factories around Cologne, Germany. Horrific as that sounds, the attack did not level the city, as RAF planners had predicted. Indeed, later studies indicated that for all the damage done, Axis productivity actually increased until the last months of the war. Still, strategic bombing disrupted Japanese and German industry, brought the war home to the civilian population, and diverted enemy forces from the front to home defense.

Raids on Dresden and on Tokyo dramatized the horrors of the new technology. Dresden, a charming German city almost untouched by the twentieth century, had largely been ignored until February 1945. The RAF hit it first; then, with fires still raging, the American bombing wave struck. A huge inferno drew all the oxygen out of the center of the city, so that victims who did not burn suffocated. The city and its 60,000 people died. In March 340 American bombers hit Tokyo with incendiary bombs. The resulting firestorms, whipped by strong winds, leveled 16 square miles, destroyed 267,000 homes, left 83,000 dead, and injured 41,000.

The B-29 bombers gave the American air force much greater range, speed, and bomb loads. The *Enola Gay* (above), named after the pilot's mother, was modified to carry the first atom bomb dropped on Hiroshima.

Dispute over Poland

Allied differences were most clearly reflected in the disagreements over Poland. For Britain, Hitler's invasion of Poland had been the flashpoint for war. It was fighting, in part, to ensure that Poland survived as an independent nation. For Stalin, Poland was the historic corridor of invasion used by Russia's enemies. After Soviet troops reentered Poland, he insisted that he would recognize only the Communist-controlled government at Lublin. Stalin also demanded that Russia receive territory in eastern Poland, for which the Poles would be compensated with German lands. That was hardly the "self-determination" called for in the Atlantic Charter. Roosevelt proposed a compromise. For the time being, Poland would have a coalition government; after the war, free elections would settle the question of who should rule. The Soviets would also receive the territory they demanded in eastern Poland, and the western boundary would be established later.

The heat was so intense that the water in canals boiled.

To ensure the success of aerial warfare, aircraft designers on both sides raced to make their planes bigger and faster. The first English raids used the Wellington bomber, a plane 65 feet long with a wing span of 86 feet and a bomb load of 1500 pounds. By contrast, the American B-29s that bombed Hiroshima and Nagasaki carried up to 10 tons on a plane that was about 50 percent larger. The Wellington flew 255 miles an hour and cruised as high as 12,000 feet, with a range of 2200 miles, whereas the new B-29s could travel more than 350 miles an hour, at altitudes up to 30,000 feet, with a range of up to 5000 miles—more than double the Wellington's. German scientists took an even more radical step. To increase the speed and range of their weaponry they produced a new V-1 pilotless "buzz bomb" (named for the sound of its jet engine) and the V-2 rocket, the first true missile used as a weapon. Launched from bases in Europe, V-1s and V-2s easily reached targets in England. For all the terror they inspired, however, they were inaccurate and the Germans could not launch them in suffi- cient quantities to mount a decisive threat.

With the development of long-range air power, the "front line" of traditional war vanished. Every civilian became a potential combatant, every village a potential target in a total war. Although air power was not decisive in the war, the creation of longer-range aircraft with heavier payloads forced Americans to rethink their ties to the world. After World War I, Americans had rejected the League of Nations and involvement in the political affairs of Europe. Arthur Vandenberg, a Republican senator from Michigan, became one of the nation's most outspoken isolationists. That was before Pearl Harbor and before Vandenberg visited London during the war. As German V-1 and V-2 missiles brought terror from the skies, the senator came to believe that an isolationist policy no longer made sense. Physical distance would never again be a safeguard from attack, because air power had reshaped the strategic map of the world. The United States was now a matter of hours, not days, away from both friends and potential enemies.

Similarly, the Allies remained at odds about Germany's postwar future. Stalin was determined that the Germans would never invade Russia again. Many Americans shared his desire to have Germany punished and its war-making capacity eliminated. At the Teheran Conference, Roosevelt and Stalin had proposed that the Third Reich be drastically dismembered, split into five powerless parts. Churchill was much less eager to bring low the nation that was the most natural barrier to Russian expansion. The era after World War I, he believed, demonstrated that a healthy European economy required an industrialized Germany.

Again, the Big Three put off making a firm decision. For the time being, they agreed to divide Germany into separate occupation zones (France would receive a zone carved from British and American territory). These four powers would jointly occupy Berlin while an Allied Control Council supervised the national government.

Dividing Germany

When the Big Three turned their attention to the Far East, Stalin held a trump card. Roosevelt believed that only a bloody invasion of Japan itself could force a surrender. He thus secured from Stalin a pledge to enter the Pacific war within three months of Germany's defeat. His price was high. Stalin wanted to reclaim territories that Russia had lost in the Russo-Japanese War of 1904–1906, including islands north of Japan as well as control over the Chinese Eastern and South Manchurian railroads.

The agreements reached at Yalta depended on Stalin's willingness to cooperate. In public Roosevelt put the best face on matters. He argued that the new world organization (which Stalin had agreed to support) would "provide the greatest opportunity in all history" to secure a lasting peace. As if to lay to rest the isolationist sentiments that had destroyed Woodrow Wilson's dream, Roosevelt told Congress, "We shall take responsibility for world collaboration, or we shall have to bear the responsibility for another world conflict." Privately the president was less optimistic. He confessed to one friend that he doubted that, "when the chips were down, Stalin would be able to carry out and deliver what he had agreed to."

The Fallen Leader

The Yalta Conference marked one of the last and most controversial chapters of Franklin Roosevelt's presidency. Critics charged that the concessions to Stalin had been too generous and a threat to American national interests. Poland had been betrayed; China sold out; the United Nations crippled at birth. Yet Roosevelt gave to Stalin little that Stalin had not liberated with Russian blood and could have taken anyway. Even Churchill, an outspoken critic of Soviet ambitions, concluded that although "our hopeful assumptions were soon to be falsified . . . they were the only ones possible at the time."

What peace Roosevelt might have achieved can never be known. He returned from Yalta visibly ill. On April 12, 1945, while sitting for his portrait at his vacation home in Warm Springs, Georgia, he complained of a "terrific headache," then suddenly fell unconscious. Two hours later Roosevelt was dead, the victim of a cerebral hemorrhage. Not since the assassination of Lincoln had the nation so grieved. Under Roosevelt's leadership government had become a protector, the president a father and friend, and the United States the leader in the struggle against Axis tyranny. Eleanor recalled how many Americans later told her that "they missed the way the President used to talk to them. . . . There was a real dialogue between Franklin and the people."

Truman becomes president

Harry S Truman faced the awesome task of replacing Roosevelt. "Who the hell is Harry Truman?" the chief of staff had asked when Truman was nominated for the vice presidency in 1944. In the brief period he served as vice president, Truman had met with Roosevelt fewer than 10 times. He knew almost nothing about the president's postwar plans and promises. When a reporter now addressed him as "Mr. President," he winced. "I wish you didn't have to call me that," he said. Sensing his own inadequacies, Truman adopted a tough pose and made his mind up quickly. People welcomed the new president's decisiveness as a relief from Roosevelt's evasive style. Too often, though, Truman acted before the issues were clear. He at least knew victory in Europe was near as Allied troops swept into Germany.

The Holocaust

The horror of war in no way prepared the invading armies for the liberation of the concentration camps. Hitler, they discovered, had ordered the systematic extermination of all European Jews as well as Gypsies, homosexuals, and others considered deviant. The

In April 1945, at the concentration camp in Buchenwald, Germany, Senator Alben Barkley of Kentucky viewed a grisly reminder of the horrors of the Nazis' "final solution." As vice president under Harry Truman, Barkley urged the administration to support an independent homeland in Israel for Jews.

SS, Hitler's security force, had constructed six extermination centers in Poland. By rail from all over Europe the SS shipped Jews to die in the gas chambers.

No issue of World War II more starkly raised questions of human good and evil than what came to be known as the Holocaust. Tragically, the United States could have done more to save at least some of the 6 million Jews killed. Until the autumn of 1941 the Nazis permitted Jews to leave Europe, but few countries would accept them—including the United States. Americans haunted by unemployment feared that a tide of new immigrants would make competition for jobs even worse. Tales of persecution from war refugees had little effect on most citizens: opinion polls showed that more than 70 percent of Americans opposed easing quotas. After 1938 the restrictive provisions of the 1924 Immigration Act were made even tighter.

American Jews wanted to help, especially after 1942, when they learned of the death camps. But they worried that highly visible protests might only aggravate American anti-Semitism. They were also split over support for Zionists working to establish a Jewish homeland in Palestine. The British had blocked Jewish emigration to Palestine and, to avoid alienating the Arabs, opposed Zionism. Roosevelt and his advisers ultimately decided that the best way to save Jews was to win the war quickly, but that strategy still does not explain why the Allies did not do more. They could have bombed the rail lines to the camps, sent commando forces, or tried to destroy the death factories.

Anti-Semitism offers a partial answer. Assistant Secretary of State Breckinridge Long, the man responsible for immigration policy, personified a tradition of gentlemanly anti-Semitism. Polite on the surface but deeply bigoted, Long used his authority over visas to place obstacles in the way of desperate Jewish refugees. But

Influence of anti-Semitism

Long went too far when he blocked a plan that both Treasury Secretary Henry Morgenthau and the president had approved to ransom Jews in Romania and 6000 Jewish children in France. Morgenthau, the only Jewish member of Roosevelt's cabinet, had at first shown little interest in the debate over Palestine and the refugees. Long's actions so disturbed him, however, that he sent Roosevelt a report entitled "The Acquiescence of this Government in the Murder of the Jews." The president immediately stripped Long of his authority. He appointed a War Refugee Board charged with saving as many Jews as possible and promised to seek the establishment of a Jewish commonwealth in Palestine. But some 18 precious "long and heartbreaking" months had been lost and with them an untold number of lives.

A Lasting Peace

After 15 years of first depression and then war, the Allies sought a new international framework for cooperation among nations. That system, many believed, needed to **Bretton Woods economic** be economic as well as political. At a 1944 meeting at Bretton Woods, a resort in **strategies** New Hampshire, Americans led the way in creating two new economic organizations: the International Monetary Fund (IMF) and the International Bank for Reconstruction and Development, later known as the World Bank. The IMF hoped to promote trade by stabilizing national currencies, and the World Bank was designed to stimulate economic growth by investing in projects worldwide. Later that sum-**Dumbarton Oaks and** mer the Allies met at Dumbarton Oaks, a Washington estate, to lay out the struc-**the UNO** ture for the proposed United Nations Organization (UNO, later known simply as the UN). An 11-member Security Council would oversee a General Assembly composed of delegates from all member nations. By the end of the first organizational meeting, held in San Francisco in April 1945, it had become clear that the United Nations would favor the Western powers in most postwar disputes.

While the United Nations was organizing itself in San Francisco, the Axis powers were collapsing in Europe. As Mussolini attempted to escape to Germany, antifascist mobs in Italy captured and slaughtered him like a pig. Adolf Hitler committed suicide in his Berlin bunker on April 30. Two weeks later General Eisenhower accepted the German surrender.

Potsdam summit In one final summit meeting, held in July 1945 at Potsdam (just outside Berlin), President Truman met Churchill and Stalin for the first time. Two issues dominated the meeting: Germany's political fate and how much the defeated nation would pay in reparations. The three leaders agreed that Germany should be occupied and demilitarized. The British and Americans, however, did not want to burden a defeated Germany once again with excessive reparations. Stalin insisted that Russia receive a minimum of $10 billion, regardless of how much it might hurt postwar Germany or the European economy. A complicated compromise allowed Britain and the United States to restrict reparations from their zones. But in large part Stalin had his way. For the foreseeable future, Germany would remain divided into occupation zones and without a central government of its own.

Atom Diplomacy

The most crucial factor affecting postwar relations never even reached the bargaining table in Potsdam. On July 16, 1945, the first atomic fireball rose from the desert in Alamogordo, New Mexico. Scientists at the Manhattan Project had successfully detonated their first explosive device. Upon receiving the news, Truman seemed a changed man—firmer, more confident. He "told the Russians just where they got on and off and generally bossed the whole meeting," observed Churchill. Several questions loomed. Should the United States now use the bomb? Should it warn Japan before dropping it? And perhaps equally vital, should Truman inform Stalin?

A few scientists had recommended not using the bomb or at least attempting to convince Japan to surrender by offering a demonstration of the new weapon's power. A high-level committee of administrators, scientists, and political and military leaders dismissed that idea, though some later regretted they did so. Nor did Truman choose to tell Stalin about the bomb. He only mentioned obliquely that the United States possessed a weapon of "awesome destructiveness." Stalin, whose spies had already informed him of the bomb, showed no surprise. He only remarked casually that he hoped the Americans would use their new weapon to good effect against Japan. Atom diplomacy had failed its first test. Stalin immediately stepped up the Russian program to build an atom bomb. After Potsdam the nuclear arms race was on.

Should the bomb be dropped?

Finally, Truman and Churchill decided to drop the first bomb with only an implied warning to the Japanese. In an ultimatum issued at Potsdam, they demanded unconditional surrender and threatened Japan with "inevitable and complete destruction" using the "full application of our military power" if it did not comply. Unaware of the warning's full meaning, officials in Tokyo made no formal reply.

The bomb as a threat to the Soviets

Truman and Churchill knew Japan was on the verge of defeat. Japan's leaders had even sent peace feelers to the Russians. Why then did the Allies insist on unconditional surrender? Some historians have charged that Secretary of State James Byrnes, a staunch anticommunist, wanted a dramatic combat demonstration of the bomb that would serve to persuade Stalin to behave less aggressively in negotiations with the British and Americans. However much Byrnes had Soviet diplomacy on his mind, most evidence indicates that Truman decided to drop the bomb in order to end the war quickly.

Before leaving Potsdam, Truman ordered crews on Tinian Island in the South Pacific to proceed to their first target as soon as weather permitted. On August 6 the *Enola Gay,* a B-29 bomber, dropped a uranium bomb (given the name of "Little Boy") that leveled four square miles of Hiroshima, an industrial and military center. The blast immediately killed nearly 80,000 people (including 20 American prisoners of war). A German priest came upon soldiers who had looked up as the bomb exploded. Their eyeballs had melted from their sockets. Another eyewitness spoke of survivors "so broken and confused that they moved and behaved like automatons." Two days later the Soviet Union declared war on Japan, and on August 9 a second atom bomb (a plutonium weapon nicknamed "Fat Man") exploded over the port of Nagasaki. Another 60,000 people were killed instantly. In both cities many

This aerial view of Hiroshima gives stark testimony to the destructive force of the atomic blast. In one of the many bitter ironies, only the shells of the western-style buildings survived.

who lived through the horror began to sicken and die as radiation poisoning claimed tens of thousands of additional lives.

The two explosions left the Japanese stunned. Breaking all precedents, the emperor intervened and declared openly for peace. On September 3 a humiliated Japanese delegation boarded the battleship *Missouri* in Tokyo Bay and signed the document of surrender. World War II had ended.

"World War II changed everything," observed one admiral long after the war. The defeatism of the Depression gave way to the exhilaration of victory. Before the war Americans seldom exerted leadership in international affairs. After, the world looked to the United States to rebuild the economies of Europe and Asia and to maintain peace. World War II had not only shown the global interdependence of economic and political systems; it had also increased that interdependence. Out of the war developed a truly international economy. At home the trends toward bigness and centralization vastly accelerated. Advances in electronics, communications, and aviation brought the world closer to every home. Government grew, too. The size of the national debt alone guaranteed that Washington would continue to dominate the economy. Americans had come to believe in a strong defense, even if that meant a large federal bureaucracy and a generous military budget.

Still, a number of fears loomed, even as victory parades snaked down the nation's main streets. Would the inevitable cutbacks in spending bring on another depression? Would Soviet ambitions undo the new global peace, much as fascism and economic instability had undone the peace of Versailles? And then there was the shadow of the atom bomb looming over the victorious as well as the defeated. The United States might control atomic technology for the present, but what if the weapon fell into unfriendly hands? With the advent of the atomic age, no one in the world, not even in the United States, was safe anymore.

chapter summary

World War II deepened the global interdependence of nations and left the United States as the greatest economic and military power in the world.

- As fascism spread in Europe and as militarism spread in Asia, Franklin Roosevelt struggled to help America's allies by overcoming domestic political isolation and the fervor for neutrality.

- Despite German aggression against Poland in 1939, France and the Low Countries in 1940, and the Soviet Union in 1941, the United States did not enter the war until the Japanese surprise attack on Pearl Harbor in December 1941.

- The alliance forged among British Prime Minister Winston Churchill, Soviet Premier Joseph Stalin, and President Franklin Roosevelt did not swerve from its decision to subdue Germany first, even though early defeats and America's lack of preparation slowed the war effort until 1943.

- At home America's factories produced enough goods to supply the domestic economy and America's allies.

  - Demands for labor created opportunities for women and minorities.

  - War hysteria aggravated old prejudices and led to the internment of Japanese Americans.

  - New Deal reform ended as "Dr. Win-the-War" replaced "Dr. New Deal."

- Although the successful landings in France on D-Day and the island-hopping campaign in the Pacific made it clear that the Allies would win the war, issues over Poland, Germany, and postwar boundaries raised doubts about the peace.

- The war ended with the atomic bombings of Hiroshima and Nagasaki, but not soon enough to limit the horrors of the Holocaust.

Significant Events

1929 — 1929 Stock market crash signals onset of world-wide economic crisis

1930 —

1931 —

1931–1932 Japan invades Manchuria; Stimson Doctrine

1932 —

1933 — 1933 Roosevelt recognizes the Soviet Union

1935 Nye Committee hearings; first Neutrality Act

1934 — 1936 Second Neutrality Act

1937 Third Neutrality Act (cash-and-carry); Roosevelt's quarantine speech; *Panay* incident

1935 — 1938 Munich meeting; settlement of Mexican expropriation crisis

1939 Fall of Czechoslovakia; Germany signs nonaggression pact with the Soviet Union; World

1936 — War II begins in Europe

1940 Germany launches blitzkrieg against Low Countries and France; Roosevelt supports prepared-ness and peacetime draft; destroyers-for-bases

1937 — deal; Roosevelt wins third term

1941 Congress adopts Lend-Lease Act; A. Philip Randolph plans march on Washington; Roosevelt

1938 — creates Fair Employment Practices Commission; Germany invades Soviet Union; Roosevelt and Churchill sign Atlantic Charter; Japan occupies

1939 — Indochina; Roosevelt imposes embargo against Japan; Pearl Harbor attacked; Hilter and Mussolini declare war on the United States

1942 Declaration of the United Nations; War Pro-duction Board (WPB) and War Labor Board created;

1940 — submarine war in the Atlantic; internment of Japanese Americans; Bataan and Corregidor fall; battles of Guadalcanal, Coral Sea, and Midway

1941 — fought; American and British troops invade North Africa; Manhattan Project begins

1943 British-American forces invade Italy; Smith-Connolly Act; Office of War Mobilization replaces

1942 — WPB; race riot in Detroit; zoot suit riots; Big Three meet at Teheran

1944 War Refugee Board created; D-Day invasion of

1943 — France; U.S. forces return to Philippines; island-hopping campaign reaches Guam; Battle of the Bulge; Dumbarton Oaks and Bretton Woods

1944 — meetings; *Smith v. Allwright;* Roosevelt wins fourth term; Allies invade Germany

1945 Yalta Conference; Roosevelt dies; Truman

1945 — becomes president; Allied troops liberate extermination camps; first United Nations Organization meeting; Germany surrenders; Potsdam Conference; atom bombs dropped on Japan; World War II ends

additional reading

For the best brief description of prewar diplomacy and isolationism, see Robert Divine, *The Reluctant Belligerent* (2d ed., 1979). Robert Dallek, *Franklin D. Roosevelt and American Foreign Policy, 1933–1945* (1979) is more comprehensive and covers the war years. John Keegan concentrates on military strategy in *The Second World War* (1989). Studs Terkel, *The Good War: An Oral History of World War II* (1984) offers the wartime recollections of a variety of Americans. David Brinkley, *Washington Goes to War* (1988) is most readable and informative on the home front, but for a broader treatment see John Blum, *"V" Was for Victory* (1976) and Richard Polenberg, *War and Society: The United States, 1941–1945* (1972).

The American decision to drop two atomic bombs on Japan has proved one of the most controversial aspects of the war. Gar Alperovitz, *Atomic Diplomacy* (1965, rev. ed., 1986) was one of the first to challenge Truman's decision. Alperovitz argued that diplomatic leverage over the Soviet Union, not victory over Japan, determined the decision to drop the bomb. Alperovitz has updated those views with new research in *The Decision to Use the Bomb* (1995). For contrasting views, see Martin Sherwin, *A World Destroyed* (1973, rev. ed., 1985) and J. Samuel Walker, *Prompt and Utter Destruction: Truman and the Use of the Atomic Bomb Against Japan* (1997). The debate surfaced again in 1994 when the Smithsonian Museum mounted an exhibition commemorating the fiftieth anniversary of the bomb. For the controversy surrounding it, see Philip Nobile, ed., *Judgment at the Smithsonian* (1995). At the same time David Holloway, *Stalin and the Bomb: The Soviet Union and Atomic Energy, 1939–1956* (1994) uses Russian sources to help explain the role of atomic diplomacy in the cold war. Students who wish to examine the documents for themselves will find many collected in Michael B. Stoff et al., *The Manhattan Project: A Documentary Introduction to the Atomic Age* (New York, 1991). For a fuller list of readings, see the Bibliography.

AFTER THE FACT
Historians Reconstruct the Past

Did the Atomic Bomb Save Lives?

When news came that the United States had exploded a powerful new atomic device over Japan, it was hard for American troops in the Pacific to contain their joy. "We whooped and yelled like mad," recalled one veteran. "We downed all the beer we'd been stashing away. We shot bullets into the air and danced between the tent rows, because this meant maybe we were going to live."

Maybe we were going to live. The GIs in the field saw immediately that if the bomb ended the war, there would be no need for a massive invasion of Japan, similar to the D-Day invasion of Europe that had cost so many lives. As the lyrics of one popular song put it, "I believe the bomb that struck Hiroshima/was the answer to a fighting boy's prayers." After the war, Winston Churchill made the same point by calling the bomb "a miracle of deliverance." To conquer Japan "yard by yard might well require the loss of a million American lives," he told Congress. President Truman's memoirs put the totals somewhat lower: he referred to military estimates of over a million *casualties*, including half a million American deaths.

To most Americans, such large numbers made sense. Japanese resistance during the Pacific campaigns had been fierce. On the island of Okinawa alone, hand-to-hand fighting claimed over 12,000 American soldiers, sailors, and marines. American troops used flamethrowers to burn Japanese out of caves and holes. Rather than surrender, several thousand Japanese soldiers threw themselves off cliffs. In the half century following World War II, most historians assumed that dropping the bomb

saved the United States from mounting a bloody invasion of the Japanese home islands.

But how did Truman, Churchill, and other participants arrive at such casualty figures? The conclusion that the United States dropped the bomb to end the war quickly and to avoid 500,000 American deaths became one of the most controversial of World War II. The debate arose, in part, because of

the horror of nuclear weaponry. Critics have suggested that Japan might well have been persuaded to surrender without an atomic attack.

That debate—which began in earnest during the 1960s—has analyzed a host of factors affecting Truman's decision (see page 891). Many navy and air corps officers believed that a naval blockade and conventional bombing were enough to force Japan's surrender without an invasion. The country, after

made use of this newly gained power. If the test should
fail, then it would be even more important to us to bring
about a surrender before we had to make a physical conquest
of Japan. General Marshall told me that it might cost half
a million American lives to force the enemy's surrender on
his home grounds.

Harry S Truman
Memoirs, page 804
an estimate of
half a million
deaths

Harry S Truman, *Memoirs,* page 804: an estimate of half a million deaths. Reprinted by permission of Margaret Truman Daniel.

all, was virtually without defense against bombing raids. Later critics have suggested that the Allies should have modified their demand for "unconditional surrender," instead allowing the Japanese to keep their revered institution of the emperor. (As events turned out, Japan surrendered only after such a guarantee was issued.) Others argue that the United States should have arranged for a demonstration of the bomb's power without actually detonating one over Japan.

Yet as the debates over these alternatives swirled during the 1960s and 1970s, no one challenged the estimates of a million-casualty invasion. That number had been put forward in 1947 by Henry Stimson, the highly respected former secretary of war. In an article for *Harper's* magazine Stimson wrote, "We estimated the major fighting would not end until the latter part of 1946 at the earliest. I was informed that such operations might be expected to cost over a million casualties, to American forces alone."

Stimson's account cast a long shadow. A few years later Harry Truman provided an air force historian with a significantly lower number. Truman recalled that General George Marshall, the Army Chief of Staff, had told him in July 1945 that in an invasion of Japan 1/4 of a million casualties would be the cost as well as an equal number of Japanese. But when a White House aide checked Truman's memory against Stimson's account, he discovered the discrepancy—one million versus only 1/4 million. "The President's casualty figure [should] be changed to conform with that of Secretary Stimson," the aide advised, "because presumably Stimson got his from Gen. Marshall; the size of the casualty figures is very important."

The last phrase is significant. Why were the numbers so important? Obviously, the higher the po-

tential casualties, the stronger the case that using the bomb saved lives. So it is worth looking a bit closer at Stimson's article.

In fact, the idea to write an article was not actually Stimson's. It came from another atomic policy maker, James Conant. Conant, the president of Harvard University, had become increasingly concerned about "the spreading accusation that it was unnecessary to use the atomic bomb at all. . . . This type

Hiroshima, August 6, 1945

of sentimentalism," he complained privately in 1946, ". . . is bound to have a great deal of influence on the next generation. The type of person who goes into teaching, particularly school teaching, will be influenced a great deal by this type of argument." Conant believed that Stimson had the prestige to counter such criticisms. One of the nation's most distinguished public servants, he had been twice a secretary of war, an ambassador, and secretary of state.

Remains of a wristwatch from the atomic blast site at Hiroshima. The bomb exploded at 8:16 a.m.

So Stimson agreed to write an article. But where did he get his casualty estimates? During the war a memo from former President Herbert Hoover had been circulated, warning that an invasion could claim anywhere from half a million to a million American lives. At the time, in June 1945, a successful test of an atomic bomb was still a month away and the possibility of an invasion loomed larger. Stimson was convinced that the war might be ended without an invasion if the Allies would only assure the Japanese that the position of emperor would be protected. Hoover's dire warning about the costs of an invasion reinforced Stimson's argument against invading.

But contrary to the aide who later helped Truman with his memoirs, Stimson did not get similarly high casualty estimates from General Marshall. Marshall's staff thought Hoover's estimates were way too high. They estimated that the first-stage invasion (of Kyushu Island) might produce American casualties of perhaps 31,000, including about 7000 to 8000 deaths. If the invasion of Japan's main island, Honshu, took place, those numbers would rise to 120,000 casualties and 25,000 deaths. Estimates by General MacArthur were slightly higher, but within the same range. For reasons that remain unclear, however, when Stimson wrote his article after the war, he chose to use the higher estimates.

Thus, intentionally or not, Stimson's article greatly overestimated the number of invasion casualties predicted by the American military. And Conant's private worries show that those who dropped the bomb were more sensitive about their decision than they wished to admit. One of the most telling illustrations of the pressure to keep the estimates high can be seen in the successive drafts of Harry Truman's own memoirs, which were finally published in 1955. The assistants who helped Truman kept revising the figure upward. Truman's recollection, in 1952, mentioned only 250,000 casualties (not deaths); that figure jumped to 500,000 casualties in the first draft; then, in the published version, to a "half-million" *lives* saved.

Do the lower figures mean that historians should condemn Truman, Stimson, and others for preferring to use the bomb rather than invade Japan? Not necessarily. After Japan's surprise attack

Japanese fighting on Okinawa and other Pacific islands produced high casualty and death rates for American forces, reinforcing the notion that an invasion of Japan would claim many American lives.

The White House
Washington   Dec. 31, 1952

My dear Professor Cate:—
Your letter of Dec. 6th 1952 has
in........been delivered to

Earlier letter from Truman to an Air Force Historian

I asked Gen. Marshall what it
would cost in lives to land on
the Tokio plane and other places
in Japan. It was his opinion that
1/4 million casualties would be
the minimum cost as well
as an equal number of the enemy.

"1/4 million casualties"

Earlier letter from Truman to an air force historian

on Pearl Harbor and its fierce resistance in the Pacific islands, American sentiments against the Japanese ran high. The atomic bomb had cost $2 billion to develop, and officials always assumed that if the bomb were successful, it would be used. Why else develop it? Truman (and most Americans) probably believed that even an invasion costing 25,000 lives would have justified using the bomb.

Even so, historians must constantly remind themselves that seemingly "impartial" accounts are influenced by the conditions under which they were created. Stimson set out not simply to tell the facts about the decision to drop the bomb. He wished to justify a decision he believed was necessary and proper. Like Conant, he understood that the record of the past is always shaped by those who do the telling. "History," he wrote in 1948, "is often not what actually happened but what is recorded as such."

BIBLIOGRAPHY. Stimson's "The Decision to Use the Bomb" appears in the February 1947 issue of *Harper's* magazine. The debate over his casualty estimates and those of Truman and Churchill was launched by Barton J. Bernstein, "A Postwar Myth: 500,000 Lives Saved," *Bulletin of the Atomic Scientists* 42 (June/July 1986) and by Rufus Miles, "Hiroshima: The Strange Myth of Half a Million Lives Saved," *International Security* 10 (Fall 1985). Bernstein provides valuable background on Stimson's 1947 article in "Seizing the Contested Terrain of Nuclear History," *Diplomatic History,* 19 (Winter 1993). Also useful is John Ray Skates, *The Invasion of Japan: Alternative to the Bomb* (1994). The debate over the projected invasion, of course, is only one aspect of the larger question of whether atom bombs should have been dropped on Japan. For readings on that topic, see the Bibliography.

THE UNITED STATES IN A NUCLEAR AGE

At Los Alamos in July 1945, during the final feverish days of work on the first atom bomb, a few scientists calculated the possible unexpected effects of an atomic blast. The strategic bombings at Dresden and Tokyo showed how a firestorm, once started, sucked oxygen from the surrounding atmosphere, feeding upon itself and enlarging the inferno. No one had ever set off an atomic explosion, and some scientists worried that an even greater chain reaction might follow, one that would not only ignite the atmosphere around it but envelop the earth's atmosphere, leaving the planet in ashes. Members of the team checked and rechecked the calculations before deciding that those fears were unwarranted.

In the half century after Hiroshima, the atomic nightmare returned repeatedly to haunt the world. The threat appeared to be not from the detonation of a single bomb but from an all-too-human chain reaction in which escalating violence leads to atomic strike and counterstrike, followed by a decades-long radioactive "nuclear winter," from which intelligent life could never fully recover.

During the heady victory celebrations of 1945, the threat of nuclear annihilation seemed distant. Although President Truman and other American leaders had become increasingly distrustful of Stalin, the United States preserved a clear atomic monopoly. The dangers from radioactive fallout impressed only a handful of officials and even fewer members of the public, who were treated to cheery fantasies of the peacetime use of

atomics. One such whimsy, featured in the May 1947 *Collier's* magazine, showed a recovered paraplegic emerging from the mushroom cloud of his atomic treatment, his wheelchair almost miraculously left behind. By 1949, when fallout from Russian explosions indicated that the Soviet Union had gained the power of atomic weapons, the grim global realignment was already well established. Two superpowers, the Soviet Union and the United States, had replaced the players in the old balance of power that had defined European politics for two centuries.

The polarization of the globe into two camps, each dominated by a superpower, would have seemed strange even 20 years earlier. But in the long view, the result was not surprising. Since the sixteenth century, the expansion of European culture and power has been most significant along the continent's peripheries, both west and east. Along the west-facing rim, the Portuguese, Spanish, Dutch, French, and English reached beyond themselves for commercial and colonial empires. By the late nineteenth century England's colonial offshoot, the United States, was coming into its own even farther west. Over these same centuries of expansion, Europe's eastern flank saw Russian settlers pushing across the steppes of Eurasia, turning grasslands into cultivated fields. Farther north, Russian fur traders were bringing the forest and tundra of Siberia into the Russian orbit, just as French and English fur traders were mastering the forests of the Canadian shield.

GLOBAL EVENTS

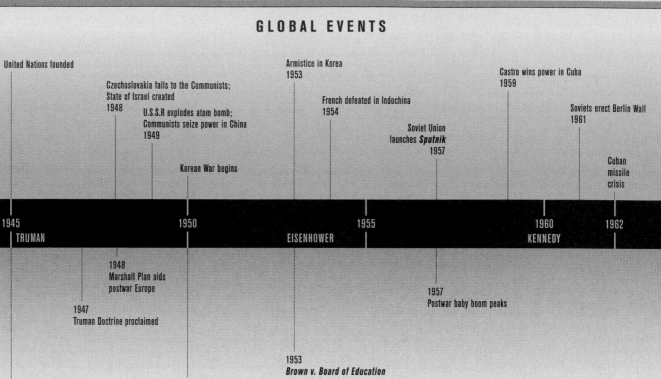

United Nations founded

Czechoslovakia falls to the Communists;
State of Israel created
1948

U.S.S.R explodes atom bomb;
Communists seize power in China
1949

Korean War begins

Armistice in Korea
1953

French defeated in Indochina
1954

Soviet Union
launches *Sputnik*
1957

Castro wins power in Cuba
1959

Soviets erect Berlin Wall
1961

Cuban
missile
crisis

| 1945 | 1950 | 1955 | 1960 | 1962 |

TRUMAN   EISENHOWER   KENNEDY

1948
Marshall Plan aids
postwar Europe

1947
Truman Doctrine proclaimed

1957
Postwar baby boom peaks

1953
Brown v. Board of Education

First atomic weapon detonated

McCarthy begins
anti-Communist campaign

AMERICAN EVENTS

In area and vastness of resources, the Soviet Union surpassed even the United States, its boundaries encompassing 12 time zones. Given the centuries-long tradition of authoritarian rule (*czar* is the Russian derivative of "caesar"), the Russian Revolution of 1917 took a firmly centralized approach to modernization. At sometimes frightful cost Stalin brought the Soviet Union to its position as superpower by the end of World War II. The peripheral powers of Europe—the United States and Russia—had become dominant. By the 1960s both relied on stockpiles of nuclear weapons to guarantee their security and power.

Deterrence—the knowledge of "mutual assured destruction"—would prevent either side from being the first to launch a missile at-

tack. So, at least, nuclear strategists suggested. Yet that strategy was frightening precisely because

the globe could not be cut neatly into communist and noncommunist halves, each with clearly unified interests. The world was riven

by ethnic, religious, and economic rivalries. When the prestige of either superpower became critically involved, such regional conflicts threatened to escalate into a full-scale nuclear war.

Both the Soviets and the Americans discovered the limits of projecting their power in regional conflicts. For more than a decade, the United States sought unsuccessfully to win a war against North Vietnam by conventional means before withdrawing in defeat. For another decade, the Soviet Union waged a similarly unsuccessful war in Afghanistan. In both cases, regional rivalries played a dominant role. In the Vietnam conflict, the Communist Ho Chi Minh was enough of a nationalist to prefer nearly any form of government, including French colonial rule, to

900

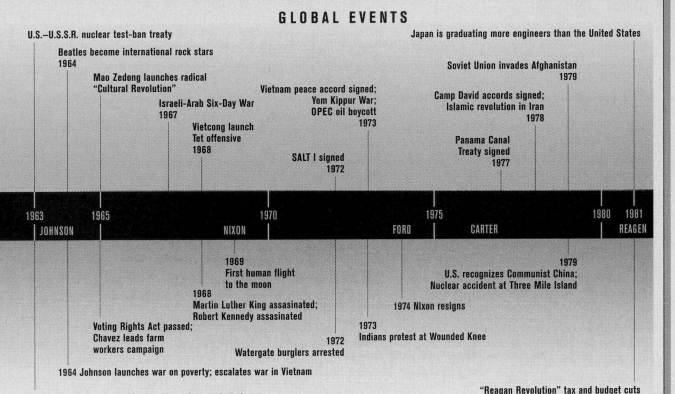

GLOBAL EVENTS

U.S.–U.S.S.R. nuclear test-ban treaty

Beatles become international rock stars
1964

Mao Zedong launches radical
"Cultural Revolution"

Israeli-Arab Six-Day War
1967

Vietcong launch
Tet offensive
1968

Vietnam peace accord signed;
Yom Kippur War;
OPEC oil boycott
1973

SALT I signed
1972

Japan is graduating more engineers than the United States

Soviet Union invades Afghanistan
1979

Camp David accords signed;
Islamic revolution in Iran
1978

Panama Canal
Treaty signed
1977

| 1963 | 1965 | 1970 | 1975 | 1980 | 1981 |
| JOHNSON | | NIXON | FORD | CARTER | REAGEN |

1969
First human flight
to the moon

1968
Martin Luther King assasinated;
Robert Kennedy assasinated

Voting Rights Act passed;
Chavez leads farm
workers campaign

1972
Watergate burglers arrested

1979
U.S. recognizes Communist China;
Nuclear accident at Three Mile Island

1974 Nixon resigns

1973
Indians protest at Wounded Knee

1964 Johnson launches war on poverty; escalates war in Vietnam

Civil rights march on Washington; Kennedy assasinated

"Reagan Revolution" tax and budget cuts

AMERICAN EVENTS

domination by Vietnam's traditional enemy, China. It did not matter that China was led by a Communist "comrade," Mao Zedong. During the war in Afghanistan, the Soviets discovered that their rebel opponents were inspired by their Islamic faith. The 1979 revolution in Iran brought the Ayatollah Khomeini to power and further demonstrated that Islamic fundamentalism would play a crucial role in the Middle East and the Saharan subcontinent. Those same religious divisions led increasingly to disputes within the Soviet Union, weakening its own empire.

In the midst of the ongoing cold war, Europe recovered from the devastation of World War II, thanks in part to aid from the United States. Over the next few decades, the peacetime economic expansion that benefited the Amer-

icans also allowed both West Germany and Japan, their former enemies, to grow into modern industrial states with robust consumer economies. That prosperity, in part, helped nurture a new generation of "baby boomers," in Europe as well as America, who became politically active during the 1960s. In Africa and Asia, old colonial regimes gave way to newly independent nations.

But the global industrial economy did not expand indefinitely. In America, the boom and development mentality of the 1950s and 1960s was tempered in the 1970s as the environmental costs of air and water pollutants, strip mining, pesticides, and a host of other abuses became obvious. Similarly, by the mid-1970s major Soviet rivers like the Ural, Volga, and Dnieper had been

polluted by industrial wastes. China, possessing coal reserves as great as those of the United States and the Soviet Union combined, had built so many coal-fired electrical plants that its northern cities were heavily polluted and damage from acid rain could be charted in neighboring regions.

By the end of the 1980s the natural limits of global growth and the strains of a nuclear standoff were becoming clear. The Soviet empire, perhaps the last of the old colonial powers, saw its Eastern European satellite nations break away. The Union of Soviet Socialist Republics itself split into a host of nations. Although some Americans cheered at having "won" the cold war, the U.S. economy was suffering from an immense budget deficit run up

GLOBAL EVENTS

Mikhail Gorbachev becomes
Soviet premier

Berlin Wall falls
1989

Gulf War in Kuwait and Iraq;
U.S.S.R. breaks up
1991

Fire at Chernobyl
nuclear reactor
1986

Outbreak of
conflict in Bosnia
1992

Financial downturn
in Asia
1997

1982   1985   1990   1995   2000

BUSH   CLINTON

1992
Riots in Los Angeles

1998
Federal budget
surplus

1986
Arms-for-hostages deal with Iran

1999
Senate acquits
Clinton of impeachment
charges

Gramm-Rudman Act passed

1991
Recession; lowest rate of job growth since World War II

AMERICAN EVENTS

in large part by military budgets aimed at checking Soviet power.

In the emerging multipolar world of the 1990s, the process of industrialization had created a truly global theater of markets, cultures, and politics. It also created such threats as a hole in the ozone layer and the possibility of a global warming trend. The United States, no longer such a dominant economic power, looked to rebuild its decayed public infrastructure, retrain displaced workers, and restore growth without further degrading the global environment. Half a millennium after the civilizations of two hemispheres achieved sustained contact, their ultimate fates have been indivisibly intertwined.

Chapter 27

7

Cold War America

preview • The roots of the cold war lay both in Stalin's aggressive posture toward Eastern Europe and in the mutual suspicions of the Americans and the Soviets toward each other's newfound power. President Truman evolved a policy of containment designed to hedge in the U.S.S.R., but even so, the cold war turned hot in Korea. At home an anticommunist crusade against suspected subversives subsided only after its reckless leader, Senator Joseph McCarthy, was censured.

he war had been over for almost five months and still troopships steamed into New York and other ports. Timuel Black was packing his duffel below decks when he heard some of the white soldiers shout, "There she is! The Statue of Liberty!" Black felt a little bitter about the war. He'd been drafted in Chicago in 1943, just after race riots ripped the city. His father, a strong supporter of civil rights, was angry. "What the hell are you goin' to fight in Europe for? The fight is here." He wanted his son to go with him to demonstrate in Detroit, except the roads were blocked and the buses and trains screened to prevent more African Americans from coming in.

Instead, Black went off to fight the Nazis, serving in a segregated army. He'd gone ashore during the D-Day invasion, survived the Battle of the Bulge, and marched through one of the German concentration camps. "The first thing you get is the stench," he recalled. "Everybody knows that's human stench. You begin to realize something terrible had happened. There's quietness. You get closer and you begin to see what's happened to these creatures. And you get—I got more passionately angry than I guess I'd ever been." He thought: if it could happen here, to the Germans, it could happen anywhere. It could happen to black folk in America. So when the white soldiers called to come up and see the Statue of Liberty, Black's reaction was, "Hell, I'm not goin' up there. Damn that." But after all, he went up. "All of a sudden, I found myself with tears, cryin' and saying the same thing [the white soldiers] were saying. Glad to be home, proud of my country, as irregular as it is. Determined that it could be better."

At the same time Betty Basye was working across the continent as a nurse in a burn-and-blind center at Menlo Park, California. Her hospital treated soldiers shipped back from the Pacific: "Blind young men. Eyes gone, legs gone. Parts of the face. Burns—you'd land with a firebomb and be up in flames." She'd joke with the men, trying to keep their spirits up, talking about times to come. She liked to take Bill, one of her favorites, for walks downtown. Half of Bill's face was gone, and civilians would stare. It happened to other patients, too. "Nicely dressed women, absolutely staring, just standing there staring." Some people wrote the local paper, wondering why disfigured vets couldn't be kept on their own grounds and off the streets. Such callousness made Basye indignant. The war was over— "and we're still here." After a time, she started dating a soldier back from the South Pacific. "I got busy after the war," she recalled, "getting married and having my four children. That's what you were supposed to do. And getting your house in suburbia."

Yet as Basye and Black soon discovered, the return to "normal" life was filled with uncertainties. The first truly global war had left a large part of Europe in ruins and the old balance of power shattered. The dramatic events occurring month

The mushroom-cloud image captured both the spectacle and the potential horror of atomic warfare. With scant regard for the effects of radioactive fallout, the Defense Department conducted above-ground tests like this one near Las Vegas, Nevada, in 1953.

after month during 1945 and 1946 made it clear that whatever new world order emerged, the United States would have a central role in building it. Isolation seemed neither practical nor desirable in an era in which the power of the Soviet Union and communism seemed on the rise. To blunt that threat the United States converted not so much to peace as to a "cold war" against its former Soviet ally.

This undeclared war came to affect almost every aspect of American life. Abroad, it justified a far wider military and economic role for the United States in areas like the Middle East and the Pacific rim nations of Asia, from Korea to Indochina. At home it sent politicians scurrying across the land in a search for Communist spies and "subversives." The red hunt led from the State Department to the movie studios of Hollywood and even into college classrooms. Preparing for war in times of peace dramatically increased the role of the military-industrial-university complex formed during World War II.

Like the return to "normalcy" after the first world war, the new postwar era was notable for what was *not* normal about it. In a time of peace, a cold war produced unprecedented military budgets, awesomely destructive weapon systems, and continued international tension. A nation that had traditionally followed an isolationist foreign policy now possessed military forces deployed across the globe. A people who had once kept government intrusion into the economy at a minimum now voted to maintain programs that ensured an active federal role. That economy produced prosperity beyond anything Americans had known before.

Effects of the cold war

The Rise of the Cold War

World War II devastated lands and people almost everywhere outside the Western Hemisphere. Once the war ended the world struggled to rebuild. Power that had once been centered in Europe shifted to nations on its periphery. In place of Germany, France, and England, the United States and the Soviet Union emerged as the world's two reigning superpowers—and as enemies. Their rivalry was not altogether an equal one. The United States ended the war with a booming economy, a massive military establishment, and the atomic bomb. By contrast, much of the Soviet Union lay in ruins.

Americans fear Soviet intentions

But the defeat of Germany and Japan left no power in Europe or Asia to block the still formidable Soviet army. And many Americans feared that desperate, war-weary peoples would find the appeal of communism irresistible. If Stalin intended to extend the Soviet Union's dominion, only the United States had the economic and military might to block him. Events in the critical years of 1945 and 1946 persuaded most Americans that Stalin did have such a plan. The Truman administration concluded that "the USSR has engaged the United States in a struggle for power, or 'cold war,' in which our national security is at stake and from which we cannot withdraw short of national suicide." What had happened that led Western leaders to such a dire view of their former Soviet allies? How did the breach between the two nations become irreparable?

Cracks in the Alliance

When Truman entered the White House, he lacked Roosevelt's easy confidence that he could manage "Uncle Joe" Stalin. The new president approached the Soviets with a good deal more suspicion. "Stalin is an SOB, but of course he thinks I'm one, too," Truman commented after their meeting at Potsdam in July 1945. Roosevelt had hoped to strike a balance between the idealism of Wilsonian internationalism and the more practical reality that the major powers would continue to guarantee their own security. Spheres of influence would inevitably continue to exist. What was not clear was just how far each sphere would extend. That uncertainty contained the seeds of conflict. Behind all the diplomatic bowing and bluffing, what were the Soviets' real intentions? Their demand that Poland's borders be adjusted was easy to understand. The new boundaries there would strengthen Soviet national security.

What were Soviet ambitions?

Stalin had also asked that Russia join Turkey in assuming joint control of the Dardanelles, the narrow straits linking Soviet ports on the Black Sea with the Mediterranean (see the map, page 911). During the war, both Roosevelt and Churchill had been willing to consider such a change, especially because Turkey had leaned toward the Axis. In the uncertain postwar atmosphere, Stalin's intentions seemed less acceptable. The Russian dictator had also suggested that the Soviet Union become trustee of Libya, Italy's former African colony. As one British diplomat at Potsdam aptly put it, the great debate was "whether Russia [is] peaceful and wants to join the Western Club but is suspicious of us, or whether she is out to dominate the world and is hoodwinking us." Truman and his advisers, like the diplomat, tended to opt for the same answer: "It always seems safer to go on the worse assumption."

American suspicions were not eased when they looked to Greece, where local Communists led the fighting to overturn the traditional monarchy. And in November 1945 Soviet forces occupying northern Iran lent support to rebels seeking to break away from the Iranian government. Asia, too, seemed a target for Communist ambitions. Russian occupation forces in Manchuria were turning over captured Japanese arms to the Chinese Communist forces of Mao Zedong. Russian troops controlled the northern half of Korea. In Vietnam leftist nationalists were fighting against the return of colonial rule. To deal with this combination of menace and disorder Harry Truman and his advisers sought to frame a policy.

The View from West and East

While postwar events heightened American suspicions of the Soviets, that mistrust had deeper roots. A deep ideological gulf had long separated the two nations. After the October Revolution of 1917, most Americans viewed Lenin's Bolshevik revolutionaries with a mixture of fear, suspicion, and loathing. In their grasp for power the Communists had often used violence, terror, and crime to achieve their ends. As Marxists they rejected both religion and the notion of private property, two institutions central to the American dream. Stalin's brutal purges during the late 1930s created a horrifying image of the Soviet Union as a totalitarian state ruled by terror. Then in 1939 Stalin had signed a cynical nonaggression pact with Germany, freeing him to divide Poland with Germany and make war on his Finnish neighbors. Would the defeat of Germany and Japan free the Soviet dictator to renew his expansion? If it did, how would the Western powers react?

Roots of the cold war

The events leading to World War II provided one lesson in what a policy of "appeasement" could mean. When Neville Chamberlain attempted to satisfy Hitler's demands in 1938, it only emboldened the Nazis to expand further. After the war, Secretary of the Navy James Forrestal applied the Munich analogy to the new situation in Europe. Giving in to Russian claims would only seem like an attempt "to buy their understanding and sympathy. We tried that once with Hitler. . . . There are no returns on appeasement." To many of Truman's advisers, the Soviet dictator seemed to be every bit as much bent on conquest as Hitler had been.

Joseph Stalin

Munich analogy

c o u n t e r p o i n t

What Were Stalin's Intentions?

What was Stalin's view of the postwar world? Because Soviet records remained secret for so many decades, historians lacked sufficient information to explain Stalin's intentions. But revisionist historians made the case that American policy makers consistently exaggerated Soviet ambitions. Over the previous two centuries, Russians had seen their lands invaded once by Napoleon (in 1812) and twice by Germany, during the two world wars. In 1945, as the Soviets struggled to rebuild their war-ravaged economy, the United States continued to gain influence and power throughout the world. When Stalin looked outward, he saw American occupation forces in Europe and Asia ringing the Soviet Union, their military might backed by a newly developed atomic arsenal. American corporations owned or controlled vast oil fields in the Middle East. Along with the French and British, the United States was a strong presence in Southeast Asia. Given that situation, revisionist historians argued, Stalin's actions after the war were primarily defensive, designed to counter what appeared to him to be a threatening American-European alliance.

More recently, some historians have used evidence from Russian archives to argue that Stalin's position was hardly as defensive as some scholars had suggested. Despite the ravages of war, Stalin recognized that in 1945 the Soviet Union was emerging as a more powerful state. With Germany and Japan defeated, Soviet borders to the east and west were secure from invasion. Only to the south did Stalin see a problem, along the border with Iran.

Further, he recognized that the people of Britain and the United States had tired of fighting. Their leaders were not about to threaten the Soviet Union with war, at least in the near term. Equally significant, Soviet spies had informed Stalin in late 1946 that the United States possessed only a few atom bombs. For the time being, the nuclear threat was more symbolic than real. These historians thus conclude that Stalin was neither a global expansionist nor a leader fearful that his nation would soon be encircled and broken apart by American imperialists. Rather, he was a political realist eager to advance the interests of the Soviet state and his own regime—so long as his actions did not risk war.

Toward Containment

The disagreements arising out of the conflicting Soviet and American points of view came to a head in the first months of 1946. For his part, Stalin announced in February that the Soviet Union would take unilateral steps to preserve its national security. In a world dominated by capitalism, he warned, future wars were inevitable. The Russian people had to ensure against "any eventuality" by undertaking a new five-year plan for economic development.

Some Americans thought Stalin was merely rallying Russian support for his domestic programs. Others saw their worst fears confirmed. *Time* magazine, an early voice for a "get tough" policy, called Stalin's speech "the most warlike pronouncement uttered by any top-rank statesman since V-J day." "I'm tired of babying the Soviets," remarked the president, who in any case seldom wore kid gloves. Even Truman's mother passed along a message: "Tell Harry to be good, be honest, and behave himself, but I think it is now time for him to get tough with someone." In March Winston Churchill warned that the Soviets had dropped an "Iron Curtain" between their satellite nations and the free world.

George Kennan's long telegram

As policymakers groped for an effective way to deal with these developments, the State Department received a diplomatic cable, extraordinary for both its length (8000 words) and its impact in Washington. The author was George Kennan, chargé d'affaires in Moscow and long a student of Soviet conduct. Kennan argued that Russian leaders, including Stalin, were so paranoid that it was impossible to reach any useful accommodations with them. This temperament could best be explained by "the traditional and instinctive Russian sense of insecurity." That insecurity, when combined with Marxist ideology that viewed capitalism as evil, created a potent force for expansion. Soviet power, Kennan explained, "moves inexorably along a prescribed path, like a toy automobile wound up and headed in a given direction, stopping only when it meets some unanswerable force."

The response Kennan recommended was "containment." The United States must apply "unalterable counterforce at every point where [the Soviets] show signs of encroaching upon the interests of a peaceful and stable world." The idea of containment was not particularly novel, but Kennan's historical analysis provided leaders in Washington with a framework for analyzing Soviet behavior. It also laid out a plan for responding to that behavior. By applying firm diplomatic, economic, and military counterpressure, the United States could block Russian aggression. Eventually, that firmness might even persuade the Soviets to reform their domestic institutions. Only with free speech, a free press, and democratic elections in the Soviet Union would a reasonable accommodation between East and West be possible. Navy Secretary Forrestal was so impressed with Kennan's "long telegram," as it came to be known, that he sent hundreds of copies to high officials in Washington as well as to American diplomats abroad. Truman wholeheartedly adopted the doctrine of containment.

The Truman Doctrine

At first it appeared that Iran, lying along the Soviet Union's southern border, would provide the first test for containment. An independent Iran seemed crucial in protecting rich fields of petroleum in the Persian Gulf region. In 1943 an oil mission sent to the area had reported that vast Middle Eastern oil fields would soon displace those in the United States as the center of world production. American oil companies had already taken a major position in the region alongside British fields established earlier in the century. During World War II the United States had adopted a far more active role in the affairs of Iran, Turkey, Saudi Arabia, and other Middle Eastern states.

At war's end, Stalin failed to respect his treaty obligation to withdraw Russian troops. The presence of those troops might force Iran to grant economic and political concessions. In March 1946 Secretary of State James Byrnes went to the United Nations, determined to force a showdown over continued Soviet occupation of northern Iran. But before he could extract his pound of Russian flesh, the Soviets reached an agreement with Iran to withdraw.

The Iranian crisis

The face-off in Iran only intensified American suspicions. In Europe severe winter storms and a depressed postwar economy threatened to encourage domestic Communist movements. A turning point in the cold war came in early 1947, when Great Britain announced that it could no longer support the governments of Greece and Turkey. Without British aid, the Communists seemed destined to win critical victories. Truman decided that the United States should provide $400 million in military and economic aid. He went before Congress in March, determined to "scare hell out of the country." The world was now divided into two hostile camps, the president warned. To preserve the American way of life, the United States must now step forward and help "free people" threatened by "totalitarian regimes." This rationale for aid to Greece and Turkey soon became known as the Truman Doctrine.

Aid to Greece and Turkey

Critics pointed out that the president had placed no limits on the American commitment. His was a proposal not simply to contain Communists in Greece and Turkey but to resist Soviet expansion everywhere. Robert Taft, once a leader of congressional isolationists, thought it was a mistake to talk about a bipolar world divided between Communist and anti-Communist camps. Congress, however, supported the new cold war crusade. It voted overwhelmingly to grant aid to Greece and Turkey.

The Truman Doctrine marked a new level of American commitment to a cold war. Just what responsibility the Soviets had for unrest in Greece and Turkey remained unclear. But Truman had linked communism with rebel movements all across

As American fears of Soviet intentions increased, journalists often described communism as though it were a disease, an inhuman force, or a savage predator. In April 1946, *Time* magazine, a particularly outspoken source of anti-Communist rhetoric, portrayed the spread of "infection" throughout Europe and Asia as the "Red Menace."

the globe. That committed Americans to a relatively open-ended struggle. In the battle between communism and freedom, the president gained expanded powers to act when unrest threatened. Occasionally Congress would regret giving the executive branch so much power, but by 1947 anticommunism had become the dominant theme in American policy, both foreign and domestic.

The Marshall Plan

For all its importance, the Truman Doctrine did not address the area of primary concern to Washington, Western Europe. Across Europe desperate people scrounged for food and coal to heat their homes. Streets stood dark at night. National treasuries lacked either capital or credit needed to reopen darkened factories. American diplomats warned that without aid to revive the European economy, Communists would seize power in Germany, Italy, and France.

In June 1947 Secretary of State George C. Marshall stepped before a Harvard commencement audience to announce a recovery plan for Europe. He invited all European nations, East or West, to request assistance to rebuild their economies. Unlike Truman, Marshall did not emphasize the communist menace. All the same, his massive aid plan was designed to eliminate conditions that produced the discontent Communists often exploited. Humanitarian aid also had its practical benefits. As Europe recovered, so would its ability to buy American goods. The secretary did not rule out Soviet participation, but he gambled that fears of American economic domination would lead the Soviets and their allies to reject his offer.

Communism in Hungary and Czechoslovakia

At first neo-isolationists in Congress argued that the United States could not afford such generosity. But when Communists expelled the non-Communists from Czechoslovakia's government, the cold war seemed to spread. Congress then approved the Marshall Plan, as it became known. And as the secretary anticipated, the Soviets blocked the efforts of Czechoslovakia and Poland to participate. The blame for dividing Europe fell, as Marshall guessed it would, on the Soviet Union, not the United States.

The Fall of Eastern Europe

The intensive American efforts to stabilize Europe and the eastern Mediterranean provoked Stalin to take countermeasures. Most shocking to the Western nations were his steps to consolidate Soviet political and military domination over Eastern Europe. In 1947 he moved against Hungary, run since 1945 by a moderate government chosen under relatively free elections. Soviet forces imposed a Communist regime dependent on Moscow. In February 1948 Communists toppled the duly elected government of Czechoslovakia. Shortly after, news came that the popular Czech foreign minister, Jan Masaryk, had fallen to his death from a small bathroom window. Suicide was the official explanation, but many suspected murder. In response to the Marshall Plan, the Soviet foreign ministry initiated a series of trade agreements tightly linking the Soviet and Eastern European economies. It also established the Cominform, or Communist Information Bureau, to assert greater political control over foreign Communist parties.

Berlin airlift

The spring of 1948 brought another clash between the Soviets and their former allies, this time over Germany. There, the United States, Great Britain, and France decided to transform their occupation zones into an independent West German state. The Western-controlled sectors of Berlin, however, lay over 100 miles to the east, well within the Soviet zone. On June 24 the Soviets reacted by blockading land access to Berlin. Truman did not hesitate to respond. "We are going to

Cold War Europe By 1956 the postwar occupation of Europe had hardened into rigid cold war boundaries. The United States reacted to the presence of Soviet conventional forces in Eastern Europe by rearming West Germany and creating the NATO alliance (1949) for the defense of nations from the North Atlantic through the Mediterranean basin. The U.S.S.R. formed a counteralliance under the Warsaw Pact (1955). Although Bonn became the de facto capital of West Germany, Berlin remained the official capital and into the 1960s the focus of the most severe cold war tensions.

stay, period." But he did say no when General Lucius Clay proposed to shoot his way through the blockade. Instead, the United States began a massive airlift of supplies that lasted almost a year. In May 1949 Stalin lifted the blockade, conceding that he could not prevent the creation of West Germany.

Stalin's aggressive actions accelerated the American effort to use military means to contain Soviet ambitions. By 1949 the United States and Canada had joined with Britain, France, Belgium, the Netherlands, and Luxembourg to establish the North Atlantic Treaty Organization (NATO) as a mutual defense pact. For the first time since George Washington had warned against the practice in his Farewell Address of 1793, the United States during peacetime entered into entangling alliances with European nations.

NATO formed

Israel recognized

Truman's firm handling of the Berlin crisis won him applause from both Democrats and Republicans. They were equally enthusiastic about another bold presidential action. Minutes after the Israelis announced their independence in May 1948, Truman recognized the new state of Israel. He had previously supported the immigration of Jews into Palestine despite the opposition of oil-rich Arab states and diplomats in the State Department. The president sympathized with Jewish aspirations for a homeland. He also faced a tough campaign in 1948 in which Jewish votes would be critical. As British Prime Minister Clement Attlee observed, "There's no Arab vote in America, but there's a heavy Jewish vote and the Americans are always having elections."

The Atomic Shield versus the Iron Curtain

The Berlin crisis forced Truman to consider the possibility of war. If it came, would atomic weapons again be used? That dilemma raised two other difficult questions. Should the decision to use atomic weapons rest in civilian or military hands? And was it possible to find a way to ease the atomic threat by creating an international system to control nuclear power?

The Atomic Energy Commission

On the question of civilian or military control of the bomb, Truman's response was firm. He was not going to have "some dashing lieutenant colonel decide when would be the proper time to drop one." In 1946 Congress seemed to have decided the issue in Truman's favor when it passed the McMahon Act. This bill established the Atomic Energy Commission (AEC) with control of all fissionable materials for both peacetime and military applications. The AEC was a civilian, not a military, agency.

But civilian control was not so complete as Truman had demanded. The wartime head of the Manhattan Project, General Leslie Groves, had been working behind the scenes to give the military a decisive voice in atomic policy. During debate over the bill, Groves had leaked information about a Canadian atomic spy ring delivering secrets to the Soviet Union. That news spread doubts that scientists and civilians could be trusted with key secrets. Thus Groves persuaded Congress to allow the military to review many civilian decisions and even severely limit their actions.

Baruch plan

The idea of international control of atomic energy also fell victim to cold war fears. Originally, a high-level government committee proposed to Truman that the mining and use of the world's atomic raw materials be supervised by an agency of the United Nations. The committee argued that in the long run the United States would be more secure under a system of international control than by relying on its temporary nuclear monopoly. But Truman chose Bernard Baruch, a staunch cold warrior, to draw up the recommendations to the United Nations in June 1946. Baruch's proposals ensured that the United States would dominate any international atomic agency. The Soviets countered with a plan calling for destruction of all nuclear bombs and a ban on their use. But Baruch had no intention of bargaining. It was either his plan or nothing, he announced. And so it was nothing. The Truman administration never seriously considered giving up the American nuclear monopoly. Stalin, for his part, gave top priority to the Soviet atomic bomb program. Failure at the United Nations thus promoted an arms race, not nuclear supremacy.

Atomic Deterrence

Ironically, because so much secrecy surrounded the bomb, many military planners knew little about it. Even Truman had no idea in 1946 how many bombs the United States actually possessed. (For the two years after Hiroshima, it was never more than two.) Military planners, however, soon found themselves relying more and more on atomic weapons. The Soviet army had at its command over 260 divisions. In contrast, the United States had reduced its forces by 1947 to little more than a single division. As the cold war heated up, American military planners were forced to adopt a nuclear strategy in face of the overwhelming superiority of Soviet forces. They would deter any Soviet attack by setting in place a devastating atomic counterattack.

"Baby Play with Nice Ball?"

LIFE OR DEATH

THE ATOM

At first, this strategy of nuclear deterrence was little more than a doomsday scenario to incinerate vast areas of the Soviet Union. A 1946 war plan, "Pincher," proposed obliterating 20 Soviet cities if the Soviets attacked Western Europe. By 1948 the war plan "Fleetwood" had raised the tally of cities to 77, with eight bombs aimed for Moscow, seven for Leningrad. Not until "Dropshot," the following year, did planners correct a major flaw in their strategy. If Moscow and Leningrad disappeared, who would be left to surrender? Dropshot recommended sparing those two cities until the second week.

By 1949, then, the cold war framed all aspects of American foreign policy. The Joint Chiefs of Staff had committed themselves to a policy of nuclear deterrence. Western Europe was on its way to economic recovery, thanks to the Marshall Plan. Soviet pressure on Greece and Turkey had abated. Many Americans had hopes that the United States might soon defeat communism.

For many scientists, the flush of success in having built the atom bomb soon gave way to fears about the stark choices atomic energy presented. British cartoonist David Low shows that the scientists' fears were widespread.

Yet success brought little comfort. The Soviet Union was not simply a major power seeking to protect its interests and expand where opportunity permitted. In the eyes of many Americans, the Soviets were determined, if they could, to overthrow the United States from either without or within. This war was being fought not only across the globe but right in America, by unseen agents using subversive means. In this way, the cold war mentality soon came to shape the lives of Americans at home much as it did American policy abroad.

Postwar Prosperity

At war's end, many business leaders feared that a sudden drop in government purchases would bring back the hard times of the 1930s. Once war production ended, wartime boom towns might become ghost towns. Hard times would offer fertile ground for subversives, like the Communists, who fed on discontent. But the hard times never came. Instead, Americans entered into the longest period of prosperity in the nation's history, lasting until the 1970s. Even the fear of communism could not dampen the simple joys of getting and spending.

Two forces drove the postwar economic boom. One was unbridled consumer and business spending that followed 16 years of depression and war. High war wages had piled up in savings accounts and war bonds. Eager consumers set off to find the new cars, appliances, and foods unavailable during the war. Despite a sharp drop in government spending (from $83 billion in 1945 to only $31 billion in 1946), the gross national product fell less than 1 percent and employment actually increased. Consumers had taken up the slack.

Sources of prosperity

Government expenditures at the local, state, and federal levels provided another boost to prosperity. The three major growth industries in the decades after World War II were health care, education, and government programs. Each of these was spurred by public spending. Equally important, the federal government poured millions of dollars into the military-industrial sector. The defense budget, which fell to $9 billion in 1947, reached $50 billion by the time Truman left office. Over the longer term, these factors promoting economic growth became clearer. In 1946, though, the road from war to peace seemed much more uncertain, especially for Americans at the margins of the economy.

Postwar Adjustments

With millions of veterans looking for peacetime jobs, workers on the home front, especially women and minorities, found themselves out of work. Cultural attitudes added to the pressure on these groups to resume more traditional roles. War employment had given many women their first taste of economic independence. As peace came, almost 75 percent of the working women in one survey indicated that they hoped to continue their jobs. But as the troops came home, male social scientists stressed how important it was for women to accept "more than the wife's usual responsibility for her marriage" and offer "lavish— and undemanding—affection" to returning GIs. One marriage counselor urged women to let their husbands know "you are tired of living alone, that you want him now to take charge."

Minority workers   For minorities, the end of the war brought a return of an old labor practice, "last hired, first fired." At the height of the war over 200,000 African Americans and Hispanics had found jobs in shipbuilding. By 1946 that number had dwindled to fewer than 10,000. The influx of Mexican laborers under the bracero program tem-

Having lived through twelve years of depression, Americans placed jobs at the top of their postwar domestic agenda. The Employment Act of 1946 shifted responsibility for a full-employment economy from the private sector to the federal government.

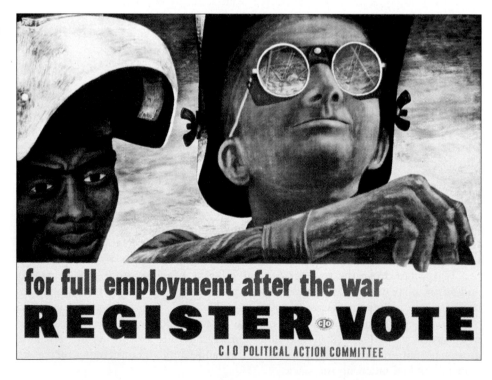

for full employment after the war
REGISTER ⊕ VOTE
CIO POLITICAL ACTION COMMITTEE

In San Antonio, Texas, Mexican American veterans helped form the Liga Pro Defensa Escolar, or School Improvement League. The huge crowd at this 1948 meeting demonstrated the interest among Hispanic Americans in tearing down the Jim Crow system of school segregation.

porarily halted. In the South, where the large majority of black Americans lived, wartime labor shortages had become surpluses, leaving few jobs available.

At the same time, many Hispanic veterans who had fought for their country during the war resented returning to a deeply segregated society. Such GIs "have acquired a new courage, have become more vocal in protesting the restrictions and inequalities with which they are confronted," noted one white Texan. When a funeral director in Three Rivers, Texas, refused to open its segregated cemetery for the burial of Felix Longoria, a Mexican American soldier killed in battle, his supporters organized. Led by Dr. Hector Garcia, a former army medical officer, the American G.I. Forum was founded in 1948 to campaign for civil rights. Longoria was finally buried in Arlington National Cemetery after the G.I. Forum convinced Congressman Lyndon Baines Johnson to intervene.

American G.I. Forum

Black veterans exerted a similar impact on the civil rights movement. Angered by violence, frustrated by the slow pace of desegregation, they breathed new energy into civil rights organizations like the NAACP and CORE (the Congress of Racial Equality). Voting rights was one of the issues they pushed. Registration drives in the South had the greatest success in urban centers like Atlanta. Other black leaders pressed for improved education. In rural Virginia, for example, a young Howard University lawyer, Spottswood Robinson, litigated cases for the NAACP to force improvement in segregated all-black schools. In one county Robinson and the NAACP even won equal pay for black and white teachers.

Black veterans and civil rights

Out in the countryside, however, segregationists used economic intimidation, violence, and even murder to preserve the Jim Crow system. White citizens in rural Georgia lynched several black veterans who had shown the determination to vote. Such instances disturbed President Truman, who saw civil rights as a key ingredient in his reform agenda. The president was especially disturbed when he learned that

Daily Lives

POPULAR ENTERTAINMENT

*Jackie Robinson
Integrates Baseball*

After World War II, Branch Rickey of the Brooklyn Dodgers was determined to break the color line in baseball. For years he had wanted to give black players the opportunity to play in the majors. Equally to the point, he was convinced that this action would improve his team. "The greatest untapped reservoir of raw material in the history of the game is the black race," he explained, adding, "The Negroes will make us winners for years to come."

In the early years of professional baseball, African Americans had played on several major league teams. In 1887, however, as Jim Crow laws spread across the South, the threat of a boycott by some white players caused team owners to adopt an unwritten rule barring black players. That ban stood for 60 years. Even the most talented black ballplayers could only barnstorm at unofficial exhibitions or play in the Negro League.

World War II created a new climate. The hypocrisy of fighting racism abroad while promoting it at home was becoming harder for team owners to ignore. "If a black boy can make it on Okinawa and Guadalcanal," Commissioner Albert "Happy" Chandler told reporters in April 1945, "hell, he can make it in baseball." Economic factors played a role as well. The African American migration to northern cities during World War II created a new, untapped audience for major league baseball. Growing cold war tensions added another factor. Even a Mississippi newspaper saw blacks in the major leagues as "a good answer to our communist adversaries who say the Negro has no chance in America."

It is not difficult to identify Jackie Robinson in this photo of the Brooklyn Dodgers celebrating a key win in the 1948 pennant race. Though Robinson had made the Dodgers a much better team, full integration of major league sports took many more years.

To Secure These Rights

police in South Carolina had gouged out the eyes of a recently discharged black veteran. Truman responded in December 1946 by appointing a Committee on Civil Rights. A year later it published its report, *To Secure These Rights*.

Discovering inequities for minorities, the committee exposed a racial caste system that denied African Americans employment opportunities, equal education, voting rights, and decent housing. But every time Truman appealed to Congress to implement the committee's recommendations, southern senators threatened to filibuster. That opposition forced the president to resort to executive authority to achieve even modest results. In his most direct attack on segregation, he issued an executive order in July 1948 banning discrimination in the armed forces. Segregationists predicted disaster, but experience soon demonstrated that integrated units fought well and exhibited minimal racial tension.

Rickey recognized the enormous hostility that the first black player would face. He found the ideal prospect in Jackie Robinson, a World War II veteran and a remarkable athlete who had lettered in four sports at UCLA. After the war Robinson had signed with the Kansas City Monarchs in the Negro League. Rickey asked Robinson to a meeting in 1945, where he laid out his proposition. But "I need a man that will take abuse, insults," he warned. Robinson would be carrying "the flag for [his] race."

Robinson was intensely proud of his people and his heritage. He had risked court-martial during the war to fight segregation. "Nobody's going to separate bullets and label them 'for white troops' and 'for colored troops,'" Robinson told a superior officer. But he let Rickey know that he would turn the other cheek. "If you want to take this gamble, I will promise you there will be no incident." Rickey assigned him to Montreal where he led the Dodgers' farm team to a championship.

When the Dodgers invited Robinson to spring training, several southern-born players circulated a petition stating their opposition to playing with a black man. But manager Leo Durocher bluntly warned them they would be traded if they refused to cooperate. Robinson would make them all rich, Durocher insisted.

On April 15, 1947, Robinson made his debut with the Dodgers at Ebbets Field. A black newspaper, the Boston *Chronicle,* proclaimed, "TRIUMPH OF WHOLE RACE SEEN IN JACKIE'S DEBUT IN MAJOR LEAGUE BALL." Half the fans in the stands that day were African Americans. They cheered wildly at everything Robinson did. Indeed, blacks everywhere instantly adopted the Dodgers as their team, showing up in large numbers when Brooklyn was on the road.

If anything, the abuse heaped on Robinson was worse than Rickey had anticipated. Opposing players shouted vicious racial epithets. Robinson received death threats, his family was harassed, and some hotels barred him from staying with the team. He secretly wore a protective lining inside his hat in case he was beaned (he was hit a record 9 times during the season, 65 times in seven years), and on several occasions he was spiked by opposing players. Through it all, Robinson kept his temper, though not without difficulty. Once when a Cubs' player kicked him, Robinson started to swing, then stopped. "I knew I was kind of an experiment," he recalled; ". . . the whole thing was bigger than me."

Robinson spoke with his glove, his bat, and his feet, not his fists. His daring base running, which he learned in the old Negro League, brought a new excitement to the game (he stole home 19 times in his career). In his first year, the Dodgers won the pennant and he was named Rookie of the Year. Two years later he was named the Most Valuable Player in the National League. After he retired in 1957, the skill and dignity he brought to the game earned him a place in baseball's Hall of Fame.

In the wake of his success, other teams added African Americans. Professional basketball and football followed baseball's lead. Still, the pace of integration was slow, and it was not until 1959 that all major league teams had a black member. Nevertheless, for once baseball had led the nation rather than followed it: the armed services were not integrated until 1948, and the Supreme Court would not strike down segregation until seven years after Robinson first played for the Dodgers. Thanks to the vision of Branch Rickey and the courage of Jackie Robinson, America's pastime had become truly a national game.

Several Supreme Court decisions gave added weight to Truman's civil rights initiatives. In cases that indicated a growing willingness to reconsider the doctrine that black facilities could be "separate but equal" (*Plessy v. Ferguson*, 1896) the Court struck down several state education laws clearly designed to create separate but inferior facilities.

For organized labor, reconversion brought an abrupt drop in hours worked and overtime paid. As wages declined and inflation ate into paychecks, strikes spread. Autoworkers walked off the job in the fall of 1945; steelworkers, in January 1946; miners, in April. In 1946 some 5 million workers struck, a rate triple that of any previous year. Antiunion sentiment soared. The crisis peaked in May 1946 with a national rail strike, which temporarily paralyzed the nation's transportation network. An angry President Truman asked, "What decent American would pull a rail strike at a time like this?"

Organized labor

At first, Truman threatened to seize the railroads and then requested from Congress the power to draft striking workers into the military. The strike was settled before the threat was carried out, but few people, whether conservative or liberal, approved the idea of using the draft to punish political foes. Labor leaders, for their part, became convinced they no longer had a friend at the White House.

The New Deal Programs Under Attack

In September 1945 Harry Truman had boldly claimed his intention to extend the New Deal into the postwar era. He called for legislation to guarantee full employment, subsidized public housing, national health insurance, and a peacetime version of the Fair Employment Practices Commission to fight job discrimination. Instead of promoting his liberal agenda, he found himself fighting a conservative backlash. Labor unrest was just one source of his troubles. The increased demand for consumer goods temporarily in short supply triggered a sharp inflation. For two years prices rose as much as 15 percent annually. Consumers blamed the White House for not doing more to manage the economy.

With Truman's political stock falling, conservative Republicans and Democrats blocked the president's attempts to revive and extend the New Deal. All he achieved was a watered-down full-employment bill, which created the Council of Economic Advisers to guide the president's policies. The bill did establish the principle that the government rather than the private sector was responsible for maintaining full employment. As the congressional elections of 1946 neared, Republicans pointed to production shortages, the procession of strikes, the mismanagement of the economy. "To err is Truman," proclaimed the campaign buttons—or, more simply, "Had Enough?" Evidently many voters had. The Republicans gained control of both houses of Congress. Not since 1928 had the Democrats fared so poorly.

Leading the rightward swing was Senator Robert A. Taft of Ohio, son of former president William Howard Taft. Bob Taft not only wanted to halt the spread of the New Deal—he wanted to dismantle it. "We have to get over the corrupting idea we can legislate prosperity, legislate equality, legislate opportunity," he said in dismissing the liberal agenda. Taft especially wished to limit the power of the unions. In

Taft-Hartley Act

1947 he pushed the Taft-Hartley Act through Congress, over Truman's veto. In the event of a strike, the bill allowed the president to order workers back on the job during a 90-day cooling-off period while collective bargaining continued. It also permitted states to adopt right-to-work laws, which banned the closed shop by eliminating union membership as a prerequisite for many jobs. Union leaders criticized the new law as a slave-labor act but discovered they could live with it, though it did hurt union efforts to organize, especially in the South.

A Welfare Program for GIs

Despite Republican gains, most Americans did not repudiate the New Deal's major accomplishments: social security, minimum wages, a more active role for government in reducing unemployment. The administration maintained its commitment to setting a minimum wage, raising it again in 1950 from 45 to 75 cents. Social security coverage was broadened to cover an additional 10 million workers. Furthermore, a growing list of welfare programs benefited not only the poor but veterans, middle-income families, the elderly, and students. The most striking of these was

The GI Bill

the GI Bill of 1944, designed to reward soldiers for their service during the war.

For veterans, the "GI Bill of Rights" created unparalleled opportunity. Those with more than two years of service received all tuition and fees plus living expenses for three years of college education. By 1948 the government was paying the college costs of almost 50 percent of all male students as more than 2 million veterans took advantage of the GI Bill. Increased educational levels encouraged a shift from blue-to white-collar work and self-employment. Although the number of jobs in areas such as mining and manufacturing increased little if at all, work in areas such as insurance, teaching, state and local governments, construction, and retailing all grew rapidly. Veterans also received low-interest loans to start businesses or farms of their own and to buy homes. By the 1950s the Veterans Administration, in charge of the program, was funding the purchase of some 20 percent of all new houses.

The GI Bill accelerated trends that would transform American society into a prosperous, heavily middle-class suburban nation. It also contributed to the economic advantages that white males held over minorities and females. Few women received benefits under the bill. Many lost their jobs or seniority to returning veterans. African Americans and Hispanics, even those eligible for veterans' benefits, were hampered by Jim Crow restrictions in segregated universities and in jobs in both the public and private sectors. The Federal Housing Administration even helped draw up "model" restrictive housing covenants. In order to "retain stability," neighborhoods were allowed to use the covenants to segregate according to "social and racial classes."

The Election of 1948

With his domestic program blocked, Harry Truman faced almost certain defeat in the election of 1948. The New Deal coalition that Franklin Roosevelt had held together for so long seemed to be coming apart. On the left Truman was challenged by Henry Wallace, who had been a capable secretary of agriculture and vice president under Roosevelt, then secretary of commerce under Truman. Wallace wanted to pursue New Deal reforms even more vigorously than Truman did, and he continually voiced his sympathy for the Soviet Union. Disaffected liberals bolted the Democratic party to support Wallace on a third-party Progressive ticket.

Henry Wallace and the progressives

Within the southern conservative wing of the party, archsegregationists resented Truman's moderate civil rights proposals for a voting rights bill and an antilynching law. When the liberal wing of the party passed a civil rights plank as part of the Democratic platform, delegates from several Deep South states stalked out of the convention. They banded together to create the States' Rights or "Dixiecrat" party, with J. Strom Thurmond, the segregationist governor of South Carolina, as their candidate.

Dixiecrats

With the Democrats divided, Republicans smelled victory. They sought to control the political center by rejecting the conservative Taft in favor of the more moderate former New York Governor Thomas Dewey. Dewey proved so aloof that he inspired scant enthusiasm. "You have to know Dewey well to really dislike him," quipped one Taft supporter. Such shortcomings aside, it seemed clear to most observers that Dewey would walk away with the race. Pollster Elmo Roper stopped canvassing the voters two months before the election.

Truman, however, did not roll over and play dead. He launched a stinging attack against the "reactionaries" in Congress: that "bunch of old mossbacks . . . gluttons of privilege . . . all set to do a hatchet job on the New Deal." From the rear platform of his campaign train, he made almost 400 speeches in eight weeks. Over and over he hammered away at the "do-nothing" 80th Congress, which, he told farmers, "had stuck a pitchfork" in their backs. Still, on election day oddsmakers favored Dewey by as much as 20 to 1. Hours before the polls closed the archconservative Chicago *Tribune* happily headlined "Dewey Defeats Truman." But the experts were

Truman fights back

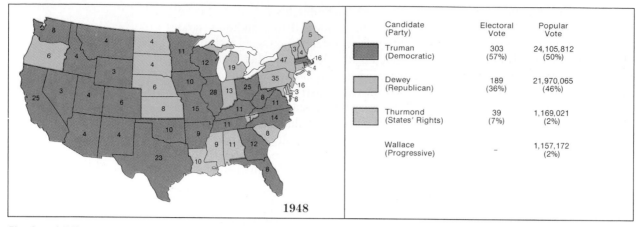

Candidate (Party)	Electoral Vote	Popular Vote
Truman (Democratic)	303 (57%)	24,105,812 (50%)
Dewey (Republican)	189 (36%)	21,970,065 (46%)
Thurmond (States' Rights)	39 (7%)	1,169,021 (2%)
Wallace (Progressive)	–	1,157,172 (2%)

1948

Election of 1948

wrong. Not only did the voters return Truman by over 2 million popular votes, they gave the Democrats commanding majorities in the House and Senate.

The defection of the liberal and conservative extremes had allowed Truman to hold the New Deal coalition together after all. Jews grateful for his stand on Israel, Catholics loyal to the Democratic party, and ethnics all supported him. He had been the first major presidential candidate to campaign in Harlem. Farmers hurt by falling prices deserted the Republicans. An easing of inflation had reminded middle-income Americans that they had benefited significantly under Democratic leadership. "I have a new car and am much better off than my parents were. Why change?" one suburban voter remarked.

The Fair Deal

As he began his new term, Harry Truman expressed his conviction that all Americans were entitled to a "Fair Deal" from their government. His agenda called for a vigorous revival of New Deal programs like national health insurance and regional TVA-style projects. Echoing an old Populist idea, Truman hoped to keep his working coalition together by forging stronger links between farmers and labor.

As before, a conservative coalition of Democrats and Republicans in Congress blocked any significant new initiatives. They voted down plans for a St. Lawrence Seaway in the Northeast, rejected national health insurance, and refused to approve federal aid to education. Furthermore, Truman could not forge a working coalition between farmers and labor. The farm bloc would not support labor in its attempts to repeal the Taft-Hartley Act, nor would labor vote to help pass farm price supports designed to encourage family farms at the expense of larger agribusinesses. On the domestic front Truman remained largely the conservator of Franklin Roosevelt's legacy.

The Cold War at Home

Bob Raymondi, a mobster serving a prison term in the late 1940s, was no stranger to extortion, racketeering, or gangland killings. In fact, he was so feared that he dominated the inmate population at Dannemora Prison. Raymondi began to make the acquaintance of a group of Communists who had been jailed for advocating the overthrow of the government. He enjoyed talking with people who had some education. When Raymondi's sister learned about his new friends, she was frantic. "My God, Bob," she told him. "You'll get into trouble."

Was something amiss? Most Americans judged it riskier to associate with Communists than with hardened criminals. Out of a population of 150 million, the Communist party in 1950 could claim a membership of only 43,000. (More than a few of those were FBI undercover agents.) But worry about Communists Americans did. In part, conscientious citizens were appalled by party members who excused Stalin's violent crimes against his own people. Millions of Russians had been executed or sent to Siberian labor camps; under those circumstances, most Americans found it outrageous to hear American Communists dismiss civil liberties as "bourgeois."

Conservatives were especially outspoken about the Communist menace. Some honestly feared the New Deal as "creeping socialism." The president's advisers, it seemed to them, were either Communist agents or their unwitting dupes. Leftists, they believed, controlled labor unions, Hollywood, and other interest groups sympathetic to the New Deal. Their outrage grew after the war as Stalin extended Soviet control in Eastern Europe and Asia. Many conservatives charged that a conspiracy within Roosevelt's administration had sold out America to its enemies. More cynical conservatives used red baiting simply to discredit people and ideas they disliked.

Conservative anticommunism

The fall of China to the Communist forces of Mao Zedong was one of two great cold war shocks of 1949. Anti-Communists joined members of the China Lobby in blaming Truman for "losing China."

The Shocks of 1949

The H-bomb

Truman won in 1948 in large part because of his strong leadership in foreign affairs. In 1949 a series of foreign policy shocks allowed Republicans to seize the anti-Communist issue. In August American scientists reported that rains monitored in the Pacific contained traces of hot nuclear waste. Only one conclusion seemed possible: the Soviet Union possessed its own atom bomb. When Truman announced the news, Congress was debating whether to spend $1.5 billion for military aid to the newly formed NATO alliance. The House stopped debating and voted the bill through, while Truman directed that research into a newer, more powerful fusion, or hydrogen, bomb continue. Senator Arthur Vandenberg, a Republican with wide experience in international affairs, summed up the reaction of many to the end of the American nuclear monopoly: "This is now a different world."

China falls to
Communists

Then in December came more bad news. The long embattled Nationalist government of Chiang Kai-shek fled mainland China to the offshore island of Formosa (present-day Taiwan). By January Communist troops under Mao Zedong swarmed into Beijing, China's capital city. Chiang's defeat came as no surprise to State Department officials, who had long regarded the Nationalists as hopelessly corrupt and inefficient. Despite major American efforts to save Chiang's regime and stabilize China, poverty and civil unrest spread in the postwar years. In 1947 full-scale civil war broke out, so Mao's triumph was hardly unexpected.

But Republicans, who had up until 1949 supported the president's foreign policy, now broke ranks. For some time, a group of wealthy conservatives and Republican senators had resented the administration's preoccupation with Europe. Time-Life publisher Henry Luce used his magazines to campaign for a greater concern for Asian affairs and especially more aid to defeat Mao Zedong. Luce and his associates, known as the "China Lobby," were supported in part with funds from the Chinese embassy. When Chiang at last collapsed, his American backers charged Democrats with letting the Communists win.

The Hiss case

Worries that subversives had sold out the country were heightened when former State Department official Alger Hiss was brought to trial in 1949 for perjury. Hiss, an adviser to Roosevelt at the Yalta Conference, had been accused by former Communist Whittaker Chambers of passing secrets to the Soviet Union during the 1930s. Though the evidence in the case was far from conclusive, the jury convicted Hiss for lying about his association with Chambers. And in February 1950 the nation was further shocked to learn that a high-ranking British physicist, Klaus Fuchs, had spied for the Russians while working on the Manhattan Project. Here was clear evidence of conspiracy at work.

The Loyalty Crusade

President Truman sought to blunt Republican accusations that he was "soft" on communism. Ten days after proposing the Truman Doctrine in March 1947, the president signed an executive order establishing a Federal Employee Loyalty Program designed to guard against the possible disloyalty of "Reds, phonies, and 'parlor pinks.'" Since the FBI could hardly find time to examine all of the 2 million government employees, the order required supervisors to review and certify the loyalties of those who worked below them, reporting to a system of federal loyalty review boards.

Loyalty Review Board

The system quickly got out of hand. Seth Richardson, the conservative who headed the Loyalty Review Board, brushed the Bill of Rights aside. In his opinion, the government could "discharge any employee for reasons which seem sufficient to the Government, and without extending to such employee any hearing whatsoever." After several years the difficulty of proving that employees were actually disloyal became clear, and Truman allowed the boards to fire those who were "potentially" disloyal or "bad security risks," such as alcoholics, homosexuals, and debtors. Suspect employees, in other words, were assumed guilty until proven innocent. After some 5 million investigations, the program identified a few hundred employees who, though not Communists, had at one time been associated with suspect groups. Rather than calm public fears, the loyalty program gave credibility to the growing red scare.

HUAC, Hollywood, and Unions

About the same time Truman established the Loyalty Review Board, the House Committee on Un-American Activities (HUAC) began to investigate Communist influence in the film industry. Hollywood, with its wealth, glamour, and highly visible Jewish and foreign celebrities, had long aroused a mixture of attraction and suspicion among traditional Americans. "Large numbers of moving pictures that come out of Hollywood carry the Communist line," charged committee member John Rankin of Mississippi. Indeed, during the Depression some Hollywood figures had developed ties to the Communist party or had become sympathetic to party causes. To generate support for the Allies during the war, Hollywood (with Roosevelt's blessing) produced films with a positive view of the Soviet Union such as *Mission to Moscow* and *Song of Russia*.

HUAC called a parade of movie stars, screenwriters, and producers to sit in the glare of its public hearings. Some witnesses, such as Gary Cooper, Robert Montgomery, and Ronald Reagan, were considered "friendly" because they answered committee questions or supplied names of suspected leftists. Others refused to inform on their colleagues or to answer questions about earlier ties to the Communist party. Eventually 10 uncooperative witnesses, known as the "Hollywood Ten," refused on First Amendment grounds to say whether they were or ever had been Communists. They served prison terms for contempt of Congress.

For all its probing, HUAC never offered convincing evidence that filmmakers were in any way subversive. About the most damning evidence presented was that one eager left-leaning extra, when asked to "whistle something" during his walk-on part, hummed a few bars of the Communist anthem the "Internationale." The investigations did, however, inspire nervous Hollywood producers to turn out films such as *The Iron Curtain* (1948), in which a Russian spy ring in the United States is exposed, and *I Was a Communist for the FBI* (1950). The studios also purged anyone suspected of disloyalty, adopting a blacklist that prevented admitted or accused Communists from finding work. Because no judicial proceedings were involved, victims of false charges, rumors, or spiteful accusations found it nearly impossible to clear their names.

Blacklisting

Suspicion of aliens and immigrants led finally to the passage, over Truman's veto, of the McCarran Act (1950). It required all Communists to register with the attorney general, forbade the entry of anyone who had belonged to a totalitarian organization, and allowed the Justice Department to detain suspect aliens indefinitely during deportation hearings. It was supported overwhelmingly in Congress. That same year a Senate committee began an inquiry designed to root out homosexuals holding government jobs. Even one "sex pervert in a Government agency tends to have a corrosive influence upon his fellow employees," warned the committee. The campaign had effects beyond government offices: the armed forces stepped up their rates of dismissal for sexual orientation, while city police more frequently raided gay bars and social clubs.

McCarran Act

The Ambitions of Senator McCarthy

By 1950 anticommunism had created a climate of fear in which legitimate concerns mixed with irrational hysteria. Joseph R. McCarthy, a Senate nonentity from Wisconsin, saw in that fear an issue with which to rebuild his political fortunes. To an audience in Wheeling, West Virginia, in February 1950 he waved a sheaf of papers in the air and announced that he had a list of 205—or perhaps 81, 57, or "a lot of"—Communists in the State Department. (No one, including the senator, could remember the number, which he continually changed.) In the following months McCarthy leveled charge after charge. He had penetrated the "iron curtain" of the State Department to discover "card-carrying Communists," the "top Russian espionage agent" in the United States, "egg-sucking phony liberals," and "Communists and queers" who wrote "perfumed notes."

It seemed not to matter that McCarthy never substantiated his charges. When examined, his lists contained names of people who had left the State Department long before or who had been cleared by the FBI. When forced into a corner, McCarthy simply lied and went on to another accusation. No one seemed beyond reach. In the summer of 1950 a Senate committee headed by Millard F. Tydings of Maryland concluded that McCarthy's charges were "a fraud and a hoax." Such candor among those in government did not last long, as "Jolting Joe" (one of McCarthy's favorite macho nicknames) in 1952 helped defeat Tydings and several other Senate critics.

McCarthy served as a blunt instrument that some conservative Republicans used to damage the Democrats. Without the support of these Republicans, McCarthy would have had little credibility. Many of his accusations came from information secretly (and illegally) funneled to him by FBI Director J. Edgar Hoover. But McCarthyism was also the bitter fruit Truman and the Democrats reaped from their own attempts to exploit the anti-Communist mood. McCarthy, more than Truman, had tapped the fears and hatreds of a broad coalition of Catholic leaders, conservatives, and neo-isolationists who harbored suspicion of things foreign, liberal, internationalist, European, or a touch too intellectual. They saw McCarthy and his fellow witch-hunters as the protectors of a vaguely defined but deeply felt spirit of Americanism.

By the time Truman stepped down as president, 32 states had laws requiring teachers to take loyalty oaths, government loyalty boards were asking employees what newspapers they subscribed to or phonograph records they collected, and a library in Indiana had banned *Robin Hood* because the idea of stealing from the rich to give to the poor seemed rather too leftish. As one historian commented, "Opening the valve of anticommunist hysteria was a good deal simpler than closing it."

Godless Communists run wild as the American flag goes up in flames in this comic book distributed by patriotic church groups. Over 4 million copies were printed to try to counter the influence of suspected subversives infiltrating American society.

From Cold War to Hot War and Back

As the cold war heated up in 1949, the Truman administration searched for a more assertive foreign policy—one that went beyond George Kennan's notion of "containment." The new policy was developed by the National Security Council (NSC), an agency created by Congress in 1947 as part of a plan to help the executive branch respond more effectively to cold war crises. The army, navy, and air force were united under a single Department of

Defense. All overseas intelligence gathering and espionage activities became the responsibility of the Central Intelligence Agency. To the National Security Council fell the job of advising the president about foreign and military policy. From the beginning, the NSC had lobbied for an active policy not just to contain the Soviets but also to win the cold war. In April 1950 it sent Truman a document, NSC-68, which came to serve as the framework for American policy over the next 20 years.

NSC-68 argued that rather than merely hold the Soviets at bay, the United States should "strive for victory." To that end NSC-68 called for an immediate increase in defense spending from $13 billion to $50 billion a year, to be paid for with a large tax increase. Most of the funds would go to rebuild conventional forces, but the NSC urged that the hydrogen bomb be developed to offset the Soviet nuclear capacity. At the same time the American people had to be mobilized to make the necessary sacrifices while the United States worked (NSC-68 never explained how) to make "the Russian people our Allies" in undermining their totalitarian government.

NSC-68

Efforts to carry out NSC-68 at first aroused widespread opposition. George Kennan argued that the Soviets had no immediate plans for domination outside the Communist bloc. Thus, NSC-68 was too simplistic and militaristic. Fiscal conservatives, both Democrat and Republican, resisted any proposal for higher taxes. Truman's own secretary of defense, Louis Johnson, warned that the new military budget would bankrupt the country. All such reservations were swept away on June 25, 1950. "Korea came along and saved us," Secretary of State Dean Acheson later remarked.

Police Action

In 1950 Korea was about the last place in the world Americans might have imagined themselves fighting a war. Since World War II the country had been divided along the 38th parallel, the north controlled by the Communist government of Kim Il Sung, the south by the dictatorship of Syngman Rhee. Preoccupied with China and the rebuilding of Japan, the Truman administration's interest had dwindled steadily after the war. When Secretary of State Acheson discussed American policy in Asia before the National Press Club in January 1950, he did not even mention Korea.

On June 24 Harry Truman was enjoying a leisurely break from politics at the family home in Independence, Missouri. In Korea it was already Sunday morning when Acheson called the president. North Korean troops had crossed the 38th parallel, Acheson reported, possibly to fulfill Kim Il Sung's proclaimed intention to "liberate" the South. Soon Acheson confirmed that a full-scale invasion was in progress. The United Nations, meeting in emergency session, had ordered a cease-fire, which the North Koreans were ignoring. With that, Truman flew back to Washington, convinced that Stalin and his Chinese Communist allies had ordered the invasion. Kim, Truman reasoned, would hardly have acted on his own. The threat of a third world war, this one atomic, seemed agonizingly real. Truman and his advisers wanted to respond firmly enough to deter aggression but without provoking a larger war with the Soviet Union or China.

The North Korean invasion

Truman did not hesitate; American troops would fight the North Koreans, though the United States would not declare war. The fighting in Korea would be a "police action" supervised by the United Nations. On June 27 the Security Council passed a U.S. resolution to send United Nations forces to Korea. That move succeeded only because the Soviet delegate, who had veto power, was absent. Six months earlier he had walked out in protest over the Council's refusal to seat

The Korean War In their opening offensive, North Korean troops almost pushed South Korean and American forces into the sea at Pusan. After MacArthur rallied UN forces, he commanded a successful landing at Inchon behind North Korean lines and then crossed the 38th parallel into North Korea. Red Chinese troops counterattacked, inflicting on U.S. troops one of the most humiliating defeats in American military history. Fighting continued for another two years.

mainland China. (Indeed, the Soviet absence from the Security Council vote undermines the idea that Stalin, rather than Kim Il Sung, had masterminded the North Korean attack.)

Truman's forceful response won immediate approval across America. Congress quickly voted the huge increase in defense funds needed to carry out the recommendations of NSC-68. American allies were less committed to the action. Though 16 nations contributed to the war effort, the United States provided half of the ground troops, 86 percent of the naval units, and 93 percent of the air force. By the time the UN forces could be marshaled, North Korean forces had pinned the South Koreans within a small defensive perimeter centered around Pusan. Then Douglas MacArthur, commander of the UN forces, launched a daring amphibious attack behind North Korean lines at Inchon, near the western end of the 38th parallel. Fighting eastward, MacArthur's troops threatened to trap the invaders, who fled back to the North.

The Chinese Intervene

MacArthur's success led Truman to a fateful decision. With the South liberated, he gave MacArthur permission to cross the 38th parallel, drive the Communists from the North, and reunite the country under Syngman Rhee. With Senator Joe McCarthy on the attack at home, the 1950 elections nearing, and the McCarran Act just passed, Truman was glad enough for the chance to vanquish the North Koreans. By Thanksgiving American troops had roundly defeated northern forces and were advancing on several fronts toward the frozen Yalu River, the boundary between Korea and China. MacArthur, emboldened by success, promised that the boys would be home by Christmas.

China, however, grew increasingly restive. Throughout the fall offensive, Premier Zhou Enlai warned that his country would not tolerate an American presence on its border. Washington officials did not take the warning seriously. Mao Zedong, they assumed, was a Soviet puppet, and Stalin had declared the Korean conflict to be merely a "civil war" and off limits. Ignoring the Chinese warnings, MacArthur launched his end-the-war offensive. Not long after, American troops captured a Chinese prisoner—as Secretary of State Acheson recalled, "you began to know at that point something was happening." On November 26 some 400,000 Chinese troops poured across the Yalu, smashing through lightly defended UN lines. At Chosan they trapped 20,000 American and South Korean troops, inflicting one of the worst defeats in American military history. Within three weeks they had driven UN forces back behind the 38th parallel. So total was the rout that Truman wondered publicly about using the atom bomb. That remark sent a frightened British Prime Minister Clement Attlee flying to Washington to dissuade the president. He readily agreed that the war must remain limited and withdrew his nuclear threat.

Marines in North Korea wait at a roadblock on December 1, 1950. American forces retreated after the Chinese crossed the Yalu. The harsh weather added to the casualties those forces suffered.

Truman versus MacArthur

The military stalemate in Korea brought into the open a simmering feud between MacArthur and Truman. The general had made no secret of his political ambitions or of his differences with Truman over American policy in Asia. He was eager to bomb Chinese and Russian supply bases across the Korean border, to blockade China's coast, and to "unleash" Chiang Kai-shek on mainland China. On March 23 he issued a personal ultimatum to Chinese military commanders demanding total surrender. To his Republican congressional supporters he sent a letter declaring, "We must win. There is no substitute for victory."

To Truman, MacArthur's insubordination threatened the tradition that military policy remained under clear civilian control. Equally alarming, MacArthur's strategy appeared to be an open invitation to another world war. Despite the general's enormous popularity, Truman made plans to discipline him. When General Omar Bradley reported that MacArthur threatened to resign before Truman could act, the irate Truman replied, "The son of a bitch isn't going to resign on me. I want him fired!" Military leaders agreed that MacArthur had to go. On April 11 a stunned nation learned that the celebrated military commander had been relieved of his duties. On his return to the states, cheering crowds gave MacArthur one of the largest ticker-tape parades in New York City's history. Truman's move seemed one of the great political mistakes of his career. Congress gave MacArthur the unprecedented opportunity to address a joint session before a national television audience and the general's most fervent supporters tried to impeach Truman and Acheson.

The Global Implications of the Cold War

Behind the scenes Truman was winning this personal clash. At stake was not simply the issue of whether he or MacArthur would prevail. Rather, the outcome would determine the future direction of American foreign policy. The cold war crisis forced American leaders to think globally. Where in the world did the nation's interests lie? What region was most critical to the future? MacArthur believed that the Pacific basin would "determine the course of history in the next ten thousand years." To avoid being swept aside, the United States should make an all-out effort, not just to contain the Communist onslaught in Korea, but to play a major role throughout Asia. "What I advocate is that we defend every place, and I say that we have the capacity to do it," insisted MacArthur. Many conservative Republicans and groups like the China Lobby shared MacArthur's view. As Senator Robert Taft put it, the United States should pursue "the same policy in the Far East as in Europe."

Europe, not Asia first

Truman and his advisers continued to see Europe as the key to American foreign policy. Western Europe in particular, they believed, remained the center of the world's economic and military power. Political scientist Hans Morgenthau argued that "he who controls Europe is well on his way toward controlling the whole world." Further, Eurocentric Americans felt that the cultural differences between the United States and Asia were so great that the battle for Asia could not be won by military might. As theologian Reinhold Niebuhr put it, using American cold war weapons against the ideology of communism would be "like the spears of the knights when gunpowder challenged their reign."

Secretary of State Acheson agreed with the Eurocentrists. Korea was to Acheson but a small link in a global "collective security sytem." The wider war in Asia that MacArthur favored would threaten American interests in Europe because American resources would be stretched too thinly. Or, as General Bradley told Congress, a war in Asia would lead to "the wrong war, at the wrong place, at the wrong time, and with the wrong enemy." In this debate the Eurocentric faction prevailed. Congressional leaders agreed with Truman that the war in Korea should remain limited and that American resources should go to rebuilding Europe's defenses.

Meanwhile, the war in Korea bogged down in stalemate. As peace negotiators argued over how to reunify Korea, the United States suffered another 32,000 casualties in an ugly war of attrition. By March 1952 Truman's popularity had sunk so low that he lost the New Hampshire presidential primary to Senator Estes Kefauver of Tennessee. With that defeat, he announced he would not run for reelection in 1952.

The Election of 1952

The Republican formula for victory in 1952 played on the Truman administration's obvious weaknesses. Republicans could capitalize on the stalemate over Korea. And several of Truman's advisers had been forced to resign for accepting mink coats and large freezers in return for political favors. The economy, however, remained remarkably healthy. Wage and price controls put in place by the administration prevented the sharp inflation that was expected to follow increased wartime spending.

The bigger problem for Republicans lay in choosing a candidate. Once General Dwight Eisenhower formally joined the Republican party, he became the choice of moderates and the northeastern establishment. Party regulars and the conservative wing were heavily committed to Robert Taft, who ran surprisingly well in the party primaries. But Ike was more popular with voters. His backers maneuvered their candidate to a first-ballot nomination. To heal the breach with the Taft delegates, the convention chose staunch anti-Communist Senator Richard Nixon as Eisenhower's running mate.

Moderates like "Ike"

With no candidate as popular as Eisenhower, the Democrats drafted Illinois Governor Adlai E. Stevenson. Few candidates could match Stevenson's eloquence, but, like Dewey before him, Stevenson lacked the common touch. Republican strategists turned his intelligence into a liability by dismissing him and his intellectual supporters as "eggheads." The GOP's campaign against communism and corruption, led by Nixon, put the Democratic candidate on the defensive. Eisenhower, meanwhile, took the high road above the mudslinging. He promised voters that if elected, he would go to Korea to seek an end to the war.

Righteous indignation over corruption mired the Republicans in a scandal of their own. Newspapers reported that a group of wealthy Californians had provided Richard Nixon with an $18,000 "slush fund" to help cover personal expenses. With his place on the ticket in peril, Nixon made an impassioned television appeal, portraying himself and his wife, Pat, as ordinary folks. Like other young couples, they had monthly payments to make on a mortgage and a car. Pat had only a sensible "Republican cloth coat," not furs. And yes, his daughter Tricia had received a cocker spaniel puppy named Checkers, but no matter what his enemies might say, his family was going to keep the dog. As soon as Nixon finished, sympathetic viewers deluged GOP headquarters with messages of support. Nixon's survival demonstrated the power of television to influence public opinion.

Nixon's Checkers Speech

The election outcome was never much in doubt. Eisenhower's broad smile and confident manner won him more than 55 percent of the vote. "The great problem of America today," Eisenhower had said during the campaign, "is to take that straight road down the middle." Most Americans who voted for him were comforted to think that was just where they were headed.

Even before taking office, Eisenhower's first priority was to end the stalemated Korean War. As president-elect, he fulfilled his campaign promise "to go to Korea"

Eisenhower and Korea

and appraise the situation firsthand. Once in office, he renewed negotiations with North Korea but warned that unless the talks made speedy progress, the United States might retaliate "under circumstances of our choosing." The carrot-and-stick approach worked. On July 27, 1953, the Communists and the UN forces signed an armistice ending a "police action" in which 54,000 Americans had died. Korea remained divided, almost as it had been in 1950. Communism had been "contained," but at a high price in human lives.

The Fall of McCarthy

It was less clear, however, whether domestic anticommunism could be contained. Eisenhower boasted that he was a "modern" Republican, distinguishing himself from what he called the more "hidebound" members of the GOP. Their continuing anti-Communist campaigns caused him increasing embarrassment. Senator McCarthy's reckless antics, at first directed at Democrats, began to hit Republican targets as well.

By the summer of 1953 the senator was on a rampage. He dispatched two young staff members, Roy Cohn and David Schine, to investigate the State Department's overseas information agency and the Voice of America radio stations. Behaving more like college pranksters, the two conducted a whirlwind 18-day witch-hunt through Western Europe, condemning government libraries for possessing "subversive" books, including volumes by John Dewey and Foster Rhea Dulles, a conservative historian and cousin of Eisenhower's secretary of state. Some librarians, fearing for their careers, burned a number of books. That action drove President Eisenhower to denounce "book burners," though soon after he reassured McCarthy's supporters that he did not advocate free speech for Communists.

The administration's own behavior contributed to the hysteria on which McCarthy thrived. The president launched a loyalty campaign, which he claimed resulted in 3000 firings and 5000 resignations of government employees. It was a godsend to McCarthyites: What further proof was needed that subversives were

The energetic and opportunistic Roy Cohn (left) served as a key strategist in the inquisition that made Senator Joseph McCarthy a figure to fear. Together with fellow staffer David Schine (right) they helped McCarthy turn a minor Senate subcommittee into a major power center.

lurking in the federal bureaucracy? Furthermore, a well-publicized spy trial had led to the conviction of Ethel and Julius Rosenberg, a couple accused of passing atomic secrets to the Soviets. Although the evidence was not conclusive, the judge sentenced both Rosenbergs to the electric chair, an unusually harsh punishment even in cases of espionage. When asked to commute the death sentence to life imprisonment, Eisenhower refused, and the Rosenbergs were executed in June 1953.

A year later the Atomic Energy Commission turned its investigative eyes on physicist J. Robert Oppenheimer. During World War II it was Oppenheimer's administrative and scientific genius that had led to the development of the atom bomb. Widely respected by his colleagues, he had raised the hackles of many politicians in 1949 when he opposed the construction of a hydrogen bomb. Despite left-wing associations from the 1930s (which army officials had known about), no one had ever accused him of passing on national security information. Nonetheless, the Atomic Energy Commission in effect suggested Oppenheimer was a traitor by barring him from sensitive research.

The case of J. Robert Oppenheimer

Once the Soviet Union developed its own nuclear capability, Americans felt vulnerable to a surprise atomic attack. This advertisement from the *New York Times* in 1954 promised consumers that their valuables could be stored deep in a mountain vault.

In such a climate—where Democrats remained silent for fear of being called leftists and Eisenhower cautiously refused to "get in the gutter with *that* guy"—McCarthy lost all sense of proportion. When the army denied his aide David Schine a commission, McCarthy decided to investigate communism in the army. The new American Broadcasting Company network, eager to fill its afternoon program slots, televised the hearings. For three weeks, the public had an opportunity to see McCarthy badger witnesses and make a mockery of Senate procedures. Soon after, his popularity began to slide and the anticommunist hysteria ebbed as well. In 1954 the Senate finally moved to censure him. He died three years later, destroyed by alcohol and the habit of throwing so many reckless punches.

McCarthy versus the army

With the Democrats out of the White House for the first time since the Depression and with right-wing McCarthyites in retreat, Eisenhower did indeed seem to be leading the nation on a course "right down the middle." Still, it is worth noting how much that sense of "middle" had changed.

Both the Great Depression and World War II made most Americans realize that the nation's economy was firmly tied to the international order. The crash in 1929, with its worldwide effects, illustrated the closeness of the links. The New Deal demonstrated that Americans were willing to give the federal government power to influence American society in major new ways. And the war led the government to intervene in the economy even more actively.

So when peace came in 1945, it became clear that the "middle road" did not mean a return to the laissez-faire economics of the 1920s or the isolationist politics of the 1930s. "Modern" Republicans supported social welfare programs such as social security and granted that the federal government had the power to lower unemployment, control inflation, and manage the economy in a variety of ways. Furthermore, the shift from war to peace demonstrated that it was no longer possible to make global war without making a global peace. Under the new balance of power in the postwar world, the United States and the Soviet Union stood alone as superpowers, with the potential capability to annihilate each other and the rest of the world.

chapter summary

In the postwar period, the cold war between the Soviet Union and the United States affected every aspect of American domestic and foreign policy and overshadowed American life.

- The cold war had roots in American suspicions of Soviet communism dating back to World War I, but Stalin's aggressive posture toward Eastern Europe and the Persian Gulf region raised new fears among American policy makers.

- In response, the Truman administration applied a policy of containment through the Truman Doc-

trine, the Marshall Plan, and NSC-68.

- The domestic transition from war to peace did not go smoothly because of inflation, labor unrest, and shortages of goods and housing, but the return of prosperity, fueled by consumer and government spending, eased the readjustment.

- Domestic fear of Communist subversion led the Truman administration to devise a government loyalty program and inspired the witch-hunts of Senator Joseph McCarthy.

- The Soviet detonation of an atomic bomb and the fall of China to the Communists, followed one year later by the Korean War, undermined the popularity of Harry Truman and the Democrats, opening the way for Dwight Eisenhower's victory in the 1952 presidential election.

Significant Events

1945	1945 Iran Crisis; civil war in Greece
1946	1946 Labor unrest; Kennan's "long telegram"; Stalin and Churchill "cold war" speeches; Republican congressional victories; McMahon Bill creates Atomic Energy Commission; Baruch plan fails at United Nations
1947	1947 Truman Doctrine; Taft-Hartley Act; Marshall announces European recovery plan; federal loyalty oath; HUAC investigates Hollywood; National Security Act creates Defense Department and CIA; Truman's Committee on Civil Rights issues *To Secure These Rights*
1948	1948 Marshall Plan adopted; Berlin blockade; Truman upsets Dewey; Truman recognizes Israel
1949	1949 Soviet atom bomb test; China falls to the Communists; NATO established; Truman orders work on hydrogen bomb
1950	1950 McCarthy's Wheeling, West Virginia, speech; Korean War begins; McCarran Act; NSC-68 adopted; Alger Hiss convicted
1951	1951 Truman fires MacArthur; peace talks in Korea
1952	1952 Richard Nixon's Checkers speech; Eisenhower defeats Stevenson
1953	1953 U.N. armistice ends police action in Korea; Rosenbergs executed
1954	1954 Army-McCarthy hearings; McCarthy censured; Robert Oppenheimer denied security clearance

additional reading

On the cold war Daniel Yergin, *Shattered Peace* (2d ed., 1989) is both readable and balanced, as are Thomas Paterson, *On Every Front* (3d ed., 1996) and Walter LaFeber, *America, Russia, and the Cold War* (8th ed., 1997). David McCullough, *Truman* (1992) combines the best of good history and popular biography. Alonzo Hamby, *Liberalism and Its Challengers* (1992) and Donald Coy, *The Presidency of Harry S Truman* (1984) are useful on the Fair Deal.

Much of the domestic red scare was fought out in and over the media. Stephen Whitfield, *The Culture of the Cold War* (1991) and John Diggins, *The Proud Decades* (1988) both provide good introductions to the tensions between popular and intellectual culture and McCarthyism. James Gilbert, *A Cycle of Outrage: America's Reaction to Juvenile Delinquency in the 1950s* (1986) shows that some critics found other forms of subversion in comic books and movies aimed at teen audiences. The special problems of Hollywood are explored in Robert Sklar, *Movie Made America: A Cultural History of American Movies* (rev. ed., 1994); Nora Sayre, *Running Time: Films of the Cold War* (1982); and Peter Biskind, *Seeing Is Believing: How Hollywood Taught Us to Stop Worrying and Love the Fifties* (1983). Erik Barnouw, *Iube of Plenty: The Evolution of American Television* (1975) argues that the same cold war tensions inhibited television programming. For a most vivid dramatic view of the witchhunt in television, see the 1976 movie *The Front,* starring Woody Allen and Zero Mostel, a blacklist victim. For a fuller list of readings, see the Bibliography.

No company epitomized the corporate culture of the 1950s more than General Motors. GM executives sought to blend in rather than to stand out. They chose their suits in drab colors—dark blue, dark gray, or light gray—to increase their anonymity. Not head car designer Harley Earl. Earl brought a touch of Hollywood into the world of corporate bureaucrats. He had a closet filled with colorful suits. His staff would marvel as he headed off to a board meeting dressed in white linen with a dark blue shirt and *blue suede shoes,* the same shoes that Elvis Presley sang so protectively about.

Mr. Earl—no one who worked for him ever called him Harley—could afford to be a maverick. He created the cars that brought customers into GM showrooms across the country. Before he came to Detroit, engineering sold cars. Advertising stressed mechanical virtues—the steady ride, reliable brakes, or, perhaps, power steering. Earl made style the distinctive feature. Unlike the boxy look other designers favored, an Earl car had a low, sleek look, suggesting motion even when the car stood still. No feature stood out more distinctively than the fins he first put on the 1948 Cadillac. By the mid-1950s jet planes inspired Earl to design ever more outrageous fins, complemented by huge, shiny chrome grills and ornaments. These features served no mechanical purpose. Some critics dismissed Earl's designs as jukeboxes on wheels.

The Suburban Era

preview • The culture of the automobile in many ways defined America at midcentury. Superhighways encouraged newly prosperous Americans to move into suburban homes boasting green lawns and new televisions. The middle-class consensus of an American dream revolved around single-family homes, religious observance of some sort, and women who cared for the family at home. And the continuing cold war cast a long shadow culminating in a confrontation over Cuba in 1962 that skirted the edge of all-out nuclear war.

To Earl and GM that did not matter. Design sold cars. "It gave [customers] an extra receipt for their money in the form of visible prestige marking for an expensive car," Earl said. The "Big Three" auto manufacturers—General Motors, Ford, and Chrysler—raced one another to redesign their annual models, the more outrageous the better. Earl once joked, "I'd put smokestacks right in the middle of the sons of bitches if I thought I could sell more cars." In the lingo of the Detroit stylists, these designs were "gasaroony," an adjective *Popular Mechanics* magazine translated as "terrific, overpowering, weird." The goal was not a better car but what Earl called "dynamic obsolescence" or simply change for change's sake. "The 1957 Ford was great," its designer remarked, "but right away we had to bury it and start another." Even a successful style had to go within a year. "We would design a car to make a man unhappy with his 1957 Ford 'long about the end of 1958." Even though the mechanics of cars changed little from year to year, dynamic obsolescence persuaded Americans in the 1950s to buy new cars in record numbers.

Fins, roadside motels, "gaseterias," drive-in burger huts, interstate highways, shopping centers, and of course, suburbs—all these were part of a culture of mobility in the 1950s. Americans continued their exodus from rural areas to cities and from the cities to the suburbs. African Americans left the South, heading for industrial centers in the Northeast, Midwest, and West Coast. Mexican Americans concentrated in southwestern cities, while Puerto Ricans came largely to New York. And for Americans in the Snowbelt, the climate of the West and South (at least when civilized by air-conditioning) made the Sunbelt irresistible to ever larger numbers.

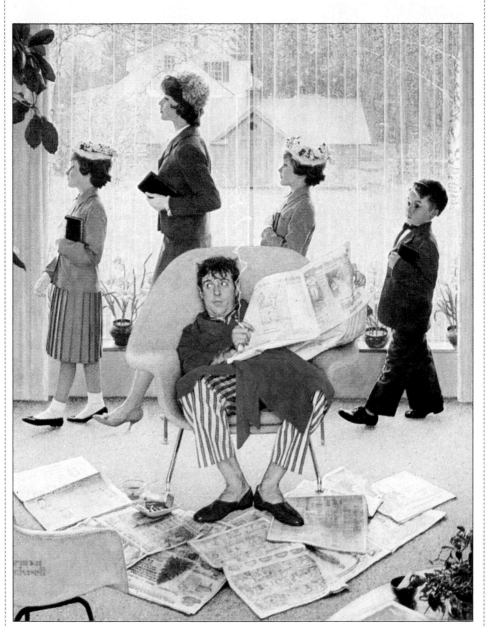

In *Easter Morning,* Norman Rockwell satirized the contrasting conformities of suburban life. This sheepish father, no doubt forced to wear suits all week, prefers a shocking red bathrobe, a cigarette, and the Sunday paper to the gray flannel lockstep of his churchbound family.

The mobility was social, too. As the economy continued to expand, the size of the American middle class grew. In an era of prosperity and peace, some commentators began to speak of a "consensus"—a general agreement in American culture, based on values of the broad middle class. In a positive light consensus reflected the agreement among most Americans about fundamental democratic values. Most citizens embraced the material benefits of prosperity as evidence of the virtue of "the American way." And they opposed the spread of communism abroad.

But consensus had its dark side. Critics worried that consensus bred a mindless conformity. Were Americans becoming too homogenized? Was there a depressing sameness in the material goods they owned, in the places they lived, and in the values they held? Besides, wasn't any notion of consensus hollow so long as racism and segregation prevented African Americans and other minorities from fully sharing in American life?

Consensus in the 1950s

The baby boomers born into this era seldom agonized over such issues. In the White House President Eisenhower radiated a comforting sense that the affairs of the nation and the world were in capable hands. That left teenagers free to worry about what really mattered: a first date, a first kiss, a first job, a first choice for college, and whether or not to "go all the way" in the back seat of one of Harley Earl's fin-swept Buicks.

The Rise of the Suburbs

The lure of the suburbs was hardly new to Americans. From the mid-nineteenth century onward, suburbs had been growing up around cities as new modes of transportation made traveling to work easier. But suburban growth accelerated sharply at the end of World War II. During the 1950s suburbs grew 40 times faster than cities, so that by 1960 half the American people lived in them. Urbanites escaping the crowding of large cities were drawn to more pastoral communities with names like Park Forest or Pacific Palisades.

Other changes in postwar society shaped the character of suburban life. With the end of the war came a baby boom and a need for new housing. With the return of prosperity came a boom in automobiles that made the suburbs accessible. But the spurt in suburban growth took its toll on the cities, which suffered as the middle class fled urban areas.

A Boom in Babies and in Housing

The Depression forced many couples to delay beginning a family. In the 1930s birthrates had reached the low point of American history, about 18 to 19 per thousand. As prosperity returned during the war, birthrates began to rise. In 1946 Americans married in record numbers, twice as many as in 1932. The new brides were also younger, most in their peak years of fertility. In a 10-year period the American population increased by 30 million, giving the United States a rate of growth comparable to that of India. By 1952 the birthrate passed 25 live births per thousand and did not peak until 1957. Ten years later it had dropped to under 18.

The boom worldwide

Historians and demographers have been hard pressed to explain this extraordinary population bulge. It was not limited to the United States. In several other industrialized nations fertility rates also soared: Australia, New Zealand, Britain, and West Germany prime among them. France and Czechoslovakia saw similar, shorter rises in the first few years after the war, but these increases seemed merely to have been a kind of catching up after the war's disruptions. Yet as the chart on page 937 indicates, the long-term trend in American fertility rates was downward, as it was in other industrialized nations. Fertility rates peaked in Australia and New Zealand in 1961, and three years later, in Great Britain and West Germany. Hence the baby boom stands as an anomaly, one that remains hard to explain.

Perhaps Americans were indeed "making up for lost time" after the war. Rising income allowed more people to afford marriage and children. But Americans should have caught up by the early 1950s, whereas the baby boom continued. Furthermore, rising standards of living do not always or even regularly go hand in hand with a baby boom. Worldwide, urbanization and higher living standards are linked to lower

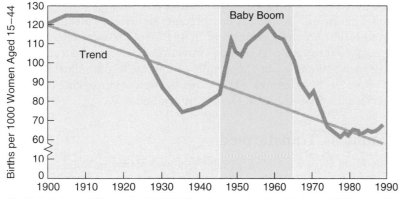

The United States Birthrate, 1900–1989 Despite periods of rapid rise and fall, the nation's birthrate has shown a steady downward trend. The Depression years showed an even sharper decline as financially strapped couples deferred child rearing. Younger marriages and postwar prosperity triggered the baby boom, but in general, affluence encourages lower birthrates.

birthrates. In 1950 the most industrialized and urban nations had a birthrate of 21.8 per thousand, while in less developed and less densely settled sub-Saharan Africa the rate was 49.8. In South Asia it was 44.8.

Whatever factors contributed to the baby boom, it had both immediate and long-term consequences for American society. In the short run, it increased demand for housing, food, consumer goods, and schools. In the long run, it made the children of the postwar era the largest population cohort in the nation. Their particular needs and expectations would have a major impact on social and political life.

Certainly, at war's end, five million American families were eagerly searching for housing, tired of living in doubled-up conditions with other families, in basements, or even in coal cellars. With the help of the GI Bill and the rising prosperity, the chance to own a house rather than rent became a reality for over half of American families. And it was the suburbs that offered the residence most idealized in American culture: a detached single-family house with a lawn and garden.

After World War II inexpensive, suburban housing became synonymous with the name of William Levitt. From building houses for war workers, Levitt learned how to use mass production techniques. In 1947 he began construction of a 17,000-house community in the New York City suburb of Hempstead. All the materials for a Levittown house were precut and assembled at a factory, then moved to the site for assembly. If all went according to schedule, a new house was erected on a cement slab every 16 minutes. Buoyed by his success in Hempstead, Levitt later built developments in Bucks County, Pennsylvania, and Willingboro, New Jersey.

Levittown, U.S.A.

The typical early Levitt house, a "Cape Codder," had a living room, kitchen, bath, and two bedrooms on the ground floor and an expansion attic, all for $7990. None had custom features, insulation, or any amenities that complicated construction. "The reason we have it so good in this country," Levitt said, "is that we can produce lots of things at low prices through mass production." Uniformity in house style extended to behavior as well. Levitt discouraged owners from changing colors or adding distinctive features to the house or yard. Buyers promised to cut the grass each week of the summer and not to hang out wash on weekends. African Americans were expressly excluded. Other suburban communities excluded Jews and ethnics through restrictive covenants that dictated who could take up residence.

In California, a state with three cars registered for every four residents, suburbs bloomed across the landscape. By 1962 it had become the nation's most populous state. Growth was greatest around Los Angeles. In 1940 city planners began building a freeway system to lure shoppers into downtown Los Angeles. Instead, white Angelinos saw the road network as an opportunity to migrate to the suburbs. Eventually one-third of the Los Angeles area was covered by highways, parking lots, and interchanges, increasing to two-thirds in the downtown areas.

Cities and Suburbs Transformed

Single-family houses on their own plots of land required plenty of open land, unlike the row houses built side by side in earlier suburban developments. That meant Levitt and other builders chose vacant areas outside major urban areas. With the new houses farther away from factories, offices, and jobs, the automobile became more indispensible than ever.

Almost all suburban activities depended on the availability of cars, cheap gasoline, and accessible roads. Shopping centers, the predecessors of more elaborate malls, exemplified the new auto-centered life. At the end of World War II the United States had just eight of these retail complexes, their clusters of stores attracting customers with convenient parking. Even a few churches and funeral homes provided drive-in facilities to attract people committed to life behind the wheel. By 1960 more than 3840 shopping centers covered as much land as the nation's central business districts.

As the population shifted to suburbs, traffic choked old country roads. To ease this congestion, the Eisenhower administration proposed a 20-year plan to build a massive interstate highway system of some 41,000 miles. Eisenhower addressed cold war fears to build support, arguing that the new system would ease evacuation of

Like a freak of evolution run riot, automotive tailfins metamorphosed from the modest stubs of a 1948 Cadillac into the monstrous protrusions of the 1959 Cadillac. With a return of prosperity, the suburban era celebrated a culture of mobility.

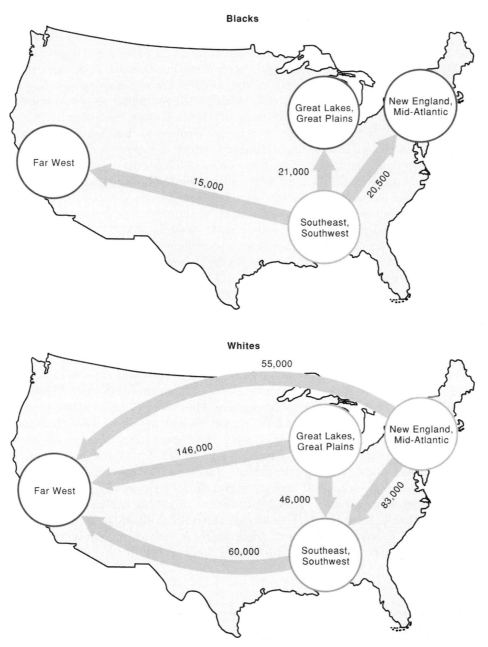

Blacks

Great Lakes, Great Plains

New England, Mid-Atlantic

Far West

21,000

20,500

15,000

Southeast, Southwest

Whites

55,000

146,000

Great Lakes, Great Plains

New England, Mid-Atlantic

Far West

46,000

83,000

60,000

Southeast, Southwest

Average Annual Regional Migration, 1947–1960 In this period, African Americans were moving in significant numbers to urban centers in the Northeast, the Midwest, and the Far West. Whites were being drawn to the increasingly diversified economy of the South as well as to the new industries, stimulated by the war, in the Far West. By the 1970s, the trend became known as the "Sunbelt" phenomenon.

cities in case of nuclear attack. In 1956 Congress passed the Interstate Highway Act, setting in motion the largest public works project in history. The federal government picked up 90 percent of the cost through a Highway Trust Fund, financed by special taxes on cars, gas, tires, lubricants, and auto parts.

The Interstate Highway Act had an enormous impact on American life. Average annual driving increased by 400 percent. Shopping centers, linked by the new roads, sprang up to provide suburbanites with an alternative to the longer trip downtown. Almost every community had at least one highway strip dotted with drive-in movies, stores, bowling alleys, gas stations, and fast-food joints.

For cities, the interstates created other problems. The new highway system featured beltways—ring roads around major urban areas. Instead of leading traffic

Interstate Highway Act of 1956

Declining cities

downtown, the beltways allowed motorists to avoid the center city altogether. As people took to their cars, intercity rail service and mass transit declined. Seventy-five percent of all government transportation dollars went to subsidize travel by car and truck; only one percent was earmarked for urban mass transit. At the same time that middle-class homeowners were moving to the suburbs, many low-paying, unskilled jobs disappeared from the cities. That forced the urban poor into reverse commuting from city to suburb. All these trends made cities less attractive places to live or do business. With fewer well-to-do taxpayers to draw on, city governments lacked the tax base to finance public services. A vicious cycle ensued that proved most damaging to the urban poor, who had few means of escape.

Much of the white population that moved to the suburbs was replaced by African Americans and Hispanics. They were part of larger migrations, especially of millions of black families leaving the South to search for work in urban centers. Most headed for the Middle Atlantic, Northeast, and Upper Midwest regions. While central cities lost 3.6 million white residents, they gained 4.5 million African Americans. Indeed, by 1960 half of all black Americans were living in central cities.

Earlier waves of European immigrants had been absorbed by the expanding urban economy. During the 1950s, however, the flight of jobs and middle-class taxpayers to the suburbs made it difficult for African Americans and Hispanics to follow the same path. In the cities fewer jobs awaited them, while declining school systems made it harder for newcomers to acculturate. In the hardest hit urban areas, unemployment rose to over 40 percent.

Minorities and suburbs

By contrast, the suburbs remained beyond reach of most minorities. Because few black or Hispanic families could afford the cost of suburban living, they accounted for less than 5 percent of the population there. The few black suburbs that existed dated from before the war and had little in common with the newer white "bedroom communities." Black suburbanites were poorer, held lower-status jobs, lived in more ramshackle housing, and had less education than urban African Americans.

Minorities who could afford the suburbs discovered that most real estate agents refused to show them houses; bankers would not provide mortgages. And many communities adopted either restrictive covenants or zoning regulations that kept out "undesirable" home buyers. One African American, William Myers, finally managed in 1957 to buy a house from a white family in Levittown, Pennsylvania, but the developers did not sell directly to African Americans until 1960.

 # The Culture of Suburbia

Suburban home ownership was popularly associated with the broad middle classes: those workers who held white- or blue-collar jobs and made enough income to afford the housing. Unlike many urban neighborhoods, where immigrant parents or grandparents might be living on the same block or even in the same apartment, single-family dwellers often left their relatives and in-laws behind. As a result, ethnic lifestyles were less pronounced in the suburbs. The restrictive immigration policies of the 1920s had also eroded ethnicity by reducing the number of newly arrived foreign-born Americans.

Class distinctions were more pronounced between suburban communities than within them. The upper middle class clustered in older developments, often centered around country clubs. Working-class suburbs sprouted on the outskirts of large manufacturing centers, where blue-collar families eagerly escaped the city to own their own homes. Within these suburbs, where differences of class and ethnicity blurred, a more homogeneous suburban culture evolved. "We see eye to eye on most things," commented one Levittown resident, "about raising kids, doing things together with your husband . . . we have practically the same identical background."

American Civil Religion

If the move to the suburbs gradually stripped many ethnics of their native customs and languages, it seldom forced them to abandon their religious identities. Religion continued to be a distinctive and segregating factor during the 1950s. Catholics, Protestants, and Jews generally married within their own faiths, and in the suburbs they kept their social distance as well.

Communities that showed no obvious class distinctions were sometimes deeply divided along religious lines. Catholics attended parochial rather than public schools, formed their own clubs, and generally did not socialize with their Protestant neighbors. Protestant and Catholic members of the same country club usually did not play golf or tennis in the same foursomes. As for Jews, social historian Richard Polenberg has remarked that whereas a gulf divided many Catholics and Protestants, Jews and Gentiles "seem to have lived on the opposite sides of a religious Grand Canyon." Even superficial signs of friendliness masked underlying mistrust and the persistence of old stereotypes.

The religious division

Although such religious boundaries remained distinct, religion was central to American life. Church membership rose to more than 50 percent for the first time in the twentieth century, and by 1957 the census bureau reported that 96 percent of the American people cited a specific affiliation when asked "What is your religion?" The religious upswing was supported in part by the prevailing cold war mood, because Communists were avowedly atheists. Cold war fervor led Congress in 1954 to add the phrase "under God" to the Pledge of Allegiance. With this phrase, commented one supporter, "we denounce the pagan doctrine of communism and declare 'under God' in favor of a free government and a free world."

Baptist Billy Graham led the revival of evangelistic denominations and sects. While his message emphasized the traditional fundamentalist themes of sin, redemption, and the Second Coming of Christ, his up-to-date methods took advantage of television, advertising, radio, and paperback books to reach the widest possible audience.

Such patriotic and anticommunist themes were strong in the preaching of clergy who pioneered the use of television. Billy Graham, a Baptist revival preacher, warned Americans to repent, for God would not long abide the sin of materialism. Graham first attracted national attention at a tent meeting in Los Angeles in 1949. Following in the tradition of nineteenth-century revivalists like Charles Finney and Dwight Moody, he soon achieved an even wider impact by televising his meetings. Though no revivalist, the Roman Catholic Bishop Fulton J. Sheen became one of television's most popular celebrities. In his weekly program he extolled traditional values and attacked communism.

The growing consensus among Americans was that *any* religious belief was better than none. President Eisenhower joined the chorus of those extolling this view. "Our government makes no sense unless it is founded on a deeply religious faith," he proclaimed, "—and I don't care what it is." Children got the message too. Every Friday afternoon kids watching *The Howdy Doody Show* were exhorted by Buffalo Bob to worship "at the church or synagogue of your choice."

Daily Lives

PUBLIC SPACE/ PRIVATE SPACE
The New Suburbia

When World War II ended, many Americans were happy to find housing of any kind. But prosperity in the 1950s brought a greater demand for houses that, like automobiles, reflected the status of those who owned them. No longer would William Levitt's standard 900-square-foot Cape Cod saltbox satisfy popular demand. Levitt's success inspired new designs, often created by builders rather than architects. Eager to please buyers rather than critics, they haphazardly mixed styles and colors.

Even so, suburban design did evolve from major architectural traditions. The most renowned of all suburban features, the picture window, traced its roots to architect Frank Lloyd Wright. Wright had come of age in the 1890s, at a time when "streetcar suburbs" were expanding around major urban areas. Wright's turn-of-the-century innovations combined open interior space, wide windows for natural lighting, and a horizontal, single-story layout. California architects translated Wright's ideas into the ranch house, where rooms flowed into each other and indoor spaces opened to the outdoors to take advantage of the mild climate. Houses with fewer walls and defined spaces discouraged formality and even privacy.

Developers across the country seized on the California "fantasy" style to conjure up dreams of informal living along with a touch of glamour. The use of picture windows allowed them to make small houses seem more spacious. Critics of suburban living suggested that the picture window was a means to ensure conformity. Why, after all, was the window most often placed looking onto the front yard, except to afford homeowners a means to keep an eye on neighbors who were watching them through their own picture windows? In truth, it made sense to have a picture window look onto the street in order to keep an eye on children. More important, the view provided about the only vantage point from which people could enjoy their front yards. Few suburbanites sat out front or actually used the lawn. But since front yards made an important statement about houses and their owners, families decorated and tended them with special care.

In the wake of the baby boom and a demand for new homes, mass-produced houses soon filled suburban developments all across the United States. By varying styles only slightly, developers were able to construct houses quickly at prices many young couples could afford.

"Homemaking" Women in the Workaday World

The growth of a suburban culture revealed a contradiction in the lives of middle-class women. Never before were their traditional roles as housewives and mothers so central to American society. Yet never before did more women join the workforce outside the home.

Most housewives found that suburban homes and growing families required increasing time and energy. With relatives and grandparents less likely to live nearby, mothering became full-time work. Dependence on automobiles made many a suburban housewife the chauffeur for her family. In the 1920s grocers or milkmen had

By 1955, economics forced developers to forsake the box shape of most suburban houses. Surveys showed that three-quarters of all would-be buyers wanted a single-story house. But with land prices rising and new zoning codes being enforced, builders could not fit enough floor space onto typical lots. To build a two-story house without seeming to, they hit upon the split-level, or "raised ranch": something, as one critic wryly noted, that "looked like a ranch-style house that had fallen out of the air and landed on something else." The front door opened onto a landing halfway between the upper and lower floors, creating an illusion that it was only half the distance from one floor to the next. The basic construction, two simple boxes side by side, was cheap to build. By placing half the living space—either the kitchen, dining, and family rooms or the bedrooms—in what would otherwise be a basement, the split level created more habitable living space at little additional cost.

Most of all, homeowners in the 1950s wanted family rooms and "live-in kitchens." One magazine described the family room as "the newest room in the house, but also the oldest," for the concept originated in the middle-class Victorian front parlor. Like it, the 1950s living room acquired more elegant furnishings for use during holidays or special entertaining. That led to the conversion of what often had been a basement "rumpus" room for the kids into a family room. Here, families sought a cozier feel with pine paneling and furniture designed for comfort and durability, with the television as the focus of the room.

The growing families of the late 1950s needed more space to prepare and eat meals. Earlier kitchens had normally been small and limited largely to food preparation. Meals were eaten in a combined living-dining area. The new larger live-in kitchens were designed, one advertiser claimed, to make "mother a member of the family again." Everyone could gather while mom cooked. The same space would also hold appliances such as dishwashers, dual ovens, and televisions, which became common kitchen features.

Clearly, suburban houses were more than "Little boxes on the hillside/Little boxes all the same," as one folk-singing critic of the 1960s complained. To the people who flocked to suburbia, their homes represented a compromise between fantasy and practicality, fulfilling the American dream, "To own your own home."

commonly delivered their goods from door to door; by the 1950s delivery services were being replaced by housewives doing "errands."

Yet between 1940 and 1960 the percentage of wives working outside the home doubled from 15 to 30 percent. Although some women took jobs simply to help make ends meet, often more than financial necessity was involved. Middle-class married women went to work as often as lower-class wives, and women with college degrees were the most likely to get a job. Two-income families were able to spend far more on extras: gifts, education, recreation, and household appliances. In addition, women found status and self-fulfillment in their jobs, as well as a chance for increased social contacts.

Working women

To housewife and mother, many suburban women of the 1950s added the role of chauffeur. Husbands who once walked to work and children who walked to school now needed to be delivered and picked up. The average suburban woman spent one full working day each week driving and doing errands.

More women were going to college, too, but that increased education did not translate into economic equality. The percentage of women holding professional jobs actually dropped between 1950 and 1960. And the gap between men's and women's wages was greater than in any other industrial nation. In the United States, the median wage for women was less than half that for men.

Media images of women

Despite women's wider roles in society, the modern media continued to portray women either as sex objects or as domesticated housewives and mothers. A typical article appearing in *Redbook* in 1957 made a heroine of Junior, a "little freckle-faced brunette" who had given up work. As the story closed, Junior nursed her baby at two in the morning, crooning "I'm glad, glad, glad I'm just a housewife." In 1950 Lynn White, the president of Mills College for women, advocated a curriculum that displaced traditional academic subjects with those that were "distinctly feminine," such as crafts or home economics.

The media trivialized women in other ways. Whereas the films of the 1930s and 1940s often starred independent, confident women, the heroines of the 1950s appeared more vulnerable. Marilyn Monroe's voluptuous sensuality, combined with a little-girl innocence, clearly appealed to male tastes. Similarly, women's fashions portrayed a male vision of femininity. In 1947 Christian Dior introduced his "new look": narrow waistlines emphasizing shapely hips and a full bosom, rarely achieved without constricting foundation garments. The heels on shoes became ever higher and the toes pointier. As historian Lois Banner concluded, "Not since the Victorian era had women's fashions been so confining."

A Revolution in Sexuality?

The suburbs themselves encouraged other changes in sexual attitudes, especially among the middle classes who lived there. Throughout the twentieth century, a trend had been under way deemphasizing the tradition that sex within marriage was primarily for the procreation of children—a duty (especially for women) to be endured rather than enjoyed. During the 1920s reformer Ben Lindsey promoted the idea of "companionate marriage," stressing personal happiness and satisfaction as primary goals. Such a marriage included the enjoyment of sex for both wife and husband.

The suburban home of the 1950s encouraged such ideals, symbolizing as it did a place of relaxation and enjoyment. Unlike city apartments, where extended families often lived in crowded conditions, the suburban single-family houses provided greater privacy and more space for intimacy.

The increased willingness to see sexual pleasure as an integral part of marriage received additional attention in 1948 with the publication of an apparently dry scientific study, *Sexual Behavior in the Human Male*. Its author, Professor Alfred Kinsey, hardly expected the storm of publicity received by that study or its companion, *Sexual Behavior in the Human Female* (1953). Kinsey began his research career as a zoologist with a zest for classifying data. During the 1940s he turned to collecting information on sexual behavior. Based on more than 10,000 interviews, Kinsey reached conclusions that were unorthodox and even startling for his day. Masturbation and premarital petting, he reported, were widespread. Women did not just endure sex as a wifely duty, they enjoyed it in much the same way men did. Extramarital sex was common for both husbands and wives. About 10 percent of the population was homosexual.

The Kinsey Report

It is difficult in more sexually liberated times to appreciate the impact of Kinsey's work and the controversy surrounding it. Commentators called his first volume "the most talked about book of the twentieth century." Social scientists, with some justice, objected that Kinsey's sample was too limited. (Most of his subjects were midwestern, middle class, and well educated.) Later studies challenged some of his figures (for example, the percentage of homosexuals in the population). Strident critics of the day charged that Kinsey was a "menace to society." These critics would have been even more outraged had they known of his private obsessions (such as filmed group sex and masochism) that may have distorted his research agenda. In public Kinsey maintained his professional posture. He had only published a "report on what people do which raises no question of what they should do." Polls indicated that most Americans felt comfortable about having such research published, perhaps partly because they found liberation in the discovery that behaviors once treated as sinful or perverse were widely practiced.

The Flickering Gray Screen

In the glow of postwar prosperity, most Americans found themselves with more leisure time and more income. In the suburbs, a yard to tend and a young family to raise determined that much of that free time would be spent around the house. The new medium of television fit perfectly into suburban lifestyles. It provided an ideal way to entertain families at home as well as sell them consumer goods.

Television viewership boomed after World War II. By 1949 Americans had bought a million sets. In only three years the figure jumped to 15 million, and by 1960, 46 million. Indeed, by then more Americans had television sets than had bathrooms. Home viewing transformed American entertainment habits, cutting sharply into pastimes like moviegoing and professional sports. In cities around the country more than 4000 neighborhood theaters closed. Many were replaced in the suburbs by popular drive-ins, which allowed whole families to enjoy movies in the comfort of their cars.

In 1948 television began its involvement in politics, covering both the Democratic and Republican conventions. Two years later, it combined entertainment, politics, and news by televising a series of hearings on organized crime chaired by Senator Estes Kefauver. Some 30 million viewers watched senators grill mobster Frank Costello about his criminal organization and its ties to city governments. Millions

Television and politics

more watched Senator Joseph McCarthy's ill-fated crusade against the army in 1954. Clearly, television demonstrated the potential to shape the political life of the nation. By the mid-1950s, however, controversy over news coverage of issues like McCarthyism led the networks to downgrade public affairs programs. As an alternative, the networks turned to Hollywood film studios, which provided them with telefilm series. By selling time to advertisers, the networks, rather than the sponsors, gained ultimate control over program content. By 1959 live television was virtually a thing of the past. Westerns, detective and quiz shows, and old movies led the ratings.

The Politics of Calm

In presiding over these changes in American society, President Dwight David Eisenhower projected an aura of paternal calm. Pursuing "modern Republicanism," the new president sought consensus, not confrontation. No longer would diehard conservatives like Herbert Hoover and Robert Taft dictate the Republican agenda. Eisenhower declared that he was "conservative when it comes to money and liberal when it comes to human beings."

Eisenhower's Modern Republicanism

Eisenhower had been raised in a large Kansas farm family. His parents, though poor, offered him a warm, caring home steeped in religious faith. In an era of organization men, Eisenhower succeeded by mastering the military's bureaucratic politics.

President Dwight D. Eisenhower

A graduate of West Point, he was neither a scholar nor an aggressive general like George Patton. In the years between the two world wars, the skills "Ike" demonstrated at golf, poker, and bridge often proved as valuable as his military expertise. Yet these genial ways could not hide his ambition or his ability to judge character shrewdly. It took a gifted organizer to coordinate the D-Day invasion and to hold together the egocentric generals who pushed east to Berlin. Eisenhower was so widely respected that both parties had considered running him in the 1948 presidential race.

In pursuing his pragmatic course, Eisenhower resisted conservative demands to dismantle New Deal programs. He even agreed to increases in social security, unemployment insurance, and the minimum wage. He accepted a small public housing program and a modest federally supported medical insurance plan for the needy. But as a conservative, Eisenhower remained uncomfortable with big government. Thus he rejected more far-reaching liberal proposals on housing and universal health care through the social security system.

To make modern Republicanism successful, Eisenhower had to woo the newly prosperous Democratic voters joining the middle class. Success in that effort hinged on how well the administration managed the economy. The Democrats of the New Deal had established a tradition of activism. When the economy faltered, deficit spending and tax cuts were used to stimulate it. Eisenhower, in contrast, wanted to reduce federal spending and the government's role in the economy. When a recession struck in 1953–1954, the administration was concerned more with balancing the budget and holding inflation in line than with reducing unemployment through government spending.

But these policies worked poorly enough (and the voters expressed their resentment in midterm elections) so that when recessions hit again in 1957–1958 and 1960–1961 the administration spoke less of balancing the budget. Indeed, Eisenhower achieved that goal in only three of eight fiscal years, and in 1959 he faced what was then the largest peacetime deficit in history. The result was that although the economy grew during the Eisenhower years, that growth remained uneven. The poor of both urban and rural areas remained largely unaffected by economic expansion.

Eisenhower followed a similar pragmatic approach in other areas. When major projects called for federal leadership, as with the Highway Act, he supported the policy. In 1954 he signed the St. Lawrence Seaway Act, which joined the United States and Canada in an ambitious engineering project to open the Great Lakes to ocean shipping. Like the highway program, the Seaway was fiscally acceptable because the funding came from user tolls and taxes rather than from general revenues.

In farm policy Eisenhower's practical approach yielded scant results. Farmers made up a major Republican voting bloc. For the president to abolish the price supports established under the New Deal was to commit political suicide. On the other hand, crop surpluses continued to fill government silos with unwanted grain. Eisenhower's secretary of agriculture, Ezra Taft Benson, proposed a system of lower support payments designed to discourage farmers from overproducing basic commodities like corn, cotton, and wheat. Benson also established a soil bank program to pay farmers for taking land out of production.

Farm policy

In the end, however, modern technology made it difficult to limit agricultural production. Automated harvesters, fertilizers, and new varieties of plants increased farm outputs even though farmers were planting fewer acres. Pressure to maximize production and profit grew as more and more small farms were being replaced by large commercial farms called agribusinesses. Modern business farmers made ever more use of artificial pesticides, herbicides, and fertilizers. Runoff of these chemicals began to poison the nation's groundwater, lakes, and rivers, but the damage went largely unnoticed. Americans in the 1950s worried more about economic growth than the quality of their environment.

Despite occasional economic setbacks Eisenhower remained popular. Even after he suffered a major heart attack in 1955, voters gladly reelected him over Adlai Stevenson in 1956. But poor economic performance took its toll on the Republican party. In the wake of the 1954 recession the Democrats gained a 29-member majority in the House and a 1-vote edge in the Senate. Never again would Eisenhower work with a Republican majority in Congress. In 1958, when recession again dragged down the economy, the Democrats took a 68-seat majority in the House and a 12-vote advantage in the Senate. Modern Republicanism did not put down deep roots beyond Eisenhower's White House.

Eisenhower reelected

counterpoint

Assessing Eisenhower

In 1962, when historians rated presidential performance, Eisenhower scored near the bottom, barely ahead of Ulysses S. Grant. As president, he had kept a low political profile. His speeches often wandered; at press conferences he sometimes seemed uninformed. Critics complained that he conceived of himself as a mere figurehead, like a constitutional monarch. Certainly, Eisenhower remained more aloof than most presidents. He seldom challenged the aggressive anticommunism of Senator Joseph McCarthy, and as we shall see, he only reluctantly moved to defend the civil rights of African Americans. Critics also attacked Eisenhower's firm belief in letting the business community chart its own course without government interference. Secretary of Defense Charles Wilson, former president of General Motors, best expressed the administration's probusiness creed when he told a Senate committee that he had always believed, "What was good for our country was good for General Motors and vice versa."

More recently, historians have been inclined to place Eisenhower among the most capable of American presidents. His aloof manner, some argue, disguised a president whose "hidden hand" acted vigorously behind the scenes. While in public Eisenhower let others speak for him (and take the heat), in private he made decisions and set directions. The garbled or rambling answers at press conferences were sometimes an act to bamboozle the press. "Don't worry," he once reassured his press secretary, "if that question comes [up] I'll just confuse them." Ike was not activist in the energetic tradition of either Roosevelt. Then again, the three presidents who followed him took "bold" actions that were quite controversial: John Kennedy's invasion of Cuba, Lyndon Johnson's war in Vietnam, and Richard Nixon's political overreaching. In this light Eisenhower's modern Republicanism no longer seems like inactive government but a mature appreciation of the limits of the presidency.

The Conglomerate World

Large corporations welcomed the administration's probusiness attitudes as well as the era's general prosperity. Wages for the average worker rose over 35 percent between 1950 and 1960. At the same time, the economic distress of the 1930s had led corporate executives to devise new ways to minimize the danger of economic downturns. Each of the approaches expanded the size of corporations in various ways in order to minimize shocks in specific markets.

One expansion strategy took the form of diversification. In the 1930s, a giant like General Electric had concentrated largely in one industrial area: equipment for generating electric power and light. When the Depression struck, GE found its markets evaporating. The company responded by entering markets for appliances, X-ray machines, and elevators—all products developed or enhanced by the company's research labs. In the postwar era General Electric diversified even further, into nuclear power, jet engines, and television. Diversification was most practical for large industrial firms, whose size allowed them to support extensive research and development.

Conglomeration often turned small companies into giants. Unlike earlier horizontal and vertical combinations, conglomerate mergers could join companies with seemingly unrelated products. Over a 20-year period International Telephone and Telegraph branched out from its basic communications business into baking, hotels and motels, car rental, home building, and insurance. Corporations also became multinational by expanding their overseas operations or buying out potential foreign competitors. Large integrated oil companies like Mobil and Standard Oil of New Jersey (Exxon) developed huge oil fields in the Middle East and markets around the free world.

One aid to managing these modern corporate giants was the advent of electronic data processing. In the early 1950s computers were virtually unknown in private industry. But banks and insurance companies saw these calculating machines

General Electric emerged as one of the great conglomerate corporate enterprises of the postwar era. It produced consumer, military, and industrial goods. To shape its public image General Electric used former movie star and television celebrity (and later president) Ronald Reagan as its spokesperson.

as an answer to their need to manipulate huge quantities of records and statistical data. Manufacturers, especially in the petroleum, chemical, automotive, and electronics industries, began to use computers to monitor their production lines, quality control, and inventory.

As corporations merged in order to increase their reach, power, and stability, corporate spokespeople praised the prosperity of business as a part of the emerging consensus over the American way. ("What was good for our country was good for General Motors.") Yet there were distinct cracks in the consensus. Intellectuals and social critics spoke out against the stifling features of a conformist corporate culture. At the fringes of American society, the beatniks rejected conformity, while the more mainstream rock and roll movement broadcast its own brand of youthful rebellion.

Cracks in the Consensus

Critics of Mass Culture

In Levittown, New Jersey, a woman who had invited her neighbors to a cocktail party eagerly awaited them dressed in newly fashionable Capri pants—a tight-fitting calf-length style. Alas, one early arriving couple glimpsed the woman through a window. What on earth was the hostess wearing? *Pajamas?* Who in their right mind would entertain in pajamas? The couple sneaked home, afraid they had made a mistake about the day of the party. They telephoned another neighbor, who anxiously called yet others on the guest list.

The neighbors finally mustered enough courage to attend the party. But when the hostess later learned of their misunderstanding, she put her Capri pants in the closet for good. Levittown was not ready for such a change in fashion.

Was America turning into a vast suburban wasteland, where the neighbors' worries over Capri pants would stifle all individuality? Many highbrow intellectuals worried openly about the homogenized lifestyle created by mass consumption, conformity, and mass media. Critics such as Dwight Macdonald sarcastically attacked the culture of the suburban middle classes: *Reader's Digest* Condensed Books, uplifting film spectacles such as *The Ten Commandments*, television dramas that pretended to be high art but in reality were little more than simplistic pontificating. "Midcult," Macdonald called it, which was his shorthand for middlebrow culture.

Other critics charged that the skyscrapers and factories of giant conglomerates housed an all-too-impersonal world. In large, increasingly automated workplaces, skilled laborers seemed little more than caretakers of machines. Large corporations required middle-level executives to submerge their personal goals in the processes and work routines of a large bureaucracy. David Riesman, a sociologist, condemned stifling conformity in *The Lonely Crowd* (1950). In nineteenth-century America, Riesman argued, Americans had been "inner directed." It was their own consciences that formed their values and drove them to seek success. In contrast, modern workers had developed a personality shaped not so much by inner convictions as by the opinions of their peers. The new "other-directed" society of suburbia preferred security to success. "Go along to get along" was its

David Riesman's *The Lonely Crowd*

motto. In a bureaucratized economy, it was important to please others, to conform to the group, and to cooperate.

William Whyte's *The Organization Man*

William Whyte carried Riesman's critique from the workplace to the suburb in *The Organization Man* (1956). Here he found rootless families, shifted from town to town by the demands of corporations. (IBM, according to one standard joke, stood for "I've Been Moved.") The typical organization man was sociable but not terribly ambitious. He sought primarily to keep up with the Joneses and the number of consumer goods they owned. He lived in a suburban "split-level trap," as one critic put it, one among millions of "haggard" men, "tense and anxious" women, and "the gimme kids," who, like the cartoon character Dennis the Menace, looked up from the litter under the Christmas tree to ask, "Is that all?"

No doubt such portraits were overdrawn. (Where, after all, did Riesman's nineteenth-century inner-directed Americans get their values, if not from the society around them?) But such critiques indicated the problems of adjustment faced by people working within large bureaucratic organizations and living in suburbs that were decentralized and self-contained.

The Rebellion of Young America

Young Americans were among suburbia's sharpest critics. Dance crazes, outlandish clothing, strange jargon, rebelliousness toward parents, and sexual precociousness—all these behaviors challenged middle-class respectability. More than a few parents and public figures warned that America had spawned a generation of rebellious juvenile delinquents. Psychologist Frederic Wertheim told a group of doctors, "You cannot understand present-day juvenile delinquency if you do not take into account the pathogenic and pathoplastic [infectious] influence of comic books." Others laid the blame on films and the lyrics of popular music.

Juvenile delinquency

The center of the new teen culture was the high school. Whether in consolidated rural school districts, new suburban schools, or city systems, the large, comprehensive high schools of the 1950s were often miniature melting pots in which middle-class students were exposed to, and often adopted, the style of the lower classes. Alarmed school administrators complained of juvenile delinquents who wore jeans and T-shirts, challenged authority, and defiantly smoked cigarettes, much like the motorcycle gang leader portrayed by Marlon Brando in the film *The Wild One* (1954).

In many ways the argument about juvenile delinquency was an argument about social class and, to a lesser degree, race. Adults who complained that delinquent teenagers dressed poorly, lacked ambition, and were irresponsible and sexually promiscuous were voicing the same arguments traditionally used to denigrate other outsiders—immigrants, the poor, and African Americans. Nowhere were these racial and class undertones more evident than in the hue and cry greeting the arrival of rock and roll.

The rise of rock and roll

Before 1954 popular music had been divided into three major categories: pop, country and western, and rhythm and blues. A handful of major record companies with almost exclusively white singers dominated the pop charts. On one fringe of the popular field was country and western, often split into cowboy musicians such as Roy Rogers and Gene Autry and the hillbilly style associated with Nashville. The music industry generally treated rhythm and blues as "race music," whose performers and audience were largely black. Each of these musical traditions grew out of regional cultures. As the West and the South merged into the national culture, so too were these musical subcultures gradually integrated into the national mainstream.

By the mid-1950s the distinctiveness of the three styles began to blur. Singers on the white pop charts recorded a few songs from country and from rhythm and blues. The popularity of crossover songs such as "Sh-boom," "Tutti-Frutti," and "Earth Angel" indicated that a major shift in taste and market was under way. Lyrics still reflected the pop field's preoccupation with young love, marriage, and happiness, but the music now vibrated with the rawer, earthier style of rhythm and blues. Country and western singer Bill Haley brought the new blend to the fore in 1954 with "Shake, Rattle, and Roll," the first rock song to reach the top ten on the pop charts.

And then—calamity! Millions of middle-class roofs nearly blew off with the appearance in 1955 of the rhythmic and raucous Elvis Presley. By background, Elvis was a country boy whose musical style combined elements of gospel, country, and blues. But it was his hip-swinging, pelvis-plunging performances that electrified teenagers. To more conservative adults, Presley's long hair, sideburns, and tight jeans seemed menacingly delinquent, an expression of hostile rebellion. What they often resented but rarely admitted was that Elvis looked lower class, sounded black, and really could sing.

The King, Elvis Presley

Beyond the frenetic rhythms of rock and roll, and even farther beyond the pale of suburban culture, flourished a subculture known as the beat generation. In rundown urban neighborhoods and college towns this motley collection of artists, intellectuals, musicians, and middle-class students dropped out of mainstream society. In dress and behavior the beatniks self-consciously rejected what they viewed as the excessive spiritual bankruptcy of America's middle-class culture. Cool urban hipsters—especially black jazz musicians like John Coltrane or Sonny Rollins—were their models. They read poetry, listened to jazz, explored Oriental philosophy, and experimented openly with drugs, mystical religions, and sex.

The beat generation

The "beats" viewed themselves as being driven to the margins of society, rejecting the culture of abundance, materialism, and conformity. "I saw the best minds of my generation destroyed by madness, starving hysterical naked," wrote Allen Ginsberg in his 1955 poem *Howl.* They had become "angelheaded hipsters . . . who in poverty and tatters and hollow-eyed and high sat up smoking in the supernatural darkness of cold-water flats floating across the tops of cities contemplating jazz." Jack Kerouac tapped the frenzied energy beneath the beatniks' cool facade in *On the Road* (1957), a novel based on his travels across the country with his friend Neal Cassady. Kerouac finished the novel in one frenetic three-week binge, feeding a 120-foot roll of paper through his typewriter and spilling out tales of pot, jazz, crazy sex, and all-night raps undertaken in a search for "IT"—the ultimate transcendental moment when mind and experience mesh.

Try as they might, the beats could not ignore the atomic menace that overshadowed American society at midcentury.

Nationalism in an Age of Superpowers

Along the Iron Curtain of Eastern Europe and across the battle lines of northern Asia, Soviet-American rivalry had settled into a stalemate. The American public shared with most foreign policy makers a view of the globe as divided between the "free world" nations and the "communist bloc." Thus the Eisenhower administration sought ways to contain the Soviets: setting up security and trade agreements, employing covert action to install governments favorable to the United States, and using the threat of nuclear war, if need be.

Not all nations viewed the world in such bipolar terms. World War II had disrupted Europe's longstanding imperial relationships. As nationalists in the Middle East, Africa, and Southeast Asia fought to gain independence from their colonial masters, new nations like India proclaimed themselves "nonaligned," independent of the Soviet Union and the United States. Nonetheless the two superpowers competed for the allegiance of emerging nations. And as crises flared in one region or another, the risk was always present that a minor conflict might escalate into the ultimate nuclear confrontation between the superpowers.

To the Brink?

John Foster Dulles

As a general who fought in a global war and as commander of NATO, Eisenhower was no stranger to world politics. Still, he shared the conduct of foreign policy with his secretary of state, John Foster Dulles. Dulles approached his job with a somber enthusiasm. Coming from a family of missionaries and diplomats, he had within him a touch of both. He viewed the Soviet-American struggle in almost religious terms: a fight of good against evil between two irreconcilable superpowers. Admirers praised his global vision; detractors saw him as "the wooliest type of pontificating American." Certainly Dulles did not lack confidence. "With my understanding of the intricate relationship between the peoples of the world," he told Eisenhower, "and your sensitiveness to the political considerations, we will make the most successful team in history."

The administration was determined to make Truman's containment strategy more forceful. Dulles, the more confrontational of the two men, wanted the United States to aid in liberating the "captive peoples" of Eastern Europe and other Communist nations. On the other hand, Eisenhower was equally determined to cut back military spending and troop levels in order to keep the budget balanced. The president, who understood well how the military services and their allies in defense industries competed for government money, was irked at the "fantastic programs" the Pentagon kept proposing. "If we demand too much in taxes in order to build planes and ships," he argued, "we will tend to dry up the accumulations of capital that are necessary to provide jobs for the million or more new workers that we must absorb each year."

The New Look in foreign policy

So Eisenhower and Dulles hit on a more economical strategy. Rather than rely on conventional forces, they would contain Soviet aggression by using the threat of massive nuclear retaliation. Dulles insisted that Americans should not shrink from the threat of nuclear war: "If you are scared to go to the brink, you are lost." As Treasury Secretary George Humphrey put it, a nuclear strategy was much cheaper— "a bigger bang for the buck." Henceforth American foreign policy would have an aggressive "New Look." Behind the more militant rhetoric, however, lay an ongoing commitment to containment.

Brinksmanship in Asia

Taiwan and mainland China

Moving from talk of "brinksmanship" to concrete action did not prove easy. When Dulles announced American intentions to "unleash" Chiang Kai-shek to attack mainland China from his outpost on Taiwan (formerly Formosa), China threatened to invade Taiwan. At that, Eisenhower ordered the Seventh Fleet into the area to pro-

Asian Trouble Spots After the Geneva Accords divided Indochina into North and South Vietnam, Secretary of State Dulles organized the Southeast Asia Treaty Organization (SEATO) to resist communist aggression in Southeast Asia. In addition to the conflict in Vietnam, tensions were fueled by the mutual hostility between mainland Communist China and Chiang Kai-shek's Taiwan as well as the offshore islands of Quemoy and Matsu.

tect rather than unleash Chiang. If the Communists attacked, he warned bluntly in 1955, "we'll have to use atomic weapons."

Nuclear weapons also figured in the American response to a crisis in Southeast Asia. There, Vietnamese forces led by Ho Chi Minh were fighting the French, who had returned to reestablish their own colonial rule. Between 1950 and 1954, the United States provided France with more than $1 billion in military aid in Vietnam. Eisenhower worried that if Vietnam fell to a Communist revolutionary like Ho, other nations of Southeast Asia would soon follow. "You have a row of dominoes set up," the president warned, "you knock over the first one. . . . You could have the beginning of a disintegration that would have the most profound influences."

Worn down by a war they seemed unable to win, the French in 1954 tried to force a final showdown with Ho's forces at Dien Bien Phu. With Vietnamese and Chinese Communist troops holding the surrounding hilltops, the French garrison of 12,000 could not have chosen a worse place to do battle. Desperate, the French government pleaded for more American aid and the Joint Chiefs of Staff responded by volunteering to relieve the besieged French forces with a massive American air raid—including the use of tactical nuclear weapons, if necessary. Dulles too recommended an air strike, but Eisenhower pulled back. After Korea, the idea of American involvement in another Asian war aroused opposition from both allies and domestic political leaders.

Collapsing under the siege, the garrison at Dien Bien Phu surrendered in May 1954. At a peace conference held in Geneva, Switzerland, Ho Chi Minh agreed to withdraw his forces north of the 17th parallel, temporarily dividing the nation into North and South Vietnam. Because of Ho's widespread popularity, he could count on an easy victory in the elections that the peace conference agreed would be held within two years. Dulles, however, viewed any Communist victory as unacceptable, even if the election was democratic. He convinced Eisenhower to support a South Vietnamese government under Ngo Dinh Diem. Diem, Dulles insisted, was not bound by the agreement signed in Geneva to hold any election. The United States became further involved by sending a military mission to train an army to keep Diem in power.

Vietnamese victory at Dien Bien Phu

The Covert Side of the New Look

Overthrowing Mossadeq

In pursuing their aggressive New Look in foreign policy, Dulles and Eisenhower sometimes authorized the Central Intelligence Agency (CIA) to use covert operations against communists or those they saw as sympathetic to Moscow. For example, in Iran in 1951 a nationalist government under Mohammed Mossadeq seized the assets of a giant British oil company. With the United States boycotting Iranian oil, Dulles worried that Mossadeq would turn to the neighboring Soviet Union for aid. Eisenhower approved a secret CIA operation to topple the Mossadeq government. Led by Teddy Roosevelt's grandson, Kermit Roosevelt, Operation Ajax recruited a mob to help Iranian armed forces drive Mossadeq from the country and return Iran's monarch, Shah Mohammad Reza Pahlavi, to his throne in August 1953.

Crushing a democracy

Seeing how cheaply American influence had been restored in Iran, Secretary Dulles looked for similar results in Guatemala. Unlike Iran, however, Guatemala had an elected democratic government under Colonel Jacobo Arbenz Guzmán. Arbenz was determined to reduce the poverty in his country by confiscating the idle farmland of rich landowners and giving it to the peasants. Guatemala's richest landowner was the Boston-based United Fruit Company. United Fruit had long supported conservative governments, paid few taxes, and shipped its profits back to the United States.

When the Guatemalan government seized 400,000 acres from United Fruit, the company's agents branded Arbenz a communist. The American ambassador to Guatemala knew that the label was not true but later explained "that the man thought like a communist and talked like a communist, and if not actually one, would do until one came along." After Communist Czechoslovakia sent Guatemala 1900 tons of small arms, Dulles ordered a CIA-trained band of Latin American mercenaries into the country, supported by American planes. Within a week the leader of the Guatemalan rebels, Carlos Castillo Armas, replaced the Arbenz democracy with a military dictatorship that quickly returned the expropriated lands to United Fruit.

Success in Iran and Guatemala greatly enhanced the reputation of the CIA. American policy makers developed a misplaced faith that covert operations could achieve dramatic results at low cost. But in overthrowing popular governments or defending unpopular ones, the United States gained a reputation in many Third

The CIA secretly helped overthrow the Guatemalan government in 1954. One plan, apparently never carried out, called for the assassination of 58 Guatemalan officials. But the CIA's chilling "Conference Room Technique" survived, a four-step plan showing how "a room containing as many as a dozen subjects can be 'purified' in about 20 seconds" by two assassins. Step 4 was to "leave propaganda," making it seem as if communists had carried out the massacre.

World countries as a foe of national liberation, popular democracy, and social reform. In 1958 the depth of anti-American feeling became obvious when angry crowds in several Latin American countries attacked Vice President Richard Nixon's car, spat at him, and pelted him with eggs and stones.

Nationalism Unleashed

Korea, Indochina, Iran, Guatemala—to Dulles and Eisenhower, the crises in all these countries could be traced back to the Soviet dictatorship. Throughout the 1950s Eisenhower's secretary of state crisscrossed the globe, setting up mutual defense pacts, patterned on NATO, to solidify American security. Yet through all this activity, it was becoming harder to decide what the motives of the Soviets themselves might be.

Joseph Stalin had died in March 1953 after becoming increasingly isolated, arbitrary, vengeful, and perhaps simply mad. Power soon fell to Nikita Khrushchev, a party stalwart with a formidable intellect and peasant origins in the farm country of the Ukraine. In some ways Khrushchev resembled another farm-belt politician, Harry Truman. Both were unsophisticated yet shrewd, earthy in their sense of humor, energetic, short-tempered, and largely inexperienced in international affairs. Khrushchev kept American diplomats off balance: at times genial and conciliatory, he would suddenly become demanding and boastful.

At home Khrushchev established a more moderate regime, gradually shifting the economy toward production of consumer goods. Internationally, he sought to ease tensions and reduce forces in Europe, hoping to make Western Europeans less dependent on the United States. Yet the growing tide of nationalism made it difficult for either superpower to pursue more conciliatory policies.

When Khrushchev began to ease Stalin's iron ways, nationalists in Soviet-controlled Eastern Europe pushed for greater independence. Riots erupted in Poland, while in Hungary students took to the streets. When the rioting spread, Moscow accepted the new Hungarian government and began to remove Soviet tanks. But Hungary announced it was withdrawing from the Warsaw Pact. The act of independence proved too threatening. In October 1956 Soviet tanks rolled back into Budapest and crushed the uprising. The U.S. state department issued formal protests but did nothing to help liberate the "captive nations." For all Dulles's tough talk, the New Look foreign policy recognized that the Soviets possessed a sphere of influence in which the United States would not intervene.

Eastern Europe was not the only nationalist crisis Eisenhower faced in 1956. That same year in Egypt, nationalist forces confronted the United States. Colonel Gamal Abdel Nasser was attempting to modernize his country and rebuild his army. Dulles had hoped to win Nasser's friendship by offering American aid to build the Aswan Dam, a massive power project on the Nile River. But when Nasser formed an Arab alliance against the young state of Israel and continued to pursue economic ties with the Warsaw bloc, Dulles decided to teach the Egyptian leader a lesson. He withdrew the American pledge on Aswan. Nasser angrily upped the ante by seizing the Suez Canal, through which tankers carried most of Europe's oil.

Events moved quickly. Israel, alarmed at Nasser's Arab alliance, invaded Egypt's Sinai peninsula on October 29—the same day Hungary announced it was leaving the Warsaw Pact. Three days later French and British forces seized the canal in an attempt to restore their own interests and prestige. Angered that his allies had not

Nikita Khrushchev

Nikita Khrushchev was by turns boisterous and somber, threatening and conciliatory. *Time*'s cover of 1958 captured the brash style that both captivated and alarmed Americans. Khrushchev smiles as he toys with the Soviets' newly launched *Sputnik*, yet he made the most of the Russian lead in the space race, joking about American failures. The Sputnik satellites were "lonely . . . waiting for American satellites to join them in space."

consulted him, Eisenhower joined the Soviet Union in supporting a UN resolution condemning Britain, France, and Israel. The two superpowers demanded an immediate cease-fire. By December American pressures forced Britain and France to remove their forces.

The Eisenhower Doctrine

Given the unstable situation in the Middle East, Eisenhower convinced Congress to grant him the authority to use force against any communist attack in that region. What became known as the Eisenhower Doctrine in effect allowed the president in times of crisis to preempt Congress's power to declare war. In 1958 he used that power to send U.S. marines into Lebanon, a small nation that claimed to have been infiltrated by Nasser's supporters. Since no fighting had yet occurred, sunbathers on the beaches of Beirut, Lebanon's capital, were startled as 5000 combat-clad marines stormed ashore. In the end the crisis blew over and the American forces withdrew. Dulles claimed that the United States had once again turned back the communist drive into the emerging nations. In reality, nationalism more than communism had been at the root of Middle Eastern turmoil.

Nationalist forces were also in ferment in Latin America, where only 2 percent of the people controlled 75 percent of the land. Repressive dictatorships exercised power, and foreign interests—especially American—dominated Latin American economies. Given the unequal distribution of wealth and a rapidly growing population, social tensions were rising. Cuba, only 90 miles south of American shores, was typical.

Castro's revolution in Cuba

The United States owned many Cuban economic resources, including 80 percent of its utilities, and operated a naval base at Guantánamo Bay. Cuban dictator Fulgencio Batista had close ties both to the American government and to major crime figures who operated gambling, prostitution, and drug rings in Havana. A disgruntled middle-class lawyer, Fidel Castro, gained the support of impoverished peasants in Cuba's mountains and in January 1959 drove Batista from power.

At first many Americans applauded the revolution and welcomed Castro when he visited the United States. But President Eisenhower was distinctly cool to the cigar-smoking Cuban. By summer Castro had filled key positions with Communists, launched a sweeping agricultural reform, and confiscated American properties. In retaliation Eisenhower placed an embargo on Cuban sugar and mobilized opposition to Castro in other Latin American countries. Cut off from American markets and aid, Castro turned to the Soviet Union.

The Response to *Sputnik*

Castro's turn to the Soviets seemed all the more dangerous because the Soviet Union in 1957 stunned America by launching the first space satellite, dubbed *Sputnik*. By 1959, the Soviets had crash-landed a much larger payload on the moon. If the Russians could target the moon, surely they could launch nuclear missiles against America. In contrast, the American space program suffered so many delays and mishaps that rockets exploding on launch were nicknamed "flopniks" and "kaputniks."

How had the Soviets managed to catch up with American technology so quickly? Some analysts blamed the schools, especially weak programs in science and math. In 1958 Eisenhower joined with Congress to enact a National Defense Education Act, designed to strengthen graduate education and the teaching of science, math, and foreign languages. At the same time, crash programs were undertaken to build basement fallout shelters to protect Americans in case of a nuclear attack. Democrats charged that the administration had allowed the United States to face an unacceptable "missile gap."

Even before the launch of *Sputnik* in 1957, Americans had begun devising fallout shelters for protection from the effects of a nuclear attack. This one was exhibited in 1955.

Thaws and Freezes

Throughout this series of crises, each superpower found it difficult to interpret the other's motives. The Russians exploited nationalist revolutions where they could—less successfully in Egypt, more so in Cuba. "We will bury you," Khrushchev admonished Americans, though it was unclear whether he meant through peaceful competition or military confrontation. More menacingly, in November 1958 he demanded that the Western powers withdraw all troops from West Berlin within six months. Berlin would then become a "free city," and the Western powers could negotiate further access to it only through East Germany, a government that the West had refused to recognize. When Eisenhower flatly rejected the ultimatum, Khrushchev backed away from his hard-line stance.

Rather than adopt a more belligerent course, Eisenhower determined to use the last 18 months of his presidency to improve Soviet-American relations. The shift in policy was made easier because the president knew from American intelligence (but could not admit publicly) that the missile gap was not real. Eisenhower, although willing to support some additional development of missile systems, also invited Khrushchev to visit the United States in September 1959. The Soviet premier undertook a picturesque tour across America, swapping comments about manure with Iowa farmers, reacting puritanically to movie cancan dancers, and grousing when his visit to the new capitalist marvel, Disneyland, was canceled for security reasons.

Eisenhower's plans for a return visit to the Soviet Union were abruptly canceled in 1960 after the Russians shot down a high-altitude U-2 American spy plane over Soviet territory. At first Eisenhower claimed that the plane had strayed off course

Berlin crisis

The U-2 incident

while doing weather research, but Khrushchev sprang his trap: the CIA pilot, Gary Powers, had been captured alive. The president then admitted that for reasons of national security he had personally authorized the U-2 overflights.

That episode ended Eisenhower's hopes that his personal diplomacy might thaw cold war tensions. Yet a less mature president might have led the United States into more severe conflict or even war. Eisenhower was not readily impressed by the promises of new weapon systems or overheated talk about a missile gap between the United States and the Soviet Union. He left office with a warning that too much military spending would lead to "an unwarranted influence, whether sought or unsought" by the "military-industrial complex" at the expense of democratic institutions.

The Cold War Along a New Frontier

The 1960 election promised to bring the winds of change to Washington. The opponents—Vice President Richard Nixon and Senator John F. Kennedy of Massachusetts—were the first major presidential candidates born in the twentieth century. At the age of 43, Kennedy would be the youngest person ever elected to the presidency, and Nixon was only four years older. The nation needed to find new challenges and "new frontiers," Kennedy proclaimed. His rhetoric was noble, but the direction in which he would take the nation was far from clear.

The Election of 1960

The Catholic issue

Jack Kennedy's biggest hurdle to election was social as much as political. He was a Roman Catholic out of Irish Boston, and no Catholic had ever been elected president. Conservative Protestants, many concentrated in the heavily Democratic South, were convinced that a Catholic president would never be "free to exercise his own judgment" if the pope ordered otherwise. Kennedy chose to confront the issue head-on. In September he entered the lions' den, addressing an

Candidate (Party)	Electoral Vote	Popular Vote
Kennedy (Democratic)	303 (56%)	34,227,096 (49.7%)
Nixon (Republican)	219 (41%)	34,107,646 (49.6%)
Byrd (Independent)	15 (3%)	501,643 (0.7%)

1960

Election of 1960

association of hostile Protestant ministers in Houston. The speech was the best of his campaign. "I believe in an America where the separation of church and state is absolute," he said, "—where no Catholic prelate would tell the President (should he be Catholic) how to act, and no Protestant minister would tell his parishioners how to vote." House Speaker Sam Rayburn, an old Texas pol, was astonished by Kennedy's bravura performance. "My God! . . . He's eating them blood raw."

Kennedy's opponent, Vice President Richard Nixon, ran on his record as an experienced leader and staunch anti-Communist, but his campaign faltered in October as unemployment rose. Nixon agreed to a series of debates with Kennedy—the first to be televised nationally. Image proved more telling than issues. According to one poll, radio listeners believed Nixon won the debate; but television viewers saw a fatigued candidate with "five o'clock shadow," because Nixon had refused to use television makeup. A relaxed Kennedy convinced many viewers that he could handle the job.

In the end religion, ethnicity, and race played decisive roles in Kennedy's triumph. One voter was asked if he voted for Kennedy because he was a Catholic. "No, because *I* am," he answered; and in key states Catholic support made a difference. "Hyphenated" Americans—Hispanic, Jewish, Irish, Italian, Polish, and German—voted Democratic in record numbers, while much of the black vote that had gone to Eisenhower in 1956 returned to the Democratic fold. Indeed, when civil rights leader Martin Luther King was imprisoned during a protest in Georgia, Kennedy attracted the support of black Americans by telephoning his sympathy to Dr. King's wife. Interest in the election ran so high that 64 percent of voters turned out, the largest percentage in 50 years. Out of 68.8 million ballots cast, Kennedy won by a margin of just 119,000.

The Hard-Nosed Idealists of Camelot

Many observers compared the Kennedy White House to Camelot, King Arthur's magical court. A popular musical of 1960 pictured Camelot as a land where skies were fair, men brave, women pretty, and the days full of challenge and excitement. With similar vigor, Kennedy brought into his administration bright, energetic advisers. He and his stylish wife, Jacqueline, invited artists, musicians, and intellectuals to the White House. Impromptu touch football games on the White House lawn displayed a rough-and-tumble playfulness, akin to Arthur's jousting tournaments of old.

In truth, Kennedy was not a liberal by temperament. Handsome and intelligent, he possessed an ironic, self-deprecating humor. In Congress he had led an undistinguished career, supported Senator Joe McCarthy, and earned a reputation as a playboy. Once Kennedy set his sights on the White House, however, he revealed an astonishing capacity for political maneuver and organization. To woo the liberals in his party, he surrounded himself with a distinguished group of intellectuals and academics.

Robert Strange McNamara typified the pragmatic, liberal bent of the new Kennedy team. Steely and brilliant, McNamara was one of the postwar breed of young executives known as the "whiz kids." As a Harvard Business School professor and later as president of Ford Motors, he specialized in using quantitative tools to streamline business. As the new secretary of defense, McNamara intended to find more flexible and efficient ways of conducting the cold war.

Robert McNamara

The urbane and energetic John F. Kennedy was associated with both King Arthur (left, played by Richard Burton in the 1960 musical) and the spy James Bond (played by Sean Connery, right). Kennedy and his advisers prided themselves on their pragmatic, hard-nosed idealism. But whereas Bond used advanced technology and covert operations to save the world, in real life such approaches had their downside, as the growing civil war in Vietnam would demonstrate.

Kennedy liked men such as McNamara—witty, bright, intellectual—because they seemed comfortable with power and were not afraid to use it. The president's leisure reading reflected a similar adventurous taste: the popular James Bond spy novels. Agent 007, with his license to kill, was sophisticated, a cool womanizer (as Kennedy himself continued to be), and ready to use the latest technology to deal with Communist villains. Ironically, Bond demonstrated that there could be plenty of glamour in being hard-nosed and pragmatic. That illicit pleasure was the underside, perhaps, of Camelot's high ideals.

The (Somewhat) New Frontier at Home

Despite campaign promises for bold initiatives, the president's domestic legislative achievements were modest. Once in the White House, Kennedy found himself hemmed in by a Democratic Congress dominated by conservatives. The modest Area Redevelopment Act of 1961 provided financial aid to depressed industrial and rural areas, and Congress raised the minimum wage to $1.25. But on key issues, including aid to education and medical health insurance, Kennedy made no headway.

He wavered too on how best to manage the economy. The president's liberal economic advisers favored increased government spending to reduce unemployment, even if that spending meant a budget deficit. Similarly, they argued that tax cuts could be used to increase consumer spending and so stimulate the economy. Kennedy toyed with both remedies, but conservatives continued to push for a balanced budget. So Kennedy moved cautiously, relieved at first to discover that the economy was growing quite nicely without a tax cut. Only in 1963 did he send a tax proposal to Congress.

Always pragmatic, Kennedy hoped to work with, not against, the leaders of big business. He firmly believed that prosperity for large firms spelled growth for the whole nation. Thus the president asked Congress to ease antitrust restrictions and grant investment credits and tax breaks—all actions that perfectly suited corporate interests. But he did believe that the government should be able to limit wages and prices for large corporations and unions. If not, an inflationary spiral might result. Wage increases would be followed by price increases followed by even higher wage demands.

Showdown with Big Steel

To prevent that, the Council of Economic Advisors proposed to stabilize prices by tying wage increases to improved productivity. In April 1962 the United Steel Workers, like most other major unions, agreed to a contract that followed those guidelines. The large steel corporations, however, broke their part of the informal bargain by raising steel prices substantially. Incensed, Kennedy called for investigations into price fixing, mounted antitrust proceedings, and shifted Pentagon purchases to smaller steel companies that had not raised prices. The intense pressure caused the big companies to drop the price hikes, but soured relations between Kennedy and the business community.

During the 1952 election, Republicans exploited the stalemate in Korea, the fall of China, and the fear of domestic commu-

Kennedy's Cold War

nism to suggest that the Democrats could not protect the nation's security. During the 1960 race for the White House, recent Soviet space triumphs and the perceived missile gap gave Kennedy the chance to turn the tables on the Eisenhower-Nixon administration. Once elected, the new president was determined not to be seen as soft on communism. The cold war contest, Kennedy argued, had shifted from the traditional struggle over Europe to the developing nations in Asia, Africa, and Latin America. The United States should be armed with a more flexible range of military and economic options.

The "Alliance for Progress," announced in the spring of 1961, indicated the course Kennedy would follow. He promised to provide $20 billion in foreign aid to Latin America over 10 years—about four times what Truman and Eisenhower had provided. In return, Latin American nations would agree to reform unfair tax policies and begin agricultural land reforms. If successful, the Alliance would discourage future Castro-style revolutions. With similar fanfare, the administration set up the Peace Corps. This program sent idealistic young men and women to Third World nations to provide technical, educational, and public health services. Under the Alliance, a majority of Peace Corps volunteers were assigned to Latin America.

Alliance for Progress and Peace Corps

To give economic programs some military muscle, the Pentagon created jungle warfare schools in North Carolina and the Canal Zone. These schools trained Latin American police and paramilitary groups to fight guerrilla wars. They also trained American special forces such as the Green Berets in the arts of jungle warfare. If the Soviets or their allies promoted "wars of liberation," United States commandos would be ready to fight back.

Kennedy believed, too, that the Soviets had made space the final frontier of the cold war. Only a few months after the president's inauguration, a Russian cosmonaut orbited the world for the first time. In response, Kennedy challenged Congress to authorize a manned space mission to the moon that would land by the end of the decade. In February 1962 John Glenn circled the earth three times in a "fireball of a ride." Gradually, the American space program gained on the Russians. In July 1969, a lunar module from the *Apollo 11* spacecraft touched down on the moon. It was a showy triumph in the cold war rivalry.

Space program

Cold War Frustrations

In more down-to-earth ways, high ideals did not translate easily into practical results. Although Latin American governments eagerly accepted aid, few welcomed the intrusive Yankee diplomats who came from north of the border to inspect their programs and press for reform. Instability remained a problem, for in the first five years of the Alliance, nine Latin American governments were overthrown by military coups.

Bay of Pigs invasion

The Peace Corps, for its part, proved a tremendous public relations success and helped thousands of Third World farmers on a people-to-people basis. But individual Peace Corps workers could do little to change corrupt policies on a national level.

Nor did Kennedy succeed in countering revolutionary "wars of liberation." His prime target was Fidel Castro's Communist regime in Cuba. After breaking diplomatic relations in 1960, the Eisenhower administration had secretly authorized the CIA to organize an invasion of that nation. The CIA assured Kennedy that its 1400-member army of Cuban exiles could inspire their compatriots in Cuba to overthrow Castro. Eager to establish his own cold war credentials, the president approved an attack. But the invasion in April 1961 turned into a disaster. The poorly equipped rebel forces landed at the swampy Bay of Pigs with no protective cover for miles. Within two days Castro's army had rounded them up. Taking responsibility for the fiasco, Kennedy suffered a bitter humiliation whose sting goaded the administration to undertake further covert operations. The CIA secretly hatched plans to destabilize the Cuban government or even murder Castro.

Kennedy and Vietnam

Kennedy's advisers took a similar covert approach in South Vietnam. There, a civil war with religious overtones was under way. The autocratic Prime Minister Ngo Dinh Diem remained in power, although he was growing more unpopular by the month. South Vietnamese Communists, known as the Vietcong, waged a guerrilla war against Diem with support from North Vietnam. Buddhist elements backed the rebellion against

The World of the Superpowers
This map shows the extent of the cold war Soviet and American military buildup. The United States established a worldwide network of bases and alliances surrounding Soviet bloc nations that extended from Japan and South Korea, South Vietnam, Pakistan, and Turkey in Asia to the nations of the NATO alliance in Europe. Soviet efforts to expand its influence in the Third World led to the creation of an outpost in Cuba. Around these strategic perimeters, hot spots and centers of crisis continued to simmer.

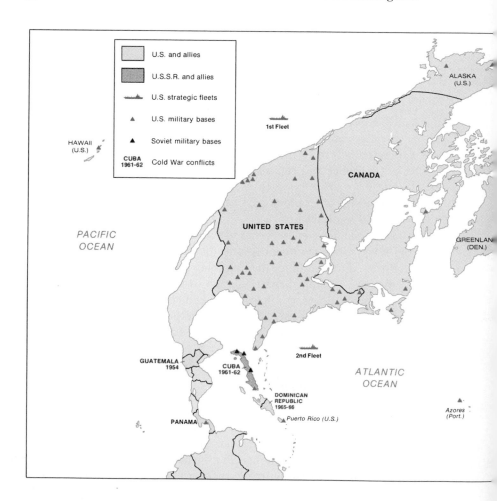

Diem, who was a Catholic. In May 1961, a month after the Bay of Pigs invasion, Kennedy secretly ordered 500 Green Berets and military advisers to Vietnam to help Diem. By 1963 the number of "military advisers" had risen to more than 16,000 soldiers. Increasingly, they were being drawn into combat with the Vietcong.

Diem falls

Diem's corruption, police state tactics, and ruthless campaign against his Buddhist opposition increasingly isolated the regime. Worse yet, he was not winning the war. As the Kennedy administration lost faith in Diem, it tacitly encouraged a military coup by other South Vietnamese military officers. To the surprise of American officials, the coup plotters not only captured Diem but shot him in November 1963. Despite Kennedy's policy of pragmatic idealism, the United States found itself mired in a Vietnamese civil war, which it had no clear strategy for winning.

Confronting Khrushchev

Vietnam and Cuba were just two areas in the Third World where Kennedy sought to battle communist forces. But the conflict between the United States and the Soviet Union soon overshadowed developments in Asia, Africa, and Latin America.

The Berlin Wall

June 1961 was the president's first chance to take the measure of Nikita Khrushchev, at a summit meeting held in Vienna. For two long days, Khrushchev was brash and belligerent. East and West Germany must be reunited, he demanded.

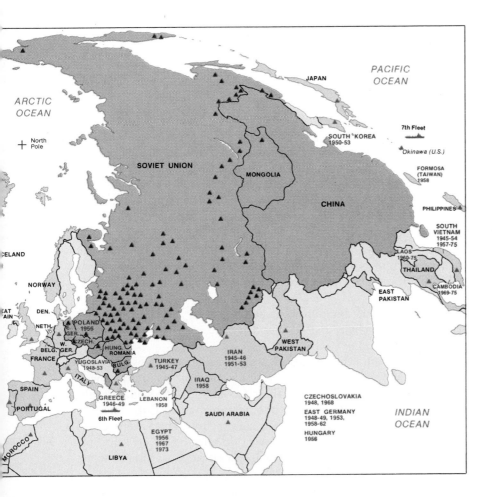

In the divided capital of Berlin, located deep within East Germany (see map, page 911), citizens from all across East Germany were crossing from the eastern sector of Berlin into the free western zone as a way of escaping communist rule. This "problem" must be settled within six months, Khrushchev insisted. Kennedy tried to stand up to Khrushchev's bullying, but he left Vienna worried that the Soviet leader perceived him as weak and inexperienced. By August events in Berlin confirmed his fears. Under cover of night, the Soviets threw up a wall sealing off any entry into West Berlin. Despite American protests, the heavily guarded Berlin Wall stayed up.

A flexible nuclear response

Tensions with the Soviet Union led the administration to rethink American nuclear strategy. Under the Dulles doctrine of massive retaliation, almost any incident threatened to trigger a launch of the full arsenal of nuclear missiles. Kennedy and McNamara sought to establish a "flexible response doctrine" that would limit the level of a first nuclear strike and therefore leave room for negotiation. In that case, however, conventional forces in Europe would have to be built up so that they could better deter aggression. McNamara proposed equipping them with smaller tactical nuclear weapons.

But what if the Soviets were tempted to launch a first-strike attack to knock out American missiles? McNamara's flexible response policy required that enough American missiles survive in order to retaliate. If the Soviets knew the United States could survive a first strike, they would then be less likely to launch a surprise attack. So McNamara began a program to place missile sites underground and to develop submarine-launched missiles. The new flexible response policies resulted in a 15 percent increase in the 1961 military budget, compared with only 2 percent increases during the last two years of Eisenhower's term. Under Kennedy, the military-industrial complex thrived.

The Missiles of October

The peril of nuclear confrontation became dramatically clear in the Cuban missile crisis of October 1962. President Kennedy had emphasized repeatedly that the United States would treat any attempt to place offensive weapons in Cuba as an unacceptable threat. Khrushchev had promised that the Soviet Union had no such intention, but bristled privately at what he perceived as a gross inequality in the cold war. "The Americans had surrounded our country with military bases and threatened us with nuclear weapons," he told high Soviet officials in May 1962. In that month he convinced them to begin building a secret nuclear base in Cuba. "Now [the Americans] would learn just what it feels like to have enemy missiles pointing at you."

Throughout the summer the buildup went undetected by Americans. But by October 14, overflights of Cuba by U-2 spy planes had uncovered the offensive missile sites. Kennedy was outraged.

A naval blockade

For a week, top American security advisers met in secret strategy sessions. Hawkish advisers urged air strikes against the missile sites, and at first Kennedy agreed. "We're certainly going to . . . take out these . . . missiles," he said. But others pointed out that the U-2 flights had not photographed all of Cuba. What if there were more concealed bases with missiles ready to fire? The Soviets could then launch an atomic attack on the United States despite the air strikes. Furthermore, if the United States attacked Cuba with no advance warning, the act would appear to the world uncomfortably like the Japanese surprise attack on Pearl Harbor in World War II.

Although the Joint Chiefs of Staff continued to press for a large air attack, Kennedy finally chose the more restrained option. The United States would impose a naval blockade to intercept "all offensive military equipment under shipment to Cuba." On October 22, word of the confrontation began to leak out. "CAPITAL CRISIS AIR HINTS AT DEVELOPMENTS ON CUBA; KENNEDY TV TALK IS LIKELY," ran *The New York Times* headline. In Moscow, Soviet leaders awaited Kennedy's speech convinced that an American invasion of Cuba was likely. "The thing is we were not going to unleash war," a nervous Khrushchev complained to his colleagues. "We just wanted to intimidate them, to deter the anti-Cuban forces." Americans were stunned that evening by the president's television address.

Over the next few days, tensions mounted as a Soviet submarine approached the line of American ships. On October 25 the navy stopped an oil tanker. Several Soviet ships reversed course. In Cuba, Soviet General Issa Pliyev felt that he had to assume the worst—that despite all the talk of a blockade, an American invasion of Cuba was being prepared. Pliyev sent a coded message to Moscow that "in the opinion of the Cuban friends [i.e., the Castro government] the U.S. air strike on our installations in Cuba will occur in the night between October 26 and October 27 or at dawn on October 27." Equally ominously, he added, "We have taken measures to disperse 'techniki' [the nuclear warheads] in the zone of operations." In other words, Pliyev was making his nuclear missiles operational.

The morning of October 27, alarmed Soviet technicians detected a U-2 plane flying over Cuba. Was this the beginning of the expected attack? General Pliyev had issued strict instructions not to use force without his authorization, but when the

The discovery of Soviet offensive missile sites in Cuba, revealed by low-level American reconnaissance flights, led to the first nuclear showdown of the cold war. For several tense days in October 1962, President Kennedy met with his National Security Council to debate alternative responses.

air defense command looked to consult him, he could not be found, and the U-2 would leave Cuban airspace momentarily. Soviet officers went ahead and shot it down, killing its pilot.

Meanwhile, Kennedy was making strenuous efforts to resolve the crisis through diplomatic channels. On October 26 he had received a rambling message from Khrushchev agreeing to remove the missiles in return for an American promise not to invade Cuba. The following day a second, more troubling message arrived with a new condition, that the United States must also dismantle its missile bases in Turkey, which bordered on the Soviet Union. As the president and his advisers debated, word came of the downed U-2. Kennedy was shocked. A policy had already been established that the United States would retaliate if the Soviets launched an attack from their Cuban bases. American planes were standing by on thirty-minute alert, ready to take off. Worried that events might quickly spiral out of control, the president put off that decision until the following morning.

Then he decided to ignore Khrushchev's second letter and accept the offer in the first: removal of Soviet missiles if the Americans pledged not to invade Cuba. Kennedy also gave private assurances that the missiles in Turkey would come out within half a year. In Moscow, Khrushchev agreed reluctantly to the deal, telling his advisers somberly that there were times to advance and times to retreat; and this time, "we found ourselves face to face with the danger of war and of nuclear catastrophe, with the possible result of destroying the human race." Thus the face-off ended on terms that saved either side from overt humiliation.

Nuclear test ban treaty

The nuclear showdown prompted Kennedy and his advisers to seek ways to control the nuclear arms race. "We all inhabit this small planet," he warned in June 1963. "We all breathe the same air. We all cherish our children's future. And we are all mortal." The administration negotiated a nuclear test ban with the Soviets, prohibiting all above-ground nuclear tests. Growing concern over radioactive fallout increased public support for the treaty. A telephone hot line was also installed, providing a direct communications link between the White House and the Kremlin for use in times of crisis. At the same time Kennedy's prestige soared for "standing up" to the Soviets.

The Cuban missile crisis was the closest the world had come to "destroying the human race," in Khrushchev's words, and it sobered both superpowers. It did not end the cold war however; indeed, both nations endured long, drawn-out regional wars before scaling back their ambitions—the United States in Vietnam and the Soviet Union in Afghanistan. Yet the intensity of confrontation—with Eisenhower and Dulles's brinkmanship, Khrushchev's provocations, and Kennedy's cold war rhetoric—began to ease. The nuclear anxieties of the 1950s, so much a part of the suburban era, yielded to different concerns in the 1960s.

In large part, that change came about because the supposed consensus of the 1950s masked a profound *lack* of consensus concerning the state of equality in America. While the suburbs flourished, urban areas decayed. While more white Americans went to college, more African Americans found themselves out of work on southern farms or desperate for jobs in northern ghettos, and still in segregated schools. As Mexican American migrant workers picked crops in California or followed the harvest north from Texas, they saw their employers resist every attempt to unionize and improve their wages. To all these Americans, the long-accepted "consensus" about opportunity in American life was no longer acceptable. The 1950s sparked a movement pursued by ordinary Americans who acted, despite the reluctance of their leaders, to bring about a civil rights revolution.

chapter summary

At midcentury, during an era of peace and prosperity, the United States began to build a new social and political agenda.

- Automobiles and the culture of the highways helped bind Americans to one another in a "consensus" about what it meant to be an American.

  - Highways made possible rapid suburban growth.

  - Suburbs proved popular with the growing white-collar middle class.

  - Consensus in suburbs blurred class distinctions and promoted the notion of "civil religion."

  - Suburban life nurtured the ideal of the woman who found fulfillment as a homemaker and a mother, even though more women began to work outside the home.

- President Eisenhower resisted the demands of conservatives to dismantle the New Deal and of liberals to extend it, in favor of moderate, or "middle of the road," Republicanism.

- Cracks in consensus appeared among discontented intellectuals and among teenagers who, through Elvis Presley and new teen idols, discovered the power of rock and roll.

- Efforts to more vigorously contain the U.S.S.R. and communist China, through a policy of "brinkmanship," proved difficult to apply because of growing Third World nationalism.

  - Eisenhower held back from using tactical nuclear weapons during crises in Vietnam and Taiwan.

  - Successful CIA operations in Iran and Guatemala encouraged American policy makers to use covert operations more frequently.

  - Post-colonial nationalism contributed to crises in Hungary, Egypt, and Cuba, where President Kennedy was embarrassed by the failure of an invasion attempt to overthrow Fidel Castro.

- Relations between the two superpowers thawed gradually but not without recurring confrontations between the United States and the Soviet Union.

  - Under Eisenhower, the Soviet success with *Sputnik* increased fears that the United States was vulnerable to missile attacks, while the U-2 spy plane incident worsened relations.

  - John F. Kennedy proved willing to use covert operations as well as diplomatic and economic initiatives like the Peace Corps and the Alliance for Progress.

  - The construction of Soviet missile bases 90 miles from American shores triggered the Cuban missile crisis of 1962, the closest the United States and the Soviet Union have ever come to nuclear war.

additional reading

No modern president's reputation has risen more among historians than Dwight Eisenhower's. Contrast the dismissive view of Eric Goldman, *The Crucial Decade and After, 1945–1960* (1960) with Stephen Ambrose, *Eisenhower: The President* (1984) or Fred Greenstein, *The Hidden Hand Presidency: Eisenhower as Leader* (1982). A similar revision has occurred in the treatment of his foreign policy, in which Eisenhower receives credit that once went to Dulles. See, for example, Robert Divine, *Eisenhower and the Cold War* (1981). On the other hand, John F. Kennedy's stock has fallen sharply since the heady days of Camelot. Contrast the reverential treatments of Kennedy in Arthur Schlesinger Jr., *The Thousand Days* (1965) and Theodore Sorenson, *Kennedy* (1965) with David Burner and Thomas West, *The Torch Is Passed: The Kennedy Brothers and American Liberalism* (1992) and Mark Stern, *Calculating Visions: Kennedy, Johnson, and Civil Rights* (1992).

For an overview of the era, see John Diggins, *The Proud Decades: America in War and Peace, 1941–1960* (1988) or the even more readable, but less analytical, David Halberstam, *The Fifties* (1993). The Cuban missile crisis is told with the aid of newly released Russian sources in Aleksandr Fursenko and Timothy Naftali, *"One Hell of a Gamble": Khrushchev, Castro, and Kennedy, 1958–1964* (1997), and the tape-recorded secret White House debates are published in Ernest R. May and Philip D. Zelikow, eds., *The Kennedy Tapes: Inside the White House during the Cuban Missile Crisis* (1997). For a fuller list of readings, see the Bibliography.

Significant Events

1947	1947 Levittown construction begins
1948	
1949	
1950	1950 David Reisman's *The Lonely Crowd* published; Kefauver crime hearings
1951	
1952	1952 Fertility rate in the United States reaches new high
1953	1953 Mossadeq overthrown in Iran
1954	1954 St. Lawrence Seaway Act; CIA overthrows Arbenz in Guatemala
1955	1955 Elvis Presley ignites rock and roll
	1956 Interstate Highway Act; Eisenhower reelected; Suez crisis
1956	1957 *Sputnik* launched; Eisenhower Doctrine
1957	1958 Richard Nixon attacked in Latin America; marines sent into Lebanon; Berlin crisis; National Defense Education Act; NASA established
1958	1959 Castro seizes power in Cuba; Khrushchev visits United States; Soviet probe hits moon
1959	1960 Soviet Union captures CIA pilot; Paris summit canceled; Kennedy-Nixon debates; Kennedy elected president
1960	1961 Eisenhower's farewell address warns of military-industrial complex; Alliance for Progress; Peace Corps begun; Alan Shepard Jr. is first American in space; Bay of Pigs invasion; Kennedy steps up U.S. role in Vietnam; Vienna Summit; Berlin Wall built; Area Redevelopment Act
1961	
1962	1962 Michael Harrington's *The Other America* published; Cuban missile crisis
1963	1963 Diem assassinated in Vietnam

Chapter 29

Six-year-old Ruby knew the lessons. She was to look straight ahead—not to one side or the other—and especially not at *them*. She was to keep walking. Above all, she was not to look back once she'd passed, because that would encourage them. Ruby's parents had instructed her carefully, but she still struggled to keep her eyes straight. The first day of school, federal marshals were there along with her parents. So were hundreds of nasty white people who came near enough to yell things like "You little nigger, we'll get you and kill you." Then she was within the building's quiet halls and alone with her teacher. She was the only person in class: none of the white students had come. As the days went by during that autumn of 1960, the marshals stopped walking with her but the hecklers still waited. And once in a while Ruby couldn't help looking back, trying to see if she recognized the face of one woman in particular.

Ruby's parents were not social activists. They signed their daughter up for the white school because "we thought it was for all the colored to do, and we never thought Ruby would be alone." Her father's white employer fired him; letters and phone calls threatened the family's lives and home. Ruby seemed to take it all in stride, though her parents worried that she was not eating the way she used to. Often she left her school lunch untouched or refused anything other than packaged food such as potato chips. It was only after a time that the problem was traced to the hecklers. "They tells me I'm going to die, and that it'll be soon. And that one lady tells me every morning I'm getting poisoned soon, when she can fix it." Ruby was convinced that the woman owned the variety store nearby and would carry out her threat by poisoning the family's food.

Over the course of a year, white students gradually returned to class and life settled into a new routine. By the time Ruby was 10, she had developed a remarkably clear perception of herself. "Maybe because of all the trouble going to school in the beginning I learned more about my people. Maybe I would have anyway; because when you get older you see yourself and the white kids; and you find out the difference. You try to forget it, and say there is none; and if there is you won't say what it be. Then you say it's my own people, and so I can be proud of them instead of ashamed."

If the new ways were hard for Ruby, they were not easy for white southerners either—even those who saw the need for change. One woman, for years a dedicated teacher in Atlanta, vividly recalled a traumatic summer 10 years earlier, when she went north to New York City to take courses in education. There were black students living in the dormitory, an integrated situation she was not used to. One day as she stepped from her shower, so did a black student from the nearby stall. "When I saw her I didn't know what to do," the woman recalled. "I felt sick all over, and frightened. What I remember—I'll never forget it—is that horrible feeling of being caught in a terrible trap, and not knowing what to do about it. I thought

Civil Rights & the Crisis of Liberalism

preview • Largely walled out from the prosperity of the 1950s, African Americans and Latinos campaigned to gain the freedoms denied them through widespread racism and, in the South, a system of segregation. As the civil rights movement blossomed, young and relatively affluent baby boomers spread the revolution to other areas of American life. Their radical goals sometimes clashed with President Lyndon Johnson's liberal strategy of using federal programs to alleviate inequality and create a Great Society.

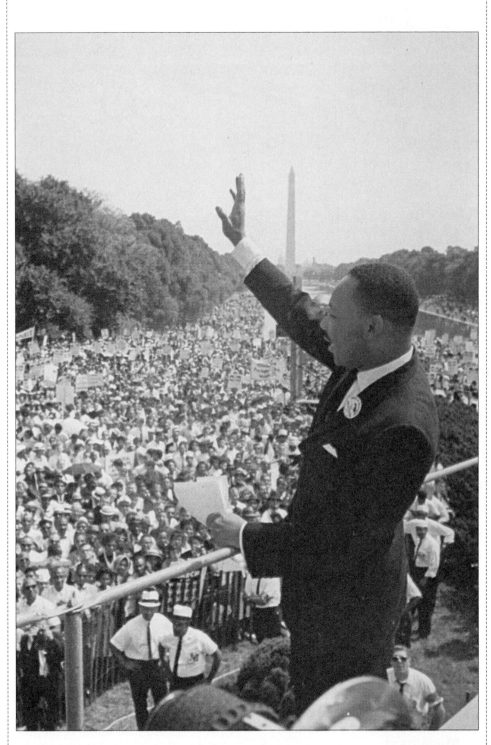

On August 28, 1963, more than 250,000 demonstrators joined the great civil rights march on Washington. The day belonged to the Reverend Martin Luther King Jr., who movingly called on black and white Americans to join together in a color-blind society.

of running out of the room and screaming, or screaming at the woman to get out, or running back into the shower. . . . My sense of propriety was with me, though—miraculously—and I didn't want to hurt the woman. It wasn't *her* that was upsetting me. I knew that, even in that moment of sickness and panic." So she ducked back into the shower until the other woman left.

Summer was almost over before she felt comfortable eating with black students at the same table. And when she returned home, she told no one about her experiences. "At that time people would have thought one of two things: I was crazy

Ruby's drawings of a white girl (left) and herself

(for being so upset and ashamed) or a fool who in a summer had become a dangerous 'race mixer.'" She continued to love the South and to speak up for its traditions of dignity, neighborliness, and honor, but she saw the need for change. And so in 1961 she volunteered to teach one of the first integrated high school classes in Atlanta, even though she had her doubts. By the end of two years she concluded that she had never spent a more exciting time teaching. "I've never felt so useful, so constantly useful, not just to the children but to our whole society. American as well as Southern. Those children, all of them, have given me more than I've given them."

 ## The Civil Rights Movement

For Americans in all walks of life, the upheavals that swept America in the 1960s were wrenching. From the schoolrooms and lunch counters of the South to the college campuses of the North, from eastern slums to western migrant labor camps, American society was in ferment.

On the face of it, such agitation seemed to be a dramatic reversal of the placid 1950s. Turbulence and change had overturned stability and consensus. Yet the events of the 1960s grew naturally out of the social conditions that preceded those years. The civil rights movement was not brought about by a group of far-sighted leaders in government, but by ordinary folk who sought change, often despite the reluctance or even fierce opposition of people in power. After World War II, grass-roots organizations like the NAACP for blacks and the American GI Forum for Latinos acted with a new determination to achieve the equality of opportunity promised by the American creed.

Thus the 1950s were a seedbed for the more turbulent revolutions of the 1960s. The booming postwar economy held out the possibility of better lives for minorities; yet systematic discrimination and racism, long embedded in American life by custom and law, prevented prosperity from spreading equally. Time and again, activists challenged the poltical system to deal with what the 1950s had done—and what had been left undone. As one friend of Martin Luther King predicted in 1958, "If the young people are aroused from their lethargy through this fight, it will affect broad circles throughout the country."

The Changing South and African Americans

The struggle of African Americans for equality during the postwar era is filled with ironies. By the time barriers to legal segregation in the South began to fall, millions of black families were leaving for regions where discrimination was less easily challenged in court. The South they left behind was in the early stages of an economic boom. The cities where many migrated had entered a period of decline. Yet, as if to close a circle, the rise of large black voting blocs in major cities created political pressures that helped force the nation to dismantle the worst legal and institutional barriers to racial equality.

After World War II the southern economy began to grow significantly faster than the national economy. The remarkable about-face began during the New Deal with federal programs like the Tennessee Valley Authority. World War II brought even more federal dollars to build and maintain military bases and defense plants. And the South attracted new business because it offered a "clean slate." In contrast to the more mature economies of the Northeast and Upper Midwest, the region had few unions, little regulation and bureaucracy, and low wages and taxes. Finally, there was the matter of climate, which later caused the region to be nicknamed the Sunbelt. Especially with improvements in air conditioning, the South grew more attractive to skilled professionals, corporate managers, and affluent retirees.

Before World War II, 80 percent of African Americans lived in the South. Most raised cotton as sharecroppers and tenant farmers. But the war created a labor shortage at home, as millions of workers went off to fight and others went to armament factories. This shortage gave cotton growers an incentive to mechanize cotton picking. In 1950 only 5 percent of the crop was picked mechanically; by 1960 at least half was. Farmers began to consolidate land into larger holdings. Tenant farmers, sharecroppers, and hired labor of both races, no longer in short supply, left the countryside for the city.

Mechanized cotton farming

The national level of wages also profoundly affected southern labor. When federal minimum wage laws forced lumber or textile mills to raise their pay scales, the mills no longer expanded. In addition, steel and other industries with strong national unions and manufacturers with plants around the country set wages by national standards. Those changes brought southern wages close to the national average by the 1960s. As the southern economy grew, what had for many years been a distinct regional economy became more diversified and more integrated into the national economy.

As wages rose and unskilled work disappeared, job opportunities for black southerners declined. Outside of cotton farming, the lumber industry provided the largest number of jobs for young black men. There, the number of black teenagers hired by lumber mills dropped 74 percent between 1950 and 1960. New high-wage jobs were reserved for white southerners, because outside industries arriving in the South made no effort to change local patterns of discrimination. So the ultimate irony arose. As per capita income rose and industrialization brought in new jobs, black laborers poured out of the region in search of work. They arrived in cities that showed scant tolerance for racial differences and little willingness or ability to hire unskilled black labor.

The NAACP and Civil Rights

In the postwar era the NAACP decided it would use the judicial system to attack Jim Crow laws. That stepped-up attack reflected the increased national political influence that African Americans achieved as they migrated in great numbers out of the South. No longer could northern politicians readily ignore the demands black leaders made for greater equality. The Swedish scholar Gunnar Myrdal had amply documented the black case in his landmark work *The American Dilemma* (1944), sponsored by the Carnegie Corporation. Presidents Roosevelt and Truman had taken small but significant steps to address the worst forms of legal and economic discrimination. And across the South black churches and colleges became centers for organized resistance to segregation.

Thurgood Marshall

Thurgood Marshall emerged as the NAACP's leading attorney. Marshall had attended law school in the 1930s at Howard University in Washington. There, the law school's dean, Charles Houston, was in the midst of revamping the school and

Overton Park Zoo in Memphis, Tennessee, was segregated like thousands of other public facilities throughout the South in the late 1950s. In the case of the zoo, Tuesdays were "colored" days, the only time when blacks could attend—except if the Fourth of July fell on a Tuesday. Then "colored" day was moved to Thursday.

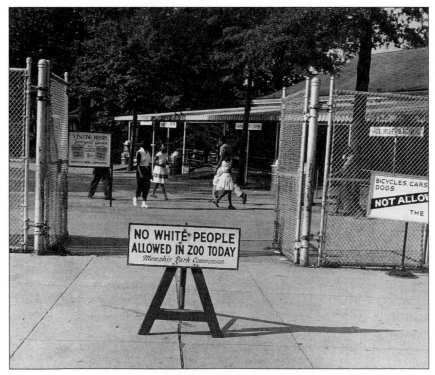

turning out sharp, dedicated lawyers. Marshall was not only sharp, he had the common touch. "Before he came along," one observer noted,

> the principal black leaders—men like Du Bois and James Weldon Johnson and Charles Houston—didn't talk the language of the people. They were upper-class and upper-middle-class Negroes. Thurgood Marshall was *of* the people. . . . Out in Texas or Oklahoma or down the street here in Washington at the Baptist church, he would make these rousing speeches that would have 'em all jumping out of their seats. . . . "We ain't gettin' what we should," was what it came down to, and he made them see that.

During the late 1930s and early 1940s Marshall toured the South (in "a little old beat-up '29 Ford"), typing out legal briefs in the back seat, trying to get teachers to sue for equal pay, and defending blacks accused of murder in a Klan-infested county in Florida. He was friendly with whites, not shy, and black citizens who had never even considered the possibility that a member of their race might win a legal battle "would come for miles, some of them on muleback or horseback, to see 'the nigger lawyer' who stood up in white men's courtrooms."

For years NAACP lawyers had worked hard to organize local chapters, to support members of the community willing to risk their jobs, property, and lives in order to challenge segregation. But they waged a moderate, pragmatic campaign. They chose not to attack head-on the Supreme Court decision (*Plessy v. Ferguson*, 1896) that permitted "separate but equal" segregated facilities. They simply demonstrated that a black college or school might be separate, but it was hardly equal if it lacked a law school or even indoor plumbing.

The *Brown* Decision

In 1950 the NAACP changed tactics: it would now try to convince the Supreme Court to overturn the separate but equal doctrine itself. Oliver Brown was one of the people who provided a way. Brown was dissatisfied that his daughter Linda had to walk past an all-white school on her way to catch the bus to her segregated black school in Topeka, Kansas. A three-judge federal panel rejected Brown's suit because the schools in Topeka, while segregated, did meet the test of equality. But the NAACP had been making headway with other cases in other courts. After two years of arguments the Supreme Court in *Brown v. Board of Education of Topeka* (1954) overturned the lower court ruling.

Marshall and his colleagues succeeded in part because of a change in the Court itself. The year before, President Eisenhower had appointed Earl Warren, a liberal Republican from California, as chief justice. Warren, a forceful advocate, managed to persuade the last of his reluctant judicial colleagues that segregation as defined in *Plessy* rested on an untenable theory of racial supremacy. The Court thus ruled unanimously that separate facilities were inherently unequal. To keep black children segregated solely on the basis of race, it ruled, "generates a feeling of inferiority as to their status in the community that may affect their hearts and minds in a way unlikely ever to be undone."

Overturning Plessy

At the time of the *Brown* decision, 21 states and the District of Columbia operated segregated school systems. All of them had to decide, in some way, how to comply with the new ruling. The Court allowed a certain amount of leeway, handing down a second ruling in 1955 that required that desegregation be carried out "with all deliberate speed." Some border states reluctantly decided to comply, but in the Deep South, many citizens called for die-hard defiance. In 1956, a "Southern Manifesto" was issued by 19 U.S. senators and 81 representatives; it declared their intent to use "all lawful means" to reestablish legalized segregation.

Latino Civil Rights

Mexican Americans also considered school desegregation as central to their campaign for civil rights. At the end of World War II, only one percent of children of Mexican descent in Texas graduated from high school. Both the American GI Forum (page 915) and the League of United Latin American Citizens (LULAC; page 816) supported legal challenges to the system.

Delgado **and segregated schools**

In a 1947 case, *Mendez et al. v. Westminster School District of Orange County,* the courts had ordered several California school districts to integrate. LULAC saw a way to apply that ruling in Texas. The superintendent in the town of Bastrop had refused a request to enroll first-grader Minerva Delgado in a nearby all-white school. Civil rights lawyer and activist Gus Garcia, a legal adviser to both LULAC and the GI Forum, helped bring a case on Minerva's behalf against the school district. Before *Delgado et al. v. Bastrop et al.* went to trial a Texas judge ordered an end to segregated schools beyond the first grade (based on the assumption that the youngest Mexican American children needed special classes to learn English). *Delgado* served notice that Mexicans would no longer accept second-class citizenship. It also served as a precedent in *Brown v. Board of Education* in 1954.

Two weeks before the Supreme Court made that landmark civil rights ruling, it also decided a case of great importance to Latinos. Unlike African Americans, Latinos did not face a Jim Crow system of laws imposing segregation. Throughout the Southwest the states recognized just two races: black and white. That left Mexican Americans in legal limbo. Though legally grouped with whites, they were by longstanding social custom barred from many public places, they could not serve on juries, and they faced widespread job discrimination. To remedy the situation, Mexican Americans had to establish themselves in the courts as a distinct class of people.

Attorney Gus Garcia (left) was one of the key leaders of the American GI Forum, founded by Mexican American veterans to pursue their civil rights. He and his colleagues successfully appealed the conviction of Pete Hernández (center) before the Supreme Court in 1954.

An opportunity arose in the case of Pete Hernández, who had been convicted of murder by an all-white jury in Jackson County, Texas. Indeed, as Mexican American lawyer Gus Garcia realized, no Mexican American had served on a Jackson jury in the previous 25 years. Garcia, one of the leaders of the American GI Forum, saw in the tactics of Thurgood Marshall and the NAACP a way to use the Hernández case to extend to Mexicans the benefits of the Fourteenth Amendment's equal protection clause.

Hernández and desegregation

The key to the case was ingenious but direct. The state argued that because Mexicans were white, a jury without Mexicans was still a jury of peers. Yet the courthouse in which Hernández was tried had two men's rooms. One said simply, "MEN." The other, labeled with a crudely hand-lettered sign, said "COLORED MEN" and below that in Spanish, "HOMBRES AQUI [MEN HERE]." As one of Gus Garcia's colleagues recalled, "In the jury pool, Mexicans may have been white, but when it came to nature's functions they were not." This and similar examples of discrimination persuaded the Supreme Court, in *Hernández v. Texas,* to throw out the state's argument. Latinos in south Texas, like African Americans across the South, were held to be a discrete group.whose members deserved equal protection under the law. "The Fourteenth Amendment is not directed solely against discrimination due to a 'two-class theory,' that is, based upon differences between 'white' and Negro," ruled Chief Justice Earl Warren. Warren's reasoning made it possible for Latinos to seek redress as a group rather than as individuals. After *Hernández,* the Mexican American community had both the legal basis and the leadership to broaden its attack against discrimination.

A New Civil Rights Strategy

Neither the *Brown* nor the *Hernández* decisions ended segregation, but they combined with political and economic forces to usher in a new era of southern race relations. In December 1955 Rosa Parks, a 43-year-old black civil rights activist, was riding the bus home in Montgomery, Alabama. When the driver ordered her to give up her seat for a white man, as Alabama Jim Crow laws required, she refused. Police took her to jail and eventually fined her $14.

Rosa Parks

Determined to overturn the law, a number of women from the NAACP, friends of Parks, met secretly at midnight to draft a letter of protest.

> Another Negro woman has been arrested and thrown into jail because she refused to get up out of her seat on the bus and give it to a white person. . . . Until we do something to stop these arrests, they will continue. The next time it may be you, or you or you. This woman's case will come up Monday. We are, therefore, asking every Negro to stay off the buses on Monday in protest of the arrest and trial.

Thousands of copies of the letter were distributed, and the Monday boycott was such a success it was extended indefinitely. Buses wheeled around the city virtually empty, losing over 30,000 fares a day. The white community, in an effort to halt the unprecedented black challenge, resorted to various forms of legal and physical intimidation. No local agent would insure cars used to carpool black workers. A bomb exploded in the house of the Reverend Martin Luther King Jr., the key boycott leader. And when that failed to provoke the violence that whites could use to justify harsh reprisals, 90 black leaders were arrested for organizing an illegal boycott. Still, the campaign continued until November 23, 1956, when the Supreme Court ruled that bus segregation was illegal.

Martin Luther King Jr.   The triumph was especially sweet for Martin Luther King Jr., whose leadership in Montgomery brought him national fame. Before becoming a minister at the Dexter Street Baptist Church, King had little personal contact with the worst forms of white racism. He had grown up in the relatively affluent middle-class black community of Atlanta, Georgia, the son of one of the city's most prominent black ministers. He attended Morehouse College, an academically respected black school in Atlanta, and Crozer Theological Seminary in Philadelphia before entering the doctoral program in theology at Boston University. As a graduate student, King embraced the pacifism and nonviolence of the Indian leader Mohandas Gandhi and the activism of Christian reformers of the progressive era. King heeded the call to Dexter Street in 1954 with the idea of becoming a theologian after he served his active ministry and finished his dissertation.

As boycott leader it was King's responsibility to rally black support without triggering violence. Because local officials were all too eager for any excuse to use force, King's nonviolent approach was the ideal strategy. King offered his audience two visions. First, he reminded them of the many injustices they had been forced to endure. The boycott, he asserted, was a good way to seek redress. Then he counseled his followers to avoid the actions of their oppressors: "In our protest there will be no cross burnings. No white person will be taken from his home by a hooded Negro mob and brutally murdered." And he evoked the Christian and republican ideals that would become the themes of his civil rights crusade. "If we protest courageously, and yet with dignity and Christian love," he said, "when the future history books are written, somebody will have to say, 'There lived a race of people, of black people, of people who had the moral courage to stand up for their rights. And thereby they injected a new meaning into the history of civilization.'"

Indeed, the African Americans of Montgomery did set an example of moral courage that rewrote the pages of American race relations. Their firm stand caught the attention of the national news media. King and his colleagues were developing the tactics needed to launch a more aggressive phase of the civil rights movement.

Little Rock and the White Backlash

The civil rights spotlight moved the following year to Little Rock, Arkansas. White officials there had reluctantly adopted a plan to integrate the schools with a most deliberate lack of speed. Nine black students were scheduled to enroll in September 1957 at the all-white Central High School. Instead, the school board urged them to stay home. Governor Orval Faubus, generally a moderate on race relations, called out the Arkansas National Guard on the excuse of maintaining order. President Eisenhower tacitly supported Faubus in his defiance of court-ordered integration by remarking that "you cannot change people's hearts merely by laws."

Still, the Justice Department could not simply let Faubus defy the federal courts. It won an injunction against the governor, but when the nine blacks returned on September 23 a mob of 1000 abusive whites greeted them. So great was national attention to the crisis that President Eisenhower felt compelled to uphold the authority of the federal courts. He sent in federal troops and took control of the National Guard. For a year the Guard preserved order until Faubus, in a last-ditch maneuver, closed the schools. Only in 1959, under pressure of another federal court ruling, did Little Rock schools reopen and resume the plan for gradual integration.

Angry white students, opposed to integration, menace black students during a recess at Little Rock's Central High. This civil rights crisis was the first covered by television; for weeks NBC correspondent John Chancellor took a chartered plane daily from Little Rock to Oklahoma City to deliver film footage for the nightly news program. Such national attention made people outside the South more sensitive to civil rights issues.

In the face of such attitudes, King and other civil rights leaders recognized that the skirmishes of Montgomery and Little Rock were a beginning, not the end. In fact, segregationist resistance increased in the wake of King's Montgomery success. From 1955 to 1959 civil rights protesters endured over 200 acts of violence in the South. Legislatures and city councils passed scores of laws attempting either to outlaw the NAACP or prevent it from functioning. Black leaders were unable to achieve momentum on a national scale until 1960. Then, a series of spontaneous demonstrations by young people changed everything.

On January 31, 1960, Joseph McNeill got off the bus in Greensboro, North Carolina, a freshman on the way back to col-

A Movement Becomes a Crusade

lege. When he looked for something to eat at the lunch counter, the waitress gave the familiar reply. "We don't serve Negroes here."

It was a refrain repeated countless times and in countless places. Yet for some reason this rebuke particularly offended McNeill. He and his roommates had read a pamphlet describing the 1955 bus boycott in Montgomery, Alabama. They decided it was time to make their own protest against segregation. Proceeding the next day to the "whites only" lunch counter at a local store, they sat politely waiting for service. "The waitress looked at me as if I were from outer space," recalled one of the protesters. Rather than serve them, the manager closed the counter. Word of the action spread. A day later—Tuesday—the four students were joined by 27 more. Wednesday, the number jumped to 63, Thursday, to over 300. Come the weekend, 1600 students rallied to plan further action.

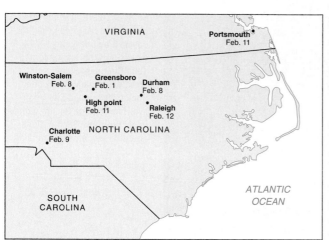

The Spontaneous Spread of Sit-ins, February 1960

On Monday, February 8, sit-ins began in nearby Durham and Winston-Salem. Tuesday it was Charlotte. Thursday, High Point and Portsmouth, Virginia. A news broadcast reassured white residents in Raleigh that black students there would not follow Greensboro's example. In response, angry black students launched massive sit-ins at variety stores in Raleigh. By Lincoln's birthday, the demonstrations had spread to Tennessee and Florida; by April, to 78 different southern and border communities. By September at least 70,000 African Americans as well as whites had participated. Thousands had been arrested and jailed.

The campaign for black civil rights gained momentum not so much by the power of national movements as through a host of individual decisions by local groups and citizens. When New Orleans schools were desegregated in 1960, young Ruby's parents had not intended to make a social statement. But once involved, they refused to back down. The students at Greensboro had not been approached by the NAACP, but acted on their own initiative.

Riding to Freedom

Newer civil rights organizations

Of course, organizations channeled these discontents and aspirations. But the new generation of younger activists also shaped and altered the organizations. Beginning in the 1960s, the push for desegregation moved from court actions launched by the NAACP and the Urban League to newer groups determined to take direct action. Since organizing the Montgomery boycott, Martin Luther King and his Southern Christian Leadership Conference (SCLC) had continued to advocate nonviolent protest: "To resist without bitterness; to be cursed and not reply; to be beaten and not hit back." A second key organization, the Congress of Racial Equality (CORE), was more willing than the SCLC to force confrontations with the segregationist system. Another group, the Student Non-Violent Coordinating Committee (SNCC, pronounced "Snick") grew out of the Greensboro sit-in. SNCC represented the more militant, younger generation of black activists who grew increasingly impatient with the slow pace of reform.

In May 1961 CORE director James Farmer led a group of black and white "freedom riders" on a bus trip into the heart of the South. They hoped their trip from Washington to New Orleans would focus national attention on the inequality of segregated facilities. Violent southern mobs gave them the kind of attention they feared. In South Carolina, thugs beat divinity student John Lewis as he tried to enter an all-white waiting room. Mobs in Anniston and Birmingham, Alabama, assaulted the freedom riders as police ignored the violence. One of the buses was burned.

President Kennedy had sought to avoid forceful federal intervention in the South. When the freedom riders persisted in their plans, he tried to convince Alabama officials to protect the demonstrators so that he would not have to send federal forces. His hopes were dashed. From a phone booth outside the bus terminal, John Doar, a Justice Department official in Montgomery, relayed the horror to Attorney General Robert Kennedy, the president's brother:

> Now the passengers are coming off. They're standing on a corner of the platform.
> Oh, there are fists, punching! A bunch of men led by a guy with a bleeding face

are beating them. There are no cops. It's terrible! It's terrible! There's not a cop in sight. People are yelling, "There those niggers are! Get 'em, get 'em!" It's awful.

Appalled, Robert Kennedy ordered in 400 federal marshals, who barely managed to hold off the crowd. Martin Luther King, addressing a meeting in town, phoned the attorney general to say that their church had been surrounded by an angry mob of several thousand—jeering, throwing rocks, and carrying firebombs. As Kennedy later recalled, "I said that we were doing the best that we could and that he'd be as dead as Kelsey's nuts if it hadn't been for the marshals and the efforts that we made."

Both Kennedys understood that civil rights was the most divisive issue the administration faced. For liberals, civil rights measured Kennedy's credentials as a reformer. Kennedy needed black and liberal votes to win reelection. Yet an active federal role threatened to drive white southerners from the Democratic party. It was for that reason that Kennedy had hedged on his promise to introduce major civil rights legislation. Through executive orders, he assured black leaders, he could eliminate discrimination in the government civil service and in businesses filling government contracts. He appointed several African Americans to high administrative positions and five, including Thurgood Marshall, to the federal courts. The Justice Department beefed up its civil rights enforcement procedures. But the freedom riders, by their bold actions, forced the Kennedys to do more.

Civil Rights at High Tide

By the fall of 1961 Robert Kennedy had persuaded SNCC to shift tactics to voter registration, which he assumed would stir less violence. Voting booths, Kennedy noted, were not like schools, where people would protest, "We don't want our little blond daughter going to school with a Negro."

As SNCC and CORE workers arrived in southern towns in the spring of 1962, they discovered that voting rights was not a peaceful issue. Over two years in Mississippi they registered only 4000 out of 394,000 black adults. Angry racists attacked with legal harassment, jailings, beatings, bombings, and murders. Terrorized workers who called on the administration for protection found it woefully lacking. FBI agents often stood by taking notes while SNCC workers were assaulted. Undaunted, SNCC workers made it clear that they intended to stay. They fanned out across the countryside to speak with farmers and sharecroppers who had never before dared to ask for a vote.

Confrontation increased when a federal court ordered the segregated University of Mississippi to admit James Meredith, a black applicant. When Governor Ross Barnett personally blocked Meredith's registration in September 1962, Kennedy faced the same crisis that had confronted Eisenhower at Little Rock in 1957. The president ordered several hundred federal marshals to escort Meredith into a university dormitory. Kennedy then announced on national television that the university had been integrated and asked students to follow the law of the land. Instead, a mob moved on campus, shooting out streetlights, commandeering a bulldozer, and throwing rocks and bottles. To save the marshals, Kennedy finally sent in federal troops, but not before 2 people were killed and 375 wounded.

James Meredith

In Mississippi, President Kennedy had begun to lose control of the civil rights issue. The House of Representatives, influenced by television coverage of the violence, introduced a number of civil rights measures. And Martin Luther King led a group to Birmingham, Alabama, to force a showdown against segregation. From a prison cell there, he produced one of the most eloquent documents of the civil rights

In Birmingham, Alabama, fire-fighters used high-pressure hoses to disperse civil rights demonstrators. The force of the hoses was powerful enough to tear bark off trees. Pictures like this one aroused widespread sympathy for the civil rights movement.

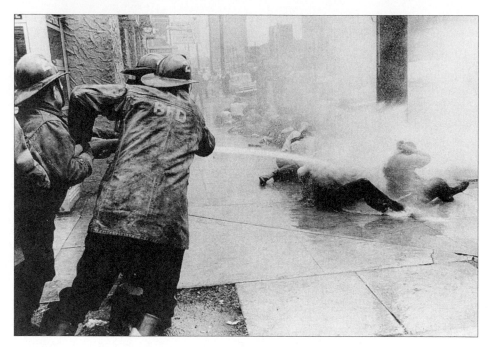

"Letter from Birmingham Jail"

movement, his "Letter from Birmingham Jail." Addressed to local ministers who had counseled an end to confrontation, King defended the use of civil disobedience. The choice, he warned, was not between obeying the law and nonviolently breaking it to bring about change; it was between his way and streets "flowing with blood," as restive black citizens turned toward more militant ideologies.

Once freed, King led new demonstrations. Television cameras were on hand that May as Birmingham police chief "Bull" Connor, a man with a short fuse, unleashed attack dogs, club-wielding police, and fire hoses powerful enough to peel the bark off trees. When segregationist bombs went off in African American neighborhoods, black mobs retaliated with their own riot, burning a number of shops and busi-nesses owned by whites. In the following 10 weeks, more than 750 riots erupted in 186 cities and towns, both North and South. King's warning of streets "flowing with blood" no longer seemed far-fetched.

Kennedy sensed that he could no longer compromise on civil rights. In phrases that, like King's, drew heavily on Christian and republican rhetoric, he asked the nation, "If [an American with dark skin] cannot enjoy the full and free life all of us want, then who among us would be content to have the color of his skin changed and stand in his place? Who among us would then be content with counsels of pa-tience and delay?" The president followed his words with support for a strong civil rights bill to end segregation and protect black voters. When King announced a massive march on Washington for August 1963, Kennedy objected that it would un-dermine support for his bill. "I have never engaged in any direct action movement which did not seem ill-timed," King replied. Faced with the inevitable, Kennedy convinced the organizers to use the event to promote the administration's bill, much to the disgust of militant CORE and SNCC factions.

The march on Washington

On August 28 some 250,000 people gathered at the Lincoln Memorial to march and sing in support of civil rights and racial harmony. Appropriately, the day be-longed to King. In the powerful tones of a southern preacher, he reminded the crowd that the Declaration of Independence was a promise that applied to all people, black and white. "I have a dream," he told them, that one day "all of God's children, black men and white men, Jews and Gentiles, Protestants and Catholics, will be able to join hands and sing in the words of the old Negro spiritual, 'Free at last! Free at last! Thank God Almighty, we are free at last!'" Congress began deliberation of the civil rights bill, which was reported out of the Judiciary Committee on October 23.

The Fire Next Time

While liberals applauded Kennedy's stand on civil rights and appreciative African Americans rejoined the Democratic party, substantial numbers of southern whites and northern ethnics deserted. The president scheduled a trip to Texas to recoup some southern support. On November 22, 1963, the people of Dallas lined the streets for his motorcade. Suddenly, a sniper's rifle fired several times. Kennedy slumped into his wife's arms, fatally wounded. His assassin, Lee Harvey Oswald, was caught several hours later. Oswald seemed a mysterious figure: emotionally unstable, he had spent several years in the Soviet Union. But his actions were never fully explained, because only two days after his arrest—in full view of television cameras—he was gunned down by a disgruntled nightclub operator named Jack Ruby. An investigative commission headed by Chief Justice Earl Warren concluded that Oswald had acted alone, a conclusion with which historians generally agree. But the commission acted so hastily that a host of critics arose and rejected its conclusions in favor of theories placing Oswald as part of various conspiracies.

Tragedy in Dallas

In the face of the violence surrounding the civil rights campaign as well as the assassination of the president, many Americans came to doubt that programs of gradual reform could hold the nation together. A few black radicals believed that the Kennedy assassination was a payback to a system that had tolerated its own racial violence—the "chickens coming home to roost," as separatist Malcolm X put it. Many younger black leaders observed that civil rights received the greatest national coverage when white, not black, demonstrators were killed. They wondered, too, how Lyndon Johnson, a consummate southern politician, would approach the civil rights programs.

The new president, however, saw the need for action. Just as the Catholic issue had tested Kennedy's ability to lead, Johnson knew that without strong leadership on civil rights, "I'd be dead before I could ever begin." On November 23, his first day in office, he promised civil rights leaders that he would pass Kennedy's bill. Despite a southern filibuster in the Senate, the Civil Rights Act of 1964 became law the following summer. The bill marked one of the great moments in the history of American reform. It barred discrimination in public accommodations such as lunch counters, bus stations, and hotels; it authorized the attorney general to bring suit to desegregate schools, museums, and other public facilities; it outlawed discrimination in employment by race, color, religion, sex, or national origin; and it gave additional protection to voting rights.

LBJ and the Civil Rights Act of 1964

Still, the Civil Rights Act did not bar the techniques that southern registrars routinely used to prevent black citizens from voting. A coalition of idealistic young black and white protesters had continued the Mississippi voting drive in what they called "Freedom Summer." In 1965 Martin Luther King led a series of demonstrations, climaxed by a 54-mile walk from Selma to Montgomery, Alabama. As pressure mounted, Johnson sent Congress a strong Voting Rights Act that was passed in August 1965. The act suspended literacy tests and authorized federal officials to supervise elections in many southern districts. With some justice Johnson called the act "one of the most monumental laws in the entire history of American freedom." Within a five-year period black registration in the South jumped from 35 to 65 percent.

Voting Rights Act of 1965

Black Power

The civil rights laws, as comprehensive as they were, did not strike at the de facto segregation found outside the South. These forms of segregation were not codified in law but practiced through unwritten custom. In large areas of America, African Americans were locked out of suburbs, kept out of decent schools, barred from exclusive clubs, and denied all but the most menial jobs. Nor did the Voting Rights Act deal with the sources of urban black poverty. The median income for urban black residents was approximately half that for white residents.

In such an atmosphere, militants sharply questioned the liberal goal of integration. Since the 1930s the Black Muslim religious sect, dedicated to complete separation from white society, had attracted as many as 100,000 members, mostly young men. During the early 1960s the sect drew even wider attention through the energetic efforts of Malcolm X. This charismatic leader had learned the language of the

Malcolm X

Malcolm X

downtrodden from his own experience as a former hustler, gambler, and prison inmate. His militancy alarmed whites, though by 1965 Malcolm was in fact moving toward a more moderate position. He accepted integration but emphasized black community action. After he broke with the Black Muslims he was gunned down by rivals.

But by 1965–1966, even CORE and SNCC had begun to give up working for nonviolent change. If black Americans were to liberate themselves fully, militants argued, they could not merely accept rights "given" to them by whites—they had to claim them. Some members began carrying guns to defend themselves. In 1966 Stokely Carmichael of SNCC gave the militants a slogan—"Black Power"—and the defiant symbol of a gloved fist raised in the air. In its moderate form, the black power movement encouraged African Americans to recover their cultural roots, their African heritage, and a new sense of identity. African clothes and natural hairstyles became popular. On college campuses black students pressed universities to hire black faculty, create black studies programs, and provide segregated social and residential space.

Black Panthers

For more militant factions like the Black Panther party of Oakland, California, violence became a revolutionary tool. Led by Huey P. Newton and Eldridge Cleaver, the Panthers called on the black community to arm. Because California law forbade carrying concealed weapons, Newton and his followers openly brandished shotguns and rifles as they patrolled the streets protecting blacks from police harassment. In February 1967 Newton found the showdown he had been looking for. "O.K., you big fat racist pig, draw your gun," he shouted while waving a shotgun. A gun battle with police left Newton wounded and in jail.

Eldridge Cleaver, who assumed leadership of the party, attracted the attention of whites with his searing autobiography, *Soul on Ice*. But even at the height of the Black Panthers' power, the group never counted more than 2000 members nationwide. Most African Americans remained committed to the goals defined by the civil rights movement: nonviolence, not armed confrontation; integration, not segregation.

Violence in the Streets

No ideology shaped the reservoir of frustration and despair that existed in the ghettos. Often, a seemingly minor incident such as an arrest or an argument on the streets would trigger widespread violence. A mob would gather, and police cars and white-owned stores would be firebombed or looted. As police and the National

Guard were ordered in, the violence escalated. Riots broke out in Harlem and Rochester, New York, in 1964, the Watts area of Los Angeles in 1965, Chicago in 1966, and Newark and Detroit in 1967. In the riot at Watts, more than $200 million in property lay in ruins and 34 people died, all of them black. It took nearly 5000 troops to end the bloodiest rioting in Detroit, where 40 died, 2000 were injured, and 5000 were left homeless.

To most whites the violence was unfathomable and inexcusable. Lyndon Johnson spoke for many when he argued that "neither old wrongs nor new fears can justify arson and murder." Martin Luther King, still pursuing the tactics of nonviolence, came to understand the anger behind it. Touring Watts only days after the riots, he was approached by a band of young blacks. "We won," they told him proudly. "How can you say you won,"

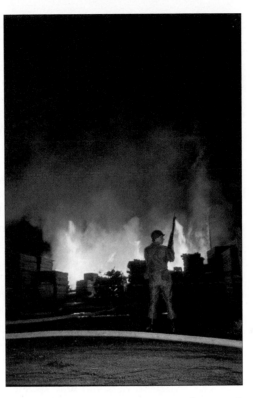

A National Guardsman watches as flames consume large areas of the Watts section of Los Angeles during the 1965 riot. Often, a seemingly trivial event set off such scenes of violence, revealing the depth of explosive rage harbored within ghettos.

King countered, "when thirty-four Negroes are dead, your community is destroyed, and whites are using the riot as an excuse for inaction?" The youngsters were unmoved. "We won because we made them pay attention to us."

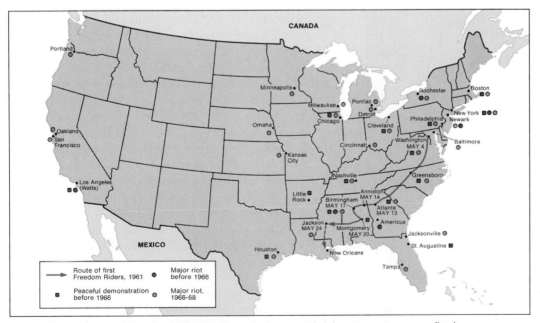

Civil Rights: Patterns of Protest and Unrest The first phase of the civil rights movement was confined largely to the South, where the freedom riders of 1961 dramatized the issue of segregation. Beginning in the summer of 1964, urban riots brought the issue of race and politics home to the entire nation. Severe rioting followed the murder of Martin Luther King Jr. in 1968, after which the worst violence subsided.

For Johnson, ghetto violence and black militance mocked his efforts to achieve racial progress. The Civil Rights and Voting Rights acts were essential parts of the Great Society he hoped to build. In that effort he had achieved a legislative record virtually unequaled by any president in the nation's history. What Kennedy had promised, Johnson delivered. But the growing white backlash and the anger exploding in the nation's cities exposed serious flaws in the theory and practice of liberal reform.

Lyndon Johnson and the Great Society

Like the state he hailed from, Lyndon Baines Johnson was in all things bigger than life. His gifts were greater, his flaws more glaring. Insecurity was his Achilles heel and the engine that drove him. If Kennedy had been good as president, Johnson would be "the greatest of them all, the whole bunch of them." If FDR won in a landslide in 1936, Johnson would produce an even larger margin in 1964. And to anyone who displeased him, he could be ruthlessly cruel. His scatological language and preoccupation with barnyard sex amused few and offended many. He counted himself among history's great figures. A visiting head of state once asked Johnson if he was born in a log cabin. "No, no," the president responded. "You have me confused with Abe Lincoln. I was born in a manger." Yet Johnson could not understand why so few people genuinely liked him; one courageous diplomat, when pressed, found the nerve to respond, "Because, Mr. President, you are not a very likable man."

The irrepressible Lyndon Johnson had difficulty playing second fiddle to anyone, even when he was vice president. But his shrewd political instincts and folksy charm, which he knew how to deploy to good effect, often allowed him to outmaneuver his opponents.

Johnson was born in Stonewall, Texas, in the hill country outside Austin, where the dry climate and rough terrain only grudgingly yielded up a living. Schooled in manners by his overbearing mother and in politics by his father and his cronies, Johnson arrived in Washington in 1932 as an ardent New Dealer who loved the political game. When he became majority leader of the Senate in 1954, he cultivated an image as a moderate conservative who knew what strings to pull or levers to jog to get the job done. Johnson knew what made his colleagues run. On an important bill, he latched onto the undecided votes until they succumbed to the famous "Johnson treatment," a combination of arguments, threats, emotional or patriotic appeals, and enticing rewards. Florida Senator George Smathers likened Johnson to "a great overpowering thunderstorm that consumed you as it closed around you." Or as Ben Bradlee of the *Washington Post* recalled, "He never just shook hands with you. One hand was shaking your hand; the other was always someplace else, exploring you, examining you."

Despite his compulsion to control every person and situation, Johnson possessed certain bedrock strengths. No one was better at hammering out compromises among competing interest groups. To those who served him well he could be loyal and generous. As president, he cared sincerely about society's underdogs. His support for civil rights, aid to the poor, education, and the welfare of the elderly came from genuine conviction. He made the betterment of such people the goal of his administration.

The Origins of the Great Society

In the first months after the assassination, Johnson acted as the conservator of the Kennedy legacy. "Let us continue," he told a grief-stricken nation. Liberals who had dismissed Johnson as an unprincipled power broker grudgingly came to respect the energy he showed in steering reform through Congress. The Civil Rights Act and tax cut legislation were only two of the most conspicuous pieces of Kennedy business Johnson quickly finished.

Kennedy had come to recognize that prosperity alone would not ease the plight of America's poor. In 1962 Michael Harrington's book *The Other America* brought attention to the widespread persistence of poverty despite the nation's affluence. Harrington focused attention on the hills of Appalachia that stretched from western Pennsylvania south to Alabama. In some counties a quarter of the population survived on a diet of flour and dried-milk paste supplied by federal surplus food programs. Under Kennedy Congress had passed a new food stamp program as well as laws designed to revive the economies of poor areas, replacing urban slums with newer housing and retraining the unemployed. Robert Kennedy also headed a presidential committee to fight juvenile delinquency in urban slums by involving the poor in "community action" programs. Direct participation, they hoped, would overcome "a sense of resignation and fatalism" that sociologist Oscar Lewis had found while studying the Puerto Rican community of New York City.

Discovering poverty

Such forces for change brought hope and energy to the liberal tradition. Like the New Dealers and the progressives before them, liberals of the 1960s did not wish to overturn capitalism. They looked primarily to tame its excesses, taking a pragmatic approach to reforming American society. Like Franklin Roosevelt, they believed that the government should play an active role in managing the economy in order to soften the boom-and-bust swings of capitalism. Like progressives from the turn of the century, liberals looked to improve society by applying the intelligence of "experts."

The liberal tradition

Liberals had confidence, at times bordering on arrogance, that poverty could be eliminated and the good society achieved. "The world seemed more plastic, more subject to human will," one liberal recalled. He and his fellow reformers believed that "the energy and commitment of multitudes could be linked to compel the enrichment of human life." That faith might prove naive, but during the 1960s such optimism was both infectious and energizing.

It fell to Lyndon Johnson to fight Kennedy's "war on poverty." By August 1964 this master politician had driven through Congress the most sweeping social welfare bill since the New Deal. The Economic Opportunity Act addressed almost every major cause of poverty. It included training programs such as the Job Corps, granted loans to rural families and urban small businesses as well as aid to migrant workers, and launched a domestic version of the Peace Corps, known as VISTA (Volunteers in Service to America). The price tag for these programs was high. Johnson committed almost $1 billion to Sargent Shriver, a Kennedy brother-in-law, who directed the new Office of Economic Opportunity (OEO). When Michael Harrington complained that even $1 billion could barely scratch the surface, Shriver tartly replied, "Maybe you've spent a billion dollars before, but this is my first time around."

The Job Corps was one strategy that Johnson used to alleviate unemployment and poverty. The idea was to train the unskilled and retrain workers whose skills were no longer needed.

The speed Johnson demanded led inevitably to confusion, conflict, and waste. Officials at OEO often found themselves in conflict with other cabinet departments as well as with state and local officials. For example, OEO workers organized voter registration drives in order to oust corrupt city officials. Others led rent strikes to force improvements in public housing. The director of city housing in Syracuse, New York, reacted typically: "We are experiencing a class struggle in the traditional Karl Marx style in Syracuse, and I do not like it." Such battles for power and bureaucratic turf undermined federal poverty programs.

The Election of 1964

In 1964, however, these controversies had not yet surfaced. Johnson's political stock remained high. To an audience at the University of Michigan in May, he announced his ambition to forge a "Great Society," in which poverty and racial injustice no longer existed. The chance to fulfill his dreams seemed open to him, for the Republicans nominated Senator Barry Goldwater of Arizona as their presidential candidate. Ruggedly handsome, Goldwater was a true son of the West who held a narrow view of what government should do, for he was at heart a libertarian. Government, he argued, should not dispense welfare, subsidize farmers, tax incomes on a progressive basis, or aid public education. At the same time, Goldwater was so anti-Communist that he championed a large defense establishment.

Goldwater's extreme views allowed Johnson to portray himself as a moderate. He chose Minnesota's liberal Senator Hubert Humphrey to give regional balance to the ticket. Only the candidacy of Governor George Wallace of Alabama marred Johnson's election prospects. In Democratic primaries, Wallace's segregationist appeal won nearly a third or more of the votes in Wisconsin, Indiana, and Maryland—hardly the Deep South. He was persuaded, however, to drop out of the race.

The election produced the landslide Johnson craved. Carrying every state except Arizona and four in the Deep South, he received 61 percent of the vote. Democrats gained better than two-to-one majorities in the Senate and House. All the same, the election was probably more a repudiation of Goldwater than a mandate for Johnson. The president realized that he had to move rapidly to exploit the momentum of his 1964 majority.

The Great Society

In January 1965 Johnson announced a legislative vision that would extend welfare programs on a scale beyond Franklin Roosevelt's New Deal. By the end of 1965, 50 bills had been passed, many of them major pieces of legislation, with more on the agenda for the following year.

Programs in education   As a former teacher, Johnson made education the cornerstone of his Great Society. Stronger schools would compensate the poor for their disadvantaged homes, he believed. Under the Elementary and Secondary School Act, students in low-income school districts were to receive educational equipment, money for books, and enrichment programs like Project Head Start for nursery-school-age children. As schools scrambled to create programs that would tap federal money, they sometimes spent more to pay middle-class educational professionals than to teach lower-income students.

Medicare and Medicaid   President Johnson also pushed through the Medicare Act to provide the elderly with health insurance to cover hospital costs. Medicare targeted the elderly, because studies had shown that older people used hospitals three times more than other Americans and generally had incomes only half as large. Because Medicare made no provision for the poor who were not elderly, Congress also passed a program called

Medicaid. Participating states would receive matching grants from the federal government to pay the medical expenses of those on welfare or too poor to afford medical care.

In many ways, Medicare and Medicaid worked. The poor and elderly received significantly more help when facing catastrophic illnesses. Over the next two decades, such aid helped to lower significantly the number of elderly poor. But as more patients used hospital services, Medicare budgets rose. In addition, nothing in the act restricted hospitals or doctors from raising their fees. The cost of the programs soared by more than 500 percent in the first 10 years.

Ten days after signing the Medicare bill, Johnson signed the Omnibus Housing Act, designed to subsidize rents for poor families unable to find adequate public housing. Four days later came the Voting Rights Act. Within two weeks Congress approved the creation of a new cabinet-level Department of Housing and Urban Development (HUD). To head it, Johnson named Robert Weaver, a former president **HUD** of the NAACP. And in the tradition of the New Deal, which had patronized the arts under the WPA, Johnson created the National Foundation of the Arts and Humanities. Colleges and their students received support for scholarships and loans, research equipment, and libraries.

The Great Society also reformed immigration policy, in ways that reflected the **Immigration reform** drastic changes in global economics and culture since the last major immigration legislation was passed in 1924. Then, the National Origins Act (page 794) had embodied the deeply Eurocentric orientation of American society and its prejudices against people of color. Almost all the annual admissions quota of 154,000 went to Northern Europeans. Asians were barred almost entirely. By the 1960s American attitudes were changing, in terms of both race and region. American soldiers, after all, had fought wars to defend Korea, the Philippines, Vietnam, Taiwan, Japan, and other Asian nations. How could it justify discriminating against citizens from those countries? President Kennedy had challenged Congress to eliminate the national origins system, which he argued "satisfies neither national need nor accomplishes an international purpose."

By 1965, with Asian economies growing, the war in Vietnam expanding, and civil rights sentiments at a peak, the need for reform took on special urgency. The Immigration Act of 1965 abolished the national origins system. It increased annual admissions to 170,000 people and put a cap of 20,000 on immigrants from any single nation. The law gave marked preference to reuniting families of those immigrants already in the United States—so much so that some observers nicknamed it the "brothers and sisters act." Asians and Eastern Europeans were among its prime beneficiaries.

The act's liberalization was offset, however, by prejudice toward Central Americans, especially Mexicans. The National Origins Act of 1924 had placed no limit on immigrants from the Americas. But by the 1960s many in Congress feared a massive influx of workers from south of the border. Widespread poverty in Latin American nations had left thousands unemployed and desperate to find work. Hence the new act capped arrivals from the Western Hemisphere at 120,000 annually. In that way immigration reform reflected the shifting balance of the global economy.

Booming economies took an increasing toll on the environment. By the mid- **The environment** 1960s many Americans had become increasingly concerned about acrid smog from factories and automobiles; about lakes and rivers polluted by detergents, pesticides, and industrial wastes; and about the disappearance of wildlife. In 1964 Congress had already passed the National Wilderness Preservation System Act to set aside 9.1 million acres of wilderness as "forever wild." Lady Bird Johnson, the president's wife, campaigned to eliminate the garish billboards and junkyards along many of the nation's roads. Congress first established pollution standards for interstate waterways and a year later provided funds for sewage treatment and water purification. Legislation also tightened standards on air pollution. Environmental reform provoked opposition from groups like mining companies, cattle-grazers, and the timber industry, who wanted to continue using the public domain for their own purposes. But the public accepted the benefits of the new regulation. Among other accomplishments, by the mid-1990s smog had declined nationwide by about a third and the number of rivers and lakes suitable for swimming and fishing had doubled.

For all he had done, Johnson wanted to do more. In 1966 he pushed through bills to raise the minimum wage, improve auto safety, aid mass transit, and develop "model cities." But in time opposition mounted. "Doesn't matter what kind of majority you come in with," Johnson had predicted early on. "You've got just one year when they treat you right, and before they start worrying about themselves." Yet as late as 1968 Johnson pushed major legislation through Congress to ban discrimination in housing (Fair Housing Act), to build public housing, to protect consumers from unfair credit practices (Truth-in-Lending Act), and to protect scenic rivers and expand the national park system.

Evaluating the Great Society

Historians have difficulty measuring the Great Society's impact. It produced more legislation and more reforms than the New Deal. It also carried a high price tag. Economic statistics suggested that general prosperity, accelerated by the tax cut bill, did more to fight poverty than all the OEO programs. And the inevitable scandals began to surface: Job Corps retrainees burglarizing homes in their off-hours, school equipment purchased that no one knew how to use. Conservatives and radicals alike objected that the liberal welfare state was intruding into too many areas of people's lives. Ethnic groups like Italian and Polish Americans objected to what they considered favoritism accorded black Americans and Hispanics under many programs.

For all that, the Great Society established the high-water mark of interventionist government, a trend that began in the progressive era and flourished during the Great Depression and in World War II. Although Americans continued to pay lip service to the notion that government should remain small and interfere little in citizens' lives, no strong movement emerged to eliminate Medicare or Medicaid. Few Americans disputed the right of the government to regulate industrial pollution or to control the excesses of large corporations or powerful labor unions. Even conservatives granted the government a role in managing the economy and providing citizens with a safety net of benefits in sickness and in old age. In this sense, the tradition of liberalism prevailed, whatever Johnson's failings.

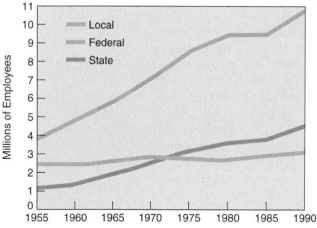

Growth of Government, 1955–1990 Government has been a major growth industry since World War II. Most people think of "big government" as federal government. But even during the Great Society, far more people worked in state and local government. Despite the antigovernment rhetoric, federal employment grew substantially in the Reagan-Bush era.

The Reforms of the Warren Court

Although Lyndon Johnson and the Congress left the stamp of liberalism on federal power during the decade, the third branch of government played a role that, in the long run, proved equally significant. Supreme Court Chief Justice Earl Warren turned

I was sentenced to the State Penitentiary by The Circuit Court of Bay County, State of Florida. The present proceeding was commenced on a petition for a Writ of Habeus Corpus to The Supreme Court of The State of Florida to vacate the sentence, on the grounds that I was made to stand Trial without the aid of counsel, and, at all times of my incarseretion. The said Court refused To appoint counsel and therefore deprived me of due process of law, and violate my rights in the Bill of Rights and the constitution of the United states.

Clarence Earl Gideon

5th day of Jan 1962 Petitioner

Laurence C Duyya

NoTary public

Noiar, Publi......

My Comai..... 1-, 1962

Bonded by AmericanSurety Co. of N. Y.

Gideon's Letter to the Supreme Court
John F. Davis, Clerk, Supreme Court of the United States

Clarence Earl Gideon (left) used this handwritten letter to bring his appeal to the attention of the Supreme Court. In the *Gideon* case the court ruled that even poor defendants have the right to legal counsel. Such incidents, while rare, restore faith in the idea of a government for the people.

what was traditionally the least activist branch of government into a center of liberal reform. His political skills, compassion, and tact had been instrumental in bringing his colleagues to a unanimous ruling on school desegregation in *Brown v. Board of Education*. And Warren continued to use these skills, until his retirement in 1969, to forge a liberal coalition of justices who handed down a series of landmark decisions in broad areas of civil liberties and civil rights.

In 1960 the rights of citizens accused of a crime but not yet convicted were often unclear. Those too poor to afford lawyers often faced trial without representation. The police and the courts seldom informed those accused of a crime of their rights guaranteed under the Constitution. In a series of decisions, the Court ruled that the Fourteenth Amendment provided broad guarantees of due process under the law. *Gideon v. Wainwright* (1963), an appeal launched by a Florida prisoner, made it clear that all citizens were entitled to legal counsel in any case involving a possible jail sentence. In *Escobedo v. Illinois* (1964) and *Miranda v. Arizona* (1966) the Court declared that individuals detained for a crime must be informed of the charges against them, of their right to remain silent, and of their right to have an attorney present during questioning. Though these decisions applied to all citizens, they were primarily intended to benefit the poor, who were most likely to be in trouble with the law and least likely to understand their rights.

Protecting due process

In *Engel v. Vitale* (1962), the Court issued a ruling that especially troubled conservative religious groups. The case involved a nonsectarian prayer written by the New York State Board of Regents that public school students were required to recite. Even if dissenting children could be excused, the Court ruled, they faced indirect pressure to recite the prayer. That violated the constitutional separation of

Banning school prayer

church and state. The following year the Court extended the ban on school prayer to cover the reading of the Bible and the Lord's Prayer.

Other decisions promoted a more liberal social climate. In *Griswold v. Connecticut* (1964) the Warren Court overturned a nineteenth-century law banning the sale of contraceptives or providing medical advice about their use. The Court demonstrated its distaste for censorship by greatly narrowing the legal definition of obscenity. A book had to be "utterly without redeeming social value" to permit censorship. The combination of decisions reforming criminal rights, prayer, free speech, and morality angered conservatives of almost all social and political backgrounds. These issues would again become a political battleground in the 1980s and 1990s.

The Court's most far-reaching decision was probably one of its least controversial, though politically most sensitive. As cities and suburbs grew, few states redrew their legislative districts to reflect the change. Rural (and generally conservative) elements continued to dominate state legislatures. In *Baker v. Carr* (1962) and a series of later cases the Court ruled that the states must apportion seats not by "land or trees or pastures," but as closely as possible by the principle of "one person, one vote."

One person, one vote

The Counterculture

In 1964 some 800 students from Berkeley, Oberlin, and other colleges met in western Ohio to be trained for the voter registration campaign in the South. Middle-class students who had grown up in peaceful white suburbs found themselves being instructed for this "Mississippi Freedom Summer" by protest-hardened SNCC coordinators. The lessons were sobering. When beaten by police, the SNCC staff advised, assume the fetal position—hands protecting the neck, elbows covering the temples. That minimized injuries from nightsticks. A few days later, grimmer news arrived. A volunteer who had left for Mississippi two days earlier had already been arrested by local police. Now he and two others were reported "missing." Six weeks later, their mangled bodies were found, bulldozed into the earthworks of a freshly finished dam. That did not stop other sobered volunteers from heading to Mississippi.

By the mid-1960s dissatisfied members of the middle class—and especially the young—had launched a revolt against the conventions of society and politics as usual. The students who returned to campus from the voter registration campaign that summer of 1964 were the shock troops of a much larger movement. They included a curious mix of political activists and apolitical dropouts, labeled hippies.

Activists on the New Left

More than a few students had become disillusioned with the slow pace of reform. Since the "establishment"—whether it was liberal or conservative—blocked meaningful change, why not overthrow it? Tom Hayden, raised in a working-class family outside Detroit, went to college at the University of Michigan, then traveled to Berkeley, and soon joined civil rights workers in Mississippi. "At first, you thought, well, the southern system is some kind of historical vestige," he recalled. "Instead, we found out that the structure of power was very tied into the structure of power in the whole U.S. You'd find that Harvard was investing in Mississippi Power and Light, which was a company that economically dominated Mississippi."

Hayden, along with Al Haber, another student at the University of Michigan, was a driving force in forming the radical Students for a Democratic Society (SDS). SDS had little sympathy with an "old left" generation of radicals who grew up in the 1930s and still debated the merits of Marxism. Action was the route to change, Hayden argued: through sit-ins, protest marches, and direct confrontation. At a meeting in Port Huron, Michigan, in 1962 the group condemned the modern bureaucratic society exemplified by the organization man of the 1950s. The Port Huron Statement called for "participatory democracy," in which large organizations run by bureaucrats would be decentralized and turned into face-to-face communities in which individual participation mattered. The Port Huron Statement did not exactly revolutionize America; only 60,000 copies of it were ever sold. It did, however, anticipate the dramatic increase in political and cultural conflict that was spreading across the nation.

SDS and Port Huron

counterpoint

What Triggered the Upheavals of the 1960s?

Historians have debated the causes of the turbulent 1960s. Some scholars have favored a generational explanation. The United States has undergone periodic cycles of reform as each new generation has come of age—about once every 30 years. Thus the twentieth century began with progressive reformers pushing for change, only to give way to the quiet "normalcy" of the 1920s, which in turn was succeeded by the activist New Deal in the 1930s. Similarly, the "consensus" decade of the 1950s preceded liberalism's high tide in the 1960s. In that light, the Port Huron Statement can be read as a call for a new cycle of reform led by the nation's young baby boomers, who grew up during the 1950s. "There had to be a critical mass of students, and enough economic fat to cushion them," suggested one historian.

Other historians are more leery of the generational approach. Consider some of the figures who played pivotal roles in the decade's social reforms: civil rights advocates like Martin Luther King and Cesar Chavez, feminist Betty Friedan, environmentalist Rachel Carson, consumer advocate Ralph Nader, drug-promoter Timothy Leary, and rock stars like Bob Dylan and the Beatles. All were born before or during World War II and were not a part of the baby boom generation. In fact, it is possible to argue that, by and large, baby boomers served mainly as foot soldiers in a crusade led by a generation that came of age during the consensus years of the 1950s.

In the end, it may be more useful to focus on specific catalytic events that bonded different generations. Mississippi Freedom Summer was such an event. Student volunteers for Mississippi underwent a kind of on-the-job boot camp, often tutored by radical "veterans" half a dozen years older who had already come to the voting rights project. The newly arrived baby boomers gave up their suburban dress for overalls and work shirts of the sort worn by poor African American laborers in the Mississippi Delta. Workers shared in the terror of frequent harassment and even possible death. Once SNCC volunteers returned to their college campuses, they themselves became catalysts for much of the turmoil that followed. They did not necessarily "cause" the rebellion of the 1960s, but they did help shape much of the discontent stirring beneath the veneer of campus conformity.

The Free Speech Movement at the University of California, Berkeley, was a case in point. To most liberals, Berkeley seemed the gem of the California state university system. Like so many other universities, it had educated a generation of GIs following World War II. But to people like Tom Hayden and the SDS, Berkeley was a bureaucratic monster, enrolling more than 30,000 students. Students at Berkeley,

The Free Speech Movement

Edie Black from Smith College was one of hundreds of middle-class students who volunteered during Freedom Summer of 1964. Here she teaches in a school at Mileston, Mississippi. Many students returned to their campuses in the fall radicalized, ready to convince others to join them in finding alternatives to "the system."

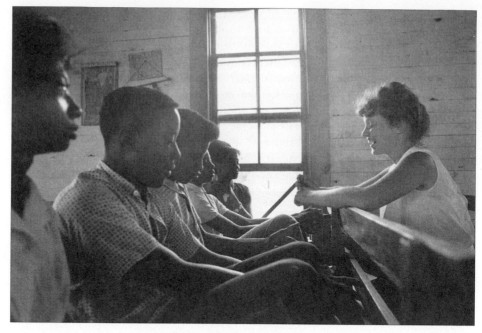

like at other large universities, filed into impersonal classrooms to hear lectures from remote professors. In the fall of 1964, Berkeley declared off limits the one small area in which political organizations had been allowed to advertise their causes. When university police tried to remove a recruiter for CORE, thousands of angry students surrounded the police car for 32 hours. They were led by a student named Mario Savio.

Before traveling south to Freedom Summer in 1964, Savio had been an undistinguished graduate student in philosophy. Mississippi changed him. "There was this single-mindedness of purpose and moral certainty that pushed him," a fellow Berkeley volunteer commented. And not just Savio. Twelve of the 21 Freedom Summer veterans at Berkeley were arrested during the protest. "In our free-speech fight," Savio proclaimed, "we have come up against what may emerge as the greatest problem of our nation—depersonalized, unresponsive bureaucracy." When the university's president, Clark Kerr, threatened to expel Savio, 6000 students took control of the administration building, stopped classes with a strike, and convinced many faculty members to join them. Kerr backed down, placing no limits to free speech on campus except those that applied to society at large. But the lines between students and administrators had been drawn. The rebellious spirit spread to other major universities such as Michigan, Yale, and Columbia and then to campuses across the nation.

The Rise of the Counterculture

Disaffection of a less political kind produced rebels who condemned an American society that they found too materialistic and shallow. These alienated students, often from conservative backgrounds, began to grope toward spiritual, nonmaterial goals. "Turn on to the scene, tune in to what is happening, and drop out of high school, college, grad school, junior executive," advised Timothy Leary, a Harvard psychology professor who dropped out himself. People who heeded Leary's call to spiritual renewal rejected politics for a lifestyle of experimentation with music, sex, and drugs. Observers labeled their movement a "counterculture."

The counterculture of the 1960s had much in common with earlier religious revival and utopian movements. It admired the quirky individualism of Henry David Thoreau, and like Thoreau, it turned to Zen Buddhism and other Oriental philosophies. Like Brook Farm and other nineteenth-century utopian communities, the new hippie communes sought perfection along the fringes of society. Communards built geodesic domes based on the designs of architect Buckminster Fuller; they "learned how to scrounge materials, tear down abandoned buildings, use the unusable," as one member of the Drop City commune put it. Sexual freedom became a means to liberate them from the repressive inhibitions that distorted the lives of their "uptight" parents. Drugs appeared to open the inner mind to a higher state of consciousness or pleasure. No longer would people be bound by conventional relationships and the goals of a liberal, bourgeois society.

The early threads of the 1960s counterculture led back to the 1950s and the subculture of the beat generation (page 951). For the beats, unconventional drugs had long been a part of the scene, but now their use expanded dramatically. Timothy Leary began experimenting with hallucinogenic mushrooms in Mexico and soon moved on to LSD. The drug "blew his mind," he announced, and he became so enthusiastic in making converts that Harvard blew him straight out of its hallowed doors.

Whereas Leary's approach to LSD was cool and contemplative, novelist Ken Kesey (*One Flew over the Cuckoo's Nest*) embraced it with antic frenzy. His ragtag company of druggies and freaks formed the "Merry Pranksters" at Kesey's home outside San Francisco. Writer Tom Wolfe chronicled their outrageous style in *The Electric Kool-Aid Acid Test,* a book that pioneered the "New Journalism." Wolfe dropped the rules of reporting that demanded objectivity and distance by taking himself and his readers on a psychedelic tour with Kesey and his fellow Pranksters. Their example inspired others to drop out.

The Rock Revolution

In the 1950s rock and roll defined a teen culture preoccupied with young love, cars, and adult pressures. One exception was the Kingston Trio, which in 1958 popularized folk music that appealed to young adult and college audiences. As the interest in folk music grew, the lyrics increasingly focused on social or political issues. Joan Baez helped define the folk style by dressing simply, wearing no makeup, and rejecting the commercialism of popular music. She joined folksinger Bob Dylan in the civil rights march on Washington in 1963, singing "We Shall Overcome" and "Blowin' in the Wind." Such folksingers reflected the activist side of the counterculture as they sought to provoke their audiences to political commitment.

Rock groups like the Grateful Dead were closely associated with the drug culture. LSD inspired the genre of psychedelic art that adorned album covers and posters with freaked-out lettering (the album is *American Beauty Rose*) that seemed to dazzle and dance even if the viewer had not inhaled or ingested.

Daily Lives

CLOTHING AND FASHION
The Politics of Dress

Three-piece suits, fur coats, berets, Grateful Dead T-shirts—clothing has always made a statement about the values of the wearer. In the 1950s that statement was conformity. The khaki slacks and brush-cut hair popular with middle-class boys hinted at military regimentation. Rock-and-rollers, lower-class kids, and farm boys often wore dungarees and T-shirts, perhaps with a cigarette pack tucked in the rolled-up sleeve. Beatniks advertised their nonconformity by adopting an exotic look: long hair, goatees, turtlenecks, and sandals.

During the 1960s nonconformity became the norm. The revolution began in earnest with the coming of the Beatles, four British rockers from working-class Liverpool. John, Paul, George, and Ringo inspired fan hysteria beyond anything seen before. Their mod-style British clothes and longish, pageboy hair caused as much commotion as their music. As young Americans embraced the Beatles and all things British, London supplanted Paris and New York as a fashion center.

Suddenly it was the young and working class, not the rich and famous, who set trends in popular style. New fashions represented a desire to break social constraints in favor of greater sensuality and freedom of expression. Nowhere was that more evident than in the costuming of the counterculture. Middle-class students began to let their hair grow. Levis and army-navy store military surplus replaced khakis and pleated skirts. The original impulse was less rebellion than a distinct youthful identity that blurred social class lines, just as rock and roll did.

Hippies added a more theatrical twist. They rejected commercial fashion, synthetic fabrics, and cosmetics in favor of a natural look. To express a return to nature, they adopted the Hispanic shawl and serape; the Indian fringed buckskin, beads, and moccasins; and the bright coloring of African, Oriental, and Caribbean cotton fabrics. This costuming became standard wear at folk and rock music festivals and be-ins as well as at political demonstrations. Much of the clothing and accessories was handcrafted and sold largely through street vendors, medieval-style craft fairs,

Men's fashions moved in two directions—toward the hippie look and, as shown here, the mod look imported from England. Bold prints, flamboyant accessories, and zany combinations replaced traditionally conservative men's styles.

The Beatles

In 1964 a new sound, imported from England, exploded on the American scene. Within a year the Beatles, four musicians from Liverpool, had generated more excitement than any previous phenomenon in popular music. Their concerts and appearances on television drove teen audiences into frenzies as the mod crooners sang "I Want to Hold Your Hand." Part of the Beatles' appeal came from their distinctly English style. With hair that was considered long in the 1960s, modish clothes, fresh faces, and irreverent wit, they looked and sounded like nothing young Americans had experienced. Their boyish enthusiasm for life captured the Dionysian spirit of the new counterculture. But the Beatles' enormous commercial success also reflected the creativity of their music. Along with other English groups such as the Rolling Stones, the Beatles reconnected white American audiences with the rhythm-and-blues roots of rock and roll.

and small shops. Often these same shops, located in college towns and artsy urban neighborhoods, did a lively business selling paraphernalia of the drug culture: water pipes, "bongs," rolling papers, roach clips, strobe lights, posters, and Indian print bedspreads.

Fashion had become a function of politics and rebellion. Traditional Americans saw beads, long hair, sandals, drugs, radical politics, and rock and roll as elements of a revolution. To them, hippies and radicals were equally threatening. To restore order, they tried to censor and even outlaw the trappings of the counterculture. Schools expelled boys when their hair was too long and girls when their skirts were too short. It became indecent to desecrate the flag by sewing patches of red, white, and blue on torn blue jeans. Short-haired blue-collar workers harassed long-haired hippies and antiwar protesters. The personal fashions of the youth rebellion came to symbolize a "generation gap" between the young and their elders.

In time, however, that gap narrowed. Men especially broke with past tradition. Sideburns lengthened and mustaches and beards flourished as they had not since the nineteenth century. Men began to wear jewelry, furs, perfume, and shoulder-length hair. Subdued tweeds and narrow lapels gave way to bell-bottoms, broad floral ties, and wide-collared, sometimes psychedelic, shirts. By the early 1970s commercial success, not legal repression, had signaled an end to the revolution in fashion. As formerly hostile blue-collar workers and GIs began to sport long hair and hip clothes, fashion no longer made such clear distinctions. Even middle-aged men and women donned boots, let their hair grow a bit fuller, and slipped into modified bell-bottoms. Feminists rejected the more extreme styles as an example of the male-dominated fashion world that treated women as sex objects. Hippie garb, which was impractical in the office, was replaced by knee-length skirts or pants suits. Before long, three-piece suits, khakis, and short hair were back, although the democratic and eclectic spirit of the 1960s persisted. The new informality provided Americans of both sexes with a wider choice in fashions.

Dylan

Until 1965 Bob Dylan was the quintessential folk artist, writing about nuclear weapons, pollution, and racism. He appeared at concerts with longish frizzy hair, working-class clothes, an unamplified guitar, and a harmonica suspended on a wire support. But then Dylan shocked his fans by donning a black leather jacket and shifting to a "folk-rock" style featuring an electric guitar. His new songs seemed to suggest that the old America was almost beyond redemption. The Beatles, too, transformed themselves. After a pilgrimage to India to study transcendental meditation, they returned to produce *Sergeant Pepper's Lonely Hearts Club Band*, possibly the most influential album of the decade. It blended sound effects with music, alluded to trips taken with "Lucy in the Sky with Diamonds" (LSD), and concluded, "I'd love to turn you on." Out in San Francisco, bands such as the Grateful Dead pioneered "acid rock" with long pieces aimed to echo drug-induced states of mind.

Soul music

The debt of white rock musicians to rhythm and blues led to increased integration in the music world. Before the 1960s black rhythm-and-blues bands had played primarily to black audiences, in segregated clubs, or over black radio stations. The civil rights movement and a rising black social and political consciousness gave rise to "soul" music. One black disc jockey described soul as "the last to be hired, first to be fired, brown all year round, sit-in-the-back-of-the-bus feeling." Soul was the quality that expressed black pride and separatism: "You've got to live with us or you don't have it." Out of Detroit came the "Motown sound," which combined elements of gospel, blues, and big band jazz. Diana Ross and the Supremes, the Temptations, Stevie Wonder, and other groups under contract to Berry Gordy's Motown Record Company appealed to black and white audiences alike. Yet although soul music promoted black consciousness, it had little to offer by way of social commentary. It evoked the traditional blues themes of workday woes, unhappy marriages, and the troubles between men and women.

The West Coast Scene

For all its themes of alienation, rebellion, and utopian quest, the counterculture also signaled the increasing importance of the West Coast in American popular culture. In the 1950s the shift of television production from the stages of New York to the film lots of Hollywood helped establish Los Angeles as a communications center. San Francisco became notorious as a center of the beat movement.

Then in 1958 the unthinkable happened. The Brooklyn Dodgers and the New York Giants baseball teams fled the Big Apple for Los Angeles and San Francisco. When Alaska and Hawaii became states in 1959, the national center of gravity shifted westward. Richard Nixon, a Californian, narrowly missed being elected president in 1960. By 1963 the "surfing sound" of West Coast rock groups like the Beach Boys and Jan and Dean had made southern California's preoccupation with surfing and cars into a national fad.

Before 1967 Americans were only vaguely aware of another West Coast phenomenon, the hippies. But in January a loose coalition of drug freaks, Zen cultists, and political activists banded together to hold the first well-publicized Be-In. The beat poet Allen Ginsberg was on hand to offer spiritual guidance. The Grateful Dead and Jefferson Airplane, acid rock groups based in San Francisco, provided entertainment. A mysterious group called the Diggers somehow managed to supply free food and drink, while the notorious Hell's Angels motorcycle gang policed the occasion. Drugs of all kinds were plentiful. And a crowd attired in a bizarre mix of Native American, circus, Oriental, army surplus, and other costumes came to enjoy it all.

The West Coast had long been a magnet for Americans seeking opportunity, escape, and alternative lifestyles; now the San Francisco Bay area staked its claim as the spiritual center of the counterculture. The more politically conscious dropouts, or "fists," gravitated toward Berkeley; the apolitical "flower children" moved into Haight-Ashbury, a run-down San Francisco neighborhood of apartments, Victorian houses, and "head shops" selling drug paraphernalia, wall posters, Indian bedspreads, and other eccentric accessories. Similar dropout communities and communes sprang up across the country. Colleges became centers of hip culture, offering alternative courses, eliminating strict requirements, and tolerating the new sexual mores of their students.

In the summer of 1969 all the positive forces of the counterculture converged on Bethel, New York, in the Catskill Mountains resort area, to celebrate the promise of peace, love, and freedom. The Woodstock Music Festival attracted 400,000 people to the largest rock concert ever organized. For one long weekend the audience and performers joined to form an ephemeral community based on sex, drugs, and rock and roll. But even then, the counterculture was dying. Violence intruded on the laid-back urban communities that hippies had formed. Organized crime and drug pushers muscled in on the lucrative trade in LSD, amphetamines, and marijuana. Bad drugs and addiction took their toll. Urban slum dwellers turned hostile to the strange middle-class dropouts who, in ways the poor could not fathom, found poverty ennobling. Free sex often became an excuse for rape, exploitation, and loveless gratification.

Much that had once seemed outrageous in the hippie world was readily absorbed into the marketplace. Rock groups became big business enterprises commanding huge fees. Slick concerts with expensive tickets replaced communal dances with psychedelic light shows. Yogurt, granola, and herbal teas appeared on supermarket shelves. Ironically, much of the world that hippies forged was co-opted by the society they had rejected.

By the late 1960s most dreams of human betterment seemed shattered—whether those dreams emanated from the promise of the march on Washington, Lyndon Johnson's Great Society, or the communal society of the hippie counterculture. Recession and inflation brought an end to the easy affluence that made liberal reform programs and alternative lifestyles seem so easily affordable. Poverty and unemployment menaced even middle-class youth who had found havens in communes, colleges, and graduate schools. Racial tensions divided black militants and the white liberals of the civil rights movement into sometimes hostile camps.

But the Vietnam War more than any other single factor destroyed the promise of the Great Society and distracted from the campaign for civil rights. After 1965 the nation divided sharply as the American military role in Southeast Asia grew. Radicals on the left looked to rid America of a capitalist system that promoted race and class conflict at home and imperialism and military adventurism abroad. Conservatives who supported the war called for a return to more traditional values like law and order. Both the left and the right attacked the liberal center. Their combined opposition helped undermine the consensus Lyndon Johnson had worked so hard to build.

chapter summary

Largely excluded from the prosperity of the 1950s, African Americans and Latinos undertook a series of grass-roots efforts to gain the legal and social freedoms denied them by racism and, in the South, by an entrenched system of segregation.

- Early postwar campaigns focused on legal challenges to the system, culminating with victories in the Supreme Court decisions of *Brown v. Board of Education* and *Hernández v. Texas*.

- Later in the 1950s, Martin Luther King and other civil rights activists used new techniques of protest, such as the boycott, to desegregate the bus system in Montgomery, Alabama.

- Continued resistance by white southerners sparked a school integration dispute in Little Rock, Arkansas.

- Beginning in 1960, widespread grassroots efforts from African American churches, students, and political groups across the South accelerated the drive for an end to segregation.

- Violence against sit-ins, freedom rides, voter registration drives, and other forms of nonviolent protest made the nation sympathetic to the civil rights cause.

- In the wake of the assassination of President Kennedy, Lyndon Johnson persuaded Congress to adopt the Civil Rights Act of 1964 and the Voting Rights Act of 1965.

- The Supreme Court under Chief Justice Earl War-ren expanded civil rights and liberties through its *Gideon, Escobedo,* and *Miranda* decisions, while also easing censorship, banning school prayer, and in-creasing voting rights.

- Lyndon Johnson delivered on the liberal promise of his Great Society through his 1964 tax cut, aid to education, Medicare and Medicaid, wilderness preservation, and urban redevelopment, and through the many programs of his war on poverty.

- Johnson's liberal reforms did not satisfy student radicals, minority dissidents, feminists, gays, and the counterculture whose members sought to trans-form America into a more just and less materialis-tic society.

Significant Events

1947	1947 *Delgado et al. v. Bastrop et al.* filed in Texas
1954	1954 *Hernández v. Texas; Brown v. Board of Education*
1955	1955 Montgomery bus boycott begun
1956	1956 "Southern Manifesto" issued
1957	1957 Little Rock Crisis
	1958 Kingston Trio popularizes folk music
1958	1960 Greensboro sit-ins
	1961 CORE freedom rides begin
1959	1962 James Meredith desegregates University of Mississippi; *Engel v. Vitale; Baker v. Carr;* SDS Port Huron Statement
1960	1963 University of Alabama desegregation crisis; Kennedy introduces Civil Rights Bill; March on Washington; *Gideon v. Wainwright;* Kennedy assassinated
1961	1964 *Escobedo v. Illinois; Griswold v. Connecticut;* Civil Rights Act passed; SNCC freedom Summer; Harlem and Rochester race riots; Johnson enacts Kennedy tax cuts; Economic Opportunity Act; VISTA established; Wilderness Preservation System Act; Johnson defeats Goldwater; Berkeley "Free Speech" Movement; Beatles introduce British rock
1962	
1963	
1964	1965 Johnson launches the Great Society; King's Selma protest; Voting Rights Act, Watts riots; Malcolm X assassinated; Medicare and Medicaid acts; Elementary and Secondary School Act; Omni-bus Housing Act; Immigration Act; escalation in Vietnam
1965	
1966	1966 *Miranda v. Arizona;* Stokely Carmichael of SNCC coins "black power" slogan; Model Cities Act; minimum wage raised
1967	1967 Black Panthers battle Oakland, California, police; first "Be-In"
1968	1968 Fair Housing Act
1969	1969 Woodstock Music Festival

additional reading

Among the many excellent studies of civil rights are Robert Weisbort, *Freedom Bound: A History of America's Civil Rights Movement* (1990); Harvard Sitkoff, *The Struggle for Black Equality* (1981); and Juan Williams, *Eyes on the Prize: America's Civil Rights Years, 1954–1964* (1987). Taylor Branch's study of Martin Luther King and the civil rights era begins with the eloquent *Parting the Waters: America in the King Years, 1954–63* (1988). *Pillar of Fire: America in the King Years, 1963–1965* (1998) is sometimes slower going. *The Autobiography of Malcolm X,* as told to Alex Haley (reissue, 1989) is a classic that provides sharp contrast to King's pacifism.

Good recent studies of the civil rights movement at the grassroots level include John Dittmer, *Local People: The Struggle for Civil Rights in Mississippi* (1994) and Stuart Burns, ed., *Daybreak of Freedom: The Montgomery Bus Boycott* (1997). Latino civil rights movements are covered in Henry A. J. Ramos, *American G.I. Forum* (1998) and F. Arturo Rosales, *Chicano! The History of the Mexican American Civil Rights Movement* (1997).

Lyndon Johnson receives a critical but evenhanded treatment in Doris Kearns, *Lyndon Johnson and the American Dream* (1976) and Robert Dallek, *Lyndon Johnson: Lone Star Rising* (1991), but is savaged in Robert Caro, *The Years of Lyndon Johnson: The Path to Power* (1982) and *Means of Ascent* (1990). On foreign policy under Kennedy and Johnson, see Walter LaFeber, *America, Russia, and the Cold War* (8th ed., 1997).

For surveys of the upheavals of the 1960s, see Allen Matusow, *The Unraveling of America* (1984) and Todd Gitlin, *The Sixties* (1987). The counterculture has received no balanced treatment yet, but Terry H. Anderson, *The Movement and the Sixties* (1995) and Edward P. Morgan, *The 60s Experience* (1991) offer much insight into political activism. For a fuller list of readings, see the Bibliography.

ietnam from afar: it looked almost like an emerald paradise. "I remember getting up on the flight deck and seeing one of the most beautiful visions I've ever seen in my life," recalled Thomas Bird, an army rifleman sent there in 1965: "A beautiful white beach with thick jungle background. The only thing missing was naked women running down the beach, waving and shouting Hello, hello, hello.'" Upon landing, Bird and his buddies were each issued a "Nine-Rule" card outlining proper behavior toward the Vietnamese. "Treat the women with respect, we are guests in this country and here to help these people."

But who were they helping and who were they fighting? When American troops sought to engage Vietcong forces, the VC generally disappeared into the jungle beyond the villages and rice fields. John Muir, a marine rifleman, walked into a typical hamlet with a Korean lieutenant. To Muir the place looked ordinary, but the Korean had been in Vietnam a while. "We have a little old lady and a little old man and two very small children," he pointed out. "According to them, the rest of the family has been spirited away... either been drafted into one army or the other. So there's only four of them and they have a pot of rice that's big enough to feed fifty people. And rice, once it's cooked, will not keep. They gotta be feeding the VC." Muir, whose only experience with rice till then had been Minute Rice or Uncle Ben's, watched as the lieutenant set the house on fire. The roof "started cooking off ammunition because all through the thatch they had ammunition stored."

GIs soon learned to walk down jungle trails with a cautious shuffle, looking for a wire or a piece of vine that seemed too straight. "We took more casualties from booby traps than we did from actual combat," recalled David Ross, a medic. "It was very frustrating because how do you fight back against a booby trap? You're just walking along and all of a sudden your buddy doesn't have a leg. Or you don't have a leg." Yet somehow the villagers would walk the same paths and never get hurt. Who was the enemy and who the friend?

The same question was being asked half a globe away, on the campus of Kent State University in May 1970. By then the Vietnam War had dragged on for more than five years and had driven President Lyndon Johnson from office. And it had embroiled his successor, Richard Nixon, in controversy when he expanded the war into Cambodia. Kent State, just east of Akron, Ohio, was one of the many campuses that flourished in the 1950s and 1960s to accommodate the children of the baby boom. Opposition to the war had become so intense in this normally apolitical community that 300 students had torn the Constitution from a history text and, in a formal ceremony, buried it. "President Nixon has murdered it," they charged. That evening demonstrators spilled into the nearby town, smashed shop windows, and returned to campus to burn down an old army ROTC building. The panicked mayor declared a state of emergency, and Governor James Rhodes ordered in 750 of the National Guard. Student dissidents were the "worst type of people we harbor in America," he announced. "We are going to eradicate the problem."

The Vietnam Era

preview • Presidents from Truman to Nixon argued that communism in Southeast Asia threatened vital American interests. But it was Lyndon Johnson who began a massive bombing campaign and sent half a million American troops to intervene in Vietnam's civil war. Amid dissent at home and continued campaigns for equality by women, gays, Latinos, and Indians, Richard Nixon gradually withdrew U.S. forces from Vietnam, signaling limits to America's influence as a superpower.

Kent State

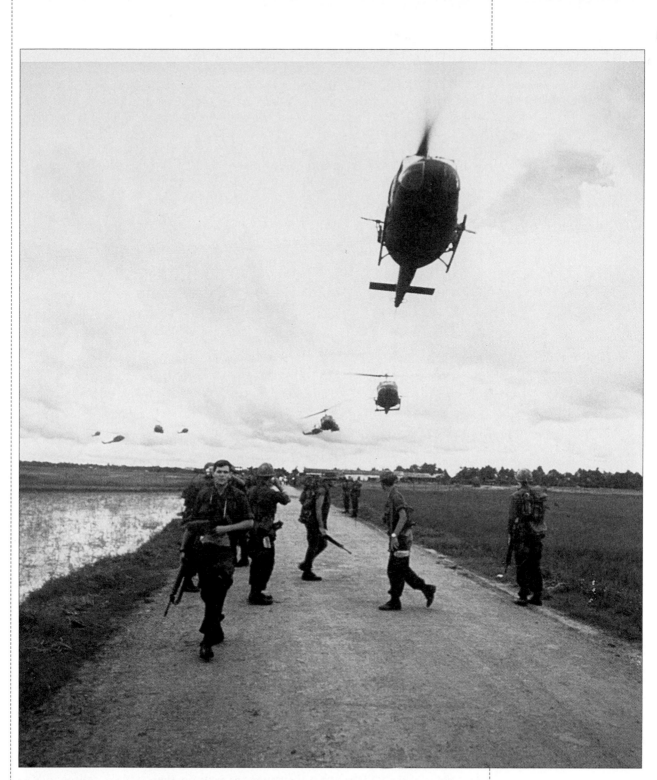

In Vietnam, helicopters gave infantry unusual mobility—a critical element in a war with no real front line, because troops could be quickly carried from one battle to another. These soldiers await a pickup amid rice paddies south of Saigon.

By background and education, the National Guard troops were little different from the students they had come to police. Almost all were white, between 18 and 30, and from Ohio. But guard veterans who fought in World War II or Korea disdained students who evaded or openly rejected their military obligation or who openly criticized their country. As his troops arrived at Kent, Guard Commander General Robert Canterbury remarked that "these students are going to have to find out what law and order is all about."

When demonstrators assembled for a rally on the college commons, the Guard ordered them to disperse, though the troops' legal right to break up a peaceful demonstration was debatable. The protesters stood their ground. Then the guardsmen advanced, wearing full battle gear and armed with M-1 rifles, whose high-velocity bullets had a horizontal range of almost two miles. Some students scattered; a few picked up rocks and threw them. The guardsmen suddenly fired into the crowd, many of whom were students passing back and forth from classes. Incredulous, a young woman knelt over Jeffrey Miller; he was dead. By the time calm was restored, three other students had been killed and nine more wounded, some caught innocently in the Guard's indiscriminate fire.

Jackson State

News of the killings swept the nation. At Jackson State, a black college in Mississippi, antiwar protesters seized a women's dormitory. On May 14 state police surrounding the building opened fire without provocation, killing two more students and wounding a dozen. In both incidents the demonstrators had been unarmed. The events at Kent State and Jackson State turned sporadic protests against the American invasion of Cambodia into a nationwide student strike. Many students believed the ideals of the United States had been betrayed by those forces of law and order sworn to protect them.

Who was the friend and who the enemy? Time and again the war in Vietnam led Americans to ask that question. Not since the Civil War had the nation been so deeply divided. As the war dragged on, debate moved off college campuses and into the homes of middle Americans, where sons went off to fight and the war came home each night on the evening news. As no other war had, Vietnam seemed to stand the nation on its head. When American soldiers shot at Vietnamese "hostiles" who could not always be separated from "friendlies," or when National Guardsmen fired on their neighbors across a college green, who were the enemies and who were the friends?

The Road to Vietnam

"The enemy must fight his battles far from his home base for a long time," one Vietnamese strategist wrote. "We must further weaken him by drawing him into protracted campaigns. Once his initial dash is broken, it will be easier to destroy him." The enemy in question was not American soldiers or the French but the Mongol invaders of 1284 C.E. For several thousand years Vietnam had struggled periodically to fight off foreign invasions. Buddhist culture penetrated eastward from India. More often Indochina faced invasion and rule by the Chinese from the north. After 1856 the French entered as a colonial power, bringing with them a strong Catholic tradition.

Ho Chi Minh was one Vietnamese who hoped to throw off French influence as well as the Chinese. In 1912, at the age of 22, Ho gave up life as a poor schoolteacher and hired out as a mess boy on a French ocean liner. By the end of World War I, he was in France when President Wilson came to Versailles calling for self-determination for small nations. Ho bought a formal pinstriped suit at a second-hand store and attended the peace conference to petition for Vietnam. When the delegates ignored his plea, he became a Communist, taking the recent Russian Revolution as his model. Visits to Moscow followed, after which he returned to the Indochina region to organize revolutionary activity.

Once Japan was defeated in 1945, Ho seized the opportunity to unite Vietnam under a nationalist government. But France moved to recover control of its old colony. Some of Ho's colleagues suggested approaching the Chinese Communists for help. But Ho was foremost a nationalist. He worried that Chinese aid might lead to permanent domination. "I prefer to smell French dung for five years rather than Chinese dung for the rest of my life," he concluded, and he accepted the French return. Soon after, negotiations for independence broke down. Ho and his forces began eight years of guerrilla war against the French, which led to victory at Dien Bien Phu in 1954 (page 953). Ho's dream of an independent Vietnam seemed at hand. He agreed at the Geneva peace conference to withdraw his forces north of the 17th parallel in return for a promise to hold free elections in both the North and the South.

The United States, however, was determined to thwart Ho. Having supported the French in what they saw as a fight to contain communism, President Eisenhower helped install Ngo Dinh Diem and then supported Diem's decision not to hold elections. Frustrated South Vietnamese Communists—the Vietcong—began their guerrilla war once again. "I think the Americans greatly underestimate the determination of the Vietnamese people," Ho remarked in 1962, as President Kennedy was committing more American advisers to South Vietnam.

Ho Chi Minh

Ngo Dinh Diem

Nguyen Ai Quoc, who became Ho Chi Minh, once worked at London's posh Carlton Hotel in the pastry kitchen of the renowned French chef Escoffier. But he was soon swept up in socialist and nationalist politics, appearing at the Versailles Peace Conference (left) to plead for an independent Vietnam. By the time the United States was increasing its involvement in Vietnam, Ho had accumulated a lifetime of anticolonialist and revolutionary activity and become a revered leader of his people. He died in 1969, six years before his dream of a united Vietnam became a reality.

Lyndon Johnson's War

The domino theory

For Kennedy, Vietnam had been just one of many anticommunist skirmishes his activist advisers wanted to fight. As attention focused increasingly on Vietnam, Kennedy accepted President Eisenhower's "domino theory": if the pro-Western Catholic government fell to the Communists, all the other nations of Southeast Asia would collapse in a row. Such an event would discredit Kennedy's claim to fight the cold war with new vigor. But even 16,000 American "advisers" had been unable to help the unpopular Diem, who was overthrown by the military in November 1963. When Kennedy was assassinated in the same month as Diem, the problem of Vietnam was left to Lyndon Johnson.

Johnson's political instincts told him to keep the Vietnam War at arm's length. He felt like a catfish, he remarked, who had "just grabbed a big juicy worm with a right sharp hook in the middle of it." Johnson's heart was in his Great Society programs. Yet fear of the political costs of defeat in Vietnam led him steadily toward deeper American involvement. He shared the assumptions of Kennedy holdovers such as National Security Advisor McGeorge Bundy and Defense Secretary Robert McNamara that Vietnam was a key cold war test. And Republican presidential candidate Barry Goldwater raised the stakes by insisting on a "let's-win" policy of total military victory.

Always preferring the middle way, Johnson wanted a policy somewhere between total commitment and disengagement. Until August 1964 American advisers had focused on South Vietnam itself: guiding the South Vietnamese army in its struggle against the Vietcong. North Vietnam, for its part, had been infiltrating modest amounts of men and supplies along the Ho Chi Minh Trail, a primitive network of jungle routes threading through Laos and Cambodia into the highlands of South Vietnam. In the summer of 1964 North Vietnam began to modernize the trail so it could handle trucks in addition to the peasants who carried supplies on their backs or used modified bicycles. At the time American officials were unaware of the change, but they realized all too well that the Vietcong already controlled some 40 percent of South Vietnam. Johnson strategists decided to relieve the South by increasing pressure on North Vietnam itself.

American ships in the Gulf of Tonkin began to patrol the North Vietnamese coast and provide cover for secret South Vietnamese raids. On August 2, three North Vietnamese patrol boats exchanged fire with the American destroyer *Maddox*—neither side hurting the other—and then the Vietnamese boats fled. An angry Johnson chided several admirals. "You've got a whole fleet and all those airplanes, and you can't even sink three little ol' PT boats?" Two nights later, in inky blackness and a heavy thunderstorm, radar operators on the *C. Turner Joy* reported a torpedo attack. But a follow-up investigation could not establish whether enemy ships had even been near the scene. "The Gulf is a very funny place," explained one communications officer. "You get inversion layers there that will give you very solid radar contacts . . . that just aren't there. That may have happened to us." The president was not pleased. "For all I know our navy might have been shooting at whales out there," he remarked privately.

Whatever his doubts, the president called the incidents "open aggression on the high sea" and ordered retaliatory air raids on North Vietnam. He did not disclose that the navy and South Vietnamese forces had been conducting secret military operations at the time. Such deception would become standard practice. It allowed Johnson to ask Congress for authority to take "all necessary measures" to "repel any armed attack" on American forces and to "prevent future aggression." Congress overwhelmingly passed what became known as the Gulf of Tonkin resolution.

Senator Ernest Gruening of Alaska, one of the two lawmakers to object, sensed danger. The Tonkin Gulf resolution gave the president "a blank check" to declare war, a power the Constitution specifically reserved to Congress. Johnson insisted—no doubt sincerely at the time—that he had no such intention. But as pressure for an American victory increased, the president exploited the powers the resolution gave him.

Tonkin Gulf incident

Rolling Thunder

In January 1965 Johnson received a disturbing memorandum from McGeorge Bundy and Robert McNamara. "Both of us are now pretty well convinced that our present policy can lead only to disastrous defeat," they said. The United States should either increase its attack—"escalate" was the term coined in 1965—or simply withdraw. In theory escalation would increase military pressure to the point at which further resistance cost more than the enemy was willing to bear. By taking gradual steps, the United States would demonstrate its resolve to win while leaving the door open to negotiations.

Escalation

The theory that made so much sense in Washington did not work well in Vietnam. Each stage of American escalation only hardened the resolve of the Vietcong and North Vietnamese. When a Vietcong mortar attack in February killed seven Marines stationed at Pleiku airbase, Johnson ordered U.S. planes to begin bombing North Vietnam. The following month Operation Rolling Thunder was launched, a systematic bombing campaign aimed at bolstering confidence in South Vietnam and cutting the flow of supplies from the North.

Air strikes

But Rolling Thunder achieved none of its goals. American pilots could seldom spot the Ho Chi Minh Trail under its dense jungle canopy. Even when bombs hit, North Vietnamese crews kept the supplies moving by quickly filling the bomb craters or improvising pontoon bridges from woven bamboo stalks. Equally discouraging,

The War in Vietnam North Vietnam established the Ho Chi Minh Trail (red arrows) through central Laos in order to supply South Vietnam's Vietcong forces. In the earlier stages of the war, supplies were transported by foot, but by 1964 the North Vietnamese were building roads and bridges that could handle heavy trucks.

South Vietnamese leaders spent their energy on political intrigue. One military government after another proved equally inept. And Ho Chi Minh refused to negotiate unless the bombing stopped and American troops went home.

Once the Americans established bases from which to launch the new air strikes, these, too, became targets for guerrilla attacks. When General William Westmoreland, the chief of American military operations in Vietnam, requested combat troops to defend the bases, Johnson sent in 3500 marines, almost without considering the implication of his decision. Until then, only military "advisers" to the South Vietnamese had been sent. Once the crucial decision to commit combat troops had been taken, the urge to shore up and protect those already there became strong. Another 40,000 soldiers arrived in May and 50,000 more by July.

Johnson, as before, deliberately downplayed the escalation, because he feared a political backlash. By the end of 1965 almost 185,000 American troops had landed— and still the call for more continued. In 1968, at the height of the war, 536,000 American troops were being supported with helicopters, jet aircraft, and other advanced military technologies. This conflict was "escalation" with a vengeance.

The impact of the war, naturally enough, fell hardest on the baby-boom generation of the 1950s. As these young people

Social Consequences of the War

came of age, draft calls for the armed services were rising. At the same time, the civil rights movement and the growing counterculture were encouraging students to question the goals of establishment America. Whether they fought in Vietnam or protested at home, supported the government or demonstrated against it, eventually these baby boomers—as well as Americans of all ages—were forced to take a stand on Vietnam.

The Soldiers' War

The social structure determining which Americans would be required to fight and which would remain civilian was the draft. The system in place generally favored the middle and upper classes because college students and graduate students at first received deferments. Thus the Vietnam War increased male enrollment in colleges. As the war escalated the draft was changed so that some students were called up through a lottery system. Still, those who knew the medical requirements might be able to produce a doctor's affidavit certifying a weak knee, flat feet, or bad eyes— all grounds for flunking the physical. About half the potential draftees flunked— two to three times the rejection rate of those called up by the NATO allies. Of the 1200 men in Harvard's class of 1970, only 56 served in the military, and only 2 of them in Vietnam.

The poorest and least educated were also likely to escape service, because the Armed Forces Qualification Test and the physical often screened them out. Thus the sons of blue-collar America were most likely to accept Uncle Sam's letter of induction, as were the sons of Latino and black Americans, who, having fewer skills, were more often assigned to combat duty. The draft also made it a relatively young man's war. The average soldier serving in Vietnam was 19, compared with 26 years old for World War II.

Most American soldiers came to Vietnam well trained and with high morale. But the physical and psychological hardships inevitably took their toll. In a war of

Body counts

continual small skirmishes, booby traps, and search-and-destroy missions, it was hard to relax. An American force would fight its way into a Communist-controlled hamlet, clear and burn it, and move on—only to be ordered back days or weeks later because the enemy had moved in again. Because success could not be measured in territory gained, the measure became the "body count": the number of Vietcong killed. Unable to tell who was friendly and who was hostile, GIs regularly took out their frustrations on innocent civilians. Their deaths helped inflate the numbers used to prove that the Americans were winning.

Other social factors affected the way soldiers fought. Only about one in nine soldiers was actually in combat; the rest supported them. Combat veterans particularly despised the rear-echelon soldiers who superintended supply depots or received combat pay for being lifeguards at beaches near Da Nang. Paradoxically, the miracles of modern technology also made the war hard to cope with. Helicopters could whisk GIs from the front lines of a steaming jungle back to Saigon, where they could catch overnight flights to Hawaii or the mainland. The sudden shift from the hell of war to civilian peace could be wrenching.

Technology and its limits

To support a technological war, American forces built the shell of a modern society in South Vietnam. By 1967 a million tons of supplies arrived in Vietnam each month—an average of a hundred pounds a day for every American in the country. South Vietnam's airports soon handled more flight traffic than New York, Rome, Tokyo, or any other city in the world. No matter where they were, ground forces could count on air strikes to strafe or bomb suspected enemy positions. Because the Vietcong routinely mixed with the civilian population, the chances for deadly error increased. Bombs of napalm (jellied gasoline) and white phosphorus rained liquid fire from the skies, coating everything from village huts to the flesh of fleeing humans. Cluster bombs, designed to explode hundreds of pellets in midair, sprayed the enemy with high-velocity shrapnel. To clear jungle canopies and expose Vietcong camps and roads, American planes spread more than 100 million pounds of defoliants such as Agent Orange. ("Only You Can Prevent Forests" was the sardonic motto of one unit assigned to the task.) The destroyed forests totaled more than

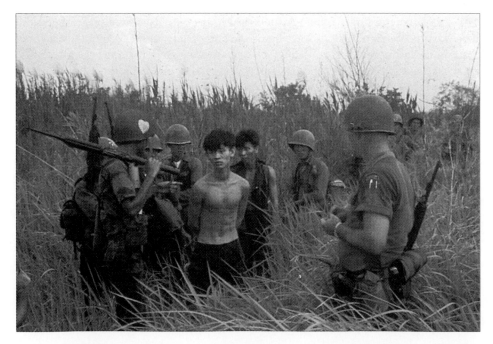

The Vietcong often fought in small groups, using the dense vegetation to cover their movements. These suspects faced a difficult interrogation as U.S. soldiers tried to learn more about the location of Vietcong units.

one-third of South Vietnam's timberlands—an area approximately the size of the state of Rhode Island. In many ways the ecological devastation was more severe than the military destruction.

By 1967 the war costs exceeded more than $2 billion a month. The United States dropped more bombs on Vietnam than it had during all of World War II. After one air attack on a Communist-held provincial capital, American troops walked into the remains, now mostly ruined buildings and rubble. "We had to destroy the town in order to save it," an officer explained. As the human and material costs of the war increased, that statement stuck in the minds of many observers. What sense was there in a war that saved people by burning their homes?

The War at Home

As the war dragged on, such questions provoked anguished debate among Americans, especially on college campuses. Faculty members held "teach-ins" to explain the issues to concerned students. Scholars familiar with Southeast Asia questioned every major assumption the president used to justify escalation. The United States and South Vietnam had brought on the war, they charged, by violating the Geneva Accords of 1954. Moreover, the Vietcong were an indigenous rebel force with legitimate grievances against Saigon's corrupt government. The war was a civil war among the Vietnamese, not an effort by Soviet or Chinese Communists to conquer Southeast Asia, as Eisenhower, Kennedy, and Johnson had claimed.

By 1966 national leaders had similarly divided into opposing camps of "hawks" and "doves." The hawks argued that America must win in Vietnam to save Southeast Asia from communism, to preserve the nation's prestige, and to protect the lives of American soldiers fighting the war. A large majority of the American people supported those views. The doves were a prominent minority. They included New Left radicals as well as respected editorialist Walter Lippmann; Senator J. William Fulbright, head of the Foreign Relations Committee; and Dr. Benjamin Spock, the physician whose child care manuals had raised the generation of baby boomers.

Hawks and doves

African Americans as a group were far less likely than white Americans to support the war. Some resented the diversion of Great Society resources from the cities to the war effort. Many black Americans' heightened sense of racial consciousness led them to identify with the Vietnamese people. Martin Luther King, SNCC, and CORE all opposed the war.

By 1967 college students and faculty turned out in crowds of thousands to express their outrage: "Hey, hey, LBJ, how many kids have you killed today?" More than 300,000 people attended the demonstration organized in April 1967 in New York City. Sixty college protesters organized by SDS leaders from Cornell University burned their draft cards in defiance of federal law. In the fall more violent protests erupted as antiwar radicals stormed a draft induction center in Oakland, California. The next day 55,000 protesters, including some prominent writers and artists, ringed the Pentagon in Washington. Again, mass arrests followed.

Student protests forced policy makers and citizens to take a sobering look at the justice of the war. But the guerrilla tactics of more radical elements alienated many. It would be hard to exaggerate the shock that university communities felt when radicals shut down Columbia University and clashed with police for a week

Lyndon Johnson shocked reporters in October 1965 when he publicly exposed his surgical scar from a gallbladder operation. Political caricaturist David Levine caught the underlying irony of the Johnson presidency by drawing the scar in the shape of Vietnam.

in 1968. The following year black militant students—bandoliers draped across their shoulders, shotguns at their sides—seized the student union at Cornell. Even more shocking, a graduate student at the University of Wisconsin was killed in his lab when a bomb exploded there. The device had been planted by radicals protesting government-sponsored defense research.

On the other hand, key moderates both within and outside the government were convinced that the United States could not win the war. Senator Fulbright was among them. Having helped President Johnson push the Tonkin Gulf resolution through the Senate, Fulbright now held hearings sharply critical of American policy. Even the strongest supporters of the war felt the pressure. Secretary of State Dean Rusk, a hard-liner throughout, was dismayed to hear his relatives back home in Cherokee County, Georgia: "Dean, if you can't tell us when this war is going to end, well then, maybe we just ought to chuck it."

McNamara loses faith

Defense Secretary McNamara became the most dramatic defector. For years the statistically minded secretary had struggled to quantify the success of the war effort. General Westmoreland duly provided body counts, number of bombs dropped, and pacification reports. For a time McNamara remained confident that there was indeed a "light at the end of the tunnel." But by 1967 the secretary had become skeptical. "The picture of the world's greatest superpower killing or seriously injuring 1,000 non-combatants a week, while trying to pound a tiny, backward nation into submission on an issue whose merits are hotly disputed, is not a pretty one," he advised.

Johnson, however, thought of himself as a moderate on the war. He weighed doves like McNamara against hawks like Senator John Stennis of Mississippi and General Westmoreland, who pressed to escalate further. Because Johnson did not want to be remembered as the first American president who lost a war, he sided more with the hawks. And so McNamara resigned.

Inflation

As the war dragged on, it had one severe economic consequence: inflation. By 1967 the cost of the war had soared to more than $50 billion a year. Medicare, education, housing, and other Great Society programs raised the domestic budget sharply, too. Through it all Johnson refused to raise taxes, for fear of losing support for his domestic programs. From 1950 to 1960 the average rate of inflation hovered at about 2 percent a year. From 1965 to 1970, as the war escalated, it jumped to around 4 percent. The economy was headed for trouble.

 The Unraveling

Almost all the forces dividing America seemed to converge in 1968. Until January of that year, most Americans had reason to believe General Westmoreland's estimate that the United States was winning the war. Johnson and his advisers, whatever their private doubts, in public painted an optimistic picture. With such optimism radiating from Washington, few Americans were prepared for the events on the night of January 30, 1968.

Tet Offensive

As the South Vietnamese began their celebration of Tet, the Vietnamese lunar new year, Vietcong guerrillas launched a series of concerted attacks. Assault targets included Saigon's major airport, the South Vietnamese presidential palace, and Hue, the ancient Vietnamese imperial capital. Perhaps most unnerving to Americans, 19 crack Vietcong commandos blasted a hole in the wall of the American embassy compound in Saigon and stormed in. They fought in the courtyard until all 19 lay dead.

Tet must rank as one of the great American intelligence failures, on a par with Pearl Harbor or China's intervention in Korea. For nearly half a year the North Vietnamese had lured American troops into pitched battles at remote outposts like Khe Sanh, Con Thien, Song Be, and Dak To. As American forces dispersed, the Vietcong infiltrated major population areas of Saigon and the delta region. A few audacious VC, disguised as South Vietnamese soldiers, even hitched rides on American jeeps and trucks. Though surprised by the Tet offensive, American and South Vietnamese troops quickly counterattacked, repulsing most of the assaults. Appearing before the American press, General Westmoreland announced that the Vietcong had "very deceitfully" taken advantage of the Vietnamese holiday "to create maximum consternation" and that their "well-laid plans went afoul."

In a narrow military sense, Westmoreland was right. The enemy had been driven back, sustaining perhaps 40,000 deaths. Only 1100 American and 2300 South Vietnamese soldiers had been killed—a ratio of more than 10 to 1 (though 12,500 civilians died). But Americans at home received quite another message. Tet created a "credibility gap" between the administration's promises and the harsh reality. Westmoreland, Johnson, and other officials had repeatedly claimed that the Vietcong were on their last legs. Yet as Ho Chi Minh had coolly informed the French after World War II, "You can kill ten of my men for every one I kill of yours . . . even at those odds, you will lose and I will win." Highly respected CBS news anchor Walter Cronkite drew a gloomy lesson of Tet for his national audience: "To say that we are mired in stalemate seems the only realistic, yet unsatisfactory, conclusion."

Stalemate

Two months later, American forces remained edgy about Vietcong attacks. At the remote hamlet of My Lai, American troops under Lieutenant William Calley swept in, rounded up the villagers, and slaughtered more than 200 men, women, and children. The dead of My Lai would have been just more figures in the "body count," except that an army photographer had taken pictures and a helicopter pilot intervened. If returning veterans were to be believed, there had been hundreds of similar incidents, though perhaps few as bloody. On the communist side, vengeance was at times even more severe. Before Hue could be retaken, the Vietcong had shot, clubbed to death, or buried alive perhaps 3000 civilians.

My Lai

The Tet offensive sobered Lyndon Johnson as well as his new secretary of defense, Clark Clifford. Clifford was a stalwart believer in the war. But as he reviewed the American position in Vietnam, he could get no satisfactory answers from the Joint Chiefs of Staff, who had requested an additional 206,000 troops. "How long would it take to succeed in Vietnam?" Clifford recalled asking them.

Levels of U.S. Troops in Vietnam (at Year End) This graph suggests one reason why protest against the war increased after 1964, peaked by 1968, and largely ended after 1972.

They didn't know. How many more troops would it take? They couldn't say. Were two hundred thousand the answer? They weren't sure. Might they need more? Yes, they might need more. Could the enemy build up [their own troop strength] in exchange? Probably. So what was the plan to win the war? Well, the only plan was that attrition would wear out the Communists, and they would have had enough. Was there any indication that we've reached that point? No, there wasn't.

Clifford decided to build a case for deescalation. To review policy, he formed a panel of "wise men," respected pillars of the cold war establishment, that included Dean Acheson, Harry Truman's secretary of state; Henry Cabot Lodge, a Republican and former ambassador to South Vietnam; and several retired generals. Johnson's advisers had led him "down the garden path" on Vietnam, the wise men concluded. The war could not be won, and he should seek a negotiated settlement.

"Clean for Gene"

Meanwhile, the antiwar forces had found a political champion in Senator Eugene McCarthy from Minnesota. McCarthy was something of a senatorial maverick who wrote poetry in his spare time. He announced that no matter what the odds, he would challenge Johnson in the 1968 Democratic primaries. Idealistic college students got haircuts and shaves in order to look "clean for Gene." Thus transformed, they canvassed New Hampshire voters. Johnson had not formally entered the 1968 presidential race, but his supporters sponsored a write-in campaign, confident of a decisive win in this opening primary. When the votes were counted, McCarthy had lost by only 300 out of 50,000 votes cast. For the president, so slim a victory was a stunning defeat. To the outrage of McCarthy supporters, Robert Kennedy, John Kennedy's younger brother, now announced his own antiwar candidacy.

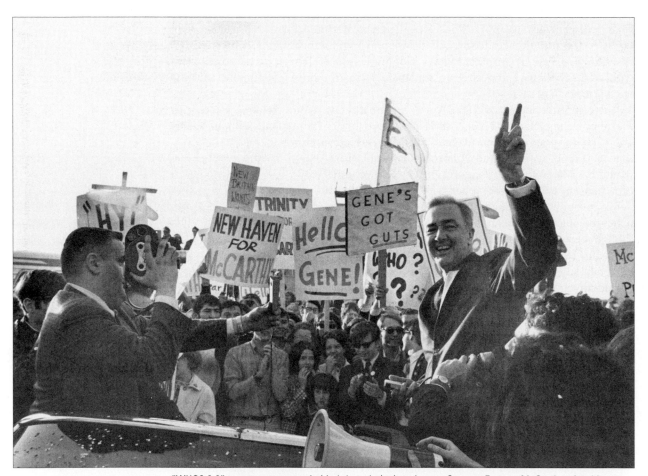

"WHO? ? ?" taunts one poster behind the relatively unknown Senator Eugene McCarthy after his strong showing against President Johnson in the New Hampshire Democratic primary. College students were among McCarthy's most fervent supporters.

"I've got to get me a peace proposal," the president told Clifford. The White House speechwriters finally put together an announcement that bombing raids against North Vietnam would be halted, at least partially, in hopes that peace talks could begin. They were still trying to write an ending when Johnson told them, "Don't worry; I may have a little ending of my own." On March 31 he supplied it, announcing: "I have concluded that I should not permit the presidency to become involved in the partisan divisions that are developing in this political year. . . . Accordingly I shall not seek, and I will not accept, the nomination of my party for another term as your president."

LBJ withdraws

c o u n t e r p o i n t

Whose War?

In the spring of 1995 Robert McNamara published a memoir that stunned long-time defenders of the war and confirmed the beliefs of those who had opposed it. The war had been a great mistake, he concluded. The Johnson administration could—and should—have avoided sending hundreds of thousands of Americans into the conflict. Moreover, McNamara implied that if Kennedy had lived, he would not have escalated the war as Lyndon Johnson had. In other words, even though presidents from Truman through Kennedy had involved the United States in Southeast Asia, Vietnam was truly Lyndon Johnson's war. Some historians have argued that by the summer of 1963, Kennedy had become convinced that American forces had to be gradually withdrawn but that politically he dared not do so until the election of 1964. "If I tried to pull out now from Vietnam," one aide recalls him saying, "we would have another Joe McCarthy red scare on our hands."

Other historians have been more skeptical. They argue that even in 1965, no official of importance was suggesting that the United States should allow Vietnam to fall to the Communists. Senators Fulbright and Mike Mansfield and Undersecretary of State George Ball, who criticized Johnson by 1968, all backed the Tonkin Gulf resolution in 1965. Further, historians have evidence that President Kennedy would have escalated the war, though perhaps not as quickly. "We want the war to be won, the Communists to be contained, and the Americans to go home," Kennedy asserted only two months before his death; ". . . But we are not there to see a war lost." As one historian concluded, "The widespread and prevailing opinion in the administration, Congress, and the press and among the mass of Americans was that the United States simply could not walk away from Vietnam and sacrifice a pro-Western country to Communist aggression." In this historian's view, Vietnam was America's war: a product of the cold war mentality that had arisen over the previous two decades, not the act of a single, stubborn president.

Whether or not Johnson's tragedy was self-inflicted, the Vietnam War had pulled down one of the savviest, most effective politicians of the modern era. North Vietnam, for its part, responded to the speech by sending delegates to a peace conference in Paris, where negotiations quickly bogged down. And American attention soon focused on the chaotic situation at home, where all the turbulence, discontent, and violence of the 1960s seemed to be coming together.

The Shocks of 1968

On April 4 Martin Luther King Jr. traveled to Memphis to support striking sanitation workers. He was relaxing on the balcony of his motel when James Earl Ray, an escaped convict, fatally shot him. King's campaign of nonviolence was overshadowed by the frustration and anger that greeted news of his death. Riots broke out that

The King and Kennedy assassinations

Enthusiastic crowds followed Robert Kennedy on his Democratic primary campaign during the 1968 presidential election. The evening of his victory in California he was assassinated by a Palestinian refugee, Sirhan Sirhan, who later claimed he admired Kennedy.

evening in ghetto areas of the nation's capital; by the end of the week, disturbances rocked 125 more neighborhoods across the country. Almost before Americans could recover, a disgruntled Arab nationalist, Sirhan Sirhan, assassinated Robert Kennedy on the evening of June 5. Running in opposition to the war, Kennedy had just won a crucial primary victory in California.

The deaths of King and Kennedy pained Americans deeply. In their own ways, both men exemplified the liberal tradition, which reached its high-water mark in the 1960s. King had retained his faith in a Christian theology of nonviolence. He sought change without resorting to the language of the fist and the gun. In the final years of his life, his campaign broadened to include the poor of all races. Robert Kennedy had begun his career as a pragmatic politician who, like his brother John, had not hesitated to use power ruthlessly. But Kennedy, like King, had come to reject the war his brother had supported, and he seemed genuinely to sympathize with the poor and minorities. At the same time, he was popular among traditional white ethnics and blue-collar workers. Would the liberal political tradition have flourished longer if these two charismatic figures had survived the turbulence of the 1960s?

Chicago

Once violence had claimed the clearest liberal voices, it became obvious that the Democrats would choose Hubert Humphrey when their convention met at Chicago in August. Humphrey had begun his career as a progressive and a strong supporter of civil rights. But as Johnson's loyal vice president he was intimately associated with the war and the old-style liberal reforms that could never satisfy radicals. Humphrey's impending nomination meant, too, that no major candidate would speak for Americans disillusioned with the war or the status quo. The Republicans had chosen Richard Nixon, a traditional anticommunist (now reborn as the "new," more moderate Nixon). As much as radicals disliked Johnson, they abhorred any Nixon, "new" or old.

Chicago, where the Democrats met, was the fiefdom of Mayor Richard Daley, long the symbol of machine politics and backroom deals. Daley was determined that the radicals who poured into Chicago would not disrupt "his" Democratic convention. The radicals were equally determined that they would. For a week the police skirmished with demonstrators: police clubs, riot gear, and tear gas versus the demonstrators' eggs, rocks, and balloons filled with paint and urine. When Daley refused to allow a peaceful march past the convention site, the radicals marched anyway. With the mayor's blessing, the police turned on the crowd in what a federal commission later labeled a police riot. In one pitched battle, many officers took off their badges and waded into the crowd, nightsticks swinging, chanting, "Kill, kill, kill." Reporters, medics, and other innocent bystanders were injured; at 3:00 A.M. police invaded candidate Eugene McCarthy's hotel headquarters and pulled some of his assistants from their beds.

With feelings running so high, President Johnson did not dare appear at his own party's convention. Theodore White, a veteran journalist covering the assemblage, scribbled his verdict in a notebook as police chased hippies down Michigan Avenue. "The Democrats are finished," he wrote.

The clashes in Chicago seemed homegrown, but they reflected a growing willingness among students worldwide to use violence to press their revolutionary causes. In 1966 Chinese students were in the vanguard of Mao Zedong's Red Guards, formed to enforce a Cultural Revolution that was purging China of all bourgeois middle-class culture. Although that revolution persecuted millions among the educated classes and left China in economic shambles, Mao became a hero to student activists in Europe and America, who also lionized other armed revolutionaries: Fidel Castro and Che Guevara of Cuba and Ho Chi Minh.

Revolutionary targets varied. In Italy students denounced the official Marxism of the Soviet Union and the Italian Communist party. French students at the Sorbonne in Paris rebelled against the university's efforts to discipline student activists as well as protested their decrepit classrooms and dormitories. Students in Czechoslovakia launched a full-scale rebellion in the Prague Spring of 1968, which the Soviets eventually crushed. Although radical agendas varied from region to region, students showed remarkable unanimity in condemning one event on the world stage: the American war in Vietnam.

Revolutionary clashes worldwide

Whose Silent Majority?

Radicals were not the only Americans alienated from the political system in 1968. Governor George Wallace of Alabama sensed the frustration among the "average man on the street, this man in the textile mill, this man in the steel mill, this barber, this beautician, the policeman on the beat." In running for president, Wallace sought the support of blue-collar workers and the lower middle classes.

Wallace had first come to national attention as he stood at the door barring integration of the University of Alabama. Briefly, he pursued the Democratic presidential nomination in 1964. For the race in 1968 he formed his own American Independent party with the hawkish General Curtis LeMay as his running mate. (LeMay spoke belligerently of bombing North Vietnam "back to the stone age.") Wallace's enemies were the "liberals, intellectuals, and long hairs [who] have run this country for too long." Wallace did not simply appeal to law and order, militarism, and white backlash; he was too sharp for that. With roots in southern Populism, he called for federal job-training programs, stronger unemployment benefits, national health insurance, a higher minimum wage, and a further extension of union rights. Polls in September revealed that many Robert Kennedy voters had shifted to Wallace. A quarter of all union members backed him.

In fact, Wallace had tapped true discontent among the working class. Many blue-collar workers despised hippies and peace marchers yet wanted the United States out of Vietnam. And they were suspicious, as Wallace was, of the upper-class "establishment" that held power. Old-style radicals of the 1930s might have tried to tap such discontent, but the leaders of the New Left by and large had given up on traditional workers. They aimed their appeal at the newer minorities: students, Latinos, African Americans, and the unorganized poor.

Richard Nixon also sought to attract traditionally Democratic voters, especially disaffected southern Democrats, away from Wallace into the Republican party. The Republicans, of course, had been reviled by the Populists of old as representatives of the money power, monopoly, and the old-line establishment. But Nixon himself had modest roots. His parents owned a general store in Whittier, California, where he had worked to help the family out. His high school grades were good enough to earn him a scholarship to Harvard, but fearing the cost of

Nixon's "silent majority"

traveling east, he turned it down in favor of nearby Whittier College. At Duke Law School he was so pinched for funds, he lived in an abandoned toolshed. If ever there had been a candidate who could claim to be self-made, it was Nixon. And he well understood the disdain ordinary laborers felt for "kids with the beards from the suburbs"—hippies who wore flags sewn to the seat of their pants—who seemed always to be insisting, protesting, *demanding*. Nixon believed himself a representative of the "silent majority," as he later described it, not a vocal minority.

He thus set two fundamental requirements for his campaign: to distance himself from President Johnson on Vietnam and to turn Wallace's "average Americans" into a Republican "silent majority." The Vietnam issue was delicate, because Nixon had generally supported the president's efforts to end the war. He told his aide Richard Whalen, "I've come to the conclusion that there's no way to win the war. But we can't say that, of course. In fact, we have to seem to say the opposite." For most of his campaign he hinted that he had a secret plan to end the war but steadfastly refused to disclose it. He pledged only to find an honorable solution, at the same time promising to promote "law and order" while cracking down on "pot," pornography, protest, and permissiveness.

The election of 1968

Hubert Humphrey had the more daunting task of surmounting the ruins of the Chicago convention. All through September antiwar protesters dogged his campaign with "Dump the Hump" posters. Finally the vice president distanced his position on Vietnam, however slightly, from that of his unpopular boss. The protests then faded, Humphrey picked up momentum, and traditional blue-collar Democrats began to return to the fold. By November his rallies were enthusiastic and well attended. But the late surge did not turn the tide. Nixon captured 43.4 percent of the popular vote to 42.7 percent for Humphrey and 13.5 percent for Wallace. More important, Nixon's "southern strategy" paid off; he and Wallace carried the entire southern tier of states except Texas. Some voters had punished the Democrats not just for the war but also for supporting civil rights. The majority of the American electorate seemed to have turned their backs on liberal reform.

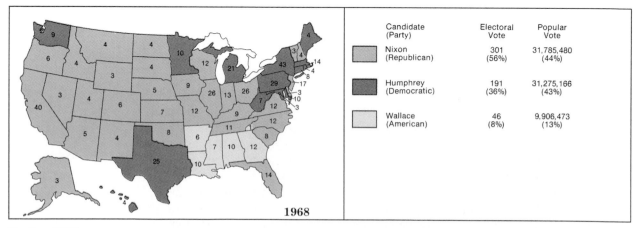

Election of 1968

In Richard Nixon, Americans had elected two men to the presidency. On the public side, he appeared as the traditional

Nixon's War

small-town, middle-class conservative who cherished individual initiative, Chamber-of-Commerce capitalism, Fourth-of-July patriotism, and Victorian mores. The private Nixon was a troubled man. His language among intimates was caustic and profane. He waxed bitter toward those he saw as enemies. Never a natural public speaker, he was physically rather awkward—a White House aide once found toothmarks on a "child-proof" aspirin cap the president had been unable to pry open. But Nixon seemed to search out challenges—"crises" to face and conquer.

The new president saw himself as a master of foreign policy. The Vietnam War stood in the way of his major goals. Hence, ending it became one of his first priorities. He found a congenial ally in National Security Adviser Henry Kissinger. Kissinger, like Nixon, had a global vision of foreign affairs. Like Nixon, he had a tendency to pursue his ends secretly, skirting the traditional channels of government such as the Department of State.

Henry Kissinger

Vietnamization—and Cambodia

To bring the Vietnam War to an end, Nixon and Kissinger wanted to negotiate a settlement that would bring American troops home, but they insisted on "peace with honor." That boiled down to preserving a pro-American South Vietnamese government. The strategy Nixon adopted was "Vietnamization," which involved a carrot and a stick. On its own initiative, the United States began gradually withdrawing troops as a way to advance the peace talks in Paris. The burden of fighting would shift to the South Vietnamese army, equipped now with massive amounts of American supplies. Critics likened this strategy to little more than "changing the color of the corpses." All the same, it helped reduce antiwar protests at home. Once the media shifted their focus from the war to the peace talks, the public had the impression that the war was winding down.

Using the stick, President Nixon hoped to drive the North Vietnamese into negotiating peace on American terms. Quite consciously, he traded on his reputation as a cold warrior who would stop at nothing. As he explained to his chief of staff, Robert Haldeman,

> I call it the Madman Theory, Bob. I want the North Vietnamese to believe that I've reached the point where I might do anything to stop the war. We'll just slip the word to them that, "for God's sake, you know Nixon is obsessed about Communists. We can't restrain him when he's angry—and he has his hand on the nuclear button"—and Ho Chi Minh himself will be in Paris in two days begging for peace.

To underline his point, Nixon in the spring of 1969 launched a series of bombing attacks against North Vietnamese supply depots inside neighboring Cambodia. Johnson had refused to widen the war in this manner, fearing domestic reaction. Nixon simply kept the raids secret.

The North Vietnamese refused to cave in to the bombing or the threats of the "Madman." Ho Chi Minh's death in 1969 changed nothing. His successors continued to reject any offer that did not end with complete American withdrawal and an abandonment of the South Vietnamese military government. Once again

Invading Cambodia

Nixon decided to turn up the heat. Over the opposition of his secretaries of defense and state, he ordered American troops into Cambodia to wipe out North Vietnamese bases there. This action was, to be sure, Johnson's old policy of escalation—precisely the opposite of the withdrawal Nixon had promised. But the Joint Chiefs argued that such an attack would buy time to strengthen the South Vietnamese army.

Nixon recognized that a storm of protest would arise. (The administration was "going to get unshirted hell for doing this," he noted.) On April 30, 1970, he announced the "incursion" of American troops into Cambodia, proclaiming that he would not allow "the world's most powerful nation" to act "like a pitiful helpless giant." The wave of protests that followed included the Kent State tragedy as well as another march on Washington by 100,000 protesters. Even Congress was upset enough to repeal the Tonkin Gulf resolution, a symbolic rejection of Nixon's invasion. After two months American troops left Cambodia, having achieved little.

Fighting a No-Win War

For a time, Vietnamization seemed to be working. As more American troops went home, the South Vietnamese forces improved modestly. But for American GIs still in the country, morale became a serious problem. Obviously the United States was gradually pulling out its forces. After Tet, it was clear there would be no victory. So why were the "grunts" in the field still being asked to put their lives on the line? The anger surfaced increasingly in incidents known as "fragging," in which GIs threw fragmentation grenades at officers who pursued the war too aggressively.

Nor could the army isolate itself from the trends dividing American society. Just as young Americans "turned on" to marijuana and hallucinogens, so soldiers in Vietnam used drugs. The Pentagon estimated that by 1971 nearly a third of American troops there had experimented with either opium or heroin, easily obtained in Southeast Asia. Nor did black GIs leave black power issues at home. Robert Rawls recalled that the brothers "used to make a shoestring that they braided up and tied around their wrist, and everywhere a whole lot of blacks used to go, they'd give a power sign." One white medic noticed that Muhammad Ali's refusal to be drafted caused the blacks in his unit "to question why they were fighting the Honky's war against other Third World people. I saw very interesting relationships happening between your quick-talking, sharp-witted Northern blacks and your kind of easygoing, laid-back Southern blacks. . . . Many Southern blacks changed their entire point of view by the end of their tour and went home extremely angry."

The problem with morale only underlined the dilemma facing President Nixon. As the troops became restive, domestic opposition to the war grew. By repealing the Gulf of Tonkin resolution, Congress itself had put the president on notice that he would have to negotiate a settlement soon. Yet the North Vietnamese refused to yield, even after the American assaults in Cambodia.

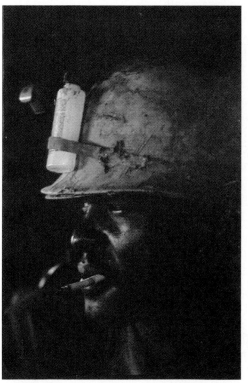

A helicopter machine gunner: cigarette dangling, a knife and "jungle juice" insect repellent stuck in his helmet. Increasingly, there were few illusions about this no-win war.

The Move toward Détente

Despite Nixon's insistence on "peace with honor," Vietnam was not a war he had chosen to fight. Both Kissinger and Nixon recognized that the United States no longer had the strength to exercise unchallenged dominance across the globe. The Soviet Union, not Vietnam, remained their prime concern. Ever since Khrushchev had backed down at the Cuban missile crisis in 1962, the Soviets had steadily expanded their nuclear arsenal. Furthermore, the growing economies of Japan and Western Europe challenged American leadership in world trade. Continued instability in Southeast Asia, the Middle East, and other Third World areas threatened the strength of the non-Communist bloc. Thus Vietnam diverted valuable military and economic resources from more critical areas.

In what the White House labeled the new "Nixon Doctrine," the United States announced it would no longer expect to fight every battle, win every war, or draw every line to keep the global peace. Instead, Americans would shift some of the military burden for containment to such allies as Japan in the Pacific, the shah of Iran in the Middle East, Zaire in central Africa, and the apartheid government in South Africa. Over the next six years American foreign military sales jumped from $1.8 billion to $15.2 billion. At the same time, Nixon and Kissinger looked for new ways to contain Soviet power not simply by the traditional threat of arms but through negotiations to ease tensions. This policy was named, from the French, détente.

To pursue détente Kissinger and Nixon used "linkages," a system of making progress on one issue by connecting it with another. They recognized, for example, how much the cold war arms race burdened the Soviet economy. To ease that pressure, they would make concessions to the Soviets on nuclear arms. The Soviets in

Nixon Doctrine

Upon seeing China's Great Wall, an ebullient Richard Nixon pronounced it a "great wall," built by a great people. Perhaps precisely because he had been so staunch an anti-Communist, Nixon appreciated the enormous departure his trip marked in Sino-American relations.

Daily Lives

TIME AND TRAVEL
The Race to the Moon

In campaigning for the presidency in 1960 John F. Kennedy chided the Republicans for creating a missile gap. While the American space program limped along, the Soviet Union had launched *Sputnik.* Only a few months after Kennedy's inauguration, Russian cosmonaut Yuri Gagarin orbited the world in a five-ton spacecraft. The first American space flight on May 6, 1961, succeeded only in carrying Commander Alan Shepard into a suborbital flight of 300 miles. Kennedy feared that if it lost the space race, the United States might lose the cold war as well.

Thus Kennedy ordered his science advisers "to shift our efforts in space from low to high gear." He announced on national television that the United States would do something truly dramatic: land a man on the moon and bring him back alive "before the decade is out." No matter how great the cost, Kennedy believed the investment was sound. "This is not merely a race," he remarked in an allusion to the Soviets' success. "Space is open to us now; and our eagerness to share its meaning is not governed by the efforts of others. We must go into space because whatever mankind must undertake, free men must fully share."

There were skeptics such as former President Eisenhower who thought anyone was "nuts" to spend billions for a space spectacular that promised little in the way of scientific discoveries. Nor was it clear that NASA could achieve such a feat in so short a time. To many members of Congress, however, the space program was a huge pork barrel, so they voted to fund Kennedy's "great new American enterprise." From then on the space program achieved a string of triumphs. In February 1962 Colonel John Glenn successfully circled the

Landing on the moon may have been one small step for a man, but NASA spent $25 billion on the project, over $2 billion for each of the 12 astronauts who took lunar walks.

return would have to limit their arms buildup and, in a linked concession, pressure North Vietnam to negotiate an end to the war. To add pressure, Nixon and Kissinger developed a "China card." The United States would stop treating Mao Zedong as an archenemy and, instead, open diplomatic relations with the Chinese. Fearful of a more powerful China, the Soviets would be more conciliatory toward the United States.

earth three times in "a fireball of a ride"; an unmanned satellite passed Venus later that year; and a Telstar communications satellite began relaying television broadcasts, launching an era of truly global mass communications.

One after another, the space spectaculars continued, much to the public's delight. In March 1965 American astronauts first maneuvered their capsule; in May Edward White took America's first space walk; the following year two vehicles met and docked for the first time. The Gemini program was followed by the Apollo missions, whose Saturn rockets powered their payloads into lunar orbit. From there, two astronauts planned to pilot a separate module to the moon's surface, while a third remained in the orbiting command module waiting for them and the return trip. By Christmas eve 1968 the *Apollo 8* mission was circling the moon. It seemed a "vast, lonely and forbidding sight," one astronaut remarked to hundreds of millions in a live telecast.

On July 20, 1969, the lunar module of *Apollo 11* at last touched down on the earth's closest neighbor. Commander Neil Armstrong, moving awkwardly in his bulky spacesuit, worked his way down a ladder to the white, chalky surface. He was not alone. Besides Edwin Aldrin, who followed him, and Michael Collins, orbiting in the command module, Armstrong brought along a quarter of the world's population, who monitored the moment live on television. "That's one small step for a man, one giant leap for mankind," he proclaimed.

For all its stunning success, the space program did not escape the political crosscurrents of the 1960s. Critics argued that those billions might better have been spent solving more earthly problems. And Richard Nixon turned *Apollo 11* into a public relations gold mine, even though Kennedy and Johnson had supported the space program against Republican attacks. "This is the greatest week in the history of the world since the Creation," Nixon told the astronauts after their capsule splashed down in the Pacific. Evangelist Billy Graham took exception to his friend's theological excess. What of Christ's birth, his death, and his resurrection, Graham wanted to know. "Tell Billy," Nixon wrote White House Chief of Staff H. R. Haldeman, "RN referred to a week not a day."

But *Apollo 11* marked the climax of a phase of exploration, not, like the Creation, a beginning. After *Apollo 17* and $25 billion in costs, Nixon predicted "this may be the last time in this century men will walk on the moon." Space travel since then has belonged largely to the space shuttles and to science fiction, where the crew of the starship *Enterprise* and their Kennedyesque captains, James T. Kirk and Jean Luc Picard, "boldly go where no one has gone before."

It took a shrewd diplomatist to sense an opportunity to shift traditional cold war policy. Conservative Republicans in particular had denounced the idea of ever recognizing Mao's government, even after 20 years. They believed that the Soviets responded only to force and that they were united with China in a monolithic communist conspiracy. Now Richard Nixon, the man who had built a career fighting communism, made overtures to the Communist powers. Kissinger slipped off to

China on a secret mission (he was nursing a stomachache, his aides assured the press) and then reappeared having arranged a week-long trip to China for the president. During that visit in early 1972, Nixon pledged to normalize relations, a move the public enthusiastically welcomed, although some conservative Republicans were angered at the idea of betraying their old ally in Taiwan, Chiang Kai-shek. Only Nixon's impeccable anti-Communist credentials had allowed him to reverse the direction of America's China policy.

A new overture to the Soviet Union followed the China trip. Eager to acquire American grain and technology, Soviet Premier Leonid Brezhnev invited Nixon to visit Moscow in May 1972. Nixon saw in the Soviet market a chance to ease American trade deficits by selling grain surpluses. The two leaders struck a major wheat deal, but the most important benefit of the meeting was the signing of the first Strategic Arms Limitation Treaty (SALT I). In the agreement, both sides pledged not to develop a new system of antiballistic missiles, which would have accelerated the costly arms race. And they agreed to limit the number of intercontinental ballistic missiles each side would deploy.

SALT I

Both the China and Moscow visits strengthened Nixon's reputation as a global strategist. Americans were pleased at the prospect of lower cold war tensions. But it was not clear that the linkages achieved in Moscow and Beijing would help extricate the United States from Vietnam.

 ## The New Identity Politics

During the 1968 campaign Richard Nixon had noticed a placard carried by a hopeful voter—"Bring Us Together." That phrase became his campaign theme. Yet in the divisive atmosphere of the 1960s, unity was an elusive goal. George Wallace had attracted a large block of voters fed up with protest and social unrest. If Nixon could add those discontented southerners and blue-collar workers to his traditional base of Republicans, his enlarged silent majority could easily return him to the White House in 1972.

Separate identities vs. assimilation

Nixon's effort to create among his followers the sense that they held the moral high ground played off a growing unease over the divided nature of American society. To the silent majority, it seemed as if the consensus of the 1950s was increasingly being ripped apart. In their campaign for civil rights, African Americans very often insisted that because they had *not* been treated equally, that therefore they necessarily belonged to a separate, oppressed group. In the 1960s activists took pride in proclaiming black power or even, like the Nation of Islam, embracing a doctrine of separation. Latinos, American Indians, Asian Americans, feminists, and gay Americans all applied much of the same critique to their own situations. Out of this increased pride in each group's distinctive values and characteristics came a new political and social assertiveness. Whereas before, Latino civil rights groups such as LULAC and World War II veterans in the American GI Forum had sought assimilation into American society, now minorities began to forge identities in opposition to the prevailing culture.

Latino Activism

Part of the increased visibility of minorities resulted from a new wave of immigration from Mexico and Puerto Rico after World War II. That wave was augmented by Cubans, after the 1959 revolution that brought Fidel Castro to power.

Historical, cultural, ethnic, and geographic differences made it difficult to develop a common political agenda among Latinos. Still, some activists did seek greater unity.

After World War II a weak island economy and the lure of prosperity on the mainland brought more than a million Puerto Ricans into New York City. As citizens of the United States, they could move freely to the mainland and back home again. That dual consciousness discouraged many from establishing deep roots stateside. Equally important, the newcomers were startled to discover that, whatever their status at home, on the mainland they were subject to racial discrimination and most often segregated into urban slums. In 1964 approximately half of all recent immigrants lived below the poverty level, according to the Puerto Rican Forum. Their unemployment was three times greater than for whites and 50 percent higher than for blacks. Light-skinned migrants escaped those conditions by blending into the middle class as "Latin Americans." The Puerto Rican community thereby lost some of the leadership it needed to assert its political rights.

Still, a shared island orientation preserved a strong group identity. By the 1960s the urban barrios gained greater political consciousness, as groups such as Aspira adopted the strategies of civil rights activists and as organizations like the Black and Puerto Rican Caucus linked with other minority groups. The Cubans who arrived in the United States after 1959—some 350,000 over the course of the decade—forged fewer ties with other Latinos. Most settled around Miami. An unusually large number came from Cuba's professional, business, and government class and were racially white and politically conservative.

Mexican Americans, on the other hand, constituted the largest segment of Latinos. Until the 1940s most were farmers and farm laborers in Texas, New Mexico, and California. But during the 1950s, the process of mechanization had affected them just as it had southern blacks. By 1969 about 85 percent of Mexican Americans had settled in cities. With urbanization came a slow improvement of the range and quality of jobs they held. A body of skilled workers, middle-class professionals, and entrepreneurs emerged.

Puerto Ricans and Cubans

Living conditions were harshest for Mexican Americans among agricultural workers. Cesar Chavez mobilized migrant workers into the United Farm Workers Union. His demands for recognition of the union by California growers led to a bitter strike (in Spanish, *huelga*) in 1966.

Cesar Chavez and the UFW

Yet Mexican agricultural workers continued to face abysmally low wages and harsh working conditions. Previous attempts to unionize them had failed partly because workers migrated from job to job and strikebreakers were easily imported. In 1963 a soft-spoken but determined farmworker, Cesar Chavez, recruited fellow organizers Gil Padilla and Dolores Huerta to make another attempt. Their efforts over the next several years led to the formation of the United Farm Workers (UFW) labor union.

Chavez, like Martin Luther King, proclaimed an ethic of nonviolence. Also like King, he was guided by a deep religious faith (Roman Catholicism in the case of Chavez and most Mexican American farmworkers). When the union's meager financial resources made it difficult to sustain a strike of Mexican and Filipino grape workers that began in the summer of 1966, Chavez rallied supporters for a 250-mile march on Sacramento. "Dr. King had been very successful" with such marches, he noted. Seeking additional leverage, the union looked to use consumers as an economic weapon by organizing a boycott of grapes in supermarkets across the nation. Combined with a 24-day hunger strike by Chavez—a technique borrowed from Gandhi—the boycott forced growers to negotiate contracts with the UFW beginning in 1970.

Chicano activists

Chavez's movement was rooted in the traditional issues of labor organizing. But just as Martin Luther King found his nonviolent approach challenged by more radical activists, a new generation of Mexican Americans forged a more aggressive brand of identity politics. Many began calling themselves Chicanos. Like blacks, Chicanos saw themselves as a people whose culture had been taken from them. Their heritage had been rejected, their labor exploited, and their opportunity for advancement denied. Of Chavez's generation, Reies Lopez Tijerina attracted wide attention as a charismatic leader. His movement in northern New Mexico ("*La Alianza*") organized armed bands to occupy federal lands that Hispanos in the region had once used for grazing livestock. In Denver, Rodolfo "Corky" Gonzales laid out a blueprint for a separatist Chicano society, with public housing set aside for Chicanos and the development of economically independent barrios in which a new cultural pride could flourish. "We are a Bronze People with a Bronze Culture," declared Gonzales. "We are a Nation. We are a union of free pueblos. We are Aztlán."

Recruits to the new activism came from both college and high school students. Like other members of the baby boom generation, Mexican Americans attended college in increasing numbers. In addition, Lyndon Johnson's Educational Opportunity Programs (EOP), part of his war on poverty, brought thousands more Latinos onto college campuses, especially in California. By 1968 some 50 Mexican American student organizations on college campuses counted at least 2000 to 3000 members among their ranks. In Los Angeles that year thousands of Chicano high school students walked out to protest substandard educational conditions. Two years later the new ethnic militancy led to the formation of

Most Mexican American migrant workers were devout Catholics. This farmworker's altar combines both religious symbols (the Crucifixion) and the UFW's red-and-black Aztec eagle (surrounded by the arms of workers of different races, showing solidarity) into designs signifying the strike and national grape boycott.

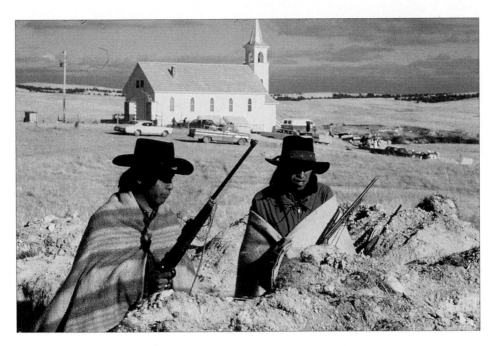

In 1890 the U.S. cavalry had killed 146 Indians at Wounded Knee, South Dakota. In 1973 these members of the American Indian Movement seized the hamlet of Wounded Knee, making it once again a symbol of conflict.

La Raza Unida (The Race United). This third-party movement sought to gain power in communities in which Chicanos were a majority and to extract concessions from the Democrats and Republicans. The more militant "Brown Berets" adopted the paramilitary tactics and radical rhetoric of the Black Panthers.

La Raza Unida

The Choices of American Indians

Like African Americans and Latinos, Indians began to protest, yet the unique situation of Native Americans (as many had begun to call themselves) set them apart from other minorities. A largely hostile white culture had in past centuries sought either to exterminate or to assimilate American Indians. Ironically, the growing strength of the civil rights movement created another threat to Indian tribal identities. Liberals came to see the reservations not as oases of Indian culture but as rural ghettos. During the 1950s liberals joined conservatives (eager to repeal the New Deal) and western state politicians (eyeing tribal resources) to adopt a policy of "termination." The Bureau of Indian Affairs would reduce federal services, gradually sell off tribal lands, and push Indians into the "mainstream" of American life.

Termination

Although most full-blooded Indians objected to the policy, some mixed bloods and Indians already assimilated into white society supported the move. The resulting relocation of approximately 35,000 Indians accelerated a shift from rural areas to cities. The urban Indian population, which had been barely 30,000 in 1940, reached more than 300,000 by the 1970s.

The social activism of the 1960s inspired Indian leaders to shape a new political agenda. In 1968 urban activists in Minneapolis created AIM, the American Indian Movement. A year later similarly minded Indians living around San Francisco Bay formed Indians of All Tribes. Because the Bureau of Indian Affairs refused to address the problems of urban Indians, more militant members of the organization dramatized their dissatisfaction by seizing the abandoned federal prison on Alcatraz Island in San Francisco Bay.

American Indian Movement

Wounded Knee

The Alcatraz action inspired a national Pan-Indian rights movement. Richard Oakes, a Mohawk Indian from New York, declared that the Alcatraz protest was not "a movement to liberate the island, but to liberate ourselves." Then in 1973, AIM organizers Russell Means and Dennis Banks led a dramatic takeover of a trading post at Wounded Knee, on a Sioux reservation in South Dakota. Ever since white cavalry had gunned down over a hundred Sioux in 1890 (see page 587), Wounded Knee had symbolized for Indians the betrayal of white promises and the bankruptcy of reservation policy. Even more, Wounded Knee now demonstrated the problems that Indian activists faced. When federal officers surrounded the trading post, militants discovered that other Indians did not support their tactics, and they were forced to leave. A Pan-Indian movement was difficult to achieve when so many tribes were determined to go their own ways as distinct, self-regulating communities. Thus even activists who supported the Pan-Indian movement found themselves splintering. During the 1970s more than 100 different organizations were formed to unite various tribes pursuing political and legal agendas at the local, state, and federal levels.

Asian Americans

In removing quotas that had discriminated against immigration from non-European nations (page 989), the 1965 Immigration Act removed one of the major affronts to Asian Americans. Further, it spurred a rapid increase in immigration from Asia to the United States. Asians who in 1960 constituted just one percent of the American population (about a million people) were by 1985 two percent (about five million). This new wave included many middle-class professionals, a lower percentage of Japanese, and far more newcomers from Southeast and South Asia. Civil rights reforms had already swept away legal barriers to full citizenship that had previously stigmatized Asians.

Many Americans treated these new immigrants as "model minorities." They brought skills in high demand, worked hard, were often Christians, and seldom protested. The 1970 census showed Japanese and Chinese Americans with incomes substantially above the median for white Americans. Such statistics hid significant fault lines within communities. Although many professionals assimilated into the American mainstream, agricultural laborers and sweatshop workers remained trapped in poverty. And no matter how much Anglos praised their industry, the distinguishing appearance of Asian Americans still amounted to what one sociologist defined as a "racial uniform." They were nonwhites in a white society.

Few Americans were aware of Asian involvement in identity politics. That was in part because the large majority of Asian Americans lived in just three states—Hawaii, California, and New York. Further, Asian Americans were less likely to join in the era's most vocal protests. Nonetheless, some Asian students on California campuses joined with African Americans, Chicanos, and Native Americans to advocate a "third world revolution" against the white establishment. Specifically, Asian activists called for a curriculum that recognized their particular histories and cultures. As the Asian population increased, so too would the demands of Asian Americans for recognition of their place in a multicultural society.

Gay Rights

In 1972, Black Panther leader Huey Newton observed that homosexuals "might be the most oppressed people" in American society. Certainly Newton was qualified to recognize oppression when he saw it. But by then a growing number of homosexuals had publicly declared their sexual identity. Growing political activism placed them among minorities demanding equal rights.

Even during the "conformist" 1950s, gay men founded the Mattachine Society (1951) to fight antihomosexual attacks and to press for a wider public acceptance of their lifestyle. Lesbians formed a similar organization, the Daughters of Bilitis, in 1955. Beginning in the mid-1960s, more radical gay and lesbian groups began organizing to raise individual consciousness and to establish a gay culture in which they felt free. One group called for "acceptance as full equals . . . basic rights and equality as citizens; our human dignity; . . . [our] right to love whom we wish."

The movement's defining moment came on Friday June 27, 1969, when New York City police raided the Stonewall Inn, a Greenwich Village bar. Such raids were common enough: gay bars were regularly harassed by the police in an attempt to control urban "vice." This time the patrons fought back, first with taunts and jeers, then with paving stones and parking meters. Increasingly, gay activists called on homosexuals to "come out of the closet" and publicly affirm their sexuality. In 1974 gays achieved a major symbolic victory when the American Psychiatric Association removed homosexuality from its list of mental disorders.

Stonewall incident

Feminism

The movement for women's rights and equality in the United States was not, of course, a creation of the 1960s. It began well before the Civil War, and the sustained political efforts of its supporters had won women the vote in 1920. But the women's movement of the 1960s and 1970s began to push for equality in broader, deeper ways.

Writer Betty Friedan was one of the first women to voice dissatisfaction with the cultural attitudes prevalent at midcentury. Even though more women were entering the job market, the media routinely glorified housewives and homemakers while discouraging those women who aspired to independent careers. In *The Feminine Mystique* (1963) Friedan identified the "problem that has no name," a dispiriting boredom or emptiness in the midst of affluent lives. "Our culture does not permit women to accept or gratify their basic need to grow and fulfill their potentialities as human beings."

The Feminine Mystique

The Feminine Mystique gave birth to a new women's rights movement. The Commission on the Status of Women appointed by President Kennedy proposed the 1963 Equal Pay Act and helped add gender to the forms of discrimination outlawed by the 1964 Civil Rights Act. Women had also assumed an important role in both the civil rights and antiwar movements. They accounted for half the students who went south for the Freedom Summers in 1964 and 1965. Living with violence and assuming heavy responsibilities, these women discovered new freedom and self-confidence.

Movement women also realized that they were themselves victims of systematic discrimination. Male reformers often limited them to behind-the-scenes services such as cooking, laundry, and fulfilling sexual needs. Casey Hayden, a veteran of SDS and SNCC, confronted the male leadership. The "assumptions of male superiority are as widespread . . . and every bit as crippling to the woman as the assumptions of white superiority are to the Negro," she wrote. By 1966 activist women were less willing to see their grievances eclipsed by other political constituencies. Friedan joined a group of 24 women and 2 men who formed the National Organization for Women (NOW). The new feminists sought to force the Johnson administration to take bolder action to eliminate discrimination in such areas as jobs and pay. When feminists argued that "sexism" was not qualitatively different from racism,

National Organization for Women

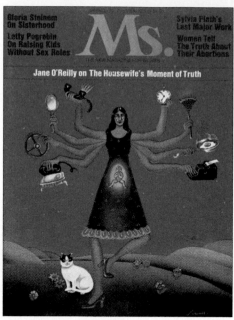

Ms. magazine, edited by feminist Gloria Steinem, gave the women's movement a means to reach a broader audience. The cover of the first issue, published in 1972, uses the image of a many-armed Hindu goddess to satirize the multiple roles of the modern housewife.

Johnson accepted the argument and in 1967 included women as well as African Americans, Hispanics, and other minorities as groups covered by federal affirmative action programs.

Broader social trends established a receptive climate for the feminist appeal. After 1957 the birthrate began a rapid decline; improved methods of contraception, such as the birth control pill, permitted more sexual freedom and smaller family size. By 1970 more than 40 percent of all women, an unprecedented number, were employed outside the home. Education also spurred the shift from home to the job market and increased consciousness of women's issues. Higher educational levels allowed women to enter an economy oriented increasingly to white-collar service industries rather than blue-collar manufacturing.

As much as women sought liberation from old restrictions, their new circumstances raised problems. Men did not readily share traditional family responsibilities with working women; obligations of a job were added to domestic routines. Because women often took part-time jobs or jobs treated as "female" work, they earned far less than men. And though greater sexual freedom implied more gender equality, the media continued to promote the image of women as sex objects.

By 1970 feminists had captured the media's attention. Fifty thousand women participated in NOW's Strike for Equality Parade down New York's Fifth Avenue. Television cameras zeroed in on signs with such slogans as "Don't Cook Dinner—Starve a Rat Today." Some newscasters reported that marchers had burned their bras to protest sexual stereotyping. "Bra burners" became the media's condescending phrase used to deny credibility to militant feminists such as Kate Millett, whose *Sexual Politics* (1970) condemned a male-dominated "patriarchal" society.

Equal Rights and Abortion

With its influence growing, the feminist movement sought to translate women's grievances into a political agenda. NOW members could agree in 1967 to a "Bill of Rights" that called for maternity leave for working mothers, federally supported day-care facilities, child care tax deductions, and equal education and job training. But they divided on two other issues: the passage of an Equal Rights Amendment to the Constitution and a repeal of all state antiabortion laws.

At first, support seemed strong for an Equal Rights Amendment that would forbid all discrimination on the basis of gender. By the 1970s public opinion polls showed that even a majority of American men were sympathetic to the idea. In 1972 both the House and the Senate passed the Equal Rights Amendment (ERA) virtually without opposition. Within a year 28 of the necessary 38 states had approved the ERA. It seemed only a matter of time before 10 more state legislatures would complete its ratification.

Many participants in the women's movement also applauded the Supreme Court's decision, in *Roe v. Wade* (1973), to strike down 46 state laws restricting a woman's access to abortion. In his opinion for the majority, Justice Harry Blackmun observed that a woman in the nineteenth century had "enjoyed a substantially broader right to terminate a pregnancy than she does in most states today." As legal abortion in the first three months of pregnancy became more readily available, the rate of maternal deaths from illegal operations, especially among minorities, declined.

But the early success of the ERA and the feminist triumph in *Roe v. Wade* masked underlying divisions among women's groups. *Roe v. Wade* triggered a sharp backlash from many Catholics, Protestant fundamentalists, and socially conservative women. Their opposition inspired a crusade for a "right to life" amendment to the Constitution. A similar conservative reaction breathed new life into the "STOP ERA" crusade of Phyllis Schlafly, an Illinois political organizer. Although Schlafly was a professional working woman herself, she believed that women should embrace their traditional role as homemakers subordinate to their husbands. "Every change [that the ERA] requires will deprive women of a right, benefit, or exemption that they now enjoy," she argued.

In the middle ground stood women (and a considerable number of men) who wanted to use the political system, rather than a constitutional amendment, to correct the most glaring inequalities between the sexes. Within a year after Congress passed the ERA, the National Women's Political Caucus conceded that the momentum to ratify was waning. Although Congress in 1979 extended the deadline for state legislatures to act for another three years, it became clear that the amendment would fail.

The Legacy of Identity Politics

The identity politics of the late 1960s and early 1970s marked a beginning, not an end. Over the next decade, African Americans, Latinos, American Indians, Asian Americans, gays, and feminists would discover that many of the issues they raised remained unresolved. White males still earned more than women or minority men. A glass ceiling barred the path to the executive suites in most corporations, professions, and politics. Many laws and social customs favored white males. The military, for example, barred women from combat and gays altogether. Being labeled a feminist, a homosexual, or a social activist carried a stigma in many areas of American society. Conservatives continued to see identity politics as a threat to national unity.

All the same, political and social activism had brought a sense of empowerment to people who had long seen themselves as "other." By speaking up, they had demonstrated how traditional ways of presenting American history and culture excluded the experience of the majority of Americans. They had opened doors to jobs, careers, and avenues of success previously closed to them. An increasing number of women and minorities won election to political office. Beyond that, identity politics forced the nation to see itself, not as Eurocentric, but as a multicultural society whose histories intersected with those of people across the globe.

Just as identity politics revealed the divisions in American society, so did the continuing debate over Vietnam. President

The End of an Era

Nixon was particularly frustrated because a settlement there still eluded him. The North Vietnamese refused any peace agreement that left the South Vietnamese government of General Nguyen Van Thieu in power. Nixon wanted to subdue his opponents through force but recognized that it would have been political suicide to send back American troops. Instead, he ordered Haiphong harbor mined and blockaded in May 1972, along with a sustained bombing campaign. Then on December 18 the president launched an even greater wave of attacks, as American planes

Women divided

dropped more bombs on the North in 12 days than they had during the entire campaign from 1969 to 1971.

Paris peace treaty

Once again, Kissinger returned to Paris, hoping that the combination of threats and conciliation would bring a settlement. Ironically the Americans' ally, General Thieu, threw up the most stumbling blocks, for he was rightly convinced that his regime would not last once the United States departed. But in January 1973 a treaty was finally arranged, smoothed by Kissinger's promise of aid to the North Vietnamese to help in postwar reconstruction, as well as a secret pledge to Thieu to send troops again if they were needed. By March the last American units were home.

"The enemy must fight his battles . . . [in] protracted campaigns," wrote the Vietnamese strategist in 1284. For all concerned, the American phase of the Vietnam War had been a bloody, wearying conflict. Between 1961 and 1973 the war claimed 57,000 American lives and left more than 300,000 wounded. The cost to Southeast Asia in lives and destruction is almost impossible to calculate. More than a million Vietnamese soldiers and perhaps half a million civilians died. Some 6.5 million South Vietnamese became refugees, along with 3 million Cambodians and Laotians. Nixon claimed the "peace with honor" he had insisted on, but experienced observers predicted that South Vietnam's days were numbered. By any real measure of military success the Vietcong peasant guerrillas and their lightly armed North Vietnamese allies had held off—and in that sense defeated—the world's greatest military power.

Vietnam and the cold war

Truman may have started the United States down the road to Vietnam by promoting a doctrine of containment all across the globe. Certainly Eisenhower and Kennedy increased American involvement and Richard Nixon ended it. But fairly or not, Vietnam is remembered as Lyndon Johnson's war. He committed both the material and human resources of the United States to defeat communism in Southeast Asia. The decision to escalate eventually destroyed the political consensus that had unified Americans since the late 1940s. That consensus was built on two major assumptions. First, it assumed that the United States must bear the burden of containing communism around the world. Second, American leaders had believed that the prosperity generated by the American economy made it possible both to fight communism abroad and to solve major social problems at home.

Liberal dreams died with Vietnam, too. The war in Southeast Asia shattered the optimism of the early 1960s: the belief that the world could be remade with the help of enough brilliant intellectuals or enough federal programs. The war also eroded the prosperity upon which the optimism of the postwar era had rested. After 1973 the economy slid into a long recession that forced Americans to recognize they had entered an era of limits both at home and abroad. Lyndon Johnson, who sought to preserve both liberal dreams and the cold war consensus, died on January 22, 1973, one day before the American war in Vietnam ended.

chapter summary

Though presents from Truman to Nixon sent American forces to Indochina, Vietnam was Lyndon Johnson's war, and the political divisions it caused ended both his presidency and his attempts to establish the Great Society.

- To force the North Vietnamese to negotiate a peace, Johnson escalated the American war effort in 1965. By 1966 American soldiers were doing most of the fighting and American warplanes subjected North Vietnam to heavy bombing.

- As the war dragged on into 1968 and as the nation divided into prowar hawks and antiwar doves, the Vietcong's Tet offensive so shocked Americans that Johnson almost lost the New Hampshire presidential primary to maverick Senator Eugene McCarthy, leading the president to abandon his campaign for a second full term.

- In the wake of the assassinations of Martin Luther King and Robert Kennedy, Hubert Humphrey be-

came the Democrats' presidential nominee. But riots at the Chicago convention so damaged Humphrey's candidacy that Richard Nixon won the election, promising a "peace with honor" in Vietnam.

- Despite Nixon's promise to "bring us together," the nation remained divided not only because of the war but also because a wide range of minorities—Latinos, Indians, Asian Americans, gays, and feminists—adopted newly assertive identity politics as a way to claim their full rights and opportunities as Americans.

  - Mexican American migrant workers led by Cesar Chavez successfully established a farmworkers' union, the UFW, while a rising generation of Latino students adopted more militant techniques for establishing a Chicano identity.

  - Though often divided by tribal diversity, militant Native Americans called attention to the discrimination faced by Indians in urban settings as well as on reservations.

  - Feminists campaigned for civil and political equality as well as to change deep-seated cultural attitudes of a "patriarchal" society.

additional reading

A number of questions have framed the debate about American involvement in Vietnam. Over the past few years, historians have paid particular attention to Lyndon Johnson's responsibility for escalating the war. Larry Berman, *LBJ's War* (1990) raised the issue, which has more recently been taken up by George Herring, *LBJ and Vietnam* (1995); Lloyd Gardner, *Pay Any Price: Lyndon Johnson and the Wars for Vietnam* (1995); and LBJ biographer Robert Dallek, *Lone Star Rising* (1991), in "Lyndon Johnson and Vietnam," *Diplomatic History* (Spring 1996).

For a broader view of the war see George Herring, *America's Longest War* (2d ed., 1986) and Marilyn B. Young, *The Vietnam Wars* (1991), two good surveys. George Kahin, *Intervention* (1986) is useful to understand the road to escalation. Melvin Small, *Johnson, Nixon, and the Doves* (1988) explains how the antiwar movement impacted Washington, and Tom Wells, *The War Within: America's Battle over Vietnam* (1994) examines the full range of antiwar protest. On Richard Nixon and his administration, see Stephen Ambrose, *Nixon, the Tri-*

umph of a Politician, 1962–1972 (1989). For an introduction to identity politics see Stewart Burns, *Social Movements in the 1960s* (1990); on Latinos F. Arturo Rosales, *Chicano! The History of the Mexican American Civil Rights Movement* (rev. ed. 1997) and Joan Moore and Harry Pachon, *Hispanics in the United States* (1985); for Asian Americans we recommend Sucheng Chan, *Asian Americans: An Interpretive History* (1991). Barry D. Adam, *The Rise of a Gay and Lesbian Movement* (1987); John D'Emilio, *Sexual Politics, Sexual Communities: The Making of a Homosexual Minority in the United States, 1940–1970* (1983); and Martin Duberman, *Stonewall* (1993) provide complementary perspectives on the emergence of gay and lesbian activism. John William Sayer, *Ghost Dancing the Law: The Wounded Knee Trials* (1997) recounts one of the most contested moments of Native American activism. Feminism and women's rights has produced a rich literature. A particularly readable and slightly irreverent work is Susan Douglas, *Where the Girls Are: Growing Up Female with the Mass Media* (1994). Sara Evans, *Personal Politics* (1980) links women's liberation to the civil rights movement and the new left. For two other significant topics see Mary Frances Berry, *Why ERA Failed: Politics, Women's Rights, and the Amending Process of the Constitution* (1986) and Amy Erdman, *Yours in Sisterhood: Ms. Magazine and the Promise of Popular Feminism* (1998). For a fuller list of readings, see the Bibliography.

Significant Events

1945	1945 Ho Chi Minh unifies Vietnam
	1947 Puerto Rico given commonwealth status
	1954 French defeated at Dien Bien Phu; Geneva accords
1955	1963 Diem assassinated; United States has 16,000 "advisers" in Vietnam
	1964 Tonkin Gulf incident; Tonkin Gulf resolution
	1965 Rolling Thunder begins bombing of North Vietnam; antiwar "teachings" on college campuses
	1966 Cesar Chavez leads national campaign on behalf of farm workers; National Organization of Women established
1960	1967 March on the Pentagon; Johnson's advisers oppose war
	1968 U.S. troop levels in Vietnam peak at 536,000; Tet offensive; My Lai massacre; peace talks begin in Paris; Eugene McCarthy challenges Johnson in New Hampshire primary; Johnson withdraws from race; Martin Luther King Jr. assassinated; Los Angeles Chicano students protest educational abuses; Robert Kennedy enters race and is assassinated; riots at Democratic Convention in Chicago; George Wallace candidacy; Nixon wins election
1965	1969 Secret bombing of Cambodia; "Vietnamization" leads to reduction of American forces; Stonewall incident, Greenwich Village; Nixon Doctrine
	1970 U.S. troops invade Cambodia; killings at Kent State and Jackson State; march on Washington; NOW organizes Strike for Equality; repeal of Tonkin Gulf resolution
1970	1972 Congress passes Equal Rights Amendment; Nixon trip to China; détente with Soviet Union; SALT I; mining of Haiphong Harbor; Christmas bombings of North Vietnam
	1973 Vietnam peace treaty; *Roe v. Wade;* AIM supporters occupy Wounded Knee

*I*n July 1969, tens of thousands of spectators gathered at Cape Kennedy to witness the launching of *Apollo 11,* the first manned space flight to the moon. Among the crowd was a mule-cart procession led by the Reverend Ralph Abernathy, a leader in the civil rights movement. Abernathy brought his Poor People's March to the moon launching to dramatize the problem of poverty. The *Saturn 5*'s thunderous ignition and fiery rocket blast proved so awesome that Abernathy instead prayed for the safety of the crew. Days later, he, too, celebrated when astronauts Neil Armstrong and Buzz Aldrin walked across a lunar landscape.

The triumph had been epochal. And yet some uncertainty lingered over what it all meant. One scientist took comfort that after *Apollo* the human race could always go elsewhere, no matter how much a mess was made of the planet earth. That was no small consideration given the increasing problems of smog, water pollution, and toxic wastes. There had been some dramatic warnings. In 1967 an oil tanker, the *Torrey Canyon,* spilled 100,000 tons of oil into the English Channel. Detergents used to clean up the spill left the area clean but without plant and animal life for years after.

Such dangers worried city officials in Santa Barbara, California, an outpost of paradise along the Pacific Coast. In the channel stretching between there and Los Angeles, 90 miles to the south, oil companies had drilled some 925 wells in the coastal tidelands. State efforts to impose stringent regulations on federal oil leases offshore had failed. The Department of Interior repeatedly assured local officials they had "nothing to fear." That changed on January 28, 1969, when Union Oil Company's well A-21 blew a billow of thick crude oil into the channel. Crews quickly capped the hole, only to discover that pressure had driven natural gas and oil through another hole. "It looked like a massive, inflamed abscess bursting with reddish-brown pus," one observer commented.

By February 1, an oil slick covered 5 miles of Santa Barbara's white beaches. In the 11 days it took workers to seal the leak, more than 200,000 barrels of oil had left a slick extending for some 800 miles. Black, tarry goo coated beaches, boats, and wildlife as far south as San Diego. "Cormorants and grebes dived into the oily swells for fish, most never to surface alive. All along the mucky shoreline, birds lay dead or dying, unable to raise their oil-soaked feathers," one reporter wrote. Despite the efforts of environmentalists, thousands of shore birds perished, and detergents claimed the entire population of limpets, abalones, lobsters, sea urchins, mussels, clams, and some fish.

Santa Barbara, not *Apollo 11,* served as a portent of the coming decade. Having reached the moon, Americans discovered more pressing concerns closer to home. War erupted in the Middle East. Arab members of the Organization of Petroleum Exporting Countries (OPEC) announced that they would embargo oil shipments to Western nations. Growing concern over environmental deterioration, the shocking revelations of the Watergate scandals, and the continuing rise of inflation eroded the

THE AGE OF LIMITS

preview • Americans in the 1970s discovered painful limits to many aspects of their society: limits to economic growth sparked by a shortage of oil, limits on the environment due to pollution and overdevelopment. Richard Nixon too met political limits, as he was forced from office by his role in campaign scandals. With the nation mired in an economic downturn, Presidents Ford and Carter steered a course that acknowledged the decline of American power.

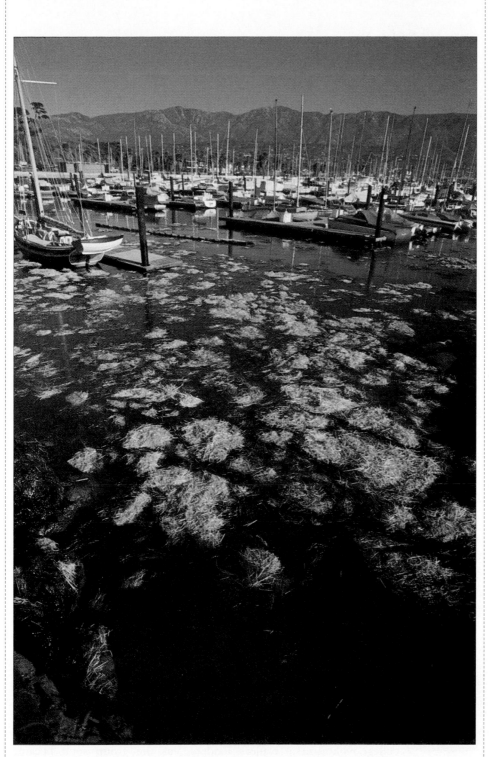

At the end of a decade in which Americans landed on the moon, a series of down-to-earth crises, such as the oil spill that fouled these waters off Santa Barbara, California, in 1969, underscored the limits of American power and technology both at home and abroad.

nation's optimism. Americans began to doubt that technological know-how could solve any problem or that economic growth was both inevitable and beneficial. Elliot Richardson, the Nixon administration's secretary of health, education and welfare, drew the appropriate lesson when he remarked, "We must recognize, as we have with both foreign affairs and natural resources, that resources we thought were boundless . . . are indeed severely limited." The United States had entered an era of limits.

The Limits of Reform

Like the space program, the reform movements of the early 1960s had sprung from an optimistic faith in the perfectibility of society. But as Vietnam dragged on, Americans had become more fragmented. America still seemed a nation in need of reforming, but as inflation dogged the economy and unemployment grew, Americans set their sights much lower. According to social observer Tom Wolfe, in the 1970s the self-obsessed "Me Generation" displaced the crusading New Left.

Amid frustrated hopes, some elements of the reform movement kept alive the idea of restructuring society. Environmentalists and consumer advocates used many of the same strategies of nonviolent protest and legal maneuver that worked so effectively in the civil rights crusade. But unlike much of the radicalism of the 1960s, these movements each had long been associated with the American reform tradition. And though they often had radical goals, their leadership most frequently came from the political mainstream and won some major victories, even if they failed to achieve the transformation they sought.

Consumerism

Ralph Nader attacks GM

In 1965 a thin, intense young man shocked the automotive world by publishing *Unsafe at Any Speed.* The author, Ralph Nader, argued that too many automobiles were unsafe even in minor accidents. Nader's particular target was the Chevrolet Corvair, a rear-engined small car built by General Motors. Crash reports indicated that the Corvair sometimes rolled over in routine turns and that drivers quickly lost control when the car skidded. Even more damning, Nader accused General Motors of being aware of the flaw from its own internal engineering studies.

GM, the corporate Goliath, at first decided that rather than defend the Corvair, it would attack Nader, this countercultural David. It sent out private investigators to dig up dirt from his personal life. They discovered no hippie disguised in a suit but the hardworking son of Lebanese immigrants who had fulfilled the American dream. Nader had graduated from Princeton and Harvard Law School, wore his hair short, and never used drugs. And when he discovered GM's underhanded tactics against him, he sued.

GM's embarrassed president, James Roche, publicly apologized, but by then Nader was a hero and *Unsafe at Any Speed* a bestseller. In 1966 Congress passed the National Traffic and Motor Vehicle Safety Act and the Highway Safety Act, which for the first time required safety standards for cars, tires, and roads. Nader used $425,000 from his successful lawsuit to launch his Washington-based Center for the Study of Responsive Law (1969) with a staff of five lawyers and a hundred college volunteers. "Nader's Raiders," as the group soon became known, investigated a wide range of consumer and political issues, lobbying against water pollution, influence-peddling in Congress, and abuses in nursing homes and in favor of consumer-oriented government agencies.

Nader's Raiders were part of a diverse consumer movement comprised of people who ranged from modest reformers to radicals. The radicals viewed the system of markets in which consumers bought goods to be deeply flawed. Only a thorough overhaul of the system, carried out by an active, interventionist government, could empower citizen-consumers. Nader suggested both the radicals' tone and their agenda

Ralph Nader's dogged, ascetic style forced corporations like General Motors to examine more seriously issues of public safety in products they produced. Nader's organization, Public Citizen, expanded its efforts on behalf of consumers to a wide range of issues.

when he called on corporations "to stop stealing, stop deceiving, stop corrupting politicians with money, stop monopolizing, stop poisoning the earth, air and water, stop selling dangerous products, stop exposing workers to cruel hazards." To pressure corporate America, Nader created the Public Interest Research Group, whose branches across the country lobbied for consumer protection.

More moderate reformers concentrated on making the existing market economy more open and efficient. To be better consumers, people needed better information. Reformers identified specific abuses: unsafe toys, dangerous food additives, the health consequences of smoking, and defective products dubbed "lemons." They brought suit against unethical marketing strategies like "bait-and-switch advertising" and hidden credit costs that plagued the poor. Many consumer organizations concentrated on a single issue, such as auto safety, smoking, insurance costs, or health care.

Diversity of goals broadened the movement's appeal but also fragmented support. Consumerism often overlapped with other causes, such as environmentalism, civil rights, and the women's movement. Nader was never able to establish consumerism as a mass political movement, finding supporters largely among the more affluent upper middle class. Furthermore, a weak economy created fears that more regulation would drive up consumer prices and thus add to inflation. Still, the consumer movement had placed its agenda in the mainstream of political debate, and powerful consumer groups continued to represent the public interest.

Environmentalism

The Santa Barbara oil spill was hardly the first warning that Americans were abusing the environment. As early as 1962 marine biologist Rachel Carson had warned in *Silent Spring* of the environmental damage done by the pesticide DDT. Though chemical companies tried to discredit her as a woman and a scientist, 40 state legislatures passed laws restricting DDT. Certainly, no one with a sense of irony could help but marvel that the oil-polluted Cuyahoga River running through Cleveland, Ohio, had burst into flames. Smog, nuclear fallout, dangerous pesticides, and polluted rivers were the not-so-hidden costs of a society wedded to technology and unbridled economic growth.

In some ways, the environmental movement echoed the concerns and approaches of both the traditional conservation movement associated with Teddy Roosevelt, Gifford Pinchot, and Harold Ickes and the preservationist philosophies of John Muir and the Sierra Club. Conservationists had always stressed the idea of proper *use* of both renewable and nonrenewable resources. Efficient use would ensure the nation's future prosperity. Engineers, lawyers, and economists shaped the conservation agenda. Preservationists shared the Romantics' vision of humankind's spiritual links to nature. They sought largely to save unique wilderness areas like Yellowstone, Yosemite, and the Grand Canyon from *any* development and commercial exploitation.

Conservation versus preservation

In addition the new environmental movement drew heavily on the field of ecology. Since the early twentieth century, this biological science had demonstrated how closely life processes throughout nature depend on one another. Barry Commoner in his book *The Closing Circle* (1971) argued that modern society courted disaster by trying to "improve on nature." American farmers, for example, had shifted from animal manures to artificial fertilizers to increase farm productivity. But the change also raised costs, left soil sterile, and poisoned nearby water sources. After laundry detergents artificially "whitened" clothes, they created foamy scum in lakes and

Barry Commoner and ecology

Daily Lives

FOOD/DRINK/DRUGS

Fast-Food America

Before the 1960s, few Americans regularly ate food prepared outside the home. The rich with access to servants, restaurants, and clubs might regularly eat food prepared by a nonfamily member. So, too, might college students or the very poor who had to take their meals in prisons, soup kitchens, or other institutional settings. By the 1970s the consumption of prepared foods and meals had become common for most Americans. Fast-food chains, school and office cafeterias, vending machines, and other public facilities served up more than 40 percent of the meals Americans ate. Many home meals consisted of packaged foods like TV dinners or frozen entrées that required nothing but heating prior to consumption. Whether at home or away, the emphasis at mealtime was less on nutrition and more on speed, convenience, and economy.

As prepared foods became more popular, meals as social occasions for families became rarer.

Common meals required the participants to foresake personal preferences and time schedules to share the same foods, served in the same order, at the same time. But in an age of fast-food chains and ethnic food takeouts, it became practical for individual family members to eat different foods at the same time or to break the "one-cook-to-one-family" pattern. In the process, eating became desocialized. The two most communal meals, breakfast and dinner, no longer brought families together. By the end of the 1970s some 75 percent of American families did not share breakfast, and the average family sat down to dinner fewer than three times a

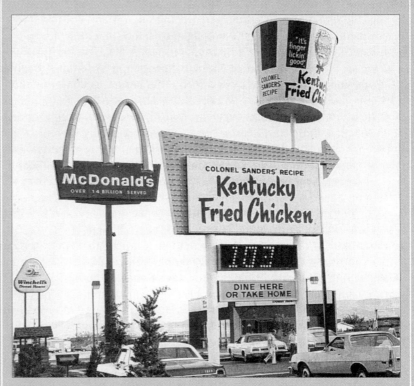

Once limited largely to hamburgers, ice cream, and pancakes, during the 1970s fast-food chains increasingly allowed Americans to bolt down indifferently synthesized varieties of ethnic and regional foods as well.

rivers while nourishing deadly algae blooms. Industry profited in the short run, Commoner argued, but in the long run the environment was going bankrupt.

By the 1970s, environmentalists had organized to implement what biologist René Dubos had called a "new social ethic." They brought a lawsuit to block the plan of a consortium of oil companies to build an 800-mile pipeline across Alaska's fragile wilderness. In addition, they successfully lobbied in Congress to defeat a bill authorizing support for the supersonic transport plane, the SST, whose high-altitude flights threatened to deplete the earth's vital ozone layer. Similarly, environmental groups fought a proposed jet airport that threatened South Florida's water supply and the ecology of Everglades National Park.

Even President Nixon, normally a friend of business and real estate interests, responded to the call for more stringent environmental regulation. His administration week. The meal seldom lasted more than 20 minutes. As formal meals lost their importance, snacking became common. Individual family members ingested food in some fashion as often as 20 times a day. More and more often, people combined the consumption of food with activities other than meals: popcorn and movies, beer and TV sports, coffee and commuting.

As important as where and how people ate were nutritional trends. In earlier societies meals had consisted largely of a core complex carbohydrate (rice, bread, potatoes, or noodles), served up with a fringe complement of meats, vegetables, and fruits, and seasoned perhaps with a sauce. The core carbohydrate provided most nutrition, calories, and satisfaction; the fringe abetted the eating of the core. In modern Western society, including the United States, that pattern reversed over time. By the 1970s the bulk of Americans' calories came from protein foods like meat and eggs and even more from foods rich in sugars and fats.

As preoccupation with slimness grew, the direct consumption of sugar declined. But because most Americans ate more prepared and precooked foods, the indirect consumption of sugar and sweeteners increased. Food manufacturers discovered that sugars and dense fats like palm and coconut oil improved flavor, texture, taste, and shelf life. Thus they included sweeteners or fats in places where most people did not expect them: table salt, coatings for fried foods, peanut butter, and "health" foods like granola. By the late 1970s the average American consumed some 130 pounds of sugar and sweeteners per year and about 40 percent of all calories in the form of animal and vegetable fats. That led to a steady increase in obesity and diet-related heart diseases and cancers.

So eating patterns suggest some basic contradictions of the 1970s. While traditionalists called for family values, most families discarded the most traditional ritual, "breaking bread together." And as the American diet, like the population, became more diverse, the basic sources of food energy became less varied. Further, while medical technologies added to life expectancy, most doctors ignored dietary patterns responsible for life-threatening diseases. In this way, the patterns of daily life may be more revealing than the great events of the era.

banned the use of DDT (though not its sale abroad) and supported the National Environmental Policy Act of 1969. The act required environmental impact statements for most public projects and made the government responsible for representing the public interest. Nixon also established the Environmental Protection Agency to enforce the law. Echoing Barry Commoner, he announced, "We must learn not how to master nature but how to master ourselves, our institutions, and our technology."

EPA established

By the spring of 1970 a healthy environment had become a widely popular cause. Senator Gaylord Nelson of Wisconsin suggested a national "Earth Day" to celebrate this new consciousness. On April 22, 1970, for at least a few hours pedestrians reclaimed downtown city streets, millions of schoolchildren planted trees and picked up litter, college students demonstrated, and Congress adjourned. The enthusiasm reflected the movement's dual appeal: it combined the rationalism of science with a

Earth Day

religious vision of life's organic unity. But at least one member of Congress recognized the movement's more radical implications: "The Establishment sees this as a great big anti-litter campaign. Wait until they find out what it really means . . . to clean up our earth."

Earth Day did not signal a consensus on an environmental ethic. President Nixon, for one, was unwilling to restrict economic development. In his own Earth Day speech he supported the oil industry's Alaskan pipeline project, which threatened huge caribou herds and the Arctic's fragile ecology. Despite a long series of court challenges construction began in 1973. "We are not going to allow the environmental issue . . . to destroy the system," he announced in 1972.

Nixon's political instincts were shrewd. Conflict between social classes underlay the environmental debate. To those he courted for his silent majority, the issue came down to jobs versus the environment. "Out of work? Hungry? Eat an environmentalist," declared one bumper sticker. During the 1960s many middle Americans came to resent the veterans of the counterculture, civil rights, and antiwar movements who now found an outlet in environmental activism. But so long as pollution threatened, the environmental movement would not go away. Whether conservative hunters in Ducks Unlimited or mainstream nature lovers in the Wilderness Society or radical groups like Greenpeace, numerous organizations continued the fight to protect the environment.

counterpoint

Interpreting the Environmental Movement

Because historians have often been sympathetic to the goals of environmentalists, they have tended to interpret the movement somewhat uncritically. Mainstream accounts often point out flattering continuities with the progressive movement, such as a reliance on the authority of science. Biology, for example, caused progressives to discard once popular theories of human exceptionalism and to see nature not as a simple warehouse of useful resources but as a series of interlinking systems. In similar ways, environmentalists have relied on ecological studies to provide a more sophisticated understanding of how those systems were interacting.

Recently some historians have become more critical of environmentalism. One confessed, "Where once I saw a movement founded in science, now I see a utopian political program." He compared modern environmentalism to the temperance crusade at the turn of the century. Although temperance advocates were divided over how to attack alcohol abuse, the more extreme factions successfully promoted prohibition and the Eighteenth Amendment. It was a utopian experiment that, in the end, was doomed to fail. Similarly, some environmental reformers have called for "global schemes of economic and political control," according to this point of view. Environmentalist Paul Ehrlich's popular book *The Population Bomb* (1968), for example, warned of the dire consequences of overpopulation. Ehrlich suggested that voluntary efforts at family planning were likely to fail and that the state might have to step in to control birthrates, especially in developing nations.

The parallel between the environmentalists and the temperance reformers is instructive. Progressivism, we have seen, displayed a mix of reform and control. Its middle-class and upper-middle-class advocates worried about what the unruly masses might do without the guidance of "experts." A similar tension can be seen in the environmental movement, whose professional, white-collar advocates during the 1960s and 1970s paid scant attention to the environmental problems specific to poor urban residents. Only in the 1980s did a number of new organizations focus greater attention on the effects of hazardous industrial sites on lower-class neighborhoods or the danger of pesticides to migrant workers.

As president, Richard Nixon saw himself as a global leader with a grand strategic vision. Domestic politics interested him

Watergate and the Politics of Resentment

far less. His instincts were often those of a pragmatist. He recognized that the popularity of issues like social security, consumer protection, or pollution control required compromise from the White House. All the same, as a conservative Republican he looked to scale back or eliminate many New Deal and Great Society programs. "After a third of a century of power flowing from the people and the states to Washington," he proclaimed, "it is time for a New Federalism in which power, funds, and responsibility will flow from Washington to the people."

Twenty-five years of cold war had given the presidency enormous power. One historian described the White House ascendance over Congress and the Judiciary as an "imperial presidency." Nixon would use the power in his office both to assert American interests abroad and to destroy his enemies at home. Despite his pragmatism, he had never overcome his resentment of liberals, the media, and the eastern establishment that had often looked slightly askance at the awkward young man from Whittier, California. Such animosities led Nixon to see himself as embattled, surrounded by enemies who conspired against him and his administration. The line between the use and abuse of presidential power would prove a thin one. Crossing it led to a third-rate burglary at the Watergate office complex in Washington, D.C., and the political downfall of Richard Nixon.

Nixon's New Federalism

Nixon envisioned his New Federalism as a conservative counter to liberal policies that had depended on the federal government to implement. His new system proposed that Washington give money in block grants to state and local governments. Rather than receiving funds earmarked for specific purposes, localities could decide which problems needed attention and how best to attack them. Congress passed a revenue-sharing act in 1972 that distributed $30 billion over the subsequent five years. A similar approach influenced aid to individuals. Liberal programs from the New Deal to the Great Society often provided specific services to individuals: job retraining programs, Head Start programs for preschoolers, food supplement programs for nursing mothers. Republicans argued that such a "service strategy" too often assumed that federal bureaucrats best understood what the poor needed. Nixon favored an "income strategy" instead, which simply gave recipients money and allowed them to spend it as they saw fit. Such grants would encourage individual initiative, increase personal freedom, and reduce government bureaucracy.

Revenue sharing

In this spirit Nixon encouraged a renegade liberal academic, Daniel Patrick Moynihan, to develop a program to replace the welfare system. His "Family Assistance Plan" stressed "workfare," not welfare; it targeted the working poor, not the undeserving poor. Poor families would be guaranteed a minimum annual income of $1600. An emphasis on family would encourage fathers to live at home. The plan also required recipients to register for employment to satisfy conservative critics who believed that too many welfare recipients were able-bodied workers addicted to handouts and too lazy to work. Though Moynihan's proposals died in Congress, they defined the general terms in which poverty and assistance to the poor would be debated into the 1990s.

Family Assistance Plan

Even if Nixon was determined to reverse the liberalism of the 1960s, critics were wrong to dismiss him as a knee-jerk conservative. His appeal to local authority and individual initiative in some ways echoed the New Left's rhetoric of "power

Nixon reforms

to the people." In 1970 he signed a bill establishing an Occupational Safety and Health Agency (OSHA) to enforce health and safety standards in the workplace. And although the president was no crusader for the environment, he did support a Clean Air Act to reduce car exhaust emissions as well as a Clean Water Act to make polluters liable for their negligence and to deal with disastrous oil spills.

Stagflation

Ironically, economic distress, aggravated by the Vietnam War, forced Nixon to adopt liberal remedies. By 1970 the nation had entered its first recession in a decade. Traditionally a recession brought a decrease in demand for goods and a rise in unemployment as workers were laid off. Manufacturers then cut wages and prices in order to preserve profit margins and encourage demand for their goods. But in the recession of 1970, while unemployment rose as economists would have expected, wages and prices were also rising in an inflationary spiral. Americans were getting the worst of two worlds: a stagnant economy combined with rising prices—or "stagflation." Unfriendly Democrats labeled the phenomenon "Nixonomics," in which "all things that should go up—the stock market, corporate profits, real spendable income, productivity—go down, and all things that should go down—unemployment, prices, interest rates—go up."

To blame the recession on Nixon was hardly fair, because Lyndon Johnson had brought on inflation by refusing to raise taxes to pay for the war and Great Society social programs. In addition, wages continued their inflationary rise partly because powerful unions had negotiated automatic cost-of-living increases into their contracts. Similarly, in industries dominated by a few large corporations, like steel and oil, prices did not follow the market forces of a recession. So prices and wages continued to rise as demand and employment fell.

Mindful that his own silent majority were the people most pinched by the slower economy, Nixon decided that unemployment posed a greater threat than inflation. Announcing "I am now a Keynesian," he adopted a deficit budget designed to stimulate the growth of jobs. More surprising, in August 1971 he announced that to provide short-term relief, wages and prices would be frozen for 90 days. For a Republican to advocate federal wage and price controls was near heresy, almost as heretical as Nixon's overtures to China. Yet the president did not hesitate. For another year federal wage and price boards enforced the ground rules for any increases; most controls were lifted in January 1973. As in foreign policy, Nixon had reversed long-cherished economic policies to achieve practical results.

Social Policies and the Court

School busing

Many of the blue-collar and southern Democratic voters Nixon also sought to attract resented the Supreme Court's use of school busing to achieve desegregation. Fifteen years after *Brown v. Board of Education* had ruled that racially separate school systems must be desegregated, many localities still had not complied. Busing to achieve racial balance aroused determined opposition from white neighborhoods. White parents resented having their children bused away from their neighborhood to more distant, formerly all-black schools. Black parents, although they worried about the reception their children might receive in hostile white neighborhoods, by and large supported busing as a means to better education.

Under President Nixon, federal policy on desegregation took a 180-degree turn. In 1969, when lawyers for Mississippi asked the Supreme Court to delay an integration plan, the Nixon Justice Department supported the state. The Court rejected that proposal, holding in *United States v. Jefferson County Board of Education* that all state systems, including Mississippi's, had an obligation "to terminate dual systems at once and to operate now and hereafter only unitary schools." Two years later, in *Swann v. Charlotte–Mecklenburg Board of Education* (1971), the Court further ruled that busing, balancing ratios, and redrawing school district lines were all acceptable ways to achieve integration.

The Warren Court's liberal activism, in decisions such as *Brown v. Board of Education, Hernandez v. Texas,* and *Roe v. Wade,* had encouraged minorities to seek redress through the courts. Nixon looked to create a more conservative judicial system. When Earl Warren resigned as chief justice in 1969, the president nominated Warren Burger, a jurist who accepted most of the Court's precedents but had no wish to break new ground. When another vacancy occurred in 1969, Nixon tried twice to appoint conservative southern judges. But because both nominees had reputations on the federal bench for opposing civil rights and labor unions, the Senate rejected them. In the end, Nixon chose Minnesotan Harry Blackmun, a moderate judge of unimpeachable integrity. In 1971 he made two additional appointments: Lewis Powell, a highly regarded Virginia lawyer, and William Rehnquist of Arizona, an extreme conservative.

The successive appointments of Burger, Blackmun, Powell, and Rehnquist effectively transformed the Court. No longer would it lead the fight for minority rights, as it had under Chief Justice Earl Warren. But neither would it reverse the achievements of the Warren Court.

Nixon and the Court

Us versus Them

In so many of his battles, as in the struggle to shape the Supreme Court, Nixon portrayed those who opposed him as foes of traditional American values. Just as Nixon had tended to equate liberal reformers with Communist "pinkos" during the 1950s, now his administration blurred the lines between honest dissent and radical criminals. In doing so, it reflected the president's tendency to see issues in terms of "us against them."

With Nixon's consent (and Lyndon Johnson's before him), J. Edgar Hoover and the FBI conducted a covert and often illegal war against dissent. The CIA and military intelligence agencies also allowed themselves to be used. Attorney General John Mitchell and his Justice Department aggressively prosecuted civil rights activists, antiwar groups like Vietnam Veterans Against the War, socially conscious members of the Catholic clergy, the Black Panthers, SDS activists, and leaders of the peace movement. In its war on the drug culture of hippies and radicals, the administration proposed a bill that would allow police to stage "no-knock" raids and use "preventive detention" to keep suspected criminals in jail without bail. It also lobbied for permission to use more phone taps and other means of electronic surveillance.

In the political arena, Vice President Spiro Agnew launched an alliterative assault on the administration's enemies. He referred to the press and television news commentators as "nattering nabobs of negativism" and "troubadours of trouble" who contributed to the "creeping permissiveness that afflicted America." Antiwar demonstrators were "an effete corps of impudent snobs." In the campaign between "us" and "them," the national press corps was clearly "them," a hostile establishment that gave the news a liberal slant.

Triumph

George McGovern

As the election of 1972 approached, Nixon's majority seemed to be falling into place, especially as the antiwar candidacy of Senator George McGovern of South Dakota became unstoppable. Under the new rules of the Democratic party, which McGovern had helped write, the delegate selection process was opened to all party members. Minorities, women, and young people all received proportional representation. No longer would party bosses handpick the delegates. McGovern's nomination gave Nixon the split between "us" and "them" he sought. The Democratic platform embraced all the activist causes that the silent majority resented. It called for immediate withdrawal from Vietnam, abolition of the draft, amnesty for war resisters, and a minimum guaranteed income for the poor. Those issues antagonized much of the traditional New Deal coalition of urban bosses, southerners, labor leaders, and white ethnic groups.

By November the only question to be settled was the size of Nixon's majority. An unsolved burglary at the Watergate complex in Washington, D.C., while vaguely linked to the White House, had not touched the president. He even captured some antiwar sentiment by announcing on election eve that peace in Vietnam was at hand. When the smoke cleared, only liberal Massachusetts and the heavily black District of Columbia gave McGovern a majority. Nixon received almost 61 percent of the popular vote. In the races for the Senate and governorships, however, the Democrats actually made gains, and they lost only 13 House seats. As one pollster concluded, "Richard Nixon's 'new American majority' was the creation of George McGovern."

Even this overwhelming victory did not bring peace to Richard Nixon. He still felt that he had scores to settle with his political opponents. "We have not used the power in the first four years, as you know," he remarked to Haldeman during the campaign. "We haven't used the Bureau [FBI] and we haven't used the Justice Department, but things are going to change now. And they are going to change and they're going to get it, right?" Haldeman could only agree.

The President's Enemies

Encouraged by his victory, Nixon determined to use the power of his office even more broadly. Members of his staff began compiling an "enemies list"—including popular television news correspondents and celebrity antiwar activists. Some on the list were targeted for audits by the Internal Revenue Service or similar harassment.

The plumbers

Then in June 1971 the *New York Times* published a secret, often highly critical military study of the Vietnam War, soon dubbed the Pentagon Papers. Nixon was so irate, he authorized his aide John Ehrlichman to organize a team known as "the plumbers" to find and plug security leaks. The government prosecuted Daniel Ellsberg, the disillusioned official who had leaked the Pentagon Papers. The plumbers also went outside the law: they burglarized the office of Ellsberg's psychiatrist in hopes of finding personally damaging material.

Impoundment

When Congress passed a number of programs Nixon opposed, he simply refused to spend the appropriated money. Some members of Congress claimed that the practice, called impoundment, violated the president's constitutional duty to execute the laws of the land. By 1973 Nixon had used impoundment to cut some $15 billion out of more than 100 federal programs. The courts eventually ruled that impoundment was illegal. But the president continued his campaign to consolidate power and reshape the more liberal social policies of Congress to his own liking.

Break-In

Nixon's fall began with what seemed a minor event. In June 1972 burglars had entered the Democratic National Committee headquarters, located in Washington's plush Watergate apartment complex. But the five burglars proved an unusual lot. They wore business suits, carried walkie-talkies as well as bugging devices and tear-gas guns, and had more than $2000 in crisp new hundred-dollar bills. One of the burglars had worked for the CIA. Another was carrying an address book whose phone numbers included that of a Howard Hunt at the "W. House." Nixon's press secretary dismissed the break-in as "a third rate burglary attempt" and warned that "certain elements may try to stretch this beyond what it is." In August, Nixon himself announced that White House counsel John Dean's own thorough investigation had concluded that "no one on the White House staff . . . was involved in this very bizarre incident. What really hurts in matters of this sort is not the fact that they occur," the president continued. "What really hurts is if you try to cover up."

Matters were not so easily settled, however. *Washington Post* reporters Bob Woodward and Carl Bernstein traced some of the burglars' money back to the Nixon re-election campaign, which had a secret "slush fund" to pay for projects to harass the Democrats. The dirty tricks included forged letters, false news leaks, and spying on Democratic campaign workers.

To the Oval Office

In January 1973 the five burglars plus former White House aides E. Howard Hunt Jr. and G. Gordon Liddy went on trial before Judge John Sirica. Sirica, a no-nonsense judge tagged with the nickname "Maximum John," was not satisfied with the defendants' guilty plea. He wanted to know whether anyone else had directed the burglars and why "these hundred dollar bills were floating around like coupons."

Facing a stiff jail sentence, one of the Watergate burglars cracked. He admitted that the defendants had been bribed to plead guilty and had perjured themselves to protect other government officials. The White House then announced on April 17 that all previous administration statements on the Watergate scandal had become "inoperative." Soon after, the president accepted the resignations of his two closest aides, H. R. Haldeman and John Ehrlichman. He also fired John Dean, his White House counsel, after Dean agreed to cooperate with prosecutors.

Over the summer of 1973 a string of administration officials testified at televised Senate hearings. Attorney General John Mitchell, it became clear, had attended meetings in 1972 in which Gordon Liddy outlined preliminary plans for a campaign of dirty tricks. Liddy and others had also worked as the plumbers under the direction of Ehrlichman in the White House. Then White House counsel John Dean gave his testimony. Young, with a Boy Scout's face, Dean declared in a quiet monotone that the president had personally been involved in the cover-up as recently as April. The testimony stunned the nation. Still, it remained Dean's word against the president's—until Senate committee staff discovered, almost by chance, that Nixon had been secretly recording conversations and phone calls in the Oval Office. The reliability of Dean's testimony was no longer central, for the tapes could tell all.

Obtaining that evidence proved no easy task. In an effort to restore confidence in the White House, the president agreed to appoint a special prosecutor, Harvard law professor Archibald Cox, to investigate the new Watergate disclosures. When Cox subpoenaed the tapes, the president refused to turn them over, citing executive privilege and matters of national security.

Senate hearings

Under the leadership of North Carolina Senator Sam Ervin (left), the Senate Committee investigating the Watergate scandal attracted a large television audience. John Dean (seated), the former White House legal counsel, provided the most damning testimony linking President Nixon to the cover-up. But only when the existence of secretly recorded White House tapes became known was there a chance to corroborate his account.

Agnew resigns

As that battle raged and the astonished public wondered if matters could possibly get worse, they did. Evidence unrelated to Watergate revealed that Vice President Spiro Agnew had systematically solicited bribes, not just as governor of Maryland but while serving in Washington. To avoid jail, he agreed to resign the vice presidency in October and to plead no contest to a single charge of federal income tax evasion. Under provisions of the Twenty-Fifth Amendment, Nixon appointed Representative Gerald R. Ford of Michigan to replace Agnew.

Meanwhile, when Special Prosecutor Cox demanded the tapes, the president offered to submit written summaries instead. Cox no longer had any reason to trust the president and rejected the offer. On Saturday night, October 20, Nixon fired

Saturday Night Massacre

Cox. Reaction to this "Saturday Night Massacre" was overwhelming. The president's own attorney general resigned in protest, 150,000 telegrams poured into Washington, and by the following Tuesday, 84 House members had sponsored 16 different bills of impeachment. The beleaguered president agreed to hand over the tapes. And he appointed Texas lawyer Leon Jaworski as a new special prosecutor. By April 1974, Jaworski's investigations led him to request additional tapes. Again the president refused, although he grudgingly supplied some 1200 pages of typed transcripts of the tapes.

Even the transcripts damaged the president's case. Littered with cynicism and profanity, they revealed Nixon talking with his counsel, John Dean, about how to "take care of the jackasses who are in jail." When Dean estimated it might take a million dollars to shut them up, Nixon replied, "We could get that. . . . You could get a million dollars. And you could get it in cash. I know where it could be gotten." When the matter of perjury came up, Nixon suggested a way out: "You can say, 'I don't remember.' You can say, 'I can't recall.'"

Even those devastating revelations did not produce the "smoking gun" demanded by the president's defenders. When Special Prosecutor Jaworski petitioned the Supreme Court to order the release of additional tapes, the Court in *United States v. Nixon* ruled unanimously in Jaworski's favor.

Resignation

The end came quickly. The House Judiciary Committee adopted three articles of impeachment, charging that Nixon had illegally obstructed justice, had abused his constitutional authority in improperly using federal agencies to harass citizens, and had hindered the committee's effort to investigate the cover-up.

The tapes produced the smoking gun. Conversations with Haldeman on June 23, 1972, only a few days after the break-in, showed that Nixon knew the burglars were tied to the White House staff, knew that his attorney general had been involved, and knew that Mitchell had acted to limit an FBI investigation. Not willing to be the first president convicted in a Senate impeachment trial, Nixon resigned on August 8, 1974. The following day Gerald Ford became president. "The Constitution works," Ford told a relieved nation. "Our long national nightmare is over."

The smoking gun

Had the system worked? In one sense, yes. The wheels of justice had turned, even if slowly. For the first time a president had been forced to leave office. Four cabinet officers, including Attorney General John Mitchell, the highest law officer in the nation, were convicted of crimes. Twenty-five Nixon aides eventually served prison terms ranging from 25 days to more than 4 years.

Yet what would have happened if Woodward and Bernstein had been less resourceful? With the exception of the *Washington Post* and one or two other newspapers, the media had accepted the administration's cover-up. Later abuses within the executive branch, such as the "Irangate" scandals under Ronald Reagan, have demonstrated that the imperial powers of the presidency are still largely unchecked. The Fair Campaign Practices Act was adopted in 1974 in an attempt to enforce greater financial accountability on campaigns. Yet special interest groups have circumvented the law by funneling money through political action committees. The system works, as the Founders understood, only when citizens and public servants respect the limits of government power.

Fair Campaign Practices Act

Gerald Ford inherited a presidential office almost crippled by the Watergate scandals. As the first unelected president, he had no popular mandate. He was little known outside Washington and his home district around Grand Rapids, Michigan. Ford's success as the House minority leader came from personal popularity, political reliability, and party loyalty, qualities that suited a member of Congress better than an unelected president.

A Ford, Not a Lincoln

Ford respected the limits of government. His easy manner came as a relief after the mercurial styles of Johnson and Nixon. By all instincts a conservative, he was determined to continue Nixon's foreign policy of cautious détente and a domestic program of social and fiscal conservatism.

Kissinger and Foreign Policy

As Nixon's star fell, that of his Secretary of State and National Security Adviser Henry Kissinger rapidly rose. Kissinger cultivated reporters, who relished his witty quips, intellectual breadth, and willingness to leak stories to the press. Kissinger viewed himself as a realist, a man for whom order and stability were more important than principle. In that way he offended idealists on the political left and right. Quoting the German writer Goethe, Kissinger acknowledged, "If I had to choose between justice and disorder, on the one hand, and injustice and order on the other, I would always choose the latter."

War Powers Act

Kissinger had struggled to prevent Vietnam and Watergate from eroding the president's power to conduct foreign policy. He believed Congress was too sensitive to public opinion and special-interest groups to pursue consistent long-term policies. But after Vietnam congressional leaders were eager to curtail presidential powers. The War Powers Act of 1973 required the president to consult Congress whenever possible before committing troops, to send an explanation for his actions within 2 days, and to withdraw any troops after 60 days unless Congress voted to retain them. Such limits often led Kissinger to take a covert approach, as he did in an attempt to quell political ferment in Chile.

Coup in Chile

In 1970 Chile ranked as one of South America's few viable democracies. When a coalition of Socialists, Communists, and radicals elected Salvador Allende Gossens as president, the Central Intelligence Agency determined that his victory created a danger to the United States. Kissinger pressed the CIA to bribe the Chilean Congress and to promote a military coup against Allende. When those attempts failed, Kissinger resorted to economic warfare between the United States and the Allende government. By 1973 a conservative Chilean coalition with CIA backing had driven the Socialists from power, attacked the presidential palace, and killed Allende. The United States immediately recognized the new government, which over the next decade deteriorated into a brutally repressive dictatorship. Kissinger argued that the United States had the right to destroy this democracy because Communists themselves threatened an even longer-term dictatorship.

Global Competition and the Limits of American Influence

Kissinger understood that the United States no longer had the economic strength to dominate the affairs of the non-Communist bloc of nations, even in areas such as Central America and the Middle East, where it had once prevailed. Soaring inflation was a major source of weakness. In addition key American industries were crippled by inefficient production, products of poor quality, and high wages. They faced mounting competition from more efficient manufacturers in Europe and in nations along the Pacific rim (Japan, South Korea, Taiwan, Hong Kong, Singapore, and the Philippines). Reacting to these changes, American-based multinational corporations moved high-wage jobs overseas to take advantage of lower costs and cheap labor. The bellwether industry of the American economy, automobile manufacturing, steadily lost sales to Japan and Germany. Speaking on behalf of its blue-collar workers, the AFL-CIO complained that the loss of high-wage manufacturing jobs would create "a nation of hamburger stands, a country stripped of industrial capacity . . . a nation of citizens busily buying and selling cheeseburgers and root beer floats."

The United States was particularly vulnerable because of its dependence on foreign oil—a dependence far greater than most Americans appreciated. With just 7 percent of the world's population, the United States consumed about 30 percent of its energy. The nation's postwar prosperity came in large part from the use of cheap energy. Inflation had already bedeviled the economy, but it would become a much more serious problem if a basic commodity such as oil rose dramatically in price.

Yom Kippur War and the energy crisis

That problem materialized the autumn of 1973, after Syria and Egypt launched a devastating surprise attack against Israel on the Jewish holy day of Yom Kippur. The Soviet Union airlifted supplies to the Arabs; the United States countered by

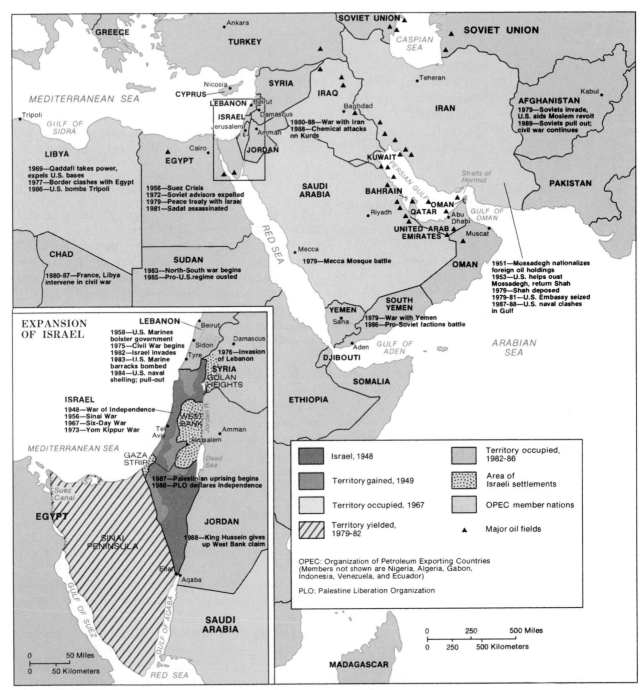

Oil and Conflict in the Middle East, 1948–1988 After World War II, the Middle East became a vital geopolitical region beset by big-power rivalry and complicated by local tribal, ethnic, and religious divisions and political instability. Much of the world's known oil reserves lie along the Persian Gulf. Proximity to the former Soviet Union and vital trade routes like the Suez Canal have defined the region's geographic importance. Revolutions in Iran and Afghanistan, intermittent warfare between Arabs and Jews, the unresolved questions of Israel's borders and a Palestinian homeland, the disintegration of Lebanon, and a long, bloody war between Iran and Iraq were among the conflicts that unsettled the region.

resupplying Israel while pressing the two sides to accept a cease-fire. The seven Arab members of OPEC backed Egypt and Syria by imposing a boycott of oil sales to countries seen as friendly to Israel. The boycott from October 1973 until March 1974 staggered the economies of Western Europe and Japan, which imported 80 to 90 percent of their oil from the Middle East. And by November 1973 President Nixon was warning the nation that it faced "the most acute shortage of energy since World War II." As the price of petroleum-based plastics soared, everything from records to raincoats cost more. In some places motorists hoping to buy a few gallons of gas waited for hours in lines miles long. As the price of oil soared, recession spread.

Shuttle Diplomacy

Kissinger believed that stability in the Middle East would ease pressures on the western economies. He wanted the Arab states to view the United States as neutral in their conflict with Israel. That would make them less likely to resort to oil blackmail. And as American prestige rose, Kissinger could reduce Soviet influence in the region. From January to April 1974 Kissinger intermittently engaged in "shuttle diplomacy" between Sadat's government in Cairo and the Israeli government of Golda Meir in Jerusalem. Flying back and forth, Kissinger persuaded Israel to withdraw its troops from the west bank of the Suez Canal. He also arranged a disengagement between Israel and Syria in the Golan Heights.

South Vietnam falls

Still, Kissinger's whirlwind efforts could not stem the erosion of American power everywhere. While the secretary of state struggled to restore order to the Middle East, the American client government in South Vietnam was near defeat by North Vietnam. President Ford asked Congress for $1 billion in aid to Vietnam, Cambodia, and Laos. This time, Congress refused to spend money on a lost cause. As North Vietnamese forces marched into Saigon in April 1973, desperate South Vietnamese civilian and military leaders rushed to escape Communist retribution.

Détente

Vietnam, Chile, and the Yom Kippur War indicated that the spirit of détente had not ended Soviet-American rivalry over the Third World. Seeking to ease tensions, Ford met with Soviet leader Leonid Brezhnev in November 1974. Since economic stagnation also dogged the Soviet Union, Brezhnev came to Vladivostok eager for more American trade; Ford and Kissinger wanted a limit on nuclear weapons that preserved the current American advantage. Though many issues could not be resolved, the two sides agreed in principle to a framework for a second SALT treaty.

Helsinki summit

A similar hope to extend détente brought Ford and Brezhnev together with European leaders at Helsinki, Finland, in August 1975. There they agreed to recognize the political boundaries that had divided Eastern and Western Europe since 1945. For the first time the United States sent an ambassador to East Germany. In return Brezhnev eased restrictions on the right of Soviet Jews to emigrate.

The erosion of American power, symbolized by Kissinger's overtures to the Soviet Union, dismayed Republican conservatives. The 1976 presidential hopeful Ronald Reagan criticized Ford and Kissinger for selling out American interests and weakening the nation's power. In an effort to subdue the critics, Ford in 1976 stripped Kissinger of his post as national security adviser.

After having won a Nobel Peace Prize in 1973 for his role in ending the Vietnam War, Henry Kissinger (left) entered the Ford administration as something of a hero. But his efforts to improve relations with the Soviet Union by strengthening détente aroused the ire of the Republican right wing, whereas liberals accused Kissinger of being too secretive and friendly to dictators. Here, he briefs President Ford on a train on the way to a 1974 summit meeting in Vladivostok in the Soviet Union.

The Limits of a Post-Watergate President

At home, Gerald Ford found himself facing a Congress determined to restrain an "imperial presidency." Because Ford himself had served in Congress for many years, he enjoyed a brief honeymoon with the legislative branch. But after only a month in office the new president granted Richard Nixon a pardon for any crimes committed during the Watergate affair. In trying to put Watergate in the past, Ford only managed to reopen the wounds. Pardon meant no prosecution, leaving charges against Nixon unanswered and crimes unpunished. The move was especially controversial because at the same time President Ford refused to provide any similar full pardon to draft resisters from the Vietnam War for any wrongdoing. Instead, the president offered them conditional amnesty after review by a government panel.

CIA and FBI abuses

If Ford was willing to forgive and forget presidential sins, Congress was not, especially after reports surfaced of misconduct by the nation's intelligence agencies. Senate investigations as well as a presidential commission appointed by Ford revealed that the CIA had routinely violated its charter by spying on American citizens at home. It had opened private mail, infiltrated domestic protest organizations—even conducted experiments on unwitting subjects using the hallucinogenic drug LSD. Abroad, the CIA had been involved in the assassination or attempted murder of foreign leaders in Cuba, Chile, South Vietnam, the Dominican Republic, and the Congo. The FBI had also used illegal means to infiltrate and disrupt domestic dissidents, including an attempt by J. Edgar Hoover to drive Martin Luther King to suicide. In an effort to bring the executive branch under control, the Senate created an oversight committee to monitor the intelligence agencies.

Fighting Inflation

By the time Ford gave Congress his first State of the Union message in January 1975, he faced the twin scourges of inflation and recession. Inflation had climbed to almost 14 percent, and unemployment exceeded 7 percent. At the heart of the economic crisis lay the problem of rising energy costs. By 1976 oil consumption had returned to 1973 levels, even though domestic oil production had fallen by more than 1 million barrels. Before the Arab oil boycott, OPEC crude oil had been selling at around $2 to $3 a barrel. In a matter of months the price had tripled; by 1976 it was averaging $12 a barrel. (And the worst was yet to come: prices would peak in 1981 at nearly $35 a barrel.)

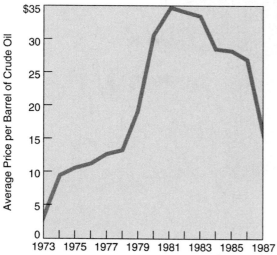

OPEC Oil Prices, 1973–1987 Prices fell even further than the chart shows after 1980 because the dollar was worth much less than in 1973. By the late 1980s gasoline was actually cheaper than in the 1950s.

Congress responded in 1975 by passing the Energy Policy and Conservation Act. It authorized the Federal Energy Administration to order utilities to burn abundant coal rather than expensive oil. In addition, the act created a strategic petroleum reserve as a hedge against future boycotts and ordered the auto industry to improve the energy efficiency of the engines it produced. And as a final—but environmentally dangerous—stopgap measure, the government encouraged the rapid development of nuclear power plants.

The energy-driven recession struck hardest at the older industrial centers of the Northeast and Upper Midwest, which imported most of their energy. Housing and plants built in the days of cheap energy proved wasteful and inefficient. Nixon's and Ford's fiscal conservatism hurt, too. Cutbacks in federal spending fell hardest on major cities with shrinking tax bases, outmoded industries, and heavy social service costs. The crisis for "rust belt" cities came to a head in October 1975 when New York City announced that it faced bankruptcy. New York's plight reflected the wrenching adjustments faced in an era of economic limits. A shrinking economic base could not support high wages and expensive public services.

The Election of 1976

In the 1976 presidential campaign the greatest debates occurred within rather than between the major parties. Ford's challenge came from former California governor, movie actor, and television pitchman Ronald Reagan. Once a supporter of Franklin

In the 1976 election African American votes provided Jimmy Carter with the crucial margin for victory. Here Carter, a born-again Christian, worships with black leaders including (to his right) Coretta Scott King, widow of Martin Luther King Jr.

Roosevelt, Reagan discovered true conservatism after his marriage to actress Nancy Davis. The polished Reagan won crowds with an uncompromising but amiable conservatism. "Under Messrs. Nixon and Ford this nation has become Number Two in military power," he would tell enthusiastic audiences. Ford barely eked out the nomination at the convention.

Before 1976 few Democrats had ever heard of presidential hopeful James Earl (Jimmy) Carter. That allowed Carter, a peanut farmer and former governor of Georgia, to run as a Washington outsider. Carter managed to address controversial issues like abortion without offending large groups on either side. (He was "personally opposed to abortion" as a Christian but against a constitutional amendment overturning *Roe v. Wade*.) As a southerner and a "born-again" Christian he appealed to voters who had recently left the Democratic party.

Because both candidates rejected Great Society activism, party loyalty determined the outcome. Most voters (80 percent of Democrats and 90 percent of Republicans) backed their party's candidate, giving Carter 50.1 percent of the vote, a popular edge of almost 1.7 million. Carter's overwhelming margin among African Americans (90 percent) carried the South and offset Ford's margin among whites, especially in the western states, which all went Republican. Resounding Democratic majorities in Congress indicated more accurately than the presidential race how much the weak economy had hurt Ford's campaign.

Jimmy Carter

Jimmy Carter: Restoring the Faith

Jimmy Carter looked to invest the White House with a new simplicity and directness. Rather than the usual Inauguration Day ride down Pennsylvania Avenue in the presidential limousine, the new president and his wife, Rosalynn, walked. Carter shunned the formal morning coat and tails for a business suit. But Congress too was determined to see that the executive branch would no longer be so imperial. Because the president and many of his staff were relative newcomers to Washington, Carter found it difficult to reach many of his goals.

The Search for Direction

Although the president possessed an ability to absorb tremendous amounts of information, too often he focused on details. His larger goals remained obscure. Carter's key appointments reflected this confusion. In foreign policy, a rivalry arose between National Security Adviser Zbigniew Brzezinski and Secretary of State Cyrus Vance. Brzezinski harbored the staunch cold warrior's preoccupation with containing the Communist menace. Vance believed negotiations with the Communist bloc were both possible and potentially profitable. Stronger economic ties would reduce the risk of superpower conflict. At different times, Carter gravitated in both directions.

The president found that it was no easy task to make government more efficient, responsive to the people, and ethical. His first push for efficiency—calling for the elimination of 19 expensive pork barrel water projects—angered many in Congress, including the leaders of his own party. They promptly threatened to bury his legislative program. Even the weather seemed to conspire against the Carter administration. The winter of 1977 was one of the most severe in modern history, as heavy snows and fierce cold forced many schools and factories to close. Supplies of heating fuels dwindled, and prices shot up. Like Ford, Carter preferred voluntary restraint to mandatory rules for conserving energy and controlling fuel costs. The nation should adopt energy conservation measures as the "moral equivalent of war," he announced in April 1977.

Carter correctly sensed that conservation was the cheapest and most practical way to reduce dependence on foreign oil. But homilies about "helping our neighbors" did not sell the president's program. Most controversial were new taxes to discourage wasteful consumption. The American way, as domestic oil producers were quick to argue, was to produce more, not live with less. Americans were too wedded to gas-guzzling cars, air conditioners, inefficient electrical appliances, and warm houses to accept limits as long as fuel was available. Although Congress did agree

Department of Energy

to establish a cabinet-level Department of Energy, it rejected most of Carter's energy taxes and proposals to encourage solar energy alternatives.

By 1978 what Carter had called the "moral equivalent of war" was sounding more like its acronym: MEOW. Renewed administration efforts resulted in a weak National Energy Act, which provided tax credits for installation of energy-saving equipment, encouraged utility conversion to coal, and allowed prices to rise for newly discovered natural gas. As a result, the nation was ill prepared for the dislocation in international oil markets that followed the 1978 revolution against the shah of Iran. Renewed shortages allowed OPEC to raise prices steeply again. Carter could only complain that such hikes were unfair while asking Americans to lower thermostats to 65 degrees, take only essential car trips, and "drive 55."

The nuclear power industry had long touted its reactors as the best alternative to buying foreign oil. But on March 28, 1979, a valve stuck in the cooling system of the Three Mile Island nuclear power plant near Harrisburg, Pennsylvania. A cloud of radioactive gas floated into the atmosphere, and for a time, officials worried that they faced a meltdown of the reactor core. About a hundred thousand nearby residents fled their homes. The debate that followed revealed that public utilities had often constructed nuclear power plants before installing adequate safeguards or solving the problem of where to dispose of the nuclear radioactive wastes generated by the plant. Large construction cost overruns and concerns about safety inspired a growing antinuclear backlash. By the time of the accident at Three Mile Island, many energy experts believed that nuclear plants could be no more than a temporary response to the nation's long-term needs.

Three Mile Island

Three Mile Island gave President Carter another opportunity to press for his energy program, most of which Congress rejected. By May motorists once again faced long lines at the gas pumps. Not until spring 1980 did Congress pass a bill taxing some windfall profits of oil companies, regulating nuclear power more stringently, and establishing a solar-energy program. Carter had promoted sacrifice as a way to "seize control of our common destiny"; Congress preferred halfhearted measures that left America's energy future in OPEC's hands.

Oil shortages in the 1970s increased American dependence on nuclear power as an alternative energy source. The danger became evident in 1979 when an accident closed a nuclear power plant at Three Mile Island near Harrisburg, Pennsylvania. The large towers pictured on this *Time* Magazine cover are part of the cooling system in which the accident occurred. Huge construction costs, the unsolved problem of nuclear waste disposal, and safety issues soon soured many Americans on nuclear energy.

A Sick Economy

Rapid OPEC price hikes dislocated an economy built on cheap energy. Inflation shot from just below 6 percent in 1976 to almost 14 percent by 1979. Federal policies added to these inflationary pressures. Government subsidies to farmers continued to keep prices artificially high, as did laws protecting key industries like steel from foreign competition. As prices rose, wages could not keep pace. Workers took home more dollars, but inflation guaranteed that those dollars, in real terms, were worth less.

Within factories, the news was no better. If workers' real income was declining, so too was their productivity. It was difficult to produce efficiently when so many industrial plants had become outdated and union rules blocked innovation. Furthermore, wage contracts with built-in cost-of-living adjustments (COLAs) lowered the competitive standing of American industry in world markets. Plants in Japan and other Pacific Rim nations were newer, labor costs were lower, and the products turned out were often better.

The plight of the automobile industry reflected this economic malaise. Americans had turned in increasing numbers to higher-quality and more fuel-efficient Japanese cars. By 1978 Chrysler Corporation, the nation's tenth largest business enterprise, stood on the brink of bankruptcy unless the government provided a billion-dollar tax credit. The threat of massive unemployment persuaded Congress to guarantee a $1.5 billion loan. New financing and concessions from union workers

The Chrysler bailout

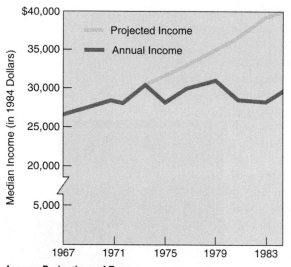

Income Projections of Two-Income Families, 1967–1984
Had the economy maintained its earlier growth, family earnings (Projected Income line) would have continued to rise. In an age of limits, family income leveled off instead. It stayed relatively even, rather than falling, only because more wives entered the workforce. Wages for individual workers fell when calculated in real dollars.

Human rights

brought Chrysler off the critical list. Still, disgruntled liberals and conservatives laughed when folk singer Tom Paxton announced,

> I'm changing my name to Chrysler.
> I'll be waiting in that great receiving line.
> So when they hand a billion grand out,
> I'll be standing with my hand out;
> Mister I'll get by.

"Hard choices," not stopgap loans, were needed to place the economy back on a competitive footing, the *Wall Street Journal* argued. Those choices might mean higher taxes and cuts in popular programs like social security or subsidies to farmers. But Carter called only for voluntary restraints on prices and wages while seeking to restore the strength of the dollar in international trade. Meanwhile, high interest rates struck hardest at American consumers addicted to installment and credit-card buying. Before Carter's economic remedies could work, OPEC began another round of oil price hikes that increased energy costs almost 60 percent. Interest rates shot up to almost 20 percent. Such high rates discouraged American consumers who bought on credit. With the Federal Reserve determined to keep interest rates high in order to dampen inflation, recession seemed to doom Carter's political future.

Leadership, Not Hegemony

Presidents battered on the domestic front often find that a strong foreign policy can restore power and prestige. Carter approached foreign policy with a set of ambitious yet reasonable goals. Like Nixon and Kissinger, he accepted the fact that in a post-colonial world, American influence could not be heavy-handed. The United States should exert "leadership without hegemony," Carter announced. Unlike Nixon and Kissinger, Carter believed that a knee-jerk fear of Soviet power and disorder had led Americans to support too many right-wing dictators simply because they professed to be anti-Communist. Carter reasserted the nation's moral purpose by giving a higher priority to preserving human rights.

Though this policy was often jeered at by foreign policy "realists," it did make a difference. At least one Argentinian Nobel Peace Prize winner, Adolfo Pérez Esquivel, claimed he owed his life to it. So did hundreds of others in countries like the Philippines, South Korea, Argentina, and Chile, where dissidents were routinely tortured and murdered. The Carter administration exerted economic pressure to promote more humane policies.

Debate over American influence in the Third World soon focused on the Panama Canal, long a symbol of American intervention in Latin America. Most Americans were under the impression that the United States owned the canal—or if it didn't, it at least deserved to. Senator S. I. Hayakawa of California spoke for defenders of the American imperial tradition when he argued, "It's ours. We stole it fair and square." In reality the United States held sovereignty over a 10-mile-wide strip called the Canal Zone and administered the canal under a perpetual lease. Since the 1960s Panamanians had resented, and sometimes rioted against, the American presence. Secretary of State Vance believed conciliation would reduce anti-American sentiment in the region. He convinced Carter in 1977 to sign treaties that would return the canal to Panama by 1999. The United States did reserve the right to defend and use the waterway.

From 1979 on, however, it was not Vance but Zbigniew Brzezinski who dominated the administration's foreign policy. Brzezinski was determined to reimpose a cold war framework, even in Latin America. Unrest troubled all the region's struggling nations, especially Nicaragua. Its dictator, Anastasio Somoza, had proved so venal and predatory that even the normally conservative propertied classes disliked him. Only the United States, at Brzezinski's urging, proved willing to support Somoza. With support from Nicaragua's business leaders, the Sandinistas toppled him. They then rejected American aid in favor of a nonaligned status and friendliness toward Communist Cuba.

Brzezinski and Central America

Revolution soon spread to neighboring El Salvador. The Carter administration also found it hard to make a case for the Salvadoran government, which had systematically murdered its own people as well as four American Catholic churchwomen. But hard-liners grew more alarmed when the Sandinistas began supplying the Salvadoran rebels. Worried about the spread of communism in Latin America, Carter agreed to assist El Salvador while encouraging the overthrow of the leftist government in Nicaragua.

The Wavering Spirit of Détente

The United States was not the only superpower with a flagging economy and problems in the Third World. The Soviet Union struggled with an aging leadership and an economy that produced guns but little butter. Even though the Russians led the world in oil production, income from rising oil prices was drained off by inefficient industries. Support for impoverished allies in Eastern Europe, Cuba, and Vietnam and attempts to extend Soviet influence in the Middle East and Africa proved costly.

Economic weakness made the Soviets receptive to greater cooperation with the United States. In that spirit President Carter and Soviet premier Leonid Brezhnev in 1977 issued a joint statement on a Middle East peace. But domestic opposition to any Soviet role as a peacemaker in the Middle East was immediate and powerful. Carter quickly rendered his understanding with Brezhnev inoperative. The Soviets then renewed arms shipments to Israel's archenemy, Syria. And in that troubled environment, Zbigniew Brzezinski flew off to Beijing to revive "the China card"— Kissinger's old hope of playing the two communist superpowers against each other. The United States extended formal recognition to China in 1979, and trade doubled within a year.

Reviving the China card

For the Russians the China card was a blow to détente. A potential Japanese-Chinese-American alliance threatened their Asian border. In an attempt to save détente Brezhnev met Carter at Vienna in 1979. Following through on the summit with President Ford, their talks produced an arms control treaty—SALT II—to limit nuclear launchers and missiles with multiple warheads. But neither the Americans nor the Soviets would agree to scrap key weapons systems. Conservative critics saw the SALT agreements as another example of the bankruptcy of détente. Nuclear "parity" (an equal balance of weapons on the American and Soviet sides) was to them yet another insulting symbol of declining American power. They successfully blocked ratification of the treaty in the Senate.

SALT II

With détente under attack Carter turned to Brzezinski and his hard-line approach to the Soviet Union. Confrontation and a military buildup replaced the Vance policy of negotiation and accommodation. The president expanded the defense budget, built

American bases in the Persian Gulf region, and sent aid to anti-Communist dictators whatever their record on human rights. The Soviet Union responded with similar hostility.

The Middle East: Hope and Hostages

Before World War I, the unstable Balkans had proved to be the spark setting off a larger conflict. For the superpowers in the 1970s and 1980s, the Middle East promised a similar threat. Oil and the Soviets' nearby southern border gave the area its geopolitical importance. Religious, tribal, national, and ethnic rivalries created chronic instability, dramatized by the wars between Israel and its Arab neighbors in 1948, 1956, 1967, and 1973. The United States had to balance its strong ties to oil-rich Saudi Arabia with its commitment to the survival of Israel.

Camp David Accords

Preservation of the peace was one key to American policy. As a result, Americans were greatly encouraged when President Anwar Sadat of Egypt made an unprecedented trip to Israel to meet with Prime Minister Menachem Begin. To encourage the peace process, Carter invited Begin and Sadat to Camp David in September 1978. For 13 days the talks waxed hot and cold, often breaking into argument and heated debate. When the marathon session ended, Carter had succeeded in helping the two long-standing rivals reach agreement. The 30-year state of war between Israel and Egypt finally ended. Israel accommodated Egypt by agreeing to withdraw from the Sinai Peninsula, which it had occupied since 1967. Carter compensated Israel by offering $3 billion in military aid. Begin and Sadat shared a Nobel Peace Prize that might just as fairly have gone to Carter for his critical role in pushing the two leaders to compromise.

The shah of Iran, with his American-equipped military forces, was another key to American hopes for stability in the Middle East. A strong Iran, after all, blocked Soviet access to the Persian Gulf and its oil. But in the autumn of 1978, the shah's regime was challenged by Iranian Islamic fundamentalists. They objected to the

It was at Camp David, in private talks sponsored by President Jimmy Carter, that Egyptian President Anwar el-Sadat (left) and Israeli Prime Minister Menachem Begin (right) hammered out a "Framework for Peace in the Middle East" as a first step toward ending decades of war and mistrust. For their efforts Begin and Sadat shared the Nobel Peace Prize of 1978, but the prize justifiably might have gone to Carter.

Western influences flooding their country, especially the tens of thousands of American advisers. Brzezinski urged Carter to support the shah with troops if necessary; Vance recommended meetings with the revolutionary leaders, distance from the shah, and military restraint.

Carter waffled between the two approaches. He encouraged the shah to use force but refused any American participation. When the shah's regime collapsed in February 1979, fundamentalists established an Islamic republic led by a religious leader, the Ayatollah Ruhollah Khomeini. The new government was particularly outraged when Carter admitted the ailing shah to the United States for medical treatment. In November student revolutionaries stormed the American embassy in Teheran, occupying it and taking 53 Americans hostage. In the face of this insult the United States seemed helpless to act. Would Muslim Shiite fundamentalists spread their revolution to neighboring Arab states? Worse yet, would the Soviets prey on a weakened Iran?

In fact, the Soviets were equally worried that religious zeal might spread to their own restless minorities, especially to Muslims within their borders. In December 1979 Leonid Brezhnev ordered Soviet troops into neighboring Afghanistan to subdue anti-Communist Muslim guerrillas. President Carter condemned the invasion, but the actions he took to protest it were largely symbolic, especially the decision to withdraw the American team from the 1980 Olympic games in Moscow. And he announced a Carter Doctrine: the United States would intervene unilaterally if the Soviet Union threatened American interests in the Persian Gulf.

A President Held Hostage

The spectacle of "America held hostage" shown on nightly newscasts dimmed Carter's hopes for another term. It did not help that Iran's turmoil led to another round of OPEC price hikes and new inflationary pressures.

Once again Carter faced a test of his leadership. Even more than the 53 Americans in Teheran, Jimmy Carter had been taken hostage by events there. His ratings in national polls sank to record lows (77 percent negative). Carter responded by reviving the cold war rhetoric of the 1950s and accelerating the development of nuclear weapons. But where the CIA in 1953 had successfully overthrown an Iranian government, an airborne rescue mission launched in 1980 ended in disaster. Eight marines died when two helicopters and a plane collided in Iran's central desert. Cyrus Vance, a lonely voice of moderation, finally resigned.

By 1980 the United States was mired in what Carter himself described as "a crisis of confidence." Visions of Vietnam, Central America, and the Middle East produced a nightmare of waning American power. Economic dislocations at home revived fears of a depression. None of these problems had begun with Jimmy Carter. The inflationary cycle and declining American productivity had their roots in the Vietnam era. And ironically, America's declining influence abroad reflected long-term success in bringing economic growth to Europe and the Pacific rim.

In that sense, Carter's failure was largely symbolic. But the uneasiness of the late 1970s reflected a widespread disillusionment with liberal social programs and even with pragmatic engineers like Carter. Had the government become a drag on the American dream? Tom Wolfe's Me Generation seemed to be rejecting Carter's appeals to sacrifice. It turned instead to promoters of self-help therapy, fundamentalist defenders of the faith, and staunch conservatives who promised both spiritual and material renewal for the 1980s.

chapter summary

In the aftermath of Vietnam, Watergate, the economic recession, and the energy crisis, the United States found itself mired in what President Jimmy Carter described as a "crisis of confidence."

- Despite the fragmentation of the left in the 1970s, consumer advocates and environmentalists kept alive the spirit of reform.

- Unpopular domestic political strategies like impoundment and the secret activities of the plumbers made Richard Nixon vulnerable to political attacks that followed relevations of White House involvement in the Watergate break-in and subsequent cover-up.

- Following a Senate investigation and the discovery of White House tapes containing the smoking gun linking the president to the cover-up, Richard Nixon resigned rather than face inevitable impeachment.

- As the nation's first unelected president, Gerald Ford inherited an office weakened by scandal, the determination of Congress to rein in an "imperial presidency," and his own decision to pardon Richard Nixon for his role in Watergate.

- Under Ford, Henry Kissinger became the real power in Washington as he pursued peace between Israel and its Arab neighbors, détente with the Soviet Union, and an easing of oil prices that burdened the American economy with high inflation.

- Jimmy Carter, unable to end the recession at home, pursued success abroad with a human rights policy and the negotiation of the Camp David Accords between Israel and Egypt—only to have the Soviet invasion of Afghanistan and the Iranian hostage crisis undermine his foreign policy.

additional reading

Of late, historians have become engaged in the debate over environmental reform. The story began with Barry Commoner, *The Closing Circle* (1971), which introduced many Americans to the core ideas of ecology. Donald Worster, *Nature's Economy* (3d ed., 1994) offers a rich history of the ideas informing environmentalism, and Samuel Hays, *Beauty, Health, and Permanence* (1987) surveys the postwar era. Charles Rubin, *The Green Crusade* (1994) challenges the methods and assumptions of some of the movement's central figures, including Rachel Carson and Commoner. Robert Gottlieb provides another critical perspective in *Forcing the Spring: The Transformation of the American Environmental Movement* (1996).

On consumerism see Robert Mayer, *The Consumer Movement* (1989). Among the books on Watergate are J. Anthony Lukas, *Nightmare* (2d ed., 1988), Stanley Kutler, *The Wars of Watergate* (1990) and *The Abuse of Power* (1997), and Stephen Ambrose, *Nixon: The Triumph of a Politician* (1989). Kissinger's own memoirs, *The White House Years* (1979) and *Years of Upheaval* (1982), contrast with the more critical studies by Walter Isaacson, *Kissinger* (1992) and Robert Schulzinger, *Henry Kissinger: Doctor of Diplomacy* (1991). For foreign policy during the Carter years, see Gaddis Smith, *Morality, Reason, and Power* (1986). Peter Carroll offers a survey of the 1970s in *It Seemed Like Nothing Happened* (1982). For a fuller list of readings, see the Bibliography.

Significant Events

1962 — 1962 Rachel Carson's *Silent Spring* published

1963 —

1964 —

1965 — 1965 Ralph Nader's *Unsafe at Any Speed* published

1966 — 1966 National Traffic and Motor Vehicle Safety Act

1967 —

1969 *Apollo 11* moon mission; Santa Barbara oil Spill; National Environmental Policy Act

1968 — 1970 First Earth Day; Environmental Protection agency created; Clean Air and Water acts; creation of OSHA; recession creates stagflation

1969 — 1971 Nixon adopts wage and price controls; *Swann v. Charlotte-Mecklenburg Board of Education;* Barry Commoner's *The Closing Circle* published; Pentagon Papers published

1970 —

1972 Woodward and Bernstein investigate Watergate burglary; Revenue Sharing Act; Nixon reelected

1971 — 1973 Ervin Committee hearings; Archibald Cox appointed special prosecutor; Spiro Agnew resigns; Saturday Night Massacre; War Powers Act; OPEC oil boycott triggers U.S. recession

1972 — 1974 *United States v. Nixon;* House adopt articles of impeachment; Nixon resigns; Ford becomes president; Fair Campaign Practices Act; Kissinger Arad-Israeli "shuttle" diplomacy; Ford-Brezhnev meeting at Vladivostok; Ford pardons Nixon

1973 —

1975 Thieu government falls in South Vietnam; Helsinki Summit; Energy Policy and Conservation Act; New York City faces bankruptcy

1974 — 1976 Carter defeats Ford

1975 —

1976 —

1977 — 1977 Panama Canal treaties

1978 — 1978 Revolution in Iran; Chrysler bailout; Camp David meetings on the Middle East

The Contested Ground of Collective Memory

Perhaps the nation's most cherished commemorative space lies along the mall in Washington, D.C. On the south side of its grassy boulevards the Smithsonian Institution holds room after room of artifacts from the nation's past. Across the way is the National Gallery of Art. And the mall's western end is dominated by memorials to Washington and Lincoln.

As the mall makes clear, a culture defines itself by the history it elevates in public places. Such markers are hardly limited to Washington. Town squares boast statues; post office murals portray the deeds of forebears; even sports arenas hang honored jerseys from the rafters. As scholars of commemoration point out, all societies find visible ways to affirm their collective values.

For the historian, the Washington mall presents one singular puzzle. Today the most frequently visited and publically acclaimed site also happens to be the least epic. Unlike Washington's 555-foot obelisk, this memorial does not soar. Unlike Lincoln's Greek temple, there are no columns evoking classical grandeur. In fact, at any reasonable distance the memorial cannot even be seen. It is simply a V of highly polished black granite incised into the ground—a V whose wide arms, each 247 feet long, converge 10 feet below the surface of the boulevard. This site is the Vietnam Veterans Memorial. Amid consider-

able controversy, the memorial was built in the wake of what was not only the nation's longest war but a divisive one that the United States lost.

Why, in a mall that takes special care to burnish the nation's proudest memories, has this memorial moved so many Americans?

That question intrigues historians, who have been drawn in recent years to the study of collective memories. Their interest is not the traditional concern over whether this or that recollection is accurate. At issue instead is the *process* of memory making: "how people together searched for common memories to meet present needs, how they first recognized such a memory and then agreed, disagreed, or negotiated over its meaning." At first, the definition seems unnecessarily complex. But the process of forging a collective memory is complex and can take years or even decades.

For example, most people today take for granted commemorative statues honoring two sworn enemies, Ulysses S. Grant and Robert E. Lee. Yet the tradition that allows us to venerate *both* generals is possible only because of a collective memory that emphasizes the heroism of all Americans who fought. That memory began to take form in the 1880s, when northern and southern veterans started to hold joint reunions.

But for African Americans of that era, Confederate leaders such as Lee symbolized slavery, making this emerging collective memory difficult to endorse. Frederick Douglass, a former slave and prominent Republican, warned that monuments honoring Lee would only "reawaken the confederacy." He argued that emancipation, not martial valor, deserved the most emphasis. To that end, he supported efforts of African Americans to erect the Freedman's Memorial Monument in Washington. The nation may "shut its eyes to the past . . ." he warned, "but the colored people of this country are bound to keep the past in lively memory till justice shall be done them." Even today the collective memories of the Civil War remain contested ground.

The same can be said for the war in Vietnam. By the 1980s the vast majority of Americans, whether they had opposed or defended American involvement in Vietnam, agreed that the war had been a mistake. How then would a nation used to celebrating success find a way to remember failure?

Vietnam veteran Jan Scruggs took an approach that was consciously apolitical. Rather than celebrate the war, Scruggs proposed a monument honoring the veterans themselves. From 1959 to 1975 over three million American men and women had served in Vietnam, of whom 75,000 returned home permanently disabled. Yet many felt their sacrifices had been lost amid the debate over the war. To promote reconciliation Congress in 1980 set aside a two-acre site on the mall, almost equidistant from the Washington and Lincoln memorials.

In the competition to select a design for the memorial over 1400 entries were submitted, all judged anonymously. The panel's unanimous choice came as a surprise: the entry of Maya Ying Lin, a Chinese American student at Yale University's School of Arts and Architecture. The idea for the design had occurred to her when she vis-

Maya Lin

ited the projected site. "I thought about what death is . . . ," Lin recalled, "a sharp pain that lessens with time, but can never heal over. A scar. Take a knife and cut open the earth, and with time the grass would heal it."

To view the monument a visitor descends a gentle incline. Because there are no steps, the handicapped have easy access. The memorial's polished black granite sets a somber tone, yet the open sky and reflection of the sun dispel any sense that this is a tomb or mausoleum. A person beginning the descent at first sees only a few names carved into the granite, but as the wall deepens, so does the procession of names. Altogether, 70 panels enumerate over 54,000 Americans who died in Vietnam. As Lin insisted, "you cannot ever forget that war is not just a victory or loss. It's really about individual lives."

The design immediately roused controversy. Some critics resented Lin's relative youth,

Despite his personal dislike of the statue (because the slave was kneeling rather than proudly standing) Frederick Douglass helped dedicate the Freedmen's Memorial Monument to Abraham Lincoln in 1876. Douglass believed emancipation was central to remembering the Civil War.

her ethnicity, and the fact that she was a woman. Others objected to the memorial's abstract and decidedly unheroic character. Lin had rejected a traditional approach in favor of a more feminine and nonwestern sensibility. "I didn't set out to conquer the earth, or to overpower it the way Western man usually does," she acknowledged. Ross Perot, a major financial supporter and later a presidential candidate, called the memorial a slap in the face to veterans. Others less politely described it as a public urinal. To them the black granite seemed a mark of shame and the descent below ground level an admission of wrongdoing.

So loud were these objections that in 1982 the secretary of the interior refused a construction permit until the memorial's sponsors agreed to add to the site a realistic sculpture by Frederick Hart. Hart, one of Lin's most outspoken critics, created three soldiers with an American flag, installed in 1984. This memorial provoked a female Vietnam veteran, Diane Carlson Evans, to lead a campaign for one additional monument, to honor the women of Vietnam.

This third sculptural piece (also realistic) portrays three nurses, one holding a wounded soldier.

Who captured the contested terrain of Vietnam commemoration? For the historian, the evidence lies in the crowds who flock to Maya Lin's memorial. Often, visitors seek out the name of someone they knew and make a rubbing of it to take with them. So many have left flowers, flags, personal objects, along with messages and poems, that the Park Service has created a museum for them. The messages vary wildly, from the hopeful and resolute to the sorrowful and disgusted:

Thank you for having the courage to fight . . .
You never would listen to anyone and you
  finally screwed up . . .
I am sorry Frankie, I know we left you,
  I hope you did not suffer too much . . .

Given such diverse reactions, Lin's choice of polished black marble was inspired. "The point," she said, "is to see yourself reflected in the names." The reflective marble and the wall's abstract design allow people to find their own meaning in the memorial.

For the historian who passes by—even a century from now—the site will always bear witness to Vietnam's contested ground. As on a real battlefield, the opposing sides stand arrayed: heroic, realistic figures on one side, challenged and ultimately outflanked by the wide embrace of that silent granite V. In aesthetic terms, traditional realism wars with abstract modernity. But that contrast only reflects a deeper cultural divide over the way we choose to remember war. Maya Lin's commemoration would have been unthinkable in 1946, when a triumphant United States was emerging as one of the world's superpowers. In an age of limits, when even superpowers falter, the gleam of black marble reflects faces that are less certain that martial valor can guarantee a nation's immortality.

BIBLIOGRAPHY. A useful introduction to the concept of collective memory is *Memory and American History* (1990), edited by David Thelen. Suzanne Vromen summarizes the controversy over Maya Lin's memorial in "The Vietnam Veterans Memorial, Washington, D.C.: Commemorating Ambivalence," *Focaal,* 25 (1995), 95–102. For more detail see Jan C. Scruggs and Joel T. Swerdlow, *To Heal a Nation* (1985), Brent Ashabranner, *Always to Remember: The Story of the Vietnam Veterans Memorial* (1988), and James Mayo's more interpretive *War Memorials as Political Landscapes* (1988). For Maya Ying Lin, see Peter Tauber, "Monument Maker," *New York Times Sunday Magazine,* February 24, 1991: 49–55, and a fine documentary film, "Maya Lin: A Strong, Clear Vision" (1995).

Chapter 32

THE CONSERVATIVE CHALLENGE

preview • As frustration mounted over an era of limits, conservatives pressed to restore traditional religious and social values. Ronald Reagan led the political charge with a program to reduce government regulations, raise military spending, and lower taxes. A newly conservative Supreme Court trimmed back more liberal rulings on civil rights, abortion, and the separation of church and state. But as the national debt rose sharply and a recession deepened, voters reined in the conservative movement.

*I*n the early 1970s San Diego city officials looked out at a downtown that was growing seedier each year as stores and shoppers fled to the suburban malls that ringed the city. Nor was San Diego an exception. Across the nation many once-thriving downtown retail centers became virtual ghost towns at the close of the business day. But San Diego found a way to bounce back. The city launched a $3 billion redevelopment plan calling for a convention center, a marina, hotels, and apartment complexes.

At the core of the redevelopment plan was Horton Plaza, a mall with the look of an Italian hill town. Stores with stucco facades fronted twisting pedestrian thoroughfares where Renaissance arches lured customers to upscale stores like Banana Republic, to jewelers, and to sporting goods shops. Jugglers and clowns wandered the streets, while guitarists serenaded passersby. Horton Plaza soon ranked just behind the zoo and Sea World as San Diego's prime tourist attraction. By 1986 it drew more than 12 million shoppers and tourists.

For all its extravagance, Horton Plaza was hardly an innovation. The first enclosed mall, Southdale Center, had been completed nearly 20 years earlier in Edina, Minnesota, near Minneapolis. Edina had good reason for enclosure: with chilling winters and 100 days a year of rain, shopping conditions were hardly ideal for outdoor strollers. The mall's planners had approached Victor Gruen, an architect seeking ways to reclaim urban downtowns from what he saw as the tyranny of the automobile. Gruen contrasted the pedestrian-dominated streets and fountain-filled squares of European villages with the acres of sterile parking lots surrounding suburban shopping centers. As he noted in his manifesto, *The Tired Heart of Our Cities,* automobiles added pollution and congestion to the urban environment. Southdale provided an alternative: a climate-controlled marketplace where shoppers could browse or get a bite to eat at a café without dodging cars or inhaling exhaust fumes.

At first retailers feared that customers who couldn't drive by their stores or park in front wouldn't stop and shop. Success dispelled those fears. By 1985, when Horton Plaza opened, Southdale had expanded to a three-level, 144-store complex, spreading over 1.1 million square feet. Nationwide, there were more shopping centers (25,000) than either school districts or hospitals. Some 2800 were enclosed, like Southdale.

With their soaring atriums, lavish food courts, and splashing fountains, malls became the cathedrals of American material culture. Shopping on Sunday rivaled churchgoing as the weekly family ritual. Whereas American youth culture centered on the high school in the 1950s and on college campuses in the 1960s, in the 1970s and 1980s it gravitated toward mall fast-food stores and video amusement arcades. For single men and women, malls became a place to find a date. Older people in search of moderate exercise discovered that the controlled climate was ideal for "mall walking." Malls even had their counterculture—"mall rats" who hung out and diverted themselves by shoplifting.

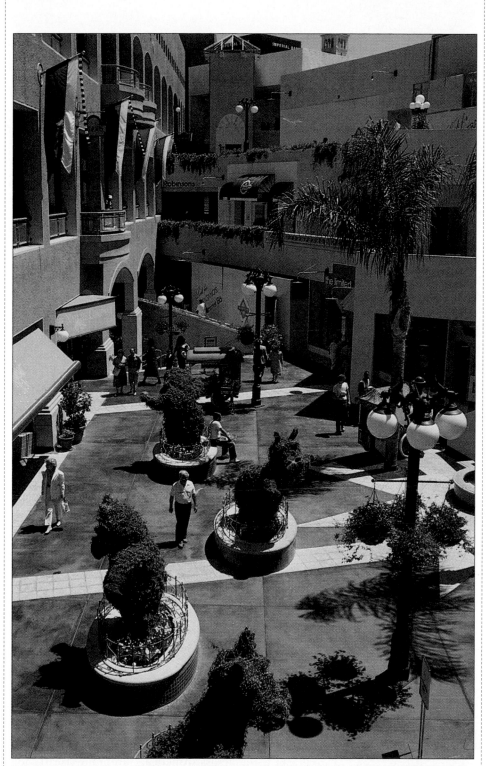

Bringing a touch of Disney World–style magic to urban redevelopment. San Diego succeeded in luring shoppers back to its downtown retail center with Horton Plaza, a replica of an Italian hill town.

**Malls as symbols
of an age**

The new cathedrals of consumption served as an appropriate symbol of a society that in the 1980s turned from protests and crusades to more private paths of spiritual fulfillment. Confronted by an age of limits, some people turned to evangelical religion, with its emphasis on the conversion of "born-again" individuals. Others extolled the virtues of the traditional family and lauded private charity and volunteerism as an alternative to the activist social policies of a modern welfare state. Along less orthodox paths, the "human potential movement" focused on techniques such as yoga, transcendental meditation, and "bioenergetics" to bring inner fulfillment.

So it was not surprising, perhaps, that in 1980 Ronald Reagan chose to evoke Puritan John Winthrop's seventeenth-century vision of an American "city on a hill"— that city Winthrop hoped would inspire the rest of the world. For conservatives, the image carried strong religious overtones. The Puritans, after all, sought to create a Christian commonwealth that was both well ordered and moral. Reagan's vision updated the Puritans', embracing nineteenth-century ideals of "manifest destiny" as well. (America should "stand tall," he insisted, as the world's number one military power.) And Reagan affirmed the laissez-faire ideals of the late nineteenth century, encouraging citizens to promote the public good through the pursuit of private wealth. "Government is not the solution to our problem," he asserted. "Government is the problem."

Critics contended that Reagan could no more succeed with his revolution than John Winthrop had been able to impose his Puritan utopia on a disorderly world. History, they argued, had shown that private enterprise was unable to prevent or regulate the environmental damage caused by acid rain, oil spills, or toxic waste dumps. Furthermore, a severely limited federal government would prove unable to cope with declining schools, urban violence, or the AIDS epidemic. To liberals the Reagan agenda amounted to a flight from public responsibility into a fantasy world no more authentic than the Italian hill town nestled in downtown San Diego. John Winthrop's austere vision risked being transformed into a city on a hill with climate control, where the proprietors of Muzak-filled walkways banished all problems beyond the gates of the parking lots.

Throughout the 1980s Americans gravitated between the born-again vision of the conservative revolution and more secular, centrist politics. Ronald Reagan and his successor George Bush both championed the causes of social conservatives, such as abortion rights, the call to allow prayer in public schools, and an end to affirmative action. But in an increasingly secular society, those social causes received less attention than Reagan's economic and military agenda: to cut taxes and increase military spending.

The Conservative Rebellion

In 1964 conservative candidate Barry Goldwater had proclaimed on billboards across America: "In Your Heart You Know He's Right." Beneath one of the billboards an unknown Democratic wag unfurled his own banner: "Yes—Extreme Right." In 1964 most citizens voted with the wag, perceiving Goldwater's platform as too conservative, too extreme, too dangerous for the times.

By 1980 rising prices, energy shortages, and similar economic uncertainties fed a growing resistance to a liberal agenda. Hard-pressed workers resented increased competition from minorities, especially those supported by affirmative action quotas and government programs. Citizens resisted the demands for higher taxes to support social welfare spending. The traditional family, too, seemed under siege as divorce rates and births to single mothers soared. Increasingly the political agenda was determined by those who wanted to restore a strong family, traditional religious values, patriotism, and limited government.

The United States was not the only nation to experience a resurgence of political conservatism, nationalism, and religious revival. The year before Ronald Reagan became president, Great Britain chose Margaret Thatcher as its first woman prime minister. Under her conservative leadership, "Thatcherism" became a synonym for cutting social programs, downsizing government, and privatizing state-controlled industries. Even within the Soviet bloc, rumblings could be felt as more citizens turned to religion after becoming disillusioned with the communist system. In China, the successors to revolutionary leader Mao Zedong introduced market capitalism into the economy during the 1980s.

The conservative tide worldwide

In some regions the conservative revival reflected a questioning of the liberal values that emerged from Europe's eighteenth-century Enlightenment. That era's faith in the rational spirit of science and technology had dominated Western thought for 200 years. Increasingly, fundamentalists were demanding that traditional religion become the center of public life. The student radicals in Iran who seized the American embassy feared that Western ideas would destroy their Islamic faith. They saw the theocracy of the Ayatollah Khomeini as a way to rid Iran of Western secularism. In Israel, religious conservatives became a political force as they too resisted secular trends in their society. And as we shall see, leadership of the Roman Catholic Church fell to Pope John Paul II, who rejected calls to liberalize doctrine on such issues as birth control, abortion, and the acceptance of female priests.

Born Again

Thus the call for a revival of religion loomed large in the conservative rebellion. That call came most insistently from white Protestant evangelicals. Fundamentalist Protestants had since the 1920s increasingly separated themselves from the older, more liberal denominations. In the decades after World War II their membership grew dramatically—anywhere from 400 to 700 percent, compared with less than 90 percent for mainline denominations. By the 1980s they had become a significant third force in Christian America, after Roman Catholics and traditional Protestants. The election of Jimmy Carter, himself a born-again Christian, reflected their new-found visibility.

Like fundamentalists of the 1920s, the evangelicals of the 1980s resisted the trend toward more secular values, especially in education. They pressed states and the federal government to adopt a "school prayer" amendment allowing officially sanctioned prayer in classrooms. They urged the teaching of "Creationism" as an acceptable alternative to Darwinian evolution. Frustrated with public schools, they created private Christian academies to insulate their children from the influence of "secular humanism." They condemned modernist notions of a materially determined world in which all truths were relative and in which circumstances rather than absolute moral precepts determined ethical behavior.

Although evangelicals denounced the modern media as secular agencies, they eagerly used broadcast technology to sell their message. Cable and satellite broadcasting allowed "televangelists" to reach national audiences. The Reverend Pat Robertson,

Evangelicals

During the late 1970s and the 1980s conservatives increasingly spoke out against abortion and in favor of the right to life for unborn fetus. Adopting the tactics of protest and civil disobedience once common to radicals in the 1960s, they clash here with pro-choice demonstrators outside Faneuil Hall in Boston.

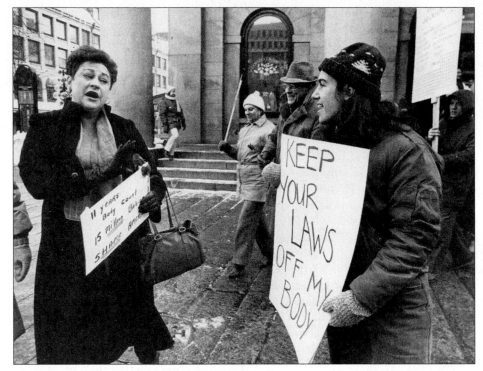

the son of a Virginia politician, introduced his "700 Club" over the Christian Broadcast Network from Virginia Beach, Virginia. His success inspired a "700 Club" regular, Jim Bakker, to launch a spin-off program called the "Praise the Lord Club"—PTL for short. Within a few years PTL had the largest audience of any daily show in the world. The content was Pentecostal in background: gospel singing, fervent sermons, faith healing, and speaking in tongues. The format, however, imitated that of sophisticated network "talk shows," including Bakker's Christian monologue, testimonials from celebrity guests, and musical entertainment.

It was the Reverend Jerry Falwell who first made the step from religious to political activism. In 1979 he formed the Moral Majority, Inc., an organization to attract campaign contributions and examine candidates around the country on issues important to Christians. America, Falwell proclaimed, possessed "more God-fearing citizens per capita than any other nation on earth." Using computerized mailing lists to identify donors and target audiences, the Moral Majority sent out more than a billion pieces of mail during the 1980 election.

The Catholic Conscience

American Catholics faced their own decisions about the lines between religion and politics. In the 1960s a social activist movement had arisen out of the church council known as Vatican II (1962–1965). Convened by Pope John XXIII and continued by his successor, Pope Paul VI, the council sought to revitalize the church and to reappraise its role in the modern world. The reforms of Vatican II reduced the amount of Latin in the mass, invited greater participation by ordinary church members, and encouraged closer ties to other Christians and to Jews.

Disturbed by these currents, Catholic conservatives found support for their views when the magnetic John Paul II assumed the papacy in 1979. Pope John Paul reined in the modern trends inspired by Vatican II. He ruled against a wider role for women in the church hierarchy and stiffened church policy against birth control. That put him at odds with a majority of American Catholics. The American church also faced a crisis as fewer young men and women chose celibate lives as priests and nuns.

Though conservative Catholics and Protestant evangelicals were sometimes wary of one another, they shared certain views. Both groups lobbied for the government to provide federal aid to parochial schools and fundamentalist academies. But it was the issue of abortion that attracted the greatest mutual support. Pope John Paul reaffirmed the church's teaching that all life begins at conception and that abortion amounts to murder of the unborn. Evangelicals, long suspicious of the power of secular technology and science, attacked abortion as another instance in which science had upset the natural moral order of life.

Pope John Paul II

c o u n t e r p o i n t

Defining the New Conservatism

It is not an easy task to pinpoint the underlying elements that unite the conservative rebellion. Some analysts, focusing on the movement's political leadership, have viewed matters cynically. Ronald Reagan, George Bush, and their ilk are simply members of the established and wealthy business elite who have tapped the resentments of ordinary people in order to attain power and provide others of their class with tax and regulatory relief. In this view, "hot button" issues like school prayer, abortion, and gun control can be used "as a means to ignite people who do not normally support Republicans," in the words of one conservative political adviser. Such an analysis emphasizes the differences within the conservative movement. On the one side, libertarians and free-enterprising businesspeople would keep the government out of regulating public morals as well as out of regulating the economy. On the other side cultural conservatives urge the government to take an active role in restoring morality.

Other historians concede the existence of this split but stress the cultural roots that unite both sides: the rejection of a liberalism that brought activism to government and a secular perspective to society at large. Conservatives of all stripes, these historians argue, hold up the values of a purer past, one free, in their view, from government interference and invigorated by a clear moral order. In 1955, when William F. Buckley Jr. began his conservative magazine, *National Review,* he proclaimed it his job to "stand athwart History and shout Stop!" In the eyes of some historians, it is this fixation on a past—an idealized one, at that—that unites the new right. "People became conservatives," suggested one analyst, "when they experienced 'the horrible feeling' that a society they took for granted might suddenly cease to exist."

The Media as Battleground

Both evangelists and political conservatives viewed the mass media as an establishment that was liberal in its politics and permissive in its tolerance of sex and violence. Because film and television had come to occupy such a prominent place in American life, they became a battleground where conservatives and liberals clashed.

By the late 1960s the film industry had left behind the strict standards of its Production Code, established in 1930 to police Hollywood's morals. Soft-core pornography with simulated sex and partial nudity had been exceeded in the 1970s

Topical sitcoms

by hard-core films. Even the traditionally inoffensive television programming became more topical. In 1971 producer Norman Lear introduced *All in the Family,* whose main character, Archie Bunker, was a rough-hewn blue-collar father. Archie treated his addlepated wife like a doormat, struggled to understand his modestly rebellious daughter, and shouted endless insults at his Polish American son-in-law. Americans were supposed to laugh at Archie's outrageous references to "Hebes," "Spics," and "Commie crapola," but many in the audience were not laughing. Some minority leaders charged that by making Archie lovable, the show legitimized the very prejudices it seemed to attack.

M*A*S*H, a popular television series launched in 1972, was more clearly liberal in its sympathies. Although the show was set in a medical unit during the Korean War, its real inspiration was Vietnam and the growing disillusionment with the war. *M*A*S*H* twitted bureaucracy, authority, pretense, bigotry, and snobbery. As newer liberal sensitivities emerged during the decade, the show adapted as well. "Hawkeye" Pierce and his fellow army doctors began as hard-drinking, womanizing foes of war and army life. Ten years later they still hated the army and war, but Hawkeye had become more vulnerable and respectful to women, while "Hot Lips" Houlihan was transformed from an overly patriotic military martinet into Margaret Houlihan, a career woman struggling for respect. For conservatives, antiauthoritarian shows like *M*A*S*H* demonstrated how deeply liberal values pervaded American life. That same bias, they believed, affected newspaper and television reporters. For their part, feminists and minority groups complained that television portrayed them as stereotypes, when it bothered to portray them at all.

Perhaps inevitably, the wars for the soul of prime time spilled into the political arena. Norman Lear, Archie Bunker's creator, went on to form People for the American Way, a lobbying group that campaigned for more diversity in American life and attempted to counteract pressure groups like the Moral Majority. Conservatives, looking to make a stronger political impact, in 1980 embraced an amiable former movie actor who had long preached their gospel.

The Election of 1980

Jimmy Carter might have been born again, but Ronald Reagan spoke the language of true conservatism. "I think there is a hunger in this land for a spiritual revival, a return to a belief in moral absolutes," he told his followers. Such a commitment to fundamentalist articles of faith was more important than the fact that Reagan actually had no church affiliation and seldom attended services.

The defection of many southern evangelical Protestants to the Republicans was just one of Jimmy Carter's problems. His rapid military buildup and cutbacks in social programs offended liberals, while rampant inflation and a weak economy alienated blue-collar voters. Preoccupied with the Iran hostage crisis, the president refrained from vigorous campaigning. When undecided voters saw Reagan as a candidate with the power to lead, the race turned into a landslide. Equally impressive, the Republicans won their first majority in the Senate since 1954. Reagan had splintered the New Deal Democratic coalition. Although his support was greatest among those who were over age 45, white, and earning more than $50,000 a year, he made striking gains among union workers, southern white Protestants, Catholics, and Jews. For the next decade and beyond, conservatives would dominate the terms of debate in public policy.

The Reverend Jerry Falwell's Moral Majority actively supported Ronald Reagan as well as other political candidates who shared the Moral Majority's social agenda.

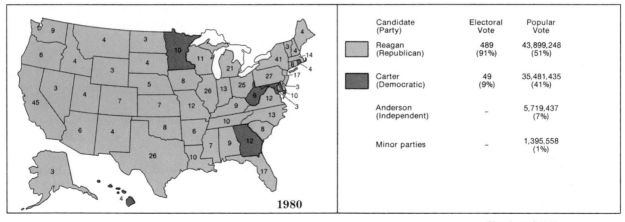

Candidate (Party)	Electoral Vote	Popular Vote
Reagan (Republican)	489 (91%)	43,899,248 (51%)
Carter (Democratic)	49 (9%)	35,481,435 (41%)
Anderson (Independent)	–	5,719,437 (7%)
Minor parties	–	1,395,558 (1%)

1980

Election of 1980

Ronald Reagan brought the bright lights of Hollywood to Washington. His managers staged one of the most extravagant

Prime Time with Ronald Reagan

inaugurations in the nation's history. Nancy Reagan became the most fashion-conscious first lady since Jackie Kennedy, while the new administration made the conspicuous display of wealth once again a sign of success and power.

The Great Communicator

Ronald Reagan came to Washington with a simple message. "It is time to reawaken the industrial giant, to get government back within its means, and to lighten our punitive tax burden," he announced on inauguration day. A strong national defense and a determined effort to revive the cold war crusade would reestablish the United States as the number one power in the world. Commentators began referring to the president as "the great communicator" because of his mastery of television and radio.

Reagan's skill as an actor obscured contradictions between his rhetoric and reality. With his jaunty wave and jutting jaw, he projected physical vitality and the charismatic good looks of John Kennedy. Yet at age 69, he was the oldest president to take office, and none since Calvin Coolidge slept as soundly or as much. Reagan had begun his political life as a New Deal Democrat, but over the next two decades he moved increasingly to the right. By the 1950s he had become an ardent anti-Communist, earning a reputation among conservatives as an engaging after-dinner speaker. General Electric made him its corporate spokesperson. In 1966 he began two terms as governor of California with a promise to pare down government programs and balance budgets. In fact, spending jumped sharply during his term in office. Similarly, he continued to champion family values, although he was divorced and estranged from some of his children.

Similar inconsistencies marked Reagan's leadership as president. Outsiders applauded his "hands-off" style: less management, not more, was what the nation needed after a succession of activist presidents from Kennedy to Carter. Reagan set the tone and direction, letting his advisers take care of the details. On the other hand, many within the administration, such as Secretary of the Treasury Donald Regan,

The Reagan style

Ronald Reagan's image as a plainspoken westerner helped build his reputation as "the great communicator."

were shocked to find the new president remarkably ignorant of and uninterested in important matters of policy. "The Presidential mind was not cluttered with facts," Regan lamented.

Nancy Reagan (aided by an astrologer) often dictated the president's schedule, helped select his advisers, and sometimes even determined the major issues the president addressed. Yet the public believed that the president was firmly in charge and, until the Iran arms scandal in 1986, consistently approved his conduct. His capacity for deflecting responsibility for mistakes earned him a reputation as the "Teflon president," because no criticism seemed to stick.

In addition, Reagan was blessed by remarkable fortune: a number of events beyond his control broke in his favor. The deaths of three aging Soviet leaders, beginning with Leonid Brezhnev in 1982, compounded that country's economic weakness and reduced Russian influence abroad. Members of the OPEC oil cartel quarreled among themselves, exceeded production quotas, and thus forced oil prices lower. The lower oil prices removed a major inflationary pressure on the American economy. The day Reagan took office, the Iranians released the American hostages, relieving the president of his first major foreign policy crisis. And when a would-be assassin shot the president in the chest on March 30, 1981, the wound was not life-threatening. His courage in the face of death impressed even his critics.

The Reagan Agenda

Reagan set out with two major goals: to reestablish the prestige of a presidency battered by Watergate and to weaken big government. His budget would become an instrument to reduce bureaucracy and to undermine activist federal agencies in the areas of civil rights, environmental and consumer protection, poverty programs, urban renewal, transportation, the arts, and education. In essence, Reagan wanted to return government to the size and responsibility it possessed in the 1950s, before the reforms of Kennedy and Johnson.

Supply-side economics

At the heart of the Reagan revolution was a commitment to supply-side economics, a program that in many ways resembled the trickle-down economic theories of the Harding-Coolidge era. Supply-side theorists argued that high taxes and government regulation stifled enterprising businesses and economic expansion. The key to revival lay in a large tax cut—a politically popular though economically controversial proposal. Such a cut threatened to reduce revenues and increase an already large deficit. Not so, argued supply-side economist Arthur Laffer. The economy would be so stimulated that tax revenues would actually rise, even though the tax rate was cut.

The president's second target for action was inflation, the "silent thief" that had burdened the economy during the Ford and Carter years. Reagan resisted certain traditional cures for inflation: tight money, high interest rates, and wage and price controls. He preferred two approaches unpopular with Democrats: higher unemployment and weakened unions to reduce labor costs.

Military Buildup

Lower public spending, a favorite Republican remedy, might have seemed one likely method of reducing inflation. But the third element of Reagan's agenda was a sharp rise in military outlays: a total of $1.5 trillion to be spent over five years. The American military would gain the strength to act unilaterally anywhere in the world to beat back communist threats. This goal was a remarkably expansive one: Presidents Nixon, Ford, and Carter had all looked to scale back American commitments, either through détente or by shifting burdens to allies in Western Europe. Reagan recognized no such limits. And rather than emphasize either nuclear defense or conventional weapons, Defense Secretary Caspar Weinberger lobbied Congress for both.

The Reagan Revolution in Practice

The administration soon found an opportunity to "hang tough" against unions when air traffic controllers went on strike, claiming that understaffing and long working hours threatened air safety. But because the controllers were civil service employees, the strike was technically illegal. Without addressing the merits of the controllers' complaints, Reagan simply fired them for violating their contract. The defeat of the air controllers signaled a broader attack on unions. When a recession enveloped the nation, major corporations wrung substantial concessions on wages and work rules. Organized labor witnessed a steady decline in membership and political power.

The president's war against government regulation took special aim at environmental rules. Conservatives, especially in the West, dismissed the environmental lobby as "nature lovers." Preservation of wild lands restricted mining, cattle grazing, farming, and real estate development—all powerful western industries. Reagan appointed westerner James Watt, an outspoken champion of this "sagebrush rebellion," to head the Interior Department. Watt, in turn, devoted himself to opening federal lands for private development, including lumbering and offshore oil drilling. A series of rash statements forced Watt to resign in 1983, but the administration continued to oppose most efforts to regulate or protect the environment. The president even refused to accept the conclusion of scientists that the smoke from coal-fired power plants in the Ohio valley was sending destructive acid rain over the lakes and forests of eastern Canada and the United States.

Environmental controversies

Most important, by the summer of 1981 Reagan had pushed his supply-side legislation through Congress. The Economic Recovery Tax Act provided a 25 percent across-the-board reduction for all taxpayers. The president hailed it, along with recently passed budget cuts, as an antidote to "big government's" addiction to spending and a stimulus to the economy. Opponents pointed out that an "equal" cut of 25 percent for all taxpayers left far more dollars in the hands of the wealthy.

Tax cuts

The Supply-Side Scorecard

The impact of Reagan's supply-side economics was mixed. By 1982 a recession had pushed unemployment above 10 percent. The Federal Reserve Board's tight money policies and high interest rates deepened the recession. But 1983 saw the beginning of an economic expansion that was to last through Reagan's presidency, thanks in part to increased federal spending and lowered interest rates. Then, too, falling energy costs and improved industrial productivity also contributed to renewed prosperity. Although many workers earned less per hour, the flow of women into the labor market kept family incomes from falling too much.

Even so, the Reagan tax cut was one of a series of policy changes that brought about a substantial transfer of wealth from poor and lower-middle-class workers to the upper middle classes and the rich. For the wealthiest Americans, the 1980s were the best of times. The top 1 percent commanded a greater share of the nation's wealth (37 percent) than at any other time since 1929. Their earnings averaged about $560,000 per year as opposed to $20,000 or less for the bottom 40 percent. What

The transfer of wealth

counterculture hippies were to the 1960s, high-salaried "yuppies" (young, upwardly mobile professionals) were to the 1980s.

On the surface, the buoyant job market seemed to signal a more general prosperity as well. By the end of Reagan's term, more than 14.5 million jobs had been created for Americans. Yet these jobs were spread unevenly by region, class, and gender. More than 2 million were in finance, insurance, real estate, and law, all services used by the wealthy, not the poor. In highly paid "Wall Street" jobs—those involving financial services—more than 70 percent went to white males, only 2 percent to African Americans. New employment for women was concentrated in the areas of health, education, social services, and government, where approximately 3 million jobs opened, most dependent on government support. New jobs for the poor (more than 3 million) were largely restricted to minimum wage, part-time, dead-end jobs in hotels, fast-food restaurants, and retail stores.

Because Reaganomics preached the virtues of free markets and free trade, the administration did little to discourage high-wage blue-collar jobs from flowing to cheap labor markets in Mexico and Asia. Furthermore, Reagan aimed the sharpest edge of his budget ax at programs for the poor: food stamps, Aid to Families with Dependent Children, Medicaid, school lunches, and housing assistance. The programs trimmed back least were middle-class entitlements like social security and Medicare. Those programs affected Americans over age 65, who, as social activist Michael Harrington observed, as a general class "are not now, and for a long time have not been, poor."

As more income flowed toward the wealthy and as jobs were lost to overseas competitors, the percentage of Americans below the poverty level rose from 11.7 percent in 1980 to 15 percent by 1982. There the level remained through the Bush administration. Reagan's successful war on inflation, which dropped to less than 2 percent by 1986, contributed to a rise in unemployment. Even during the recovery, the figure dropped below 6 percent of the workforce only in the months before the 1988 election. (By contrast, the highest rate under Jimmy Carter was 5.9 percent.) Thus the Reagan boom was an uneven one despite continued economic expansion.

Poverty in America, 1970–1993 Social security and other income supplements to older Americans reduced their rate of poverty. For all other traditionally impoverished groups the prosperity of the Reagan-Bush years left them slightly worse off than in 1980.

The Military Buildup

At the core of the Reagan revolution was a sharp rise in military spending. Outlays rose from less than $200 billion under Presidents Ford and Carter to almost $300 billion in 1985, when growing opposition led to some restraint. The largest increases were for expensive strategic nuclear weapons systems. The Reagan administration argued that a nuclear buildup would strengthen the position of American negotiators during arms reductions talks.

Huge costs were not the only source of criticism. When Reagan's tough-talking defense planners spoke about "winning" a nuclear exchange, they revived the

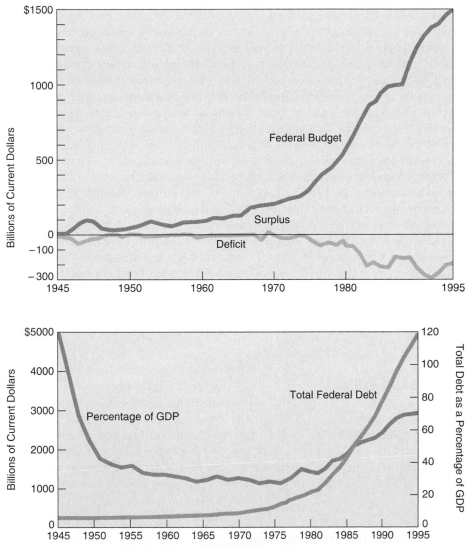

The Federal Budget and Surplus/Deficit, 1945–1995 Despite Reagan's campaign pledge to reduce federal spending, the federal deficit soared higher during his presidency than at any other time in the nation's history. During the Bush presidency the deficit continued to climb despite the restrictions of the Gramm-Rudman Act, passed in 1985. The size of the national debt became a central issue in the 1992 presidential election.

antinuclear peace movement across Europe and America. The bishops of the American Catholic church felt moved to announce their opposition to nuclear war, and scientists warned that the debris in the atmosphere from an atomic exchange might create a "nuclear winter" fatal to all life on earth. Equally vocal critics singled out the cost of the Pentagon's armament list. Stories of $600 toilet seats and $7000 coffeepots made headlines, but more serious were the failures of entire multi-billion-dollar weapons systems. One of the president's favorite programs was the Strategic Defense Initiative, or SDI. Nicknamed "Star Wars" after a popular science fiction film, the program spent billions of dollars trying to establish a space-based missile system that would be merely "defensive." Most scientists contended that the project was as fantastic as the movie.

Star Wars

The combination of massive defense spending and substantial tax cuts left the federal government awash in red ink. Annual deficits soared to more than $200 billion. By the end of his term, Reagan had run up more debt within eight years than the federal government had accumulated in its entire 200-year history. Furthermore, with interest rates so high, the value of the dollar soared on world markets. The strong dollar pushed up the cost of American exports in foreign markets. As American exports declined, imports from abroad (such as Japanese autos) captured a larger market share in America. From the end of World War I until the beginning of the Reagan years, the United States had been the world's leading creditor nation. By 1986 it had become the world's largest debtor.

The spending excesses of the Reagan agenda would come to haunt his conservative successors. For the time being, however, Ronald Reagan's popularity seemed unassailable. In 1984 he easily won a second term, gaining 59 percent of the vote in his run against Democrat Walter Mondale of Minnesota. (Mondale's running mate, Geraldine Ferraro of New York, was the first female candidate for the vice presidency.) Reagan remained his sunny, unflappable self, seeming to enjoy the presidency immensely. "The 75-year-old man is hitting home runs," rhapsodized *Time* magazine at the beginning of his second term. In reality, Reagan would soon be tested by a series of crises arising out of his more aggressive stance toward foreign policy.

Standing Tall in a Chaotic World

Reagan brought to the conduct of foreign policy the same moral stance that shaped his approach to domestic affairs. Reagan wanted the United States to stand tall: to adopt a policy that drew bold, clear lines as a means of restoring American prestige. But turmoil abroad demonstrated that bold policies were not always easy to carry out. And because the president remained indifferent to most day-to-day details, he was at the mercy of those officials who put into effect his aggressive anti-Communist foreign policy.

Terrorism in the Middle East

In the Middle East, the passions of religious factions demonstrated how difficult it was to impose order, even for a superpower like the United States. In 1982 President Reagan sent American Marines into Lebanon as part of a European-American peacekeeping force. His hope was to bring a measure of stability to a region torn by civil war. But in trying to mediate between Lebanon's religious and political sects, the American "peacekeepers" found themselves dragged into the fighting. Terrorists retaliated by blowing up a U.S. Marine barracks in October 1983, killing 239. The president then ordered American troops withdrawn.

Just as hostage-taking in Iran had frustrated the Carter administration, terrorist attacks by Islamic fundamentalists bedeviled Reagan. In 1985 terrorists took additional hostages in Lebanon; others hijacked American airline flights, killed an American hostage on a Mediterranean cruise ship, and bombed a nightclub where American soldiers met in West Germany. In such situations, the president's public response was always uncompromising: "Let terrorists beware: . . . our policy will be one of swift and effective retribution."

But against whom should the United States seek revenge? American intelligence agencies found it extremely difficult to collect reliable information on the many political and terrorist factions. In 1986 the president sent bombers to attack targets in Libya, whose anti-American leader, Colonel Muammar al-Qadhafi, had links to terrorists. But so did the more powerful states of Syria and Iran.

Mounting Frustrations in Central America

At first, a policy of standing tall seemed easier closer to home. In 1983, the administration launched an invasion of Grenada, a small Carribbean island whose government was challenged by pro-Castro revolutionaries. U.S. forces crushed the rebels and succeeded in protecting several hundred American medical students attending school there. But the invasion was largely a symbolic gesture.

Grenada invasion

More frustrating to the president, Nicaragua's left-wing Sandinista government had established increasingly close ties with Cuba. In 1981 Reagan extended aid to the antigovernment "Contra" forces. When critics warned that Nicaragua could become another Vietnam, the president countered that the Contras were "freedom fighters," battling in the spirit of America's Founding Fathers. Although the Contras did include some moderate democrats and disillusioned Sandinistas, most of their leaders had served the brutal Somoza dictatorship that the Sandinistas had toppled in 1979.

Reagan might have sought a negotiated settlement between the Contras and the Sandinistas. Instead he allowed the CIA to help the Contras mine Nicaraguan harbors in hopes of overthrowing the Sandinistas outright. When some of the mines exploded, damaging foreign ships in violation of international law, even some conservative senators were dismayed. Congress adopted an amendment sponsored by Representative Edward Boland of Massachusetts, explicitly forbidding the CIA or "any other agency or entity involved in intelligence activities" from spending money to support the Contras "directly or indirectly." The president signed the Boland Amendment, though only grudgingly.

Boland Amendment

The Iran-Contra Connection

Thus by mid-1985 Reagan policy makers felt two major frustrations. First, Congress had forbidden any support of the Contras in Central America, and second, Iranian-backed terrorists continued to hold hostages in Lebanon. In the summer of 1985 a course of events was set in motion that eventually linked these two issues.

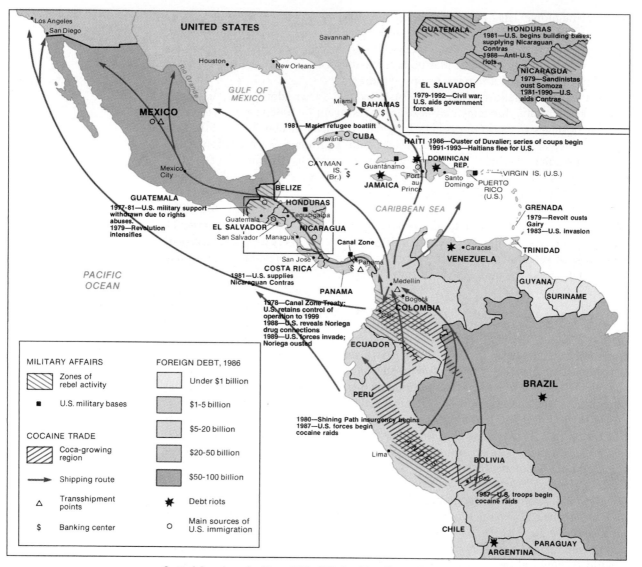

Central American Conflicts, 1974–1990 President Reagan's attempts to overthrow the Sandinista government in Nicaragua and to contain communism focused American attention on Latin America. So too did the staggering debts Latin countries owed to banks in America and elsewhere. Equally distorting to the hemisphere's social and economic fabric was the sharp rise in the drug trade organized by criminal syndicates. Most notorious was the Medellín cartel, which operated from a remote region in Colombia, shipping drugs through havens in Panama and the Bahamas into the United States while depositing its enormous profits in banks in Miami and offshore banking centers such as the Cayman Islands. The war on drugs led President Bush to invade Panama in December 1989.

Arms for hostages deal

The president made it increasingly clear that he wanted to find a way to free the remaining hostages. National Security Adviser Robert McFarlane, eager to please, suggested opening a channel to "moderate factions" in the Iranian government. If the United States sold Iran a few weapons, the grateful moderates might use their influence in Lebanon to free the hostages. But an agreement to exchange arms for hostages would violate the president's often-repeated vow never to pay ransom to

Oliver North successfully took the offensive in his testimony before the congressional committee investigating the Iran-Contra scandals. Here he delivers a pro-Contra lecture to his interrogators.

terrorists. Still, Reagan apparently approved the initiative. Over the following year, four secret arms shipments were made to Iran. One hostage was set free.

Reagan's secretaries of state and defense both had strongly opposed the notion of trading arms for hostages. "This is almost too absurd to comment on," Defense Secretary Weinberger commented when he was first told of the proposal. Surprisingly, however, both men were kept largely uninformed of the shipments, precisely because their opposition was well known. McFarlane's successor as national security adviser, Admiral John Poindexter, had the president sign a secret intelligence "finding" that allowed him and his associates to pursue their mission without informing anyone in Congress or even the secretaries of defense and state. Because the president ignored the details of foreign policy, McFarlane, Poindexter, and their aides had assumed the power to act on their own.

The man most often pulling the strings seemed to be Lieutenant Colonel Oliver "Ollie" North, a junior officer under McFarlane and later Poindexter. A Vietnam veteran with a flair for the dramatic, North was impatient with bureaucratic procedures. He and McFarlane had already discovered a way to evade the Boland Amendment in order to secretly aid the Contras. McFarlane told Saudia Arabia and several other American allies that the Contras desperately needed funds. As a favor, the Saudis deposited at least $30 million in Swiss bank accounts set up to launder the money. North then used the cash to buy weapons that were delivered to Central America.

The two strands of the secret missions came together in January 1986, when North hit upon the idea that the profits made selling arms to Iran could be siphoned off to buy weapons for the Contras. The Iranian arms dealer who brokered the deal thought it a great idea. "I think this is now, Ollie, the best chance, because . . . we never get such good money out of this," he laughed, as he was recorded on a tape North himself made. "We do everything. We do hostages free of charge; we do all terrorists free of charge; Central America free of charge."

Cover Blown

Through the fall of 1986, both operations remained hidden from view. That changed abruptly when reports of the Iranian arms deal were leaked to a Lebanese newspaper. Astonished reporters besieged the administration, demanding to know how secret arms sales to a terrorist regime benefited the president's antiterrorist campaign. As the inquiry continued, the link between the arms sales and the Contras was discovered. Attorney General Edwin Meese moved so slowly to investigate that North and his secretary had time to shred crucial documents. Still, enough evidence remained to make the dimensions of the illegal operations clear.

Irangate

The press nicknamed the scandal "Irangate," comparing it to Richard Nixon's Watergate affair. But Irangate raised more troubling issues. Watergate sprang from political tricks that ran amok. The president had led the cover-up to save his own political skin. But the Iran-Contra congressional hearings, held during the summer of 1987, left the role of President Reagan unexplained. Poindexter testified that he had kept Reagan in ignorance "so that I could insulate him from the decision and provide some future deniability for the president if it ever leaked out. . . . On this whole issue, you know, the buck stops here, with me." In that way, Iran-Contra revealed a presidency out of control. An unelected segment within the government had taken upon itself the power to pursue its own policies beyond legal channels.

As one analyst noted, Reagan's ideological approach to foreign policy tended to give his aides an "absolute certainty of their own rightness." Because they were operating with "pure hearts," they found it all too easy to justify working with "dirty hands." In doing so, however, they subverted the constitutional system of checks and balances.

From Cold War to Glasnost

Because few members of Congress wanted to impeach a genial president, the hearings came to a sputtering end. Reagan's popularity returned, in part because of substantial improvement in Soviet-American relations. By the 1980s the Soviet Union

Soviet Premier Mikhail Gorbachev (right) used his summits with Ronald Reagan to reduce Soviet-American tensions, although the spirit of *glasnost* did not ease the skirmishes between his wife, Raisa, and Nancy Reagan, who waged a quiet war over fashion and ideology. Gorbachev came to rival Reagan as a "great communicator," with many Americans applauding his efforts to reform Soviet society and to slow the arms race.

was far weaker than American experts, including the CIA, had ever recognized. The Soviet economy stagnated; the Communist party was mired in corruption. The war in Afghanistan had become a Russian Vietnam. By accelerating the arms race, Reagan placed additional pressure on the Russians.

In 1985 a fresh spirit entered the Kremlin. Unlike the aged leaders who preceded him, Mikhail Gorbachev was young and saw the need for reform within the Soviet Union. Gorbachev's fundamental restructuring, or perestroika, set about improving relations with the United States. He reduced military commitments and adopted a policy of openness (glasnost) about problems in the Soviet Union. In October, the two leaders held their second summit in Reykjavík, Iceland. Gorbachev dangled the possibility of abolishing all nuclear weapons. Reagan seemed receptive to the idea, apparently unaware that if both sides eliminated all nuclear weapons, Soviet conventional forces would far outnumber NATO troops in Europe. In the end, the president refused to sacrifice his Star Wars system for so radical a proposal.

Mikhail Gorbachev

Despite the immediate impasse, negotiations continued after the summit. In December 1987 Reagan traveled to Moscow, where he signed the Intermediate Nuclear Force treaty, which eliminated an entire class of nuclear missiles with ranges of 600 to 3400 miles. Both sides agreed to allow on-site inspections of missile bases and the facilities where missiles would be destroyed.

The Election of 1988

Thus as the election of 1988 approached, the president could claim credit for improved relations with the Soviet Union. Loyalty to Ronald Reagan made Vice President George Bush the Republican heir apparent. Bush appealed most to party professionals, white Protestants, and the affluent middle class that had benefited from Reaganomics.

The Democratic challenger, Governor Michael Dukakis of Massachusetts, tried to call attention to weaknesses in the American economy. An alarming number of savings and loan institutions had failed, and Dukakis recognized that poor and even many middle-class Americans had lost ground during the 1980s. But Bush put the lackluster Dukakis on the defensive. With the economy reasonably robust, Bush won by a comfortable margin, taking 54 percent of the popular vote. The Reagan agenda remained on track.

President George Herbert Walker Bush was born to both privilege and politics. The son of a Connecticut senator, he

An End to the Cold War

attended an exclusive boarding school and then the ivy-league Yale University. That background made him part of the East Coast establishment often scorned by more populist Republicans. Yet once the oil business lured Bush to Texas, he moved to the right, becoming a Goldwater Republican when he ran for the Senate in 1964. Although he once supported Planned Parenthood and a woman's right to abortion, Bush eventually adopted the conservative right-to-life position. In truth, foreign policy interested him far more than domestic politics. But in the end, inattention to domestic issues proved his undoing as the economy slid into recession.

A Post–Cold War Foreign Policy

To the astonishment of most western observers, Mikhail Gorbachev's reform policies led not only to the collapse of the Soviet empire but to the breakup of the Soviet Union itself. In December 1988, Gorbachev spoke in the United Nations of a "new world order." To that end he began liquidating the Soviet cold war legacy, as the last Russian troops began leaving Afghanistan and then Eastern Europe.

The fall of communism

Throughout 1989 Eastern Europeans began to test their newfound freedom. In Poland, Hungary, Bulgaria, Czechoslovakia, and most violently in Romania, Communist dictators fell from power. Nothing more inspired the world than the stream of celebrating East Germans pouring through the Berlin Wall in November 1989. Within a year the Wall, a symbol of Communist oppression, had been torn down and Germany reunified. Although Gorbachev struggled to keep together the 15 republics that made up the U.S.S.R., the forces of nationalism and reform pulled the Soviet Union apart. The Baltic republics—Lithuania, Latvia, and Estonia—declared their independence in 1991. Then in December, the Slavic republics of Ukraine, Belarus, and Russia formed a new Commonwealth of Independent States. By the end of December eight more of the former Soviet republics had joined the loose federation. Boris Yeltsin, the charismatic president of Russia, became the Commonwealth's dominant figure. With no Soviet Union left to preside over, Gorbachev resigned as president.

The Berlin Wall had stood since August 1961 as a symbol of cold war tensions. Thus, Americans joined these Germans in celebrating the Wall's destruction. At long last, the cold war seemed to have ended.

President Bush's response to these momentous changes was cautious: a policy of "status quo plus," one aide called it. Although the president increasingly supported Gorbachev's reforms, even if he had wished to aid Eastern Europe and the new Commonwealth states, soaring deficits at home limited his options. The administration seemed to support the status quo in Communist China, too. When in June 1989 China's aging leadership crushed students rallying for democratic reform in Beijing's Tiananmen Square, Bush muted American protests.

The fall of the Soviet Union signaled the end of a cold war that, more than once, had threatened a nuclear end to human history. At a series of summits with Russian leaders, the United States and its former rivals agreed to sharp reductions in their stockpiles of nuclear weapons. The Strategic Arms Reduction Treaty (or START), concluded in July 1991, far surpassed the limits negotiated in earlier SALT talks. By June 1992 Bush and Yeltsin had agreed to even sharper cuts.

The Gulf War

With two superpowers no longer facing off against each other, what would the "new world order" look like? If anything, regional crises loomed larger. President Bush moved to project American power more forcefully in the Middle East. But civil wars in Eastern Europe and Africa demonstrated that a world order beyond the shadow of the cold war might be more chaotic and unpredictable than ever.

Instability in the Middle East brought Bush's greatest foreign policy challenge. From 1980 to 1988 Iran and Iraq had battered each other in a debilitating war. During those years the Reagan administration assisted Iraq with weapons and intelligence, until at last it won a narrow victory over Iran's fundamentalists. But Iraq's ruthless dictator, Saddam Hussein, had run up enormous debts. To ease his financial crisis, Saddam cast a covetous eye on his neighbor, the small oil-rich sheikdom of Kuwait. In August 1990, 120,000 Iraqi troops invaded and occupied Kuwait, catching the Bush administration off guard. Would Saddam stop there?

Saddam Hussein

"We committed a boner with regard to Iraq and our close friendship with Iraq," admitted Ronald Reagan. Embarrassed by having supported the pro-Iraqi policy, Bush was determined to thwart Saddam's invasion of Kuwait. The president successfully coordinated a United Nations–backed economic boycott. Increasing the pressure further, he deployed half a million American troops in Saudi Arabia and the Persian Gulf. By November Bush had won a resolution from the Security Council permitting the use of military force if Saddam did not withdraw.

On January 17, 1991, planes from France, Italy, Britain, Saudi Arabia, and the United States began bombing Baghdad and Iraqi bases. Operation Desert Storm had begun. After weeks of merciless pounding from the air, ground operations shattered Saddam's vaunted Republican Guards in less than 100 hours. In an act of spite, Saddam resorted to ecoterrorism. His forces set Kuwait's oil fields ablaze and dumped huge quantities of crude oil into the rich Persian Gulf ecosystem. It did him no

Operation Desert Storm

War with Iraq: Operation Desert Storm When Saddam Hussein invaded oil-rich Kuwait on August 2, 1990, the United States formed a coalition to force out the Iraqis. (Although Turkey was not a formal member, it allowed its airfields to be used. Israel remained uninvolved to avoid antagonizing Arab coalition members.) The coalition launched Operation Desert Storm in January 1991; land forces invaded on February 24 (Operation Desert Saber), routing Iraqi troops, who left Kuwait in ruin and its oil fields aflame.

good: by the end of February Kuwait was liberated, and nothing stood between Allied forces and Iraq's capital, Baghdad. Bush was unwilling to advance that far—and most other nations in the coalition agreed. If Hussein were toppled, it was not clear who in Iraq would fill the vacuum of power. But long after the war ended, sanctions had still not driven the dictator from power. And with tensions still high between Israel and its Arab neighbors, the Middle East remained a volatile region.

Domestic Doldrums

Victory in the Gulf War so boosted the president's popularity that aides brushed aside the need for any bold domestic program. "Frankly, this president doesn't need another single piece of legislation, unless it's absolutely right," asserted John Sununu, his cocky chief of staff. "In fact, if Congress wants to come together, adjourn, and leave, it's all right with us." That attitude suggested a lack of direction that proved fatal to Bush's reelection hopes.

At first, Bush envisioned a domestic program that would soften the harsher edges of the Reagan revolution. He promised to create a "kinder, gentler" nation. Yet pressures from conservative Republicans kept the new president from straying too far in the direction of reform. Although he appointed a well-respected conservationist, William Reilly, to head the Environmental Protection Agency, Reilly often found his programs opposed by other members of the administration. When delegates from 178 nations met at an "Earth Summit" in Rio de Janeiro in 1992, the president opposed efforts to draft stricter rules to lessen the threat of global warming. Bush did sign into law the sweeping Clean Air Act passed by Congress in 1990. But soon after, Vice President Dan Quayle established a "Council on Competitiveness" to rewrite regulations that corporations found burdensome.

Environmental issues

Similarly, the president called for reform of an educational system whose quality had declined through the 1980s. But while he convened a well-publicized "Education Summit" in 1989, the delegates issued a modest set of goals only after the president was urged to do so by his cochair at the summit, Governor Bill Clinton of Arkansas. Secretary of Housing and Urban Development Jack Kemp searched for ways to improve the plight of the homeless and empower poor urban communities by promoting economic "free enterprise zones." But Kemp too found himself frustrated by the president's unwillingness to push hard for any of his programs.

The Conservative Court

Although Presidents Reagan and Bush both spoke out against abortion, affirmative action, the banning of prayer in public schools, and other conservative social issues, neither made action a legislative priority. Even so, both presidents shaped social policy through their appointments to the Supreme Court. Reagan placed three members on the bench, including in 1981 Sandra Day O'Connor, the first woman to sit on the high court. Bush nominated two justices. As more liberal members of the Court retired (including William Brennan and Thurgood Marshall), the decisions handed down became distinctly more conservative.

On two occasions, the Senate challenged this trend. In 1987, it rejected Robert Bork, a nominee whose opposition to long-established Court policies on privacy and civil rights led even some Republicans to oppose him. But this fight proved so exhausting that the Senate quickly approved President Reagan's alternate choice, Antonin Scalia. In the end, Scalia proved to be one of the Court's most conservative members.

In 1991 the Senate also hotly debated President Bush's nomination of Clarence Thomas, an outspoken black conservative and former member of the Reagan administration. The confirmation hearings became even more heated when Anita Hill, a woman who had worked for Thomas, testified that he had sexually harassed her. Because Hill was a professor of law and herself a Reagan conservative, her often graphic testimony riveted millions of television viewers. Suddenly the hearings raised new issues. Women's groups blasted the all-male Judiciary Committee for keeping Hill's allegations private until reporters uncovered the story. Thomas and his defenders accused his opponents of using a disgruntled woman to help conduct a latter-day lynching. In the end the Senate narrowly voted to confirm, and Thomas joined Scalia as one of the Court's most conservative members.

Evidence of the Court's changing stance came most clearly in its attitude toward affirmative action—those laws that gave preferred treatment to minority groups in order to remedy past discrimination. State and federal courts and legislatures had used techniques such as busing and the setting of quotas such as to overturn past injustices. In 1978, however, the Court began to set limits on affirmative action. In *Bakke v. Regents of the University of California* (1978), the majority ruled that college admissions staffs could not set fixed quotas, although they could still use race as a guiding factor in trying to create a more diverse student body. Increasingly, the Court made it easier for white citizens to challenge affirmative action programs. At the same time it set higher standards for those who wished to put forward a claim of discrimination. "An amorphous claim that there has been past discrimination in a particular industry cannot justify the use of an unyielding racial quota," wrote Justice O'Connor in 1989. By 1996 a federal circuit court had gone so far as to claim (in *Hopwood v. State of Texas et al.*) that race could not be a factor in college admissions.

Court decisions on abortion and religion in public schools demonstrated a similar desire to set limits on the established precedents. *Planned Parenthood v. Casey* (1992) upheld a woman's constitutional right to an abortion, but it also allowed states to place new restrictions on the procedure. Other Court decisions let stand

The Clarence Thomas hearings

Justice Clarence Thomas survived a bitter Senate battle during his Supreme Court confirmation hearings. Here, he is sworn in by Chief Justice William Rehnquist as Thomas's wife and President George Bush and Barbara Bush look on. Thomas's conservative views on abortion and affirmative action were later confirmed by the votes he cast as a justice.

Daily Lives

PUBLIC AND PRIVATE SPACE

Life in the Underclass

During the 1880s Jacob Riis "discovered" a class of people he described as invisible. They were "individuals who have lost connection with home life, or never had any, or whose homes had ceased to be sufficiently separated, decent, and desirable to afford what are regarded as ordinary wholesome influences of home and family." A century later investigators for the *Chicago Tribune* discovered in American cities "a lost society dwelling in enclaves of despair and chaos that infect and threaten the communities at large." This ghetto world of dilapidated housing, poverty, and despair was home to as many as 5 million Americans. Yet while many of its spaces and avenues were public, it too was invisible, except when its private behavior became so violent or criminal that the news forced the broad middle class to pay attention.

Like Riis the *Tribune* reporters portrayed this urban blight through the story of individual lives. Dorothy Sands was one. In 1957 Dorothy,

her mother, Ora Streeter, and the rest of her family lived in a one-room shack in rural Mississippi. Conditions there had improved little since the days of Reconstruction. The shack had neither electricity nor indoor plumbing. Ora finally decided to escape the South, her job, and her abusive husband. She took six small children to Chicago, where her mother lived. For her daughter Dorothy, "It was something like going to a new world."

Life in Chicago imposed disappointments and cruelties of its own. For several years Streeter struggled to make a decent life for her family. Arthritis finally prevented her from working and forced her to sign up for public assistance. Dorothy, the oldest child, assumed responsibility for the household. With what little time she had for herself, she reached the ninth grade. But at age 15 her dream of a nursing career ended when she discovered she was pregnant. In 1965, after her mother died, Dorothy began a relationship with Carra Little, a man who promised he could not get her pregnant. Within a year, Dorothy had her second child. She asked the doctors to sterilize her, but they refused. And the children kept arriving—four more

of them. "When you are young, you don't really think about the future," Dorothy recalled. "You say, 'If I have another baby, then I have another child.'"

After Little died suddenly of a heart attack in 1976, the household disintegrated. Dorothy's oldest daughter, Barbara, like her mother and grandmother before

The bleak spaces of public housing in the "Chicago projects" and in other decaying urban areas made life difficult for residents.

laws restricting abortions and even abortion counseling by clinics or hospitals receiving federal funds. And while the Court affirmed that religious teachings or prayer could have no official status in public schools, it allowed students to engage in voluntary prayer as well as to form religious clubs meeting after school.

Disillusionment and Anger

Ronald Reagan had given a sunny face to conservatism. He had assured voters that if taxes were cut, the economy would revive and deficits would fall. He promised that if "big government" could be scaled back, there would be a new "morning in America." Yet after a decade of conservative leadership, with its hands-off approach, the deficit had ballooned and state and local governments were larger than ever. A her, became pregnant at age 15. By 1985 Dorothy was suffering from chronic depression and considered suicide. She was a 37-year-old grandmother living in a three-room apartment with five of her six children, her daughter LaWanda's new boyfriend, two grandchildren ages 7 and 2, and two teenage runaways. In 20 years, the family had never been off welfare and no one in the household had held a regular job. Only one of her children attended school other than briefly.

With public assistance money Dorothy could afford only rooms in a dilapidated three-story building on Chicago's West Side. Each evening people pried open the building's front door to do "crack" or drink 100 percent grain alcohol. Sometime in 1985 the family stopped bathing because every time they turned on the water, plaster fell into the tub. The building manager reneged on his promise to make repairs. So the children just stood over the sink and washed their clothes by hand. An electrical wire attached to a bare bulb doubled as a clothesline. Only Dorothy had a room of her own. The girls slept on canvas cots in one room, while the boys took turns between cots and a mattress on the living room floor. Meals were irregular affairs, because money was scarce and no one liked to cook. For two weeks each month the family splurged on eggs for breakfast and Spam for dinner. More often they got by on hot dogs, rice, and beans.

Of the neighborhood's 61,500 people, more than half received some form of welfare. People lucky enough to find work quickly moved away. The social agencies that existed to help people in trouble had largely stopped trying. One government official described "a caste of people almost totally dependent on the state, with little hope of breaking free." By the late 1980s murders, drive-by shootings, and guns in school had become commonplace. For the rest of the American people, more fortunate in their circumstances, a question persisted: how could the problems of the largely invisible underclass be solved before the violence and desperation of their private world overwhelmed the city streets? As rioting swept Los Angeles in the spring of 1992 Americans had to wonder if that question had gone too long unanswered.

growing number of Americans felt that the institutions of government had come seriously off track. Indeed, such cynicism was fueled by the attacks on big government by Reagan and Bush.

A series of longer-term crises contributed to this sense of disillusionment. One of the most threatening centered on the nation's savings and loan institutions. By the end of the decade these thrifts were failing at the highest rate since the Great Depression. To help increase bank profits, the Reagan administration and Congress had agreed to cut back federal regulations. That move allowed savings and loan institutions to invest their funds more speculatively. Few depositors noticed or cared, because their money was insured by the Federal Savings and Loan Insurance Corporation. The government, however, had to pay depositors if these banks failed. Reagan's advisers as well as members of Congress ignored the warnings that fraud and

S&L crisis

mismanagement were increasing sharply. Only during the Bush administration did it become clear that the cost of rebuilding the savings banks and paying off huge debts might run into hundreds of billions of dollars.

The late 1980s also brought a public health crisis. Americans were spending a higher percentage of their resources on medical care than were citizens in other nations, yet they were no healthier. New technologies that improved care also burdened the system with heavy expenses. Doctors complained of excessive paperwork. As medical costs soared, more than 30 million Americans had no health insurance. The crisis was worsened by a fatal disorder that physicians began diagnosing in the early 1980s: acquired immunodeficiency syndrome, or AIDS. With no cure available, the disease threatened to take on epidemic proportions not only in the United States but across the globe. Yet because the illness at first struck hardest at the male homosexual community and intravenous drug users, many groups in American society were hesitant to address the problem.

As the AIDS epidemic spread in the 1980s, quilts such as these expressed sorrow for lost friends and loved ones. The quilts also served to raise public awareness of the need for a more effective policy to aid the afflicted and fight the disease.

Bank failures, skyrocketing health costs, anger over poverty and discrimination—none of these problems by themselves had the power to derail the conservative rebellion. Still, the various crises demonstrated how pivotal government had become in providing social services and limiting the abuses of powerful private interests in a highly industrialized society. Neither the Reagan nor the Bush administration had developed a clear way to address such problems without the intervention of government—the sort of intervention envisioned by a more activist Republican, Teddy Roosevelt, at the turn of the century.

The Election of 1992

In the end, George Bush's inability to rein in soaring government deficits proved most damaging to his reelection prospects. "Read my lips! No new taxes," he had pledged to campaign audiences in 1988. But the president and Congress were at loggerheads over how to reach the holy grail of so many conservatives: a balanced budget. In 1985 Congress had passed the Gramm-Rudman Act, establishing a set of steadily increasing limits on federal spending. These limits were meant to force Congress and the president to make hard choices needed to reach a balanced budget. If they did not, automatic across-the-board cuts would go into effect. By 1990 the law's automatic procedures were threatening programs like Medicare, which Republicans and Democrats alike supported. Facing such unpopular cuts, Bush agreed to a package of new taxes along with budget cuts. Conservatives felt betrayed, and in the end, the deficit grew larger all the same.

Gramm-Rudman Act

White-collar unemployment

As the election of 1992 approached, unemployment stood at more than 8 percent, penetrating to areas of the economy not affected by most recessions. Statistics showed that wages for middle-class families had not increased since the early 1970s and had actually declined during Bush's presidency. Many Reagan Democrats seemed ready to return to the party of Franklin Roosevelt, who had mobilized an activist government in a time of economic depression. Other disillusioned voters were drawn to the maverick candidacy of Texas computer billionaire H. Ross Perot. The blunt-talking, jug-eared Perot (he, too, made fun of his ears) demanded a government run like a business but free of big-business lobbyists. He declared his willingness to administer the bitter medicine needed to lower the deficit.

Meanwhile, the Democrats gave their nomination to Governor Bill Clinton of Arkansas. Clinton had personal hurdles to surmount: he was dogged by reports of marital infidelity, by his lame admission that he had tried marijuana while a student (but had not inhaled), and by his youthful opposition to the war in Vietnam. Still, he gained ground by hammering away at Bush for failing to revive the economy. "It's the economy, stupid!" read the sign tacked up at his election headquarters to remind Clinton workers of the campaign's central theme. Clinton painted himself as a new kind of Democrat: moderate, willing to work with business, and not a creature of liberal interest groups.

"It's the Economy . . ."

The Bush campaign miscalculated by allowing the most conservative members of the party to dominate the Republican convention. Middle-of-the-road voters turned to Perot and Clinton. Clinton himself proved a resourceful campaigner, even willing to play his saxophone on MTV. On Election Day, he captured 43 percent of the popular vote (to Bush's 38 and Perot's 19) in the largest turnout—55 percent—in 20 years. The election of four women to the Senate, including the first African American woman, Carol Moseley Braun, indicated that gender had become an electoral factor.

The 1992 election left the fate of the conservative revolution unresolved. Under Reagan and Bush the economy had grown and inflation had subsided. Yet prosperity benefited mostly those at the upper end of the income scale. The majority of Americans saw their financial situation stagnate or grow worse. Reagan and Bush both had supported a conservative social agenda that sought to restrict abortion rights, return prayer to the schools, and end affirmative action, but neither had done much to put that agenda into action. Both presidents significantly weakened the capacity of the federal government to implement social programs. No longer did Americans expect Washington to solve all the issues of the day. How then would the nation meet the future needs of the increasing numbers of poor, minority, elderly, and immigrant Americans?

Reagan and Bush had also presided over the end of the cold war. Despite a growing isolationist sentiment among Democrats and Republicans, both presidents had shown a willingness to assert American power—in Libya, in Lebanon, in Nicaragua, in Panama, in Somalia, in the Persian Gulf—though these were situations in which no major conflict threatened. What role would the United States play in the post–cold war era, when it stood as the lone superpower in the world arena? That was a question for William Jefferson Clinton as he sought to lead the United States into the twenty-first century.

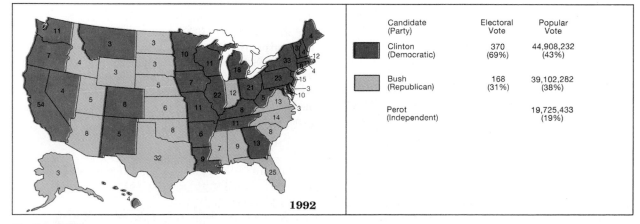

Candidate (Party)	Electoral Vote	Popular Vote
Clinton (Democratic)	370 (69%)	44,908,232 (43%)
Bush (Republican)	168 (31%)	39,102,282 (38%)
Perot (Independent)		19,725,433 (19%)

1992

Election of 1992

chapter summary

During the years of the Reagan and Bush administrations, the nation's political and social agenda was increasingly determined by a conservative movement, including newly politicized evangelical Christians, that sought to restore traditional religious and family values, patriotism, and a more limited role for government.

- Ronald Reagan led the conservative tide with a program to limit the power of labor unions, reduce government regulation, lower taxes, and sharply increase spending on the military.

- Despite a revived economy, Reaganomics had two undesirable outcomes: huge government budget deficits and a growing gap in income between the rich and poor.

- Conservative appointments to the federal judiciary and the Supreme Court led to decisions increasing limits on government intervention in the areas of civil rights, affirmative action, abortion rights, and the separation of church and state.

- Reagan's efforts to "stand tall" in foreign policy led to the Iran-Contra scandal, which revealed a broad pattern of illegal arms shipments to right-wing rebels in Nicaragua and the trading of arms to Iran in an unsuccessful attempt to win the release of hostages in Lebanon—actions for which the president was sharply criticized but not impeached.

- Both Reagan and George Bush welcomed reforms set in motion by Mikhail Gorbachev that led by 1991 to the breakup of the Soviet Union, reductions in nuclear arms, and an end to the cold war.

- In the post–cold war era, regional conflicts proved more troublesome as Iraq's invasion of Kuwait led Bush to form a UN coalition that routed the forces of Saddam Hussein in Operation Desert Storm.

- For George Bush, a continuing recession, high budget deficits, and high unemployment undermined his bid for reelection.

additional reading

During Ronald Reagan's political career, the public knew little about the man or his inner thoughts. That remains true even after the publication of Edmund Morris, *Dutch* (1999), despite the author's unprecedented access to Reagan in the White House. Unable to penetrate Reagan's outer shell, Morris resorted to fiction to bring more light to his subject. Even less credible have been the efforts of Reagan's conservative supporters to turn him into a political giant. See, for example, Dinesh D'Souza, *Ronald Reagan* (1999). Haynes Johnson, *Sleep Walking through History: America in the Reagan Years* (1991); Jane Mayer and Doyle McManus, *Landslide: The Unmaking of the President, 1984–1988* (1988); and Gary Wills, *Reagan's America* (1987) still offer readers more insight, as does David Stockman's White House memoir, *The Triumph of Politics: The Inside Story of the Reagan Revolution* (1986). Godrey Hodgson, *The World Turned Right Side Up: A History of the Conservative Ascendancy in America* (1996) puts the conservatism of the 1980s into a wider perspective.

George Bush has inspired no major biography, but his *All the Best, George Bush: My Life and Other Writings* (1999) and with Brent Scowcroft, *A World Transformed* (1999) give a picture of the person and his foreign policy. Thomas Friedman, *From Beirut to Jerusalem* (1988) offers many insights into Middle East politics, and Dilip Hiro, *Desert Shield to Desert Storm: The Second Gulf War* (1992) treats the war from a non-American perspective. Frank Levy, *The New Dollars and Dreams* (rev. ed. 1999) analyzes the patterns of income inequality. Racial currents of the decade are powerfully conveyed in Nicholas Lemann, *The Promised Land* (1991). Ronald Takaki, *Strangers from a Different Shore* (1989) discusses changing trends in immigration.

Significant Events

1978	1978 *Bakke v. Regents of the University of California*
1979	1979 Moral Majority established; Sandinistas overthrow Somoza in Nicaragua
1980	1980 Reagan defends Carter
1981	1981 Reagan breaks air traffic controllers' strike; recession sets in; Economic Recovery Tax Act; United States begins aiding Nicaraguan Contras
1982	1982 Attack on U.S. Marine barracks in Lebanon
1983	1983 Reagan proposes the Strategic Defense Initiative; invasion of Grenada
1984	1984 Boland Amendment passed; Reagan defeats Mondale
1985	1985 Gramm-Rudman Act sets in motion a plan to balance budget; United States begins secret arms-for-hostages negotiations with Iran
1986	1986 Reykjavík summit; Iran-Contra scandal breaks
1987	
1988	1988 Congress passes drug and welfare reform bills; Bush elected president
1989	1989 Eastern Europe nations break with Soviet Union; China crushes revolt in Tiananmen Square; Berlin Wall taken down
1990	1990 Iraq invades Kuwait; Clean Air Act; Bush agrees to higher taxes in budget agreement with Congress
1991	1991 Operation Desert Storm launched; Strategic Arms Reduction Treaty (START) concluded; Clarence Thomas hearings; 11 former republics of the Soviet Union become the Commonwealth of Independent States
1992	1992 *Planned Parenthood v. Casey* sets new restrictions on abortion; Clinton defeats Bush and Perot

*J*uan Chanax had never been far from San Cristobal, a small village in the Guatemalan highlands. In that region, some two thousand years earlier, his Mayan ancestors had created one of the world's great civilizations. During the twentieth century, San Cristobal had escaped the political upheavals that disrupted much of Guatemala. Still, by the 1970s Chanax, a weaver, struggled to support his young family. Work at a nearby American textile factory brought steady wages, but scarcely enough to survive on. The coming of the factory alerted him to a larger world outside his mountain village. In 1978 he decided that the only way he could help his sick son and improve himself—to *"superarme,"* as he put it—was to go north. He told his wife "the United States was a place where people could work and make their own lives." So began a journey that changed the destiny of Juan Chanax, San Cristobal, and the multicultural community in America.

Reaching his destination was not easy. Several times Chanax was robbed. Twice border guards turned him away. On his third attempt he successfully eluded the border patrol and made his way to Houston, Texas, with little more than a letter introducing him to several Guatemalans. Through them he learned of a maintenance job at a Randall's supermarket.

NATION OF NATIONS IN A GLOBAL COMMUNITY

preview • A renewed wave of immigration in the last decades of the century was only one way in which global ties increased both diversity in the United States' and the nation's interdependence with the rest of the world. The rise of the Internet signaled a revolution in global communications and commerce as well. Amid the decade's robust economic expansion, the Clinton administration sparred with Republicans over how best to define the multicultural contours of a nation of nations.

In the late 1970s, high oil prices had brought a boom to Houston. And as the city grew, Randall's expanded with it. That expansion meant plenty of low-wage jobs for people like Chanax, even though he had almost no education and had entered the United States illegally. Randall's did not want just any low-wage workers. The chain specialized in high-priced goods in fancy suburban stores. Its upscale customers received valet parking, hassle-free shopping, and service from uniformed employees. Shortly before Chanax began working at Randall's, one of its managers had a falling out with several African American employees. When the manager criticized their work, they argued heatedly, until one employee finally threw a mop at the manager and quit.

That incident proved to be Chanax's opportunity. Unlike the worker who stormed out, Chanax was happy to do any job without complaint. The minimum wage was more than twice what he earned in Guatemala. Within several weeks he began to wire money home to his family. And when the manager said Randall's would soon need more workers, Chanax arranged for his brother-in-law and an uncle to come north. Over time Randall's began to hire Guatemalans exclusively. Shortly before a new store opened, the managers would tell Chanax how many maintenance people they needed. He would then recruit more Mayans from San Cristobal.

As the newcomers arrived, Chanax and the experienced Mayans prepared them for the job. Preparation meant more than learning to clean and stack. The recruits were also told to arrive on time, work hard, disrespect no one, and use proper manners. If a problem arose, they were not to go to a Randall's manager, but to another Guatemalan. "That way," as Chanax observed, "if there was any problem, if a man was sick or had to leave work early or anything, we would solve it ourselves." As each store opened, the Guatemalans would have the entire maintenance department staffed and ready to work 24 hours a day, seven days a week.

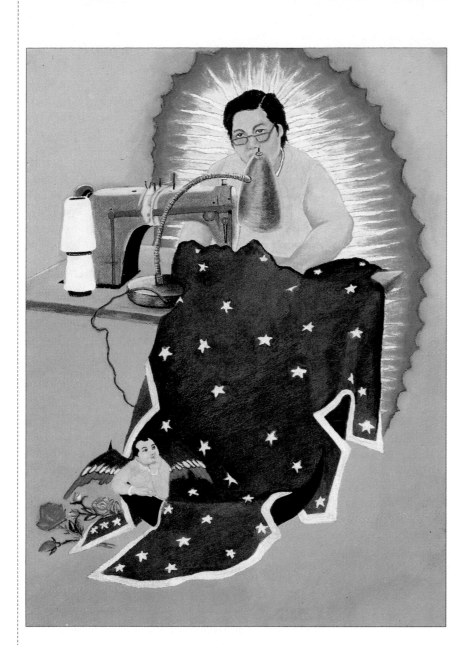

By 1995 over a quarter of a million laborers worked in Southern California's garment industry, many of them recently arrived immigrants from Mexico and Central America. "Very often we work until eight or nine at night the six days and then work a half day Sunday," commented one. Here Chicano artist Yolanda López celebrates the virtues of a hardworking seamstress by portraying her as the Virgin of Guadalupe, the traditional patron saint of Mexico.

Within five years after Chanax reached Houston, over a thousand Mayans from San Cristobal were working at Randall's. A single person had created what scholars call a migration chain. Through Chanax, Randall's had found access to a minimum wage workforce who would perform willingly—in the company's words—as "cheerful servants." The Mayans, in turn, found opportunities unavailable in Guatemala. In the process Chanax and other early immigrants had become department managers and supervising assistants. Many of their wives worked as maids and servants in the homes of Houston's rapidly growing upper-income communities.

In many ways, Juan Chanax and his fellow Guatemalans mirrored the classic tale of immigrants realizing the American dream. In suburban Houston they formed their own community in an area that came to be known as *Las Americas*. There, various Central American immigrant groups established churches and social clubs amid some 90 apartment complexes that a decade or two earlier had housed mostly young, single office workers. On weekends and evenings rival soccer teams played in the

Migration chain

nearby park. (Juan, also the soccer league's president, helped new teams fill out the forms required by the parks department to use its fields.) The growth of *Las Americas* in the late twentieth century echoed the pattern of immigrants who had come to the United States at the century's opening.

Changes in the patterns of global immigration

Yet those patterns had changed in important ways, too. Although cities remained the mecca of most immigrants, Juan and many newcomers of the 1980s and 1990s settled in suburban areas, particularly in the West and Southwest. Industrial factories provided the lion's share of work in the 1890s, but a century later the service industries—grocery stores, fast-food chains, janitorial positions—absorbed many more of the new arrivals. Even the faces had changed, as European immigrants found themselves outnumbered by Latinos from Mexico and Central America as well as by Asians from the Philippines, China, Korea, Southeast Asia, and the Indian subcontinent, not to mention increasing numbers of Arabs from the Middle East and Africans. This broad geographic range reflected perhaps the most important shift in immigration: its truly global character. Transportation and communications networks tied immigrants to their home countries more strongly than in the past, allowing immigrants like Juan to keep regularly in touch with their former neighbors and relatives by phone as well as mail. Immigrants continued to participate in home-country politics more easily; they could wire money instantly to relatives and even build homes thousands of miles away where one day they planned to retire.

The global nature of immigration was only one aspect of an American society more tightly linked to the world community. For half a century the cold war had shaped American responses to the wider world. With the fall of the Soviet Union, attention shifted toward the need to manage regional conflicts. International economic ties linked the United States with the rest of the world in equally important ways, because the effects of a recession or financial collapse in Russia or Thailand could spread to other countries in a matter of weeks or months. Finally, the 1990s witnessed a communications revolution as the Internet tied together correspondents, consumers, manufacturers, and information systems. In short, the movement of people, financial capital, and data around the globe forced a nation of nations to adapt itself to an increasingly global community.

@ The New Immigration

The Immigration Act of 1965 (page 989) altered the face of American life—perhaps more significantly than any piece of legislation among Lyndon Johnson's Great Society programs. The lawmakers who passed the act did not expect such far-reaching changes, for they assumed that Europeans would continue to predominate among newcomers. Yet reform of the old quota system opened the way for a wave of immigrants unequaled since the beginning of the century.

Economic political causes of immigration

Turmoil abroad pushed many immigrants toward the United States, beginning in the 1960s with Fidel Castro's revolution in Cuba and unrest in the Dominican Republic. The war in Vietnam and its aftermath produced more than 500,000 refugees in the 15 years after 1975. Revolutionary conflicts in Central America during the 1980s launched new streams. Yet economic factors played as great a role as the terrors of war. Although some Filipinos fled the repressive regime of Ferdinand Marcos, many more came to the United States in a more straightforward search for economic prosperity. When Mexico suffered an economic downturn in the 1980s, emigration there rose sharply.

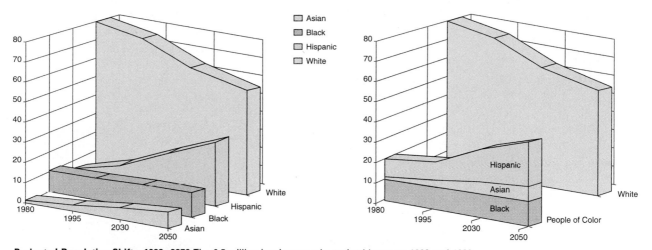

Projected Population Shifts, 1980–2050 The 6.5 million immigrants who arrived between 1990 and 1998 accounted for 32 percent of the increase in the total U.S. population. Census figures have projected an increasing racial and ethnic diversity. White population was projected to drop from 80 percent in 1980 to about 53 percent in 2050, with the nation's Latino population rising most sharply. Which graph presents the data most effectively?

In all, about 7 million immigrants, both legal and illegal, arrived in the United States between 1975 and 1995. The nation's foreign-born population rose to 9 percent, the highest proportion since World War II. The tide rose even more sharply in the 1990s, with the Latino population increasing by over 35 percent to about 30.3 million by 1999. The Asian American population grew at an even faster rate, to about 10.8 million. Through the decade a steadily expanding economy made immigrants a welcome source of new labor. Prosperity, in turn, reduced—though it did not eliminate—conflict among longstanding residents, new immigrants, and people on the margin of the labor market.

The New Look of America—Asian Americans

In 1970, 96 percent of Asian Americans were Japanese, Chinese, or Filipino. By the year 2000, those same three groups comprised barely over half of all Asian Americans. As the diversity of Asian immigration increased, Asian Indians, Koreans, and Vietnamese came to outnumber Japanese Americans. The newcomers also varied dramatically in economic background, crowding both ends of the economic spectrum.

The higher end included many Chinese students who, beginning in the 1960s, sought out the United States for a college education, then found a job and stayed, eventually bringing in their families. "My brother-in-law left his wife in Taiwan and came here as a student to get his Ph.D. in engineering," explained Subi Lin Felipe. "After he received his degree, he got a job in San Jose. Then he brought in a sister and his wife, who brought over one of her brothers and me. And my brother's wife then came." Amy Tan, in her novel *The Joy Luck Club*, described the migration of upwardly mobile Chinese professionals to upscale urban and suburban neighborhoods. Asian Indians were even more acculturated upon arrival because about two-thirds entered the United States with college degrees already in hand. Indian engineers played a vital role in the computer and software industries. Similarly, Korean and Filipino professionals took skilled jobs, particularly in medical fields.

Prosperous newcomers

Daily Lives

TIME AND TRAVEL

Motels as an Ethnic Niche

For Americans who traveled by car in the 1950s, the end of the day meant a stop at a motel. These motels were mostly mom-and-pop businesses in rural towns or along highways into the nation's cities. Because the motel industry had no standards, a motorist never knew what to expect. A flashy sign might lure the unsuspecting tourist into a rattrap. Some motels catered to the hot sheet trade, offering privacy for a midday tryst. Still, the majority provided clean sheets, a decent bed, and a hot shower at an affordable price.

By the 1960s, with the completion of the main links of the interstate highway system, the motel business changed. The interstates brought drivers to major exchanges. There, large chains like Ramada, Sheraton, and Holiday Inns were ready to provide travelers with accommodations that were familiar whether they were in California or Maine. Holiday Inn's slogan was, "At Holiday Inn the best surprise is no surprise." The rise of the major motel chains spelled financial disaster for the mom-and-pop operations, which were often built in older, less desirable locations that by the 1970s were showing signs of decay.

A ray of hope came from an unexpected source. For reasons that remain far from clear, immigrants from India began to go into the lodging business. One Indian motel owner cited an ancient Sanskrit phrase, *Atithi devo bhava*—the guest is God. "Hospitality is in our culture," he concluded. But there were other reasons, more practical. After the Immigration Reform Act of 1965 Indians, along with other Asians, came to the United States in large numbers. Newcomers of modest means saw motels as an attractive opportunity. Because many of the new Indians were professionals who did not "like working for other people," as one owner recalled, motels supplied an independent business. They also provided housing without the need to tie up capital in a home. Prejudice played a role too. More affluent Indians who approached the large chains learned quickly that "the big brands didn't really want us."

By the mid-1980s Indians owned 50 percent of all the non-chain motels in the country. Even more remarkable, 70 percent of those Indians shared the same name—Patel. A common joke among them was that "in some American small

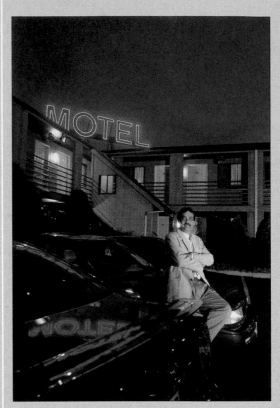

Dinu Patel, the owner of a motel in Branford, Connecticut. By 1999 a little over 50 percent of all American motels were owned by people of Indian origin.

Blue-collar Asians

Yet Asian immigrants also included those on the lower rungs of the economic ladder. Among the new wave of Chinese immigrants, or *San Yi Man*, many blue-collar workers settled in the nation's Chinatowns, where they worked in restaurants or sewed in sweatshops. Without education and language skills, often in debt to labor contractors, most have remained trapped in Chinatown's ethnic economy. Refugees from war and revolution in Southeast Asia often made harrowing journeys. Vietnamese families crowded into barely seaworthy boats, sometimes only to be terrorized by pirates, other times, nearly drowned in storms before reaching poorly equipped Thai refugee camps. By 1990 almost a million refugees had arrived in the United States, three-quarters of them from Vietnam, most of the others from Laos or Kampuchea (formerly Cambodia). California and Texas absorbed the greatest number, with significant populations in Pennsylvania, Washington, and Minnesota.

towns they think that 'Patel' is an Indian word for 'motel.'" In fact, the name identified them as the members of one of India's four principal castes—the *vaishyas,* or traders. Among Indians, Patel was as common a name as Smith was to Americans. When the many Patels emigrated to the United States, they brought their experience in commerce with them.

A closer look at the motel phenomenon makes the story a bit less unusual. Sociologists have defined such occupational clustering as a "nonlinear ethnic niche." After the early pioneers from a group discover the opportunities in a particular enterprise or profession, they attract fellow ethnics to it. What Indians did with motels, Arabs in greater Detroit did with gas stations, Koreans with groceries, and Vietnamese in Los Angeles with fingernail salons.

Once an ethnic group achieved dominance in a niche, other groups found it difficult to move in. Indians kept close track of any motel properties that came up for sale. Hotel brokers, in turn, learned that they were among the most reliable prospects. "If it's a motel with less than 60 rooms," one broker commented, "the likely buyers will be Indians 98 times out of 100. And why not? They run them better than anyone else." All that was needed, one owner recalled, was financing, which relatives and other Indians generally provided, and "the will to work long hours." One Indian who moved from London to Hickory, North Carolina, in 1990 bought a motel for $713,000. His father gave him $50,000 and his in-laws another $50,000 to cover the down payment. At first he thought Hickory was "Hicksville." "The whole town sat out on the porch in rocking chairs," he recalled. The culture shock soon wore off and Hickory became home. Careful management and shrewd investment paid large dividends. In 1999 the property was appraised at almost $2 million.

Among Indians this motel success story is more the norm than an exception. By the late 1990s Indian motels employed over 800,000 people and had property valued at close to $40 billion. In fact, Indians provided 37 percent of all the hotel rooms in America. Twenty five years ago, "the hotel establishment . . . didn't want to know about us," one owner remarked. "But now we are the establishment."

Among such populations, poor language skills and cultural differences locked workers into low-wage jobs and recurring cycles of unemployment.

Thus the profile of Asian immigration resembled an hourglass, with the most newcomers either relatively affluent or extremely poor. Even so, such statistics could be misleading. Although more Asian Americans made over $50,000 per year than any other racial or ethnic group, more than half of all Asian American families lived in just five metropolitan areas—Honolulu, Los Angeles, San Francisco, Chicago, and New York—where the cost of living ranked among the nation's highest. High prices meant real earnings were lower. On a per capita basis, only the Japanese and Indians among Asian Americans made above the national average in 1990.

Further, a close examination of employment patterns in those five cities showed that more Asians than whites worked in low-status, low-income jobs.

Within professions like dentistry, nursing, and health technology where Asians found work, they often held the lower-paying positions. Those Asians who worked in sales were more often retail clerks than insurance agents or stockbrokers. A glass ceiling blocked many Asians from reaching the highest rungs in corporate management. As the *Wall Street Journal* reported, "the same companies that pursue them for technical jobs often shun them when filling managerial and executive positions."

Asian downward mobility

Finally, Asian Americans experienced two forms of downward mobility. First, highly educated Asian immigrants often found it difficult or impossible to land jobs in their professions. To American observers, Korean shopkeepers seemed examples of success, when in fact such owners often enough had been former professionals forced into the risky small-business world. One Filipino doctor noted that strict state licensing standards prevented him from opening up his own medical practice. Instead, he found himself working as a restaurant meat cutter, for employers who had no idea of his real occupation. "They thought I was very good at separating meat from the bone," he commented ironically. Second, schools reported significant numbers of Asian American students who were failing. This "lost generation" were most often the children of families who entered the United States with little education and few job skills. Still others were middle-class children, who found it difficult to adjust to a new culture.

The New Look of America—Latinos

Like Asian Americans, Latinos in the United States constituted a diverse mosaic, reflecting dozens of immigrant streams. Although the groups shared a language, they usually settled in distinct urban and suburban barrios across the United States. Such enclave communities provided support to newcomers and an economic foothold for newly established businesses. Money circulated within a community; the workers and owners of an ethnic grocery, for example, spent their wages at neighboring stores, whose profits fueled other immigrant businesses in a chain reaction.

The Dominicans of Washington Heights

Washington Heights, at the northern tip of New York City, followed that path as nearly a quarter of a million Dominicans settled there during the 1970s and 1980s. A hundred blocks to the south, Manhattan's downtown skyscrapers seemed distant; shopkeepers' stereos along the major thoroughfares boomed music of trumpets and congas, while peddlers pushed heavily loaded shopping carts through busy streets, crying "¡A peso! ¡A peso!" ("For a dollar!"). In addition Dominican social clubs planned dances or hosted political discussions. Sports clubs competed actively. Similarly, in Miami and elsewhere in South Florida, Cuban Americans created their own self-sustaining enclaves. A large professional class and strong community leadership brought them prosperity and political influence.

East Los Angeles

Along the West coast, Los Angeles was the urban magnet for many Latino (and Asian) immigrants. Mexican immigrants had long flocked to East Los Angeles, and in the 1990s it remained convenient to the jobs in factories, warehouses, and railroad yards across the river. Many Mexican Americans now owned their own businesses and homes, whose neatly kept backyards were filled with blooming bougainvillea. But beginning in the mid-1980s and 1990s the neighborhood of MacArthur Park became the focal point for the newest immigrants from Mexico and Central America. MacArthur Park was less developed as a community, and many of its residents were transient, passing quickly to other neighborhoods or jobs. Vendors of pirated audiocassettes competed with dice games and the occasional evangelist preacher, while hand-lettered signs in windows offered services to parents working long hours: "SE CUIDAN BEBÉS" (babysitting).

As more factories and service industries became decentralized, locating themselves beyond urban downtowns, the barrios followed as well. *Las Americas* near Houston, where Juan Chanax lived, was one example; but suburban barrios could be found dotted all across the nation, from Rockville, Maryland, to Pacoima, California, near Burbank. Pacoima's bungalows housed well-kept working-class Mexican Americans who had lived in California for decades. But the front lawns of many residences were often paved over to hold the cars of additional workers or families, and the garages were converted to dormitories with a sink and toilet, where four or five newcomers from Central America could rent a spot to lay a bedroll on the cement floor.

Illegal Immigration

Because Mexico and the United States shared such a long common border—and an equally long history of intermingling of peoples and cultures—many Mexicans entered the United States illegally. But the number of illegal immigrants increased during the 1980s as Central Americans joined the northward flow, along with Mexicans escaping a sharp economic downturn in their own country. By 1985, the number of illegal immigrants in the United States was estimated at anywhere from 2 to 12 million.

Congress attempted to stem that flow by passing the Immigration and Control Act of 1986. Tightened border security was coupled with a new requirement that American employers bear the responsibility of certifying their workers as legal residents of the United States. At the same time, those illegal immigrants who had arrived before 1986 were granted amnesty and allowed to become legal residents. In the end, however, the terms of the law failed to create the clean slate Congress had hoped for. California's fruit and vegetable growers, who worried that they would not have enough laborers under the new rules, lobbied for exceptions to the rules, which allowed over 1.7 additional illegal immigrants to gain amnesty. Furthermore, the many immigrants who suddenly became legal under the terms of the law quickly sought to reunite their families, bringing in wives and children illegally. Reluctantly, the federal government decided it could not break up these families, and it allowed them to live illegally in the United States while they applied for visas. By 1995 the backlog in applications had soared to over 800,000 newcomers.

Thus by 1996, the illegal population of Latinos in the United States stood at about 5 million people—about the same number as in 1986 when the immigration reform act was passed. Thus legal immigrants continued to be intertwined with illegals in a host of different ways: as relatives helping loved ones make the transition to living in the United States, as landlords boarding newcomers until they could get on their feet, as links with communities in the home country—just as Juan Chanax continued to be after he received amnesty from the act in 1986.

Immigration and Control Act of 1986

Links with the Home Country

Because systems of communication and transportation drew the world closer, the new immigrants found it easier to maintain links with their points of origin. Chanax, we have seen, regularly wired money back to relatives in Guatemala, and he was hardly alone in the practice. Pacoima, the suburban barrio outside Burbank, California, boasted only a small town center. But along that half-mile stretch of Van Nuys Boulevard, 13 different currency exchanges were open for business to handle immigrant funds. By 1992, the amount of funds sent worldwide was so great that it was surpassed in volume only by the currency flows of the global oil trade.

And not just money traveled these routes. An immigrant entering La Curaçao, a furniture store in Los Angeles's MacArthur Park, could sign up to buy a bedroom suite on the installment plan. When the payments were completed, the furniture was released—not in Los Angeles but at a branch warehouse in El Salvador, where relatives could pick up the purchase. Cultural ties remained strong as well. Young Mexican immigrants flocked on Saturday night to popular dance halls like the Lido in Los Angeles to hear a variety of music known as *banda*. Women wore tight tank tops and jeans or skirts, while the men's cowboy outfits were distinguished by their *cuarta,* a small riding whip at the belt, and by a kerchief hanging from the right hip pocket, with the the name of the wearer's native Mexican state embroidered proudly for all to see. State by state, the band leader would call out a welcome to *"nuestros amigos"* ("our friends") from the various states such as Sinaloa or Jalisco. In return, each region's group of immigrants would cheer and stomp their approval.

Banda music

Religious Diversity

The global nature of the new immigration also reshaped the religious faiths of America. During the 1950s, most Americans' sense of religious diversity encompassed the mainline Protestant churches, Roman Catholicism, and Judaism. But immigrants brought with them not only their own brands of Christianity and Judaism but also Buddhist, Hindu, and Islamic beliefs. By 1999 there were perhaps 5 to 6 million Muslims in the United States. Many had emigrated from Arab states, but adherents from South Asia made up an even greater number. Buddhists and Hindus numbered about a million each.

Mainline Protestants and Catholics changed as well. The Presbyterian Church (U.S.A.) increased its Korean-speaking congregations from about 20 in 1970 to over 350. In New York City, Episcopalian services were held in 14 different languages. And Catholic Churches increasingly found themselves celebrating mass in both English and Spanish. Such arrangements took place not only in urban congregations such as the Church of the Nativity in South Central Los Angeles (where

At Our Lady of Guadalupe Catholic Mission, a family in the growing Mexican and Central American community of Muscatine, Iowa, held a *quinceañera*—a celebration of a girl's 15th birthday. Even towns in rural southeastern Iowa reflected the growing diversity of immigrant religious life.

Latinos alternated services with African Americans) but increasingly even in rural areas like Columbus Junction, Iowa, whose Catholic church was energized by Mexican Americans working in a nearby meat-processing plant.

The religious and cultural diversity of the new immigrant streams broadened the ties between the United States and the rest of the world. Despite the end of the cold war, the future of that world remained as uncertain as ever. Regional conflict in Vietnam, Central America, the former Yugoslavia, and elsewhere became an increasing source of unrest. Such political unrest had driven many immigrants to America. Economic pressures around the world had encouraged many more to come. The nation's newest immigrants often linked the United States to the conflicts that presented the greatest challenge to American leadership in the post–cold war world.

With the presidential inauguration of 1992, William Jefferson Clinton became the first baby boomer to occupy the

The Clinton Presidency: Managing a New Global Order

@

White House. His wife, Hillary Rodham Clinton, would be the most politically involved presidential wife since Eleanor Roosevelt. Like so many couples of their generation, the Clintons were a two-career family. Both trained as lawyers at Yale University during the tumultuous 1960s. Bill chose politics as his career, while Hillary mixed private practice with public service. Their marriage had not been easy. Revelations of Clinton's sexual affairs as governor of Arkansas almost ruined his campaign for the presidency. The first couple seemed, however, more intent on making public policy than in defending their private lives.

As a young man, Bill Clinton had met John Kennedy, an event that inspired him to enter politics. Like Kennedy, Clinton envisioned himself as an activist president, not a more detached leader like Reagan. But Clinton's desire for major legislative initiatives ran up against the election results of 1992. He had received just 43 percent of the popular vote, while the Republicans had narrowed the Democratic majorities in Congress. Still, Clinton believed that an activist executive could achieve much, "even a president without a majority mandate coming in, if the president has a disciplined, aggressive agenda."

Clinton: Ambitions and Character

Certainly, the agenda was ambitious. The new president pledged to revive the economy and rein in the federal deficit that had grown so enormously during the Reagan years. Beyond that, he called for systematic reform of the welfare and health care systems as well as measures to reduce the increasing violence that too often had turned urban neighborhoods like *Las Americas* into war zones.

Clinton agenda

What often seemed missing in the White House was the "disciplined, aggressive" approach needed to move legislation through Congress. As one of his first presidential acts, Clinton attempted to eliminate a rule that banned homosexuals from serving in the military, fulfilling a campaign pledge to the gay community. Resistance from conservatives and the military led Clinton to accept a compromise position satisfactory to no one: "Don't ask; don't tell." So long as gay soldiers kept their sexual orientation private, they could serve their country. Clinton had also promised to appoint a cabinet reflecting the gender and racial diversity of the nation. When several nominees provoked controversy, he withdrew his support.

Don't ask; don't tell

These early failures could be set down partly to the stumbles of a newcomer learning his way around the office. But larger issues of character could not be dismissed. Despite the president's considerable intellectual abilities, he seemed driven sometimes by a need to be popular. (As governor of Arkansas, Clinton was "someone who require[d] the constant love of an entire state," commented his friend Webster Hubbell.) The president's habit of relying on opinion polls to shape policy led even some supporters to fear that he would not find it in himself to make hard choices. Others questioned his personal discipline. One observer shrewdly noted that there were two Bill Clintons—the idealistic young man from Hope, Arkansas (his hometown), and the boy from Hot Springs (his mother's home). The latter was a resort town associated with the seamier side of Arkansas high life. With increasing frequency, the leadership mustered by the idealistic politician from Hope seemed to be undermined by the character flaws of the boy from Hot Springs.

Although Clinton's conservative opponents disliked his politics, it was the president's moral lapses that they most deeply resented. Critics nicknamed him "Slick Willie," and sought continually to expose discreditable or illegal dealings from his past. Accusations were published that, when Clinton was governor in the early 1980s, both he and his wife had received special treatment from a failed real estate venture known as Whitewater. An air of mystery deepened when Vince Foster, a White House advisor and close friend of Hillary Clinton's from Arkansas, committed suicide. (The Clintons' most vocal critics suggested that the verdict of suicide was merely a murder cover-up, although the best evidence suggested depression as a cause.) Rumors also abounded about Clinton's womanizing, fanned in 1994 when a former Arkansas state employee, Paula Jones, filed a sexual harassment suit against the president. Under pressure from Congressional conservatives, Attorney General Janet Reno appointed former judge Kenneth Starr as a special prosecutor to investigate Whitewater. But during Clinton's first term, investigations by Starr as well as two Senate committees produced no evidence that the Clintons had acted illegally.

Whitewater

The New World Disorder

Determined to focus on domestic issues, Clinton hoped to pay less attention to foreign affairs. He discovered that the "new world order," hailed by both Mikhail Gorbachev and George Bush, seemed more like a world of regional disorders. The United States depended heavily on Russian President Boris Yeltsin to bring order out of chaos, yet market reforms failed to revive Russia's stagnant economy. Although Yeltsin maintained his own grip on power, he suffered from chronic ill health and routinely dismissed rivals for power. Elsewhere in the world, rampant ethnic and nationalist movements provoked a number of regional crises. By using American power in a limited way, Clinton gained considerable public support.

In sub-Saharan Africa, corruption and one-party rule severely weakened most economies, tribal violence mounted, and AIDs became epidemic. Brutal civil wars broke out in both Somalia and Rwanda. As a presidential candidate, Clinton had supported President Bush's decision in December 1992 to send troops to aid famine-relief efforts in Somalia. But attempts to install a stable government proved difficult. Tragically, the United States as well as European nations failed to intervene in Rwanda before over a million people were massacred in 1994.

Instability in Haiti pushed the president to take a bolder approach closer to home. In 1991 Haitian military leaders had forced their country's elected president, Jean-Bertrand Aristide, into exile. The harsh rule that followed prompted over 35,000 refugees to flee toward the United States, often in homemade boats and rafts. When a UN-sponsored economic embargo failed to oust the military regime, the Security Council in 1994 approved an invasion of Haiti by a multinational force. American troops proved crucial in convincing the military to leave. A smaller UN force stayed on to maintain order as new elections returned Aristide to the presidency.

Americans in Haiti

Yugoslavian Turmoil

Europe's most intractable trouble spot proved to be Yugoslavia, a nation divided by ethnic rivalries within a number of provinces, including Serbia, Croatia, and Bosnia. After 1991 Bosnia and Croatia declared their independence from Yugoslavia, which was dominated by Serbia and its leader, Slobodan Milosevic. Milosevic urged the Serbian minorities within Bosnia and Croatia to take up arms, and he sent in Serbian troops to aid them. The Croats had sufficient military force to drive the Serbs out, but in Bosnia the population mix was more complex and resistance less organized.

Conflicts in Bosnia and Croatia

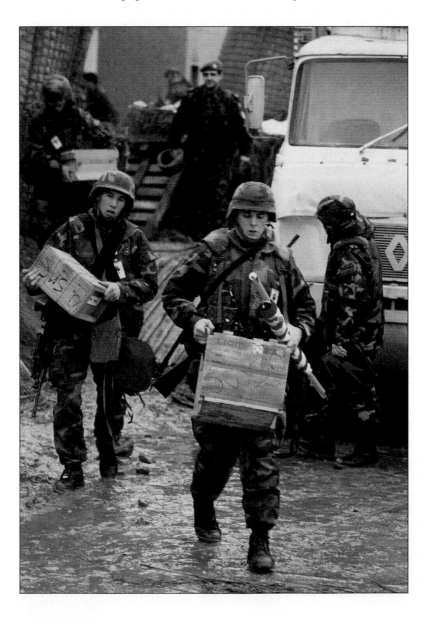

American troops were part of the NATO peacekeeping force sent to Bosnia after the Dayton Accords of 1995. This female marine (center) was among the first arrivals, who encountered chill, wet weather.

Serbs, Bosnians, and Muslims had lived side-by-side and intermarried for generations. After Bosnia became independent in 1992 both sides, but especially the Serbs, resorted to what was euphemistically referred to as "ethnic cleansing"—the massacre of rival populations—to secure control. Serbs even set up rape camps where they brutalized Muslim women. The Serbian military began the systematic bombing of Sarajevo, Bosnia's capital city that had been declared a safe haven.

The United States initially viewed the civil war in Yugoslavia as Europe's problem. But as the civilian death toll mounted to a quarter of a million, the conflict became difficult to ignore. Nobel Peace Prize winner and Holocaust survivor Elie Wiesel beseeched President Clinton to "stop the bloodshed. . . . Something, anything, must be done" to end the horror in Bosnia. Still, the ghosts of Vietnam loomed. Many members of Congress feared the prospect of American troops bogged down in a distant civil war. By 1995 Clinton had committed the United States to support NATO bombing of Serb forces, and when Bosnian and Croatian forces began to win back territory, the Serbs agreed to peace talks at a meeting in Dayton, Ohio. The

Dayton Accords

Dayton Accords created separate Croatian, Bosnian, and Serbian nations. Some 60,000 NATO troops, including 20,000 Americans, moved into Bosnia to enforce the peace. Clinton had intervened successfully without the loss of American lives, though five years later U.S. troops remained in Bosnia.

Intervention in Kosovo

Having lost Croatia and Bosnia, Milosevic was determined not to lose Kosovo, a province in which the Serb minority ruled over a mostly Albanian population. In 1998 attacks by Albanian rebels (who called themselves the Kosovo Liberation Army) provided Milosevic an excuse to send in troops. Along with Serbian police and militia groups, they committed widespread atrocities against civilians. Hundreds of thousands of Albanian refugees poured into the surrounding countries. In the spring of 1999 Clinton committed U.S. forces to a NATO bombing campaign that hit targets both in Serbia and Kosovo. They destroyed much of Serbia's industrial, military, and transportation infrastructure. Without admitting defeat, Milosevic finally agreed to a NATO occupation of Kosovo. Once again, American troops entered as peacekeepers. The inclusion of troops from Russia, Serbia's traditional ally, helped prevent the revival of cold war tensions.

Middle East Peace

Steps forward in Haiti and the Balkans could not quiet fears of a new Middle East crisis. Sporadic protests and rioting by Palestinians in the Israeli-occupied territories of Gaza and the West Bank gave way in the 1990s to negotiations. At a ceremony hosted by President Clinton in 1993, Palestinian leader Yasir Arafat and Israeli Prime Minister Itzak Rabin signed a peace agreement permitting self-rule for Palestinians in the Gaza Strip and in Jericho on the West Bank. In 1995 Arafat became head of the West Bank Palestinian National Authority.

Middle East peace negotiations

Still, a full settlement remained elusive. As Clinton pursued negotiations, he found he had limited leverage to broker a lasting peace. The assassination of Prime Minister Rabin in 1995, by an angry Orthodox Jew, began a period of increased suspicion on both sides as extremists sought to derail the peace process. Even when Clinton engaged in nine days of marathon sessions with the two sides at Wye River, Maryland, in 1998, the agreement hammered out there was largely ignored by a more conservative Israeli government under Prime Minister Benjamin Netanyahu. Only in 1999, after Netanyahu was replaced by the more moderate Ehud Barak, did hopes rise for a more stable peace. Whether in the Middle East, Eastern Europe, Africa, or the Caribbean, such regional crises demonstrated that a new global "world order" would be difficult to maintain.

Global Financial Disorder

Yet crises in such distant regions could not be ignored, because the world's political and economic systems had become so closely intertwined. The effects from a calamity in one area of the world rippled outward in unpredictable ways. In 1997 and 1998 a series of shocks nearly brought the world financial system to its knees.

Thai crisis sets off an Asian recession

The crisis began along the Pacific Rim, where the economies of Japan, South Korea, the Philippines, Thailand, and other East Asian nations had propelled global prosperity during the 1980s. That boom faltered in the mid-1990s when the Japanese economy slid into a long recession that slowed growth throughout the world. Then in December 1997 the government of Thailand suddenly announced it was closing 56 of the nation's 58 banks. Surmising that the economy was on the verge of collapse, world currency speculators tried to profit by betting that the value of the *baht,* Thailand's currency, would drop sharply. When it did, so did the value of many loans made by Thai banks, bringing the building boom to a standstill. Quickly the Thai crisis spread to South Korea, Indonesia, and Hong Kong, causing foreign investors to withdraw their capital from the region. Prices of stocks on Asian exchanges fell precipitously. A popular sweatshirt announced its wearer "Formerly Rich."

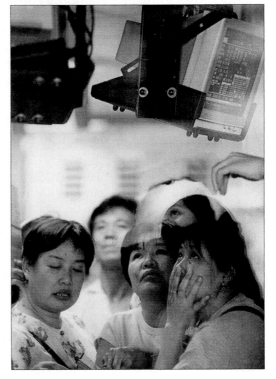

Now Asian economies were no longer consuming large quantities of raw materials. As demand slackened for commodities such as oil, for example, prices fell, hurting exporting nations as widespread as Venezuela, Saudi Arabia, and Russia. Russia was especially hard hit, because the Yeltsin government had developed no effective system for collecting taxes, relying instead on the sale of commodities such as oil to finance its operations. To make up the deficit, the Russians borrowed heavily from foreign investors, offering attractive interest rates as high as 70 percent. In August 1998 the jerry-built Russian financial structure collapsed when the Yeltsin government defaulted—refused to pay—much of its debt.

Hong Kong residents anxiously scan monitors displaying plummeting stock prices during the Asian recession of 1997 and 1998.

That default should not have had a severe effect on the global financial system—except that Russia's interest rates had been so tempting that many speculators had borrowed money to take advantage of them. To repay their creditors, these investors were forced to sell bonds they held from reasonably strong economies such as Israel, Egypt, Mexico, and Brazil. As those bonds lost value, yet other investors, worried that the chain reaction might continue, fled to the safe haven offered by U.S. Treasury bonds. Brazil's currency in particular found itself under severe pressure.

Financial crisis at home

At first the United States had seemed insulated from these crises. But over the previous year, one large and respected investment fund, Long-Term Capital Management (LTCM), had bet an immense sum—about $120 billion—that the price of U.S. Treasuries would fall and those of currencies in emerging markets like Russia's would rise. Unfortunately, the crisis that had spread from Thailand through Russia to Brazil sent prices and interest rates in exactly the opposite direction. LTCM suddenly faced bankruptcy—and many large American banks and investment firms had put large sums of their own money into LTCM. Fearing a financial crisis, Federal Reserve Chair Alan Greenspan intervened. He arranged for LTCM's creditors to take over the embattled fund.

Similarly the International Monetary Fund (IMF) organized loans and credits that pumped $115 billion into Asia, then $10.2 billion into Russia, $50 billion into Mexico (of which the United States supplied $20 billion), and yet another $41.5 billion for Brazil. Although Russia remained largely insolvent, Brazil recovered and the Asian economy began to turn around. But the resources of the IMF had been stretched dangerously thin in order to escape a full-blown world crisis. The fragile underpinnings of global financial markets had been exposed.

 The Clinton Presidency on Trial

Throughout Clinton's presidency the nation experienced a powerful economic expansion. Despite low unemployment, there was little inflation. Prosperity allowed the president to eliminate the budget deficits that had soared during the 1980s. It also kept his popularity high despite recurring scandals. But soaring government revenues did not persuade Congress to support Clinton's reform agenda.

Recovery without Reform

Clinton program

In his first speech to Congress, Clinton proposed a program that began reducing the deficit but also provided investments to stimulate the economy and repair the nation's decaying public infrastructure. By contrast, Presidents Reagan and Bush had cut funds to rebuild schools, roads, dams, bridges, and other public structures. In August 1993 a compromise budget bill passed by only a single vote in the Senate, with Republicans blocking the stimulus portion of Clinton's program. Still, deficit reduction was a significant achievement. During the Reagan-Bush years deficits had risen sharply, despite conservative rhetoric about balancing the budget.

NAFTA

The victory in the budget battle provided Clinton with some momentum. In the fall he hammered together a bipartisan coalition to pass NAFTA, the North American Free Trade Agreement. With the promise of greater trade and more jobs, the pact linked the United States economy more closely with Canada and Mexico. The president also helped supporters of gun control overcome the powerful opposition of the National Rifle Association to pass the Brady Bill, which required a five-day waiting period on gun purchases. And with inner-city violence and drive-by shootings making headlines, the president pushed through a compromise crime bill in September 1994.

Health care reform

Health care reform topped Clinton's legislative agenda. A task force led by Hillary Rodham Clinton developed a plan to provide health coverage for all Americans, including the 37 million who in 1994 remained uninsured. The plan rejected a more sweeping single payer system, in which the government would act as the central agency reimbursing medical expenses. At the same time, it proposed more far-reaching changes than did a Republican plan merely to reform insurance laws in order to make private medical coverage more readily available. But a host of interest groups attacked the proposal, especially small businesses who worried that they would bear the brunt of the system's financing. Despite last-minute lobbying, even a compromise bill lacked the votes needed to win approval.

If the Clintons' plan had passed, the president and the Democratic majority in Congress might have staked their claim to a government that was actively responding to some of the long-term problems facing American society. But the failure of health care reform heightened the perception of an ill-organized administration and

President Clinton's most ambitious attempt at reform was to overhaul the nation's health care system to provide all Americans with basic health care (along with a card to guarantee it). But medical interest groups defeated the proposal, arguing it would create yet another huge and inefficient bureaucracy. In 1996 Congress passed a more modest medical reform bill that made it easier for workers to retain health insurance if they lost or changed jobs.

an entrenched Congress content with the status quo. Republicans, sensing the level of public frustration, stepped up their opposition to other Democratic legislation. The partisan battle only increased the sense of stalemate.

The Conservative Revolution Reborn

The 1994 midterm elections confirmed the public's anger over political gridlock. For the first time since the Eisenhower years, Republicans captured majorities in both the House and the Senate. The combative new Speaker of the House, Newt Gingrich of Georgia, proclaimed himself a "genuine revolutionary" and vowed to complete what Ronald Reagan had begun. Gingrich used the first hundred days of the new Congress to bring to a vote ten proposals from his campaign document "The Contract with America." The contract proposed a balanced budget amendment, tax cuts, and term limits for all members of Congress. To promote family values, its anticrime package included a broader death penalty and welfare restrictions aimed at reducing teen pregnancy. Although the term limits proposal did not survive, the other nine proposals were passed by the House.

The Contract with America

The whirlwind performance was impressive. "When you look back five years from now," enthused Republican Governor Tommy Thompson of Wisconsin, "you're going to say 'they came, they saw, they conquered.'" But the Senate was less eager to enact the House proposals. And as Republicans assembled a more comprehensive budget, it became clear that the public was increasingly worried about the Gingrich revolution. Fiscally, the Republicans set out to balance the federal budget in the year 2002 while still cutting taxes by $245 billion. To do that, they proposed scaling back Medicare expenditures by $270 billion and allowing Medicare premiums to double. Republicans also sought to roll back environmental legislation that had been passed over the previous quarter century. Their proposals reduced protection for endangered species, relaxed pollution controls set up by the Clean Water Act, and gave mining, ranching, and logging interests greater freedom to develop public lands.

"I am a genuine revolutionary," House Speaker Newt Gingrich proclaimed, and the newly elected Republican freshmen in Congress led the charge to complete the Reagan revolution. By clothing Newt's followers as stiff-armed, flag-waving militarists, illustrator Anita Kunz recalls Mussolini's overzealous Brown Shirts. Enough of the public agreed, forcing the Republicans to backpedal.

Government shutdown

When President Clinton threatened to veto the Republican budget, first-year Republicans (among Gingrich's most committed troops) pushed the Speaker toward confrontation. Rather than compromise, Republicans twice forced the federal government to shut down. The result was a disaster for the self-proclaimed revolutionaries. Most of the public viewed their stance as intransigent, and the Congress was forced to back down. At the same time, right-wing extremists were linked to the bombing of a federal building in Oklahoma City that killed 169 men, women, and children. The incident made Americans aware of the many right-wing militia groups operating on the fringes of American society. Though these groups ranged from religious cults to survivalists, anti-Semites, skinheads, and rabid nationalists, what did seem to unite them was a profound mistrust of the federal government.

At the same time, President Clinton moved steadily to preempt the Republican agenda. In his earlier efforts at reducing public debt, he had been willing to settle for a $200 billion annual budget deficit. (It had run as high as $290 billion under George Bush.) By 1995, he was proposing his own route toward a balanced budget by 2002. Similarly, in 1996 the president signed into law a sweeping reform of welfare. The law owed as much to Republican ideas as it did to the president's. For the first time in 60 years, the social welfare policies of the liberal democratic state were being substantially reversed. The bill ended guarantees of federal aid to poor children, turning over such programs to the states. Food stamp spending was cut, and

Welfare reform

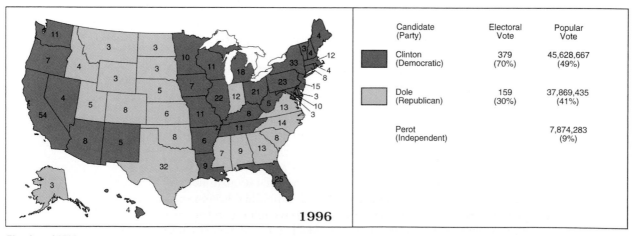

Candidate (Party)	Electoral Vote	Popular Vote
Clinton (Democratic)	379 (70%)	45,628,667 (49%)
Dole (Republican)	159 (30%)	37,869,435 (41%)
Perot (Independent)		7,874,283 (9%)

1996

Election of 1996

the law placed a five-year limit on payments to any family. Most adults receiving payments were required to find work within two years.

Thus as the election of 1996 approached, the Republican revolution had been either dampened or co-opted by the president. "By popular demand," one reporter joked, Newt Gingrich had become "a political hermit." Following a lackluster primary campaign, the Republicans nominated former Senator Bob Dole, an aging party loyalist, to run for president. Dole sought to stir excitement with promises of a 15 percent tax cut. But the economy was robust, and skeptical voters doubted he could balance the budget and still deliver his tax cut. In November Bill Clinton became the first Democrat since Franklin Roosevelt to win a second term in the White House.

Conservatives and the Feminist Agenda

Conservatives aimed some of their most bitter barbs at Hillary Clinton. Throughout her career she had supported liberal causes disdained by most conservatives, including the Children's Defense Fund, the American Bar Association's commission on women, and educational reform in Arkansas. Hillary Clinton also used her influence to promote opportunity for women and to draw attention to feminist issues. Bill Clinton shared many of his wife's concerns. During the election he told voters that he had "learned that building up women does not diminish men." In that spirit he appointed Ruth Bader Ginsburg to the Supreme Court and three women to his cabinet, including Janet Reno as attorney general. In 1997 he named Madeleine Albright as the first female secretary of state.

Both Clintons had supported a woman's right to control her decisions on reproduction, an issue that remained hotly contested during the 1990s. Because antiabortion conservatives had been unable to secure the repeal of *Roe v. Wade,* they sought to limit its application as much as possible by proposing to make illegal a procedure they referred to as "partial birth" late-term abortion. Doctors seldom performed the procedure and did so only to save a mother's life. Twice President Clinton vetoed bills that would criminalize the procedure.

More problematic for feminists was the legacy of the Supreme Court decision in the 1991 case of *UAW v. Johnson Controls.* Since *Muller v. Oregon* in 1908 (page 710), the Court had accepted as constitutional laws that gave women special protection based on their biological differences from men. Using this standard, Johnson Controls had established a policy of not hiring women workers to manufacture batteries, because the lead fumes in the workplace might damage a pregnant woman's unborn fetus. The workers' union challenged the policy, noting that fertile men who faced reproductive risks in the workplace were not restricted. The Court agreed with the union, ruling that the emphasis on biological differences denied women an "equal employment opportunity." Justice Harry Blackmun wrote that a woman's decision as to whether her "reproductive role is more important to herself and her family than her economic role" was one for her to make on her own.

UAW v. Johnson Controls

Many feminists hailed the decision as a step toward workplace equality. Feminist scholar Cynthia Daniels saw it as more ambiguous. Should laws recognize biological difference, or should they uphold equality? As Daniels argued, "To ignore difference is to risk placing women in a workplace designed by and for men, with all of its hazards and lack of concern for the preservation of life and health." Yet rules that recognized difference had in the past reinforced "those assumptions and economic structures which form the foundation of women's inequality." Throughout the 1990s feminists struggled with how to balance gender neutrality with gender justice.

Contrasting views of feminism

"For some, feminism necessarily means the promotion of equality between men and women," historian Elizabeth Fox Genovese wrote. "For others, it just as necessarily means the celebration of differences between women and men."

Scandal

Almost every two-term president has faced some crisis in his second term. Franklin Roosevelt squandered an enormous electoral mandate with his plan to pack the Supreme Court. Watergate brought down Richard Nixon, whereas the Iran-Contra controversy tarnished Reagan. Bill Clinton's scandal was in some ways more puzzling. At once smaller and more personal, it nonetheless threatened his presidency with the American political system's ultimate sanction: impeachment, conviction, and removal from office.

The Lewinsky affair

By four years into the Whitewater investigation, Special Prosecutor Kenneth Starr had spent $30 million and produced only the convictions of several of the president's former business partners. (The Watergate investigation, by contrast, lasted just over two years.) Starr dismissed the grand jury in Arkansas without filing charges against either of the Clintons on Whitewater; still, he pursued several other investigations while the sexual harassment suit brought by Paula Jones kept alive allegations of Clinton's sexual misconduct. Then in January 1998, Starr hit what looked like the jackpot. Linda Tripp, a disgruntled federal employee with links to the Bush administration and to a conservative literary agent, produced audiotapes of phone conversations in which a 21-year-old White House intern, Monica Lewinsky, talked of an intimate relationship with the president.

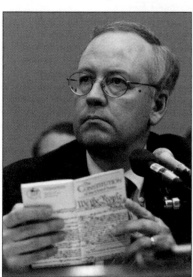

Special Prosecutor Kenneth Starr, holding a copy of the Constitution during House Judiciary hearings.

Starr succeeded in preventing Clinton from learning of the tapes before the president and Lewinsky testified in depositions to Paula Jones's attorneys that they had not had "sexual relations." When word of the tapes leaked out several days later, the news media predicted ominously that the president must resign or face impeachment—if not for his personal conduct, at the very least for lying under oath. Other evidence emerged over the following six months that Clinton had denied the affair to members of his Cabinet and perhaps even offered Lewinsky a job to buy her silence. That summer Starr subpoenaed the president to appear before a Washington grand jury. Four hours of testimony was taken on videotape, and in September Starr made public his report to the House of Representatives, recommending that the president be impeached on the grounds of perjury, obstruction of justice, and witness tampering.

Impeachment

To the astonishment of the news media, polling indicated that the public did not support the Republican calls for impeachment. Although Clinton had clearly engaged in behavior most Americans found inappropriate or even repugnant, they seemed to draw a line between public and private actions. Furthermore, Starr's report went into such lurid detail that many Americans questioned the special prosecutor's motives. Nonetheless, the Republicans pressed their attack. Along strict party lines, a majority in the House voted three articles of impeachment for lying to the grand jury, suborning perjury, and orchestrating a cover-up. In January 1999 the matter went to the Senate for trial, with Chief Justice of the United States William Rehnquist presiding.

In a month-long hearing, the House managers presented the case against the president. But unlike the Watergate scandals, in which Richard Nixon resigned because a bipartisan consensus had determined that impeachment was necessary, the accusers and defenders of Bill Clinton had always divided along strongly partisan lines. The Senate voted to acquit, with five Republicans joining all 45 Senate Democrats in the decision.

Acquittal

counterpoint

The Significance of Impeachment

Did the impeachment of Bill Clinton signify a major constitutional crisis? That question is one on which historians are unlikely to concur, unless they can agree first on the seriousness of the president's offenses. Were Clinton's misdeeds essentially personal—brought onto the public stage only because his enemies were determined to pursue him, even to the point of entrapment? If so, the process leading to impeachment could be said to be little more than a vendetta by a partisan majority in Congress. And surely the Founders did not intend Congress to overrule the decision that voters had made in a presidential election. From this perspective, if a zealous Congress had succeeded in removing the president from office, the nation might have faced a threat to the traditional separation of powers erected by the Constitution.

Such arguments reflect the conviction of most historians that Clinton's actions did not constitute an impeachable offense. But what if the case was not simply "just about sex" but—as Republicans charged—a matter of the rule of law being violated because the chief executive of the United States had committed perjury and abused the powers of his office to protect himself? Such abuses had proven sufficient grounds to set in motion the impeachment of Richard Nixon. Was the true Constitutional crisis, then, a failure of political principle and conscience on the part of Senate Democrats?

No one, including the president himself, defended his personal conduct. On the other hand, the fervid pursuit of his accusers seemed excessive to many observers. Given the ambiguity of the situation, the debate over the meaning of the Clinton impeachment will undoubtedly continue for years to come.

The Politics of Surplus

The impeachment controversy left the president weakened, but hardly impotent. Throughout the political tempest the nation's economy had continued to grow strongly, leading pollsters to suggest that the general prosperity accounted for Clinton's popularity. By 1999 the rate of unemployment had dropped to 4.1 percent, the lowest in nearly 30 years, while the stock market reached new highs. Furthermore, as the economy expanded, federal tax receipts grew with it. By 1998 Bill Clinton faced a situation that would have seemed improbable a few years previous—a budget surplus. Much of that surplus had more to do with accounting practices than with real excess revenue. Nonetheless, by balancing the budget the president had appropriated a key Republican issue. Political debate shifted to what to do with the surplus.

Clinton sought to revive much of his initial agenda. He wanted the money spent on education, paying down the national debt, and protecting social security and Medicare funds from predicted future deficits. The deficits seemed sure to arise because an entire generation of graying baby boomers was heading toward retirement beginning around the year 2010. During the 1990s six workers paid taxes for each retiree collecting benefits; thus for years the government had been able to borrow excess revenues from the social security trust fund to help reduce annual deficits. But projections indicated that by around 2030, only three workers would be paying taxes for each person collecting benefits. That ratio threatened fiscal disaster.

Social security crisis

Clinton thus argued that the budget surplus could best be used to ensure the solvency of social security and Medicare.

For Republicans in Congress, tax relief remained the highest priority. They viewed it both as a means of reducing progressive tax rates, which they had long resented, and a way to downsize the federal government, because reduced revenues would mean fewer and smaller government social programs. Republicans launched a campaign for a large tax cut in the summer of 1999 but found to their surprise that the public showed scant interest. So Clinton succeeded in controlling the terms of the debate, which ended with both parties trying to claim credit for protecting social security.

Defeat of nuclear test ban treaty

As the presidential campaign of 2000 loomed, the Senate unexpectedly took up debate on a treaty banning underground nuclear testing by the 44 nations of the world considered to have nuclear capabilities. Clinton had signed the treaty in 1996, but Senate Republicans refused to ratify it, claiming that it could be neither verified nor enforced. Democrats pressed for a vote, underestimating the degree of opposition. When Republicans called the Democrats' bluff, the treaty was voted down in October 1999, far short of the two-thirds support needed to ratify. It was the first time a treaty of that magnitude had been rejected since the Senate voted down the Versailles agreement ending World War I. Although some Republicans known as internationalists opposed the treaty, others in the party reflected a rising strain of isolationism. House Republican Dick Armey captured that spirit when he remarked, "I've been to Europe once. I don't have to go again."

 ## The United States in a Networked World

In 1988 economist Lawrence Summers was working on the presidential campaign of Michael Dukakis. At a meeting in Chicago, the staff assigned him a car with a telephone. Summers was so impressed, he recalled, that "I used it to call my wife to tell her I was in a car with a phone." A decade later as deputy treasury secretary in the Clinton administration, he visited the Ivory Coast in Africa to help launch an American-supported health project. One village on his itinerary could be reached only by dugout canoe. As Summers stepped into the canoe for his return trip, an aide handed him a cell phone. "Washington has a question for you," the aide said. The same man who once marveled at a phone in his car in Chicago ten years later expected one in his dugout canoe in the interior of Africa.

The Internet Revolution

Like Summers, Americans at the end of the twentieth century had become linked to a global communications network almost wherever they went. Computers, cell phones, pagers, and other electronic devices provided almost instant contact with the wider world. The process of connection had been driven by a revolution in microchip technologies.

The Galactic Network and ARPANET

Although the Internet communications revolution gained global momentum and widespread public attention only after 1995, its roots could be traced to the early 1960s. In 1962 J. C. R. Licklider of the Massachusetts Institute of Technology wrote a series of memos laying out the concept of what he grandly termed a "Galactic Network": computers all across the world connected in order to share data and programs. But the technology for sending data back and forth efficiently along phone lines was still primitive. Computer technicians cobbled together a network between four host computers in 1969. Known as the ARPANET, it allowed university and Department of Defense researchers to share computer capacity more efficiently as well as to create a communications system that could survive a nuclear attack. Managers discovered that many of the researchers with access to the network used it to send personal messages. E-mail had been born.

A second phase of the revolution began in the 1970s when a Harvard dropout named Bill Gates helped write software to operate personal computers. Most computing was then done on what were called mainframes, massive and hugely expensive machines found only in large businesses, universities, and government agencies. Gates was among a growing group of technically minded visionaries who saw that the technologies of miniaturization would make personal computers useful in everyday life.

Most software writers made their work freely available to anyone wanting to use it. Gates perceived that software had commercial potential because it was a key to making computers accessible to a mass public. He created the Microsoft Corporation to exploit that promise. In 1980 International Business Machines Corporation (IBM) adopted Microsoft's program, MS-DOS, to operate IBM personal computers. MS-DOS became a standard for the computer industry. By the mid-1980s small businesses, homes, and schools were using personal computers for word processing, graphic design, and spreadsheets that tracked personal and financial data. Other manufacturers used microprocessors on silicon chips to operate complex mechanical systems ranging from watches to jet aircraft. By the 1990s desktop computers could boast more power than the mainframes of just forty years earlier.

The personal computer

The Internet (successor to the ARPANET) was growing too. By 1985 it linked about 1000 host computers. To help users connect, sites were given domain names instead of a faceless string of numbers. Taking the next step in the evolutionary process, British-born physicist Tim Berners-Lee wrote software that created the World Wide Web as a facet of the Internet. Berners-Lee saw the possibility for a universal system with access to anything that was information. He applied the hypertext link (http:\\) that allowed users to move freely from one site to sites of related interest, each with its own Web address, or URL (Uniform Resource Locator).

The World Wide Web

Berners-Lee shared the democratic vision common among software programmers and Internet pioneers. They saw the Web as open and free to all. Users could communicate without restriction and find access to any form of information. Such openness was the bane of authoritarian governments, which found it difficult to control public opinion in a world in which information flowed freely. The unregulated format of the Web raised substantial legal, moral, and political questions in the United States as well. People with products or ideas to promote could establish their own Web sites for a nominal cost. By 1999 five million sites were in operation—among them were sites promoting pornography, hate speech, and even instructions on how to build atomic bombs. A number of politicians and civic groups called for the censorship of the more extreme Web content. But the system's openness, coupled with the opposition of a majority of Web users, made censorship extremely difficult to effect.

One of Berners-Lee's central visions was based on the Web's capacity for interactivity. "The Web," he said, "will still be a universal space but one in which people feel more creative, less like couch potatoes." Interactivity also gave the Web enormous commercial potential. With Web browsers, developed in the mid-1990s, seekers and finders increasingly became buyers and sellers. Early sites such as CDNow and The Onion tended to offer goods—music CDs, financial information, news, and games—favored by young, technically sophisticated Web surfers. After 1995

Use of the Internet broadened sharply after 1995. As of May 1998, the number of pieces of mail handled daily by the U.S. Postal service was 630 million. The average number of e-mails sent daily was 2.1 billion. This graphic by Stephen G. Eick, of Bell Laboratories, plotted worldwide Internet traffic.

E-commerce

business on the Web, or e-commerce, grew at over 175 percent per year as more and more people went "online." By 1999 over 200 million people internationally and 100 million Americans used the Web to buy over $300 billion in goods. Economists estimated that over the near-term future, Internet business would double every nine months.

The revolution in microchip technologies contributed substantially to the economic expansion of the 1990s. In 1998 e-commerce alone generated some 482,000 jobs. Whereas in 1965 business committed just 3 percent of their spending to high technology, they committed 45 percent in 1996. That increase in spending contributed to a significant rise in labor productivity. Improved productivity in turn proved to be a critical factor behind economic growth.

American Workers in a Two-Tiered Economy

The benefits of prosperity have not been evenly distributed, however. Economists described the United States in the 1990s as a two-tiered labor market in which most increases in earning went to people at the top of the wage scale. Thus despite the computer revolution and the decade's prosperity, the median income of American families was barely higher in 1996 than in 1973. Indeed, the earnings of the average white male worker actually fell. Only because so many women entered the job market did the family standard of living remain the same. In the early 1970s some 37 percent of women worked outside the home; in 1999 about 57 percent did.

Education was a critical factor in determining winners in the computer economy. Families with college-educated parents were three times more likely to have home access to the Web than were those families in which parents' education ended with high school. Because average education levels were relatively lower among African Americans and Latinos (and relatively higher among Asian Americans), the computer divide took on a racial cast as well. But the implications went beyond mere access to the Web and its cornucopia of information and commerce. More important, the high-wage sector of the computer economy required educated workers, and the demand for them drove up those workers' salaries.

Wage stagnation

By contrast, most semiskilled and unskilled workers saw little growth in earnings despite full employment. The choices facing the nation's half-million long-haul truck drivers was a case in point. Typically, drivers piloting these eighteen-wheel rigs—on the road for two to three weeks at a time—made as much as $35,000 a year in the mid-1990s, about the same as they had in the 1970s. To keep their earnings that high, drivers needed to log around 3000 hours a year—50 percent more than the average work-year in America. Because the motor freight business was so competitive, trucking firms did not grant wage increases that would have to be passed on to their customers. And because most drivers did not belong to a union, they could not bargain effectively for higher wages. (Membership in the Teamsters, which represented truck drivers, fell from 30 percent in the 1970s to 10 percent by 1999.) So rather than make less money or strike, the drivers stayed on the road longer. In 1998 they averaged 65 hours every seven days. To skirt regulations limiting the amount of time on the job, drivers logged loading and unloading time as rest periods. Accidents involving the big rigs increased.

If the hours were long and conditions grueling, why did so many truckers continue to drive? In essence, they had no appealing alternative. The highest-paid unskilled workers in the United States averaged 2000 hours per year at about $14 per hour, or $28,000 a year—an effective pay cut of $7000. "So there [was] a lot of movement between companies," one executive observed, but few drivers were willing to quit. Unlike computer programmers or corporate executives who were in high demand, low-skill workers like the truckers were not able to increase their earnings simply by switching jobs. Some economists concluded that "the most important economic division is not between races, or genders, or economic sectors, but between the college-educated and the noncollege-educated."

Diverging income levels

Certainly, the spread in the incomes of American workers widened sharply during the 1990s. The highest-paid Americans saw their pay grow twice as fast as that of the middle class and even more than that of blue-collar workers. In 1982, corporate executives made 42 times more than factory workers; in 1998 they made 419 times more. High-wage college graduates were also more likely to invest in the stock market; thus the run-up in stock values since the early 1990s produced enormous wealth for people at the top of the economic pyramid. As of 1995, the top one-half of one percent of all American households (500,000) held just under 28 percent of all net worth. That figure translated into $11.7 million per household. At the top of this pyramid stood Microsoft's Bill Gates, whose personal worth in July 1999 briefly exceeded $100 billion. In fact, in 1998 Gate's wealth was greater than the gross domestic product of all but 41 of the world's nations, falling between Egypt and Pakistan.

Effects of prosperity

The booming economy in the last three years of the twentieth century brought a small decrease in that inequality. Wages rose slightly, boosting the median American income to $38,885 in 1998. The number of Americans living in poverty dropped by a million in 1998, to a decade low. Once again, earnings differences between white, black, and Latino males began to narrow. Governments showed new willingness to spend money on education and transportation, services most vital to the poor. Even the Republican Congress restored some spending cuts on housing, urban development, and social welfare, all programs that increased the well-being of the poorest Americans.

The prosperity of the late 1990s produced an interesting dilemma. On the one hand, it eased many social tensions that long divided the nation. Inner-city crime rates fell; the poor began to experience a marked improvement in their economic situation; consumer confidence reached an all-time high. But over the longer term, the boom's statistics were not encouraging. Despite the decline in the poverty rate, it remained above the rate for any year in the 1970s. If the strongest economy in 30 years left the poverty rate higher than the inflation-plagued years of the 1970s, what would happen if the economy faltered? Most likely, those Americans on the lower end of the two-tier economy would be the major losers. Government funding for services they most needed—education, day care, transportation, and health care—would likely decline. Surpluses targeted for social security and Medicare reform might disappear. Would the two-tier economy become a permanent fixture, with those people born into the bottom tier destined to stay there?

Multiculturalism and Contested American Identity

No state more fully represented the multicultural and global complexion of late-twentieth-century America than California. More of the nation's recently arrived immigrants from Asia, Central America, and Mexico settled there than in any other state. By 1990, fully 33 percent of the residents of Los Angeles county were foreign born, a figure rivaling the high-water mark of 40 percent set by New York City in 1910. Predictably, then, it was California that so often led the national debate over multiculturalism. Californians put forth election propositions challenging the policies of affirmative action, proposed to make English an official language, and sought to restrict welfare, education, and other social benefits for immigrants and aliens. A recession there sharpened the debate in the early 1990s, as did several explosive legal cases raising the issue of racism. The battles over race, immigration, and multiculturalism suggest that in an era of internationally linked economies and global migrations, the United States remains a nation of nations seeking to accommodate distinctive identities along lines of race, ethnicity, and national origins.

African Americans and the Persistence of the Racial Divide

In the 1990s the highest-paid celebrity in the world was an African American—Michael Jordan. Oprah Winfrey, also an African American, was the highest-paid woman in America. African American lawyer Vernon Jordan ranked as one of President Clinton's most trusted friends and advisers. Both political parties eyed former General Colin Powell as a possible presidential candidate. Millions of white as well as black Americans expressed outrage when an all-white jury acquitted four Los Angeles police officers charged with beating Rodney King, a black American man. Yet when a largely black jury acquitted football star O. J. Simpson of murder in a 1994 trial, polls indicated that whites and blacks sharply disagreed over Simpson's guilt or innocence. Although the situation of African Americans had improved vastly compared with their position in the 1950s, race still mattered.

Rodney King and the Los Angeles riots

In 1991 Los Angeles police arrested a black motorist, Rodney King, for speeding and drunken driving. The police were all white; King was African American. As he lay on the ground, four officers proceeded to beat him with nightsticks more than 50 times. When blacks complained about such brutality at the hands of largely white police, public officials often dismissed their complaints. This case was different. A man in a nearby apartment videotaped the beating, which the news media repeatedly broadcast to the entire nation. But the following year, an all-white suburban jury acquitted the officers, concluding that King had been threatening and that the officers had acted within their authority.

The verdict enraged the African American community in Los Angeles, where widespread riots erupted for three days, making the violence the worst civil disturbance in Los Angeles history. By the time police and the National Guard restored order, nearly 2000 people had been injured, 40 people had died, over 4500 fires burned, and $500 million of property had been looted, damaged, or destroyed.

At first glance the riot appeared to be much like the one that had decimated Watts, a poor area of Los Angeles, in 1965. Poor African Americans had lashed out in frustration at white racism. In fact, the 1992 riots were multiracial in character, exposing divisions in Los Angeles's multicultural communities. Rioters, both black and Latino, damaged over 2000 small groceries, liquor stores, and other businesses run by Korean American immigrants. African Americans also attacked Latinos; and after the first day, Latinos also joined in the disturbances. But there was a revealing pattern. In the more established Latino communities of East Los Angeles, where families had more to lose, residents remained quiet or worked actively to maintain the peace. By contrast, fires and looting destroyed many businesses in the MacArthur Park area, where the newest Latino immigrants lived. "Everybody said, 'How can they destroy their neighborhoods, their jobs . . . ?'" commented a Latino demographer from UCLA. "Well, my answer is that they did not consider it to be their own." Thus the 1992 riots exposed tension and competition among ethnic groups.

Complexity of the riots

In quite another way the case of O. J. Simpson revealed the persistence of a racial divide. Born into a ghetto family, Simpson had become first a football legend, then a movie star and television personality. He seemed to defy all notions that race prejudice restricted African Americans. But in 1994 police charged Simpson with the brutal murders of his white ex-wife, Nicole, and her friend Ron Goldman. Millions of television viewers watched with rapt attention as Simpson's attorneys transformed what seemed to be a strong prosecution case into a trial of the Los Angeles police. Their client had been framed, his attorneys suggested, by racist police officers. Defense lawyers revealed that the lead officer in the case had lied on the stand about his own prejudice and about his use of racial slurs.

The O. J. Simpson case

After a trial lasting almost a year, a jury of nine African Americans, two whites, and one Mexican American took just four hours to acquit Simpson. Regardless of his guilt or innocence, the verdict revealed a racial fault line dividing Americans. The vast majority of whites believed the evidence against Simpson allowed just one verdict—guilty. Most African Americans were equally persuaded that Simpson had been framed. Why? Both groups had watched the same trial; yet each brought to it significantly different personal experiences of the American system of justice. Black Americans who had all too often found themselves stopped arbitrarily by police or pulled over while driving in white neighborhoods disagreed fundamentally over whether that system applied equally to all people regardless of race.

African Americans in a Full-Employment Economy

In 1966 the African American community of North Lawndale, on Chicago's West Side, was one of the worst slums in America. At the time, Martin Luther King Jr. rented an apartment there, hoping to draw attention to its plight. When he was assassinated two years later, rioters burned down much of the neighborhood. Over the next 20 years half the population moved away from the endemic crime, drug addiction, and violent gangs.

By the late 1990s North Lawndale had undergone a rebirth. African American professionals had returned to the neighborhood. Homes that once stood deserted now sold for over $250,000. What happened in North Lawndale reflected new circumstances for many African Americans across the country during a decade of economic expansion. Home ownership reached 46 percent and employment increased from around 87 percent in 1980 to nearly 92 percent in 1998. African Americans

Inner-city renewal

in increasing numbers rose up the ladder in corporate America. Many started their own businesses. Test scores for reading and math proficiency also improved, and more African Americans, though fewer males, attended college.

Economic success brought new hope to the nation's inner cities. Crime and poverty decreased significantly, especially rates of murder and violence. Births to unwed mothers reached a postwar low. Fewer blacks lived below the poverty level and fewer were on welfare. The most hard-core block of the unemployed—males between 16 and 24—found many more jobs. The gap between wages for whites and blacks narrowed as well. Life expectancy increased substantially—from 63.8 years for African American males in 1980 to 66.1 in 1996 (white males were 70.7 and 73.8).

Yet many African Americans were reserved in their reaction to such statistics. "To the extent that you proclaim your success," one community leader remarked, "people forget about you." Furthermore, an economic downturn might reverse those gains, especially if employers resorted to the traditional practice of "last hired, first fired."

Proposition 209 against affirmative action

Civil rights leaders were most concerned about the continued assault on affirmative action. In 1996 California voters passed a ballot initiative, Proposition 209, that eliminated racial and gender preferences in hiring and college admissions. Ironically, the leading advocate for Proposition 209 was a conservative black businessman, Ward Connerly. Connerly argued that racial preferences demeaned black and other minority students by setting up a double standard that patronizingly assumed minorities could not compete on an equal basis. In any case, Proposition 209 had a striking effect. Enrollments of Latinos and blacks at the elite California university campuses and professional schools dropped sharply: down 57 percent for black students at Berkeley and 34 percent for Latinos. What remained was a student body that was only 3 percent black and 9 percent Latino, in a state in which African Americans constituted 7 percent and Latinos 29 percent of the population. A ballot initiative banning racial preference in admissions had a similar impact on the University of Washington. Enrollment for African Americans there dropped 40 percent and for Hispanics some 30 percent, while whites and Asians had small percentage increases. Major state universities in Texas and Michigan experienced similar declines after passing similar laws.

Opponents of affirmative action pointed out that total enrollments for blacks, Native Americans, and Latinos remained almost constant within the California university system. Minority students flocked to California's second- and third-tier university campuses, where they could benefit from smaller class sizes and a less competitive environment. But defenders of affirmative action remained skeptical. "Students' aspirations are very much shaped by the aspirations of their peers," wrote Derek Bok, a former president of Harvard University. "When you go to a very selective school, you probably set your sights higher." Other critics added that the decline of minority students at the elite campuses reduced ethnic and cultural diversity there to the detriment of other students' education.

Persistent poverty

Although African Americans had made undoubted gains, the census figures still challenged the notion that the playing field had been leveled enough for blacks to compete equally. Although joblessness among young black males fell by nearly a third between 1985 and 1998, unemployment remained twice as high among blacks (8.9 percent in 1998) as among whites (3.9 percent). A remarkably high percentage of black males were, in the language of the street, on "some kind of paper"—meaning they were in jail, on parole, or on probation. Some 13 percent, or 1.4 million, could not vote because they had been convicted of a felony. Such disparities suggested that even in the booming 1990s, race remained an evident dividing line along which inequalities persisted.

Global Pressures in a Multicultural America

Clearly the enormous changes wrought by immigration and the new global economy affected not just the immigrant enclaves but American culture as a whole. Salsa rhythms became part of the pop culture mainstream, and Latino foods competed with Indian curries, Japanese sushi, and Thai takeout for the loyalties of two-career families whose parents lacked the time to cook. In 1999 the first baseball player ever to hit over 60 home runs in two seasons was Sammy Sosa, a Dominican and only one of many Latino stars in the game.

But the mix of cultures was not always benign. Throughout the course of American history, when immigration flows increased, members of the dominant culture often reacted defensively. The Know-Nothings of the 1850s took as their slogan, "Americans should rule America," and nativists of the early twentieth century succeeded in sharply restricting immigration. During the 1990s the debate continued over how diverse the United States could become without losing its central identity.

Restriction again became a goal of those citizens worried about American identity. In 1916 Madison Grant had written *The Passing of the Great Race* to warn that unrestricted immigration might lead to racial suicide. In 1990 Lawrence Auster published *The Path to National Suicide,* in which he complained of the "browning of America." The new restrictionists in Congress proposed the Immigration and Stabilization Act of 1993, but neither the Democrats, who controlled Congress, nor President Clinton supported major changes in immigration policy. The following year, restrictionists used a different strategy in California, where their Proposition 187 ballot initiative denied health, education, and welfare benefits to illegal aliens. Despite the opposition of most major religious, ethnic, and educational organizations, the measure passed with a lopsided 59 percent of the vote. In the end, though, the proposition was not put into effect because a federal judge ruled unconstitutional the provision denying education to children of illegal aliens.

Proposition 187 and illegal aliens

A movement to make English the official language of the United States received broader support. As early as 1981 California Senator S. I. Hayakawa had urged Congress to adopt an English language amendment to the Constitution. The proposal

English as an official language

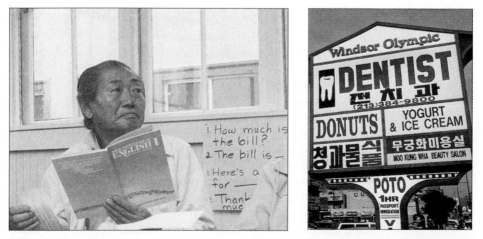

Both native-born Americans and immigrants debated whether English should be made an official language. Such ballot initiatives and legislation were often supported by newcomers who, like this Korean woman, were eager to learn English.

forbid the use of foreign languages in government documents and sought to eliminate bilingual education from public schools. Speaking a native tongue in the privacy of the home was acceptable, one English-only supporter granted, but "English is the 'glue' that helps keep America culture vibrant and dynamic."

Unable to move Congress to act, Hayakawa lent his support to a voter initiative to make English California's official language. There, state forms were often printed in Spanish, and San Francisco printed ballots in three languages—Chinese, Spanish, and English. Asian and Latino organizations, along with the Democratic Party and many state officials, opposed the proposition. They saw it as an attack on a liberal immigration policy and an effort to eliminate bilingual education. Nonetheless, in 1986 73 percent of Californians voted for the measure. Similarly, as a new wave of Cuban immigrants flooded southern Florida during the 1980s, voters of Dade County adopted an initiative making English the county's official language. Cubans resented the initiative as an attempt to restrict their culture and in 1993 they pressured county officials into repealing it. The same year, however, Florida voters approved an English-only referendum for the state. By 1996 23 states had adopted either resolutions or laws declaring English their official language.

Traditionally, nativist conflicts pit the dominant majority culture against the minority cultures of more recent arrivals. But in a multicultural society, such polar opposites often break down. In 1998 yet another ballot initiative passed in California (Proposition 227), mandating that schools phase out all their bilingual education programs. Students would be granted only one year of English-language immersion courses before receiving all instruction in English. In this instance both white and Latino voters approved the proposition by nearly the same margin, within one or two points of 62 percent. And the measure itself had been proposed after a group of Spanish-speaking parents boycotted their elementary school until it agreed to teach their children to read and write in English.

The pressures of global migration also increased tensions between minorities, as the Los Angeles riots of 1992 demonstrated. As recently as 1980 blacks and Latinos seldom competed directly in California's economy. African Americans had made gains in older industries and in the public sector. Latinos were more likely to work in agriculture or the low-wage service sector. But those economic boundaries were always changing. In the 1980s, for example, a great many of the janitors working in the downtown office buildings of Los Angeles were African American. As union members, their wages and benefits came to more than $12.00 an hour. By 1990 most had been replaced by nonunion Latino immigrants, usually illegals, working for only about $5.00 an hour with no contract, no benefits or health insurance, and no vacation time. That same dynamic had caused Juan Chanax and his fellow villagers from Guatemala to replace African Americans at Randall's supermarkets in Houston.

Libertad by Ester Hernandez

For the time being, the prosperity of the late 1990s muted the tensions arising from such conflicts. High employment meant ample work for both blacks and Latinos, though often in low-paid and unskilled jobs. And even after the heavy influx of immigrants, foreign-born residents accounted for less than 10 percent of the total U.S. population. If prosperity continued to be fueled by the productivity sparked by the computer revolution and the interconnections of the Web, the benefits of the two-tier economy might spread.

Yet the long-term trend remains unchanged. Since the peoples of Europe, Africa, and Asia made contact with the Americas half a millennium ago, the cultures and economies of the world have been drawn ever more tightly together. With the arrival of an information superhighway and the acceleration of international migrations, the United States will necessarily remain what it has always been: a nation of nations whose political system continues to evolve new ways of democratically encompassing a diversity that now reflects the world.

Epilogue, November 1999: Outside the Food Emporium on New York City's West Side, Lillian Winston, a woman in her eighties, emerged with four grocery bags. A young man approached promptly, dressed in a crisp white shirt, tie, and brightly polished shoes—one of the store's delivery workers. He was not Guatemalan, like Juan Chanax. He came from the continent that, during the first three centuries after the arrival of Columbus in the Americas, supplied four times as many immigrants as any other land. His name was Gasel Lii and he hailed from the Congo. The number of sub-Saharan Africans such as Lii living in New York City had almost doubled, from 44,000 in 1990 to about 84,000 in 1999. Like earlier immigrants from Europe, Asia, and Latin America, these newcomers arrived willing to work for a better life. Lii was putting in 12 hours a day, six days a week, for pay that averaged out to $2.50 an hour, or $107 a week. He supported a wife and children who still lived in Africa. "We thought life in America was going to be easier," commented one of his fellow workers, from Gabon, who added sardonically, "Maybe we watched too much *Dynasty*." Gasel Lii picked up the grocery bags, two in each hand, and headed down the street.

chapter summary

During the 1990s the United States became increasingly tied to a worldwide network of economic, financial, and demographic relationships that increased both the nation's diversity and its interdependence.

- The Immigration Act of 1965 opened the United States to a new wave of immigration in the 1980s and 1990s, different from the influx earlier in the century because of its truly global diversity.

  - Immigrants from Asia—hailing from South and Southeast Asia as much as from China, Japan, and the Philippines—crowded both ends of the economic spectrum in an hourglass profile.

- Both legal and illegal immigrants from Mexico, Cuba, and Central America contributed to the growing Latino population, settling in both urban and suburban barrios.

- Many immigrants retained closer financial, political, and emotional ties with their home countries.

- Immigration changed the shape of religion in America, adding an increased presence of Muslim, Buddhist, and Hindu faiths.

- During the Clinton presidency, regional conflicts in the Middle East, Eastern Europe, Africa, and the Caribbean replaced cold war rivalries as the central challenge of foreign policy.

- The world financial crisis of 1997, spreading from Asia to Russia to Brazil and beyond, demonstrated how American and other world economies were closely linked.

- President Clinton's ambitious political agenda included rebuilding the nation's infrastructure, improving education, and reforming the health care system.

  - A divided and (after the elections of 1994) increasingly hostile Congress limited the president's legislative program.

  - The campaign of Republican Congressional conservatives to impeach President Clinton ended when the Senate failed to adopt the three articles of impeachment.

- The growth of the Internet, the World Wide Web, and e-commerce was part of a revolution in communications and information management made possible by advances in microchip and computer technology. But those advances also threatened to create a permanent two-tiered economy divided by levels of education and literacy.

- The political battles of the 1990s over race, immigration, and multiculturalism suggest that the United States will remain a nation in which distinctive identities along lines of race, ethnicity, social class, and religion continue to be both a source of strength and of political conflict.

additional reading

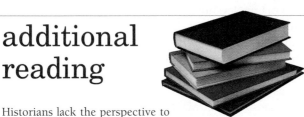

Historians lack the perspective to write effectively about the most recent past. Most often they rely on journalists and social scientists to provide analysis for what count as current events. Two early studies—Elizabeth Drew, *On the Edge: The Clinton Presidency* (1994) and Bob Woodward, *The Agenda: Inside the Clinton White House* (1994)—offer insight into the Clinton presidency in its first five years. The memoirs of two administration insiders, Robert Reich, *Locked in the Cabinet* (1997) and George Stephanopoulos, *All Too Human: A Political Education* (1999) help fill out the picture. Federal judge Robert Posner, *An Affair of State: The Investigation and Trial of President Clinton* (1999) analyzes the legal issues in the impeachment trial. On the Republican revolutionaries, see Dan Balz and Ronald Brownstein, *Storming the Gates: Protest Politics and the Republican Revival* (1996) as well as Elizabeth Drew's incisive *Showdown: The Struggle between Gingrich and the Clinton White House* (1996).

A useful portrait of the global economy in the Internet era is Thomas Friedman, *The Lexus and the Olive Tree* (1999). Michael Lewis takes readers inside the new world of the Internet and e-commerce in his readable *The New New Thing: A Silicon Valley Story* (1999). The problem of income inequality is carefully examined in Frank Levy, *The New Dollars and Dreams* (1999). For the debate over multiculturalism and diversity, see Lawrence Levine, *The Opening of the American Mind* (1996) and Alan Wolf, *One Nation, After All* (1998). David Reimers, *Unwelcome Strangers: American Identity and the Turn against Immigration* (1999) places the recent debates on immigration in historical context. Roberto Suro provides a sensitive examination of Latino cultures in the 1990s in *Strangers Among Us: How Latino Immigration Is Transforming America* (1998). For profiles of the new Asian immigration, see the final chapters of Ronald L. Takaki, *Strangers from a Different Shore* (revised edition, 1998) and Sucheng Chan, *Asian Americans* (1991) as well as Gary Okihiro, *Margins and Mainstreams* (1995). Nicholas Lemann, *The Big Test* (1999) takes a broad historic look at the SATs and affirmative action. For a fuller list of readings, see the Bibliography.

Significant Events

1965 — 1965 Immigration Reform Act

1969 ARPANET created

1970 —

1986 Immigration and Control Act; Proposition 63

1992 Whitewater scandal surfaces; Rodney King verdict; Los Angeles riots; Bill Clinton elected

1985 — 1993 Controversy over gays in the military; NAFTA passed; Peace agreement between Israel and Palestinians; Clinton's deficit reduction budget adopted

1994 U.S. troops sent to Haiti; health care reform fails; Paula Jones initiates lawsuit; Kenneth Starr appointed special prosecutor; Rwanda massacres; Republicans win control of Congress; California's Proposition 187 denies benefits to illegal aliens

1990 — 1995 Oklahoma City bombing; O. J. Simpson acquitted; Dayton Accords; GOP government shutdowns; U.S. troops in Bosnia; e-commerce boom begins

1996 Welfare reform adopted; Clinton defeats Dole; California passes Proposition 209 against affirmative action

1997 Pacific Rim financial collapse

1995 — 1998 Lewinsky scandal; Starr issues report recommending impeachment; federal budget surplus

1999 Senate acquits Clinton of impeachment charges; NATO planes bomb Serbia; American troops enter Kosovo as NATO peacekeepers; Senate rejects nuclear test ban treaty

Appendix The Declaration of Independence

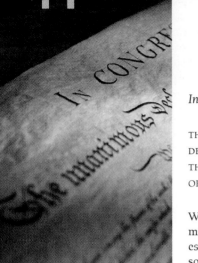

In Congress, July 4, 1776,

THE UNANIMOUS
DECLARATION OF THE
THIRTEEN UNITED STATES
OF AMERICA

When, in the course of human events, it becomes necessary for one people to dissolve the political bands which have connected them with another, and to assume, among the powers of the earth, the separate and equal station to which the laws of nature and of nature's God entitle them, a decent respect to the opinions of mankind requires that they should declare the causes which impel them to the separation.

We hold these truths to be self-evident, that all men are created equal; that they are endowed by their Creator with certain unalienable rights; that among these, are life, liberty, and the pursuit of happiness. That, to secure these rights, governments are instituted among men, deriving their just powers from the consent of the governed; that, whenever any form of government becomes destructive of these ends, it is the right of the people to alter or to abolish it, and to institute a new government, laying its foundation on such principles, and organizing its powers in such form, as to them shall seem most likely to effect their safety and happiness. Prudence, indeed, will dictate that governments long established, should not be changed for light and transient causes; and, accordingly, all experience hath shown, that mankind are more disposed to suffer, while evils are sufferable, than to right themselves by abolishing the forms to which they are accustomed. But, when a long train of abuses and usurpations, pursuing invariably the same object, evinces a design to reduce them under absolute despotism, it is their right, it is their duty, to throw off such government and to provide new guards for their future security. Such has been the patient sufferance of these colonies, and such is now the necessity which constrains them to alter their former systems of government. The history of the present King of Great Britain is a history of repeated injuries and usurpations, all having, in direct object, the establishment of an absolute tyranny over these States. To prove this, let facts be submitted to a candid world:

He has refused his assent to laws the most wholesome and necessary for the public good.

He has forbidden his governors to pass laws of immediate and pressing importance, unless suspended in their operation till his assent should be obtained; and, when so suspended, he has utterly neglected to attend to them.

He has refused to pass other laws for the accommodation of large districts of people, unless those people would relinquish the right of representation in the legislature; a right inestimable to them, and formidable to tyrants only.

He has called together legislative bodies at places unusual, uncomfortable, and distant from the depository of their public records, for the sole purpose of fatiguing them into compliance with his measures.

He has dissolved representative houses repeatedly for opposing, with manly firmness, his invasions on the rights of the people.

He has refused, for a long time after such dissolutions, to cause others to be elected; whereby the legislative powers, incapable of annihilation, have returned to the people at large for their exercise; the state remaining, in the meantime, exposed to all the danger of invasion from without, and convulsions within.

He has endeavored to prevent the population of these States; for that purpose, obstructing the laws for naturalization of foreigners, refusing to pass others to encourage their migration hither, and raising the conditions of new appropriations of lands.

He had obstructed the administration of justice, by refusing his assent to laws for establishing judiciary powers.

He has made judges dependent on his will alone, for the tenure of their offices, and the amount and payment of their salaries.

He has erected a multitude of new offices, and sent hither swarms of officers to harass our people, and eat out their substance.

He has kept among us, in time of peace, standing armies, without the consent of our legislatures.

He has affected to render the military independent of, and superior to, the civil power.

He has combined, with others, to subject us to a jurisdiction foreign to our Constitution, and unacknowledged by our laws; giving his assent to their acts of pretended legislation:

For quartering large bodies of armed troops among us:

For protecting them by a mock trial, from punishment, for any murders which they should commit on the inhabitants of these States:

For cutting off our trade with all parts of the world:

For imposing taxes on us without our consent:

For depriving us, in many cases, of the benefit of trial by jury:

For transporting us beyond seas to be tried for pretended offences:

For abolishing the free system of English laws in a neighboring province, establishing therein an arbitrary government, and enlarging its boundaries, so as to render it at once an example and fit instrument for introducing the same absolute rule into these colonies:

For taking away our charters, abolishing our most valuable laws, and altering, fundamentally, the powers of our governments:

For suspending our own legislatures, and declaring themselves invested with power to legislate for us in all cases whatsoever.

He has abdicated government here, by declaring us out of his protection, and waging war against us.

He has plundered our seas, ravaged our coasts, burnt our towns, and destroyed the lives of our people.

He is, at this time, transporting large armies of foreign mercenaries to complete the works of death, desolation, and tyranny, already begun, with circumstances of cruelty and perfidy scarcely paralleled in the most barbarous ages, and totally unworthy the head of a civilized nation.

He has constrained our fellow citizens, taken captive on the high seas, to bear arms against their country, to become the executioners of their friends, and brethren, or to fall themselves by their hands.

He has excited domestic insurrections amongst us, and has endeavored to bring on the inhabitants of our frontiers, the merciless Indian savages, whose known rule of warfare is an undistinguished destruction of all ages, sexes, and conditions.

In every stage of these oppressions, we have petitioned for redress, in the most humble terms; our repeated petitions have been answered only by repeated injury. A prince, whose character is thus marked by every act which may define a tyrant, is unfit to be the ruler of a free people.

Nor have we been wanting in attention to our British brethren. We have warned them, from time to time, of attempts made by their legislature to extend an unwarrantable jurisdiction over us. We have reminded them of the circumstances of our emigration and settlement here. We have appealed to their native justice and magnanimity, and we have conjured them, by the ties of our common kindred, to disavow these usurpations, which would inevitably interrupt our connections and correspondence. They, too, have been deaf to the voice of justice and consanguinity. We must, therefore, acquiesce in the necessity which denounces our separation, and hold them as we hold the rest of mankind, enemies in war, in peace, friends.

We, therefore, the representatives of the United States of America, in general Congress assembled, appealing to the Supreme Judge of the world for the rectitude of our intentions, do, in the name, and by the authority of the good people of these colonies, solemnly publish and declare, that these united colonies are, and of right ought to be, free and independent states: that they are absolved from all allegiance to the British Crown, and that all political connection between them and the state of Great Britain is, and ought to be, totally dissolved; and that, as free and independent states, they have full power to levy war, conclude peace, contract alliances, establish commerce, and to do all other acts and things which independent states may of right do. And, for the support of this declaration, with a firm reliance on the protection of Divine Providence, we mutually pledge to each other our lives, our fortunes, and our sacred honor.

The foregoing Declaration was, by order of Congress, engrossed, and signed by the following members:

JOHN HANCOCK

New Hampshire	New York	Delaware	North Carolina
Josiah Bartlett	William Floyd	Caesar Rodney	William Hooper
William Whipple	Philip Livingston	George Read	Joseph Hewes
Matthew Thornton	Francis Lewis	Thomas M'Kean	John Penn
	Lewis Morris		

Massachusetts Bay	New Jersey	Maryland	South Carolina
Samuel Adams	Richard Stockton	Samuel Chase	Edward Rutledge
John Adams	John Witherspoon	William Paca	Thomas Heyward, Jr.
Robert Treat Paine	Francis Hopkinson	Thomas Stone	Thomas Lynch, Jr.
Elbridge Gerry	John Hart	Charles Carroll, of Carrollton	Arthur Middleton
	Abraham Clark		

Rhode Island
Stephen Hopkins
William Ellery

Connecticut
Roger Sherman
Samuel Huntington
William Williams
Oliver Wolcott

Pennsylvania
Robert Morris
Benjamin Rush
Benjamin Franklin
John Morton
George Clymer
James Smith
George Taylor
James Wilson
George Ross

Virginia
George Wythe
Richard Henry Lee
Thomas Jefferson
Benjamin Harrison
Thomas Nelson, Jr.
Francis Lightfoot Lee
Carter Braxton

Georgia
Button Gwinnett
Lyman Hall
George Walton

Resolved, That copies of the Declaration be sent to the several assemblies, conventions, and committees, or councils of safety, and to the several commanding officers of the continental troops; that it be proclaimed in each of the United States, at the head of the army.

The Constitution of the United States of America[1]

We the People of the United States, in Order to form a more perfect Union, establish Justice, insure domestic Tranquility, provide for the common defence, promote the general Welfare, and secure the Blessings of Liberty to ourselves and our Posterity, do ordain and establish this CONSTITUTION for the United States of America.

ARTICLE I

Section 1. All legislative Powers herein granted shall be vested in a Congress of the United States, which shall consist of a Senate and House of Representatives.

Section 2. The House of Representatives shall be composed of Members chosen every second Year by the People of the several States, and the Electors in each State shall have the Qualifications requisite for Electors of the most numerous Branch of the State Legislature.

No Person shall be a Representative who shall not have attained to the Age of twenty-five Years, and been seven Years a Citizen of the United States, and who shall not, when elected, be an Inhabitant of that State in which he shall be chosen.

[Representatives and direct Taxes[2] shall be apportioned among the several States which may be included within this Union, according to their respective Numbers, which shall be determined by adding to the whole Number of free Persons, including those bound to Service for a Term of Years, and excluding Indians not taxed, three fifths of all other Persons.][3] The actual Enumeration shall be made within three Years after the first Meeting of the Congress of the United States, and within every subsequent Term of ten Years, in such Manner as they shall by Law direct. The Number of Representatives shall not exceed one for every thirty Thousand, but each State shall have at Least one Representative; and until such enumeration shall be made, the State of New Hampshire shall be entitled to chuse three, Massachusetts eight, Rhode-Island and Providence Plantations one, Connecticut five, New York six, New Jersey four, Pennsylvania eight, Delaware one, Maryland six, Virginia ten, North Carolina five, South Carolina five, and Georgia three.

When vacancies happen in the Representation from any State, the Executive Authority thereof shall issue Writs of Election to fill such Vacancies.

The House of Representatives shall chuse their Speaker and other Officers; and shall have the sole Power of Impeachment.

Section 3. The Senate of the United States shall be composed of two Senators from each State, chosen by the Legislature thereof, for six Years; and each Senator shall have one Vote.

Immediately after they shall be assembled in Consequence of the first Election, they shall be divided as equally as may be into three Classes. The Seats of the Senators of the first Class shall be vacated at the Expiration of the second Year, of the second Class at the Expiration of the fourth Year, and of the third Class at the Expiration of the sixth Year, so that one-third may be chosen every second Year; and if Vacancies happen by Resignation, or otherwise, during the Recess of the Legislature of any State, the Executive thereof may make temporary Appointments until the next Meeting of the Legislature, which shall then fill such Vacancies.

No Person shall be a Senator who shall not have attained to the Age of thirty Years, and been nine Years a Citizen of the United States, and who shall not, when elected, be an Inhabitant of that State for which he shall be chosen.

The Vice President of the United States shall be President of the Senate, but shall have no vote, unless they be equally divided.

The Senate shall chuse their other Officers, and also a President pro tempore, in the absence of the Vice President, or when he shall exercise the Office of President of the United States.

The Senate shall have the sole Power to try all Impeachments. When sitting for that purpose they shall be on Oath or Affirmation. When the President of the United States is tried, the Chief Justice shall preside: And no person shall be convicted without the Concurrence of two thirds of the Members present.

Judgment in Cases of Impeachment shall not extend further than to removal from Office, and disqualification to hold and enjoy any Office of honor, Trust, or Profit under the United States: but the Party convicted shall nevertheless be liable and subject to Indictment, Trial, Judgment, and Punishment, according to Law.

Section 4. The Times, Places and Manner of holding Elections for Senators and Representatives, shall be prescribed in each State by the Legislature thereof; but the Congress may at any time by Law make or alter such Regulations, except as to the Places of Chusing Senators.

---

[1]This version follows the original Constitution in capitalization and spelling. It is adapted from the text published by the United States Department of the Interior, Office of Education.

[2]Altered by the Sixteenth Amendment.

[3]Negated by the Fourteenth Amendment.

The Congress shall assemble at least once in every Year, and such Meeting shall be on the first Monday in December, unless they shall by Law appoint a different Day.

Section 5. Each House shall be the Judge of the Elections, Returns and Qualifications of its own Members, and a Majority of each shall constitute a Quorum to do Business; but a smaller number may adjourn from day to day, and may be authorized to compel the Attendance of absent Members, in such Manner, and under such Penalties, as each House may provide.

Each House may determine the Rules of its Proceedings, punish its Members for disorderly Behaviour, and, with the Concurrence of two thirds, expel a Member.

Each House shall keep a Journal of its Proceedings, and from time to time publish the same, excepting such Parts as may in their Judgment require Secrecy; and the Yeas and Nays of the Members of either House on any question shall, at the Desire of one fifth of those Present, be entered on the Journal.

Neither House, during the Session of Congress, shall, without the Consent of the other, adjourn for more than three days, nor to any other Place than that in which the two Houses shall be sitting.

Section 6. The Senators and Represeratives shall receive a Compensation for their Services, to be ascertained by Law, and paid out of the Treasury of the United States. They shall in all Cases, except Treason, Felony, and Breach of the Peace, be privileged from Arrest during their Attendance at the Session of their respective Houses, and in going to and returning from the same; and for any Speech or Debate in either House, they shall not be questioned in any other Place.

No Senator or Representative shall, during the Time for which he was elected, be appointed to any civil Office under the Authority of the United States, which shall have been created, or the Emoluments whereof shall have been increased, during such time; and no Person holding any Office under the United States shall be a Member of either House during his continuance in Office.

Section 7. All Bills for raising Revenue shall originate in the House of Representatives; but the Senate may propose or concur with Amendments as on other bills.

Every Bill which shall have passed the House of Representatives and the Senate, shall, before it become a Law, be presented to the President of the United States; If he approve he shall sign it, but if not he shall return it, with his Objections, to that House in which it shall have originated, who shall enter the Objections at large on their Journal, and proceed to reconsider it. If after such Reconsideration two thirds of that House shall agree to pass the bill, it shall be sent, together with the objections, to the other House, by which it shall likewise be reconsidered, and if approved by two thirds of that House, it shall become a Law. But in all such Cases the Votes of both Houses shall be determined by Yeas and Nays, and the Names of the Persons voting for and against

the Bill shall be entered on the Journal of each House respectively. If any Bill shall not be returned by the President within ten Days (Sundays excepted) after it shall have been presented to him, the Same shall be a Law, in like Manner as if he had signed it, unless the Congress by their Adjournment prevent its Return, in which Case it shall not be a Law.

Every Order, Resolution, or Vote to which the Concurrence of the Senate and House of Representatives may be necessary (except on a question of Adjournment) shall be presented to the President of the United States; and before the Same shall take Effect, shall be approved by him, or being disapproved by him, shall be repassed by two thirds of the Senate and House of Representatives, according to the Rules and Limitations prescribed in the Case of a Bill.

Section 8. The Congress shall have Power To lay and collect Taxes, Duties, Imposts and Excises, to pay the Debts and provide for the common Defence and general Welfare of the United States; but all Duties, Imposts and Excises shall be uniform throughout the United States;

To borrow money on the credit of the United States;

To regulate Commerce with foreign Nations, and among the several States, and with the Indian Tribes;

To establish an uniform rule of Naturalization, and uniform Laws on the subject of Bankruptcies throughout the United States;

To coin Money, regulate the Value thereof, and of foreign Coin, and fix the Standard of Weights and Measures;

To provide for the Punishment of counterfeiting the Securities and current Coin of the United States;

To establish Post Offices and post Roads;

To promote the Progress of Science and useful Arts, by securing for limited Times to Authors and Inventors the exclusive Right to their respective Writings and Discoveries;

To constitute Tribunals inferior to the Supreme Court;

To define and punish Piracies and Felonies committed on the high Seas, and Offenses against the Law of Nations;

To declare War, grant Letters of Marque and Reprisal, and make Rules concerning Captures on Land and Water;

To raise and support Armies, but no Appropriation of Money to that Use shall be for a longer Term than two Years;

To provide and maintain a Navy;

To make Rules for the Government and Regulation of the land and naval forces;

To provide for calling forth the Militia to execute the Laws of the Union, suppress Insurrections and repel Invasions;

To provide for organizing, arming, and disciplining the Militia, and for government such Part of them as may be employed in the Service of the United States, reserving to the States respectively, the Appointment of the Officers, and the Authority of training the Militia according to the discipline prescribed by Congress;

To exercise exclusive Legislation in all Cases whatsoever, over such District (not exceeding ten Miles square) as may, by Cession of particular States, and the acceptance of Congress, become the Seat of the Government of the United States, and to exercise like Authority over all Places purchased by the Consent of the Legislature of the State in which the Same shall be, for the Erection of Forts, Magazines, Arsenals, Dockyards, and other needful Buildings;—And

To make all Laws which shall be necessary and proper for carrying into Execution the foregoing Powers, and all other Powers vested by this Constitution in the Government of the United States, or in any Department or Officer thereof.

Section 9. The Migration or Importation of such Persons as any of the States now existing shall think proper to admit, shall not be prohibited by the Congress prior to the Year one thousand eight hundred and eight, but a tax or duty may be imposed on such Importation, not exceeding ten dollars for each Person.

The privilege of the Writ of Habeas Corpus shall not be suspended, unless when in Cases of Rebellion or Invasion the public Safety may require it.

No bill of Attainder or ex post facto Law shall be passed.

No capitation, or other direct, Tax shall be laid unless in Proportion to the Census or Enumeration herein before directed to be taken.

No Tax or Duty shall be laid on Articles exported from any State.

No Preference shall be given by any Regulation of Commerce or Revenue to the Ports of one State over those of another: nor shall Vessels bound to, or from, one State, be obliged to enter, clear, or pay Duties in another.

No Money shall be drawn from the Treasury, but in Consequence of Appropriations made by Law; and a regular Statement and Account of the Receipts and Expenditures of all public Money shall be published from time to time.

No Title of Nobility shall be granted by the United States: And no Person holding any Office of Profit or Trust under them, shall, without the Consent of the Congress, accept of any present, Emolument, Office, or Title, of any kind whatever, from any King, Prince, or foreign State.

Section 10. No State shall enter into any Treaty, Alliance, or Confederation; grant Letters of Marque and Reprisal; coin Money; emit Bills of Credit; make any Thing but gold and silver Coin a Tender in Payment of Debts; pass any Bill of Attainder, ex post facto Law, or Law impairing the Obligation of Contracts, or grant any Title of Nobility.

No State shall, without the Consent of the Congress, lay any Imposts or Duties on Imports or Exports, except what may be absolutely necessary for executing its inspection Laws; and the net Produce of all Duties and Imposts, laid by any State on Imports or Exports, shall be for the use of the Treasury of the United States; and all such Laws shall be subject to the Revision and Control of the Congress.

No state shall, without the Consent of Congress, lay any duty of Tonnage, keep Troops, or Ships of War in time of Peace,

enter into any Agreement or Compact with another State, or with a foreign Power, or engage in War, unless actually invaded, or in such imminent Danger as will not admit of delay.

ARTICLE II

Section 1. The executive Power shall be vested in a President of the United States of America. He shall hold his Office during the Term of four years, and, together with the Vice President, chosen for the same Term, be elected, as follows:

Each State shall appoint, in such Manner as the Legislature thereof may direct, a Number of Electors, equal to the whole Number of Senators and Representatives to which the State may be entitled in the Congress: but no Senator or Representative, or Person holding an Office of Trust or Profit under the United States, shall be appointed an Elector.

[The Electors shall meet in their respective States, and vote by Ballot for two persons, of whom one at least shall not be an Inhabitant of the same State with themselves. And they shall make a List of all the Persons voted for, and of the Number of Votes for each; which List they shall sign and certify, and transmit sealed to the Seat of the Government of the United States, directed to the President of the Senate. The President of the Senate shall, in the Presence of the Senate and House of Representatives, open all the Certificates, and the Votes shall then be counted. The Person having the greatest Number of Votes shall be the President, if such Number be a Majority of the whole Number of Electors appointed; and if there be more than one who have such Majority, and have an equal Number of Votes, then the House of Representatives shall immediately chuse by Ballot one of them for President; and if no Person have a Majority, then from the five highest on the List the said House shall in like Manner chuse the President. But in chusing the President, the Votes shall be taken by States, the Representation from each State having one Vote; a quorum for this Purpose shall consist of a Member or Members from two-thirds of the States, and a Majority of all the States shall be necessary to a Choice. In every Case, after the Choice of the President, the Person having the greatest Number of Votes of the Electors shall be the Vice President. But if there should remain two or more who have equal votes, the Senate shall chuse from them by Ballot the Vice President.][4]

The Congress may determine the Time of chusing the Electors, and the Day on which they shall give their Votes; which Day shall be the same throughout the United States.

No person except a natural-born Citizen, or a Citizen of the United States, at the time of the Adoption of this Constitution, shall be eligible to the Office of President; neither shall any Person be eligible to that Office who shall not have attained to the Age of thirty-five years, and been fourteen Years a Resident within the United States.

In Case of the Removal of the President from Office, or of his Death, Resignation, or Inability to discharge the Powers and

---

[4]Revised by the Twelfth Amendment.

Duties of the said Office, the same shall devolve on the Vice President, and the Congress may by Law provide for the Case of Removal, Death, Resignation, or Inability, both of the President and Vice President, declaring what Officer shall then act as President, and such Officer shall act accordingly, until the disability be removed, or a President shall be elected.

The President shall, at stated Times, receive for his Services a Compensation, which shall neither be increased nor diminished during the Period for which he shall have been elected, and he shall not receive within that Period any other Emolument from the United States, or any of them.

Before he enter on the execution of his Office, he shall take the following Oath or Affirmation:—"I do solemnly swear (or affirm) that I will faithfully execute the Office of President of the United States, and will, to the best of my Ability, preserve, protect, and defend the Constitution of the United States."

Section 2. The President shall be Commander in Chief of the Army and Navy of the United States, and of the Militia of the several States, when called into the actual Service of the United States; he may require the Opinion, in writing, of the principal Officer in each of the executive Departments, upon any subject relating to the Duties of their respective Offices, and he shall have Power to Grant Reprieves and Pardons for Offenses against the United States, except in Cases of Impeachment.

He shall have Power, by and with the Advice and Consent of the Senate, to make Treaties, provided two-thirds of the Senators present concur; and he shall nominate, and by and with the Advice and Consent of the Senate, shall appoint Ambassadors, other public Ministers and Consuls, Judges of the supreme Court, and all other Officers of the United States, whose Appointments are not herein otherwise provided for, and which shall be established by Law: but the Congress may by Law vest the Appointment of such inferior Officers, as they think proper, in the President alone, in the Courts of Law, or in the Heads of Departments.

The President shall have Power to fill up all Vacancies that may happen during the Recess of the Senate, by granting Commissions which shall expire at the End of their next Session.

Section 3. He shall from time to time give to the Congress Information of the State of the Union, and recommend to their Consideration such Measures as he shall judge necessary and expedient; he may, on extraordinary occasions, convene both Houses, or either of them, and in Case of Disagreement between them, with respect to the Time of Adjournment, he may adjourn them to such Time as he shall think proper; he shall receive Ambassadors and other public Ministers; he shall take care that the Laws be faithfully executed, and shall Commission all the Officers of the United States.

Section 4. The President, Vice President and all civil Officers of the United States, shall be removed from Office on Impeachment for, and Conviction of, Treason, Bribery, or other high Crimes and Misdemeanors.

ARTICLE III

Section 1. The judicial Power of the United States, shall be vested in one supreme Court, and in such inferior Courts as the Congress may from time to time ordain and establish. The Judges, both of the supreme and inferior Courts, shall hold their Offices during good Behaviour, and shall, at stated Times, receive for their Services, a Compensation, which shall not be diminished during their Continuance in Office.

Section 2. The judicial Power shall extend to all Cases, in Law and Equity, arising under this Constitution, the Laws of the United States, and Treaties made, or which shall be made, under their Authority;—to all Cases affecting ambassadors, other public ministers and consuls;—to all cases of admiralty and maritime Jurisdiction;—to Controversies to which the United States shall be a Party;—to Controversies between two or more States;—between a State and Citizens of another State;[5]—between Citizens of different States—between Citizens of the same State claiming Lands under Grants of different States, and between a State, or the Citizens thereof, and foreign States, Citizens, or Subjects.

In all Cases affecting Ambassadors, other public Ministers and Consuls, and those in which a State shall be Party, the supreme Court shall have original Jurisdiction. In all the other Cases before mentioned, the supreme Court shall have appellate Jurisdiction, both as to Law and Fact, with such Exceptions, and under such Regulations as the Congress shall make.

The trial of all Crimes, except in Cases of Impeachment, shall be by Jury; and such Trial shall be held in the State where the said Crimes shall have been committed; but when not committed within any State, the Trial shall be at such Place or Places as the Congress may by Law have directed.

Section 3. Treason against the United States, shall consist only in levying War against them, or in adhering to their Enemies, giving them Aid and Comfort. No Person shall be convicted of Treason unless on the Testimony of two Witnesses to the same overt Act, or on Confession in open Court.

The Congress shall have power to declare the Punishment of Treason, but no Attainder of Treason shall work Corruption of Blood, or Forfeiture except during the Life of the Person attainted.

ARTICLE IV

Section 1. Full Faith and Credit shall be given in each State to the public Acts, Records, and judicial Proceedings of every other State. And the Congress may by general Laws prescribe the Manner in which such Acts, Records and Proceedings shall be proved, and the Effect thereof.

---

[5]Qualified by the Eleventh Amendment.

Section 2. The Citizens of each State shall be entitled to all Privileges and Immunities of Citizens in the several States.

A Person charged in any State with Treason, Felony, or other Crime, who shall flee from Justice, and be found in another State, shall on demand of the executive Authority of the State from which he fled, be delivered up, to be removed to the State having Jurisdiction of the crime.

No Person held to Service or Labour in one State, under the Laws thereof, escaping into another, shall, in Consequence of any Law or Regulation therein, be discharged from such Service or Labour, but shall be delivered up on Claim of the Party to whom such Service or Labour may be due.

Section 3. New States may be admitted by the Congress into this Union; but no new State shall be formed or erected within the Jurisdiction of any other State; nor any State be formed by the Junction of two or more States, or parts of States, without the Consent of the Legislatures of the States concerned as well as of the Congress.

The Congress shall have Power to dispose of and make all needful Rules and Regulations respecting the Territory or other Property belonging to the United States; and nothing in this Constitution shall be so construed as to Prejudice any Claims of the United States, or of any particular State.

Section 4. The United States shall guarantee to every State in this Union a Republican Form of Government, and shall protect each of them against Invasion; and on Application of the Legislature, or of the Executive (when the Legislature cannot be convened) against domestic Violence.

ARTICLE V

The Congress, whenever two-thirds of both Houses shall deem it necessary, shall propose Amendments to this Constitution, or, on the Application of the Legislatures of two-thirds of the several States, shall call a Convention for proposing Amendments, which, in either Case, shall be valid to all Intents and Purposes, as part of this Constitution, when ratified by the Legislatures of three-fourths of the several States, or by Conventions in three-fourths thereof, as the one or the other Mode of Ratification may be proposed by the Congress; Provided that no Amendment which may be made prior to the Year One thousand eight hundred and eight shall in any Manner affect the first and fourth Clauses in the Ninth Section of the first Article; and that no State, without its Consent, shall be deprived of its equal Suffrage in the Senate.

ARTICLE VI

All Debts contracted and Engagements entered into, before the Adoption of this Constitution, shall be as valid against the United States under this Constitution, as under the Confederation.

This Constitution, and the Laws of the United States which shall be made in Pursuance thereof; and all Treaties made, or which shall be made, under the Authority of the United States, shall be the supreme Law of the Land; and the Judges in every State shall be bound thereby, any Thing in the Constitution or Laws of any State to the Contrary notwithstanding.

The Senators and Representatives before mentioned, and the Members of the several State Legislatures, and all executive and judicial Officers, both of the United States and of the several States, shall be bound by Oath or Affirmation to support this Constitution; but no religious Tests shall ever be required as a qualification to any Office or public Trust under the United States.

ARTICLE VII

The Ratification of the Conventions of nine States shall be sufficient for the Establishment of this Constitution between the States so ratifying the same.

Done in Convention by the Unanimous Consent of the States present the Seventeenth Day of September in the Year of our Lord one thousand seven hundred and Eighty seven, and of the Independence of the United States of America the Twelfth. In Witness whereof We have hereunto subscribed our Names.[6]

GEORGE WASHINGTON
PRESIDENT AND DEPUTY FROM VIRGINIA

New Hampshire	**New Jersey**	**Delaware**	**North Carolina**
John Langdon	William Livingston	George Read	William Blount
Nicholas Gilman	David Brearley	Gunning Bedford, Jr.	Richard Dobbs Spaight
	William Paterson	John Dickinson	Hugh Williamson
	Jonathan Dayton	Richard Bassett	
		Jacob Broom	

---

[6]These are the full names of the signers, which in some cases are not the signatures on the document.

Massachusetts	**Pennsylvania**	**Maryland**	**South Carolina**
Nathaniel Gorham	Benjamin Franklin	James McHenry	John Rutledge
Rufus King	Thomas Mifflin	Daniel of St. Thomas Jenifer	Charles Cotesworth Pinckney
	Robert Morris	Daniel Carroll	Charles Pinckney
Connecticut	George Clymer		Pierce Butler
William Samuel Johnson	Thomas FitzSimons	**Virginia**	
Roger Sherman	Jared Ingersoll	John Blair	**Georgia**
	James Wilson	James Madison, Jr.	William Few
New York	Gouverneur Morris		Abraham Baldwin
Alexander Hamilton			

Articles in Addition to, and Amendment of, the Constitution of the United States of America, Proposed by Congress, and Ratified by the Legislatures of the Several States, Pursuant to the Fifth Article of the Original Constitution[7]

[AMENDMENT I]

Congress shall make no law respecting an establishment of religion, or prohibiting the free exercise thereof; or abridging the freedom of speech, or of the press; or the right of the people peaceably to assemble, and to petition the Government for a redress of grievances.

[AMENDMENT II]

A well regulated Militia, being necessary to the security of a free State, the right of the people to keep and bear Arms shall not be infringed.

[AMENDMENT III]

No Soldier shall, in time of peace, be quartered in any house, without the consent of the Owner, nor in time of war, but in a manner to be prescribed by law.

[AMENDMENT IV]

The right of the people to be secure in their persons, houses, papers, and effects, against unreasonable searches and seizures, shall not be violated, and no Warrants shall issue, but upon probable cause, supported by Oath or affirmation, and particularly describing the place to be searched, and the persons or things to be seized.

[AMENDMENT V]

No person shall be held to answer for a capital or otherwise infamous crime, unless on a presentment or indictment of a Grand Jury, except in cases arising in the land or naval forces, or in the Militia, when in actual service in time of War or public danger; nor shall any person be subject for the same offence to be twice put in jeopardy of life or limb; nor shall be compelled in any criminal case to be a witness against himself, nor be deprived of life, liberty, or property, without due process of law; nor shall private property be taken for public use, without just compensation.

[AMENDMENT VI]

In all criminal prosecutions, the accused shall enjoy the right to a speedy and public trial, by an impartial jury of the State and district wherein the crime shall have been committed, which district shall have been previously ascertained by law, and to be informed of the nature and cause of the accusation; to be confronted with the witnesses against him; to have compulsory process for obtaining witnesses in his favour, and to have the Assistance of Counsel for his defence.

[AMENDMENT VII]

In suits at common law, where the value in controversy shall exceed twenty dollars, the right of trial by jury shall be preserved, and no fact tried by a jury, shall be otherwise reexamined in any Court of the United States, than according to the rules of the common law.

[AMENDMENT VIII]

Excessive bail shall not be required, nor excessive fines imposed, nor cruel and unusual punishments inflicted.

[AMENDMENT IX]

The enumeration of the Constitution, of certain rights, shall not be construed to deny or disparage others retained by the people.

[AMENDMENT X]

The powers not delegated to the United States by the Constitution, nor prohibited by it to the States, are reserved to the States respectively, or to the people.

[Amendments I–X, in force 1791.]

[AMENDMENT XI][8]

The Judicial power of the United States shall not be construed to extend to any suit in law or equity, commenced or

---

[7]This heading appears only in the joint resolution submitting the first ten amendments, known as the Bill of Rights.

[8]Adopted in 1798.

prosecuted against one of the United States by Citizens of another State, or by Citizens or Subjects of any Foreign State.

[AMENDMENT XII][9]

The Electors shall meet in their respective States and vote by ballot for President and Vice-President, one of whom, at least, shall not be an inhabitant of the same State with themselves; they shall name in their ballots the person voted for as President, and in distinct ballots the person voted for as Vice-President, and they shall make distinct lists of all persons voted for as President, and of all persons voted for as Vice-President, and of the number of votes for each, which lists they shall sign and certify, and transmit sealed to the seat of the government of the United States, directed to the President of the Senate;—The President of the Senate shall, in the presence of the Senate and House of Representatives, open all the certificates and the votes shall then be counted;—The person having the greatest number of votes for President, shall be the President, if such number be a majority of the whole number of Electors appointed; and if no person have such majority, then from the persons having the highest numbers not exceeding three on the list of those voted for as President, the House of Representatives shall choose immediately, by ballot, the President. But in choosing the President, the votes shall be taken by states, the representation from each state having one vote; a quorum for this purpose shall consist of a member or members from two-thirds of the states, and a majority of all the states shall be necessary to a choice. And if the House of Representatives shall not choose a President whenever the right of choice shall devolve upon them, before the fourth day of March next following, then the Vice-President shall act as President, as in the case of the death or other constitutional disability of the President.—The person having the greatest number of votes as Vice-President, shall be the Vice-President, if such number be a majority of the whole number of Electors appointed, and if no person have a majority, then from the two highest numbers on the list, the Senate shall choose the Vice-President; a quorum for the purpose shall consist of two-thirds of the whole number of Senators, and a majority of the whole number shall be necessary to a choice. But no person constitutionally ineligible to the office of President shall be eligible to that of Vice-President of the United States.

[AMENDMENT XIII][10]

Section 1. Neither slavery nor involuntary servitude, except as a punishment for crime whereof the party shall have been duly convicted, shall exist within the United States, or any place subject to their jurisdiction.

Section 2. Congress shall have power to enforce this article by appropriate legislation.

[9]Adopted in 1804.
[10]Adopted in 1865.

[AMENDMENT XIV][11]

Section 1. All persons born or naturalized in the United States, and subject to the jurisdiction thereof, are citizens of the United States and of the State wherein they reside. No State shall abridge the privileges or immunities of citizens of the United States; nor shall any State deprive any person of life, liberty, or property, without due process of law; nor deny to any person within its jurisdiction the equal protection of the laws.

Section 2. Representatives shall be apportioned among the several States according to their respective numbers, counting the whole number of persons in each State, excluding Indians not taxed. But when the right to vote at any election for the choice of electors for President and Vice-President of the United States, Representatives in Congress, the Executive and Judicial officers of a State, or the members of the Legislature thereof, is denied to any of the male inhabitants of such State, being twenty-one years of age, and citizens of the United States, or in any way abridged, except for participation in rebellion, or other crime, the basis of representation therein shall be reduced in the proportion which the number of such male citizens shall bear to the whole number of male citizens twenty-one years of age in such State.

Section 3. No person shall be a Senator or Representative in Congress, or elector of President and Vice-President, or hold any office, civil or military, under the United States, or under any State, who, having previously taken an oath, as a member of Congress, or as an officer of the United States, or as a member of any State legislature, or as an executive or judicial officer of any State, to support the Constitution of the United States, shall have engaged in insurrection or rebellion against the same, or given aid or comfort to the enemies thereof. But Congress may by a vote of two-thirds of each House, remove such disability.

Section 4. The validity of the public debt of the United States, authorized by law, including debts incurred for payment of pensions and bounties for services in suppressing insurrection or rebellion, shall not be questioned. But neither the United States nor any State shall assume or pay any debts or obligation incurred in aid of insurrection or rebellion against the United States, or any claim for the loss or emancipation of any slave; but all such debts, obligations, and claims shall be held illegal and void.

Section 5. The Congress shall have the power to enforce, by appropriate legislation, the provisions of this article.

[11]Adopted in 1868.

[AMENDMENT XV][12]

Section 1. The right of citizens of the United States to vote shall not be denied or abridged by the United States or by any State on account of race, color, or previous condition of servitude—

Section 2. The Congress shall have power to enforce this article by appropriate legislation.

[AMENDMENT XVI][13]

The Congress shall have power to lay and collect taxes on incomes, from whatever source derived, without apportionment among the several States, and without regard to any census or enumeration.

[AMENDMENT XVII][14]

The Senate of the United States shall be composed of two Senators from each State, elected by the people thereof, for six years; and each Senator shall have one vote. The electors in each State shall have the qualifications requisite for electors of the most numerous branch of the State legislatures.

When vacancies happen in the representation of any State in the Senate, the executive authority of such State shall issue writs of election to fill such vacancies: *Provided,* That the legislature of any State may empower the executive thereof to make temporary appointments until the people fill the vacancies by election as the legislature may direct.

This amendment shall not be so construed as to affect the election or term of any Senator chosen before it becomes valid as part of the Constitution.

[AMENDMENT XVIII][15]

Section 1. After one year from the ratification of this article the manufacture, sale, or transportation of intoxicating liquors within, the importation thereof into, or the exportation thereof from the United States and all territory subject to the jurisdiction thereof for beverage purposes is hereby prohibited.

Section 2. The Congress and the several States shall have concurrent power to enforce this article by appropriate legislation.

Section 3. This article shall be inoperative unless it shall have been ratified as an amendment to the Constitution by the legislatures of the several States, as provided in the Constitution, within seven years from the date of the submission hereof to the States by the Congress.

[AMENDMENT XIX][16]

The right of citizens of the United States to vote shall not be denied or abridged by the United States or by any State on account of sex.

Congress shall have power to enforce this article by appropriate legislation.

[AMENDMENT XX][17]

Section 1. The terms of the President and Vice-President shall end at noon on the 20th day of January, and the terms of Senators and Representatives at noon on the 3d day of January, of the years in which such terms would have ended if this article had not been ratified; and the terms of their successors shall then begin.

Section 2. The Congress shall assemble at least once in every year, and such meeting shall begin at noon on the 3d day of January, unless they shall by law appoint a different day.

Section 3. If, at the time fixed for the beginning of the term of the President, the President elect shall have died, the Vice-President elect shall become President. If a President shall not have been chosen before the time fixed for the beginning of his term or if the President elect shall have failed to qualify, then the Vice-President elect shall act as President until a President shall have qualified; and the Congress may by law provide for the case wherein neither a President elect nor a Vice-President elect shall have qualified, declaring who shall then act as President, or the manner in which one who is to act shall be selected, and such person shall act accordingly until a President or Vice-President shall have qualified.

Section 4. The Congress may by law provide for the case of the death of any of the persons from whom the House of Representatives may choose a President whenever the right of choice shall have devolved upon them, and for the case of the death of any of the persons from whom the Senate may choose a Vice-President whenever the right of choice shall have devolved upon them.

Section 5. Sections 1 and 2 shall take effect on the 15th day of October following the ratification of this article.

Section 6. This article shall be inoperative unless it shall have been ratified as an amendment to the Constitution by the legislatures of three-fourths of the several States within seven years from the date of its submission.

[12]Adopted in 1870.

[13]Adopted in 1913.

[14]Adopted in 1913.

[15]Adopted in 1918.

[16]Adopted in 1920.

[17]Adopted in 1933.

[AMENDMENT XXI][18]

Section 1. The eighteenth article of amendment to the Constitution of the United States is hereby repealed.

Section 2. The transportation or importation into any State, Territory, or possession of the United States for delivery or use therein of intoxicating liquors, in violation of the laws thereof, is hereby prohibited.

Section 3. This article shall be inoperative unless it shall have been ratified as an amendment to the Constitution by conventions in the several States, as provided in the Constitution, within seven years from the date of the submission hereof to the States by the Congress.

[AMENDMENT XXII][19]

No person shall be elected to the office of the President more than twice, and no person who has held the office of President, or acted as President, for more than two years of a term to which some other person was elected President shall be elected to the office of the President more than once.

But this Article shall not apply to any person holding the office of President when this Article was proposed by the Congress, and shall not prevent any person who may be holding the office of President, or acting as President, during the term within which this Article becomes operative from holding the office of President or acting as President during the remainder of such term.

This article shall be inoperative unless it shall have been ratified as an amendment to the Constitution by the legislatures of three-fourths of the several states within seven years from the date of its submission to the states by the Congress.

[AMENDMENT XXIII][20]

Section 1. The District constituting the seat of Government of the United States shall appoint in such manner as the Congress may direct:

A number of electors of President and Vice-President equal to the whole number of Senators and Representatives in Congress to which the District would be entitled if it were a State, but in no event more than the least populous State; they shall be in addition to those appointed by the States, but they shall be considered, for the purpose of the election of President and Vice-President, to be electors appointed by a State; and they shall meet in the District and perform such duties as provided by the twelfth article of amendment.

Section 2. The Congress shall have power to enforce this article by appropriate legislation.

[AMENDMENT XXIV][21]

Section 1. The right of citizens of the United States to vote in any primary or other election for President or Vice-President, for electors for President or Vice-President, or for Senator or Representative in Congress, shall not be denied or abridged by the United States or any state by reason of failure to pay any poll tax or other tax.

Section 2. The Congress shall have the power to enforce this article by appropriate legislation.

[AMENDMENT XXV][22]

Section 1. In case of the removal of the President from office or of his death or resignation, the Vice-President shall become President.

Section 2. Whenever there is a vacancy in the office of the Vice President, the President shall nominate a Vice President who shall take office upon confirmation by a majority vote of both Houses of Congress.

Section 3. Whenever the President transmits to the President Pro Tempore of the Senate and the Speaker of the House of Representatives his written declaration that he is unable to discharge the powers and duties of his office, and until he transmits to them a written declaration to the contrary, such powers and duties shall be discharged by the Vice-President as Acting President.

Section 4. Whenever the Vice-President and a majority of either the principal officers of the executive departments or of such other body as Congress may by law provide, transmit to the President Pro Tempore of the Senate and the Speaker of the House of Representatives their written declaration that the President is unable to discharge the powers and duties of his office, the Vice President shall immediately assume the powers and duties of the office as Acting President.

Thereafter, when the President transmits to the President Pro Tempore of the Senate and the Speaker of the House of Representatives his written declaration that no inability exists, he shall resume the powers and duties of his office unless the Vice President and a majority of either the principal officers of the executive departments or of such other body as Congress may by law provide, transmit within four days to the President Pro Tempore of the Senate and the Speaker of the House of Representatives

---

[18]Adopted in 1961.

[19]Adopted in 1961.

[20]Adopted in 1933.

[21]Adopted in 1964.

[22]Adopted in 1967.

their written declaration that the President is unable to discharge the powers and duties of his office. Thereupon Congress shall decide the issue, assembling within forty-eight hours for that purpose if not in session. If the Congress, within twenty-one days after receipt of the latter written declaration, or, if Congress is not in session, within twenty-one days after Congress is required to assemble, determines by two-thirds vote of both Houses that the President is unable to discharge the powers and duties of his office, the Vice President shall continue to discharge the same as Acting President; otherwise, the President shall resume the powers and duties of his office.

[AMENDMENT XXVI][23]

Section 1. The right of citizens of the United States, who are eighteen years of age or older, to vote shall not be denied or abridged by the United States or by any State on account of age.

Section 2. The Congress shall have power to enforce this article by appropriate legislation.

[AMENDMENT XXVII][24]

No law, varying the compensation for the services of the Senators and Representatives, shall take effect, until an election of Representatives shall have intervened.

---

[23]Adopted in 1971.

[24]Adopted in 1992.

Presidential Elections

Year	Candidates	Parties	Popular Vote	% of Popular Vote	Electoral Vote	% Voter Participation
1789	**George Washington**				69	
	John Adams				34	
	Other candidates				35	
1792	**George Washington**				132	
	John Adams				77	
	George Clinton				50	
	Other candidates				5	
1796	**John Adams**	Federalist			71	
	Thomas Jefferson	Dem.-Rep.			68	
	Thomas Pinckney	Federalist			59	
	Aaron Burr	Dem.-Rep.			30	
	Other candidates				48	
1800	**Thomas Jefferson**	Dem.-Rep.			73	
	Aaron Burr	Dem.-Rep.			73	
	John Adams	Federalist			65	
	Charles C. Pinckney	Federalist			64	
	John Jay	Federalist			1	
1804	**Thomas Jefferson**	Dem.-Rep.			162	
	Charles C. Pinckney	Federalist			14	
1808	**James Madison**	Dem.-Rep.			122	
	Charles C. Pinckney	Federalist			47	
	George Clinton	Dem.-Rep.			6	
1812	**James Madison**	Dem.-Rep.			128	
	DeWitt Clinton	Federalist			89	
1816	**James Monroe**	Dem.-Rep.			183	
	Rufus King	Federalist			34	
1820	**James Monroe**	Dem.-Rep.			231	
	John Quincy Adams	Indep.-Rep.			1	
1824	**John Quincy Adams**	Dem.-Rep.	108,740	31.0	84	26.9
	Andrew Jackson	Dem.-Rep.	153,544	43.0	99	
	Henry Clay	Dem.-Rep.	47,136	13.0	37	
	William H. Crawford	Dem.-Rep.	46,618	13.0	41	
1828	**Andrew Jackson**	Democratic	647,286	56.0	178	57.6
	John Quincy Adams	National Republican	508,064	44.0	83	
1832	**Andrew Jackson**	Democratic	688,242	54.5	219	55.4
	Henry Clay	National Republican	473,462	37.5	49	
	William Wirt	Anti-Masonic	101,051	8.0	7	
	John Floyd	Democratic			11	
1836	**Martin Van Buren**	Democratic	765,483	50.9	170	57.8
	William H. Harrison	Whig			73	
	Hugh L. White	Whig	739,795	49.1	26	
	Daniel Webster	Whig			14	
	W. P. Mangum	Whig			11	

Year	Candidates	Parties	Popular Vote	% of Popular Vote	Electorial Vote	% Voter Participation
1840	**William H. Harrison**	Whig	1,275,016	53.0	234	80.2
	Martin Van Buren	Democratic	1,129,102	47.0	60	
1844	**James K. Polk**	Democratic	1,338,464	49.6	170	78.9
	Henry Clay	Whig	1,300,097	48.1	105	
	James G. Birney	Liberty	62,300	2.3		
1848	**Zachary Taylor**	Whig	1,360,967	47.4	163	72.7
	Lewis Cass	Democratic	1,222,342	42.5	127	
	Martin Van Buren	Free Soil	291,263	10.1		
1852	**Franklin Pierce**	Democratic	1,601,117	50.9	254	69.6
	Winfield Scott	Whig	1,385,453	44.1	42	
	John P. Hale	Free Soil	155,825	5.0		
1856	**James Buchanan**	Democratic	1,832,955	45.3	174	78.9
	John C. Fremont	Republican	1,339,932	33.1	114	
	Millard Fillmore	American	871,731	21.6	8	
1860	**Abraham Lincoln**	Republican	1,866,452	39.8	180	81.2
	Stephen A. Douglas	Democratic	1,375,157	29.5	12	
	John C. Breckinridge	Democratic	847,953	18.1	72	
	John Bell	Constitutional Union	590,631	12.6	39	
1864	**Abraham Lincoln**	Republican	2,206,938	55.0	212	73.8
	George B. McClellan	Democratic	1,803,787	45.0	21	
1868	**Ulysses S. Grant**	Republican	3,013,421	52.7	214	78.1
	Horatio Seymour	Democratic	2,706,829	47.3	80	
1872	**Ulysses S. Grant**	Republican	3,596,745	55.6	286	71.3
	Horace Greeley	Democratic	2,843,446	43.9	66	
1876	**Rutherford B. Hayes**	Republican	4,036,298	48.0	185	81.8
	Samuel J. Tilden	Democratic	4,300,590	51.0	184	
1880	**James A. Garfield**	Republican	4,453,295	48.5	214	79.4
	Winfield S. Hancock	Democratic	4,414,082	48.1	155	
	James B. Weaver	Greenback-Labor	308,578	3.4		
1884	**Grover Cleveland**	Democratic	4,879,507	48.5	219	77.5
	James G. Blaine	Republican	4,850,293	48.2	182	
	Benjamin F. Butler	Greenback-Labor	175,370	1.8		
	John P. St. John	Prohibition	150,369	1.5		
1888	**Benjamin Harrison**	Republican	5,477,129	47.9	233	79.3
	Grover Cleveland	Democratic	5,537,857	48.6	168	
	Clinton B. Fisk	Prohibition	249,506	2.2		
	Anson J. Streeter	Union Labor	146,935	1.3		
1892	**Grover Cleveland**	Democratic	5,555,426	46.1	277	74.7
	Benjamin Harrison	Republican	5,182,690	43.0	145	
	James B. Weaver	People's	1,029,846	8.5	22	
	John Bidwell	Prohibition	264,133	2.2		
1896	**William McKinley**	Republican	7,104,779	52.0	271	79.3
	William J. Bryan	Democratic	6,502,925	48.0	176	
1900	**William McKinley**	Republican	7,218,491	51.7	292	73.2
	William J. Bryan	Democratic; Populist	6,356,734	45.5	155	
	John C. Wooley	Prohibition	208,914	1.5		

Year	Candidates	Parties	Popular Vote	% of Popular Vote	Electoral Vote	% Voter Participation
1904	**Theodore Roosevelt**	Republican	7,628,461	57.4	336	65.2
	Alton B. Parker	Democratic	5,084,223	37.6	140	
	Eugene V. Debs	Socialist	402,283	3.0		
	Silas C. Swallow	Prohibition	258,536	1.9		
1908	**William H. Taft**	Republican	7,675,320	51.6	321	65.4
	William J. Bryan	Democratic	6,412,294	43.1	162	
	Eugene V. Debs	Socialist	420,793	2.8		
	Eugene W. Chafin	Prohibition	253,840	1.7		
1912	**Woodrow Wilson**	Democratic	6,293,454	42.0	435	58.8
	Theodore Roosevelt	Progressive	4,119,538	28.0	88	
	William H. Taft	Republican	3,484,980	24.0	8	
	Eugene V. Debs	Socialist	900,672	6.0		
	Eugene W. Chafin	Prohibition	206,275	1.4		
1916	**Woodrow Wilson**	Democratic	9,129,606	49.4	277	61.6
	Charles E. Hughes	Republican	8,538,221	46.2	254	
	A. L. Benson	Socialist	585,113	3.2		
	J. Frank Hanly	Prohibition	220,506	1.2		
1920	**Warren G. Harding**	Republican	16,143,407	60.4	404	49.2
	James M. Cox	Democratic	9,130,328	34.2	127	
	Eugene V. Debs	Socialist	919,799	3.4		
	P. P. Christensen	Farmer-Labor	265,411	1.0		
1924	**Calvin Coolidge**	Republican	15,718,211	54.0	382	48.9
	John W. Davis	Democratic	8,385,283	28.8	136	
	Robert M. La Follette	Progressive	4,831,289	16.6	13	
1928	**Herbert C. Hoover**	Republican	21,391,381	58.2	444	56.9
	Alfred E. Smith	Democratic	15,016,443	40.9	87	
1932	**Franklin D. Roosevelt**	Democratic	22,821,857	57.4	472	56.9
	Herbert C. Hoover	Republican	15,761,841	39.7	59	
	Norman Thomas	Socialist	881,951	2.2		
1936	**Franklin D. Roosevelt**	Democratic	27,751,597	60.8	523	61.0
	Alfred M. Landon	Republican	16,679,583	36.5	8	
	William Lemke	Union	882,479	1.9		
1940	**Franklin D. Roosevelt**	Democratic	27,307,819	54.8	449	62.5
	Wendell L. Wilkie	Republican	22,321,018	44.8	82	
1944	**Franklin D. Roosevelt**	Democratic	25,606,585	53.5	432	55.9
	Thomas E. Dewey	Republican	22,014,745	46.0	99	
1948	**Harry S Truman**	Democratic	24,105,812	50.0	303	53.0
	Thomas E. Dewey	Republican	21,970,065	46.0	189	
	J. Strom Thurmond	States' Rights	1,169,021	2.0	39	
	Henry A. Wallace	Progressive	1,157,172	2.0		
1952	**Dwight D. Eisenhower**	Republican	33,936,234	55.1	442	63.3
	Adlai E. Stevenson	Democratic	27,314,992	44.4	89	
1956	**Dwight D. Eisenhower**	Republican	35,590,472	57.6	457	60.6
	Adlai E. Stevenson	Democratic	26,022,752	42.1	73	
1960	**John F. Kennedy**	Democratic	34,227,096	49.7	303	62.8
	Richard M. Nixon	Republican	34,107,646	49.6	219	
	Harry F. Byrd	Independent	501,643		15	
1964	**Lyndon B. Johnson**	Democratic	43,129,566	61.1	486	61.7
	Barry M. Goldwater	Republican	27,178,188	38.5	52	

Year	Candidates	Parties	Popular Vote	% of Popular Vote	Electorial Vote	% Voter Participation
1968	**Richard M. Nixon**	Republican	31,785,480	44.0	301	60.6
	Hubert H. Humphrey	Democratic	31,275,166	42.7	191	
	George C. Wallace	American Independent	9,906,473	13.5	46	
1972	**Richard M. Nixon**	Republican	47,169,911	60.7	520	55.2
	George S. McGovern	Democratic	29,170,383	37.5	17	
	John G. Schmitz	American	1,099,482	1.4		
1976	**Jimmy Carter**	Democratic	40,830,763	50.1	297	53.5
	Gerald R. Ford	Republican	39,147,793	48.0	240	
1980	**Ronald Reagan**	Republican	43,899,248	51.0	489	52.6
	Jimmy Carter	Democratic	35,481,432	41.0	49	
	John B. Anderson	Independent	5,719,437	7.0	0	
	Ed Clark	Libertarian	920,859	1.0	0	
1984	**Ronald Reagan**	Republican	54,451,521	58.8	525	53.3
	Walter Mondale	Democratic	37,565,334	40.5	13	
1988	**George Bush**	Republican	48,881,221	53.9	426	48.6
	Michael Dukakis	Democratic	41,805,422	46.1	111	
1992	**William J. Clinton**	Democratic	44,908,254	43.0	370	55.9
	George H. Bush	Republican	39,102,343	37.4	168	
	H. Ross Perot	Independent	19,741,065	18.9	0	
1996	**William J. Clinton**	Democratic	47,401,185	49.3	379	49
	Robert Dole	Republican	39,197,469	40.7	159	
	H. Ross Perot	Reform	8,085,294	8.4	0	

Presidential Administrations

The Washington Administration (1789–1797)

Office	Name	Years
Vice President	John Adams	1789–1797
Secretary of State	Thomas Jefferson	1789–1793
	Edmund Randolph	1794–1795
	Timothy Pickering	1795–1797
Secretary of Treasury	Alexander Hamilton	1789–1795
	Oliver Wolcott	1795–1797
Secretary of War	Henry Knox	1789–1794
	Timothy Pickering	1795–1796
	James McHenry	1796–1797
Attorney General	Edmund Randolph	1789–1793
	William Bradford	1794–1795
	Charles Lee	1795–1797
Postmaster General	Samuel Osgood	1789–1791
	Timothy Pickering	1791–1794
	Joseph Habersham	1795–1797

The John Adams Administration (1797–1801)

Office	Name	Years
Vice President	Thomas Jefferson	1797–1801
Secretary of State	Timothy Pickering	1797–1800
	John Marshall	1800–1801
Secretary of Treasury	Oliver Wolcott	1797–1800
	Samuel Dexter	1800–1801
Secretary of War	James McHenry	1797–1800
	Samuel Dexter	1800–1801
Attorney General	Charles Lee	1797–1801
Postmaster General	Joseph Habersham	1797–1801
Secretary of Navy	Benjamin Stoddert	1798–1801

The Jefferson Administration (1801–1809)

Office	Name	Years
Vice President	Aaron Burr	1801–1805
	George Clinton	1805–1809
Secretary of State	James Madison	1801–1809
Secretary of Treasury	Samuel Dexter	1801
	Albert Gallatin	1801–1809
Secretary of War	Henry Dearborn	1801–1809
Attorney General	Levi Lincoln	1801–1805
	Robert Smith	1805
	John Breckinridge	1805–1806
	Caesar Rodney	1807–1809
Postmaster General	Joseph Habersham	1801
	Gideon Granger	1801–1809
Secretary of Navy	Robert Smith	1801–1809

The Madison Administration (1809–1817)

Office	Name	Years
Vice President	George Clinton	1809–1813
	Elbridge Gerry	1813–1817
Secretary of State	Robert Smith	1809–1811
	James Monroe	1811–1817
Secretary of Treasury	Albert Gallatin	1809–1813
	George Campbell	1814
	Alexander Dallas	1814–1816
	William Crawford	1816–1817
Secretary of War	William Eustis	1809–1812
	John Armstrong	1813–1814
	James Monroe	1814–1815
	William Crawford	1815–1817
Attorney General	Caesar Rodney	1809–1811
	William Pinkney	1811–1814
	Richard Rush	1814–1817
Postmaster General	Gideon Granger	1809–1814
	Return Meigs	1814–1817
Secretary of Navy	Paul Hamilton	1809–1813
	William Jones	1813–1814
	Benjamin Crowninshield	1814–1817

The Monroe Administration (1817–1825)

Office	Name	Years
Vice President	Daniel Tompkins	1817–1825
Secretary of State	John Quincy Adams	1817–1825
Secretary of Treasury	William Crawford	1817–1825
Secretary of War	George Graham	1817
	John C. Calhoun	1817–1825
Attorney General	Richard Rush	1817
	William Wirt	1817–1825
Postmaster General	Return Meigs	1817–1823
	John McLean	1823–1825

Secretary of Navy	Benjamin Crowninshield	1817–1818
	Smith Thompson	1818–1823
	Samuel Southard	1823–1825

The John Quincy Adams Administration (1825–1829)

Vice President	John C. Calhoun	1825–1829
Secretary of State	Henry Clay	1825–1829
Secretary of Treasury	Richard Rush	1825–1829
Secretary of War	James Barbour	1825–1828
	Peter Porter	1828–1829
Attorney General	William Wirt	1825–1829
Postmaster General	John McLean	1825–1829
Secretary of Navy	Samuel Southard	1825–1829

The Jackson Administration (1829–1837)

Vice President	John C. Calhoun	1829–1833
	Martin Van Buren	1833–1837
Secretary of State	Martin Van Buren	1829–1831
	Edward Livingston	1831–1833
	Louis McLane	1833–1834
	John Forsyth	1834–1837
Secretary of Treasury	Samuel Ingham	1829–1831
	Louis McLane	1831–1833
	William Duane	1833
	Roger B. Taney	1833–1834
	Levi Woodbury	1834–1837
Secretary of War	John H. Eaton	1829–1831
	Lewis Cass	1831–1837
	Benjamin Butler	1837
Attorney General	John M. Berrien	1829–1831
	Roger B. Taney	1831–1833
	Benjamin Butler	1833–1837
Postmaster General	William Barry	1829–1835
	Amos Kendall	1835–1837
Secretary of Navy	John Branch	1829–1831
	Levi Woodbury	1831–1834
	Mahlon Dickerson	1834–1837

The Van Buren Administration (1837–1841)

Vice President	Richard M. Johnson	1837–1841
Secretary of State	John Forsyth	1837–1841
Secretary of Treasury	Levi Woodbury	1837–1841
Secretary of War	Joel Poinsett	1837–1841
Attorney General	Benjamin Butler	1837–1838
	Felix Grundy	1838–1840
	Henry D. Gilpin	1840–1841
Postmaster General	Amos Kendall	1837–1840
	John M. Niles	1840–1841
Secretary of Navy	Mahlon Dickerson	1837–1838
	James Paulding	1838–1841

The William Harrison Administration (1841)

Vice President	John Tyler	1841
Secretary of State	Daniel Webster	1841
Secretary of Treasury	Thomas Ewing	1841
Secretary of War	John Bell	1841
Attorney General	John J. Crittenden	1841
Postmaster General	Francis Granger	1841
Secretary of Navy	George Badger	1841

The Tyler Administration (1841–1845)

Vice President	None	
Secretary of State	Daniel Webster	1841–1843
	Hugh S. Legaré	1843
	Abel P. Upshur	1843–1844
	John C. Calhoun	1844–1845
Secretary of Treasury	Thomas Ewing	1841
	Walter Forward	1841–1843
	John C. Spencer	1843–1844
	George Bibb	1844–1845
Secretary of War	John Bell	1841
	John C. Spencer	1841–1843
	James M. Porter	1843–1844
	William Wilkins	1844–1845
Attorney General	John J. Crittenden	1841
	Hugh S. Legaré	1841–1843
	John Nelson	1843–1845
Postmaster General	Francis Granger	1841
	Charles Wickliffe	1841
Secretary of Navy	George Badger	1841
	Abel P. Upshur	1841
	David Henshaw	1843–1844
	Thomas Gilmer	1844
	John Y. Mason	1844–1845

The Polk Administration (1845–1849)

Vice President	George M. Dallas	1845–1849
Secretary of State	James Buchanan	1845–1849
Secretary of Treasury	Robert J. Walker	1845–1849
Secretary of War	William L. Marcy	1845–1849
Attorney General	John Y. Mason Nathan Clifford Isaac Toucey	1845–1846 1846–1848 1848–1849
Postmaster General	Cave Johnson	1845–1849
Secretary of Navy	George Bancroft John Y. Mason	1845–1846 1846–1849

The Taylor Administration (1849–1850)

Vice President	Millard Fillmore	1849–1850
Secretary of State	John M. Clayton	1849–1850
Secretary of Treasury	William Meredith	1849–1850
Secretary of War	George Crawford	1849–1850
Attorney General	Reverdy Johnson	1849–1850
Postmaster General	Jacob Collamer	1849–1850
Secretary of Navy	William Preston	1849–1850
Secretary of Interior	Thomas Ewing	1849–1850

The Fillmore Administration (1850–1853)

Vice President	None	
Secretary of State	Daniel Webster Edward Everett	1850–1852 1852–1853
Secretary of Treasury	Thomas Corwin	1850–1853
Secretary of War	Charles Conrad	1850–1853
Attorney General	John J. Crittenden	1850–1853
Postmaster General	Nathan Hall Sam D. Hubbard	1850–1852 1852–1853
Secretary of Navy	William A. Graham John P. Kennedy	1850–1852 1852–1853
Secretary of Interior	Thomas McKennan Alexander Stuart	1850 1850–1853

The Pierce Administration (1853–1857)

Vice President	William R. King	1853–1857
Secretary of State	William L. Marcy	1853–1857
Secretary of Treasury	James Guthrie	1853–1857
Secretary of War	Jefferson Davis	1853–1857
Attorney General	Caleb Cushing	1853–1857
Postmaster General	James Campbell	1853–1857
Secretary of Navy	James C. Dobbin	1853–1857
Secretary of Interior	Robert McClelland	1853–1857

The Buchanan Administration (1857–1861)

Vice President	John C. Breckinridge	1857–1861
Secretary of State	Lewis Cass Jeremiah S. Black	1857–1860 1860–1861
Secretary of Treasury	Howell Cobb Philip Thomas John A. Dix	1857–1860 1860–1861 1861
Secretary of War	John B. Floyd Joseph Holt	1857–1861 1861
Attorney General	Jeremiah S. Black Edwin M. Stanton	1857–1860 1860–1861
Postmaster General	Aaron V. Brown Joseph Holt Horatio King	1857–1859 1859–1861 1861
Secretary of Navy	Isaac Toucey	1857–1861
Secretary of Interior	Jacob Thompson	1857–1861

The Lincoln Administration (1861–1865)

Vice President	Hannibal Hamlin Andrew Johnson	1861–1865 1865
Secretary of State	William H. Seward	1861–1865
Secretary of Treasury	Samuel P. Chase William P. Fessenden Hugh McCulloch	1861–1864 1864–1865 1865
Secretary of War	Simon Cameron Edwin M. Stanton	1861–1862 1862–1865
Attorney General	Edward Bates James Speed	1861–1864 1864–1865

Postmaster General	Horatio King	1861
	Montgomery Blair	1861–1864
	William Dennison	1864–1865
Secretary of Navy	Gideon Welles	1861–1865
Secretary of Interior	Caleb B. Smith	1861–1863
	John P. Usher	1863–1865

The Andrew Johnson Administration (1865–1869)

Vice President	None	
Secretary of State	William H. Seward	1865–1869
Secretary of Treasury	Hugh McCulloch	1865–1869
Secretary of War	Edwin M. Stanton	1865–1867
	Ulysses S. Grant	1867–1868
	Lorenzo Thomas	1868
	John M. Schofield	1868–1869
Attorney General	James Speed	1865–1866
	Henry Stanbery	1866–1868
	William M. Evarts	1868–1869
Postmaster General	William Dennison	1865–1866
	Alexander Randall	1866–1869
Secretary of Navy	Gideon Welles	1865–1869
Secretary of Interior	John P. Usher	1865
	James Harlan	1865–1866
	Orville H. Browning	1866–1869

The Grant Administration (1869–1877)

Vice President	Schuyler Colfax	1869–1873
	Henry Wilson	1873–1877
Secretary of State	Elihu B. Washburne	1869
	Hamilton Fish	1869–1877
Secretary of Treasury	George S. Boutwell	1869–1873
	William Richardson	1873–1874
	Benjamin Bristow	1874–1876
	Lot M. Morrill	1876–1877
Secretary of War	John A. Rawlins	1869
	William T. Sherman	1869
	William W. Belknap	1869–1876
	Alphonso Taft	1876
	James D. Cameron	1876–1877

Attorney General	Ebenezer Hoar	1869–1870
	Amos T. Ackerman	1870–1871
	G. H. Williams	1871–1875
	Edwards Pierrepont	1875–1876
	Alphonso Taft	1876–1877
Postmaster General	John A. J. Creswell	1869–1874
	James W. Marshall	1874
	Marshall Jewell	1874–1876
	James N. Tyner	1876–1877
Secretary of Navy	Adolph E. Borie	1869
	George M. Robeson	1869–1877
Secretary of Interior	Jacob D. Cox	1869–1870
	Columbus Delano	1870–1875
	Zachariah Chandler	1875–1877

The Hayes Administration (1877–1881)

Vice President	William A. Wheeler	1877–1881
Secretary of State	William M. Evarts	1877–1881
Secretary of Treasury	John Sherman	1877–1881
Secretary of War	George W. McCrary	1877–1879
	Alex Ramsey	1879–1881
Attorney General	Charles Devens	1877–1881
Postmaster General	David M. Key	1877–1880
	Horace Maynard	1880–1881
Secretary of Navy	Richard W. Thompson	1877–1880
	Nathan Goff Jr.	1881
Secretary of Interior	Carl Schurz	1877–1881

The Garfield Administration (1881)

Vice President	Chester A. Arthur	1881
Secretary of State	James G. Blaine	1881
Secretary of Treasury	William Windom	1881
Secretary of War	Robert T. Lincoln	1881
Attorney General	Wayne MacVeagh	1881
Postmaster General	Thomas L. James	1881

Secretary of Navy	William H. Hunt	1881
Secretary of Interior	Samuel J. Kirkwood	1881

The Arthur Administration (1881–1885)

Vice President	None	
Secretary of State	F. T. Frelinghuysen	1881–1885
Secretary of Treasury	Charles J. Folger	1881–1884
	Walter Q. Gresham	1884
	Hugh McCulloch	1884–1885
Secretary of War	Robert T. Lincoln	1881–1885
Attorney General	Benjamin H. Brewster	1881–1885
Postmaster General	Timothy O. Howe	1881–1883
	Walter Q. Gresham	1883–1884
	Frank Hatton	1884–1885
Secretary of Navy	William H. Hunt	1881–1882
	William E. Chandler	1882–1885
Secretary of Interior	Samuel J. Kirkwood	1881–1882
	Henry M. Teller	1882–1885

The Cleveland Administration (1885–1889)

Vice President	Thomas A. Hendricks	1885–1889
Secretary of State	Thomas F. Bayard	1885–1889
Secretary of Treasury	Daniel Manning	1885–1887
	Charles S. Fairchild	1887–1889
Secretary of War	William C. Endicott	1885–1889
Attorney General	Augustus H. Garland	1885–1889
Postmaster General	William F. Vilas	1885–1888
	Don M. Dickinson	1888–1889
Secretary of Navy	William C. Whitney	1885–1889
Secretary of Interior	Lucius Q. C. Lamar	1885–1888
	William F. Vilas	1888–1889
Secretary of Agriculture	Norman J. Colman	1889

The Benjamin Harrison Administration (1889–1893)

Vice President	Levi P. Morton	1889–1893
Secretary of State	James G. Blaine	1889–1892
	John W. Foster	1892–1893
Secretary of Treasury	William Windom	1889–1891
	Charles Foster	1891–1893
Secretary of War	Redfield Proctor	1889–1891
	Stephen B. Elkins	1891–1893
Attorney General	William H. H. Miller	1889–1893
Postmaster General	John Wanamaker	1889–1893
Secretary of Navy	Benjamin F. Tracy	1889–1893
Secretary of Interior	John W. Noble	1889–1893
Secretary of Agriculture	Jeremiah M. Rusk	1889–1893

The Cleveland Administration (1893–1897)

Vice President	Adlai E. Stevenson	1893–1897
Secretary of State	Walter Q. Gresham	1893–1895
	Richard Olney	1895–1897
Secretary of Treasury	John G. Carlisle	1893–1897
Secretary of War	Daniel S. Lamont	1893–1897
Attorney General	Richard Olney	1893–1895
	James Harmon	1895–1897
Postmaster General	Wilson S. Bissell	1893–1895
	William L. Wilson	1895–1897
Secretary of Navy	Hilary A. Herbert	1893–1897
Secretary of Interior	Hoke Smith	1893–1896
	David R. Francis	1896–1897
Secretary of Agriculture	Julius S. Morton	1893–1897

The McKinley Administration (1897–1901)

Vice President	Garret A. Hobart	1897–1901
	Theodore Roosevelt	1901
Secretary of State	John Sherman	1897–1898
	William R. Day	1898
	John Hay	1898–1901
Secretary of Treasury	Lyman J. Gage	1897–1901

Secretary of War	Russell A. Alger	1897–1899
	Elihu Root	1899–1901
Attorney General	Joseph McKenna	1897–1898
	John W. Griggs	1898–1901
	Philander C. Knox	1901
Postmaster General	James A. Gary	1897–1898
	Charles E. Smith	1898–1901
Secretary of Navy	John D. Long	1897–1901
Secretary of Interior	Cornelius N. Bliss	1897–1899
	Ethan A. Hitchcock	1899–1901
Secretary of Agriculture	James Wilson	1897–1901

The Theodore Roosevelt Administration (1901–1909)

Vice President	Charles Fairbanks	1905–1909
Secretary of State	John Hay	1901–1905
	Elihu Root	1905–1909
	Robert Bacon	1909
Secretary of Treasury	Lyman J. Gage	1901–1902
	Leslie M. Shaw	1902–1907
	George B. Cortelyou	1907–1909
Secretary of War	Elihu Root	1901–1904
	William H. Taft	1904–1908
	Luke E. Wright	1908–1909
Attorney General	Philander C. Knox	1901–1904
	William H. Moody	1904–1906
	Charles J. Bonaparte	1906–1909
Postmaster General	Charles E. Smith	1901–1902
	Henry C. Payne	1902–1904
	Robert J. Wynne	1904–1905
	George B. Cortelyou	1905–1907
	George von L. Meyer	1907–1909
Secretary of Navy	John D. Long	1901–1902
	William H. Moody	1902–1904
	Paul Morton	1904–1905
	Charles J. Bonaparte	1905–1906
	Victor H. Metcalf	1906–1908
	Truman H. Newberry	1908–1909
Secretary of Interior	Ethan A. Hitchcock	1901–1907
	James R. Garfield	1907–1909
Secretary of Agriculture	James Wilson	1901–1909

Secretary of Labor and Commerce	George B. Cortelyou	1903–1904
	Victor H. Metcalf	1904–1906
	Oscar S. Straus	1906–1909
	Charles Nagel	1909

The Taft Administration (1909–1913)

Vice President	James S. Sherman	1909–1913
Secretary of State	Philander C. Knox	1909–1913
Secretary of Treasury	Franklin MacVeagh	1909–1913
Secretary of War	Jacob M. Dickinson	1909–1911
	Henry L. Stimson	1911–1913
Attorney General	George W. Wickersham	1909–1913
Postmaster General	Frank H. Hitchcock	1909–1913
Secretary of Navy	George von L. Meyer	1909–1913
Secretary of Interior	Richard A. Ballinger	1909–1911
	Walter L. Fisher	1911–1913
Secretary of Agriculture	James Wilson	1909–1913
Secretary of Labor and Commerce	Charles Nagel	1909–1913

The Wilson Administration (1913–1921)

Vice President	Thomas R. Marshall	1913–1921
Secretary of State	William J. Bryan	1913–1915
	Robert Lansing	1915–1920
	Bainbridge Colby	1920–1921
Secretary of Treasury	William G. McAdoo	1913–1918
	Carter Glass	1918–1920
	David F. Houston	1920–1921
Secretary of War	Lindley M. Garrison	1913–1916
	Newton D. Baker	1916–1921
Attorney General	James C. McReynolds	1913–1914
	Thomas W. Gregory	1914–1919
	A. Mitchell Palmer	1919–1921
Postmaster General	Albert S. Burleson	1913–1921
Secretary of Navy	Josephus Daniels	1913–1921

Secretary of Interior	Franklin K. Lane	1913–1920
	John B. Payne	1920–1921
Secretary of Agriculture	David F. Houston	1913–1920
	Edwin T. Meredith	1920–1921
Secretary of Commerce	William C. Redfield	1913–1919
	Joshua W. Alexander	1919–1921
Secretary of Labor	William B. Wilson	1913–1921

The Harding Administration (1921–1923)

Vice President	Calvin Coolidge	1921–1923
Secretary of State	Charles E. Hughes	1921–1923
Secretary of Treasury	Andrew Mellon	1921–1923
Secretary of War	John W. Weeks	1921–1923
Attorney General	Harry M. Daugherty	1921–1923
Postmaster General	Will H. Hays	1921–1922
	Hubert Work	1922–1923
	Harry S. New	1923
Secretary of Navy	Edwin Denby	1921–1923
Secretary of Interior	Albert B. Fall	1921–1923
	Hubert Work	1923
Secretary of Agriculture	Henry C. Wallace	1921–1923
Secretary of Commerce	Herbert C. Hoover	1921–1923
Secretary of Labor	James J. Davis	1921–1923

The Coolidge Administration (1923–1929)

Vice President	Charles G. Dawes	1925–1929
Secretary of State	Charles E. Hughes	1923–1925
	Frank B. Kellogg	1925–1929
Secretary of Treasury	Andrew Mellon	1923–1929
Secretary of War	John W. Weeks	1923–1925
	Dwight F. Davis	1925–1929
Attorney General	Henry M. Daugherty	1923–1924
	Harlan F. Stone	1924–1925
	John G. Sargent	1925–1929
Postmaster General	Harry S. New	1923–1929
Secretary of Navy	Edwin Derby	1923–1924
	Curtis D. Wilbur	1924–1929

Secretary of Interior	Hubert Work	1923–1928
	Roy O. West	1928–1929
Secretary of Agriculture	Henry C. Wallace	1923–1924
	Howard M. Gore	1924–1925
	William M. Jardine	1925–1929
Secretary of Commerce	Herbert C. Hoover	1923–1928
	William F. Whiting	1928–1929
Secretary of Labor	James J. Davis	1923–1929

The Hoover Administration (1929–1933)

Vice President	Charles Curtis	1929–1933
Secretary of State	Henry L. Stimson	1929–1933
Secretary of Treasury	Andrew Mellon	1929–1932
	Ogden L. Mills	1932–1933
Secretary of War	James W. Good	1929
	Patrick J. Hurley	1929–1933
Attorney General	William D. Mitchell	1929–1933
Postmaster General	Walter F. Brown	1929–1933
Secretary of Navy	Charles F. Adams	1929–1933
Secretary of Interior	Ray L. Wilbur	1929–1933
Secretary of Agriculture	Arthur M. Hyde	1929–1933
Secretary of Commerce	Robert P. Lamont	1929–1932
	Roy D. Chapin	1932–1933
Secretary of Labor	James J. Davis	1929–1930
	William N. Doak	1930–1933

The Franklin D. Roosevelt Administration (1933–1945)

Vice President	John Nance Garner	1933–1941
	Henry A. Wallace	1941–1945
	Harry S Truman	1945
Secretary of State	Cordell Hull	1933–1944
	Edward R. Stettinius Jr.	1944–1945
Secretary of Treasury	William H. Woodin	1933–1934
	Henry Morgenthau Jr.	1934–1945
Secretary of War	George H. Dern	1933–1936
	Henry A. Woodring	1936–1940
	Henry L. Stimson	1940–1945

Attorney General	Homer S. Cummings	1933–1939
	Frank Murphy	1939–1940
	Robert H. Jackson	1940–1941
	Francis Biddle	1941–1945
Postmaster General	James A. Farley	1933–1940
	Frank C. Walker	1940–1945
Secretary of Navy	Claude A. Swanson	1933–1940
	Charles Edison	1940
	Frank Knox	1940–1944
	James V. Forrestal	1944–1945
Secretary of Interior	Harold L. Ickes	1933–1945
Secretary of Agriculture	Henry A. Wallace	1933–1940
	Claude R. Wickard	1940–1945
Secretary of Commerce	Daniel C. Roper	1933–1939
	Harry L. Hopkins	1939–1940
	Jesse Jones	1940–1945
	Henry A. Wallace	1945
Secretary of Labor	Frances Perkins	1933–1945

The Truman Administration (1945–1953)

Vice President	Alben W. Barkley	1949–1953
Secretary of State	Edward R. Stettinius Jr.	1945
	James F. Byrnes	1945–1947
	George C. Marshall	1947–1949
	Dean G. Acheson	1949–1953
Secretary of Treasury	Fred M. Vinson	1945–1946
	John W. Snyder	1946–1953
Secretary of War	Robert P. Patterson	1945–1947
	Kenneth C. Royall	1947
Attorney General	Tom C. Clark	1945–1949
	J. Howard McGrath	1949–1952
	James P. McGranery	1952–1953
Postmaster General	Frank C. Walker	1945
	Robert E. Hannegan	1945–1947
	Jesse M. Donaldson	1947–1953
Secretary of Navy	James V. Forrestal	1945–1947
Secretary of Interior	Harold L. Ickes	1945–1946
	Julius A. Krug	1946–1949
	Oscar L. Chapman	1949–1953

Secretary of Agriculture	Clinton P. Anderson	1945–1948
	Charles F. Brannan	1948–1953
Secretary of Commerce	Henry A. Wallace	1945–1946
	W. Averell Harriman	1946–1948
	Charles W. Sawyer	1948–1953
Secretary of Labor	Lewis B. Schwellenbach	1945–1948
	Maurice J. Tobin	1948–1953
Secretary of Defense	James V. Forrestal	1947–1949
	Louis A. Johnson	1949–1950
	George C. Marshall	1950–1951
	Robert A. Lovett	1951–1953

The Eisenhower Administration (1953–1961)

Vice President	Richard M. Nixon	1953–1961
Secretary of State	John Foster Dulles	1953–1959
	Christian A. Herter	1959–1961
Secretary of Treasury	George M. Humphrey	1953–1957
	Robert B. Anderson	1957–1961
Attorney General	Herbert Brownell Jr.	1953–1958
	William P. Rogers	1958–1961
Postmaster General	Arthur E. Summerfield	1953–1961
Secretary of Interior	Douglas McKay	1953–1956
	Fred A. Seaton	1956–1961
Secretary of Agriculture	Ezra T. Benson	1953–1961
Secretary of Commerce	Sinclair Weeks	1953–1958
	Lewis L. Strauss	1958–1959
	Frederick H. Mueller	1959–1961
Secretary of Labor	Martin P. Durkin	1953
	James P. Mitchell	1953–1961
Secretary of Defense	Charles E. Wilson	1953–1957
	Neil H. McElroy	1957–1959
	Thomas S. Gates Jr.	1959–1961
Secretary of Health, Education, and Welfare	Oveta Culp Hobby	1953–1955
	Marion B. Folsom	1955–1958
	Arthur S. Flemming	1958–1961

The Kennedy Administration (1961–1963)

Vice President	Lyndon B. Johnson	1961–1963
Secretary of State	Dean Rusk	1961–1963
Secretary of Treasury	C. Douglas Dillon	1961–1963
Attorney General	Robert F. Kennedy	1961–1963
Postmaster General	J. Edward Day John A. Gronouski	1961–1963 1963
Secretary of Interior	Stewart L. Udall	1961–1963
Secretary of Agriculture	Orville L. Freeman	1961–1963
Secretary of Commerce	Luther H. Hodges	1961–1963
Secretary of Labor	Arthur J. Goldberg W. Willard Wirtz	1961–1962 1962–1963
Secretary of Defense	Robert S. McNamara	1961–1963
Secretary of Health, Education, and Welfare	Abraham A. Ribicoff Anthony J. Celebrezze	1961–1962 1962–1963

The Lyndon Johnson Administration (1963–1969)

Vice President	Hubert H. Humphrey	1965–1969
Secretary of State	Dean Rusk	1963–1969
Secretary of Treasury	C. Douglas Dillon Henry H. Fowler	1963–1965 1965–1969
Attorney General	Robert F. Kennedy Nicholas Katzenbach Ramsey Clark	1963–1964 1965–1966 1967–1969
Postmaster General	John A. Gronouski Lawrence F. O'Brien Marvin Watson	1963–1965 1965–1968 1968–1969
Secretary of Interior	Stewart L. Udall	1963–1969
Secretary of Agriculture	Orville L. Freeman	1963–1969
Secretary of Commerce	Luther H. Hodges John T. Connor Alexander B. Trowbridge Cyrus R. Smith	1963–1964 1964–1967 1967–1968 1968–1969
Secretary of Labor	W. Willard Wirtz	1963–1969
Secretary of Defense	Robert F. McNamara Clark Clifford	1963–1968 1968–1969
Secretary of Health, Education, and Welfare	Anthony J. Celebrezze John W. Gardner Wilbur J. Cohen	1963–1965 1965–1968 1968–1969
Secretary of Housing and Urban Development	Robert C. Weaver Robert C. Wood	1966–1969 1969
Secretary of Transportation	Alan S. Boyd	1967–1969

The Nixon Administration (1969–1974)

Vice President	Spiro T. Agnew Gerald R. Ford	1969–1973 1973–1974
Secretary of State	William P. Rogers Henry A. Kissinger	1969–1973 1973–1974
Secretary of Treasury	David M. Kennedy John B. Connally George P. Shultz William E. Simon	1969–1970 1971–1972 1972–1974 1974
Attorney General	John N. Mitchell Richard G. Kleindienst Elliot L. Richardson William B. Saxbe	1969–1972 1972–1973 1973 1973–1974
Postmaster General	Winton M. Blount	1969–1971
Secretary of Interior	Walter J. Hickel Rogers Morton	1969–1970 1971–1974
Secretary of Agriculture	Clifford M. Hardin Earl L. Butz	1969–1971 1971–1974
Secretary of Commerce	Maurice H. Stans Peter G. Peterson Frederick B. Dent	1969–1972 1972–1973 1973–1974
Secretary of Labor	George P. Shultz James D. Hodgson Peter J. Brennan	1969–1970 1970–1973 1973–1974
Secretary of Defense	Melvin R. Laird Elliot L. Richardson James R. Schlesinger	1969–1973 1973 1973–1974
Secretary of Health, Education, and Welfare	Robert H. Finch Elliot L. Richardson Caspar W. Weinberger	1969–1970 1970–1973 1973–1974

Secretary of Housing and Urban Development	George Romney James T. Lynn	1969–1973 1973–1974
Secretary of Transportation	John A. Volpe Claude S. Brinegar	1969–1973 1973–1974

The Ford Administration (1974–1977)

Vice President	Nelson A. Rockefeller	1974–1977
Secretary of State	Henry A. Kissinger	1974–1977
Secretary of Treasury	William E. Simon	1974–1977
Attorney General	William Saxbe Edward Levi	1974–1975 1975–1977
Secretary of Interior	Rogers Morton Stanley K. Hathaway Thomas Kleppe	1974–1975 1975 1975–1977
Secretary of Agriculture	Earl L. Butz John A. Knebel	1974–1976 1976–1977
Secretary of Commerce	Frederick B. Dent Rogers Morton Elliot L. Richardson	1975–1976 1975–1976 1976–1977
Secretary of Labor	Peter J. Brennan John T. Dunlop W. J. Usery	1974–1975 1975–1976 1976–1977
Secretary of Defense	James R. Schlesinger Donald Rumsfeld	1974–1975 1975–1977
Secretary of Health, Education, and Welfare	Caspar Weinberger Forrest D. Mathews	1974–1975 1975–1977
Secretary of Housing and Urban Development	James T. Lynn Carla A. Hills	1974–1975 1975–1977
Secretary of Transportation	Claude Brinegar William T. Coleman	1974–1975 1975–1977

The Carter Administration (1977–1981)

Vice President	Walter F. Mondale	1977–1981
Secretary of State	Cyrus R. Vance Edmund Muskie	1977–1980 1980–1981
Secretary of Treasury	W. Michael Blumenthal G. William Miller	1977–1979 1979–1981
Attorney General	Griffin Bell Benjamin R. Civiletti	1977–1979 1979–1981
Secretary of Interior	Cecil D. Andrus	1977–1981
Secretary of Agriculture	Robert Bergland	1977–1981
Secretary of Commerce	Juanita M. Kreps Philip M. Klutznick	1977–1979 1979–1981
Secretary of Labor	F. Ray Marshall	1977–1981
Secretary of Defense	Harold Brown	1977–1981
Secretary of Health, Education, and Welfare	Joseph A. Califano Patricia R. Harris	1977–1979 1979
Secretary of Health and Human Services	Patricia R. Harris	1979–1981
Secretary of Education	Shirley M. Hufstedler	1979–1981
Secretary of Housing and Urban Development	Patricia R. Harris Moon Landrieu	1977–1979 1979–1981
Secretary of Transportation	Brock Adams Neil E. Goldschmidt	1977–1979 1979–1981
Secretary of Energy	James R. Schlesinger Charles W. Duncan	1977–1979 1979–1981

The Reagan Administration (1981–1989)

Vice President	George Bush	1981–1989
Secretary of State	Alexander M. Haig George P. Shultz	1981–1982 1982–1989
Secretary of Treasury	Donald Regan James A. Baker III Nicholas Brady	1981–1985 1985–1988 1988–1989
Attorney General	William F. Smith Edwin A. Meese III Richard Thornburgh	1981–1985 1985–1988 1988–1989
Secretary of Interior	James Watt William P. Clark Jr. Donald P. Hodel	1981–1983 1983–1985 1985–1989
Secretary of Agriculture	John Block Richard E. Lyng	1981–1986 1986–1989

Secretary of Commerce	Malcolm Baldrige	1981–1987
	C. William Verity Jr.	1987–1989
Secretary of Labor	Raymond Donovan	1981–1985
	William E. Brock	1985–1987
	Ann D. McLaughlin	1987–1989
Secretary of Defense	Caspar Weinberger	1981–1987
	Frank Carlucci	1987–1989
Secretary of Health and Human Services	Richard Schweiker	1981–1983
	Margaret Heckler	1983–1985
	Otis R. Bowen	1985–1989
Secretary of Education	Terrel H. Bell	1981–1985
	William J. Bennett	1985–1988
	Lauro F. Cavazos	1988–1989
Secretary of Housing and Urban Development	Samuel Pierce	1981–1989
Secretary of Transportation	Drew Lewis	1981–1983
	Elizabeth Dole	1983–1987
	James H. Burnley	1987–1989
Secretary of Energy	James Edwards	1981–1982
	Donald P. Hodel	1982–1985
	John S. Herrington	1985–1989

The Bush Administration (1989–1993)

Vice President	J. Danforth Quayle	1989–1993
Secretary of State	James A. Baker III	1989–1992
Secretary of Treasury	Nicholas Brady	1989–1993
Attorney General	Richard Thornburgh	1989–1991
	William P. Barr	1991–1993
Secretary of Interior	Manuel Lujan	1989–1993
Secretary of Agriculture	Clayton K. Yeutter	1989–1991
	Edward Madigan	1991–1993
Secretary of Commerce	Robert Mosbacher	1989–1992
	Barbara Franklin	1992–1993
Secretary of Labor	Elizabeth Dole	1989–1991
	Lynn Martin	1991–1993
Secretary of Defense	Richard Cheney	1989–1993
Secretary of Health and Human Services	Louis W. Sullivan	1989–1993
Secretary of Education	Lauro F. Cavazos	1989–1991
	Lamar Alexander	1991–1993

Secretary of Housing and Urban Development	Jack F. Kemp	1989–1993
Secretary of Transportation	Samuel K. Skinner	1989–1992
	Andrew H. Card Jr.	1992–1993
Secretary of Energy	James D. Watkins	1989–1993
Secretary of Veterans Affairs	Edward J. Derwinski	1989–1993

The Clinton Administration (1993–   )

Vice President	Albert Gore	1993–
Secretary of State	Warren Christopher	1993–1997
	Madeleine Albright	1997–
Secretary of Treasury	Lloyd Bentsen	1993–1995
	Robert E. Rubin	1995–1999
	Lawrence H Summers	1999
Attorney General	Janet Reno	1993–
Secretary of Interior	Bruce Babbitt	1993–
Secretary of Agriculture	Michael Espy	1993–1995
	Dan Glickman	1995–
Secretary of Commerce	Ronald Brown	1993–1996
	Mickey Kantor	1996
	William Daley	1997–
Secretary of Labor	Robert B. Reich	1993–1997
	Alexis Herman	1997–
Secretary of Defense	Les Aspin	1993–1994
	William J. Perry	1994–1997
	William Cohen	1997–
Secretary of Health and Human Services	Donna Shalala	1993–
Secretary of Housing and Urban Development	Henry G. Cisneros	1993–1997
	Andrew Cuomo	1997–
Secretary of Education	Richard W. Riley	1993–
Secretary of Transportation	Federico Peña	1993–1997
	Rodney Slater	1997–
Secretary of Energy	Hazel R. O'Leary	1993–1997
	Federico Peña	1997
	Bill Richardson	1998–
Secretary of Veterans Affairs	Edward J. Derwinski	1993–
	Togo D. West Jr.	1998–

Justices of the Supreme Court

	Term of Service	Years of Service	Life Span		Term of Service	Years of Service	Life Span
John Jay	1789–1795	5	1745–1829	William B. Woods	1880–1887	7	1824–1887
John Rutledge	1789–1791	1	1739–1800	Stanley Matthews	1881–1889	7	1824–1889
William Cushing	1789–1810	20	1732–1810	Horace Gray	1882–1902	20	1828–1902
James Wilson	1789–1798	8	1742–1798	Samuel Blatchford	1882–1893	11	1820–1893
John Blair	1789–1796	6	1732–1800	Lucius Q. C. Lamar	1888–1893	5	1825–1893
Robert H. Harrison	1789–1790	—	1745–1790	*Melville W. Fuller*	1888–1910	21	1833–1910
James Iredell	1790–1799	9	1751–1799	David J. Brewer	1890–1910	20	1837–1910
Thomas Johnson	1791–1793	1	1732–1819	Henry B. Brown	1890–1906	16	1836–1913
William Paterson	1793–1806	13	1745–1806	George Shiras Jr.	1892–1903	10	1832–1924
*John Rutledge**	1795	—	1739–1800	Howell E. Jackson	1893–1895	2	1832–1895
Samuel Chase	1796–1811	15	1741–1811	Edward D. White	1894–1910	16	1845–1921
Oliver Ellsworth	1796–1800	4	1745–1807	Rufus W. Peckham	1895–1909	14	1838–1909
Bushrod Washington	1798–1829	31	1762–1829	Joseph McKenna	1898–1925	26	1843–1926
Alfred Moore	1799–1804	4	1755–1810	Oliver W. Holmes	1902–1932	30	1841–1935
John Marshall	1801–1835	34	1755–1835	William R. Day	1903–1922	19	1849–1923
William Johnson	1804–1834	30	1771–1834	William H. Moody	1906–1910	3	1853–1917
H. Brockholst Livingston	1806–1823	16	1757–1823	Horace H. Lurton	1909–1914	4	1844–1914
Thomas Todd	1807–1826	18	1765–1826	Charles E. Hughes	1910–1916	5	1862–1948
Joseph Story	1811–1845	33	1779–1845	*Edward D. White*	1910–1921	11	1845–1921
Gabriel Duval	1811–1835	24	1752–1844	Willis Van Devanter	1911–1937	26	1859–1941
Smith Thompson	1823–1843	20	1768–1843	Joseph R. Lamar	1911–1916	5	1857–1916
Robert Trimble	1826–1828	2	1777–1828	Mahlon Pitney	1912–1922	10	1858–1924
John McLean	1829–1861	32	1785–1861	James C. McReynolds	1914–1941	26	1862–1946
Henry Baldwin	1830–1844	14	1780–1844	Louis D. Brandeis	1916–1939	22	1856–1941
James M. Wayne	1835–1867	32	1790–1867	John H. Clarke	1916–1922	6	1857–1945
Roger B. Taney	1836–1864	28	1777–1864	William H. Taft	1921–1930	8	1857–1930
Philip P. Barbour	1836–1841	4	1783–1841	George Sutherland	1922–1938	15	1862–1942
John Catron	1837–1865	28	1786–1865	Pierce Butler	1922–1939	16	1866–1939
John McKinley	1837–1852	15	1780–1852	Edward T. Sanford	1923–1930	7	1865–1930
Peter V. Daniel	1841–1860	19	1784–1860	Harlan F. Stone	1925–1941	16	1872–1946
Samuel Nelson	1845–1872	27	1792–1873	*Charles E. Hughes*	1930–1941	11	1862–1948
Levi Woodbury	1845–1851	5	1789–1851	Owen J. Roberts	1930–1945	15	1875–1955
Robert C. Grier	1846–1870	23	1794–1870	Benjamin N. Cardozo	1932–1938	6	1870–1938
Benjamin R. Curtis	1851–1857	6	1809–1874	Hugo L. Black	1937–1971	34	1886–1971
John A. Campbell	1853–1861	8	1811–1889	Stanley F. Reed	1938–1957	19	1884–1980
Nathan Clifford	1858–1881	23	1803–1881	Felix Frankfurter	1939–1962	23	1882–1965
Noah H. Swayne	1862–1881	18	1804–1884	William O. Douglas	1939–1975	36	1898–1980
Samuel F. Miller	1862–1890	28	1816–1890	Frank Murphy	1940–1949	9	1890–1949
David Davis	1862–1877	14	1815–1886	*Harlan F. Stone*	1941–1946	5	1872–1946
Stephen J. Field	1863–1897	34	1816–1899	James F. Brynes	1941–1942	1	1879–1972
Salmon P. Chase	1864–1873	8	1808–1873	Robert H. Jackson	1941–1954	13	1892–1954
William Strong	1870–1880	10	1808–1895	Wiley B. Rutledge	1943–1949	6	1894–1949
Joseph P. Bradley	1870–1892	22	1813–1892	Harold H. Burton	1945–1958	13	1888–1964
Ward Hunt	1873–1882	9	1810–1886	*Fred M. Vinson*	1946–1953	7	1890–1953
Morrison R. Waite	1874–1888	14	1816–1888	Tom C. Clark	1949–1967	18	1899–1977
John M. Harlan	1877–1911	34	1833–1911	Sherman Minton	1949–1956	7	1890–1965
				Earl Warren	1953–1969	16	1891–1974

*Appointed and served one term, but not confirmed by the Senate.

Note: Chief justices are in italics.

	Term of Service	Years of Service	Life Span
John Marshall Harlan	1955–1971	16	1899–1971
William J. Brennan Jr.	1956–1990	33	1906–1997
Charles E. Whittaker	1957–1962	5	1901–1973
Potter Stewart	1958–1981	23	1915–1985
Bryon R. White	1962–1993	31	1917–
Arthur J. Goldberg	1962–1965	3	1908–1990
Abe Fortas	1965–1969	4	1910–1982
Thurgood Marshall	1967–1991	24	1908–1992
Warren C. Burger	1969–1986	17	1907–1995
Harry A. Blackmun	1970–1994	24	1908–1999
Lewis F. Powell Jr.	1972–1987	15	1907–

	Term of Service	Years of Service	Life Span
William H. Rehnquist	1972–1986	14	1924–
John P. Stevens III	1975–	—	1920–
Sandra Day O'Connor	1981–	—	1930–
William H. Rehnquist	1986–	—	1924–
Antonin Scalia	1986–	—	1936–
Anthony M. Kennedy	1988–	—	1936–
David H. Souter	1990–	—	1939–
Clarence Thomas	1991–	—	1948–
Ruth Bader Ginsburg	1993–	—	1933–
Stephen Breyer	1994–	—	1938–

A Social Profile of the American Republic

Year	Population	Percent Increase	Population Per Square Mile	Population Percent Urban/ Rural	Percent Male/ Female	Percent White/ Nonwhite	Persons Per Household	Median Age
1790	3,929,214		4.5	5.1/94.9	NA/NA	80.7/19.3	5.79	NA
1800	5,308,483	35.1	6.1	6.1/93.9	NA/NA	81.1/18.9	NA	NA
1810	7,239,881	36.4	4.3	7.3/92.7	NA/NA	81.0/19.0	NA	NA
1820	9,638,453	33.1	5.5	7.2/92.8	50.8/49.2	81.6/18.4	NA	16.7
1830	12,866,020	33.5	7.4	8.8/91.2	50.8/18.1	81.9/18.1	NA	17.2
1840	17,069,453	32.7	9.8	10.8/89.2	50.9/49.1	83.2/16.8	NA	17.8
1850	23,191,876	35.9	7.9	15.3/84.7	51.0/49.0	84.3/15.7	5.55	18.9
1860	31,443,321	35.6	10.6	19.8/80.2	51.2/48.8	85.6/14.4	5.28	19.4
1870	39,818,449	26.6	13.4	25.7/74.3	50.6/49.4	86.2/13.8	5.09	20.2
1880	50,155,783	26.0	16.9	28.2/71.8	50.9/49.1	86.5/13.5	5.04	20.9
1890	62,947,714	25.5	21.2	35.1/64.9	51.2/48.8	87.5/12.5	4.93	22.0
1900	75,994,575	20.7	25.6	39.6/60.4	51.1/48.9	87.9/12.1	4.76	22.9
1910	91,972,266	21.0	31.0	45.6/54.4	51.5/48.5	88.9/11.1	4.54	24.1
1920	105,710,620	14.9	35.6	51.2/48.8	51.0/49.0	89.7/10.3	4.34	25.3
1930	122,775,046	16.1	41.2	56.1/43.9	50.6/49.4	89.8/10.2	4.11	26.4
1940	131,669,275	7.2	44.2	56.5/43.5	50.2/49.8	89.8/10.2	3.67	29.0
1950	150,697,361	14.5	50.7	64.0/36.0	49.7/50.3	89.5/10.5	3.37	30.2
1960	179,323,175	18.5	50.6	69.9/30.1	49.3/11.4	88.6/11.4	3.33	29.5
1970	203,302,031	13.4	57.4	73.5/26.5	48.7/51.3	87.6/12.4	3.14	28.0
1980	226,545,805	11.4	64.0	73.7/26.3	48.6/51.4	86.0/14.0	2.76	30.0
1990	248,709,873	9.8	70.3	NA	48.7/51.3	80.3/19.7	2.63	32.9
2000*	276,382,000	7.1	75.8	NA	48.9/51.5	82.6/17.4	NA	NA

NA = Not available.

*Projections.

Vital Statistics (rates per thousand)					
Year	Births	Year	Births	Deaths*	Marriages*	Divorces*
1800	55.0	1900	32.3	17.2	NA	NA
1810	54.3	1910	30.1	14.7	NA	NA
1820	55.2	1920	27.7	13.0	12.0	1.6
1830	51.4	1930	21.3	11.3	9.2	1.6
1840	51.8	1940	19.4	10.8	12.1	2.0
1850	43.3	1950	24.1	9.6	11.1	2.6
1860	44.3	1960	23.7	9.5	8.5	2.2
1870	38.3	1970	18.4	9.5	10.6	3.5
1880	39.8	1980	15.9	8.8	10.6	5.2
1890	31.5	1990	16.7	8.6	9.8	4.6

NA = Not available.

*Data not available before 1900.

Year	Total Population	Life Expectancy (in years)		White Males	Nonwhite Males
		White Females	Nonwhite Females		
1900	47.3	48.7	33.5	46.6	32.5
1910	50.1	52.0	37.5	48.6	33.8
1920	54.1	55.6	45.2	54.4	45.5
1930	59.7	63.5	49.2	59.7	47.3
1940	62.9	66.6	54.9	62.1	51.5
1950	68.2	72.2	62.9	66.5	59.1
1960	69.7	74.1	66.3	67.4	61.1
1970	70.9	75.6	69.4	68.0	61.3
1980	73.7	78.1	73.6	70.7	65.3
1990	75.4	79.3	76.3	72.6	68.4

The Changing Age Structure

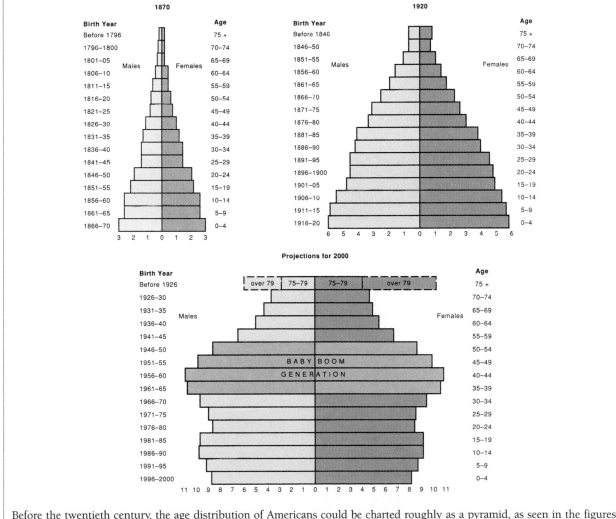

Before the twentieth century, the age distribution of Americans could be charted roughly as a pyramid, as seen in the figures for 1870 and 1920. High birthrates create a broad base at the bottom, while mortality rates winnow the population to a small tip of elderly. But by the year 2000, the pyramid has been transformed more nearly into a cylinder. Over the past two centuries fertility rates have undergone a steady decline, pulling in the base of the pyramid, while higher living standards have allowed Americans to live longer, broadening the top. Only the temporary bulge of the baby boom distorts the shape.

Years	Total Number of Immigrants	Regional Origin of Immigrants (percent) EUROPE				Western Hemisphere	Asia
		Total Europe	North and West	East and Central	South and Other		
1821–1830	143,389	69.2	67.1	—	2.1	8.4	—
1831–1840	599,125	82.8	81.8	—	1.0	5.5	—
1841–1850	1,713,251	93.8	92.9	0.1	0.3	3.6	—
1851–1860	2,598,214	94.4	93.6	0.1	0.8	2.9	1.6
1861–1870	2,314,824	89.2	87.8	0.5	0.9	7.2	2.8
1871–1880	2,812,191	80.8	73.6	4.5	2.7	14.4	4.4
1881–1890	5,246,13	90.3	72.0	11.9	6.3	8.1	1.3
1891–1900	3,687,546	96.5	44.5	32.8	19.1	1.1	1.9
1901–1910	8,795,386	92.5	21.7	44.5	6.3	4.1	2.8
1911–1920	5,735,811	76.3	17.4	33.4	25.5	19.9	3.4
1921–1930	4,107,209	60.3	31.7	14.4	14.3	36.9	2.4
1931–1940	528,431	65.9	38.8	11.0	16.1	30.3	2.8
1941–1950	1,035,039	60.1	47.5	4.6	7.9	34.3	3.1
1951–1960	2,515,479	52.8	17.7	24.3	10.8	39.6	6.0
1961–1970	3,321,677	33.8	11.7	9.4	12.9	51.7	12.9
1971–1980	4,493,300	17.8	4.3	5.6	8.4	44.3	35.2
1981–1990	7,338,000	10.4	5.9	4.8	1.1	49.3	37.3

Dash indicates less than 0.1 percent.

Recent Trends in Immigration (in thousands)					PERCENT		
	1961–1970	1971–1980	1981–1990	1991	1961–1970	1971–1980	1981–1990
All countries	3,321.7	4,493.3	7,338.0	1,827.2	100.0	100.0	100.0
Europe	1,123.5	800.4	761.5	146.7	33.8	17.8	10.4
Austria	20.6	9.5	18.9	3.5	0.6	0.2	0.3
Hungary	5.4	6.6	5.9	0.9	0.2	0.1	0.1
Belgium	9.2	5.3	6.6	0.7	0.3	0.1	0.1
Czechoslovakia	3.3	6.0	5.4	0.6	0.1	0.1	0.1
Denmark	9.2	4.4	2.8	0.6	0.3	0.1	0.1
France	45.2	25.1	92.1	4.0	1.4	0.6	1.3
Germany	190.8	74.4	159.0	10.9	5.7	1.7	2.2
Greece	86.0	92.4	31.9	2.9	2.6	2.1	0.4
Ireland	33.0	11.5	67.2	4.6	1.0	0.3	0.9
Italy	214.1	129.4	12.3	30.3	6.4	2.9	0.2
Netherlands	30.6	10.5	4.2	1.3	0.9	0.2	0.1
Norway	15.5	3.9	83.2	0.6	0.5	0.1	1.1
Poland	53.5	37.2	40.3	17.1	1.6	0.8	0.5
Portugal	76.1	101.7	20.5	4.6	2.3	2.3	0.3
Spain	44.7	39.1	11.1	2.7	1.3	0.9	0.2
Sweden	17.1	6.5	8.0	1.2	0.5	0.1	0.1
Switzerland	18.5	8.2	57.6	1.0	0.6	0.2	0.8
USSR	2.5	39.0	18.7	31.6	0.1	0.9	0.3
United Kingdom	213.8	137.4	159.2	16.8	6.4	3.1	2.2
Yugoslavia	20.4	30.5	37.3	2.8	0.6	0.7	0.5
Other Europe	9.1	18.9	7.7	1.2	0.2	0.2	0.0

Recent Trends in Immigration (in thousands)							
					PERCENT		
	1961–1970	1971–1980	1981–1990	1991	1961–1970	1971–1980	1981–1990
Asia	427.6	1,588.2	2,738.1	342.2	12.9	35.2	37.3
China	34.8	124.3	298.9	24.0	1.0	2.8	4.1
Hong Kong	75.0	113.5	98.2	15.9	2.3	2.5	1.3
India	27.2	164.1	250.7	42.7	0.8	3.7	3.4
Iran	10.3	45.1	116.0	9.9	0.3	1.0	1.6
Israel	29.6	37.7	44.2	5.1	0.9	0.8	0.6
Japan	40.0	49.8	47.0	5.6	1.2	1.1	0.6
Korea	34.5	267.6	333.8	25.4	1.0	6.0	4.5
Philippines	98.4	355.0	548.7	68.8	3.0	7.9	7.5
Turkey	10.1	13.4	23.4	3.5	0.3	0.3	0.3
Vietnam	4.3	172.8	281.0	14.8	1.1	3.8	3.8
Other Asia	36.5	176.1	631.4	126.4	1.1	3.8	8.6
America	1,716.4	1,982.5	3,615.6	1,297.6	51.7	44.3	49.3
Argentina	49.7	29.9	27.3	4.2	1.5	0.7	0.4
Canada	413.3	169.9	158.0	19.9	12.4	3.8	2.2
Colombia	72.0	77.3	122.9	19.3	2.2	1.7	1.7
Cuba	208.5	264.9	144.6	9.5	6.3	5.9	2.0
Dominican Rep.	93.3	148.1	252.0	42.4	2.8	3.3	3.4
Ecuador	36.8	50.1	56.2	10.0	1.1	1.1	0.8
El Salvador	15.0	34.4	213.5	46.9	0.5	0.8	2.9
Haiti	34.5	56.3	138.4	47.0	1.0	1.3	1.9
Jamaica	74.9	137.6	208.1	23.0	2.3	3.1	2.8
Mexico	453.9	640.3	1,655.7	947.9	13.7	14.3	22.6
Other America	264.4	373.8	639.3	128.4	7.9	8.3	8.7
Africa	29.0	80.8	176.8	33.5	0.9	1.8	2.4
Oceania	25.1	41.2	45.2	7.1	0.8	0.9	0.6

Figures may not add to total due to rounding.

American Workers and Farmers						
Year	Total Number of Workers (thousands)	Percent of Workers Male/Female	Percent of Female Workers Married	Percent of Workers in Female Population	Percent of Workers in Labor Unions	Farm Population (thousands)	Farm Population as Percent of Total Population
1870	12,506	85/15	NA	NA	NA	NA	NA
1880	17,392	85/15	NA	NA	NA	21,973	43.8
1890	23,318	83/17	13.9	18.9	NA	24,771	42.3
1900	29,073	82/18	15.4	20.6	3	29,875	41.9
1910	38,167	79/21	24.7	25.4	6	32,077	34.9
1920	41,614	79/21	23.0	23.7	12	31,974	30.1
1930	48,830	78/22	28.9	24.8	7	30,529	24.9
1940	53,011	76/24	36.4	27.4	27	30,547	23.2
1950	59,643	72/28	52.1	31.4	25	23,048	15.3
1960	69,877	68/32	59.9	37.7	26	15,635	8.7
1970	82,049	63/37	63.4	43.4	25	9,712	4.8
1980	108,544	58/42	59.7	51.5	23	6,051	2.7
1990	117,914	55/45	58.4	44.3	16	4,591	1.8

Year	Gross National Product (GNP) (in billions)*	FOREIGN TRADE (in millions) The Economy and Federal Spending			Federal Budget (in billions)	Federal Surplus/Deficit (in billions)	Federal Debt (in billions)
		Exports	Imports	Balance of Trade			
1790	NA	$20	$23	$−3	$0.004	$+0.00015	$0.076
1800	NA	71	91	−20	0.011	+0.0006	0.083
1810	NA	67	85	−18	0.008	+0.0012	0.053
1820	NA	70	74	−4	0.018	−0.0004	0.091
1830	NA	74	71	+3	0.015	+0.100	0.049
1840	NA	132	107	+25	0.024	−0.005	0.004
1850	NA	152	178	−26	0.040	+0.004	0.064
1860	NA	400	362	−38	0.063	−0.01	0.065
1870	$7.4	451	462	−11	0.310	+0.10	2.4
1880	11.2	853	761	+92	0.268	+0.07	2.1
1890	13.1	910	823	+87	0.318	+0.09	1.2
1900	18.7	1,499	930	+569	0.521	+0.05	1.2
1910	35.3	1,919	1,646	+273	0.694	−0.02	1.1
1920	91.5	8,664	5,784	+2,880	6.357	+0.3	24.3
1930	90.7	4,013	3,500	+513	3.320	+0.7	16.3
1940	100.0	4,030	7,433	−3,403	9.6	−2.7	43.0
1950	286.5	10,816	9,125	+1,691	43.1	−2.2	257.4
1960	506.5	19,600	15,046	+4,556	92.2	+0.3	286.3
1970	992.7	42,700	40,189	+2,511	195.6	−2.8	371.0
1980	2,631.7	220,783	244,871	+24,088	590.9	−73.8	907.7
1990	5,743.8	394,030	495,042	−101,012	1,253.1	$−220.5	3,266.0
1998	8,511.0	931,315	1,099,902	−168,587	1,652.	69	5,555.5

*For 1990 and after, gross domestic product (GDP) is given.

	U.S. Military Personnel (thousands)	American Wars Personnel as % of Population	U.S. Deaths	U.S. Wounds	Direct Cost 1990 Dollars (millions)
American Revolution					
Apr. 1775–Sept. 1783	184–250	9–12	4,004	6,004	$100–140
War of 1812					
June 1812–Feb. 1815	286	3	1,950	4,000	87
Mexican War					
May 1846–Feb. 1848	116	0.5	13,271	4,102	82
Civil War: Union	3,393	14	360,222	275,175	2,302
Civil War: Confederacy					
Apr. 1861–Apr. 1865	1,034	11	258,000	NA	1,032
Spanish-American War					
Apr. 1898–Aug. 1898	307	0.4	2,446	1,662	270
World War I					
Apr. 1917–Nov. 1918	4,714	5	116,516	204,002	32,740
World War II					
Dec. 1941–Aug. 1945	16,354	12	405,399	670,846	360,000
Korean War					
June 1950–June 1953	5,764	4	54,246	103,284	50,000
Vietnam War					
Aug. 1964–June 1973	8,400	4	47,704	219,573	140,644
Persian Gulf War					
Jan. 1991–Feb. 1991	467	0.1	293	467	NA

Bibliography

Chapter 17: Reconstructing the Union

General Histories James McPherson, *Ordeal by Fire: The Civil War and Reconstruction* (1982); Kenneth M. Stampp, *The Era of Reconstruction, 1865–1877* (1965).

National Politics Herman Belz, *Emancipation and Equal Rights: Politics and Constitutionalism in the Civil War Era* (1978); Michael Les Benedict, *A Compromise of Principle: Congressional Republicans and Reconstruction* (1974); W. R. Brock, *An American Crisis: Congress and Reconstruction, 1865–1867* (1963); John and LaWanda Cox, *Politics, Principles, and Prejudice, 1865–1866* (1963); Laura F. Edwards, *Gendered Strife and Confusion: The Political Culture of Reconstruction* (1997); William C. Harris, *With Charity for All: Lincoln and the Restoration of the Union* (1997); James M. McPherson, *The Struggle for Equality: Abolitionists and the Negro in the Civil War and Reconstruction* (1964); Hans L. Trefousse, *The Radical Republicans: Lincoln's Vanguard for Racial Justice* (1969); Xi Wang, *The Trial of Democracy: Black Suffrage and Northern Republicans, 1860–1910* (1997).

Reconstruction and the Constitution William Gillette, *The Right to Vote: Politics and the Passage of the Fifteenth Amendment* (1965); Harold M. Hyman, *A More Perfect Union: The Impact of the Civil War and Reconstruction on the Constitution* (1973); Joseph James, *The Framing of the Fourteenth Amendment* (1956); William E. Nelson, *The Fourteenth Amendment: From Political Principle to Judicial Doctrine* (1988).

The Black Experience in Reconstruction James D. Anderson, *The Education of Blacks in the South, 1860–1935* (1988); Herbert G. Gutman, *The Black Family in Slavery and Freedom, 1750–1925* (1976); Janet Sharp Hermann, *The Pursuit of a Dream* (1981); Howard Rabinowitz, ed., *Southern Black Leaders in Reconstruction* (1982); Vernon L. Wharton, *The Negro in Mississippi, 1865–1890* (1947); Joel Williamson, *After Slavery: The Negro in South Carolina during Reconstruction* (1966).

Reconstruction in the South Richard N. Current, *Those Terrible Carpetbaggers: A Reinterpretation* (1988); William C. Harris, *Day of the Carpetbagger: Republican Reconstruction in Mississippi* (1979); Michael Perman, *Reunion without Compromise: The South and Reconstruction, 1865–1868* (1973); George C. Rable, *But There Was No Peace: The Role of Violence in the Politics of Reconstruction* (1984); Ted Tunnell, *Crucible of Reconstruction: War, Radicalism, and Race in Louisiana, 1862–1877* (1974); Allen Trelease, *White Terror: The Ku Klux Klan Conspiracy and Southern Reconstruction* (1967); Sarah Woolfolk Wiggins, *The Scalawag in Alabama Politics, 1865–1881* (1977).

Social and Economic Reconstruction Paul A. Cimbala, *Under the Guardianship of the Nation: The Freedmen's Bureau and the Reconstruction of Georgia, 1865–1870* (1997); Steven Hahn, *The Roots of Southern Populism: Yeoman Farmers and the Transformation of the Georgia Upcountry, 1850–1890* (1983); Jacqueline Jones, *Soldiers of Light and Love: Northern Teachers and Georgia Blacks, 1865–1873* (1980); Claude F. Oubre, *Forty Acres and a Mule: The Freedmen's Bureau and Black Landownership* (1978); Lawrence N. Powell, *New Masters: Northern Planters during the Civil War and Reconstruction* (1984); Roger L. Ransom and Richard Sutch, *One Kind of Freedom: The Economic Consequences of Emancipation* (1977); Mark W. Summers, *Railroads, Reconstruction, and the Gospel of Prosperity* (1984).

The End of Reconstruction Keith Ian Polakoff, *The Politics of Inertia: The Election of 1876 and the End of Reconstruction* (1973); C. Vann Woodward, *Reunion and Reaction: The Compromise of 1877 and the End of Reconstruction* (1951).

Biographies Fawn M. Brodie, *Thaddeus Stevens: Scourge of the South* (1959); David Donald, *Charles Sumner and the Rights of Man* (1970); William S. McFeely, *Yankee Stepfather: General O. Howard and the Freedmen* (1968) and *Grant: A Biography* (1981); Brooks D. Simpson, *Let Us Have Peace: Ulysses S. Grant and the Politics of War and Reconstruction, 1861–1868* (1991); Hans L. Trefousse, *Andrew Johnson: A Biography* (1989).

Chapter 18: The New South and the Trans-Mississippi West

The New South: History, Politics, and Culture Edward L. Ayers, *The Promise of the New South: Life after Reconstruction* (1992) and *Southern Crossing: A History of the American South, 1877–1906* (1995); Orville Vernon Burton, *In My Father's House* (1985); W. J. Cash, *The Mind of the South* (1941); Thomas D. Clark and Albert Kirwan, *The South since Appomattox* (1967); David L. Carlton, *Mill and Town in South Carolina, 1880–1920* (1982); John M. Cooper, *Walter Hines Page: The Southerner as American, 1855–1918* (1977); Pete Daniel, *Breaking the Land: The Transformation of Cotton, Tobacco, and Rice Cultures since 1880* (1985); Carl N. Degler, *The Other South: Southern Dissenters in the Nineteenth Century* (1974); Robert Durden, *The Self-Inflicted Wound: Southern Politics in the Nineteenth Century* (1985); John S. Ezell, *The South since 1865* (1975); Paul Gaston, *The New South Creed: A Study in Southern Mythmaking* (1970); Richard Gray, *Writing the South: The Idea of an American Region* (1986); Patrick H. Hearden, *Independence and Empire: The New South's Cotton Mill Campaign, 1865–1920* (1982); J. Morgan Kousser, *The Shaping of Southern Politics: Suffrage Restriction and Establishment of the One Party South* (1974); J. Morgan Kousser and James McPherson, eds., *Region, Race, and Reconstruction* (1982); Lawrence Karsen, *The Rise of the Urban South* (1985); I. A. Newby, *Plain Folk in the New South: Social Change and Cultural Persistence, 1880–1915* (1989); Raymond B. Nixon, *Henry W. Grady: Spokesman of the New South* (1969); Ted Ownby, *Subduing Satan* (1990); David M. Potter, *The South and the Concurrent Majority* (1972); Allen Tullos, *Habits of Industry: White Culture and the Transformation of the Carolina Piedmont* (1989); Marjorie Spruill Wheeler, *New Women of the New South: The Leaders of the Woman Suffrage Movement in the Southern States* (1993); Charles R. Wilson, *Baptized in Blood: The Religion of the Lost Cause, 1865–1920*

B-1

(1980); C. Vann Woodward, *Tom Watson: Agrarian Rebel* (1938), and *The Origins of the New South* (1951).

The Southern Economy and Race   David Carlton, *Mill and Town in South Carolina, 1880–1920* (1982); Pete Daniel, *Breaking the Land: The Transformation of Cotton, Tobacco, and Rice Cultures since 1880* (1985); Glenda Gilmore, *Gender and Jim Crow: Women and the Politics of White Supremacy in North Carolina, 1896–1920* (1996); Steven Hahn, *The Roots of Southern Populism: Yeoman Farmers and the Transformation of the Georgia Upcountry, 1850–1890* (1983); Louis T. Harlan, *Booker T. Washington: The Making of a Black Leader, 1865–1901* (1972); Robert Higgs, *Competition and Coercion: Blacks in the American Economy, 1865–1890* (1977); Gerald David Jaynes, *Branches without Roots: Genesis of the Black Working Class in the American South, 1862–1882* (1986); Neil R. McMillen, *Dark Journey: Black Mississippians in the Age of Jim Crow* (1989); J. M. McPherson, *The Abolitionist Legacy: From Reconstruction to the NAACP* (1975); August Meier, *Negro Thought in America, 1880–1915: Racial Ideologies in the Age of Booker T. Washington* (1963); Howard Rabinowitz, *Race Relations in the Urban South, 1865–1890* (1978); Roger Ransom and Richard Sutch, *One Kind of Freedom: The Economic Consequences of Emancipation* (1977); Donald Spivey, *Schooling for the New Slavery: Black Industrial Education* (1978); J. F. Stover, *The Railroads of the South* (1955); Edward Wheeler, *Uplifting the Race: The Black Minister in the New South, 1865–1902* (1986); Joel Williamson, *The Crucible of Race: Black-White Relations in the American South since Emancipation* (1984) and *After Slavery* (1965); C. Vann Woodward, *The Strange Career of Jim Crow,* 3d rev. ed. (1974); Gavin Wright, *Old South, New South: Revolutions in the Southern Economy since the Civil War* (1986).

Opening of the West   Walton Bean, *California* (1978); Thomas Berger, *Little Big Man* (1964); Ray A. Billington, *Westward Expansion* (1967); Thomas D. Clark, *Frontier America,* rev. ed. (1969); William Cronon, *Nature's Metropolis: Chicago and the Great West* (1991); William Cronon, George Miles, and Jay Gitlin, *Under an Open Sky: Rethinking America's Western Past* (1992); Sarah Deutsch, *No Separate Refuge: Culture, Class, and Gender on an Anglo-Hispanic Frontier in the American Southwest, 1880–1940* (1987); Robert Hine, *The American West,* 2d rev. ed. (1984); Paul Hutton, ed., *Soldiers West: Biographers from the Military Frontier* (1987); Howard Lamar, *The Reader's Encyclopedia of the American West* (1977) and *The Far Southwest, 1846–1912* (1966); Patricia Nelson Limerick, *The Legacy of Conquest: The Unbroken Past of the American West* (1987); Leo Marx, *The Machine in the Garden* (1964); Gerald McFarland, *A Scattered People: An American Family Moves West* (1985); Donald W. Meinig, *The Southwest: Three People in Geographical Change, 1600–1970* (1971); Frederick Merk, *History of the Westward Movement* (1978); Clyde A. Milner II, *A New Significance: Re-Envisioning the History of the American West* (1996); Clyde A. Milner II, Carol A. O'Connor, and Martha A. Sandweiss, eds., *The Oxford History of the American West* (1994); Roderick Nash, *Wilderness and the American Mind,* 3d ed. (1982); Earl Pomery, *The Pacific Slope* (1968); Richard Slotkin, *The Fatal Environment: The Myth of the West in the Age of Industrialization* (1985) and *Gunfighter Nation: The Myth of the Frontier in Twentieth-Century America* (1992); Wallace Stegner, *Beyond the Hundredth Meridian: John Welsey Powell and the Second Opening of the West* (1954); Henry Nash Smith, *Virgin Land* (1950); Jane Tompkins, *West of Everything: The Inner Life of Westerns* (1992); Mark Twain, *Roughing It* (1872); Elliott West, *The Way to the West: Essays on the Central Plains* (1995); Richard White, *"It's Your Misfortune and None of My Own": A New History of the American West* (1992); Donald Worster, *Rivers of Empire: Water, Aridity, and the Growth of the American West* (1992) and *Under Western Skies: Nature and History in the American West* (1992).

The Peoples of the West   Rodolfo Acuña, *Occupied America: A History of Chicanos* (1981); Ralph Andrist, *The Long Death: The Last Days of the Sioux Nation* (1964); Robert Athearn, *In Search of Canaan: Black Migration in Kansas, 1879–1880* (1978); Gunther Barth, *Bitter Strength: A History of the Chinese in the United States, 1850–1870* (1964); Gretchen Bataille and Charles Silet, *The Pretend Indians: Images of Native Americans in the Movies* (1980); Beverly Beeton, *Women Vote in the West: The Woman Suffrage Movement, 1869–1896* (1986); Robert Berkhofer Jr., *The White Man's Indian* (1978); Dee Brown, *Bury My Heart at Wounded Knee: An Indian History of the American War* (1970); Anne M. Butler, *Daughters of Joy, Sisters of Misery: Prostitutes in the American West, 1865–1890* (1985); Colin G. Calloway, ed., *Our Hearts Fell to the Ground: Plains Indian Views of How the West Was Lost* (1996); Edward Curtis, *The North American Indian* (1972); David Dary, *Cowboy Culture* (1981); Everett Dick, *Sod House Frontier* (1954); Carol Fairbanks, *Prairie Women: Images in American and Canadian Fiction* (1986); John Mack Faragher, *Women and Men on the Overland Trail* (1979); Christine Fisher, ed., *Let Them Speak for Themselves: Women in the American West, 1849–1900* (1977); Joe B. Frantz and Julian Choate, *The American Cowboy: The Myth and Reality* (1955); Carl Guarneri and David Alvarez, *Religion and Society in the American West* (1987); Julie Roy Jeffrey, *Frontier Women: The Trans-Mississippi West, 1840–1880* (1979); Alvin Josephy, *The Indian Heritage in America* (1969); William Katz, *The Black West* (1971); Polly W. Kaufman, *Women Teachers on the Frontier* (1984); William Leckie, *The Buffalo Soldiers: A Narrative History of the Negro Cavalry* (1967); Frederick Luebke, *Ethnicity on the Great Plains* (1980); Janet A. McDonnell, *The Dispossession of the American Indian, 1887–1934* (1991); M. S. Meier and Feliciano Rivera, *The Chicanos: A History of the Mexican Americans* (1972); David Montejano, *Anglos and Mexicans in the Making of Texas, 1836–1986* (1987); Sandra Myres, *Western Women and the Frontier Experience, 1880–1915* (1982); James S. Olsen and Raymond Wilson, *Native Americans in the Twentieth Century* (1984); Nell Painter, *The Exodusters: Black Migration to Kansas after Reconstruction* (1976); Peggy Pascoe, *Relations of Rescue: The Search for Female Moral Authority in the American West, 1874–1939* (1990); Paul Prucha, *American Indian Policy in Crisis* (1976); Harriet and Fred Rochlin, *Pioneer Jews: A New Life in the Far West* (1984); Mari Sandoz, *Cheyenne Autumn* (1954); William Savage, *The Cowboy Hero: His Image in American History and Culture* (1979) and as ed., *Cowboy Life* (1975); Kent Steckmesser, *The Western Hero in History and Legend* (1965); Elinor Pruitt Stewart, *Letters of a Woman Homesteader* (1913, 1914); Joanna Stratton, *Pioneer Women: Voices of the Kansas Frontier* (1981); John Tebbel and Keith Jennison, *The American Indian Wars* (1960); Robert Utley, *High Noon in Lincoln: Violence on the Western Frontier* (1987), *The Indian Frontier of the American West, 1846–1890* (1984), and *Frontier Regulars: The United States Army and the Indian, 1866–1890* (1984); Sylvia Van Kirk, *Many Tender Ties: Women in Fur Trade Society* (1983); Wilcomb Washburn, *The Indian in America* (1975).

The Western Economy   Lewis Atherton, *Cattle Kings* (1961); Gunther Barth, *Instant Cities* (1975); Edward Dale, *The Range*

Cattle Industry, rev. ed. (1969); David Dary, *Entrepreneurs of the Old West* (1986); Alan Derickson, *Workers' Health, Workers' Democracy: The Western Miners' Struggle, 1891–1925* (1988); Robert Dykstra, *The Cattle Towns* (1968); Gilbert Fite, *The Farmer's Frontier* (1966); David Emmons, *The Butte Irish: Class and Ethnicity in an American Mining Town, 1875–1925* (1989); Paul Gates, *History of Public Land Development* (1968); William Greever, *The Bonanza West: The Story of the Western Mining Rushes* (1963); Gene M. Gressley, *Bankers and Cattlemen* (1966); Robert West Howard, *The Great Iron Trail: The Story of the First Transcontinental Railroad* (1963); Donald Jackson, *Gold Dust* (1980); Richard Lingenfelter, *The Hardrock Miners: A History of the Mining Labor Movement in the American West, 1863–1893* (1974); Rodman Paul, *The Far West and the Great Plains in Transition, 1865–1900* (1988); Gunther Peck, *Reinventing Free Labor: Padrones and Immigrant Workers in the North American West, 1880–1930* (2000); Mari Sandoz, *Old Jules* (1962) and *The Buffalo Hunters: The Story of the Hide Men* (1978); Fred A. Shannon, *The Farmer's Last Frontier, 1860–1897* (1945); J. M. Skaggs, *The Cattle Trailing Industry* (1973); George R. Taylor and Irene Neu, *The American Railroad Network, 1861–1890* (1956); James Ward, *Railroads and the Character of America, 1820–1887* (1986); Walter Prescott Webb, *The Great Plains* (1931); Donald Worster, *Rivers of Empire* (1985); Mark Wyman, *Hard Rock Epic: Western Miners and the Industrial Revolution, 1860–1910* (1979).

Chapter 19: The New Industrial Order

General Histories   Daniel Boorstin, *The Americans: The Democratic Experience* (1973); John A. Garraty, *The New Commonwealth* (1968); Ray Ginger, *The Age of Excess* (1963); Samuel P. Hays, *The Response to Industrialism, 1885–1914* (1957); Edward C. Kirkland, *Industry Comes of Age: Business, Labor, and Public Policy, 1860–1897* (1967); Martin V. Melosi, *Coping with Abundance: Energy and Environment in Industrial America* (1985); Robert Wiebe, *The Search for Order, 1877–1920* (1968).

The Economy   Frederick Lewis Allen, *The Great Pierpont Morgan* (1949); W. Elliot Brownlee, *Dynamics of Ascent: A History of the American Economy*, rev. ed. (1979); Stuart Bruchey, *Growth of the Modern American Economy* (1975); Milton Friedman and Anna Schwartz, *Monetary History of the United States, 1867–1960* (1963); Robert L. Heilbroner, *The Economic Transformation of America* (1977); Robert Higgs, *The Transformation of the American Economy, 1865–1914* (1971); Susan Previant Lee and Peter Passell, *A New Economic View of American History* (1979); Harold G. Vatter, *The Drive to Industrial Maturity: The United States Economy, 1860–1914* (1975).

The Railroads   Alfred D. Chandler Jr., *The Railroads: The Nation's First Big Business* (1965); Robert Fogel, *Railroads and American Economic Growth* (1964); Julius Grodinsky, *Jay Gould* (1957); Gabriel Kolko, *Railroads and Regulation, 1877–1916* (1965); Albro Martin, *James J. Hill and the Opening of the Northwest* (1976) and *Railroads Triumphant: The Growth, Rejection, and Rebirth of a Vital American Force* (1992); John F. Stover, *American Railroads* (1970).

The Rise of Big Business   Alfred Chandler Jr., *Strategy and Structure: Chapters in the History of American Industrial Enterprise* (1962), *The Visible Hand: The Managerial Revolution in American Business* (1977), and *Scale and Scope: The Dynamics of Industrial Capitalism* (1990); Thomas Cochrane, *Business in American Life* (1972); Naomi Lamoreaux, *The Great Merger Movement in American Business, 1895–1904* (1985); Harold C. Livesay, *Andrew Carnegie and the Rise of Big Business* (1975); Alan Nevins, *Study in Power: John D. Rockefeller*, 2 vols. (1953); Glenn Porter, *The Rise of Big Business* (1973); Martin J. Sklar, *The Corporate Reconstruction of American Capitalism, 1890–1916: The Market, Law and Politics* (1988); Richard Tedlow, *The Rise of the American Business Corporation* (1991); Alan Trachtenberg, *The Incorporation of America* (1982); Joseph Wall, *Andrew Carnegie* (1970); Olivier Zunz, *Making America Corporate, 1870–1920* (1990).

Invention and Industry   Robert Bruce, *Alexander Graham Bell and the Conquest of Solitude* (1973); Ron Chernow, *Titan: The Life of John D. Rockefeller, Sr.* (1998); Robert Conot, *A Streak of Luck* (1979); Ruth Schwartz Cowan, *A Social History of American Technology* (1996); Siegfried Giedion, *Mechanization Takes Command* (1948); David Hounshell, *From the American System to Mass Production, 1800–1932* (1984); Robert Kanigel, *The One Best Way: Frederick Winslow Taylor and the Enigma of Efficiency* (1997); John F. Kasson, *Civilizing the Machine* (1976); Carolyn Marvin, *When Old Technologies Were New: Thinking about Electric Communication in the Late Nineteenth Century* (1988); David Nye, *Electrifying America: Social Meanings of a New Technology, 1890–1940* (1990); Harold Passer, *The Electrical Manufacturers, 1875–1900* (1953); Leonard S. Reich, *The Making of Industrial Research: Science and Business at GE and Bell, 1876–1926* (1985); Nathan Rosenberg, *Technology and American Economic Growth* (1972); Peter Temin, *Iron and Steel in Nineteenth Century America* (1964); Frederick A. White, *American Industrial Research Laboratories* (1961).

Capitalism and Its Critics   Robert Bannister, *Social Darwinism: Science and Myth in Anglo-American Social Thought* (1979); Robert H. Bremner, *American Philanthropy* (1988); Carl N. Degler, *In Search of Human Nature: The Decline and Revival of Darwinism in America* (1991); Sidney Fine, *Laissez Faire and the General Welfare State: A Study of Conflict in American Thought, 1865–1900* (1956); Louis Galambos, *The Public Image of Big Business in America, 1880–1940: A Quantitative Study of Social Change* (1975); Richard Hofstadter, *Social Darwinism in American Thought*, rev. ed. (1955); Edward C. Kirkland, *Dream and Thought in the Business Community, 1860–1900* (1956); Ellen Condliffe Lagemann, *The Politics of Knowledge: The Carnegie Corporation, Philanthropy, and Public Policy* (1989); T. Jackson Lears, *No Place of Grace: Antimodernism and the Transformation of American Culture, 1880–1920* (1981); George E. Pozzetta, ed., *Americanization, Social Control, and Philanthropy* (1991); John Thomas, *Alternative America: Henry George, Edward Bellamy, Henry Demarest Lloyd, and the Adversary Tradition* (1983).

The Culture of Work   American Social History Project, *Who Built America? Working People and the Nation's Economy, Politics, Culture, Society*, vol. 2: *From the Gilded Age to the Present* (1992); Cindy Sondik Aron, *Ladies and Gentlemen of the Civil Service: Middle-Class Workers in Victorian America* (1987); James R. Barrett, *Work and Community in the Jungle: Chicago's Packinghouse Workers, 1894–1922* (1990); John Bodnar, *Immigration and Industrialization: Ethnicity in an American Mill Town* (1977); John T. Cumbler, *Working Class Community in Industrial America: Work, Leisure, and Struggle in Two Industrial Cities, 1880–1930* (1979); David Emmons, *The Butte Irish: Class and Ethnicity in an American Mining Town, 1875–1925* (1989); Michael Frisch and Daniel Walkowitz, eds., *Working-Class America: Essays on Labor,*

Community, and American Society (1983); James R. Green, *World of the Worker: Labor in Twentieth Century America* (1980); Herbert Gutman, *Work, Culture, and Society in Industrializing America: Essays in American Working-Class History* (1976); Tamara Hareven, *Family, Time, and Industrial Time: The Relationship between the Family and Work in a New England Industrial Community* (1982); William H. Harris, *The Harder We Run: Black Workers since the Civil War* (1982); Jacqueline Jones, *Labor of Love, Labor of Sorrow: Black Women, Work, and the Family, from Slavery to the Present* (1985); Susan Kennedy, *If All We Did Was to Weep at Home: A History of White Working Class Women in America* (1979); Walter Licht, *Working for the Railroad: The Organization of Work in the Nineteenth Century* (1983); Joanne J. Meyerowitz, *Women Adrift: Independent Wage Earners in Chicago, 1880–1930* (1988); David Montgomery, *Workers' Control in America: Studies in the History of Work, Technology, and Labor Struggles* (1979); Daniel Nelson, *Managers and Workers: Origins of the New Factory System* (1975); Richard Jules Oestreicher, *Solidarity and Fragmentation. Working People and Class Consciousness in Detroit, 1875–1900* (1986); Daniel T. Rodgers, *The Work Ethic in Industrial America, 1850–1920* (1978); Stephan Thernstrom, *The Other Bostonians: Poverty and Progress in the American Metropolis, 1880–1970* (1973).

The Labor Movement   Eric Arnesen, *Waterfront Workers of New Orleans: Race, Class, and Politics, 1863–1923* (1991); Paul Avrich, *The Haymarket Tragedy* (1984); Mary H. Blewett, *Men, Women, and Work: Class, Gender, and Protest in the New England Shoe Industry, 1880–1910* (1988); Jeremy Brecher, *Strike!* (1977); Mari Jo Buhle, *Women and American Socialism, 1870–1920* (1981); Melvyn Dubofsky, *Industrialism and the American Worker, 1865–1920* (1975) and *We Shall Be All: A History of the Industrial Workers of the World* (1969); Philip Foner, *Women and the American Labor Movement*, 2 vols. (1979); James R. Grossman, *Land of Hope: Chicago, Black Southerners, and the Great Migration* (1989); William H. Harris, *The Harder We Run: Black Workers since the Civil War* (1982); Stuart Kaufman, *Samuel Gompers and the Origins of the American Federation of Labor* (1973); Paul Krause, *The Battle for Homestead: Politics, Culture and Steel* (1992); Susan Levine, *Labor's True Women: Carpet Weavers, Industrialization, and Labor Reform in the Gilded Age* (1984); Gwendolyn Mink, *Old Labor and New Immigrants in American Political Development: Union, Party, and State, 1875–1920* (1986); David Montgomery, *The Fall of the House of Labor: The Workplace, the State, and American Labor Activism, 1865–1925* (1987); Leon Fink, *Workingmen's Democracy: The Knights of Labor and American Politics* (1983); Alice Kessler-Harris, *Out to Work: A History of Wage-Earning Women in the United States* (1982); Nick Salvatore, *Eugene V. Debs: Citizen and Socialist* (1982); David Shannon, *The Socialist Party* (1955); Sheldon Stromquist, *A Generation of Boomers: The Pattern of Railroad Labor Conflict in Nineteenth-Century America* (1987); Lloyd Ulman, *The Rise of the National Trade Union: The Development and Significance of Its Structure, Governing Institutions, and Economic Policies* (1955).

Chapter 20: The Rise of an Urban Order

General Histories   Howard B. Chudacoff, *The Evolution of American Urban Society*, rev. ed. (1981); William Cronon, *Nature's Metropolis: Chicago and the Great West* (1991); Charles Glabb and A. Theodore Brown, *A History of Urban America*, rev.

ed. (1976); Blake McKelvey, *The Urbanization of America, 1860–1915* (1963); Allan Pred, *Spatial Dynamics of U.S. Urban Growth, 1800–1914* (1971); John Stilgoe, *Borderland: The Origins of the American Suburb, 1820–1929* (1988); Stephan Thernstrom and Richard Sennett, eds., *19th Century Cities: Essays in the New Urban History* (1969); Sam Bass Warner Jr., *Streetcar Suburbs* (1962) and *The Urban Wilderness* (1972).

Immigration and Immigrants   John Bodnar, *The Transplanted: A History of Immigrants in Urban America* (1985); Josef Barton, *Peasants and Strangers: Italians, Rumanians, and Slovaks in an American City* (1975); John J. Bukowczyk, *And My Children Did Not Know Me: A History of Polish Americans* (1987); Sucheng Chan, *Asian Americans: An Interpretive History* (1991); Jack Chen, *The Chinese of America* (1970); Roger Daniels, *Coming to America: A History of Immigration and Ethnicity in American Life* (1990); Hasia A. Diner, *Erin's Daughters in America: Irish Immigrant Women in the Nineteenth Century* (1983); Leonard Dinnerstein, Roger Nichols, and David Reimers, *Natives and Strangers* (1979); John Duff, *The Irish in the United States* (1971); Mario Garcia, *Desert Immigrants: The Mexicans of El Paso, 1880–1920* (1981); Susan A. Glenn, *Daughters of the Shtetl: Life and Labor in the Immigrant Generation* (1990); Richard Griswold del Castillo, *La Familia: Chicano Families in the Urban Southwest, 1848 to the Present* (1984); Irving Howe, *World of Our Fathers: The Journey of the East European Jews to America and the Life They Found and Made* (1976); Yuji Ichioka, *The Issei: The World of the First Generation Japanese Americans, 1885–1924* (1988); Jenna Weissman Joselit, *The Wonders of America: Reinventing Jewish Culture, 1880–1950* (1994); Edward Kantowicz, *Polish-American Politics in Chicago* (1975); Thomas Kessner, *The Golden Door: Italian and Jewish Immigrant Mobility in New York City, 1880–1915* (1977); Alan M. Kraut, *The Huddled Masses: The Immigrant in American Society, 1880–1921* (1982); Michael La Sorte, *La Merica: Images of Italian Greenhorn Experience* (1985); Joseph Lopreato, *Italian Americans* (1970); Kerby A. Miller, *Emigrants and Exiles: Ireland and the Irish Exodus to North America* (1985); Ewa Morawska, *For Bread and Butter: The Life-Worlds of East Central Europeans in Johnstown, Pennsylvania, 1890–1940* (1985); James Stuart Olsen, *The Ethnic Dimension in American History*, vol. 2 (1979); Moses Rischin, *The Promised City: New York's Jews* (1962); Jacob Riis, *How the Other Half Lives* (1890); Howard M. Sachar, *A History of Jews in America* (1992); Ronald Takaki, *Strangers from a Different Shore: A History of Asian Americans* (1989) and *A Different Mirror: A History of Multicultural America* (1993); Philip Taylor, *The Distant Magnet: European Emigration to the U.S.A.* (1971); Virginia Yans-McLaughlin, *Family and Community: Italian Immigrants in Buffalo, 1880–1930* (1977), and as ed., *Immigration Reconsidered: History, Sociology, Politics* (1990); Anzia Yezierska, *Bread Givers* (1925); Olivier Zunz, *The Changing Face of Inequality: Urbanization, Industrial Development, and Immigrants in Detroit, 1880–1920* (1982).

Nativism and Race   Leonard Dinnerstein, *Anti-Semitism in America* (1994); Louis Harlan, *Booker T. Washington: The Making of a Black Leader, 1856–1901* (1972) and *Booker T. Washington: The Wizard of Tuskegee, 1901–1915* (1983); John Higham, *Strangers in the Land: Patterns of American Nativism, 1880–1925* (1955) and *Send These to Me* (1975); Kenneth Kusmer, *A Ghetto Takes Shape: Black Cleveland, 1870–1930* (1976); Stanley Lieberson, *A Piece of the Pie: Blacks and White Immigrants since 1880* (1980); Gilbert Osofsky, *Harlem: The Making of a Ghetto* (1966); Joel Perlman, *Ethnic Differences: Schooling and Social Structure* among the Irish, Italians, Jews, and Blacks in an American City, 1880–1935 (1988); Elizabeth Hafkin Pleck, *Black Migration and Poverty, Boston, 1865–1900* (1979); Allan H. Spear, *Black Chicago* (1967); Donald Spivey, *Schooling for the New Slavery: Black Industrial Education, 1868–1915* (1978).

Politics and Poverty John Allswang, *Bosses, Machines, and Urban Voters* (1977); Robert H. Bremmer, *From the Depths: The Discovery of Poverty in the United States* (1956); Alexander B. Callow, ed., *The City Boss in America* (1976); Lyle Dorsett, *The Pendergast Machine* (1968); Steven P. Erie, *Rainbow's End: Irish-Americans and the Dilemmas of Urban Machine Politics, 1840–1985* (1988); Leo Hershkowitz, *Tweed's New York: Another Look* (1977); Zane Miller, *Boss Cox's Cincinnati* (1968); James T. Patterson, *America's Struggle against Poverty* (1981); Thomas Philpott, *The Slum and the Ghetto* (1978); William L. Riordon, *Plunkitt of Tammany Hall* (1963); Lloyd Wendt and Herman Kogan, *Bosses in Lusty Chicago*, 2d ed. (1971).

Reform Jane Addams, *Twenty Years at Hull-House* (1910); Ruth Bordin, *Woman and Temperance: The Quest for Power and Liberty, 1860–1900* (1981); Paul Boyer, *Urban Masses and Moral Order in America, 1820–1920* (1978); Allen Davis, *Spearheads for Reform: The Social Settlements and the Progressive Movement, 1890–1914* (1967) and *American Heroine: The Life and Legend of Jane Addams* (1973); Marvin Lazerson, *Origins of the Urban School* (1971); Eric Monkonnen, *Police in Urban America, 1860–1920* (1981); David Pivar, *Purity Crusade: Sexual Morality and Social Control, 1868–1900* (1973); James Reed, *The Birth Control Movement and American Society: From Private Vice to Public Virtue* (1983); Barbara Rosencrantz, *Public Health and the State* (1972); Martin Schiesl, *The Politics of Efficiency: Municipal Administration and Reform in America* (1977); David Tyack, *The One Best System: A History of American Urban Education* (1974); Morris Vogel, *The Invention of the Modern Hospital: Boston, 1870–1930* (1980); James C. Whorton, *Crusaders for Fitness: The History of American Health Reformers* (1982).

Urban Life, Work, and Culture Cindy Aron, *Ladies and Gentlemen of the Civil Service: Middle Class Workers in Victorian America* (1987); Gunther Barth, *City People: The Rise of Modern City Culture in 19th Century America* (1980); Susan Porter Benson, *Counter Cultures: Saleswomen, Managers, and Customers in Department Stores, 1890–1940* (1986); Allan Brandt, *No Magic Bullet: A Social History of Venereal Disease in the United States Since 1880*, rev. ed. (1985); Robert Cross, *The Church and the City* (1967); Ronald Davies, *A History of Music in American Life*, vol. 2: *The Gilded Years, 1865–1920* (1980); Lewis A. Erenberg, *Steppin' Out: New York Nightlife and the Transformation of American Culture, 1890–1930* (1981); Ellen Garvey, *The Adman in the Parlor: Magazines and the Gendering of Consumer Culture, 1880s to 1910s* (1996); James Gilbert, *Perfect Cities: Chicago Utopias of 1893* (1991); Thomas J. Gilfoyle, *City of Eros: New York City, Prostitution, and the Commercialization of Sex, 1790–1920* (1992); Tamara K. Hareven and Randolph Langenbach, *Amoskeag: Life and Work in an American Factory* (1978); Neil Harris, *Humbug: The Art of P. T. Barnum* (1973); Lawrence Kasson, *Amusing the Million: Coney Island at the Turn of the Century* (1978) and *Rudeness and Civility: Manners in Nineteenth-Century Urban America* (1990); William Leach, *Land of Desire: Merchants, Power, and the Rise of a New American Culture* (1993); Lawrence Levine, *Highbrow/Lowbrow: The Emergence of Cultural Hierarchy in America* (1988); Richard Lingeman, *Theodore Dreiser: At the Gates of the City, 1871–1907* (1986); John Lucas and Ronald Smith, *Saga of*

American Sport (1978); Henry F. May, *Protestant Churches and Urban America* (1949); Katherine Morello, *The Invisible Bar: The Woman Lawyer in America, 1638 to the Present* (1986); Joseph Musselman, *Music in the Cultured Generation: A Social History of Music in America, 1870–1900* (1971); David Nasaw, *Schooled to Order: A Social History of Public Schooling in the United States* (1979), *Children of the City: At Work and at Play* (1986), and *Going Out: The Rise and Fall of Public Amusements* (1993); Kathy Peiss, *Cheap Amusements: Working Women and Leisure in Turn-of-the-Century New York* (1986); Roy Rosenzweig, *Eight Hours for What We Will: Workers and Leisure in an Industrial City, 1870–1920* (1983); Russel Nye, *The Unembarrassed Muse: The Popular Arts in America* (1970); Thomas J. Schlereth, *Victorian American: Transformations in Everyday Life, 1876–1915* (1991); Robert H. Walker, *Life in the Age of Enterprise, 1865–1900* (1967).

Women, Family, and Social Mores Elaine S. Abelson, *When Ladies Go A-Thieving: Middle-Class Shoplifters in the Victorian Department Store* (1990); Allan M. Brandt, *No Magic Bullet: A Social History of Venereal Disease since 1880* (1985); John D'Emilio and Estelle B. Freedman, *Intimate Matters: A History of Sexuality in America* (1988); Harvey Green, *The Light of the Home: An Intimate View of the Lives of Women in Victorian America* (1983); John S. Haller and Robin M. Haller, *The Physician and Sexuality in Victorian America* (1986); N. Ray Hiner and Joseph Hawes, eds., *Growing Up in America: Children in Historical Perspective* (1985); David Katzman, *Seven Days a Week: Women and Domestic Service in Industrializing America* (1978); Judith Leavitt, *Brought to Bed: Childbearing in America, 1750–1950* (1988); Elizabeth Lunbeck, *The Psychiatric Persuasion: Knowledge, Gender, and Politics in Modern America* (1994); Elaine May, *Great Expectations: Marriage and Divorce in Post-Victorian America* (1980); Steven Mintz, *A Prison of Expectations: The Family in Victorian Culture* (1983); Steven Mintz and Susan Kellogg, *Domestic Revolutions: A Social History of American Family Life* (1988); Ellen Rothman, *Hands and Hearts: A History of Courtship in America* (1984); Gar Scharnhorst, *Charlotte Perkins Gilman* (1985); Carroll Smith-Rosenberg, *Disorderly Conduct: Visions of Gender in Victorian America* (1986); Susan Strasser, *Never Done: A History of American Housework* (1983).

Chapter 21: The Political System under Strain

General Histories James Bryce, *The American Commonwealth*, 2 vols. (1888); Sean Cashman, *America and the Gilded Age: From the Death of Lincoln to the Rise of Theodore Roosevelt* (1984); John Dobson, *Politics in the Gilded Age* (1978); Harold Faulkner, *Politics, Reform, and Expansion, 1890–1900* (1959); John Garraty, *The New Commonwealth, 1877–1890* (1968); Richard Hofstadter, *The Age of Reform: From Bryan to FDR* (1955); Nancy Eleanor Flexner, *Century of Struggle: The Women's Rights Movement in the United States* (1959); Morton Keller, *Affairs of State: Public Life in the Late 19th Century America* (1977); H. Wayne Morgan, *From Hayes to McKinley: National Party Politics, 1877–1896* (1969), and as ed., *The Gilded Age* (1970); Nell Irvin Painter, *Standing at Armageddon: The United States, 1877–1919* (1987); Stephen Skowronek, *Building a New American State: The Expansion of National Administrative Capacities* (1982); Robert Wiebe, *The Search for Order, 1877–1929* (1967).

Ideology and Politics Kenneth Davison, *The Presidency of Rutherford B. Hayes* (1972); Margaret Forster, *Significant Sisters:*

The Grassroots of Active Feminism, 1839–1939 (1986); Lewis Gould, *The Presidency of William McKinley* (1981); David C. Hammack, *Power and Society: Greater New York at the Turn of the Century* (1982); S. P. Hirshon, *Farewell to the Bloody Shirt: Northern Republicans and the Southern Negro, 1877–1893* (1962); Ari Hoogenboom, *Rutherford B. Hayes: Warrior and President* (1995); Richard Jensen, *The Winning of the Midwest: Social and Political Conflict, 1888–1896* (1971); David Jordan, *Roscoe Conkling of New York* (1971); Paul Kelppner, *The Cross of Culture: A Social Analysis of Midwestern Politics, 1850–1900* (1970) and *The Third Electoral System, 1853–1892: Voters, Parties, and Political Cultures* (1979); Robert Marcus, *Grand Old Party: Political Structure in the Gilded Age* (1971); Robert McCloskey, *American Conservatism in the Age of Enterprise* (1951); Michael McGerr, *The Decline of Politics: The American North, 1865–1928* (1988); Allan Nevins, *Grover Cleveland: A Study in Courage* (New York, 1932); Arnold Paul, *Conservative Crisis and the Rule of Law: Attitudes of Bar and Bench, 1887–1895* (1969); Allan Peskin, *Garfield* (1978); Thomas Reeves, *Gentlemen Boss: The Life of Chester Alan Arthur* (1975); Martin Ridge, *Ignatius Donnelly* (1962); David Rothman, *Politics and Power: The United States Senate, 1869–1901* (1966); Martin J. Sklar, *The Corporate Reconstruction of American Capitalism, 1890–1916* (1988); Homer E. Socolofsky and Allan B. Spetter, *The Presidency of Benjamin Harrison* (1987); Richard Welch, *The Presidencies of Grover Cleveland* (1988); R. Hal Williams, *Years of Decision: American Politics in the 1890s* (1978).

Protest and Reform   Geoffrey Blodgett, *The Gentle Reformers* (1966); William Dick, *Labor and Socialism in America* (1972); John Diggins, *The American Left in the Twentieth Century* (1973); Louis Harlan, *Booker T. Washington: The Making of a Black Leader, 1856–1901* (1972) and *Booker T. Washington: The Wizard of Tuskegee* (1983); Ari Hoogenboom, *Outlawing the Spoils: A History of the Civil Service Movement, 1865–1883* (1961); John Laslett, *Labor and the Left* (1970); Charles Lofgren, *The Plessy Case: A Legal-Historical Interpretation* (1987); Walter Nugent, *Money and American Society* (1968); Theda Skocpol, *Protecting Soldiers and Mothers: The Political Origins of Social Policy in the United States* (1992); John Sproat, *The Best Men: Liberal Reformers in the Gilded Age* (1968); Irwin Unger, *The Greenback Era: A Social and Political History of American Finance, 1865–1879* (1964); C. Vann Woodward, *The Strange Career of Jim Crow*, 3d rev. ed. (1974).

Populism   Peter Argersinger, *Populism and Politics: William Alfred Peffer and the People's Party* (1974); Gene Clanton, *Populism: The Humane Preferences, 1890–1900* (1991); Gerald H. Gaither, *Blacks and the Populist Revolt* (1977); Lawrence Goodwyn, *Democratic Promise: The Populist Movement in America* (1976) and *The Populist Moment: A Brief History of the Agrarian Revolt* (1978); Steven Hahn, *The Roots of Southern Populism: Yeoman Farmers and the Transformation of the Georgia Upcountry* (1983); Sheldon Hackney, *Populism to Progressivism in Alabama* (1969); John Hicks, *The Populist Revolt* (1931); Robert W. Larson, *Populism in the Mountain West* (1986); Robert C. McMath Jr., *Populist Vanguard: A History of the Southern Farmers' Alliance* (1975) and *American Populism: A Social History, 1877–1898* (1993); Scott G. McNall, *The Road to Rebellion: Class Formation and Kansas Populism, 1865–1900* (1988); Theodore R. Mitchell, *Political Education in the Southern Farmers' Alliance, 1887–1900* (1987); Bruce Palmer, *Man over Money* (1980); Norman Pollack, *The Populist Response to Industrial America* (1962) and *The Just Polity: Populism, Law, and Human Welfare* (1987); Theodore Sa-

loutos, *Farmer Movements in the South, 1865–1933* (1960); Barton Shaw, *The Wool-Hat Boys: Georgia's Populist Party* (1984); John L. Shover, *First Majority–Last Minority: The Transforming of Rural Life in America* (1976); Lala Carr Steelman, *The North Carolina Farmers' Alliance* (1985); C. Vann Woodward, *Tom Watson, Agrarian Rebel* (1938); Allan Weinstein, *Prelude to Populism: Origins of the Silver Issue* (1970).

The Depression of 1893 and the Election of 1896   Paolo Coletta, *William Jennings Bryan*, 3 vols. (1964–1969); Robert F. Durden, *The Climax of Populism: The Election of 1896* (1965); Ray Ginger, *Altgeld's America* (1958); Paul W. Glad, *McKinley, Bryan, and the People* (1964) and *The Trumpet Soundeth* (1960); Charles Hoffman, *The Depression of the Nineties: An Economic History* (1970); J. Rogers Hollingsworth, *The Whirligig of Politics: The Democracy of Cleveland and Bryan* (1963); Stanley Jones, *The Presidential Election of 1896* (1964); Louis Koenig, *Bryan* (1971); Samuel McSeveney, *The Politics of Depression* (1972); Carlos A. Schwantes, *Coxey's Army: An American Odyssey* (1985).

The New American Empire   Richard Bannister, *Social Darwinism* (1979); Robert Beisner, *From the Old Diplomacy to the New, 1865–1900* (1975); Charles Campbell, *The Transformation of American Foreign Relations, 1865–1900* (1976) and *From Revolution to Rapprochement: The United States and Great Britain, 1783–1903* (1974); Richard Challener, *Admirals, Generals, and American Foreign Policy, 1889–1914* (1973); John Dobson, *America's Ascent: The United States Becomes a Great Power, 1880–1914* (1978); John Lewis Gaddis, *Russia, the Soviet Union, and the United States*, 2d ed. (1990); John A. S. Grenville and George Young, *Politics, Strategy, and American Diplomacy* (1967); Richard Hofstadter, *Social Darwinism in American Thought*, rev. ed. (1959); Michael Hunt, *Ideology and American Foreign Policy* (1984); Ronald Jensen, *The Alaska Purchase and Russian-American Relations* (1970); Walter LaFeber, *The New Empire: An Interpretation of American Expansion, 1860–1898* (1963) and *The American Age* (1989); David Pletcher, *The Awkward Years* (1962); Emily Rosenberg, *Spreading the American Dream* (1982); Tom Terrill, *The Tariff, Politics, and American Foreign Policy, 1874–1901* (1973); Mira Wilkins, *The Emergence of the Multinational Enterprise* (1970); William A. Williams, *The Tragedy of American Diplomacy*, rev. ed. (1962) and *Empire as a Way of Life: An Essay on the Causes and Character of America's Present Predicament* (1982).

The Question of Imperialism   David Anderson, *Imperialism and Idealism: American Diplomats in China, 1861–1898* (1986); William Becker, *The Dynamics of Business-Government Relations* (1982); Robert L. Beisner, *Twelve against Empire* (1968); Phillip Darby, *Three Faces of Imperialism: British and American Approaches to Asia and Africa, 1870–1970* (1987); Philip S. Foner, *The Spanish-Cuban-American War and the Birth of American Imperialism*, 2 vols. (1972); Frank Friedel, *The Splendid Little War* (1958); Willard Gatewood Jr., *Black Americans and the White Man's Burden, 1898–1903* (1975); Kenneth Hagan, *American Gunboat Diplomacy, 1877–1889* (1973); David Healy, *U.S. Expansionism* (1970); Michael Hunt, *Ideology and U.S. Foreign Policy* (1987); Frederick Merk, *Manifest Destiny and Mission in American History* (1963); Wolfgang Mommsen and Jurgen Osterhammel, eds., *Imperialism and After* (1986); H. Wayne Morgan, *America's Road to Empire: The War with Spain and Overseas Expansion* (1965); Thomas J. Osborne, *Empire Can Wait: American Opposition to Hawaiian Annexation, 1893–1898* (1981); Ernest Paolino, *The Foundations of American Empire* (1973); Thomas Paterson, ed., *Imperialism and Anti-Imperialism* (1973); Bradford Perkins, *The Great Rapprochement* (1968); Julius Pratt, *The Expansionists of 1898* (1936); Tony Smith, *The Pattern of Imperialism: The United States, Great Britain and the Late Industrializing World since 1815* (1982); Richard Turk, *The Ambiguous Relationship: Theodore Roosevelt and Alfred Thayer Mahan* (1987).

The United States and Asia   David Anderson, *Imperialism and Idealism: American Diplomacy in China, 1861–1898* (1985); Jong-suk Chay, *Diplomacy of Asymmetry: Korean-American Relations to 1910* (1990); Warren Cohen, *America's Response to China*, rev. ed. (1980); Michael Hunt, *The Making of a Special Relationship: The United States and China to 1914* (1983); Jane Hunter, *The Gospel of Gentility: American Women Missionaries in Turn-of-the-Century China* (1984); Akira Iriye, *Across the Pacific* (1967) and *Pacific Estrangement: Japanese and American Expansion, 1897–1911* (1972); Stanley Karnow, *In Our Image* (1989); Yur-Bok Lee and Wayne Patterson, eds., *One Hundred Years of Korean-American Relations, 1882–1982* (1986); Brian M. Linn, *The U.S. Army and Counterinsurgency in the Philippine War, 1899–1902* (1989); Ernest May and John Fairbanks, eds., *America's China Trade in Historical Perspective* (1986); Glenn May, *Social Engineering in the Philippines* (1980); Thomas McCormick, *China Market: America's Quest for Informal Empire, 1893–1901* (1968); Charles Neu, *The Troubled Encounter* (1975); Gary Okihiro, *Cane Fires: The Anti-Japanese Movement in Hawaii, 1865–1945* (1991); Peter Stanley, *A Nation in the Making: The Philippines and the United States* (1974); Randall Stross, *The Hard Earth: American Agriculturalists on Chinese Soil, 1898–1937* (1986); James Thomson, Peter Stanley, and John Perry, *Sentimental Imperialists: The American Experience in East Asia* (1981); Robert Welch Jr., *Response to Imperialism: The United States and the Philippine-American War, 1899–1902* (1979); Marilyn B. Young, *Rhetoric of Empire: American China Policy, 1895–1901* (1968).

The United States and the Americas   Robert Brown, *Canada's National Policy, 1883–1900* (1964); Kenneth Bourne, *Britain and the Balance of Power in North America, 1815–1908* (1967); Walter LaFeber, *Inevitable Revolutions: The United States in Central America*, rev. ed. (1993); Lester Langley, *The Banana Wars* (1983) and *The United States and the Caribbean, 1900–1970* (1980); Louis Perez Jr., *Cuba under the Platt Amendment, 1902–1934* (1986) and *Cuba between Empires, 1878–1902* (1983); Dexter Perkins, *The Monroe Doctrine, 1867–1907* (1937); Ramon Ruiz, *Cuba* (1968); Karl Schmitt, *Mexico and the United States, 1821–1973* (1974); Josefina Vazquez and Lorenzo Meyer, *The United States and Mexico* (1985).

Chapter 22: The Progressive Era

General Histories   John Chambers II, *The Tyranny of Change: America in the Progressive Era, 1900–1917* (1980); John M. Cooper Jr., *The Pivotal Decades: The United States, 1900–1920* (1990); Alan Dawley, *Struggles for Justice: Social Responsibility and the Liberal State* (1991); Steven J. Diner, *A Very Different Age: Americans of the Progressive Era* (1998); Arthur Ekrich, *Progressivism in America* (1974); Peter Filene, "An Obituary for 'the Progressive Movement,'" *American Quarterly* 22 (1970); Lewis Gould, ed., *The Progressive Era* (1974); Richard Hofstadter, *The Age of Reform: From Bryan to FDR* (1955); James T. Kloppenberg, *Uncertain Victory: Social Democracy and Progressivism in European and American Thought, 1870–1920* (1986); Gabriel Kolko,

The Triumph of Conservativism (1963); Arthur Link and Richard L. McCormick, *Progressivism* (1985); William O'Neill, *The Progressive Years* (1975); Dan Rogers, "In Search of Progressivism," *Reviews in American History* 10 (1982); James Weinstein, *The Corporate Ideal in the Liberal States, 1900–1918* (1969); Robert Wiebe, *Businessmen and Reform: A Study of the Progressive Movement* (1962).

The Progressive Impulse   Daniel Aaron, *Men of Good Hope: A Story of American Progressives* (1951); Richard Abrams, *The Burdens of Progress* (1978); Walter M. Brasch, *Forerunners of Revolution: Muckrakers and the American Social Conscience* (1990); Robert H. Bremner, *From the Depths: The Discovery of Poverty in the United States* (1956); Mina Julia Carson, *Settlement Folk: Social Thought and the American Settlement Movement, 1885–1930* (1990); David Chalmers, *The Social and Political Ideas of the Muckrakers* (1964); Clarke Chambers, *Paul U. Kellog and the Survey* (1971); Robert Crunden, *Ministers of Reform: The Progressives' Achievements in American Civilization, 1889–1920* (1982); Charles Forcey, *The Crossroads of Liberalism: Croly, Weyl, Lippmann, and the Progressive Era, 1900–1925* (1961); William Hutchinson, *The Modernist Impulse in American Protestantism* (1976); Rivka Shpak Lissak, *Pluralism and Progressives: Hull House and the New Immigrants, 1890–1919* (1989); Roy Lubove, *The Professional Altruist: The Emergence of Social Work as a Career, 1880–1930* (1965); D. W. Marcell, *Progress and Pragmatism: James, Dewey, Beard, and the American Idea of Progress* (1974); Daniel Nelson, *Frederick W. Taylor and the Rise of Scientific Management* (1980); David Nobel, *The Progressive Mind, 1890–1917*, rev. ed (1981); Martin Schiesl, *The Politics of Efficiency: Municipal Administration and Reform in America, 1880–1920* (1977); Robert B. Westbrook, *John Dewey and American Democracy* (1991); Morton White, *Social Thought in America: The Revolt against Formalism* (1949); Harold Wilson, *McClure's Magazine and the Muckrakers* (1970).

Social Reform, Radical Politics, and Minority Rights   Mari Jo Buhle, *Women and American Socialism, 1870–1920* (1981); Allen F. Davis, *American Heroine: The Life and Legend of Jane Addams* (1973); James R. Green, *Grass-Roots Socialism: Radical Movements in the Southwest, 1895–1943* (1978); Louis Harlan, *Separate and Unequal: Public School Campaigns and Racism in the Southern Seaboard States, 1900–1915* (1968); Charles F. Kellogg, *NAACP: A History of the National Association for the Advancement of Colored People, 1909–1920* (1967); David L. Lewis, *W. E. B. Dubois: Biography of a Race* (1994); Roy Lubove, *The Progressives and the Slums: Tenement House Reform in New York City* (1962); James McPherson, *The Abolitionist Legacy: From Reconstruction to the NAACP* (1975); David Musto, *The American Disease: Origins of Narcotics Control* (1973); Elliot M. Rudwick, *W. E. B. DuBois* (1968); Nick Salvatore, *Eugene V. Debs: Citizen and Socialist* (1982); James Timberlake, *Prohibition and the Progressive Campaign* (1963); John D. Weaver, *The Brownsville Raid* (1970); James Weinstein, *The Decline of Socialism in America, 1912–1925* (1967); Nancy Weiss, *The National Urban League, 1910–1940* (1974).

Women's Rights, Gender, and Sexuality   Paula Baker, *Gender and the Transformation of Politics: Public and Private Life in New York, 1870–1930* (1989); George Chester, *Gay New York: Gender, Urban Culture, and the Making of the Gay Male World, 1890–1940* (1994); Ellen Chesler, *Woman of Valor: Margaret Sanger and the Birth Control Movement in America* (1992); Nancy F. Cott, *The Grounding of Modern Feminism* (1987); Nancy Dye, *As Equals and*

Sisters: Feminism, the Labor Movement, and the Women's Trade Union League of New York (1980); Linda Gordon, Woman's Body, Woman's Right: A Social History of Birth Control (1976), Heroes of Their Own Lives: The Politics and History of Family Violence, 1880–1960 (1988), and Pitied but Not Entitled: Single Mothers and the History of Welfare (1994); David Kennedy, Birth Control in America: The Career of Margaret Sanger (1970); Aileen Kraditor, Ideas of the Woman Suffrage Movement (1965); Ellen Lagemann, A Generation of Women: Education in the Lives of Progressive Reformers (1979); Christine Lunardini, From Equal Suffrage to Equal Rights: Alice Paul and the National Women's Party (1986); David Morgan, Suffragists and Democrats: The Politics of Woman Suffrage in America (1972); Robyn Muncy, Creating a Female Dominion in American Reform, 1890–1935 (1991); William O'Neil, Divorce in the Progressive Era (1967); Dorothy Richardson, The Long Day: The Story of a New York Working Girl (1905); Ruth Rosen, The Lost Sisterhood: Prostitutes in America, 1900–1918 (1982); Rosalind Rosenberg, Beyond Separate Spheres: Intellectual Roots of Modern Feminism (1982); Anne Firor Scott, Natural Allies: Women's Associations in American History (1992); Anne Firor Scott and Andrew MacKay Scott, One Half the People: The Fight for Woman Suffrage (1982); Meredith Tax, The Rising of the Women: Feminist Solidarity and Class Conflict, 1880–1917 (1980).

Education, the New Professionalism, and Entertainment   Burton Bledstein, The Culture of Professionalism (1976); Darlene Clark Hine, Black Women in White: Racial Conflict and Cooperation in the Nursing Profession, 1890–1950 (1989); Lawrence Cremin, The Transformation of the School: Progressivism in American Education (1961); John DiMeglio, Vaudeville U.S.A. (1973); Lewis Erenberg, Steppin' Out: New York Nightlife and the Transformation of American Culture, 1890–1930 (1981); James Farrell, Inventing the American Way of Death, 1830–1920 (1980); Thomas Haskell, The Emergence of Professional Social Science (1977); Bruce Kuklick, The Rise of American Philosophy (1977); Martin Laforse and James Drake, Popular Culture and American Life: Selected Topics in the Study of American Popular Culture (1981); Cathy Peiss, Cheap Amusements: Working Women and Leisure in Turn-of-the-Century New York (1986); Robert Sklar, Movie-Made America: A Social History of the American Movies (1975); Paul Starr, The Social Transformation of American Medicine (1982); David Tyack and Elizabeth Hansot, Managers of Virtue: Public School Leadership in America, 1820–1980 (1982); Lawrence Vesey, The Emergence of the American University (1970).

Local and State Reform   Richard Abrams, Conservatism in a Progressive Era: Massachusetts Politics, 1900–1912 (1964); John D. Buenker, Urban Liberalism and Progressive Reform (1973); Thomas E. Cronin, Direct Democracy: The Politics of Initiative, Referendum, and Recall (1989); James Crooks, Politics and Progress: The Rise of Urban Progressivism in Baltimore, 1895–1911 (1968); Dewey Grantham, Southern Progressivism: The Reconciliation of Progress and Tradition (1983); Melvin Holli, Reform in Detroit: Hazen S. Pingree and Urban Politics (1969); J. Joseph Huthmacher, "Urban Liberalism and Progressive Reform," Mississippi Valley Historical Review (1962); Jack Kirby, Darkness at Dawning: Race and Reform in the Progressive South (1972); Richard L. McCormick, From Realignment to Reform: Political Change in New York State, 1893–1910 (1981); George Mowry, The California Progressives (1951); Bradley Rice, Progressive Cities: The Commission Government Movement in America, 1901–1920 (1977); Jack Tager, The Intellectual as Urban Reformer:

Brand Whitlock and The Progressive Movement (1968); David P. Thelen, The New Citizenship: Origins of Progressivism in Wisconsin (1972).

National Politics and Public Policy   Donald Anderson, William Howard Taft (1973); John M. Blum, The Republican Roosevelt (1954) and Woodrow Wilson and the Politics of Morality (1954); John Milton Cooper Jr., The Warrior and the Priest: Woodrow Wilson and Theodore Roosevelt (1983); Stephen R. Fox, The American Conservation Movement: John Muir and His Legacy (1981); John Gable, The Bull Moose Years (1978); Alexander George and Juliette George, Woodrow Wilson and Colonel House: A Personality Study (1956); Lewis Gould, Reform and Regulation: American Politics, 1900–1916 (1978) and The Presidency of Theodore Roosevelt (1991); Samuel P. Hays, Conservation and the Gospel of Efficiency: The Progressive Conservation Movement, 1890–1920 (1959); James Holt, Congressional Insurgents and the Party System (1969); Arthur Link, Woodrow Wilson, 5 vols. (1947–1965); Albro Martin, Enterprise Denied: Origins of the Decline of American Railroads, 1897–1917 (1971); Robert T. McCulley, Banks and Politics during the Progressive Era: The Origins of the Federal Reserve System (1992); David McCullough, Mornings on Horseback (1981); Michael McGerr, The Decline of Popular Politics: The American North, 1865–1928 (1986); Edmund Morris, The Rise of Theodore Roosevelt (1979); George Mowry, The Era of Theodore Roosevelt (1958); James Penick, Progressive Politics and Conservation: The Ballinger-Pinchot Affair (1968); Harold Pinkett, Gifford Pinchot: Private and Public Forester (1970); Edwin Weinstein, Woodrow Wilson and Colonel House: A Personality Study (1956); Craig West, Banking Reform and the Federal Reserve, 1863–1923 (1977); Clifton Yearley, The Money Machines (1970).

Chapter 23: The United States and the Old World Order

General Histories   Paul Abrahams, The Foreign Expansion of American Finance and Its Relationship to Foreign Economic Policies of the United States, 1907–1921 (1976); Robert Beisner, From the Old Diplomacy to the New, 1865–1900 (1975); John Dobson, America's Ascent: The United States Becomes a Great Power, 1880–1914 (1978); Morrell Heald and Lawrence Kaplan, Culture and Diplomacy (1977); Peter Karsten, The Naval Aristocracy (1972); Robert Osgood, Ideals and Self-Interest in America's Foreign Relations (1953); Emily Rosenberg, Spreading the American Dream: American Economic and Cultural Expansion, 1890–1945 (1982); Robert Schulzinger, American Diplomacy in the Twentieth Century (1984); Tom Terrill, The Tariff, Politics, and American Foreign Policy, 1874–1901 (1973); Rubin Weston, Racism and U.S. Imperialism, 1865–1946 (1971); Mira Wilkins, The Emergence of the Multinational Enterprise (1970).

Roosevelt, Taft, and Wilson   Howard K. Beale, Theodore Roosevelt and the Rise of America to World Power (1956); David Burton, Theodore Roosevelt: Confident Imperialist (1968); Robert W. Cherney, A Righteous Cause: The Life of William Jennings Bryan (1985); Richard H. Collin, Theodore Roosevelt, Culture, Diplomacy, and Expansion (1985); John Cooper Jr., Walter Hines Page (1977); Lloyd Gardner, Wilson and Revolutions, 1913–1921 (1976) and William Jennings Bryan: Missionary Isolationist (1983); Arthur Link, Wilson: The Diplomatist (1957) and

Woodrow Wilson: Revolution, War, and Peace (1968); Frederick Marks III, *Velvet on Iron: The Diplomacy of Theodore Roosevelt* (1979); Ralph E. Minger, *William Howard Taft and United States Foreign Policy* (1975).

Asia, the Pacific, and Latin America   Warren Cohen, *America's Response to China*, rev. ed. (1980); David Healy, *Gunboat Diplomacy in the Wilson Era: The U.S. Navy in Haiti, 1915–1916* (1976) and *Drive to Hegemony: The United States in the Caribbean, 1898–1917* (1988); Akira Iriye, *Pacific Estrangement: Japanese and American Expansion, 1897–1911* (1972); Jerry Israel, *Progressivism and the Open Door: America and China, 1905–1921* (1971); Lester Langley, *Struggle for the American Mediterranean* (1980) and *The United States and the Caribbean, 1900–1970* (1980); Glenn May, *Social Engineering in the Philippines* (1980); Robert McClellen, *The Heathen Chinese: A Study of American Attitudes toward China* (1971); David McCullough, *The Path between the Seas: The Creation of the Panama Canal, 1870–1914* (1977); Dana Munro, *Intervention and Dollar Diplomacy in the Caribbean, 1900–1920* (1964); Charles Neu, *The Troubled Encounter* (1975); Robert Smith, *The United States and Revolutionary Nationalism in Mexico, 1916–1932* (1972); Peter Stanley, *A Nation in the Making: The Philippines and the United States, 1899–1921* (1974).

From Neutrality to War   Thomas Baily and Paul Ryan, *The Lusitania Disaster* (1975); John Coogan, *The End of Neutrality: The United States, Britain, and Maritime Rights, 1899–1915* (1981); John Cooper, *The Vanity of Power: American Isolationism and the First World War* (1969); Patrick Devlin, *Too Proud to Fight: Woodrow Wilson's Neutrality* (1974); Ross Gregory, *The Origins of American Intervention in the First World War* (1977); Burton Kaufman, *Efficiency and Expansion: Foreign Trade Organization in the Wilson Administration* (1974); Roland Marchand, *The American Peace Movement and Social Reform, 1898–1918* (1972); Ernest R. May, *The World War and American Isolation, 1914–1917* (1957); Jeffrey Safford, *Wilsonian Maritime Diplomacy* (1977).

The First World War Abroad   Arthur Barbeau and Henri Florette, *The Unknown Soldiers: Black American Troops in World War I* (1974); J. Gary Clifford, *The Citizen Soldiers* (1972); Edward Coffman, *The War to End All Wars: The American Military Experience in World War I* (1968); Frank Freidel, *Over There: The Story of America's First Great Overseas Crusade* (1964); Paul Fussell, *The Great War and Modern Memory* (1975); John Gifford, *The Citizen Soldiers* (1972); Otis Graham, *The Great Campaigns* (1971); Maurine Greenwald, *Women, War, and Work* (1980); James Joll, *The Origins of the First World War* (1984); N. Gordon Levin Jr., *Woodrow Wilson and World Politics: America's Response to War and Revolution* (1968); Laurence Stallings, *The Doughboys: The Story of the AEF, 1917–1918* (1963); David F. Trask, *The AEF and Coalition Warmaking, 1917–1918* (1973); Frank Vandiver, *Black Jack: The Life and Times of John J. Pershing*, 2 vols. (1977); Russell Weigley, *The American Way of War* (1973).

The Home Front   Daniel R. Beaver, *Newton D. Baker and the American War Effort, 1917–1919* (1966); John W. Chambers, *To Raise an Army: The Draft Comes to Modern America* (1987); Valerie Jean Connor, *The National War Labor Board: Stability, Social Justice, and the Voluntary State in World War I* (1983); Robert Cuff, *The War Industries Board: Business-Government Relations during World War I* (1973); Maurine W. Greenwald, *Women, War, and Work* (1980); Keith Grieves, *The Politics of Manpower, 1914–1918* (1988); Frank L. Grubb, *Samuel Gompers and the Great War* (1982); Carol Gruber, *Mars and Minerva: World War I and the*

Uses of Higher Learning in America (1975); Ellis Hawley, *The Great War and the Search for Modern Order* (1979); Robert Haynes, *A Night of Violence: The Houston Riot of 1917* (1976); David M. Kennedy, *Over Here: The First World War and American Society* (1980); Gina Bari Kolata, *Flu: The Story of the Great Influenza Pandemic of 1918 and the Search for the Virus That Caused It* (1999); Seward Livermore, *Politics Is Adjourned: Woodrow Wilson and the War Congress, 1917–1918* (1966); Frederick Luebke, *Bonds of Loyalty: German Americans and World War I* (1974); Paul Murphy, *World War I and the Origins of Civil Liberties* (1979); Richard Polenberg, *Fighting Faiths: The Abrams Case, the Supreme Court, and Free Speech* (1987); Walton Rawls, *Wake Up America! World War I and the American Poster* (1987); Ronald Schaffer, *America in the Great War: The Rise of the War Welfare State* (1991); Jordan Schwarz, *The Speculator: Bernard M. Baruch in Washington, 1917–1965* (1981); Dale N. Shook, *William G. McAdoo and the Development of National Economic Policy, 1913–1918* (1987); Barbara Steinson, *American Women's Activism in World War I* (1982); John A. Thompson, *Reformers and War: Progressive Publicists and the First World War* (1987); Joe William Trotter Jr., ed., *The Great Migration in Historical Perspective* (1991); Stephen Vaughn, *Holding Fast the Inner Lines: Democracy, Nationalism, and the Committee on Public Information* (1979); James Weinstein, *The Decline of Socialism in America, 1912–1923* (1967); Neil A. Wynn, *From Progressivism to Prosperity: World War I and American Society* (1986).

Versailles   Thomas Bailey, *Woodrow Wilson and the Great Betrayal* (1945) and *Woodrow Wilson and the Lost Peace* (1944); Robert Ferrell, *Woodrow Wilson and World War I* (1985); Inga Floto, *Colonel House at Paris* (1980); John Gaddis, *Russia, the Soviet Union, and the United States* (1978); Lloyd Gardner, *Safe for Democracy: The Anglo-American Response to Revolution, 1913–1923* (1984); Thomas J. Knock, *To End All Wars: Woodrow Wilson and the Quest for a New World Order* (1992); Arno Mayer, *Politics and Diplomacy of Peacemaking: Containment and Counterrevolution at Versailles* (1965); Charles Mee Jr., *The End of Order, Versailles, 1919* (1980); Ralph Stone, *The Irreconcilables: The Fight against the League of Nations* (1970); William C. Widenor, *Henry Cabot Lodge and the Search for an American Foreign Policy* (1980).

Aftermath   David Brody, *Labor in Crisis: The Steel Strike of 1919* (1965); Stanley Coben, *A. Mitchell Palmer: Politician* (1963); Stanley Cooperman, *World War I and the American Mind* (1970); Roberta Feuerlicht, *Justice Crucified* (1977); Dana Frank, *Purchasing Power: Consumer Organizing, Gender, and the Seattle Labor Movement, 1919–1929* (1994); Robert Murray, *The Red Scare* (1955); Burl Noggle, *Into the Twenties* (1977); Stuart Rochester, *American Liberal Disillusionment in the Wake of World War I* (1977); Francis Russell, *A City in Terror* (1975); William Tuttle Jr., *Race Riot: Chicago in the Red Summer of 1919* (1970); Stephen Ward, ed., *The War Generation: Veterans of the First World War* (1975).

Chapter 24: The New Era

General Histories   Frederick Lewis Allen, *Only Yesterday: An Informal History of the 1920s* (1931); John Braeman et al., eds., *Change and Continuity in Twentieth Century America: The 1920s* (1968); Ann Douglas, *Terrible Honesty: Mongrel Manhattan in the 1920s* (1995); Lynn Dumenil, *Modern Temper: American Culture* and Society in the 1920s (1995); Ellis Hawley, *The Great War and the Search for a Modern Order* (1979); John Hicks, *The Republican Ascendancy, 1921–1933* (1960); Isabel Leighton, ed., *The Aspirin Age* (1949); William Leuchtenburg, *The Perils of Prosperity, 1914–1932* (1958); Donald McCoy, *Coming of Age* (1973); Geoffrey Perrett, *America in the Twenties* (1982); Arthur Schlesinger Jr., *The Crisis of the Old Order* (1957); David Shannon, *Between the Wars: America, 1919–1940* (1979).

Economics, Business, and Labor   Irving Bernstein, *The Lean Years: A History of the American Worker, 1920–1933* (1960); David Brody, *Steelworkers in America* (1960) and *Workers in Industrial America* (1980); Lizabeth Cohen, *Making a New Deal: Industrial Workers in Chicago, 1919–1939* (1990); Alfred D. Chandler Jr., *Strategy and Structure: Chapters in the History of American Industrial Enterprise* (1962); Ed Cray, *Chrome Colossus: General Motors and Its Times* (1980); Gilbert Fite, *George Peek and the Fight for Farm Parity* (1954); James Flink, *The Car Culture* (1975); Louis Galambos, *Competition and Cooperation* (1966); James Gilbert, *Designing the Industrial State* (1972); Allan Nevins and Frank Hill, *Ford*, 3 vols. (1954–1963); Jim Potter, *The American Economy between the Wars* (1974); John Rae, *American Automobile* (1965) and *The Road and the Car in American Life* (1971); George Soule, *Prosperity Decade* (1947); Keith Sward, *The Legend of Henry Ford* (1948); Leslie Woodcock Tentler, *Wage Earning Women: Industrial Work and Family Life in the United States, 1900–1930* (1979); Bernard Weisberger, *The Dress Maker* (1979); Robert Zieger, *Republicans and Labor, 1919–1929* (1969) and *American Workers, American Unions, 1920–1980* (1986).

Mass Society and Mass Culture   Erick Barnouw, *A Tower of Babel: A History of American Broadcasting in the United States to 1933* (1966); A. Scott Berg, *Lindbergh* (1998); Daniel Boorstin, *The Americans: The Democratic Experience* (1973); Paul Carter, *Another Part of the Twenties* (1977); Robert Creamer, *Babe* (1974); Kenneth Davis, *The Hero: Charles A. Lindbergh* (1954); Stuart Ewen, *Captains of Consciousness: Advertising and the Social Roots of the Consumer Culture* (1976); Richard Wrightman Fox and T. J. Jackson Lears, eds., *The Culture of Consumption: Critical Essays in American History, 1880–1980* (1983); T. J. Jackson Lears, *Fables of Abundance: A Cultural History of Advertising in America* (1994); Robert Lynd and Helen Lynd, *Middletown: A Study in Modern Culture* (1929); Roland Marchand, *Advertising the American Dream: Making Way for Modernity, 1920–1940* (1985); Lary May, *Screening Out the Past* (1980); Leonard Mosley, *Lindbergh: A Biography* (1976); Otis Pease, *The Responsibilities of American Advertising* (1959); Daniel Pope, *The Making of Modern Advertising* (1983); Randy Roberts, *Jack Dempsey, The Manassa Mauler* (1979); Philip Rosen, *The Modern Stentors: Radio Broadcasting and the Federal Government, 1920–1933* (1980); Robert Sklar, *Movie-Made America: A Cultural History of American Movies* (1975); Kevin Starr, *Material Dreams: Southern California through the 1920s* (1990); Susan Strasser, *Satisfaction Guaranteed: The Making of the American Mass Market* (1990).

High Culture   Carlos Baker, *Hemingway* (1956); Malcolm Cowley, *Exile's Return* (1934); Robert Crunden, *From Self to Society: Transition in Modern Thought, 1919–1941* (1972); Frederick Hoffman, *The Twenties* (1949); Arthur Mizner, *The Far Side of Paradise* (1951); Roderick Nash, *The Nervous Generation: American Thought, 1917–1930* (1969); Mark Shorer, *Sinclair Lewis* (1961); Marvin Singleton, *H. L. Mencken and the "American Mercury" Adventure* (1962).

Women, Youth, and Minorities   Lois Banner, *American Beauty* (1983); Susan D. Becker, *The Origins of the Equal Rights Amendment* (1981); Kathlenn M. Blee, *Women of the Klan: Racism and Gender in the 1920s* (1991); Dorothy M. Brown, *Setting a Course: American Woman in the 1920s* (1987); William Chafe, *The American Woman: Her Changing Social, Economic, and Political Roles, 1920–1970* (1972); Nancy Cott, *The Grounding of Modern Feminism* (1987); David Cronon, *Black Moses: The Story of Marcus Garvey* (1955); Melvin Patrick Ely, *The Adventures of Amos 'n' Andy: A Social History of an American Phenomenon* (1991); Paula Fass, *The Damned and Beautiful: American Youth in the 1920s* (1977); Linda Gordon, *Woman's Body, Woman's Right: A Social History of Birth Control in America* (1976); Peter Gottlieb, *Making Their Own Way: Southern Blacks' Migration to Pittsburgh, 1916–1930* (1987); Florette Henri, *Black Migration: Movement North, 1900–1920* (1975); Nathan Huggins, *Harlem Renaissance* (1971); Jacqueline Jones, *Labor of Love, Labor of Sorrow: Black Women, Work, and Family, from Slavery to the Present* (1985); J. Stanley Lemons, *The Woman Citizen: Social Feminism in the 1920s* (1973); David Levering Lewis, *When Harlem Was in Vogue* (1981); Glenna Matthews, *"Just a Housewife!" The Rise and Fall of Domesticity in America* (1987); Cary D. Mintz, *Black Culture and the Harlem Renaissance* (1988); Wilson Moses, *The Golden Age of Black Nationalism, 1850–1925* (1988); Kathy H. Ogren, *The Jazz Revolution: Twenties America and the Meaning of Jazz* (1989); Arnold Rampersed, *The Life of Langston Hughes,* 2 vols. (1986–1988); Ricardo Romo, *East Los Angeles: History of a Barrio* (1983); Vicki L. Ruiz, *From Out of the Shadows: Mexican Women in Twentieth Century America* (1998); George J. Sánchez, *Becoming Mexican American: Ethnicity, Culture, and Identity in Chicano Los Angeles, 1900–1945* (1993); Lois Scharf, *To Work and to Wed* (1980); Virginia Scharff, *Taking the Wheel: Women and the Coming of the Motor Age* (1991); Alan Spear, *Black Chicago* (1967); Judith Stein, *The World of Marcus Garvey: Race and Class in Modern Society* (1986); Joe William Trotter Jr., *Black Milwaukee: The Making of an Industrial Proletariat* (1985); Theodore Vincent, *Black Power and the Garvey Movement* (1971); Winifred Wandersee, *Women's Work and Family Values, 1920–1940* (1981).

Political Fundamentalism   Paul Avrich, *Sacco-Vanzetti: The Anarchist Background* (1991); David Burner, *The Politics of Provincialism* (1968); David Chalmers, *Hooded Americanism: The History of the Ku Klux Klan* (1965); Norman Clark, *Deliver Us from Evil* (1976); Robert Divine, *American Immigration Policy* (1957); Norman Furniss, *The Fundamentalist Controversy, 1918–1933* (1954); Ray Ginger, *Six Days or Forever? Tennessee v. John Scopes* (1958); Joseph Gusfeld, *Symbolic Crusade* (1963); John Higham, *Strangers in the Land: Patterns of American Nativism, 1860–1925* (1955); Kenneth Jackson, *The Ku Klux Klan in the City, 1915–1930* (1967); Don Kirschner, *City and Country: Rural Responses to Urbanization in the 1920s* (1970); Edward J. Larson, *Summer of the Gods: The Scopes Trial and America's Continuing Debate over Science and Religion* (1997); Shawn Lay, ed., *The Invisible Empire in the West: Toward a New Historical Appraisal of the Ku Klux Klan of the 1920s* (1992); Nancy MacLean, *Behind the Mask of Chivalry: The Making of the Second Ku Klux Klan* (1994); George Maraden, *Fundamentalism and American Culture* (1980); Leonard J. Moore, *Citizen Klansmen: The Ku Klux Klan in Indiana, 1921–1928* (1991); Andrew Sinclair, *Prohibition: The Era of Excess* (1962); William Wilson, *Coming of Age: Urban America, 1915–1945* (1974).

Politics, Public Policy, and the Election of 1928   Kristi Andersen, *The Creation of a Democratic Majority* (1979); Paula

Edler, *Governor Alfred E. Smith: The Politician as Reformer* (1983); James Giglio, *H. M. Daugherty and the Politics of Expediency* (1978); Oscar Handlin, *Al Smith and His America* (1958); Ellis Hawley, *Herbert Hoover as Secretary of Commerce: Studies in New Era Thought and Practice* (1974); Robert Himmelberg, *The Origins of the National Recovery Administration: Business, Government, and the Trade Association Issue, 1921–1933* (1976); J. Joseph Huthmacher, *Massachusetts People and Politics, 1919–1933* (1959); Alan Lichtman, *Prejudice and the Old Politics* (1979); Richard Lowitt, *George Norris,* 2 vols. (1971); Donald McCoy, *Calvin Coolidge* (1967); Robert Murray, *The Harding Era* (1969) and *The Politics of Normalcy* (1973); Burl Noggle, *Teapot Dome* (1962); Elisabeth Perry, *Belle Moskowitz: Feminine Politics and the Exercise of Power in the Age of Alfred E. Smith* (1987); George Tindall, *The Emergence of the New South* (1967); Eugene Trani and David Wilson, *The Presidency of Warren G. Harding* (1977).

Chapter 25: The Great Depression and the New Deal, 1929-1939

General Histories Frederick Lewis Allen, *Since Yesterday* (1939); John Braeman et al., *The New Deal,* 2 vols. (1975); Paul Conkin, *The New Deal* (1967); Steve Fraser and Gary Gerstle, eds., *The Rise and Fall of the New Deal Order, 1930–1980* (1989); John A. Garraty, *The Great Depression* (1987); Otis Graham Jr., *Encore for Reform: The Old Progressives and the New Deal* (1967); Barry Karl, *The Uneasy State* (1983); David Kennedy, *Freedom from Fear: The United States, 1933–1945* (1999); William Leuchtenburg, *Franklin D. Roosevelt and the New Deal, 1932–1940* (1963); Robert McElvaine, *The Great Depression: America, 1929–1941* (1984); Broadus Mitchell, *Depression Decade* (1947); Gerald Nash, *The Great Depression and World War II* (1979); Arthur Schlesinger Jr., *The Crisis of the Old Order* (1957); Harvard Sitkoff, ed., *Fifty Years Later: The New Deal Evaluated* (1985); T. H. Watkins, *The Great Depression: America in the 1930s* (1991).

The Great Crash and the Origins of the Great Depression Michael A. Bernstein, *The Great Depression: Delayed Recovery and Economic Change in America, 1929–1939* (1987); Lester Chandler, *America's Greatest Depression, 1929–1941* (1970); Milton Friedman and Ana Schwartz, *The Great Contraction, 1929–1933* (1965); John Kenneth Galbraith, *The Great Crash,* rev. ed. (1988); Susan Kennedy, *The Banking Crisis of 1933* (1973); Charles Kindleberger, *The World in Depression* (1973); Robert Sobel, *The Great Bull Market: Wall Street in the 1920s* (1968); Peter Temin, *Did Monetary Forces Cause the Great Depression?* (1976); Gordon Thomas and Max Morgan-Witts, *The Day the Bubble Burst: The Social History of the Wall Street Crash of 1929* (1979).

Depression Life Edward Anderson, *Hungry Men* (1935); Robert Angel, *The Family Encounters the Depression* (1936); Ann Banks, *First Person America* (1980); Caroline Bird, *The Invisible Scar* (1966); The Federal Writers' Project, *These Are Our Lives* (1939); John Garraty, *Unemployment in History: Economic Thought and Public Policy* (1978); Mirra Komarovsky, *The Unemployed Man and His Family* (1940); Robert Lynd and Helen Lynd, *Middletown in Transition* (1937); Robert McElvaine, ed., *Down and Out in the Great Depression* (1983); Harvey Levenstein, *Paradox of Plenty: A Social History of Eating in Modern America* (1993); H. Wayne Morgan, *Drugs in America: A Social History, 1800–1980* (1981); David Musto, *The American Disease, Origins of Narcotics Control,* rev. ed. (1988); Lois Scharf, *To Work and to Wed: Female Employment, Feminism, and the Great Depression* (1980); Tom Terrill and Jerrold Hirsch, eds., *Such as Us: Southern Voices of the Thirties* (1978); Studs Terkel, *Hard Times: An Oral History of the Great Depression* (1970); Winifred Wandersee, *Women's Work and Family Values, 1920–1940* (1981); Susan Ware, *Holding Their Own: American Women in the 1930s* (1982); Jeane Westin, *Making Do: How Women Survived the '30s* (1976).

Ethnicity and Race Rodolfo Acuña, *Occupied America: A History of Chicanos* (1981); Ralph Bunche, *The Political Status of the Negro in the Age of FDR* (1973); Dan Carter, *Scottsboro: A Tragedy of the American South* (1969); Sarah Deutsch, *No Separate Refuge: Culture, Class, and Gender on an Anglo-Hispanic Frontier in the American Southwest, 1880–1940* (1987); Abraham Hoffman, *Unwanted Mexican-Americans in the Great Depression* (1974); Richard Polenberg, *One Nation Divisible: Class, Race, and Ethnicity in the United States since 1938* (1980); Bernard Sternsher, ed., *The Negro in Depression and War* (1969); Robert Weisbrot, *Father Divine and the Struggle for Racial Equality* (1983); Nancy Weiss, *The National Urban League* (1974); Raymond Wolters, *Negroes and the Great Depression* (1970).

Depression Culture Daniel Aaron, *Writers on the Left* (1961); James Agee, *Let Us Now Praise Famous Men* (1941); Andrew Bergman, *We're in the Money: Depression America and Its Films* (1971); Eileen Eagan, *Class, Culture and the Classroom* (1981); Neal Gabler, *An Empire of Their Own: How the Jews Invented Hollywood* (1988); Lawrence Levine, *The Unpredictable Past: Explorations in American Cultural History* (1993); Jeffrey Meikle, *Twentieth Century Limited: Industrial Design in America, 1925–1939* (1979); Richard Pells, *Radical Visions and American Dreams: Culture and Social Thought in the Depression Years* (1973); Thomas Schatz, *The Genius of the System: Hollywood Filmmaking in the Studio Era* (1988); John Steinbeck, *The Grapes of Wrath* (1939); William Stott, *Documentary Expressionism and Thirties America* (1973); Warren Susman, *Culture as History: The Transformation of American Society in the Twentieth Century* (1984); Twelve Southerners, *I'll Take My Stand: The South and the Agrarian Tradition* (1937).

Radicalism and Protest Irving Bernstein, *The Lean Years: A History of the American Worker, 1920–1933* (1960); Robert Cohen, *When the Old Left Was Young: Student Radicals and America's First Mass Student Movement, 1929–1941* (1993); Roger Daniels, *The Bonus March* (1971); John Hevener, *Which Side You On? The Harlan County Coal Miners, 1931–1939* (1978); Harvey Klehr, *The Heyday of American Communism: The Depression Decade* (1984); Donald Lisio, *The President and Protest: Hoover, Conspiracy, and the Bonus Riot* (1974); Mark Naison, *Communists in Harlem during the Depression* (1983); Theodore Saloutos and John Hicks, *Twentieth Century Populism: Agrarian Protest in the Middle West, 1900–1939* (1951); John Shover, *Cornbelt Rebellion: The Farmers' Holiday Association* (1965).

The Hoover Years David Burner, *Herbert Hoover: A Public Life* (1979); Roger Daniels, *The Bonus March* (1971); Martin Fausold, *The Presidency of Herbert C. Hoover* (1985); Martin Fausold and George Mazuzun, eds., *The Hoover Presidency* (1974); George Nash, *The Life of Herbert Hoover* (1983); James Olson, *Herbert Hoover and the Reconstruction Finance Corporation* (1977); Albert Romasco, *The Poverty of Abundance: Hoover, the Nation, the Depression* (1965); Elliot A. Rosen, *Hoover, Roosevelt, and the Brains Trust: From Depression to New Deal* (1977); Jordan Schwarz, *The Interregnum of Despair* (1970); Joan Hoff Wilson, *Herbert Hoover: Forgotten Progressive* (1975).

Franklin and Eleanor   James Burns, *Roosevelt: The Lion and the Fox* (1956); Rochelle Chadakoff, ed., *Eleanor Roosevelt's My Day: Her Acclaimed Columns, 1936–1945* (1989); Blanche Wiesen Cook, *Eleanor Roosevelt, Volume 1884–1933* (1992) and *Eleanor Roosevelt: Volume 1933–1938* (1999); Kenneth Davis, *FDR*, 4 vols. (1972–1993); Frank Freidel, *Franklin D. Roosevelt*, 4 vols. (1952–1973) and *Franklin D. Roosevelt: A Rendezvous with Destiny* (1990); Joseph Lash, *Eleanor and Franklin* (1971); Ted Morgan, *FDR: A Biography* (1985); Eleanor Roosevelt, *This Is My Story* (1937) and *This I Remember* (1949); Lois Scharf, *Eleanor Roosevelt: First Lady of American Liberalism* (1987); Arthur Schlesinger Jr., *The Age of Roosevelt*, 3 vols. (1957–1960); Rexford Tugwell, *The Democratic Roosevelt: A Biography of Franklin D. Roosevelt* (1957); Geoffrey Ward, *Before the Trumpet: Young Franklin Roosevelt* (1985) and *A First Class Temperament: The Emergence of Franklin Roosevelt* (1989).

The New Deal and New Dealers   Anthony J. Badger, *The New Deal: The Depression Years, 1933–1940* (1989); Barton J. Bernstein, "The New Deal: The Conservative Achievements of New Deal Reform," in Barton J. Bernstein, ed., *Towards a New Past: Dissenting Essays in American History* (1968); Michael Beschloss, *Kennedy and Roosevelt: The Uneasy Alliance* (1980); John Blum, *From the Morgenthau Diaries*, 3 vols. (1959–1965); Harold Ickes, *The Secret Diaries of Harold L. Ickes*, 3 vols. (1953–1954); Peter Irons, *The New Deal Lawyers* (1982); Joseph Lash, *Dealers and Dreamers: A New Look at the New Deal* (1988); Katie Lockheim, ed., *The Making of the New Deal: The Insiders Speak* (1983); Richard Lowitt, *George W. Norris: The Triumph of a Progressive, 1933–1944* (1978); George Martin, *Madame Secretary: Frances Perkins* (1976); George McJimsey, *Harry Hopkins: Ally of the Poor and Defender of Democracy* (1987); Raymond Moley, *After Seven Years* (1939); Frances Perkins, *The Roosevelt I Knew* (1946); Samuel Rosenman, *Working for Roosevelt* (1952); Jordan Schwarz, *Liberal: Adolf A. Berle and the Vision of an American Era* (1987) and *The New Dealers: Power Politics in the Age of Roosevelt* (1993); Robert Sherwood, *Roosevelt and Hopkins: An Intimate History* (1948); Bernard Sternsher, *Rexford Tugwell and the New Deal* (1964); Susan Ware, *Beyond Suffrage: Women and the New Deal* (1981) and *Partner and I: Molly Dewson, Feminism, and New Deal Politics* (1987); T. H. Watkins, *The Righteous Pilgrim: The Life and Times of Harold L. Ickes* (1990).

Recovery and Reform   Bernard Belush, *The Failure of the NRA* (1975); Donald R. Brand, *Corporatism and the Rule of Law: A Study of the National Recovery Administration* (1988); Walter L. Creese, *TVA's Public Planning: The Vision, the Reality* (1990); Colin Gordon, *New Deals: Business, Labor, and Politics in America, 1920–1935* (1994); Ellis Hawley, *The New Deal and the Problems of Monopoly* (1966); Barry Karl, *Executive Reorganization and Reform in the New Deal* (1963); Susan E. Kennedy, *The Banking Crisis of 1933* (1973); Mark Leff, *The Limits of Symbolic Reform: The New Deal and Taxation, 1933–1939* (1984); Thomas McCraw, *TVA and the Public Power Fight* (1970); James Olson, *Saving Capitalism: The RFC and the New Deal, 1933–1940* (1988); Michael Parrish, *Securities Regulation and the New Deal* (1970); Richard Polenberg, *Reorganizing Roosevelt's Government* (1966); Albert Romasco, *The Politics of Recovery: Roosevelt's New Deal* (1983).

Agriculture and Conservation   Sidney Baldwin, *Poverty and Politics: The Rise and Decline of the Farm Security Administration* (1967); David Conrad, *The Forgotten Farmers: The Story of Sharecroppers in the New Deal* (1965); James Gregory, *American Exo-dus: The Dust Bowl Migration and Okie Culture in California* (1989); Richard Kirkendall, *Social Scientists and Farm Politics in the Age of Roosevelt* (1966); Richard Lowitt, *The New Deal and the West* (1984); Percy H. Merrill, *Roosevelt's Forest Army: A History of the Civilian Conservation Corps, 1933–1942* (1981); Paul Mertz, *The New Deal and Southern Rural Poverty* (1978); Van Perkins, *Crisis in Agriculture* (1969); Donald Worster, *Dust Bowl: The Southern Plains in the 1930s* (1979) and *Rivers of Empire: Water, Aridity, and the Growth of the American West* (1986).

Relief and the Rise of the Semi-Welfare State   Searle Charles, *Minister of Relief* (1963) [about Harry Hopkins]; Paul Conkin, *FDR and the Origins of the Welfare State* (1967); Phoebe Cutler, *The Public Landscape of the New Deal* (1986); Linda Gordon, *Pitied but Not Entitled: Single Mothers and the History of Welfare* (1994); Richard Lowitt and Maurine Beasley, eds., *One Third of a Nation: Lorena Hickok Reports on the Great Depression* (1981); Roy Lubove, *The Struggle for Social Security* (1968); Jerre Mangione, *The Dream and the Deal: The Federal Writers' Project, 1935–1943* (1972); Jane deHart Matthews, *The Federal Theater, 1935–1939* (1967); Richard McKinzie, *The New Deal for Artists* (1973); Barbara Melosh, *Engendering Culture: Manhood and Womanhood in New Deal Public Art and Theater* (1991); Francis O'Connor, ed., *Art for the Millions: Essays from the 1930s by Artists and Administrators of the WPA Federal Art Project* (1973); Karen Benker Orhn, *Dorothea Lange and the Documentary Tradition* (1980); Marlene Park and Gerald Markowitz, *Democratic Vistas: Post Offices and Public Art in the New Deal* (1984); John Salmond, *The Civilian Conservation Corps* (1967); Bonnie Schwartz, *The Civil Works Administration, 1933–1934* (1984).

Dissent and Protest   Alan Brinkley, *Voices of Protest: Huey Long, Father Coughlin, and the Great Depression* (1982); Donald Grubbs, *Cry from Cotton: The Southern Tenant Farmers Union and the New Deal* (1971); Abraham Holzman, *The Townsend Movement* (1963); Glen Geansonne, *Gerald L. K. Smith: Minister of Hate* (1988); Robin D. G. Kelly, *Hammer and Hoe: Alabama Communists during the Great Depression* (1990); R. Alan Lawson, *The Failure of Independent Liberalism, 1930–1941* (1971); Greg Mitchell, *The Campaign of the Century: Upton Sinclair's Epic Race for Governor of California and the Birth of Media Politics* (1992); Mark Naison, *Communists in Harlem during the Depression* (1983); Leo Ribuffo, *The Old Christian Right: The Protestant Far Right from the Great Depression to the Cold War* (1983); Vicki Ruiz, *Cannery Women/Cannery Lives: Mexican Women, Unionization, and the California Food Processing Industry, 1930–1950* (1987); Charles Tull, *Father Coughlin and the New Deal* (1965); T. Harry Wiliams, *Huey Long* (1969); Frank Warren, *Liberals and Communism: The "Red Decade" Revisited* (1966) and *An Alternative Vision: The Socialist Party in the 1930s* (1976); George Wolfskill, *Revolt of the Conservatives: A History of the American Liberty League, 1934–1940* (1962).

Labor   Jerold Auerback, *Labor and Liberty: The La Follette Committee and the New Deal* (1966); John Barnard, *Walter Reuther and the Rise of the Auto Workers* (1983); Irving Bernstein, *Turbulent Years: A History of the American Worker, 1933–1941* (1969); Lizbeth Cohen, *Making a New Deal: Industrial Workers in Chicago, 1919–1939* (1990); Melvyn Dubofsky and Warren Van Tine, *John L. Lewis: A Biography* (1977); Sidney Fine, *Sit-Down: The General Motors Strike of 1936–1937* (1969); Steven Fraser, *Labor Will Rule: Sidney Hillman and the Rise of American Labor* (1991); Peter Friedlander, *The Emergence of a UAW Local* (1975); Nelson Lichenstein, *"The Most Dangerous Man in Detroit": Walter*

Reuther and the Fate of American Labor (1995); August Meier and Elliott Rudwick, *Black Detroit and the Rise of the UAW* (1979); David Milton, *The Politics of U.S. Labor: From the Great Depression to the New Deal* (1980); Ronald Schatz, *The Electrical Workers* (1983); Robert H. Zieger, *John L. Lewis* (1988).

New Deal Politics   John Allswang, *The New Deal in American Politics* (1978); Frank Freidel, *FDR and the South* (1965); J. Joseph Huthmacher, *Senator Robert Wagner and the Rise of Urban Liberalism* (1968); Gregg Mitchell, *The Campaign of the Century: Upton Sinclair's Race for Governor and the Birth of Media Politics* (1992); James Patterson, *Congressional Conservatism and the New Deal* (1967) and *The New Deal and the States* (1969); William Leuchtenburg, "The Origins of Franklin D. Roosevelt's 'Court Packing' Plan," in Philip Kurland, ed., *The Supreme Court Review* (1966).

African Americans, American Indians, and Latinos   Camille Guerin-Gonzales, *Mexican Workers and American Dreams: Immigration, Repatriation, and California Farm Labor, 1900–1939* (1994); Laurence Kelly, *The Assault on Assimilation: John Collier and the Origins of Indian Policy Reform, 1920–1954* (1983); Harry A. Kersey Jr., *The Florida Seminoles and the New Deal, 1933–1942* (1989); John Kirby, *Black Americans in the Roosevelt Era: Liberalism and Race* (1980); Carey McWilliams, *North from Mexico* (1949); Donald Parman, *The Navajoes and the New Deal* (1976); Kenneth Philp, *John Collier's Crusade for Indian Reform, 1920– 1934* (1977); Francis Prucha, *The Indians in American Society: From the Revolutionary War to the Present* (1985); Mark Reisler, *By the Sweat of Their Brow: Mexican Immigrant Labor in the United States, 1900–1940* (1976); Harvard Sitkoff, *A New Deal for Blacks* (1978); Raymond Walters, *Negroes and the Great Depression: The Problem of Economic Recovery* (1970); Graham D. Taylor, *The New Deal and American Indian Tribalism: The Administration of the Indian Reorganization Act, 1934–1945* (1980); Derva Weber, *Dark Sweat, White Gold: California Farm Workers and the New Deal* (1994); Nancy Weiss, *Farewell to the Party of Lincoln: Black Politics in the Age of FDR* (1983); Robert Zangrando, *The NAACP Crusade against Lynching* (1980).

Chapter 26: America's Rise to Globalism

The Roosevelt Era and the Coming of World War II   Dorothy Borg, *The United States and the Far Eastern Crisis of 1933–1938* (1964); James MacGregor Burns, *Roosevelt: The Lion and the Fox* (1956); Wayne S. Cole, *Roosevelt and the Isolationists, 1932–1945* (1983); Robert Dallek, *Franklin D. Roosevelt and American Foreign Policy, 1932–1945* (1979); Charles DeBenedetti, *The Peace Reform Movement in American History* (1980); John Findling, *Close Neighbors, Distant Friends: United States–Central American Relations* (1987); Lloyd Gardner, *Economic Aspects of New Deal Diplomacy* (1964) and *The Great Powers Partition Europe, from Munich to Yalta* (1993); Irwin Gellman, *Good Neighbor Diplomacy* (1979); Patrick Headen, *Roosevelt Confronts Hitler: America's Entry into World War II* (1987); Edwin Herzstein, *Roosevelt and Hitler: Prelude to War* (1989); Akira Iriye and Warren Cohen, eds., *American, Chinese, and Japanese Perspectives on Asia, 1931– 1949* (1990); Warren Kimball, *The Most Unsordid Act: Lend Lease, 1939–1941* (1969); Walter LaFeber, *Inevitable Revolutions: The United States in Central America* (1993); Douglas Little, *Malevolent Neutrality: The United States, Great Britain, and the Origins of the Spanish Civil War* (1985); Arnold Offner, *The Origins of the Second World War* (1975); Gordon Prange, *At Dawn We Slept* (1981); Linda Schott, *Reconstructing Women's Thoughts: The Women's International League for Peace and Freedom before World War II* (1997); Michael Slackman, *Target: Pearl Harbor* (1990); John Toland, *Infamy* (1982); Jonathan Utley, *Going to War with Japan, 1937–1941* (1985); Roberta Wohlstetter, *Pearl Harbor: Warning and Decision* (1962); Bryce Wood, *The Making of the Good Neighbor Policy* (1961); David Wyman, *The Abandonment of the Jews* (1984).

War and Strategy   Stephen Ambrose, *Citizen Soldiers* (1997); Tom Brokaw, *A Time for Giants* (1999); John Dower, *War without Mercy: Race and Power in the Pacific War* (1986); David Eisenhower, *Eisenhower at War, 1943–1945* (1986); Richard B. Frank, *Guadalcanal* (1990); B. H. Liddell Hart, *History of the Second World War* (1970); Max Hastings, *Overlord: D-Day and the Battle of Normandy* (1984); Akira Iriye, *Power and Culture: The Japanese-American War, 1941–1945* (1981); D. Clayton James with Anne Sharp Wells, *A Time for Giants: Politics of the American High Command during World War II* (1987); John Keegan, *The Second World War* (1989); Warren Kimball, *Forged in War: Roosevelt, Churchill, and the Second World War* (1997); Eric Larabee, *Commander in Chief: Franklin Delano Roosevelt, His Lieutenants, and Their War* (1987); Gerald Linderman, *The World within War: American Combat Experience in World War II* (1997); William Manchester, *American Caesar* (1979); Karal Ann Marling and John Wetenhall, *Iwo Jima* (1991); Ken McCormick and Hamilton Perry, *Images of War: The Artists' Vision of World War II* (1990); Nathan Miller, *War at Sea: A Naval History of World War II* (1995); Samuel Eliot Morison, *The Two Ocean War* (1963); Bernard C. Nalty, *Strength for the Fight: A History of Black Americans in the Military* (1986); Geoffrey Perret, *There's a War to Be Won: The United States Army and World War II* (1991) and *Winged Victory: The American Air Force in World War II* (1993); Forrest Pogue, *George C. Marshall*, 3 vols. (1963–1975); Paul P. Rogers, *The Good Years: MacArthur and Sutherland* (1990); Ronald Schaffer, *Wings of Judgment: American Bombing in World War II* (1985); Michael Sherry, *The Rise of American Air Power* (1987); Bradley Smith, *The Shadow Warriors: O.S.S. and the Origins of the C.I.A.* (1983); Ronald Spector, *The Eagle against the Sun: The American War with Japan* (1985); James Stokesbury, *A Short History of World War II* (1980); Barbara Brooks Tomlin, *G.I. Nightingales: The Army Nurse Corps in World War II* (1996).

The Home Front at War   Michael Adams, *The Best War Ever: Americans and World War II* (1994); Karen T. Anderson, *Wartime Women: Sex Roles, Family Relations, and the Status of American Women during World War II* (1981); Matthew Baigall and Julia Williams, eds., *Artists against War and Fascism* (1986); M. Joyce Baker, *Images of Women on Film: The War Years, 1941–1945* (1981); David Brinkley, *Washington Goes to War* (1988); John Costello, *Virtue under Fire: How World War II Changed Our Social and Sexual Attitudes* (1985); George Q. Flynn, *The Draft, 1940–1973* (1993); Paul Fussell, *Wartime* (1989); Sherna Berger Gluck, *Rosie the Riveter Revisited: Women, the War, and Social Change* (1987); Doris Kearns Goodwin, *No Ordinary Time, Franklin and Eleanor Roosevelt: The Homefront in World War II* (1994); Susan Hartmann, *The Home Front and Beyond: American Women in the 1940s* (1982); Maurice Isserman, *Which Side Were You On? The American Communist Party during the Second World War* (1982); Clayton Koppes and Gregory Black, *Hollywood Goes to War* (1987); Molly Merryman, *Clipped Wings: The Rise and Fall of the Women Airforce Service Pilots (WASPs) of World War II*

(1998); Ruth Milkman, *Gender at Work: The Dynamics of Job Segregation by Sex during World War II* (1987); Gerald Nash, *The American West Transformed: The Impact of the Second World War* (1985); Richard Polenberg, *War and Society: The United States, 1941–1945* (1972); David Robertson, *Sly and Able: A Political Biography of James F. Byrnes* (1994); George H. Roeder Jr., *The Censored War: American Visual Experience during World War II* (1993); Studs Turkel, *The Good War: An Oral History of World War II* (1984); William Tuttle, *Daddy's Gone to War: The Second World War in the Lives of America's Children* (1993); Harold Vatter, *The American Economy in World War II* (1985).

Minorities and the War   Robert Abzug, *Inside the Vicious Heart: Americans and the Liberation of the Nazi Concentration Camps* (1985); Allan Bérubé, *Coming Out under Fire: Gay Men and Women in World War Two* (1990); Richard Breitman and Alan Kraut, *American Refugee Policy and European Jewry, 1933–1945* (1987); A. Russell Buchanan, *Black Americans in World War II* (1977); Dominic Capeci Jr., *Race Relations in Wartime Detroit* (1984) and *The Harlem Race Riot of 1943* (1977), Clete Daniel, *Chicano Workers and the Politics of Fairness: The Fair Employment Practices Commission and the Southwest 1941–1945* (1990); Roger Daniels, *Concentration Camps U.S.A.* (1981) and *Prisoners without Trials: The Japanese-Americans in World War II* (1993); Leonard Dinnerstein, *America and the Survivors of the Holocaust* (1982); Masayo Umezawa Duus, *Unlikely Liberators: The Men of the 100th and 442nd* (1987); Henry Feingold, *Bearing Witness: How America and Its Jews Responded to the Holocaust* (1995); Lee Finkel, *Forum for Protest: The Black Press during World War II* (1975); Peter Irons, *Justice at War: The Story of the Japanese American Internment Cases* (1983); Deborah Lipstadt, *Beyond Belief: The American Press and the Coming of the Holocaust, 1933–1945* (1986); Mauricio Mazon, *The Zoot Suit Riots* (1984); Phillip McGuire, ed., *Taps for a Jim Crow Army: Letters from Black Soldiers in World War II* (1982); Sandra Taylor, *Jewel of the West: Japanese-American Internment at Topaz* (1993); Patrick Washburn, *A Question of Sedition: The Federal Government and the Investigation of the Black Press during World War II* (1986); Neil Wynn, *The Afro-American and the Second World War* (1976); Norman Zucker and Naomi Flink Zucker, *The Guarded Gate: The Reality of American Refugee Policy* (1987).

Atoms and Diplomacy   Gar Alperovitz, *The Decision to Use the Bomb* (1995); Edward M. Bennett, *Franklin D. Roosevelt and the Search for Victory: American-Soviet Relations, 1935–1945* (1990); Henry Blumenthal, *Illusion and Reality in Franco-American Diplomacy, 1914–1945* (1982); McGeorge Bundy, *Danger and Survival: Choices about the Atom Bomb in the First Fifty Years* (1988); James MacGregor Burns, *Roosevelt: The Soldier of Freedom* (1970); Winston Churchill, *The Second World War,* 6 vols. (1948–1953); Herbert Feis, *Roosevelt, Churchill, Stalin: The War They Waged and the Peace They Sought* (1957), *Between War and Peace: The Potsdam Conference* (1960), and *The Atomic Bomb and the End of World War II* (1966); John L. Gaddis, *The United States and the Origins of the Cold War* (1972); Fraser J. Harbutt, *The Iron Curtain: Churchill, America, and the Origins of the Cold War* (1986); George Herring, *Aid to Russia, 1941–1946* (1977); John Hersey, *Hiroshima* (1946); Richard Hewlett and Oscar Anderson, *The New World* (1962); "Hiroshima in History and Memory: A Symposium," *Diplomatic History,* 19, no. 2 (spring 1995), 197–365; Godfrey Hodgson, *The Colonel: The Life and Wars of Henry Stimson* (1990); Warren Kimball, ed., *Churchill and Roosevelt: The Complete Correspondence, 1939–1945* (1984); Gabriel Kolko, *The Politics of War* (1968); William Roger Louis, *Imperialism at Bay: The United States and the Decolonization of the British Empire, 1941–1945* (1978); Mark H. Lytle, *The Origins of the Iranian-American Alliance, 1941–1953* (1987); David Painter, *Oil and the American Century: The Political Economy of U.S. Foreign Oil Policy, 1941–1954* (1986); Richard Rhodes, *The Making of the Atomic Bomb* (1986); Keith Sainsbury, *Roosevelt, Stalin, Churchill, and Chiang Kai-shek, 1943: The Moscow, Cairo, and Tehran Conferences* (1985); Gaddis Smith, *American Diplomacy during the Second World War, 1941–1945* (1985); Michael B. Stoff, *Oil, War, and American Security: The Search for a National Policy on Foreign Oil, 1941–1947* (1980) and as ed., *The Manhattan Project: A Documentary Introduction* (1991); J. Samuel Walker, *Prompt and Utter Destruction: Truman and the Use of the Atomic Bomb against Japan* (1997); Randall B. Woods, *A Changing of the Guard: Anglo-American Relations, 1941–1946* (1990).

Chapter 27: Cold War America

The Postwar Era   Paul Boyer, *By the Bomb's Early Light* (1986); H. W. Brands, *The Devil We Knew: America and the Cold War* (1993); Robert Ferrell, *Harry S Truman: A Life* (1994); Eric Goldman, *The Crucial Decade and After* (1960); Margot Henriksen, *Dr. Strangelove's America: Society and Culture in the Atomic Age* (1997); Landon Jones, *Great Expectations: America and the Babyboom Generation* (1980); George Lipsitz, *Class and Culture in Postwar America* (1981); James O'Connor, ed., *American History/American Television* (1983); William O'Neill, *American High* (1986); Richard Pells, *The Liberal Mind in a Conservative Age* (1985); Dana Polan, *Power and Paranoia: History, Narrative, and the American Cinema, 1940–1950* (1986); Leila Rupp and Verta Taylor, *Survival in the Doldrums: The American Women's Rights Movement, 1945 to the 1960s* (1987); Mark Silk, *Spiritual Politics: Religion and America since World War II* (1988); Jules Tygiel, *Baseball's Great Experiment: Jackie Robinson and His Legacy* (1983); Martin Walker, *The Cold War: A History* (1994).

The Cold War in the West   Dean Acheson, *Present at the Creation* (1969); Stephen Ambrose, *The Rise to Globalism* (1983); Douglas Brinkley, ed., *Dean Acheson and the Making of American Foreign Policy* (1993); Richard Wightman Fox, *Reinhold Niebuhr: A Biography* (1985); Richard Freeland, *The Truman Doctrine and the Origins of McCarthyism* (1970); John L. Gaddis, *Strategies of Containment* (1982), *The Long Peace: Inquiries into the History of the Cold War* (1987), and *We Now Know* (1997); Lloyd Gardner, *Architects of Illusion* (1970); Gregg Herken, *The Winning Weapon* (1980); Michael Hogan, *The Marshall Plan: America, Britain, and the Reconstruction of Western Europe, 1947–1952* (1987); Walter Isaacson and Evan Thomas, *The Wise Men* (1986); Fred Kaplan, *The Wizards of Armageddon* (1983); Laurence Kaplan, *The United States and NATO* (1984); George Kennan, *Memoirs,* 2 vols. (1967, 1972); Bruce Kuniholm, *The Origins of the Cold War in the Near East* (1980); Mark H. Lytle, *The Origins of the Iranian-American Alliance, 1941–1953* (1987); James Miller, *The United States and Italy, 1940–1950* (1986); Ronald Pruessen, *John Foster Dulles* (1982); Cheryl Rubenberg, *Israel and the American National Interest* (1986); Gaddis Smith, *The Last Years of the Monroe Doctrine, 1945–1993* (1994); Lawrence Wittner, *American Intervention in Greece, 1943–1949* (1982); Randall B. Woods and Howard Jones, *Dawning of the Cold War* (1991).

The Cold War in Asia   Robert Blum, *Drawing the Line: The Origin of the American Containment Policy in East Asia* (1982); Bruce Cumings, *The Origins of the Korean War* (1980) and vol. 2 (1990), and as ed., *Child of Conflict: The Korean-American Relationship, 1943–1953* (1983); William Head, *America's China Sojourn* (1983); Gary Hess, *The United States' Emergence as a Southeast Asian Power, 1940–1950* (1987); Akira Iriye, *The Cold War in Asia* (1974); Burton Kaufman, *The Korean War* (1986); Michael Schaller, *The United States and China in the Twentieth Century* (1979) and *The American Occupation of Japan: The Coming of the Cold War to Asia* (1985); John W. Spanier, *The Truman-MacArthur Controversy and the Korean War* (1959); William Stueck Jr., *The Road to Confrontation* (1981) and *The Korean War: An International History* (1995); Nancy Tucker, *Patterns in the Dust: Chinese-American Relations and the Recognition Controversy, 1949–1950* (1983).

The Domestic Cold War   Michael Belknap, *Cold War Political Justice: The Smith Act, the Communist Party, and American Civil Liberties* (1977); David Caute, *The Great Fear* (1978); Bernard F. Dick, *Radical Innocence: A Critical Study of the Hollywood Ten* (1988); Stanley I. Kutler, *The American Inquisition: Justice and Injustice in the Cold War* (1982); Robert Lamphere and Tom Shachtman, *The FBI-KGB War* (1986); Victor Navasky, *Naming Names* (1980); Robert Newman, *Owen Lattimore and the "Loss" of China* (1992); William O'Neill, *A Better World: Stalinism and the American Intellectuals* (1983); Michael Oshinsky, *A Conspiracy So Immense: The World of Joe McCarthy* (1983); Ronald Radosh and Joyce Radosh, *The Rosenberg File* (1983); Thomas Reeves, *The Life and Times of Joe McCarthy* (1982); Richard Rovere, *Senator Joe McCarthy* (1959); Ellen Shrecker, *No Ivory Tower: McCarthyism and the Universities* (1984) and *Many Are the Crimes: McCarthyism in America* (1998); Athan Theoharis, *Seeds of Repression: Harry S Truman and the Origins of McCarthyism* (1971); Allen Weinstein, *Perjury: The Hiss-Chambers Case* (1978); Robert Williams, *Klaus Fuchs: Atom Spy* (1987).

The Truman Administration   Jack Ballard, *The Shock of Peace: Military and Economic Demobilization after World War II* (1983); James Chace, *Acheson* (1998); Clark Clifford with Richard Holbrooke, *Counsel to the President, A Memoir* (1991); Richard Dalfiume, *Desegregation of the U.S. Armed Forces* (1969); Robert Ferrell, *Harry S Truman and the Modern American Presidency* (1983); Donald Fixico, *Termination and Relocation: Federal Indian Policy, 1945–1960* (1986); David Goldfield, *Black, White, and Southern: Race Relations and Southern Culture* (1990); Allen Matusow, *Farm Politics and Policies in the Truman Years* (1967); Donald McCoy, *The Presidency of Harry S Truman* (1984); Donald McCoy and Richard Ruetten, *Quest and Response: Minority Rights and the Truman Administration* (1973); Merle Miller, *Plain Speaking* (1973); Richard Miller, *Truman: The Rise to Power* (1986); Allen Yarnell, *Democrats and Progressives: The 1948 Presidential Election as a Test of Postwar Liberalism* (1974).

Chapter 28: The Suburban Era

General Histories   Alan Brinkley, *Liberalism and Its Discontents* (1998); Paul Carter, *Another Part of the Fifties* (1983); John Diggins, *The Proud Decades: America in War and Peace, 1941–1960* (1988); James Gilbert, *A Cycle of Outrage* (1986); Godfrey Hodgson, *America in Our Time* (1976); Martin Jezer, *The Dark Ages: Life in the United States, 1945–1960* (1982); William Leuchten-berg, *A Troubled Feast* (1979); Douglas Miller and Marion Nowak, *The Fifties: The Way We Really Were* (1977); Ronald Oakley, *God's Country: America in the 1950s* (1986); Jon R. Stone, *On the Boundaries of American Evangelicalism* (1997); Steven Watts, *The Magic Kingdom: Walt Disney and the American Way of Life* (1997); Stephen Whitfield, *The Culture of the Cold War* (1991).

American Life and Culture   Erik Barnouw, *Tube of Plenty: The Evolution of American Television* (1975); James L. Baughman, *The Republic of Mass Culture: Journalism, Filmmaking, and Broadcasting in America since 1941* (1992); Daniel Bell, *The End of Ideology* (1960); Carl Belz, *The Story of Rock* (1972); Wini Breines, *Young, White, and Miserable: Growing Up Female in the Fifties* (1992); Victoria Byerly, *Hard Times Cotton Mill Girls* (1986); Stephanie Coontz, *The Way We Never Were: American Families and the Nostalgia Trap* (1992); John D'Emilio and Estelle Freedman, *Intimate Matters: A History of Sexuality in America* (1988); Colin Escott, *Good Rockin' Tonight: Sun Records and the Birth of Rock and Roll* (1991); Betty Friedan, *The Feminine Mystique* (1963); Neil Gabler, *Winchell: Gossip, Power, and the Culture of Celebrity* (1994); John Kenneth Galbraith, *The Affluent Society* (1958); Herbert Gans, *The Levittowners* (1967); Carol George, *God's Salesman: Norman Vincent Peale and the Power of Positive Thinking* (1994); Serge Gilbaut, *How New York Stole the Idea of Modern Art* (1983); Charlie Gillett, *The Sound of the City: The Rise of Rock and Roll* (1970); William Graebner, *Coming of Age in Buffalo: Youth and Authority in the Postwar Era* (1990); Will Herberg, *Protestant-Catholic-Jew* (1956); Thomas Hine, *Populux* (1986); Kenneth Jackson, *Crabgrass Frontier: The Suburbanization of the United States* (1985); James H. Jones, *Alfred Kinsey: A Public/Private Life* (1997); Wendy Kozol, *Life's America: Family and Nation in Postwar Photojournalism* (1994); William Martin, *A Prophet with Honor: The Billy Graham Story* (1991); C. Wright Mills, *The Power Elite* (1956) and *White Collar* (1951); George Nash, *The Conservative Intellectual Movement in America* (1976); David Potter, *People of Plenty* (1956); David Riesman, *The Lonely Crowd* (1950); Lynn Spiegel, *Make Room for TV: Television and the Family Ideal in Postwar America* (1992); Gaye Tuchman et al., eds., *Hearth and Home: Images of Women in the Mass Media* (1978); Brian Ward, *Just My Soul Responding: Rhythm and Blues, Black Consciousness, and Race Relations* (1998); Ed Ward et al., *Rock of Ages: The Rolling Stone History of Rock and Roll* (1986); Carol Warren, *Madwives: Schizophrenic Women in the 1950s* (1987); William Whyte, *The Organization Man* (1956).

Foreign Policy in the Eisenhower-Kennedy Era   Graham Allison, *Essence of Decision: Explaining the Cuban Missile Crisis* (1971); Stephen Ambrose, *Ike's Spies: Eisenhower and the Espionage Establishment* (1981); Michael Beschloss, *The Crisis Years, Kennedy and Khrushchev, 1960–1963* (1991); Blanche Weisen Cook, *The Declassified Eisenhower* (1981); Campbell Craig, *Destroying the Village: Eisenhower and Thermonuclear War* (1998); Robert Divine, *Eisenhower and the Cold War* (1981) and *Blowin' in the Wind: The Nuclear Test Ban Debate, 1954–1960* (1978); Aleksandr Fursenko and Timothy Naftali, *"One Hell of a Gamble:" Khrushchev, Castro, and Kennedy, 1958–1964* (1997); Trumbell Higgins, *Perfect Failure: Kennedy, Eisenhower, and the Bay of Pigs* (1987); Elizabeth Hoffman, *All You Need Is Love: The Peace Corps and the Spirit of the 1960s* (1998); Townsend Hoopes, *The Devil and John Foster Dulles* (1973); Richard Immerman, *The CIA in Guatemala* (1982); Madeline Kalb, *The Congo Cables: The Cold War in Africa from Eisenhower to Kennedy* (1982); Frederick Marks III, *Power and Peace: The Diplomacy of John Foster Dulles* (1993); Ernest May and

Philip Zelikow, *The Kennedy Tapes: Inside the White House during the Cuban Missile Crisis* (1997); Richard Melanson and David Mayers, eds., *Reevaluating Eisenhower: American Foreign Policy in the 1950s* (1987); Thomas Paterson, *Contesting Castro: The United States and the Triumph of the Cuban Revolution* (1994); Brenda Gayle Plummer, *Rising Wind: Black Americans and U.S. Foreign Policy, 1935–1960* (1996); Richard Rhodes, *Dark Sun: The Making of the Hydrogen Bomb* (1995); Gerald Rice, *The Bold Experiment: JFK's Peace Corps* (1985); R. B. Smith, *An International History of the Vietnam War: The Kennedy Strategy* (1985); Evan Thomas, *The Very Best Men—Four Who Dared: The Early Years of the CIA* (1995); Richard Welch Jr., *Response to Revolution: The United States and the Cuban Revolution, 1954–1961* (1985).

Domestic Politics   Stephen Ambrose, *Eisenhower the President* (1984); Piers Brendon, *Ike* (1986); Jeff Broadwater, *Eisenhower and the Anti-Communist Crusade* (1992); David Burner and Thomas West, *The Torch Is Passed: The Kennedy Brothers and American Liberalism* (1984); Larry Burt, *Tribalism in Crisis: Federal Indian Policy, 1953–1961* (1982); Barbara Clowse, *Brainpower for the Cold War: The Sputnik Crisis and the National Defense Education Act of 1958* (1981); Donald Fixico, *Termination and Relocation: Federal Indian Policy, 1945–1960* (1986); John Giglio, *The Presidency of John F. Kennedy* (1991); Fred Greenstein, *The Hidden Hand Presidency: Eisenhower as Leader* (1982); Seymour Hersh, *The Dark Side of Camelot* (1997); Chester Pach, *The Presidency of Dwight D. Eisenhower* (1991); Thomas Reeves, *A Question of Character: A Life of John F. Kennedy* (1992); Mark Rose, *Interstate Express Highway Politics, 1939–1989* (1991); Arthur Schlesinger Jr., *The Thousand Days* (1965) and *Robert Kennedy and His Times* (1978); Mary Ann Watson, *The Expanding Vista, American Television in the Kennedy Years* (1990); Theodore White, *The Making of the President, 1960* (1961); Gary Wills, *Nixon Agonistes* (1970).

Chapter 29: Civil Rights and the Crisis of Liberalism

General Histories   John M. Blum, *Years of Discord: American Politics and Society, 1961–1974* (1991); David Faber, *The Age of Great Dreams: America in the 1960s* (1994), and as ed., *The Sixties: From Memory to History* (1994); Richard Goodwin, *Remembering America: A Voice from the Sixties* (1988); Godfrey Hodgson, *America in Our Time* (1976); Maurice Isserman and Michael Kazin, *America Divided: The Civil War of the 1960s* (1999); Edward P. Morgan, *The 60s Experience: Hard Lessons about Modern America* (1991); David Steigenwald, *The Sixties and the End of the Modern Era* (1995); Lawrence Wright, *The New World: Growing Up in America, 1960–1984* (1988).

The Civil Rights Revolution   Michael Belknap, *Federal Law and Southern Order: Racial Violence and Constitutional Conflict in the Post-Brown South* (1987); Derrick Bell, *And We Are Not Saved: The Elusive Quest for Racial Justice* (1987); Jack Bloom, *Class, Race, and the Civil Rights Movement* (1987); Taylor Branch, *Parting the Waters: America in the King Years, 1954–1963* (1988) and *Pillar of Fire: America in the King Years, 1963–65* (1998); Eric Burner, *And Gently He Shall Lead Them: Robert Parris Moses and Civil Rights in Mississippi* (1994); Stokely Carmichael and Charles Hamilton, *Black Power* (1967); Clayborne Carson, *In Struggle: SNCC and the Black Awakening of the 1960s* (1981); Dan T. Carter, *The Politics of Rage: George Wallace and the New Con-servatism* (1995); William Chafe, *Civilities and Civil Rights* (1980); Claude Clegg III, *An Original Man: The Life and Times of Elijah Muhammad* (1997); John Dittmar, *Local People: The Struggle for Civil Rights in Mississippi* (1994); James Duram, *Moderate among Extremists: Dwight D. Eisenhower and the School Desegregation Crisis* (1981); Michael Eric Dyson, *Making Malcolm: The Myth and Meaning of Malcolm X* (1995); Seth Forman, *Blacks in the Jewish Mind* (1998); David Garrow, *The FBI and Martin Luther King* (1981) and *Bearing the Cross* (1986); Henry Louis Gates Jr., *Colored People: A Memoir* (1994); Hugh Davis Graham, *Civil Rights and the Presidency: Race and Gender in American Politics, 1960–1972* (1992); David Halberstam, *The Children* (1988); Vincent Harding, *There Is a River: The Black Struggle for Freedom in America* (1981); Elizabeth Huckaby, *The Crisis at Central High: Little Rock, 1957–1958* (1980); Otto Kerner et al., *The Report of the National Advisory Commission on Civil Disorders* (1968); Richard Kluger, *Simple Justice: The History of Brown v. Board of Education and Black America's Struggle for Equality* (1975); Anthony Lewis et al., *Portrait of a Decade* (1964); Doug McAdam, *Freedom Summer* (1988); Malcolm X (with Alex Haley), *The Autobiography of Malcolm X* (1966); August Meier and Elliott Rudwick, *CORE: A Study in the Civil Rights Movement, 1942–1968* (1975); Adam Nossiter, *Of Long Memory: Mississippi and the Murder of Medgar Evers* (1994); Stephen Oates, *Let the Trumpet Sound: The Life and Times of Martin Luther King, Jr.* (1982); Bruce Perry, *Malcolm* (1992); Bernard Schwartz, *Inside the Warren Court* (1983); Harvard Sitkoff, *The Struggle for Black Equality, 1954–1992* (1993); Mark Stern, *Calculating Visions: Kennedy, Johnson, and Civil Rights* (1992); Harris Wofford, *Of Kennedy and Kings* (1980); Juan Williams, *Eyes on the Prize: America's Civil Rights Years, 1954–1965* (1987); Eugene Wolfenstein, *The Victims of Democracy: Malcolm X and the Black Revolutionaries* (1981); Miles Wolff, *Lunch at the 5 & 10* (1990); C. Vann Woodward, *The Strange Career of Jim Crow* (1974).

The Counterculture and New Left   John Andrew III, *The Other Side of the Sixties: Young Americans for Freedom and the Rise of Conservative Politics* (1997); Howard Brick, *Age of Contradiction: American Thought and Culture in the 1960s* (1998); Serge Denisoff, *Great Day Coming: Folk Music and the American Left* (1971); Morris Dickstein, *The Gates of Eden* (1976); Robert S. Ellwood, *The Sixties Spiritual Awakening* (1994); James Farrell, *The Spirit of the Sixties: The Making of Postwar Radicalism* (1997); Thomas Frank, *The Conquest of the Cool: Business Culture, Counterculture, and the Rise of Hip Consumerism* (1997); Todd Gitlin, *The Whole World Is Watching: The Mass Media in the Making and Unmaking of the New Left* (1981); Richard Goldstein, *Reporting the Counterculture* (1989); Paul Goodman, *Growing Up Absurd* (1960); Emmett Grogan, *Ringolevio* (1972); Maurice Isserman, *If I Had a Hammer . . . : The Death of the Old Left and the Birth of the New Left* (1987); Judy Kaplan and Linn Shapiro, *Red Diaper Babies: Children on the Left* (1985); Martin Lee and Bruce Shlain, *Acid Dreams: The CIA, LSD, and the Sixties Rebellion* (1985); Christine Mamiya, *Pop Art and the Consumer Culture: American Super Market* (1992); Timothy Miller, *The Hippies and American Values* (1991); W. J. Rorabaugh, *Berkeley at War: The 1960s* (1989); Doug Rossinow, *The Politics of Authenticity: Liberalism, Christianity, and the New Left in America* (1998); Theodore Roszak, *The Making of a Counter Culture* (1969); Kirkpatrick Sale, *SDS* (1973); Mark Spitz, *Dylan: A Biography* (1989); Students for a Democratic Society, *The Port Huron Statement* (1962); Hunter Thompson, *Hell's Angels* (1967) and *Fear and Loathing in Las Vegas* (1971); Ed Ward et al., *Rock* of Ages: The Rolling Stone History of Rock and Roll (1986); Tom Wolfe, Electric Kool-Aid Acid Test (1968).

Politics and Foreign Policy in the Great Society   James Anderson and Jared Hazelton, Managing Macroeconomic Policy: The Johnson Presidency (1986); Michael Beschloss, ed., Taking Charge: The Johnson White House Tapes, 1963–1964 (1997); H. W. Brands, The Wages of Globalism: Lyndon Johnson and the Limits of American Power (1994); Warren Cohen, Dean Rusk (1980); Robert Dallek, Flawed Giant (1998); Hugh Graham Davis, Uncertain Trumpet (1984); Greg Duncan, Years of Poverty, Years of Plenty (1984); Morton Horowitz, The Warren Court and the Pursuit of Justice (1998); Diane Kunz, ed., The Diplomacy of the Crucial Decade: American Foreign Policy in the 1960s (1995); Richard Mahoney, JFK: Ordeal in Africa (1983); Alan Matusow, The Unraveling of America: A History of Liberalism in the 1960s (1984); Walter McDougall, . . . The Heavens and the Earth: A Political History of the Space Age (1985); Charles Murray, Losing Ground: American Social Policy, 1950–1980 (1984); Thomas Noer, Cold War and Black Liberation: The United States and White Rule in Africa, 1948–1968 (1985); Earl Warren et al., The Report of the Warren Commission (1964); Bryce Wood, The Dismantling of the Good Neighbor Policy (1985).

Chapter 30: The Vietnam Era

The United States and the Vietnam War   Christian Appy, Working Class War: American Combat Soldiers and Vietnam (1993); Loren Baritz, Backfire: A History of How American Culture Led Us into Vietnam and Made Us Fight the Way We Did (1985); Larry Berman, Planning a Tragedy (1982), Larry Cable, Conflict of Myths: The Development of American Counterinsurgency Doctrine and the Vietnam War (1986); Mark Clodfelter, The Limits of Airpower (1989); Francis Fitzgerald, Fire in the Lake (1972); Lloyd Gardner, Pay Any Price: Lyndon Johnson and the War for Vietnam (1995); Leslie Gelb and Richard Betts, The Irony of Vietnam: The System Worked (1979); Mike Gravel et al., The Pentagon Papers (1975); David Halberstam, The Best and the Brightest (1972) and The Making of Quagmire (1987); Le Ly Hayslip, When Heaven and Earth Changed Places (1989); Le Ly Hayslip and James Hayslip, Child of War, Woman of Peace (1993); George Herring, LBJ and Vietnam (1994); George Kahin, Intervention (1986); Stanley Karnow, Vietnam (1983); Gabriel Kolko, Anatomy of a War (1985); Andrew Krepinevich Jr., The Army and Vietnam (1986); David Levy, The Debate Over Vietnam (1991); Kathryn Marshall, In the Combat Zone: An Oral History of Women in the Vietnam War, 1966–1975 (1987); H. R. McMaster, Dereliction of Duty: Lyndon Johnson, Robert McNamara, the Joint Chiefs of Staff, and the Lies That Led to Vietnam (1997); Harold G. Moore and Joseph Galloway, We Were Soldiers Once . . . and Young (1992); Tim Page, Nam (1983); Bruce Palmer Jr., The 25-Year War (1984); Archimedes Patti, Why Viet Nam? (1983); Norman Podhoretz, Why We Were in Vietnam (1982); Al Santoli, Everything We Had: An Oral History of the Vietnam War by Thirty-Three American Soldiers Who Fought It (1981); Neil Sheehan, A Bright Shining Lie: John Paul Vann and America in Vietnam (1988); Ronald Spector, The United States Army in Vietnam (1983) and After Tet: The Bloodiest Year in Vietnam (1993); Harry Summers Jr., On Strategy: A Critical Analysis of the Vietnam War (1981); Wallace Terry, Bloods: An Oral History of the Vietnam War by Black Veterans (1984); William Turley, The Second Indochina War: A Short Political and Military History (1986); James Westheider, Fighting on

Two Fronts: African Amerians and the Vietnam War (1997); Jim Wilson, The Sons of Bardstown (1994).

Dissent against the War   William Berman, William Fulbright and the Vietnam War (1988); David Caute, The Year of the Barricades, 1968 (1988); Charles DeBenedetti and Charles Chatfield, An American Ordeal: The Antiwar Movement and the Vietnam Era (1990); David Farber, Chicago '68 (1988); Myra MacPherson, Long Time Passing: Vietnam and the Haunted Generation (1984); Norman Mailer, Armies of the Night (1968) and Miami and the Siege of Chicago (1969); Kim McQuaid, The Anxious Years (1989); James Miller, Democracy Is in the Streets (1987); Melvin Small, Covering Dissent: The Media and the Anti–Vietnam War Movement (1994); William Strauss, Chance and Circumstance (1978); Amy Swerdlow, The Women's Strike for Peace: Traditional Motherhood and Radical Politics in the 1960s (1993); Lawrence Wittner, Rebels against War: The American Peace Movement, 1933–1983 (1984); Nancy Zaroulis and Gerald Sullivan, Who Spoke Up? American Protest against the War in Vietnam (1984).

Identity Politics   Rodolfo Acuña, Occupied America (1981); Barry D. Adam, The Rise of a Gay and Lesbian Movement (1987); Rae Andre, Homemakers: The Forgotten Workers (1981); Mario Barerra, Race and Class in the Southwest (1979); Peter Berger and Brigitte Berger, The War over the Family: Capturing the Middle Ground (1983); Mary Frances Berry, Why ERA Failed: Politics, Women's Rights, and the Amending Process of the Constitution (1986) and The Politics of Parenthood: Childcare, Women's Rights, and Feminism (1993); Susan Brownmiller, Against Our Will: Men, Women, and Rape (1975); John Burma, ed., Mexican-Americans in the United States (1970); Albert Camarillo, Hispanics in a Changing Society (1979); Tony Castro, Chicano Power (1974); Robert Coles and Geoffrey Stokes, Sex and the American Teenager (1985); Angela Davis, Women, Race, and Class (1981); Vine Deloria, Behind the Veil of Broken Treaties (1974); John D'Emilio, Sexual Politics, Sexual Communities: The Making of a Homosexual Minority in the United States, 1940–1970 (1983); Susan Douglas, Where the Girls Are: Growing Up Female with the Mass Media (1994); Martin Duberman, Stonewall (1993); Andrea Dworkin, Right-Wing Women (1983); Barbara Ehrenreich, The Hearts of Men: American Dreams and the Flight from Commitment (1983); Amy Erdman, Yours in Sisterhood: Ms. Magazine and the Promise of Popular Feminism (1998); Susan Esterbrook, If All We Did Was to Weep at Home: A History of White Working-Class Women in America (1979); Shulamith Firestone, The Dialectic of Sex: The Case for the Feminist Revolution (1970); Jo Freeman, The Politics of Women's Liberation (1975); Patrick Gallagher, The Cuban Exile (1980); David Garrow, Liberty and Sexuality: The Right and Privacy in the Making of Roe v. Wade (1994); Carol Gilligan, In Another Voice: Psychological Theory and Women's Development (1982); Germaine Greer, The Female Eunuch (1972); Alice Kessler Harris, Out to Work (1982); Hazel W. Hertzberg, The Search for an American Indian Identity: Modern Pan-Indian Movements (1971); Gloria Hull et al., But Some of Us Are Brave: Black Women's Studies (1982); Peter Iverson, The Navajo Nation (1981); Christopher Lasch, Haven in a Hostile World (1979); Kristen Luker, Abortion and the Politics of Motherhood (1984); Norma McCorvey, I Am Roe: My Life, Roe v. Wade, and Freedom of Choice (1994); Darcy Mc-Nickle, Native American Tribalism (1973); Kate Millett, Sexual Politics (1970); Steven Mintz and Susan Kellogg, Domestic Revolutions: A Social History of American Family Life (1988); Joan Moore and Harry Pachon, The Hispanics in the United States

(1985); Joan Moore et al., *Homeboys* (1978); Robin Morgan, ed., *Sisterhood Is Powerful: An Anthology* (1970); Maureen Muldoon, *Abortion Debate in the United States and Canada: A Source Book* (1991); Roger Nichols, *The American Indian: Past and Present* (1986); James Olsen and Raymond Wilson, *Native Americans in the Twentieth Century* (1984); Hugh Pearson, *The Shadow of the Panther: Huey Newton and the Price of Black Power in America* (1994); A. Petit, *Images of the Mexican-American in Fiction and Film* (1980); La Frances Rodgers-Rose, ed., *The Black Woman* (1980); John William Sayer, *Ghost Dancing the Law: The Wounded Knee Trials* (1997); Gloria Steinem, *Outrageous Acts and Everyday Rebellions* (1983); Roger Streitmatter, *Unspeakable: The Rise of the Gay and Lesbian Press in America* (1995); Ronald Taylor, *Chavez and the Farm Workers* (1975); Arnulfo Trejo, ed., *The Chicanos: As We See Ourselves* (1979); Karl Wagenheim, *Puerto Rico: A Profile* (1975).

Chapter 31: The Age of Limits

Environmentalism   Edward Abbey, *The Monkey Wrench Gang* (1975); Rachel Carson, *Silent Spring* (1962); Barry Caspar and Paul Wellstone, *Powerline* (1981); Barry Commoner, *The Closing Circle* (1971); Albert Cowdry, *This Land, This South: An Environmental History* (1983); Irene Diamond and Gloria Feman Orenstein, *Reweaving the World: The Emergence of Ecofeminism* (1990); Thomas Dunlap, *DDT: Scientists, Citizens, and Public Policy* (1981); Robert Booth Fowler, *The Greening of Protestant Thought* (1995); Robert Gottlieb, *Forcing the Spring: The Transformation of the American Environmental Movement* (1993); Linda Lear, *Rachel Carson: Witness for Nature* (1997); Daniel Martin, *Three Mile Island* (1980); Robert N. Mayer, *The Consumer Movement* (1989); Ian McHarg, *Design with Nature* (1969); Lester Milbrath, *Environmentalists: Vanguard for a New Society* (1984); Roderick Nash, *The Rights of Nature* (1989); Marc Reisner, *Cadillac Desert: The American West and Its Disappearing Water* (1986); Charles Rubin, *The Green Crusade: Rethinking the Roots of Environmentalism* (1994); Kirkpatrick Sale, *The Green Revolution: The American Environmental Movement, 1962–1993* (1993); Philip Shabecoff, *A Fierce Green Fire: The American Environmental Movement* (1993); Andrew Szasz, *EcoPopulism: Toxic Waste and the Movement for Environmental Justice* (1994); James Trefethen, *An American Crusade for Wildlife* (1975); Donald Worster, *Rivers of Empire: Water, Aridity, and the Growth of the American West* (1985).

American Society and the Economy in the 1970s   Barry Bluestone and Bennett Harrison, *The Deindustrialization of America* (1982); Paul Boyer, *When Time Shall Be No More: Prophecy Belief in Modern American Culture* (1992); Peter Calleo, *The Imperious Economy* (1982); Barry Commoner, *The Politics of Energy* (1979); Ronald Formisano, *Boston against Busing: Race, Class, and Ethnicity in the 1960s and 1970s* (1991); Christopher Lasch, *The Culture of Narcissism* (1978); Michael Lienesch, *Redeeming America: Piety and Politics in the New Christian Right* (1993); J. Anthony Lukas, *Common Ground: A Turbulent Decade in the Lives of Three American Families* (1986); George Marsden, *Fundamentalism and Evangelicalism* (1991); Martin Melosi, *Coping with Abundance: Energy and Environment in Industrial America* (1985); Timothy O'Neill, *Bakke and the Politics of Equality* (1985); Daniel Yergin, *The Prize* (1991).

Richard Nixon and Watergate   Stephen Ambrose, *Nixon, The Triumph of a Politician, 1962–1972* (1989) and *Nixon: Ruin and*

Recovery, 1973–1990 (1991); John Dean, *Blind Ambition* (1976); John Erlichmann, *Witness to Power* (1982); H. R. Haldeman, *The Haldeman Diaries: Inside the Nixon White House* (1994); Seymour Hersh, *The Price of Power: Kissinger in the Nixon White House* (1983); Stanley Kutler, *The Wars of Watergate* (1990) and *Abuse of Power* (1997); J. Anthony Lukas, *Nightmare: The Underside of the Nixon Years* (1988); Richard Nixon, *RN* (1978); John Sirica, *To Set the Record Straight* (1979); Theodore White, *Breach of Faith* (1975); Tom Wicker, *One of Us: Richard Nixon and the American Dream* (1991); Bob Woodward and Carl Bernstein, *All the President's Men* (1974) and *The Final Days* (1976).

Politics and Diplomacy in the Age of Limits   James Bill, *The Eagle and the Lion: The Tragedy of American-Iranian Relations* (1987); Zbigniew Brzezinski, *Power and Principle* (1983); William Bundy, *A Tangled Web: The Making of Foreign Policy in the Nixon Presidency* (1998); James Cannon, *Time and Chance: Gerald Ford's Appointment with History, 1913–1974* (1993); Peter Carroll, *It Seemed Like Nothing Happened* (1982); Jimmy Carter, *Keeping the Faith* (1982); Rosalynn Carter, *First Lady from Plains* (1984); John Dumbull, *The Carter Presidency: A Reevaluation* (1993); Gary Fink and Hugh Graham Davis, eds., *The Carter Presidency* (1998); Gerald Ford, *A Time to Heal* (1979); Raymond Garthoff, *Détente and Confrontation: American-Soviet Relations from Nixon to Reagan* (1985); Millicent Gates and Bruce Geelhoed, *The Dragon and the Snake: An American Account of the Turmoil in China, 1976–1977* (1986); Michael Hogan, *The Panama Canal in American Politics* (1986); Walter Isaacson, *Kissinger* (1992); Henry Jackson, *From the Congo to Soweto: U.S. Foreign Policy toward Africa since 1960* (1982); Burton Kaufman, *The Presidency of James Earl Carter Jr.* (1993); Henry Kissinger, *The White House Years* (1979) and *Years of Upheaval* (1982); Walter LaFeber, *The Panama Canal*, rev. ed. (1989); Robert Litwack, *Détente and the Nixon Doctrine* (1984); Alan Matusow, *Nixon's Economy: Booms, Busts, Dollars, and Votes* (1998); Morris Morley, *The United States and Chile* (1975); Richard Pipes, *U.S.-Soviet Relations in the Era of Détente* (1981); William Quandt, *Camp David* (1986); A. James Reichley, *Conservatives in an Age of Change: The Nixon and Ford Administrations* (1981); Robert Schulzinger, *Henry Kissinger: Doctor of Diplomacy* (1989); William Shawcross, *Sideshow: Nixon, Kissinger, and the Destruction of Cambodia* (1978); Gary Sick, *All Fall Down* (1985); Gaddis Smith, *Morality, Reason, and Power* (1986); Robert Sutter, *The China Quandary* (1983); Seth Tillman, *The U.S. in the Middle East* (1982); Cyrus Vance, *Hard Choices* (1983); Theodore White, *The Making of the President, 1968* (1969).

Chapter 32: The Conservative Challenge

American Society   Bruce Bawer, *A Place at the Table: The Gay Individual and American Society* (1994); Robert Bellah et al., *Habits of the Heart: Individualism and Commitment in American Life* (1985) and *The Good Society* (1991); Dallas Blanchard, *The Anti-Abortion Movement* (1994); Stephen Carter, *The Culture of Disbelief: How American Law and Politics Trivialize Religious Devotion* (1993); William Dietrich, *In the Shadow of the Rising Sun: The Political Roots of American Economic Decline* (1991); Thomas Byrne Edsall, *The New Politics of Inequality* (1984); Barbara Ehrenreich, *Fear of Falling: The Inner Life of the Middle Class* (1989) and *The Worst Years of Our Lives* (1990); Susan Faludi, *Backlash: The Undeclared War against American Women* (1991);

Elizabeth Fee and Daniel Fox, eds., *AIDS: The Burdens of History* (1992); Henry Louis Gates Jr., *Loose Canons: Notes on the Culture Wars* (1993); Michael Goldfield, *The Decline of Organized Labor in the United States* (1987); Otis Graham Jr., *Losing Time: The Industrial Policy Debate* (1992); Michael Harrington, *The New American Poverty* (1984); Richard Herrnstein and Charles Murray, *The Bell Curve: Intelligence and Class Structure in American Life* (1994); Godfrey Hodgson, *The World Turned Right Side Up: A History of the Conservative Ascendancy in America* (1996); Robert Hughes, *Culture of Complaint: The Fraying of America* (1993); Paul Krugman, *Peddling Prosperity: Economic Sense and Nonsense in the Age of Diminished Expectations* (1994); Frank Levy, *Dollars and Dreams: The Changing American Income Distribution* (1987); Steve Levy, *Insanely Great: The Life and Times of Macintosh, the Computer That Changed Everything* (1994); Jane Maysbridge, *Why We Lost the ERA* (1986); Ruth Milkman, *Farewell to the Factory: Autoworkers in Late Twentieth Century America* (1997); Joseph Nocera, *A Piece of the Action: How the Middle Class Joined the Money Class* (1994); Juliet Schor, *The Overworked American: The Unexpected Decline of Leisure* (1991); Studs Terkel, *The Great Divide* (1988); Thomas Toch, *In the Name of Excellence: The Struggle to Reform the Nation's Schools* (1991).

Conservative Politics   Ken Auletta, *The Underclass* (1982); Earl Black and Merle Black, *The Vital South: How Presidents Are Elected* (1992); Sidney Blumenthal, *The Rise of the Counter-Establishment from Conservative Ideology to Political Power* (1988); Sidney Blumenthal and Thomas Byrne Edsall, eds., *The Reagan Legacy* (1988); Paul Boyer, ed., *Reagan as President: Contemporary Views of the Man, His Politics, and His Policies* (1990); William Brennan, *America's Right Turn from Nixon to Bush* (1994); Barbara Bush, *Barbara Bush: A Memoir* (1994); Michael Deaver, *Behind the Scenes* (1987); Theodore Draper, *A Very Thin Line: The Iran-Contra Affairs* (1991); Ken Gross, *Ross Perot: The Man behind the Myth* (1992); David Hoeveler Jr., *Watch on the Right: Conservative Intellectuals in the Reagan Era* (1991); Peter Irons, *Brennan vs. Rehnquist: The Battle for the Constitution* (1994); Jonathan Kwitny, *The Crimes of Patriots: A True Tale of Dope, Dirty Money, and the CIA* (1987); Jonathan Lash, *A Season of Spoils: The Story of the Reagan Administration's Attack on the Environment* (1984); Theodore Lowi, *The End of the Republican Era* (1995); Kevin Phillips, *The Politics of Rich and Poor: Wealth and the American Electorate in the Reagan Aftermath* (1990) and *Boiling Point: Republicans, Democrats, and the Decline of Middle Class Prosperity* (1993); John Podhoretz, *Hell of a Ride: Backstage at the White House Follies, 1989–1993* (1993); Dan Quayle, *Standing Firm: A Vice-Presidential Memoir* (1994); Donald Regan, *For the Record* (1988); Tom Rosenstiel, *Strange Bedfellows: How Television and the Presidential Candidates Changed American Politics, 1992* (1993); Randy Shilts, *And the Band Played On: Politics, People, and the AIDS Epidemic* (1987); David Stockman, *The Triumph of Politics: The Inside Story of the Reagan Revolution* (1986); Stephen Vaugh, *Ronald Reagan in Hollywood: Movies and Politics* (1994); Gary Wills, *Reagan's America* (1987); Daniel Wirls, *The Politics of Defense in the Reagan Era* (1992).

Foreign Policy into the 1990s   Michael Beschloss and Strobe Talbott, *At the Highest Levels: The Inside Story of the End of the Cold War* (1993); Raymond Bonner, *Weakness and Deceit: U.S. Policy and El Salvador* (1984); William Broad, *Teller's War: The Top Secret Story behind the Star Wars Deception* (1992); Bradford Burns, *At War with Nicaragua* (1987); Leslie Cockburn, *Out of Control* (1987); Christopher Coker, *The United States and South Africa, 1968–1985* (1986); Thomas Friedman, *From Beirut to Jerusalem* (1989); John Lewis Gaddis, *The United States and the End of the Cold War* (1992); Roy Gutman, *Banana Diplomacy* (1988); Alexander Haig Jr., *Caveat: Realism, Reagan, and Foreign Policy* (1984); Delip Hiro, *Desert Shield to Desert Storm* (1992); Bruce Jentleson, *Pipeline Politics: The Complex Political Economy of East-West Trade* (1986); Robert Kaplan, *Balkan Ghosts* (1993); Walter LaFeber, *Inevitable Revolutions* (1993); William LeoGrande, *Our Own Backyard: The United States in Central America, 1977–1992* (1998); John Mueller, *Policy and Opinion in the Gulf War* (1994); Robert Pastor, *Condemned to Repetition: The United States and Nicaragua* (1987); Jonathan Schell, *The Fate of the Earth* (1982); David Schoenbaum, *The United States and the State of Israel* (1993); Strobe Talbott, *Deadly Gambits: The Reagan Administration and the Stalemate in Nuclear Arms Control* (1984); Sanford Ungar, *Africa* (1985); William Vogele, *Stepping Back: Nuclear Arms Control and the End of the Cold War* (1994); Thomas Walker, ed., *Reagan versus the Sandinistas* (1987); Bob Woodward, *Veil: The Secret Wars of the CIA* (1987).

Minorities and American Culture   Roger Daniels et al., eds., *Japanese-Americans: From Relocation to Redress* (1986); Reynolds Farley and Walter Allen, *The Color Line and the Quality of Life in America* (1987); Lawrence Fuchs, *The American Kaleidoscope: Race, Ethnicity, and the Civic Culture* (1990); Douglas Glasgow, *The Black Underclass* (1980); Andrew Hacker, *Two Nations: Black and White, Separate, Hostile, Unequal* (1992); Denis Heyck, ed., *Barrios and Borderlands: Cultures of Latinos and Latinas in the United States* (1993); Bill Ong Hing, *Making and Remaking Asian America through Immigration Policy, 1850–1990* (1993); Christopher Jencks, *The Homeless* (1994); Jonathan Kozol, *Savage Inequalities: Children in America's Schools* (1991); Joan Moore and Harry Pachon, *Hispanics in the United States* (1985); Adolph Reed, *The Jesse Jackson Phenomenon: The Crisis of Purpose in Afro-American Politics* (1986); Sam Roberts, *Who Are We? A Portrait of America Based on the Latest U.S. Census* (1994); Arthur Schlesinger Jr., *The Disuniting of America* (1991); Peter Skerry, *Mexican-Americans: The Ambivalent Minority* (1993); Robert C. Smith, *Racism in the Post–Civil Rights Era: Now You See It, Now You Don't* (1995); The Staff of the Chicago Tribune, *The American Millstone: An Examination of the Nation's Permanent Underclass* (1986); Shih-Shan Henry Tsai, *The Chinese Experience in America* (1986); William Wei, *The Asian American Movement* (1993).

Chapter 33: Nation of Nations in a Global Community

Domestic Politics in the Clinton Era   Charles Allen, *The Comeback Kid: The Life and Times of Bill Clinton* (1992); Elizabeth Drew, *Whatever It Takes: The Struggle for Political Power in America* (1997) and *The Corruption of American Politics: What Went Wrong and Why* (1999); Theodore Lowi, *The End of the Republican Era* (1995); David Maraness, *First in His Class: The Biography of Bill Clinton* (1996) and *The Clinton Enigma* (1998); Mary Matlin and James Carville, *All's Fair in Love and Running for President* (1994); Joyce Milton, *The First Partner: Hillary Rodham Clinton* (1999); Roger Morris, *Partners in Power: The Clintons and their America* (1999); *The New Yorker*, "Special Politics Issue," October 21 & 28, 1996; Mark Rosell, ed., *The Clinton*

Scandel and the Future of American Government (2000); James Stewart, *Bloodsport: The President and His Adversaries* (1997); James Trabor and Eugene Gallagher, *Why Waco? Cults in the Battle for Religious Freedom* (1995); Bob Woodward, *The Agenda: Inside the Clinton White House* (1994) and *Shadow: Five Presidents and the Legacy of Watergate* (1999).

Foreign Policy in the 1990s   G. Pope Atkins and Lamar Wilson, *The Dominican Republic and the United States* (1998); Richard Barnet and John Cavanaugh, *Global Dreams: Imperial Corporations and the New World Disorder* (1996); Wayne Bert, *The Reluctant Superpower: The United States Policy in Bosnia* (1997); Steven Burg and Paul Shoup, *The War in Bosnia-Herzegovina* (1999); Michael Cox, *U.S. Foreign Policy after the Cold War* (1995); James Cronin, *The World the Cold War Made* (1996); Michael Dobbs, *Madeline Albright* (1999); H. Richard Frimen, *NarcoDiplomacy* (1996); David Fromkin, *Kosovo Crossing: American Ideals Meet Reality in the Balkan Battlefield* (1999); George W. Grayson, *The North American Free Trade Agreement* (1995); William Greider, *Fortress America* (1998); Avigdor Haselkorn, *The Continuing Storm: Iraq, Poisonous Weapons, and Deterrence* (1999); John Hirsch and Robert Oakley, *Somalia and Operation Restore Hope* (1995); Stanley Hoffman, *World Disorders* (1999); Robert Kaplan, *The Ends of the Earth: A Journey to the Frontiers of Anarchy* (1996); Walter LaFeber, *The Clash: U.S.-Japan Relations throughout History* (1997); Noel Malcolm, *Bosnia* (1994); John Martz, *United States Policy in Latin America* (1995); Julie Mertus, *Kosovo: How Myths and Truths Started a War* (1999); Ilan Pape, *The Israel/Palestine Question* (1999); Randall Ripley and James Lindsey, eds., *U.S. Foreign Policy after the Cold War* (1997); Stephen Schwartz, ed., *Atomic Audit* (1998); Ronald Steele, *Temptations of a Superpower* (1995); Lawrence Susskind, *Environmental Diplomacy* (1994); Robert Thomas, *The Politics of Serbia* (1999); Susan Woodward, *Balkan Tragedy* (1995).

The Global Economy and Environment in the 1990s   Janet Abbate, *Inventing the Internet* (1999); Paul Andrews, *How the Web Was Won* (1999); Sharon Beder, *Global Spin: The Corporate Assault on the Environment* (1998); Tim Berners-Lee, *Weaving the Web: The Original Design and Ultimate Destiny of the World Wide Web by the Inventor* (1999); Mark Bowie, *Losing Ground: American Environmentalism at the Close of the Twentieth Century* (1996); Charles Ferguson, *High Stakes and No Prisoners: A Winner's Tale of Greed and Glory in the Internet Wars* (1999); David Helvarg, *The War against the Greens: "The Wise-Use" Movement, the New Right, and Anti-Environmental Violence* (1997); Charles Johnson, *The Evolution of Wired Life: From the Alphabet to the Soul-Catcher Chip* (1999); Jason Olim et al., *The CDnow Story: Rags to Riches on the Internet* (1999); Robert Reid, *Architects of the Web: 1,000 Days That Built the Future of Business* (1997); Robert Solomon, *Money on the Move: The Revolution in International Finance since 1980* (1999); Kara Swisher, *aol.com: How Steve Case Beat Bill Gates, Nailed the Netheads, and Made Millions in the War for the Web* (1998); Brian Tokar, *Earth for Sale: Reclaiming Ecology in the Age of Corporate Greenwash* (1997); Art Wolinsky, *The History of the Internet and the World Wide Web* (1999).

Multicultural America   Lawrence Auster, *The Path to National Suicide: An Essay on Immigration and Multiculturalism* (1990); Frank Bean et al., *At the Crossroads: Mexico and U.S. Immigration Policy* (1998); Roy Beck, *The Case against Immigration* (1996); Richard Bernstein, *Multiculturalism and the Battle for America's Future* (1994); Peter Brimelow, *Alien Nation: Common Sense about America's Immigration Disaster* (1995); Ellis Cose, *A Nation of Strangers: Prejudice, Politics, and the Populating of America* (1992) and *The Rage of a Privileged Class: Why Are Middle-Class Blacks Angry?* (1994); Jose Cruz, *Identity and Power: Puerto Rican Politics and the Challenge of Ethnicity* (1998); Timothy Dunn, *The Militarization of the U.S.-Mexico Border* (1996); Susan Faludi, *Stiffed: The Betrayal of the American Man* (1999); Joshua Gamson, *Fresh Talk Back: Tabloid Talk Shows and Sexual Nonconformity* (1998); Garrett Hardin, *The Immigration Dilemma: Avoiding the Tragedy of the Commons* (1995); Richard Herrnstein and Charles Murray, *The Bell Curve: Intelligence and Class Structure in American Life* (1994); David Hollinger, *Postethnic America: Beyond Multiculturalism* (1995); Robert Lee, *Orientals: Asian Americans in Popular Culture* (1999); Maxine Margolis, *An Invisible Minority: Brazilians in New York City* (1998); Oscar Martinez, *Border People: Life and Society in the U.S.-Mexico Borderlands* (1994); Joel Millman, *The Other Americans: How Immigrants Renew Our Country, Our Economy, and Our Values* (1997); Juan Perea, eds., *Immigrants Out: The New Nativism and Anti-Immigration Impulse in the United States* (1997); Peter Slains, *Assimilation American Style* (1997); Alex Stepick, *Pride against Prejudice: Haitians in the United States* (1998); Michael S. Teitelbaum and Myron Wiener, eds., *Threatened Peoples, Threatened Borders* (1995); Sanford Ungar, *Fresh Blood: The New American Immigrants* (1995); Bernard Wong, *Ethnicity and Entrepreneurship: The New Chinese Immigrants in the San Francisco Bay Area* (1998); Jun Xing, *Asian Americans through the Lens* (1998).

Photo Credits

533 Winslow Homer, "A Visit from the Old Mistress," 1876. Oil on canvas, 18×24 1/8″. National Museum of American Art, Smithsonian Institution, Washington, DC, USA. Gift of William T. Evans. **535** Library of Congress **536** General Research Division, New York Public Library, Astor, Lenox and Tilden Foundations **537** Library of Congress **541** Library of Congress Theodor Kaufmann, "Portrait of Hiram Rhoades Revels," 1870. Oil on millboard, 12″ × 10″. Courtesy of the Herbert F. Johnson Museum of Art, Cornell University, Ithaca. NY. Transferred from the Olin, [69.170]. **544** Library of Congress **546** The New-York Historical Society **548** Corbis Images **553** Sophie Smith Collection, Smith College **554** The Granger Collection, New York **555** Rutherford B. Hayes Presidential Center **558** Library of Congress **561** By Permission of The British Library, London, [p.p. 5270] **562** Library of Congress **563** Erich Lessing/Art Resource, NY **566** Kansas State Historical Society, Topeka,KS ., [E185.1878*1] **567** Idaho State Historical Society, [349] **569** Thomas Anshutz, "Cabbages," 1879. Oil on canvas. 24 × 17″. The Metropolitan Museum of Art, Morris K. Jesup Fund, 1940. [40.40]. Photo © 2000 The Metropolitan Museum of Art, New York **571** National Archives at College Park [NWDNS–102-LH-462] **572** T.E. Armitstead Collection, University of South Alabama Archives **575** Courtesy of the Billy Graham Center Museum **576** LSU in Shreveport, Noel Memorial Library, Archives and Special Collections **580** Library of Congress **587** The Institute of Texan Cultures, San Antonio, Texas **592** Huntington Library/ SuperStock, Florida **593** Clara McDonald Williamson, "Old Chisholm Trail." The Roland P. Murdock Collection, Wichita Art Museum, [M124.54] **596** (top) The Kansas State Historical Society, Topeka, KS [ГK2.R6.75.B*2]; (bottom) The Kansas State Historical Society, Topeka, KS [FK2.R6.75.B*1] **597** University of Oregon Library **598** Copyright, Colorado State University Photographic Services **603** Library of Congress **604** (top) Karl Bodmer, "Hidatsa Buffalo Robe." Joslyn Art Museum, Omaha, Nebraska; Gift of the Enron Art Foundation; (bottom) Karl Bodmer, "Piegan Blackfeet Man." Joslyn Art Museum, Omaha, Nebraska; Gift of the Enron Art Foundation. **605** From: William M. Harlow, "Inside the Wood: Masterpiece of Nature" (Washington DC, 1970) p.6 fig.7 **609** Collection of New York Public Library, Astor, Lenox and Tilden Foundations **612** Corbis Images **614** Culver Pictures, Inc. **617** Library of Congress **619** Smithsonian Institution, Washington, D.C. National Museum of American History, Warsaw Collection of Business Americana, [#83-30065-11] **622** Library of Congress **626** The Carnegie Library of Pittsburgh **629** Thomas Anschutz, "The Ironworkers' Noontime,"1880. Oil on canvas. Fine Arts Museums of San Francisco, Gift of Mr. and Mrs. John D. Rockefeller 3rd, [1979.7.4]; (overlay) Courtesy Strong Museum, Rochester, New York © 2000. **631** (top) Library of Congress; (bottom) Courtesy, MetLife Archives **635** Deutsches Historisches Museum **636** Culver Pictures, Inc. **641** George Wesley Bellows, "Cliff Dwellers," 1913. Los Angeles County Museum of Art, Los Angeles County Fund **644** (top left) Brown Brothers; (top right) National Archives; (middle overlay) Library of Congress National Archives **648** Collection of The New York Public Library, Astor, Lenox and Tilden Foundations. **650** Photo Courtesy of The Newberry Library, Chicago **651** George Bellows, "The Sawdust Trail,"1916. Oil on canvas, 63 × 45 1/8 in. Milwaukee Art Museum, Layton Art Collection **654** Reproduced by permission of Chinn Family, San Francisco, CA. **655** Courtesy of the Colorado Historical Society, from the Lillybridge Collection. Gift of John Werness **659** Winslow Homer, "Blackboard," 1877. Watercolor on wove paper; laid down (19 3/4 × 12 3/4).Gift (Partial and Promised) of Jo Ann and Julian Gans, Jr., in honor of the 50th Anniversary of the National Gallery of Art, © 2000 Board of Trustees, National Gallery of Art, Washington **661** Courtesy Strong Museum, Rochester, NY. © 2000. **662** Horace Bonham, "Nearing the Issue at the Cockpit", 1870–78. Oil on canvas, 20 1/4 × 27 1/8 in. In the Collection of The Corcoran Gallery of Art, Museum Purchase, [99.6] **669** Chicago Historical Society **671** Courtesy of the Colorado Historical Society **672** From, "Harper's Weekly" (April 30, 1881) **675** (top) Culver Pictures, Inc.; (bottom) Courtesy of the California History Room, California State Library, Sacramento, California **677** Courtesy of Cornell University Library, Ithaca, NY **679** The Kansas State Historical Society, Topeka, KS **682** Library of Congress **685** Library of Congress **687** Ramsayer Presidential Research Library, McKinley Museum of History, Science, and Industry of the Stark County Historical Society, Canton, Ohio. **690** Fred Pansing, "Naval Parade, August 20, 1898." Oil on canvas. Courtesy of the Museum of the City of New York **692** Philip P. Choy, Professor of Asian American Studies at San Francisco State University **694** Hawaii State Archives **696** Chicago Historical Society **697** Huntsville Public Library **707** Library of Congress **708** Brown Brothers **710** Corbis Images **713** The San Diego Historical Society, Ticor Collection **715** Library of Congress **718** "Gondolas in Venice Canal, Venice, California." Photograph by Pacific Novelty Co. California Historical Society, San Francisco, [FN-29415] **720** Library of Congress **721** National Portrait Gallery, Washington, D.C./Art Resource, NY **722** Culver Pictures, Inc. **724** (left) Brown Brothers; (right) Library of Congress **725** Library of Congress **728** The Bancroft Library, University of California, Berkeley **729** Culver Pictures, Inc. **732** Culver Pictures, Inc. **739** Horace Pippin, "The End of the War; Starting Home," c. 1931. Philadelphia Museum of Art: Given by Robert Carlen **740** Theodore Roosevelt Collection, Harvard College Library **745** Brown Brothers **746** Childe Hassam, "Avenue of the Allies: Great Britain, 1918 (The Flags of the Colonies: Canada and Anzac; Brazil and Belgium Beyond)," The Metropolitan Museum of Art, Bequest of Miss Adelaide Milton de Groot (1876–1967), 1967 [67.187.127]. Photo © 2000 The Metropolitan Museum of Art, New York **752** Culver Pictures, Inc. **753** (top and bottom) Trustees of the Imperial War Museum, London. **754** Read Collection, Private Papers, Folder 54a, Series II, Ellis & Jenkins, 1892–1920, Box #9, Serial Number 8425, WWI, Felix Sanchez Photo Number 7224. Courtesy New Mexico State Records Center & Archives, Santa Fe, New Mexico **756** National Archives, U.S. War Department **759** Art Department of the Imperial War Museum. Trustees of

son Agency **1065** (bottom) Courtesy of The Lincoln Museum, Ft. Wayne, IN., [#748]; (top) AP/Wide World Photos **1066** (top) Frank Fournier/Contact Press Images; (bottom) Sandra Baker/Liaison Agency **1069** Robert Landau/CORBIS **1072** (top) Corbis Images; (bottom) AP/Wide World Photos **1076** Corbis Images **1083** AP/Wide World Photos **1084** Fred Ward/Black Star **1086** Patrick Piel/Liaison Agency **1089** Dirck Halstead/Liaison Agency **1090** Leonard Freed/Magnum Photos Inc. **1092** Brad Markel/Liaison Agency **1097** © Yolanda M. Lopez **1100** Diane Cook & Len Jenshel **1104** Buzz Orr **1107** Tom Haley/SIPA **1109** Vincent

Yu/AP/Wide World Photos **1111** Wally McNamee/CORBIS **1112** Illustration by Anita Kunz for the "New Yorker Magazine." Anita Kunz Limited. Reproduced by permission of the artist. **1114** Win McNamee/Reuters Newmedis Inc./Corbis Images **1118** Stephen G. Eick, Visual Insights **1123** (left) Shulee Ong; (right) Alon Reininger/Contact Press Images **1124** Ester Hernandez, "Libertad,"1976. Etching, 16 1/8 × 10 1/8 in. Collection of the Artist. Photo Courtesy UCLA at the Armand Hammer of Art and Cultural Center, Los Angeles, CA. Reproduced by permission of the artist.

Index

Note: Page numbers in *italics* indicate illustrations and their captions; page numbers followed by (m) indicate maps; page numbers followed by (n) indicate footnotes.

AAA (Agricultural Adjustment Administration), 828, 842
ABC powers, 745
Abernathy, Rev. Ralph, 1036
Abilene, Kansas, 592, 593
Abortion
    Carter's stand on, 1055
    in late 19th century, 657
    right-to-life movement and, *1072*, 1085
    Supreme Court decisions, 1030–1031, 1089–1090
Abrams, Jacob, 758
Abrams v. United States (1919), 758
Acheson, Dean, 925, 927, 928–929, 1014
Acid rock, 997
ACLU. *See* American Civil Liberties Union
Acquired immunodeficiency syndrome (AIDS), 1092, *1092*, 1106
Adams, Charles Francis, Jr., 680
Adams, Henry, *672*
Adams, Samuel Hopkins, 727
Addams, Jane, 652, 709, 712, 714, 717, 720–721, *721*, 750
Adventures of Tom Sawyer, The (Twain), 615
Advertising, 757–758, 783–784, 934, 1039
AEC (Atomic Energy Commission), 912, 931
Affirmative action, 1089, 1122
Afghanistan
    revolution in, 1051(m)
    Soviet invasion of (1979), 1061, 1085
    unsuccessful war in, 900, 901
AFL (American Federation of Labor), 633–634
AFL-CIO, 1050
Africa. *See also* North Africa
    European expansion, 688, 689(m)
    sub-Saharan, 1106, 1125
African Americans
    during Reconstruction
        black codes, 536, *536*, 537–538
        Davis Bend plantations, 532–533, 557–558, *558*
        education, *548*, 548–549
        experience of freedom, 545–547
        families, 547–548
        Freedmen's Bureau and, 537, 538, 548, 549, 550–551
        planters and, 551–552
        religion, 549
        sharecropping, *546*, 546–547, 550, *550*
        voting rights, 537, 542–543, *543*
        working conditions, 549–550, *550*
    in late 19th century
        Alliance Movement and, 678
        buffalo soldiers, 583
        education of, 659, 660
        exodusters, 566–567, 578
        field labor and, *569*
        Jim Crow politics and, 684–685, *685*, 685–686
        middle class, *655*
        migration to cities, 617–618

African Americans—*Cont.*
    professional baseball and, 662
    segregation and (*See* Segregation)
    sharecropping, 569, 570
    in Spanish-American War, 697, *697*
    in timber industry, *572*
    voting rights, 671
    in workplace, 631
    in early 20th century
        in automobile industry, 780
        black pride, 791–792, *792*
        Harlem Renaissance, 777, 792
        jazz music, 663, 790–791
        in World War I, 754
    during Great Depression
        in Federal Theater Project, 841
        limits of New Deal, 834–836, *835*
        unemployment, 816–817, *817*
    during and after World War II
        GI Bill and, 919
        labor practices, *914*, 914–915
        mobility of, 876
        race riots, 880–881
        segregation (*See* Segregation)
        women in war work, 875
    in later 20th century
        Black Power movement, 984, *984*, 1020
        changes in South and, 973–974
        Civil War commemoration and, 1064–1065, *1065*
        education levels, 1118
        full-employment economy and, 1121–1122
        migrations of, *939*, 940
        politics and, 1024, *1055*
        racial divide and, 1120–1121
        restrictive housing covenants, 919, 937, 940
        Vietnam War and, 1011
African Methodist Episcopal (AME) Church, 549
Afro-American Realty Company, 647
Agent Orange, 1010
Agnew, Spiro, 1045, 1047
Agribusiness, 947
Agricultural Adjustment Act (1933), 828, *846*
Agricultural Adjustment Act (1938), 829
Agricultural Adjustment Administration (AAA), 828, 842
Agriculture. *See also* Domestic animals; Farming; *specific crops*
    Eisenhower's farm policy and, 947
    during Great Depression, 773
        agricultural strikes, 838, *838–839*
        Dust Bowl, 814–815, *815*
        planning for, *828*, 828–829, 842, *846*
    in 19th century
        commercial, 562
        cotton-dominated economy, 568–569
        crop-lien system, 569–570, 570(m)
        peanuts, 569
        sharecropping, *546*, 546–547, 550, *550*
Aguinaldo, Emilio, 699
AIDS (acquired immunodeficiency syndrome), 1092, *1092*, 1106
Aid to Families with Dependent Children, 1078
AIM (American Indian Movement), 1027, *1027*, 1028

Aircraft
    in early 20th century, 752, 789
    during World War II
        aircraft industry production, 871
        female pilots, 870
        improved air power, *886*, 886–887
        naval aviation, 866
    use in Vietnam
        helicopters, *1003*, 1020
        systematic air strikes, 1007, 1010, 1031–1032
Air traffic controllers' strike, 1077
Alabama
    Montgomery bus boycott, 977–978, *979*
    Tuskegee Institute, 569, *685*, 686
Alabama, University of, 1017
Alaska, 687, 693, 998, 1040, 1042
Albee, Edward, 665
Albright, Madeleine, 1113
Alcatraz Island, 1027, 1028
Alcoa Aluminum, 798
Alcohol consumption
    alcoholism in city slums, 648
    in early 20th century, 718–719
    temperance movement and, 656–657, 672
Aldrin, Edwin "Buzz," 1023, 1036
Alexander II, Czar of Russia, 645
Algonquin, sinking of, (1917), 751
Ali, Muhammad, 1020
La Alianza, 1026
Alien Land Law (1887), 599–600
All-American Canal (1938), 834
Allen, Fred, 788
Allen, Frederick Lewis, 776, 777, 784
Allen, Gracie, 813–814
Allende Gossens, Salvador, 1050
Alliance Exchanges, 678
Alliance for Progress (1961), 961
Allied Control Council, 887
Allies. *See* World War II
All in the Family (sitcom), 1074
Altgeld, Gov. John Peter, 636, 669
Amendments to Constitution. *See* Constitution, U.S.
American Bar Association, 1113
American Baseball League (1901), 662
American Beauty (Grateful Dead), *995*
American Birth Control League, 785
American Broadcasting Company, 931
American Civil Liberties Union (ACLU), 795–796
American Dilemma, The (Myrdal), 974
American Expeditionary Force (WWI), 758, 764
American Federation of Labor (AFL), 633–634, 756, 783, 787, 839
"American Frankenstein, The" 677
American GI Forum, 973, 976, 1024
American Independent party (1968), 1017
American Indian Defense Association, 837
American Indian Movement (AIM), 1027, *1027*, 1028
American Liberty League (1934), 829
American Museum (NYC), 786
American Negro Exposition (1940), *817*
American Plan (1921), 782–783
American Psychiatric Association, 1029

American Railway Union, 637
American Red Cross, 868–869
American Sugar Refining Company, 726
American Telephone and Telegraph Company, 613
American Tobacco Company, 571
American Union Against Militarism (1914), 750
American Woman Suffrage Association, 553
Las Americas neighborhood (Houston), 1097–1098, 1103, 1105
Ames, Gov. Adelbert, 556
Amiens, Battle of (1918), 759, 759(m)
Amnesty, 1053, 1103
Amnesty Act (1872), 553
Amos 'n' Andy, 788, 830
Amusement parks, 656, 663, 718, 718–719
Anarchists, 636, 768
Anderson, Marian, 834
Angel Island (San Francisco), 644, 644–645
Angelus Temple, 776
Anglo-Chinese War (1856–1860), 643
Anthony, Susan B., 553, 715
Anthracite coal strike (1902), 725
Anthrax, 764
Anti-Comintern Pact (1937), 858
Anticommunism
    conservative, 921
    McCarthyism, 924, 924, 927, 930, 930–931, 931
Antifusionists, 683
Anti-imperialists, 700
Antilynching crusade, 685–686
Anti-Saloon League (1893), 672, 719
Anti-Semitism, 645, 889–890
Anti-Trust Division (Justice Department), 799
Antitrust suits, 627, 725–726
    railroad trusts, 726
    Sherman Antitrust Act and, 625, 627, 676, 725–726
    under Taft administration, 729–730, 733
    U.S. Steel suit, 729–730
Apache Indians, 579, 587
Apollo 8 (1968), 1023
Apollo 11 (1969), 961, 1022, 1023, 1036
Appeasement policy, 858, 907
Applied Christianity (Gladden), 651
Arab alliance (Nasser), 955–956
Arafat, Yasir, 1108
Arbenz Guzmán, Col. Jacobo, 954
Architecture. *See also* Housing, residential
    dumbbell tenements, 648, 648
    shopping malls, 1068, 1069, 1070
    skyscrapers, 647, 647–648
    suburban residential, 942, 942–943, 945
    Vietnam Veterans Memorial, 1064–1066, 1064–1067
Area Redevelopment Act (1961), 960
Argentina, 1058
Aristide, Jean-Bertrand, 1106
Arizona, 600, 715, 725
Arizona (U.S. battleship), 852
Armed forces. *See also* Army, U.S.; National Guard; Navy, U.S.; Warfare; *specific wars*
    buffalo soldiers, 583
    discrimination banned (1948), 916
    homosexuals and, 869–870, 1031, 1105
    in World War I
        army life, 764, 764–765
        battles, 758–760, 759(m), 759
        influenza pandemic (1918–1919), 760, 760–762
    in World War II
        army life, 868, 868
        recruits, 868–870, 869

Armed forces—*Cont.*
    in World War II—*Cont.*
        segregation in, 868–869, 869, 904
        women, 870
    in Vietnam War
        morale, 1020, 1020
        social class and, 1009–1011, 1010
        troop levels, 1013
Armed Forces Qualification Test, 1009
Armey, Rep. Dick, 1116
Arms race, 747
Arms sales during Vietnam War, 1021
Armstrong, Comdr. Neil, 1022, 1023, 1036
Army, U.S. *See also* Armed forces; Navy, U.S.; Warfare; *specific wars*
    Bonus army and, 821
    desegregation and, 978, 981
    in early 20th century
        army life, 764, 764–765, 768
        Army War College, 740
        Brownsville incident (1906), 724
        draft lottery and volunteers, 753–754, 754
        preparedness advocates and, 750–751
        sent to end strikes, 725
    in late 19th century
        Ninth and Tenth Cavalry, 583, 697, 698
        quelling strikes, 636, 636
        Seventh Cavalry, 584, 585
        Spanish-American War, 696
    McCarthy's investigation of, 931
Army Quartermaster Market Center, 870
ARPANET, 1116–1117
Art(s). *See also* Popular culture and entertainment
    architecture (*See* Architecture)
    commercial product design, 934
    film (*See* Motion pictures)
    music (*See* Music; *specific kinds of music*)
    New Deal and
        muralists, 811, 841
        WPA arts program, 840–841, 869, 989
    painting
        Ashcan School, 641, 712
        murals, 811, 841, 842, 842–843
        naturalism in, 712
    photography, 712, 841
    psychedelic, 995
    sculpture, 1065, 1065, 1066, 1066
    Vietnam Veterans Memorial, 1064–1066, 1064–1067
Art Deco, 814
Arthur, Chester A., 674
Ashcan School of art, 641, 712
Asia. *See also specific countries*
    in early 20th century
        missionary diplomacy in, 744
        progressive diplomacy in, 741–742
        spread of democracy, 771
    immigration from
        Angel Island facility, 644, 644–645
        factory labor, 642–643
Asian Americans
    demographics of, 1099–1102
    education levels, 1118
    political activism of, 1028
    projected population of, 1099
Aspira, 1025
Assassination
    of Archduke Franz Ferdinand, 748
    CIA abuses, 1054
    Conference Room Technique, 954
    of Garfield, 673, 674
    of Itzak Rabin, 1108
    of J.F.K., 983, 1006

Assassination—*Cont.*
    of Martin Luther King, 1015–1016
    of McKinley, 723
    of Robert Kennedy, 1016, 1016
"Assembly centers" for Nisei, 877–878
Assembly line, 771, 780
Assimilation
    of immigrants, 655, 816
    Indian assimilation movement, 586
Associationalism, 798–800, 799, 818
Aswan Dam (Egypt), 955
Atatürk, Kemal, 771
Atchison, Topeka and Santa Fe Railroad, 588
Atlanta, Georgia, 718
Atlanta (U.S. warship), 690
Atlanta Compromise, 686
Atlanta Constitution (newspaper), 568
Atlantic Charter (1941), 861, 886
Atlantic City, New Jersey, 786, 786–787
Atom bomb, 886. *See also* Nuclear weapons
    atom diplomacy and, 890–892, 891
    calculating effects of, 899
    Manhattan project, 872, 873, 890, 912, 922
    WWII casualty estimates and, 895–898, 895–898
Atomic Energy Commission (AEC), 912, 931
Atomic research, 872, 873, 890, 912, 922
Attlee, Clement, 889, 912, 927
Auster, Lawrence, 1123
Australia, 884(m)
Australian (secret) ballot, 650
Austria, 716
Austria-Hungary, 748
Automobile(s), 771, 934, 938, 1068
    auto safety legislation (1966), 990
    suburban homemakers and, 942–943, 944
    suburban lifestyle and, 938, 938–940, 939
    during World War II, 871
Automobile industry
    boom in manufacturing, 779–780, 780, 781
    Chrysler bailout, 1057–1058
    global competition and, 1050
    strikes in, 917
Autry, Gene, 950
Axis powers (WWII), 854, 865

Babbitt (Lewis), 791
Babcock, Orville, 554
Baby boom, 936–938, 937
Baby boomers, 901, 993, 1009, 1115–1116
Bach, Johann Sebastian, 841
Back Home: April 1865 (mural), 842, 842
Baez, Joan, 995
Baker, George, 817
Baker, Newton, 764
Baker v. Carr (1962), 992
Bakker, Jim, 1072
Bakke v. Regents of the University of California (1978), 1089
Ball, George, 1015
Ballinger, Richard, 729
Baltic republics, 1086
Bananas, 661
Banda music, 1104
Bankers' buying pools, 804
Banking Act (1935), 832
Banks, Dennis, 1028
Banks and banking
    in late 19th century
        bank networks, 614–615
        farm credit and, 677
    in early 20th century, 733, 804, 805, 806
    Federal Reserve System, 733, 806
    during Great Depression

Banks and banking—*Cont.*
  during Great Depression—*Cont.*
    "bank holidays," 824
    efforts to save, 824–825
    Nye Committee (1935), 856
    investment banks, 621, 625
  in later 20th century
    Cayman Islands, 1082(m)
    S&L failures, 1085, 1091–1092
    Thailand bank closures, 1109
Banner, Lois, 944
Baptism, adult, *575*
Baptist church, 575, *575,* 795, 941, *941*
Bara, Theda, 787
Barak, Ehud, 1108
Barbados, 540
Barbed wire fencing, 595
Barkley, Sen. Alben, *889*
Barnett, Gov. Ross, 981
Barnum, P. T., 786
Barrios, 794
Barron's (newspaper), 773
Baruch, Bernard, 755, 912
Baseball, 790
  color barrier in, *916,* 916–917
  development of, 662
  during Great Depression, 813
  multiculturalism in, 1123
  Negro League, 916, 917
Basketball, invention of, 663
Basye, Betty, 904
Bataan, fall of (1942), 865
Batista, Fulgencio, 956
Battle of Running Bulls, 840
Bay of Pigs invasion (1960), 962
B-29 bombers, *886,* 887, 891
Beach Boys, 998
Bear market, 803
Beat generation, 951, 995, 996
Beatles, The 993, 996, 997
Beauty contests, *786,* 786–787
Becky Sharp (film), 814
Beecher, Henry Ward, 681
Beethoven, Ludwig van, 841
Begin, Menachem, 1060, *1060*
Beijing, China, 702
Be-In, 998
Beirut, Lebanon, 956
Belarus, 1086
Belgium, 688, 689(m), 860
Belknap, William W., *554*
Bell, Alexander Graham, 613, 614
Bellamy, Edward, 626
Belleau Wood, Battle of (1918), 759, 759(m)
Bell Laboratories, *1118*
Bellows, George, *641, 651,* 712
Bell Telephone Company, 613
Beltways, 939–940
Benevolent associations, 818
Benny, Jack, 814
Benson, Ezra Taft, 947
Berkeley (University of California), 993–994
Berlin airlift, 910–911
Berlin wall, 963–964, 1086, *1086*
Berners-Lee, Tim, 1117
Bernstein, Carl, 1047, 1049
Berryman, John, *844*
Bessemer process, *609,* 611, 623
Bethel, New York, 998–999
Bethlehem Steel Company, 782
Bethune, Mary McLeod, 834–835
Bethune-Cookman College, 835
Beveridge, Sen. Albert, 702
BIA (Bureau of Indian Affairs), 837, 1027

Bible, interpretation of, 795–796
Bicycling, *655,* 662
Big business. *See* Industrial systems
Big Four, 762
"Big stick" policy, 741
Bilingual education, 1124
Bill of Rights for women (1967), 1030
Bird, Thomas, 1002
Birmingham, Alabama
  demonstrations in, 982, *982*
  "Letter from Birmingham Jail," 981–982
  steel industry in, 572–573
Birth control, 713–714, 785, *785*
Birth Control Review, 785
Birthrates
  baby boom, 936–938, *937*
  decline after 1957, 1030
  in late 19th century, 569, 654
  during World War II, 875
Bison. *See* Buffalo
Black, Edie, *994*
Black, Timuel, 904
Black and Puerto Rican Caucus, 1025
Black blizzards, 814, *815*
Black Cabinet, 835
Black codes, 536, *536,* 537–538
Black colleges, 660
Blackfoot Indians, *604,* 605
Black graft, 640
Black Hills (South Dakota), 580, 584, *585*
Black Kettle (Cheyenne chief), 583
Blacklisting, 923
Blackmun, Harry, 1030, 1045, 1113
Black Muslims (1931), 817
Black Panther party, 984, 1027, 1028, 1045
Black Power movement, 984, *984,* 1020
Black Star Line, 792
Black Thursday, 804
Blaine, Sen. James G., 674, 693, 694
Bland-Allison Act (1878), 674
Blitzkrieg, 860, 886
Block grants, 1043
"Blowin' in the Wind" (song), 995
Blue Flame, The (film), 787
Blues (Motley), 777
Board games, 813
Board of Indian Commissioners (1869), 586
Bok, Derek, 1122
Boland, Rep. Edward, 1081
Boland Amendment (1981), 1081, 1083
Bolivia, 855
Bolshevik government (Russia), 751–752, 753, 760, 767
Bombings
  anarchist bombings, 768
  atom bomb, *886,* 890–892, *891,* 895–898, 895–898
  in Vietnam, 1007, 1010
  in WWII air war, 886–887
Bonanza farms, 595
Bonham, Horace, *662*
Bonneville Dam, 834
Bonsack, James, 570
Bonus Army (1932), 821–822
Boodle, 640
Boom-and-bust business cycle, 624, *627,* 627–628, 680, 692
"Boomers," 595
Booth, John Wilkes, 534
Border Patrol, creation of, 794
Bork, Robert, 1088
Bosnia
  civil war in, *1107,* 1107–1108
  World War I and, 748

Bosses. *See* Ward bosses
Boston (U.S. warship), 690
Boston, Massachusetts, 614, 646, 664, 711–712, 718
Boston *Chronicle,* 917
Boston University, 978
Boulder Dam, 833–834
Boxer Rebellion (1899), 702
Boxing, 663, 790
Boycotts
  economic, of Iraq, 1087
  of grapes, 1025, *1026*
  Montgomery bus boycott, 977–978, 979
  OPEC oil embargo, 1036, 1052, 1054
Bra burners, 1030
Bracero program, 879
Bradlee, Ben, 986
Bradley, Gen. Omar, 928, 929
Bradley, Tom, 852
Brady Bill, 1110
Brains Trust, 824
Brandeis, Louis, 710, 733
Brand name products, 656
Brando, Marlon, 950
Braun, Carol Moseley, 1093
Brazil, 1088
Bread Givers (Yesierska), 655
Bread lines, *681,* 811, 812
Brennan, William, 1088
Bretton Woods meeting (1944), 890
Brezhnev, Leonid, 1024, 1052, 1059, 1061, 1076
Brice, Fanny, 665
Bridges, 647
Brierfield Plantation, 532–533, 558
Brinkmanship, 952–953, 953(m)
Britain, Battle of (1940), 860, 886
British Guiana, 693
Brokers' loans, 803
Bronson House (1900), 652
Brook Farm, 995
Brooklyn Bridge, 647
Brooklyn Dodgers (baseball), 917, 998
Brotherhood of Sleeping Car Porters, 879
Brown, John, 566
Brown, (Mrs.) Jonas, *567*
Brown Berets, 1027
Brownsville, Texas, 724
Brown v. Board of Education of Topeka (1954), 975–976, 977, 991, 1044, 1045
Brucellosis, 605
Bryan, William Jennings, *682,* 728, 733
  anti-imperialism of, 700
  Cross of Gold speech, 683
  Scopes trial, 796
  as secretary of state, 744
  on sinking of *Lusitania,* 749–750
Brzezinski, Zbigniew, 1056, 1059, 1061
Buchanan, James, 674
Buchanan Dam, 834
Buchenwald concentration camp, *889*
Buckley, William F., Jr., 1073
Buffalo (bison), *603–605,* 603–606
  destruction of, 583–584
  Native American hunting, 579, *580*
"Buffalo" Bob, 941
Buffalo soldiers, 583
Bulgaria, 1086
Bulge, Battle of (1944), 883, 904
Bull market, 803
"Bull Moose" (Progressive) party (1912), 708, 730, *730,* 731(m)
Bundy, McGeorge, 1006, 1007
Bureaucracy, 755–756, 782, 847
Bureau of Indian Affairs (BIA), 837, 1027

Bureau of Reclamation, U.S., 834
Bureau of Standards, U.S., 799
Bureau of the Budget (1921), 798
Burger, Warren, 1045
Burleson, Albert, 768
Burnham, Daniel, 647
Burns, George, 813–814
Burton, Richard, *960*
Bush, Barbara, *1089*
Bush, George, 1073, *1089*, 1110
    background of, 1085
    election of 1988 and, 1085
    election of 1992 and, 1092–1093, 1093(m)
    presidency of
        budget, 1110, 1112
        disillusionment with, 1090–1092, *1092*
        domestic agenda, 1088, 1091
        foreign policy, 1086, *1086*, 1106
        Gulf War and, 1086–1088, 1087(m)
        invasion of Panama, 1082(m)
        Supreme Court and, 1088–1090, *1089*
Business and commerce. *See also* Corporations;
        Industrialization; Trade
    big business (*See* Industrial systems)
    in 19th century
        American expansion and, 693–694
        business leaders, 628
        forms of ownership, 615–616
        railroads (*See* Railroads)
    in 20th century
        associationalism, 798–800, *799*
        expansion of, *948*, 948–949
        impersonality of, 949
        Kennedy administration, 960–961
        renewed respect for, 782
        stimulated by construction industry, 779
Busing for racial balance, 1044
Butler v. U.S. (1936), 828
Byrnes, James F., 871, 891, 909

C. Turner Joy (ship), 1007
Cadillac automobile, 934, 938
Caldwell, Charles, 552
Caldwell, Erskine, 841
California. *See also specific cities*
    Asian Americans in, 1028
    counterculture in, 998
    English as official language, 1124
    Free Speech Movement, 993–994
    freeway system, 938
    during Great Depression, 814–815, 829
    immigration to, 1100
    Ku Klux Klan in, 797
    legislation, 1122, 1123, 1124
    multiculturalism in, 1120
    in 19th century, 578
    woman suffrage (1911), 715
California, University of (Berkeley), 993–994
Calley, Lt. William, 1013
Cambodia (Kampuchea), 1019, 1020, 1100
"Camelot" (Kennedy administration), 959, *960*
Camera, invention of, 612
Camp David Accords (1978), 1060, *1060*
Canada, 561
Cannery and Agricultural Workers Industrial
        Union (CAWIU), 838
Cannon, Joseph, 729
Canterbury, Gen. Robert, 1004
Cape Cod houses, 937, 942
Capital deepening, 614
Capitalism
    industrial capitalism, 627
    market capitalism in China, 1071
    welfare capitalism, 756, 782–783, *783*, 800
Capone, Al ("Scarface"), 795
Carbohydrates in American diet, 1041

Cardozo, Benjamin, 828
Caribbean islands, 540, 741, 742, 743(m)
Carmichael, Stokely, 984
Carnegie, Andrew, *609*, 618, 625, 628, 632, 700
    philanthropy of, 625, 626, *626*, 686, 750
    steel industry and, *622–623*, 623–624, 679
Carnegie Corporation, 974
Carnegie Endowment for Peace, *626*
Carnegie Hall, 790–791
Carpenters union, 839
Carpentier, Georges, 790
Carpetbaggers, 543, 544, 545
Carranza, Venustiano, 744, 745
Carson, Pirie, and Scott department store, 648
Carson, Rachel, 993, 1039
Carter, James Earl (Jimmy):
    fundamentalism of, *1055*, 1071, 1074
    presidency of
        détente and, 1059–1060
        economic problems, 1057–1058, *1058*,
            1078
        foreign policy, 1058–1059
        hostage crisis, 1061
        Middle East crises, 1060–1061, *1061*
        military spending, 1076, 1079
        search for direction in, 1056–1057, *1057*
Carter Doctrine, 1061
Carver, George Washington, 569
Cash-and-carry neutrality, 858
Cassady, Neal, 951
Castillo Armas, Carlos, 954
Cast iron, in buildings, 647
Castle Garden (immigrant facility), 644
Castro, Fidel, 956, 962, 1017, 1024, 1098
Catalog shopping, 598, *619*, 661
Cat and Mouse Act, 715
Catron, Thomas, 588
Catt, Carrie Chapman, 715
Cattle industry, 592–594, *593*, 599
CAWIU (Cannery and Agricultural Workers In-
        dustrial Union), 838
Cayman Islands, 1082(m)
Cayuse Indians, 583
CCC (Civilian Conservation Corps), 826, *846*,
        881
CD-Now (Web site), 1117
Celebrities, mass interest in, 788–789
Censorship, 814, 992, 1117
Census, U.S.
    of 1890, 600
    of 1930, 794
    African Americans and, 1122
    mobility of population, 876
    projected population shifts, *1099*
Center for the Study of Responsive Law (1969),
        1038
Central America
    conflicts in, 1082(m), 1083
    immigration from, *1097*, 1097–1098, 1103
    U.S. foreign policy and, 1081
Central Intelligence Agency (CIA)
    assassination, *954*, 1054
    Bay of Pigs invasion (1960), 962
    in Chile (1970), 1050
    during Cold War, 925
    during Eisenhower administration, *954*, 954–
        955
    involvement in Nicaragua, 1081
    Nixon's use of, 1045
    Senate investigation of, 1053
    weakness of Soviet Union and, 1084–1085
Central Pacific Railroad, 591–592, *592*
Century of Dishonor, A (Jackson), 586
Chadwick, Edwin, 561
Chain stores, 661, 782
Chamberlain, Neville, 858, 907

Chamber of Commerce, 782
Chambers, Whittaker, 922
Chanax, Juan, 1096–1098, 1103, 1124, 1125
Chancellor, John, *979*
Chandler, Albert ("Happy"), 916
Charities, 818
Charleston (dance), 790
Château-Thierry, Battle of (1918), 759, 759(m)
Chattanooga, Tennessee, 572
Chavez, Cesar, 815–816, 993, 1025, 1026, *1026*
Chavez, Dennis, 836
Chesapeake, Ohio, and Southwestern Railroad,
        685
Chevrolet Corvair, 1038
Cheyenne, Wyoming, 592, 593
Cheyenne Indians, 579, 580, 582
    Chivington massacre, 583
    at Little Big Horn, 584, *585*
    starvation of, 604–605
Chiang Kai-shek, 774, 854, 876, 884(m), 922,
        928, 952–953, 953(m), 1024
Chicago (U.S. warship), 690–691
Chicago, Illinois
    in late 19th century
        architecture, 647, 648
        Haymarket Square Riot (1886), 636
        Hull House (1889), 652
        meatpacking industry, 611, 622
        municipal government, 649
        as railroad hub, 620(m)
        trolley cars, 646
        World's Columbian Exposition (1893),
            668–669, *669*, 719
    in 20th century
        alcohol consumption in, 718
        American Negro Exposition (1940), *817*
        Asian Americans in, 1101
        Democratic convention (1968),
            1016–1017, *1018*
        graft, 720–721, *721*
        inner-city life, *1090*, 1090–1091
        protests (1933), *812*
        racial violence in, 757, 985
        steelworkers' strike (1937), 840
        urban renewal, 1121–1122
Chicago *Defender,* 757
Chicago school of architecture, 647–648
Chicago *Tribune,* 919, 1090
Chicago Vice Commission (1910), 720
Chief Joseph (Nez Percé), 584
Children. *See also* Families and family life
    child labor legislation, 713, 713(n), 733
    factory labor, *571*, 630, *631*, 681
    working during WWII, 873
Children's Bureau (1912), 714, 723
Children's Defense Fund, 1113
Chile, 1050, 1054
China
    in late 19th century
        American missionaries and, 692, *692*
        Boxer Rebellion (1899), 702
        open door policy, 701–702
    in 20th century, 774, *1021*
        Cultural Revolution, 1017
        dollar diplomacy, 742
        fall to Mao Zedong, *921*
        intervention in Korean War, 927, *927*
        invasion from Taiwan, 952–953, 953(m)
        Japanese aggression in, 854–855, 858, 862
        market capitalism in, 1071
        migrations during WWII, 876
        Nixon's relations with, *1021*, 1022–1024
        open door policy, 854
        Tiananmen Square rally (1989), 1086
        Treaty of Portsmouth (1905), 741
China card, 1022, 1059

China Lobby, *921, 922, 928*
China Victory (U.S. warship), 871
Chinese Americans, 869
Chinese Exclusion Act (1882), 651
Chinese immigrants *(San Yi Man), 675*
   college students, 1099
   factory work and, 643
   immigration restriction and, 651, 654
   as Nativist targets, 651
   railroad workers, 591–592
   urban ghettos, 653, 654, *654*
Chinn, Thomas, 870
Chinook Indians, 580
Chisholm Trail, 593
Chivington, Col. John, 583
Chosan, Battle of (1950), 927
Christian Broadcast Network, 1072
Chrysler Corporation, 871, 934, 1057–1058
Chuco dialect, 653
Churches. *See also* Religion; *specific denominations*
   in 19th century
      African American, 549
      in New South, 573, 575, *575*
   in 20th century
      fundamentalism, 795–796
      immigrant groups and, *1104,* 1104–1105
      rising membership in 1950s, 941
Churchill, Winston
   Argentia meetings with Roosevelt, 861, *861*
   atom diplomacy and, 890–891, 895, 908
   in Big Three, 865, 866, 885–888, 906
   feelings about Pearl Harbor, 863
   war strategies of, 863–864
Church of Jesus Christ of Latter-Day Saints
   (Mormon), 652(n)
CIA. *See* Central Intelligence Agency
Cigarette-rolling machine, 570
Cigarettes, 570–571, 784
Cigar Makers' Union, 634
Cigars, 571, 634
Cincinnati Red Stockings (1869), 662
CIO (Congress of Industrial Organizations),
   839–840
Cities and urbanization. *See also specific cities*
   in late 19th century
      arts and entertainment, *641,* 663–665
      bridges, 647
      consumer culture, 660–661, *661*
      corruption, 650
      higher education, 659–660
      immigrant life, 652(n), 652–655, *654*
      leisure pursuits, 661–663, *662*
      middle-class life, *655,* 655–656
      migrating labor pool and, 642–645, *643,*
         644, 654
      municipal government, 649
      patterns of settlement, 645, *646*
      population explosion, 642
      progressivism and, 707
      public education, 658–659, *659*
      revivals and reform, 651, *651*
      role of railroads in, 592
      settlement house movement, 652, 714
      skyscrapers, *647,* 647–648
      sources of work, 617
      tenements, 648, *648*
      unconventional lifestyles, 657–658
      urban planning, 561–562, 597–598
      urban transport, *646,* 646–647
      vaudeville, *664,* 664–665
      Victorianism and, 656–657
      ward bosses, 640–641, 649–650, *650*
      in West, *597,* 597–598
   in 20th century (*See also* Suburban era,
      Specific cities)
      "average" Americans, 776–777

Cities and urbanization—*Cont.*
   in 20th century—*Cont.*
      decline of cities, 940
      Native American population, 1027
      relief efforts during Great Depression, 818
      urban blight, *1090,* 1090–1091
      urban redevelopment, 1068, *1069,* 1070,
         1121–1122
      ward bosses, 720–721, *721*
Citizenship, 538, 869
Citizens' League for Fair Play (1933), 835
City-manager plan, 721
Civilian Conservation Corps (CCC), 826, *846,*
   881
Civil liberties, 758, 768
Civil rights. *See also* Civil rights movement
   anti-Klan laws and, 556
   black codes and, 536, *536,* 537–538
   legal standing of Mexican Americans,
      976–977
   loyalty review boards and, 922–923
   New Deal and, 836
   Roosevelt administration and, 876, 877, 879,
      974
   Supreme Court and, 990–991, *991*
   Truman administration and, 915–916, 974
   during World War I, 758
   during World War II, 876–881
      internment camps, 877–879, *878*
      Italian Americans, 877
      Jim Crow and, 880–881
      minorities at work, 879–880
      opposition to Roosevelt, 881, *881*
Civil Rights Act (1866), 576
Civil Rights Act (1875), 554
Civil Rights Act (1964), 983, 986, 987, 1029
Civil Rights Cases (1883), 576–577
Civil rights movement. *See also* Liberalism
   activism
      antilynching crusade, 685–686
      of Mexican Americans, 915, *915*
      "new left" activists, 992–994, *994*
   counterculture and
      catalytic events, 993
      "new left" activists, 992–994, *994*
      rise of, 994–995
   desegregation, 970–972, *972*
   growth of
      at high tide, 981–983, *982*
      Kennedy assassination and, 983
      militants in, 984, *984*
      new organizations, *980,* 980–981
      sit-ins, 979–980, 980(m), *980*
      violence and, 984–986, 985(m), *985*
   social conflict and, 972–979
      black veterans and, 915
      Brown decision and, 975–976
      Latinos and, *976,* 976–977
      Little Rock, 978–979, *979*
      NAACP and, 973, *974,* 974–975
      new strategies, 977–978
      in South, 973–974
Civil Service Act (1883), 673, 674
Civil service reform, 672, 673
Civil war
   in Africa, 1106
   in Haiti, 1106–1107
   Spanish Civil War, 857
   in Yugoslavia, *1107,* 1107–1108
Civil War, American
   commemoration of, 1064–1065, *1065*
   political legacy of, 672
   prewar industrialization, 610
Civil Works Administration (CWA; 1933), 826,
   846
Clark, Maurice, 621

Clarke, Dr. Edward, 660
Clay, Gen. Lucius, 911
Clayton Antitrust Act (1914), 733
Clayton-Bulwer Treaty (1850), 693
Clean Air Act (1990), 1044, 1088
Clean Water Act, 1044, 1111
Cleaver, Eldridge, 984
Clemenceau, Georges, 760, 762, *763*
Clemens, Samuel (Mark Twain), 615, 700
Clergy. *See also* Churches; Religion
   televangelists, 1071–1072, *1072*
   view of melting pot, 664–665
Cleveland, Grover, 700
   election of 1884 and, 674
   election of 1888 and, *675*
   election of 1892 and, 679–680
   presidency of, 674–675
      Coxey's Army and, 681–682
      Cuban revolt and, 695
      depression of 1893 and, 681
      immigration restriction and, 651
      opening of world's fair, 668, 680
      Pullman Strike (1894), 637
      refusal to annex Hawaii, 694
      repeal of silver purchases, 682
      Venezuelan boundary dispute, 693
Cleveland, Ohio, 648, 718, 721, 1039
Cliff Dwellers (Bellows), *641*
Clifford, Clark, 1013, 1014, 1015
Clinton, Hillary Rodham, 1105, 1106, 1110,
   1113
Clinton, William Jefferson, 1120
   background and character, 1105–1106
   election of 1992 and, 1070, 1092–1093,
      1093(m)
   as governor of Arkansas, 1088
   presidency of
      budget surplus, 1115–1116
      conservatism and, 1111–1113, *1112*
      domestic agenda, 1105
      feminist agenda and, 1113–1114
      global economy and, *1109,* 1109–1110
      immigration issue, 1123
      international conflict and, 1106–1107
      legislative agenda, 1110–1111, *1111*
      Middle East peace, 1108
      scandals in, *1114,* 1114–1115
      two-tiered economy, 1118–1120
      Yugoslavia, division of, *1107,* 1107–1108
      Whitewater case and, 1106, 1114
Closing Circle, The (Commoner), 1039–1040
Clothing and fashion
   beauty contests, *786,* 786–787
   glasnost and, *1084*
   of Mexican immigrants, 1104
   in mid-20th century, 944, 949
   mods and hippies, *996,* 996–997
   of 1920s, 776–777, 784–785, *788*
   shirtwaist blouses, 660
"Cloudscrapers," 647
Cluster bombs, 1010
"Coal Caravan" (1932), 820
Coal mining, 636, 725
Cockfighting, 574, 662
Coeur d'Alene, Idaho, 591, *597,* 636
Cohan, George M., 665
Cohn, Roy, 930, *930*
COLAs (cost-of-living adjustments), 1057
Cold war, 904–931
   beginnings of
      atomic deterrence, 912–913, *913*
      containment policy, 907, 908, 924, 1032
      control of nuclear energy, 912
      fall of Eastern Europe, 910–912, 911(m)
      Marshall Plan and, 910, 913
      roots of mistrust, 907, *907*

Cold war—*Cont.*
  beginnings of—*Cont.*
    spheres of influence, 906–907
    Stalin's intentions, 907–908
    Truman doctrine, *909,* 909–910
  continuation of, 924–931
    Chinese intervention in Korea, *927,* 927
    election of 1952 and, 929–930, 961
    end of McCarthyism, *930,* 930–931, *931*
    global implications of, 928–929
    police action in Korea, 925–926, 926(m)
    Truman-MacArthur conflict, 928
  effects in U.S., 905, 920–924, *921,* 941
    foreign affairs and, 922
    HUAC investigations, 923
    loyalty review boards, 922–923
    McCarthyism, 924, *924,* 927
  end of, 1093
  postwar prosperity and, 913–920
    election of 1948 and, 919–920, 920(m)
    Fair Deal, 920
    New Deal programs and, 918
    social adjustments, *914,* 914–918, *915*
    welfare programs for GIs, 918–919
  in suburban era
    Cuban missile crisis, 964–966, *965*
    frustrations of, 961–963,
      962(m)–963(m)
    Soviet-American relations, 963–964
Colleges and universities
  affirmative action and, 1089
  Carnegie endowments, 625, *626*
  Chinese immigrants in, 1099
  Proposition 209 and, 1122
  rise of professional and, 659–660
  student protests in
    guerilla tactics, 1011–1012
    Kent State, 1002, 1004, *1004*
    worldwide, 1017
Collier, John, 837
Collier's magazine, 899, *899*
Collier's Weekly, 727
Collins, Michael, 1023
Cologne, Germany, 886
Colombia, 1082(m)
Colorado, 583, 600, 679, 725
Colored Citizen, The (newspaper), 566
Colored Farmers' National Alliance and Cooper-
  ative Union (1886), 678
Coltrane, John, 951
Columbia Park Boys Band, *654*
Columbus, New Mexico raid (1916), 745
Comanche Indians, 579
Comfort women (Korean), 876
Comic book propaganda, *924*
Cominform (Communist Information Bureau;
  1948), 910
Comintern (1919), 767
Commission for Relief in Belgium (1914), 755
Commission on the Status of Women, 1029
Commission on Training Camp Activities, 754
Committee for Industrial Organization. *See*
  Congress of Industrial Organizations
Committee on Civil Rights (1946), 916
Committee on Public Information (CPI), 757,
  758, 783
Commodity Credit Corporation, 828
Commoner, Barry, 1039–1040, 1041
Commonweal Army of Christ, 681–682
Commonwealth of Independent States (1991),
  1086
Communications
  global networks, 561, 1116–1118, *1118*
  immigrant networks, 1098, 1103–1104

Communications—*Cont.*
  intercity, 614
  Internet technology, 1116–1118, *1118*
  in late 19th century, 613, *614,* 614–615
  Telstar satellite, 1023
Communism
  in early 20th century
    in Asia, 771
    democracy and, 772
    Red scare, 766–767, *766*–769
  in Castro's Cuba, 956, 962
  Cold War and
    ambitions after WWII, 906–907
    baseball and, 916
    espionage, 922
    fear of communists, 920–921
    Hollywood, investigation of, 923
    Truman doctrine and, 909–910
Communist Information Bureau (Cominform;
  1948), 910
Communist Labor Party (1919), 767–768
Communist party, U.S., 820–821, *821*
Companionate marriage, 944
Company unions, 782–783
Competition, business
  critics of, *626,* 626–627
  defenders of, 625–626
  railroads, 619–620
Compromise of 1877, 557
Computers, 948–949, 1117
Comstock, Anthony, 657
Comstock Law (1873), 657
Comstock Lode (silver), 591
Conant, James, 896, 897
Concentration, policy of, 582
Concentration camps
  Nazi camps, 865, 888–890, *889*
  U.S. internment camps, 877–879, *878*
Concerts, 663
Coney Island, 663, 718, 719
Conference Room Technique, *954*
Confiscation Act, second (1862), 541
Conformity
  in home design, *942,* 942–943
  in suburban era, 935, *935,* 949
Conglomerate mergers, corporate, 948
Congo, 1054, 1125
Congregational Church, 651
Congress, U.S. *See also* House of Representatives,
    U.S.; Senate, U.S.
  congressional hearings
    HUAC hearings, 923
    Iran-Contra hearings, 1084
    Kefauver hearings, 945–946
    McCarthy hearings, 931, 946
    on Watergate, 1047–1048, *1048*
  during Reconstruction
    break with Johnson, *537,* 537–538
    corruption in, 553
    end of Freedmen's Bureau, 551
    impeachment of Johnson, *541,* 541–542, 552
    Reconstruction program, 539–542, 540(m)
    white supremacy and, *555,* 555–556
  in late 19th century
    balance of power in, 670, *670*
    "Billion Dollar Congress," 676
    Cuban revolt and, 695
    debate over tariffs, 673
    environmental legislation, 591
    immigration restriction by, 651
    naval improvement, 690–691
    regulation of commerce, 678
  in 20th century
    conflicts with Ford, 1054

Congress, U.S.—*Cont.*
  in 20th century—*Cont.*
    conflict with Nixon, 1046
    conservative revolution in, 1070
    denies aid to South Vietnam, 1052
    farm bloc in, 800
    food stamp program, 987
    immigration restriction, 717, 1123
    medical reform bill (1996), *1111*
    New Deal legislation, 831–832
    Pledge of Allegiance, 941
    Republican control of, 798
    restrains CIA, 1081
    support of McCarran Act, 923
    Truman's initiatives and, 920
Congressional Union (1914), 716
Congress of Industrial Organizations (CIO),
  839–840
Congress of Racial Equality (CORE), 880–881,
  915, 980, 981, 984, 994, 1011
Congress party (India), 771
Conkling, Roscoe, 674
Connerly, Ward, 1122
Connery, Sean, *960*
Connor, "Bull," 982
Conrad, Fred, 788
Consensus (on American life), 935, 966
Conservation, 727–728, *728,* 729, 1039–1042
Conservatism. *See also* Bush, George; Reagan,
    Ronald
  anticommunism and, 921, 924
  Catholicism, 1072–1073
  Clinton administration and, 1111–1113, *1112*
  defining, 1073
  in election of 1980, 1074, 1075(m)
  fundamentalism, 1071–1072, *1072*
  media and, 1073–1074
  STOP ERA crusade, 1031
  urban redevelopment, 1068, *1069,* 1070
  worldwide, 1070–1071
Constitution, U.S., amendments to
  Eighteenth (1920), 794–795, 1042
  English language amendment, proposed, *1123,*
    1123–1124
  Equal Rights Amendment, proposed, 786, 1030
  Fifteenth (1870), *544,* 552–553, *553*
  First (1791), 923
  Fourteenth (1866), 538, 539, 553, 558, 576,
    991
  Nineteenth (1920), 716
  Seventeenth (1913), 722
  Sixteenth (1913), 729, 732–733
  Thirteenth (1865), 535, 536
  Twenty-Fifth, 1048
Constitution Hall (DAR), 834
Construction industry, 779
Consumer culture, 771, 783–784
Consumer goods (products)
  in late 19th century, 600
    culture of consumption, 660–661, *661*
    growth in, 621–623
    middle-class homemaker and, 656
  in 20th century
    design of, 934
    post-WWII spending, 913
    1920s technology and, 778–779
Consumerism, *1038,* 1038–1039
Containment policy
  in cold war, 907, 908, 924
  Eisenhower administration, 951–952, 1032
Con Thien (Vietnam), 1013
Contraception, 657, 713–714, 785, *785*
Contraceptives, sale of, 992
Contract bridge (game), 813

Contract With America, 1111
Contra forces (Nicaragua), 1081, 1083
Coolidge, Calvin, 1075
    associationalism, 798–800, *799*, 818
    decisiveness of, 798
    dispute with Mexico (1927), 855
    foreign and domestic problems, 800–801
    pardons Marcus Garvey, *792*
    refuses to run, 801
Coolidge, Grace, *799*
Cooper, Gary, 923
Copland, Aaron, 841
Coral Sea, Battle of (1942), 866
CORE (Congress of Racial Equality), 880–881,
        915, 980, 981, 984, 994, 1011
Cornell University, 663, 1011, 1012
Corporations. *See also* Business and commerce;
        Industrialization; Industrial systems;
        Trade
    associationalism and, 799–800
    conglomerate mergers, 948
    corporate abuses, 725–726
    defenders of, 625–626, *626*
    Great Depression and, 806
    mergers, 622, 624–625, *707*, 725
    oligopolies, 782
    rise of, 615–616
Corregidor, fall of (1942), 865
Corrido (ballad), 592, 784
Corruption
    in 19th century
        bribery, 545
        during Reconstruction, 553–554, *554*
    in late 19th century, *672*
        in Army supply, 696
        election fraud, 650
        graft, 640, 650, 696
        railroad competition and, 619
        timber industry and, 572
    in 20th century
        Agnew bribery scandal, 1048
        Harding administration, 798
        Nixon's "Checkers" speech and, 929
        Watergate scandal, 1047, 1084, 1114–1115
        Whitewater case, 1106, 1114
Corvair (Chevrolet), 1038
Costello, Frank, 945–946
Cost-of-lifing adjustments (COLAs), 1057
Cotton cultivation, 532, 552, 568–569, 588, 973
Coughlin, Fr. Charles, 830, 832
Council of Economic Advisors, U.S., 960
Counterculture (1960s)
    activists of new left, 992–994, *994*
    catalytic events, 993
    clothing and fashion, *996*, 996–997
    rise of, 994–995
    rock revolution, *995*, 995–998
    West coast scene, 998–999
Countercyclical action in economy, 844–845
Country clubs, 941
Court of Indian Affairs, 837
Courts. *See also* Crime; Law enforcement;
        Supreme Court, U.S.; *specific cases*
    in late 19th century
        antitrust suits, 627, 725–726
        circuit courts, rural, 574
        Molly McGuires and, 635
    in 20th century
        juvenile courts, 710, 780
        reform of lower courts, 844
Courtship, in New South, 574, 575
Cowboys, 592, *593*
Cow towns, 592, 593
Cox, Archibald, 1047, 1048

Coxey, "General" Jacob, 681–682
Coxey's Army, 681–682
CPI (Committee on Public Information), 757,
        758, 783
Crafts, Dr. Wilber, 792
Craftworkers, 632, 634
Crawford, William, 803
Crazy Horse (Sioux chief), 584
Creationism, 1071
Credibility gap, 1013
Credit
    in late 19th century
        crop-lien system and, 570
        department stores and, 661
        farmers' problems and, 677
    in 20th century
        consumer culture and, 783
        consumer debt and, 805
        GI Bill loans, 919
        installment buying, 784, 805
        rapid expansion of, 779
        stock market and, 803
Creel, George, 757
Creole Jazz Band, 790
Crime. *See also* Courts; Law enforcement
    in late 19th century
        Chinese gangs, 654
        street toughs, 648
    in 20th century
        anticrime legislation, 1110
        death penalty, 931
        Nixon's burglaries, 1046, 1047
        poverty and, 1122
        Sacco and Vanzetti, 793
        Simpson murder, 1120, 1121
        S&L fraud, 1091–1092
        spy cases (*See* Espionage)
"Crime of '73," 674
Crisis of confidence, 1061
Croatia, 1107
Crocker, Charles, 591
Croker, "Boss" Richard, 649
Cronkite, Walter, 1013
Crop-lien system, 569–570, 570(m)
Croquet, 661–662
"Cross of Gold" speech, 683
Crow Indians, 582
Crozer Theological Seminary, 978
Cuba
    Bay of Pigs invasion (1960), 962
    Castro's revolution in (1959), 956, 1024, 1100
    CIA abuses, 1054
    immigration from, 1024, 1025
    missile crisis (1962), 964–966, *965*
    Platt Amendment and, 741
    Spanish-American War in
        naval blockade, 696
        revolt in (1895), 694–695
        San Juan Hill, Battle of, *697*, 697–698
        Santiago Bay, Battle of, 738
        sinking of *Maine*, 695, *696*
        Treaty of Paris (1898), 700
Cuban Giants baseball team, 662
Cultural Revolution (China), 1017
Cultures, regional
    effect of missionaries on, 691–692, *692*
    suburban (*See* Suburban era)
    of trans-Mississippi West, 579
    tribal cultures, destruction of, 583
Currency
    Asian, 1109
    devaluation of, 804
    gold *versus* silver standard, 673–674, *682*,
        682–684, 683(n), 684(m)

Currency—*Cont.*
    greenbacks, 673–674
    international currency flows, 1103
    in McKinley's presidency, 687, *687*
    money supply, 803
    Panic of 1873 and, 555
Custer, Col. George Armstrong, 584, *585*
CWA (Civil Works Administration), 826
Czechoslovakia, 858, 910, 954, 1017, 1086
Czolgosz, Leon, 723

Dade County, Florida, 1124
Dak To (Vietnam), 1013
Daley, Richard, 1016
Dallas, Texas, 983
Da Nang (Vietnam), 1010
Dancing, 790
Daniels, Cynthia, 1113
Dannemora Prison, 920
DAR (Daughters of the American Revolution), 834
Darrow, Clarence, 796
Darwin, Charles, 625, 692
Darwinism, 709
    fundamentalism and, 795–796, 1071
    Social Darwinism, 625–626, 692
Daugherty, Harry, 798
Daughters of Bilitis (1955), 1029
Daughters of the American Revolution (DAR),
        834
Davies, Jeff, 873
Davies, "Little Bob," 650
Davis, Jefferson, 532, 557, 558, *558*
Davis, Joseph, 532, 558
Davis, Rep. Henry Winter, 534
Davis Bend plantations, 532–533, 557–558, *558*
Dawes, Charles G., 800
Dawes Severalty Act (1887), 586, 837
Dayton Accords (1995), 1107
D-Day (Normandy landing), 859(m), *882*, 883,
        885, 946
DDT, 873, 1040–1041
Dean, John, 1047, 1048, *1048*
DeAnda, James, 977
Death penalty, 931
Death rates
    from disease, 873
    in industrial accidents, 629
    influenza pandemic, 761
    in intercollegiate football, 663
Debs, Eugene V., 637, 726, 731, 731(m), 758,
        767
Debt peonage, 570
Declaration of Independence, 982–983
De Leon, Daniel, 626
Delgado, Minerva, 976
Delgado et al. v. Bastrop et al., 976
de Lôme letter, 695
Deloria, Vine, Jr., 876
Democracy, *771*, 771–774, *773*, 847
Democratic party
    elections
        of 1876, *555*, 555–556
        of 1896, 683
        of 1912, *730*, 730–731, 731(m)
        of 1928, 801(m), 801–802
        of 1932, 822, 822(m)
        of 1936, 832–833
        of 1952, 929–930
        of 1964, 988
        of 1972, 1046
        of 1976, 1054–1055, *1055*
        of 1980, 1074, 1075(m)
        of 1988, 1085
        of 1992, 1092–1093, 1093(m)

Democratic party—*Cont.*
  in 19th century
    balance of power and, *670,* 670–671
    Farmers' Alliance and, 679
    loyalty to, 671
    Mississippi plan and, 556
    during Reconstruction, 539
    on tariffs, 673
    Tweed Ring, 545
  in 20th century
    all-white primary outlawed, 881
    Chicago convention (1968), 1016–1017,
      1018
    Democratic National Committee, 830, 837,
      1046, 1047
    growth of, 847
    preparedness for peace issue, 751
    Supreme Court packing and, 844
    women in, 837
Demonstrations. *See* Protests and violence
Dempsey, Jack, 790
Dendrochronology, 605, *605*
Denmark, 860
Denver, Colorado, 592, 593, 597–598
Denver Pacific Railroad, 597
Department of Commerce, U.S., 726, 799
Department of Defense, U.S., 924–925, 1117
Department of Energy, U.S., 1056
Department of Housing and Urban Development
      (HUD; 1965), 989
Department of Interior, U.S., 1036
Department stores, 648, 661, *661*
Deportation, of Mexican Americans, 815
Depression, economic. *See also* Great Depression
  of 1893, 669, 680–681, *681,* 708
  Panic of 1873 and, 554–555
Derleth, August, 778
Desegregation, 970–972, *972*
  Brown ruling and, 975–976
  school busing and, 1044
Détente
  Carter administration and, 1059–1060
  Ford administration and, 1052, *1053*
  Vietnam War and, *1021,* 1021–1024
Detroit, Michigan, 721, 880, 985, 998
Devanter, Justice Willis Van, 844
Devastation (Brit. warship), 690
Dewey, Adm. George, 696
Dewey, Alice, 710
Dewey, John, 709–710, *710,* 930
Dewey, Thomas E., 881, 919–920, 920(m)
De Witt, Gen. John, 877
Dewson, Mary W. ("Molly"), 837
Dexter Street Baptist Church, 978
Díaz, Porfirio, 744
Dick, Alfred, 615
Dickens, Charles, 712
Dickson, Donald, 868
Dictatorships, 954, 956, 1050, 1058, 1059
Dien Bien Phu (1954), 953, 953(m), 1005
Diet and nutrition. *See also* Food and drink
  starvation
    of Cheyenne Indians, 604–605
    during Great Depression, 812
    in 1920s Soviet Union, 805
  in 19th century
    in city slums, 648
    New England Kitchen (1890), 711–712
  in 20th century
    effects of fast food, 1041
    malnutrition, 812
    new dietary habits of 1920s, 800
    poverty and, 1091
    for WWII military, 870

Diggers, 998
Dingley Tariff (1897), *675,* 687
Dior, Christian, 944
Diplomacy. *See also* Foreign policy
  Native American, 605
  in 20th century
    atom diplomacy, 890–892, *891,* 895, 908
    Big Three and, 885–888
    in Cuban missile crisis, 966
    Good Neighbor policy, 855, *855*
    Iran hostage crisis (1979), 1061, 1074,
      1081–1082
    isolationism, 855–856
    Mexican Revolution and, 745
    moral diplomacy, 743–745
    progressivism and, 740–742
    shuttle diplomacy, 1052
Disarmament, 801
Disasters
  flooding, control of, *826,* 826–827
  Galveston tidal wave, 721
  natural, on Great Plains, 596
  Triangle Shirtwaist fire (1911), 706–707, *708,*
    722
Discrimination. *See* Prejudice and discrimination;
      Racism
Disease. *See also* Health and sanitation; Medicine
  in 19th century
    cholera epidemic (1848), 561
    in city slums, 648
    of domestic animals, 594, 605
    germ theory of, 561
    during Spanish-American War, 696
  in 20th century
    AIDS, 1092, *1092,* 1106
    anthrax, 764
    during Great Depression, 812, *836*
    influenza pandemic (1918–1919), *760,*
      760–762
    poliomyelitis, 823, *824*
    during World War II, 868, 873
    yellow fever, 738
Disenfranchisement, 576, *576–577, 578,*
      684–685
Distinguished Flying Cross, 869
Diversification, corporate, 948
Divine, M. J. ("Father Divine"), 817
Divorce, 813
Dixiecrat (States' Rights) party, 919–920, 920(m)
Doar, John, 980–981
Dodd, Samuel C. T., 624, 625
Dodge, Gen. Grenville, 591
Dodge City, Kansas, 593
Dole, Sen. Bob, 1113
Dollar diplomacy, 742
Dolphin (U.S. dispatch boat), 690, 744–745
Domestic animals. *See also* Agriculture; Farming
  cattle industry, 592–594, *593,* 599
  diseases carried by, 594, 605
  in New York City, 648
  sheep raising, 593
Domestic policy
  under Bush, 1088
  under Clinton, 1105–1106
  under Kennedy, 960–961
  under Reagan, 1076–1077
Domestic science courses, 660
Domestic service
  during Great Depression, 813
  middle class and, 655–656
  strikes and protest, 635–636
  women employed in, 618, 631
Dominican Republic, 1054, 1098
"Don't ask; don't tell" policy, 1105

Doughboys. *See* Armed forces, in World War I
Douglass, Esther, 549
Douglass, Frederick, 1065, *1065*
Draft, military
  deferments, 1009
  draft lottery (1917), 753–754, 764
  to punish political foes, 918
Draft card burning, 1011
Draft lottery (1917), 764
Dreadnought (Brit. warship), 691
Dreiser, Theodore, 712
Dresden, Germany, 886
Drew, Charles, 869
Drew, Daniel, 619
Drive-in businesses, 938
Drop city commune, 995
"Dropshot" deterrence plan (1949), 913
Drugs
  AIDS crisis and, 1092, *1092*
  Latin American drug trade, 1082(m)
  Nixon's war on, 1045
  1960s counterculture and, 995, 997, 998, 999
  in Vietnam War, 1020
Du Bois, W. E. B., 686, 975
Dubos, René, 1040
Ducks Unlimited, 1042
Dukakis, Gov. Michael, 1085, 1116
Duke, James, 571
Duke, Washington, 571
Dulles, Foster Rhea, 930
Dulles, John Foster, 952, 953, 954, 966
Dumbarton Oaks meeting (1944), 890
"Dumbbell" tenements, 648, *648*
Dunkirk, evacuation from, 860
Durant, William, 803
Durocher, Leo, 917
Dust Bowl, 814–815, *815*
Dutch East Indies, 876
Dylan, Bob, 993, 995, 996
Dynamic obsolescence, 934

Eads, James B., 610, 637
Earl, Harley, 934, 936
"Earth Angel" (song), 951
Earth Day (1970), 1041–1042, *1042*
Earth Summit (1992), 1088
Easter Morning (Rockwell), *935*
Eastern Europe. *See also specific countries*
  communist domination of, 910–911, 911(m)
East Los Angeles, California, 1102–1103
Eastman, George, 612
Eastman Kodak Company, 612
East St. Louis, Missouri, 757
Ecology. *See also* Environment
  in late 19th century
    disappearance of bison and, 604–605
    effect of cities on, 642
    European expansion and, 688
    Native Americans and, 580, *580*
  in 20th century
    Agent Orange and, 1010–1011
    Commoner's view of, 1039–1040
    Dust Bowl, 814–815, *815*
    ecoterrorism, 1087–1088
    oil spills, 1036, *1037,* 1039
Economic Opportunity Act (1964), 987
Economic Recovery Tax Act (1981), 1077
Economy. *See also* Depression, economic
  during Reconstruction, 545
  in late 19th century
    boom-and-bust cycle, 624, *627,* 627–628,
      680
    boom economies, 567–568
    cattle economy, 594

Economy—*Cont.*
  in late 19th century—*Cont.*
    effect on political system, 669
    family economy, *598,* 598–599
    foreign investments, 599–600
    world economy, 599–600, 654
  in early 20th century
    automobile and, 779–780, *780, 781*
    business and, 782
    construction industry and, 779
    consumer culture and, 783–784
    consumer spending, 778–779
    defects in, 805
    economic ignorance, 806
    Great Crash, 804
    progressive diplomacy and, 740
    welfare capitalism and, 756, 782–783, *783,*
      800
    World War I and, 755–756, 768
  during Great Depression (*See* Great Depression)
  after World War II
    international strategies, 890
    recession of 1953–1954, 946
    sources of prosperity, 913–914
  in late 20th century
    effects of prosperity, 1119
    immigration and, 1098
    inflationary pressures, 1057–1058, *1058*
    stagflation, 1044
    supply-side economics, 1076, 1077–1078,
      1078, 1079
    two-tiered, 1118–1120
    Vietnam War and, 1012
    world financial system, *1109,* 1109–1110
Economy Act (1933), 825
Ecoterrorism, 1087–1088
Edison, Thomas Alva, 612, *612,* 614, *619,* 646
Edison Electric Light Company, 612
Education. *See also* Colleges and universities
  private
    Christian academies, 1071
    parochial schools, 659, 941, 1073
    women's colleges, 660
  public schools, 549, 658–659, *659,* 1089
  teachers
    desegregation and, 970–972
    in late 19th century, 659, *659*
  in 19th century
    for African Americans, *548,* 548–549, *578,*
      685
    first kindergartens, 659
    parochial schools, 659
    public schools, 549
    Southern poverty and, 573
    urban public education, 658–659, *659*
  in 20th century
    affirmative action, 1089, 1122
    after World War II, 919, 944 .
    Asian Americans and, 1102
    bilingual, elimination of, 1124
    business schools, 782
    computer economy and, 1118
    desegregation (*See* Desegregation)
    Deweyism, 709–710, *710*
    feminism and, 1030
    Great Society programs, 988, 989
    high schools, 950
    for Mexican Americans, 1026–1027
    National Defense Education Act (1958), 956
    parochial schools, 941
    school prayer, 1071
    service in Vietnam and, 1009
    state reforms, 1113
    women and, 713, 785

Educational Opportunity Programs (EOP), 1026
Education Summit (1989), 1088
Efficiency, in business, *619,* 780
Egypt
  attack on Israel (1973), 1050, *1051*(m), 1052
  nationalist crisis in, 955
  shuttle diplomacy and, 1052
  during World War II, 864
Ehrlich, Paul, 1042
Ehrlichman, John, 1046, 1047
Eick, Stephen G., *1118*
Eighteenth Amendment (1920), 794–795, 1042
Einstein, Albert, 873
Eisenhower, Dwight D., 961, 964, 966, 1011
  election of 1952 and, 929–930
  heart attack (1955), 947
  presidency of
    assessment of, 947–948
    Berlin crisis, 957
    conflict in Asia, 952–953, 953(m), 1005,
      1032
    containment of Soviets and, 951–952, 1032
    domino theory, 1006
    end of McCarthyism, *930,* 930–931, *931*
    foreign policy of, 952
    interstate highway system, 938–940
    judicial appointments, 975
    loyalty campaign, 930–931
    middle road, 931, 936
    modern Republicanism, *946,* 946–947
    probusiness policies, *948,* 948–949
    religion and, 941
    response to *Sputnik,* 956, *957*
    support of Faubus, 978, 981
  on space program, 1022
  as WWII general
    German surrender, 890
    Normandy landing (D-Day), *882, 883,* 946
    in North Africa, 867
Eisenhower Doctrine, 956
Elections
  Australian (secret) ballot, 650
  campaigning, *670,* 670–671
  congressional
    of 1866, 538–539
    of 1874, 555
    of 1890, 679
    of 1894, 682
    of 1914, 733
    of 1918, 763
    of 1932, 822, 822(m)
    of 1938, 845
    of 1946, 918
    of 1976, 1055
    of 1994, 1111
    direct election of senators, 722
  direct primary laws, 722
  municipal, 650
  presidential
    of 1800, 683(n)
    of 1828, 683(n)
    of 1860, 683(n)
    of 1872, 657
    of 1876, 556(m), 556–557, 674
    of 1880, 674
    of 1884, 674
    of 1888, *671, 675, 675*
    of 1892, 679
    of 1896, *682,* 682–684, 683(n), 684(m),
      687, *687*
    of 1904, 726
    of 1908, 728
    of 1912, *730,* 730–731, 731(m)
    of 1916, 733, 750(m), 750–751

Elections—*Cont.*
  presidential—*Cont.*
    of 1928, 683(n), 801(m), 801–802
    of 1932, 822, 822(m)
    of 1936, 832–833
    of 1944, 881
    of 1948, 919–920, 920(m)
    of 1952, 929–930
    of 1956, 947
    of 1960, 958, 958(m), 959, 961
    of 1964, 988
    of 1968, *1014,* 1014–1015, 1016
    of 1972, 1046
    of 1976, 1054–1055, *1055*
    of 1980, 683(n), 1074, 1075(m)
    of 1984, 1080
    of 1988, 1085
    of 1992, 1092–1093, 1093(m)
    of 1996, 1112(m), 1113
    pivotal elections, 683(n)
  Seventeenth Amendment and, 722
Electoral College, 556, 675
Electricity, 612, 646
Electric Kool-Aid Acid Test, The (Wolfe), 995
Electronic data processing, 948–949
Elementary and Secondary School Act (1965),
  988
Eliot, T. S., 791
Elkins Act (1903), 726
Ellet, Elizabeth F., *661*
Ellis Island, 644, *644*
Ellsberg, Daniel, 1046
Ellsworth, Kansas, 593
El Paso, Texas, 597, 653
El Salvador, 1059, 1104
Embargo
  OPEC oil embargo, 1036, 1052, 1054
  proposed on arms sales, 856
  on trade with Japan, 862
Emergency Banking Act (1933), 824
Emergency Relief and Construction Act (1932),
  820
Emergency Relief Appropriation Act (1935), 831,
  846
Emigration during Great Depression, 812
Emmons, Gen. Delos, 877
Empire State Building (1931), 779
Employment. *See* Work and workers
Employment Act (1946), 914
Employment Service, U.S., 880
End of the War: Starting Home, The (Pippin), *739*
"End Poverty in California" campaign, 829
Energy conservation, 1056
Energy Policy and Conservation Act (1975),
  1054
Enganchistas, 816
Engel v. Vitale (1962), 991
English, as official language, *1123,* 1123–1124
Enlightenment, The 1071
Enola Gay (B-29 bomber), *886,* 891
Enterprise (U.S. aircraft carrier), 866–867
Entrepreneurship, 649
Environment. *See also* Ecology
  in late 19th century
    in cattle kingdom, 594
    cities and, 642
    hydraulic mining and, *567, 591,* 611
    industrial operations and, 611
    logging operations and, *572, 572*
    Native Americans and, *580, 580*
    in West, 581(m), 582
  in 20th century
    agribusiness and, 947
    Bush administration and, 1088

Environment—*Cont.*
  in 20th century—*Cont.*
    controversies under Reagan, 1077
    deterioration of, 1036
    Great Society programs, 989–990
    industrialization and, 901, 902
Environmentalism, 1039–1042
Environmental Protection Agency, 1041, 1088
EOP (Educational Opportunity Programs), 1026
Episcopal church, 1104
Equal employment opportunity, 1113
Equal Pay Act (1963), 1029
Equal Rights Amendment (ERA; 1972), 786, 1030
Equal Rights party, 657
Erdman Act (1898), 687
Erie Railroad, 619
Erie Wars (railroad), 619–620
Ervin, Sen. Sam, *1048*
Escalation, 1007, 1020
Escobedo v. Illlinois (1964), 991
Escoffier, *1006*
Espionage
  in Cuban missile crisis, 964
  Hiss case, 922
  Rosenberg case, 931
  U-2 spy plane incident, 957–958
Espionage Act (1917), 758
Estonia, 1086
Ethics, 827
Ethnic charities, 818
Ethnic cleansing, 1107
Ethnicity. *See also* Prejudice and discrimination
  in late 19th century
    ethnic and racial tensions, 588–589
    political affiliation and, 671
  in 20th century
    nonlinear ethnic niche, 1101
    role in Los Angeles Riots (1992), 1121,
      1124
    suburban lifestyle and, 940
Ethnic neighborhoods, 653
Euclid Beach Park, 718
Eugenics, 717
Eurocentrists, 928–929
Europe. *See also* Eastern Europe; *specific countries*
  in late 19th century
    immigration from, 643, 644, *644*
    worldwide expansion, 688, *688*
  in 20th century
    effects of Great Depression, 773, 774,
      804–805, *805*
    expansion of culture and power, 899
    Marshall Plan, 910, 913
    spread of democracy, 771
    Treaty of Versailles, 762–766, *763*, 768,
      854, 857, 858
  World War I in (*See* World War I)
  World War II in (*See* World War II)
Evangelicalism. *See also* Fundamentalism
  in late 19th century, 575, 597
  in 20th century, 1071–1072
Evans, Diane, 1066
Evans, Gov. John, 583
Everest, Wesley, 768
Everglades National Park, 1040
Evolution, Darwinian theories of. *See* Darwinism
Executive Order 9066, 877
Exodusters, 566–567, 578, 815
Expatriate writers, 791
Exxon (Standard Oil of New Jersey), 948

Factories. *See also* Industrialization; Industrial
    systems
  child and immigrant labor in, 570, 571, *571*,
    630, *631*

Factories—*Cont.*
  migrating labor pool, 642–645, *643, 644*
  women workers, 630–631
Fair Campaign Practices Act (1974), 1049
Fair Deal, 920
Fair Employment Practices Commission (FEPC),
    879, 918
Fair Housing Act (1968), 990
Fair Labor Standards Act (1938), *846*
Fall, Sen. Albert, 798
Fallout shelters, *957*
Falwell, Rev. Jerry, 1072, *1072*
Families and family life. *See also* Children; Mar-
    riage
  in 19th century
    child-rearing theories, 655
    freedmen's families, 547–548
    Grange movement and, 678
    married women workers, 630–631
    of working-class immigrants, 653
  in 20th century
    effects of fast food, *1040,* 1040–1041
    family earnings, *1058*
    during Great Depression, 812–813
    inner-city existence, *1090,* 1090–1091
    suburban home design and, *942,* 942–943
Family Assistance Plan, 1043
Family room, 943
FAP (Federal Arts Project), 841, *869*
Farewell to Arms, A (Hemingway), 791
Farm Credit Administration, 829
Farm entertainments, 574
Farm equipment, 595
Farmer, James, 980
Farmers. *See* Farming
Farmers' Alliance
  growth of, 678–679, *679*
  origins of, 677–678
Farm Holiday Association, 820
Farming. *See also* Agriculture; Domestic animals;
    Farmers' Alliance
  in 19th century
    agrarian revolt, 676–680
    agricultural ladder and, 569–570
    Farmers' Alliance, 677–679, *679*
    on Great Plains, 595
    hired hands, 569
    Indian resistance to, 580
    targets of farm anger, 677
    in West, 592, 593
  in 20th century
    commercial, ecology and, 814–815
    Eisenhower's farm policy, 947
    farm bloc in Congress, 800
    farm subsidies, 828–829
    mechanized cotton farming, 973
Farm Security Administration (1937), 829, *846,*
    881
Fasci di Combattimento, 772
Fascism, 772, 855, 857
Fast-food restaurants, *1040,* 1040–1041
"Fat man" (atom bomb), 891
Faubus, Gov. Orval, 978
FBI (Federal Bureau of Investigation), 981, 1045,
    1046
Federal Arts Project (FAP), 841, *869*
Federal Bureau of Investigation (FBI), 981, 1045,
    1046, 1054
Federal Deposit Insurance Corporation (1933),
    825, *846*
Federal Emergency Relief Act (1933), *846*
Federal Emergency Relief Administration
    (FERA), 825–826, 838
Federal Employee Loyalty Program (1947),
    922–923

Federal Energy Administration, 1054
Federal government. *See also specific branches of*
    federal government
  budget
    balanced, 1092
    budget deficit, 947, 952
    Clinton program for, 1110, 1111
    Gingrich proposals, 1111–1112
    under Reagan, 1076, 1078, *1079,* 1080
    surplus, 1115–1116
  in 19th century
    aid to railroads, 620, 621
    black officeholders, 543, *543*
    spoils system, 673
  in 20th century
    bureaucracy, 755–756
    government contracts, 756
    post-WWII spending, 914
    wage and price freezes, 1044
Federal Housing Administration, 919
Federal Music Project (FMP), 841
Federal One (WPA), 840–841
Federal Reserve Act (1913), 733
Federal Reserve Board, 803, 832, 1077
Federal Reserve System, 733, 806
Federal Savings and Loan Insurance Corpora-
    tion, 1091
Federal Theater Project (FTP), 841
Federal Trade Commission Act (1914), 733
Federal Writers Project (FWP), 841
Federation of Jewish Charities, 818
Feeder lines (railroad), 618
Feminine Mystique, The (Friedan), 1029
Feminism. *See also* Women's rights movement
  Clinton administration and, 1113–1114
  political activism and, 1029–1030, *1030*
Feminization of workforce, 631, 785
Fencing, barbed wire, 595
FEPC (Fair Employment Practices Commission),
    879, 918
FERA (Federal Emergency Relief Administra-
    tion), 825–826, 838
Ferguson, Gov. Miriam ("Ma"), 785
Ferguson, Robert, 608
Fermi, Enrico, 873
Ferraro, Geraldine, 1080
Fertilizers, 568
Fessenden, William Pitt, 537
Fifteenth Amendment (1870), *544,* 552–553, *553*
Filipino soldiers (WWII), 869
Finance
  investment capital, 613–615
  railroad building and, 620–621
  world financial system, *1109,* 1109–1110
  World War I spending, 755–756
  World War II spending, *881*
Finney, Charles, 941
Fireside chats (Roosevelt), 824
Firestorms, 886, 899
First Amendment (1791), 923
Fisher Body plant (GM), 840
Fisk, James, Jr., 619
Fitzgerald, F. Scott, 791
Five-Power Agreement (1921), 801
Flagg, James, 757–758
Flanagan, Hallie, 841
Flappers, 784–786, *785*
Flatiron Building, 647, *647*
Fleetwood deterrence plan (1948), 913
Flexible response doctrine, 964
Florida
  Cuban Americans in, 1102
  Enlish language initiative, 1124
  Everglades National Park, 1040
Flower children, 998

FMP (Federal Music Project), 841
Folk music, 995, 997
Food Administration (WWI), 755, 798
Food and drink. *See also* Diet and nutrition
    army food, 765
    fast food, *1040,* 1040–1041
    on Great Plains, *598,* 598–599
    new foods, *661*
Food stamps, 1078
Football, intercollegiate, 662–663, 790
Foraker Act (1900), 701
Force Act (1870), 555–556
Ford, Gerald R., 1076, 1079
    appointed vice president, 1048
    election of 1976 and, 1054–1055, *1055*
    as House minority leader, 1049
    Nixon's resignation and, 1049
    presidency of
        détente, 1052, *1053*
        foreign policy, 1049–1050
        global competition, 1050, 1051(m), 1052
        inflation, 1050, 1054, *1054*
        Nixon pardoned, 1053
        post-Watergate limits, 1053–1054
        shuttle diplomacy, 1052
Ford, Henry, 755, 771, 779–780, *780,* 790, 820,
    840
Ford, John, 841
Ford Motor Company (1903), 779–780, 820,
    871, 934, 959
Foreign investments, 599–600
Foreign-language newspapers, 653
Foreign policy
    "big stick" policy, 741
    under Bush, 1086, *1086*
    under Carter, 1058–1059
    under Clinton, 1106–1107
    during Cold War
        assertiveness of, 924–925
        global implications, 928–929
        NSC-68, 925, 926
    declaration of war and, 752
    Kissinger and, 1049–1050
    open door policy, 693, 701–702
    under Reagan, 1080–1081
Foreign Relations Committee (Senate), 763
Foreman, Clark, 834
Formosa. *See* Taiwan
Forrestal, James, 907, 908
Fort Laramie, Treaty of (1868), 584
Foster, Vince, 1106
Foster, William Z., 822
Four Freedoms, 861
Four Policemen, 885
Foursquare gospel, 776
Fourteen Points (Wilson), 759–760, 762, 7
    65
Fourteenth Amendment (1866), 538, 539, 553,
    558, 576, 991
Fourtune, Henry, 634
Fourtune, Malvina, 634
Fragging, 1020
France
    territorial expansion, 688, 689(m)
    in 20th century
        student protests in (1968), 1017
        ties to U.S., 748, 749
        trench warfare, 753, *753*
        in Vietnam, 907, 953, 953(m)
    during World War II
        Hitler's invasion of, 860
        Normandy landing (D-Day), 859(m), *882,*
        883, 885
Franco, Francisco, 857
Franklin, Benjamin, 645

Franz Ferdinand, Archduke of Austria-Hungary,
    748
Free blacks. *See* African Americans
Freedman's Memorial Monument, 1065, *1065*
Freedmen's Bureau (1865), 537, 538, 548, 549,
    550–551
Freedmen's Courts, 551
Freedom riders, 980–981
Freedom Summers, 983, 992, 993, 994, *994,* 1029
Free Speech Movement, 993–994
Freud, Sigmund, 785
Friedan, Betty, 993, 1029
Frontier, 578, 579
Frowne, Sadie, 628, 637
FTP (Federal Theater Project), 841
Fuchs, Klaus, 922
Fuel Administration (WWI), 755
Fulbright, Sen. J. William, 1011, 1012, 1015
Fuller, Buckminster, 995
Fundamentalism, 1071
    conservatism and, 1071–1072, *1072*
    Islamic, 901, 1061, 1081
    social structure and, 795–796
Fundamentals, The (Stewart & Stewart), 795
Furniture, manufacture of, 572
FWP (Federal Writers Project), 841

Gagarin, Yuri, 1022
Galactic Network, 1116
Galveston, Texas, 721
Gambling, 574, 648, *662*
Games and sports. *See* Sports
Gandhi, Mohandas K., 771, 880–881, 978, 1025
Garcia, Gus, 976
Garcia, John, 852
Gardens, *569,* 598, 872
Garfield, James, 673, 674
Garment industry
    during Great Depression, 813
    immigrants in, 653, *1097*
    Triangle Shirtwaist fire (1911), 706–707, *708,*
    722
Garner, John Nance, 858
Garvey, Marcus, 791–792, *792*
Gassed (Sargent), 759
Gates, Bill, 1117, 1119
Gay rights activism, 1028–1029
Gaza, 1108
General Assembly, U.N., 890
General Electric Company, 612, 782, 948, *948,*
    1075–1076
General Federation of Women's Clubs, 713, 723
General Motors Acceptance Corporation, 784
General Motors Corporation, 780, 840, 871, 934,
    948, 949, 1038, *1038*
Geneva Accords, 953(m)
Genovese, Elizabeth Fox, 1114
Gentlemen's agreement, 742
Geodesic domes, 995
Geological Survey, U.S., 582
George, Henry, 626, 665
George Washington (U.S. warship), 762
Georgia, 539–540, 550(m)
Germany
    in late 19th century
        in Pacific, 699(m)
        territorial expansion, 688, 689(m)
    in early 20th century
        Dawes plan and, 800
        effects of influenza pandemic, 761
        Great Depression in, 773
        Keynesian economics in, 844–845
        Nazi party in (*See* National Socialist (Nazi)
        Party)

Germany—*Cont.*
    in early 20th century—*Cont.*
        U.S. view of, 748–749
        votes for women (1919), 716
        war reparations, 800, 890
        Weimar Republic, 800
        World War I, 758–760, 759(m), *759*
    during World War II
        air power, 860, 886, 887
        Big Three plans for, 887
        fall of Third Reich, *882,* 882–883
        submarine warfare (*See* Submarines,
        German)
        use of captive labor, 876
    during Cold War
        Berlin airlift, 910–911
        Berlin wall, 963–964, 1086, *1086*
Ghost Dance religion, 586–587
Gibbons, Floyd, 746, 747
GI Bill of Rights (1944), 915, 918–919, 937
Gibson, Charles Dana, *664, 681*
Gibson, Katherine, 595–596
Gideon, Clarence Earl, 991, *991*
Gideon v. Wainwright (1963), 991, *991*
Gilman, Charlotte Perkins, 713, 750
Gilpin, William, 581, 582, 591
Gingrich, Newt, 1070, 1111, 1112, *1112,* 1113
Ginsberg, Allen, 951, 998
Ginsburg, Ruth Bader, 1113
Gladden, Washington, 651
Glasnost, *1084,* 1084–1085
Glass ceiling, 1031
Glass-Steagall Banking Act (1932), 820
Glass-Steagall Banking Act (1933), 825
Glenn, Col. John, 961, 1022–1023
Glidden, Joseph, 595
Goering, Hermann, 860
Goethe, Johann, 1049
Gold, 693, 803
Goldman, Ron, 1121
Gold rush, 581, 589
Gold standard
    abandoned in Europe, 804
    silver standard and, 673–674, *682,* 682 684,
    683(n), 684(m)
Goldwater, Sen. Barry, 988, 1006, 1070
Gompers, Samuel, 633–634, 787
Gonzales, Rodolfo ("Corky"), 1026
Good Neighbor policy, 855, *855*
Goodyear Tire and Rubber Company, 840
Gorbachev, Mikhail, *1084,* 1085, 1086, *1106*
Gorbachev, Raisa, *1084*
Gordy, Berry, 998
Gorgas, Dr. William, 738
Gorman, Margaret, *786,* 787
Las Gorras Blancas (White Caps), 588
Gospel of wealth, 625
Gould, Jay, 619, 620
Government(s). *See also* Elections; Political
    parties; Politics
    cities (*See* Municipal government)
    federal (*See* Federal government)
    growth of, *990*
    hands off approach to, 1090–1091
    state (*See* States)
Graduated income tax, 729, 732–733
Grady, Henry, 568, 572
Graham, Rev. Billy, 941, *941,* 1023
Gramm-Rudman Act (1985), 1092
Grand Army of the Republic, 672
Grand Coulee Dam, 834
Grange movement
    growth of, 678–679, *679*
    origins of, 677–678
Grant, Madison, 717, 1123

Grant, Ulysses S., 947
　campaign for president, 544
　commemorative statue, 1064
　election of 1868 and, 552
　presidency of
　　Comstock Law (1873), 657
　　election of 1872, 554
　　relations with Indians, 584, 586
　　scandals, 553–554, 554, 672, 673
Grapes of Wrath, The (film), 841
Grapes of Wrath, The (Steinbeck), 815
Grateful Dead, 995, 996, 997, 998
Graveyard vote, 650
Great American Desert, 579, 594
Great Atlantic and Pacific Tea Company, 661,
　782
Great Basin, environment of, 594
Great Britain
　in late 19th century
　　Anglo-Chinese War, 643
　　naval power of, 690, 691
　　territorial expansion, 688, 689(m)
　　Venezuelan boundary dispute and, 693
　in 20th century
　　espionage in, 922
　　gold standard abandoned, 804
　　"Great Slump" in, 845
　　Thatcherism, 1071
　　ties to U.S., 748, 749
　　woman suffrage, 715, 716
　in World War II
　　Battle of Britain (1940), 860, 886
　　lend-lease program, 860–861, 861
Great Crash, 804
Great Depression, 810–811, 811
　causes of, 805–806
　corporate diversification and, 948
　economy and, 844–845, 845
　effects on Europe, 773, 774, 804–805, 805
　global perspective of, 804–805, 805
　Hoover and (See Hoover, Herbert)
　human impact of, 811–817, 812
　　African Americans and, 816–817, 817
　　ecological disaster, 814–815, 815
　　hard times, 812–813
　　Mexican Americans and, 815–816
　　radio and film, 813–814, 814
　Keynesian economics and, 844–845, 845
　New Deal and (See New Deal)
Greater East Asia Co-Prosperity Sphere, 856
Great Plains
　agriculture in, 579
　buffalo hunting, 603–604
　Dust Bowl, 814–815, 815
Great Railroad Strike (1877), 635, 681
Great Society programs, 988–990, 990, 999,
　1026, 1100
　Nixon's conservatism and, 1043
　origins of, 987, 987–988
　Vietnam War and, 1012
Great Train Robbery, The (film), 788
Great Wall of China, 1021
Great White Fleet, 742
Greece, 906, 909
Greeley, Horace, 554, 658
Green, William, 839
Greenback party (1874), 672
Greenbacks, 673–674
Greenpeace, 1042
Greenspan, Alan, 1109
Grenada, invasion of (1983), 1081
Grimes, James W., 553
Griswold v. Connecticut (1964), 992
Groves, Gen. Leslie, 912
Grower-Shipper Vegetable Association, 878

Gruen, Victor, 1068
Gruening, Sen. Ernest, 1007
Guadalcanal, battle of (1942), 867
Guam, 699(m), 700, 862
Guatemala, 954, 954, 1098, 1103
Guevara, Che, 1017
Guiteau, Charles, 673
Gulf of Tonkin resolution (1965), 1007, 1012,
　1015, 1020

Habeas corpus, writ of, 556
Haber, Al, 993
Haddon, Briton, 788
Haight-Ashbury, 998
Haiphong harbor (Vietnam), 1031
Haiti, 540, 1106–1107
Haldeman, H. Robert, 1019, 1023, 1046, 1047,
　1049
Haley, Bill, 951
Half-Breeds (Republican), 674
Hanna, Marcus Alonzo, 683
Hanson, Ole, 767, 768
Harding, Warren G.:
　presidency of, 771, 797, 798, 818
　as senator, 768
Harlem (New York City), 646–647, 835
　Harlem Renaissance, 777, 792
　race riots (1964), 985
Harper's magazine, 896
Harrington, Michael, 987, 1078
Harrison, Benjamin
　election of 1888 and, 671, 675, 675
　election of 1892 and, 679–680
Harrison, William Henry, 675
Hart, Frederick, 1066, 1066
Harvard University, 660, 782, 823, 896, 959,
　1122
Hassam, Childe, 746
Haussmann, Baron Georges, 561–562
Havana, Cuba, 695, 696
Hawaii
　American expansion and, 694, 694
　annexation of (1898), 699, 699(m)
　Asian Americans in, 1028
　Japanese Americans in, 877
　Pearl Harbor attack, 852, 853, 854, 862–863
　statehood (1959), 998
"Hawks" and "doves," 1011
Hay, John, 694, 695, 702
Hayakawa, Sen. S. I., 1058, 1123, 1124
Hayden, Casey, 1029
Hayden, Tom, 992, 993
Hayes, Rutherford B.
　election of 1876 and, 556, 672
　presidency of
　　civil service reform and, 674
　　first White House telephone, 613
　　Great Railroad Strike (1877), 635
Haymarket Square Riot (1886), 636
Hay-Pauncefote Treaty (1901), 694
Health and sanitation. See also Disease; Medicine
　in late 19th century
　　examination of immigrants, 644, 644–645
　　in major cities, 561, 561
　　Pasteur's discovery, 642
　　water and sewage systems, 648
　in 20th century
　　drugs and pesticides, 873, 947, 1039
　　health care reform, 1110–1111, 1111
　　Panama Canal building and, 738
　　progressive reform, 722
　　public health crisis, 1092
　　pure food and drug bills, 727
Hearst, William Randolph, 695, 880
Helicopters, use in Vietnam, 1003, 1020

Hell's Angels, 998
Helsinki summit (1975), 1052
Hemingway, Ernest, 791
Hensley, Josephine ("Chicago Jo"), 590
Hepburn Railway Act (1906), 726
Hernandez, Ester, 1124
Hernández, Pete, 977
Hernández v. Texas, 977, 1045
Herrera, Juan José, 588
Hickok, Lorena, 810
Hidatsa Indians, 604
Highway Act, 947
Highways
　beautification program, 989–990
　California freeway system, 938
　interstate highway system, 938–940
Highway Safety Act (1966), 1038
Highway Trust Fund, 939
Hill, Anita, 1089
Hippies, 996–997, 998, 999
Hirabayashi, Gordon, 878
Hiroshima, Japan, 886, 887, 892, 892–893, 896,
　897, 899
Hispanics. See Latinos; Mexican Americans
"Hispanos," 578, 587, 587–588
Hiss, Alger, 922
History of the Standard Oil Company (Tarbell),
　711
Hitler, Adolf, 772–773, 820
　air power and, 886
　Allied strategy and, 859(m)
　American neutrality legislation and, 857
　conquest of Czechoslovakia (1939), 858
　control of Third Reich, 855–856
　death of, 890
　declares war on U.S., 863
　invasion of Poland (1939), 858–860, 859(m)
　Keynesian economics and, 844–845
　mass politics and propaganda, 857
　nonaggression pact with Soviet Union,
　　858–859, 861, 907
Hitler Youth, 857
Hoboes of America, 873
Ho Chi Minh, 771, 900–901, 953, 1005, 1006,
　1009, 1013, 1017, 1019
Ho Chi Minh Trail, 1006–1007, 1008(m)
Hohokam Indians, 580
Holiday Inn, 1100
Holland, Hitler's invasion of, 860
Hollywood. See Motion pictures
Hollywood Ten, 923
Holmes, Oliver Wendell, Jr., 710, 758
Holocaust, 865, 888–890, 889
Home Insurance Building (1885), 647
Homelessness, 812, 812
Home Owners' Loan Act (1934), 825, 846
Homer, Winslow, 533
Home Relief Station (Ribak), 818
Homestead, Pennsylvania. See Pittsburgh
Homestead Act (1862), 582, 595
Homosexuality. See also Sexuality
　AIDS crisis and, 1092, 1092
　gay rights activists, 1028–1029
　military service and, 869–870, 1105
　in urban community, 657–658
Hong Kong, 1109
Honolulu, Hawaii
　Asian Americans in, 1101
　Pearl Harbor attack, 852, 853, 854, 862–863
Hoover, Herbert, 798–799, 946
　casualty estimates by (WWII), 897
　election of 1928 and, 801(m), 801–802
　election of 1932 and, 822, 822(m), 839
　presidency of, 810
　　Bonus Army, 821–822

Hoover, Herbert—*Cont.*
    presidency of—*Cont.*
        conflict over China, 854–855
        criticisms of, 817–818, 820, 823
        depression program, *819*, 819–820
        discontent during, 820–821, *821*
        failure of relief and, *818*, 818–819
        Good Neighbor policy, 855
        Hoovervilles, *812*
Hoover, J. Edgar, 924, 1045, 1054
Hoovervilles, *812*
Hopkins, Harry, 810, 825–826, 829, 831
Hopkins, Johns, 660
Hopwood v. State of Texas et al (1996), 1089
Horizontal growth
    of business, 622, 624
    of unions, 634
Hornet (U.S. aircraft carrier), 866–867
Horton Plaza, 1068, *1069*
House, Edward M., 744, 751
Houseman, John, 841
House of Morgan, 804
House of Representatives, U.S. *See also* Congress,
        U.S.; Senate, U.S.
    civil rights measures, 981
    Democratic control of, 555, 670
    Nixon impeachment, 1049
    Puerto Rican representation, 701
    Starr report, 1114
House Un-American Activities Committee
        (HUAC), 841, 923
Housing, residential. *See also* Architecture
    in 19th century
        on Great Plains, 598–599
        sharecroppers' cabins, *546*, 546–547, 550
        slave cabins, 547
        sod houses, 595–596, *596*, 599
    in 20th century
        federal assistance, 1078
        minority housing, 880
        residential construction, 779
        suburban housing boom, 937, *942*,
            942–943
        urban blight, *1090*, 1090–1091
Houston, Charles, 974–975
Houston, Texas, 754, 1097–1098, 1103, 1105
Howard, John Langley, *811*
Howdy Doody Show, The 941
Howl (Ginsberg), 951
HUAC (House Un-American Activities
        Committee), 841, 923
Hubbell, Webster, 1106
HUD (Department of Housing and Urban
        Development; 1965), 989
Hudson, T. S., 608, 610, 618, 637
Hue, Vietnam, 1012
Huerta, Dolores, 1025
Huerta, Victoriano, 744, 745
Hughes, Charles Evans, 751, 768, 798
Hughes, Langston, 792
Hull, Cordell, 857, 862
Hull House (1889), 652, 714, 720, *721*, 817
Human potential movement, 1070
Human rights issues, 1058
Humphrey, George, 952
Humphrey, Sen. Hubert, 988, 1016, 1018
Hungary
    breakup of Soviet Union and, 1086
    Hungarian uprising (1956), 955
Hunger strikes, 1025
Hunt, E. Howard, 1047
Hunting, 574, 583–584, 603–604
Huntington, Collis, 686
Hurricane Plantation, 532–533, 558
Hurston, Zora Neale, 792

Hussein, Saddam, 1087, 1087(m)
Hutcheson, "Big Bill," 839
Hyden, Kentucky, 777, 778
Hydrogen bomb, 922, 925, 931
Hypertext links, 1117

IBM (International Business Machines
        Corporation), 950, 1117
ICC (Interstate Commerce Commission), 678,
        726
Iceland, 1085
Ickes, Harold, 827, 834, 835, *844*, 874, 1039
"If We Must Die" (McKay), 792
Illegal aliens, 1096–1098, 1103, 1123
Illinois (battleship), 668
Illinois Vice Commission (1916), 720
IMF (International Monetary Fund), 890, 1110
Immigrant aid societies, 653
Immigration
    as global issue, 1096–1105, *1099*
        Asian Americans, 1099–1102
        illegal aliens, 1096–1098, 1103, 1123
        Latinos, 1102–1103
        links with home country, 1103–1104
        "new" immigration, 1098–1099, *1099*
        religious diversity and, *1104*, 1104–1105
    restriction of
        Chinese immigrants, 651, 654
        LULAC support of, 816
        nativism and, 651, 717, 793–794
        Taft's veto of, 700–701
    in late 19th century
        assimilation, 655
        city life and, 652(n), 652–655, *654*
        education, 659
        in Europe, 561
        factory labor, 571, 600, 642–645, *643*, *644*
        international labor pool, 616–618, *617*
        from Mexico, 588
        profile of immigrants, 645
        railroad workers, 591
    in 20th century
        after World War II, 1024
        Johnson's immigration reform, 989
        of Latinos, 1024–1025
        social control of, 716, 717
        social education, 717
        Triangle Shirtwaist fire (1911), 706–707,
            708, 722
Immigration Act (1924), 889
Immigration Act (1965), 989, 1028, 1098
Immigration and Control Act (1986), 1103
Immigration and Stabilization Act (1993), 1123
Immigration Reform Act (1965), 1100
Immigration Restriction League, 651, 717
Impeachment
    of Andrew Johnson, *541*, 541–542
    of Clinton, 1114–1115
    of Nixon, 1049, 1115
    significance of, 1115
Imperialism, 687–694. *See also* Spanish-
        American War
    age of, 562–564
    American imperialism, 688–693, 689(m), *692*
    commercial empire, 693–694
    European expansion, 688, *688*
    "new" navy and, *690*, 690–691
    in Pacific, 694, *694*
Imperial Valley, California, 815, 816
Inchon, Korea, 926, 926(m)
Income tax, graduated, 729, 732–733
Index of American Design, 841
India, 563, 771, 1099, *1100*, 1100–1101
Indiana, 924
Indiana (U.S. battleship), 690

Indianapolis, Indiana, 797
Indian Reorganization Act (1934), 837
Indian Rights Association, 586
Indians of All Tribes, 1027
Indochina (French), 862, 953, 953(m), 1005
Indonesia, 1109
Industrial capitalism, 627
Industrialism, progressivism and, 709
Industrialization. *See also* Business and
        commerce; Corporations; Trade; *specific
        industries*
    after World War II, 827–828, 901, 902
    before Civil War, 610
    industrial recovery, planning for, 827 828
    industrial systems (*See* Industrial systems)
    regional identity and, 600
    in South
        effects of, 561–564, *561–564*
        in late 19th century, 570–571, *571*
        poverty and, 573
        during Reconstruction, 545
        women's work and, 631, *631*
    during World War II (*See* World War II, war
        production)
Industrial systems. *See also* Business and
        commerce; Corporations;
        Industrialization; Trade
    assembly line and, 771, 780
    development of, 610–618
        corporations, rise of, 615–616
        finance capital, 613–615
        information systems, *614*, 614–615
        international labor pool, 616–618, *617*
        invention, 611–612, *612*
        rail systems, 608, 610
        resources and technology, 610–611, *611*
        steel industry, 609
        transportation and communication,
            612–613
    effects of protests and violence, 634–637, *635*,
        636
    growth of big business, 621–628
        business leaders, 628
        consumer goods, 621–623
        corporate mergers, 622, 624–625, *707*, 725,
            782
        costs of doing business, 627, 627–628
        critics of, 626–627
        defenders of, 625–626, *626*
        steel industry, 622–623, 623–624
        trusts, 624
    labor unions (*See* Labor unions)
    railroads as (*See* Railroads)
    workers (*See* Work and workers)
Industrial Workers of the World (IWW), 758
"Inebriate's Express," *720*
Inflation
    after World War II, 918
    fear of, 673
    under Ford, 1050, 1054, *1054*
    under Reagan, 1076
    Vietnam War and, 1012, 1044
    in Weimar Republic, 800
Influence of Sea Power upon History, The (Mahan),
        689–690
Influenza pandemic (1918–1919), *760*, 760–762
Infrastructure
    effects of New Deal on, *811*
    Public Works Administration and, 827, 835,
        837
    public works under Hoover, 819–820
    Tennessee Valley Authority, *826*, 826–827
    water conservation projects, 833–834
Initiative (introduction of legislation), 722
Insurance, 1110–1111, *1111*

Integration. *See* Desegregation
Intelligence gathering. *See* Central Intelligence
     Agency; Espionage
Intelligence (IQ) tests, 754, 1009
Intercollegiate football, 662–663, 790
Interior Department, U.S., 1077
Internal combustion engine, 611
Internal Revenue Service, 873, 1046
International Bank for Reconstruction and
     Development (World Bank), 890
International Business Machines Corporation
     (IBM), 950, 1117
International Monetary Fund (IMF), 890, 1110
International Telephone and Telegraph, 948
Internet, 1116–1118, *1118*
Internment camps, 877–879, *878*
Interstate Commerce Commission (ICC; 1887),
     678, 726
Interstate Highway Act (1956), 939
Interstate highway system, 938–940
*Intoxicating Drinks and Drugs in All Lands and
     Times* (Crafts and Crafts), 792
Intracity transportation, 562, 598
Invention factories, 612
Inventions
     basketball, 663
     camera, 612
     cigarette-rolling machine, 570
     industrial technology, 611–612, *612*
     internal combustion engine, 611
     mimeograph, 615
     safety razor, 764
Investment capital, 599–600, 613–615
Invisible Empire. *See* Ku Klux Klan
Iowa, 676, *1104,* 1105
Iran
     arms-for-hostages scandal, 1076, 1081–1083,
          1082(m), *1083*
     hostage crisis (1979), 1061, 1074, 1081–1082
     Operation Ajax (1951), 954
     revolution in, *1051*(m), 1056
     under Shah, 954, 1021, 1056, 1060–1061
     Stalin's plans for, 906
     war with Iraq, 1086
Irangate scandals, 1049, 1083–1084
Iraq, 1086–1087
     ecoterrorism by, 1087–1088
     Persian Gulf War, 1086–1088, *1087*(m)
     war with Iran, 1086
Irish, The 634–635, 674
Iron Curtain, 908
Iron Curtain, The (film), 923
Iroquois Indians, *836*
Islamic fundamentalism, 901, 1061, 1081
Isolationism, 855–856, 860–861, *861*
Israel
     invasion of Sinai (1956), 955–956
     recognition of (1948), 912
     shuttle diplomacy and, 1052
     Yom Kippur War (1973), 1050, *1051*(m),
          1052
Issei (Japanese aliens), 877
Italglish dialect, 653
Italian Americans, 877
Italy
     Allied invasion of (1943), 882
     attack on Ethiopia (1935), 857
     fascism in, 772, 855
     student protests in (1968), 1017
"I Want to Hold Your Hand" (Beatles), 996
I Was a Communist for the FBI (film), 923
IWW (Industrial Workers of the World), 758

Jackson, Andrew, 683(n), 690
Jackson, Helen Hunt, 586
Jackson State University, 1004

Jamaica, 540
James, William, 709
Jan and Dean, 998
Japan
     in late 19th century, 643, 688, 689(m)
     in 20th century
          aggression in China, 854–855, 858
          democracy and, 772
          League of Nations and, 855, 856
          Treaty of Portsmouth (1905), 741
          Twenty-One Demands (1915), 744
          use of captive labor, 876
          World War II and
               Hiroshima and Nagasaki, *886,* 887, *892,*
                    892–893, *896,* 897, 899
               industrialization following, 901
               Pearl Harbor attack, 852, *853,* 854, 862–863
               prewar expansion in Pacific, 862–863
               proposed invasion of, 897
               surrender of, 892
Japanese Americans, 877–879, *878*
Japanese immigrants, 643, 742
Jaworski, Leon, 1048
Jazz Age, 777
Jazz music, 663, 790–791, 951
Jazz Singer, The (film), 814
J. Edgar Thomson Mills, *622–623,* 623
Jefferson, Thomas, 743
Jefferson Airplane, 998
Jenney, William LeBaron, 647
Jewish Daily Forward (newspaper), 653
Jews
     in late 19th century
          cigar makers, 571
          immigration of, 645, 652
          as ward bosses, 641
     in 20th century
          during Great Depression, 818
          Holocaust, 865, 888–890, *889*
          immigration of, restricted, 889
          restrictive housing covenants, 919, 937
          social divisions, 941
Jim Crow system
     black response to, *685,* 685–686
     laws, 577, 754, 916, 974, 977
     legal standing of Latinos and, 976–977
     NAACP efforts against, 974
     politics, 684–685
     World War II and, 880–881
Job Corps, 987, *987,* 990
John XXIII, Pope, 1072
John Paul II, Pope, 1071, 1073
Johns Hopkins University (1873), 660, 783
Johnson, Andrew, 693
     break with Congress, *537,* 537–538
     on confiscation laws, 541
     elections of 1866 and, 538–539
     failure of program, *536,* 536–537
     Fourteenth Amendment and, 538, 539, 553,
          558
     impeachment, 532, *541,* 541–542, 552, 672
     Reconstruction plan, 535, *535*
Johnson, Hugh, 827
Johnson, James Weldon, 975
Johnson, Lady Bird, 989–990
Johnson, Louis, 925
Johnson, Lyndon B., 948, 1011, *1011,* 1045, 1076
     background and character, 986, *986*
     death of, 1032
     election of 1964 and, 988
     election of 1968 and, 1014, *1014,* 1016
     presidency of
          Civil Rights Act (1964), 983
          evaluation of, 990, *990*
          Great Society, 988–990, *990,* 999, 1012,
               1026, 1100

Johnson, Lyndon B.—*Cont.*
     presidency of—*Cont.*
          inflation, 1044
          Kennedy legacy and, 987, *987*–988
          origins of Great Society, 987, *987*–988
          racial violence and, 985, 986
          Supreme Court and, 990–992, *991*
          Supreme Court reform, *991*
          Vietnam War and, 1002, 1006–1007, 1009,
               1013, 1015, 1018, 1020, 1032
          women's rights and, 1029–1030
Johnson, Rev. John H., 835
Johnson, Sen. Hiram, 794
Johnson, Tom, 721
Joint Chiefs of Staff, U.S., 965, 1013
Joint Committee on Reconstruction, 538
Jones, Amy, *836*
Jones, Mary, 551
Jones, Paula, 1106, 1114
Joplin, Scott, 663
Jordan, Michael, 1120
Jordan, Vernon, 1120
Journalism. *See also* Magazines; *specific
     publications*
     in late 19th century, 653, 695
     in 20th century
          African American newspapers, 757
          coverage of zoot suit riots, 880
          effect on public opinion, 922
          muckrakers, 710–711
          "New Journalism," 995
          newspaper chains, 788
          war correspondents, 860, 868
Joy Luck Club, The (Tan), 1099
Judiciary Committee, U.S., 1089
Jungle, The (Sinclair), 727
Justice Department, U.S.:
     Anti-Trust Division, 799
     antitrust suits, 627, 726
     civil rights, 981
     Nixon and, 1046
Juvenile courts, 710, 780
Juvenile delinquency, 950, 987

Kaiser, Henry J., 871
Kampuchea (Cambodia), 1019, 1020, 1100
Kansas, 566–567, 678, 715
Kansas City Monarchs, 917
Kansas Pacific Railroad, 597
Kasserine Pass, Battle of (1943), 867
KDKA radio, 788
Keating-Owen Child Labor Act (1916), 714,
     714(n), 733
Keegan, Bill, 852
Keegan, Dennis, 852
Kefauver, Sen. Estes, 945–946
Kefauver hearings, 945–946
Keith, Benjamin Franklin, 664, 665
Keith-Albee vaudeville circuit, 665
Kelley, Florence, 714
Kelley, Oliver Hudson, 677
Kellogg, Frank, 801
Kellogg-Briand Pact (1928), 801
Kemp, Jack, 1088
Kennan, George, 908, 924, 925
Kennedy, Jacqueline, 959, 1075
Kennedy, John F., 948, 989, 1011, 1014, 1016,
     1075, 1076, 1105
     assassination of, 983, 1006
     election of 1960 and, 958(m), 958–959, 961
     presidency of
          as "Camelot," 959–960, *960*
          civil rights and, 980–981
          cold war frustrations, 961–963,
               962(m)–963(m)
          Cuban missile crisis, 964–966, *965*

Kennedy, John F.—*Cont.*
 presidency of—*Cont.*
  domestic agenda, 960–961
  U.S.-Soviet tensions, 963–964
  Vietnam War and, 1005, 1006, 1015, 1032
  war on poverty, 987
  women's rights and, 1029
Kennedy, Robert, 1014, 1017
 assassination of, 1016, *1016*
 as Attorney General, 980–981, 987
Kent State University (1970), 1002, 1004, *1004*
Kerouac, Jack, 951
Kerr, Clark, 994
Kesey, Ken, 995
Keynes, John Maynard, 844–845
Keynesian economics, 844–845, 1044
Keystone Kops, 787
Khe Sanh (Vietnam), 1013
Khomeini, Ayatollah Ruhollah, 901, 1061, 1071
Khrushchev, Nikita
 Berlin wall, 963–964
 change from Stalin, 955, *955*
 Cuban missile crisis and, 964–966, *965*, 1021
 Soviet-American relations and, *957*, 957–958
Kim Il Sung, 925
Kindergartens, 659
King, Coretta Scott, *1055*
King, Rev. Martin Luther, Jr., *971*, 973, 979, 993,
  1011, *1055*, 1120
 assassination of, 1015–1016
 election of 1960 and, 959
 ethic of nonviolence, 1025
 FBI and, 1054
 "I have a dream" speech, 983
 "Letter from Birmingham Jail," 981–982
 march from Selma to Montgomery, 983
 march on Washington, *971*, 982–983
 Montgomery bus boycott, 977, 978
 SCLC, 980
 on Watts riots, 985, 985(m), *985*
King, Rodney, 1120
King Ranch (Texas), 594
Kingston Trio, 995
Kinsey, Alfred, 945
Kinsey Report, 945
Kinship groups, 580
Kiowa Indians, *604*, 605
Kipling, Rudyard, 563, 692
Kissinger, Henry, 1019, 1023–1024, 1032
 détente and, 1052, *1053*
 foreign policy and, 1049–1050
 shuttle diplomacy, 1052
Kiss-Me Clubs, 782–783
Kitchens, 943
Knights of Labor (1869), 633
Know-Nothings, 1123
Knox, Philander, 726, 742
Kodak camera, 612
Koehler, Robert, *635*
Konoye, Fumimaro, 862
Korea. *See also* Korean War; North Korea; South
  Korea
 immigration from, 1099
 Japanese domination of, 854
 slave labor in WWII, 876
Korean Americans, 869, 1104, 1121
Korean War
 Chinese intervention, 927, *927*
 Eisenhower and, 929–930
 global implications of, 928–929
 MacArthur relieved, 928
 M*A*S*H (tv program), 1074
 North Korean invasion, 925–926, 926(m)
Korematsu, Fred, 878, 879
Korematsu v. United States (1944), 879
Kosovo, intervention in, 1107

Kosovo Liberation Army, 1107
Krupp (arms manufacturer), 668
Ku Klux Klan (1866)
 after World War I, *796*, 796–797
 during Great Depression, 817
 during Reconstruction, *555*, 555–556
 during World War II, 880
Ku Klux Klan Act (1871), 555–556
Kuwait, 1086–1088, 1087(m)

Labor. *See* Work and workers
Labor contractors, 551, 616–617, 757, 816
Labor Department, U.S., 756
Labor unions. *See also* Strikes; Work and workers
 in late 19th century, 632–637
  American Federation of Labor, 633–634
  early unions, 632–633
  Knights of Labor, 633
  management's response to, *636*, 636–637
  protests and violence, 634–637, *635*, *636*
  vocational education and, 659
 in 20th century
  company unions, 782–783
  immigrant labor and, 1124
  Reagan attack on, 1077
  during World War II, 874, *874*
 during Great Depression
  migrant workers' unions, 816, 838
  rise of, 838–839, *838–839*
 yellow dog contracts and, 637, 782
Laconia, sinking of (1917), 746–747
Ladies Home Journal, The 806
Laffer, Arthur, 1076
La Fleche, Susette, 586
La Follette, Robert ("Battle Bob"), 722, *722*, 726,
  733
La Follette's Magazine, 722
Land
 redistribution of, 540–541
 speculation in, 586, 588
Landis, Judge Kenesaw Mountain, 790
Land League (1914), 589
Landon, Gov. Alfred, 833
Language, 653, *1123*, 1123–1124
Laos, 1100
Lasker, Albert, 784
Lathrop, Julia, 714
Latin America, in 20th century. *See also* Central
  America; *specific countries*
 American imperialism and, 687–688
 effects of Great Depression in, 804–805
 Good Neighbor policy in, 855, *855*
 instability in, 961
 nationalism in, 956
Latinos
 civil rights of, *976*, 976–977
 education levels, 1118
 enclave communities of, 1102–1103
 Mexican Americans (*See* Mexican Americans)
 migrations of, *939*, 940
 pachucos, 880
 political activism of, 1024–1027, *1026*
 projected population of, *1099*
 union jobs and, 1124
 during World War II, 879, 880
Latvia, 1086
Laundresses, 635–636
Laundries, Chinese, 653
Law enforcement. *See also* Courts; Crime
 in 20th century
  Chicago police riot (1968), 1016
  creation of Border Patrol, 794
  Nixon's war on dissent and, 1045
  "no-knock" police raids, 1045
  Palmer raids, 768
  Simpson murder and, 1121

Law enforcement—*Cont.*
 vigilante committees, 597
Lawrence, Jacob, *869*
Law schools, 660
LCTM (Long-Term Capital Management), 1109
League for the Protection of the Family (1896),
  681
League of Nations, 763, 855, 856
League of United Latin American Citizens
  (LULAC; 1929), 815, 816, 976, 1024
League of Women Voters, 856
Lear, Norman, 1074
Leary, Timothy, 993, 994–995
Lease, Mary Elizabeth, 679, *679*
Lebanon
 Iran hostage crisis (1979), 1061, 1074,
  1081–1082
 U.S. invasion of (1958), 956
 U.S. Marines in, 1080–1081
Lee, Gen. Robert E., 1064
Legion of Decency (1933), 814
Legislation. *See also* Congress, U.S.; Supreme
  Court, U.S.
 anti-alcohol laws, 720
 Great Society and (*See* Great Society pro-
  grams)
 Jim Crow laws, 577
 labor codes, 707
 to limit corporations, 626–627
 mandatory education laws, 658
 New Deal programs (*See* New Deal)
Leisure pursuits. *See* Popular culture and
  entertainment; Sports
LeMay, Gen. Curtis, 1017
Lend-Lease Act (1941), 860
Lend-lease aid to Britain, 860–861, *861*
Lenin, Vladimir I., 753, 772, 907
Lenoir, Etienne, 611
Levine, David, *1011*
Levitt, William, 937, 938, 942
Levittown communities, 937, 940, 941, 949
Lewinsky, Monica, 1114
Lewis, John, 980
Lewis, John L., 839, 840, 874, *874*
Lewis, John Solomon, 569, 570
Lewis, Oscar, 987
Lewis, Sinclair, 791
Lexington (U.S. aircraft carrier), 866
Leyte Gulf, Battle of (1944), 883, 884
Liberalism
 conservative resistance to, 1070–1071
 Great Society programs, *986*, 986–992, 999,
  1012, 1026, 1100
 Nixon's conservatism and, 1043–1044
 view of Reagan, 1070
Liberal Republican party, 554
Liberdad (Hernandez), *1124*
Liberty bonds, 755
Libraries, 625, *626*
Libya, 1081
Lice, 765
Licklider, J. C. R., 1116
Life magazine, 715
Liga Pro Defensa Escolar, *915*
Lii, Gasel, 1125
Liliuokalani, Queen of Hawaii, 694
Lin, Maya Ying, *1065*, 1065–1067
Lincoln, Abraham, 683(n), 693, 888
 commemorative statue, 1065, *1065*
 presidency of, 533, 534, 535, 583
Lincoln Memorial, 834
Lindbergh, Charles, 789
Lindsey, Ben, 710, 944
Linkages, détente and, 1021–1022
Lippmann, Walter, 784, *1011*

Literacy, *548, 658*
Literacy tests, 651, 717
Literature. *See also specific works*
  banning and burning, 924, 930
  Harlem Renaissance, 792
  James Bond novels, 960, *960*
  naturalism in, 712
  nihilism in, 791
  reflection of society, 815
Lithuania, 1086
Little, Cara, 1090
Little Big Horn, Battle of (1874), 584, *585*
"Little boy" (atom bomb), 891
Little Rock, Arkansas, 978–979, *979*
Liu, Harold, 869
Living Newspapers, 841
Lloyd George, David, 762, *763*
Lobbies, 677, 750
Locke, Alain, 792
Lodge, Sen. Henry Cabot, 695, 763, 765, 766,
  794, 1014
Logging, 571–572, *572,* 974
Lombardo, Guy, 814
Lôme, Enrique Dupuy de, 695
London, England, 752
London *Morning Post,* 742
Lonely Crowd, The (Reisman), 949–950
Long, Breckinridge, 889–890
Long, Sen. Huey P. ("Kingfish"), 830, *830,* 831
Long telegram, 908
Long-Term Capital Management (LCTM), 1109
Looking Backward (Bellamy), 626
Lopez, Yolanda, *1097*
Lord and Thomas (advertising firm), 784
Lorentz, Pare, 841
Los Angeles, California
  in late 19th century, 592, 597, 642
  in 20th century
    Asian Americans in, 1101
    effects of freeway system, 938
    Mexican Americans in, 1102–1105
    riots in (1992), 1120–1121, 1124
    settlement houses, 652, 714
    Venice Beach Amusement Park, 718, *718,* 719
    Watts race riots (1965), 985, 985(m), *985*
  during World War II
    Pearl Harbor attack and, 852, *853*
    war industries in, 871
Louisiana
  Huey Long and, 830, *830*
  integration requirement, 544
  Plessy v. Ferguson (1896), 577, 659, 917, 975
Louisiana (U.S. battleship), 738
Louis XIV, King of France, 762, *763*
Low, David, *913*
Loyalty Leagues, 758
Loyalty oaths, 535, 924
Loyalty Review Board, 922–923
LSD, 995
Luce, Henry R., 788, 922
Lucky Strike cigarette ads, 784
"Lucy in the Sky with Diamonds" (Beatles), 997
Ludendorf, Gen. Eric von, 761
Luftwaffe, 886
Luks, George, *708*
LULAC. *See* League of United Latin American
  Citizens
Luna Park (Coney Island), 663, 718, 719
Lusitania, sinking of (1915), 749–750
Lyles, Aubrey, 788
Lynching
  in late 19th century, 578
    Colored Farmers' Alliance (1891), 678
    Jim Crow politics and, 685

Lynching—*Cont.*
  in 20th century
    after World War I, *796*
    after World War II, 915
    campaign against, 835
    during Great Depression, 817

McAdoo, William Gibbs, 755
MacArthur, Gen. Douglas, 821, 865, 882
  casualty estimates by, 897
  in Korean War, 926, 926(m), 927
  relieved of command, 928
  return to Philippines, 883–884, 884(m)
MacArthur Park, 1102, 1104
MacAuliffe, Gen. Tony, 883
Macbeth (Shakespeare), 841
McCallum, Daniel, 618–619
McCarran Act (1950), 923, 927
McCarthy, Sen. Eugene, 1014, *1014,* 1015, 1016
McCarthy, Sen. Joseph R., 946, 947, 959
  fall of, *930,* 930–931, *931*
  rise of, 924, *924,* 927
McClure's magazine, 710–711
McCombs, William, 731
McCormick, Cyrus, 687
McCormick Harvester Company, 622–623, 636
Macdonald, Dwight, 949
McFarlane, Robert, 1082, 1083
McGovern, Sen. George, 1046
McGuffey's Reader, 659
Machine guns, 753
Machine politics, 649–650, *650,* 722
McIlhenny, Edward, 574
McKay, Claude, 792
McKellar, Sen. Kenneth, 767
McKinley, William, 724
  assassination of, 723
  election of 1896 and, *682,* 682–684, 683(n),
    684(m), *687*
  presidency of
    Boxer Rebellion (1899), 702
    Cuban revolt and, 695, *696*
    legislation, 687
    Spanish-American War and, 696, 697, 699
  as senator, 673
McKinley Tariff (1890), 673, 676, 694
McMahon Act (1946), 912
McNamara, Robert Strange, 959, 960, 964, 1006,
  1007, 1012, 1015
McPherson, Aimee Semple, 776, 778, *778,* 795
McTeague (Norris), 712
Macune, Dr. Charles W., 678, 679
Maddox (U.S. destroyer), 1007
Madera, Francisco, 744
Madison, James, 542
Magazines. *See also specific publications*
  muckrakers, 710–711
  women's rights movement and, 657
Mahan, Alfred Thayer, 689–690, 702
Mail order sales, *619,* 661
Maine, USS (battleship), 695, *696*
Main Street (Lewis), 791
Major Bowes' Amateur Hour, 813
Malcolm X, 983, 984, *984*
Mall rats, 1068
Malnutrition, 812
Management, corporate
  administrative techniques, 624
  new managerial elite, 618–619, *619*
  as organization model, 710
  personnel management, 756
  response to strikes, *636,* 636–637
  as salaried bureaucracy, 782
Manchuria (Manchukuo), 854–855, 907

Manhattan Project, *872,* 873, 890, 912, 922
Manifest Destiny, 687, 693, 740
Mann Act (1910), 720
Mansfield, Sen. Mike, 1015
Manzanar, California, *878*
Mao Zedong, 901, 907, *921,* 922, 927, 1017,
  1022, 1023, 1071
"Maple Leaf Rag" (Joplin), 663
Marcos, Ferdinand, 1098
Margin requirements (stocks), 803
Marines, U.S., 1080–1081
Market system, 561, 599
Marne River, Battle of (1918), 759, 759(m)
Marquis of Queensbury rules, 663
Marriage. *See also* Families and family life
  companionate, 944
  effects of Great Depression, 812–813
  of freedpeople, 547–548
  picture brides, 653
Marshall, Gen. George C., 874, 896, 897, 910
Marshall, Thurgood, 974–975, 977, 981, 1088
Marshall Plan, 910, 913
Martí, José, 694
Marx, Karl, 564, 988
Marxism, 772
Masaryk, Jan, 910
*M*A*S*H* (tv program), 1074
Massachusetts, 676, 793
Massachusetts (U.S. battleship), 690
Massachusetts Institute of Technology, 711, 713,
  1116
Mass culture, 719, 949–950
Mass media
  conservative rebellion and, 1037–1074
  in early 20th century, 787–789, *788, 789*
  effects on world culture, 771–772, 773–774
  images of women in, 944
Mass production
  assembly line, 771, 780
  of consumer goods, 660
  of housing, 937, *942,* 942–943
Mass transit legislation (1966), 990
Materialism, 557, 771
Matsu, 953(m)
Mattachine Society (1951), 1029
Means, Russell, 1028
Meat Inspection Act (1906), 727
Meatpacking industry, 611, 622, 727
Medellin drug cartel, 1082(m)
Medicaid Program (1965), 988–989, 990, 1078
Medical schools, 660
Medicare, 990, 1092, 1111
Medicare Act (1965), 988, 989
Medicine. *See also* Disease; Health and sanitation
  condemnation of homosexuality, 658
  home remedies, 599
  nursing, 904
  women in, 785
Meese, Edwin, 1084
Me Generation, 1038, 1061
Meir, Golda, 1052
Mellon, Andrew, 798–800, *799,* 806
Melting Pot, The (Zangwill), 664
Melting pot, views of, 664–665
Memoirs (Truman), 896
Memphis (U.S. warship), 789
Memphis, Tennessee, 539, *974*
*Mendez et al. v. Westminster School District of
  Orange County* (1947), 976
Mercenaries, in Guatemala, 954
Merchant marine, 798
Merchants, 590–591, 598
Meredith, James, 981

Mergers, corporate
  big business and, 622, 624–625, *707*, 725
  Supreme Court on, 725–726
Merry Pranksters, 995
Methodist church, 549
Metro-Goldwyn-Mayer, 814
Mexican Americans
  in late 19th century
    Anglos and, *587*, 587–588
    cowboys, 592
    racial conflict, 588–589
  in early 20th century
    labor migrations, 757
    nativism and, 794
    traditional views, 784
    in World War I, 754, *754*, 757
  during Great Depression
    federal efforts to help, 836
    muralists, 840
    repatriation, 815–816
  World War II and
    activism following, 915, *915*
    bracero program, 879
    in military, 869
  in later 20th century
    Chicanos, 1026
    legal standing of, 976–977
    in Los Angeles, 1102–1103
    political activism of, 1025–1026, *1026*
Mexican Revolution (1910), 744–745, *745,*
  843
Mexico
  in late 19th century
    immigration from, 588
    states bordering, *587*, 587–588
    transnational labor pool, 617
  in early 20th century
    disputes with U.S., 855
    U.S. intervention in, 744–745, *745*
    Zimmerman telegram, 751
  in late 20th century
    immigrants from, *1097*
    Immigration Act of 1965, 989
Miami, Florida, 1102
Michigan, University of, 992, 993
Michigan Salt Association (1869), 621–622
Microchip technology, 1118
Microsoft Corporation, 1117
"Midcult," 949
Middle class. *See also* Social class; Suburban
    era
  in late 19th century
    urban, *655*, 655–656
    vaudeville and, 665
  in early 20th century
    progressivism and, 711
    women's sphere, 712–714, *713*
  in mid-20th century
    homemakers, 942–944, *944*
    sexual attitudes of, 944–945
    suburban culture, 940–941
Middle East. *See also specific countries*
  Camp David Accords, 1060, *1060*
  chronic instability of, 1060
  oil fields in, 909, 1051(m)
  peace negotiations, 1108
  Persian Gulf War, 1086–1088, 1087(m)
  shuttle diplomacy in, 1052
  terrorism in, 1080–1081
  U.S.-Soviet peace statement (1977), 1059
  war in (1969), 1036
Middle managers, 619, *619*
Midway, Battle of (1942), 866–867, *866–867*
Midway Island, 693, 699(m)

Migration(s)
  of African Americans to cities, 617–618
  regional migrations in 1950's, *939, 940*
  from South to North, 793(m), 817
  World War I labor migrations, 757
  World War II labor migrations, 876
Migration chains, 616–618, 1096–1098
Migratory labor
  during Great Depression, *811,* 836
  worldwide, 616, 642–645, *643, 644*
Milholland, Inez, 714–715
Military-industrial sector, 914
Military preparedness, 750–751, 753–754, *754*
Military spending
  during Cold War, 925
  depression and, 845
  Eisenhower's warning on, 958
  under Reagan, 1076–1077, 1079–1080
Miller, Flournoy, 788
Miller, Jeffrey, 1004
Millett, Kate, 1030
Mills College, 944
Milosevic, Slobodan, 1107–1108
Mimeograph, invention of, 615
Minimum wage bill (1966), 990
Mining
  in late 19th century, 562
    coal mining, 636, 725
    gold and silver, 581, 589
    hydraulic, *567,* 591, 611
    mining camps, 589–591, 590(m)
  in 20th century, 917
Minneapolis, Minnesota, 641
Minnesota, 625, 652, 1068, 1100
Miranda v. Arizona (1966), 991
Miss America contest, 786, 786–787
Missiles
  Cuban missile crisis (1962), 964–966, *965*
  V-1 and V-2 missiles, 887
Missionary diplomacy, 743–744
Missions and missionaries, 691–692, *692,* 702
Mission to Moscow (film), 923
Mississippi
  Freedom Summers, 983, 992, 993, 994, *994,*
    1029
  during Reconstruction, *543,* 684
  in 19th century, 536, 540
Mississippi, University of, 981
Mississippi Plan (1875), 556
Missouri (U.S. battleship), 892
Mitchell, Albert, 760, 761
Mitchell, John (Attorney General), 1045, 1047,
    1049
Mitchell, John A. (UMW president), 725
Mobility
  downward mobility, 1102
  1950s culture of, 934–935, *938*
  social mobility, 632, 935
  World War II and, 875, 876
Mobil Oil Corporation, 948
Model cities legislation (1966), 990
Model T Ford, 780
Mod-style clothing, 996, *996*
Mohawk Indians, 1028
Molly McGuires, 634–635
Mondale, Walter, 1080
Money supply, 803
Monopoly (game), 813
Monroe, James, 843
Monroe, Marilyn, 944
Monroe Doctrine (1823), 687–688, 693, 741,
    855
Montana, 600
Montgomery, Alabama, 977–978, 979

Montgomery, Benjamin, 532–533, 557–558, *558*
Montgomery, Gen. Bernard, 867
Montgomery, Robert, 923
Moody, Dwight Lyman, 651, 941
Moon landing, *1022,* 1023
Moorehead v. Tipaldo (1936), 843
Moral diplomacy, 743–745
Morality, 754, 814, 1106
Moral Majority, Inc., 1072, *1072,* 1074
Morehouse College, 978
Morgan, J. C., 837
Morgan, J. Pierpont, 624–625, 726, 729
Morgenthau, Hans, 928
Morgenthau, Henry, 844, 873, 890
Morill Act (1862), 659–660
Mormon Church. *See* Church of Jesus Christ of
    Latter-Day Saints
Morse, Samuel F. B., 613, 615
Morse code, 615
Morton, Gov. Oliver, 539
Morton, Levi P., 675
Moss, Thomas, 685
Mossadeq, Mohammed, 954
Motel industry, *1100,* 1100–1101
Motion pictures
  declining standards in, 1073–1074
  effects of television on, 945, 946
  during Great Depression, 814
  HUAC and, 923
  lavish movie houses, *789*
  Production Code (1930), 1073
  propaganda value of, 773
  in 1920s, 787–788
Motley, Archibald, Jr., 777
Motown Record Company, 998
Moynihan, Daniel Patrick, 1043
Ms. magazine, *1030*
MS-DOS, 1117
MTV, 1093
Muhammad, Elijah (Poole), 817
Muir, John, 1002
Muir, John (naturalist), 727, *728,* 1039
Muller, Curt, 710
Muller v. Oregon (1908), 710, 1113
Multiculturalism
  full-employment economy and, 1121–1122
  global pressures and, *1123,* 1123–1125,
    1124
  racial divide and, 1120–1121
Munich analogy, 907
Munich Pact (1938), 858, 907
Municipal government. *See also* Cities and
    urbanization
  in late 19th century
    boss rule, 640–641, 649–650, *650*
    graft and corruption, 650, *650*
    National Municipal League (1895), 676
    need for reform, 649
  in 20th century, 940
    garbage collection, 720–721, *721*
    progressive reform of, 721
Munn v. Illinois (1877), 678
Murals, *811,* 841, *842,* 842–843
Murphy, Gov. Frank, 840
Murray, Philip, 840
Muscatine, Iowa, *1104*
Museums, 786, 1066
Music
  banda music, 1104
  Beatles, The 993, 996, 997
  country and western, 950, 951
  folk music, 995, 997
  during Great Depression, 813, 814
  jazz, 663, 790–791, 951

Music—*Cont.*
neighborhood bands, *654*
rhythm and blues, 950, 951, 998
rock and roll, 950–951, *951, 995,* 995–998
surfing sound, 998
Woodstock Music Festival (1969), 998–999
Mussolini, Benito, 761, 772, 773, 845, 855, 857, 877, 882, 890
Mutual assured destruction, 900
Mutualistas, 818
"My Day" (E. Roosevelt), 824
Myers, William, 940
My Lai (1968), 1013
Myrdal, Gunnar, 974

NAACP. *See* National Association for the Advancement of Colored People (NAACP)
Nader, Ralph, 993, *1038,* 1038–1039
Nader's Raiders, 1038
NAFTA (North American Free Trade Agreement), 1110
Nagasaki, Japan, *886,* 887, *892,* 892–893
Naismith, Dr. James, 663
Napalm bombs, 1010
Napoleon Bonaparte, 907
NASA (National Aeronautics and Space Administration), 1022
Nasser, Col. Gamal Abdel, 955, 956
Nast, Thomas, *650, 672*
Nation (journal), 541
National Aeronautics and Space Administration (NASA), 1022
National American Woman Suffrage Association (1890), 715, 716
National Association for the Advancement of Colored People (NAACP), 686, 835, 879, 880
after World War II, 915
Montgomery bus boycott, 977–978, 979
push for desegregation, 980
social conflict and, 973, *974,* 974–975
National Association of Colored Women (1896), 686, 713
National Association of Manufacturers, 693, 782
National Baseball League, 916–917
National Birth Control League, 785
National Civil Service Reform League (1881), 673
National Consumers' League, 711, 714, 723
National Defense Education Act (1958), 956
National Energy Act (1978), 1056
National Environmental Policy Act (1969), 1041
National Farmers' Alliance (1880), 678
National Farmers' Alliance and Industrial Union, 678
National Foundation of the Arts and Humanities (1965), 989
National Gallery of Art, 1064
National Guard. *See also* Army, U.S.; Navy, U.S.
in auto industry strikes, 840
in Detroit (1943), 880
at Kent State, 1002, 1004, *1004*
Los Angeles riots (1992), 1120–1121
at Tulsa race riots (1921), *796*
urban race riots and, 984–985, 985(m), *985*
National Industrial Recovery Act (NIRA; 1933), 827, *846*
Nationalism
in mid-20th century, 951–958
World War I and, *746,* 747, 758
National Labor Relations Act (1935), 832, *846*
National Labor Relations Board (NLRB), 832
National Labor Union (NLU), 633
National League of Professional Baseball Clubs (1876), 662

National Municipal League (1895), 676
National Negro Business League (1900), 686
National Organization for Women (NOW; 1966), 1029, 1030
National Origins Act (1924), 794, 989
National Park Service, U.S., 1066
National park system, 727
National Police Gazette, The 663
National Press Club, 925
National Public Housing Act (1937), *846*
National Recovery Administration (NRA; 1933), 827–828, 837–838, 842
National Resources Planning Board, 881
National Review, 1073
National Rifle Association, 1110
National Security Council (NSC), 924, 925
National Socialist (Nazi) Party (1933), 772–773, 844
concentration camps, 865, 888–890, *889*
growing menace of, 858
Nazism, 820–821
National Traffic and Motor Vehicle Safety Act (1966), 1038
National Union for Social Justice (1934), 830
National War Labor Board (NWLB; 1918), 756
National Wilderness Preservation System Act (1964), 989
National Woman's party (1917), 716, 786
National Woman Suffrage Association (1890–1920), 553, 672, 786
National Women's Political Caucus, 1031
National Youth Administration, 831, 881
National Youth Congress, 847
Nation of Islam, 1024
Native Americans. *See also specific tribes and leaders*
of late 19th century
policy of concentration, 582
relations with whites, 583–584
religion, 586–587, 597
reservations, 584, 586
treaties and legislation, 586–587
wars with whites, 584, 585(m), *585*
western environment and, 580, *580*
of 20th century
during Great Depression, *836,* 836–837
political activism of, *1027,* 1027–1028
during World War II, 876
Nativism
immigration restriction and, 651, 717, 793–794, 1123
Know-Nothings and, 1123
progressivism and, 716, 717
support of Prohibition, 794
NATO. *See* North Atlantic Treaty Organization
Natural resources, 562
industrial technology and, 610–611, *611*
search for, in West, 599
timber resources, 571–572, *572*
water resources, 581(m), 582
Navajo Indians, 587, 837
Navy, U.S.
in late 19th century
American imperialism and, 689–691
improved naval power, *690,* 690–691
Spanish-American War, 696
in 20th century
blockade of Cuba, 964–965
Guantánamo naval base, 956
preparedness advocates and, 750–751
Seventh Fleet in Asia, 952–953
during World War II
naval aviation, 866
Pearl Harbor attack, 852, *853,* 854
war in Pacific, 866–867, *866–867,* 883, 884(m), 888

Navy, U.S.—*Cont.*
during World War II—*Cont.*
zoot suit riots, 880
Nazism. *See* National Socialist (Nazi) Party
Nearing the Issue at the Cockpit (Bonham), *662*
Nebraska, 600
Negro Baptist Church, 549
"Negro Speaks of Rivers, The" (Hughes), 792
Nelson, Donald M., 871
Nelson, Sen. Gaylord, 1041
Nesters, 593
Netanyahu, Benjamin, 1108
Neutrality
diplomacy of, 749–750
pre–World War II laws, 856–858, *857*
U.S. declaration of, 748–749
Neutrality Act (1935), 856–857
Neutrality Act (1936), 857
Neutrality Act (1937), 858
Nevada, 591
Newark, New Jersey, 985
"New Captain in the District, A," 732
New Cathay Boys Club Band, *654*
New Deal
assessment of, 847
early years of (1933–1935)
agriculture, planning for, *828,* 828–829
banks, aid to, 824–825
industrial recovery planning, 827–828
Roosevelts and, 823–824, *824*
unemployed, relief for, 817, 820, 825(m), 825–827, *826*
effects of
arts projects, 840–841, *842,* 842–843, *869*
limited reach of, 834–836, *835*
on Native Americans, *836,* 836–837
organized labor and, *838–839,* 838–840
rural electrification, 833
western water and, 833–834
on women, 837–838
final years of (1937–1940), 841
Keynesian economics, 844–845, *845*
legacy of, 845–847, *846*
Supreme Court and, 842–844, *844*
legislation of, *846*
perceptions of, 810–811
Second New Deal (1936–1936)
election of 1936 and, 832–833
legislation, *831,* 831–832
protests during, 829–831, *830*
Truman's extension of, 918
World War II and, 881, *881*
New England Kitchen (1890), 711–712
New Federalism, 1043–1044
New frontier
domestic agenda, 960–961
election of 1960, 958(m), 958–959
Kennedy's presidency, 959–960, *960*
New Haven, Connecticut, 613
New Jersey, 625, 732
Newlands, Sen. Frederick, 727
New Mexico, 580, 600, 745
New nationalism (Roosevelt), 730, 733, 734, 755
New Negro, The (Locke), 792
New Orleans, Louisiana, 539, *646,* 980
New Orleans *Tribune,* 551
New Republic, The, 771, 817
New South. *See* The South, in late 19th century
Newspapers. *See* Journalism
New Theatre (Boston), 664
Newton, Huey P., 984, 1028
New York and Erie Railroad, 618
New York Central Railroad, 619, 620(m)

New York City
  in late 19th century
    architecture, 647, *647*
    Central Park created, 718–719
    dominance of, 642
    graft, 650, *650*
    homosexual community, 658
    immigrant processing facilities, 644, *644*
    intercity communications, 614
    as railroad hub, 620(m)
    settlement houses, 652
    subway, 646
    tenements and slums, 648, *648*
    vaudeville, 664
  municipal politics
    graft, 650, *650*
    Tammany Hall, 640–641, 649
    Tweed Ring, 545
  in 20th century
    Asian Americans in, 1101
    Dominicans in, 1102
    immigrant jobs in, 1125
    multiculturalism in, 1120
    potential bankruptcy (1975), 1054
    racial violence in (1919), 757
    starvation during Great Depression, 812
    Triangle Shirtwaist fire (1911), 706–707, *708*, 722
    Union Square protest (1930), *821*
New Yorker magazine, *789*
New York Giants (baseball), 998
New York Journal, 695
New York State, 797, 1028
New York State Board of Regents, 991–992
New York Stock Exchange (1792), 615, 621, 804
New York *Sun* (newspaper), 699
New York Times, 634, 650, *931*, 965, 1046
Nez Percé Indians, 583, 584
Ngo Dinh Diem, 953, 962–963, 1005, 1006
Nguyen Ai Quoc. *See* Ho Chi Minh
Nguyen Van Thieu (Gen.), 1031, 1032
Niagara movement (1905), 686
Nicaragua
  Contra forces, 1081, 1083
  dollar diplomacy, 742
  missionary diplomacy, 744
  Sandinista government, 1059, 1081, 1082(m)
  Somoza dictatorship, 1059
  U.S. involvement in, 1081
Nicholas II, Czar of Russia, 752
Nickelodeons, 787
Niebuhr, Reinhold, 928
Nihilism, in literature, 791
Nimitz, Adm. Chester, 883, 884, 884(m)
Nineteenth Amendment (1920), 716
Ninth Cavalry (U.S. Army), 583, 698
NIRA (National Industrial Recovery Act; 1933), 827, *846*
Nissei (Japanese Americans), 877
Nixon, Pat, 929
Nixon, Richard M., 948, 998, 1076
  character of, 1019
  election of 1952 and, 929–930
  election of 1960 and, 958, 958(m), 959
  election of 1968 and, 1016, 1017–1018, 1018(m), 1024
  election of 1972 and, 1046
  pardoned by Ford, 1053
  presidency of, 1044, 1045, 1046
    environmentalism and, 1040–1041, 1042, 1044
    morale in Vietnam and, 1020
    move toward détente, *1021*, 1021–1024
    New Federalism, 1043–1044
    resignation, 1049
    Senate hearings, 1047–1048, *1048*

Nixon, Richard M.—*Cont.*
  presidency of—*Cont.*
    social policies, 1044–1045
    Vietnamization, 1019–1020
    Vietnam War and, 1002, 1031
    Watergate scandal and, 1047, 1084, 1114–1115
  as vice-president, 955
Nixon, Tom, 603–604
Nixon, Tricia, 929
Nixon Doctrine, 1021
NLRB (National Labor Relations Board), 832
N.L.R.B. v. Jones and Laughlin Steel Corporation (1937), 844
NLU (National Labor Union), 633
Nobel Prize
  for literature, 791
  Peace Prize, 741, 1058, 1060, *1060*, 1107
Noble and Holy Order of the Knights of Labor (1869), 633
"No-knock" police raids, 1045
Nonlinear ethnic niche, 1101
Nonviolence, 978
"Normalcy," 797, 798
Normal schools, 659
Normandy landing (D-Day), 859(m), *882*, 883, 885, 946
Norris, Frank, 712
Norris, Sen. George W., *826*, 856
North, The, 554–555, 671
North, Lt. Col. Oliver, 1083, *1083*
North Africa (WWII):
  Allied strategy in, 859(m)
  El Alamein (1942), 867
  Operation Torch (1942), 866, 867, 882
  Rommel's Afrika Korps, 864
North American Free Trade Agreement (NAFTA), 1110
North Atlantic Treaty Organization (NATO; 1949), 911, 911(m), 922, 962(m)–963(m), 1085, 1107, 1108
North Carolina, 572, 979–980, 980(m), *980*
North Dakota, 600
North Korea, 907. *See also* Korea; Korean War
  invasion of South Korea, 925–926, 926(m)
North Vietnam, 900–901, 953, 953(m)
Northwestern University, 656
Norway, Hitler's invasion of, 860
NOW (National Organization for Women; 1966), 1029, 1030
Noyes, Alexander, 803
NRA (National Recovery Administration; 1933), 827–828, 837–838, 842
NSC (National Security Council), 924, 925
NSC-68, 925, 926
Nuclear deterrence strategy, 912–913, *913*
Nuclear power, 899, 1057, *1057*
Nuclear test ban treaty (1963), 966
Nuclear test ban treaty (rejected; 1999), 1116
Nuclear weapons
  civilian *versus* military control of, 912
  deterrence and, 912–913, *913*
  flexible response doctrine, 964
  hydrogen bomb, 922, 925, 930
  Korean War and, 927
  limits on, 1052
  mutual assured destruction, 900
  Reykjavik summit and, 1085
  threat of retaliation, 952
Nuclear winter, 1080
Nursing, 904
NWLB (National War Labor Board; 1918), 756
Nye, Sen. Gerald P., 856
Nye Committee (1935), 856

Oakes, Richard, 1028
Oak Ridge, Tennessee, *872*
Ocala Demands (1890), 679
Occupational Safety and Health Agency (OSHA; 1970), 1044
O'Connor, Sandra Day, 1088, 1089
Office of Economic Opportunity (OEO), 987–988
Office of War Mobilization (OWM), 871
Oil. *See* Petroleum industry
Okies, 815
Okinawa, 895, *896*
Oklahoma, 584, 594–595, 600, *812*, 815
Oklahoma (U.S. battleship), 852
Oklahoma City bombing, 1112
Old Age Revolving Pensions, Limited (1934), 830
Olds, Sarah, 599
Oliver, Joe ("King"), 790
Olympic Games (1980), 1061
Omaha, Nebraska, 757
Omnibus Housing Act (1965), 989
One Flew over the Cuckoo's Nest (Kesey), 995
101st Airborne Division, 883
Onion, The (Web site), 1117
Only Yesterday (Allen), 776, 777
On the Origin of Species (Darwin), 692
On the Road (Kerouac), 951
OPEC. *See* Organization of Petroleum Exporting Countries
"Open door" notes, 702
Open door policy, 693, 701–702, 741
Operation Ajax (1951), 954
Operation Desert Saber (1991), 1087(m)
Operation Desert Storm (1991), 1087(m), 1087–1088
Operation Overlord (D-Day), 859(m), *882*, 883, 885, 946
Operation Rolling Thunder (1965), 1007
Operation Torch (1942), 866
Opium Wars (1839–1842), 643
Oppenheimer, J. Robert, 931
Oregon, 578, 715
Oregon (U.S. battleship), 690, 738
Organization Man, The (Whyte), 950
Organization of Petroleum Exporting Countries (OPEC), 1036, 1076
  oil embargo, 1036, 1052, 1054
  oil prices and, *1054*, 1056–1057, 1058, 1061
  Yom Kippur War and, 1052
Original Dixieland Jazz Band, 790
Orlando, Vittorio, 762
Orozco, José Clemente, 841
OSHA (Occupational Safety and Health Agency; 1970), 1044
Oshima, Dunks, 878
Ostrogorski, Moisei, 670
Oswald, Lee Harvey, 983
Other America, The (Harrington), 987
"Our Stumbling Block" (Nast), 672

Pachucos, 880
Pacific islands
  American imperialism in, *694*
  American interests in, 854–855
  in late 19th century, 694, *694*, 699(m)
  during World War II (*See* World War II; *specific islands*)
Pacific Northwest, 580, 583
Pacific Rim, 1109
Pacifism, 750, 752
Packard automobile, *781*
Pacoima, California, 1103
Padilla, Gil, 1025
Pago Pago, 694
Pahlavi, Shah Mohammad Reza, 954, 1021, 1056, 1060–1061

Paiute Indians, 580, 587
Palestine, 889, 912
Palmer, A. Mitchell, 768
Panama, Republic of, 738, 1082(m)
Panama Canal, 693, 738–740, 739(m), 740
Panama Canal Zone, 1058–1059
Pan American Conference (1933), 855
Pan-American Conference (1936), 855
Pan-American Union, 693
Panay (U.S. gunboat), 858
Panic of 1873, 554–555
Panic of 1893, 669, 680
Pankhurst, Christabel, 715
Pankhurst, Emmeline, 715
Pankhurst, Sylvia, 715
Paper sons, 654
Paragon Amusement Park, 718
Pardons, 534, 792, 1053
Paris, Treaty of (1898), 700
Paris peace treaty (1973), 1032
Parker, Alton B., 726
Parks, Rosa, 977
Parliament, English, 715
Parochial schools, 659, 941, 1073
Parr, "Boss" Archie, 649
Passing of the Great Race, The (Grant), 717, 1123
Pasteur, Louis, 642
Pastor, Tony, 664
Patel, Dinu, 1100
Patent Office, U.S., 611
Paternalism, 708, 743
Path to National Suicide, The (Auster), 1123
Patrons of Husbandry (1867), 677
Patton, Gen. George S., 867, 883, 946
Paul, Alice, 715–716, 786
Paul VI, Pope, 1072
Pauncefote, Julian, 694
Pavisto Indians, 580
Paxton, Tom, 1058
Payroll deduction system, 873
Peabody Fund, 660
Peace Corps (1961), 961, 962
Peanuts, cultivation of, 569
Pearl Harbor attack, 852, 853, 854, 862–863
Peirce, Charles, 709
Pendleton Act (1883), 673
Pennsylvania. *See also* Philadelphia; Pittsburgh
    immigration to, 1100
    Molly McGuires, 634–635
    steel industry in, 622–623, 623–624
Pennsylvania (U.S. battleship), 852
Pennsylvania Railroad, 618, 623
Pensions, 832
Pentagon, 961
Pentagon Papers, 1046
People for the American Way, 1074
People's party. *See* Populist party
People's Party (in Southwest), 588
Pepperell textile mills, 618
Perkins, Frances, 837
Perot, H. Ross, 1065, 1092, 1093
Pershing, Gen. John ("Black Jack"), 745, 745, 746, 758
Persian Gulf, 1061
Persian Gulf War, 1086–1088, 1087(m)
Personal computers, 1117
Pesticides, 873, 947, 1039, 1040–1041
Petroleum industry
    Alaska oil pipeline, 1040, 1042
    conglomerate mergers in, 948
    distilling methods, 611
    falling prices (1998), 1109
    Iraqi ecoterrorism, 1087–1088
    oil in Middle East, 909
    oil spills, 1036, 1037, 1039
    Opec oil embargo, 1036, 1052, 1054

Petroleum industry—*Cont.*
    OPEC prices, 1054, 1056–1057, 1058, 1061
    Teapot Dome scandal, 798
    Yom Kippur War and, 1050–1051
Peyton, Philip A., 647
Philadelphia, Pennsylvania, 676, 818
Philadelphia and Reading Railroad, 669
Philanthropy
    of Carnegie, 625, 626, 626
    to colleges and universities, 660
    Tuskegee Institute and, 686
Philippine Islands, 862
    Filipino insurrection, 699, 699(m), 700, 701
    immigration from, 1098, 1099
    Marcos regime, 1098
    Spanish-American War, 696, 697, 698, 700
    during World War II, 883, 883–884, 884(m)
        fall to Japanese, 865
        Japanese attack on, 862
        MacArthur's return, 883–884, 884(m)
Phonograph records, 663
Photography, 712, 841
Picketing, for woman suffrage, 714–715
Picture brides, 653
Picture windows, 942
Pilgrim's Progress (Bunyan), 711
Pima Indians, 580
"Pincher" deterrence plan (1946), 913
Pinchot, Gifford, 727, 729, 1039
Pingree, Hazen, 721
Pinkerton agency, 636
Pippin, Horace, 739
Pittsburgh, Pennsylvania
    first radio station, 788
    steel industry in, 609
        steel mills, 622–623, 623, 629
        strike (1892), 636, 679, 710
Pittsburgh Bessemer Steel Company, 629
Plains Indians, 579, 580, 580
Planned Parenthood v. Casey (1992), 1089
Plantations, 532–533, 533
Planters, 551–552
Plate glass windows, 647
Platt Amendment (1902), 741, 855
Pledge of Allegiance, change in (1954), 941
Pleiku airbase (1965), 1007
Plessy v. Ferguson (1896), 577, 659, 917, 975
Pliyev, Gen. Issa, 963–964
"Plumbers," 1046
Plunkitt, George Washington, 640–641, 649, 650
Pocahontas, 685
Pocket veto, 534, 534(n)
Poetry, 791, 951
Pogroms, 645
Poindexter, Adm. John, 1083
Poison gas, 753, 759
Poland, 858–860, 859(m), 886, 1086
Polenberg, Richard, 941
Polish National Alliance, 653
Political campaigns, 929
Political cartoons, 554, 626, 644, 650, 672, 675, 677, 682, 692, 715, 732, 828, 913, 1011
Political parties. *See also specific parties*
    balance of power, 670, 670–671
    loyalty to, 671, 671–672, 672
Political system, 668–702, 669
    agrarian revolt and, 676–680
        Farmers' Alliance movement (*See* Farmers' Alliance)
        Populist party (*See* Populist party)
        targets of farm anger, 677, 677
    imperialism and (*See* Imperialism)
    paralysis of, 670–676
        balance of power, 670, 670–671
        issues, 672–674
        political parties and, 671, 671–672, 672

Political system—*Cont.*
    paralysis of—*Cont.*
        presidency, 674–676, 675
        states and cities, 676
        welfare state, origins of, 672
    realignment of, 680–687
        African Americans and, 685, 685–686
        beginning of unrest, 681–682
        depression of 1893 and, 680–681, 681
        Jim Crow politics and, 684–685
        McKinley's presidency and, 687, 687
        monetary standards and, 682, 682–684, 683(n), 684(m)
Political upheaval, 1098
Politicians, professional, 650
Politics
    identity politics
        Asian Americans, 1028
        equal rights and abortion, 1030–1031
        feminism, 1029–1030, 1030
        gay rights, 1028–1029
        Latino activism, 1024–1027, 1026
        legacy of, 1031
        Native Americans, 1027, 1027–1028
    in late 19th century, 563–564 (*See also* Political system)
        cockfight as symbol for, 662
    in 20th century
        Carter administration, 1056–1061
        Ford administration, 1049–1055
        influence of television on, 945–946
        Ku Klux Klan in, 797
        "modern Republicanism," 946–949
        Nixon administration, 1043–1049
        women in, 785–786
Ponce de Leon Park, 718
Poole, Elijah (Muhammad), 817
Pooling, 620, 624
Pope, Gen. John, 583
Popular culture and entertainment. *See also* Art(s); Motion pictures; Television
    farm entertainments, 574
    in late 19th century
        amusement parks, 656
        in immigrant neighborhoods, 654
        social life, 663–665
        vaudeville, 664, 664–665
    in early 20th century
        amusement parks, 718, 718–719
        car culture, 780, 781
        jazz music, 663, 790–791
        mass media, 787–789, 788, 789
        sports (*See* Sports)
    multiculturalism and, 1123
Popular Front (Spain), 857
Popular Mechanics, 934
Population
    in late 19th century, 597, 642, 643
    in 20th century, 793(m), 936–938, 937, 1042, 1099
Population Bomb, The (Ehrlich), 1042
Populist party (1892), 564, 672
    in election of 1892, 679–680
    in election of 1896, 682, 683
    formation of, 679
Pornography, in films, 1073–1074
Port Huron Statement (1962), 993
Portland, Oregon, 597
Port Moresby, New Guinea, 866
Portsmouth, Treaty of (1905), 741
Post, Louis, 768
Postal Service, U.S., 657, 842, 842–843, 1118
Potsdam summit (1945), 890, 906
Pound, Ezra, 791
Poverty
    in 19th century, 573, 648, 648

Poverty—*Cont.*
  in 20th century
    inner-city life and, *1090*, 1090–1091
    origins of Great Society and, 987
    persistence of, 1122
    under Reagan, 1077–1078, *1078*
    in strong economy, 1119–1120
    urban poor, 712, 940
Powderly, Terence V., 633, 634
Powell, Gen. Colin, 1120
Powell, John Wesley, 582, 586
Powell, Lewis, 1045
Powers, Gary, 959
Powers, Johnny, 721
Pragmatism, 709, 847, 946
Prague Spring (1968), 1017
Prairie Cattle Company, 599
Praise the Lord Club (PTL), 1072
Pregnancy, 713–714, 785, *785*
Prejudice and discrimination
  by DAR, 834
  against immigrants (*See* Nativism)
  in New Deal programs, 835
  against Okies, 815
  racial (*See* Racism)
  against women, 713
Presbyterian Church, 1104
Preservationism, 727, 1039–1042, 1077
Presidency. *See also specific presidents*
  FDR's effect on, 846
  female candidate for, 657
  "imperial," 1049, 1053
  powers of, 1007, 1043, 1049, 1053
  weakness of, 672, 674–676, *675*
Presley, Elvis, 934, 951, *951*
Preventive detention, 1045
Princeton University, 662–663, 732
Proclamation of Amnesty and Reconstruction
    (1863), 534
Proctor, F. F., 664
Production Code (motion pictures), 1073
Professionals, 650, 659–660, 711
Professional schools, 660
Professions
  downward mobility of Asians, 1102
  feminization of, 631
  prejudice against women, 713
  social work, 712
  women in, 713, 785
Progress and Poverty (George), 626
Progressive party, 564, 708, 730, *730*, 731(m),
    919–920, 920(m)
Progressivism, 706–734
  defined, 709
  environmental movement and, 1042
  in federal government
    conservation, 727–728, *728*
    consumer protection, 727
    election of 1912 and, *730*, 730–731, 731(m)
    Roosevelt, Theodore, 723–724, *724–725*,
      729–730
    Square Deal, 724–726
    Taft, William Howard, 728–729, *729*
  governmental reform
    municipal, 720–721, *721*
    state, 721–723, *722*
  New Deal and, 811
  politics of morality and
    labor and social reform, 733
    limits of progressive reform, 734
    new freedom, *732*, 732–733
    Wilson, Woodrow, 731–732
  roots of progressive reform, 708
    beliefs, 709
    pragmatism, 709–710, *710*
    progressive method, 710–711

Progressivism—*Cont.*
  social control
    immigrants, 716–717
    prostitution and, 720
    temperance movement, 717–720, *720*
  social reform, 711
    poverty and, 712
    social welfare, 714, 714(n), 722
    woman's sphere and, 712–714, *713*
    woman suffrage, 714–716, *715*, 716(m)
  World War I and, 754
Prohibition, 777, 794–795, 802
Prohibition party (1869), 672
Project Head Start (1965), 988, 1043
Promontory Point, Utah, 592
Propaganda, 757–758, 768, 783, *924*
Proposition 209, 1122
Prostitution, 589–590, 648, 654, 657, 720
Proteins, in American diet, 1041
Protests and violence. *See also* Strikes;
    Terrorism
  Chicago Democratic convention, 1016,
    1018
  in late 19th century
    depression of 1893 and, 681–682
    Haymarket Square Riot (1886), 636
    industrial systems and, 634–636, *635*
    management response to, *636*, 636–637
    Populist rhetoric, 680
    range wars, 593
  in early 20th century
    anarchist bombings, 768
    Klan terrorism, 797
    labor unrest, 766–767, *767*
    militant suffragists, 715
  during Great Depression, 820–821, *821*
    anti-government protest, 829–831, *830*
    hunger riot (1931), *812*
  marches
    Bonus Army (1932), 821–822
    civil rights march (1963), *971*, 982–983
    hunger march (1931), 821
    on Sacramento, 1025
    from Selma to Montgomery, 1025
    Tramps' March, 681–682
    during World War II, 879
  race riots (*See* Racial violence)
  against Vietnam War
    antiwar sentiments, *1011*, 1011–1012
    Jackson State, 1004
    Kent State, 1002, 1004, *1004*
Proximity fuse, 872
Psychology, 710, 813
Public accommodations, *974*
Public assistance, 672, 681
Public Citizen, *1038*
Public Interest Research Group, 1039
Public relations, 824, *824*, 827
Public schools, 549, 658–659, *659*, 1089
Public Utilities Holding Company Act (1935),
    832, *846*
Public Works Administration (PWA; 1933), 827,
    835, 837
Pueblo Indians, 837
Puerto Rican Forum, 1025
Puerto Rico, 698–699, 700, 701, 1024, 1025
Pujo, Arsene, 733
Pullman, George, 637
Pullman Palace cars, 610, 637
Pullman Strike (1894), 637
Pure Food and Drug Act (1906), 727
Puritans, 1070
Pusan, Korea, 926, 926(m)
PWA (Public Works Administration; 1933), 827,
    835, 837
Pyle, Ernie, 868

Qadhafi, Col. Muammar al-, 1081
Quay, Matthew, *675*
Quayle, Dan, 1088
Quemoy, 953(m)
Quinceañera, 1104

Rabin, Itzak, 1108
Race
  imperialism and, 563
  in New West, 588–589
  segregation and (*See* Segregation)
Racial violence
  Birmingham (1961), 982, *982*
  Jim Crow politics and, 685
  in late 20th century, 984–986, 985(m), *985*
  Los Angeles (1992), 1120–1121, 1124
  Memphis, Tennessee (1866), 539
  National Guard in Tulsa (1921), *796*
  New Orleans (1866), 539
  during Reconstruction, 539
  during Reconstruction (1866), 539
  Watts (1965), 985, 985(m), *985*
  in World War I, 754, 757
  during World War II, 880–881
Racism. *See also* Ku Klux Klan; Prejudice and
    discrimination
  of Andrew Johnson, 535
  anti-Semitism, 645
  against Chinese, 653
  failure of Reconstruction and, 557–558, *558*
  Filipino insurrection and, 700, *701*
  imperialism and, 700
  white supremacists and, *555*, 555–556
Radicalism
  Red scare, 766–767, 766–769
  Wobblies, 758
Radical Republicans. *See also* Republican party
  Johnson's Reconstruction plan and, 535, *537*,
    537–538
  land redistribution and, 541
  power of, 539, 542, 552
  woman suffrage and, 553
Radio
  effects of, 772
  first broadcasting station, 788
  during Great Depression, 813–814, *814*
  "Radio Priest," 830
  Reagan and, 1075
  religious, 776
  revival of dancing and, 790
  Roosevelt's fireside chats, 824
  Scopes trial broadcast, 796
  Voice of America, 930
RAF (Royal Air Force), 852, 860, 886
Railroad Administration, U.S. (WWI), 755, 756
Railroads
  as industrial systems, 618–621
    competition and consolidation, 619–620,
      620(m)
    finance capital for, 620–621
    managerial revolution and, 618–619, *619*
  in late 19th century, 570
    bridge-building by, 647
    buffalo hunting and, 604
    cross-country travel, 608, 610
    development of mining and, 590(m)
    farmers' anger over rates, 677, *677*
    growth of cities and, 642
    railroad brotherhoods, 632
    rate wars, 619–620
    transcontinental, 582, 591–592, *592*, 693
  in 20th century
    regulation of, 726
    in World War I, 755
    WWII strikes, 874

Rainford, Rev. William, 651
Raised-ranch houses, 943
Ramada Inn, 1100
Ranch-style houses, 942
Randall's supermarkets, 1096–1098, 1124
Randolph, A. Philip, 879
Range wars, 593
Rankin, Jeannette, 752, *752*
Rankin, John, 923
Rate wars (railroads), 619–620
Rawls, Robert, 1020
Ray, James Earl, 1015
Rayburn, Rep. Sam, 959
Raymondi, Bob, 920–921
La Raza Unida, 1026–1027
REA (Rural Electrification Administration), 833, *846*
Reader's Digest Condensed Books, 949
Ready-made clothing, 660
Reagan, Nancy, 1055, 1075, 1076, *1084*
Reagan, Ronald, 683(n), *948*, 1073, *1076*, 1088, 1105, 1110, 1111
    election of 1976 and, 1054–1055, *1055*
    election of 1980 and, 1074, 1075(m)
    election of 1984 and, 1080
    election of 1988 and, 1085
    as governor of California, 1075
    at HUAC hearings, 923
    presidency of
        Central America and, 1081, 1082(m)
        domestic agenda, 1076–1077, 1091
        foreign policy issues, 1080–1085
        glasnost and, *1084*, 1084–1085
        Iran-Contra scandal, 1076, 1081–1083, 1082(m), *1083*, 1114
        Irangate, 1049, 1083–1084
        leadership style, 1075–1076
        Middle East terrorism, 1080–1081
        military spending, 1076, 1079–1080
        supply-side economics, 1076, 1077–1078, *1078, 1079*
    Puritan ideals of, 1070
Rebellion and unrest. *See* Protests and violence
Recall (removal of officials), 722
Recessions, economic. *See also* Depression, economic; Economy; Great depression
    of 1982, 1077
    Asian (1998), 1109
    OPEC oil embargo and, 1036, 1052, 1054
    in 1950s and 1960s, 946–947
    1970s stagflation, 1044
Reconstruction
    abandonment of
        election of 1876 and, *556*, 556–557
        election of Grant and, 552–553, *553*
        Grant administration, 553–554, *554*
        Northern disillusionment and, 554–555
        political violence, 552
        racism and, 557–558, *558*
        white supremacy and, *555*, 555–556
    congressional, 539–540, 540(m)
        Caribbean and, 540
        Johnson's impeachment and, *541*, 541–542
        land issue and, 540–541
    freedpeople
        education, *548*, 548–549
        experience of freedom, 545–547
        families, 547–548
        Freedmen's Bureau and, 537, 538, 550–551
        landowners, 532–533
        planters and, 551–552
        religion, 549
        sharecropping, *546*, 546–547, 550, *550*
        working conditions, 549–550, *550*
    presidential
        Congress and, *537*, 537–538

Reconstruction—*Cont.*
    presidential—*Cont.*
        Elections of 1866 and, 538–539
        failure of Johnson's program, *536*, 536–537
        Fourteenth Amendment and, 538, 539, 553, 558
        Johnson's plan, 535, *535*
        Lincoln's plan, 534
        Southern hostility to, 534–535
    in South
        attitudes of whites, 534–535
        black office holding, 542–543, *543*
        economy and corruption in, 545
        new state governments and, 544, 544(n), *544*
        white Republicans and, 543–544
Reconstruction Acts (1867 & 1868), 539
Reconstruction Finance Corporation (RFC; 1932), 820
Recycling, during World War II, 872
Red baiting, 921
Redbook magazine, 944
Redeemer governments, 576
Redeemers, 557
Red Guards, 1017
Red Menace, *909*
Reed, Thomas, 676
Referendum (enactment or repeal), 722
Reform movements. *See also specific issues and organizations*
    in late 19th century
        education and, 658–659
        Indian assimilation movement, 586
        Knights of Labor as, 633
        political organizations of, 671–672
        revivalism and, 651, *651*
        settlement house movement, 652
        temperance movement, 656–657
        Victorianism and, 656–657
    progressive reform (*See* Progressivism)
    in 20th century
        causes of, 993
        consumerism, *1038*, 1038–1039
        environmentalism, 1039–1042
        limits of, 1038–1042
        poverty and, 712
        1960's counterculture (*See* Counterculture)
        settlement house movement, 714
        under Wilson administration, 733, 734
Regan, Donald, 1075–1076
Regional communities, 588
Regulation of commerce
    in late 19th century
        of corporations, 626–627
        "Granger" cases, 678
        of industry, 676
    in 20th century
        demise of NRA and, 828, 842
        progressive reform and, 722
        railroads, 726
        under Wilson administration, 733
Rehnquist, William, 1045, *1089*, 1114
Reilly, William, 1088
Reisman, David, 949–950
Reliance Building (1890), 647
Relief efforts (Great Depression):
    failure of, *818*, 818–819
    migrant families and, 815
    state efforts, 819, 823
    for unemployed, 817, 820, 825(m), 825–827, *826*
    work relief, 826
Religion. *See also* Churches; *specific denominations*
    in late 19th century
        labor unions and, 633

Religion—*Cont.*
    in late 19th century—*Cont.*
        political affiliation and, 671
        rural, 575, *575*
        western hardships and, 597
    Native American, 580, 586–587
    in 20th century
        "born-again" Christians, 1055, 1074
        fundamentalism, 795–796, 1071–1072, *1072*
        immigrant groups and, 1104–1105
        Islamic fundamentalism, 901, 1061, 1081
        revivalism, 776, 777, 778
        in suburban era, 941, *941*
Remington Arms Company, 615
Reno, Janet, 1106, 1113
Republican party
    conservatism in (*See* Conservatism; Reagan, Ronald)
    elections
        of 1916, 751
        of 1928, 801(m), 801–802
        of 1932, 822, 822(m)
        of 1936, 833
        of 1952, 929–930, 961
        of 1964, 988
        of 1968, 1017–1018, 1018(m)
        of 1976, 1054–1055, *1055*
        of 1980, 1074, 1075(m)
        of 1988, 1085
        of 1992, 1092–1093, 1093(m)
        of 1996, 1112(m), 1113
        congressional, of 1994, 1111
    during Reconstruction, 533
        black southern Republicans, *544*
        Panic of 1873 and, 555
        white southern Republicans, 543–544
    in late 19th century
        balance of power and, *670*, 670–671
        Farmers' Alliance and, 679
        loyalty to, 671
        McCarthyism, 924
        "Stalwarts" and "Half-Breeds," 674
        on tariffs, 673
    in 20th century
        economic policy, 798–800, *799*
        economic unrest, 800–801
        election of 1928 and, 801–802
        modern Republicanism, *946*, 946–947
        Progressive party and, *730*, *730*, 731(m)
        return to "normalcy," 797, 798
        in 1920s, 797–802
Republic Steel Company, 840
Research laboratories, 612
Resettlement Administration (1935), 829, 841
Restraint of trade, 625
Restrictive housing covenants, 919, 937, 940
Reuben James, sinking of (1941), 751
Reuther, Walter, 840
Revels, Hiram, *543*
Revenue Act (1935), 832, *846*
Revenue Act (1942), 873
Revenue sharing act (1972), 1043
Revivalism
    in late 19th century, 651, *651*
    in early 20th century, 776, 778, *778*
    in mid-20th century, 941, *941*
Reykjavik summit (1985), 1085
RFC (Reconstruction Finance Corporation; 1932), 820
Rhee, Syngman, 925, 927
Rhino ferry, *882*
Rhodes, Gov. James, 1002
Rhythm and blues music, 950, 951, 998
Ribak, Louis, *818*
Rice cultivation, 552

Richards, Ellen, 711–712, 713
Richardson, Elliot, 1037
Richardson, Seth, 922–923
Rickey, Branch, 916, 917
Riefenstahl, Leni, 773
"Right to life" amendment, 1031
Right-to-life movement, 1072, 1085
Riis, Jacob, 712, 1090
River, The (documentary film), 841
Rivera, Diego, 841, 843
Robber barons, 615, 628
Roberts, Peter, 717
Robertson, Rev. Pat, 1071–1072
Robeson, George M., 554
Robin Hood (banned book), 924
Robinson, Jackie, 916, 917
Robinson, Spottswood, 915
Roche, James, 1038
Rochester, New York, 985
Rock and roll
    advent of, 950–951, 951
    counterculture and, 995, 995–998
Rockefeller, John D., 621, 624, 628, 687, 726,
    768
Rockwell, Norman, 935
Roebling, John, 647
Roebling, Washington, 647
Roebuck, Alvah C., 661
Roe v. Wade (1973), 1030–1031, 1045, 1055
Rogers, Roy, 950
Rogers, Will, 665
Rolling Stones, 996
Rollins, Sonny, 951
Roman Catholic Church
    in late 19th century, 597, 659
    in 20th century
        activist priests, 1045
        anti-Catholicism and, 802
        antinuclear stance, 1080
        community divisions and, 941
        conservatism in, 1071, 1073
        election of 1960 and, 958(m), 958–959
        immigrant groups and, 1104, 1104–1105
        Legion of Decency (1933), 814
        Mexican Americans in, 1026
        Radio Priest, 830
        Vatican II (1962–1965), 1072, 1073
Romania, 1086
Rommel, Gen. Erwin ("Desert Fox"), 859(m),
    864, 867
Roosevelt, Eleanor, 823, 824, 834, 837, 847, 870,
    888, 1105
Roosevelt, Franklin D., 871, 919, 948, 987,
    1054–1055, 1092, 1113
    background and character, 823–824, 824
    death of, 888
    declining health, 881
    election of 1932 and, 822, 822(m)
    election of 1944 and, 881
    as governor of New York, 823
    inauguration of, 823
    opinion of Hoover, 821–822
    presidency of
        Argentina meetings, 861, 861
        in Big Three, 865, 885–888, 906
        civil rights and, 876, 877, 879, 974
        compromise over Poland, 886
        fireside chats, 824
        Good Neighbor policy and, 855, 855
        hope for recovery and, 810–811, 811
        lend-lease aid to Britain, 860–861, 861
        MacArthur and, 883
        Morgenthau report, 889–890
        New Deal programs (See New Deal)
        Pearl Harbor attack and, 862–863
        pro-Soviet films and, 923

Roosevelt, Franklin D.—Cont.
    presidency of—Cont.
        quarantine speech, 858
        second hundred days, 831, 831–832
        Spanish Civil War and, 857
        Supreme Court and, 842–844, 844, 858,
            1114
        war strategies, 863–864
Roosevelt, Kermit, 954
Roosevelt, Theodore, 683, 702, 708, 732, 823,
    954, 1092
    character and background, 723–724, 724–725
    Cuban revolt and, 695
    election of 1912 and, 730, 730–731, 731(m)
    election of 1916 and, 751
    on muckrakers, 711
    new nationalism of, 730, 733, 734, 755
    presidency of
        assassination of McKinley and, 723
        on business concentration, 726
        conservation, 727–728, 728, 1039
        consumer protection, 727
        naval power and, 691
        Nobel Peace Prize (1906), 741
        Panama Canal and, 738–740, 739(m), 740
        Square Deal, 724–726
    return to politics, 729–730
    on sinking of Lusitania, 749
    in Spanish-American War, 697, 698, 723
    on Taft, 729, 729
"Roosevelt Corollary" to Monroe Doctrine, 741,
    855
Root, Elihu, 741
Roper, Elmo, 919
Rosenberg, Ethel, 931
Rosenberg, Julius, 931
Rosie the Riveter, 875
Ross, David, 1002
Ross, Diana, 998
Ross, Gov. Nellie, 785
Ross, Prof. Edward A., 716
Rough Riders, 697, 698, 723
Round Lick Association of Primitive Baptists,
    795
Rowland, Charles, 869
Roxy Theater (1926), 789
Royal Air Force (RAF), 852, 860, 886
Rubber supply, during WWII, 871
"Ruby," 970–972, 972, 980
Ruby, Jack, 983
Rum, Romanism, and Rebellion, 674
Rumpus room, 943
Rural Electrification Administration (REA), 833,
    846
Rural environment, 574
Rusk, Dean, 1012
Russell Sage Foundation, 712
Russia. See also Soviet Union
    in 19th century
        immigration to, 561
        Jewish immigration from, 645
        territorial expansion, 688, 689(m)
    in early 20th century
        Bolshevik government, 760, 762, 767
        Russian Revolution (1917), 751–752, 753,
            900, 907
    post-Soviet Union
        economic collapse, 1109
        independence of (1991), 1086
        stagnant economy of, 1106
Russian Revolution (1917), 751–752, 753, 900,
    907
Russo-Japanese War (1904–1906), 888
Rutgers University, 662–663
Ruth, George Herman ("Babe"), 790
Rwanda, 1106

Sacco, Nicola, 793
Sachs, Sadie, 714
Sac Prairie, Wisconsin, 777, 778
Sacramento, California, 591
Sacramento River Commission (1893), 591
Sadat, Anwar, 1052, 1060, 1060
Safety razor, invention of, 764
Sagebrush rebellion, 1077
Saigon, Vietnam, 1012
St. George's Episcopal Church, 651
St. Lawrence Seaway Act (1954), 947
St. Lawrence Seaway project, 920
St. Louis, Missouri, 566, 641, 648, 659
St. Louis Exposition, 786
Saint-Mihiel, Battle of (1918), 759, 759(m), 759
Saloons, 663, 664–665, 718
SALT I (1972), 1024
SALT II (1979), 1052, 1059
Salt producers, 621–622
Salvation Army, 651
Samoa, 694, 699(m)
Sampson, Adm. William, 696
San Antonio, Texas, 587, 593, 597
Sanchez, Felix, 754
Sand Creek massacre, 583
San Diego, California, 871, 1068, 1069, 1070
Sandinistas (Nicaragua), 1059, 1081, 1082(m)
Sands, Dorothy, 1090, 1091
San Francisco, California, 589, 646
    Angel Island facility, 644, 644–645
    Asian Americans in, 1101
    conservation in, 727
    counterculture in, 998
    earthquake and fire (1906), 654
    entertainment in, 654
    during Great Depression, 818, 829
    homosexual community, 658
    Pearl Harbor attack and, 852
    ward bosses, 641
Sanger, Margaret, 713–714, 717, 785, 785
San Juan Hill, Battle of (1898), 697, 697–698
Santa Barbara, California, 1036, 1037, 1039
Santee Sioux Indians, 583
Santiago Bay, Battle of (1898), 738
San Yi Man. See Chinese immigrants
Sargent, John Singer, 759
Saturday Night Massacre, 1048
Saturn 5 rocket, 1036
Saudi Arabia, 1083
Savings and loan failures, 1085, 1091–1092
Savio, Mario, 994
Sawdust Trail, The (Bellows), 651
Sawmills, 572
Scalawags, 543–544
Scalia, Antonin, 1088
Schecter Poultry Corp. v. United States (1935),
    828
Schenk v. United States (1919), 758
Schine, David, 930, 930, 931
Schlafly, Phyllis, 1031
Schneiderman, Rose, 707
School busing, 1044
School Improvement League, 915
School lunches, 1078
School of Pedagogy (Dewey; 1896), 710
School prayer issue, 991–992
Science and technology. See also specific
        technological advances
    communications, 1116
    dissatisfaction with, 1036–1037
    in early 20th century, 778–779
    industrial technology
        Bessemer process, 609, 611, 623
        petroleum distillation, 611
    Internet, 1116–1118, 1118
    microchip technology, 1118

Science and technology—*Cont.*
  military technology
    improved naval power, *690,* 690–691
    during World War II, *872,* 872–873
Scientific management techniques, 782
SCLC (Southern Christian Leadership
    Conference), 980
Scopes, John T., 795–796
Scottsboro boys, 817
Scruggs, Jan, 1065
SDI (Strategic Defense Initiative; "Star Wars"),
    1080, 1085
SDS (Students for a Democratic Society), 993,
    1011, 1029, 1045
Sears, Richard W., 661
Sears Roebuck, 598, 615, 661
SEATO (Southeast Asia Treaty Organization),
    953(m)
Seattle, Washington, 646, *812,* 871
Second New Deal. *See* New Deal
Secret (Australian) ballot, 650
Secret Service, 824
Secrettown trestle, 591, *592*
Securities Exchange Act (1934), 825, *846*
Security Council, U.N., 890, 925–926, 1107
Sedalia, Missouri, 592, 593
Sedition Act (1918), 758
Segregation, 574. *See also* African Americans;
    Desegregation
  in late 19th century
    accommodation to, 686
    in churches, *575*
    in New South, 576–578, *576–578*
    in New West, 588
    as psychological separation, 551–552
  in 20th century
    de facto segregation, 984
    during Great Depression, 834
    of Japanese immigrants, 742
    progressivism and, 717
    public accommodations, *974*
  during World War II
    in military, 868–869, *869,* 904
    in war work, 879–880
Selassie, Emperor Haile, 857
Selective Service Act (1917), 753
Senate, U.S. *See also* Congress, U.S.; House of
    Representatives, U.S.
  censure of McCarthy, 931
  Clinton impeachment trial, 1114–1115
  first black senator, *543*
  Gingrich proposals and, 1111
  investigation of CIA, 1053
  Kefauver hearings, 945–946
  League of Nations defeated, 763
  Republican control of, 670
  Supreme Court appointees and, 1088
  Watergate hearings, 1047–1048, *1048*
Seneca Falls Convention (1848), 715
Sennett, Mack, 787
Separate but equal doctrine, 576–577, 659, 917,
    975
Serbia, 748, 1107–1108
Sergeant Pepper's Lonely Hearts Club Band
    (Beatles), 997
Service industries, 1098, *1100,* 1100–1101
Settlement houses, 652, 714
700 Club, 1072
Seventeenth Amendment (1913), 722
Seventh Cavalry (U.S. Army), 584, *585*
Seward, William Henry, 693
Sewing machine, 692
Sex in Education (Clarke), 660
Sexism, 1029–1030
Sexual Behavior in the Human Female (Kinsey),
    945

Sexual Behavior in the Human Male (Kinsey),
    945
Sexual harassment, 1089
Sexuality
  in late 19th century
    homosexuality (*See* Homosexuality)
    women's attitudes toward, 657
  in 20th century
    army sex education, 754
    birth control and, 713–714, 785, *785*
    changes in attitudes, 944–945
    counterculture and, 995
    Freudian psychology and, 785
    premarital sex, 790
Sexual Politics (Millett), 1030
"Shake, Rattle, and Roll" (song), 951
Shakespeare, William, 841
Sharecropping
  cabins, *546,* 546–547, 550
  development of, 550, *550*
  in Great Depression, 810
  in late 19th century, 569, 570
Share Our Wealth proposal, 830
Shasta Dam, *811*
Shaw (U.S. warship), 852
Shaw, Pauline, 711
"Sh-boom" (song), 951
Sheen, Bishop Fulton J., 941
Sheep raising, 593
Shepard, Alan, 1022
Sheppard-Towner Federal Maternity and Infancy
    Act (1921), 786, 802
Sheraton Inn, 1100
Sherman Antitrust Act (1890), 625, 627, 676,
    725–726
Sherman Silver Purchase Act (1890), 674, 675,
    682
Shipping Out (Lawrence), *869*
Ships and boats. *See also* Navy, U.S.
  British troop carriers, 764, *764*
  Liberty ships, 871
  submarines (*See* Submarines)
Shirer, William, 860
Shirtwaist blouses, 660
Sholes, C. Latham, 615
Shopping centers, 938
Shopping malls, 1068, *1069,* 1070
Shoshone Indians, 580
Shriver, Sargent, 987
"Sick" industries, 806
Sierra Club (1892), 727, *728,* 1039
Silent majority, 1017–1018, 1018(m)
Silent Sentinels, 714–715, 716
Silent Spring (Carson), 1039
Silver standard (currency), 673, 674, *682,*
    682–684, 683(n), 684(m)
Simpson, Nicole, 1121
Simpson, O. J., 1120, 1121
Sims, Bill, 566, 567
Sinclair, Upton, 727, 829, 830, 831
Singer, Isaac, 692
Singer Sewing Machine Company, 622–623
Single tax clubs, 626
Sioux Indians, *580,* 582, 583, *1027,* 1028
  at Little Big Horn, 584, *585*
  Sioux War, 584
  at Wounded Knee, 587
Sirhan Sirhan, 1016, *1016*
Sirica, John ("Maximum John"), 1047
Sister Carrie (Dreiser), 712
Sit-ins, 979–980, 980(m), *980*
Sitting Bull (Sioux medicine man), 584
Six Companies (Chinese charity), 818
Sixteenth Amendment (1913), 729, 732–733
Skyscrapers, 647, *647*
Slater Fund, 660

Slavic republics, 1086
Sloan, Alfred, 784
Sloan, John, 712
Slums, 645, 648, *648*
Slush funds (Nixon), 929, 1047
Smathers, Sen. George, 986
Smith, Al, 683(n), 801(m), 801–802
Smith, Alfred E., 722
Smith, "Buffalo" Bob, 941
Smith, Capt. John, 685
Smith-Connally Act (1943), 874
Smith v. Allwright (1944), 881
Smohalla (Wanapun chief), 580
Smoot-Hawley Tariff (1930), 819
SNCC (Student Non-Violent Coordinating
    Committee), 980, 981, 984, 992, 993,
    1011, 1029
Soap operas, radio, 814
Social class. *See also* Middle class
  Indian castes, 1101
  in 19th century
    in Hispanic society, *587,* 587–588
    poor whites in South, 555
    urban social stratification, 652
  in 20th century
    automobile as status symbol, *781*
    distinctions in suburbs, 940–941
    jobs *versus* environment, 1042
    juvenile delinquency and, 950
    Prohibition and, 795
Social conflict
  in 19th century
    in cattle kingdom, 593
    industry and (*See* Industrial systems)
  in 20th century (*See also* Protests and violence)
    civil rights movement (*See* Civil rights
      movement)
    fashion of counterculture and, 997
    multiculturalism and, 1125
    prosperity and, 1119
Social control, 716–720
Social Darwinism, 625–626, 692
Social Gospel, 651
Socialism, big business and, 626, 637
Socialist Labor party (1877), 626
Socialist Party of America (1901), 626, 726, 731,
    731(m), 758
Socialization, to consumer culture, 661
Social mobility, 632, 935
Social reform. *See* Reform movements
Social Security, 837, *1078,* 1115–1116
Social Security Act (1935), 832, 844, *846*
Social structure
  during Reconstruction
    Davis Bend plantations, 532
    ideology of segregation, 551–552
    social equality, 544
  in late 19th century
    effect on political system, 669
    imperialism and, 563–564
    segregation and social custom, 577–578
  in 1920s
    African Americans, 791–792, *792*
    arts and literature, 791
    beauty contests, 786, 786–787
    entertainment, 790–791
    fundamentalism and, 795–796
    immigration restriction, 793–794
    Ku Klux Klan and, *796,* 796–797
    mass media and, 787–789, *788, 789*
    mass society, 784
    New Woman and, 784–786, *785*
    Prohibition, 777, 794–795, 802
    significance of change in, 802
    traditional views and, 784, 792–797
    youth culture, 789–790

Social structure—*Cont.*
  in later 20th century
    divided nature of, 1024
    effects of 1920s on, 802
    post-WWII adjustments, *914,* 914–918, *915*
    revolution in fast food, *1040,* 1040–1041
    strain of industrial society, 707–708
    wartime stresses, 875
    youth culture, 950–951, *951*
Social welfare
  for GIs (*See* GI Bill of Rights)
  progressivism and, 714, 714(n), 722
Social work, 712, 785
Society for the Protection of Italian Immigrants, 653
Sociological jurisprudence, 710
Sodbusters, 592
Sod houses, 595–596, *596,* 599
Soil bank program, 947
Soil Conservation and Domestic Allotment Act (1936), 828
Solomon Islands, battle of (1942), 867
Somalia, civil war in, 1106
Somme River, Battle of (1916), 753
Somoza, Anastasio, 1059, 1081
Sonar, 872
Song Be (Vietnam), 1013
Song of Russia (film), 923
"Sooners," 595
Sosa, Sammy, 1123
Soul music, 998
Soul on Ice (Cleaver), 984
Souls of Black Folk, The (Du Bois), 686
Soup kitchens, 812
Sousa, John Philip, 663
South, The
  in late 19th century
    agriculture in, 568–569
    churches, role of, 575, *575*
    Democratic party in, 671
    economy of, 567–568
    industry in, 570–571, *571,* 600
    New South, 568, 573–574
    poverty in, 573
    response to Jim Crow politics, *685,* 685–686
    rural life in, 574
    segregation in, 576–578, *576–578*
    tenancy and sharecropping, *569,* 569–570, 570(m)
    timber and steel, 571–573, *572*
  1960s economy, 973–974
South Carolina, 536, 543, 544, 544(n)
South Dakota, 600
Southdale Center, 1068
Southeast Asia. *See also specific countries*
  refugees from, 1098
Southeast Asia Treaty Organization (SEATO), 953(m)
Southern Alliance (1875), 678
Southern Christian Leadership Conference (SCLC), 980
Southern Literary Messenger, 608
Southern Manifesto (1956), 976
South Korea. *See also* Korea; Korean War; North Korea
  financial crisis (1998), 1109
  North Korean invasion, 925–926, 926(m)
South Vietnam. *See also* North Vietnam; Vietnam; Vietnam War
  CIA abuses, 1054
  fall of (1973), 1052
  fall of French and, 953, 953(m)
  Kennedy policy in, 962–963
Southwest, The, *587,* 587–588

Soviet Union. *See also* Russia
  in early 20th century
    Great Depression avoided, 805
    totalitarianism in, 772
    U.S. recognition of (1933), 856
  during World War II
    Churchill's view of, 885
    invasion of Finland, 859, 861
    labor migrations, 876
    nonaggression pact with Hitler (1939), 858–859, 861, 907
    second front and, 865
    Stalingrad, Battle of (1942–1943), 867–868
    Yalta Conference (1945), 885–886
  cold war and
    ambitions of, 906–907
    atomic weapons, 899
    disintegration of, 901–902
    nuclear deterrence strategy, 912–913, *913*
  in later 20th century
    breakup of (1988), 1086
    Carter's hard-line approach, 1059–1060
    economic difficulties, 1059
    glasnost, *1084,* 1084–1085
    invasion of Afghanistan (1979), 1061
    under Khrushchev, 955, *955,* 957, 963–964, 1021
    Nixon's overtures to, 1024
    perestroika, 1085
    space program, *955,* 956, *957,* 1022
    Yom Kippur War (1973), 1050, 1051(m), 1052
Space program
  American
    Apollo series, 961, *1022,* 1023, 1036
    growth of, *1022,* 1022–1023
    under Kennedy, 961, 1022
  Soviet, *955,* 956, *957,* 1022
Space satellites
  Sputnik, 955, 956, *957,* 1022
  Telstar, 1023
Spain, 857
Spanish-American War
  naval battles, 696
  open door in China and, 701–702
  peace and empire, 698–700, 699(m)
  prewar tensions, 695, *696*
  rebellion in Philippines, 700–701, *701*
  revolt in Cuba, 694–695
  war in Cuba, *697,* 697–698, 698(m)
Spanish Civil War (1936–1939), 857
Speakeasies, 795
Spectator sports, 662–663, 790
Speculation, financial, 803, 1109
Spencer, Herbert, 625, 626, 692
Spicer, Laura, 548
Spirit of St. Louis, 789
Split-level houses, 943
Spock, Dr. Benjamin, 1011
Spoils system, *672,* 673
Sporting News, The, 813
Sports. *See also specific sports and activities*
  bicycling, *655,* 662
  in early 20th century, 790
  in late 19th century, 661–663, *662*
  Olympic Games (1980), 1061
  tennis, 661
Sports agents, 790
Sprague, Frank Julian, 646
Springfield, Massachusetts, 663
Sputnik, 955, 956, *957,* 1022
SST (supersonic transport plane), 1040
Stagflation, 1044
Stalin, Joseph, 772, 955
  American suspicions about, 906
  atom diplomacy and, 891, 899, 900

Stalin, Joseph—*Cont.*
  Berlin airlift and, 910–911
  in Big Three, 865, 866, 885–888
  designs on Poland, 886
  offensive in Eastern Europe, 859(m)
Stalingrad, Battle of, 859(m)
Stalwarts (Republican), 674
Standard Oil Company, 621, 624, 687, 948
Stanford, Leland, 591, 660
Stanford University (1890), 660, 818
Stanton, Edwin, 540–541
Stanton, Elizabeth Cady, 553
Starr, Kenneth, 1106, 1114, *1114*
Stars and Stripes, 874
START (Strategic Arms Reduction Treaty; 1991), 1086
Starvation
  of Cheyenne Indians, 604–605
  in 1920s Soviet Union, 805
"Star Wars" (Strategic Defense Initiative; SDI), 1080, 1085
State capacity (bureaucracy), 847
States
  during Reconstruction
    black officeholders, 543
    Compromise of 1877, 556
    domination of party politics, 553
    Johnson's plan and, 535
    new constitutions, 544, 544(n)
    readmission to Union, 539–540, 540(m)
  in late 19th century
    aid to railroads, 620
    corporate regulation, 626–627
    regulation of industry, 676
    statehood for territories, 600
  in 20th century
    medical licensing, 1102
    progressive reform, 721–723, *722*
    Red scare and, 768
    relief efforts in Depression, 819
    woman suffrage granted, 715
States' Rights ("Dixiecrat") party, 919–920, 920(m)
Statue of Liberty, 904
Staunton, Virginia, 721
Steam-powered ships (Navy), *690,* 690–691
Steel, use in building, 647, *647*
Steel industry
  in late 19th century
    Bessemer process, *609,* 611, 623
    Carnegie's success, *622–623,* 623–624
    corporate mergers, 625
    Homestead strike (1892), 636, 679, 710
    in New South, 572–573
    production figures, *611*
  in 20th century
    Kennedy's showdown with, 960–961
    steelworkers' strike (1919), *766–767*
    steelworkers' strike (1946), 917
Steel Workers' Organizing Committee, 839, 840
Steffens, Lincoln, 649, 710–711
Steinbeck, John, 815
Steinem, Gloria, *1030*
Stennis, Sen. John, 1012
Stephens, Alexander, 536
Stephens, Uriah, 633
Stephenson, David, 797
Stevens, Gov. Isaac, 583
Stevens, Rep. Thaddeus, 537, *537,* 541
Stevenson, Gov. Adlai E., 929–930, 947
Stewart, Helen Wiser, 593
Stewart, Lyman, 795
Stewart, Milton, 795
Stieglitz, Alfred, 712
Stimson, Henry, 854–855, 856, 862, 863, 896, 897, 898
Stimson Doctrine, 855

Stock market. *See also* Great Depression; Wall Street
  in late 19th century
    investments in, 623
    railroad building and, 620–621
    watered stock, 619–620
  new highs under Clinton, 1115
  in 1920s
    bull market, 803, *803*
    Great Crash, 804
Stone, Lucy, 553, *553*
Stonewall Inn riot (1969), 1029
Strategic Arms Limitation Treaty (SALT I; 1972), 1024
Strategic Arms Limitation Treaty (SALT II; 1979), 1052, 1059
Strategic Arms Reduction Treaty (START; 1991), 1086
Strategic Defense Initiative (SDI; "Star Wars"), 1080, 1085
Streetcars, 646, *646*
Streetcar suburbs, 647
Streeter, Ora, 1090
Stretch-outs, 783
Strike, The (Koehler), *635*
Strikebreakers
  African American, 631
  Great Railroad Strike (1877), 635
  Red scare and, 766–767
Strike for Equality Parade (1970), 1030
Strikes. *See also* Labor Unions; Work and workers
  in late 19th century
    Colored Farmers' Alliance (1891), 678
    Great Railroad Strike (1877), 635
    Homestead strike (1892), 636, 679, 710
    industrial, 631
    labor unions and, 633
    miners' strike (1892), 591
    spontaneous, 634, *635*
  in 20th century
    after World War I, 782
    after World War II, 917
    agricultural strikes, 838, *838–839*
    air traffic controllers, 1077
    anthracite coal strike (1902), 725
    Gastonia strike (1927), 783
    during Great Depression, 820, 829, 838, *838–839*
    sit-down strikes, 840
    steelworkers' strike (1919), *766–767*
    of United Farm Workers (1966), *1026*
    during World War I, 756
    during World War II, 874
Strong, Rev. Josiah, 651
Stryker, Roy, 841
Student Non-Violent Coordinating Committee (SNCC), 980, 981, 984, 992, 993, 1011, 1029
Student protests
  Chicago Democratic convention, 1016, 1018
  guerilla tactics, 1011–1012
  Kent State and Jackson State, 1002, 1004, *1004*
  worldwide, 1017
Students for a Democratic Society (SDS), 993, 1011, 1029, 1045
Submarines, American, 872, 964
Submarines, German (U-boats)
  in World War I
    sinking of *Algonquin* (1917), 751
    sinking of *Laconia* (1917), 746–747
    sinking of *Lusitania* (1915), 749–750
    unrestricted warfare, 750, 751
  in World War II
    Allied antisubmarine warfare, 868
    sinking of *Reuben James* (1941), 751
    toll on Allied shipping, 864(m), 864–865

Subsistence income, 812–813
Subtreasury system (Populist), 679
Suburban era
  Cold War and
    Cuban missile crisis, 964–966, *965*
    frustrations of, 961–963, 962(m)–963(m)
    Soviet-American relations, 963–964
  culture of suburbia, 940–946
    architecture and, *942*, 942–943
    baby boom and, 936–938, *937*
    religion, 941, *941*
    role of television, 945–946
    sexual attitudes, 944–945
    women in, 942–944, *944*
  nationalism, 951–958
    Asian conflict and, 952–953, 953(m)
    CIA and, *954*, 954–955
    foreign policy and, 952
    international crises and, *955*, 955–956
    response to *Sputnik*, 956
    Soviet-American relations, *957*, 957–958
  new frontier
    domestic agenda, 960–961
    election of 1960, 958(m), 958–959
    Kennedy's presidency, 959–960, *960*
  political climate
    business and, *948*, 948–949
    modern Republicanism, *946*, 946–947
  social criticism
    of mass culture, 949–950
    young Americans, 950–951, *951*
Suburbs
  automobile and, 934–935, *938*, 938–940, *939*
  in late 19th century, 645
Subways, 646
Suez Canal, 739, 864, 955–956, 1051(m)
Sugar, 694, *694*, 1041
Sullivan, Louis H., 647–648
Summers, Lawrence, 1116
Sumner, Charles, 537
Sumner, William Graham, 626, 692
Sun Also Rises, The (Hemingway), 791
Sunbelt phenomenon, *939*
Sunday, William Ashley ("Billy"), *651*
Superpowers, 906
Supersonic transport plane (SST), 1040
Supreme Court, U.S. *See also* Legislation; *specific cases*
  on abortion, 1030–1031, 1089–1090
  on affirmative action, 1089
  antitrust suits (*See* Antitrust suits)
  appointment of Ginsburg, 1113
  on apportionment, 992
  on black voting rights, 881
  Bush's conservative appointees, 1088–1090, *1089*
  on censorship, 992
  on child labor legislation, 714(n)
  on civil liberties in WWI, 758
  on corporate mergers, 725–726
  desegregation rulings, 975–976, 1044, 1045
  "Granger" cases, 678
  on legal standing of Latinos, 976–977
  on limits to working hours, 710
  on minimum wage, 843
  on Native Americans, 586
  Nixon's conservative appointees, 1045
  Nixon tapes, 1048, 1049
  outlaws sit-down strikes, 840
  on protection for women, 1113
  reforms of Warren court, 990–992, *991*, 1045
  on regulation of agriculture, 828
  regulation of commerce, 828, 832
  on rights of Japanese Americans, 878–879
  Roosevelt's attempt to pack court, 842–844, *844*, 858

Supreme Court, U.S.—*Cont.*
  on school prayer, 991–992
  on Scottsboro boys, 817
  separate but equal doctrine, 576–577, 659, 917, 975
  on Sherman Antitrust Act, 627, 725–726
  on trade associations, 799–800
  on Wagner Act, 844
Supremes, The, 998
Surfing sound, 998
Sussex pledge (1916), 750
Swann v. Charlotte—Mecklenburg Board of Education (1971), 1045
Swift, Gustavus, 622
Swift and Company, 622
Synthetic rubber, *871*
Syria, 1050, 1051(m), 1052
Szilard, Leo, 873

Taft, Sen. Robert A., 856, 860, 909, 918, 928, 929, 946
Taft, William Howard, 918
  character of, 728–729, *729*
  as governor of Philippines, 700–701
  presidency of
    antitrust suits, 729–730, 733
    Chinese railroad project, 744
    dispute over conservation, 729
    on dollar diplomacy, 742
    election of 1912, 730, 730(m)
    veto of immigration restriction, 700–701
Taft-Hartley Act (1947), 918, 920
Taiwan (Formosa), 922, 952–953, 953(m)
Tammany Hall, 640–641, 649, 722
Tampa, Florida, 697, *697*
Tan, Amy, 1099
Tanks, in World War I, 753
Taos Indians, 580
Tarbell, Ida M., 711
Tariffs
  in late 19th century
    congressional debate over, 673
    Dingley tariff bill (1897), *675*, 687
    election of 1888 and, 675
    farmers' anger over, 677
    McKinley Tariff (1890), 673, 676, 694
  in 20th century
    Great Depression and, 804, *805*, 806, 819
    Wilson's reforms and, 732–733
Tasmanian dodge, 650
Taxation
  in late 19th century, 626
  in 20th century
    under Bush, 1092
    under Coolidge, 799, 806
    energy conservation and, 1056, 1057
    graduated income tax, 729, 732–733, 873
    during Great Depression, 819
    Kennedy administration and, 960
    payroll taxes, 832
    under Reagan, 1076, 1077
    Social Security, 832
    state income tax, 722
    during World War II, 873
Taylor, Frederick W., 630
Taylorism, 630
Teachers, 659, *659*, 970–972
Teamsters Union, 1119
Teddy's Texas Tarantulas, *697*, 698
Teflon president. *See* Reagan, Ronald
Teheran Conference (1943), 885, 887
Telegraph, 613, 615
Telephone, 613, 614, *614*, 1116
Televangelists, 1071–1072, *1072*

Television
  "Christian" television, 1071–1072
  influence on public opinion, 929
  McCarthy hearings, 931, 946
  news programs, 979
  Reagan and, 1075
  religious uses of, 941, 941
  in suburban lifestyle, 945–946
Teller Amendment (1895), 695, 698
Telstar communications satellite, 1023
Temperance movement
  in late 19th century, 656–657, 672
  in 20th century
    parallel with environmentalism, 1042
    progressivism and, 718–720, 720
    Prohibition, 777, 794–795, 802
    in World War I, 754
Temporary Emergency Relief Administration
    (TERA; 1931), 819, 823
Temptations, The, 998
Tenant farming, 569–570, 570(m)
Ten Commandments, The (film), 949
Tenements, 648, 648
Tennessee, 538
Tennessee Coal, Iron, and Railway Company
    (TCI), 572
Tennessee Coal and Iron Company, 728,
    729–730
Tennessee Valley Authority (TVA; 1933), 826,
    826–827, 834, 835, 872, 973
Tennis, 661
Ten percent plan, 534
Tenth Cavalry (U.S. Army), 583, 697, 698
Tenure of Office Act (1867), 541
TERA (Temporary Emergency Relief
    Administration; 1931), 819, 823
Termination policy, 1027
Terrorism
  Iran hostage crisis (1979), 1061, 1074,
    1081–1082
  Iraqi ecoterrorism, 1087–1088
  by Ku Klux Klan, 797
  in Middle East, 1080–1081
  Molly McGuires, 634–635
  Oklahoma City bombing, 1112
  voter registration and, 981, 992
Tesla, Nikola, 612
Tet offensive (1968), 1012–1015, 1013, 1014
Texas
  in 19th century, 540, 589, 593, 594, 678
  in 20th century, 797, 1100
Texas and Pacific Railroad, 633
Textile industry, 570, 571, 783, 1098
Thailand, bank closures, 1109
Thatcher, Margaret, 1071
Theater, 663, 665
There Were No Crops (White), 817
Third Reich. See Germany
Third world revolution, 1028
Thirteenth Amendment (1865), 535, 536
This Side of Paradise (Fitzgerald), 791
Thomas, Clarence, 1089, 1089
Thomas, Norman, 822
Thompson, Gov. Tommy, 1111
Thoreau, Henry David, 995
Three Mile Island, 1057, 1057
Thurman, Allen B., 675
Thurmond, J. Strom, 919
Tiananmen Square rally (1989), 1086
Tijerina, Reies Lopez, 1026
Tilden, Samuel, 556
Timber resources, 571–572, 572
Time, 618–621, 755
Time-Life, 922
Time magazine (1923), 788, 908, 909, 955, 1057,
    1080

Tin Can Tourists Association, 780
Tired Heart of Our Cities, The (Gruen), 1068
Tobacco industry. See also Cigarettes; Cigars
  in New South, 570–571, 571
Tobacco Road (Caldwell), 841
Tojo, Gen. Hideki, 862
Tokyo, Japan, 886
Tonkin, Gulf of, 1007
Tonkin resolution (1965), 1007, 1012, 1015,
    1020
Too Many, Too Close, Too Long (Dickson), 868
Torrey Canyon (oil tanker), 1036
To Secure These Rights (report), 916
Towns and villages, 574, 663
Townsend, Dr. Francis, 830
Trade. See also Business and commerce
  in late 19th century
    American expansion and, 692–693
    export-import balance, 688
    importance of naval power to, 689–690
  in early 20th century
    collapse of world trade, 805
    missionary diplomacy and, 744
    progressive diplomacy and, 740
Trade associations, 799
Tramps' March on Washington, 681–682
Trans-Mississippi West, 578, 579
Transportation, 562, 598, 612–613
Transportation networks, 561, 1098, 1103–1104
Travel
  automobile tourism, 780
  cross-country rail travel, 608, 610
  improved naval power, 690, 690–691
  information systems and, 614, 614–615
  trans-Atlantic, 613
Treasury Department, U.S., 842, 842, 873
Trench warfare, 747(m), 752–753, 753
Triangle Shirtwaist Company fire (1911),
    706–707, 708, 722
Tripp, Linda, 1114
Trolleys, 598, 646, 718
Truck drivers, 1118–1119
Truman, Harry S, 881, 889, 955, 961, 1014
  death of Roosevelt and, 888
  election of 1948 and, 919–920, 920(m), 922
  memoirs of, 896, 897
  presidency of
    atom bomb and, 890–892, 891, 895–898,
      895–898, 899
    civil rights, 915–916, 974
    cold war and, 906
    executive orders, 916
    extension of New Deal, 918
    Fair Deal, 920
    foreign policy, 928–929, 1032
    Korean War, 925–926, 926(m), 927, 927,
      928
    "loss" of China, 921
    loyalty crusade, 922–923
    MacArthur relieved of command, 928
    McCarthyism and, 924
    postwar spending, 914
    Potsdam summit (1945), 890
    Truman doctrine, 909, 909–910
Truman Doctrine (1947), 922
Trumbull, Lyman, 537
Trunk lines (railroad), 618
Trusts (business), 624
  antitrust suits (See Antitrust suits)
  progressive reform and, 725–726
Truth, Sojourner, 880
Truth-in-Lending Act (1968), 990
Tuberculosis, 605
Tugwell, Rexford, 841
Tulsa, Oklahoma, 796
Turkey, 906, 909

Turkish Republic, 771
Turner, Frederick Jackson, 579
Tuskegee Institute, 569, 685, 686
"Tutti-Frutti" (song), 951
TVA. See Tennessee Valley Authority
TV dinners, 1040
Twain, Mark. See Clemens, Samuel
Tweed, "Boss" William, 650, 650
Tweed Ring, 545
Twenty-Fifth amendment, 1048
Twenty-One Demands (Japan; 1915), 744
Tydings, Millard F., 924
Typewriter, 615

UAW (United Auto Workers), 839, 840
UAW v. Johnson Controls (1991), 1113
UFW (United Farm Workers), 1025, 1026
Ukraine, 1086
UMW (United Mine Workers), 725, 839
Underwood-Simmons Tariff (1913), 732–733
Unemployment, 634
  depression of 1893 and, 680–681, 681
  Great Depression and, 811, 820, 831
    African Americans, 816–817
    relief for, 817, 820, 825(m), 825–827, 826
  in later 20th century
    Nixonomics and, 1044
    under Reagan, 1078
    record lows, 1115
  in 1920s, 806
  in 1990s, 1122
  white-collar, 1092
UNIA (Universal Negro Improvement
    Association), 791–792, 792
Uniform Resource Locator (URL), 1117
Union Oil Company, 1036
Union Pacific Corporation, 591–592, 592
Union Square protest (1930), 821
United Auto Workers (UAW), 839, 840
United Farm Workers (UFW), 1025, 1026
United Farm Workers of America, 816
United Fruit Company, 954
United Mine Workers (UMW), 725, 839
United Nations (UN)
  Baruch plan, 912
  economic boycott of Iraq, 1087
  General Assembly, 890
  intervention in Haiti, 1107
  North Korean invasion and, 925–926, 926(m)
  planning for, 890
  Security Council, 890, 925–926, 1107
  Suez Canal crisis, 956
United Nations Organization (UNO). See United
    Nations
United Rubber Workers Union, 840
United States Steel Corporation, 573, 625, 728,
    729–730, 840
United States v. E. C. Knight Co. (1895), 627,
    725–726
United States v. Jefferson County Board of
    Education (1969), 1045
United States v. Nixon (1974), 1048
United Steel Workers, 960–961
Universal Negro Improvement Association
    (UNIA), 791–792, 792
Universal Pictures, 814
University of Michigan, 663
Unsafe at Any Speed (Nader), 1038
Urbanization. See Cities and urbanization
Urban League, 835, 980
Urban liberalism, 722–723
URL (Uniform Resource Locator), 1117
U.S. Rubber Company, 612
U-2 spy plane, 957–958, 964, 965
Utah, 592, 600, 652, 652(n)
Ute Indians, 580

Vance, Cyrus, 1056, 1058, 1059, 1061
Vandenberg, Sen. Arthur, 887, 922
Vanderbilt, Cornelius, 615, 619
Vanzetti, Bartolomeo, 793
Vatican II (1962–1965), 1072, 1073
Vaudeville, *664*, 664–665, 788
Vaughn, Dr. Victor, 761
V-1 "buzz bomb," 887
VC (Vietcong), 962–963, 1002, 1005
Venezuela, 693, 741
Venice Beach Amusement Park, 718, *718*, 719
Versailles, Treaty of (1918), 762–766, *763*, 768, 854, 857, 858
Versailles peace conference, 762, 763, *763*, 1005, *1006*
Vertical growth (business), 622–623
Veterans, military, 672
Veterans Administration, 919
Veterans' Bureau scandal, 798
Veto power
    Cleveland's use of, 651, 675
    Johnson's use of, 537–538, 539
    Lincoln's pocket veto, 534, 534(n)
Victoria, Queen of England, 656
Victorianism, 656–657
Victory bonds, 755
Victory gardens, 872
Vienna summit (1961), 963–964
Vienna summit (1979), 1059
Vietcong (VC), 962–963, 1002, 1005
Vietnam. *See also* North Vietnam; South Vietnam
    Dien Bien Phu (1954), 953, 953(m)
    French colonial rule, 907
Vietnam era
    end of, 1031–1032
    identity politics in, 1024–1031
    protest in, 1002, 1004, *1004*
Vietnamization, 1019
Vietnam Veterans Against the War, 1045
Vietnam Veterans Memorial, *1064–1066*, 1064–1067
Vietnam War, 999, 1002, *1003*
    *M*A*S*H* (tv program) and, 1074
    Nixon's war
        détente and, *1021*, 1021–1024
        no-win situation, 1020, *1020*
        Vietnamization, 1019–1020
    origins of, 1005, *1006*, 1015
        Johnson and, 1006–1007
        military advisers, 1006, 1009
        Operation Rolling Thunder, 1007, 1008(m), 1009
    Paris peace treaty (1973), 1032
    protests against
        antiwar sentiments, *1011*, 1011–1012
        Jackson State, 1004
        Kent State, 1002, 1004, *1004*
    refugees after 1975, 1098
    setbacks in
        election of 1968 and, 1017–1018, 1018(m)
        King and Kennedy assassinations, 1015–1016, *1016*
        Tet offensive, 1012–1015, *1013*, *1014*
        violence in Chicago, 1016–1017
    social consequences
        at home, *1011*, 1011–1012
        for soldiers, 1009–1011, *1010*
Villa, Francisco ("Pancho"), 745, *745*
Virginia, 540
Visit from the Old Mistress, A (Homer), *533*
VISTA (Volunteers in Service to America), 987
Vladivostok meetings (1974), 1052, *1053*
V-2 missile, 887
Vocational education, 659, *685*, 686
Voice of America, 930
Volunteerism, 711

Volunteers, military, 754
Volunteers in Service to America (VISTA), 987
Voters, 671, 802, 992
Voting rights
    disenfranchisement of blacks, 576, *576–577*
    Fifteenth Amendment and, *544*, 552–553, *553*
    post-World War II activism, 915
    during Reconstruction, 537, 542–543, *543*, *544*
    voter registration in South, 981
    woman suffrage
        Populist party and, 678, 679
        progressivism and, 714–716, *715*, 716(m)
        rejected, 553, *553*
Voting Rights Act (1965), 983, 986, 989

Wade, Sen. Benjamin, 534, 537
Wade-Davis bill (1864), 534, 534(n)
Wages, in 20th century, 778. *See also* Work and workers
    COLAs, 1057
    education level and, 1119
    Five-Dollar Day, 780
    frozen by Nixon, 1044
    Great Depression, 843
    minimum wage, 843, 918
    rising real wages, 780
    semiskilled and unskilled workers, 1118–1119
    1990s income levels, 1118, 1119
    Southern labor and, 973
    wage gap for women, 1030
    welfare capitalism and, 783
Wagner, Robert F., 722
Wagner, Sen. Robert, 832
Wagner Act, 840
Wainwright Building (1890), 648
Wald, Lillian, 750
"Walking cities," colonial, 645
Wallace, Gov. George, 988, 1017, 1018, 1024
Wallace, Henry C., 798, 881, 919
Walla Walla Indians, 580, 583
Wall Street. *See also* Great Depression; Stock market
    electrification of, 612
    financial services jobs, 1078
    Great Crash, 804
    panic of 1907, 728
    telephone and, *614*
Wall Street Journal, 800, 1058, 1102
Walsh, Christy, 790
Wanapun Indians, 580
Ward, Aaron Montgomery, 661
Ward bosses
    graft and, 720–721, *721*
    life of, 640–641
    political machine and, 649–650, *650*
War Department, U.S., 870, 877
Ware, James E., 648
Warfare. *See also* Armed forces; *specific wars*
    air war
        in early 20th century, 752
        in Vietnam, *1003*
    atrocities against civilians, 1107
    casualties of
        "body count" in Vietnam, 1010
        WWII estimates, 895–898, *895–898*
    guerilla warfare
        in late 19th century, *701*
        in Vietnam, 962–963, 1002
    jungle warfare schools, 961
    trench warfare, 747(m), 752–753, *753*
War Industries Board (WIB), 755
War Labor Board (WLB; 1942), 874
Warmoth, Gov. Henry, 545
War of the Worlds, The (Wells), 814

War Powers Act (1973), 1050
War Production Board (WPB), 871
Warren, Earl, 880, 975, 977
    Kennedy assassination and, 983
    liberal reforms, 990–992, *991*, 1045
Warren Commission, 983
Warsaw Pact, 955
Washing Society (1881), 636
Washington, Booker T., 569, *685*, 686, 724
Washington, D. C.
    Coxey's Army, 681–682
    homosexual community, 658
    racial violence in (1919), 757
    Vietnam Veterans Memorial, *1064–1066*, 1064–1067
Washington, George, 758, 911
Washington, University of, 1122
Washington Post, 986, 1047
Washington state, 600, 715, 1100
Waste Land, The (Eliot), 791
Watergate burglary (1972), 1046, 1047, 1053
Watergate hearings, 1047–1048, *1048*
Water resources, in West, 581(m), 582
Watson, John B., 710, 783
Watson, Tom, 679, 680, 683, 684–685
Watt, James, 1077
Watts (Los Angeles), 985, 985(m), *985*
WAVEs, 870
WCTU (Women's Christian Temperance Union; 1874), 656, 672
Wealth
    birthrate and, *937*
    industrial capitalism and, 627
    unequal distribution of, 632, 652, 830, 1077–1078
"Wealth Tax" Act (1935), 832, *846*
Weapons. *See also* Atom bomb; Nuclear weapons
    Brady Bill, 1110
    machine guns, 753
    manufacture of, *756*
    in World War I, 753
    during World War II
        in air war, *886*, 886–887
        military technology, *872*, 872–873
Weather
    blizzards, 594, 596, *614*, 1056
    drought cycles, 605, *605*
    on Great Plains, 596
Weaver, Gen. James B., 679, 680
Weaver, Robert C., 834, 989
Weimar Republic, 771, 800
Weinberger, Caspar, 1077, 1083
Weisel, Elie, 1107
Welfare capitalism, 756, 782–783, *783*, 800
Welfare system
    Block grants, 1043
    boss rule as, 649–650
    origins of welfare state, 672, 846–847
    programs for GIs, 918–919
    reform of (1996), 1112–1113
    Social Security and, 832, 837
    welfare state, origins of, 672
Welles, Ida B., 685–686
Welles, Orson, 814, 841
Wellington bomber, 887
Wells, H. G., 814
Wertheim, Frederic, 950
"We Shall Overcome" (song), 995
West, The
    in late 19th century, 578
        border states, *587*, 587–588
        cattle ranching, 592–594, *593*
        conflict in, 583–584
        economy of, 567–568
        ethnic and racial tensions, 588–589
        farming on plains, 595

West, The—*Cont.*
  in late 19th century—*Cont.*
    food and drink, *598,* 598–599
    mining in, 589–591, 590(m)
    Native Americans (*See* Native Americans)
    Oklahoma land rush, 594–595
    sod houses, 595–596, *596,* 599
    transcontinental railroad, 582, 591–592,
      592, 693
    urbanization in, *597,* 597–598
    varied environments in, 578, 579
    whites and, 581(m), 581–582
    world economy and, 598–600
  in 20th century
    conservation in, 727–728, *728*
    water resources, 833–834
West, Mae, 665
West Bank (Palestine), 1108
West Bank Palestinian National Authority, 1108
Western Federation of Miners, 591
Western Union Company, 613
West Germany, 901
Westinghouse, George, 612
Westinghouse Electric Company, 612, 788
Westmoreland, Gen. William, 1009, 1012, 1013
West Virginia (U.S. battleship), 852
Weyler, Valeriano ("Butcher"), 694, 695, 700
Whalen, Richard, 1018
Wheat, 594, 595
Whiskey Ring scandal, *554*
White, Charles, *817*
White, Edward, 1023
White, Lynn, 944
White, Theodore, 1016
White Caps (*Gorras Blancas*), 588
White collar work, 630, *631*
White House, 714–715, 716
Whiteman, Paul, 790–791
"White Man's Burden," 692, 700
Whites, in late 19th century
  conflict with Indians (*See* Native Americans)
  in South, 539, 552
  in West, 581(m), 581–582
White Shadows (McKay), 792
White slave trade, 720
White supremacy, *555,* 555–556, 684, 717
Whitewater case, 1106, 1114
Whyte, William, 950
WIB (War Industries Board), 755
Wichita, Kansas, 597
Wilderness Society, 1042
Wild One, The (film), 950
Wiley, Harvey, 727
Wilhelm II, Kaiser of Germany, 747, 751, 760
Willard, Frances, 656–657
Williamson, Clara, *593*
Willkie, Wendell, 860
Wilson, Charles, 948
Wilson, Edith Bolling, 765
Wilson, Woodrow, 708, 771, 888
  background and early career, 731–732, 743
  election of 1912 and, *730,* 730–731, 731(m)
  inauguration protest, 715–716
  presidency of, 797, 834
    conservation, 727
    declaration of neutrality, 748
    declaration of war, 752
    ends dollar diplomacy, 742
    Fourteen Points speech, 759–760, 762, 765
    government reform, 732, 732–733
    influenza pandemic, 761
    intervention in Mexico, 744–745, *745,* 746,
      754
    missionary diplomacy and, 743(m),
      743–744
    "peace offensive" of, 751–752, *752*

Wilson, Woodrow—*Cont.*
  presidency of—*Cont.*
    propaganda, 757
    submarine warfare and, 749–750
    Treaty of Versailles and, 762–766
    at Versailles peace conference, 762, 763,
      763, 1005
    veto of immigration restriction, 700–701
    wartime economy and, 755–756, 874
    war work and, 756, *756,* 768
  suffers stroke, 764–765
Windfall profits, taxation of, 1057
Winfrey, Oprah, 1120
Winston, Lillian, 1125
Winthrop, John, 1070
WIS (Women in Industry Service; 1917), 756
Wisconsin, 652, 722, *722,* 820
Wisconsin, University of, 722, 1012
WLB (War Labor Board; 1942), 874
Wobblies, 758
Wolfe, Tom, 995, 1038, 1061
Woman suffrage
  Populist party and, 678, 679
  progressivism and, 714–716, *715,* 716(m)
  rejected, 553, *553*
Women. *See also* Feminism; Women's rights
    movement
  African American
    first U.S. senator, 1093
    marriages, 547–548
    in reform movements, 686
    social networks, 549
  in late 19th century
    attitudes toward sexuality, 657
    cattle ranchers, 593
    depression of 1893 and, 681
    factory work, 630–631
    in Farmers' Alliance, 678–679, *679*
    as home manager, 655–656
    lesbianism, 657–658
    life on Great Plains, 595–596, *596, 598,*
      598–599
    participation in sports, 662
    private colleges, 660
    public education of, 658
    as teachers, 549
    Victorianism and, 656–657
    voting rights, 671
    white collar work, 614, 631, *631*
  Native American, 586
  in early 20th century
    changes in 1920s, 776–777
    flappers, 784–786, *785*
    in labor force, 785
    limits to working hours, 710
    progressivism and, 712–714, *713*
    Triangle Shirtwaist fire (1911), 706–707,
      708, 722
    war work, 756, *756*
  during Great Depression, 813, 837–838
  World War II and
    GI Bill and, 919
    in military service, 870
    pressure toward traditional roles, 914
    war work, 874–875, *875*
  in mid-20th century, 942–944, *944*
  in late 20th century
    abortion issue, 1030–1031
    Clinton's appointments, 1113
    feminist movement, 1029–1030, *1030*
    first Supreme Court justice, 1088
    first vice-presidential candidate, 1080
    glass ceiling, 1031
    legal protections for, 1113
    in Vietnam War, 1066
Women and Economics (Gilman), 713

Women in Industry Service (WIS; 1917), 756
Women of the Ku Klux Klan, 797
Women's Army (Auxiliary) Corps (WACs), 870
Women's Christian Temperance Union (WCTU;
    1874), 656, 672
Women's International League for Peace and
    Freedom (1914), 750, 856
Women's Loyal League, 553
Women's National Indian Association (1874),
    586
Women's organizations, 713
Women's rights movement. *See also* Feminism;
    Women
  Prohibition and, 795
  temperance movement and, 657
  woman suffrage (*See* Woman suffrage)
Women's Service Section (Railroad
    Administration), 756
Wonder, Stevie, 998
Woodhull, Victoria, 657
Woodhull & Claflin's Weekly (magazine), 657
Woodstock Music Festival (1969), 998–999
Woodward, Bob, 1047, 1049
Work and workers. *See also* Industrialization;
    Strikes
  freedpeople, 546, 549–550, *550*
  industrial systems and, 628–632
    American dream and, 632
    children, women, and blacks, 630–631, *631*
    working conditions, 628, *629,* 629–630
  labor systems (*See* Labor unions)
  in late 19th century
    control of work and, 630
    factory labor, 570, 571, *571*
    free blacks, 549–550, *550*
    industrial transformation and, 610
    international labor pool, 616–618, *617*
    labor contracting, 551, 616–617
    migratory labor, 588
    Southern poverty and, 573
  in 20th century
    Asian American patterns, 1101–1102
    Asian immigrants, 1100–1101
    financial services jobs, 1078
    full-employment economy, 1121–1122
    glass ceiling, 1031
    minority workers, *914,* 914–915
    Proposition 209, 1122
    semiskilled and unskilled workers,
      1118–1119
    sick economy and, 1057
    war work, 756, *756,* 768
    working women, 713, 813, 943
  during World War II
    disabled workers, 873
    minority workers, 879–880
    segregation in war work, 879–880
    war industry productivity, 871–872
    women workers, 874–875, *875*
Workers' compensation laws, 722
Workfare, 1043
Working conditions
  Freedmen's Bureau and, 550–551
  for freedpeople, 549–550, *550*
  industrial work, 628, *629,* 629–630
Works Progress Administration (WPA), 831,
    835, 840–841, 842, *869,* 989
World Bank, 890
World's Columbian Exposition (1893), 668–669,
    669, 680, 719
World War I, 738–769
  background of, *746,* 746–752
    American neutrality, 748–749
    causes of war, 747(m), 747–748
    diplomacy of neutrality, 749–750
    election of 1916 and, 750(m), 750–751

World War I—*Cont.*
  background of—*Cont.*
    reasons for U.S. entry into, 752
    sinking of *Laconia,* 746, 746–747
    Wilson's peace offensive, 751–752, *752*
  contributions of women, 716
  end of
    German reparations, 800
    Paris peace conference, 762
    ratification battle, 763–766
    Red scare and, *766–767,* 766–769
    Treaty of Versailles, 762–766, *763,* 768,
      854, 857, 858
  military action
    battles, 758–760, 759(m), *759*
    influenza pandemic, *760,* 760–762
    soldiers (*See* Armed forces)
    trench warfare, 747(m), 752–753, *753*
  moral diplomacy and
    Mexican Revolution, 744–745, *745*
    missionary diplomacy, 743(m), 743–744
  progressive diplomacy and, 740–742
    in Caribbean, 741
    dollar diplomacy, 742
    in Far East, 741–742
  society and
    civil liberties, 758, 768
    economic changes, 755–756
    labor migrations, 757, 794
    military preparedness, 753–754, *754*
    propaganda, 757–758, 768
    war work, 756, *756,* 768
World War II
  Allies, 854
    coordination of strategy, 859(m)
    strengths of, 865–866
  Axis powers, 854, 865
  civil rights and, 876–881
    internment camps, 877–879, *878*
    Italian Americans, 877
    Jim Crow and, 880–881
    minorities at work, 879–880
    opposition to Roosevelt, 881, *881*

World War II—*Cont.*
  framework for peace, 890
    Big Three diplomacy, 885–888
    Yalta Conference and, 885–888
  as global war
    Big Three and, 865–866, 885–888
    in Europe, 867–868
    gloomy prospects for, 864(m), 864–865
    naval war in Pacific, 866–867, *866–867,*
      883, 884(m), 888
    strategies for, 863–864
  postwar period
    Cold War (*See* Cold War)
    return to "normal" life, 904–905
  prewar period
    Good Neighbor policy, 855, *855*
    growing Nazi menace, 858
    invasion of Poland, 858–860, 859(m)
    isolationism, 855–856
    lend-lease, 860–861, *861*
    neutrality laws, 856–858, *857*
    Pearl Harbor attack, 852, *853,* 854,
      862–863
    U.S. interests in Pacific, 854–855
  soldiers (*See* Armed forces)
  war production, 870–876
    global labor migrations, 876
    industry, *871,* 871–872
    mobility and, 875, 876
    organized labor and, 874, *874*
    prosperity and, 873
    science and technology, *872,* 872–873
    women workers, 874–875, *875*
  winning the war
    air war, *886,* 886–887
    atom bomb and, *886,* 890–892, *891,*
      895–898, *895–898*
    death of Roosevelt and, 888
    estimating casualties, 895–898, *895–898*
    fall of Third Reich, *882,* 882–883
    Holocaust, 865, 888–890, *889*
    Philippines, *883,* 883–884, 884(m)
World Wide Web, 1117–1118

Wounded Knee, 587, *1027,* 1028
Wovoka (Paiute prophet), 587
WPA. *See* Works Progress Administration
WPB (War Production Board), 871
Wright, Frank Lloyd, 942
Wye River peace negotiations (1998), 1108
Wyoming, 600

X, Malcolm, 983, 984, *984*

Yakima Indians, 580, 583
Yale University, 1065, 1105
Yalta Conference (1945), 885–886
Yamamoto, Adm. Isoruku, 866–867, *866–867*
Yellow dog contracts, 637, 782
Yellow fever, 738
Yeltsin, Boris, 1086, 1106, 1109
Yesierska, Anzia, 655
YMCA (Young Men's Christian Association), 651,
    663, 717, 754
Yom Kippur War (1973), 1050, 1051(m), 1052
Yorktown (U.S. aircraft carrier), 866–867
Young Men's Christian Association (YMCA), 651,
    663, 717, 754
Youth culture
  in mid-20th century, 950–951, *951*
  in 1920s, 789–790
  shopping malls and, 1068
Yugoslavia, *1107,* 1107–1108
Yuppies, 1078
Yurok Indians, 580

Zangwill, Israel, 664
Zapata, Emiliano, 745
Zen Buddhism, 995
Zhou Enlai, 927
Zimmerman, Arthur, 751
Zionists, 889
Zola, Emile, 661
Zone of emergence, 645
Zoot suit riots, 880